BLACK LITERATURE

C R I T I C I S M

SUPPLEMENT

Guide to Gale Literary Criticism Series

For criticism on	Consult these Gale series
Authors now living or who died after December 31, 1959	**CONTEMPORARY LITERARY CRITICISM (CLC)**
Authors who died between 1900 and 1959	**TWENTIETH-CENTURY LITERARY CRITICISM (TCLC)**
Authors who died between 1800 and 1899	**NINETEENTH-CENTURY LITERATURE CRITICISM (NCLC)**
Authors who died between 1400 and 1799	**LITERATURE CRITICISM FROM 1400 TO 1800 (LC)** **SHAKESPEAREAN CRITICISM (SC)**
Authors who died before 1400	**CLASSICAL AND MEDIEVAL LITERATURE CRITICISM (CMLC)**
Black writers of the past two hundred years	**BLACK LITERATURE CRITICISM (BLC) AND BLACK LITERATURE CRITICISM SUPPLEMENT (BLCS)**
Authors of books for children and young adults	**CHILDREN'S LITERATURE REVIEW (CLR)**
Dramatists	**DRAMA CRITICISM (DC)**
Hispanic writers of the late nineteenth and twentieth centuries	**HISPANIC LITERATURE CRITICISM (HLC)**
Native North American writers and orators of the eighteenth, nineteenth, and twentieth centuries	**NATIVE NORTH AMERICAN LITERATURE (NNAL)**
Poets	**POETRY CRITICISM (PC)**
Short story writers	**SHORT STORY CRITICISM (SSC)**
Major authors from the Renaissance to the present	**WORLD LITERATURE CRITICISM, 1500 TO THE PRESENT (WLC)**
Major authors and works from the Bible to the present	**WORLD LITERATURE CRITICISM SUPPLEMENT (WLCS)**

BLACK LITERATURE

C R I T I C I S M

SUPPLEMENT

Excerpts from Criticism of the Most Significant Works
of Black Authors over the Past 200 Years

Jeffrey W. Hunter
Jerry Moore
Editors

GALE GROUP

Detroit
New York
San Francisco
London
Boston
Woodbridge, CT

Library of Congress Catalog Card Number 98-27492
ISBN 0-8103-8574-0

Printed in the United States of America
10 9 8 7 6 5 4 3

Contents

Introduction ix

Acknowledgments xiii

Introduction

A Comprehensive Information Source on Black Literature

*B*lack Literature Criticism Supplement (*BLCS*) extends the coverage of *Black Literature Criticism* (*BLC*; 1992), a three-volume set designed for high school, college, and university students as well as for the general reader interested in learning more about literature. The *Supplement* presents a broad selection of the best criticism of works by twenty-six major black writers of the past one hundred years. Among the authors included in *BLCS* are: Barbadian poet, essayist, and critic Edward Kamau Brathwaite; Jamaican-born American novelist and poet Michelle Cliff; Guadeloupean novelist, critic, and dramatist Maryse Condé; American poet, dramatist, short story writer, and novelist Rita Dove; American critic and essayist Henry Louis Gates, Jr.; American film writer and director Spike Lee; American philosopher Alain Locke; Nigerian novelist Flora Nwapa; Jamaican novelist and essayist Orlando Patterson; English novelist Caryl Phillips; South African novelist Sol T. Plaatje; and Guadeloupean novelist and dramatist Simone Schwarz-Bart. The scope of *BLCS* is wide, with authors spanning several genres and representing Barbados, Guadeloupe, Jamaica, Nigeria, Senegal, South Africa, the United States, and other nations.

Coverage and Inclusion Criteria

This *Supplement* was developed in response to numerous requests from students, librarians, and other readers for information on major black authors not covered in the original *BLC* series. Authors were selected for inclusion in *BLCS* based on the range and amount of critical material available as well as on the advice of leading experts on black literature. A special effort was made to identify important new writers and to give the greatest coverage to the authors most frequently studied in academic programs.

Each author entry in *BLCS* presents a historical survey of critical response to the author's works. Typically, early criticism is offered to indicate initial responses, later selections document any rise or decline in literary reputations, and retrospective analyses provide modern views. Every endeavor has been made to include the seminal essays on each author's work along with recent commentary providing current perspectives. Interviews and author statements are also included in many entries. Thus, *BLCS* is both timely and comprehensive.

Organization of Author Entries

Information about authors and their works is presented through eight key access points:

■The **Author Heading** cites the name under which the author most commonly wrote, followed by birth and death dates. Uncertain birth or death dates are indicated by question marks. Name variations, including full birth names when available, are given in parentheses on the first line of the **Biographical and Critical Introduction.**

■The **Biographical and Critical Introduction** contains background information about the life and works of the author. Emphasis is given to four main areas: 1) biographical details that help reveal the life, character, and personality of the author; 2) overviews of the major literary interests of the author--for example, novel writing, autobiography, social reform, documentary, etc.; 3) descriptions and summaries of the author's best-known works; and 4) critical commentary about the author's achievement, stature, and importance.

■Most *BLCS* entries include an **Author Portrait.**

■The **List of Principal Works** is chronological by date of first book publication and identifies the genre of each work. For non-English language authors whose works have been translated into English, the title and date of the first English-language edition are given in brackets beneath the foreign language listing. Unless otherwise indicated, dramas are dated by first performance rather than first publication.

■**Criticism** is arranged chronologically in each author entry to provide a useful perspective on changes in critical evaluation over the years. Entries include book reviews, studies of individual works, and comparative examinations. To ensure timeliness, current views are most often presented, but never to the exclusion of important early pieces. For the purpose of easy identification, the critic's name and the date of the critical work are given at the beginning of each piece of criticism. Unsigned criticism is preceded by the title of the source in which it appeared. Within the criticism, titles of works by the author are printed in boldface type. Publication information (such as publisher names and book prices) and certain numerical references (such as footnotes or page and line references to specific editions of works) have been deleted at the editor's discretion to provide smoother reading of the text.

■Critical essays are prefaced by **Explanatory Notes** as an additional aid to readers of *BLCS*. These notes may provide several types of valuable information, including: 1) the reputation of the critic; 2) the perceived importance of the critical work; 3) the commentator's approach to the author's work; 4) the purpose of the criticism; and 5) changes in critical trends regarding the author.

■ A complete **Bibliographical Citation** of the original essay or book precedes each piece of criticism.

■ An annotated **Further Reading List** appears at the end of each entry and suggests resources for additional study. In addition, boxed text directs readers to other Gale series containing information about the author.

Other Features

BLCS contains three distinct indexes to help readers find information quickly and easily:

The **Cumulative Author Index** lists all the authors appearing in *BLC* and *BLCS*. To ensure easy access, name variations and name changes are fully cross-indexed.

The **Cumulative Nationality Index** lists all authors featured in *BLC* and *BLCS* by nationality. For expatriated authors and authors identified with more than one nation, multiple listings are offered.

The **Cumulative Title Index** lists in alphabetical order all individual works by the authors appearing in *BLC* and *BLCS*. English-language translations of original foreign-language titles are cross-referenced to the foreign titles so that all references to a work are combined in one listing.

Citing *Black Literature Criticism Supplement*

When writing papers, students who quote directly from BLCS may use the following general forms to footnote reprinted criticism. The first example is for material drawn from periodicals, the second for material reprinted from books.

Andrew Delbanco, "Talking Texts," *The New Republic,* 200, Nos. 2 and 3, (9 and 16 January 1989), 28-34; excerpted and reprinted in *Black Literature Criticism Supplement,* eds. Jeffrey W. Hunter and Jerry Moore (Farmington Hills, MI: Gale Research, 1999), pp. 142-47.

Arlene Elder, "Ama Ata Aidoo and the Oral Tradition: A Paradox of Form and Substance," *Women in African Literature Today* (Africa World Press, 1987); excerpted and reprinted in *Black Literature Criticism Supplement,* eds. Jeffrey W. Hunter and Jerry Moore (Farmington Hills, MI: Gale Research, 1999), pp. 5-9.

Acknowledgments

The editors wish to acknowledge the valuable contributions of the many librarians, authors, and scholars who assisted in the compilation of *BLCS* with their responses to telephone and mail inquiries. Special thanks are offered to the three chief advisors for *BLCS*: Todd Duncan, Professor of English and Africana, Wayne State University; Christine Guyonneau, Reference Librarian, Krannert Memorial Library, University of Indianapolis; and Ricardo Cortez Cruz, Associate Professor of English, Southern Illinois University at Carbondale.

Comments Are Welcome

The editors hope that readers will find *BLCS* to be a useful reference tool and welcome comments about the work. Send comments and suggestions to: Editors, *Black Literature Criticism Supplement,* 27500 Drake Road, Farmington Hills, MI, 48331-3535.

Acknowledgments

The editors wish to thank the copyright holders of the excerpted criticism included in this volume and the permissions managers of many book and magazine publishing companies for assisting us in securing reproduction rights. We are also grateful to the staffs of the Detroit Public Library, the Library of Congress, the University of Detroit Mercy Library, Wayne State University Purdy/Kresge Library Complex, and the University of Michigan Libraries for making their resources available to us. Following is a list of the copyright holders who have granted us permission to reproduce material in this volume of *BLCS*. Every effort has been made to trace copyright, but if omissions have been made, please let us know.

COPYRIGHTED EXCERPTS IN *BLCS*, WERE REPRODUCED FROM THE FOLLOWING PERIODICALS:

African American Review, v. 26, 1992 for "Two Black Intellectuals and the Burden of Race" by Clarence E. Walker; v. 27, Spring, 1993 for "Yusef Komunyakaa:The Unified Vision--Canonization and Humanity" by Alvin Aubert; v. 28, Summer, 1994 for "Journey into Speech-A Writer Between Two Worlds: An Interview with Michelle Cliff" by Opal Palmer Adisa. Copyright © 1992, 1993, Indiana State University. Copyright (c)1994 by Opal Palmer Adisa. All reproduced by permission of the respective authors.—*The American Book Review*, March/May, 1995. Copyright © 1995 by *The American Book Review*. Reproduced by permission.—*American Visions*, April, 1991. Reproduced by permission.—*Ariel: A Review of International English Literature*, v. 25, October, 1994 for "Crisscrossing the River: An Interview with Caryl Phillips" by Carol Margaret Davison. Copyright © 1994 The Board of Governors, The University of Calgary. Reproduced by permission of the publisher and the author.—*Arizona Quarterly*, v. 42, Spring, 1986 for "The Voices of Misery and Despair in the Fiction of James Alan McPherson" by William Domnarski. Copyright © 1986 by the Regents of the University of Arizona. Reproduced by permission of the publisher and the author.—*Black American Literature Form*, v. 18, Summer, 1984 for "Connections, Links and Extended Networks: Patterns in Octavia Butler's Science Fiction" by Sandra Y. Govan. Copyright © 1984 by the author. Reproduced by permission of the publisher and the author.—*Chicago Tribune-Books*, August 2, 1992. Copyright © 1992 Chicago Tribune-Books. All rights reserved. Reproduced by permission./August 7, 1994 for "Ceaseless Remaking" by Andy Solomon. Copyright © 1994 Chicago Tribune-Books. All rights reserved. Reproduced by permission of the author.—*Cineaste*, v. 19, 1993. Copyright © 1993 by Cineaste Publishers, Inc. Reproduced by permission.—*CLA Journal*, v. 25, March, 1982; v. XL, September, 1996. Copyright © 1982, 1996 by The College Language Association. Both used by permission of The College Language Association.—*Commentary*, v. 75, April, 1983 for "The Unfree" by Robert Nisbet; August, 1993 for "Immoderate Moderate" by Arch Puddington. Copyright (c)1983, 1993 by the American Jewish Committee. All rights reserved. Both reproduced by permission of the publisher and the respective authors.—*Contemporary Literature*, v. 36, Spring, 1995. Reproduced by permission.—*Film Comment*, v. 22, September-October, 1986 for "Lee Way" by Marlaine Glicksman; v. 33, January-February, 1997 for "The Invisible Man: Spike Lee" by Kent Jones. Copyright © 1986, 1997 by Film Comment Publishing Corporation. Both reproduced by permission of the respective authors.—*Harper's Magazine*, v. 239, December, 1969. Copyright © 1969 by Harper's Magazine. All rights reserved. Reproduced by permission./ v. 295, July, 1997. Copyright © 1997 by Vince Passaro. All rights reserved. Reproduced by permission of Georges Borchardt, Inc., for the author.—*Journal of Black Studies*, v 22, March, 1992. Reproduced by permission.—*Journal of Commonwealth Literature*, v. VIII, June, 1973. Reproduced with the kind permission of Bowker-Saur, a part of Reed Business Information Ltd.—*The Journal of Interdisciplinary History*, v. 25, Summer, 1994. © 1994 by the Massachusetts Institute of Technology and *The Journal of Interdisciplinary History*. Reprinted with the permission of the editors of *The Journal of Interdisciplinary History* and The MIT Press, Cambridge, Massachusetts.—*Journal of Social History*, v. 26, Summer, 1993. Reproduced by permission.—*L'Esprit Createur*, v. XXXIII, Summer, 1993. Reproduced by permission.—*London Review of Books*, March 20, 1997 for "Its Own Dark Styx" by Marina Warner. Appears here by permission of the *London Review of Books* and the author.—*Modern Fiction Studies*, v. 34, Autumn, 1988. Copyright © 1988. Reproduced by permission of The Johns Hopkins University Press.—*New Literary History*, v. 22, Autumn, 1991. Copyright © 1991 by *New Literary History*. Reproduced by permission of The Johns Hopkins University Press.—*Obsidian II: Black Literature in Review*, v. 5, Winter, 1990 for "The Historical Novel in Africa: The Example of Two South African Novelists" by Chinyere Nwahunanya. Reproduced

COPYRIGHTED EXCERPTS IN *BLCS,* WERE REPRODUCED FROM THE FOLLOWING BOOKS:

PHOTOGRAPHS AND ILLUSTRATIONS APPEARING IN *BLCS,* WERE RECEIVED FROM THE FOLLOWING SOURCES:

BLACK LITERATURE
C R I T I C I S M

SUPPLEMENT

Ama Ata Aidoo

1942-

(Full name Christina Ama Ata Aidoo) Ghanian novelist, poet, dramatist, and short story writer.

INTRODUCTION

Best known for her short stories and novels, Aidoo embraces the devices of African oral tradition in her writing. Her works reflect a feminist and nationalist consciousness that link Africa's social problems and the decline of its oral tradition to past European colonial rule and the present neocolonial economy. Different aspects of this history, particularly its legacy of slavery, are the subject of her stories. A controversial element of Aidoo's work is her exploration of the marginalization of educated African women. Her fiction features women who defy the stereotype of the submissive African woman by becoming strong despite male opposition and abuse. Aidoo received a short story prize in a Mbari Press competition and another from *Black Orpheus* for the title story of her collection *No Sweetness Here* (1970).

Biographical Information

Born to Chief Nana Yaw Fama of the Fanti town of Abeadzi Kyiakor, Ghana, and his wife Maame Abba Abasema, Aidoo was raised in a royal household. This environment exposed her to traditional lore and ritual which would strongly influence her later writings. She was educated in a Western manner, attending Wesley Girls' School in Cape Coast and graduating with an honors degree in English from the University of Ghana at Legon in 1964. The university included a school of drama and a writing workshop; consequently Aidoo's first publications were plays. The publication of *The Dilemma of a Ghost* (1965) one year after its first performance, and her second play, *Anowa* (1970), established her reputation as a rising playwright. Since then, she has published a number of essays, novels, poems, reviews, plays, and short stories. However, it is in her short stories that her dramatic skills are most evident. The collection *No Sweetness Here* represents her best efforts at integrating African oral techniques and Western literary conventions. This collection also best expresses her feminist concerns. Several years elapsed between the publication of *No Sweetness Here* and her first novel, *Our Sister Killjoy* (1977). Her long silence was due in part to the repressive political regime in Ghana at the time, characterized by military brutality and the indiscriminate incarceration of Ghana's intelligentsia. Aidoo taught English literature at the University of Ghana, Cape Coast, from 1970 to 1983, and was a consulting professor in the ethnic studies program of the Phelps-Stokes Fund from 1974 to 1975. From 1982 to 1983, Aidoo served as Minister of Education in Ghana. She has traveled extensively in Africa, the United States, and Eastern and Western Europe, and has presented lectures at universities throughout Africa and North America. She lives in Harare, Zimbabwe, where she chairs the Zimbabwe Women Writers Group. She is a full-time writer and mother of one daughter.

Major Works

The publication of Aidoo's first plays, *The Dilemma of a Ghost* and *Anowa,* established her reputation as an emerging author. *Dilemma* focuses on culture conflict. A young Ghanaian, Ato Yawson, educated in America, returns home with his African-American wife, Eulalie Rush, whom he has married without forewarning his family. The strength and wisdom of Ato's mother helps to assuage a bitter confrontation between Western individual values and African communal ones. In *Anowa,* a beautiful, talented young woman marries Kofi Ako, the man of her choice, against her parents' wishes, and discovers they have nothing in common. The story deals with questions pertaining to the role and identity of women and is based on a familiar folktale in which a girl marries a disguised monster. *No Sweetness Here* is Aidoo's most impressive work, a collection of eleven short stories that emphasize Aidoo's feminist concerns. Aidoo treats such diverse issues as sexism, degradation, budding girlhood, and the ways in which modernization affects both rural and urban women. Each story profiles a different female protagonist. *Our Sister Killjoy* is Aidoo's first novel, a mix of prose, poetry, and epistolary form. Consisting of a prologue and three chapters, it records the protagonist Sissie's impressions of present-day Germany and England in comparison to their colonial history and their governments' role as oppressors of African peoples. In 1985, the College Press of Zimbabwe published *Someone Talking to Someone,* the first collection of Aidoo's poetry, which contains 44 works. *Changes: A Love Story* (1991) is a novel that looks at options in love and marriage for modern African women. Through the female protagonist, Esi, Aidoo examines such issues as career choices, marital rape, monogamy, polygamy, and the role of compromise in relationships. Aidoo has also written for children, in *The Eagle and the Chickens and Other Stories* (1986), a book of children's fiction, and *Birds and Other Poems* (1987), a book of children's poetry.

Critical Reception

Critical assessment of Aidoo's literary canon has been generally positive. However, freedom to pursue her writing has been limited by the restrictions of Ghana's intermittent political and social unrest. An example of this occurred during the period from 1970 to 1977, when political turmoil prevented Aidoo from publishing her work. *The Dilemma of a Ghost* attracted praise from critics, despite negative comments about structural weaknesses and the attempt to blend African oral and Western literary elements. Critic Dapo Adelugba remarked that its "success in creating levels of language, in matching literary grace with veracity of characterization, [and] in suiting . . . the action to the word, the word to the action, is commendable." Eldred Jones lauded *Anowa* for reaching myth-like dimensions while retaining social relevance. *No Sweetness Here* drew Daniele Stewart's comment that Aidoo's sympathy for her characters raises her stories to a universal level rarely seen in contemporary literature. Chikwenye O. Ogunyemi has compared Aidoo's style in *Our Sister Killjoy* to that of James Baldwin in *The Fire Next Time* and Jean Toomer's in *Cane*. While most reviewers have agreed on Aidoo's impact as a social critic, some have expressed uneasiness over what they describe as pointed attacks against the Western world in *Our Sister Killjoy*.

PRINCIPAL WORKS

The Dilemma of a Ghost (play) 1965
Anowa (play) 1970
No Sweetness Here (short stories) 1970
Our Sister Killjoy: or, Reflections from a Black-Eyed Squint (novel) 1977
Someone Talking to Someone (poetry) 1985
The Eagle and the Chickens and Other Stories (short stories) 1986
Birds and Other Poems (poetry) 1987
Changes: A Love Story (novel) 1991

CRITICISM

Brenda F. Berrian (essay date March 1982)

SOURCE: "African Women as Seen in the Works of Flora Nwapa and Ama Ata Aidoo," in *CLA Journal*, Vol. 25, No. 3, March, 1982, pp. 331-9.

[*In the following essay, Berrian identifies Nwapa and Aidoo as two African authors whose female protagonists defy the stereotype of the submissive African woman.*]

It has been commonly assumed that West African women

wish to dominate their spouses, be good mothers and providers, and remain faithful and submissive to their husbands. Such myths have been perpetuated largely by West African male writers and, to some extent, by foreigners who have contributed and supported these myths in African-oriented studies. In short, the contemporary African woman has been defined, by and large, by her countrymen and by foreign researchers.

One of the factors which has contributed to the perpetuation of myths about African women has been the near-absence of female African writers and, when they exist, their low profile in African literary anthologies. Thus, African women writers are not as well known as their male counterparts: Achebe, Soyinka, Ngugi, and Ousmane. Despite the neglect of women writers, Flora Nwapa of Nigeria and Ama Ata Aidoo of Ghana have managed to attract the attention of literary critics and publishing companies. Recently, teachers of African literature have been exposed to the works of these women writers.

A subject treated by Flora Nwapa and Ama Ata Aidoo is the myths about the role of African women. The image that African women writers portray of themselves differs from the one created by the male writers. This is particularly true with Nwapa and Aidoo's portraiture of the wife, the mother, the traditional (rural) women, and the changing educated (urban) woman. Whether writing about the traditional woman or the changing educated woman, Nwapa and Aidoo place their women characters in situations where their values conflict with those of the men and their milieu. Nwapa's exploration of women in her short stories, *This Is Lagos and Other Stories* (1971), and Aidoo's depiction of women in her short story collection, *No Sweetness Here* (1971), are the subject of this paper.

Ama Ata Aidoo treats the theme of childhood in her story **"No Sweetness Here."** The central theme revolves around Maami Ama's intense attachment and love for her son, Kwesi. This statement assures the mother's claim to womanhood-through-motherhood and compensates for her loneliness, vulnerability, and imposed limitations in a society where male prerogatives prevail. The male prerogatives are underlined by the fact that Maami Ama and Kodjo Fi's divorce proceedings are modeled on traditional customs, run by the male elders who favor male privileges. The divorce proceedings do not allow Maami Ama a recourse against her inconsiderate husband's exclusive claims on *his* son: "The boy belongs to his mother's family, in this community, but he must be of some service to his father too."

Maami Ama clings to her son after the break-up of her marriage to Kodjo Fi, and mothering becomes her primary reason for living. The narrator of the story, Kwesi's teacher, is as fond of the boy as his mother, and frequently taunts

Maami Ama by saying in a joking manner: "Kwesi is so handsome. If ever I am transferred from this place, I will kidnap him." Maami Ama would look scandalised, pleased, and voice her alarm: "Please Chicha, I always know you are making fun of me, but promise me you won't take Kwesi away with you. . . . What will I do Chicha, what would I do, should something happen to my child?" The fear of losing custody of her child makes Maami Ama more protective and possessive of her son. Possessiveness of Kwesi by his mother replaces the failure of marriage and camouflages loneliness. As the date of the court case nears, Kwesi becomes dearer to his mother, and she calls him "My husband, my brother, my father, my all-in-all."

As fate would have it, Maami Ama loses custody of Kwesi. When Kwesi's teacher learns that the mother has lost the case, she identifies with the woman's suffering: I became sad at the prospect of a possible separation from the mother who loved him so much and whom he loved. From infancy, they had known each other, a lonely mother and a lonely son.

This decision of the elders exhibits how vulnerable Maami Ama, as a woman, is in her relationship with a selfish man like Kodjo Fi. When Kwesi dies from a fatal snake bite, a neighbor is so moved that she remarks on the unfairness of life: "And he was his mother's only child. She has no one now. We do not understand it. Life is not sweet."

There are two major issues here: (1) a son too precious to live and (2) the fragility of motherhood. Maami Ama's vulnerability is exhibited in her relationship with Kodjo Fi and the verdict of the elders. Kodjo Fi is left with two wives and children, while Maami Ama goes home to an empty house. The beauty of the mother-son relationship is well expressed by Ms. Aidoo, and she also confronts the significance of an individual woman's total commitment to motherhood to compensate for the lack of a substantial male-female relationship.

Another issue which is raised in this story is how much a woman should invest in a marriage when the husband neglects and bullies her. When Maami Ama complains to a female relative about her husband's ill-treatment of her, she is told that in marriage a woman must sometimes be a fool. However, Maami Ama no longer wants to be a fool but rather to live with some self-respect. Therefore, she instigates the divorce proceedings.

The importance of children in an Igbo marriage and the ambivalent role of a wife is examined in Flora Nwapa's short story, "The Child Thief." The story details the metamorphosis of Agnes, the protagonist. Before her marriage Agnes is gay, thin, and lively, with sophisticated ideas of marriage (according to Bisi, the narrator). Ten years later in Lagos, Nigeria, Agnes and Bisi meet by chance. Years of marriage have left their toil upon Agnes, who is now fat, careless about her appearance, and unhappy. The unhappiness stems from her inability to bear a child.

This inability has impacted negatively on Agnes' and Mike's marriage. Mike indulges in an extramarital affair which produces two children, while Agnes goes to extremes to learn why she cannot physically have a child. For Agnes the only source of happiness is to have children. She believes that her husband would treat her better if she could have a child for him.

Here the African woman's ambiguous situation is stressed in terms of Agnes' perception of herself and her relationship with her husband. In spite of her misfortunes and an unhappy marriage, Agnes still thinks that she is "slightly better than Bisi because of her marital state." Bisi is single, slim, and a working woman unhampered by domestic problems.

The tragedy of the story occurs when Agnes thinks that she is pregnant only to learn that she has a tumor. With shame she leaves Lagos to undergo an operation in a village. Rather than tell her husband the truth, she kidnaps a baby from the hospital nursery and pretends that he is hers. Her rationale for the kidnapping is: "Now that her husband wanted and needed her, she should not disappoint him. She must take a baby to him at all costs." Agnes stole the baby in order to stay in the good graces of her husband. Her prophecy that her husband would come back to her once she became pregnant was true no matter how short-lived.

The sad plight of the Ghanian women's daily struggle to survive covers the pages of Ama Ata Aidoo's short stories. Some of the most interesting stories are about the effects of a changing urban society upon the women who flock to it. In **"Two Sisters"** Ama Ata Aidoo recognizes the attraction of the cities with jobs, cars, and divertissements, but she also condemns the city for its victimization of young women through the characterizations of two sisters. Mercy, the younger sister, is an unmarried typist who drifts into successive affairs with wealthy, married politicians. She is attracted by the politicians' chauffeured American cars, large bank accounts, and expensive gifts. In addition, Mercy's notions of liberated womanhood are linked with sexy clothes and the driving of a car close to the sea.

The misguided aspirations of some urban middle-class African women are studied by Aidoo through the older sister, Connie, in the story **"Two Sisters."** Connie, the elder sister, stubbornly believes that her tottering marriage to a "woman chasing" husband will be restored with the arrival of the second baby. As for Mercy, she continues repeating old habits by being the temporary girlfriend to an older married politician at the story's end—knowing that the prospects of a permanent relationship are dismal.

Deborah Pellow, author of *Women in Accra,* notes that in West African society there is a double standard which governs the conduct of married couples. A married woman owes obedience to her husband (as Connie illustrates) and is expected to be faithful to him. Men, in contrast, can have several wives if they can afford them. In addition, the men can acceptably have "girlfriends" with whom they appear in public, rather than with their wives.

Male concern with chasing women and mistreatment of wives is treated in Flora Nwapa's "Jide's Story." While studying in England, Jide attends a school dance, where he meets Rose, a girl from his home village in eastern Nigeria. As the story progresses, the two young people marry. Shortly afterwards, Jide leaves for home with the mutual agreement that Rose is to follow him later. On the boat home Jide has an affair with a woman named Maria who is scheduled to work in Ibadan. Maria changes her job site to Lagos and is located in the same building as Jide.

Maria is depicted as a possessive, unbalanced woman who changes jobs whimsically. Nwapa sympathetically explains that Maria is mentally unbalanced because she was a victim of beatings and other cruelties inflicted upon her by her husband in England. Rather than take her to a hospital for psychiatric treatment, Jide begins to shun Maria and indulges in short-lived affairs with other women, until Rose arrives in Lagos.

Rose, like other Nwapa female characters, is a model wife who has written to her husband faithfully every Sunday, while he was leading a decadent life in Lagos. Jide recognizes Rose's goodness and vows to mend his ways, but he is too caught up in new opportunities and the spirited life of Lagos. He begins and aborts other affairs, until he meets a drunken and erratic Maria at his apartment door early one morning. Rose acts unconcerned about Maria; this lack of interest on her part causes Jide to suspect her of unfaithfulness.

The reader can only assume that Rose is not pleased with her husband's conduct, but she endures it in silence. The old idea that patience and silence will blow away the problem is alluded to here. On the other hand, the heroine's veiled displeasure is a cause of her husband's future conduct. The story ends with Jide succumbing to guilty feelings and transferring his guilt to Rose:

> For days I thought Rose would ask questions, but she did not. What was at the back of her mind? Was she being liberal? Why did she behave in that superior manner? Was she making a fool of me? I was told that when a married woman had affairs with men, it was her husband who was the last to know. I became jealous. I began suspecting every man that

came to our house, even our friends. But it was no good.

Rose makes a choice to try to save her marriage with Jide by ignoring his nightly absences from home, whereas Agnes in "The Child Thief" first cries and then asks her husband to let her take care of his children by his mistress. Female unhappiness in both Aidoo's and Nwapa's short stories is almost always the result of their husbands' irresponsible conduct.

In Flora Nwapa's "The Delinquent Adults" it is a young widow's brother-in-law who torments her about her deceased husband's money and deepens her grief. The death of Ozoemena's husband brings about an abrupt change in her life style. Accustomed to being dependent on her deceased husband, Chukwuma, she now must take complete charge of her two sons. Before Ozoemena can properly mourn her husband, her in-laws ask her about her husband's property and money. In Igbo society a widow has no inheritance rights; therefore, her husband's property is returned to his family. However, a widow has the option of marrying her brother-in-law, but Ozoemena cares not to assent to do so. Instead, her primary concern is whether or not she, being a widow, will suffer.

Ozoemena's question is answered soon when she learns that her neighbor has been spreading evil gossip about her. Her grief is also increased when she hears that she is being accused of her husband's death in a lorry accident, not only by the neighbor but by her brother-in-law. To hurt her even more, Uzonwane, the brother-in-law, harasses her about the ten pounds left in the bank account. Uzonwane is quite confident that Chukwuma has left a large sum of money, which Ozoemena must be hiding. Ozoemena finally reaches a nervous crisis in which she asks, "Was she getting off her head? If she was not, then all the people around her were getting off their heads too."

Ozoemena loved her husband, who did not shirk his responsibilities to his family. Because of Chukwuma's kindness, she tried to reciprocate by being a good mother and a good wife. The only dark spot was that she discontinued her studies to marry Chukwuma despite the warnings of her friends and school principal. Not possessing the necessary qualifications to apply for a job during her widowhood, Ntianu, Ozoemena's mother, secretly makes arrangements for her daughter to be a concubine to an older man. When Ozoemena fully comprehends the situation and her mother's plotting, she cries out to the astonishment of the man in question:

> Why should you insult me in this way? . . . What is my sin? Why do you want to exploit me because I lost my husband, and it would seem, have no

means of livelihood. Haven't you a grown daughter? Would you like her to be thus treated if she married and lost her husband in a motor accident?

No answers are brought forth, and the story ends on a grim note with the brother-in-law's message that Ozoemena must swear to the gods if all of Chukwuma's money cannot be found.

On the other hand, Ama Ata Aidoo's **"In the Cutting of a Drink"** ends on an optimistic note. To tell this story, as Lloyd W. Brown—author of two articles on female African writers—so aptly states, Aidoo utilizes the storyteller's techniques and the traditional values of the rural audience. The storyteller is a young man who describes his search for his sister, Mansa, who left for Accra twelve years earlier. He goes to Accra to learn that his sister has become bound up with both the changes of urban life and its fast pace by becoming a prostitute.

The storyteller/narrator's search for Mansa also turns out to be an educational trip, for he learns about his own sexuality and comprehends Mansa's choice of occupation. The narrator dances with "bad" women in a bar, watches his cousin's girlfriend "cut beer like a man," and sees women wearing "skin-tight dresses." The "bad" women's unrestricted sexuality arouses the narrator's puritanism but prepares him for the inevitable meeting with Mansa:

> What is there to weep about? I was sent to find a lost child. I found a woman.
>
> Cut me a drink. . . .
>
> Any kind of work is work. . . . That is what Mansa told me with a mouth that looked like clotted blood.

"Bad" city women are symbols of uprootedness and are not perceived within the familial context. During her twelve-year stay in Accra, Mansa develops the attitude that rural people have no right to question her about her line of work, and she calls her brother a "villager" when he does question her. Contrariwise, "good" rural women stay within the extended family structure and adhere to customs. Therefore, Mansa's brother believes that she will come home for Christmas, for he cannot totally accept her moral value system. If Mansa has not returned home in twelve years, it is doubtful that she will come now, but her brother cannot help but hope.

On the whole, Flora Nwapa and Ama Ata Aidoo avoid presenting idealized Western images of African women. After all, Maami Ama and Ozoemena do fight back when they are compromised or placed in a delicate situation. However, the most liberated women in the towns—Connie and Mansa—are not presented in the most admirable or moral terms ei-

ther. These two are prostitutes, but their state of uprootedness and the mentioning of misplaced values are hinted at by their author, Ama Ata Aidoo.

The behavior expected of women varies among ethnic groups, but the image of the faithful wife and the good mother remains constant. With the disruption of traditional society through colonialism and the cultural changes which occur, women find new roles as teachers, nurses, typists and librarians. These new roles are a continuation of the roles held during the colonial times. Due to the fast pace of urban life, some women do become the mistresses of wealthy men and others postpone marriage by enjoying single life longer than usual.

This problem of moving from colonialism to postcolonialism with a changing and dynamic culture also creates problems of generational conflict between mothers and daughters or brothers and sisters, i.e., Ozoemena and her mother, Ntianu, or the unidentified storyteller and his sister, Mansa. These generational conflicts can also be translated into terms of cultural tensions between African traditions and Western influences. Both Flora Nwapa and Ama Ata Aidoo insist that although the African woman may be vulnerable to men, she does not play a subordinate role. This view is truly contrary to the one projected by male African and Western writers. She does, however, want sexual fulfillment by choice, not by coercion. She is also preoccupied with her own definition of who and what she is. Buchi Emecheta, a female Nigerian writer, sums up how the African woman seeks to define herself:

> She must clarify her notions of home and family, of freedom and identity. She must, finally, choose her own life, or at least her own master.

Arlene Elder (essay date 1987)

SOURCE: "Ama Ata Aidoo and the Oral Tradition: A Paradox of Form and Substance," in *Women in African Literature Today,* Africa World Press, 1987, pp. 109-18.

[*In the following essay, Elder discusses Aidoo's novel* Our Sister Killjoy, *which argues that European colonization has all but destroyed African artistic literary traditions.*]

In 1967, the Ghanaian writer, Ama Ata Aidoo asserted:

> I totally disagree with people who feel that oral literature is one stage in the development of man's artistic genius. To me it's an end in itself . . .

We cannot tell our stories maybe with the same expertise as our forefathers. But to me, all the art of the speaking voice could be brought back so easily. We are not that far from our traditions.

This comment has served readers well in clarifying Aidoo's aesthetic and cultural concerns and providing a key to her style. Certainly, her plays, *The Dilemma of a Ghost* (1965) and *Anowa* (1969), and collection of short stories, *No Sweetness Here* (1972) all demonstrate her allegiance to oral performance and her skillful re-creation of the traditional unity of performer and audience.

Her most recent work, *Our Sister Killjoy: or, Reflections from a Black-eyed Squint* (1979), is most interesting, however, because, paradoxically, it utilizes the very devices of Ghanaian oral literature to suggest that colonialism has fractured African society so severely that art is no longer both 'a form of aesthetic expression and a mode of communication', solidly rooted in 'underlying social, cultural and religious values', as J.H. Kwabena Nketia describes traditional drama. Instead, the contemporary African artist, in Aidoo's view, is unsure of, even rebuffed by, his audience. His attempts at communal expression are stifled; his fate, ironically, is like that of his Western counterpart: to speak in isolation, most often in defiance and frustration. It is nothing less than a *tour de force* that Aidoo successfully employs traditional oral techniques to present us with such a non-traditional conclusion.

The book jacket announces that *Our Sister Killjoy* is a novel, but at first glance, it appears to be a *mélange* of fictional episodes in both prose and verse mixed with sections of political speculation and social criticism. The book is divided into four parts: **'Into A Bad Dream', 'The Plums', 'From Our Sister Killjoy',** and **'A Love Letter'.** Briefly, the story is of 'our Sister', Sissie, who is selected by officials in Ghana to accompany other young Africans to a youth hostel in Germany. There, she develops a troubling relationship with a discontented and lonely German housewife and learns something about connections between women and, particularly, about her own predicament as an African woman. She then travels to London and comes face-to-face with others like herself who had left Africa for the promises of Western education. In the end, she returns to Africa, but only after arguing with her compatriots and alienating her lover because of her outspoken political beliefs.

Aidoo tells this story in the third person, using the omniscient narrator common to many Western novels, but the narrative proper does not begin until page 8. Preceding the story are several pages of curiously spaced, conversational observations about neo-colonial, 'moderate' blacks and, 'academic-pseudo-intellectuals'. Page 6 is only three-quarters filled with prose; pages 5 and 7 are shaped like poems; and pages 3 and 4 consist of only one line apiece.

In addition to this unusual typography, the feature that suggests that Aidoo has something other than the conventional novel in mind is the conversational nature of these passages. She begins with the reassurance, 'Things are working out', as though the reader already knows what these 'Things' are. This casual, imprecise beginning establishes a dynamic between reader and writer essential to Aidoo's overall goal.

First, as every good story-teller must, she whets her reader's curiosity to discover what has been happening to her speaker, what it is that might be in doubt of 'working out'. Second, by beginning in the middle of the action, she establishes a bond of prior acquaintanceship with her reader. When the narrator then calls him, 'my brother', he is transformed from a stranger, a distant reader of a novel on a cold, printed page, interested privately in a good story, perhaps, into a member of her community involved in the very situation confronting the main character. Moreover, the style in these first pages tends toward the epistolary, a technique she will make explicit in the fourth section, thus enhancing the intimacy between writer and reader, between speaker and listener. In a very real sense, because Aidoo has defined her audience so carefully, both by the conversational style and by the designation, 'my brother', we, as readers, become participants and, at least temporarily, part of her society, confronting the dilemmas of one of our own kind whose experiences and decisions hold meaning for our own lives. Such is the traditional dynamic between the African poet and his audience.

Aidoo enhances this effect by shaping her narrative with other traditional techniques. Throughout the story, for example, there are passages written in poetic form, like the songs interspersed throughout the oral performance of a folk tale. 'In the evenings', reports Okechukwu Mezu in *African Writers on African Writing,*

> When children gather to listen to stories, yarns and fairy-tales from their grandparents, they listen to pieces interspersed with rhymes, lyrics and choruses . . . One of the most interesting aspects of traditional African civilization is the unity of the art forms.

In form and substance, Aidoo's verse in this book most resembles the type of traditional poetry described by Kofi Antubam in *Ghana's Heritage of Culture* as 'Abentia Munsem', that is, very short verses that:

> often are reminders to chiefs of a certain calamity that had befallen their state or community in the past. Sometimes, too, they warn them of either their responsibilities as head of their state or first member of the royal family. Where no trouble has come

in the way of a state or community, its chief ABENTIA player serves as the secret guide of his master, and forewarns him when he is about to meet some trouble and fall into the hands of his enemies.

African writers rooted in their traditions strive for an integration of established and changing social customs and combine, in critic Lloyd Brown's words, 'a sense of permanence with a process of continual change.' Like the verses of the Abentia player of old, Aidoo's songs confront her listeners with their sense of political calamity, in this instance, colonialism, but her awareness of historical change demands that they be intended as warnings for the common people, her 'brothers', not the neo-colonial heads of state whom she mistrusts.

An example of this poetry occurs in the second section, **'The Plums'**, when Sissie is recounting her tour of Upper Volta to her new German friend, Marija. 'Was Upper Wolta also beautiful' Marija asks:

> She did not know she thought so then.
> She was to know.
>
> The bible talks of
> Wilderness
> Take your eyes to see
> Upper Volta, my brother-
> Dry land. Thorn trees. Stones.
>
> The road from the Ghana border to
> Ouagadougou was
> Out-of-sight!
>
> The French, with
> Characteristic contempt and
> Almost
> Childish sense of
> Perfidy had
> A long time ago, tarred two
> Narrow
> Strips of earth for motor vehicles.
> Each wide enough for
> One tyre.

A prose section follows, recounting a near disaster occurring to three travellers as a result of the shoddy paving of the road and highlighting the French indifference to such accidents. Then, the verse continues:

> A sickening familiar tale.
> Poor Upper Volta too.
>
> There are
> Richer, much

> Richer countries on this continent
> Where
> Graver national problems
> Stay
> Unseen while
> Big men live their
> Big lives
> Within . . .

The first section of the book, **'Into A Bad Dream'**, is connected to **'The Plums'** by three pages containing one word each: 'Where', 'When', 'How'. These words are not presented as questions, but as statements. They are the equivalent of the narrator saying something like: 'Now, I will tell you *where* Sissy went, when she returned, and how her time in Europe progressed.' Therefore, they serve as a bridge in the narrative and are not really conversational; rather, they are like subject headings in a notebook.

Nevertheless, almost immediately, she reestablishes the oral quality of her narrative by introducing first, a poetic passage inspired by Sissie's visiting a German castle and reflecting on the misuse of power by the nobility and secondly, another moving prose vignette about the plight of some naive Asians, ignorant of the discrimination in the West against people with dark skin. Such alternation of prose features with poetic narrative and reflection is the pattern of the first three sections of the work and illustrates Aidoo's adherence to the similar structure of African oral performance. As Mezu observes, 'side by side with [the] unity of the art forms is the element of repetition . . . a litany that says the same thing in various ways . . .

The third section, **'From Our Sister Killjoy'**, serves a dual purpose: to expose the self-delusion and dishonesty of the 'been-tos' and to characterize Sissie as perceiving the discrepancies between what she has been told of the life of Africans abroad and what she actually confronts in England: 'Sissie bled as she tried to take the scene in. The more people she talked to, the less she understood'. When she sees again and again the pitiful condition of the Africans in London, whatever their claims or expectations, her first reaction is to weep and then to rage. Aidoo uses the third-person narrator to judge Sissie's growth at various points in the book, for one way to look at this novel is as a story of maturation. 'Our poor sister', the narrator laments,

> So touchingly naive then . . .
> She wondered why they never told the truth of
> their travels at home.
> Not knowing that if they were to keep on being
> something in their own eyes, then they could not
> tell the truth to their own selves or to anyone else.

'So when they eventually went back home as "been-tos",'

like Ato of the author's first play, they returned 'the ghosts of the humans that they used to be . . . '

This third section ends with the satiric episode of Sissie's meeting with a typical 'been-to', Kunle. Their disagreement about a current news item, the first heart transplants, demonstrates Aidoo's ability to satirize and identify a prominent figure she feels worthy of criticism without actually naming him, a skill valued in traditional oral performance. In *Yes and No, the Intimate Folklore of Africa,* Alta Jablow points out that in oral performance:

> Often, in addition to the traditional stories and legends, topical items are recounted though disguised as fiction with sly humor and sarcasm. The pretentious, the wily and dishonest are thus often criticized publicly. If the talent of the narrator is such that the personalities involved can be recognized, though he is avoiding specific reference to them, so much the better.

After Sissie and Kunle's disagreement, in which it is revealed that the first hearts transplanted were from Coloured South Africans to white South Africans, the narrator remarks:

> That was some years
> Before
> A colleague described
> The Christian Doctor's nth triumph as being
> 'Dangerously close to outright
> experimentation.'
>
> . . . .
>
> Meanwhile
> One or two more
> Idealistic
> Young
> Refugees
> Have gone totally
> Mad—or got themselves killed on
> the Zambezi.
> The Christian Doctor has
> Taken a couple of press pictures
> In the company of a
> Movie Queen
>
> Divorced
> Mrs. Christian Doctor
>
> Acquired another
> Mrs. Christian Doctor
> and a couple of rand
> Millions
> Effected quite a few more

> Heart transplantations.
> He is the only one
> Who seems
> Now to be doing well;
> The rest?
> A veritable catalogue of
> Death and just plain
> Heartbreak.

The futility of the 'been-tos' like Kunle who support whatever they find in the West, heart transplants, for instance, no matter how barbaric such 'advances' may actually be, and the frequently dashed dreams of those awaiting their return are emphasized by Kunle's mother's letter to him at the end of the third part.

The device of the epistle is extended in the concluding section, **'A Love Letter'.** The form here—first-person narration of a letter Sissie is writing on her plane back to Africa—reinforces the conversational emphasis of the preceding chapters and allows us an even greater intimacy with Aidoo's heroine through direct contact with her innermost thoughts expressed in her own voice. Appropriately, it is here in her own words that Sissie expresses her own and, no doubt, Aidoo's reservations about language and the possibility of communication. Such questioning raises the very serious issue of the possibility of traditional art in a neo-colonial society. 'First of all, there is this language!', she begins in complaint, 'This language . . . so far, I have only been able to use a language that enslaved me, and therefore, the messengers of my mind always come shackled . . . '

Language, then, like everything else she discovers on her odyssey, carries political overtones which affect individuals as well as societies. Her letter is to a man she still loves but who considers her too politically radical for him and, like the heroine of Aidoo's second play, *Anowa,* not womanly enough. He has decided to remain in London, not return to Africa.

Sissie reads and rereads the letter, like the reader, acquainting herself with her new ideas and refining her new perceptions. If the story had ended here, the book's reliance on traditional oral performance would have been in keeping with Aidoo's earlier works. As listeners, we would have been drawn into the action more intimately with each succeeding section and, possibly, would have been affected like the traditional audience to the point that the story would have reflected and perpetuated our own moral and cultural values. However, most of the fictional 'brothers' Sissie meets do not share her concern about selling themselves for the fool's gold of the West, thus betraying Africa; and we, her readers in the West can only be her 'brothers' ideologically, at best, not culturally. The distancing technique Aidoo uses at the end of the fourth section, which will be discussed below, suggests that she realizes the isolating effect that colonialism has brought to the storyteller and the resulting change in the power of his art.

Analyzing the historical context of African poetry, Okechukwu Mezu explains:

> African traditional poetry can . . . be described as a collective experience initiated by an individual in a group and shared by the rest. It is a conscious and finalistic attempt to verbalize, vocalize or orchestrate notions, themes and/or events for enjoyment, parody, or veneration with a view to artistic recreation, group catharsis or supernatural contemplation.

Modern African poetry—Mezu is particularly concerned with revolutionary poetry—like Western poetry, however, is personal:

> From a group catharsis, modern African poetry became an experiment in self-exorcism. Because he can no longer speak to his people, the modern African poet has chosen to sing, chant, shout, be angry, rave, curse, condemn and praise when occasion demands it in the interests of his people.

Unlike the audience for whom the revolutionary poet writes, Sissie's 'brothers' do not seem to want to overthrow their psychological and political 'bosses'. All the compatriots she meets in London offer her multiple rationalizations as to why they should remain there. She knows that even the man she loves would react to her letter by saying:

> There you go again, Sissie, you are so serious;
> Dear Lord, all you radicals make me sick. How oversensitive do you people want to be?;

and:

> There goes Sissie again. Forever carrying Africa's problems on her shoulders as though they have paid her to do it.

She realizes he might not even be listening to her and has to ask him in Swahili, 'Unasika, Mpenzi Wangu?', which is 'Are you listening, my love?'

Finally, she decides not to mail the letter. The last few pages of this section return to the voice of the third-person narrator, distancing us from Sissie, as she feels herself distanced from all but the beautiful continent of Africa itself, which inspires and nourishes her; ' . . . she was back in Africa. And that felt like fresh wild honey on the tongue . . . '

Colonialism has broken the circle of singer and listener, ora-

tor and audience. Sissie learns that she cannot speak to her 'brothers' in any tongue: 'I hadn't been aware that I was making a speech,' she remembers a particularly unpleasant confrontation with them: 'when I paused the silence made itself heard.' Nor can she speak for them: 'Listen, Sister. You cannot make these blanket statements,' they inform her.

In the end, she speaks only to and for herself:

> 'Oh, Africa. Crazy old continent . . .'

> Sissie wondered whether she had spoken aloud to herself. The occupant of the next seat probably thought she was crazy. Then she decided she didn't care anyway.

Sissie's travels have led to her growth in understanding and self-confidence, but unlike her predecessors, the Abentia players of old, she is isolated, without an audience, without a community of shared values.

And so, in search of unity of meaning, at least, we circle back with the narrator's voice to the first statements in the work and realize that, despite her pessimism, as embodied in Sissie's failure to send the letter and her sense of isolation and defiance, Aidoo does not despair. 'Things are working out', the narrator has promised,

> towards their dazzling conclusions . . .

> . . . so it is neither here nor there,
> what ticky-tackies we have
> saddled and surrounded ourselves with,
> blocked our views,
> cluttered our brains.

The narrator, always superior to Sissie in understanding, provides structural unity for the narrative and, at the same time, establishes Aidoo's paradoxical role as an artist attempting to continue the moral function of the communal oral performer in an individualistic, materialistic present. While, like Africa itself, art, culture, morality continue, despite attacks on them, Aidoo has demonstrated that the communication of these verities has become increasingly difficult. The artist's unifying and strengthening role is diminished, and the bond between singer and audience is broken. One may revitalize the forms of traditional culture as Aidoo demonstrates so skillfully in all of her work, but history has guaranteed that the substance, the ethical bond between artist and audience, will probably never return.

Sara Chetin (essay date 1993)

SOURCE: "Reading from a Distance: Ama Ata Aidoo's *Our Sister Killjoy*," in *Black Women's Writing,* St. Martin's Press, 1993, pp. 146-59.

[*In the following essay, Chetin discusses Aidoo's attempt to construct a new language for the African woman in* Our Sister Killjoy.]

> But how can I help being so serious? Eh, my Love, what positive is there to be, when I cannot give voice to my soul and still have her heard? Since so far, I have only been able to use a language that enslaved me, and therefore, the messengers of my mind always come shackled?

A modern dilemma tale—directed at an African man but written in the form of a letter that never gets sent. The Western-educated African woman has so 'great a need to communicate' that it leads her to attempt to engage her African male counterparts despite knowing, from experience, that it will be misconstrued, laughed at or silenced. An open dialogue aborted, Ama Ata Aidoo closes her novel *Our Sister Killjoy* with the heroine alone, flying back to Africa from Europe, reflecting on the difficulty of finding an authentic female voice that will be heard by her African brothers, but also a voice that will not be appropriated by a Western audience:

> So you see, My Precious Something, all that I was saying about language is that I wish you and I could share our hopes, fears and our fantasies, without feeling inhibited because we suspect that someone is listening. As it is, we cannot write to one another, or speak across the talking cables or converse as we travel on a bus or a train or anywhere, but we are sure they are listening, listening, listening.

An African woman writer's dilemma tale—directed at an African audience but written within a Western structure that deviates from the conventional, unified shape of the novel. A product of a Western education, the modern African woman writer creates a fragmented voice that reflects the alienated experiences of an African woman who is in search of a new language, a new way of conceptualising these experiences that ultimately aim to synthesise the fragmented consciousness of an uprooted people, her people:

> This is why, above all, we have to have our secret language. We must create this language. It is high time we did. We are too old a people not to. We can. We must. So that we shall make love with words and not fear of being overheard.

This secret language that Ama Ata Aidoo searches for in *Our Sister Killjoy* highlights the complex issue of the writer's re- lationship to her audience. The novel, both structurally and thematically, resists identification with Western male literary traditions, but Aidoo also appears to be implicitly questioning the ways in which the First World feminist reader can enter African female-centred realities and interpret the unfamiliar codes produced by the text. We are attracted to a story about an 'African New Woman' whose journey into Europe's 'heart of darkness' turns the exotic, reified image of womanhood on its head and explores the growing consciousness of a woman coming to terms with her own identity and means of self-fulfilment. But does this signal a common terrain for female identification? As non-Africans, we are reminded that our 'listening-in' is intrusive and prevents Aidoo from speaking directly to her own people. Like other African women writers, such as Bessie Head and Buchi Emecheta, Aidoo purposely wants to keep her 'outsider' audience at a self-conscious distance—a political and literary device that makes the First World feminist reader all the more aware of her limited vision and need to resist universalising female experience and expectations which are not only culturally specific but politically charged.

In *Our Sister Killjoy* Ama Ata Aidoo makes a forceful plea to her African compatriots who are transplanted on a spiritually barren foreign soil to return home. Their moral and cultural values are misdirected and fragmented, and her adoption of the modern 'novel' form reflects these Western concerns. But Aidoo, in an attempt to articulate the modern dilemmas facing her people, has combined both poetry and prose as a means of juxtaposing the political against the personal. A satirical, political voice serves as a backdrop to highlight the personal adventures and inner feelings, narrated in the third person, of the main character, Sissie, as she goes to Europe and experiences what it means to be a Black woman in an alien environment. The naïve Sissie embarks on a journey of self-discovery and returns home to Africa a much stronger, more independent and self-assured woman who realises, despite the pain and bitterness it causes, what her responsibility to her people—and ultimately herself—entails. As Sissie's consciousness develops, Aidoo weaves in poetry that resembles the form of a song with its chorus-like structure and variations on a theme. The poetry/song is echoing Sissie's individual experiences on a wider more generalised landscape. The poetry parts of the novel resemble the function and structure of the epic tale which, originally based on oral improvisation and connected to preliterate cultures, has a cyclical structure that evokes a journey motif. Aidoo's African epic, tragic in character and moral in tone, has an impersonal, dignified narrative style which is more remote and objective than Sissie's personal narrative but is none the less closely connected as Aidoo weaves a fine line between subjective and objective responses, between personal dilemmas and political concerns. In this novel Sissie emerges as the female version of the epic hero who wants to fight for the honour and survival of her people.

So why does Aidoo end her novel with a letter? After two plays and several short stores that draw on the tradition of oral storytelling, is Aidoo now ominously warning of the death of communal art, of her own art? Despite her intention to engage her audience, is 'our sister' so disillusioned that she is gloomily forecasting, in true 'killjoy' fashion, the end of her role as a storyteller? Or is Aidoo hinting at another type of closure that wants to leave behind, to exclude all those who do not share her African female-centred consciousness, a consciousness turned in on itself as a means of resisting attempts to appropriate an image of African womanhood for needs other than the writer's own?

Perhaps the answers lie in the epic form itself: the opening lines of the novel point to the cyclical nature of Sissy's voyage where she sets off alone to rescue her people and returns home alone, the tragedy being that her people wanted to be left behind. But her own needs become visible as she refuses to compromise with both her African brothers and Western demands. The woman warrior retains a sense of her integrity as she searches for a language that cannot betray her, a language that rejects 'so much of the softness and meekness . . . all the brothers expect of me and the sisters . . . which is really western', as well as a language that would affirm her own self worth and is more honourable than a compromise with a 'private white audience for whom [the superior monkey] performs his superior tricks'. Nameless to others, the archetypal Sissie names a new African female identity that does not merely define itself in relation to others, but an identity which values its relationship to itself.

The opening five pages of **Our Sister Killjoy** indicate the way Aidoo envisions the relationship between form and content. The irony of the opening lines: 'Things are working out / towards their dazzling conclusions' which are placed on the stark background of two otherwise empty pages, emphasise both the irrelevancy of the 'ticky-tackies' that 'surround', 'block' and 'clutter' lives/pages and the frightening prophecy that 'things are working out', seemingly against one's control. But Aidoo's carefully controlled language attacks that very premise that 'talks of universal truth, universal literature and the Gross National Product'. These are the ideas that have made her people lose touch with their sense of history, a history that evokes 'the massive walls of slave forts standing along our beaches'. The empty opening pages symbolise both the loss of language and the uselessness of a false language as spoken by the 'moderate' and 'academic-pseudo-intellectual' Africans who, like dogs, chase the 'latest crumbs' being thrown at them by defending interests that 'are not even [their] own'. Aidoo's novel is addressed primarily to her African 'brothers' who, not wanting to confront their victimisation, are only perpetuat-

ing it, unaware of how they are hurting their own people. As an educated African, Aidoo shares some of her brothers' experiences and thus understands their dilemmas abroad; but as a woman, her experiences have placed her outside of their reality as well.

The full title of the novel, **Our Sister Killjoy: or, Reflections from a Black-Eyed Squint,** establishes Sissy's perception of her brothers—or rather their ironic view of her—as well as her attitude to the world in general. Whose 'sister' is she? Obviously her fellow Africans recognise her as one of them, as 'belonging to the elite, whatever that is', as one of the 'migrant birds of the world'. But through her use of irony, Sissy clearly indicates she is buying no part of their dreams, a true killjoy who recognises that 'migrations are part of the general illusion of how well an unfree population think they can do for themselves'. Her criticisms and anger directed at her own people leave them defensive and her full of despair. Despite the numerous references to her own naïveté, the self-conscious Sissy, 'from knowledge gained since', is able to see the world more clearly through her black-eyed squint. What she sees is neither joyful nor hopeful, for until her brothers realise how much they are needed at home, Sissy will distinctly remain a lost sister and a lost lover—her need for Africa greater than her need for romance.

After the initial five pages of the novel, Sissy leads us 'into a bad dream' where she journeys into that unreal, foreign territory of nightmarish Europe. The opening chapter serves as a type of chorus, a prologue which frames the action of the rest of the novel. The recurring symbols like food, archetypal 'Sammys' and consumer goods are juxtaposed against feelings of distaste, distress and powerlessness as Sissy begins to gain a self-conscious awareness about 'where', 'when' and 'how' her people lost control of their own lives and found themselves without a language to fill the blank spaces on the page. Her sarcasm and satire reveal a political awareness that doesn't uphold the supremacy of Western values, an awareness which essentially mocks the hypocrisy of those who want 'to make good again'. Sissy had been chosen to go to Europe, something that 'her fellow countryman' had seen as a kind of 'dress rehearsal for a journey to paradise'. This man, whose real name she was never to discover, was referred to by her European hosts as 'Sammy'. His enthusiasm, eagerness to please and familiarity with them 'made her feel uneasy' and her distaste would never disappear as 'Time was to bring her many many more Sammys. And they always affected her in the same way'.

Sissy's journey of self-development continues when she is made conscious of her Blackness, ironically by someone speaking a language she barely understands, and 'for the rest of her life, she was to regret this moment when she was made to notice the difference in human colouring'. The harsh reality of 'Power, Child, Power' is a nightmare from which Sissy can't escape as she 'came to know that someone somewhere would always see in any kind of difference, an excuse to be mean'. The episode ends with a kind of epic simile that evokes the relationship between power and exploitation, between 'any number of plums' and the suffering of the powerless.

The second and longest chapter, **'The Plums',** recounts Sissy's personal experiences as a Black woman working with an international youth group planting Christmas trees in southern Germany. The absurdity of the Bavarian widows who were attempting to purge their guilt and fill in the gaps of their own lives left damaged by a war they wanted to forget was not lost to the black-eyed squint. Against this background Sissy meets a German woman, Marija, who comes to symbolise everything that was unnatural and tragic about the isolation of life in Europe. Marija is in a sense also a widow, a victim of a society that had destroyed bonds between people. Forced into a stultifying existence where looking after her son was her one pleasure, Marija lives her life through her son, hoping her Little Adolph would make it, 'would go to university, travel and come back to tell her all about his journeys'. Forced to think about her own mother, the African Mother, Sissy reflects on the universal loneliness of motherhood and the contradictions women are faced with when they are denied lives of their own but feel guilty when they desire 'to be alone. . . . Just for a very little time . . . may be?':

> It is
> Heresy
>
> In Africa
> Europe,
> Everywhere.
>
> This is
> Not a statement to come from a
> Good mother's lips-
>
> . . .
>
> Yet
> Who also said that
> Being alone is not like
> Being
> Alone?

These lines, like the other poetic passages in the novel, although not part of the action, reflect Aidoo's internal comments which are triggered off by the action in the story. The poetry attempts to place the personal conflicts in a broader context to illustrate that suffering and powerlessness are not isolated, individual problems but part of a whole system that continues to survive by feeding off individual misery. The poetic voice is more Aidoo than Sissy, but in the last chapter, as Sissy returns home, the separation between poetry and prose disappears. Sissy's and Aidoo's voices merge to reconstruct 'that secret language', the only hope left for their people. Marija is distinctly excluded from this language, although her life epitomises what it means to be a woman anywhere in the world:

> Any good woman
> In her senses
> With her choices
> Would say the
> Same
>
> In Asia
> Europe
> Anywhere:
>
> For
> Here under the sun,
> Being a woman
> Has not
> Is not
> Cannot
> Never will be a
> Child's game
>
> From knowledge gained since
> So why wish a curse on you child
> Desiring her to be a female
> ?
> Beside, my sister
> The ranks of the wretched are
> Full,
> Are full.

Although in theory Aidoo speaks of a shared sisterhood, Sissy, the woman warrior, believes that her first priority is to honour her own people. Her interactions with Marija force her to examine her own life and she comes to learn that a shared loneliness does not create a sustaining life-force: Sissy has much empathy for Marija's fate but their world views and cultural differences artificially bring them together and naturally pull them apart. Aidoo explores the cultural differences through the use of food and the women's misreadings of each other's concept of hospitality. Food, that universal symbol of sharing and nourishment, is also a symbol of hospitality turned sterile and unnatural.

The symbolic significance of food emerges in **'The Plums'** chapter as Aidoo establishes not only the relationship between women and food production, as represented by Marija's generous sharing of food and Sissy's 'The Bringer-of-Goodies-After-Lights-Out' role, but also depicts the obscenity of food surplus in the West where people stuff themselves in an attempt to satisfy other unfulfilled desires. This is symbolised through the depiction of Marija's sexual frustrations and the hypocrisy of foreign aid and the Third World rulers who feed themselves 'intravenously' with riches, oblivious to the poverty in their own peoples' lives. Against Aidoo's angry poetic voice we see Sissy and her companions 'benefiting' from Western hospitality as they 'were required to be there, eating, laughing, singing, sleeping and eating. Above all eating,' Their function was purely symbolic: why should they worry about anything, 'even if the world is rough, it's still fine to get paid to have an orgasm . . . or isn't it?'.

The tinned, synthetic, unnatural food represents Europe itself where those who embrace it end up ghosts of their former slaves:

> Brother
> The internal logic is super-cool:
> The only way to end up a cultural
> Vulture
> Is to feed on carrion all the way . . .

Sissy is initially seduced by the overabundance and the novelty of the food, particularly the plums, which represent her desire to experience a new world. But 'in knowledge gained since', Sissy is able to reflect back on the nature of Marija's hospitality which placed Sissy in the dangerous position of being the object of someone else's dreams and desires.

Marija's preoccupation with feeding Sissy reveals the frustrated, unnatural life Marija is forced to live where she is deprived of a community of human activity. Her life-giving past, which reminds Sissy of her own background, makes a sharp contrast to her sterile present:

> They grew in her mother's garden. The black currants did. Plenty, plenty. And every summer since she was little, her one pleasure had been preserving black currants—making its jam, bottling its juices. And she still went home to help. Or rather, she went to avail herself of the pleasure, the beauty, the happiness at harvest time: of being with many people, the family. Working with a group. If they had met earlier, she could have taken Sissy home for that year's harvest.

The 'plenty, plenty' of her childhood community is now a nostalgic memory that she tries to reproduce by giving all of herself to Sissy who represents everything the German woman lacks in her own life. Though flattered, Sissy recognises that Marija's loss of her sense of self is born out of a 'kind of loneliness overseas which is truly bad', a disease like 'the cold loneliness of death' which is slowly killing Aidoo's own people whom she fears will also become ghosts of their former selves.

As well as using Marija as a vehicle for forcing Sissy to examine her own life, Aidoo also uses the relationship between the two women to explore gender roles and note specific contrasts between Western women's and African women's lives. When she arrives on foreign soil, Sissy detects that it is not at all 'normal' 'for a young / Hausfrau to / Like / Two Indians / who work in / supermarkets', and realises that Marija 'was too warm for Bavaria, Germany' where prying neighbours thought that a friendship between a Black woman and a white woman who didn't even speak the same language was something perverse: 'SOMEONE MUST TELL HER HUSBAND'. Despite Sissy sensing 'a certain strangeness about Marija', she had no reason to question whether ulterior motives lay behind her hospitality. When Marija makes sexual advances, the surprised Sissy is able to empathise with Marija's tear-shaped

> L
> O
> N
> E
> L
> I
> N
> E
> S
> S

'like a rain cloud over the chimneys of Europe', that has forced her into the alienated position of sexually desiring other women. In this context, Aidoo appears to perceive lesbianism as a reaction against a culturally specific type of isolation but does not accept it as an alternative for a better world: it remains a symptom of a woman's pain in an unhealthy society where individuals' sexually repressed desires force them into extreme behavior patterns. 'How then does one / Comfort her / Who weeps for / A collective loss?'.

Before Sissy is confronted with Marija's motives (whether Marija herself is conscious or unconscious of a sexual longing remains ambiguous), she plays with the idea of being a man and imagines 'what a delicious love affair she and Marija would have had if one of them had been a man':

> Especially if she, Sissie had been a man. She had imagined and savoured her tears, their anguish at knowing that their love was doomed. But they would make promises to each other which of course would not stand a chance of getting fulfilled. She could see Marija's tears. . . .

Although only a 'game', this type of gender-role-playing lets

Aidoo explore male/female relationships and question why Black men become involved with European women when it is clear 'The Guest Shall Not Eat Palm-Nut Soup'. Despite the exceptional 'successes' of such relationships, most end up leaving the black men 'lost', 'Changed into elephant-grey corpses. . . . Their penises cut.' Racist societies have no compassion and Sissy is determined not to forget this. But later, when Marija hears of Sissy's imminent departure, Sissy finds herself enjoying the pain she was causing the German woman:

> It hit her like a stone, the knowledge that there is pleasure in hurting. A strong three-dimensional pleasure, an exclusive masculine delight that is exhilarating beyond all measure. And this too is God's gift to man? She wondered.

Aidoo is attempting to make a parallel between racial and sexual exploitation. Sissy is able to exploit Marija as long as Marija continues to be the masochistic female just as the white man is able to exploit the Black man as long as the Black man continues to play the scapegoat. Sissy in many ways becomes impatient with Marija's 'femaleness', but having the humanity and insight due to her own recognised vulnerability, Sissy reflects: 'Whoever created us gave us too much capacity for sorrow'. It is the socially constructed systems that force people into unhealthy behaviour patterns, and Aidoo makes it clear that gender divisions, like racial divisions, must be exposed for their absurd and frightening distortion of human potential. The intolerant and incompassionate environment of the cold European nightmare affects all people in different ways, and as Sissy leaves Marija, taking with her memories of the tragedies of wasted possibilities in the form of some plums, Aidoo's poetic voice can be heard echoing through layers of Sissy's consciousness:

> We are the victims of our History and our Present.
> They place too many obstacles in the Way of Love.
> And we cannot enjoy even our Differences in peace.

In the third chapter, Our Sister shifts her ground to explore the alienation of her own people living in the 'cold strange land where dogs and cats eat better than many children'. Having sympathetically understood the isolation of Western women's lives, the African Sissy does not need the rallying cry 'Sisterhood is powerful': her own experiences and history force her to see 'group survival' from another angle. Arriving in England, she is astonished at the number of wretched Black people and 'wondered why they stayed'. She remarks that the women were especially pitifully dressed in tattered, cheap clothes and knows that 'in a cold land, poverty shows as nowhere else'. But she begins to articulate her anguish at hearing the feeble excuses and outrageous lies her people have invented in order to justify their betrayal of their own families: 'We have all fallen victim, / Sometime or / Other'.

As Sissy dismisses the ignorance of those non-Africans she meets who think the thing that 'binds the Germans, the Irish and the African—in that order naturally—together' is 'OPPRESSION', she is forced to examine the attitudes of her own people and realises 'every minute, every day . . . Ghana opened a dance of the masquerades called Independence, for Africa'. The consciousness that shapes the African experience abroad takes the form of Kunle in this chapter, another 'Sammy' who defends 'science' without grasping a moral sense of his own history as witnessed by his justification of the Christian doctor who used a South African Black man's heart to save a white man:

> Yet she had to confess she still had not managed to come round to seeing Kunle's point: that cleaning the bassa's chest of its rotten heart and plugging in a brand-new, palpitatingly warm kaffirheart, is in the surest way to usher in the Kaffirmillennium.

Kunle ends up 'killed by the car for which he had waited for so long', and Sissy mourns for him and all the others who symbolically are killed by false Western promises and tricked into embracing the 'security' offered by their ex-colonial masters:

> although the insurance policy had been absolutely comprehensive, the insurance people had insisted it did not cover a chauffeur driving at 80 M.P.H. on the high road. . . . He had taken out his policy with a very reliable insurance company . . . Foreign, British, terribly old and solid, with the original branch in London and cousins in Ottawa, Sydney, Salisbury and Johannesburg. . . .

The novel ends with Sissy's letter—to that one special brother, to all her African brothers, but ultimately to herself. It speaks about the importance of language, of group survival and of reconstructing the future. It celebrates Sissy's strength as a woman but mourns what she has lost as a result of her newly defined womanhood. The letter is full of pain and compassion and to me is one of the most moving personal statements found in African literature today.

Aidoo's and Sissy's voices merge to explain how language still remains a collective creation that can only have value if people recognise what Sissy's 'killjoy' function serves:

> Of course, we are different. No, we are not better than anybody else. But somewhere down the years, we let the more relaxed part of us get too strong. So that the question was never that of changing into something that we have never been. No, we only

need to make a small effort to update the stronger, the harder, the more insensitive part of ourselves.

Sissy recognises the dialectic between the past and the present, between the 'loss of perspective' and the language that will recapture it: 'the question is not just the past or the present, but which factors out of both the past and the present represent for us the most dynamic forces for the future'. Sissy empathises with her people who 'have been caught at the confluence of history and that has made ignorant victims of some of us', but condemns her people for remaining 'past masters for fishing out death', for staying in Europe where all they have learned is 'how to die':

> To come all this way just to learn how to die from a people whose own survival instincts have not failed them once yet. . . . I do not laugh enough . . . I remember how my old friends and I used to scream with mirth at home, looking at how we were all busy making fools of ourselves. . . . Maybe it was the sun and the ordinary pleasure of standing on our own soil. . . . Our beautiful land? One wonders whether it is still ours. And how much longer it will continue to be. . . .
>
> A curse on all those who steal continents!

By attempting to reconstruct a new language in the hope of communicating with her people, Sissy also reclaims her lost identity as an African woman. Yet she can only do this by not sending the letter: her initial intention in writing the letter was to tell her brother how much she missed him, how much she needed and loved him, 'whatever that means'. But she gives up romance in favour of her own dignity and self-integrity. Aidoo's closure, which appears to destroy the communal function of language, really marks the birth of a new female African identity that has rejected its 'otherness' and returned home, the letter being an affirmation of how much Sissy is worth to herself.

As Aidoo's fictional character returns to its source, the difficult journey of the African woman writer continues. Ama Ata Aidoo speaks openly about the hardships she encounters in her own patriarchal culture that ignores or silences women's voices, voices that want, above all, to be heard at home, from their own centre:

> I am convinced that if *Killjoy* or anything like it had been written by a man, as we say in these parts, no one would have been able to sleep a wink these last couple of years, for all the noise that would have been made about it. If *Killjoy* has received recognition elsewhere, it is gratifying. But that is no salve for the hurt received because my own house has put a freeze on it.'

Aidoo goes on to recount the story of how one of her own colleagues at an African university appeared to dismiss women's literature as not being of importance in Africa:

> Dialogue, January 1980: My head of department (a good friend and a well-known writer himself) and I are discussing the latest edition of the book which had just then come out in New York. We are both going on about how well laid out it is, the beautiful type used, etc. Then I remark that unfortunately my impression is that the publishers don't seem to care much whether they sell it or not.
>
> 'What a shame,' says he, 'because there are all these women's-studies programs springing up in universities all over the United States. Surely *they* would be interested in it . . .'
>
> And I bled internally. Because although the protagonist of the story is a young woman, anyone who read the book would realize that her concerns are only partially feminist, if at all. In any case, what if they are? Feminism is about half of the human inhabitants of this earth!

At First World feminists, we 'listen-in' from an unprivileged position in an attempt to understand the kind of parameters that determine African women's writing, parameters that highlight the political difficulties of deconstructing feminism in an international context.

FURTHER READING

Criticism

Afzal-Khan, Fawzia. Review of *No Sweetness Here and Other Stories,* by Ama Ata Aidoo. *World Literature Today* 71, No. 1 (Winter 1997): 205-6.
    Praises Aidoo for portraying women who learn to be strong in the face of men's fickleness and abuse.

Owusu, Kofi. "Canons under Siege: Blackness, Femaleness, and Ama Ata Aidoo's *Our Sister Killjoy." Callaloo* 14, No. 2 (Spring 1990): 341-63.
    Probes the unusual structure and symbolism of Aidoo's novel.

Wilentz, Guy. "The Politics of Exile: Ama Ata Aidoo's *Our Sister Killjoy." Studies in Twentieth Century Literature* 15, No. 1 (Winter 1991): 159-73.
    Praises Aidoo for confronting those who have forgotten their duty to rebuild their homeland.

Additional coverage of Aidoo's life and career is contained in the following sources published by Gale: *Black Writers,* Vol. 1; *Contemporary Authors,* Vol. 101; and *Dictionary of Literary Biography,* Vol. 117.

Mariama Bâ

1929-1981

Senegalese novelist.

INTRODUCTION

Senegalese novelist Mariama Bâ did not publish her first book—*Une si longue lettre* (*So Long a Letter;* 1980)—until she was fifty-one. That book and *Un chant ecarlate* (*Scarlet Song*), which was released in 1981, after Bâ's death, are the author's only published books. Both novels depict African women struggling against an oppressive society, an issue which Bâ often addressed publicly in her lifetime. Bâ also expressed concern for such issues as women's education, polygamy, child custody, and women's legal rights in marriage. Despite the short span of her writing career, Bâ is widely viewed as an influential author who contributed to the understanding and appreciation of the unique challenges faced by African women; she was honored with the first Noma Award for *So Long a Letter.*

Biographical Information

Bâ was born in 1929 in Dakar, Senegal. Her mother died when Bâ was very young, and Bâ was sent to live with her maternal grandparents, although she maintained a relationship with her father, whose duties as a politician and civil servant (he was the first Senegalese Minister of Health) required him to travel extensively. Although Bâ was reared in a traditional Muslim family and environment, she also attended school and was recognized as an exceptional student. Bâ's academic gifts led to her secondary education at the École Normale, a rare privilege for a young Senegalese in the 1940s. Following her graduation from the École Normale, Bâ worked as a teacher for twelve years, beginning with a job at the School of Medicine in Dakar, where she became a regional school inspector. Bâ's own family experiences informed her writings. She often acknowledged the positive influence of her father, who encouraged her to read and to speak French, and her grandmother, from whom Bâ learned dedication to her religion and spirituality as well as a firm devotion to living a virtuous, honorable life. Bâ married a politician, Obeye Diope, with whom she had nine children; they eventually divorced. Bâ died following a long illness in 1981.

Major Works

So Long a Letter relates the story of Ramatoulaye, whose husband abandons her to pursue a relationship with a younger woman. Ramatoulaye's story is revealed as she writes a letter to her friend, Aissatou, while she mourns her husband's death for the lengthy period dictated by Islamic law. As Ramatoulaye reflects on her life, the reader is introduced to Aissatou, whose husband also married a second time. She, unlike Ramatoulaye, who remained in Senegal, chose to go against tradition and leave her husband, establishing a life and career independent of him. Ramatoulaye, contemplating the condition of women in her society, is roused to fury when her brother-in-law, fulfilling his duty according to tradition, asks her to marry him. Expressing her anger and frustration with being viewed by society as property, Ramatoulaye refuses his proposal, asserting, "You forget that I have a heart and a head, that I am not just an object that one passes from one hand to the next." Although she does not choose divorce, Ramatoulaye demonstrates that her ideas about her role and her value as a woman have evolved by the novel's end. In *Scarlet Song,* Bâ again depicts the story of a woman whose husband marries a second time. Mireille, a French woman, marries Ousmane, her Senegalese classmate. Her father rejects her because she has married a black man. Mireille and Ousmane return to Africa after the marriage, but the relationship soon deteriorates due to their cultural differences. Ousmane abandons Mireille and their son for Ouleymatou, a traditional Senegalese woman. Powerless and rejected by both her husband and her family, Mireille goes insane. Realizing that her son will not gain societal acceptance just as she has not, Mireille kills him in a rage; later that evening, she attacks and wounds Ousmane. At the end of the book, Mireille is in the custody of the French Embassy.

Critical Reception

Critics responded favorably to Bâ's novels, lauding them as moving and effective portrayals of the plight of women in traditional African society. Charles Ponnuthurai Sarvan characterized *So Long a Letter* as a feminist novel, and noted its demonstration of how women affect each other's lives. "Women play a significant role in breaking up Ramatoulaye's and Aissatou's respective marriages," he wrote. Likewise, Nancy Topping Bazin felt that Ba's depiction of relations between African women is an important feature in *So Long a Letter.* One of the reasons Ramatoulaye refuses to wed her suitor is that he is already married—she does not want to inflict on his wife the same suffering she experienced. Bazin suggested that Ramatoulaye's decision illustrates that "this is the kind of female solidarity that can defeat polygamy." Sarvan noted that Ramatoulaye demonstrates her transcendence of the bounds of her society by her ability to support her unmarried, pregnant daughter in spite of the disapproval expressed over her condition by traditional society. Sarvan declared that *Scarlet Song* depicts Africa as a more "vibrant and real" world than European culture and identified the conflict between Mireille and Ouleymatou "as a conflict between principle and passion, between Europe and Africa, rather than between individuals." Bazin, on the other hand, asserted that the novel emphasizes the need for change to a better and more equal society. Bazin maintained that *Scarlet Song* demonstrates that "love can only thrive in an egalitarian relationship, and egalitarian relationships are rare in a context of patriarchal customs." She explained, "The powerlessness of the African female within her own home and within her husband's family is matched . . . [in *Scarlet Song*] by the portraits of the French mother and daughter." Mireille and her mother, though part of different societies, are equally powerless, each suffering in her own world of pain and loneliness. Both of Bâ's books deal with the problems faced by women in Senegalese society, a society laden with traditional values. In Bazin's opinion, the extent to which these women accept the customs of their society also determines the limitations they place on the choices available to them. Sarvan noted that in Bâ's novels "the position of women is an element in a total culture." Thus, while aware of the need for change in an oppressive society, Bâ also shows a concern about the effect of these changes on the uniqueness of African culture. Therefore, Sarvan stated, Bâ's novels "are questioning and explorative rather than radical and imperative."

PRINCIPAL WORKS

Une si longue lettre [*So Long a Letter*] (novel) 1980
Un chant ecarlate [*Scarlet Song*] (novel) 1981

CRITICISM

Charles Ponnuthurai Sarvan (essay date Autumn 1988)

SOURCE: "Feminism and African Fiction: The Novels of Mariama Bâ," in *Modern Fiction Studies*, Vol. 34, No. 3, Autumn, 1988, pp. 453-64.

[*In the following essay, Sarvan examines Bâ's handling of women's life experiences within African cultures.*]

In Chinua Achebe's *No Longer at Ease*, Obi is asked the meaning of his name on the assumption that "all African names mean something." With a modesty and an incisiveness more characteristic of the author than of his fictional

creation, Obi replies, "Well, I don't know about African names—Ibo names, yes." Obi, although a Nigerian, doesn't feel able to make comments about Nigeria (much less Africa) but only about his own people, the Igbos. So too, one cannot speak about feminism and *African* literature, especially in a journal article, and hence the immediate limitation in the title above. The focus here will be on the contradictions and tensions in Mariama Bâ's novels. Africa is a vast and varied continent, and one can generalize only in glib fashion, as if regional, cultural, and class factors did not influence the position of women. For example, M.G. Marwick, in describing the matrilineal cewa, states that at marriage a man goes to live in his wife's village and that the maternal uncle has greater authority over a child than even the father. As Ramatoulaye, the first-person narrator of *So Long a Letter* reflects, Africa is diverse: even within a single country there are changes in attitudes as one moves from north to south and east to west. The cultural significance attached to the fact of a person being female changes not only from country to country, but, at any given time, *within* it. For example, in contemporary Africa, whether one lives in a town or in a remote village, whether one belongs to the new elite or to the urban proletariat, little has changed since independence.

African writers such as Chinua Achebe and Ngugi Wa Thiong'o have long enjoyed an international reputation, and Wole Soyinka won the Nobel Prize last year in recognition of his work as dramatist, poet, novelist, and critic. The works of Olive Schreiner, Doris Lessing, and Nadine Gordimer are also famous, but black women novelists have yet to gain an equal repute and readership—with the possible exception of the late Bessie Head. Mariama Bâ's *So Long a Letter* broke new ground and won the Noma award; even if one wished to, it would be difficult now to ignore the female condition and feminist black African writing. Growing critical attention is attested by the many conferences and discussions that are taking place both within and outside Africa and by the number of journals that devote attention to topics on women writers.

Before proceeding to Mariama Bâ's work, we must mention certain facts about Senegal relevant to a discussion of these novels. The country was a French colony and subjected to its imperial policy of assimilation—the effort to turn Africans into (black) French men and women. In this endeavor, everything African was condemned as barbaric so that the African, being ashamed, would abandon the old and take to the new (French) ways. The whites projected themselves as powerful, wise, and good people who had brought peace to warring tribes, formal education to illiterates, and medical facilities and knowledge to those who didn't know the basics of hygiene. Nonwhites were made to feel it was both a misfortune and a humiliation that one was not white, and because skin color cannot be changed, the individual was condemned to life-long feelings of inferiority and unhappiness.

> Africa
> This rich granary
> Of taboos, customs,
> Traditions . . .
> Mother, mother,
> Why
> Why was I born
> Black?

In practice, however, little attempt was made to educate the broad mass of Africans: the focus, instead, was on a small minority, an elite who, cutting itself off from the people, would collaborate with Western commercial interests. (The British adopted the policy of "indirect rule" through local chiefs, their excuse being that the natives were being prepared for self-government although, of course, the "natives" had been governing themselves before the arrival of European technological and, therefore, military superiority.) The reaction to assimilation often came from the assimilated: partly because their education enabled them to penetrate the fraud, partly because the elite found that despite a fluency in French language and French ways, they would never, because of their visually distinguishing color, be fully accepted. Further, the prestige accorded to European technological power meant that Europeans were treated in the colonies with greater deference than the native elite, much to the latter's chagrin.

Senegal became independent in June 1960 and was ruled by Leopold Senghor until the end of 1980 when he voluntarily handed over power to his nominee, Abdou Diouf. Senghor has been described as "one of the most highly assimilated of French Africans" [Michael Crowder, *Senegal: A Study in French Assimilation,* 1962] and almost more French than the French. Coming from a wealthy family, Senghor developed the argument that class divisions existed not within African countries but between rich (Western) and poor nations. Discouraging mass politicization and participation, he called for "national unity"—a ploy adopted by dictators, "Life-presidents," and one-party states. (It was partly a ploy, partly an idealization of the African past—a vision of an idyllic, communal past, partly a refusal to accept that under his rule class divisions had widened.) "Senghor was committed to an elitist approach" [Irving Markovitz, *Senghor and the Politics of Negritude,* 1969], and the gulf between the privileged and the disinherited is vast. Another writer claims that corruption is endemic in Senegal, working always to "the advantage of a privileged elite" [Donald Cruise O'Brien, *Saints and Politicians,* 1975]—in a poor country, arid and without valuable minerals. The population today is about seven million, with the rate of illiteracy being over seventy percent. Life expectancy in 1984 was forty-five years for males and

forty-eight for females. Although Senghor is a Christian, ninety-one percent of the population is Moslem. Only a small minority work in paid, regular employment; the majority of people depend precariously on subsistence farming. The country's budget deficit, running into billions of Senegalese francs, has increased with each passing year. Mariama Bâ's father was Minister of Health, and her husband, from whom she was divorced after bearing nine children, was Minister of Information. She died in 1981 at the age of 52 after a long illness; her second novel was published posthumously.

In *So Long a Letter,* a short epistolary novel, Ramatoulaye writes to her friend Aissotou who works as an interpreter in the Senegalese Embassy in the United States. When Aissotou's husband, Mawdo, took a second wife, Nabou, she left him, studied at the School of Interpreters, and made an independent life for herself and the children. When Modou Fall, after thirty years of married life and twelve children, does the same, Ramatoulaye, unlike Aissotou, decides to remain, even though Modou Fall marries Binetou, the classmate and friend of one of their daughters. Modou Fall had courted Binetou in secret, deceiving Ramatoulaye and the children and, lacking courage, sent the priest and friends to inform Ramatoulaye after the marriage ceremony was over. The *Koran* warns that a man may marry again, but he must treat all his wives equally; but Modou Fall neglects Ramatoulaye and the children completely, neither visiting nor sending them money. Now, five years later, he is dead of a sudden heart attack, releasing memories, bitterness, and love in Ramatoulaye. The four months and ten days of seclusion imposed on widows gives her the opportunity to write a long letter to her absent friend Aissotou.

The novel is feminist, right from the dedication to all women and, additionally, to men of goodwill. Even at the death of a husband, the widow is subjected to various observances and customs, including the possibility that she will be inherited by one of her late husband's brothers. (The *Koran* urges men in general to marry widows; it was a man's obligation to marry his late brother's widow, thus affording her and her children protection and care.) A woman is abandoned or exchanged as if she were a commodity; married or single, she has little liberty: no "decent" woman can go out, for example to the cinema, unescorted. She is frequently the victim of physical assault; husbands, unable to win an argument, produce a knife to secure silence and obedience.

In Naruddin Farah's *From A Crooked Rib,* an illiterate peasant girl, Ebla, hardly more than a child when the novel opens, obscurely but strongly feels that the lot given to her by traditional Moslem society is unjust. Hers is an instinctive rebellion unlike that of the mature, wealthy, educated Ramatoulaye. The latter is a trained teacher feminized by her European headmistress, a woman who destined Ramatoulaye, Aissotou, and the other girls for the mission of female emancipation. The word "sisters" is the rallying term, like the socialist "comrades," for the new Africa and its new women. Formal education itself was a European import, and the elite were highly Westernized: for example, although believing and practicing Moslems, Ramatoulaye and her friends organize Christmas eve parties, and the old dances they revive turn out to be not traditional African dances but the rumba and the tango. Feminism with Ramatoulaye, unlike that of Elba, is both via and an aspect of assimilation.

The wealth and social position of the family becomes clear at the funeral of Modou Fall with which the novel commences. The procession consists of official and private cars, buses, and lorries, and most of those who come to condole are dressed in expensive clothes. It is the duty of the dead man's sisters to buy the widows' mourning clothes, and the sum raised, in this instance, is 200,000 francs. In 1980, around the time in which the novel is set, the average lowest income of someone in public employment was 29,587 francs per month whereas the highest was 231,288 [*Statistik Des Auslandes: Ländebericht Senegal 1987,* 1987]. Modou Fall had bought a villa for Binetou—the furniture had been imported from France—and two sports cars. At the age of 50, Ramatoulaye experienced for the first time in her life the tribulation of having to use public transport. Ramatoulaye's reaction to joining the long lines of people waiting for public transport is one of self-pity; her experiences do not lead to a broadening of sympathy. Fortunately, Aissotou comes to the rescue by paying for a new car; Ramatoulaye and her children can once again drive in comfort and dignity. In 1985, only 11.5 persons per thousand possessed cars [*Statistik*]. The much-admired Daouda Dieng sees national development not as a matter of self-reliance and mass participation but of "behaving" in such a way that confidence is inspired and foreign aid attracted. This class then is the one of which Ramatoulaye is a member.

From this elite perspective, huts almost become picturesque to Ramatoulaye—as to some visiting tourist who sees in them the "real" Africa but does not see the discomfort of actually living in them. The words of Ocol are apposite:

> We will not just
> Breach the wall
> Of your mud hut
> To let in the air . . .
> We will set it ablaze
> This lair of backwardness.
>
> [Okot p'Bitek, *Song of Ocol,* 1970]

Ramatoulaye and her friends buy cottages by the sea to escape from the city. On holiday, she envies the freedom of the naked and snotty-nosed children of the fisher-folk playing on the beach: it is the "freedom" of poverty, the freedom of children who have no clothes or toys and who are not able to attend school. Ramatoulaye idealizes poverty so as to avoid confronting it and, on the other hand, romanticizes physical labor. The fishermen, come ashore after hours spent in open boats under the hot sun, are cheerful; the sea air alone is sufficient to intoxicate the poor with health.

Despite the feminism of the novel, women play a significant role in breaking up Ramatoulaye's and Aissotou's respective marriages. In the latter's case, the royal mother-in-law, unable to accept that her son has married a goldsmith's daughter, schemes to have him married to Nabou whom she adopts and raises for that sole purpose. When she judges both the time and the girl "ripe," the royal lady simply presents her son with a second wife, warning that shame kills faster than disease. In Ramatoulaye's case, Binetou was reluctant to marry a man so much older than herself, but her mother, coming from a hut made of zinc sheets and with a face long faded in the smoke from the wood fire, begs Binetou to marry Modou so that she, the mother, can experience some material comfort before dying. Significantly, Ramatoulaye has a grudging admiration for Aissotou's royal mother-in-law but only contempt for Binetou and her mother whom she sees as parvenus, the latter particularly as she wallows in her new-found luxury, eating from the trough of good food, modern comforts, and amenities. In one of her novels, Nadine Gordimer ironically describes a women's liberation meeting in South Africa, organized by a white woman (Flora), to which black women are also invited. The white ladies are determined that the meeting will have "nothing to do" with politics, although it is apartheid politics that causes most of the country's problems. However, the economic gap, and therefore the educational and social gap, between white and black women proves too great, despite Flora's insistence on the unifying and "common possession of vaginas, wombs and breasts" [Nadine Gordimer, *Burger's Daughter,* 1979]. In *So Long a Letter,* the gap is not between white and black women but between black women who belong to two widely distanced classes.

Ramatoulaye's anger is because the wealth that should have flowed to her and her children has been diverted to a different destination. As in Achebe's *No Longer At Ease,* cooperate, communal living is being replaced by competition, the traditional, "extended" family by the nuclear family. The elite—educated, confident, self-sufficient—does not need that social insurance that the meticulous discharge of "extended family" obligations purchases in the Third World. On the contrary, it wishes to break free from such duties and demands, but a capitalist-orientated nuclear family finds it difficult to function in a polygamous society, for polygamy itself is an extension of the family. Modou Fall, a technical advisor and trade-union leader, a man on a fixed monthly salary, was able to buy sports cars and build villas. How and from where did he get such wealth? Rather than question closely, Ramatoulaye admires Modou for effecting minor improvements in the workers' lot and for leading them into compromise and collaboration. Husband and wife emphasized "national unity" and were against foreign ideologies, despite so much that was foreign in their thinking and lifestyle. Ramatoulaye, adopting an odd stance for a declared feminist, eschews politics, although political means are the surest ways to change laws and an unjust social order.

Part of Ramatoulaye's refusal to have anything to do with politics and public life stems from her wish not to endanger a system that, by and large, favored her class though not her sex. If women agitate overtly and aggressively, will not the poorer classes follow suit? (Just a few months ago—February 1988—President Diouf declared a state of emergency because of widespread unrest.) On balance, the economic and social loss might be greater than the feminist gain. Similarly, in South Africa where skin color and class coincide, Olive Schreiner is unusual because white female writers, for different reasons, have not often taken a feminist stand. Sarah Millin did not understand feminism—a call to loneliness, in her opinion—because she moved in the highest circles of a highly privileged (white) group; Doris Lessing, in her African phase, was a Marxist demanding the political enfranchisement of the black majority, and Nadine Gordimer sees all too clearly where the prime cause of the troubles besetting her country lie.

Ramatoulaye is a paradox, a conservative in revolt. She may endorse the European headmistress's exhortation to leave the bog of superstition, custom, and tradition, a call that equates African tradition with superstition and consigns both to the rubbish heap, but a part of her remains cautious, conservative, and "patriotic." The harshness and contempt reserved for the lower class that Binetou and her mother represent, and the very different treatment accorded to Mawdo's royal mother and Nabou, has already been mentioned. The latter are associated with Africa's heroic past: the retributive violence of the warrior, his reckless courage, his dusty combat, and thoroughbred horses. Of course, it is courage conceived of in aristocratic rather than in democratic terms. Like Camara Laye, Ramatoulaye regrets that traditional crafts decline into mere tourist art as the young artists choose European-run or European-modeled schools. In nonindustrialized countries, formal schooling and "paper qualifications" are sure avenues to well-paid jobs in the public sector. And as the individual rises, so does the extended family. Formal education is one means to an upward economic and social mobility, but traditional Ramatoulaye sees in young students only that lack of sensitivity to honor that leads to physical retaliation and assault. She who spoke about the bog of tradition also applauds the fierce resistance put up by old virtues against the inroads of imported vices. During the Algerian war of independence, the French attempted to compel Algerian women to discard their veils, but they clung to them: what was traditional was also national and, therefore, to be protected and preserved against foreign attack. Polygamy, which Ramatoulaye opposes, is sanctioned by Islam, a traditional religion, unlike Christianity. This is yet another contradiction and tension in devout, traditional, feminist Ramatoulaye. The conservative aspect of her character is also revealed in some of her opinions: for example, that cleanliness is one of the essential qualities of a woman and that a woman's mouth should be fragrant: but don't these qualities apply to men as well? Unwittingly, she casts women in the role of sex objects, attracting and seducing men into marriage. In spite of the decline in the conduct of young women, Ramatoulaye will not give her daughters immunity in pleasure. The price of sin is an unwanted pregnancy; such a pregnancy indicates theft, theft of virginity and of family honor. A woman who exposes any part of her body, like a woman who smokes, exposes a jaunty shamelessness.

And so Ramatoulaye the rebel becomes afraid of progress. (The negritude cry was "Assimilate but don't get assimilated," that is, assimilate elements but not to such an extent that you lose your distinctive and essential "Africanness"). Ramatoulaye's caution and skepticism seem to extend to Aissotou, her dear and faithful friend: Has Aissotou, because of her stay in the United States, become too Westernized? Will she insist on eating with a fork and knife, rather than with the hand? Will she wear trousers? And so Ramatoulaye continues to write her letter even after hearing that her old friend will return home on holiday, to write even on the very day before Aissotou's arrival. The letter has now become a diary, a form suggesting greater loneliness, beginning and ending with oneself.

In *So Long a Letter* we have one section of the elite (female) demanding fuller emancipation, insufficiently aware of the majority of women (and men and children) who lead very poor and difficult lives. It is interesting to contrast *So Long a Letter* with Sembene Ousmane's *God's Bits of Wood*, particularly since both are by Senegalese writers. The latter describes the wives of striking railway workers: Moslem women, most of them illiterate, wives of polygamous husbands, inhabiting little dwellings, living in close proximity and cooperation. Theirs is a hard existence and, with the strike, they and their children experience hunger and starvation. In such circumstances, they fight not against polygamy but for class emancipation. They bravely and fiercely stand with their husbands in the struggle for better wages, a measure of social security and pensions.

But to say that a greater injustice lies elsewhere is not to deny the injustice suffered by women such as Ramatoulaye. Besides, in Algeria, Kenya, and Zimbabwe (in historical order) women fought alongside the men in military and political struggles only to find that freedom meant a reimposition of traditional culture that, in turn, meant they were relegated to the old ways and excluded from power-sharing, except for the few token women in high government offices. From the perspective of a Western feminist, Mariama Bâ may not be a radical, for she does not attempt to "overthrow" the entire "system" that produces women's oppression and sexism, but, situated within her cultural context, Ramatoulaye takes a step in the right direction, and, although it is but a step, her daughters immediately follow and quickly go beyond. As Ramatoulaye reflects, the ground gained by her generation is not much and, in the face of male egoism, is difficult to retain, but she remains optimistic. Her caution does not mean a lack of courage, and although Ramatoulaye may fear that freedom can degenerate into immorality and license, she is remarkably flexible. There is perhaps no greater shame in a Moslem society than for a young, unmarried girl to become pregnant; yet, when this happens to her daughter, Ramatoulaye overcomes traditionally prescribed reactions (indignation, shame, revenge) and reaches out in support and love. In this way, she is willing to reexamine her values and attitudes, to accept the logical, further development of her stand by the Ramatoulayes and Aissotous of the next generation, and to relinquish leadership to them.

In *So Long a Letter,* Jacqueline from the Ivory Coast marries a Senegalese and returns with him to Senegal only to find herself abandoned. She suffers a breakdown and is admitted to the hospital's psychiatric ward. *Scarlet Song* elaborates on this story with the difference that the foreign woman, unlike Jacqueline, is white. Ousmane meets Mireille, daughter of a French diplomat, at school. They fall in love, but Monsieur Jean de La Vallée, Mireille's father, learns of their relationship and hustles his daughter out of the country. The pair are separated for five years, during which time each completes the M. A. in Philosophy. Ousmane is unable to forget Mireille; their love is in no way diminished by distance, time, intervening events, and travels to Paris. They are married in a registry and, according to Moslem rites, they return to Dakar where they both work as teachers. When the marriage strains, Ousmane meets Ouleymatou, his adolescent love, and marries her, unknown to Mireille, and gradually spends more and more time in the house he has set up for her and her family. Eventually and inevitably Mireille learns his secret and, after a struggle to encounter the situation, loses her sanity. Mireille gives their little son a fatal does of sleeping tablets and, when Ousmane comes home in the early hours of the morning, she attacks him with a kitchen knife. He is wounded but survives, and the police contact the French embassy to take charge of the deranged Mireille.

The tension in this novel is not within a fictional character but arises from conflicting sympathies for Ousmane as an *African* and Mireille as a *woman* who suffers greatly and undeservedly. Ousmane's marriage to a white woman is received as a misfortune, a reaction which he, a student of phi-losophy, does not examine but accepts. Wole Soyinka said that inasmuch as a tiger does not need to prove its tigritude, there was no necessity for Africans to proclaim and assert their negritude: it was self-evident. But Ousmane feels his marriage will call his credentials—as a Moslem, a male, an African—into question. He is torn between two worlds perceived to be mutually exclusive. The conflict within Ousmane is there in the text. Despite the evident effort, the author fails to create credible European characters, modes of conduct, and culture. For example, although Ousmane's father emerges as a pious, sincere human being, Mireille's father is the stereotype of the suavity that hides authoritarianism and racism. Mireille has golden hair; she is beautiful—and as distant as a film star. (Before their marriage, photographs of her in Ousmane's room were mistaken to be those of some film star. Ousmane's mother never accepts Mireille as a human being, as another woman's loved and cared for daughter; to her, she is unreal, a bewitching spirit. Notions of honesty, justice, and compassion do not enter into her treatment of Mireille. Foreigners, simply because they are foreigners, can be treated differently.) So too, Mireille's clothes are pretty, and she prepares dainty but "spiceless" and insubstantial meals. In contrast, Ouleymatou's figure is repeatedly described with delight and pride, and in sensual detail. Her layers of clothes are described down to the beads she wears around her waist for sexual titillation. The description of Ouleymatou's elaborate cooking includes her purchases and the entire process in savory detail. The baptism of Ousmane's and Mireille's son was a brief, staid matter; that of Ousmane's son with Ouleymatou, a colorful, extravagant ceremony marked by music, feasting, a procession, and the exchange of gifts. The African world, as in Laye's *The Radiance of the King,* is so vibrant and real, it seems right for Ousmane to abandon (Western) Mireille for (black African) Ouleymatou.

Mireille had not married Ousmane out of some obscure impulse to rebellion; she was genuinely in love with him. For his part, Ousmane once attributed his success to Mireille. While Ouleymatou had not completed primary school, Mireille was his intellectual equal and the ideal companion and "soul-mate." But those aspects that had once attracted now provoke disaffection; her ability to engage in discussion is seen as the Western urge to argue and dissect; her attempt to keep a clean and pleasing home seems obsessive fastidiousness. These criticisms of Ousmane—including his dishonesty—are made, but there is a strong undercurrent of sympathy for him, a sympathy trembling on the verge of vindication. The "competition" between the two women for Ousmane's love is seen as a conflict between principle and passion, between Europe and Africa, rather than between individuals. The scrupulous rationality and justice of the text is subverted by the heart of feeling for Ousmane, Ouleymatou, and things African.

This tug-of-war within the text leads to unintended ironies. A young French couple live in the same block of flats, and although they are on cordial terms with Ousmane and Mireille, the husband, Guillaume, privately refers to them as beauty and the beast. Ousmane's treatment of Mireille ironically appears to vindicate Guillaume's racist position that Africans cannot be trusted and that European women should not marry them. The portrayal of Africans as careless of cleanliness and order, warm-hearted, sensuous, and experienced in the arts of love is in keeping with the colonial view of Africans as simple, passionate children of nature. In marrying Ouleymatou, Ousmane sees himself as a cultural prodigal returning home, going back to his roots. But this return to Africa is accompanied by deceit, cruelty, and selfishness. (Mireille had brought her savings from France and opened a joint account; Ousmane secretly withdraws the money and lavishes it on Ouleymatou, her family and friends, and on his mother who is given to ostentatious living.) Loyalty, love, courage, and sacrifice are all reposed in Mireille in whom there is no trace of racism. The text appears unaware of its own implications. Senegalese men of the older generation who had married European women are taunted with the fact that they help in the house, the suggestion being that European women dominate and emasculate their husbands. Yet Ramatoulaye in *So Long a Letter* had approvingly observed that in her daughter's generation, young black Senegalese men were beginning to share in the work in the house.

In Mireille we see woman in one of the most vulnerable of situations: in a foreign country, in a culture that expresses considerable rejection and contempt, abandoned by her husband who had brought her there. She feels her son will not be accepted by her parents and their society; so there are no avenues of retreat, no paths of escape for her. It is exploitation at its unkindest.

In the novels of Mariama Bâ we see that feminism may at times overlook that economic inequality that affects the majority of women, children, and men. In the Third World, this inequality is great and the suffering of the poorer classes very real. In turn, this oversight may lead to the charge that feminism is lacking in breadth of sympathy (see Femi Ojo-Ade, "Still a Victim?," *African Literature Today,* 1982). Secondly, feminism here enters via European education and influence. The position of women is an element in a total culture: how can one alter an element and not affect the traditional African whole? But there is also the awareness that change is not only inevitable but welcome, that societies and cultures should not be static but dynamic. But at what speed and to which extent is change to be instituted? In ridding society of an undoubted injustice in its fabric, there is the danger of setting in motion centrifugal forces, of losing things that are essential to and distinctive of African culture, things of great value. Mariama Bâ does not write from a clear and cat-egorical standpoint; her novels are questioning and explorative rather than radical and imperative.

Rashidah Ismaili Abubakr (essay date 1993)

SOURCE: "The Emergence of Mariama Bâ," in *Essays on African Writing 1: A Re-Evaluation,* edited by Abdulrazak Gurnah, Heinemann, 1993, pp. 24-37.

[*In the following essay, Abubakr analyzes both* So Long a Letter *and* Scarlet Song, *considering Bâ's rendering of the challenges faced by African and Islamic women in their marriages, their sense of personal identity, and their difficulties with society in general.*]

Mariama Bâ emerges from a society that is both African and Islamic. She was born in Senegal in 1929, and died in 1981. Her writing takes women out of the parenthesis, and offers a direct and clear account to replace the variations which imply the pitiable position of African women in general and Islamic women in particular. The subject of *So Long a Letter* is a Senegalese marriage, while *Scarlet Song* is about a racially mixed one. Decline of personal and public morals, and betrayal of dreams and love echo in both. In her first novel betrayal leads to divorce and abandonment. The second novel has loss of self and culture, leading finally to madness and violence.

Mariama Bâ centres her work on individual figures whose lives are then elaborated with references which place their chronologies and histories. Both novels focus on women figures and their marriages as the means of opening up a wider debate on social and religious structures. Ramatoulaye in *So Long a Letter* is constantly aware that she is an African and Muslim woman, and is self-conscious about these aspects of her identity. Mireille in *Scarlet Song* suffers the consequences of her alienation and exclusion from her husband's Muslim African community. As Senegambian scholar Mbye B. Cham has said: 'In few other places in the creative traditions of sub-Saharan Africa is the factor of Islam more prominent and influential than in Senegal. Clearly Islam is central and forms a core around and through which Mariama Bâ 'tells her story'.

So Long a Letter takes the form of a 'long letter' from Ramatoulaye to her 'milk sister', Aissatou. The two women both married for love and were both later abandoned by their husbands. Ramatoulaye's letter carefully establishes her relationship to Aissatou as well as contextualising the events which befall them:

> I conjure you up. The past is reborn, along with its procession of emotions. I close my eyes. Ebb and

tide of feeling: heat and dazzlement, the woodfires, the sharp green mango, bitten into in turns, a delicacy in our greedy mouths. I close my eyes. Ebb and tide of images: drops of sweat beading your mother's ochre-coloured face as she emerges from the kitchen, the procession of young wet girls chattering on their way back from the spring.

Ramatoulaye begins her letter after the death of her estranged husband, Modou Fall. Through it we come to understand the power of definition of place and gender. Her rootedness in her culture enables Ramatoulaye to sit out the wearying funeral rituals with dignity despite the presence of the young co-wife and a greedy new mother-in-law: 'Comforting words from the Koran fill the air; divine words, divine instructions, impressive promises of punishment or joy, exhortations to virtue, warnings against evil, exaltations of humility, and faith'. This rootedness is significant in the contextualisation of her criticism. It asserts both allegiance and the right to speak strongly, and also enables Ramatoulaye to settle into the monotony of the expected four-month retreat:

> I hope to carry out my duties fully. My heart concurs with demands of religions. Reared since childhood on their precepts, I expect not to fail. The walls that limit my horizon for four months and ten days do not bother me. I have enough memories for me to ruminate upon. And these are what I am afraid of, for they smack of bitterness.

> May their evocation not soil the state of purity in which I must lie.

The burden of her letter is these 'memories', evoked in a searchingly introspective manner: memories of the marriages of Ramatoulaye and Modou Fall, and Aissatou and Mawdo Bâ. Aissatou's and Ramatoulaye's lives parallel each other in their long marriages, each over twenty years. Both women fulfil what has become an overworked appellation of definition: 'mother'. Ramatoulaye becomes the mother of twelve children, Aissatou four—and Aissatou's are all males!

Each woman is undone by the trickery of a mother-in-law. In Aissatou's case, her mother-in-law accepts her only reluctantly, despite her intellectual brilliance and beauty. Her father is a goldsmith and she is marrying into a noble family. She leaves her husband after he takes a second wife. Ramatoulaye elects to stay with her husband when *he* takes a second wife, despite the protests of her children. The young wife Modou marries is a school friend of his daughter Daba, a fact which disgusts his children. Daba says to Ramatoulaye: 'Break with him, mother . . . He has respected neither you nor me. Do what Aunty Aissatou did, break with him'. But Ramatoulaye does not break with him, and in her letter reflects on and analyses her decision:

I told myself what every betrayed woman says: if Modou was milk, it was I who had had all the cream—the rest, well, nothing but water with a vague smell of milk. But the final decision lay with me . . . Leave? Start again at zero, after living twenty-five years with one man after having borne twelve children? . . . Did I have enough energy to bear alone the weight of this responsibility which was both moral and material? Leave? Draw a clean line through the past—turn over a page on which not everything was bright, certainly, but at least all was clear.

Ramatoulaye debates the options available to women in her circumstances: she chooses to stay, Aissatou to leave, and the outcome of Jacqueline's marriage (another friend) remains uncertain. Modou's action is defended as the right of a Muslim man—by the Imam, by his brother Tamsir and by his friend Mawdo Bâ. Ramatoulaye argues that this action is not Islamic. Many suras were written to clarify the point of privilege men claimed at the expense of women, and the specific conditions which allow for multiple wives. The usual reasons for a new wife are barrenness on the part of the woman and 'protection' of the second wife. All of this has to be negotiated openly, and win the first wife's consent.

There are restrictions placed on the man. He must be able to provide for the second wife and he must be *fair* and equal in his affection and treatment of each woman. If he fails to keep his part of the bargain, the wives can seek redress and even divorce. Both Mawdo Bâ, Aissatou's husband, and Ramatoulaye's husband Modou Fall transgress these dictates by marrying without the consent of their first wives. That they were each aided by their mothers or, as in the case of Modou, also by an older woman's plot to insert her young daughter as his wife, is an example of women's complicity in their oppression.

As we have seen, Aissatou divorces Mawdo for his betrayal. She denies Mawdo excuses by reminding him of his former words of endearment:

> You want to draw a line between heartfelt love and physical love. I say there can be no union of bodies without the heart's acceptance, however little that may be . . .

> I am stripping myself of your love, your name. Clothed in my dignity, the only worthy garment, I go my way.

The disrobing in the 'stripping myself' is encoded. Aissatou becomes herself by disrobing. She takes off Mawdo's honour and refuses his reasons as hypocritical and dishonest. On his part, Mawdo is left 'completely disoriented'. His justification for his action is that in addition to obeying his mother's wish that he should marry again, 'the force of instincts in man' cannot be resisted. Ramatoulaye, the old friend to whom he offers these excuses, rejects them contemptuously.

In the brief tale of Jacqueline from Côte d'Ivoire, Ramatoulaye reflects on yet another response to abandonment. Jacqueline marries a Muslim. His family refuse her as their daughter because she remains faithful to her Protestant religion. This is even though Muslim law allows men to marry women of the Books (Jews and Christians), while forbidding women from doing the same. The pressure for Jacqueline to conform is enormous. Her estrangement, when it comes, is too much for her and leads to a nervous breakdown. With the help of a kind doctor, she faces her illness and that becomes the key to recovery and to knowledge.

Ramatoulaye gradually 'becomes' her own self too after Modou's marriage. She is still 'clothed' in her husband's honour but assumes all responsibility. She finds a way back to herself, and is reborn taking small baby steps:

> I was surviving. In addition to my former duties, I took over Modou's as well . . . I survived. I overcame my shyness at going alone to cinemas; I would take a seat with less and less embarrassment as the months went by—people stared at the middle-aged lady without a partner. I would feign indifference, while anger hammered against my nerves and the tears I held back welled up behind my eyes.

> From the surprised looks, I gauged the slender liberty granted to women . . . What a great distraction from distress is the cinema! I survived.

However, as Ramatoulaye re-creates her self ('disrobes' her self), she realises she was not 'divorced' but 'abandoned': 'a fluttering leaf that no hand dares to pick up'. In her self-analysis she comes to understand her complicity in her own oppression and finds ample examples:

> I gave freely, gave more than I received. I am one of those who can realise themselves fully and bloom only when they form part of a couple . . . I have never concéived of happiness outside marriage . . . I mobilised day and night in his service, I anticipated his slightest desire.

These are the virtues of both an African and a Muslim wife, elaborated as the sanctions of patriarchal society.

No less emphatic as an expression of patriarchal authority is Tamsir's announcement of his right to marry his brother's widow, Ramatoulaye, but she defies him: 'My voice has known thirty years of silence, thirty years of harassment. It burst out, violent, sometimes sarcastic, sometimes contemptuous'. Her denial subverts Tamsir's plan to acquire her and her inheritance. She shames him with his inability to provide even for his current wives, and mocks him for his greed. Her denial of Tamsir is a disgusted refusal to be treated as property for men to dispose of. In finding her voice, she liberates herself from the burden of obedience which had kept her silent for decades, and also finds the strength to refuse Daouda Dieng as well: 'My heart does not love Daouda Dieng. My mind appreciates the man. But heart and mind often disagree'. Ramatoulaye denies him marriage but offers her friendship. She refuses to inflict the same betrayal she had suffered on Dieng's wife Aminata.

Ramatoulaye's daughters are offered as a vision of the future. Not only are they allies to their mother as she comes to grips with her new existence, but the possibilities in their lives reflect on what had been possible for Ramatoulaye and Aissatou in their generation. Daba, the eldest, and her husband manage her legal affairs and are able to retrieve money and property that Modou had given to his second wife illegally. But Daba and her husband also live as 'equals', in a kind of relationship unavailable to Ramatoulaye and Aissatou, even with their own 'love' marriages. Young Aissatou, another of Ramatoulaye's daughters, becomes pregnant, and though Ramatoulaye is appalled by this, she forces herself to respond calmly and helpfully, and is rewarded by the responsible behaviour of the young people.

So Long a Letter shows Ramatoulaye slowly emerging through her tunnel of custom, tradition and gender stratification with the realisation that 'all women have almost the same fate, which religions or unjust legislation have sealed'—yet, she remains 'persuaded of the inevitable and necessary complementarity of men and women'. She argues for fairness and harmony, 'as the harmony of multiple instruments creates a pleasant symphony'. Her final prediction is 'The success of a nation therefore depends inevitably on the family'. Finally she expresses a simple and profound faith: 'hope still lives on within me. The word "happiness" does indeed have meaning, doesn't it? I shall go out in search of it. Too bad for me if once again I have to write you so long a letter . . .'

When Mariama Bâ was writing *Scarlet Song,* a novel which deals with the consequences of an inter-racial marriage, she knew that she was dying. The novel begins with Ousmane being woken by his mother, Yaye Khady, on the morning he is to start university. His father, Djibril Gueye, a devout man, is on his way to the mosque. These details are established precisely and early, and will become significant later. The family live in a suburb of Dakar, respectable and not too poor. Ousmane is the archetypal male child-hero, the pride of his parents, industrious, ambitious. He is a 'continuation' of his father, who in the context of his time achieved more than many others. The father has been 'delivered' from the yoke of a religious teacher when he joined the French colonial army. The war he went to fight 'broadened his horizons'—Djibril Gueye 'had seen Paris', and, more importantly, married a 'beautiful young wife'.

The father is an inspiration to Ousmane, who loves and respects his parents, and 'was grateful to his father for having resisted the temptation to take more wives'. Djibril tries to live his life as the Koran dictates—'like an evenly balanced scale'. Ousmane is pleased to be from his family: 'Yaye Khady's heart is like a pitcher of fresh water from which, for as long as I can remember, only father and I have drunk.' Ousmane is 'her arms and legs'—he fetches water and coal for her. The father makes comments that reflect typical gender responses of men to their first-born son—'you'll turn the lad into a sissy'—but otherwise our attention is drawn firmly to his obedience of the law.

This warm and sustaining family huddle contains discords, but they are muted at this stage. The mother works hard all day while the father plays the noble patriarch. Even the image of the mother as a pitcher is an ambivalent one. It is an object of use, in service to others, belonging only to father and son. The high but unspecified ambitions of the parents for their son invite disappointment. Ousmane's glowing 'idealism' about education, hard work and achievement appears naive. In time all these warning murmurs come to be significant.

The heart of the novel is the story of Mireille, the daughter of a French official serving in Dakar. Ousmane meets her at the university and they are attracted to each other:

> They were enriched by their differences. Each worried about the other over the smallest thing: a slight temperature, a scratched pimple, a bad cold. Low marks for a test, failure to understand a lecture upset their serenity. They wanted their happiness to be perfect.

The portrayal of their relationship does not progress far beyond these chaste expressions at this stage, but in the process cultural nuances are exposed. For example Mireille shows Ousmane a pictorial history of herself when she was four: 'I'd just finished reading that book I'm holding. I could read when I was four. What about you? . . . Look at me in my ballet tutu. Here I'm playing the piano. . . . These are my paternal grandparents. . . . That's a picture of our family home'. She has a grasp of the rich complexity of her circumstances and their sources, and an openness which hints at generosity.

Ousmane says in lieu of photographs: 'I will never speak of my family or let you into the secret garden of my origins

until I am ready to ask you to be my wife'. It is not difficult to see guilt and self-contempt in the evasiveness of this response, and anxious bravado in the proposal of marriage. Mireille marvels at her 'fate': 'I can't explain my feelings. Why should it have to be you?' she asks. The answer is 'fate', but she comes from a culture which has ceased to think of that as an explanation. Mireille's parents, however, discover what is going on and hurriedly pack their daughter off to France.

Ousmane's despair over her absence from school, and the anxiety he cannot hide, causes his mother to take note of his withdrawal without being able to discover the reason. Unlike the French household, the African home is quiet and still apparently locked in its huddle. Ousmane develops ways to camouflage his anguish. By placing her photograph in his textbook he can give the appearance of studiousness while fantasising over his lost romance. While Ousmane grieves, it is Mireille who takes decisive action in her letter to him. She writes:

> I'm not asking you for anything you don't want to tell me. But in order to fight, I must know what I am fighting for.
>
> Just tell me what to do and nothing else except you will matter.

At the crossroads of decision, Ousmane lets his own history flow through him. For him history is both Yaye Khady and Djibril Gueye, the culture of his Dakar suburb and his religion. Ousmane realises that: 'Yaye Khady's love was echoed in the hearts of all the women of the neighbourhood, all mothers by proxy,' and he cannot imagine a way to extricate himself from their caring. What should he do? Reject Usine Niari Talli, the small impoverished district, with its stench and open ditches?

> No longer heed the pointing finger of his father's respected fellow Muslims, directing him towards God's royal road? Never more to be moved to meditation at the sound of the muezzin, under the minaret of a mosque bathed in the purple glow of dawn? Shred the thousand pages of his ancestral heritage? Decry pride in one's birth? Die for love and not for honour?

The debate is rendered in the familiar, polarised form of the 'culture clash', and in this case 'love' triumphs. He decides to write back, but obviously 'love' here carries the seeds of profounder implications, symbolised in the looming opposition of entrenched fathers. Over the next years there is a semblance of order. The young people write to each other, acquire education and degrees, solidifying their relationship through disclosures in their letters.

Much of Mireille's years seem focused on her budding sense of politics. She rebels in 1968 with her classmates. Leading a double life, she engages in an antagonistic internal dialogue as she listens to her father. She is in revolt against him, his class and much of her culture. She sees her mother as a parrot who uses all her father has said previously to 'inform' her peers the next day at coffee or at the beauty salon. All the while Mireille documents these events and dispatches them to Ousmane, detailing the nihilism of her society. She feels protected by her secret romance from the pitfalls of a 'good' marriage to the 'right' type. Mireille can bear this time, waiting for the moment when life will really begin.

Ousmane also takes part in the student revolt in Dakar, where the issues at stake and the responses of the authority are brutally simpler. He is arrested and released, finishes university and responds to Mireille's weekly reportage. But, unlike her, Ousmane has not been able to loosen himself from his parents and culture. His success is shared with his family. With his first pay cheque he purchases his father's ticket to Mecca, paying the traditional tribute of the prodigal. But he avoids local girls, keeping his romance sacred. His deception deepens as pictures and letters from France accumulate and he is forced to avoid conversation which would lead him into lying.

Finally, Ousmane decides it is time to make his move. He announces one day that he is going to Paris. His mother warns him: 'white women are on the look out for black men. Be on your guard. Don't bring us back one of them'. Laden with gifts, Ousmane sets off to Paris to his 'fairy princess', and in their brief moment of re-encounter, he concludes: 'His fairy princess was more bewitching than ever, here in her own environment.' Mireille finds: 'She had left an adolescent. She discovered a man.'

The narrative does not dwell on their reunion, whisking them off to a small mosque where Mireille takes her most important first step away from her culture: the Shahadah—converting to Islam. After this Mireille hurriedly seals an episode in her life by becoming the wife of an African Muslim, and the narrative locks her into the tragedy which has been prepared for her. The directness of the narrative also describes the innocence of the young people, who themselves apparently act with an uncomplicated openness. They have, in reality, been deceiving everyone for years, and it will soon be clear that they have been deceiving themselves as well.

Once again, as in describing the growth of the relationship between Mireille and Ousmane, and in portraying Ramatoulaye's introspection in *So Long a Letter,* letter-writing as a form of disclosure at a moment of crisis becomes a useful tool. Both Ousmane and Mireille write letters to their respective parents to announce their marriage, and it is interesting to compare the parents' separate responses to the news. Ousmane's letter to his father is written in 'foreign' words, an act of affiliation which adequately explains itself. It falls to his younger brother, Babacar, to read this letter. He, of 'constant chatter' as he describes himself, hesitates and falters because: 'My brother's French is too difficult for me.' In other words, he refuses to accept the role of intermediary in an act of self-betrayal. Another interpreter is called. He is a school teacher and through his lips comes the awful truth. Ousmane describes the years of longing, the desire for free choice in love, his inescapable destiny:

> She loves me for myself and has renounced her own religion to become my wife. You have the delicate task of informing my Mother. When you do so, lay stress on the fact that she is not 'losing me'. When you do so, think of the destiny of every creature that is in the hands of Allah, the All-Powerful.

> Nothing can alter the deep feeling that I have for you. We shall be seeing you soon.

When the father arrives home with his difficult news, Yaye Khady 'was in tears already, without knowing what she was weeping for'. The couple go back and forth, inside and outside images, reproach themselves for not reading the signs properly. In the end they arrive at an explanation which makes the matter bearable: 'Since this woman has embraced Islam, we must simply accept her into the bosom of our family. In the framework of Morality, he has the right to do what he pleases with his own life'. That is the father. The mother has other disappointments:

> A *Toubab* can't be a proper daughter-in-law. She'll only have eyes for her man. We'll mean nothing to her. And I who dreamt of a daughter-in-law who'd live here and relieve me of the domestic work by taking over the management of the house, and now I'm faced with a woman who's going to take my son away from me. I shall die on my feet, in the kitchen.

While the young people have their own naive satisfactions in mind, the old feel a more uncomplicated anguish and some practical regrets.

Mireille's letter to her parents opens with confrontation: 'When you receive this letter, posted just before my departure, I shall already be far away from you starting my new life with my Senegalese family'. M de La Vallée, her father, hears the echo of his own words about Africans and we are invited to share the daughter's delectable revenge: 'Primitive, hideous half-wits'. His nightmare image of the gentle daughter in rough black hands has found fulfilment as a means of her rejection of him and the ethos he lives by. Reading her plea for understanding and forgiveness, which we can only read as gloating for the sake of observing the form, predictably only serves to harden his heart against her. Mireille sends the letter to his office, and he leaves for home in a rage to break the news to his wife. His wife's entire morning is spent making 'paella for lunch', another criticism of the empty hedonism of bourgeois life. M de La Vallée's incoherent rage and his wife's sudden despair contrast vividly with the African family's response. Despite the latter's feeling of loss, they find a form of words which will enable compromise while the European family succumbs to a self-indulgent sense of tragedy.

When Mireille and Ousmane return to Senegal, they are met by a proud father bedecked with war medals, but Yaye Khady quietly begins a campaign to get rid of Mireille. Ousmane reassures Mireille with calm self-importance: 'She feels frustrated. You must forgive her. She feels she has lost me. That I now belong to you'.

Slowly, they begin to grow apart. Once again the conflict takes the form of 'culture clash' polarities. Ousmane attacks a loyal friend and cousin, Lamine, for abandoning his culture to live in the western world of his wife. Mireille, on the other hand, finds Lamine's marriage enviable. Both parents approve of their daughter Pierrett's choice, and come every winter to visit them. The more Mireille points out how Lamine seems more at ease than him, the more Ousmane parades his Africanity. On one occasion he says to Lamine:

> You don't realise that you are betraying your true self. You live like a *Toubab,* you think like a *Toubab*. If it weren't for your skin you wouldn't be an African anymore. You know you're deserting our ranks, just when we need trained men.

It is at this time of accelerating crises of identity that an old friendship plays an important role.

On the first morning we meet him, at the beginning of the novel, Ousmane is reflecting on his first friendship with a girl, and how disastrously it turned out. Her name was Ouleymatou, the sister of his 'hut-brother'. He helped her with her French grammar but she seemed more interested in another boy. When he spoke to Ousseynou, his 'hut-brother', about her, the latter said: 'My sister doesn't want a boy who sweeps the house, fetches buckets of water and smells of dried fish.' Now this old friendship with Ousseynou is revived. Ousmane's new Peugeot and elegant clothes make quite an impression on the family as Ouleymatou, his old love, serves drinks. Though many years older and divorced, she is still beautiful, and upon seeing Ousmane she plots his seduction. She is on hand at her younger brother's when Ousmane visits. She visits Yaye Khady at washing time and offers to be her hands. Everyone knows Yaye Khady and her son's 'white wife' are not on good terms. Finally her campaign works and Ousmane succumbs. Later she becomes pregnant and Ousmane marries her without telling Mireille.

Mireille finds out soon enough, though, and now the crisis for her has reached the critical moment. By now she is thoroughly alienated from her surroundings, of course, but the possibility of returning to France also seems unattractive. There is her son. The de La Vallées will never accept this brown-skinned grandchild. In the earlier response of her parents, which also represented that of their sub-culture, lies a criticism of European racism and its ungenerous individualism.

Ousmane, on his part, feels guilt for Mireille, and goes to see a *bilodja* for medicine which would cool his passion for Ouleymatou. The man tells him: 'A woman is bringing you bad luck,' and 'bathes' him in water. However, the bath does not cool his desire for Ouleymatou but drives him further into his own sense of being connected to Africa.

When he arrives home he finds Mireille dishevelled and naked. She has killed their son—'The Gnouloule Khessoul is dead' ('The *neither-black-nor-white* is dead')—and stabs Ousmane twice before he escapes. Mireille makes the tragic journey from the courageous and generous young lover to the alienated and rejected outsider, in the process losing her own sense of identity. The culture she marries into rejects her, and she herself has already rejected her own. Her story shows that it is the woman who has to sacrifice in such marriages, for while she concedes to her new circumstances, Ousmane does not. In fact, his marriage has only left him with a greater need to assert his affiliations to Africa, in case his 'love' of a European woman should seem like self-contempt. As in *So Long a Letter,* it is through the exploration of marriages that Mariama Bâ demonstrates the patriarchal indulgences of Senegalese society. In both novels, the taking of a second wife is the fullest expression of the inequality between men and women, and the point of crisis beyond which her protagonists cannot acquiesce. Ramatoulaye chooses to stay with Modou, of course, but as a result is forced to reappraise herself and her society. Mireille's circumstances are already more dramatic in the first place, and her alienation, when it comes, unhinges her completely.

Deborah G. Plant (essay date Summer 1996)

SOURCE: "Mythic Dimensions in the Novels of Mariama Bâ," in *Research in African Literatures,* Vol. 27, No. 2, Summer, 1996, pp. 102-111.

[*In the following essay, Plant explains how Bâ illustrates the economic, intellectual, political, moral, cultural, and other contributions African women have made and continue to make to their countries in both* So Long a Letter *and* Scarlet Song, *and demonstrates Bâ's positive depiction of women's friendships and motherhood.*]

The nostalgic songs dedicated to African mothers which express the anxieties of men concerning Mother Africa are no longer enough for us. The Black woman in African literature must be given the dimension that her role in the liberation struggles next to men has proven to be hers, the dimension which coincides with her proven contribution to the economic development of our country.
[Mariama Bâ, quoted in *Ngambika, Studies of Women in African Literature,* by Anne Adams Graves, 1986, p. xi]

Such is the mandate of Mariama Bâ. Full to surfeit with romantic accolades that work more to stifle than to uplift and empower Black women thus, Africa. Mariama Bâ demands that women be recognized as actual beings who not only exist in a physical reality, but who also have made and are making actual contributions to the welfare of that reality. Niara Sudarkasa ["Female Employment and Family Organization in West Africa," *The Black Woman Cross-Culturally,* 1981] documents the African woman's proven economic contribution to the struggle for survival, liberation, and a better quality of life for African peoples. "Moreover," she writes, "during the pre-colonial period in many West African societies, women had important political and religious roles that entailed their working extensively 'outside the home.'" This legacy continues in contemporary society where "virtually all adult females are engaged in some type of money-making activity."

Sudarkasa details the African woman's economic as well as socio-political contributions. In spite of these contributions, the spread of institutionalized religions beginning in the eleventh century, the European invasion beginning in the fifteenth century—both with their attendant patriarchal ideologies—and, later, industrial capitalism served to undermine the esteem of woman and erode her "place" in society. The cataclysmic upheavals traditional societies suffered as a result of their collision with an insidious modernity forced transformations of social structure and worldviews which are yet to be dealt with in a manner beneficial to African peoples. These religious and socio-political forces would relegate woman to a tangential and marginal relationship with and within her society and a corresponding relationship in the literature of Africa. That relationship, however, is not, as Sudarkasa's article among others bears out, a representative one. Though there are notable exceptions regarding the depiction of African women in literature, Mariama Bâ's clarion call for a depiction of woman's role beyond the one-dimensional still resounds.

Mariama Bâ's own literary work is a response to that call. In her first novel, *So Long a Letter* (*Une si longue lettre*), there are a number of women characters who function beyond the typical "role-categories such as girlfriends, mistresses, and prostitutes," Their well-wrought delineations mark their multi-dimensionality. Their economic power and contributions are also well detailed, as is their physical, intellectual, and spiritual strength. In *So Long a Letter* the main character, Ramatoulaye Fall, teaches school. Her income, placed in a joint account with her husband Modou, supported their family, which included twelve children. After Modou's abandonment of the family, Ramatoulaye shouldered "both moral and material" responsibility for the family. Her friend, Aissatou, found herself likewise situated. Choosing to divorce her husband Mawdo rather than continue in a polygynous marriage, Aissatou supported herself and her four sons. The wives of Tamsir, Modou Fall's brother, worked to meet the family's needs. "To help you out with your financial obligation," Ramatoulaye tells him, "one of your wives dyes, another sells fruit, the third untiringly turns the handle of her sewing machine." Mariama Bâ recognizes and praises all of woman's work. Whereas an industrial-capitalistic system would divide labor into remunerative and non-remunerative categories, the former valued and the latter valueless, Mariama Bâ recognizes no distinctions. Her narrator declares, "Those women we call 'house'-wives deserve praise. The domestic work which they carry out, and which is not paid in hard cash, is essential to the home."

Mariama Bâ's characters represent and bring to the foreground not only the economic and socio-political contributions but also the moral and spiritual contributions of African women to the development of their countries. As depicted in her fiction, the African woman is not only complex and multi-dimensional, she is, indeed, mythic; and her role in Mariama Bâ's fiction is, though subtly drawn so, of mythic dimensions. In view of Africa's woman-centered history and in light of more profound definitions of "myth," a sober analysis of the mythic African woman goes beyond nostalgic and romantic "sweet-nothings" while not making of her a "superwoman." Referring to a photograph of an African woman in traditional dress, sitting before her home while holding a baby, Joseph Campbell writes [in *Transformations of Myth through Time,* 1990]:

This woman with her baby is the basic image of mythology. The first experience of anybody is the mother's body. . . . The earth and the whole universe, as our mother, carries this experience into the larger sphere of adult experience. When one can feel oneself in relation to the universe in the same complete and natural way as that of the child with the mother, one is in complete harmony and tune with the universe. Getting into harmony and tune with the universe and staying there is the principal function of mythology.

Many scholars agree that Africa is the beginning of human existence and the birth-place of human civilization and culture. In addition, these scholars maintain that ancient African civilizations were woman-centered. Larry Williams and Charles S. Finch [in "The Great Queens of Ethiopia," *Black Women in Antiquity,* 1984] write to that effect:

> *The matriarchy, probably the oldest form of social organization, appears to have evolved first in Africa. Even when the patriarchy emerged and began to supplant the older social organization, matriarchal social forms in Africa have thrived in whole or part up to the present.* (emphasis in original)

John Henrik Clarke [in "African Warrior Queens," *Black Women in Antiquity,* 1984] also relates his findings regarding woman-centered societies:

> In Africa the woman's "place" was not only with her family; she often ruled nations with unquestionable authority. Many African women were great militarists and on occasion led their armies in battle. Long before they knew of the existence of Europe the Africans had produced a way of life where men were secure enough to let women advance as far as their talent would take them.

Given the antiquity of her societies and given her power in those societies, the Black woman, asserts Filomina Chioma Steady [in "The Black Woman Cross-Culturally: An Overview," *The Black Woman Cross-Culturally,* 1981], "is to a large extent the original feminist." She is the archetypal womanist. And, as Diedre Badéjò attests [in "The Goddess Osun as a Paradigm for African Feminist Criticism," *Sage,* Vol. 6, No. 1, 1989], "femininity and power are central to the definition of womanist/feminist." From her analysis of Osun mythology, she draws these conclusions:

> (1) that women's power evolves from The Source of all power; (2) that some women have this power innately; (3) that social order cannot proceed without active participation of the female principle; and (4) that Olódùmarè ["the Infinite Being"] envisions a universal order in which balance and reciprocity prevail between the genders.

Mariama Bâ's vision of the ideal society also demands a balance predicated on the principle of complementarity, on cooperation as opposed to the co-opting of power. Ramatoulaye, the protagonist, who gradually feels her innate power, questions the repression of the feminine principle and also desires and envisions a restoration of reciprocity and balance in relationships. Thus, in *So Long a Letter,* Ramatoulaye rebuts her suitor Daouda Dieng who, defending his "feminist" stance and speeches in the National Assembly, triumphantly states that "there are women in the Assembly." She exclaims, "Four women, Daouda, four out of a hundred deputies. What a ridiculous ratio! Not even one for each province." Daouda Dieng, though a member of "that male Assembly," professes, proudly conveying to Ramatoulaye his progressive politics: "Women should no longer be decorative accessories, objects to be moved about, companions to be flattered or calmed with promises." He continues, "Women are the nation's primary, fundamental root, from which all else grows and blossoms. Women must be encouraged to take a keener interest in the destiny of the country. . . . " Ramatoulaye acknowledges Daouda's efforts and the "notable achievements" that have aided the forward momentum of women's struggles. "But Daouda," she contends, calling him three times, "the constraints remain; but Daouda, old beliefs are revived; but Daouda, egoism emerges, scepticism rears its head in the political field. You want to make it a closed shop and you huff and puff about it."

As opposed to any recognition of the need to balance feminine and masculine principles and work in cooperation for the welfare of African society as a whole, Daouda speaks of the need to encourage fuller political participation from women so that women can protect their own interests. "If men alone are active in the parties," he declares, "why should they think of the women? It is only human to give yourself the larger portion of the cake when you are sharing it out. If men alone are active in the parties why should they think of women?" The welfare of women and children is reduced to a portion of cake. Given Daouda Dieng's insight into the mindset of many of his cronies, given the industrial-capitalistic division of labor and its inherent inequities, and given the artificial schism between domestic and public spheres, one can appreciate the standpoint of Ramatoulaye's daughter, Daba: "I don't want to go into politics; it's not that I am not interested in the fate of my country and, most especially, that of woman. But when I look at the fruitless wranglings even within the ranks of the same party, when I see men's greed for power, I prefer not to participate." Though "men will continue to have the power of decision," she counters, "everyone knows that polity should be the affair of women." Daba prefers to work for change through her own associations and organizations, a realm outside the ostensibly political one. But, given the overlap of "public" and "domestic" arenas as analyzed by Sudarkasa, that does not mean her actions are any less political or any less militant and effective.

When, where, how, why did men lose the security they had which allowed them to see woman as their equal, to respect and encourage her militancy as they would her meekness, her firmness as her femininity? When, where, how, why has woman been taught that "the first quality in a woman is docility," that "a woman does not need too much education," as Aunty Nabou teaches young Nabou whom she prepared to be a wife for her son, Mawdo? Why is woman taught that she is powerless—powerless before what has become some men's "instincts" and appetites as Mawdo harangues Ramatoulaye:

> I saw a film in which the survivors of an air crash survived by eating the flesh of the corpses. This fact demonstrates the force of the instincts in man, instincts that dominate him, regardless of his level of intelligence. . . . You can't resist the imperious laws that demand food and clothing for man. These same laws compel the "male" in other respects. . . .
>
> Driven to the limits of my resistance, I satisfy myself with what is within reach. It's a terrible thing to say. Truth is ugly when one analyses it.

Such rationalizations decree that woman be powerless before the finicky nature of those men who can, with little or no compunction, take up one woman while abandoning another and sheepishly ascribe their actions to nature, to culture—as in the case of Ousmane Guèye in Bâ's second novel, *Scarlet Song*—to fate, or to Allah. When Modou Fall secretly marries Binetou, the *Imam* chants to Ramatoulaye: "There is nothing one can do when Allah the almighty puts two people side by side. . . . God intended him to have a second wife, there is nothing he can do about it." Nothing she can do about it; nothing he can do about it. Powerless.

When, where, how, why was woman displaced from her central position as giver, nurturer, protector of life to become "a worn-out or out-dated *boubou*," "a plate of food," a "good luck" *piece,* a bouncing ball at fate's whim with "no control over where it rolls and even less over who gets it," a thing, "a fluttering leaf that no hand dares to pick up"—a thing disdained? "Truth is ugly when one analyses it." Mawdo, of course, is right. Why the imbalance between the masculine and the feminine principles? Why the one valorized at the expense of the other? This African woman, why is she told, "Shut up! Shut up!" When Tamsir, Modou's brother, decides he will inherit Ramatoulaye after she comes out of mourning, Ramatoulaye is insulted, wounded, and outraged: "You forget that I have a heart, a mind, that I am not an object to be passed from hand to hand. You don't know what marriage means to me: it is an act of faith and of love, the total surrender of oneself to the person one has chosen and who has chosen you. (I emphasized the word 'chosen')." "Stop! Stop!" protests Mawdo. "But you can't stop once you've let your anger loose." Ramatoulaye could not "tame all that anger down." "My voice has known thirty years of silence, thirty years of harassment. It bursts out, violent, sometimes sarcastic, sometimes contemptuous," she confides to

Aissatou. Thirty years. In Africa, where the spoken word had primacy, where the procreative power of the spoken word was recognized and revered, this woman remained silent for thirty years. The Word, the *sine qua non* of being, was denied her. She was, in the most basic and profound sense rendered powerless: "Shut up!"

Modou's total abandonment of Ramatoulaye, then later his death, left Ramatoulaye alone with the moral and material responsibility of her children and herself. "I was surviving," she writes Aissatou. "In addition to my former duties, I took over Modou's as well." She fixed broken doors and windows, managed a meager budget, and cared for her children. Interspersed in the recounting of her duties is the signifying refrain, "I survived. . . . I survived. . . . I survived. . . ." Her survival was nothing short of miraculous. Women similarly abandoned, like Jacqueline, suffered nervous breakdowns. Others, like Mireille in *A Scarlet Song,* became insane. Still others were hurled to early graves. Ramatoulaye found her tongue. By speaking for her *self* she moved from a state of psycho-spiritual non-existence to one of existence, of being. Prior to her abandonment, Ramatoulaye lived on the periphery of her own life, always trying to please and placate others. The greater portion of her physical, psychological, and spiritual energies were spent in meeting the expectations of her husband, her children, her "family-in-law," and the laws and customs of her religion and society. "I try to spot my faults in the failure of my marriage," Ramatoulaye ponders in a letter to Aissatou:

> I loved my house. You can testify to the fact that I made it a haven of peace where everything had its place, that I created a harmonious symphony of colours. You know how softhearted I am, how much I loved Modou. You can testify to the fact that, mobilized day and night in his service, I anticipated his slightest desire.
>
> I made peace with his family. Despite his desertion of our home, his father and mother and Tamsir, his brother, still continued to visit me often, as did his sisters. My children too grew up without much ado. Their success at school was my pride, just like laurels thrown at the feet of my lord and master.

In all this, she was dutifully submissive and self-effacing. And it was there, in the eyes of others, that she garnered her sense of self and self-worth. When she began to speak, however, and on her own behalf, she gave voice to ideas, beliefs, and feelings which expressed her true self and acknowledged her inherent self-worth. She became profoundly aware of herself as an autonomous, complex, and significant entity who had a choice, a say, in how she would live. This self, in its incipient stages of life, she nurtured. The African woman, praised also for her procreative power, her fecundity, is the giver of life. Like Isis, of Egyptian mythology, she is not only procreative, but self-created, autogenetic. It is through the miracle of autogenesis that Ramatoulaye comes into her own. She experiences again what Campbell describes as the first experience: the mother's body. She seeks again balance and harmony. The void created in the house by Modou's absence became her womb. Images symbolic of gestation and fecundity are prevalent in *So Long a Letter:* "I lived in a vacuum," she tells Aissatou. And it is within the womb of the cinema that she was distracted from the void in this vacuum and learned "lessons of greatness, courage, and perseverance." It was there, in the darkness that she was enlightened and gained a "vision of the world." "The cinema, an inexpensive means of recreation," helped her to re-create herself. Ramatoulaye emerged from its dark maw renewed. And in the sleepless, solitary night, pregnant with loneliness, Ramatoulaye writes that "music lulled my anxiety. I heard the message of old and new songs, which awakened hopes. My sadness dissolved."

Ramatoulaye's ritual acts of "rememory" were the birthpangs of her travail. To recall her thirty silent years, to acknowledge and articulate them, the ebb and flow of them, was to begin to understand and heal self. In expressing her trials of abandonment and, as well, the trials of her friend Aissatou, Ramatoulaye knows the pain her words evoke: "I know that I am shaking you, that I am twisting a knife in a wound hardly healed; but what can I do? I cannot help remembering in my forced solitude and reclusion." Ramatoulaye's ritual of rememory evokes her mythic self, allowing her recreated self to issue forth. She is reborn.

When Modou chose to marry Binetou, Ramatoulaye reconciled herself to be a "co-wife": "I had prepared myself for equal sharing, according to the precepts of Islam concerning polygamic life. I was left with empty hands." But emerging from the womb of her solitude and seclusion, she learned, like Aissatou, the necessity of taking one's life into one's own hands. Aissatou would not reconcile herself to polygynous life, as she could not accept Mawdo's "absurd divisions" between "heartfelt love and physical love." She left. She took her life and the lives of her children into her own hands. Ramatoulaye writes that books saved Aissatou. They created for her a womb of fertile interiority as did the films at the cinema for Ramatoulaye. But Aissatou's development was nurtured by Ramatoulaye's presence and encouragements. As she was midwife at the rebirth of Aissatou, so Aissatou was midwife to her friend. And it is to friendship that Ramatoulaye sings hosannas throughout the novel. Though Aissatou chose to live the "single life" of the "modern, liberated woman," she respected Ramatoulaye's choice to remain in her marriage and her desire and hope to some day marry again. As E. Imafedia Okhamafe argues in "African Feminism(s) and the Question of Marital and Non-Marital Loneliness and Intimacy" [*Sage*, Vol. 6, No. 1, 1989], it is not often that respect is accorded women who make choices seen as contrary to feminist ideologies. She observes:

> . . . [S]elf-esteem does not come by telling women to develop androphobia or manophobia since many of these single or divorced or abandoned women would still want to develop intimate relationships with some other men. . . . What I am saying is that women should have such an option without being made to feel guilty if they choose to exercise it.

Bâ's novel also attests that mutual respect—reciprocity and balance—is essential to friendship, as it is to any other relationship. Ramatoulaye writes Aissatou, "Even though I understand your stand, even though I respect the choice of liberated women, I have never conceived of happiness outside marriage." As Ramatoulaye's choice was not a judgment against Aissatou, Aissatou's choice never rose to condemn her friend. Rather than abandoning her sister-friend, who chose a way different from hers, Aissatou supported her. Abandoned and left without a means of transportation, Ramatoulaye and her children had to rely on unreliable public transportation. Aissatou responded to her friend's plight with the gift of a ear: "I shall never forget your response, you, my sister, nor my joy and my surprise when I was called to the Fiat agency and was told to choose a car which you had paid for, in full." This gift never became for Aissatou a vehicle for pronouncements and dictates against her friend. It never granted Aissatou the right to impose upon Ramatoulaye an ideology that would be, for her, incongruous. Because of Aissatou's disinterested support, Ramatoulaye's self-esteem escalated. Their friendship and sisterhood reinforced her strength to be and become.

Mariama Bâ's metaphors of birth, recreation, and fecundity come to their fruition in Young Aissatou's pregnancy. Metaphors of the mythic African woman are also fully realized at this point. Young Aissatou, Ramatoulaye's second oldest daughter and the namesake of her friend, becomes pregnant while unmarried and still in school. Tradition and convention, epitomized in the character of "the *griot* woman" Farmata, dictated that Ramatoulaye vehemently upbraid her daughter. Young Aissatou standing before her, pregnant, Ramatoulaye was surprised, angered, disappointed, and hurt. Checking herself, Ramatoulaye stood for immeasured time, figuring her response. At the crossroads of a moment, where mythic and historical time dialogued with actual time to comment on its future, Ramatoulaye remembered: "Remembering, like a lifebuoy, the tender and consoling attitude of my daughter during my distress, my long years of loneliness, I overcame my emotion. . . ." She painfully felt her responsibilities:

> To make my being a defensive barrier between my daughter and any obstacle. At this moment of con-

frontation, I realized how close I was to my child. The umbilical cord took on new life, the indestructible bond beneath the avalanche of storms and the duration of time. I saw her once more, newly sprung from me, kicking about, her tongue pink, her tiny face creased under her silky hair. I could not abandon her, as pride would have me do. Her life and her future were at stake, and these were powerful considerations, overriding all taboos and assuming greater importance in my heart and in my mind. The life that fluttered in her was questioning me. It was eager to blossom. It vibrated, demanding protection.

Giver, nurturer, protector, and preserver of life, Ramatoulaye's ritual act of rememory called forth her mythic self: "I took my daughter in my arms. Painfully, I held her tightly, with a force multiplied tenfold by pagan revolt and primitive tenderness. She cried. She choked on sobs." This is the most moving, most powerful, most profound moment in Ramatoulaye's existence. A primordial knowledge was called up from and echoed back to the timeless, mythic spiral of life: "I took myself in hand with superhuman effort. The shadows faded away. Courage! The rays of light united to form an appeasing brightness. My decision to help and protect emerged from the tumult. It gained strength as I wiped the tears, as I caressed the burning brow."

Ramatoulaye's erstwhile empty hands teemed with life—her life, the cumulation of countless lives before her, her child's life, her grandchild's life and beyond. Ramatoulaye emerged from her tumult with a mythic conception of motherhood which determined her momentous response. The potential for such growth is aborted in Bâ's *Scarlet Song*. Where Ramatoulaye could "face the Hood," Mathilde de La Vallée could not—though she desperately desired to. Her husband, Jean de La Vallée, saw their daughter's marriage to Ousmane, "her nigger," as an "attack on his honour," an "assault on his dignity," and an insufferable disgrace before his French compeers. With the exclamation of "Snake-in-the-grass! Slut!" he banished his daughter Mireille to oblivion. Mathilde, like Ramatoulaye, remembered:

> Finally, she read the letter [of Mireille's elopement]. As a mother, she could share her child's despair as she was driven to this drastic measure. Reading between the lines, she could appreciate her dreadful dilemma. She was heartsick at the thought of the wrench her daughter's decision must have caused her. She was moved by the sincerity of her cry from afar. She forgave her. She opened her arms to cradle her child. . . . [H]er maternal instinct was reborn. Must she forgo the possibility of becoming a grandmother?

Having made her husband her life, Mathilde had no sister-friend in whom she could confide and with whom she could express herself. Her remembering, alone, was not enough. She needed more to overcome, like Ramatoulaye, thirty hushed years. Mathilde's silent scream noiselessly echoed about the infertile caverns of her deliberations to issue forth stillborn:

> And then, out of habit—thirty years during which she had not had a thought of her own, no initiative, no rebellion, thirty years during which she had simply moved in the direction in which she was pushed, thirty years during which it had been her lot to agree and to applaud—then, out of habit rather than conviction, she sobbed, "Snake-in-the-grass! Slut!" and fell into a faint.

Overwhelmed in face of patriarchal convention, Mathilde could not summon the courage to help and protect her child.

The umbilical cord cut, isolated and otherwise abandoned in her adopted home of Senegal, Mireille, unable to cope with her external reality, was driven inward. Interiority is dangerous when there is no connection with external reality to keep one grounded. Mireille, insane, murdered her son, stabbed her husband, his blood a scarlet song which sang a confused and strangled rhythm. Soukeyna, Mireille's sister-in-law, tried to be a sister-friend, a midwife to see Mireille through her mother-in-law's total rejection of her and her husband's abandonment of her. But Mireille, who "no longer spoke," had not understood, like Ramatoulaye, "that confiding in others allays pain."

Ramatoulaye knows what treasure she has in Aissatou. She appreciates the possibilities of and sees the need for friendship and sisterhood. As she writes Aissatou, "Instruments for some, baits for others, respected or despised, often muzzled, all women have almost the same fate, which religions or unjust legislation have sealed." Ramatoulaye knows also that when women suffer, they do not suffer alone. With the repression of the feminine principle, there can be no balance, no order.

"The material of myth is the material of our life, the material of our body, and the material of our environment, and a living, vital mythology deals with these in terms that are appropriate to the nature of knowledge of the time" (Campbell). One function of myth is to explain the inexplicable. This, Ramatoulaye concludes, is what mothers do: "one is a mother in order to understand the inexplicable. One is a mother to lighten the darkness. One is a mother to shield when lightning streaks the night, when thunder shakes the earth, when mud bogs one down. One is a mother in order to love without beginning or end." Given her knowledge of the tumultuous times in which she lives and her children grow, she knows she must give them a "living, vital mythology" to help ensure their harmonious existence in the universe. By example and precept, she transmits to her children her mythic concepts of balance and harmony, equanimity and complementarity, flexibility and change.

Ramatoulaye sees herself and Aissatou as "true sisters" with a "mission of emancipation." Ramatoulaye awaits an eagerly anticipated visit from Aissatou. She ponders what effect the changes each has made will have on the other and what discussions they will have about their "search for a new way." "Reunited, will we draw up a detailed account of our faded bloom, or will we sow new seeds for new harvests?" She warns Aissatou, "I have not given up wanting to refashion my life. Despite everything—disappointments and humiliations—hope still lives on within me. It is from the dirty and nauseating humus that the green plant sprouts into life, and I can feel new buds springing up in me." When these two women meet, what then? What then? What then?

FURTHER READING

Biography

Staunton, Cheryl Wall. "Mariama Bâ: Pioneer Senegalese

Woman Novelist." *CLA Journal* 37, No. 3 (March 1994): 328-35.
> Surveys Bâ's life and career.

Criticism

Cham, Mbye Baboucar. "The Female Condition in Africa: A Literary Exploration by Mariama Bâ." *A Current Bibliography on African Affairs* 17, No. 1 (1984-85): 29-52.
> Examines Bâ's treatment of the impact of male-female relationships and female-female relationships on society, and studies her narrative technique.

King, Adele. "The Personal and the Political in the Work of Mariama Bâ." *Studies in 20th Century Literature* 18, No. 2 (Summer 1994): 177-88.
> Surveys Bâ's treatment of both the personal issues of women and the political concerns of Senegal in her works.

Rueschmann, Eva. "Female Self-definition and the African Community in Mariama Bâ's Epistolary Novel *So Long a Letter*." In *International Women's Writing: New Landscapes of Identity,* edited by Anne E. Brown and Marjanne E. Goozé, pp. 3-18. Westport, CT: Greenwood Press, 1995.
> Considers Bâ's portrayal of the social status of Senegalese women, their personal qualities, and the challenges they face.

Additional coverage of Bâ 's career can be found in the following source published by Gale: *Black Writers,* **Vol. 2.**

Edward Kamau Brathwaite

1930-

(Born Lawson Edward Brathwaite) Barbadian poet, essayist, historian, and critic.

INTRODUCTION

One of the West Indies' leading authors and scholars, Brathwaite has devoted much of his career to encouraging the development of an indigenous Caribbean culture as an alternative to the prevailing colonial tradition, which emphasizes European influences. Brathwaite's poetry, for which he is best known, traces the transition in the West Indies from colonialism to independence and attempts to establish a new Caribbean identity based on the area's African heritage. As a literary and cultural historian, Brathwaite has made in-depth studies of creolization and has sought to recover the elements of the Caribbean past that were repressed because of European domination. Brathwaite's literary and academic focus, combined with his impressive and moving oral performances of his poetry, have led many West Indians to revere him as the guru of the new Caribbean nationalism.

Biographical Information

Brathwaite was born in 1930 in Bridgetown, Barbados, a Caribbean island populated almost entirely by people of African descent, at the height of the island's British colonial rule. In the late 1940s, Brathwaite enrolled at Harrison College, where he and a few of his friends started a school newspaper, the *Harrisonian.* Several of Brathwaite's earliest poems appeared in the *Harrisonian* as well as in *Bim,* a pioneering and well-respected literary journal which was the major forum for Brathwaite's poems and essays until the late 1960s. Another outlet for his early work was the British Broadcasting Corporation's *Caribbean Voices* program, which aired more than fifty of his poems between 1953 and 1958. After leaving Harrison College, Brathwaite attended Pembroke College, Cambridge, on a scholarship, and received a B.A. in history in 1953 and a Diploma of Education the following year. In 1955 Brathwaite moved to for Africa, where he worked in Ghana's Ministry of Education from 1955-62. While on a leave of absence in Barbados in 1960, he met and married Doris Monica Welcome, a teacher and librarian with whom he had one child; she died in 1986. From 1965 to 1968 Brathwaite worked on his doctoral degree at the University of Sussex in England, at the same time composing the greater portion of the work that established his international reputation—*The Arrivants* (1973), which includes *Rights of Passage* (1967), *Masks* (1968) and *Islands*

(1969). In 1966 Brathwaite played a key role in forming the Caribbean Artists Movement; he became a founding editor of its journal, *Savacou,* in 1970. In 1972, under the auspices of a Guggenheim fellowship, Brathwaite began work on his second poetic trilogy, which includes *Mother Poem* (1977), *Sun Poem* (1982), and *X/Self* (1987). Since moving to the United States in 1991 to assume a position with the Department of Comparative Literature at New York University, Brathwaite has published several more volumes of poetry. In 1994, his contributions to literature were honored with the prestigious Neustadt International Prize for Literature.

Major Works

Brathwaite's reputation as a writer rests on his poetry. His two trilogies, along with such other well-known collections as *Other Exiles* (1975) and *Black and Blues* (1976), constitute a cultural history of African peoples in the Caribbean as well as a deeply personal account of Brathwaite's exploration of his own identity as a black writer living in the West Indies. *The Arrivants* moves back and forth in space and time as Brathwaite describes the alienation experienced by the first African slaves who made the middle passage to the West Indies and North America (*Rights of Passage*); moves on to tell of a modern Caribbean poet's pilgrimage to Africa in search of his roots (*Masks*); and then returns his speaker to the New World, where he searches for remnants of the African past that can be rebuilt into a new "home" culture (*Islands*). Brathwaite's second trilogy continues the themes of identity, exile, dispossession, and belief in a redemptive force, but with a more specific focus on Barbados. Essential to Brathwaite's concept of an indigenous Caribbean culture is his belief that West Indian writers should chiefly rely on native sources and folk material for creative inspiration. Throughout his own poetry Brathwaite continually experiments with language and form in an effort to reproduce the sounds and rhythms characteristic of the speech of the Caribbean folk communities. He makes use of assonance, enjambment, puns, and neologisms; he fragments multisyllabic words and creates curious line formations; and in his later poems, such as those collected in *Barabajan Poems, 1492-1992* (1994), he exploits computer technology, varying fonts, ink emphasis, and page layout to create what he refers to as a "video style."

Critical Reception

Discussions of Brathwaite's poetry generally focus on his themes and technique. Critics frequently comment on his dual persona: Brathwaite, the individual black West Indian whose perspective on culture has been altered by his experiences in Africa; and Brathwaite, the symbolic voice of the emerging Caribbean nationalism. Brathwaite's use of water, earth, and sun imagery is viewed as particularly effective in conveying his themes of exile and rebirth and his idea that the Caribbean writer's creative inspiration is best found in native surroundings. Critics also discuss the spiritual context of Brathwaite's poetry, often in connection with his concept of *nam,* which he defines as "the survival potential, the irreducible spirit" of the African people in the Caribbean and "atomic core" of their cultural identity. Reaction to Brathwaite's linguistic and formal innovations has been mixed. While some critics applaud his reproduction of Caribbean dialects—what Brathwaite calls "nation languages"— as an ingenious means of bringing the African oral tradition to print, others complain that his eccentric style creates far too much ambiguity and places inordinate demands on readers. According to Brathwaite, the time he spent in Africa was the most significant influence on his career. Critics agree that Brathwaite's quest to reclaim the Caribbean's African cultural roots has had an enormous impact on both West Indian literature and on the ways in which West Indians perceive themselves. In the minds of most critics, Brathwaite has successfully "de-educated" himself—and a significant number of West Indians—by breaking down colonial tradition and reconstructing Caribbean culture using African models.

PRINCIPAL WORKS

Jazz and the West Indian Novel (essay) 1967
Rights of Passage (poetry) 1967
Masks (poetry) 1968
Islands (poetry) 1969
Creative Literature of the British West Indies During the Period of Slavery (criticism) 1970
Folk Culture of the Slaves in Jamaica (history) 1970
The Development of Creole Society in Jamaica (1770-1820) (history) 1971
*The Arrivants: A New World Trilogy (poetry) 1973
The African Presence in Caribbean Literature (essay) 1974
Other Exiles (poetry) 1975
Black and Blues (poetry) 1976
Mother Poem (poetry) 1977
Gods of the Middle Passage (essay) 1982
Sun Poem (poetry) 1982
History of the Voice (history) 1984
X/Self (poetry) 1987
Barabajan Poems (poetry) 1994

*Contains *Rights of Passage, Masks,* and *Islands.*

CRITICISM

J. Michael Dash (essay date 1979)

SOURCE: "Edward Brathwaite," in *West Indian Literature,* edited by Bruce King, The MacMillan Press Ltd., 1979, pp. 210-27.

[*In the following essay, Dash traces the progress of style and theme in Brathwaite's work, and considers it in the context of patterns of development in the work of other Caribbean writers.*]

Probably the best introduction to the poetry of Edward Brathwaite is his largely autobiographical essay entitled **'Timehri'.** In this account of his own experiences and how they combined to form an awareness of certain literary and cultural problems, the poet attempts to situate himself in terms of the evolution of West Indian writing. In tracing various tendencies among his fellow writers, Brathwaite isolates two important phases in a gradual movement from an initial sense of dispossession and fragmentation towards a more recent attempt to go beyond this sense of disintegration and to envisage the positive forces of creolisation in the Caribbean context:

> The problem of and for West Indian artists and intellectuals is that having been born and educated within this fragmented culture, they start out in the world without a sense of 'wholeness'. . . . The achievement of these writers was to make the society conscious of the cultural problem. The second phase of West Indian and Caribbean artistic and intellectual life, on which we are now entering, having become conscious of the problem, is seeking to transcend and heal it.

There is no attempt by Brathwaite to disown any of the writers who preceded him and whose preoccupations he sees as different from his. What he is taking care to outline is a crucial shift in sensibility within recent West Indian writing. The evolution is away from that obsessive sense of loss, that once fed the violent protest or inveterate cynicism of the earlier phase, towards a newer more speculative vision of 'wholeness' in the Caribbean situation. He not only identifies closely with the second phase but sees it as a way of resolving the problems posed in the work of his literary forebears.

Indeed this notion of estrangement from one's community and landscape becomes in Brathwaite's various critical articles or surveys of West Indian writing the main criterion for judging individual Caribbean writers. For instance, Claude McKay's ability to visualise Bita Plant's reintegration into Banana Bottom makes him a precursor of the second phase. In contrast to the vision of V. S. Naipaul, McKay presents a positive world from which one was not tempted to escape. In this progression Wilson Harris emerges as the artist whose work represents a conscious investigation of the previously overlooked creolising forces or 'native consciousness' in the Caribbean experience.

An insight into Brathwaite's formative literary experiences can be had from the early poems published in the literary journal *Bim* in the 1950s. In what must be one of the first poems published by Brathwaite, **'Shadow Suite',** we have a private, contemplative mood which has obviously drawn on the abstract metaphysical brooding of T. S. Eliot for inspiration:

> You who expect the impossible
> Know that here you will see
> Only what you have already seen
> What you hear
> is only what you have already heard
> For life is an eternal pattern.

This sombre, meditative verse does not indicate the poet's alienation from reality; it illustrates the introspective quality present in his early period of literary apprenticeship which also directly informs his later vision of the New World.

A pattern emerges from this poetic contemplation of the human condition. What the poet seems to be doing is linking a fundamentally religious notion with the process of artistic creativity. Brathwaite seems to consider reality in general in terms of a world fallen from grace; the poet's special role revolves around his awareness of this fall and his capacity to recapture the lost state through his vision. For instance, the poem **'South'** which first appears in *Bim* in 1959 (and is later included in an edited form in ***Rites of Passage***) concerns the poet's ability to transform this fallen world through his creative imagination. The poem's very first line indicates the difference between the vision and the ordinary world: 'But today I recapture the islands.' This poetic fantasy comes to a climax with: 'And gulls, white sails slanted seawards, / fly into the limitless morning before us.' The restoration of a state of grace is seen as fragile and tentative in the 1959 version. The ending, which he later removed, suggests a world which easily relapses into its former state as the vision fades:

> Night falls and the vision is ended.
> The drone of the groaners is ended.

The same is true of the poem **'The Leopard'** which when it later appears in *Islands* can be made to suggest the Black Panther organisation and certainly a more militant context. The caged animal in the first version of **'The Leopard'** be-

comes a metaphor of betrayal with obvious religious overtones. It connects with the poet's concern for a world heedless of spiritual values and vainly attempting to tame or shut out a deeper dimension to human existence:

> We breed our haggard rages
> And lock Christ up, a leopard
> in cold unheeded cages.

A final illustration of this quality in Brathwaite's early work is seen in the short poem **'The Vision'.** This might be considered a poetic manifesto as it stresses the need for restoring that lost hallowed quality to the world, what he would later term 'wholeness'. The poet's role in this process of recreating a sense of wonder before reality is made explicit here:

> Without fear or faces. There
> should be places where the roots
> can grow, where green shoots
> Sing, where the gold blown pollen
> Blossoms. But feet that walk
> the rootless walk, find no way here
> No water. And so the blind eyes, wells,
> Lack tears, lack pity, lack their proper use.

The poem is a prototype for the world of Brathwaite's trilogy. The very images of roots, pollen, green shoots are to recur in the later work as symbols of a world restored. The blind eyes that 'lack their proper use' relate to the inhibited and insensitive world that has lost its sense of the fantastic which can only be regained through a poetic consciousness.

The recent appearance of ***Other Exiles*** completes the pattern we have been examining. This collection of miscellaneous poems has no dominant theme. Many of the poems are largely personal poems of his early period, and their inclusion seems to be based on their success in evoking certain impressions or moods. For instance, a love poem such as **'Schooner'** reveals Brathwaite's ability to use sustained imagery to suggest, in this case, a relationship between two individuals. The collection is given some coherence by being enclosed by two poems that allude to the theme of recreation and that awesome moment of wonder in which communion is made with the spiritual. The first poem, **'Ragged Point',** refers to the east coast of Barbados where the landscape is untamed and is easily linked with the idea of freshness associated with the dawn light, and the new year:

> We watched what there was to watch
> saw the cold rocks come clearer
> sky rise.

The vision cannot be sustained:

Next morning the weather was clear
we'd forgotten our notions.

The final poem, **'New Year Letter'**, symbolises the same moment of intense revelation:

So softly now this moment fills
the darkness with its difference.
Earth waits, trees touch
the dawn.

Brathwaite's work can be seen as a slow progression towards this moment when the vision of 'wholeness' is established.

In his early work Brathwaite conceives of the poetic imagination as a superior way of perceiving the world. The poetic reconstruction of the world could redeem reality from its fallen state. In another early poem in **Other Exiles** Brathwaite expresses the need for 'words to refashion futures like a healer's hand'. The same line recurs in the trilogy as the poet is attempting to liberate the region from its sterile fallen state. The poet's public voice has its roots in this early recognition of the role of art as a means of discovering unconscious figurative meanings behind the concrete and the visible. What was essentially a private literary quest for the young Brathwaite later becomes the point of departure for an aesthetic exploration of the Caribbean that transcends the historical stereotype of pluralism and fragmentation.

Even though Brathwaite situates himself in a new vanguard of West Indian writing, his actual career and experiences are not unlike those of the generation of the 'first phase'. Born in Barbados in 1930 he follows the familiar pattern of metropolitan exile and an eventual return to the West Indies. He receives his higher education in Cambridge in the early fifties and becomes in his own words 'a roofless man of the world' before returning to the Caribbean. As is the case with most artists who underwent this sequence of experiences, the odyssey served to heighten the poet's sensitivity to the dilemma of alienation which plagued West Indian intellectuals in exile.

During this period of exile Brathwaite's work reflects his various experiences. For instance, **'The day the first snow fell'** (1953) is basically about the poet's disappointment at discovering his estrangement in Britain from a world which he thought he could possess. The frustration normally expected at this point in the career of the exiled artist, when all worlds appear strange to him, never really emerges in Brathwaite's work. We have an important departure from the sense of dispossession that comes with exile, in the poet's eight-year stay in Ghana (1955-62). It is here that he discovers that sense of the sacred so crucial to the poetic imagination. He discovers a world which he cannot adopt but one

which seems to retain a communion with the mysterious and numinous which is absent in the historically disadvantaged New World. His awareness of the customs and language of the Ghanaian people is seen in his adaptation of *Antigone* to a Ghanaian context in **Odale's Choice** (1962). This does not represent an original project since the adaptation of classical drama to local situations was not unknown, but it does show a closeness to the environment in which he found himself, which is central to his dramatisation of this experience in his trilogy.

Brathwaite returned to the Caribbean in 1962 and began work on the trilogy, **The Arrivants,** which meant a coming to terms with his European and African experiences. The earlier, more introspective mode would now yield to an epic reconstruction of the cultural and historical situation of the Caribbean. The first section of this long work, **Rites of Passage** (1967), evokes the sterility and dispossession inspired by his own experiences growing up in Barbados and his awareness of Caribbean history. **Masks** (1968) draws heavily on the world observed during his stay in Ghana and is a marked contrast to the fragmented and desecrated world of the previous section. The final part, **Islands** (1969), treats the poet's physical and spiritual return to the Caribbean and attempts to restore that vision of grace that was absent in his first negative picture of waste and sterility.

When one considers the epic and dialectical structure of Brathwaite's trilogy, a comparison is inevitable with Aimé Césaire's *Cahier d'un retour au pays natal*. Essentially the same pattern emerges in both these poets—from an initial evocation of devastation in the Caribbean, the poem moves to a concluding vision of renascence. This progression can be shown by the following examples.

The *Cahier* first presents the islands 'shipwrecked in the mud of this bay' and later returns to the islands as 'scars upon the water . . . waste paper torn and strewn upon the water'. The movement is from the static and pathetic to an image which, while retaining the sense of absurdity and tragedy, suggests new possibilities. Brathwaite in his long poem locates the progression in his work in the same way. The cabin presents Old Tom as a casualty of history, his suffering forgotten by his descendants. The later section, **Islands,** contains the poem **'Anvil'** which evokes a less resigned Tom: 'But from the edge / of dark, defeated silence, / what watchful patience glitters.' Césaire's poem could easily have had some influence on Brathwaite. The *Cahier* is an unprecedented attempt to deal with the Caribbean region on such a scale and with such insight. Indeed, solely on the evidence on the literary activity in *Bim* in the 1950s, there was obviously an awareness of the literary renascence in the French-speaking Caribbean. Translations of Haitian and French West Indian poets are present as early as 1953, and in a review of Harris's poetry in 1960 Brathwaite mentions 'the influence of Césaire and French West Indian poets on modern French writing'. Yet it would be a simplification to present **The Arrivants** as an English version of the *Cahier*. The *Cahier* may have presented identical issues a few decades earlier than Brathwaite's poem and was in general a shaping force on the younger poet, but the latter work can be more usefully interpreted in terms of a response to certain issues raised within Anglophone West Indian writing.

These issues touch on two important areas—the history of the New World and the problems of the literary imagination in such a context. V. S. Naipaul, because of his outspoken views, can easily illustrate what these ideas meant. The tension between Naipaul and Brathwaite has been overworked but it is important to see the distance between these writers in order to state the point of departure of **The Arrivants**. The two stereotypes that emerge in Naipaul's essays hinge upon a particular attitude to the absurdity of the New World situation. In *The Middle Passage* the Caribbean is presented as uncreative and philistine:

> The history of the islands can never be satisfactorily told. Brutality is not the only difficulty. History is built around achievement and creation; and nothing was created in the West Indies.

Brathwaite's trilogy can be conceived as a demonstration of how the writer can emerge from such a despairing attitude to the Caribbean. The second notion which follows on this one concerns the enormous difficulty faced by the writer who attempts to use such an environment as a source for literary creation. Naipaul is perceptive on the question of the problems faced by such a writer attempting to repossess this experience and landscape:

> Fiction or any work of the imagination, whatever its quality, hallows its subject. To attempt . . . to give a quality of myth to what was agreed to be petty and ridiculous . . . required courage.

Brathwaite as a writer of the second phase saw it as his duty to resolve this question. For him George Lamming started this process with *In the Castle of My Skin* (1953) in his attempts to 'hallow' the commonplace and the petty. **The Arrivants** can be read as a metaphor of the literary process, namely an attempt to redeem through literary means a world thought to be trivial and debased. This latter preoccupation neatly ties in with the attempts to retrieve a communion with the spiritual values present in Brathwaite's earlier work. The poet's own literary development is now tied in with our ideological debate and is the prime motivation for the literary and psychic journey traced in his trilogy.

The poems of **Rites of Passage** are clustered around the theme of spiritual dispossession. They are an attempt to re-

move the amnesia about historical events in the West Indian psyche and create an awareness of the historical injustice perpetrated in the region and the blind materialism of the present. In this instance, the actual historical events in the New World are symbolically related to the Fall of Man; one of the most effective fantasies describes the arrival of Columbus in the West Indies. This arrival is an important hieroglyph for the poet as it marks the transition from a state of grace to a desecrated and profane reality. It is one of the few instances when images of decay and waste are not used to describe the Caribbean. Columbus first sees an untainted world:

> Columbus from his after-
> deck watched stars, absorbed in water,
> melt in liquid amber drifting.

'Liquid amber' suggests a state of sustained harmony existing before Columbus's intrusion. The latter is portrayed as an innocent, not fully aware of the horrors this encounter would precipitate:

> What did this journey mean, this
> new world mean: dis-
> covery? Or a return to terrors
> he had sailed from, known before?

Brathwaite's reconstruction of this moment is not done as a strident protest against the European conquest, but rather he imagines it in terms of a process of desecration that makes the Spaniard no different from self-seeking politicians, from Mammon.

This section is devoted to a recall of the violations that are part of the New World heritage. In the same way that Césaire shattered the picture of an exotic, fun-loving Caribbean, Brathwaite undermines such superficiality with a sustained tableau of absurdity and frustration. This is interestingly done in **'Calypso'** as the tragic consequences of the Imperialist Adventure emerge. The contrast lies between the glorification of the adventure and the awesome truth of what took place. The light-hearted jingle of the following lines emphasises the irony of what is suggested:

> O it was a wonderful time
> an elegant benevolent redolent time
> and young Mrs P.'s quick irrelevant crime
> at four o'clock in the morning.

This picture of 'the hurt of history' is continued in the numerous references to the historical suffering of the black race. This is a repeated theme of the negritude writers and the Harlem Renaissance; Brathwaite adds his voice to tracing the journeys of 'the wretched of the earth' or in his words, 'Columbus' coursing Kaffirs'. Poems such as *'Didn't he ramble'*, *'The Journeys'*, *'The Emigrants'*, all suggest the sufferings and humiliations of the black diaspora.

The images that dominate **Rites of Passage** convey the atmosphere of desolation the poet sees around him. In **'Prelude'** these images are introduced as engraved in the landscape:

> Dust glass grit
> the pebbles of the desert:
> Sands shift
> across the scorched
> world water ceases
> to flow.

These lines recur in **'Epilogue'** with the same suggestion of a sordid, barren world: 'desert / sands still shift'.

The religious associations of this sterile world become clear in a poem such as **'Mammon'**. The title is significant in itself and the poem deals with a profane world trapped in a blind materialism. The Caribbean of the present makes no attempt to retrieve the spiritual, or to establish traditions, but forges 'brilliant concrete crosses'. This ties in with the general picture of a paralysing materialism in the Western world not unlike the dry, sterile Europe of Senghor and Césaire. New York epitomises this tendency, 'soilless, stainless, nameless'.

The following sequence, **Masks,** is a contrast to the first in that it is an evocation of serenity and reverence totally absent in the violated New World. It is tempting to locate Brathwaite's vision of Africa as part of the mythical, nostalgic picture evident in such poets as Senghor, to cast Brathwaite in the role of the prodigal son returning to his roots. However, it is significant to note the section is entitled **Masks** and not 'Africa' and to see the extent to which we witness something more complex than blind romanticising of the ancestral past.

What Brathwaite does is situate his quest for a hallowed world in the Ghanaian experience. There he makes contact with a world where there is still communion with the spiritual. So **Masks,** as the word implies, represents a borrowed way of interpreting the world, of making contact with the numinous:

> So for my hacked
> heart, veins' memories, I wear this
> past I borrowed.

Three hundred years have made him a stranger and the agony of this recognition is felt in a poem such as **'The New**

Ships'. **Masks** is not a reintegration into the African past. It is a significant stop on the way back to the New World.

Masks is also used to provide a corrective to the traditional myth of savagery and primitivism in African societies. It describes the kingdoms of Ghana, Mali, Songhai and the growth of these civilisations with the historian's eye for setting the record straight. Central to **Masks,** however, is the poet's encounter with this universe and his initiation into a world of rituals and mystery. **'The Forest'** describes such a recognition of a hallowed state. The images of desolation in the previous section are replaced by a sense of awe and calm appropriate to an unfallen world, the poet's 'wom'd heaven':

> This
> was the pistil journey in-
> to moistened gloom. Dews
> dripped, lights twink-
> led, crickets chirped and still
> the dark was silence, still
> the dark was home.

This vision of 'wholeness' is not permanent. It is the preparation for the final stage of the poet's return. It is the attempt to restore such a moment of stillness and contemplation in his own broken landscape that represents the fundamental movement of the trilogy.

The analogy with Césaire's *Cahier* is useful in discussion of the final phase, **Islands.** In the Martinican poet's work we find that the process of return and fashioning a new poetic vision draws on Rimbaud and Surrealist technique as literary antecedents. The *Cahier* even more than an ideological 'prise de position' is an attempt to dislocate the traditional meanings of words so as to set the poetic imagination free. It was through such directed anarchy that language could be cleansed and become the poet's miraculous weapon for reconstructing the world after the flood. This is precisely what the poet is referring to when he speaks of 'the madness that sees'. Brathwaite's 'the eye must be free / seeing' also suggests this feature of modern poetry as he wishes to reach beyond the static and sterile to retrieve his world through his poetic vision. In this, an important literary ancestor is T. S. Eliot.

Eliot is as important to Brathwaite's creative imagination as the overwhelming moment of revelation in the African experience. To this extent Eliot's poetry almost becomes the literary pre-text for the Caribbean poet's trilogy. This is not to say that Brathwaite supports Eliot's religious and ideological dogma; what he does endorse is the latter's plea for the restoration of the numinous and his indictment of man's enslavement to materialism. In the same way that Eliot criticises modern man's attempt to fix time—indeed, his servitude to linear time, 'the enchainment of past and future', and the accompanying notions of material progress—so Brathwaite attempts to defy such a view of the New World which would make it an uncreative adjunct to Imperial expansion.

At this point Brathwaite the poet upstages Brathwaite the historian, in that he feels the need to go beyond the formal recorded history to a more open and speculative view of the New World experience. This is one way to avoid the knowledge that falsifies, to rediscover in myth a new, liberating sense of self and of possibilities in the Caribbean. When this intense moment of revelation is attained, the poet begins to see his community and landscape for the first time. It is his poetic vision that has the redemptive force of defying the tragic, mutilated, historical stereotype. Brathwaite is alluding to this moment of quasi-mystical illumination when he explains:

> Like a worshipper possessed at shango or vodun,
> as with a jazz musician, time past and time future
> speak to the community in the trapped and hunting
> [sic] moment of awareness.

The artist / shaman in this creative trance becomes a medium, the community's link with a world of mystery which involves a new potency for change.

Islands casts the poet in such a role and can be seen as the *raison d'être* of the trilogy. It begins by restating the sterile, materialistic world of *Rites of Passage.* In **'Homecoming'** this initial state is made explicit:

> To this new doubt
>
> and desert I return,
> expecting nothing.

The universe to which the poet returns represents a harsh encounter with a lifeless, secular reality: God 'is glass with his type- / writer teeth'; the land 'has lost the memory of the most secret places' and the people 'float round and round . . . without hope of the hook / of the fisherman's tugging-in root'. This state is poignantly evoked in the epigrammatic poem **'Pebbles'** which in a sustained image presents a world which is barren and unheeding:

> But my island is a pebble.
> . . .
> It will slay
> giants
>
> but never bear children.

The humpbacked turtle of **'Francina'** is a symbol of the past, of the sacred (like Eliot's river in 'The Dry Salvages') which is ignored and unpropitiated by an insensitive, complacent world. Francina's quiet, daring act of retrieval is mocked by a world that cannot comprehend such an act.

For the poet to accomplish his mission he must find the poetic equivalent to Francina's act. He must reinstate a sense of the sacred in this empty, destructively secular world. Ideology and political solutions are not adequate for this level of restoration. Yet this spiritually impoverished world resists the poet. The poetic word in its full literary and religious significance is the only means of redemption but the poet is daunted by the task. The 'word has been destroyed / and cannot live among us', and the poet has difficulty restoring the word to its real importance. The way in which this strange, desecrated waste-land defies the poet is referred to in such lines as 'the stars / remain my master's / property' and 'they'd rob the world I ruled.' The world is at least temporarily possessed by the Other. It can only be retrieved by an imagination and a language that have been set free.

Some of the poems in *Islands* can be seen as an allegory of the poetic act, namely the act of retrieving and renaming the landscape. A poem such as **'Veve'** suggests this process of 'hallowing' as the fisherman's net or poetic vision falls gently over reality and retrieves it. The lyricism of the poem revolves around the invoking of this state of 'wholeness' and images of rebirth: 'The black eye travels to the brink of vision: / look, the fields are wet, / the sea sits gentle on the dawn.' Significantly placed towards the end of *Islands,* this poem represents the end of the quest, the attainment of this transcendental vision. The final poem, **'Jou'vert'**, is more than an attempt to re-use a local ritual—the carnival. It also represents the dawn of the risen god / word and the poetic vision retrieved with all its positive and healing resonances.

Brathwaite has included himself in the 'second phase' of West Indian writing because his work is so deeply involved in an aesthetic renascence. It is interesting to see how this vision of salvation for the Caribbean has certain implications for the poet's role. The relationship of the poet to his community becomes more complex than that of a poet-politician. It is no longer a question of a readily accessible ideal of commitment which would inspire some collective action. Central to Brathwaite's conception of the poet is the element of possession. Even though he identifies closely with his community, his superior vision inevitably isolates him. Each metaphor of the artist as he appears in Brathwaite's work is presented in terms of a sensitive but essentially lonely figure. For instance, **'Ananse'** suggests such characteristics, 'creator / dry stony world-maker, word breaker' who survives with his memories in the 'dark attic'. The same is true of **'Littoral'** with the frequently used image of the solitary fisherman / artist; 'his head / sleeps in the surf's / drone, his crossed / legs at home / on the rough sand.' He shares the same spiritual resources of Ananse—a voice in the dark—'his fingers knit as the dark rejoices / but he has many voices.' The distance between this creative consciousness and the materialistic world around it is made clear in **'Ogun'.** Ordinarily he appeared to be nothing but a carpenter making 'what the world preferred' but secretly he is a divine craftsman shaping the block of wood 'that would have baffled them . . . breathing air . . . still tuned to roots and water'. This sombre communion with the spiritual has little to do with the rhetorical gesture and iconoclasm of protest poetry. The contemplative state which frees the creative imagination creates an overwhelming kind of self-awareness in the poet. As the trilogy progresses, Brathwaite focuses more intensely on the relocation of his vision of the Caribbean in an artistic consciousness and not in the external history of the region.

So far we have treated literary preoccupations in Brathwaite's work and the emergence of a poetic self-consciousness. Such a resumé of his poetry would seem adequate if he simply saw himself as a cerebral poet, but even the most casual reading of Brathwaite's verse would reveal different or even conflicting voices in his work. The voice we have examined so far is easily recognised as the product of various literary concerns of his initiation into poetry. The other voice that is apparent is more direct and closely linked to the speech patterns and rituals of the folk.

Along with the use of sustained visual imagery and the dislocation of words, Brathwaite favours the use of speech patterns for purposes of irony or to bring immediacy to what he is saying. These intonations that often relieve the apparent plainness of his verse are frequently drawn from local dialects. This has both ideological and literary implications. Brathwaite accepts the need for a writer to be part of a tradition, indeed to be its growing edge. He has sought such a tradition in the creolised cultures of the Caribbean. The use of dialect (like the use of various deities and rituals) is his articulation of the consciousness of those who survived in the New World. The literary significance of what the poet is doing presents a more complicated problem.

The use of dialect in poetry is never considered just another literary device which a poet can exploit to dramatise certain features in his work. It has traditionally been seen as part of an anti-intellectual rejection of formalism in poetry. The spontaneity and simplicity of folk poetry did not seek academic acclaim—in the case of Langston Hughes it meant a defiance of the literary establishment—and so was apparently exempt from critical evaluation. However, it would be a simplification to see Brathwaite's use of dialect as a gratuitous rejection of formal poetic devices, especially with his own closeness to the conventions of modern poetry. The seriousness with which he considers this issue is revealed in a series of articles written in 1967 entitled **"Jazz and the West Indian Novel."** The analogy between the novel form and jazz may be overdone but the point is that Brathwaite sees Caribbean writing in terms of literary improvisation, which explains the comparison with music. This improvisation is also part of a general shift away from traditional literary models towards the articulation of indigenous cultural forms. Repeatedly stressed is the need to bring the literary work closer to speech and the community experience. What is never really discussed is the inevitable differences between speech and the language of poetry.

Essentially any language in poetry is subjected to the conventions of the genre in that the language of everyday speech undergoes a process of transformation. The language of poetry moves beyond the familiar to a new mode that brings new ambiguities, new clusters of resonances and a certain atemporality to what is expressed. Brathwaite in his more successful poems subjects the English language to this process. The same should apply to his use of dialect. Brathwaite's better dialect verse is subjected to enough of a formal re-ordering and control that it rises above the commonplace to become the language of poetry. The poem **'Dust'**, which recounts the explosion of Mont Pelée in Martinique in 1902, effectively captures a feeling of deep-seated terror as well as the notion of a world that has become contingent, where bewildering things occur 'widdout rhyme / widdout reason'. The metaphor of the dust from the volcanic eruption is used with its full biblical resonance to suggest a world where the people 'can't pray to no priest or no leader / an' God gone and darken the day'. Similarly the cricket match of 'Rites' is more than a celebration of a certain community ritual. It becomes an insight into a debilitating passivity which afflicts the crowd. When a poet uses a language in his work he makes it his own. Dialect is a tool for exploring the Caribbean landscape and is moulded by the poet's creative authority. It is in this way also part of the conscious process of repossession.

Any attempt to extract either cultural or political prescriptions from Brathwaite's work takes us onto treacherous ground. The poetic concept of 'wholeness' and the importance of myth and ritual can become distorted when converted into ideological formulae. Brathwaite does not opt for the simplification of cultural decolonisation and does not see the colonial past as a complete void. He has attempted to discover tangible evidence for his essentially poetic perception of reality in the investigation of the continuing process of creolisation in Caribbean society. His historical work, *The Development of Creole Society in Jamaica (1770-1820)*, is original in its attempts to substantiate the integrating creole features which he sees at work in Jamaican society. He has more recently returned to this refutation of cultural plurality in his monograph, *Contradictory Omens: Cultural diversity and integration in the Caribbean.* This work, which sets out to be an objective account of the creolising forces in the Caribbean, becomes somewhat impenetrable as the language moves further away from historical documentation towards the poetic imagination. Brathwaite's main thesis is that

> In spite of efforts to socialize individuals into separate racial groupings as demanded by the ethos of slavery, the ramifications of personal relationships . . . brought new, unexpected exchanges into each group's repertoire of behaviour. This slow uncertain but organic process (from initiation/imitation to invention) . . . is what we mean by creolisation.

Art sometimes offers a way of seeing reality which may be left out of account in other kinds of investigation. *Contradictory Omens* is an attempt to combine poetry and history. The difficulties of such an endeavour are apparent in the obscure and paradoxical nature of this text.

In contrast to this monograph, Brathwaite's most interesting recent work, *Mother Poem,* is a more appropriate medium for articulating his intuition of an authentic creole presence in the Caribbean. The monograph ends 'Unity is submarine' and the main theme and dominant imagery of *Mother Poem* are drawn from this idea. This is the continuation of the process begun in *Islands* as the poet returns to Barbados to discover the 'ancient watercourses' secreted in its limestone landscape. The collection presents a specific focus on Brathwaite's own beginnings and the landscape of Barbados. To this extent it is different from the more panoramic trilogy. We have a narrowing down of the same act of retrieval, the same desire to transcend a dehumanised, materialistic world and restore a sense of the past and a sense of 'wholeness'. The mother, however, is neither Europe nor Africa; the Caribbean poet is no longer a provincial. The image of 'black Sycorax', like the old Amerindian women of Wilson Harris's stories, is that of an ancestral, hidden symbol of survival from which the poet derives his vision.

To conceive of Brathwaite as either a folk poet or a political poet is to limit and even distort what has emerged from his creative imagination. Perhaps the most important single idea behind Brathwaite's work is the rejection of man as a product of ideology. His ability to shift back and forth between a palpably desolate world and the realm of the imaginative, and his consistently anti-materialistic position suggest that for him art has provided a way of liberating the individual from the confining grip of privation and brutality that cloud the documented, external history of the New World. It is this subversion of the traditional myths of an uncreative past and fragmented present that provides the crucial transition to the 'second phase' and enables the artist to conceive of the possibilities of growth and an authentic creole culture in the Caribbean experience.

Velma Pollard (essay date Spring 1980)

SOURCE: "Language in the Poetry of Edward Brathwaite," in *World Literature Written in English,* Vol. 19, No. 1, Spring, 1980, pp. 62-74.

[In the following essay, Pollard considers Brathwaite's "conquest of language," and its role in the poet's handling of voice and themes.]

Since the publication of *Rights of Passage* in 1967, Edward Brathwaite's work has received considerable attention from critics with an interest in Caribbean literature, and the significance of his contribution to the development of that literature as an important branch of literature written in English is now nowhere in doubt. While much of this criticism has centred around the themes he explores (there are very few aspects of Caribbean life that have not received his attention) and the inspired use of complementary rhythms, his use of language has been treated only as an inevitable part of considerations of rhythm, which in turn has been explored within the context of his highly innovative use of the sounds of black music. While it is admittedly difficult and frequently unnecessary to separate language from music, additional perspective may possibly be gained by isolating his creative use of language for specific attention. This article discusses the interrelation of language and theme in this poet's work, having special regard to the importance of language in any description of total behaviour.

It is fitting that a consideration of language in Caribbean poetry should focus on Brathwaite's themes, for he of all the Caribbean poets has stuck most doggedly to themes and images that reflect essentially Caribbean realities or foreign realities of more than passing interest to Caribbean people. In addition, his keen ear for detail and his intense identification with the physical as well as the emotional landscape have constantly stimulated his audience's involvement from idea to idea, from image to image. Visual and aural stimuli complement each other; image is accompanied by sound of word and music of word arrangement so that each unit offers a kind of multidimensional sensation to the reader/listener. Within this vortex of sensation, the creative use of language allows insight into nuances of meaning where sometimes many truths must be told by one phrase, puts the final touch of reality on every image, and identifies the environment and individual character types within it. And this is as it should be, for language is perhaps the most powerful agent at work in our recognition of similarities and differences between ourselves and the people with whom we interact, between our orientation and theirs.

In Brathwaite's trilogy (*Rights of Passage, Masks, Islands*), the main persona, identifiable as the archetypal Caribbean man, moves through various phases of identification and nonidentification with the "manscape" as he travels to the United States and to Europe, to Africa and back to the Caribbean Islands. Language identifies people in all these places and sometimes underlines the prevailing attitudes. In Europe and the U.S. the "Spade" feels dislocated and lonely in cities so vast their "ears have ceased to know / a simple human sound"; where people's attitudes leave no room for doubt that he represents "they," the obvious outsider. His response to the countless negatives offered him is made in the language that is part of his personal behaviour. He asks a number of rhetorical questions in the English of the Caribbean, with its unmistakeable local intonation, as strange and unexpected there as the "Spade" himself:

> So what to do, man?
> Ban the Bomb, Bomb
> the place down?

One representative of the "we" of that environment uses English words to ask in a different tongue:

> Have you no language of your own
> no way of doing things . . . ?

and the "Spade," describing the reaction of another class of that hostile "we," parodies the voice of their language:

> The chaps who drive the City busses
> don't like us clipping for them much;
> in fact, make quite a fuss.

Language is more than mere words. It is, among other things, a way with words. If you try to repeat the second or third quotation using Caribbean intonation or the first quotation using English intonation, the language difference that renders the second ironical should become clear.

In the actual Caribbean environment there is at the artist's disposal an entire language continuum ranging from an almost pure Creole to some local equivalent of standard English. Language usage along the continuum is related to social class and to speech situation, and among people on the islands the acceptance of this reality is almost subconscious. Brathwaite explores the possibilities of this language situation where he describes environment and character on the islands and strives for the same effortlessness that characterizes its normal use. Brotherman the Rasta man in **"Wings of a Dove"** for example, is described at first with the narrator's detachment in the language of the privileged. He is poor and he lives in depressed circumstances where he

> watched the mice
> come up through the floor—
> boards of his down-

town, shanty-town kitchen.

Later the narrator attempts to move into Brotherman's skin. He uses the "I" which is the most obvious feature of Brotherman's language and the most frequently borrowed by outsiders who need, for whatever reason, a temporary identification with him. But one feature does not make a system. The total effect is far too close to standard English. It is still the voice of the observer that speaks:

> And I
> Rastafar-I
>
> In Babylon's boom
> town, crazed by the moon
> and the peace of this chalice. . . .

The true body and spirit of Rasta is only revealed when Brotherman's feelings are made known in his own highly marked version of Jamaica Creole:

> Them doan mean it, yuh know,
> them cahn help it
> but them clean-face browns in
> Babylon town is who I most fear
> an' who fears most I. . . .

Brotherman's social and religious positions are both visible in these words. He is a particular unit of Caribbean man: he is a member of the Rastafari religious/social group in Jamaica.

Less highly marked, more generally representative is the language in the mouths of the "little" women of the Caribbean in **"The Dust."** They come together in a small-goods shop, recognizable the length and breadth of the islands. Here they take groceries on credit and here they enjoy the social interaction so necessary to meaningful living. The sounds behind their reactions to local news and their deep philosophizing about reality are folk and calypso; the language is the language of the Caribbean man in the street, in this case a mild Barbadian Creole easily understood by speakers from other anglophone islands and not so difficult that a non-Caribbean listener feels lost. Brathwaite is totally faithful to the important if routine event he reproduces in this poem. The idea that poor people in the Caribbean (like their equivalents elsewhere) find some philosophical framework into which the irrationalities of everyday living are made to fit would lose credibility if the philosopher had been asked to use anything but the language that is her natural response to her environment:

> When uh hear things so;
> is make me wonder an'
> pray; 'cause uh say

to meself: Olive, chile,
you does eat an' sleep
an' try to fuhget

some o' de burdens
you back got to bear;
. . . .

ev'ry day you see the sun
rise, the sun
set; God sen' ev'ry month

a new moon, Dry season
follow wet season again
an' the green crop follow the rain.

The philosophy of these women may be simplistic by twentieth-century Western standards but it is by no means unreasonable and does represent the kind of philosophizing that is still frequently heard in the Caribbean environment, particularly when unusual events take place.

Completely unrecognizable to Caribbean man is the environment he meets when he journeys to Africa. It is stranger to him than Europe or the United States because it is not the place from which his education emanated; nothing has prepared him for what he finds. It is only at the gut level that he can respond to this environment. The world of his mind has constantly omitted this landscape. *Masks,* the second book of the trilogy, describes the journey to Africa and exposes the reader to a wealth of historical information on the kingdoms of this continent under the guise of re-educating the ex-African.

The first lesson is about the **"Making of the Drum."** The next lesson is even more important: that you must *listen* to the drum. This Africa is a landscape of sound. In the oral Akan tradition, the talking drum is an instrument of speech, not a background of sound to support other instruments; Twi language tones are in fact represented on these drums. There are visual images here, but the overriding sense is that of hearing:

The gong-gong's
iron eyes
of music
walk us through the humble
dead to meet
the dumb
blind drum
where Odomankoma speaks

Kon Kon kon kon
kun kun kun kun
Funtumi Akore

Twenebon Akore. . . .

The beautiful sound-shapes of the Akan words, striking in the spoken rendering of the poem, are effective even on the cold page. Here language places the significant touch on the description of environment so the reader receives a total impression. Slowly the words of the language of our understanding replace the Akan words, but the sounds are not English. The shapes continue to mesmerise:

Tweneboa Akore
Spirit of the Cedar Tree
Spirit of the Cedar Tree
Tweneboa Kodia . . .

. . . .

we are addressing you
ye re kyere wo

listen
let us succeed. . . .

In the sequencing of *Masks,* the sense of sound on the African landscape balloons slowly. **"Atumpan,"** the one dimensional talking drum, is followed by **"Mmenson,"** the orchestra of elephant horns (this is the same music of elephant horns that is later used to join Africa with black America). But no more language is heard until people (as opposed to historical figures) appear on the landscape. They greet the returning brother in voices "smooth . . . like pebbles / moved by the sea of their language. . . ." The sounds are incomprehensible but they are sweet. The reader is not, however, left to accept the poet's judgement on trust. The actual words are presented with their English meanings:

Akwaaba they smiled
meaning welcome

Akwaaba they called
aye koo. . . .

The text continues in English but again the intonation is faithful to the environment:

well have you walked
have you journeyed

welcome

The thematic consideration here is that the brother returning "after three hundred years" will understand that his future cannot be contained in this present; that the whole experience of the Middle Passage and its consequences have rendered him something of a misfit in these surroundings.

The psychic refrain ("do you remember?") prepares us for his doubt and eventual despair. But nothing is explicit; this is the language of gentle suggestion. Brathwaite is using an interesting strategy here: he uses the language of the elders in Akan country to express the arrivant's doubt:

> I walked in the bush
> but my cut-
> lass cut
> no path;
> returned
> from the farm
>
> but could not hear
> my children
> laugh. . . .

Notice that this motif is one that has been retained in Caribbean Creoles, if in fragmented form, from the African parent. Compare the style of that quotation with the following lines from a Caribbean folk song:

> mi trow mi caan a grong
> mi no caal no fowl far i
> you com pick i up
> an i run you belly . . .
>
> (I threw my corn on the ground; I didn't call any
> fowls for it; you came and picked it up; and it gave
> you diarrhoea)

The man who remembers fragments of food and of comfort remembers also fragments of language form. In a number of ways he is "half-home." It is not the intention here to suggest that this particular linguistic style belongs exclusively to the African continent or even that Brathwaite's awareness of its possibilities is less the result of his eurocentric book-learning than of his African experience. What is important here is that he has exploited a pattern of language and uses it in the same way that he uses patterns of music to extend the subordinate theme of African continuities.

Language as a marker of cultural difference, not cultural similarity, is most blatantly used in **"Nametracks,"** a studied, if biased, discussion of the education system. This aspect of Caribbean life and a certain resentment of its obvious eurocentricity appears in nearly every volume of Brathwaite's work so far. Here he selects with creditable precision a symbol of playtime in any primary school (perhaps not of the seventies), the game Ogrady, which is a kind of follow-the-leader. In the actual practice of the game, Ogrady gets back what he gives. In **"Nametracks"** the leader constantly sees the possibility that his orders will be interpreted in an unexpected and totally unacceptable way by the would-be follower. Brathwaite is playing with a language in which many of the jokes across social barriers are based on misinterpretations of words with identical sounds but quite different meanings:

> say
> i
> ogrady says
> say
> i
> not
> eye
> globe
> seeing word
> blue priest
> green voodoo doctor. . . .

The images after "eye" accept the connotations Caribbean folk know for words associated with "seeing." If you suspect that something supernatural is affecting you, you go to "look"—you go to the "see-er man." This aspect of Caribbean life represents disorganized fragments of African religions here used as symbols of the world Ogrady wishes his follower to reject:

> say
> i
> am your world
>
> you must not
> break
> it. . . .

The conflict continues throughout this very long poem. Ogrady continues to use the English "I" and receives, later, not an incorrect interpretation of the word but a repetition of its Creole translation "me," which allows it the additional gloss of "my":

> say
> i
> Ogrady
>
> say
> aei
>
> but
>
> me muh
> me muh
> mud
> me mudda
>
> brek
> de word

. . .

an she te an she teach an she teach mih. . . .

The total message of this poem is too vast and too important to be treated as part of a commentary such as this. It is sufficient to note here how Ogrady loses his temper and rushes into his follower/pupil's ideolect to facilitate comprehension and how the follower, obstinate and resisting, suggests that he give up the struggle:

> i learn
> says ogrady
> what she bell you
>
> but i doan want no oo
> ma nor congolese mudda
> to hell i in here
> leh me quell yuh
>
> so is i
> says ogrady
> say i
>
> says ogrady
> say i
>
> . . . .
>
> but me head hard ogrady
> an me doan give a damn
>
> me back to me belly
> an me dun dead a'ready. . . .

Ogrady's speech reverses a stylistic device used with considerable effect in earlier Brathwaite where words on the page carry echoes of similar words which serve to reinforce the atmosphere of the poem or to signify the narrator's attitude. Here it is the word on the page that gives the attitude while the echo gives the sense of the phrase. Perhaps the attitude is too important here to be left to chance. In any case it is a very economical device and this poet has obviously learned how to control it. Look for example at the words "bell," "hell" and "quell" in the quotation above. All are echoes of the verb "tell," but in the first case, the mother tells it, constantly repeating it like a bell; in the second case "hell" reflects Ogrady's view of the Congo and its paraphernalia; and "quell" is what Ogrady truly hopes to do to the influence from which this unfortunate follower is so obviously suffering. Ogrady's failure is reported in the final lines in the mouth of the follower:

> but e nevver *maim* what me
>   mudda me name
> an a nevva *nyam* what me

mane.

(Emphasis added.) After this comes the refrain heard earlier, the calypsonian singing lines taken from a well-known calypso here suggesting that if, as Ogrady says, the mother culture is hell, then the follower is quite irretrievably there, and is not particularly unhappy about it:

> uh doan give a damn
> uh dun dead a'ready. . . .

In this poem, as in a number of other serious poems by Brathwaite, the music of the lines is so seductive that one feels that one could pass over much of the message of the poem without losing enjoyment of the lines. This perhaps indicates that one should read first for music and then again for meaning so that the same script is both words and "version."

Brathwaite's conquest of language for Caribbean poetry has been a very important triumph. Perhaps it is also very self-conscious, for he himself has, in another context, commented on the attitude to the word in folk cultures, where language "was and is a creative act in itself." The writer in the Caribbean has at his disposal not merely the sleights of language of the skilled monodialectal artist but also the freedom of the entire afro-european continuum, with all its niceties of reference, that is his linguistic heritage. That he has explored this language in his poetry, maintaining the fine balance required to present linguistic honesty without making his work inaccessible to a wider audience, is particularly praiseworthy.

Joan Dayan (review date 9 April 1988)

SOURCE: "The Beat and the Bawdy," in *The Nation,* April 9, 1988, pp. 504-07.

[*In the following review of* X/Self, *Dayan examines the elements of culture and history that are embedded in Braithwaithe's epic poem.*]

In 1982 Morris Cargill, a white Jamaican, writing in Jamaica's largest newspaper, the *Daily Gleaner,* condemned what he called "the tastelessness and idiocy of the current pop and Reggae 'culture'":

> That the mass of people have vulgar and uneducated tastes is nothing new. What is new is that we are forced into approval of it. . . . We are in effect told that Yellow Man is a superior artist to Beethoven, and that almost any horrid noise made by some group of unattractive louts is our "cultural heritage."

Cargill called upon Jamaicans to "take heart and speak up, and not allow themselves to be overrun by the barbarians."

What happens when an "educated" poet of the West Indies chooses to write for and with the "masses," to reclaim a history and a heritage based not on the monumental, colonial myth but on the realities of racism and class oppression? Edward Kamau Brathwaite, a respected historian and critic, editor of *Bim,* one of the earliest and most important literary magazines in the West Indies, and of *Savacou,* a journal of the Caribbean Artists' Movement, which he founded in 1966, became a source of embarrassment and discomfort to his academic colleagues with the publication of **Rites of Passage** in 1967. In the first book in what would become his moving trilogy of the black diaspora, **The Arrivants,** Brathwaite turned to those voices long neglected by Eurocentric scholarship, the disenfranchised and silenced in urban ghetto and countryside.

One Jamaican poet and critic responded to the presence in **Rites of Passage** of the jiving "spade," "fuck-in' negro" and "Brother Man the Rasta" with the taunt, "Niggers, niggers, everywhere." Another reviewer, perhaps disconcerted by the rhythms of blues and jazz, gospel, work song and dialect, more prudently relegated certain passages to the less demanding (and implicitly mindless) status of oral performance pieces: "Sections which on close scrutiny seem to grow only more unrewarding and 'gimmicky' would come into their own in the onward, unreflective press of speaking."

Since that time, in spite of the ambivalent responses of the Caribbean literary establishment, Brathwaite has continued to write a poetry that engages in social history, in voices other than poetic. With its cultural urgency and desire to build from the ground up, literally forging a national language out of the common voice, his poetry is unique for committing itself to West Indian reality and to the often submerged origins of that reality. Throughout this poetry of reconnection, Brathwaite labors to see the journey from Africa to the New World not only as "a traumatic, destructive experience, separating the black from Africa, disconnecting their sense of history and tradition, but a pathway or channel between this tradition and what is being evolved, on new soil, in the Caribbean." His struggle to give voice to "the drum, the beat, and the bawdy," to base his work in an "alternative" or "folk" tradition that remains for him the surest trace of history, redefines and broadens the bounds of what we deem "poetic."

Black & Blues (1976), his bitter response to the end of the Black Power movement in America and its collapse in the Caribbean, won the Casas de las Americas Prize, and his recent **X/Self** has been awarded the British Commonwealth Award. Brathwaite may well be the most original poet now writing in English. He has not, however, been claimed or praised by Anglo-American academic critics, a fate, it seems, reserved for Derek Walcott, the other major epic voice in the Caribbean. And yet, the opposition between Walcott and Brathwaite, constructed primarily by Caribbean critics, is more apparent than real.

To pit Walcott against Brathwaite, the visionary "noble rider" against the earthbound historian of the "local," is to diminish and marginalize the particularity of the Caribbean experience. Any reductive Prospero/Caliban opposition ignores a reciprocal and fertile dialogue (uniquely Caribbean in its materials and inspiration) in the name of something called "universality." When critics compare Walcott with Lowell, Auden or Stevens, and completely ignore his reaction to, and dialogue with Brathwaite, they obscure the evolution of national expression. As the discerning Jamaican critic Sylvia Wynter wrote, "the dilemma of being either West Indian or European is a false one. To be a West Indian is to accept all the facets of one's being."

Brathwaite and Walcott discussed their poetry for the first time together in a colloquy at Yale University this February. Though the quality of language in their poetry differs, both poets attempt to reimagine a history. In the composite world of the West Indies, where Coca-Cola and transplanted African gods coexist, the "drum and trumpet" history of empire is subsumed in a new kind of writing that might well be the ground for a new myth. In between any New World/Old World antagonism stands Brathwaite's "computer conjur man" or Walcott's very down-to-earth, fast-talking Odysseus, his "Shabine," who summons and is transformed by the memory of the footloose, golden Caribs.

X/Self is the unsettling, final book of another trilogy, which includes the "calm histories" of **Mother Poem** (1977) and **Sun Poem** (1982). While **The Arrivants** deals with transmigration, a movement from Africa to New York or England and back to the West Indies, Brathwaite's second trilogy focuses on a "landscape of emergence," a place the gods might once again inhabit. **Mother Poem** is a tribute to his native land, the coral and limestone island of Barbados. The poet listens for the "ancient watercourses," the "echo of river, trickle, worn stone / the sunken voice." And out of a "cracked fragmented landscape," of "bricks and cement blocks," he miraculously gains a voice: "the stone wrinkled, cracked and gave birth to water." It is not so much naming but remembering that matters, the effort to recall what has been unnamed, submerged and violated. In **Sun Poem,** the son of the woman / island Barbados journeys to the rough, northeastern part of the island. Here, in the most compelling passage of the poem, he sees Legba: Once the Dahomean god of procreative energy, the New World "Legba-of-the-Old-Bones," the Haitian god of the crossroads, is now suffering and broken. Going beyond mere nostalgia for a phantom Africa, Brathwaite brings the god to life on Cattlewash beach, where he howls, rages and falls to his death:

> And when his raving was done he had stood on a cliff called hackletons cliff and gazing full at the sun that was beating tormenting drums in his head he had raised his head in a shout . . . and his cry grew greater as the pain of the world grew black for him and he staggered and fell slipped staggered and fell down hackletons cliff down past the few bent coconut trees.

Brathwaite's search for "the lineaments of Legba" in the Americas becomes a terrible rite of passage to Guinea, the legendary home of the gods, and it marks the poet's turn to his own lost history and identity: "Turning my face down / wards to my approaching past."

In *X/Self* Brathwaite can no longer present the Akan mysteries, the beat of the *atumpan* ("talking drums"), the African icons given voice in his early *Masks* (1968). Now those things are broken against the sound waves of CNN broadcasts. Speaking as prophet, *houngan,* DJ, father and son, Brathwaite turns on his own language; and that language of return and renovation is made out of what others might judge as shards and remnants. He risks a lot by refusing to eliminate (or purify his text of) those odds and ends, the tokens of conflicting histories that deter, fragment and exhaust. This cleansing, this latest "sunsong," has nothing to do with Judeo-Christian ideals of hierarchy or privilege. It cannot afford to encase the teachings of Walcott's "absent masters" in the beauties of verse. For this long road to Guinea leads not to whiteness but "towards / young Caliban howling for his tongue / . . . towards / red tacky bleeding in the west."

Even in the final, exuberant **"Xango,"** Brathwaite speaks unashamedly for and with an unprivileged majority. His song is rooted in popular experience and serves popular needs. Here, he recalls the early language experiments of his first epic poem, ***Rites of Passage.*** After wandering from Rome through the remnants of Old and New World civilizations in *X/Self,* Brathwaite returns to the "blue note" of the trumpeter/poet:

> after so many twists
> after so many journeys
> after so many changes
> bop hard bop soul bop funk
> new thing marley soul rock skank
> *bunk johnson is ridin again*

The legendary New Orleans jazz trumpeter is the god of thunder and lightning, Shango, and Brathwaite brings the African past into the presence of a sound that can "shatter outwards to your light and calm and history / your thunder has come home."

X/Self is a vexed poem, fragmentary and uneven. Courting his own failure ("& / a fine / a cyaan get nutten / write / a cyaan get nutten really / rite"), Brathwaite bluntly disavows the role of poet as the "antennae of the race" or "legislator of mankind." Unlike Walcott, or his own self-image in ***Sun Poem,*** he cannot be Adam, blessed and elated, as Walcott writes, by "Adam's task of giving things their names." For Brathwaite's *X/Self* turns out to be more than the Caribbean self unselved: "you make of me mysteries foundationless histories / child drake athlete moor." Its title recalls a crucial scene in Aimé Césaire's *Une Tempête* (1969), his remarkable adaptation of Shakespeare's *Tempest* for a "black theater." The play turns upon Caliban's interrogation of history, his call for origins and demand for remembrance. Césaire gives Caliban the power to choose another name; he announces, "I will no longer be Caliban." How about Cannibal, jokes Prospero, restoring the name to its origin. Or Hannibal, "They all love historic names!" Caliban chooses X for his missing past: "Every time you call me I am reminded that you've stolen everything from me: even my identity!" Caliban's problem with naming Brathwaite applies to his title as well: "Why a callin it / X? / a doan writely / know."

In a profound reassessment of the meaning of history, Brathwaite fixes *X/Self* somewhat uncomfortably in between opposing worlds: Mount Blanc/Europe confronts Kilimanjaro/Africa, as Ogoun/Caliban fights against and within Western history. He tells the stories of those peoples oppressed and confounded since the breakup of the Roman Empire and the beginning of Western European civilization. The poem's language, sometimes verging on incoherence, articulates the pathos of the two-way linguistic inheritance of the West Indies: the givens of an alien, dominant lexicon (the imported, educated *langue de culture*) and the remnants of African usages still existing in the islands. Here is Brathwaite in *X/Self,* thinking about how to begin, how to get into the "language thing":

> & what is de bess weh to seh so/so
> it doan sounn like
>
> brigg
> flatts nor hervokitz
>
> nor de pisan cantos nor de souf sea
> bible

This rough dream of beginnings is asked in the letter X/Self writes to his "mamma." Punctuated with stops and starts, marred by misspellings and grammatical blunders, the letter is beat out on a new computer. Caliban's retaliatory curse, his project of turning the gift of language against his master, turns out to be nothing more than the wiles of the computer cursor: "for not one a we should responsible if prospero get curse / wid im own / curser."

The labor of poetry remains as hard a task for Brathwaite, given neocolonial impositions that slowly erode the *nyam*—life force, food, gut or word—of indigenous local cultures, as slaving in the cane fields, working someone else's land, reading someone else's history. Living in Kingston, and teaching at the University of the West Indies, Brathwaite witnesses the Jamaica of Edward Seaga and Ronald Reagan while never allowing us to forget the promise of the Manley years. In **"Mai Village"** Brathwaite looks back to a revolutionary time (1968-1976) in Jamaica, feared by "the master gunners in the sweating three piece suits," and now lost:

> there was a fear
> for a time that marcus malcolm martin
>   & mahatma one of the sooth
> say/ers from among the youth might
>   have boiled
> over boys will be boils they say
>
> but they chew gum sitting on the wall
>   in sunshine or in sha. a. dow
> steer clear of politricks letting the future
>   pray
> unto itself with garbage

Brathwaite makes us respond to this time of quiet unselving, of de-historicizing, where history—or any attempt to retrieve a history—is buried under a pile-up of recycled images, media hype and satellite dishes, "micro / maniacs and preachers harps." The question he asks again and again—is this a time of recognition?—staggers in a world of voices where recognition has lost meaning. In this poem even disavowal fails.

Confronting the realities of recolonization, Brathwaite sees a new Middle Passage (the slaves journey from Africa to America), devised by the tempting importations coming to the islands from the north: "how dangerous were the generosities wrapped up in cellophane." The Amerindian past bucks up against TV, word processor and dinette set. Tourism becomes the link between the early conquistadors and the new colonizers: "there will be / buildings rushing upwards on a scream of sand." Brathwaite's effort is no false nostalgia or rant but an attempt to confront the West Indian embarrassment about their past, their choosing to forget slavery and to revel instead in the acquisitions of "civilization." A dramatic attack on the elites, whom Césaire once described as the most powerful allies of the neocolonialist, Brathwaite's poem alternately accommodates and defies the

antagonistic forces identified primarily as the savants, mercantilists, politicians and clergy.

Brathwaite's personal experiences, growing up in Barbados and reading Caesar's *Gallic Wars* in his uncle's library, lead to this surreal tour through civilizations and conquests. Caesar's *Gallic Wars* seen through a child's eyes and war reprocessed as the transmission of language in *Kennedy's Latin Primer* confront the mud, memory and breath of "the flare of drum," "swahili laughter," "the sunlights and sunrise of the east." Although much in the poem might first appear as nothing more than the stereotype of an oppression, with condemnations as pernicious in their extremes as any idealized sentiment can be, Brathwaite maintains a tension between things and times in whatever site he chooses. He makes sure that the opposition between Caliban's push and Prospero's rigidity is no easy antithesis but a mutual infiltration: "rome burns / and our slavery begins"; "chad sinks / and forest trees crash down"; "in the alps . . . glacier of god / chads opposite . . . as it rises / chad sinks"; "far out across the lake of galilee / the aztecs wheel around their painted whips."

Brathwaite moves through breakdown to something like clarity, from "rome burns / and our slavery begins / herod herodotus the tablets of moses are broken" to the tentative glories of **"Sunsong"** and **"Xango."** Yet most of the poetry records a disintegration unalleviated by any saving landscape or envisioned harmony. *X/Self* most often reads as if the poet were composing frantically at the edge of an apocalypse of consumption: "we have been visited by goddesses and loan sharks from across the / water." And in words recalling the "contra naturam" of Pound's Usura Canto:

> there will be
> no more sonny rollins . . . there will be
> no more magic lanthorn lilies
>
> no fra angelico annunciations
>
> no herb nor obi bush nor blue nor
> susumba no canefield doctor in
> the back dam
>
> glow
>
> no lla lla llaaa illllalla and malcolm is
> his profit

Both reticent and wild, the language of *X/Self* takes on the meaning of writing and living in conditions of terror and violence, in the daily reminder that "independence" is a mere word. The poem asks us to think about how words *mean* at all in a language that historically blinds, manipulates and deadens. Brathwaite utters the now empty jargon, the sad fact of the worn-out phrase, "an you young and gifted": "i just can't get / up stand / up stand / up for i rights bob," before he finally gains a voice, the "hail," "huh," "hah" of his final hymn to Africa, **"Xango."** The poem thus redefines the epic for the Caribbean—and its medium of "bone and riddim" is not a poetry of transcendence. It would not be appreciated by Joseph Brodsky, who limits Walcott's tentative and multivoiced efforts to a "supreme version" of language—a "language . . . greater than its masters or its servants." Brathwaite's epic tells the story of the colonizing of minds, the costuming of souls, "the guile of velvet and the plumes of pride."

If there is any victory celebrated in *X/Self,* it is no easy synthesis but a jangling, cavorting Jamaican/African, New World/Old World embrace, the grip of the "computer conjur man." After journeying through Charlemagne's France, Henri Christophe's Haiti, T. S. Eliot's London, Reagan's America and Botha's South Africa, Brathwaite offers us a composite triumph. The triumph lies in repeating words partly remembered from Césaire's *Cahier d'un retour au pays natal* ("Notebook of a Return to the Native Land"): "i would leave dross / i would still say with cesaire. spark / i would say. storm. olodumare's conflagration / i would speak sperm. and twinkle." Strength returns in the annunciation of the Rasta "bongo man," the rebel who revolts by changing the uses of the Hausa word "bungu," which in Jamaica had come to mean not only "crude, ugly, or loutish" but "black-and-ugly": "*bongo man a come / bongo man a come / bruggadung / bruggadung /* . . . and we rise / . . . rising / rising / burning / soon."

Brathwaite's remembering of history in this remarkable sequence of poems demands a breakdown of the word and the fragmentation of identity. Whose word, how to say it, how to know it? The word imposed, the word in histories that kills, the word that will not come, broken, stuttered, regained.

> who dat speaking
> I is who
> I-self
>
> I was trying to say what my name

A moving response and sequel to Walcott's perpetuation of Adam's task.

H.H. Anniah Gowda (essay date Autumn 1994)

SOURCE: "Creation in the Poetic Development of Kamau Brathwaite," in *World Literature Today,* Vol.68, No.4, Autumn, 1994, pp. 683-96.

[*In the following essay, Gowda investigates Brathwaite's use of "nation language" as a means of expressing a postcolonial West-Indian perspective.*]

There are not many historians who have distinguished themselves as poets and prose writers, who can recite poetry with rhythm and melody, not many who have endeavored to create "nation language" and make poetry truly native. Kamau Brathwaite, who has now become the Neustadt Prize laureate for 1994, has all these attributes and accomplishments, as well as the great honor of freeing poetry in English from the tyranny of dying of ossified main tradition. In his 1982 lectures at the Centre for Commonwealth Literature and Research in Mysore, India, he emphasized a "true alternative to Prospero's offering." "What happened in Shakespeare," he said, "what happened to Caliban in *The Tempest* was that his alliances were laughable, his alliances were fatal, his alliances were ridiculous. He chose the wrong people to make God. And if he had understood the nature of the somatic norm, it is possible that he would have chosen a different set of allies for his rebellion. So that is the first thing I want to present to you, the notion of the alternative, the image of the alternative, which resides in the figure of Caliban, not the Caliban who is concerned with metaphysical revolt, the revolt of the spirit, the reconstitution of the mind, which is something that becomes much more crucial in the development of the Third World than simple physical revolt." He considered Sycorax, Caliban's mother, "a paradigm for all women of the Third World, who have not yet, despite all the effort, reached that trigger of visibility which is necessary for a whole society."

This is the main theme that underlies the prose and poetry of Brathwaite, a major Caribbean poet with a large reputation and world stature. He insists on the sense and value of the inheritance of the West Indies and continuity with Africa; he is keen on discovering the West Indian voice in creative arts and emerges a creator of words. He has waged a war against the English language, which had allowed itself to be shackled into a verse system borrowed from the Latin language which did not go in for hammer blows of the West Indian Creole. His legacy was to work in "the English which is so subtly deformed, so subtle a subversion of English." Hence he draws freely on all the riches of the Caribbean multicultural inheritance and has created "the semantic image, where you begin to conceive of the metaphor, also an alternative to that of Prospero." His essays and speeches offer very interesting insights into his own creative writing and the situation of the writer in the Third World and newly independent nations. He has evolved a critical system using critical values different from what one would find in the *Times Literary Supplement.* As a historian, he traces the background to the evolution of West Indian writing and its structural conditions and the diversity of languages in a plural society. He wants the language, the new language, to embody "the syllables, the syllabic intelligence, to describe the hurricane, which is our own experience."

The early Walcott, Brathwaite, and others have endeavored to create a nation language and confidently communicate with the audience. They use language in its most intense, rich, nuanced, and vital forms, outgrowing the sophisticated and artificial language of the colonizers. They use dialect and local detail and express the voice of the community. In their hands we see the strangeness of the English language. We are aware of Walcott's use of speech rhythms—"O so Yu is Walcott? / You is Robby brother? / Teacher Alix son?" (*Sea Grapes,* 1976)—but this mission is up to a point in Walcott, who seems alternately ardent and cold in the desire to be outside English literature—English literature in a hierarchical sense. The angst of the important poems "The Spoiler's Return" and "North and South" in *The Fortunate Traveller* suggest an American infection. But it is zeal that makes him return to the Caribbean in theme and vocabulary in his epic *Omeros* (1992), which demonstrates his philosophy to "ground with West Indian people." Salman Rushdie in 1982 argued that the English language "grows from many roots; and those whom it once colonized are carving out large territories within the language themselves." It is the genius of the English language that it adapts to strange climates and strange people.

Brathwaite, who has not wavered in his determination, is very close to Indian poets who try to make their content Indian, even while their drapery is English. In his views on "nation language," exploration and exile, and the drudgery and loneliness of Negro slaves, he seeks and seeks "but finds no one to speak," and prayers do not go "beyond our gods / or righteousness and mammon."

Brathwaite, who now rides the tide of literary innovation freeing poetry "from the tyranny of the pentameter," is distinguished in his use of nation language. He is deeply immersed in writing about the frustration of a West Indian and of his critical experience of the black sage and the New World. In 1970 he said, "The problem of and for West Indian artists and intellectuals within this fragmented culture, they start out in the world without a sense of wholeness." Having mastered and bent Prospero's language to suit his purpose, as a poet he concentrates on "Europe coming to the Caribbean," or what he calls "the after-Renaissance of Europe coming with an altered consciousness." Therefore his poetry deals with the Maroon, the artist, the Negro slave, the reconstruction of fragments into something much more humane: a vision of a man-world. Brathwaite's ability lies in discovering the sense of wholeness. He has produced a metaphor for West Indians as a dispossessed people and has tried to invent his own esthetics for representing the Caribbean consciousness.

How does Brathwaite, who feels the need to liberate himself from inherited colonial cultural models, seek to distance his work from the pentameter of Chaucer? By attempting to develop a system that more closely and intimately approaches the experience common to all ex-colonies. He has expanded the treasures of his native talent in adapting and deepening his hold on the English language, making of it an instrument upon which he is able to play to perfection a greater variety of melodies than any other West Indian.

The West Indies, like many Third World countries, has colonial problems, but unlike India, the region does not have a long and rich literary heritage. In spite of many invasions, India retained her cultural riches; she was neither humiliated nor dispossessed even when ruled by foreigners. In the New World, on the contrary, blacks and West Indians had to endure slavery, indentured labor, and also an apparent discontinuity with their native cultures in Africa and India: "We have had a history of slavery and colonialism for the last four hundred years and very little else." In such a situation a heavy burden is placed on the writer. He must create not only awareness but a tradition, what Eliot termed "the historical sense-indispensable." Hence Brathwaite endeavors hard to create a usable past for his fragmented region.

Having lived in Ghana for nine years and felt his stay there to be something of a homecoming, Brathwaite sees "its" culture as continuous with the West Indian diaspora. In order to drive home this important point, he uses the words of a revolutionary and composes poetry characterized first and foremost by its self-conscious and formal lexical contrast to standard English. He uses "music and rhythm" as bases of his verse, and also "kinesis and possession." *Kinesis* is a term which refers to the use of energy, and it derives here from the African religious culture, where worship is best expressed in kinetic energy. The idea is that the more energy "you can accumulate and express, the nearer you will come to God." The poet's heart bleeds at the predicament of the Negro slave in the New World. His prayers are the common prayers of all who underwent imperialism but still possess the "mother's milk of language to fall back on."

Brathwaite began his poetic career on the assumption that he was cut off from civilization, that he was in exile. He even gave his earliest poems the suggestive collective title *Other Exiles.* A desire for change in social values is evident there in the juxtaposition of folk images and historical elements: "he watched the seas of noon-dragged aunts and mothers / black galley slaves of prayer // but all his thoughts were chained / which should have sparked and hammered in his brain" (**"Journeys"**).

In many multilingual countries creation in a foreign language is considered inferior to creation in one's mother tongue. Unlike India, which possesses a rich cultural heritage and a strong epic tradition, the Caribbean had no alternative to Prospero's offering. Hence Brathwaite's attempts to overcome that obstacle, to "leap the saddle" and "reach the moon" (**"Journeys"**). The medium is English but the subject is Caribbean. Very early the poet discarded the classical meters of English verse as incapable of effectively expressing, for example, the havoc of the hurricane. In **"Arrival"** he speaks of how his islands inspire him, and he hugs them, "stuffed away in his pockets / the fingers tightly clenched, / around a nervousness."

Brathwaite conceives of ancestral cultures from the Caribbean perspective—that is, the American culture, the European culture which formed the modern Caribbean beginning in 1492, and the cultures of Africa and Asia which constitute the basis of Caribbean society. One culture impinges on the other. Therefore, he says, "he unpacked the wired apparatus of his eyes // So that he could assess not only surfaces / but doubts and coils" (**"Arrival"**). His images are distinct. In one of his early poems, **"Cat,"** he writes that the poet must create with the sensitivity of the cat, an integral element of African history which imparts authenticity to the Caribbean. The sensibility of **"Cat"** yields to a new type of poetic sensibility which adumbrates the folk culture of the slaves; that folk culture, in turn, contributes a certain continuity to the development of modern-day society. As a historian, Brathwaite asserts that the folk culture of the ex-African slaves still persists in the life of contemporary folk.

The Arrivants: A New World Trilogy—comprising the earlier collections *Rights of Passage* (1967), *Islands* (1969), and *Masks* (1968)—is an epic which explores the pathos and frustration of a nation on an epic scale. Its opening lines are suggestive:

> Drum skin whip
> lash, master sun's
> cutting edge of
> heat, taut
> surfaces of things
> I sing
> I shout
> I groan
> I dream
> about
>
> Dust glass grit
> the pebbles of the desert

The short lines and strong rhythm express pain and anguish.

African migration to the New World and the consciousness of the slaves become integral elements in the poetry of Kamau Brathwaite. They form the underlying basis of *Rights*

of Passage, which is considered an epic of a civilization. "Prelude," whose first twelve lines are cited above, is characteristic of Brathwaite's effort in composing new verse for the consciousness of an ignored soul. That poem continues:

> sands shift:
> across the scorched
> world water ceases
> to flow.
> The hot
> wheel'd caravan's
> carcases
> rot.
> Camels wrecked
> in their own
> shit
> resurrect butter-
> flies that
> dance in the noon
> without hope
> without hope
> of a morning.

Brathwaite's verse deals with the history of rootlessness, folk aspirations, and exile. Hence it is a kind of an "Iliad for Black People." *Rights of Passage* demonstrates Brathwaite's preoccupations not only with the poetic form but also with content: the experiences of the black diaspora and its links to the new archetypal themes of exile, journey, and exploration of the New World. Of the Maroon he says: "The Maroon is not an antiquity, lost and forgotten, an archeological relic. Maroons are alive and their patterns are still there for us to learn from. You can still learn the art of carving from Maroons. You can still learn the poetry of religious invocation from the Maroons. You can still learn techniques, if we need them, of guerrilla warfare from the Maroons, so that we have a very living alternative culture on which we could draw." Therefore he says in **"Tom"**:

> the paths we shall never remember
> again: Atumpan talking and the harvest branches,
> all the tribes of Ashanti dreaming the dream
> of Tutu, Anokye and the Golden Stool, built
> in Heaven for our nation by the work
> of lightning and the brilliant adze: and now
> nothing

This reference to heritage is relevant to all Third World countries where an older or existing civilization is destroyed by imperialism. There is a correspondence between the poet's sense of tradition and his vision which gives *The Arrivants* its epic quality. "Tom" the old slave is a symbol of the continuity of the tradition of the poet as visionary and as representative voice in all oppressed Third World countries.

not green alone
not Africa alone
not dark alone
not fear
alone
but Cortez
and Drake
Magellan
and that Ferdinand
the sailor
who pierced the salt seas to this land.

The mask is also an important symbol in Brathwaite's poetry. It can conceal the real nature behind it, but it can also
act as a bridge. *Masks* (1968) contains elegiac poetry. The
adventure of an epic character through "tunnelling termites,"
"monuments, graves," and **"The Making of the Drum"**
through ruins and cities ends on an interrogative.

So the god,
mask of dreamers,
hears lightnings
stammer, hearts
rustle their secrets,
blood shiver like leaves
on his branches. Will
the tree, god
of path-
ways, still
guide us? Will
your wood lips speak
so we see?

The poet's voice and concerns are those of all West Indians. Like most poets of the Commonwealth, Brathwaite
seems to have been influenced early by English poets, for
several of whom he has expressed clear admiration: "What
T. S. Eliot did for Caribbean poetry and Caribbean literature was to introduce the notion of the speaking voice, the
conversational tone." Soon he outgrew this influence, however, and developed his own forms and style of expression.
In his 1968 essay **"Jazz and the West Indian Novel"** he
delineated what he saw as a new and more relevant esthetic
for the assessment of West Indian writing.

Brathwaite is of the earth, earthy, and creates a history which
links the West Indies to Africa. As we read the three constituent parts of *The Arrivants,* we see the Maroons resurrected and given a voice as "the first alternative settlers in
the Caribbean, the first successful alternative communities
in the Caribbean." We hear of the untold sufferings of the
slave, the Maroon, the peasant, and the unemployed; we are
taken into the Caribbean past, into West Indian culture as
represented by the calypso singer, the Rastafarian, and the
black radical. In **"Volta"** (from *Masks*) we read:

I know, I know.
Don't you think that I too know
these things? Want these things?
Long for these soft things?

Ever since our city was destroyed
by dust, by fire; ever since our empire
fell through weakened thoughts, through
quarrelling, I have longed for

markets again, for parks
where my people may walk,
for homes where they may sleep,
for lively arenas

where they may drum and dance.
Like all of you I have loved
these things, like you
I have wanted these things.

But I have not found them yet.
I have not found them yet.
Here the land is dry, the bush
brown. No sweet water flows.

Can you expect us to establish houses here?
To build a nation here? Where
will the old men feed their flocks?
Where will you make your markets?

In Brathwaite we find a unique combination of poet, historian, and creator of critical theories. *Mother Poem* (1977),
all about "my mother, Barbados," is an attempt to document
his native island in verse and place it in the context of the
historical experience of tribal Africa and of the deracinated
African in the New World. For Brathwaite the historian, his
poetry is to a considerable degree an abstract of racial and
historical experience. History seems to reinforce and fulfill
the poetry. As he says in the preface to *Mother Poem,* Barbados is the "most English of West Indian islands, but at the
same time nearest, as the slaves fly, to Africa. Hence the
protestant pentacostalism of its language, interleaved with
Catholic bells and kumina."

Compared to the other islands of the West Indies, Barbados
is plain, ordinary, unexotic, even dry. *Mother Poem* begins
in the southerly parish, with its wide, bleak, wind-beaten
plain; the opening lines of the very first poem, **"Alpha,"** suggest the mood: "The ancient watercourses of my island / echo
of river, trickle, worn stone, / the sunken voice of glitter inching its pattern to the sea, / memory of form, fossil, erased
beaches high above the eaten boulders of st philip // my
mother is a pool." The poet makes a kind of grim sense of
the country when he goes on to speak of his mother's "grey
hairs" and "green love" and her association with nature: "she

waits with her back / slowly curving to mountain / from the deeps of her poor soul."

In political terms Brathwaite's ability to envision a wholeness amid the fragments of postcolonial societies can be clearly seen here. The landscape of Barbados becomes a vehicle of his mood to depict "[slavery's] effect upon the manscape." The island's history is condensed for us in the story of Sam Lord, a kind of English pirate, in lines that echo the Twenty-third Psalm: "The lord is my shepherd / he created my black belly sheep // he maketh me to lie down in green pastures / where the spiders sleep." The images contained in such titles as **"Bell," "Fever," "Lix,"** and **"Cherries"** evoke the various African cults of the West Indies and their permutations over time, and the poems document the experience and practices of the slaves who kept such traditions alive, often within the confines of their cabins and always in spite of their "unhappiness" and servitude. In one hymn it is suggested, "let unhappiness come / let unhappiness come / let unhappiness come." The plague of 1854 killed about 20,000 in Barbados alone. To describe the havoc of such events, the poet cleverly uses the image of a black dog "blinding the eye balls" and "prowling past the dripping pit latrines." In such lines and poems Caribbean culture and history are vividly brought to life.

Mother Poem is an exhilarating exploration of the land and people of Barbados, in a vocabulary that blends standard English and "Bajan," but in a larger sense it represents the poet's continued movement toward a concept of West Indian identity. In almost kinesthetic terms he says, "so she dreams of michael who will bring a sword / ploughing the plimpler black into its fields of stalk, / of flowers on their stilts of future rising / who will stand by the kitchen door and permit no stranger entrancement."

Sun Poem (1982) has the ring of authority and the sureness of rhythm of *The Arrivants.* It supplements *Mother Poem,* exploring the male history of Barbados. The opening poem, "Red Rising," seems to be universal in the broadest sense of that term: "When the earth was made / when the wheels of the sky were being fashioned / when my songs were first heard in the voice of the coot of the owl / hillaby soufriere and kilimanjaro were standing towards me with water with fire." There is a change in the method here, for the lines can be set to music. The swiftly growing "sun" moves from one generation to the next, from grandfather to father to son, the relationships realized through the imagery of the seven colors of the rainbow. With sprinklings of Barbadian dialect, the clearly fascinated poet describes sunsets and sunrises around the world. *Sun Poem* shows Brathwaite's ability to recast biography into poetry; it is built principally around his childhood and youth and his relations with his father: "this pic- / ture shows him always suited dressed for work hat / on his head no light between his him and me."

The collection has poems in both prose and verse, all suggesting a certain naturalness. On seeing the Krishnaraja Sagar illumination at Mysore, Brathwaite expressed the thought that some civilizations create things for the enjoyment of others whereas some are selfish, money-minded. What strikes one most is how flexible and beautiful Brathwaite's writing often is, and how different in word and feeling individual pieces are from one another. *Sun Poem* deals with Rastafarianism and Ethiopia, with Yoruba traditions and the black New World God, with landscapes both African and Caribbean. Truly the historian is seen here as a poem of great authenticity. "History, after all," wrote Carlyle, "is the true poetry. Reality; if rightly interpreted, is greater than Fiction; nay, even in the right interpretation of Reality and History does genuine poetry lie." This statement seems to find a true exponent in Kamau Brathwaite. Neither history nor poetry is repudiated at the cost of the other in his work, as *Sun Poem* amply illustrates.

Brathwaite, who has used the metaphor of Caliban to depict the subjugation of the West Indies, is now like Prospero, whose "charms are all o'erthrown," supplanted by the sweetness and harmony of **"Son,"** where "my thrill- / dren are coming up coming up coming up coming up / and the sun // new." The later Brathwaite writes a bare kind of poetry, with lines that are austere but images that are real, as in this selection from *Jah Music,* a collection of poems of incomparable music and rhythm:

> He grows dizzy
> with altitude
>
> the sun blares
>
> he hears
> only the brass
> of his own mood
>
> if he could fly
> he would be
> an eagle
>
> he would see
> how the land
> lies softly
>
> in contours
> how the fields
> lie striped
>
> how the houses fit into the valleys
>
> he would see cloud
> lying on water
> moving like the hulls of great ships over the land

but he is only
a cock
he sees

Brathwaite has faced the problem of creating a nation language and has worked steadily to arrive at a solution. The problem is one which has beset many countries as they have thrown off the yoke of English imperialism. Indian poets have moved from Toru Dutt and Sarojini Naidu to Nissim Ezekiel, Leel Dharma Raj, A.K. Ramanujan, and other moderns whose work is characterized by quick, deft touches and a style that renders native idiom and nuance perfectly. Nissim Ezekiel's hymns are distinctively native. The late Ugandan writer Okot p'Bitek, the unique author of the long dramatic monologue *Song of Lawino,* gave voice to the dispossessed, the urban vagrant prisoner, and the ubiquitous *malaya* (Swahili for prostitute) and became a social reformer in verse. In New Zealand both Maori and Pakeha (white European-descended) poets have searched for a broad "symbolic language" natural to the indigenous people of the land. Thus writers of the new lands have gone beyond the inherited modes of English and modern European poetry and have de-educated themselves, escaping the tyranny of the sonnet in an effort to be more genuine, more true to their medium and milieu. The new poetry of the Commonwealth is no longer the prisoner of the colonizer but instead has found the rhythmic audacity and wherewithal to express local realities and, in so doing, has become a part of world poetry. Kamau Brathwaite, a towering poet, has moved from the margins of language and history, from the peripheral realm of "the other exiles," to the center of civilization, effecting a renaissance of oral poetry and remaking the poetic world.

Emily Allen Williams (essay date September 1996)

SOURCE: "Whose Words Are These? Lost Heritage and Search for Self in Edward Brathwaite's Poetry," in *CLA Journal,* Vol. XL, No. 1, September, 1996, pp.104-108.

[*In the following essay, Williams considers the personal and social heritage and identity expressed in Brathwaite's poetry.*]

Born in Barbados in 1930, Edward Kamau Brathwaite is well known as a poet having received a number of prestigious awards, including a Guggenheim Foundation Fellowship, for his poetic efforts. He remains, perhaps, the most important person in Caribbean literary studies to promote a scholarly approach to the Caribbean poetic tradition with a methodical look at the importance of the oral and scribal traditions; his poetry is illustrative of his comfort with the use of Caribbean dialect and standard English as well as a creative mingling of the two.

Brathwaite's poetry is particularly evocative to the literary scholar in that it moves the reader historically, socially, and psychologically through a world of dichotomized existence brought on by the ravages of European colonization. In his book *The Colonial Legacy in Caribbean Literature* Amon Saba Saakana offers a perspective of the colonization of Caribbean peoples:

A society which educates its people away from its own history and environment is a colonial society. The Caribbean has been a basin of colonialism since the traumatic adventure of Columbus in search of a new route to Asia. The Spaniards, the Dutch, the French, the English, have all invaded the region, meticulously depopulated the aboriginal settlers, transformed a self-sustaining economy to that of a sugar economy for export to Europe, and consequently instituted the gravest holocaust that history has ever known. The removal of millions of Africans under the threat of the gun, the brutality that was experienced by the African under the lash, the whip, the hot iron, the chain, the rack, was all for one purpose: the prosperity of individual Europeans, the mercantilists and the monarchy. When slavery was abolished, under the persistent ravaging destruction of rebellion, a new form of control was instituted: education. Creole-speaking Caribbeans were told that their ancestors were Gauls: the British were subtler, they simply removed any historical record of the existence of African society before the period of colonization. In its stead, they taught English history, English language (with an emphasis on English literature), French, Spanish, Latin, etc., which had the desired effect of inculcating into the consciousness of the emerging Afro and Indo-Caribbean intelligentsia the belief that the world was centred in Europe. This psychological programming was responsible for the schizophrenic attitudes, neurosis, mental trauma, and double consciousness of the Caribbean writer.

Brathwaite's poetic language moves pursuant to a search for self in his attempt to make sense of the past in terms of living in the present. His work is painfully illustrative of the double consciousness and dichotomy present in many Caribbean writers' work. His work simultaneously shows a detachment from curiosity about his African and Caribbean heritage along with an affinity for European values and ideals. Brathwaite, however, exhibits a vehement frustration with both sides of his "self" as he searches for identity:

To hell
with Af-
Rica
To hell

with Eu-
rope too,
just call my blue
black bloody spade
a spade.

Brathwaite's anger stemming from his lack of knowledge about his heritage is directed to the institution of colonization and its devastating effects on the Caribbean people in the here and now. In **"Starvation and Blues,"** the speaker laments:

This is no white man lan'
an yet we have ghetto here
we have place where man cyaan live good
we have place where man have to sweat shit
we have place where man die wid im eye-water
dry up
where he cyaan even cry tribulation
where de dry river rocks clog im in

i did swim into dis worl' from a was a small bwoy
an i never see harbour yet
ship cyaan spot no pilot light
i burnin through dis wall o silence
wid me dread.

Brathwaite's poetry examines the longevity of the devastation of colonization and the wasted souls left behind in its wake. Many of the people lacked (and still lack) the spirit, energy, and passion to forge a new relationship with themselves and their land; such disassociation with the source of pain, for many, culminated (and still does) in flight to Europe or America. J. Edward Chamberlin in *Come Back to Me My Language* talks about Brathwaite's trilogy, ***The Arrivants,*** which deals with this socio-psychological "baggage" which many Caribbeans constantly carry:

The first of the books of the trilogy, ***Rights of Passage,*** appeared in 1967. It chronicled the generations from slavery to the years of desperation in the grim factories and slum cities and lonesome roads of freedom in the new world, and on to a time when the question "where then is the nigger's home?" expressed the spirit of restlessness epitomized in what Brathwaite called "great nigration" of the 1950's, when West Indians went on the move.

Brathwaite's **"Starvation and Blues"** does not simply mirror the historic displacement of the Caribbeans; it presents an inside view of the "modern face" of colonization—the commercialization of the Caribbean with few economically meaningful opportunities for the Caribbeans. The speaker in the poem prophesies an end to the pillaging of the foreign power-brokers:

i waitin here:
one day de grass going green,
de tyre dem goin shred thru to de rim

de sheraton hotel goin flash
out all it light,
it money-makin room goin resurrect dem
self back down to gravel
an babylon gwine hear an
crash down to de groun'.

The constant yearning for "home" pervades Brathwaite's work, whether he looks back to the past or forward to the future; the duality of dispossession and dislocation are ever present as in **"Red Rising"**:

So that for centuries now have i fought against
these
opposites
how i am sucked from water into air
how the air surrounds me blue all the way

from ocean to the other shore
from halleluja to the black hole of hell

from this white furnace where i burn
to those green sandy ant-hills where you grow
your yam

you would think that i would hate eclipses
my power powdered over as it were.

Yet Brathwaite does not emerge as a pessimistic poet prophesying an endless dichotomized existence; he suggests that selfhood can be retrieved from the ashes of the past. He successfully utilizes poetic language to impart a sense of order to a life he presents in his poetry as dichotomized yet manageable. His poem "Miss Own" is illustrative of the dauntless resolve of many Caribbeans:

Selling calico cloth on the mercantile shamrock,
was one way of keeping her body and soul-seam
together
surrounded by round-shouldered backras on broad
street by
cold-shouldered jews on milk.

Through an intricate weaving of words, Brathwaite works through a fragmented existence as he sheds light on a past that cannot be rectified in moving toward a present and future that must be made manageable through knowledge of the past. In the *Dark Ancestor,* Dathorne asserts:

Brathwaite's world is secure, even with its uncertainties, as in **"Islands"**—

The Word Becomes
again a god and walks among us
look, here are his rags,
here is his crutch and his satchel
of dreams, here is his love and his
rude implements
on this ground
on this broken ground.

Brathwaite's poetry is a bitter-sweet looking back to a cloudy history. It is also a song for the disenfranchised and dispossessed to take forth in their hearts and minds and on their tongues in coming to terms with the past in creating and shedding light on the present as the journey is made into the future. In so doing, Brathwaite's "words" help make the transition less painful:

i will never i now know make it over the atlantic
of that
nebula

but that you may live my fond retreating future
i will accept i will accept the bonds that blind me
turning my face down/wards to my approaching
past these
morning chill/dren.

FURTHER READING

Criticism

Aiyejina, Funso. "The Death and Rebirth of African Deities in Edward Brathwaite's *Islands.*" *World Literature Written in English* 23, No. 2 (Spring 1984): 397-404.
　　Argues the pervasive presence of African numinism and myth in Brathwaite's work.

Gikandi, Simon. "E. K. Brathwaite and the Poetics of the Voice: The Allegory of History in *Rights of Passage.*" *Callaloo* 4, No. 3 (1991): 727-36.
　　Considers the implications of the use of Creole in the work of Brathwaite, particularly in *Rights of Passage.*

Ismond, Patricia. "Walcott Versus Brathwaite." In *Critical Perspectives on Derek Walcott,* edited by Robert D. Hamner, pp.220-36. Washington D.C.: Three Continents Press, 1993.
　　An elaboration of a dichotomy in West Indian experience and its embodiment in the work of Derek Walcott and Edward Brathwaite.

Wallace, Milverton. "A Black Blossoming." *The Times Literary Supplement* (27 November 1992): 27.
　　An informative review of Anne Walmsley's *The Caribbean Artists Movement, 1966-1972,* a history of the influential group of artists that included Edward Brathwaite.

Additional coverage of Brathwaite's life and career is contained in the following sources published by Gale: *Black Writers,* Vol. 2; *Contemporary Authors,* Vols. 25-28R; *Contemporary Authors New Revision Series,* Vols. 11, 26, and 47; *Contemporary Literary Criticism,* Vol. 11; *Dictionary of Literary Biography,* Vol. 125; and Discovering Authors Modules: Poets.

Octavia Butler
1947-

(Full name Octavia Estelle Butler) American novelist, short story writer, and essayist.

INTRODUCTION

Best known as the author of the Patternist series of science fiction novels, which involves a society whose inhabitants have developed telepathic powers over several centuries, Butler explores themes that have been given only cursory treatment in the genre, including sexual identity and racial conflict. Butler's heroines are black women who are powerful both mentally and physically. While they exemplify the traditional gender roles of nurturer, healer, and conciliator, these women are also courageous, independent, and ambitious. They enhance their influence through alliances with or opposition to powerful males. Butler has earned many accolades, including a Hugo Award, a Nebula Award, and a *Locus* Award, all for her 1985 novella, "Bloodchild," which was later published in the collection *Bloodchild and Other Stories* (1995).

Biographical Information

Butler spent her youth in a racially mixed neighborhood in Pasadena, California. Her father died when she was very young, and her mother worked as a maid to support the two of them. Butler has written memoirs of her mother's sacrifices, which included buying Butler a typewriter of her own when she was ten years old, and paying a large fee to an unscrupulous agent so Butler's stories could be read. Butler entered student writing contests as a teenager and, after attending such workshops as the Writers Guild of America West's "open door" program during the late 1960s and the Clarion Science Fiction Writer's Workshop in 1970, she sold her first science fiction stories. This early training brought her into contact with a range of well-known science fiction writers, including Joanna Russ and Harlan Ellison, who became Butler's mentor.

Major Works

Four of Butler's novels—*Patternmaster* (1976), *Mind of My Mind* (1977), *Survivor* (1978), and *Wild Seed* (1980)—revolve around the Patternists, a group of mentally superior beings who are telepathically connected to one another. These beings are the descendants of Doro, a four thousand-year-old Nubian male who has selectively bred with humans throughout time with the intention of establishing a race of superhumans. He prolongs his life by killing others, includ-

ing his family members, and inhabiting their bodies. The origin of the Patternists is outlined in *Wild Seed*, which begins in seventeenth-century Africa and spans more than two centuries. The novel recounts Doro's uneasy alliance with Anyanwu, an earth mother figure whose extraordinary powers he covets. Their relationship progresses from power struggles and tests of will to mutual need and dependency. Doro's tyranny ends when one of his children, the heroine of *Mind of My Mind*, destroys him and unites the Patternists with care and compassion. *Patternmaster* and *Survivor* are also part of the Patternist series. The first book is set in the future and concerns two brothers vying for their dying father's legacy. The pivotal character in the novel, however, is Amber, one of Butler's most heroic women, whose unconventional relationship with her brother is often analyzed within feminist contexts. In *Survivor*, set on an alien planet, Butler examines human attitudes toward racial and ethnic differences and their effects on two alien creatures. Alanna, the human protagonist, triumphs over racial prejudice and enslavement by teaching her alien captors tolerance and respect for individuality. *Kindred* (1979) departs from the Patternist series yet shares its focus on male/female relationships and racial matters. The protagonist, Dana, is a contemporary writer who is telepathically transported to a pre-Civil War plantation. She is a victim both of the slave-owning ancestor who summons her when he is in danger and of the slave-holding age in which she is trapped for increasingly lengthy periods. *Clay's Ark* (1984) reflects Butler's interest in the psychological traits of men and women in a story of a space virus that threatens the earth's population with disease and genetic mutation. In an interview, Butler commented on how Ronald Reagan's vision of a winnable nuclear war encouraged her to write more dystopic material. This shift in focus is most evident in *Parable of the Sower* (1993), a novel which depicts a religious sea-change, set against the backdrop of a strife-ridden inner city in 2025. Butler has also authored three novels—*Dawn* (1987), *Adulthood Rites* (1988), and *Imago* (1989)—known collectively as the Xenogenesis Trilogy; the trilogy has been interpreted as a positive analysis of an evolutionary society in which things are in a constant state of change. Butler's acclaimed novella, "Bloodchild," examines the topic of patriarchal society, and is set in a world inhabited by human-like beings called Terrans who live on "Preserves" which are provided for them by a government run by a monstrous race of creatures known as Tlics. The Terran families are valued by the Tlics because each of them is forced to sacrifice at least one of its sons to the Tlics to function as a "host" for Tlic eggs; the process produces highly desirable offspring but results in the death of the host. The central relationship in the novella is that between T'Gatoi, a government official who manages the Preserves, and Gan, the Terran boy who serves as the host for her eggs. Elyce Rae Halford has observed: "Through these and other characters, and the setting in which Butler places them, we experience a text which simultaneously explores outer space—in its focus on extraterrestrials and human adventures beyond planet Earth—and inner space, through metaphoric figures which illustrate and invite comment upon the construction of identity."

Critical Reception

Critics have often applauded Butler's lack of sentimentality, and have responded favorably to her direct treatment of subjects not previously addressed in science fiction, such as sexuality, male/female relationships, racial inequity, and contemporary politics. Frances Smith Foster has commented: "Octavia Butler is not just another woman science fiction writer. Her major characters are black women, and through her characters and through the structure of her imagined social order, Butler consciously explores the impact of race and sex upon future society."

PRINCIPAL WORKS

Patternmaster (novel) 1976

Mind of My Mind (novel) 1977
Survivor (novel) 1978
Kindred (novel) 1979
Wild Seed (novel) 1980
Clay's Ark (novel) 1984
Dawn (novel) 1987
*Adulthood Rites** (novel) 1988
*Imago** (novel) 1989
Parable of the Sower (novel) 1993
Bloodchild and Other Stories (novella, short stories, and essays) 1995

*Known collectively as the Xenogenesis Trilogy.

CRITICISM

Sandra Y. Govan (essay date Summer 1984)

SOURCE: "Connections, Links, and Extended Networks: Patterns in Octavia Butler's Science Fiction," in *Black American Literature Forum,* Vol. 18, No. 2, Summer, 1984, pp. 82-7.

[*In the following essay, Govan explores and commends Butler's innovations in narrative technique, plot, setting, and characters, and focuses particularly on the importance of power as a unifying theme in Butler's works.*]

> He was suddenly able to see the members of the Pattern not as starlike parts of light but as luminescent threads. He could see where the threads wound together into slender cords, into ropes, into great cables. He could see where they joined, where they coiled and twisted together to form a vast sphere of brilliance, a core of light that was like a sun formed of many suns. That core where all the people came together was Rayal.
>
> [*Patternmaster*]

Nearing Forsyth, ancestral home of all Patternists, Teray, the second most powerful son of Patternmaster Rayal and destined to become the Patternmaster, has just had an epiphany. He has recognized precisely the way in which all Patternists, the powerful psionically enhanced mutant humans of a future Earth society, are linked to each other through the Pattern. Science-fiction fans and discriminating others discovering and savoring Octavia Butler's full canon may experience a revelation similar to Teray's. The four published novels of the Patternist saga—*Patternmaster* (1976), *Mind of My Mind* (1977), *Survivor* (1978), and *Wild Seed* (1980)—, the projected *Clay's Ark* (publication scheduled for March 1984), and *Kindred* (1979), an ostensibly mainstream fiction outside the series, are all connected, and not simply by story line. To paraphrase Teray's revelation, the core at which all comes together in Butler's universe is the delineation of power, "I began writing about power," Butler has said, "because I had so little." Her fascination with the politics of power encouraged her to "imagine new ways of thinking about people and power" and gave her license to place her characters into adversarial situations which challenged their bid for control or authority in alternative speculative societies in which "men and women [were] honestly considered equal . . . where people [did] not despise each other because of race or religion, class or ethnic origin." Janice Bogstad has argued that, specifically, *Mind of My Mind* and *Patternmaster* "can be characterized in terms of power relationships and their effects on individual existence of very normal people [whereas] *Survivor* is more about the establishment of a power equilibrium"; similar modes are operative in *Wild Seed* and *Kindred.*

Power, then, is clearly at the center of Butler's novels. But illuminating that central core are the threads, cords, ropes, and cables wrapped around it. Power relationships are detailed by the pattern of conflicts animating Butler's characters; by their distinctive markings, especially those of her women; by the shaped plots and structural devices; and by the shared thematic concerns connecting all the novels.

In each of the published novels, the implicit struggle for power revolves around explicit conflicts of will and the contests of survival a heroine endures. The struggle of Anyanwu, a three-hundred-year-old Onitsha priestess of the Igbo people, against the domination of Doro, a four-thousand-year-old Nubian with the awesome power of instantaneous transmigration of his psychic essence, illustrates these tests. Doro and Anyanwu first come together in *Wild Seed,* the "prequel" to the Patternist saga. They are seeming immortals, and each is powerful, though their respective powers, drives, and goals are different. Both are mutants. Although Doro is not a telepath, he can sense and "track" people who have latent or nascent psychic gifts, those who are the witches or outcasts of their own kind. According to Butler, he is attracted to these people and encourages their reproduction because "he enjoys their company and, sadly, because they provide his most satisfying kills." Within her community, Anyanwu's power is so omnipresent that several times during her "various youths," villagers have mistakenly accused her of witchcraft. Not a witch, Anyanwu serves and enriches her people as an oracle and, occasionally, a god. Anyanwu is also a regenerative healer and a shape-shifter who can analyze and alter her skeletal, biochemical, and cellular structure.

Although she has lived as a powerful, feared, and respected independent woman in her community for generations,

Anyanwu, to Doro, is only potentially valuable "wild seed," an offshoot from his well-nurtured, carefully husbanded, seed communities of mutant families. Initially, he wants her with him to add her genes to his breeding stock because her power is a factor he covets. Her longevity, her special healing abilities, and her physical strength can strengthen immeasurably "any line he bred her into." Ironically, their destined linkage has been foreshadowed by their names: "'As though,'" Anyanwu says, "'we were intended to meet.'" *Doro* means "'the east—the direction from which the sun comes,'" and *Anyanwu* means "'the sun.'" Once he has seen what Anyanwu has to contribute, Doro is determined to entice her away from her village and to one of his New World communities. He has already begun the selective breeding process in an effort to build outcasts "'into a strong new people.'" Butler adds that, at this point, Doro is building his colonies to "amuse himself. He seeks to create more benign versions of himself—the closest he can hope to come to true progeny. He assures the availability of congenial, controllable companions, and, he breeds food." Although he early lays the foundations, Doro's serious interest in race building (eventually he will found a superior race of psychically sensitive human beings bred for their prowess with telepathy, telekinesis, psychometry, and the ability to perform regenerative healing) comes later. For now, he wants to persuade Anyanwu to join him and so makes veiled threats against the safety of her many children while offering as an inducement the idea that she should be with her "own kind" and that, someday, he will show her children "'she will never have to bury. . . . A mother,'" he says, "'should not have to watch her children grow old and die. If you live, they should live. . . . Let me give you children who will live!'" An almost satanic manipulator, Doro has decided he must have the use of Anyanwu; when her usefulness is finished, he will kill her.

Anyanwu, however, thwarts Doro's design on her life because of her survival skills (when she takes the form of a bird or beast, he cannot track her) and her strength of will. His is the more terrible power; he kills instantaneously whenever he takes a host body. But hers is the nurturing healing power of the archetypal earth mother. Doro can maintain his life-force indefinitely by transferring from host to host; but, he will eventually be living, as a son warned, alienated and alone, with only a vestige of humanity left. Butler argues that it is not the "*changing* that diminishes him; it is the need to regard humans as food. It is the fact that everyone dies and leaves him (until Anyanwu). It is the reality that no matter what he does, *he cannot die.*" A century passes before Doro recognizes his vulnerability, before he knows the reason that he cannot simply take Anyanwu's life or take for granted her submission to his will. They are not, nor will they ever be, *alike*; but they do complement one another. Without Anyanwu there is no pleasure, no companionship, no one with whom to share his long life. Finally, sickened by his insensitivity, by his gross gratification of his immediate needs whatever the costs to others, Anyanwu moves to sever their linkage by taking her own life. Her resolve makes Doro reckon with a will he cannot control. Anyanwu forces him to recognize love, to reveal love; through love, she forces him to change. He cannot stop killing, but he will be more selective. He will not kill her close relatives, and he will cease the casual killing of those who have served him best when their "usefulness" has ended. Anyanwu makes Doro salvage what humanity he has remaining, and that is no small victory.

Neither the historical framing nor the extended chronological movement in **Wild Seed** are particularly new structural devices in science fiction. Butler's innovation comes with setting and character, it comes with the movement of black characters through time, coupled to travel through Africa and to locales central to the African diaspora. Science fiction as genre has seldom evoked an authentic African setting or employed non-stereotypical blacks as characters (Robert Heinlein's *Farnham's Freehold* [1964] and Ray Bradbury's "Way Up in the Middle of the Air" [1950] offer noteworthy examples.) In a recent essay Butler exposes what has been the rule of thumb for science-fiction writers: They were (are?) told not to use "any black characters . . . unless those characters' blackness was somehow essential to the plot." The argument alleged that "the presence of blacks . . . changed the focus of the story—drew attention away from the intended subject" [**"Lost Races of Science Fiction,"** *Transmission,* Summer, 1980, pp. 17-18].

Doro's machinations are raceless. He will take any "host," black or white, young or old, male or female; yet, neither his nor Anyanwu's racial heritage is mere fluff. They are a black Adam and Eve, and those whom they beget shall themselves beget a new race. In the meantime, Butler's artfully didactic sketches of seventeenth-century West African cultural history and social anthropology (one can see the influence of Chinua Achebe's *Things Fall Apart* and hear the echoes of Aye Armah's *2000 Seasons*) are important because they illustrate the longevity, continuity, and richness of African civilization; they also give us a present context, and they foreshadow the structural basis of the Patternist society to come. Anyanwu's voice has the deep intonations of the griot reciting the ancient history of the clan: "'We crossed [the Niger] long ago. . . . Children born in that time have grown old and died. We were Ado and Idu, subject to Benin before the crossing. Then we fought with Benin and crossed the river to Onitsha to become free people, our own masters.'" Patternists centuries removed from Anyanwu's village will find themselves repeating this cycle. The significance of the initial setting is also that we witness the repetitive brutality of the internal and external slave trade, and we see some portion of the hor-

rors of the Middle Passage. These are icons shabbily treated in most science-fiction texts, if they appear at all.

Whether we focus on Wheatley, the eighteenth-century New England "seed" village Doro brings Anyanwu to, or the nineteenth-century antebellum Louisiana plantation Anyanwu creates and manages, through time shifts and the replication of each historically definite place, we ingest a wealth of historical and anthropological data which utilizes an Afro-centric point of view. The kinship networks that strengthened family ties in West African society survived the Middle Passage and are brought to the New World. Both Doro and Anyanwu use the kinship social model as each collects his/her people, black and white, into vast extended families linked by blood, by psionic ability, and by their difference from the world outside their sheltered communities. The cultural norms of the age occasionally raise the specter of racial discord within the family group; but, in the controlled environments which Doro oversees, racial prejudice is not tolerated. Genes and bloodlines are important not as they bear on race or sex but as they bear on the development of psychic identity, on the enhancement of psionic talent.

Generations later; the key to that ultimate enhancement lies in Doro's daughter Mary, the twentieth-century heroine of **Mind of My Mind.** Mary is a direct descendant of Anyanwu, now called Emma (meaning grandmother or ancestress as her private joke). Like Emma, Mary is a survivor and a fighter; like Emma, she possesses a unique potential Doro wants. And like Emma, she is a woman Doro underestimates.

Rather than using history or anthropology to tell Mary's story, Butler uses contemporary sociology. The abused child of a latent mother, Mary undergoes "transition," the rite of passage from the intense suffering imposed by unrestrained latent psionic ability (pretransition telepaths cannot shield themselves against the reception of anyone else's emotional or physical pain) to "active" adult. When she emerges from transition, she emerges in total control of the six most powerful telepaths, having linked them all in an unbreakable telepathic union. Mary is the center of their newly formed "pattern" and is the genesis, the mother, of the new race Doro has worked toward. Mary and the members of her Pattern form a "family," the "First Family." Gradually, they move more and more people from latent to active, extending the family, creating new families, and thus building the Patternists' hierarchical structure; they save the latents suffering and anguish while augmenting the power of the Pattern. Mary's growing power forces the inevitable confrontation with Doro, her father (whom she has loved as child and lover) and now the "grandfather" of the Patternists; she has not relished the contest of wills, but, like Emma/Anyanwu, Mary cannot passively submit and allow Doro to destroy her as he has in the past destroyed uncontrollable, errant "experiments." Mary and Doro are alike because they both need the life force of others for sustenance; but Doro is, in effect, a vampire, and Mary is "a symbiont, a being living in partnership with her people. She gave them unity, they fed her, and both thrived. She was not a parasite. . . . And though she had great power, she was not naturally, instinctively, a killer. He was." Despite Doro's killer instinct, and knowing what his victory would do to her people, Mary survives Doro's attempt to "take" her, and, drawing on the combined power of all her Patternists, she snares him within the Pattern and destroys him.

Mary's "difference"—that she is the symbiont, not the vampire—is what saves her from Doro. Difference is what initially draws Doro to Anyanwu in **Wild Seed. *Patternmaster*'s** Amber is forced into a nomadic life outside the typical structure of Patternist society because she rejects a would-be suitor. Alanna, the Afro-Asian heroine of ***Survivor,*** has the hostile attention of three separate social groups examining her, questioning her loyalties, because of her racial, social, and presumed biological differences. And an undefined "difference" in Dana, ***Kindred*'s** heroine, links her to the activities of her distant ancestors—a white slave owner and the slave he rapes. Difference, adaptability, change, and survival are thematic threads connecting Butler's books as tightly as the first pattern held by Mary linked the Patternists.

Each of Butler's heroines is a strong protagonist paired with, or matched against, an equally powerful male. This juxtaposition subtly illustrates differences in feminine/masculine values, differences in approaches to or conceptions of power, differences in the capacity to recognize and exercise social or personal responsibility. In each story, a physical, psychic, or attitudinal difference associated with the heroine sets her apart from society and often places her in jeopardy; each survives because her "difference" brings with it a greater faculty for constructive change.

Emma/Anyanwu coexisted with Doro; discovering his strength and learning how to challenge him, through her ability to adapt. In her long life, she weds many men, holds varied positions within a traditional African society, and moves fluidly from Old World to New and past to present, changing shape and relationships as circumstances warrant. Even her death is by her choice and expresses a refusal to adapt any further.

Mary, too, learns to adapt. In her pre-transition state, her survival depends on her ability to surmount the limitations of her environment. Strength of will keeps her from becoming the prostitute her mother was; bending her will to Doro's wishes keeps him from destroying her when she is vulnerable. Doro forces a marriage between Mary and one of his sons, his strongest telepath. Their union initially reinforces their differences: Mary is weak, black, and poor; her environment is riddled by chaotic, casual violence. Karl is strong,

white, and wealthy; his lifestyle is orderly, restrained, and controlled. Mary and Karl clash, but unlike other telepaths whom Doro has forced together, they don't lose themselves by "merging into each other uncontrollably," nor do they try to kill each other to defend their individuality. Until her transition, Mary compromises, and, though hostile, she copes with the forced alliance and even learns to appreciate it. After transition, Mary becomes the strongest telepath, and because of her power, she can bring mutually antagonistic people together for the first time, mitigating their natural antipathy. The "difference" bred into her becomes her greatest asset; she adapts easily to controlling others and alters conditions for all of Doro's people, latent and active. With the creation of the Pattern, they become *her* people. Karl resists acknowledging the dramatic change in Mary's status, but she realizes early that the newly established, unbreakable Pattern "represented power. Power that I had and that he would never have. And while that wasn't something I threw at him, ever, it wasn't something I denied either." Their forced liaison becomes a real marriage, and Karl, conscious not only of her power but also of her efforts to use it constructively to save rather than destroy, changes too. He becomes Mary's staunch supporter and ally.

***Patternmaster*'s** Amber, a distant descendant of Emma/Anyanwu, is an "independent," a migrant healer with no attachments to any particular House; thus, she is outside the semi-feudal hierarchical structure of the far future's Patternists. Though she is far more experienced, more sophisticated, and more ruthless than Teray, the novel's hero, she nevertheless joins him to escape Coransee, Teray's ambition-ridden brother, to go to Forsyth and the Patternmaster. Their journey is arduous. They must avoid other Patternists, as capture would mean return to Coransee; and they must avoid or kill Clayarks, mutated man-beasts who prey upon Patternists. Hostile environments are old for Amber. She has survived as an independent since her transition a few years after puberty. At the outset of the trek, Teray grudgingly acknowledges that it is Amber's survival skills which keep them alive. Eventually though, Amber is able to teach Teray some of her knowledge, and he proves an apt pupil. She teaches him about healing and, more importantly, about killing, quickly, like a healer, without draining all his psionic energy or the energy drawn from others he is linked to. Taking too much through the link can be fatal.

Teray and Amber are close to each other in the Pattern; they are compatible personalities. Frequently, they "link" themselves to establish a conduit or canopy of instantaneous awareness and perception; if one senses danger, the other is immediately aware of it. The link also allows for the sharing of intimate personal thoughts and feelings, for the probing of both conscious and subconscious thoughts. Neither Amber nor Teray abuses the link's possibilities however; while it is more beneficial than a simple connection for protection, it binds neither of them. It does permit them to get to know each other—they respect each other, they grow to love each other, they conceive a child; yet, none of these facts sways Amber, a rather androgynous heroine, from her determination to establish her own House and be its master. Amber and Teray are allies at the start of their journey, and allies they will remain in a perfectly balanced complementary relationship. Patternmaster Rayal's benediction to the pair is that Amber will *"always be a better healer"* whereas Teray will always be a stronger healer; theirs is *"the right combination of abilities."*

Teray would not have survived his final battle with Coransee had he not taken heed of Amber, had he not learned from her. The heroine of *Survivor,* Alanna, does not have the same success with the Missionaries she tries to aid. Alanna's Missionaries are refugees from Earth. They are not Patternists but "mutes"—in Patternist terms, humans without any psionic ability. They have fled an Earth virtually partitioned by Patternists as one kind of predator and Clayarks as another. They flee to their new world accompanied by Alanna, a human wild child whom they have captured, "converted," and adopted. Alanna's conversion to the Missionaries' theology (they believe their holy Mission is to "preserve and to spread the sacred God-image of humankind," to see a God figure only in the image of man) is principally chameleon coloration. On Earth the orphaned girl, also psychically mute, had lived alone from the age of eight until she was fifteen by savage skill, stealth, and cunning. A hostile environment necessitated a vicious struggle for survival. Alanna fought and killed to stay alive; once among the Missionaries, though, she understood that she had to adopt their ways or be exiled back to the wild. Not surprisingly, Alanna's wilderness background has sharpened her perceptive ability and honed her instinct for potentially dangerous conflicts; she is easily the most astute member of the Missionary party.

When the Missionaries find themselves caught between the Garkohn and Tehkohn peoples (the Kohn peoples are large, fur-covered beings ranked by clans and activities according to the coloring in their fur), Alanna is the first to recognize the failings of the Missionaries' practice of cultural egoism, their refusal to learn alien ways, their refusal to accept differences. Alanna learns the language and the customs of both the Garkohn and the Tehkohn, and this enables her to become the Missionaries' emissary to the Tehkohn and permits her to enlist their aid. She is also able to expose Garkohn duplicity to the Missionaries. And, though it was not originally her intent, Alanna proves to the Missionaries that humankind may come in different shapes and textures and still be part of the human family. Outer differences pale to insignificance.

Alanna's strength is drawn from her own resources. Her wits are the product of an outsider's constant vigil. The force of

her will can be measured by her determination to live, her determination to exact retribution for any wrong done to her. That had been Alanna's survival code until it was tempered by the Missionaries, and the code serves her again when she is captured by the Tehkohn, whom she lives among for two years. Alanna's status with the Tehkohn gradually changes from prisoner to partner, not because she betrays the Missionaries, but because she overcomes an immediate impulse to strike and allows herself to weigh differences, examine values, see merit, beauty, and strength in the cultural norms of others. Butler is able to establish her theme poignantly here because in *Survivor,* as in *Mind of My Mind,* the novel's point of view shifts. We move between Alanna and Diut, the Tehkohn leader, seeing what Alanna is learning and how she is being taught; in fact, we also have a sympathic omniscient narrator with our two participant narrators, enabling us to see more of the psychological spacing in the novel.

Alanna is not bound by Missionary prejudices (often directed at her because of her heritage and background), nor is she bound by Missionary traditions or conceits—all Kohn peoples are "animals." In fact, the Tehkohn hunt an animal related to them, but, unlike man and the great ape, they acknowledge their "relative." The Tehkohn have a structured society more egalitarian than the Missionaries. Although Alanna is furless, once she has proven herself, she is accepted more easily among the Tehkohn than she had ever been among the Missionaries. When she confirms to the Verricks, her adoptive Missionary parents, that she has married and born a child by Diut, all the Missionaries, including the Verricks, reject her and, with her, the fact that crossbreeding between themselves and the Kohn is possible. They cannot tolerate the idea, and their intolerance forces them to deny fact rather than face it. At the novel's end, although Mrs. Verrick makes an effort to understand what has happened to her daughter, the Missionaries march off, seeking to start their Mission life afresh, isolated from Garkohn and Tehkohn. In doing so, they leave behind unacknowledged Garkohn-Missionary children and Alanna, who elects to remain with the Tehkohn where she is valued as a fighter, a judge, a wife, a survivor, and an individual.

Alanna's loyalty to the Missionaries rests on her sense of social responsibility and her sense of kinship, whereas in the more direct Patternist tales, social grouping is by family or house. In *Survivor,* despite dissension, the stubborn, bigoted Missionaries function as Alanna's family. Diut commands Alanna to try to make peace with the Verricks before they depart because, "among the Kohn, a kinsman was a kinsman no matter how foolishly he behaved." She tries, but Jules Verrick's beliefs are too deeply entrenched.

Alanna's experience with the Missionaries, the energy she expends on behalf of recalcitrant kin, is roughly analogous to Dana's predicament in *Kindred*. But whereas Alanna is permitted to resolve her difficulties in a world whose order she understands, a world in which there is a support network broad enough to teach her and adopt her, Dana has no such advantages. She undergoes several harrowing experiences before she can begin to understand what has happened to her. And though she eventually comes to understand the *what,* she never does learn *why.*

Essentially, the plot of *Kindred* follows a twentieth-century black woman from California pulled mysteriously through time and space to early nineteenth-century Maryland, ancestral soil of her family tree. How Dana moves is undefined. An inexplicable psychic phenomenon links her life to that of a young white boy. Whenever Rufus, the child, is endangered, he can "call" Dana to him for help. On her second rescue mission (once Dana saves a five-year-old Rufus from drowning; mere hours later, from her time reference, she saves an eight-year-old Rufus from a fire), Dana makes some startling discoveries. She finds herself in 1815 Maryland, a strange "nigger" without "papers" in a slave state. She discovers that Rufus is destined to become her ancestor, if he lives long enough to father the black woman who is to become Dana's great-great-grandmother. She also discovers the full ramifications of her peculiar situation—a twentieth-century black woman suddenly confronted by the chattel slavery system to find herself, like any other slave, a virtually powerless victim. She is at the mercy of white men—patrollers, overseers, or plantation owners—and white women; she has no freedom, no options, no rights any white person is bound to respect. Whatever happens to her during the time she is trapped in the past, actually happens. The whippings and beatings are painfully real, and the pain travels with her from past to present and back. She learns that, while Rufus can call her back, the catalyst which hurls her forward to her own time is the sincerity of her belief that her own life is in jeopardy. (There is a "catch-22" with this time mechanism: The longer Dana lives on Rufus' plantation, the more she learns, empirically, about pain and suffering, and endurance despite pain. Once equipped with the knowledge that a brutal beating may not kill, her fear can no longer give impetus to her flight back to the twentieth century. She must struggle, like any other slave.) Time, for Dana, is subverted; she may lose seconds or minutes, later hours or weeks, out of her present life while time passes at its usual pace in the past.

Dana makes other discoveries as well. Try as she might, she is unable to teach the maturing Rufus enough about respect, responsibility, or compassion to prevent him from adopting the behavioral patterns of his class and race. She discovers firsthand the brutal effects of slavery on black and white alike. She learns that, to live in the past of her kin, she must find reservoirs of strength. Dana's movement through so alien a setting, yet one so palpably real, heightens the story's

tension and our understanding of Dana's fear as she experiences the horror of her people's history.

Dana's problems appear all the more striking because they are cast as an anomaly in the fabric of authentic historic context, as opposed to distant, extrapolative, "pretend" reality. Actually, however, the conflicts Dana surmounts are no more remarkable than those endured by thousands of slave women or those facing Butler's other heroines. Like all Butler's women, Dana is an outsider who must establish her own power base or personal territorial boundaries if she is not to be destroyed. Like the rest, she finds it a necessity either to adapt to the strange and unknown or to yield and die. Her survival skills and her determination to live are tested constantly. And, like Butler's other women, Dana's capacity to love and nurture is also examined (her relation ship to Rufus and Alice suggests another archetypal earth mother image). A bittersweet irony tinctures her power to love. Though Anyanwu and Mary have known Doro in black and white hosts, and Mary becomes Karl's wife, Dana's marriage to Kevin, a young white writer, must stand the test of disapproval in the present and denial in the past. Compounding the problem, while stranded in the past away from Kevin, Dana serves as both a mother figure to Rufus and, as the other half of a doppelganger, the object of his sexual interest. Initially, she provides him only intellectual stimulation; Alice, her double, meets his physical needs. But when Alice, whom Rufus loves but cannot marry, kills herself, he transfers all of his attention to Dana, seeing her as "the same woman" and, therefore, capable of fulfilling all his needs. Finally, Dana has the same acute sense of social responsibility that her sister heroines exhibit. Her attempts at reforming Rufus are for the good of the entire plantation, an enclosed community which is akin to the extended family structure. Like the others, too, Dana's battle is against tremendous odds, and she does not survive without paying heavy costs.

Though Butler denies that *Kindred* is in any way related to the Patternist novels, one is tempted to see yet another connection binding Dana to Anyanwu, Mary, and Amber. The process by which Dana returns to Rufus remains unexplained, but the implicit suggestion is that they are linked by telepathic union; certainly they are linked by blood. Caring for family, however extended, is a theme that resonates consistently through all the novels.

To return to Teray's epiphany, the "luminescent threads" binding Butler's books are probably far more numerous than those just cited. When looking at the novels, one invariably sees new links, new connections, new variations in the pattern. We could talk about Butler's feminist stance or about the mythic cast of her tales; we could talk about her androgynous characters, her characters as classic archetypes, or the unique status her characters have as coequal heroic partners.

We could also, as Thelma S. Shinn has suggested, "read Butler's fiction metaphorically . . . turning inward to discover powers inherent in the self has sound psychological validity; so too does the unity Butler establishes between people through empathy and interdependence." We could talk as well about Butler's sense of cultural nationalism or her brilliant adaptation of the classic slave narrative form in *Kindred* (Dana experiences slavery, witnesses brutal punishment, attempts escape, suffers betrayal and capture, experiences brutal punishment) or her similar adaptation of the historical novel form for *Wild Seed.* The threads are ubiquitous. In my mind, it is signally important that we see Octavia Butler as an exceptional writer, as a strong black voice helping to forge a black presence in science fiction, and as a woman determined to weave from spangled cloth new patterns of her own design.

Thelma J. Shinn (essay date 1985)

SOURCE: "The Wise Witches: Black Women Mentors in the Fiction of Octavia E. Butler," in *Conjuring: Black Women, Fiction, and Literary Tradition,* edited by Marjorie Pryse and Hortense J. Spillers, Indiana University Press, 1985, pp. 203-15.

[*In the following essay Shinn surveys Butler's novels, discussing various critical analyses of her works, and analyzing Butler's use of "archetypal patterns" and wise female characters in her narratives.*]

Being born black and female in contemporary urban America has taught Octavia Butler much about the uses—and abuses—of power. "To comprehend a nectar/Requires sorest need," Emily Dickinson has written, and Butler's understanding of social power certainly fits that definition. On the other hand, her recognition of personal power—survival power—comes from more direct experience. "The Black women I write about aren't struggling to make ends meet," Butler explains, "but they are the descendants of generations of those who did. Mothers are likely to teach their daughters about survival as they have been taught, and daughters are likely to learn, even subconsciously" ["Futurist Woman: Octavia Butler," *Essence,* April, 1979]. Not only have her black women learned "about survival," but also they transform that personal power into social power by teaching others.

Exploring what "mothers are likely to teach their daughters" brings Butler's fiction inevitably into comparison with the novels of other women. Annis Pratt [with Barbara White, Andrea Loewenstein, and Mary Wyer, in *Archetypal Patterns in Women's Fiction,* 1981] has defined archetypal patterns,

common to three centuries of women's fiction, which preserve female knowledge within the enclosure of patriarchal society as follows:

> It gradually became clear that women's fiction could be read as a mutually illuminative or inter-related field of texts reflecting a preliterary repository of feminine archetypes, including three particularly important archetypal systems—the Demeter/Kore and Ishtar/Tammuz rebirth myths, Arthurian grail narratives, and the Craft of the Wise, or witchcraft.

Each of these patterns can be found in Butler's fiction, providing a framework for the transfer of knowledge, although one pattern governs each of the novels. Her first work, *Patternmaster* (1976), carefully follows the grail quest, leading the quester Teray to Forsyth, California, where he must accept the role of Patternmaster from his dying father, Rayal. "The Quest," Pratt quotes Jean Markale, "is an attempt to re-establish a disciplined sovereignty, usurped by the masculine violence of the despoiling knight, while the kingdom rots and the king, the head of the family . . . is impotent." The quester must be compassionate, even "androgynous," and must "restore a kingdom punished for violating women." The grail itself, "as container of beneficence, feeder of the tribe, and locus of rebirth," symbolizes feminine power: "As 'mother pot,' 'magic cauldron' (with which Persephone can regenerate the dead heroes and heal the sick), golden bowl of healing, etc., this archetype expresses women's generative and regenerative powers." In *Patternmaster,* Teray's older brother Coransee is the "despoiling Knight," violating Teray's prospective wife Iray, demanding his Housemaster's right to sexual favors from the independent healer Amber who accompanies Teray on his journey and allowing the mistreatment of those under his care, as Teray discovers when the beaten and abused Suliana comes to him for help. Rayal, suffering from Clayark's disease (a "gift" from the first returning starship which decimated the population of Earth and left mutants in its wake), is impotent to stop the stronger Coransee, who is also his son by his lead wife and sister Jansee. Teray is recognizable as the appropriate successor by his "androgynous" qualities: his protection of Suliana and others like her; his willingness to recognize the humanity in the feared and hated mutants the Clayarks; his unwillingness to kill except for survival. Yet Teray is young, lacking the necessary knowledge and skills to succeed in his quest. For these he must turn to the first of Butler's black women mentors, Amber. Amber's knowledge has literally been transferred to her and her healing skill has been brought through transition to a useful tool by her friend and lesbian lover, the Housemaster Kai, suggesting an archetypal Demeter/Kore pattern of "uniting the feminine generations." She seems to symbolize the grail in herself, literally regenerating Teray's body after his final fight with Coransee.

Butler's next two novels, *Mind of My Mind* (1977) and *Survivor* (1978), follow the pattern of rebirth and transformation myths. *Mind of My Mind* can be seen as what Pratt calls a "novel of development," and young Mary struggles against much of the poverty and violence common to "the multiple alienation of sex, class, and race" which "intensifies physical and psychological suffering for the young Black woman." She grows up in a California ghetto with a prostitute mother and finds it necessary at times to protect herself from unwanted men by wielding a cast-iron skillet. But Mary is exceptional; her "transition" from adolescence to selfhood leaves her an active telepath, controlling minds of others like her through a Pattern. In giving birth to the Pattern, Mary gives birth to a new society in which she is the most powerful figure and gives rebirth to thousands of "latent" telepaths who have been suffering from their uncontrollable reception of human pain from everyone around them. However reluctantly, Mary has learned survival from her female heritage—from her mother Rina and her ancestress Emma (whose name means grandmother)—and she is ready to become another black woman mentor, leading "her people" to constructive utilizations of their individual skills.

Although Frances Smith Foster argues that Mary, despite her name, cannot fit the stereotype of the Black Madonna as defined in Daryl Dance's essay "Black Eve or Madonna: A Study of the Antithetical Views of the Mother in Black American Literature," she must admit later that Mary combines the traits "not only of Eve and Madonna, but also of God and Satan" into "a new kind of female character in both science fiction and Afro-American literature." That new character has been defined by Phyllis J. Day as follows:

> The new women of science fiction, then, whether witch or Earthmother, are real people, strong people, and they are integral to and often protectresses of Earth and ecology. Moreover, they are part of an organic whole, a return to our premechanistic past, and they represent a force against man in his assumption of the right to dominate either women or Earth/Nature ["Earthmother/Witchmother: Feminism and Ecology Renewed," *Extrapolation*, Spring, 1982].

Much of this applies to Mary, daughter of the godlike Doro and descendant of Emma (whose African name Anyanwu means "sun," as does Doro), combining the male and female principles represented by these two and ending the domination of Doro by absorbing his life into her Pattern, allowing herself to offer rebirth to those dependent on her: "Karl lived. The family lived. . . . Now we were free to grow again—we, his children." In her new role, Mary is the archetypal

female defined by Pratt: "the mothers and daughters in women's fiction seem also to be enacting the various aspects of the triple goddess, who was virgin, maternal figure, and old woman at one and the same time. The third figure of the triad, who has often been gynophobically perceived as 'devouring mother' or 'crone,' represents the wise older mother's knowledge of the best moment to fledge or let go of her children, a moment that, if precipitous or delayed, can lead the maternal element to become destructive." So it is with Mary. Her third aspect becomes apparent when she draws strength from her people through the Pattern. If she lets go too late, she kills them. But unlike Doro, whose power depended upon killing his victims, Mary discovers that she doesn't have to destroy: "I'm not the vampire he is. I give in return for my taking." Doro finally recognizes that Mary is whole, "a complete version of him":

> She was a symbiont, a being living in partnership with her people. She gave them unity, they fed her, and both thrived. She was not a parasite, though he had encouraged her to think of herself as one. And though she had great power, she was not naturally, instinctively, a killer. He was.

As such, Mary fits Day's description of witch, as do the other "wise witches" of Butler's fiction:

> These capable women with power are most often called witches and considered deviant from their society. They are usually feared and hated by other tamed women, as well as by men. They are healers, wise women, religious leaders, or focal points for natural or preternatural powers. Their power is usually antimachine, though not always anti-technology—that is, they may use technologies but in a nondeterministic manner in which nature is enhanced rather than destroyed.

In her role as Patternmaster, Mary will enhance what Doro has neglected by bringing the latent telepaths through transition, by providing unity for all Patternists, and by teaching individuals how to use their powers for the betterment of the community. Although Mary is hated at first, Butler reminds us that "people who must violate their long-held beliefs are rarely pleasant. I don't write about heroes; I write about people who survive and sometimes prevail." Mary must kill Doro, but she does survive and she does prevail—teaching others to make the most of what they have and giving rebirth to the rejects of the society into which she was born. Through her, Butler can transmute her Afro-American heritage into archetypal human heritage and achieve her aim by bringing "together multi-racial groups of men and women who must cope with one another's differences as well as with new, not necessarily controllable, abilities within themselves."

Alanna's rebirth in *Survivor* (1978) is personal rather than communal, following the structure Pratt provides for woman's spiritual quest into the self:

> Phase I: Splitting off from family, husbands, lovers
>
> Phase II: The green-world guide or token
>
> Phase III: The green-world lover
>
> Phase IV: Confrontation with parental figures
>
> Phase V: The plunge into the unconscious

Butler's only novel set on another planet, *Survivor* offers alternatives to today's prejudices for those who do not fit into the Pattern she has created, to the nontelepathic "mutes." Unfortunately, the mutes have carried their prejudices with them. As Missionaries of Humanity, they have fought the Clayark threat by deifying the human image. Consequently, they are blind to humanity in any other guise—to the humanity of the native Kohn, furlike creatures of various hues who live in tune with their environment. Except for a few, their prejudice extends as well to Alanna, an Afro-Asian who had survived as a "wild human" after her parents had died protecting her from a Clayark attack. Alanna had been adopted by the leader of the colony, Jules Verrick, and his wife, Neila, despite the prejudices that would allow these religious people to kill wild humans as if they were animals and would further lead them to suggest that Alanna at least be put with a black family. Clearly, hers is at best an uneasy relationship with her society, making her a perfect candidate for a quest or rebirth journey which, Pratt asserts, can "create transformed, androgynous, and powerful human personalities out of socially devalued beings."

Phase I is accomplished for Alanna when she is kidnapped with some other Missionaries and some of the Garkohn natives with whom they peacefully coexisted. The kidnappers are the Tehkohn, a native group bluer in color than the predominately green-furred Garkohn. Phase II is realized by something taken from rather than given to Alanna, as is the usual pattern. This "ordinary phenomenon that suddenly takes on extraordinary portent" is the meklah fruit, which has become the staple diet of the Missionaries as it is for the Garkohn. Meklah, however, is addictive; withdrawal from it is so difficult that only Alanna, owing probably to her wild human brushes with starvation and her incredible will to survive, is alive when the five-day "cleansing period" ends.

Alanna has learned that not all is good in the green world—Nature can offer poison as well as life. She needs to discover Phase III, "an ideal, nonpatriarchal lover who sometimes appears as an initiatory guide and often aids at difficult points in the quest." Her lover turns out to be the leader of the Tehkohn, their Hao Diut. Diut rules because he is the darkest blue; before him, the Hao Tahneh, a female, had ruled. However, though Diut can offer her knowledge of and participation in a society which lives in tune with its environment—constructing dwellings which "mimicked the mountains around it in its interior as well as its exterior," fighting without weapons, even recognizing the animal jehruk "as their wild relative and they took pride in its ferocity"—he must also learn from her the limits he must put on his power before they can have a relationship "where differences existed, but were ignored." "We're not children squabbling in the inner corridors," she tells him. "You need not prove your strength or your coloring to me. We can talk to each other. Or we can go away from each other!"

Drawing on her memories of survival on Earth, Alanna is able to fit into this alien society much better than she could with the Missionaries. The shared knowledge of the green world, of working with rather than against nature, is lost on the Missionaries, whose walled settlement mars the natural landscape and who see all Kohn as animals. But Alanna is "rescued" from her new home, and in the process the life she has created there—a daughter Tien—is destroyed. She is forced into Phase IV, and her confrontation with her foster parents is bittersweet. While Neila could accept the changes in her daughter, Jules cannot condone the blasphemy of mating with "animals." Alanna must come to terms with her parents by doing all she can to enable them to survive, but then she must be rejected by them.

This rejection initiates the final phase, the plunge into the unconscious where Alanna must face her own actions and define her self. "I'm a wild human," she tells her foster parents. "That's what I've always been."

> She glanced at Jules. "I haven't lost my self. Not to anyone." And again to Neila. "In time, I'll also be a Tehkohn judge. I want to be. And I'm Diut's wife and your daughter. If . . . you can still accept me as your daughter."

Alanna has completed the quest for self and chosen that self above any social identity that would limit or enclose her, transforming even Diut through her personal integrity. Unfortunately, she is not able to share her survival skills with the Missionaries. While she is willing to teach, risking her life for them, they are not willing to learn. Their prejudices limit their humanity and their possibilities for survival.

Butler's next novel, *Kindred* (1979), is a departure from the science fiction mode which has enabled her to fantasize societies accepting of her strong and independent black women. If the feminine archetypes provided a framework for her own mythos, that mythopoeic vision was allowed room to expand by the possibilities inherent in the contemporary mythological form. [In "Science Fiction Myths and their Ambiguity," in *Science Fiction: Contemporary Mythology*, edited by Patricia Warrick, Martin H. Greenberg, and Joseph Olander, 1978] Patricia Warrick has identified three ways in which science fiction offers this expansion. First,

> The radical element in all the myths is their setting in the future. They describe a future time that will be different from the present in at least one significant way. In contrast, traditional myths typically are set outside time; they reflect all that is conceived to be eternal and unchanging in the universe.

Second,

> It seems safe to assume that in previous myths both the teller and the listener believed the story to be true. In contrast, the participants in a science fiction myth are very conscious that the story is not true; however, they do believe that in the future it just might be true.

And third,

> These earlier myths tend to be very clear in their meanings and their concepts of good and evil. . . . But science fiction myths have a quality of ambiguity about them. They are much less certain of what man's relationship to the natural world around him and to the cosmos is. Good and evil can no longer be easily labeled.

Besides the acceptance of change and ambiguity in a probable future, science fiction also provides Butler with the one aspect her heritage neither as a black nor as a woman seemed to provide—freedom. This concept, central to everything she has written, drew her to the literary form where, as she explains,

> I was free to imagine new ways of thinking about people and power, free to maneuver my characters into situations that don't exist. For example, where is there a society in which men and women are honestly considered equal? What would it be like to live in such a society? Where do people not despise each other because of race or religion, class or ethnic origin?

Patternist society fits this description, but such a change is not without ambiguous results. The timelessness of the feminine archetypes and the experiences of the black woman have penetrated even Butler's fantasies to show that human beings will find new categories of prejudice—assigning sub-

human status to mutes and Clayarks—and new abuses for power unless it is limited. Her communal solutions remain dependent on the humanity of its individual members: the compassion of the Patternmaster, the determination of others to preserve their freedom even if they must kill or die to accomplish this, and the willingness of all members of the society to overcome prejudice and accept differences. Only Tehkohn society seems potentially utopian, although the power hierarchy and stress on fighting separate it from most utopias.

Borrowing the vehicle of time travel from her science fiction, Butler turns in *Kindred* to apply her new understanding of power to the Afro-American experience today and yesterday. Dana, her contemporary black woman, finds herself mentor and healer to her own white slave-holder ancestor Rufus when he pulls her back through time over and over again to save him. Certainly feminine archetypes again underlie Butler's fiction, as Dana "controls death and rebirth," not only that of Rufus but her own as his descendant. This rebirth myth most closely relates to Pratt's Ishtar/Tammuz pattern, as "the hero can be released from death only through feminine power." That feminine power can also be used to destroy, and is so used when Rufus has concluded the rape through which Dana's ancestress is conceived and furthermore has ignored the limits set on his power. "I'm not property, Kevin," Dana had assured her contemporary white husband. "I'm not a horse or a sack of wheat. If I have to seem to be property, if I have to accept limits on my freedom for Rufus's sake, then he also has to accept limits—on his behavior toward me. He has to leave me enough control of my own life to make living look better to me than killing and dying." So too had Alanna set limits on Diut in *Survivor:*

> "And I have your bow and your arrows." She looked at me for a long time, her face already bruised and swollen, her eyes narrowed, the knife steady in her hand. "Then use them to kill me," she said. "I will not be beaten again."

Diut accepts and both survive; Rufus tests his limits once too often. The first time, he hits Dana when she objects to his selling a field hand out of jealousy: "And it was a mistake. It was the breaking of an unspoken agreement between us—a very basic agreement—and he knew it." In retaliation, Dana cuts her wrists, and the threat to her life returns her to the present. The next betrayal, attempted rape, forces her to overcome her compassion finally: "I could accept him as my ancestor, my younger brother, my friend, but not as my master, and not as my lover. He had understood that once." At the cost of her left arm, she kills him.

Dana is not a victim, as Beverly Friend concludes [in "Time Travel as a Feminist Didactic in Works by Phyllis Eisenstein,

Marlys Millhiser, and Octavia Butler," *Extrapolation,* Spring, 1982] when she compares **Kindred** with novels by Eisenstein and Millhiser. Butler recognizes some truth in Friend's other conclusion "that contemporary woman is not educated to survive, that she is as helpless, perhaps even more helpless, than her predecessors," at least inasmuch as Dana accepts "that educated didn't mean smart. He had a point. Nothing in my education or knowledge of the future had helped me to escape." But Dana has learned to heed women's knowledge; as Kai had fed Amber all she knew in **Patternmaster,** Dana seeks out the cookhouse because

> sometimes old people and children lounged there, or house servants or even field hands stealing a few moments of leisure. I liked to listen to them talk sometimes and fight my way through their accents to find out more about how they survived lives of slavery. Without knowing it, they prepared me to survive.

And, although Dana suffers a share of what her ancestors had endured in slavery and loses her arm in saving her life, she never becomes an object; she maintains control of her life and acts out of a sense of responsibility even while she recognizes the irony of her position as Rufus's mentor:

> I was the worst possible guardian for him—a black to watch over him in a society that considered blacks subhuman, a woman to watch over him in a society that considered women perennial children. I would have all I could do to look after myself. But I would help him as best I could. And I would try to keep friendship with him, maybe plant a few ideas in his mind that would help both me and the people who would be his slaves in the years to come.

Dana may, as Friend submits, be as much a slave as the heroines of the other two novels, but she does have heritage on her side—black women have survived slavery before.

Kindred shows that Butler's wise witches, her compassionate teachers armed with knives and cast-iron skillets, have survived and will survive, whether or not they are accepted by their society. Her consciousness of "the adaptations women with power must make in a patriarchal society," however, adds an African archetype to her mythology in her most recent novel, **Wild Seed** (1980). In **Mind of My Mind,** where we first met Emma/Anyanwu, Doro had told Mary that "Emma was an Ibo woman"; so it seems particularly fitting that Sir James G. Frazer [in *The New Golden Bough,* 1959] has specifically attributed the belief in shape shifting to her kinspeople: "They think that man's spirit can quit his body for a time during life and take up its abode in an animal. This is called *ishi anu,* 'to turn animal.' "Anyanwu, a wild

seed growing free in nature—not, until the beginning of this novel, under the control of Doro—has learned through an inner quest how to change her body, aging and becoming young again, hunting as a leopard or swimming as a dolphin. Symbolizing the adaptations she had made for survival in a patriarchy headed by Doro, four-thousand-year-old patriarch of what would become the Patternists, Anyanwu's shape shifting is the prototype for Alanna's chameleon ability, which she draws on in **Survivor** to save the Missionaries: "But deception is the only real weapon we have. We face physical chameleons. To survive, we must be mental chameleons." Alanna accurately labels this awareness "survival philosophy."

Shape shifting is also the source of the healing power that Anyanwu will hand down to the Patternists, ultimately to Amber and Teray of **Patternmaster.** Anyanwu heals herself by turning inward and changing the shape of the injured or diseased part until it is again healthy. The archetypal witch most reflective of its designation by Pratt as "Craft of the Wise," Anyanwu is clearly the female principle of life itself. This Great Mother has already been living three hundred years when Doro tracks her down and coerces her into his selective breeding program by threatening to use her children if she refuses. Typical of the black women who will follow her, however, she stays not out of fear of Doro or acceptance of slavery but out of compassion. In time she comes to recognize the truth in what her husband and Doro's son Isaac tells her: "I'm afraid the time will come when he [Doro] won't feel anything. If it does . . . there's no end to the harm he could do. . . . You, though, you could live to see it—or live to prevent it. You could stay with him, keep him at least as human as he is now." When Anyanwu comes to feel that Doro is past learning from her, past feeling, she is ready to let herself die rather than be used by him. As Dana has challenged Rufus, as Alanna has challenged Diut, Anyanwu challenges Doro with the one thing beyond his control—her own life. Doro can destroy her, but he cannot make her live if she chooses not to. It is only when he sincerely recognizes and admits his need for her and his feeling for her that she decides to stay with him.

As much as Anyanwu offers her daughters as the Great Mother, she is not limited as this figure usually is. A living woman (**Wild Seed** begins in 1690, which puts her birth around 1390), she still fits Aldous Huxley's definition of "the principle of life, of fecundity, of fertility, of kindness and nourishing compassion; but at the same time she is the principle of death and destruction." She, however, prefers not to kill and feels great remorse when she finds it necessary to do so. Nor is she an irrational force. Even science fiction, usually more open to ambiguity and change, has stereotyped men and women, as Scott Sanders observes [in "Woman as Nature in Science Fiction," in *Future Females: A Critical Anthology,* edited by Marleen S. Barr, 1981]:

In much of the genre, women and nature bear the same features: both are mysterious, irrational, instinctive; both are fertile and mindless; both inspire wonder and dread in the hero; both are objects of male conquest. . . . Men belong to the realm of mind; women and nature, to no-mind. Women are the bearers of life; men are life's interpreters and masters.

Yet Anyanwu, not the male principle Doro, is the source of "logic, reason, the analytical workings of the mind" in **Wild Seed.** She has achieved her shape-shifting knowledge by careful, systematic inner quests, where she has studied herself down to the atoms. She learns what nature can provide— what foods are beneficial, which are poisonous—by ingesting small quantities and watching her bodily reactions. She can "clone" an animal or fish only after she has eaten some of it and studied within her its genetic makeup. She is both the scientist and the laboratory. Even then, she must consciously decide to shift her shape, and the process is painstaking as each part of her is absorbed or transformed.

Doro, on the other hand, is as much a life and death source as Anyanwu. He can be compared to the Nuban myth recounted by Frazer of the taboo person:

> The divine person who epitomizes the corporate life of his group is a source of danger as well as blessing; he must not only be guarded, he must be guarded against. . . . Accordingly the isolation of the man-god is quite as necessary for the safety of others as for his own. His magical virtue is in the strictest sense contagious; his divinity is a fire which, under proper restraints, confers endless blessings, but, if rashly touched or allowed to break bounds, burns and destroys what it touches.

Doro is described as "a small sun" and seeks people who are "good prey," who will satisfy his appetite when he devours their life and assumes their body. He can exercise some control over his appetite if he has fed recently; otherwise his action is instinctual, irrational. He occupies the nearest body. Even his seemingly scientific quest for the right people for his selective breeding program is determined by his appetite for them—latent telepaths and people with other potential mental talents are "good prey." In fact, he began his breeding program originally as one would raise cattle—for food. He still uses his settlements for this, and the followers who love and fear him have come to accept the human sacrifices his appetite demands. Doro provides a frightening version, of patriarchy; only the matriarchal balance which Anyanwu, whom he calls Sun Woman, chooses to provide him keeps Doro human in any way, as Isaac had predicted. It is from these roots that Mary eventually evolves, encompassing the ambiguities of both principles in herself and

thereby giving birth to a society in which men and women can be equal.

Butler's archetypal frameworks allow us to see how seemingly insurmountable differences can be recognized as artificial polarizations of human qualities. By combining Afro-American, female, and science fiction patterns, she can reveal the past, the present, and a probable future in which differences can be seen as challenging and enriching rather than threatening and denigrating and in which power can be seen as an interdependence between the leader and those accepting that leadership, each accepting those limits on freedom that still allow for survival of the self. Within the archetypes, embodying them, are wise witches, black women willing to share their survival skills out of compassion and a sense of responsibility with those of us who are still willing to learn.

FURTHER READING

Criticism

Helford, Elyce Rae. "Would You Really Rather Die than Bear My Young?: The Construction of Gender, Race, and Species in Octavia E. Butler's 'Bloodchild.'" *African American Review* 28, No. 2 (Summer 1994): 259-71.
> Examines "Bloodchild" in terms of Butler's treatment of issues of gender, race, and species; provides a laudatory assessment of the story and of Butler's works in general.

Kenan, Randall. "An Interview with Octavia Butler." *Callaloo* 14, No. 2 (1991): 495-504.
> Butler discusses her approach to writing, themes in her works, and reveals the people, places, and events which inform her novels.

Miller, Jim. "The Technology Fix." *American Book Review* 17, No. 3 (February/March 1996): 28.
> Offers a highly favorable review of *Bloodchild and Other Stories.*

Salvaggio, Ruth. "Octavia Butler and the Black Science-Fiction Heroine." *Black American Literature Forum* 18, No. 2 (Summer 1984): 78-81.
> Studies Butler's black female heroines and their responses to racism and sexism.

White, Eric. "The Erotics of Becoming: XENOGENESIS and *The Thing.*" *Science Fiction Studies* 20, Part 3, No. 61 (November 1993): 394-408.

Analyzes the Xenogenesis Trilogy and John Carpenter's *The Thing* as "evolutionist narratives."

Zaki, Hoda M. "Utopia, Dystopia, and Ideology in the Science Fiction of Octavia Butler." *Science Fiction Studies* 17, Part 2, No. 51 (July 1990): 239-51.
Illustrates the "dynamic interplay of utopian, dystopian, and ideological elements in Butler's works" and compares Butler's works to those of other "utopia-generating" feminist science-fiction writers.

Additional coverage of Butler's life and career is contained in the following sources published by Gale: *Authors and Artists for Young Adults,* **Vol. 18;** *Black Writers,* **Vol. 2;** *Contemporary Authors,* **Vols. 73-76;** *Contemporary Authors New Revision Series,* **Vols. 12, 24, and 38;** *Contemporary Literary Criticism,* **Vol. 38;** *DISCovering Authors Modules: Multicultural Authors* **and** *Popular Fiction and Genre Authors; Dictionary of Literary Biography,* **Vol. 33;** *Major 20th-Century Writers;* **and** *Something about the Author,* **Vol. 84.**

Michelle Cliff
1946-

Jamaican-born American poet, novelist, short story writer, and editor.

INTRODUCTION

In her novels, poetry, and short stories—primarily set in Jamaica—Cliff examines how an individual's family, and the politics, social norms, and economic history of the community in which that individual resides, affect personal development. She has twice been named a fellow by the National Endowment for the Arts, and in 1988 was awarded a Fulbright Fellowship. Simon Gikandi has commented: "The uniqueness of Cliff's aesthetics lies in her realization that the fragmentation, silence and repression that mark the life of the Caribbean subject under colonialism must be confronted not only as a problem to be overcome but also as a condition of possibility—as a license to dissimulate and to affirm difference—in which an identity is created out of the chaotic colonial and postcolonial history."

Biographical Information

Cliff was born November 2, 1946, in Kingston, Jamaica, but moved to New York City with her family in 1949. In 1969 Cliff graduated from Wagner College, where she completed a bachelor's degree in European history. Following graduation she worked for publisher W. W. Norton in New York City before travelling to London, where she earned a master of philosophy degree from the Warburg Institute. Cliff returned to New York City in 1974, and again worked for W. W. Norton, beginning as a copy editor and later serving as a manuscript and production editor. She left W. W. Norton in 1979, and from 1981 to 1983 served as editor and co-publisher (with Adrienne Rich) of the feminist journal *Sinister Wisdom*; Cliff has also been a member of the editorial board of the journal *Signs* and a contributing editor of *American Voice*. In addition to her work as a writer and editor, Cliff has been a member of the faculties of several American colleges and universities, including the University of Massachusetts, Amherst, Hampshire College, Norwich University, Vista College, San Jose State University, University of California at Santa Cruz, Stanford University, and Trinity College.

Major Works

Cliff has remarked: "In my writing I am concerned most of all with social issues and political realities and how they affect the lives of people. Because I am a Jamaican by birth,

heritage, and indoctrination, born during the time the island was a British Crown Colony, I have experienced colonialism as a force first-hand. Thus colonialism—and the racism upon which it is based—are subjects I address in most of my writing." Indeed, conflict resulting from differences—perceived or actual—in race, culture, and gender are central to Cliff's works, including her first volume of poetry, *Claiming an Identity They Taught Me to Despise* (1980). In the title prose poem the speaker, a Jamaican woman, explores her own feelings of displacement and confusion that result from being the lightest-skinned member of her family. In addition to presenting the speaker's personal struggle, the poem examines the colonial system in Jamaica, which afforded special privileges to light-skinned Creoles. This first work, and Cliff's subsequent works, are autobiographical in a variety of ways, particularly in that they feature female characters who, like Cliff herself, possess attributes (predominantly white ancestry and light skin color) which grant them membership privileges in two disparate cultures. *Abeng* (1984), Cliff's first novel, is a *bildungsroman* that features the relationship between two adolescent girls, twelve-year-old Clare Savage and her playmate, Zoe; through her relationship with Zoe and through suffering the consequences of some of her actions, Clare learns about the barriers of class and color which exist in the rural Jamaican community in which she lives with her grandmother. In her poetry and prose collection *The Land of Look Behind* (1985) Cliff treats the topics of prejudice and colonialism; in the section entitled "If I Could Write This in Fire, I Would Write This in Fire" she depicts the alienation imposed upon Jamaican mulattos. Her novel *No Telephone to Heaven* (1987) is a sequel to *Abeng* set in Jamaica during the late 1970s. It traces the experiences of an adult Clare Savage as she attempts to find a connection with her Jamaican heritage after having lived in the United States and Europe for many years. When she returns to Jamaica, Clare discovers that the country is in the midst of a period of great political and social upheaval. Struggling to come to terms with her own painful past, Clare encounters other characters who are faced with a similar struggle, including Harry/Harriet, a homosexual cross-dresser who communicates the pain he feels as a result of being ridiculed and rejected by society both through the jokes he makes to disguise his misery and through the frank, direct statements he makes regarding the political, economic, and social strife which affect his life. *Bodies of Water* (1990) is a collection of ten short stories, each of which, according to Elizabeth Nunez-Harrell, "tells a tale of abandonment, sometimes motivated purely by callousness, sometimes by racism, sexism or homophobia, sometimes for the good of the child. Regardless of the reason, it is the abandonment that leaves such individuals damaged and scarred; these are the people Ms. Cliff celebrates." Cliff's novel *Free Enterprise* (1993) is a retelling of the story of Mary Ellen Pleasant, who financed John Brown's attempted raid of Harper's Ferry that took place before the start of the American Civil War. Cliff uses letters, poems, prose, and dialogues to present the stories of people who were left out of the original account of the event, and constructs a narrative that differs from the official record in a variety of ways. According to Cliff, she wrote *Free Enterprise* to "correct received versions of history. . . . It seems to me that if one does not know that one's people have resisted, then it makes resistance difficult."

Critical Reception

Cliff has received high praise from critics for creating narratives that have resonance for readers independent of culture, class, and gender, but still manage to comment upon issues defined and shaped by such categories. In addition, critics have lauded her technical skills in crafting characters whose dialects range from standard English to Jamaican Creole and for using terms and phrases unique to Caribbean cultures. Commenting on the capacity of the characters in *Abeng* to use standard English and Creole with equal dexterity, Françoise Lionnet stated: "this move from Standard English to Creole speech is meant to underscore class and race differences among protagonists, but it also makes mani-

fest the double consciousness of the postcolonial, bilingual, and bicultural writer who lives and writes across the margins of different traditions and cultural universes." Many critics have noted and applauded Cliff's ability to transcend the traditional boundaries of culture, class, and gender, and honor the contributions of individuals to history by presenting stories rooted firmly in family and community. This ability has invited comparisons between Cliff's works and the works of Toni Morrison. Lemuel A. Johnson has noted that the titles of Cliff's works "suggest her way of working with seemingly extravagant but foundational events in the making of the Americas; . . . [she] insists on a vision of history as blood/lines."

PRINCIPAL WORKS

The Winner Names the Age: A Collection of Writing by Lillian Smith [editor] (prose) 1978
Claiming an Identity They Taught Me to Despise (poetry) 1980
Abeng (novel) 1984
The Land of Look Behind: Prose and Poetry (poetry and prose) 1985
No Telephone to Heaven (novel) 1987
Bodies of Water (short stories) 1990
Free Enterprise (novel) 1993
The Store of a Million Items (short stories) 1998

CRITICISM

Jewelle Gomez (review date May 1984)

SOURCE: "Coming of Age in Jamaica," in *The Women's Review of Books,* Vol. 1, No. 8, May, 1984, pp. 5-6.

[*In the following review, Gomez provides a positive assessment of* Abeng, *comparing it to Toni Morrison's novel,* Sula.]

I've been in love with women/girls since I can remember: my Aunt Doris, the crossing guard, Diane, the tough girl next door when I was eight, my grandmother, and all three Barbaras on the Girls' High School varsity basketball team. Each palpitation of my heart and delicate fantasy seemed slightly melodramatic (which I often was as a child) but my emotional attachments never felt less than natural to me. I'm sure this has been true for millions of girls through the ages; some of whom were lesbian, others not. Youth makes the world wide open, tempestuous and brim full with the possibilities that lie ahead. The dark edges of the forbidden remain alluring.

That open world—and its dark edges—is recreated for me by Michelle Cliff in her first novel, *Abeng.* In it Clare Savage, the very fair-skinned daughter of a Jamaican family, comes of age in the 1950s. Within this simple narrative outline Cliff explores what, for her and all of us, are core issues: the nature of woman-bonding, the colorist attitudes of both the white and the black communities, and the dynamics of colonialism.

With a sharp talent for immediacy, Cliff constructs a bond between young Clare and a variety of women both living and legend: Nanny, the warrior/obeah woman who led a rebellion against British imperialists in the early 1700s; Inez, the Indian-African mistress of Clare's slave-holding great-great-great-grandfather; the young girl, Kitty, who grows up to be Clare's mother; Anne Frank, whose diary inflames Clare with questions about loneliness and victimization; and, more directly, Zoe, the daughter of a woman who is a tenant on Clare's grandmother's land.

Zoe, a bit poorer and darker than Clare, is designated as playmate during summer vacations by Clare's grandmother, and they become inseparable for two months of every year. Through them, Cliff expresses her understanding of the nature, both complex and simple, of relationships between young women:

> They had a landscape which was wild and real and filled with places in which their imaginations could move. Their friendship over these years was expanded and limited in this wild countryside—the place where they kept it. It was bounded by bush and river and mountain. Not by school or town . . . They did not yet question who each was in this place . . . For now they spoke to each other through games and codes, secrets and enemies.

The two ten-year-olds meet each other on uncertain ground. One is dark, the other light. One is poor, the other middle-class. British colonialism has given them a place in society at opposite ends of the spectrum. Although they develop a deep love for each other they can never totally escape the differences wedged between them.

When Zoe asks to wear Clare's new bathing-suit, she refuses. Clare does not consciously understand why this particular favor would provoke harsh disapproval from her grandmother; her response to Zoe is instinctual and cutting. The bond between them is momentarily broken. The roles society has cast them in are abruptly made more important than their actual lives.

For them, as children, the breach is not impassable. So Clare picks a red hibiscus blossom for Zoe's hair and pronounces her princess and herself consort. She dresses Zoe in flow-

ers and palm fronds to make up for the rejection, and their world is safe again for the moment. The tangled nature of their relationship is not something for them to analyze. Adults do that for them. Zoe's mother prepares her for her role when she learns of her daughter's disappointment about the bathing-suit: "Clare is the granddaughter of Miss Mattie. Dem is rich people. Dem have property. Dem know say who dem is . . . Sweetie, must not get too close to *buckra* [white or white-identified] people dem."

Because there is not yet an abundance of material on black women and the relationships between them is almost inevitable that Clare and Zoe be compared to Nel and Sula in Toni Morrison's brilliant 1973 novel, *Sula.* While comparison is frequently a limited approach to analysis, here it should not be avoided.

The Morrison novel has been looked at by numerous other critics, most importantly Barbara Smith in "Toward a Black Feminist Criticism" (*Confessions Two,* 1977). In it Smith describes the story of *Sula* as "suffused with an erotic romanticism," as indeed it is. The poverty and violence of Ohio in the 1920s are tempered for Nel and Sula by their rich imaginations and the luxurious pleasure they take in each other. They are, as Smith indicates, "actually complementary aspects of the same sensuous fairytale." Yet this element remains unspoken between the characters and denied by their creator.

That Sula and Nel remain unconscious of this aspect of their relationship is not unrealistic nor is the author's unwillingness to speak about it unexpected. Finding suitable words to put to love between women is no less difficult now than it was ten or a hundred years ago. Perhaps because traditionally only men have been acknowledged to be possessors of sexuality as a natural element of who they are individually and as a group, the expression of women's sexuality is just now beginning to take shape.

At the end of Morrison's novel, when Nel realizes she has been longing, not for her husband, but for Sula, there are no words for her except "We were girls together," and there is no one to hear her cries except the trees. Similarly in *Abeng,* Clare does not categorize her feelings for Zoe as "funny" or "queer." Her only knowledge of that kind of relationship comes from hushed conversations about her Uncle Robert and his sailor friend. They are called "battymen," but there is no word for women who feel that way about each other.

It is in explicating this and the other issues that Cliff's definitive style is so important. Cliff is a historian as well as a novelist. She weaves her story like a giant tapestry. The threads of social, economic and political circumstances are multi-colored and multi-layered; it is a Dickensian density that she evokes. The narrative voice in *Abeng* sets the stage and asks the questions Clare would not consciously consider:

> Lying beside Zoe on the rock. She had felt warm. Safe, Secluded. She felt that this was something she had wanted all along. She decided that she would never be selfish again . . . She wanted on the rock to tell Zoe what she meant to her . . . she had wanted to lean across Zoe's breasts and kiss her.

This unencumbered desire is not scrutinized by Clare but it is in the narration:

> If Clare felt anything was wrong with her feelings about Zoe and her concern about losing Zoe's friendship—that those feelings should be guarded from family, for example—that would have originated in what she had been taught and what she had absorbed about loving someone darker than herself.

Because there has been no acknowledgement of the existence of such feelings by their community there is no guilt for Clare.

The issue of color, on the other hand, is well defined. It is as simple as the rhyme taught to me by other black playmates in my Boston neighborhood in the 1950s: "If you're black get back: if you're brown, stick around; if you're light, all right!" That on an island inhabited by an African people the question of color can be a predominant influence in life is a paradox wrought by colonialism and slavery. Clare's father, 'Boy' Savage, nurtures the white roots of his family, taking pride in his near-white color and dismissing the influence of Africa on his blood-line.

When Clare and her father visit the ruins of the big house on a plantation which had belonged to his great-great-grandfather, a judge, for him in is a return to his ancestral home. He takes pride in the past, the long gone furnishings, crystal and wallpaper. He does not acknowledge the full reality. He can not say that this judge, his distant relative, had, in addition to appointing his home elegantly with Carrara marble and Royal Doulton, also set fire to the homes of sleeping slaves in a fit of rage, killing scores of men, women and children. The deaths included that of a one-breasted conjure woman who helped Inez escape from the judge's sexual enslavement. Inez disappeared into the hills to join the fight against colonialists. While Boy clings only to what be considers glorious in his dappled past, " . . . the danger to Clare was that the background could so easily slide into the foreground."

When Clare questions Boy about the Holocaust: How could it have happened? Are Jews safe now? Boy still can not bring himself to admit the dangers of supremacist attitudes.

He dismisses the anxiety his daughter feels as if the words of Anne Frank, which have moved Clare, should have no meaning in their lives. She soon becomes aware that she will be required to choose which reality will be hers: the white explorers or the black freedom fighters.

The character Clare faces a decision much like that confronted by Michelle Cliff, who is a light-skinned Jamaican. In her previous book, ***Claiming an Identity They Taught Me to Despise*** (Persephone Press, 1980), Cliff explores what she calls the "camouflage" that society projects onto us and our ability to be lost inside of one color or another. Using the prose-poem form. Cliff creates a moving prelude to ***Abeng.*** The conflict presented to a black woman who might easily "pass" is not only the stuff of abolitionist melodrama: it is an insidious trauma faced by thousands of blacks and Hispanics every day. In a culture that still relentlessly extols white values and appearance and blatantly denies the validity of any other standard it is not an idle consideration of

Clare's mother, Kitty Freeman Savage, is herself of mixed parentage, a fact she accepts with a complex uneasiness. Like her husband she must live with the legacy of colonialism but her focus is on the enslaved of the past and the present. Fair-complexioned and beautiful, Kitty is also kind in a mysterious and tentative way. She knows the African ways of her people and refuses to bury their value beneath disdain. She has learned to articulate her racial pride from an elementary school teacher who was a Garveyite in New York, but the confusion of allegiance (to black/white, colonialist/enslaved) leaves Kitty emotionally distant from her concern for social ills and her fair-skinned daughter. While she intimately knows the hymns and hearts of the descendants of former slaves she cannot totally deny the privilege her skin color provides for her. Her connection to the other island blacks remains confined to her disbursement of second-hand clothes to the needy and an occasional burst of anger at her husband's belittling remarks about the blacks around them. History has left both Boy and Kitty Savage crippled by racism and self-hatred. It is up to Clare to pick her way through the entanglements of the past and to speak up for her own future.

The narration consistently brings those strands of history and knowledge together for us, to provide us with a perspective much broader than that explicitly defined by the characters themselves. It is this voice which allows Cliff to move through history with such case. The connections she makes in the unconscious of her characters are clear and unimpeachable.

The sorceress, Nanny, who used her skills to battle the British in the War of the Maroons until she was killed in 1733 by a slave faithful to the white planters, is a secret source of pride to Jamaicans. Her life and death are emblematic of the effects of colonialism and slavery. Nanny is a powerful figure in the liberation of her people, yet because one faction of those enslaved will always cast their lot with their enslaves she is killed by one of her own.

Later in the book, when Clare breaks all rules, first by handling a weapon, then accidentally killing her grandmother's bull, she is sure no amount of explanation of the circumstances will ameliorate the harshness of her punishment. Unlike her male cousins whose pranks are winked at, "she had stepped out of line, no matter what, in a society in which the lines were unerringly drawn. She had been caught in rebellion. She was a girl. No one was impressed with her." Clare cannot emulate Nanny or her other heroines in this world.

The islands remain beset by such dichotomies. The Savage family regularly attends two churches. The first is spare and clean, inhabited by an out-of-tune harpsichord imported from England that is not designed for island life. The displaced English pastor implores his congregation to sing softer so the ill-suited instrument might be heard. The Queen hovers over the spirit of everyone's faith. The second church, Clare's mother's choice, is a cement-block building that rocks with the unrestrained singing of saved souls, mostly women. In it the spirit of blackness is sanctified and rebellious.

In 1958 this lush, colorful island with its pungent black soul is officially ruled by two figures: a white British queen and a white colonial governor. But the land they rule is dark with the bones and blood of slaves. It will not be quieted by harpsichord music and dictums from the "mother country." The slaves killed by the judge's flames do not sleep alone; the habit of murder was not peculiar to him. And the Maroons, who hid in the Blue Mountains, waging war against the whites for more than 80 years, lie beneath that soil. Their legend, just beginning to surface, gives birth to an independence movement.

Cliff weaves the distant and not-so-distant past with such an immediacy that I understand why Clare can't help but heed the spiritual call of the *abeng,* an African word for the large sea shell once used to call slaves to the canefields and later by Maroon warriors to communicate their messages of rebellion. The spirit of other black women, long dead, urges her forward.

Sitting now on the corner of my desk is an abeng, "queen conch" as it is called by the island friend who gave it to me. Its outside is rough and textured; inside it is smooth and pearlized. If I hold it to my ear there is the whisper of the ocean. Held to my lips it still gives the call of freedom. It is a sound more inspiring than a trumpet and as compelling to

me as the name of my childhood best friend, the first woman I loved.

Michelle Cliff with Opal Palmer Adisa (interview dates December 1989 and September 1993)

SOURCE: "Journey into Speech—A Writer Between Two Worlds: An Interview with Michelle Cliff," in *African American Review,* Vol. 28, No. 2, Summer, 1994, pp. 273-81.

[*In the following interview which integrates two separate interviews conducted in December, 1989, and September, 1993, Cliff discusses her life and works.*]

Among the subjects Jamaican born writer Michelle Cliff explores in her writings are ancestry, the impact of colonization on the Caribbean, the relationships among and interconnection of African people in the diaspora, racism, and the often erroneous way in which the history of black people is recorded. In her latest novel, *Free Enterprise* (1993), Cliff attempts to rewrite the story of Mary Ellen Pleasant, the African American woman who supplied money with which John Brown bought arms for the raid at Harper's Ferry. Her other two novels, *No Telephone to Heaven* (1987) and *Abeng* (1984), are semi-autobiographical and explore the life of Clare Savage, a fair-skinned girl raised between Jamaica and North America, who must reconcile her mixed heritage in a changing society. Other works by Cliff include *Bodies of Water* (1990), *The Land of Look Behind* (1985), and *Claiming an Identity They Taught Me to Despise* (1980).

The following text is based on two separate interviews: one done in person in Albany, California, in December 1989, and the other conducted over the telephone in September 1993.

[*Adisa:*] *When did you find your voice, when did you decide that you wanted to be a writer?*

[Cliff:] I always wanted to write. Actually there was a terrible incident. I don't know if I should tell you, but I will. When I was at Saint Andrews, I was keeping a diary. I had been very influenced by *The Diary of Anne Frank,* and as a result of seeing the movie and reading her diary, I got a diary of my own. I wasn't living with my mother and father at this time; I was living with my aunt in Kingston [Jamaica] and going to Saint Andrews. This aunt also had a house in Saint Ann, where we used to stay on the weekends. Anyway, my parents broke into my bedroom in Kingston when we were not at the house. They went into my room, broke open my drawer, took out and broke the lock on my diary, and read it. Then they arrived at the other house. My father and mother had my diary in their hands and sat down and read it out loud in front of me, my aunt, and everybody else. My sister was there. There were very intimate details; there were a lot of things about leaving school and not going to class and playing hookey, but there was also the experience of the first time I menstruated, and I remember just being shattered. My father read it, and my mother was in total collaboration. (Pause.) Anyway I remember just crying and being sad and whatnot. I spoke to my sister about it once, and she remembered, even though she was seven at the time. And she said, "Don't you remember screaming and saying, 'Don't I have any rights?'" (Pause.) That incident really shut me down as a writer. I had wanted to be a writer from a very early age; I always wanted to write. The subject I liked most in school was English, and I read an enormous amount as a kid. But that really shut me down until quite late.

How late?

Until the mid-seventies. The only thing I wrote after the diary was my dissertation. Then I wrote **"Notes on Speechlessness."** The reason I wrote **"Speechlessness"** was . . . I guess it was all working inside of me for a while. I was involved with a group of women in New York who got together and discussed their works. We met once a month, and each person had to present something—and it was my turn. I was terrified, and I had a hell of a time just speaking. I was shy and tongued-tied a lot of the time. I didn't know what to do, so I thought I'd write something and just read it, because that would be easier than speaking. So I wrote this thing about feeling speechless. I wrote that in 1977.

So that is your first piece towards being a writer.

That was the first piece, and that led me to **"Obsolete Geography."** For a long time I hadn't thought about what it meant to be a Jamaican, even though I was going back there a lot. I was sort of creating myself but not really dealing with a lot of different things.

You mentioned that growing up you read Anne Frank *and* Great Expectations, *and that you loved literature. What else did you read?*

Everything! I loved Hemingway, and I loved F. Scott Fitzgerald. That was when I was quite young. I read a lot of poetry.

What were you thinking as you read all of these works? How did they influence you?

I think I used reading almost totally as an escape when I was young. I used to long for Saturday afternoons so I could go to the library and take out all these books, and then I would sit and read them all. I was very isolated. I was alone much of the time, and if it wasn't the library, then it was the mov-

ies. I was absolutely addicted. I still love movies, but, as a kid, they would lead me into a completely other world. I used to go to matinees, and I remember that when I would come out it would still be light, and I would feel totally disoriented.

Your work is very detailed, vivid. What impact have the movies had on your writing?

A lot. My writing is very visual. And I find movies coming into it a lot, using movies as an idea, and the effects of movies. Growing up in Jamaica movies were one of the only contacts with the outside world for many people.

You left Jamaica around 1960, then didn't return until you were a teenager. What was it like living in New York, then going back to Jamaica every summer?

It's hard to describe fully. First of all, we never assimilated into America at all. Most of the time my mother was employed by the British government and my father by various businesses, but they only socialized with Jamaicans. And whenever they had to socialize with Americans there was huge tension in the house. They never fit in, and I think one of the reasons they were very uncomfortable was because of racism. Even though both of them are very light-skinned and could pass easily, they were never comfortable with that kind of thing at all, and they always felt that white Americans were very sick. So you went back to get recharged, then came to this cold place, then returned to get recharged again. It was two completely different lives.

What was it like growing up in your family? You say both your parents are light. What was the whole attitude toward color in your family? Did your family pass? Did you?

They passed until we were with black people. It was a weird situation. We never would have passed in Jamaica because it never would have been an option.

In Jamaica wouldn't you have been considered "local" white?

Yes, exactly, or reds. So you're passing not because you want to be white but for self-protection—but it's strange and very schizophrenic.

Was there a sense in your family that white was better?

No, but there was that awful color sense which is almost unspoken—the closer you are to white the better things are. They hated the English, and they hated the Americans.

What are the images that come to mind when you think of growing up between here and Jamaica?

I feel that I had much more freedom in Jamaica than here—and I felt that when I was in my grandmother's place in Clarendon and we had no running water, no electricity, but there was this extraordinary landscape and these long days to wander in it.

What does Jamaica mean to you? You say you feel close through the writing.

It is an incredibly provincial and oppressive place. There are things about it like the landscape, and some of the people, that I really love, but I hate the classism that I grew up with. I hate the system of oppressing other people of color. I hate pettiness, obsession with appearance, what things look like, how you appear to the outside world. It's such a waste of time. I hate the sexism, the extraordinary double standards. It's unbelievable! See, I experienced a lot of it as a negative place, but also it breaks my heart when I think what might have been.

And what perhaps still might be.

I hope so. God, if they could have something just turn things around, it could be wonderful.

When people say Michelle Cliff, Jamaican writer, does that feel comfortable to you?

Well, I think I'm more of a Jamaican than an American writer.

Is it because you write about Jamaica primarily?

Well, it is my nationality, and my family roots go back to slaves and slave owners. I grew up in a family that was obsessed with the past. They were constantly talking about the past as though we were living it. I guess it was keeping them alive somehow. I also feel very much American. I feel this is my adopted country, and I care a lot about what happens in here.

Let's talk about your first book, **Claiming an Identity They Taught Me to Despise**. *Is this autobiographical?*

Some places are close, others are rough.

What about the title, what identity are you claiming?

It's from a piece in the book about being a Creole and about being neither one nor the other. And, basically, the identity is Jamaican and black. This is the first time that I was breaking the silences of my childhood in the book about race, class, sex, and all of those things. And about the secrets in the family and violence and whatnot. There's a lot of rough stuff in this book, so I'm claiming there—in a way, demanding—to be a whole person.

To identify yourself, to name yourself?

Exactly, and not to deny any piece of who I am.

Your first novel, **Abeng,** *seems to chronicle your life somewhat.*

It's not autobiographical per se, but I wanted to show somebody like me growing up partly in Jamaica (except I wanted Clare to have her whole life there)—how much of the past was kept from me, from such a character, how much she did not know.

So this was your attempt to write your own history?

Reconstruct it . . . what had been deconstructed.

Your next novel, **No Telephone to Heaven,** *is set in the late 1970s, when Jamaica was going through a lot of political, social, and violent upheaval. I was home between 1976 and 1979, and one incident in this novel that rings so true is of the gardener killing those people. I remember reading reports in* The Gleaner *and hearing stories of such murders. Was the incident in the novel based on newspaper articles?*

I was there when all of that was happening. In fact, the family of a girl I went to school with was killed, herself included. But I wanted to show how someone like Christopher [the gardener] could become who he was. And if anything, in this book I want people to have compassion for the character. He does a terrible thing, but you can understand why he would do it. At least that was my intention.

How do you see Harry/Harriet, the homosexual character, functioning in this novel?

I wanted to portray a character who would be the most despised character in Jamaica, and show how heroic he is. The homophobia in Jamaica has always appalled me; I have often wondered what the source is. Why is it such an homophobic place? Does it go back to slavery? Is it something that has its roots in slavery? Were the slaves used in that way? Anyway, he really loves his people. He is there helping, yet if they knew what he really was, they would kill him. I also wanted him to have endured what a woman in the culture endures, especially a woman like his mother, who has been a maid. When he talks about his rape, and then his mother's rape . . . he is the most complete character in the book.

This novel is about change, self-determination. You seem to be saying that Caribbean people have to work actively to free themselves from neo-colonialism.

First of all they're on this truck named No Telephone to Heaven. They cannot depend on anybody to free them from their situation. They have to get out of it themselves. I have Clare on the truck because I want to show her inching toward wholeness.

Do you think Clare's journey in the novel was somewhat influenced by the 1960s movement? You were in high school in New York during that period. What impact did the '60s have on you?

A lot.

Did you get involved in any of the marches or demonstrations?

I did when I was older. I was in high school when the Birmingham bombings happened in '63, and because our family was so nuclear and so non-assimilated, it was also very stifling. My parents were very strict about access and where you could go. I really wanted to go to a demonstration in New York after the Birmingham bombings, but my father and mother didn't want me to go. And it was this weirdly reasoned excuse that this is not our country, it is not our business, you don't want to get involved in it. But I got much more involved in civil rights activities in college and went to marches on Washington against the war in Vietnam. It had a good effect on me.

It made you more aware politically?

Thinking politically more.

What do you mean "thinking politically more"?

Seeing politically reasons why things happened, becoming conscious of the fact that certain people are not destined to be oppressed. It's pretty simple. During the '60s, I was spending a lot of time in Jamaica also, and the attitude expressed in my family a lot was, "Well, of course, Jamaica isn't racist. So that kind of thing is never going to happen here."

But it does. Your work fits into the post-colonial literature genre. You write about Jamaica as a colonial society. What does it mean to be a colonized person? What does it mean to have been colonized?

It's very complicated. I think if you're a girl, and you're growing up in a colonized country . . . when I was growing up in Jamaica it was still a colony, and the teachers I had at Saint Andrews were, for the most part, white women or light-skinned Jamaican women who believed in white supremacy and English supremacy—the Empire. The Jamaicans were somehow to feel ashamed of Jamaica, and the English were horrendously superior. You felt inadequate. I don't know how else to put it. You were taught to worship something you could never really be a part of, and you were taught to be grateful to these people. But I always hated this. It was hard not to hate them.

In the late 1960s, when you were coming of age, the feminist movement was beginning to gain momentum. What contact, if any, did you have with this movement, and how did you feel about a women's movement?

The main contact I had was through reading. I was disillusioned by what had happened in the 1960s—for example, the crackdown on the Panthers and other progressive groups—so I went to England and tried to lose myself. My first real contact was through Kate Millett's *Sexual Politics* (1970) and *The Female Eunuch* (1971) by Germaine Greer. But I've always been interested in women as historical figures. In my family I bucked against what was expected of me: marriage and children. So I found the feminist movement liberating, to discover that there were other women who thought like me. It meant I was not a freak. My fate in Jamaican society as seen by my family and the middle-class community was to marry an upper-class Jamaican man and have children. My role was to become a collaborator, and in Jamaican society that would mean collaborating in the oppression of other people of color as well as myself as a female. I think that liberation has to begin with oneself. The feminist movement allowed me certain things, like choosing to live alone, which was frowned on in the world in which I lived. Feminism for me was a way of looking in a mirror and seeing possibilities. It gave me support for my choices. One of these choices ultimately was to become a writer, which was something not at all encouraged in the world in which I grew up.

Do you consider yourself a feminist?

I consider myself a feminist in the way I chose to define feminism. That is, a world view which focuses on the experiences of women. It doesn't mean excluding men. I have real problems with that idea. Feminism should be inclusive, not exclusive. It should concern itself with the liberation of all people.

How has the feminist movement influenced your writing?

The focus of my writing would have been different if it hadn't been for contact with feminist writings, particularly with the idea of foregrounding women's lives. One of the things feminism has allowed me to do has been to focus on the experiences of women. In my novels *Abeng* and *No Tele-*

phone to Heaven, I have been able to focus on the oppression of women with regards to class and race as well as gender, and I've also been able to focus on the resistance of women with regard to class and race and gender. Both of these things are equally important to me.

Some black women have problems with the term feminist. *For example, Alice Walker uses the word* womanist. *Do you object to the term* feminist?

No. It's not important to me, but I don't have a quarrel with anyone who wants to use another term. Historically there have been black feminists in this country and the rest of the world. I would rather foreground those women like Sojourner Truth and Francis E. W. Harper, even though Harper had some limitations, like advocating the idea of the Talented Tenth. I also consider Zora Neale Hurston a feminist. I think too much of the time we get caught up in quibbles over terms. That bothers me.

Do you think the feminist movement is doing enough to embrace women of color and working-class white women?

I don't think we can look at one mainstream movement. There are quite a few different movements. The value of the feminist movement is that it has made women's lives important, and it has made us take notice of what happens to women. That idea really didn't exist that much before. But there is great strength in grassroots feminist movements throughout this country, especially in terms of health issues—for example, The Black Women's Health Project out of Atlanta. But there also has been a degree of self-involvement where I see self-help issues taking precedence over political action. That is, I do not want feminism to become consumed by the recovery industry.

What changes have you witnessed since the 1960s? We're almost into another century. Is the conflict between blacks and whites, is racism still intense?

I think it will never change until people realize where it comes from, and how deep it goes. You cannot eliminate it by changing a couple of laws which then are changed back, anyway. It's an existential thing. Racism goes very, very deep in people, and it's historically complex. I mean, it's a huge subject. I was teaching a course, the main theme of which was racism, how it is supported by the same thing that supports anti-semitism, that supports oppression of any group of people. People have simply got to, first of all, want to change, then take the steps to do so.

What are some of the steps that need to be taken?

You mean as far as whites are concerned? They have to educate themselves. They have to really want to change. They have to realize that they are not just damaging black people when they are being racist; they are damaging and diminishing themselves. It's like amputating a piece of yourself to hate another human being for no reason. I think that the problem with America is the dissonance between the myth of this country and the reality. To have to contend all the time with unraveling the myth of America is very difficult. And a lot of students, and I am speaking particularly of white students, find it very, very hard to deal with the idea that America is a difficult place for non-white people—to put it mildly. Du Bois hit the nail on the head when he said that racism was going to be the problem of the century. And it's going to go beyond this century unless it's dealt with.

What do you think you and others can do to help bring about change?

Talk about it, for one thing. I talk about it constantly. When I was teaching this course, I could hear myself saying these things over and over again, so I said, "Oh, Michelle, give it a break. Everything can't be racist." But then I pick up the paper and I read about the bombings and killing, so I say to myself, I really wasn't exaggerating, racism is really all around us, constantly. So educate, educate. Constantly bring it up.

And deal with it as a central theme in your work.

Well, it's something that deeply concerns me. It's not like it's an imposition. I often wonder what would it be like to live a day without it. Can you even imagine it? It's unimaginable.

Your new novel, **Free Enterprise,** *is based on the life of Mary Ellen Pleasant, who lived in San Francisco. When did you first learn or read about her, and how has living in California influenced the writing of this novel?*

I heard about Pleasant when I read *The Salt Eaters* (1980) by Toni Cade Bambara. Bambara has a glancing reference in there about Pleasant. Then I spoke to Toni Cade about Pleasant, but that was a while ago. Next, I found an article in *Ebony* by Lerone Bennett about Mary Ellen Pleasant. The whole idea of her intrigued me. When I moved to California in 1984, I went to San Francisco and saw the eucalyptus trees that Pleasant planted on Octavia Street. It was incredible to see tangible evidence of her existence. I'd been taking notes all along and have long been intrigued by the black woman's role in revolution historically, whether it was Nanny in Jamaica, or wherever. I have always been taken by the role African American people played in opening the West. I went to Pleasant's grave in Napa in 1990 when I was writing the novel, and her chosen epitaph says, as I say in the novel, "She was a friend of John Brown."

I know you admire Toni Morrison, and reading **Free Enterprise,** *I was reminded of Morrison's work. How, or in what ways, has Morrison influenced you writing?*

Enormously. I don't think I could have written this novel if she hadn't written *Beloved.* Her imagining of that period, of slavery and its aftermath, opened up my imagination with regard to the rewriting of history, revising the history we've all been taught. And there are touches in my novel that would have been impossible without Morrison's having taken on the whole idea of bondage and resistance.

It seems to me that your book is not a novel in the traditional sense of that genre. I have been examining how African, Caribbean, African American, and Latin American writers have been extending the boundary of this genre. Your novel is a combination of letters, poetry, prose, and even a sense of drama, dialogue. Can you speak about the novel form in relation to your writing?

I think part of it is that I come out of an oral tradition, and I come out of a colonial tradition in which we are taught that the "novel" was defined in such and such a way—a rigid definition. We come from an oral tradition that encompasses the telling of history, dreams, family stories, and then we also have the European idea of what the novel is. I have always written in a non-linear fashion. Another thing I owe to Morrison is her statement in *Beloved* that everything is now. Time is not linear. All things are happening at the same time. The past, the present, and the future coexist.

What do you want the reader to learn, to think after reading Free Enterprise? *I mean, you seem to be on a mission. Some might say you are political writer. Can you speak to this issue?*

I started out as an historian; I did my graduate work in history. I've always been struck by the misrepresentation of history and have tried to correct received versions of history, especially the history of resistance. It seems to me that if one does not know that one's people have resisted, then it makes resistance difficult.

From her very first novel, Brown Girl, Brownstones *(1954), Paule Marshall has been exploring the relationship between Caribbean and African American people, and in her latest novel,* Daughters *(1992), she makes this link more direct. Ursa, the protagonist, is the daughter of a Caribbean man and an African American woman, and raised in both countries. In your novel, Annie Christmas, from Jamaica, joins Mary Ellen Pleasant. What are you saying by joining these two women?*

Christmas and Pleasant are the two main characters who come together in this revolutionary moment, but there are

other characters from other parts of the world who also represent resistance, other revolutionary moments. I want to show that national boundaries evaporate, that people can reach each other across distances and resist. One of the things I am trying to do in this book is adjust the lens, to re-vision history.

The novel is very vivid. I can see it being made into a movie. Would you like to see that happen?

(Laughter.) I'd love to see it made into a movie. Whoopi Goldberg would be great as Mary Ellen Pleasant. I would love to see an African American filmmaker do it, yes.

What are you working on now? What will you be working on in the future?

Right now I am working on a long essay on June Jordan's work, and a new novel called *Art History.* It's set in the 1970s in England and is about a group of art historians. That's all I know now, but these things change as they evolve.

Fiona R. Barnes (essay date Spring 1992)

SOURCE: "Resisting Cultural Cannibalism: Oppositional Narratives in Michelle Cliff's *No Telephone to Heaven,*" in *The Journal of the Midwest Modern Language Association,* Vol. 25, No. 1, Spring, 1992, pp. 23-31.

[*In the following essay, Barnes analyzes* No Telephone to Heaven *as "resistance literature," illustrating the author's treatment of various political, cultural, social, and ideological issues in the novel.*]

> Resistance literature calls attention to itself, and to literature in general, as a political and politicized activity. The literature of resistance sees itself furthermore as immediately and directly involved in a struggle against ascendant or dominant forms of ideological and cultural production. [Barbara Harlow, *Resistance Literature,* 1987]

Michelle Cliff's novel **No Telephone to Heaven** both enacts and describes the multiple struggles against cultural cannibalism and for decolonization on literary and geographical terrain in Jamaica. On the individual level, the female protagonist, Clare Savage, learns to oppose the domination of Eurocentrist history and culture, and returns to Jamaica to unearth what Edward Said [in "Orientalism Reconsidered," *Cultural Critique,* Vol. 1, 1985] calls the "repressed or resistant history" of her native land. On the collective level, the novel begins (and ends) with the deployment of a small band of freedom fighters, made up of all colors and classes of Jamaicans, who intend to sabotage the neo-colonial activities of a Western film crew on the island. On the narratological level, Cliff both extends and critiques the traditional *bildungsroman* form by transforming the individualistic bourgeois quest plot into a collective struggle for social justice. Such a nexus of resistant narratives makes *No Telephone to Heaven* a difficult text for the reader to categorize or contain within a single Western theoretical paradigm, which is another important way that Cliff's novel qualifies as resistance literature—in its metafictional opposition to "ascendant or dominant forms of ideological and cultural production."

Cliff constructs *No Telephone to Heaven* as a heteroglossic Caribbean narrative in order to counter the hegemonic and monolithic scripts of various Western experts (historians, economists, literary cities/theorists and politicians). The novel's multiple scripts of resistance also serve to expose the newest and subtlest form of neo-colonialism in the Caribbean: cultural cannibalism. Jamaica, like so many so-called "Third World" countries, has become the "exotic" raw cultural material upon which the jaded palates of the First World feed, and hence it appears that the comfort and sustenance of both masses and elite in the Western world depend cannibalistically on the disinheritance and/or assimilation of the once-colonized masses.

One of the more important resistant figures in the narrative, Harry/Harriet, a homosexual cross-dresser committed to political liberation struggles in Jamaica and an influential mentor in the protagonist's political awakening, explains Jamaica's artificial place in the international arena with the remark that "Our homeland is turned to stage set too much." In reaction to this commodification of Jamaica, Cliff explodes the idyllic myths of tropical paradise that Jamaican travel posters promise: "JAMAICA, A WORLD OF CULTURE WITHOUT BOUNDARIES," and exposes the imperialistic moves in the advertisements that suggest tourists should "Make it [Jamaica] your own." The Jamaica portrayed in *No Telephone to Heaven* is certainly not a world "without boundaries," but a complex land split by rigid divisions of race, class, and gender; Cliff is relentless in her demythification of the prevailing Western romantic images of the Caribbean culture and her insistence on the presence of multiple competing scripts subsumed within every dominant narrative.

The gap between suppressed indigenous historical scripts and the dominant colonial versions is addressed in Michel Foucault's interview for the journal *Screen,* where he analyzes the role of contemporary French films in fabricating what he terms a "fake archaeology of history" ["Film and Popular Memory: An Interview with Michel Foucault," *Radical Philosophy,* Vol. 11, 1975]. Such a fake archaeol-

ogy provides a glamorized and comfortable version of the past that is commodified into a fashion fad for mass culture. These false media scripts, Foucault asserts, are "one way of *reprogramming* popular memory"—a reprogramming designed to contain past and future resistance by rewriting the memories of the past. In order to resist this erasure and distortion of popular memory, he claims "It was and is necessary to confront it with a genuine archaeology; that popular memory of struggles (and of all their forms) which has never really found expression—which has never had the power to do so—and which must be refreshed, faced with forces which are constantly striving to stifle it, and silence it for good." Michelle Cliff's novel weaves together the submerged stories of past and present popular resistance struggles in Jamaica in order to confront the fake Western archaeology of the country's history with a more "genuine" or inclusive one.

At the center of the novel lies the struggle for the power to narrate and interpret Jamaica's history. As all the history books on former colonies were written from the colonizer's perspective, an integral part of the decolonization process is the unearthing of repressed indigenous histories. In order to eradicate the effects of what Frantz Fanon termed colonialism's "cultural estrangement" [in *The Wretched of the Earth,* 1968], all erstwhile colonies must reassert their rights to a place in history, for in Amilcar Cabral's words:

> The national liberation of a people is the regaining of the historical personality of that people, it is their return to history through the destruction of the imperialist domination to which they have been subjected. [*Unity and Struggle: Speeches and Writings of Amilcar Cabral,* 1979]

In *No Telephone to Heaven* Cliff reveals that this task of historical reclamation is not an easy one, and that an uncontaminated "return to history," given the violent intervention of colonial history in the Caribbean, may well be impossible. In *No Telephone to Heaven* Cliff foregrounds the story of Nanny, a legendary Maroon woman warrior in Jamaican history, in order to show how indigenous culture and history are cannibalized in Western hands. *No Telephone to Heaven* traces the progress of a Western film crew that has come to Jamaica to film Nanny's life story. This movie project graphically illustrates the neo-colonial appropriation of "exotic" foreign locations and cultures, and Cliff exposes the deliberate de-politicization and Westernization of autochthonous histories in order to suit the tastes of American and European viewers. The film script of Nanny's life bears no resemblance to the version told by Cliff that weaves its way in and out of *No Telephone to Heaven* and its predecessor, *Abeng,* initially conceived as counterpoint and then as a parallel to the life story of Clare Savage.

Cliff's version of Nanny's life as a Maroon resistance fighter against British colonialism is, like Clare's, based on island folklore and oral history. Nanny was a magician and a rebel Windward Maroon leader who led her forces in guerrilla warfare against the British occupying forces from 1655 until her assassination by a slave in 1733. She attempted to unite her forces with those of Cudjoe, the red-skinned leader of the Leeward Maroons, but he rejected her advances and sold out to the British soon after. Despite her legendary status—she was supposed to be able to "catch a bullet between her buttocks and render the bullet harmless" (*Abeng*)—there is no doubt of her existence, and Clare visits the well-hidden remains of her Nanny-town that still exist in Jamaica today. The following description of a scene from the film of Nanny's life dramatically exposes the "fake archaeology" constructed by the foreign filmmakers:

> Two figures stood out in the costumed group. One, a woman, the actress called in whenever someone was needed to play a Black heroine, any Black heroine, whether Sojourner Truth or Bessie Smith, this woman wore a pair of leather breeches and a silk shirt—designer's notion of the clothes that Nanny wore. Dear Nanny, the Coromantee warrior, leader of the Windward Maroons, whom one book described as an old woman naked except for a necklace made from the teeth of whitemen—sent by the orishas to deliver her people. Wild Nanny, sporting furies through the Blue Mountains. Old, Dark, Small. But such detail was out of the question, given these people even knew the truth. Or cared. Facing the elegant actress was a strapping man, former heavyweight or running back, dressed as Cudjoe, tiny humpbacked soul.

> These two spoke back and forth, exchanging phrases of love in the screen-writer's version of Coromantee—which was, for all intents and purposes, pidgin. The dialogue coach a retired civil servant.

> Clare was lying flat in a bitterbrush.

This film superimposes a paradigmatic Western romantic narrative on the original indigenous history, making Nanny and Cudjoe into beautiful and universal romantic lovers. The bastardization of the indigenous language, Coromantee, into a debased colonial form of pidgin English, is fittingly accomplished by "a retired civil servant," no doubt British. This effacing and redirecting of indigenous historical narratives displays the hegemonic nature of what Fredric Jameson [in *The Political Unconscious: Narrative as a Socially Symbolic Act,* 1981] called "master codes" or "Ur-narratives." In pandering to the tastes of Western popular

culture, such films impose Western narrative and artistic conventions on "native" stories, denying the specificity of these histories and assimilating them into yet more imperial "master narratives."

[In *Critical Perspectives in East Asian Literature,* 1981] Masao Miyoshi warns Western critics of non-Western literary texts against just such assimilationist moves, calling these attempts to colonize and dominate the unfamiliar literary territory "domestication." On the other hand, we must also be wary of what Miyoshi terms "neutralization," a strategy which simply rejects the significance of the unfamiliar, and therefore ignores the literary contributions of other traditions and countries. The Western critic must therefore attempt to follow a middle path, taking cognizance of the innovations and differences of post-colonial literature while resisting the urge to contain resistant elements in a universal Western literary narrative. Cliff's symbolic reading of the Western film-maker's imperialist and cannibalistic appropriation of "Third World" raw materials should certainly act as a timely warning to the Western literary critic who attempts to appropriate *No Telephone to Heaven* as her text. As privileged literary critics we need to operate from the foundations of a critical sense of place, or what Adrienne Rich [in *Blood, Bread, and Poetry: Selected Prose 1979-1985,* 1986] has so resonantly termed "the politics of location," in order to be aware of the hegemonic status of Western theoretical and critical discourse, and therefore to remain sensitive to the dangers of adopting precisely those colonizing moves that the filmmakers in *No Telephone to Heaven* employ. Indeed the multiple narratives in the novel make it difficult for the Western critic to codify or enclose the novel in the "strategies of containment" that Jameson exposes as being both repressive and appropriative of the text.

Yet Cliff does not simplify the difficulty of resistance for the post-colonial subject. The impossibility of altogether evading such hegemonic Western scripts and their theatricality is depicted in the activities and make-up of Clare's band of resistance fighters, which show that no one in a post-colonial country can escape contamination by neo-colonial economic and cultural forces. While the resistance fighters are clearly aligned with the global anti-colonial revolutionary struggle, the group is equipped with black market American weapons supplied in return for Jamaican marijuana. They are dressed in surplus American army camouflage jackets, with the American soldiers' names still taped to the pockets—the wearers even assume these names with the jackets. Their accoutrements reveal them as American look-alikes, who base their identity on old U.S. war movies portraying "GIs fortified with Camels talking about baseball while stalking the silent, treacherous Jap." Such anomalies of dress and attitude dramatically expose the dependence of such postcolonial countries as Jamaica on the cultures and economies of imperialist Western powers:

> The camouflage jackets, names and all, added a further awareness, a touch of realism, cinematic vérité, that anyone who eyed them would believe they were faced with *real* soldiers. True soldiers—though no government had ordered them into battle—far from it. But this is how the camouflage made them feel. As the gold and green and black knitted caps some wore—a danger because the bright gold would sing out in the bush—made them feel like real freedom fighters, like their comrades in the ANC—a cliché, almost screen-played to death, *Viva Zapata!* and all that—but that *is* what they were, what they *felt* they were, what they *were* in fact. Their reason emblazoned in the colors of their skulls. *Burn!*

The confusion and sense of inferiority exhibited by the resistance fighters in their burning desire for the appearance, at least, of being "*real* soldiers" despite their anti-government stance, exposes their entrapment in the stereotypical Western movie images of soldiers that haunt them. Cliff problematizes the nationalistic desire to return to origins and indigenous culture by showing that even "real" nationalist freedom fighters, like the ANC, have become media property and hence clichés. How is it then possible to return to a "real" or "genuine" history without contamination? This extract clearly epitomizes the conflicting loyalties and impulses of nationalist movements in neo-colonial countries worldwide: while these countries are dependent on Western technology and financial aid for their continued existence, they long for a return to traditional cultural forms and the dignity of self-determination. Bruce King contends [in *The New English Literatures: Cultural Nationalism in a Changing World,* 1980] that this dual focus is ultimately self-defeating and doomed to failure, for resistance struggles follow the scripts controlled by Western imperial powers in global nationalist dramas "almost screenplayed to death":

> It is the conflict within nationalism between modernisation and authenticity which produces the well-known phenomenon in developing nations of wanting western industry, science and material goods while rejecting European culture or the kind of secular, rational, sceptical mentality that has usually accompanied industrialisation. But as its claim to authenticity is the defense of traditional culture, and as it needs the symbols of tradition to obtain and remain in power, a nationalist movement will find itself imprisoned in a paradox which in turn provides its dynamism, its despair and its outbursts of rage.

Clare Savage has herself lived out this paradoxical duality of desire, in her conflicting ties to her parents. Her development has been marked by the struggle between her love for her strong but silent mother, whose powerful love for her homeland caused her to abandon both her husband and Clare in the United States and return to Jamaica, and her identification with her class-conscious and lighter-skinned father, whose legacy to Clare was Western education and culture and her light skin. Manifesting the same cultural schizophrenia that pervades the Caribbean world, and attempting to heal this split, Clare returns to Jamaica in a dual quest for her lost dead mother and the heritage of her motherland. As her political loyalties clarify, Clare abandons her English university graduate work in the European Renaissance in favor of teaching reading, writing, and indigenous Jamaican history to secondary school children in Jamaica. Clare allies herself with indigenous culture against Western models, thereby attempting to evade co-optation by Western master narratives. Cliff portrays Clare's increasing politicization in contrast with the Western film script's strategy of domestication. Clare's resistance of conventional Western romance life-scripts is seen as a counterpoint to the film's domestication and romanticization of Nanny's life of resistance, as Nanny is assimilated into a typical Western quest-romance tale of womanhood. In this portrayal of Clare's rebellion, Cliff resists the domination of the "master codes" of literary genres and/or historical narratives, and constructs new narrative paradigms for post-colonial subjects.

Cliff reveals the twofold task of cultural reconstruction in Clare's life, and thereby also in narrative form. The first task is to break free from the Western "master narratives" that control and suppress resistant narratives. These controlling narratives maintain the place of indigenous cultures at the bottom level of the cannibalistic neo-colonial food chain, and therefore must be overthrown to clear the way for cultural reconstruction to occur. The second and following task is to construct new and challenging cultural forms which build on indigenous traditions. While this dual process obviously pertains to Cliff's multiple narrative reconstructions of history in *No Telephone to Heaven,* it also affects the novel's narrative structure. Jameson describes genre as yet another form of hegemonic literary script, which he terms a "master code" or "narrative":

> . . . in its emergent strong form a genre is essentially a socio-symbolic message, or in other terms, that form is immanently and intrinsically an ideology in its own right. When such forms are reappropriated and refashioned in quite different social and cultural contexts, this message persists and must be functionally reckoned into the new form . . . The ideology of the form itself, thus sedimented, persists into the later, more complex structure, as a generic message which coexists—either as a contradiction or, on the other hand, as a

mediatory or harmonizing mechanism—with elements from later stages.

Built on the European generic foundations of the *bildungsroman, No Telephone to Heaven* consequently carries with it, in however sedimented a form, the individualistic bourgeois values of that Western literary tradition. Yet the novel also belongs to the post-colonial literary tradition of the "been-to" narrative, in which the protagonist travels to the center of empire and back, thus gaining a privileged perspective on her country's status in the global power system, but also frequently becoming alienated from both indigenous and imperial cultures in the process. This post-colonial form of the *bildungsroman* not only "indigenizes" the Western sub-genre, but also politicizes it. Since the 1950s Caribbean literature has had a powerful tradition of novels portraying their child protagonists' development as paralleling the political and social awakening of their countries; *No Telephone to Heaven* extends that heritage to encompass the era of post-colonial resistance to continued Western oppression.

Indeed, *No Telephone to Heaven*'s hybrid literary form mirrors the cultural hybridism of Jamaica, and the tensions of such a synthesis both extend and critique the novel form. The Western individualistic emphasis of the *bildungsroman* subgenre frequently shifts to a collective one in the post-colonial novel. In *No Telephone to Heaven* Clare Savage's narrative and middle-class fortunes are intertwined even in death with two other characters who compel our attention and sympathy, and whose presences in the narrative consequently partially undercut or decenter the reader's complete identification with Clare's *bildung*. Harry/Harriet, who was raped as a boy by a British officer in an act that symbolizes imperialist exploitation of Jamaica, searches throughout the novel for free expression of his/her sexual and political identity. It is Harry/Harriet who draws Clare back to Jamaica and makes her aware of her responsibility to her people, while his decision to become a woman, to teach himself old native healing arts and so become a nurse, and then to join an active resistance movement, are examples of courage which greatly influence Clare's future actions.

The other narrative tells of the misfortunes of the destitute and haunted Christopher, an orphaned gardener who murdered his middle-class employer and family as symbols of the society that denies his grandmother a burial plot. He is an outcast, a mad wanderer known to all as "De Watchman," whose life expresses complete rejection of and by conventional middle-class Jamaican society. Ironically he is employed as an extra in the foreign film about Nanny, and his enscripted wails are the signals for the government attack on Clare and her band. He is also killed in the rain of gunfire. Class and color may have excluded Clare from the material effects of political exploitation, but Cliff exposes the

full spectrum of suffering in Jamaica by paralleling Christopher's isolated personal revolt against a classist system with Clare's gradual movement towards collective popular resistance. These multiple plot-lines serve the dual purpose of undermining linear narrative development and also of broadening the political perspectives of the novel.

The tragic ending of the novel, in which Harry/Harriet, Clare, and Christopher are mowed down by government troops, determinedly resists the reader's utopian desires and undermines the expectations of organic seamless development or "successful" socialization encouraged by the conventional *bildungsroman*. Yet it also seems to deny the hope of new literary or historical narratives for post-colonial resistance groups or literatures. The surprise betrayal of the resistance fighters (the script played out for them in earlier Jamaican history when Nanny and her band are betrayed by a loyalist slave) and their destruction by the Jamaican army, who operate in collusion with the foreign film crew, portrays the triumph both of neo-colonial forces and it seems, of European literary conventions in the narrative. With this apocalyptic narrative ending Michelle Cliff dramatically demonstrates what Helen Tiffin [in "Post-Colonialism, Post-Modernism and the Rehabilitation of Post Colonial History," *Journal of Commonwealth Literature,* 1988] calls "the complicity of politics and text in capture and containment explored in so many post-colonial works."

Yet while Cliff's post-colonial text seems to enact the continuing hegemonic control and cannibalism of cultural imperialism, it encodes various resistance strategies within this Ur-narrative. While the dominant literary and political narratives still appear to impede the development of completely independent resistant forms, the hybridization and multiplication of narrative forms undermine any attempts at totalization or containment by Western critics. While feminist critics, for example, may be dismayed at what seems a retreat by Cliff into the nineteenth-century binary option of marriage or death for women protagonists of the quest romance, the strategy is in fact very different. Clare does not die as an outcast from society because she has flouted conventional gender roles. Instead she dies at a moment of personal triumph, when her life-long struggle for a sense of place and family is consummated in the unification of her personal and communal goals. Cliff has addressed the objections of readers to the cataclysmic ending of her novel, in an essay entitled "Clare Savage as a Cross-roads Character" [*Caribbean Women Writers,* edited by Selwyn R. Cudjoe, University of Massachusetts Press, 1990], that makes clear the positive oppositional intent of her narrative act of destruction:

> At the end of *No Telephone to Heaven,* Clare Savage has cast her lot, quietly and somewhat tentatively, but definitely. She ends her life burned into

the landscape of Jamaica, literally, as one of a small band of guerrillas engaged in a symbolic act of revolution.

Many readers of this novel think this is an unhappy ending; they do not want the character to die. Though essentially tragic, for her life has been so, I see it, and envisioned it, as an ending that completes the circle, or rather triangle, of the character's life. In her death she has complete identification with her homeland; soon enough she will be indistinguishable from the ground. Her bones will turn to potash, as did her ancestors' bones.

These words demonstrate clearly the groundedness of Cliff's politics in a revolutionary concept of home. While rejecting foreign control of their lives and their nation, resistance groups such as Clare's strive to create new definitions and configurations of "home," much as Michelle Cliff strives in *No Telephone to Heaven* to create a text that enacts the struggle of emergent literary and political forms to create a place for themselves in the global cultural economy.

Thomas Cartelli (essay date Spring 1995)

SOURCE: "After *The Tempest:* Shakespeare, Postcoloniality, and Michelle Cliff's New, New World Miranda," in *Contemporary Literature*, Vol. 36, No. 1, Spring, 1995, pp. 82-102.

[*In the following excerpt, Cartelli illustrates how Cliff challenges Western readers with her West Indian narrative in* No Telephone to Heaven, *and explains how the novel rewrites Shakespeare's* The Tempest, *particularly with regard to the character of Clare Savage, whose similarities to Shakespeare's Miranda are discussed.*]

No Telephone to Heaven (1987), a novel by the Jamaican-American writer Michelle Cliff, represents perhaps the most ambitious recent attempt by a contemporary West Indian to work through and master the impulse to write back to the center. Rather than choose to ignore the circumstances of interdependency and belatedness that condition West Indian textuality, Cliff turns them to the advantage of an emergent creolized sensibility, countercolonizing the established plots of a still dominant, but imaginatively exhausted, imperial master narrative. Cliff's novel speaks in many voices—literary English, colloquial "American," Jamaican patois—and positions them in a manner that requires its "centered" Western readers to assemble a mental glossary of names and definitions that the printed glossary at the back of the book only partially satisfies. By speaking casually and knowingly of familiar Jamaican places, people, and events, Cliff challenges the Western reader's confidence in his or her ability to map

West Indian experience, placing that reader in the position of a disoriented tourist reliant on a guidebook that speaks too inwardly and elliptically to be easily apprehended, much less mastered. Cliff's novel is also one of the few postcolonial works to claim an epigraphic authority for other postcolonial writers and for the traces of precolonial cultures. Her chapter headings are studded with quotations from fellow West Indians like Derek Walcott and Aimé Césaire, from Yoruba hymns and Jamaican proverbs. And her text often alludes to the work of Jean Rhys, C.L.R. James, and the dub-poet Linton Kwesi Johnson, among others.

Canonical Western writing, however, maintains a hold on the novel from beginning to end, most obviously in its protagonist's pivotal encounter with Jane Eyre. Cliff's protagonist, Clare Savage, encounters Jane at a moment of weakness when the temptation to merge her subjectivity with Jane's is strong. Alone in London, where she "passes" as white in a deeply polarized society, Clare finds that "The fiction had tricked her. Drawn her in so that she became Jane." This at least is her first response. Her second response is more complex:

> Comforted for a time, she came to. Then, with a sharpness, reprimanded herself. No, she told herself. No, she could not be Jane. Small and pale. English . . . No, my girl, try Bertha. Wild-maned Bertha. . . . Yes, Bertha was closer the mark. Captive, Ragôut. Mixture, Confused. Jamaican. Caliban. Carib. Cannibal. Cimarron. All Bertha. All Clare.

What Clare "comes to" here is a more densely textualized and historicized identification with Jane Eyre's West Indian other. Clare's identification with Bertha is clearly negotiated by Cliff's own reading of Jean Rhys's *Wide Sargasso Sea*, a book that both encourages and enables the West Indian reader to appropriate as central what is arguably marginal to the novel *Jane Eyre*. But it is also negotiated, at least within the confines of the novel itself, by Clare's readiness to accept what has been rendered marginal by others as central to her own experience. What Cliff seems to be after, both here and elsewhere in her novel, is to have Clare act out, in the life of her fiction, what Rhys has previously enacted on the level of textuality. Cliff effectively attempts to take charge of the process that has made West Indians "creatures of books and inventions fashioned by others" by demonstrating how a newly emergent postcolonial textuality may help to engender new subject positions for West Indians to inhabit.

Much the same effort appears to motivate Clare's associative identification with Caliban. This is the first and only time that the novel makes the characteristic postcolonial move of explicitly identifying Caliban with past and present inhabitants of the West Indies. But it provides a key that opens up the novel's less explicit, but more sustained, appropriation and rewriting of *The Tempest.* Cliff herself has remarked that Caliban's famous response to Prospero—"You taught me language, and my profit on't / Is, I know how to curse"—immediately brings to my mind the character of Bertha Rochester, wild and raving ragout, as Charlotte Brontë describes her, cursing and railing, more beast than human" ["Clare Savage as a Crossroads Character," *Caribbean Women Writers: Essays from the First International Conference,* edited by Selwyn Cudjoe, 1990]. In the same essay, Cliff also speaks of herself as "a writer of Afro-Caribbean (Indian, African, and white) experience and heritage and Western experience and education (indoctrination)," who attempts, "by inventing my own peculiar speech, . . . to draw together everything I am and have been, both Caliban and Ariel and a liberated and synthesized version of each." Cliff, however, fails to remark that although her investment in Caliban and Ariel makes its presence felt in the course of her novel, it is Miranda—like Cliff herself a product of Western experience, education and indoctrination—who plays a more prominent role in underwriting Clare Savage's subjective development and evolution into an agent of social and political change.

Unlike the majority of those of her silent or silenced postcolonial sisters who have been identified as socially or politically updated versions of *The Tempest's* Miranda, Clare Savage is presented as the self-determining agent of her own education who refuses to use the advantage of pale skin and privileged class-standing either to "pass" or to deny the Caliban within. Abandoned by her defiantly Jamaican mother, raised in exile in New York by her Americanized father (who is perhaps too coyly named Boy Savage and functions, both here and in Cliff's earlier novel, *Abeng,* as a deeply flawed Prospero figure), tutored in Renaissance studies at a university in London, this New World Miranda rejects father and London alike in order to return to Jamaica, where she attempts to redeem her grandmother's homestead and, with it, a sense of "basic, assumed life." In the process of her transit between New York, Europe, and Jamaica, she has casual sex with Paul H., a spoiled prince of the Jamaican economic aristocracy; enters into a consciously restorative relationship with a physically and psychically maimed Caliban, a black American veteran of Vietnam who has had his childhood dreams of "catching shrimp with [his] mother . . . gathering okra, and dodging the snakes" permanently invaded by nightmares of dismemberment; and allies herself in "sisterhood" with an androgynous Ariel who doubles as a Jamaican nationalist. Her New World consciousness raised by a chance discovery of the grave of Pocahontas in England, Clare/Miranda eventually turns her inherited land over to the cause of nationalist rebels and dies with them, victim of an airborne tempest conjured up by the new, New World magic of American money.

As formulaic as my synopsis makes it sound, the novel seamlessly incorporates and, more to the point, extends the New World typologies of earlier rewritings of *The Tempest.* It does so most distinctly with respect to Clare's sexually and politically collaborative contact with its American Caliban and Jamaican Ariel figures; rejection of her father and the Euro-American structures of respectability to which he would have her aspire; and decisive return to her native land. The novel also extends its *Tempest* applications to an early scene of mass murder perpetrated by Christopher, a native-born Caliban, against the family of Paul H.—which rather degradingly fulfills the potential of Caliban's foiled attempt to despoil Prospero and Miranda in *The Tempest*—and a description by Harry/Harriet, the androgyne Ariel, of his sodomy-rape at the hands of a white colonial policeman. Deformed by a malnourished childhood lived in the heart of the "dungle," Kingston's slum of cardboard snacks, Christopher is presented without glamour or approval (though with a good deal of sympathetic understanding) as the denatured product of independent Jamaica's reproduction of colonial inequity. Like *Jane Eyre*'s Bertha, Christopher roars and bellows, haunted, Caliban-like, by "duppies," and seeks to bury his demons in the bellies and genitals of people with lighter skin who live in houses where he is set to work.

A homosexual who can "pass" as man or woman, Harry/Harriet initially frames his boyhood violation in the broader context of the colonialist violation of Jamaica. But as the novel's most insistent advocate of social and political change, he notably resists clothing himself in a language of colonial signifiers that has kept Jamaica in unacknowledged bondage to the past. As he states:

> we *are* of the past here. So much of the past that we punish people by flogging them with cat-o'-nine-tails. We expect people to live on cornmeal and dried fish, which was the diet of the slaves. We name hotels Plantation Inn and Sans Souci. . . . A peculiar past. For we have taken the master's past as our own. That is the danger.

Cliff arguably courts the same danger in allowing her narrative to be overrun by a promiscuous intertextuality that threatens to reestablish her writing's dependence on the master narrative of colonialism. But like Harry/Harriet, Cliff also resists the impulse to represent Jamaican experience in a strictly deterministic manner. She does so, in this instance, through her character's insistence on both the singularity and collectivity of his personal history:

> I have been tempted in my life to think *symbol*—that what he did to me is but a symbol for what they did to all of us, always bearing in mind that some of us, many of us, also do it to each other. But that's not right. I only suffered what my mother suffered—no more, no less. Not symbol, not allegory, not

something in a story or a dialogue by Plato. No, man, I am merely a person who felt the overgrown cock of a big whiteman pierce the asshole of a lickle Black bwai—there it is. That is all there is to it.

The claim for singularity is made in the brutally specific words Cliff chooses to isolate the act suffered by her character from a more rhetorically (and politically) expansive interpretation. The claim for collectivity is made in Harry/Harriet's association of the material circumstances of his rape with his mother's sufferance of economic violations that Jamaica's postcolonial status has done nothing to diminish. Of course, the phallic language and Jamaican diminutives—"lickle Black bwai"—also enhance our sense of the uncontestable power of the "big whiteman" who continues to tower, literally and symbolically, over the narrative and both sponsors and stages the destructive conflagration with which the novel—and the fictional lives of its *Tempest* surrogates—ends.

Each of these sequences indicates the restrictive hold that the neocolonial present maintains even over what may be ventured on the level of postcolonial narrative. It is in this respect, among others, that Cliff's attempt to master the impulse to write back to the center should, perhaps, be considered only a qualified success. But by extending the range and resonance of her appropriations of *The Tempest* into the province of contemporary social history, especially with respect to such concerns as underclass deracination, dissident sexualities, and feminist self-assertion, Cliff's rewritings of the roles of Caliban, Ariel, and Miranda move beyond the meanings of both Shakespeare's *Tempest* and the often predictable, and arguably circular, rewritings of Retamar, Lamming, and Césaire.

One of the obvious ironies of the postcolonial fascination with *The Tempest* has been its acceptance of the play's limited cast of characters as representative of enduring colonial(ist) configurations, as if Shakespeare had immutably fixed the only available attitudes of master, servant, and rebel at a comparatively early and ill-defined moment in the imperial enterprise. Even in the act of critique and appropriation, writers like Retamar and Césaire accept positional stereotypes whose only real claim to legitimacy is their continued circulation. There are, of course, moments in each writer's work that move beyond the host plot of *The Tempest,* that introduce variations on, and complications of, the originally configurations. The dialogue between Ariel and Caliban in 2.1 of Césaire's *A Tempest,* for example, stages at least the possibility of a future alliance between opportunistic and defiant participants in the colonialist configuration, one that is literally "colored" by later stages of political development and, hence, may be said to historicize the relationship of differently unequal parties to colonialist exploitation. This scene, however, remains locked in a parasitic relationship to Shakespeare's play, which itself can claim only the most negligible application to the wildly variegated nature of colonial experience in the Caribbean.

What is needed to break the spell of *The Tempest* on West Indian writing that chooses to confront it is a narrative that disenchants *The Tempest*'s monopoly on the available forms of postcolonial identity by reconfiguring the fixed subject positions established by both the play itself and its appropriators. The fact that *The Tempest* operates less as a plot than as a residual presence in **No Telephone to Heaven** allows both new plots and new subject positions to emerge in the novel. Cliff is particularly successful in moving her work a stage beyond that of those of her West Indian predecessors whose "subject," as George Lamming writes, was "the migration of the West Indian writer, as colonial and exile, from his native kingdom, once inhabited by Caliban, to the tempestuous island of Prospero's and his language" [*The Pleasures of Exile,* 1960].

For Lamming, the absence of an "extraordinary departure which explodes all of Prospero's premises" implicitly cedes possession of "Caliban and his future" to Prospero. Although no revolutionary change is imminent even in her novel's construction of history, Cliff's decision to have her potentially mobile protagonists reject migration and exile in an effort to regenerate a sense of "basic, assumed life" in Jamaica leaves them largely unsubjugated both to Prospero's symbolic authority and to the need to contest that authority which is usually associated with Caliban. In effecting the release both of her characters and the language she constructs for them from what Lamming terms "the prison of Prospero's gift," Cliff engages in exactly the kind of "revisionist metaphoric activity" that Gay Wilentz [in "English Is a Foreign Anguish: Caribbean Writers and the Disruption of the Colonial Canon," *Decolonizing Tradition: New Views of Twentieth-Century "British" Literary Canons,* edited by Karen R. Lawrence, 1992] considers necessary to heal the "isolating and subjugating" rupture "in the correlation of language and accepted reality" that Hearne describes and that characterizes Caliban's possession.

Nor is this the only "extraordinary departure" from "Prospero's premises" recorded in the novel. The patriarchal authority exercised by Prospero yields, in **No Telephone to Heaven,** to the attempt by the children of postcoloniality to negotiate an authority of their own, grounded in the recovery of what has survived the sustained tempest of colonialism and colonial self-hatred. The parables of escape, denial, and determinacy that the novel's native-born Prosperos tell these children are countered not only by the predictable rage of a servant-monster who inscribes his frustration on the bodies of his patrician masters, but by Clare's mother-centered recovery of her cultural and racial identity, and by Harry/Harriet's rejection of the authority of symbols in the process of his regendering. Indeed, what most distinguishes the novel from both its colonial and postcolonial forebears is its own fairly wholesale rejection and denial of the very notion of patriarchal authority embodied either in Prospero or in a successfully mated and politically redeemed Caliban figure.

In this novel, patriarchal power and authority operate effectively only in a violently displaced, corporate manner, as an army bought and paid for by an American film company ultimately has its way with Clare and her confederates, summarily erasing the latest attempted intervention in Jamaica's ongoing (neo)colonization. In the end, the magical power of American money even has its way with language—as articulate speech dissolves under the joint onslaught of artillery and animal sounds—but not before an alternative history of rebellion and resistance has been reconstructed and reevoked in the fictional present by characters who have either been exiled from, or have exiled, their fathers.

The weakness, recessiveness, or dispersion of paternal authority into corporate engines of power in **No Telephone to Heaven** is countered by the strength, persistence, and clearly defined commitments of the novel's female characters, most notably Clare and her mother. Yet neither of these women qualifies, or consents, to play the role that constitutes, in Sylvia Wynter's terms [in "Beyond Miranda's Meanings: Un/silencing the 'Demonic Ground' of Caliban's 'Woman,'" *Out of the Kumbla: Caribbean Women and Literature,* edited by Carole Boyce Davies and Elaine Savory Fido, 1990], "the most significant absence of all" in Shakespeare's play, namely, that of "Caliban's Woman." Wynter conspicuously rejects the possibility of a West Indian appropriation of Miranda as one of its own, identifying her solely in terms of her relationship to Prospero, with whom she forms a racially based and morally valorized "population-group." According to Wynter, Miranda serves as "both a co-participant, if to a lesser *derived* extent, in the power and privileges generated by the empirical supremacy of her own population; and as well, the beneficiary of a mode of privilege unique to her, that of being the metaphysically invested and 'idealized' object of desire of all classes (Stephano and Trinculo) and all population-groups (Caliban)." As such, Miranda shuts off the possibility of Caliban's mate appearing "as an alternative sexual-erotic model of desire; as an alternative source of an alternative system of meanings."

Wynter's intervention in what could be called the technology of *Tempest* appropriations would appear to require a critical reexamination of my reading of Miranda into and out of **No Telephone to Heaven,** in addition to indicating why *The Tempest*'s Miranda cannot, without substantial transformation of the play itself, sustain the interpretive effort to mate her with Caliban. In *The Tempest,* of course, Miranda is already (happily) betrothed to Ferdinand—her "brave new world" has only people like him in it—and operates within the same cultural field that frames Peter Greenaway's unrelievedly Eurocentric construction of the play in his recent film *Prospero's Books.* In order to divorce Miranda from Ferdinand and satisfactorily remate her with Caliban, one would have to dispense with *The Tempest* entirely or, as in the case of Césaire's *A Tempest,* enlist a vigorously revised version of the play in the cause of a racialized conception of West Indian nationalisms. To satisfy Wynter's objections, a revised *Tempest* might also require the continued consignment of Miranda to a subordinate position in a postcolonial power complex dominated by Caliban and an ethic of male sexual possessiveness signaled by the phrase "Caliban's Woman."

Cliff, however, is committed to a process of creolization in the racially mixed construction of her Miranda figure, as well as to a reconfiguring of both power and gender relations in the social economy of her novel. She also appears to recognize, as Laura Donaldson has argued [in "The Miranda Complex: Colonialism and the Question of Feminist Reading," *Diacritics,* Vol. 18, No. 3, 1988], that "Miranda—the Anglo-European daughter—offers us a feminine trope of colonialism, for her textual and psychological selflessness in *The Tempest* exposes the particular oppression of women under the rule of their biological and cultural Fathers." Moreover, as if in answer to Wynter's objections, Cliff has her Miranda consciously reject her capacity to "pass" as the "metaphysically invested and 'idealized' object of desire of all classes" in favor of serving "as an alternative source of an alternative system of meanings." Cliff specifically has Clare reject her role as a coparticipant in a Prospero-Miranda racial complex by having her choose to "become" black after her father chooses to become white. Clare's consciously crafted divorce from her father is effected so that she might establish a similarly deliberative (if clearly belated) relationship with another figure who is conspicuously absent in Shakespeare's *Tempest,* namely, Miranda's mother, Prospero's wife. And although Cliff in her own words, as in the words she delegates to Clare, rhetorically affiliates herself with Caliban, she also adds a significantly feminist twist to the transaction by reconfiguring a *Tempest* in which Miranda chooses not to mate at all.

In his own essay on appropriations of *The Tempest* ["Caribbean and African Appropriations of *The Tempest,*" *Critical Inquiry,* Vol. 13, 1987], Rob Nixon describes the alleged fading out of "*The Tempest*'s value for African and Caribbean intellectuals" in the 1970s and attributes it to the play's lack of "a sixth act which might have been enlisted for representing relations among Caliban, Ariel, and Prospero once they entered a postcolonial era." He adds, "The play's declining pertinence to contemporary Africa and the Caribbean has been exacerbated by the difficulty of wresting from it any role for female defiance or leadership in a period when protest is coming increasingly from that quarter." But it is precisely the awakened defiance of the dramatically silenced Miranda that Cliff wrests from *The Tempest* at an even later moment in the "play's declining pertinence" to postcolonial writers. Instead of writing a sixth act for a postcolonial *Tempest* that will, once and for all, separate the boys from the man, she writes a thoroughly creolized and womanized novel in which the new, New World Miranda effectively replaces both Prospero and Caliban as an agent of self-determination and cultural change. In the process, Cliff may be said to have engendered a second life for *The Tempest* at a stage of postcoloniality when, as [the play] *Shakespeare Wallah* suggests, "every third thought" is Prospero's grave.

FURTHER READING

Criticism

Edmonson, Belinda. "Race, Privilege, and the Politics of (Re)Writing History: An Analysis of the Novels of Michelle Cliff." *Callaloo* 16, No. 1 (1993): 180-91.
>   Examines Cliff's treatment of race, class, and history in *Abeng* and *No Telephone to Heaven*.

Nunez-Harrell, Elizabeth. "Abandoned For Their Own Good." *The New York Times Book Review* (23 September 1990): 22.
>   A favorable review of *Bodies of Water*.

Sethuraman, Ramchandran. "Evidence-Cum-Witness: Subaltern History, Violence, and the (De)Formation of Nation in Michelle Cliff's *No Telephone to Heaven*." *Modern Fiction Studies* 43, No. 1 (Spring 1997): 249-87.
>   Analyzes *No Telephone to Heaven* in terms of its treatment of culture, psychology, postcolonialism, race, history, location, nationality, and violence in film.

Additional coverage of Cliff's life and career is contained in the following sources published by Gale: *Black Writers*, **Vol. 2;** *Contemporary Authors*, **Vol. 116;** *Contemporary Authors New Revision Series*, **Vol. 39; and** *Dictionary of Literary Biography*, **Vol. 157.**

Maryse Condé
1937-

(Born Maryse Boucolon) Guadeloupean novelist, critic, dramatist, short story writer, essayist, and author of children's books.

INTRODUCTION

Condé is considered one of the most successful and important figures in contemporary Afro-Caribbean literature. She has won critical acclaim for articulating a distinctively black female perspective unmarked by the influences of imperialism and colonial oppression in the West Indies. Also lauded for her works of literary criticism, Condé often focuses—in her fiction and her nonfiction—on the relationship between the individual and society, particularly in the societies of Guadeloupe, other Caribbean locales, and equatorial Africa.

Biographical Information

Born in Guadeloupe into a well-known family of academics and entrepreneurs, Condé was raised in an atmosphere of strong racial and familial pride. At the age of sixteen, she left to study in France, where she was the victim of severe racial prejudice. After being expelled from one school, Condé eventually completed her studies at the Sorbonne, where she was the winner of a short story writing contest among West African students. Thereafter, she traveled briefly in Europe and took a teaching position in the Ivory Coast. Between 1960 and 1968, Condé taught and lived in a number of African nations, including Guinea, Ghana, and Senegal. She returned to France in 1970 in order to earn a doctorate from the Sorbonne, which she accomplished in 1976. Condé remained at the Sorbonne as a lecturer for nearly ten years, and during this time published some of her best-known works. In 1986 she returned to Guadeloupe and established a permanent residence there. She has since taught and lectured at a number of American universities, most often at the Los Angeles and Berkeley campuses of the University of California.

Major Works

Condé is known for critical works that examine Francophone literature and feminist issues—notably *La civilisation du bossale* (1978), *La parole des femmes* (1979), and *Tim tim? Bois sec!* (1980)—and for fictional accounts of life in the Third World, primarily in the Antilles and West Africa—as in *Hérémakhonon* (1976; *Heremakhonon*), *Une saison à Rihata* (1981; *A Season in Rihata*), *La vie scélérate* (1987; *Tree of Life*), and *Traversée de la mangrove* (1990; *Cross-*

ing the Mangrove). *Heremakhonon,* a semi-autobiographical novel, is set in an unidentified West African country and details the adventures of a Paris-educated Guadeloupe woman. The protagonist unwittingly becomes embroiled in the nation's political turmoil through her relationships with a bureaucrat and a radical schoolmaster. Condé's second novel, *A Season in Rihata,* again focuses on an African nation beset by internal problems in order to relate the story of a prominent family threatened by corruption and antigovernment sentiments. In her next two novels, *Ségou: Les murailles de terre* (1984; *Segu*) and *Ségou: La terre en miettes* (1985; *The Children of Segu*), Condé combines historical fact with fiction to recreate events in the West African kingdom of Ségou, which is now Mali, between 1797 and 1860. These works chronicle the experiences of members of a royal family whose lives are destroyed by such developments as European colonization, the slave trade, and the introduction of Islam and Christianity into Ségou's largely animistic culture. *Tree of Life,* set in Guadeloupe in the 1870s, details the life of a black nationalist patriarch and his scattered family, who, though haunted by loneliness, despair, and suicide, struggle for survival. Other novels by

Condé include *Moi, Tituba, sorcière noire de Salem* (1986; *I, Tituba, Black Witch of Salem*), the fictionalized biography of a Barbadian slave who was executed for practicing witchcraft in colonial Massachusetts, and *Les derniers rois mages* (1992; *The Last Magi*), the tale of the ghost of an African king who pays a visit to his relatives in contemporary South Carolina. Condé has also published several plays, collections of short stories, and works for children.

Critical Reception

Response to Condé's work has been generally positive. She has won numerous literary awards and fellowships, including the Prix littéraire de la femme in 1986 for *I, Tituba, Black Witch of Salem* and the Guggenheim fellowship in 1987. Charlotte and David Bruner have commented that Condé, in drawing on her experiences in Paris, West Africa, and her native Guadeloupe, has created several novels that "attempt to make credible on an increasingly larger scale the personal human complexities involved in holy wars, national rivalries, and migrations of peoples." Hal Wylie has called Condé's "ambitious insistence upon seeking the links between generations, and between the ethnic groups" to be "a quest for the meaningful factors of our time." Many critics have lauded Condé for her knowledge of African history, while others focus their praise on her struggle to create an independent identity for the Afro-Caribbean woman. Some critics, however, find Condé's plots convoluted and overburdened by details. Miller Newman has noted that, in *I Tituba, Black Witch of Salem,* Condé's use of apparitions and wraiths is "bizarre" and "tests the reader's patience." In discussing *Segu,* Phiefer L. Browne has stated that the work has "a sometimes confusing welter of characters" and "it ends abruptly, leaving its various plot strands hanging." Although some critics have taken exception to Condé's literary style, many share David Bruner's opinion that "Maryse Condé's work has been that of a major writer of our age."

PRINCIPAL WORKS

Anthologie de la littérature africaine d'expression française [editor] (fiction) 1966

Dieu nous l'a donné [*God Given*] (drama) [first publication] 1972

Mort d'Oluwemi d'Ajumako [*Death of a King*] (drama) 1973

Hérémakhonon [*Heremakhonon*] (novel) 1976

La poésie antillaise [editor] (criticism) 1977

Le roman antillais [editor] (criticism) 1977

La civilisation du bossale: Réflexions sur la littérature orale de la Guadeloupe et de la Martinique (essays) 1978

Notas sobre el Enriquillo (criticism) 1978

Le profil d'une oeuvre: Cahier d'un retour au pays natal (essays) 1978

La parole des femmes: Essais sur des romancières des Antilles de langue français (essays) 1979

*Tim tim? Bois sec! Bloemlezling uit de Franstalige Caribsche literatuur (criticism) 1980

Une saison à Rihata [*A Season in Rihata*] (novel) 1981

Un gout de miel (short stories) 1984

Ségou: Les murailles de terre [*Segu*] (novel) 1984

Pays mêlé suivi de Nanna-ya (short stories) 1985

Ségou: La terre en miettes [*The Children of Segu*] (novel) 1985

Moi, Tituba, sorcière noire de Salem [*I, Tituba, Black Witch of Salem*] (novel) 1986

Haiti Chérie (juvenile) 1987

La vie scélérate [*Tree of Life*] (novel) 1987

Pension les Alizés (drama) 1988

An tan revolisyon (drama) 1989

Traversée de la mangrove [*Crossing the Mangrove*] (novel) 1989

Victor et les barricades (juvenile) 1989

The Hills of Massabielle (drama) 1991

Les derniers rois mages [*The Last Magi*] (novel) 1992

La colonie du nouveau monde (novel) 1993

La migration des couers (novel) 1995

*This work contains revised and translated editions of *Le roman antillais* and *La poésie antillaise.*

CRITICISM

Howard Frank Mosher (review date 25 October 1992)

SOURCE: "Staying Alive," in *The New York Times Book Review,* October 25, 1992, pp. 11-12.

[*Mosher is an American novelist and short story writer whose works include* Where the Rivers Flow North *(1978) and* A Stranger in the Kingdom *(1989). In the following review of* I, Tituba, Black Witch of Salem *and* Tree of Life, *he praises Condé's sense of history and compassion, stating that "it is impossible to read her novels and not come away from them with both a sadder and more exhilarating understanding of the human heart."*]

In the final chapter of *Segu,* Maryse Condé's historical novel of 19th-century tribal West Africa, the youthful Muhammad, scion of one of the great families along the Upper Niger, is about to take part in a huge and terrifying battle. As blue-turbaned horsemen gallop toward him brandishing lances, as sabers clash and iron balls whirl on chains, he thinks fleetingly of his mother. "Then," Ms. Condé writes, in the last sentence of the novel, "he set his teeth and didn't think of anything except staying alive."

The world's literature has always abounded with great survivors. And although contemporary American fiction may offer readers fewer heroes than the notable novels of earlier generations, there are still plenty of first-rate novelists, here and abroad, whose characters not only survive the worst that life can throw at them but also often prevail, on their own terms, against overwhelming odds. The brilliant and prolific Maryse Condé—born in Guadeloupe, a longtime resident of Paris and now a professor of French at the University of California, Berkeley—is just such a writer. And with the appearance this fall of uniformly excellent English translations of *I, Tituba, Black Witch of Salem* and *Tree of Life,* readers in this country will have the considerable pleasure of acquainting themselves with more of her durable survivors.

Ms. Condé's Tituba is based loosely on the black slave woman who was tried for witchcraft in Salem, Mass., in 1692. In Ms. Condé's fictional rendition of the story, Tituba is born to an African mother who was raped by an English sailor on the deck of a slave ship called Christ the King. In Barbados, Tituba's childhood abruptly ends when, at the age of 7, she watches her mother try to fight off a rapist; the child hands her the cutlass with which she defends herself. Tituba's mother is hanged in the presence of all the other slaves. "I watched her body swing from the lower branches of a silk-cotton tree," Tituba says. "She had committed a crime for which there is no pardon. She had struck a white man."

Tituba's luck improves when she is driven off the plantation and adopted by an old woman who knows the secrets of spells and herbs and how to communicate with the dead. But although her years learning Mama Yaya's lore are happy ones, the teen-age Tituba succumbs to the temptations of the outside world and marries a happy-go-lucky slave named John Indian. Brought back into slavery by love, Tituba falls afoul of her new mistress and is sold to a tyrannical Puritan minister named Samuel Parris, who takes Tituba and her husband to New England.

What a fanatical sect Ms. Condé's Puritans turn out to be: sadists and murderers, rabid misogynists and racists who hang and torture women, imprison tiny children, burn Jewish families out of their homes and regularly accuse black slaves of being in league with Satan. Tituba offers an ingenuous appraisal of their doctrine of eternal damnation: "Perhaps it's because they have done so much harm to their fellow beings, to some because their skin is black, to others because their skin is red, that they have such a strong feeling of being damned?" At the same time, Tituba has a few shortcomings of her own—including a blindly passionate sexual dependence on the feckless John Indian—which make her a fully believable and very appealing character.

In less sure hands, this short, powerful novel, which won France's Grand Prix Littéraire de la Femme in 1986, might well have become merely an extended denunciation of a perverted and evil society. What makes it larger and richer are Ms. Condé's gift for storytelling and her unswerving focus on her characters, combined with her mordant sense of humor, (Hester Prynne, from *The Scarlet Letter,* makes a cameo appearance when she's imprisoned with Tituba, lamenting that her new friend will never be much of a feminist.)

Miraculously, Tituba manages to extricate herself from her tormentors and return to Barbados, where she becomes a legendary figure to the black population. However, in the final irony of the story, she is brought up for execution by an official eager to make an example of rebellious slaves. Her life seems about to end in martyrdom, just as her mother's did.

Or does it? With the help of some ghosts from Tituba's past, Maryse Condé has fashioned a marvelous final surprise for her readers. Part historical novel, part literary fable, part exploration of the clash of irreconcilable cultures *I, Tituba, Black Witch of Salem* is most of all an affirmation of a courageous and resourceful woman's capacity for survival.

The forces of good and evil are not so sharply differentiated in *Tree of Life,* Ms. Condé's passionate, multigenerational novel (originally published in France in 1987) about the endlessly intriguing family of Albert Louis, born on Guadeloupe in the early 1870's, a patriarch as morally complex as he is simply stubborn. A devout disciple of the American black nationalist Marcus Garvey, Albert doesn't hesitate to wring every last cent from the impoverished black families who dwell in the wretched tenement houses he owns. He's a man of deep contradictions and still deeper gloom. Yet, in his own way, Albert is nearly as tough a survivor as Tituba.

As a young boy, Albert manages to escape harm after taking a long plunge "from the main limb of a breadfruit tree, for he had taken it into his head to fly." A few years later, he boldly strikes out from Guadeloupe to Panama, where the Americans are "tampering with the very structure of the world and cutting continents in two." As a member of a daring explosives team at work on the Panama Canal, he emerges relatively unscathed from all kinds of potential disasters, until the loss of his wife, Liza, in childbirth almost drives him mad. After taking his infant son home to his mother in Guadeloupe, Albert heads for San Francisco, hoping his luck will change. After all, aren't the mountains of California glittering with gold nuggets, free for anyone who wants to bend over and pick them up?

Like their forebear, many of Albert's descendants range out to far-flung destinations beyond their native country, including New York and Paris, both of which Ms. Condé renders with great vivacity. Best of all, though, are her vivid evocations of Guadeloupe. She can even make a cemetery seem enticing: "Situated at the town gates, the graveyards of Guadeloupe are cities of the dead, where the *filau,* the beautiful beefwood tree, keeps weeping watch over the departed. There marble, glass and carefully whitened concrete strive to outdo each other. Ornamental bowls, flowers, crosses or crowns of pearls are placed on the graves. Votive lamps are kept lit on each side of a picture of the deceased, their tenacious and fragile flames symbolizing the affection of the living."

The family of Albert Louis is haunted by suicide, as expatriates succumb to loneliness and desperation. They are also stricken with grief, retreating into prolonged and impenetrable states of despair. Somehow, though, most endure—occasionally as thoroughly appealing ghosts.

In one of the funniest episodes of this immensely entertaining novel, the fiercely jealous spirit of Albert's first wife, Liza, torments her son, Bert, with the most explicit sexual fantasies about his stepmother, Elaise. Only after Elaise dies and becomes a ghost herself do Albert's wives become friends—preparing breakfast together for their brooding old husband, chatting companionably with him on the veranda in the evening. They discreetly look the other way when Albert takes his early-morning nip. "A little rum never hurt anyone. It's even the best remedy for life."

Other memorable survivors in *Tree of Life* include Albert's son Jean, who spends seven and a half years writing a folk history entitled *Unknown Guadeloupe,* which eventually becomes a national classic after being virtually ignored in its author's lifetime; Thécla, Albert's scholarly, lovelorn granddaughter, and Coco, Thécla's troubled daughter, the narrator of the novel, whose destiny it is to recount the amazing story of her family.

From 18th-century Africa to the America of the Rev. Dr. Martin Luther King Jr. and Malcolm X, Maryse Condé has chronicled in her wonderful fiction the lives of a series of remarkable individuals and the families that surround them. It is impossible to read her novels and not come away from them with both a sadder and more exhilarating understanding of the human heart, in all its secret intricacies, its contradictions and marvels.

Leah D. Hewitt (essay date Winter 1993)

SOURCE: "Inventing Antillean Narrative: Maryse Condé and Literary Tradition," in *Studies in 20th Century Literature,* Vol. 17, No. 1, Winter, 1993, pp. 79-96.

[*In the following essay, Hewitt examines the tension between nativism and colonialism in Condé's novels.*]

For Guadeloupean author Maryse Condé, the writer's major role is to disturb ("inquiéter") her readers. Her own novels, from her earliest, *Heremakhonon* (1976), to *Traversée de la mangrove* (1989), bear witness to this attempt to disrupt or trouble comfortable, normative positions, whether they be ideological or aesthetic. At the same time, the distinctiveness of Condé's literary contributions, as well as her affinity with other contemporary writers, can be traced through her double identity quest: to discover her role as a black woman and as a representative of an Antillean literature. Understanding the way these two projects coincide—unsettling norms, affirming postcolonial identities through writing—involves taking stock of the literary and biographical confluences that have shaped Condé's writing over the years. Condé's early years in Guadeloupe, her college education in Paris, her ten years in West Africa, her teaching appointments in France and then the USA, and her return to Guadeloupe in 1986, all feed into her fictional trajectory as she repeatedly works through the notion of an Antillean identity marked by race and gender. Her work also openly draws upon the intertexts of world literature. For Condé, Antillean literature speaks through several countries, several cultures, several languages. This black woman "tiraillée entre la tradition et le modernisme" 'torn between tradition and modernity' creates a literary amalgam that successfully mixes traditional and modern concerns.

Condé straddles two literary generations: one that has kept to conventional narrative forms, the other that has launched into novelistic experiments. Through formal experimentation, her recent *Traversée de la mangrove* accounts for and enacts a polymorphous Antillean culture, thereby relaxing barriers between textual self-consciousness and a social referentiality. Using forms from both popular and "high" literature, *Traversée de la mangrove* performs a postcolonial investigation revealing the connections between the past of the Antilles and the ever-changing faces of its modernity. For Condé, the feminine paradox is implicit, although paramount: it is through female voices that social transformations are most strongly articulated, but it is also through them that the link between past and future is maintained. Before discussing Condé's version of the postmodern in *Traversée de la mangrove,* I would like to consider the evolution of her writing.

Literary Antecedents and the Rebellious Daughter

In many ways, Condé embodies Simone de Beauvoir's image of the original writer who attracts precisely because she shocks or scandalizes. Unsatisfied with tidy oppositions of saints and sinners, victims and persecutors, her fiction finds the difference within any simple or pure identity. All idealism in Condé's work is tinged with ironic, self-conscious overtones that belie the writer's own bouts with colonial politics, as well as with race and gender issues. None of her characters is ever constructed unequivocally: idols reveal their weaknesses; the meek show their strength. And while racial, sexual and political oppressions are always denounced, Condé is more often concerned with tracing their complications and intersections than with the clarity of their definitions. In a 1988 interview, Condé assigns this inclination more to women writers than to men: (we) women try to "explorer les profondeurs de nos sociétés sans trop nous concentrer sur les divisions (noir/blanc, race, racisme) que les auteurs hommes tendent à amplifier" 'explore the depths of our societies without concentrating too much on the divisions (Black/White, race, racism) that male authors tend to amplify'. While one may contest the generality of such a statement, it does account for the way Condé's novels sound the depths of social interactions, going beyond clear-cut oppositions. Rather than pitting White against Black, man against woman, in direct confrontation, Condé focuses more on internecine battles, the struggles of people of color within themselves, among themselves, or on the psycho-social restrictions that shape men's and women's choices for interaction.

Condé's particular attention to issues of gender and race has tended to set her at odds with orthodox positions of the Left and the Right (in her fiction as well as in her essays). In her book on black women writers of the French Antilles, Condé refuses any unqualified alignment with white feminists stressing black women's oppression, or with Africans idealizing black women's traditional roles. Her early protagonists are exemplary as sets of problems, rather than as models to emulate. In a 1984 interview with a journalist from *Jeune Afrique,* Condé takes her distance from African literature (as the model for black writers) by proclaiming her dislike of Léopold Senghor's works and her love of those of V. S. Naipaul and of black women novelists in the United States, such as Paule Marshall and Alice Walker. Condé turns away from black African writers espousing "negritude" (such as Senghor) and the premises of the "Black is beautiful" movement, in favor of a group of Anglophone (racially diverse) writers who bring a less celebratory, more critical eye to their societies' particularities. They are the "contestataires," as she appreciatively calls a Naipaul, a Faulkner, or a Philip Roth. Criticism (of oneself, of others) and autobiographical fiction go hand in hand here. Condé shakes up complacent thinking about what a black Antillean woman writer is supposed to think and with whom she might identify. She is most attracted to *critical* constructions of identity.

But Condé's ambivalence about becoming the obedient black daughter embracing an African lineage or an African literary affiliation does not make her turn any more to France for her literary or cultural identifications. In her 1988 inter-

view, Condé speaks of reacting against all things French; coming from the Guadeloupean black bourgeoisie which revered French culture and proclaimed the black pride of negritude in the same uncomfortable breath, Condé uses references to France (particularly in *Heremakhonon*) that display the paradox of rejecting a culture while ironically using its linguistic and cultural codes.

The only French author with whom Condé seems to find any affinity is Francois Mauriac. It might seem surprising that a black feminist writer from the Antilles should relate her efforts to a Frenchman who is part of the classical, conservative French canon. But given Mauriac's sharply critical view of French provincial society, one can readily see how he fits in with writers like Roth, Walker, and Faulkner, whom Condé respects. Her work has been passably untouched by (post) structuralist French influences involving self-enclosed literary phenomena such as those of the New Novel. I will be showing later, however, that certain parallels can be drawn between her most recent work and some of the New Novel's formal experiments.

Condé has, on the other hand, actively promoted and analyzed French Antillean literature over the years. Although she professes an intense dislike for the idea of becoming "a national writer" (i.e. "representing Guadeloupe"), she does believe in the shared concerns of the Antilles. The one Francophone writer (from the previous generation) for whom she has consistently expressed her greatest admiration is Aimé Césaire, to whose *Cahiers d'un retour au pays natal* Condé devoted an extended commentary. Condé reads Césaire's poetic account of his return to his native Martinique not as a surrealist work under French influence, but as a specifically Antillean creation that enacts the renaissance of a people, with its faults and strengths, over and against its colonial background. What sets Condé apart from Césaire is in her emphasis on female characters: she portrays black women as the most oppressed, but also as the most active and possessing the potential to change social mores for the better.

Condé belongs to the generation of Antilleans (and Africans) whose work always reminds us of the experience of colonialism, of being taught French history, geography and civilization instead of the culture of one's home. Condé's work can be considered in three phases. In the first phase of Condé's literary career, being Guadeloupean entails a profound alienation common to many writers of the Antilles. In *Heremakhonon* and *Une saison à Rihata* (1980), black Guadeloupean characters act out the alienation of the female slave descendent, who unsuccessfully seeks in Africa (and through men) some trace of an original (authentic) identity reminiscent of a precolonial time and place in which racial dichotomies and hierarchies would not have been operative. The failure of these quests will eventually cause the author and her characters to focus again on the Antilles and on an identity link through a female lineage rather than a male one.

In a second phase, Condé creates fictive histories that document a legitimating past for the Antillean. And although Condé avoids idealizing the collective heritage she researches and (re)creates, this is nevertheless an affirmative stage of her writing, one in which she traces in fiction the possibility of black histories and an intercontinental network in which Antilleans would have a sense of their own syncretic culture. She thus moves away from the "image négative de la culture antillaise" 'negative image of Antillean culture' inherited from her parents' generation. Condé's *Ségou* (1984, 1985), the two-volume saga of the fall of the Bambara empire and the African diaspora, blends fiction and historical document, in effect creating the very ancestry that her previous heroines had longed for. In *Moi, Tituba, sorcière noire de Salem* (1986), Condé fictively rescues from historical oblivion a Barbadian female slave imprisoned during the Salem witch trials in the colonial United States. In *La vie scélérate* (1987), she turns to the fictive genealogy of an Antillean family (based on Condé's own) through several generations and with a staggering cast of characters who come and go in and out of the Antilles at a dizzying pace.

Crucial differences in attitude, genre and style distinguish these two phases of Condé's work. First, the reader notices a gradual shift from an emphasis on the individual's alienated quest for identity to a collective, more harmonized perspective on Antillean distinctiveness. (Even the *Ségou* novels seem to prepare this.) Condé's particular version of a return to her native land has caused her to focus more and more on the range of physical and social attributes of the Antilles (their social structures, plants, language, religious beliefs and politics) and less on the psychology of the individual protagonist. This new view of the Antilles, from the inside out, is less estranged, more comfortable with its syncretism as a form of value (rather than as a negative sign of imitation). Concurrently, Condé's novels and stories of the second phase change optic: from a certain tough-spirited postmodern view that emphasizes the fragmented, *alienated* quality of *contemporary* discourse and life via an alienated black female subject, Condé moves more toward the *historical* epic that underlines the vast *collective* movements of past societies. Even *Moi, Tituba, sorcière noire de Salem*, which focuses on a particular historical figure, takes care to emphasize *typical* traits of Antillean lore, its myths and magic as they are marked by the feminine. And instead of portraying the Barbadian female slave as a pitiful victim, as the character Véronica Mercier might have done in *Heremakhonon*, Condé's later novel gives voice to a resourceful survivor and heroic resister of oppression. Alienation for the black Antillean woman thus becomes less a matter of *internal* conflict than of social inequity (one that is shown in *Moi, Tituba*

to be greater for a black woman than for a black man). Like Jean Rhys's *Wide Sargasso Sea*, Condé's *Moi, Tituba* rewrites the shadowy figure of a "master narrative" (*Jane Eyre* and the Salem witch trials, respectively) and reinstitutes value in the culture of the Caribbean as it is specifically enacted by a woman (in Condé's case by a *black* woman).

Traversée de la mangrove

Traversée de la mangrove belongs to a new third phase in which Condé plays more consciously with the formal possibilities of literary invention. She appears less concerned with a conventional historical treatment of the Antilles in itself than with complex negotiations between the region's present and past. How do technology, evolving race and gender relations, and in general the trappings (good and bad) of a modern, multicultural society interact with tradition, local superstition, and a distinct Antillean environment (climate, geography, etc.)? As in *Heremakhonon,* the plot of *Traversée* takes place in a present that is understood through the memories of the individual. But like the second phase novels, *Traversée* does not limit its focus to one or two characters; rather, it gives expression to the individuals of an entire community. Antillean culture (like a language) is articulated in a double move: individuals provide detailed examples of the specific dynamics (*parole,* speech, first person narrative) that are staged in a framework of collective beliefs, mores, social and physical structures that exceed the individual (*langue,* language, third person narrative). *Traversée*'s formal gymnastics allow a critique of the social characteristics of Guadeloupe as an Antillean culture of intersections and paradoxes.

Condé's own return to Guadeloupe is anything but an idealized rediscovery of a lost paradise. In fact, in her 1988 interview she speaks of it as a humbling experience for the writer. She notes that Guadeloupean culture is "une expérience vécue plutôt qu'écrite" 'a lived experience rather than a written one', which tends to place her avocation in the margins. Despite the fact that some of the offensive social hierarchies based on race and cultural origin have loosened their hold over the years, the returning writer is by definition an outsider or foreigner, in fact doubly so: the language spoken by most is Creole, and it is the language associated with the politics of autonomy and independence from France. To speak French (not to mention writing it) is thus to align oneself implicitly with the colonizer—so much so that after a radio talk upon her return, listeners phoned in to ask if this French-speaking Maryse Condé were White. Condé's alienation from her island must have felt all the more wrenching because she considers Antillean culture to be actively generated by women more than by men: "Aux Antilles, ce sont les femmes qui élèvent, qui éduquent, qui prennent les responsabilités, qui voyagent, qui vont, qui viennent et les hommes qui sont à l'arrière plan" 'In the

Antilles, it is women who raise, who educate, who take responsibility, travel, come and go, and it is men who are in the background'. In *Traversée,* Condé will reconcile her own "foreign" activity with the struggles of women of color torn between tradition and modern life.

The Antillean New Novel, with a Difference

In writing *Traversée de la mangrove,* Condé is, as we have seen, alert to the evolving, ambivalent relationship between formal literature and a popular (oral) culture. Like the popular detective story, *Traversée* is structured around the death of one character, Francis Sancher, whose shadowy identity and enigmatic death are presented as two puzzles to be solved. As in a classical tragedy, the plot is clearly limited in time and space: the action takes place in one night in the small town of Rivière au Sel (Guadeloupe): the corpse is discovered in the evening, a wake lasts during the night—the time for all to reflect on Sancher's effect in their lives—finally, the town's inhabitants disperse in the early morning. But underneath the deceptively simple plot structure teems an abundance of perspectives, desires and hidden stories of social and personal frustration. As in so many French New Novels, the reassuring format of the murder mystery and the classical time frame are undercut: Condé multiplies the number of perspectives to the point that there can be no single overriding truth (or even a synthesized one) about who Francis Sancher was or how he died. In fact, these questions do not even remain central as the characters multiply: the dead Sancher is more a *catalyst* that triggers memories and eventual change than a conventional character. We are soundly ensconced in the "era of suspicion," meaning here not just a questioning of literary forms and their adequacy to render reality, but also a questioning of what constitutes the real. The detective story leads us to the recognition of the plurality of meaning: between the narrative's first and last chapters there are twenty short chapters representing nineteen different characters' points of view about Francis Sancher. At the end of the novel, the reader has many pieces of information concerning the dead man, many of which challenge our first impressions, but the narrative is still too sketchy and contradictory to provide a definitive explanation of Sancher.

The mangrove of the title, which Francis Sancher was crossing when he mysteriously died, provides a metaphor for the reader's situation and for Guadeloupe, where it is indigenous vegetation. The mangrove's tree branches that send out in all directions a tangle of roots, new trunks and branches, are a physical equivalent to the jumble of stories that overlap, intersect and crisscross one another. In the mangrove's thick growth it is difficult to tell roots from trunks and branches, origins from effects, beginnings from ends. Similarly, the entanglement of contradictory facts, beliefs and attitudes undermines the reader's desire to get to a univocal truth concerning the "root" or "origin" of Sancher's identity and the cause of his death. There are too many clues, too many competing interpretations, too many questions. Did Sancher die of natural causes as the autopsy stated? Was there a mysterious curse on him and his elders (all of whom died at the age of fifty) for the past sins of ancestors who were white slave owners? Did someone kill him for his money (that disappeared)? Was his death the revenge of one of the village inhabitants? Supernatural and rational explanations compete equally for our attention.

On a more general level, the mangrove, as a profusion of tropical growth, corresponds to the rich spectrum of cultures and races that makes up the population of Rivière au Sel: descendants of East Indians (the most recent arrivals) and of white plantation owners, mestizos, Blacks, Asians, Haitians. All coexist in this small town, and they bring to it the vestiges of other languages and cultures. The mangrove thus offers the image of a complex, sometimes confused, arrangement ("roots" grow off branches and produce new "trunks") that parallels the hodgepodge of cultures. Condé's image of the mangrove as novelistic and cultural model recalls Deleuze's and Guattari's "rhizome" which has neither beginning nor end and eschews the hierarchical regime of trees and their roots. In both cases, there are "déformations anarchiques" 'anarchic deformations,' for example aerial roots. Like the rhizome that is "une antigénéalogie" 'an antigenealogy' proceeding "par variation, expansion, conquête, capture" 'through variation, expansion, conquest, capture,' the cultural mangrove of Rivière au Sel emphasizes the loss of a pure origin—racial or cultural—leaving only a complex intertwining of lines that rely on obscure pasts. The crisscrossing, multiple perspectives that fuel Condé's novel are analogous to the "plateaux" of Deleuze and Guattari, segments (of writing) that allow for unexpected exchanges from one to the other and generate new meanings through their interaction or "alliance." Condé's novel belongs to a generation of works that imagine new ways of formulating a cultural (hi)story that eludes strict hierarchy (placing one value system *over* another) and teleology. Antillean culture, as Condé reads it, would appear exemplary of an open-ended postmodern conceptualization.

Condé's title also comes into play as a self-referential literary device. It involves a *mise en abyme,* for Francis Sancher had planned to write a book called *Traversée de la mangrove.* Again akin to the New Novel (one thinks of Nathalie Sarraute's *Les Fruits d'or* about a novel with the same title) Condé's book playfully suggests commentary about her own work via the title. The pretensions of Sancher's title are deflated (and his own fate indirectly recognized) when a young woman character, Vilma, shrugs and comments on the title's inaccuracy: "On ne traverse pas la mangrove. On s'empale sur les racines des palétuviers. On s'enterre et on étouffe dans la boue saumâtre" 'You don't cross the mangrove. You get caught on the roots of its trees. You get buried and suffocate in the brackish mud'. The mangrove is a dangerous quagmire, whether one is referring to the tropical swamp of Guadeloupe or to the verbal quicksand in which the writer or reader risks bogging down. As in Sarraute's novel, the words of the title are used to name the book *and* describe its contents. But the crucial difference between the New Novel's title and Condé's is that the latter evokes both a literary (self-) reference *and* a nonverbal object. There are mangroves outside the work, and their physical existence is an important landscape feature for the people, whereas the fictitious novel *Les Fruits d'or* inside Sarraute's novel remains a literary, verbal construct, not an extralinguistic object.

For Condé, literature's self-referentiality plays off its mimetic functions. Describing the Spanish Caribbean novel, essayist and novelist Julieta Campos (born in Cuba, living in Mexico) notes a peculiar Caribbean literary focus that could also apply to Condé's fiction. It involves "una porosidad capaz de absorber y almacenar al máximo sensaciones que se fijan en una atmósfera interior en estrecha simbiosis con lo de afuera" 'a porousness capable of absorbing and storing to the maximum sensations that are fixed in an interior atmosphere in close symbiosis with that of the outside'. The literary mangrove marks the line of contact between cultural insides and natural outsides. And despite Condé's claims to the contrary, her special blend of historically bound scenarios and supernatural possibilities for explaining those scenarios aligns her fiction with the magical realism of her Latin American counterparts (García Márquez, Cortázar, Fuentes). Octavio Paz's definition of magical art obtains: the universe is conceived of "como un todo en el que las partes están unidas por una corriente de secreta simpatía" 'as a whole in which the parts are united by a current of secret sympathy'. Condé leaves her readers to ponder whether unexplained coincidences (such as all Sancher's male forbears dying at age fifty) are rooted in superstition or the real.

Intertextualities

Because self-conscious irony is one of Condé's trademarks, it is not surprising that playful self references abound in *Traversée* (as they do in the New Novel). This self-consciousness is particularly endemic to *Traversée* because we are dealing with the Guadeloupean author analyzing her "own" culture. (I place "own" in quotation marks because the returning writer feels rather like a foreigner.) In several ways, the dead man, Francis Sancher, is Condé's double. Like Condé, Francis Sancher is a disillusioned idealist of about fifty when he shows up in Rivière au Sel to write *his* novel. Sancher has traveled all over the world and has a foreign accent (in his case a Spanish one, in Condé's a French one) and is clearly considered an outsider although he claims to be a native. Sancher's sense of simultaneous estrangement

from *and* connection to the island allows for a seesaw movement of identification with and distance from the community—a movement that Condé enacts in all her writing. Sancher's disenchantment with Guadeloupe's desire for independence, with Marxist revolution, with committed literature (capable of changing the world), make him the critical but sympathetic sounding board for the inhabitants of Rivière au Sel, the image of the author who willingly accepts a marginal (if potentially beneficial) role in Guadeloupean society.

In *Traversée,* the self references can also be critical. The character, Lucien Evariste, a revolutionary sympathizer and aspiring writer, remembers being delighted to meet Francis Sancher (whom he thinks is Cuban), because he has been starved for discussions with writers:

> Lucien bondit, songeant à Alejo Carpentier et José Lezama Lima et se voyant déjà discutant style, technique narrative, utilisation de l'oralité dans l'écriture! En temps normal, pareilles discussions étaient impossibles, les quelques écrivains guadeloupéens passant le plus clair de leur temps à pérorer sur la culture antillaise à Los Angeles ou à Berkeley.

> Lucien jumped up, dreaming of Alejo Carpentier and José Lezama Lima and seeing himself already discussing style, narrative technique, the use of oral speech in writing! Under normal circumstances, such discussions were impossible, because the few Guadeloupean writers there were spent most of their time giving speeches on Antillean culture in Los Angeles or Berkeley.

Condé is playfully describing and criticizing her own frequent departures for the West Coast of the United States where she has held regular teaching appointments. But the topics of the longed-for conversations are precisely those that would preoccupy any politically sensitive Guadeloupean writer (including Condé). Lucien Evariste's friends counsel him to write in Creole, a political choice, but like Condé, it is not the language in which he feels comfortable. Near the end of the novel, Evariste decides to brave the possible criticisms of those who might compare him unfavorably to Martiniquan novelist Patrick Chamoiseau, who deconstructs "le français-français" 'French French' in order to write a history of Francis Sancher. Another character, Emile Etienne, an amateur historian, is encouraged by Sancher to write a history of the island that would be rooted in the oral accounts of its inhabitants. One senses here that the import of the discussions about writing—the topics, the style, the relationship between oral and written stories—goes well beyond any vacuous game of self-reference. At stake is Condé's belief in her own activity.

Condé's exploration of her literary relationship to Antillean culture is in earnest, even if it entails a good dose of self-deriding humor. Mimicking the detective story format is in fact an ingenious way of portraying this ambivalent attitude toward Antillean identity: while the search for (extratextual) cultural truths is carried out, the text playfully acknowledges its own fabrications and constructions through the self-references. Significantly enough, Patrick Chamoiseau's 1988 novel, *Solibo magnifique,* also mimics the crime story in a self-conscious study of Antillean oral culture in its relationship to Creole and French. But Chamoiseau's fiction remains more "realistic" and hence more hermetic for the non-Antillean than Condé's: Creole dialogue and regional colloquialisms in Chamoiseau's novel are most often left intact, leaving readers unfamiliar with them to fend for themselves. Condé's work, on the other hand, provides explanatory notes of Creole and regionalisms for French readers. In either case, the author's relationship to his or her readers remains problematic.

For whom does one write? No answer is entirely satisfying for the Antillean novelist. Condé insists on opening up her works to both local Antillean references and worldwide intertexts as they articulate the cultural phenomena that interest her. In one passage, the young Carmélien Ramsaran quotes from his school readings of Jacques Roumain's classic Haitian novel, *Gouverneurs de la Rosée.* Carmélien remembers that as a boy he adopted for his own account (as his textual "source") the Haitian novel's quest for natural springs ("sources") and eventually found one. Ironically, this successful search for a "source" in nature is carried out by a boy who has lost most of his cultural "sources" (origins). With ancestors from India, Carmélien nevertheless has little knowledge of Indian culture: "A Bordeaux, les gens le prenant pour un Indien des Indes, lui parlaient de Satyajit Ray, don't il n'avait vu aucun film" 'In Bordeaux, people took [Carmélien] for an Indian from India and talked to him about Satyajit Ray, whose films he had never seen'. As she does with the "mangrove," Condé interweaves the multiple resonances of "sources," ranging from the intertextual "source" (Roumain), to the cultural (origin, identity), and the natural (life-giving fountain). Antillean literature's viability relies on its ability to juggle its multiple sources.

Although the reference to Roumain is textually explicit, others are less so, with the result that the novel's intertexts may sometimes exceed a given reader's knowledge. But if some of Condé's readers do not recognize an ironic allusion to Joyce's Stephen Dedalus when Sancher remarks that history is his nightmare, it does not stop them from appreciating the comment in Condé's context. On the other hand, understanding intertextual references does enlarge the novel's field of vision, creating links with other texts and other cultures. In *Traversée,* Vilma, a young woman of East Indian descent, is unloved by her mother and emphasizes this fact with the elliptical remark: "Elle ne m'a jamais tenu la main" 'She never held my hand'. This quotation is uncannily close to the original manuscript title of Violette Leduc's French autobiography: "Ma mère ne m'a jamais donné la main" 'My Mother Never Took My Hand'. While it is not necessary to know the Leduc reference, it does create certain implications: the supposedly "unnatural" quality of a mother not loving her daughter crosses racial and cultural boundaries (thereby de-naturalizing a "universal" while creating a common ground between Antillean and French cultures). Such overarching ties among women are confirmed when Sancher, a good listener of local woes, murmurs gently to the unhappy woman, Dinah, that women's suffering at the hands of men transcends geographical boundaries and race: "Les Blanches en métropole souffrent pareillement. . . . Nous sommes nés bourreaux" 'The white women in the metropolis [France] suffer in the same way. . . . We [men] are born brutes,' notes Sancher sadly.

Traversée's implicit references also pay homage to Faulkner. One of the children Francis Sancher sires in Rivière au Sel is named Quentin—recalling the multiple characters who share the name "Quentin" in *The Sound and the Fury.* This tribute to the repeated name is rendered in Condé's text as a series of coincidences: Quentin's birth coincides with his father's (Sancher's) death and with the spiritual rebirth of his mother, Mira. To add to the parallelism, Mira's own mother had died at *her* birth. It is as if Mira were freed of (an imagined) responsibility for her mother's death through Sancher's death and Quentin's birth. Inside the text, the name "Quentin" becomes the sign of a mysterious cultural linkage, of repeated life patterns that take on the aura of a destiny that cannot be explained with a strictly rational, "sensible" logic. (Quentin is born at the stroke of midnight and will thus have "affaire avec les esprits" 'dealings with the spirits'). As an intertextual device, the name brings into contact two texts (from Guadeloupe and the American South) about the passing from an old world to a new one.

Between Tradition and Modernity

In Condé's fiction, subjectivity is always tied to the ability to tell a story, particularly one's own. Unlike Faulkner, Chamoiseau, and most New Novelists who either choose male narrating subjects or construct anonymous voices for which gender markings are only incidental, Condé gives voice to her female characters in a privileged way in *Traversée.* Whereas her male characters' lives are for the most part recounted by an omniscient third person narrator who first quotes a few lines from the character before telling his life story and ties to Sancher, *the female characters all tell their own stories in the first person.* They are not merely the objects of discourse, desire or a rigid social system inhibiting their education, movement, aspirations, and sense of self. By becoming active subjects, the female characters, thinking to themselves during the wake, symbolically break the silence about their personal disappointments and regrets and eventually become prepared to escape from some of the constraints that have shackled them. Their sufferings stem from arranged marriages, the handicap or death of a child, fraternal incest, the lack of love from a mother, the rejection of an only suitor, as well as from the implicit pain of being unheard. (Sancher's role is crucial because he was the first to listen to them.) Each woman emerges from her reflection about Sancher with resolve, and the meditation brings the promise of major transformations: to leave the island, to start afresh, to seek forgiveness, principally for each to free herself from a suffocating past. The character Mira affirms: "Ma vraie vie commence avec sa mort" 'My real life begins with his death', as if to confirm the Christ-like role Sancher fills (as the man mysteriously destined to die because of his ancestors' "original" sin). Because the women's pains are primarily private ones that female social roles have imposed on them, the first person narrative seems all the more appropriate to portray these unheard voices. In contrast, the male characters' lives are stereotypically turned more to public life (politics, public image, making money) and for the most part, they are less inclined to reflect on Sancher's death in terms of a transformative event. It is the women who are most clearly poised for change at the novel's end.

But having suggested a methodical opposition between male and female discourse in *Traversée,* I must immediately backtrack, because Condé's gender lines are never so clear. First, the third person narratives of the male characters are often recounted in indirect discourse which places the reader almost as close to the character as first person narrative would. And several of the male characters have also suffered racial and cultural discrimination. Next, some of the men experience Sancher's presence and death as a liberation for their personal lives just as the women do (for example, Carmélien Ramsaran, Lucien Evariste, Emile Etienne). Finally, among the twelve male characters (and eight female), there are two males whose discourse is recounted in the first person: Joby Lameaulnes, a small boy who hates his rich and powerful father, and Xantippe, the local vagabond madman (or prophet?) who lost his family in a fire, and who seems to know the secret of Sancher's life and death. Both characters are marginal to the men in power and are thus in positions similar to the women.

One might then be tempted to rethink the male/female opposition as one of oppressor/oppressed, but this easy declension does not quite work either. For example, in portraying the somewhat improved racial climate in Guadeloupe, Condé notes critically that the Haitian laborer—the character Désinor, who is darker than most of the locals—is treated as the new inferior, disenfranchised in Guadeloupean society. But the passage pertaining to Désinor is told in *third-*

person narrative rather than in the first person. As we noted earlier, Condé's works resist simple oppositions and pigeon-holing. But while there are no *absolute* lines separating male and female characters, the consistent first person privilege of the female voice does place the common plights of women in a sympathetic (although not uncritical) light.

In the struggles between the past and present in Rivière au Sel, it is the women who are most often designated to be the support of tradition; marriage, childraising, religion, herbal medicine and healing, school teaching are their domains. At the same time, they try to elude the tradition's more onerous burdens. Masculine models tend to be associated more with the encroaching images of modern technological society, although there is some overlapping of gender roles. Condé's characters note that if the symbols of the Antillean past are sugar cane and the strict racial hierarchy of the plantation, contemporary (male) values revolve around money, power and a growing consumer society. With her usual talent for juxtaposing unexpected cultural items, Condé gleefully sprinkles her text with the icons of foreign influence in ways that unsettle categorical divisions between traditional and modern Antillean life. Next to the local color of a hut ("case"), a Creole maxim, or a remark about the actions of invisible spirits, the reader will find a Toyota (a BMW if it's the local doctor's), or a man sipping his Glenfiddich as he prepares to listen to a compact disc, which he manipulates with "les précautions d'une sage-femme maniant un nouveau-né" 'the precautions of a midwife handling a newborn'! Condé slyly and comically puts on a par the man's technology and the woman's childbearing, with "culture" and "nature" feeding off each other's metaphors (as we have already seen in the instances of the mangrove and the source).

Condé does not dismiss traditional social roles, nor does she unequivocally condemn the modern. Humor, hope and skepticism—about the improvement of the world and the people who share it—blend together in a literature that is both specific to the Antilles and in dialogue with literatures from several continents. And although writing may be considered as a male activity in this oral culture—in fact it is barely thought of as an activity at all by Rivière au Sel's standards—Condé transgresses categorical boundaries between the (female) oral and the (male) written. As the female characters envision new possibilities for action like better education, travel, the hope to cure a handicapped child, they reach outside their community and the reader senses that these changes go hand in hand with the women's assumption of their own voices. Taking up what Césaire said fifty years earlier about the Caribbean writer who must be "la bouche de ceux qui n'ont pas de bouche, la voix de ceux qui n'ont pas de voix" 'the mouth of those who have no mouth, the voice of those who have no voice,' Condé gives her women characters a voice. At the same time, she resists turning literature into a simple matter of advocacy. The retention of third-person narrative and the multiple voices allow her to modulate her commentary on Antillean culture, to be both inside and outside it. Ultimately, we recognize Condé's paradoxical status as "native foreigner" exemplary of the writer, both critical and playful, combining ethical imperatives and flights of literary fancy. The strength of this black feminist novelist lies in her refusal either to make her work subservient to a political cause or to forget its social anchorings. If, as Condé sometimes laments, literature cannot transform the world, it can, perhaps, create new ways of reading its dilemmas and taking advantage of its paradoxes.

Hal Wylie (essay date Autumn 1993)

SOURCE: "The Cosmopolitan Condé, or Unscrambling the Worlds," in *World Literature Today,* Vol. 67, No. 4, Autumn, 1993, pp. 763-68.

[*In the following essay, Wylie discusses the "universality" and "cosmopolitanism" of Condé's recurrent themes, including gender, nationality, and generational differences.*]

Maryse Condé is a transcendental person and restless, but unlike many wanderers, she does not dissipate herself butterflying about. Instead, she is able to marshal her forces to draw upon the many places and episodes of her own Od yssey to forge a new unity by showing symbolist *correspondances* between the parts of the scrambled postmodern landscape. We know from published biographical information that she has lived in Guadeloupe, France, Guinea, the Ivory Coast, Ghana, Senegal, Kenya, Jamaica, and Manhattan. Extrapolation from her works indicates that she has probably also spent some time in Mali, Barbados, Panama, South Carolina, Haiti, and Dahomey. She sees no contradiction between being Antillean and a wanderer. She has stated [in her **"Notes d'un retour au pays natal"**]: "Etre Antillais, finalement, je ne sais toujours pas très bien ce que ca veut dire! . . . Est-ce qu'un écrivain ne pourrait pas être constamment errant, constamment à la recherche d'autres hommes?" She shares many of the attributes of the traditional literary figures of the knight errant, the troubadour, and perhaps the Wandering Jew.

Early readers realized that the relation between the Antilles and Africa was an important concern, as *Hérémakhonon* (1976; Eng. *Heremakhonon*) and *Une saison à Rihata* (1981; Eng. *A Season in Rihata*) showed the problems her protagonists from the West Indies had in adapting to life in Africa. *Ségou* (1984; Eng. *Segu* and *Children of Segu*) sent her African characters to Jamaica and Brazil in the New World, but when she tackled the United States in *Moi, Tituba, sorcière . . . noire de Salem* (1986; Eng. *I, Tituba,*

Black Witch of Salem), a new dimension was added. Two of her most recent works have gone beyond *Tituba* in exploring the connections between the Caribbean and the U.S., by analyzing this relation throughout a prolonged period of time and by adding more places into the equation.

Is it fair to say that most of the universal classics of literature explore one place in depth, and that the concentration derived from unity of place is a major technique to increase literary density? (Of course there is *The Odyssey,* but even that explores the mythic Mediterranean of the Greeks.) The psychology of assimilation and culture shock seems to be a modern theme, one that has perhaps been most thoroughly explored by Francophone writers, especially in the Negritude tradition by such writers as Fanon, Césaire, Senghor, Camara Laye, Mongo Béti, and Sembène.

We may have arrived, however, at a new phase of transcultural and intercultural exploration with the works of V. S. Naipaul and Salman Rushdie, which seem to transcend the colonizer/colonized dichotomy to take a global approach to the problem. Jonathan Ngate has compared Condé to Naipaul in his article "Maryse Condé and Africa: The Making of a Recalcitrant Daughter." After noting Condé's "toughmindedness" and "her clear sense of history," he attacks her hostility toward Negritude and her preference for Naipaul, citing her statement that "Naipaul . . . est un esprit très contestataire, *très négatif, très nihiliste.*" He focuses on the importance of negativity, ambiguity, and irony for both writers. Both may be seen as relishing the role of devil's advocate and a refusal to acquiesce in accepting the slogans and simple theories that characterize the early politicizations of intercultural conflict. Naipaul, Rushdie, and Condé insist upon taking their analysis a step or two deeper, to go beyond simple dualities like black/white, male/female, or First World/Third World to examine the swarming multiplicity of realities, situations, positions in the vast panoply of the social world, where many nations, many cultures, many religions, many personality types clash and try to harmonize. Their works tend to stretch out and grow longer in the effort to synthesize all the nuances of the truth in all its overwhelming variegation. For them it is impossible to separate the political from the literary. For instance, in *La vie scélérate* (1987; Eng. *Tree of Life*) Condé furnishes many examples of the harm caused by a too-rapid understanding of a problem, the central one being the death of the second Albert Louis, "killed" by his own father for fathering a half-breed child. We might state that these writers see their political contribution as purely a literary analysis, except that even this is too simplistic, it seems, now that apparently Maryse Condé has consented to run for office on an "independence" ticket.

Condé's transcendental cosmopolitanism may have its roots in a certain ambiguity of class, in that, like Rimbaud and

Zola, she experienced a major shift in the family fortune when she was quite young (although in the opposite direction). Like Arthur and Emile, she might be said to have experienced both working-class and bourgeois cultures and be unable to see reality through one or the other. Her interview in *Callaloo* with Vèvè A. Clark brought to light much fascinating information, including the fact that her father's change of profession from teacher to banker made the family rich. Condé also talked about her own family politics and her special situation as an "enfant gâté." This seems of interest given the attention she lavishes on family politics in her novels. She also admits in the interview to "un penchant pour la controverse" and to being "douée pour la caricature." Of course this early understanding of the great complexity of human reality was enriched by her study in France and her marriage in Africa, where her daughters were born.

It seems Condé might accept the view that everything is political in her awareness of the political aspect of family life, culture, economics, religion, and the relations between the sexes. Her works insist on the complexities of the interrelations among all these domains. One reason she may have waited so long to write about her own island while examining Africa is that she may have felt unable to cope with all the ramifications known from in-depth experience and may have preferred to describe the more distanced material of Africa, which she could handle with more objectivity, though the tantalizingly bizarre character of Véronica (in *Hérémakhonon*)—which she labeled as a sort of "anti-moi"—impinges on Caribbean culture.

The first two international surprises in Condé's works were the difficulties experienced in Africa by her Caribbean heroines in *Hérémakhonon* and *Une saison à Rihata* and the opening out of the African world of *Ségou* to the Anglophone world of the Gold Coast and Jamaica. Many had insisted on the unity of Africa before, but not many writers had involved their characters in both Francophone and Anglophone worlds. When the focus shifted back home to the Caribbean, readers were surprised by the emphasis on the U.S. Perhaps we should have been less surprised, since clearly the Caribbean has been an "American lake" in the twentieth century, and neocolonial lines of force leading to the U.S. have supplanted the old colonial ties to a large extent.

Condé is a writer who reminds one of Voltaire, in several ways. 1) She prefers to study cultures, generations, and worlds rather than limit her focus to one individual. Her big works are all genealogical studies of generations and family histories, showing how an individual reflects an evolutionary pattern deriving from family and culture in history. 2) She keeps her distance from her inventions, her characters, and is not averse to subjugating them to shocking and sadistic treatment, to using them like marionettes so that by

pulling strings she can dramatize certain abstract points. Some have characterized her works as soap operas. 3) She may be seen as something of a social philosopher, concerned with certain abstract social patterns that can only be understood across a large expanse of time and space. 4) She seems to like to conduct rather outrageous social experiments. Where Voltaire can see what might happen if a Saturnian came to Earth, Condé can try out what would happen if an African king visited his kinsmen in the New World (*Les derniers rois mages* [*The Last Magi*; 1992]).

All of Condé's works seem to manifest the openmindedness of the empirical scientist conducting an experiment, but the earlier works displayed more reliance on preconceived ideas and theories. There is not much theory describing the social results of late-twentieth-century immigration to the United States and/or the impact on French and Creole speakers arriving here. Francophone writers have not by and large, related to the States; Léon Damas is the note-worthy exception. So it is a rather original experiment for Condé to bring herself here to explore the intercultural territory, and even more original to send her characters on their way to America. Condé seems to be defining herself increasingly through the active dialogue in American literary journals like *Callaloo* and through her interactions with her "network of loyal friends in the U.S.," mostly literary scholars. What might be some of the factors in this choice?

One surely is the desire to strike out into new literary territory and to avoid repeating what others have done. Francophone African literature is full of interesting stories of Africans' and West Indians' adventures in France. Another seems to be a desire to break out of established limits of the Francophone world, to become a "universal" or world writer. Another might be to look for those dramatic encounters of a little-expected kind based on bringing vastly different beings together. New surprises, new colors, new permutations are produced. One last explanation might be the necessity to bring back into play historical facts lost for many years in the archives Condé loves to frequent. *La vie scélérate* and *Les derniers rois mages* both seem sustained meditations on just how relevant is history. Are we determined or obsessed by history? One example is the Panama Canal. The building of the canal can be seen as a dead fact. It also seems to have provided a certain inspiration for the writing of *La vie scélérate.* The political relevance of the information Condé puts before us (the use of Third World workers to build the canal and their dying like flies in the effort) to the America of today and its involvement in Panama, Iraq, Haiti, Somalia, et cetera—this relevance seems obvious. The racism of America in the 1920s and the lynchings deserve reconsideration in the 1990s, thinks our author. (It is the gratuitous "lynching" of his friend Jacob in the San Francisco bar that sends patriarch Albert back to Guadeloupe to found his dynasty.) Marshall McLuhan said that electronic communications had woven the world together into a tribal village, and Condé wants to get to the central switchboard.

Perhaps it is too early to come up with generalizations about the postmodern, postindustrial, postcolonial relations between the Third World and the United States, but certain items may be noted in Condé's literary experiments. We must be patient, however, because, like André Gide, Condé is more concerned with asking the right question than providing an answer, especially when one considers the rapid proliferation of social and literary theory in the late days of the twentieth century, when we are so aware of the multiplicity of variables to take into account: race, class, and sex, of course, but also identity, language, culture, religion, family, roles and professions, and even sexual persuasions. [In a review of *Moi, Tituba, sorcière ... noire de Salem*], Charlotte Bruner has noted that all of "Condé's major fiction is rooted in a study of power," and Condé herself has stated in an interview that the Carribean islands are always affected by American policy and that "c'est à cause de l'Amérique que plusieurs îles ont des problèmes." In the interview she calls upon Americans to familiarize themselves with the culturally rich island peoples to their south. Writers are more aware than those who gain their information about the world from TV news and journalism that power is not merely military and economic but has its foundation in ideas and beliefs, in symbols and myths. Condé is aware of the power of Hollywood, Madison Avenue, and America's dominance in the area of international photojournalism. Two minor works give us clues to her own attitudes, which tend to be hidden behind those of her characters in the major novels.

One strange link between her island and the U.S. was Hurricane Hugo of 1989, which left such an impact on Condé that she made a children's book, *Hugo le terrible,* from it. The storm may also have led her to choose South Carolina as the setting for *Les derniers rois mages.* Characters in *Hugo* debate the nature and desirability of going to the States. America's "marvelous" democracy, skyscrapers, and technology are opposed to its oppressed minorities and homelessness in the debate of "les opinions les plus contradictoires sur ce pays." The most telling detail, however, is an aspect of the plot dealing with how information from the Third World is gathered and disseminated to the world. At the outset of the story photographers arrive to cover the hurricane, admitting that they play the role of "voyeurs." The most interesting subplot involves an adolescent boy who takes advantage of the chaos and steals a camera in order to take pictures to send to France. He ends up selling them, however, for a thousand francs to an American photographer who has flown in from New York. In germinal form many of the U.S./Third World connections are demonstrated here: the redirection of Third World energies and attitudes by American economic and journalistic power; the

selective nature of the American *regard* directed toward the Third World, which looks only for sensation and disaster there; the imposition of this American vision on the people of the Third World themselves; and the perverse nature of the whole process. (The native photographer has access to realities the international outsider does not and does not hesitate to intrude into the misery of his neighbors.)

Condé's view of the nature of this informational struggle is further revealed in another minor and surprising work, a seemingly official tourist-promotion book, *Guadeloupe,* with beautiful photographs by Jean de Boisberranger, wherein Condé seems to have decided to collaborate in a suspect genre in order to redirect its message and slant. Instead of fighting tourism, her attitude seems to be to use the genre to educate and inform the tourist of the social realities as seen by the permanent resident, while also furnishing the tour information needed. She elevates journalism to the status of literature. Or it might be better to say she sees journalism as an important form of popular literature, with an important power that must be redirected.

Condé begins her text by listing a number of "idées reçues à balayer" and leads the reader through a social and cultural description of the island, eventually plunging right into the critical politics of the struggle for independence, a very controversial and divisive matter for both Martinique and Guadeloupe. She concedes that only 3 percent have voted for independence candidates, but sees the option as much more important than that figure would indicate. She speaks directly to the tourist-reader in a friendly tone of equality, with the implication that the cooperative collaboration of rich and poor from the First and Third Worlds be in everyone's mutual interest. Her last words describe the sadness of "Les Saintes" islanders (part of Guadeloupe) because of the "hemorrhaging" of their population as young people leave for the imperial centers.

Micheline Rice-Maximin and I invited Maryse Condé to speak in San Antonio and Austin in April of 1986. The French Department lounge at University of Texas in Austin was packed when she addressed us on the women writers of her island. She told us she was resigning her professional position at the University of Paris and was going to live in Guadeloupe and write for Guadeloupe. Some of us were therefore surprised thereafter when we learned she was teaching at Berkeley, but she has indeed made an effort to write specifically for Guadeloupe. Françoise Lionnet interprets *Traversée de la mangrove* (*Crossing the Mangrove;* 1989) as the major effort to express literarily this "return to her native land," which was also a return to writing about the present. Another example is more specific: *An tan revolisyon,* a play financed and published by the Conseil Régional (of Guadeloupe). Contrasting this work with the cosmopolitan novels is revealing.

Although the title is in Creole, the text is in French, but with a note that Creole may be used "partout où voudra, sauf pour le conteur." The title seems to mean "Longtemps révolution" (Longtime Revolution). Although it would be difficult to evaluate the success of this play showing the French Revolution from the Guadeloupean standpoint, it seems likely that it was received favorably in Guadeloupe. The book form seems less successful. The typesetting and printing are disappointing, and distribution was undoubtedly quite limited. Condé must have enjoyed working with the local people to produce the play, but any clearheaded person, especially one interested in power, could derive obvious conclusions about the objective, material facts of the natures of these two kinds of literature (i.e., writing for a local audience versus publishing with international publishing houses texts designed for transnational consumption). Condé seems to be very lucid about her own talents and work and must consider addressing the issue of the loss of Third World youth (the ones on whom the play is least likely to have made an impact) in the international arena more important than the development of a purely local literature. In directly addressing the problem of immigration (and other international connections) in her cosmopolitan writings, she undoubtedly feels she can have a greater political impact in both the local and international arenas.

Just as we are drowned in information amid the din of radio and TV and the deluge of paper, we are overwhelmed by historical detail. The question is to find that which is relevant and meaningful and to apply it correctly to our lives. I believe literature is the tool we use to carry out this operation. Marshall McLuhan says one of the roles of the writer is to warn us of the perils of the future by interpreting the past. *Les derniers rois mages* surprises by adding a new element, antithetical to the earlier conception of history in Condé's works. The protagonist comes to view himself as having been victimized by history and its cultivation, and he rebels. We might say that the novel takes up historiography as a theme. It seems that Condé is refining her understanding of the importance and nature of history.

We are all obviously victims of history, predestined to inherit a biological form, predispositions, a family, an ethnic, religious, and national culture, a language, and an economic situation. There is little we can do to modify them when we are children, during our formative years. To rebel against this history is foolish. But Spéro, the protagonist of *Les derniers rois mages,* becomes critical of the tendency to focus on knowing the past to the extent of becoming fixated on it, which weakens the ability to live in the present, to see the freedom and freshness of the existential moment. There are many qualities in Spéro that make him different from his ancestors and from his wife Debbie, from those who tend to make of the past a fetish. He is an artist, whose eye seeks the essence of the object precisely in the way in which the existing object transcends its determinants, who prefers the light touch of water-color and its power to capture transitory, ephemeral qualities and who loves to paint the old buildings of Charleston and children's faces, even though the houses were those of the slaveholders and represent historically a system based on slavery and oppression. Debbie, in her insistence upon imposing a political interpretation, a priori, on his art, has ruined its spontaneity, so that the resultant oil paintings are mere illustrations of historical points.

Debbie is the antagonist and antithesis to her husband Spéro. In this bad marriage, doomed by her bad faith from the start, she represents all that is wrong about history, or a certain use of it. She married the uneducated Guadeloupean because he was the descendant of an African king. Unlike most African Americans in the United States, he could trace his genealogy. In fact, his father had made this history into a cult and ritual based upon the "Cahiers" (notebooks) written by his father in an effort to fixate the fragmentary remembrances of *his* father, the African king in exile in Martinique. The image of these West Indian princes of Africa is a source of derision and alienation, related to the males' dependence on women in this lineage and their inability to affirm their male existence. While repeating the pattern, Spéro comes closest to breaking out of the rut. Ironically, his daughter does, to a certain extent, by finally going back to Dahomey, now Bénin. Unfortunately, we never find out how she does there and if this return is a true break or more of the same.

Debbie is a historian, one who has seemingly lost control of her materials and is now drowning in the flotsam of oral history, endlessly tape-recording the senile reminiscences of an egoistic elder and enmeshing those around her in her oppressive web. She compulsively imposes a moralistic reading on the story of her ancestors and on the history of her race.

That is my reading of this problematic story, which I realize may be seen as one-sided. One of the virtues of Condé's storytelling technique is that she (like Rushdie) tells such good stories that they resemble those drawn directly from life: they have all the ambiguity, realism, resistance to interpretation of lived experience. Would Condé go so far as to agree with the husband in this couple? With the philandering male, the unproductive, undisciplined father who hates Mickey Mouse and wonders if he might have been tempted to sexually abuse his own daughter? The novel ends with his attempted suicide as he judges himself quite severely, but his judgment, as judge, seems the most clear and perceptive of all the characters (he is Guadeloupean, after all). His mind has the dialectical play of the author's. He knows a higher form of history, one not marked by a revisionist interpretation that falsifies the story by imposing a "logical" reading. He understands history as a nonlinear, multifarious, ambiguous, contradictory entity, often displeasing to the theorist.

The story of the African king, partly told in the "Cahiers," reads like a cruel joke (although we must remember the framing of this story within a story). This king is descended from the panther whose "enormous scarlet erection seemed like a barbarous flower" to the African maiden destined to become his wife and mother of the dynasty. We learn that the funerals of these kings involved the death of scores of wives and hundreds if not thousands of slaves. Condé's satiric re-creation of the African kingdom is mocking; the last king, Spéro's greatgrandfather, is shown to have been happiest wandering in the woods after the loss of his power and property to the French. It seems clear Condé does not like African kings.

In the public lecture given just before the opening of the Puterbaugh Conference at the University of Oklahoma on 25 March 1993, Maryse Condé talked about how we are haunted by history. The use of ghosts has become more forceful as it has evolved from *Ségou* to *Tituba,* from *La vie scélérate* to *Les derniers rois mages.* In *Tituba* and *La vie scélérate* the ghosts are literal and seem used mainly for melodramatic impact as a kind of narrative shorthand. In *Les derniers rois mages* they are metaphorically woven into the narrative framework. The last king and his son and grandson all lose themselves in schizophrenic mythomania in which they become their ancestor(s). Spéro, while disidentifying with his predecessors, is haunted by crabs swarming over and attacking his body in a repeated nightmare associated with his self-critique and loss of nerve, which recapitulates the story of the third "Cahier" entitled "Totem and Taboo" that describes the role of the "genies" or spirits of the animals, which both protect and punish. Spéro comes to see his alienation from Debbie as derived from "all the cadavers between them."

The postmodern writer needs ghosts and sorcery and all the magic of "marvelous realism" to cope with the complexities of our late-twentieth-century reality. Condé, for whom "Africa is no longer in Africa" and "America is no longer America," for whom the essence of present-day Guadeloupe is impossible to know, uses ironic reversals (e.g., the daughter of the actual African prince in *La vie scélérate,* abandoned by father and mother, is brought up by a simple Breton [white] wet nurse) and feedback loops (back and forth across the Atlantic, from Africa to America in *Ségou* and *Les derniers rois mages,* from the U.S. to Guadeloupe in *La vie scélérate*) to short-circuit history and get right to essential meanings. The presence of a significant outsider in a foreign culture (Spéro in South Carolina, Albert Louis in San Francisco, Tituba in Salem) quickly throws certain values

into relief. They may be seen as living ghosts and further explain the cosmopolitan tendency in Condé.

Condé's two recent epic novels show a synthesis that goes beyond the first-level history of *Tituba* and *Ségou,* which deal only with the relatively distant past. They both attempt to integrate the past with the present by tracing all connections right through to the present. The result, however, is another paradox: the past seems clearer, more interesting, more meaningful, and of course more literary. Perhaps it is endemic to the genre that the ancestors always emerge as the Titans; perhaps that is history, but Albert Louis looms above all the others in *La vie scélérate,* even over the narrator, whose life might be seen as equally interesting. Perhaps we tend to devalue our own time as banal and prosaic.

Still, Condé's ambitious insistence upon seeking the links between the generations, and between the ethnic groups, must be seen as a quest for the meaningful factors of our time. We must learn how to make the ghosts work for us rather than being haunted by them. At one point in *Les derniers rois mages* Spéro wonders about the significance of being black and concludes, "Pourtant, cela a-t-il encore une signification?" Both *La vie scélérate* and *Les derniers rois mages* analyze the evolution of racial identity in the complexities of time and space and effect a kind of demystification of identity. Condé seems to be groping beyond identity to look for the universal meaning, the touchstone values that may have been lost sight of or even that may remain to be defined. Africa, America, and Guadeloupe have changed; they are no longer themselves in the sense that their old myths are no longer functional in defining the geographic or social realities. Spéro and Claude "Coco" Elaïse Louis, the storyteller of *La vie scélérate,* are lost souls, unable to assert an identity comparable to those of their ancestors of the Titan generation, but they may be better guides for us in our days of whimper, when *everything,* indeed, does fall apart. Nothing is to be gained by inventing a new myth of Africa or positing a new identity for Guadeloupe apart from the global reality. We must now look at all the scrambled pieces and try to assemble a new image of totality and harmony capable of reflecting the complex interactions of a multicultural and multifarious entity.

Lawrence Thornton (review date 16 July 1995)

SOURCE: "The Healer," in *New York Times Book Review,* July 16, 1995, p. 17.

[*In the following review, Thornton offers praise for the multilayered story of* Crossing the Mangrove.]

Francis Sancher, aka Francisco Alvarez-Sanchez, lies snug

in his coffin, his face framed by a glass window that allows friends and enemies one last look at the mystery man of Rivière au Sel, a country village on the Caribbean island of Guadeloupe.

Though we meet him first in death, Francis Sancher is quickly resurrected in the memories of those who are attending his wake at the house of Sylvestre Ramsaran, a local dignitary whose daughter, Vilma, was one of Francis' many conquests. "Seeing such a crowd you might have concluded they were being hypocritical," notes the narrator of Maryse Condé's novel [*Crossing the Mangrove*]. "For all of them, at one time or another, had called Francis a vagabond and a cur, and isn't the fate of a cur to die amid general indifference?"

The contradictory answers to this question, presented in the speeches and internal monologues that make up *Crossing the Mangrove,* reveal images of a powerful and mysterious man who has liberated, oppressed, frightened and given solace to those who have gathered to bid him goodbye.

Elegantly translated into English by the author's husband, Richard Philcox, the narrative achieves its hypnotic effects through the intimate recollections of the villagers. They are a varied lot, ranging from Moïse the postman to the old seer Mama Sonson, from the historian Emile Etienne to Xantippe, the village idiot.

These characters' memories of their sometimes painful encounters with Francis reveal a willful stranger who took control of the village through the force of his personality. At the same time, he was a man of deep melancholy, capable of recognizing their pain even before they themselves were aware of it.

Together, the villagers and the intruder inhabit a world of unstable facts. Francis is said to have fought with Castro in the Sierra Maestra. But after seeing his brother lying in his own blood, he hadn't had "a minute's peace from all the suffering accidents and deaths." Such agonies apparently forced him to lay his weapons aside and become a *curandero,* a wandering healer.

But there are other possibilities. Moïse confidently asserts that Francis' "family comes from here and he's trying to trace them. They were white Creoles who fled after abolition." This version of his story is put into question by Emile Etienne's wife when she asserts that Francis' planter ancestor might have been "cursed by his slaves," and that Francis could be a ghost who "had come back to haunt the scenes of his past crimes."

In the translator's preface, Mr. Philcox says that the model he had in mind for the "tone and register of voice" of *Cross-ing the Mangrove* was Virginia Woolf's *To the Lighthouse.* It is hard not to see his logic, since Ms. Condé (whose other novels include *Segu* and *Tree of Life*) manipulates her narrative in ways that are reminiscent of Woolf and moves almost as effortlessly into and out of her characters' minds.

Nevertheless, the structure as well as the tone of the novel seem closer to Gabriel Garcia Márquez's *Chronicle of a Death Foretold,* whose myriad voices reveal the fate of Santiago Nasar. There are also similarities between the effects Francis has on those who meet him and the reactions of the characters who encounter Kurtz in Conrad's *Heart of Darkness.*

All these protagonists are known to us from hearsay, revealed through the distorting lens of memory. This is not to say that Francis is a brother to Conrad's prince of the dark. Unlike Kurtz the destroyer, Francis is a healer, a man who tries to bring light and possibility into lives distorted by suffering and indifference.

In the end, of course, the villagers' recollections reveal more about Rivière au Sel than about Francis Sancher. The most intriguing image in *Crossing the Mangrove* is the window of the dead man's coffin, which reflects the storytellers' faces superimposed upon his. Everyone at the wake is bound by this doubleness, by this meeting in the glass. The multiple interpretations offered by the living reveal Rivière au Sel as a protean community, changed and changing still because of one man's brief sojourn there.

FURTHER READING

Criticism

Chamoiseau, Patrick. "Reflections on Maryse Condé's *Traversée de la mangrove.*" *Callaloo* 14, No. 2 (Winter 1991): 389-95.

> Recounts the author's impressions of *Traversée de la mangrove* when Condé asked him to read the manuscript.

Ngate, Jonathan. "Maryse Condé and Africa: The Making of a Recalcitrant Daughter?" *A Current Bibliography of African Affairs* 19, No. 1 (1986-87): 5-20.

> Examines Condé's literary response to the problem of Afro-Caribbean identity.

Nyatetu-Waigwa, Wangari wa. "From Liminality to a Home of Her Own? The Quest Motif in Maryse Condé's Fiction." *Callaloo* 18, No. 3 (1995): 551-64.

> Argues that Condé's "Caribbean novels" represent a personal as well as a literary quest for the writer.

Smith, Arlette M. "Maryse Condé's *Hérémakhonon:* A Triangular Structure of Alienation" in *International Women's Writing: New Landscapes of Identity,* edited by Anne E. Brown and Marjanne E. Goozé, pp. 63-9. Westport, Conn.: Greenwood Press, 1995.

> Contends that the protagonist's journey in *Hérémakhonon* is not a failure, as other critics have asserted.

Additional coverage of Condé's life and works is contained in the following sources published by Gale: *Black Writers,* **Vol. 2;** *Contemporary Authors,* **Vol. 110;** *Contemporary Authors New Revision Series,* **Vols. 30, 53;** *Contemporary Literary Criticism,* **Vols. 52, 92; and** *DISCovering Authors Modules: Multicultural Authors.*

Rita Dove

1952-

(Full name Rita Frances Dove) American poet, dramatist, short story writer, and novelist.

INTRODUCTION

Best known for *Thomas and Beulah* (1986), for which she received the 1987 Pulitzer Prize in poetry, Dove is considered one of the leading poets of her generation. In her work she draws upon personal perception and emotion while integrating an awareness of history and social issues. These qualities are best evidenced in *Thomas and Beulah,* which commemorates the lives of her grandparents and offers a chronicle of the collective experience of African Americans during the twentieth century. In awarding Dove the United States poet laureateship in 1993, James H. Billington praised her as "an accomplished and already widely recognized poet in mid-career whose work gives special promise to explore and enrich contemporary American poetry."

Biographical Information

Dove was born in Akron, Ohio, into a highly educated family. An excellent student, Dove was a Presidential Scholar, ranking nationally among the best high school students of the graduating class of 1970. After obtaining a bachelor's degree from Miami University of Ohio in 1973 and then studying in Germany, Dove enrolled at the Iowa Writers' Workshop. She married German writer Fred Viebahn in March, 1979; they have one daughter. Dove published her first full-length collection of poetry, *The Yellow House on the Corner,* in 1980. She holds the distinction of being the first African American as well as the youngest individual to hold the post of United States poet laureate. As poet laureate, Dove expressed a desire to make poetry more appealing to the general reader. She has observed: "Given the choice between watching television and reading a book, it is a difficult battle. You have to find ways to show people the pleasure of reading, and that it is something continual and deepening—not a quick bite." Dove subsequently communicated her hope to "break down the ivory tower. . . . I want to reduce the anxiety that people have about poetry."

Major Works

Dove's poetry is characterized by a tight control of words and structure, an innovative use of color imagery, and a tone that combines objectivity and personal concern. Although many of her poems incorporate black history and directly address racial themes, they also present issues, such as preju-

dice and oppression, that transcend racial boundaries. Dove has explained: "Obviously as a black woman, I am concerned with race. . . . But certainly not every poem of mine mentions the fact of being black. They are poems about humanity, and sometimes humanity happens to be black." In *The Yellow House on the Corner,* for example, a section is devoted to poems about slavery and freedom. "Parsley," a poem published in *Museum* (1983) recounts the massacre of thousands of Haitian blacks who were killed because they allegedly could not pronounce the letter "r" in *perejil,* the Spanish word for parsley. *Thomas and Beulah* similarly combines racial concerns with historical and personal elements. Loosely based on the lives of Dove's maternal grandparents, *Thomas and Beulah* is divided into two sections. "Mandolin," the opening sequence of poems, features the viewpoint of Thomas, a former musician haunted since his youth by the death of a friend. "Canary in Bloom," the other sequence, features the perspective of Beulah, Thomas's wife, and portrays her outwardly placid domestic existence from childhood to marriage and widowhood. Through allusions to events outside the lives of Thomas and Beulah—including the Great Depression, the black migration from the rural

South to the industrial North, the civil rights marches of the 1960s, and the assassination of President John F. Kennedy—Dove emphasizes the couple's place in and interconnectedness with history. *Grace Notes* (1989) contains autobiographical poems that delineate Dove's role as a mother, wife, daughter, sister, and poet. "Pastoral," for instance, describes Dove's observations and feelings while nursing her daughter, and "Poem in Which I Refuse Contemplation" relates a letter from her mother that Dove received while in Germany. Dove's first novel, *Through the Ivory Gate* (1992), incorporates elements often considered typical of her poetry. The story of a young black artist named Virginia King, *Through the Ivory Gate* has a structure that relies heavily on the characters' memories and storytelling abilities. Documenting the protagonist's acceptance of her black identity in a society that devalues her heritage, the novel relates Virginia's attempts to reconcile herself to events and prejudices experienced and learned in her childhood, adolescence, and early adulthood. Classical myths inform two of Dove's later works, one a book of poetry and the other a verse-drama. The former, *Mother Love* (1995), treats the myth of Demeter and Persephone, and examines the often turbulent relationships between mothers and daughters. The latter, *The Darker Face of the Earth* (1994), draws upon the tragedy of Oedipus around which Dove constructs a story that uncovers some of the atrocities committed in service of slavery in the American South. The drama relates the tale of Amalia LaFarge, the wife of Lewis, a white plantation owner, who gives birth to a black son, named Augustus, who is sold into slavery by the doctor who attends his birth. By the end of the play, which spans twenty years, Dove, according to Deirdre Neilen, "skillfully brings her characters to their fated ends. Augustus kills Hector [Amalia's lover] and Louis; Amalia kills herself to save him. . . . This Oedipus, then, is carried off in triumph . . . , but his eyes can see only death and pain."

Critical Reception

Critics have consistently acclaimed Dove's innovation, technical mastery, and ability to capture a variety of thoughts, events, and perspectives and distill them into insightful and intricate works of poetry and prose. Arnold Rampersad has asserted: "[W]ith the consistently accomplished work of . . . Rita Dove, there is at least one clear sign if not of a coming renaissance of poetry, then at least of the emergence of an unusually strong new figure who might provide leadership by brilliant example." Critics point to Dove's impressive range of subject, mood, character, and setting in her works as evidence of her talent and an assurance that the best work of her career may not yet be written.

PRINCIPAL WORKS

Ten Poems (poetry) 1977
The Only Dark Spot in the Sky (poetry) 1980
The Yellow House on the Corner (poetry) 1980
Mandolin (poetry) 1982
Museum (poetry) 1983
Fifth Sunday (short stories) 1985
Thomas and Beulah (poetry) 1986
The Other Side of the House (poetry) 1988
Grace Notes (poetry) 1989
Through the Ivory Gate (novel) 1992
Selected Poems (poetry) 1993
The Darker Face of the Earth: A Verse Play in Fourteen Scenes (play) 1994
Mother Love (poetry) 1995

CRITICISM

Robert McDowell (essay date Winter 1986)

SOURCE: "The Assembling Vision of Rita Dove," in *Conversant Essays: Contemporary Poets on Poetry,* edited by James McCorkle, Wayne State University Press, 1990.

[*In the following essay, which was originally published in* Callaloo *in Winter, 1986, McDowell illustrates how Dove assembles various details from history and uses her unique brand of wordplay to present these details in an original, thought-provoking manner in her poetry.*]

Rita Dove has always possessed a storyteller's instinct. In *The Yellow House on the Corner* (1980), *Museum* (1983), and *Thomas and Beulah* (1985), this instinct has found expression in a synthesis of striking imagery, myth, magic, fable, wit, humor, political comment, and a sure knowledge of history. Many contemporaries share Dove's mastery of some of these, but few succeed in bringing them together to create a point of view that, by its breadth and force, stands apart. She has not worked her way into this enviable position among poets without fierce commitment.

Passing through a graduate writing program (Iowa) in the mid-1970s, Dove and her peers were schooled in the importance of sensation and its representation through manipulation of The Image. The standard lesson plan, devised to reflect the ascendancy of Wallace Stevens and a corrupt revision of T. S. Eliot's objective correlative, instructed young writers to renounce realistic depiction and offer it up to the province of prose; it promoted subjectivity and imagination-as-image; it has strangled a generation of poems.

How and why this came to pass is less important, really, than admitting that it is so. Literary magazines are gorged with poems devoid of shapeliness and scope. Imagistic, cramped, and confessional, they exist for the predictably surprising, climactic phrase. A historically conscious reader, aware of literary tradition, might understandably perceive an enormous cultural amnesia as the dubiously distinguishing feature of such poems. Such a reader will rue the fact that the writing and interpretation of poetry has diminished to a trivial pursuit, a pronouncement of personal instinct. If this is the dominant direction of a discouraging Moment, then Rita Dove distinguishes herself by resolutely heading the other way.

Unlike the dissembling spirit indicted above, Dove is an assembler who gathers the various facts of this life and presents them in ways that jar our lazy assumptions. She gives voice to many positions and many characters. Like the speaker/writer of classic argumentation, she shows again and again that she understands the opposing sides of conflicts she deals with. She tells all sides of the story. Consider the titles of her books, their symbolic weight. The personal turning point *House on the Corner* evolves, becoming the public Museum (symbol of preserved chronology); that, in turn, gives way to the names of two characters whose lives combine and illustrate the implicit meanings of the personal House and the public Museum.

The Yellow House on the Corner first of all, is a showcase for Dove's control of the language. This is our first encounter with the powerful images we have come to associate with her work:

> The texture of twilight made me think of
> Lengths of dotted Swiss.
>
> As the sun broke the water into a thousand needles
> tipped with the blood from someone's finger . . .
>
> This nutmeg stick of a boy in loose trousers!

These are the observations of original sight.

There is also the rich and heavily symbolic use of color—red, orange, blue, yellow, and black and white. They usually appear as adjectives, but her adjectival preoccupation comes across with a difference. For example, while repeatedly employing *black* as an adjective ("black place," "black table," "prune-black water," "horses black," "black tongues," "my black bear"), she never settles for quick agreement based on obvious connotations. Instead, she injects the adjectives with tantalizing ambiguity and new meanings based on their relationships to other words. She redefines our connotative relationship to them. She outdistances most poets simply because she understands that adjectives enhance nouns by better defining them; they are part of the equations we are born to cope with, not substitutes for weak noun counterparts.

The Yellow House also introduces the poet's devotion to myth, her determination to reveal what is magical in our contemporary lives.

"This Life"

> The green lamp flares on the table.
> You tell me the same thing
> as that one,
> asleep, upstairs.
> Now I see: the possibilities
> are golden dresses in a nutshell.
>
> As a child, I fell in love
> with a Japanese woodcut
> of a girl gazing at the moon.
> I waited with her for her lover.
> He came in while breeches and sandals.
> He had a goatee—he had
>
> your face, though I didn't know it.
> Our lives will be the same—
> your lips, swollen from whistling
> at danger,
>
> and I a stranger
> In this desert,
> nursing the tough skins of figs.

In this poem, **"The Bird Frau," "The Snow King," "Beauty and the Beast,"** and others, she echoes, distorts, and revises ancient myths; in **"Upon Meeting Don L. Lee in a Dream"** and **"Robert Schumann, Or: Musical Genius Begins with Affliction,"** she focuses on characters whose actual lives have been the stuff of myths.

These and a number of short love poems comprise one side of Dove's Grand Equation. Travelogue poems (consistent throughout her work) erect a transitional bridge between her myth-making component and the historical, public side of the equation: poems examining race relations in America. At their best, poems from the myth-making category are lyrical and mysterious; poems from the latter category are heartbreakingly honest and inescapable. Though these last poems are placed throughout the volume, the third section is made up entirely of them, a fact which makes it the most relentless and coherent segment of the book.

In these poems, Dove makes the reader aware of the relationship between private and public events. **"The Transport of Slaves from Maryland to Mississippi,"** for example, is based on an incident of 1839 in which a slave woman thwarts the escape of a wagonload of slaves by helping the driver regain his horse. The narrative point of view shifts three times, revealing the complexity of the incident and of the characters involved in it. No prescriptive strategy limits expression, as the woman's opening monologue makes clear. Describing the driver she says, "his eyes were my eyes in a yellower face. . . . He might have been a son of mine." The justification of her act is poignant even though its consequences are disastrous for her fellows.

This section of **The Yellow House** is bold and beautifully elegiac, presenting the motives and gestures of all of the dramatic players. The poet's wise utterance peels back the rhetorically thick skin of injustice and exposes Man's inhumanity for what it is: unbearable, shameful, unforgettable.

> Well,
> that was too much for the doctor.
> Strip 'em! he ordered. And they
> were slicked down with bacon fat and
> superstition strapped from them
> to the beat of the tam-tam. Those strong enough
> rose up too, and wailed as they leapt.
> It was a dance of unusual ferocity.
>
> ("**Cholera**")

That final grim understatement intensifies the reader's outrage.

Dove's synthesis of a historical consciousness, devotion to myth, and virtuoso manipulation of parts of speech convey us into the world of her major thematic preoccupation. In one poem she writes "My heart, shy mulatto," which informs the closing lines of a later poem like "**Adolescence—III.**"

> . . . I dreamed how it would happen:
> He would meet me by the blue spruce,
>
> A carnation over his heart, saying,
> "I have come for you, Madam;
> I have loved you in my dreams."
> At his touch, the scabs would fall away.
> Over his shoulder, I see my father coming toward
> us:
> He carries his tears in a bowl,
> And blood hangs in the pine-soaked air.

This poem, and this volume's cumulative thrust, redefines the poet's need to reconcile the conventional, Romantic American wish (that life be a fairy tale) with the cruel facts of Black America's heritage.

Museum begins with travelogues, which prepare the reader for travel poems that eclipse the personal by introducing overlooked historical detail. "**Nestor's Bathtub,**" a pivotal poem in this respect, begins with the lines "As usual, legend got it all wrong." This announces a dissatisfaction with the conventional ordering of events and an intention to rejuvenate history by coming up with new ways of telling it. In successive poems ("**Tou Wan Speaks to Her Husband, Lu sheng,**" "**Catherine of Alexandria,**" "**Catherine of Siena,**" "**Boccaccio: The Plague Years,**" and its companion piece, "**Fiammetta Breaks Her Peace**"), Dove adopts a variety of personae that bear witness to the struggles of victimized women in societies in which men are dubiously perceived as gods.

This strategy continues into the book's second section, though the subjects and personae are primarily male ("**Shakespeare Say,**" "**Banneker,**" "**Ike**"). Here is the narrator in "**Reading Holderlin on the Patio with the Aid of a Dictionary**":

> The meaning that surfaces
> comes to me aslant and
> I go to meet it, stepping
> out of my body
>   word for word, until I am
> everything at once.

As in **The Yellow House,** in **Museum** Dove focuses on characters, and chooses characters to speak through, from the historical rosters of those whose lives have been the stuff of fable. Toward the end of this section, her identification with historical and mysterious male-female consciousness is most complete in "**Agosta the Winged Man and Rasha the Black Dove.**" In this poem she tells the story of a pair of German circus performers, an inscrutable deformed man and an equally inscrutable black woman who dances with snakes. These characters are performers, who like the poet, look at the world in unique ways.

> Agosta in
> classical drapery, then,
> and Rasha at his feet.
> Without passion. Not
> the canvas
>
>   but their gaze,
>   so calm,
> was merciless.

The poem that follows, "**At the German Writers Conference in Munich,**" examines and exploits this preoccupation from another angle. In the poem another art—another way of performing—is described. The calm, stiff characters of a tapestry are not outwardly grotesque as they are the characters in the preceding poem. Nevertheless, they appear to be out of step with their woven environment, existing as they do in a world of flowers. The two poems, together, illustrate a brilliant shifting of focus, a looking out of the eyes of characters, then a merciless looking into them.

The third section of *Museum* contains a focusing down of this strategy in a tight group of family poems in which the father is the dominant character. He is perceived by the innocent narrator as the teacher, the bearer of all that is magical in the world.

> I've been trying
> to remember the taste,
> but it doesn't exist.
> Now I see why
> you bothered,
> father.

                                        (**"Grape Sherbet"**)

Whether he is making palpable an impalpable taste or miraculously rescuing roses from beetles (**"Roses"**) or deftly retrieving what is magical from a mistake (**"My Father's Telescope"**) he is clearly the narrator's mentor, inspiring a different way of meeting the world:

> this
> magician's skew of scarves
> issuing from an opaque heart.

            (**"A Father Out Walking On the Lawn"**)

But even in this tender, celebratory section, Dove includes one poem, **"Anti-Father,"** which satisfies her self-imposed demand that she tell all sides of the story.

> Just between
>
> me and you,
> woman to man,
>
> outer space is
> inconceivably
>
> Intimate.

The innocent narrator, now a knowledgeable woman, reverses roles here, contradicting the father but offering magical insight in doing so.

The closing section of Rita Dove's second volume summarizes all that has preceded it, and in two remarkable poems anticipates *Thomas and Beulah*. The narrator of **"A Sailor in Africa"** spins off from a Viennese card game (circa 1910) and unravels the adventures of the characters in the game. A black slave, who is actually a sea captain, outwits his captors and takes over their ship. He is shipwrecked later, only to discover great wealth in his isolation. This effortless storytelling combines Dove's great strengths—memorable images, wit, travelogue, fable, complex representation of motive and gesture, historical awareness—in a groundbreaking poem.

It is balanced and rivaled by **"Parsley,"** the book's concluding poem, which tells the story of a dictator who orders the annihilation of 20,000 blacks because they cannot pronounce the letter "r." The poem is constructed in two parts. The first, a villanelle, presents the entire drama; it is all the more terrifying because the facts smash against the stark and beautiful container of the form itself. In the second part of the poem, a third-person narrator examines the dictator's relationship to his mother, who can "roll her 'r's' like a queen."

> As he paces he wonders
> who can I kill today . . .
>
>   Someone
> calls out his name in a voice
> so like his mother's, a startled tear
> splashes the tip of his right boot.
> My mother, my love in death.

As she often does, Dove unerringly combines private and public political history in this and in many other poems in *Museum*. It is a direction that flourishes on a book-length scale in *Thomas and Beulah*.

"These poems tell two sides of a story and are meant to be read in sequence." So begins *Thomas and Beulah*. Their story is told twice: from Thomas's point of view in the twenty-three poems of "Mandolin," and from Beulah's point of view in the twenty-one poems of "Canary in Bloom." The time, according to an extensive Chronology at book's end, covers the years from 1919 to 1968. Most of the story takes place in Akron, Ohio, a city, which the Chronology also tells us, had a Negro population of 11,000 (out of a total population of 243,000) in 1940.

The chief narrative method employed, the story twice-told, does not rely so much on action; it relies on reactions of characters to events and circumstances that affect them even though they are wholly beyond them. The questions generated by this approach are chilling and clean if two characters, deeply involved with one another, interpret events (inner and outer, private and public) so differently, what does this suggest about our manipulation of history; what does it say about our reliability as witnesses, as teachers of successive generations; what is true?

Truth in *Thomas and Beulah* is found in the characters themselves. In **"The Event,"** the first poem in the section entitled "Mandolin," Thomas leaves Tennessee for the riverboat life. He travels with a good friend, Lem, and a magical symbol, a talisman which gathers pain and wards it off—his mandolin. In a turn that explodes the deliberate echo of Mark Twain's *Huck Finn*, Lem dives overboard to collect chestnuts on a passing island and drowns. This tragedy, at the outset of his journey, will haunt Thomas for the rest of his life. We observe his arrival in Akron in 1921, deftly and desperately playing his mandolin for pay. He is a driven figure, confronting his guilt and his second-class citizenship in a racially divided country. His half-hearted attempts to sell himself in such a country will drive the more sheltered Beulah to find fault in him. It is a key element of his tragedy that he faults himself for it, too:

> He used to sleep like a glass of water
> held up in the hand of a very young girl.

and later,

> To him work is a narrow grief
> and the music afterwards
> like a woman
> reaching into his chest
> to spread it around.

                                   (**"Straw Hat"**)

After their marriage, the promise of equality and upward mobility is profoundly betrayed. The world is threatening, malicious after all. In **"Nothing Down,"** they buy a new car for a trip to Tennessee, but the symbol and the dream it represents are destroyed when they're passed by a carload of jeering whites; in **"The Zeppelin Factory,"** Thomas lands construction work, laboring on the largest building in the world without interior supports (another appropriate, unforgettable symbol for the world we make) and hates it; Thomas ponders the impending birth of a third daughter against the backdrop of union violence (**"Under the Viaduct"**); Thomas walks out of a movie house to witness a splendid natural phenomenon (**"Aurora Borealis"**), but even this double-barreled symbolic magic is overpowered by the grim facts of the world around him. Finally, he finds even his oldest companion, his mandolin, estranged:

> How long has it been. . . ?
> Too long. Each note slips
> into querulous rebuke, fingerpads
> scarred with pain, shallow ditches
> to rut in like a runaway slave
> with a barking heart. Days afterwards
> blisters to hide from the children.
> Hanging by a thread. Some day,
> he threatens, I'll just
> let go.
>   (**"Definition in the Face of Unnamed Fury"**)

Only in his own good heart is Thomas vindicated, and the physical manifestation of his goodness is his family. In **"Roast Opossum,"** he spins two tales for his grandchildren: hunting opossum for Malcolm, a tale of horses for the girls. This tender poem makes a case for salvation implicit in one generation's nurturing another by gathering and making pal-

pable history and myth, fact and fiction. In such ritual we discover our one defense against the inhuman things we do to one another.

The section concludes with three elegiac poems covering the events of Thomas's declining health and eventual death. **"The Stroke"** contains a lovely memory of Beulah during pregnancy and his certainty that the pain he feels is Lem knocking on his chest. In the end, Thomas appropriately suffers his final heart attack behind the wheel of his car (**"Thomas at the Wheel"**).

Whereas Thomas's life is a perpetual scramble toward definition, Beulah's, as presented in "Canary in Bloom," is preordained. She will marry; she will bear children. These restrictions force her to develop an inward, private life. For example, her fear and distrust of male figures is established early in **"Taking in Wash."** Her father comes home drunk:

> Tonight
>
> every light hums, the kitchen arctic
> with sheets, Papa is making the hankies
> sail. Her foot upon a silk
> stitched rose, she waits
> until he turns, his smile sliding all over.

This is the seed of her reaction to her suitor and future husband. She would prefer a pianola to his mandolin; she hates his yellow scarf. When they marry, "rice drumming / the both of them blind," she sees Thomas as "a hulk, awkward in blue serge." Her father places her fingertips in Thomas's hand, and men in collusion have delivered her up to her fate.

From this point on, Beulah's story seeks the form, the shape, of meditation. In **"Dusting"** she fondly remembers a boy at a fair, comparing that magical location and meeting with the hard news of her life. In **"Weathering Out"** she daydreams through her seventh month of pregnancy, glad to be rid of Thomas as he daily hunts for work. In the sad **"Daystar"** she reclines in the backyard while the children nap and dreams of a place where she is nothing. In **"The Great Palace of Versailles"** she works in a dress shop, frequents the library, and temporarily loses the facts of her own life in the magic of lords and ladies.

Beulah's development of a rich inner life is the result of meditation with an outward eye. Throughout her long battle with the prescribed role she was born to play, she continues to cope admirably and compassionately with the world outside. She manages her family; she feeds transients during the Depression; she shows kindness to the daughter of a prejudiced neighbor. As the poems progress her wisdom deepens. Her attitude toward Thomas softens, too. While sweeping she recalls the drive to Tennessee, how

Even then
he was forever off in the woods somewhere in
search
of a magic creek.

(**"Pomade"**)

And later, addressing him in **"Company"**:

Listen: we were good,
though we never believed it,

If she does not change her life, Beulah through wisdom comes to understand it. She also comprehends the lives of her daughters. At their husbands' company picnic—a segregated picnic—Beulah remembers the march on Washington and its effects on the lives of her children. Her meditative impulse blossoms. Her preferred inner life squares off against the world of iniquity, and the succeeding generation is better off for it.

When I consider the discouraging Moment I mentioned at the beginning of this article, when I despair of it, I turn to only a few poets of my generation and am revitalized. Rita Dove's development through three volumes reminds us of the necessity for scope in poetry. A wide range of talent in service to an assembling vision is the tonic we need for discouragement.

Akasha (Gloria) Hull (review date May 1994)

SOURCE: "When Language Is Everything," in *The Women's Review of Books,* Vol. XI, No. 8, May, 1994, pp. 6-7.

[*In the following review, Hull provides a highly favorable assessment of* Selected Poems *and* The Darker Face of the Earth: A Verse Play in Fourteen Scenes, *applauding in particular Dove's ability to create verse that enables readers to identify with and understand her characters and learn and grow from their shared experiences.*]

When Thomas—the title character of Rita Dove's third book of poems, **Thomas and Beulah**—comes North to Ohio in 1921, a fine young black man sporting earrings and strumming a mandolin, he cuts a dazzling figure:

. . . gold hoop
from the right ear jiggling
and a glass stud, bright blue

in his left. The young ladies
saying *He sure plays*

that tater bug

like the devil!

sighing their sighs
and dimpling.

Though we may not sigh or dimple (and then again, we might), we come away from a reading of Dove's poetry with the same singular admiration: she sure writes some hell-a-fied poems!

There is remarkable agreement about this fact. Commentators as diverse as Helen Vendler, Arnold Rampersad and reviewers in *Time* magazine and the *Christian Science Monitor* unanimously praise her "pure shapes," "brilliant mind," "effortless economy and exactness of language," "chorus of voices" and "most impressive technical skills." *Essence* magazine hails her as "one of America's finest poets," while *The Nation*—with a Thomas-like flourish—announces: "This, ladies and gentleman, is a . . . writer worth knowing."

This unmistakable talent won Rita Dove the 1987 Pulitzer Prize for poetry—the first African American recipient since Gwendolyn Brooks in 1950, a gap that she says reveals "the nature of cultural politics in this country." In 1993, she was appointed Poet Laureate of the United States, a black "first" that she and everyone else believes might change public perception. As she told *Time* magazine, "I'm hoping that by the end of my term people will think of a poet laureate as someone who's out there with her sleeves rolled up and working, not sitting in an ivory tower looking out at the Potomac." As a black woman married to a white German man and mother of their mixed, "cream" daughter; as an American whose love of travel has taken her all over the world; as an energetic poet who writes intimate racial truth and traditional universals in both vernacular and villanelles, she is uniquely equipped to carry out her diversifying, activist project.

Selected Poems republishes her first three books in their entirety. **The Yellow House on the Corner** (1980) shows the wide-ranging eclecticism of a young poet—poems of courtship and romance, travel poems, dream sequences and fragments, a wonderful series on US slavery, childhood poems. **Museum** (1983) is unified by her desire to deal with artifacts, defined as "anything that becomes frozen by memory, or by circumstance or by history." The reader encounters not only a fish in a stone but long-dead historical figures, old authors, vignettes about her father, a moment of flirtation.

In a departure from the discrete, lyrical poems in these two works, **Thomas and Beulah** (1986) is a verse cycle, a narrative loosely based on her grandparents' lives that tells first one and then the other side of their story. It focuses intensely on their inner existence, with twentieth-century America as backdrop. Dove has also published **Fifth Sunday** (short stories, 1985), **Grace Notes** (poems, 1989) and **Through the**

Ivory Gate (a novel, 1992). Her first full-length play, ***The Darker Face of the Earth,*** further indicates just how seriously she holds that "there's no reason to subscribe authors to particular genres": "I'm a writer, and I write in the form that most suits what I want to say."

What she wishes to say in this fifteen-scene play is that chattel slavery in the United States was as humanly and fatefully tragic as any classical Greek drama. It transfers the Oedipal myth of patricide and maternal incest to antebellum South Carolina, and though we can guess the end from the very beginning, we read with continuing interest, sustained by Dove's poetic dialogue and curiosity about the particular details she will invent.

Amalia Jennings is an attractive young white woman who "exhibits more intelligence and backbone than is generally credited to a southern belle." From a liaison with her male slave, Hector, she births a son. Her infuriated but weak husband, Louis, teams with the doctor to kill the child: they maintain that he died after just one cry and spirit him away in a fancy sewing basket. But the boy lives; twenty years later, as Augustus Newcastle, he is purchased by Amalia, despite his notorious record as an educated and rebellious slave whose back is so "laced with scars / it's as rutted as a country road."

The Cassandra figure is Scylla, a mature slave woman who gains the power of second sight during Augustus' birth, though her conjure and predictions are discredited. Amalia—estranged for all these years from both her husband and the grief-deranged Hector—takes Augustus as her lover. Meanwhile, he plots insurrection with a group of radical conspirators, fueled by his hatred for some unknown white master whom he has been led to believe was his father. Returning from one of the midnight planning meetings, he is obliged to choke Hector to death to stifle an outcry he begins to raise. Later, at the height of the revolt, he confronts Louis, who finally realizes that this is the child Amalia bore. Interpreting Louis' confused, emotional response as proof of his paternity, Augustus kills him. Going next to Amalia, whom he has also been assigned to murder, he demands to know the identity of his mother, who he still believes was a black slave woman. Amalia responds:

> So you want to know, do you?
> You want to know your mother?
> I have one more story for you—
> and when I have finished,
> You will wish
> you had never set your man's foot
> on this plantation.
> You will wish
> you had not stroked my hair or
> touched my breasts or

> lain with me in that bed.
> You will wish
> you had no eyes to see
> or ears to hear
> or mouth to kiss.
> You will wish
> you had never been born.

In the hysterical aftermath of the moment of truth, the conspiracy leaders burst in. Seeing Augustus clutched in an anguished embrace with Amalia, they shoot him, thinking he is a traitor, and also kill her. As the slaves yell, "We're free! We're free!" Scylla takes one last, long look at the heap of bodies.

On two or three occasions, the high drama edges into melodrama, but overall the play's selectivity of incident, judicious sparseness, clean lines, even, dignified tone and simple staging keep it operating successfully as a modernization of the classic Greek tragic mode. Throughout the play, the slaves sit on benches as spectators when they are not acting, to function as a chorus. Dove dedicates the play: "For our daughter, Aviva Chantal Tamu Dove-Viebahn"—drawing a line of connection between the horrible miscegenation of the slave past and what we can assume is a much more fortunate contemporary uniting of races.

Notwithstanding her stretches into other genres, it is Dove as poet that I find most impressive. She has a poet's (prejudiced) belief in the absolute necessity of language. In **"Kentucky, 1833,"** she writes: "On Sundays, something hangs in the air, a hallelujah, a skitter of brass, but we can't call it by name and it disappears." Elsewhere she says: "Language is everything . . . emotion is useless if there's no way to express it." Even though I personally know there are nonverbal ways to express inarticulable feelings, as an aspiring poet I can fully appreciate the overweening faith in words that impels Dove's creativity and manifests itself so strikingly in her images, particularly the similes, supposedly the most elementary kind of metaphor to make: "while their mistress sleeps like an ivory toothpick"; "the wine, like a pink lake, tipped"; "eyes as round / As dinner plates and eyelashes like sharpened tines"; a bathtub that "stands, tiny and voluptuous / as a gravy dish"; "He used to sleep like a glass of water / held up in the hand of a very young girl"; "shallow ditches / to rut in like a runaway slave / with a barking heart."

Dove, an early and omnivorous reader, began writing in the third grade. Her Master of Fine Arts degree from the University of Iowa bespeaks rigorous training and much time spent in workshops, and she revises incessantly. Yet her poetic process, she has said, is a deeply subconscious one that she refuses to probe. As she explains in **"Reading Hölderlin on the Patio with the Aid of a Dictionary":**

The meaning that surfaces

comes to me aslant and
I go to meet it, stepping
out of my body
word for word, until I am

everything at once: the perfume
of the world in which
I go under,
a skindiver
remembering air.

Such a process yields the graspable mystery and rippling images of a poem like **"Catherine of Alexandria":**

Deprived of learning and
the chance to travel,
no wonder sainthood
came as a voice

in your bed—
and what went on
each night was fit
for nobody's ears

but Jesus'. It is
breath of a lily.
His spiraling
pain. Each morning

the nightshirt bunched
above your waist—
a kept promise,
a ring of milk.

Here, the colloquial "fit for nobody's ears" following from the plain beginning cascades into the accelerating lyricism of the second half of the poem—the collective eroticism of breath, lily and pain, and the final metaphors for the nightshirt (itself concretely visualized) yielding half-elusive and multiple meanings.

Very few commentators complain that Dove is difficult or obscure, for she walks a comfortable margin between general accessibility and high, esoteric art. One of her least transparent poems is **"Thomas at the Wheel,"** which begins:

This, then, the river he had to swim.
Through the wipers the drugstore
shouted, lit up like a casino,
neon script leering from the shuddering
asphalt.

Then the glass doors flew apart
and a man walked out to the curb
to light a cigarette. Thomas thought
the sky was emptying itself as fast
as his chest was filling with water.

But its position at the conclusion of a sequence, the associations for "river" as transition, the fact that Thomas' best friend, who haunts him throughout, had died by drowning (upon a dare from Thomas) and the preternatural heightening of the diction-images—all alert the reader to the fact that the hero is dying of a heart attack as he drives down the street in the rain. Lying across the car seat—"a pod set to sea, / a kiss unpuckering"—the last sound he hears is sirens "as the keys swung, ticking." Dove's endings are always strong and elegant.

For convenience or for political purposes, Rita Dove could be categorized—as black poet, woman poet, black woman poet, or simply poet. From a racial point of view, her work lacks the overt allegiance, criticism and protest that mark poets as diverse as lucille clifton or Thylias Moss. Her critique of white hegemony is usually implicit, impersonal, peripheral, or historically distant, and given "the nature of cultural politics in this country," this may factor into her wide success.

Dove considers herself a feminist, although she says that when she walks into her room to write, "I don't think of myself in political terms." Her work features males as well as females and reveals the gender-constructed plights of both (though one notices an absence of poems about her mother, compared to the substantial number about her father). Beulah's side of the "Thomas and Beulah" story presents some of her most feminist understandings. From a girlhood certainty that "she would make it to Paris one day," Beulah never even gets to Chicago. Her fate is to hide out behind the garage to gain "a little room for thinking" in the hour that the children nap, and to feel, as she cooks Sunday greens, that:

She wants to hear
wine pouring.
She wants to taste
change.

In the last analysis, Dove inhabits to varying extents all of these spaces, and does so in such a fluidly simultaneous and unself-conscious way that to isolate any one becomes an analytical exercise, finally reductive of the totality of who she is, how she writes and the cumulative impression that she makes. She gives meaning to each category as she breaks down the boundaries between them. In the guise of poet, she becomes many types of women and men, and takes us readers into their consciousnesses, helping us to feel whatever it is we all share that makes those journeys possible.

Helen Vendler (review date 15 May 1995)

SOURCE: "Twentieth-Century Demeter," in *The New Yorker,* Vol. LXXI, No. 12, May 15, 1995, pp. 90-2.

[*In the following review, Vendler analyzes the poems in* Mother Love, *and offers a primarily positive assessment of the collection.*]

Rita Dove, the United States Poet Laureate (occupying a post that used to be called, more accurately, Consultant in Poetry to the Library of Congress), has recently published **Mother Love,** her sixth book of poems. (Her previous works include the Pulitzer Prize-winning **Thomas and Beulah.**) In these books, Dove, who is black, has in part carried on a lyric tradition that explicitly treats themes of blackness, but she has also written many poems outside that tradition—poems of childhood and family life, of travel, of motherhood, and of aesthetic experience itself. These draw upon the events of her life but do so with remarkable objectivity. She was born in 1952 in Akron, Ohio, and educated at Miami University in Ohio. A Fulbright brought her to Tübingen; after that, she took an M.F.A. at the Iowa Writers' Workshop and is now Commonwealth Professor of English at the University of Virginia. She is married to the German novelist Fred Viebahn, and they have a daughter, Aviva.

Mother Love is not the first of Dove's volumes to address motherhood. The theme was evident—and very originally handled—in some poems in **Grace Notes,** a volume published in 1989. There she observed motherhood in a detached manner. If she did not go so far as Blake in seeing a baby as "a fiend hid in a cloud," she did say, memorably:

> We
> give our children dolls, and
> they know just what to do—
>
> line them up and shoot them.

She was equally unsentimental about the houses in which family life takes place:

> Each house notches into its neighbor
> and then the next, the whole row
>   scaldingly white,
> unmistakable as a set of bared teeth.

Now in **Mother Love** (dedicated: "For my mother / To my daughter") Dove brings into close focus the pained relation between mothers and daughters. The book takes as its central myth the story of Demeter and Persephone, the archetypal story of mother love, which was invented to explain the origins of seasonal change. When Persephone is abducted by Hades, the king of the Underworld, her mother, Demeter, who is the goddess of agriculture, ceases, in her grieving, to attend to the crops, and everything withers. Finally, the gods restore Persephone, but, because she has eaten six pomegranate seeds while she was in Hades' kingdom, she can remain with her mother only six months of the year. This myth has already been used, notably by Tennyson to represent Demeter's sorrow and by the contemporary poet Jorie Graham to explore the predicament of a woman who is both daughter of her mother and mother of a daughter. In Dove's hands, the story is used to investigate the value of myth as a perennial interpretative device.

Dove has always liked to approach any complex subject from a variety of perspectives. **Mother Love** opens with a poem about the rape from Hades' point of view, and that is followed almost immediately by a poem showing a mother's mixed feelings as she inflicts a first party dress on her mutinous but blushing daughter. Later, the social anomalousness of the bereaved mother (an object half of sympathy, half of blame) is contrasted with her inward trauma. And there is even the poem of the innocent bystander, witness to the rape.

The most realistic of these poems is a long sequence in which Dove translates the mother's loss into modern terms: an American girl has gone to live in Paris and has become involved in an affair with an older man; they have opened a gallery to sell his dubious paintings and souvenirs of Paris to unsuspecting tourists. The sequence—a narrative in seven parts followed by four poems in sonnet form—succeeds, by and large, with the mother and daughter but makes the abductor a stage villain. At the cocktail party where he meets Persephone, he is shown musing:

> God, humans are a noisy zoo. . . .
>
> I need a *divertissement:*
> The next one through that gate,
> woman or boy, will get
> the full-court press of my ennui.

He has only to twirl his mustache to become a cartoon. Demeter is more subtly revealed. Meeting her daughter at "The Bistro Styx" in Paris ("She was thinner, with a mannered gauntness / as she paused just inside the double / glass doors"), the mother is appalled:

> I saw she was dressed all in gray,
> from a kittenish cashmere skirt and cowl
>
> down to the graphite signature of her shoes.

"Sorry I'm late," she panted, though
she wasn't, sliding into the chair, her cape

tossed off in a shudder of brushed steel.
We kissed. Then I leaned back to peruse
my blighted child, this wary aristocratic
    mole. . . .

                        He'd convinced

her to pose nude for his appalling canvases,
faintly futuristic landscapes strewn
with carwrecks and bodies being chewed

by rabid cocker spaniels. . . .

        She did look ravishing,
spookily insubstantial, a lipstick ghost on
    tissue. . . .

I've lost her, I thought, and called for the bill.

Dove's foreword alerts her readers to her use of the sonnet (in various irregular and half-rhyme forms) in *Mother Love:*

> I like how the sonnet comforts even while its prim
> borders . . . are stultifying; one is constantly bump-
> ing up against Order. The Demeter/Persephone cycle
> of betrayal and regeneration is ideally suited for this
> form since all three—mother-goddess, daughter-
> consort and poet—are struggling to sing in their
> chains.

In one interpretation, the myth embodies the natural depar-ture of the daughter from the mother so that she may enter the realm of sexuality; the mother sees this as betrayal (for-getting her own earlier participation in the cycle), and in the mother's version of the story Hades is the abductor, the se-ducer of the innocent. But the daughter knows better; and several of Dove's poems examine Persephone's complicity in her own disappearance. In **"Rusks,"** done in black demotic, Persephone views her abductor as the proverbial half a loaf that is better than none:

> Let someone else have
> the throne of blues for a while,
> let someone else suffer mosquitoes.
> As my mama always said:
> half a happiness is better
> than none at goddam all.

I admire Dove's willingness to slant the myth upward to sub-limity, downward to the ordinary, and—at her best—outward to the uncanny. Here is the sonnet **"Missing,"** where the voices of Persephone and Demeter melt together in the mod-ern story of the lost adolescent:

> I am the daughter who went out with the girls,
> never checked back in and nothing marked my
> "last
> known whereabouts," not a single glistening petal.
>
> Horror is partial; it keeps you going. A lost child is
> a fact hardening around its absence, a knot in the
> breast purring *Touch, and I will*
>
> *come true.* I was "returned," I watched her
> watch as I babbled *It could have been worse.* . . .
> Who can tell
> what penetrates? Pity is the brutal
> discipline. Now I understand she can never
> die, just as nothing can bring me back—
>
> I am the one who comes and goes;
> I am the footfall that hovers.

The elegance of this ending is the mark of Dove's best work. Persephone comes and goes; Demeter waits and hovers.

Mother Love is an unsparing book. It observes both the van-ity of mother love ("duty bugles and we'll / climb out of ex-haustion every time") and the cliché of its appeal ("Any woman knows the remedy for grief / is being needed"). These sardonic remarks appear in the title poem of the vol-ume, which tells the story of Demeter's transmutation into a monster. What, Dove asks, must have happened inwardly to Demeter as a result of Persephone's abduction? The Greek myth shows the mother resigned to her yearly loss, annu-ally withdrawing from and resuming her aid to agriculture; but Dove tells a counter-myth, one in which Demeter goes mad, consumed with rage against maleness and subject to a savage mourning. In Dove's poem, a woman, pitying the be-reft Demeter, offers her a male child to nurse, thinking that it will console her. Instead, Demeter decides to "save" the baby from the vicissitudes of experience by burning him to death. This is Dove's gothic tale of maternal grief gone wrong:

> Each night
> I laid him on the smoldering embers,
> sealing his juices in slowly so he might
>   be cured to perfection. Oh, I know it
> looked damning: at the hearth a muttering crone
>   bent over a baby sizzling on a spit
> as neat as a Virginia ham. Poor human—
>   to scream like that, to make me
>   remember.

If this is mother love, it is a force that can distort personality like few others. A book taking on such a subject is not neat—for all Dove's wish to be neat—nor can it be, in an ordinary sense, beautiful. It is often harsh and often lurid. It is at times sentimental in wanting to be lurid. But it is an energetic book—one that throws motherhood into the arena of the mind and says, "Look at it."

It is typical of Dove's moral even-handedness that, having thought so much about the relation between mothers and daughters, she has also explored the subject of sons. In a play called ***The Darker Face of the Earth,*** which will have its première in 1996, she has moved the Oedipus myth into a Southern slave setting. And it is typical of Dove's literary restlessness that, after writing poems, stories, and a novel, she decided to try her hand at a play. She is not the first writer to refresh poetry at the wells of fiction and drama; but Rita Dove is first and foremost a poet, one whose laser glance exposes and cauterizes its subjects in new and disturbing ways.

Kevin Stein (essay date 1996)

SOURCE: "Lives in Motion: Multiple Perspectives in the Poetry of Rita Dove," in his *Private Poets, Worldly Acts: Public and Private History in Contemporary American Poetry,* Ohio University Press, 1996, pp. 108-26.

[*In the following essay, Stein explores Dove's treatment of the events depicted in her poetry, specifically examining how she presents a variety of perspectives on any one event or subject and then creates her own context for and approach to it.*]

In Rita Dove's poetry collections, ***The Yellow House on the Corner*** (1980), ***Museum*** (1983), and ***Thomas and Beulah*** (1986), history is figured as a continuum of ostensibly discrete and quiescent events that, in actuality, shudder against each other, thus quaking the solid ground of our present moment. For Dove, nothing about history is static, stitched in place like the pages of a high school history textbook; nothing about it is placidly "objective," dependable, and *real.* Dove envisions history as motion itself, something, like the stars, constantly in flux, always coming toward or receding from those of us who inhabit the evanescent present. History, thus, necessarily produces multiple perspectives, various vantage points from which the same event can be seen and interpreted in vastly different ways. As a poet, Dove distrusts the complacency of Leopold Ranke's much-quoted remark that history can show a past event *"wie es eigentlich gewesen"*—"as it actually was," as it actually happened. She understands that historical accounts, whether written or oral, familial or public, are often undependable narrations of what happened to whom, for what reason, and to what end. Those

accounts contain the subtly encoded conscious and unconscious prejudices of the author, for as Jurij Lotman succinctly explains in *Universe of the Mind,* any "text is always created by someone for some purpose and events are presented in the text in encoded form."

What then is left for a poet like Dove, one who openly admits to the allure of an "ultimate—and ultimately unanswerable" question regarding personal and communal origins: "How does where I come from determine where I've ended up?" The answer lies in acknowledging one's essential connection to history's multiple perspectives and encodings, its constant flux, its reverberations. For a poet enamoured of the point of intersection of public and private history, as Dove clearly is, the poet's primary task becomes to attend to (and thus "decode") both the realm of public history, supposedly factual and objective, and that of private history, woven from the subjective thread of familial and individual memory. Just as importantly, Dove then re-encodes these accounts, using poetic imagination to infuse bare "fact" with the flash of insight and human emotion. In essence, Dove takes a "fact" and imagines a universe for it to inhabit. The result is a poem itself deeply encoded, as Lotman would have it, by the workings of poetic invention, a text which seeks poetic "truth" neither historical nor ahistorical, neither wholly true nor wholly invented.

That is why Dove's poems dealing with history show an equal interest in origins and endings; that is, she's as much concerned with how things began as with how events happened to end in, or lead to, the present. This mix of concerns creates a compelling tension in which her poetry borrows from forms as disparate as the historical novel and the mythological text. Here's how Lotman distinguishes between the orientation—and intentions—of these two forms:

> Historical narrative and novels associated with it are subject to temporal and causal sequence and as such are oriented towards the end. The main structural meaning is concentrated at the end of the text. The question 'how did it end?' is typical of our perception both of the historical episode and of the novel. Mythological texts which tell of the act of creation and of legendary originators are oriented towards the beginning. We see this . . . in the persistent question 'where did it come from?'. . . .

Dove balances these competing urges, seeking to examine both the origins of certain ideas or incidents and the repercussions they exert on present events—a condition perhaps most evident in ***Thomas and Beulah*** but prevalent in her other work as well. The poet's imagination continually moves backward from the present and forward from the past. The action is reflexive and restless, borne of the conviction that history is in flux and thus the poet must move with it.

It's no wonder, then, that so many of Dove's poems dealing with historical subjects show the subjects themselves in motion. Dove thus implies that life itself is choice in motion. **"The Abduction,"** for example, recounts the story of freed slave Solomon Northrup, who, along with his "new friends Brown and Hamilton," travels the circuit playing fiddle while the other two dance and collect pennies from the audience. Restless, but enlivened by his freedom of travel, Northrup falls prey to the treachery of his new "friends" and awakens, after a night of drinking wine, to find himself "in darkness and in chains," sold downriver into slavery. Likewise, **"Corduroy Road"** uses historical fact to underscore the relative peril of any foray into the wild and uncharted. That death attends every step of those who clear a *"track two rods wide / From Prairie du Chien to Fort Howard at Green Bay"* elicits this revelation:

> The symbol of motion is static, finite,
> And kills by the coachload.

The most poignant of these poems is surely **"The Transport of Slaves from Maryland to Mississippi."** Dove opens the poem with a one-sentence summary of its narrative content, which would, were her intentions purely narrative, make the poem that follows almost unnecessary: "(On August 22, 1839, a wagonload of slaves broke their chains, killed two white men, and would have escaped, had not a slave woman helped the Negro driver mount his horse and ride for help.)" But Dove is interested not so much in the incident as in the emotions and attitudes involved, those forces which have come to shape accounts of "what actually happened." Accentuating multiple perspectives, she divides the poem into three sections, based variously on historical fact or poetic invention. Dove recognizes the indeterminacy of historical fact, much as does Claude Lévi-Strauss in *The Savage Mind,* and includes in her poem conflicting versions of the incident which illustrate the disturbing distance among historial accounts of an event. Each of these is "biased," as Lévi-Strauss explains, "even when it claims not to be," simply for the reason that to answer the question, "Where did anything take place?", proves to be a knotty problem. Lévi-Strauss posits that one answer to this question must be simply "in the mind" of witness and participant, as well as in the mind of the historian who records and interprets these events. He makes his point by suggesting: "Each episode . . . resolves itself into a multitude of individual psychic moments. Each of these moments is the translation of unconscious development, and these resolve themselves into cerebral, hormonal, or nervous phenomena, which themselves have reference to the physical or chemical order. Consequently, historical facts are no more *given* than any other. It is the historian, or the agent of history, who constitutes them in abstraction. . . ."

As both poet and "agent of history," Dove imagines the first

section spoken in the voice of the slave woman. This section offers a rationale for the woman's behavior, as the following shows:

> The skin across his cheek bones
> burst open like baked yams—
> deliberate, the eyelids came apart—
> his eyes were my eyes in a yellower face.
> Death and salvation—one accommodates the
> other.
> I am no brute. I got feelings.
> He might have been a son of mine.

Denied her humanity by slavery, she nonetheless displays it through her compassionate actions, though she fatefully dooms both her fellows and herself to further slavery. She sees in the driver's "yellower" face, its color perhaps testifying to sex between master and slave, a version of her own fate, of her own victimization.

The other two sections of the poem suggest entirely different perspectives on the incident, perspectives more in keeping with "traditional" historical texts and the presumed reaction of white victims. The second section suggests that Dove, for the sake of contrast, is drawing from a found text—a more historically "objective" account of the incident—that is, history written by those in power: white citizens. The entire five-line section, composed in elevated as opposed to spoken dialect, is enclosed within quotation marks. The text details how the "Negro Gordon, barely escaping with his life" alerted the plantation owners, led a search, and thus ended "this most shocking affray and murder." It's the final section, however, that demonstrates clearly the intellectual distance separating the attitudes of the participants that August day in 1839. Hearing the commotion, baggage man Petit rushes to the wagon, thinking, *"some nigger's laid on another one's leg,"* and is surprised to see the slaves loose. Petit believes the slaves will fall passive before the snap of his whip and screams, *"Hold it!":* "but not even the wenches stopped. To his right Atkins dropped under a crown of clubs. They didn't even flinch. *Wait. You ain't supposed to act this way."*

Tremors emanating from the kind of racial stereotyping evident in Petit's remarks confound communication between the races to this day. One group "knows" another largely through the shifting ground of suspicion and prejudice, denying in each other a shared humanity which the poem's slave woman tragically embodies. Clearly the idea of "transport" operative in the poem rises beyond the literal to a metaphorical notion of movement toward knowledge of Self and Other. The slave owners, and to curious extent the Negro driver, unquestionably regard their payload as chattel, as property no more accorded human rights than cattle or hogs bound for market. They have been taught by law, custom, and social practice to consider slaves as less then human—a misconception at root in Petit's surprised "You ain't supposed to act this way." Petit and Atkins are instructed, though fatally so, in the confoundingly unpredictable quality of human nature these slaves share with them. The slaves' will to rise up, to refuse to "flinch" in the face of his whip teaches Petit a belated and deadly lesson in respect. However, that the slaves' response to their situation is not merely violent—witness the old woman's selfless act—underscores the humane sensibility of a people repressed by those held to be morally and intellectually superior. Thus, on one level, the "transport" Dove's poem alludes to involves movement toward greater understanding of what it means to be human. Through public and historical fact long since fallen silent, Dove reconnects her readers to the past and amplifies its message to the present.

Elsewhere in *Yellow House,* Dove's speaker herself becomes the traveler, the one in "transport" whose quest for knowledge of origins and endings demands that she set out to see things for herself. The result is a peripatetic poem, a walking tour of the fractured world, during which the speaker ruminates on and then postulates reasons for the unreasonable things she encounters. The best, **"Sight-seeing,"** concerns a speaker who has come upon a European church and its inner courtyard of statues damaged during World War II. The villagers have chosen to leave the dismembered statues exactly as they found them after the Allies departed. "Come here," the speaker asks the reader at the poem's beginning, "I want to show you something":

> What a consort
> of broken dolls! Look, they were mounted
> at the four corners of the third floor terrace
> and the impact from the cobblestones
>
> snapped off wings and other appendages.
> The heads rolled the farthest.

Realizing the scene engenders strong but various reactions, the speaker plays upon that ambiguity to establish a dialectic between the mongers of despair and belief, distrusting either extreme. The villagers who locked the gates in the face of this "terrible sign" overlook what the speaker does not: that good indeed did prevail over evil in the war, that civilization did indeed reestablish order over such chaos. To the speaker, heavenly intervention, or heavenly retribution, seems hardly the point. To clarify these multiple perspectives, the speaker first invokes Yeats' "The Second Coming" and then delineates the virtues of both remembering and forgetting:

> But all this palaver about symbols and
>
> "the ceremony of innocence drowned" is—

> as you and I know—civilization's way
> of manufacturing hope. Let's look
> at the facts. Forget they are children of angels
>
> and they become childish monsters.
> Remember, and an arm gracefully upraised
>
> is raised not in anger but a mockery of gesture.
> The hand will hold both of mine. . . .

This careful balancing of opposites, her playfulness with history's multiple perspectives, is characteristic of Dove's work. It accounts for why what is viewed by the speaker instructively as the "vulgarity / / of life in exemplary size" can be merely "a bunch of smashed statues" in the eyes of two drunks who take in the same scene at the poem's close.

The great distance between the levels of language cited above—the "smashed statues" and the "vulgarity / / of life in exemplary size"—emphasizes the role language has not only in expressing but also in ordering our lives. We come to know experience itself through language; we ponder and arrange and comprehend our lives through language. In other words, meaning is not just *reflected* in language but also something *produced* by it. Which is to say, we are forever confronting its enabling and limiting aspects. Moreover, one's sense of self, and implicitly the constraints and possibilities one finds in fashioning that self, are bound up in language. What we can—and cannot—say or think is a function of language, of having the words to say or think those things. Who cannot remember the elation of finding the word for a previously inarticulate idea or feeling, and the corollary rush of validation which accrued to that idea or feeling once there was a word for it? Or the sense of possibility one feels upon learning a new word, that door opening into a field abloom with flowers? To the contrary, who cannot remember the experience of having a word forced upon oneself, being "named" and thus having borders erected around the self which one may never escape.

As a poet examining public and private history, Dove must necessarily pay attention to language, the shared medium through which filter both public events and our private lives. It's not surprising that two of her most important poems focus on language's ability either to free or to enchain us. The first of these, **"Ö,"** from *Yellow House,* begins:

> Shape the lips to an o, say a.
> That's island.
> One word of Swedish has changed the whole
> neighborhood.
> When I look up, the yellow house on the corner
> is a galleon stranded in flowers.

The exotic sound and feel of the word on her lips, the sensual awareness of the Other transforms and intoxicates the speaker. It's almost as if, in that one word, she has also the *world* on her lips, lively as any lover's kiss, erotic as only words can be. Freed by language and thus no longer place bound, the speaker imagines a complementary world where motion is possibility and distance collapses before the power of language. Where historical time subsides in sea breezes, where the house on the corner might take off "over marsh- land" and neither the speaker nor her neighbor "would be amazed." In knowledge, in one word "so right / / it trembles," the speaker has found a way to alter her concep- tion of her Self and the possibilities her life might bring— transforming equally the present and the future she imagines:

> You start out with one thing, end
> up with another, and nothing's
> like it used to be, not even the future.

But if language can thus liberate and unify, Dove also ac- knowledges its counter ability to subjugate and divide. The haunting poem, **"Parsley,"** from *Museum,* recounts the story of Rafael Trujillo (1891-1961), dictator of the Dominican Republic, who, Dove tells us in an endnote, "ordered 20,000 blacks killed because they could not pronounce the letter 'r' in *perejil,* the Spanish word for parsley." The terrible asso- ciations of that one word counter the romantic exigency found in **"Ö."** Dove examines the abuses of power and vio- lence that stem from the idea of a dominant language, a so- called pure language that demarcates the empowered from the disempowered. Surely Dove, as an African-American, is conversant with the tension existing between a culture's dominant language and its dialects, and with the ways lan- guage is used to exclude some from membership in the domi- nant culture. Although history is not language itself, it comes to us—and thus we come to know it—through words, as Dove implies: ". . . the word [parsley], or the Haitians' ability to pronounce it, was something that created history. But his- tory is also the way we perceive it, and we do perceive it through words. . . . And language does shape our percep- tions. . . . the way we perceive things is, of course, circum- scribed by our ability to express those things."

Again Dove employs multiple perspectives to juxtapose dif- fering ways to inhabit the historical reality of these events; one lense is focused on experiences in the "Cane Fields" and the other on what happens in the "Palace." The poem's first section—a melodious villanelle—conveys the feelings of the field workers. Its horrific content seems to "smash," as Rob- ert McDowell asserts [in "The Assembling Vision of Rita Dove," *Callaloo,* Winter, 1986], "against the stark and beau- tiful container of the form." Here's the opening movement:

> There is a parrot imitating spring
> in the palace, its feathers parsley green.
> Out of the swamps the cane appears

to haunt us, and we cut it down. El General searches for a word; he is all the world there is. Like a parrot imitating spring

> we lie down screaming as rain punches through
> and we come up green. We cannot speak an R . . .

On the other hand, the poem's second section, a third-per- son narrative, traces the general's warped thought processes in language markedly different from that of the villanelle. The parrot, the green cane fields, the rain, and other lyric elements of the first section reappear, but this time they're couched in flat, declarative sentences that highlight the sur- real quality of the general's stream of consciousness:

> It is fall, when thoughts turn
> to love and death; the general thinks
> of his mother, how she died in the fall
> . . . . he stomps to
> her room in the palace, the one without
> curtains, the one with a parrot
> in a brass ring. As he paces he wonders
> Who can I kill today. . . .
>
> the general sees the fields of sugar
> cane, lashed by rain and streaming.
> He sees his mother's smile, the teeth
> gnawed to arrowheads. He hears
> the Haitians sing without R's . . .

Soon the general's love for his dead mother, who could "roll an R like a queen," becomes linked with his "love in death" and the sprig of parsley villagers wore to "honor the birth of a son." In name of the dominant language, in memory of his neurotic (and incestuous?) love for his mother, the gen- eral orders the killings "for a single, beautiful word." Thus, the poem offers a meditation on history examined through the powers and permutations of language.

The balancing of perspectives I've identified in Dove's work operates also within some of her most personal narratives, as in **"My Father's Telescope,"** where her father fails in his attempt to make the impossible become tangible:

> The oldest joke
> in the world,
> a chair on three legs. . . .
>
> After
> years of cupboards
> and end tables, after
> a plywood Santa
> and seven elves
> for the lawn in snow,

he knows.
He's failed, and
in oak.

Balance is so important to Dove it's no wonder she would focus on her father's efforts to level the chair's three legs; instead of achieving balance, the chair simply "shrinks" beneath the father's saw.

The chair is an apt symbol for Dove's sense of historical perspective, the seeking of which is perhaps the world's "oldest joke." History, like the chair, can't offer a solid and unmoving foundation; it shifts and lurches, tossing the unwary unceremoniously on their backsides. Two of its legs—public and private history—are notoriously unreliable and perhaps unmeasurable. The third, one's sense of self, much of which is necessarily intuitional and invented, requires a balanced negotiation between the other two. History therefore resides less in the physical event than in memory and language—intangible things that hold but cannot be held. It cannot literally be "made" like a chair. History, if made at all, is made only in the living of it; we have no way of extracting ourselves or history from the swirling events around us. We are, as Heidegger believed, intimately wrapped up in being-in-the-world, inextricably tied to it through our relations with our fellows.

The father's Christmas present for himself and his son, a telescope, redeems him in the speaker's eyes, for implicitly he comes to see that historical perspective demands a restless searching outside of the self. One needs such a telescope to see what happened, what is, and providently, what will be. The telescope also figures prominently in **"Anti-Father,"** a poem in which the now mature speaker dares to contradict both the Big Bang theory and her father's explanation that the "stars / are far apart":

> Rather
> they draw
>
> closer together
> with years. . . .
>
>   Stars
>
> speak to a child.
> The past
> is silent. . . .
> Just between
> me and you,
> woman to man,
>
> outer space is
> inconceivably

intimate.

That physical and historical space outside the self should appear intimately connected to the self ought not to surprise any reader of Dove's work. But the notion that the past is "silent" hardly seems to be the case for Dove, especially given her achievement in imaginatively tracing the lives of her grandparents in *Thomas and Beulah.* In fact, *Thomas and Beulah* can be seen as the culmination of Dove's poetic interest in history as lives in motion, for she draws freely from both public and familial history, supplementing these accounts, where the fabric of fact frays, with the whole cloth of poetic invention.

Thomas and Beulah, as the title implies, is foremost the story of two lives caught amidst the cascading events of the early-to mid-twentieth century United States. Dove organizes the book in keeping with what by now ought to be her familiar devotion to multiple perspectives, dividing it into two sections, each relating the life and personal perspective of one title character. If one should doubt the importance of these multiple perspectives, Dove opens the book with the following invocation: "These poems tell two sides of a story and are meant to be read in sequence." Two sides of a single story, two angles which proceed ineluctably from the intersection of lives in fact and happening; one story interwoven of two distinct threads. It is tempting to consider such an arrangement dialogic, but to do so is to elevate form over substance. Thomas and Beulah don't so much as speak *to* each other as *about* each other, and their stories are told in the third person, refusing the intimacy (and narrative complications) of first person. True enough, their versions of one event often diverge, and those differing views, as we shall see, reveal much about one character's view of the other. Still, the dialogue is implicit, restrained, and understated.

However, these two lives are placed in dialogue with larger historical reality. To emphasize this dialogic historical context, Dove appends a chronology that lists both familial and public events such as the births of children and the 1963 Civil Rights March on Washington. In an aesthetic sense, it performs a necessary function, filling in the gaps which the elliptical form of the poems often leaves unspoken. If there's a shortcoming to the book, it lies in the reliance on slow accrual to gradually provide narrative facts omitted from individual poems. It's difficult to discern, for example, in the poem **"The Oriental Ballerina,"** that Beulah's blurred and nearly opaque view of her bedroom results from glaucoma—unless one consults the next to last item in the chronology. In another, largely historical sense, Dove has other intentions for the chronology: "It's a very eccentric chronology, so you can see what was happening in the social structure of midwest America at the time this couple was growing up." Just how thoroughly Dove envisions history as lives in motion is made clear in the book's first poem. When we meet

Thomas in **"The Event,"** he stands upon the deck of a riverboat heading north from Tennessee. This initial "fact" of the book has its source in familial oral history, handed down from one generation to the next like a precious heirloom, as Dove explains: "My grandmother had told me a story that had happened to my grandfather when he was young, coming up on a riverboat to Akron, Ohio, my hometown. But that was all I had basically. And the story so fascinated me that I tried to write stories about it." But this fact soon becomes insufficient. When family history evaporates, Dove discovers another wellspring to feed her story: ". . . because I ran out of real fact, in order to keep going, I made up facts for this character, Thomas." Through the workings of imagination, through "made up facts," Dove's grandfather becomes something larger than the reality of his life. He becomes "this character, Thomas," embodying not only himself but also others whose lives have gone unexamined and unrecounted. George Garrett summarizes the difficulty and reward of thus imagining history [in "Dreaming with Adam: Notes on Imaginary History," in *New Directions in Literary History,* 1974]: "To write imaginary history is to celebrate the human imagination. Not one's own. . . . The subject is the larger imagination, the possibility of imagining lives and spirits of other human beings, living or dead, without assaulting their essential and, anyway, ineffable mystery, to dream again in recapitulation the dream of Adam, knowing, as he did until he awoke, that it is true; for Adam dreamed in innocence. We can only imagine that condition."

This is especially true if one considers how Dove uses poetic invention to meld private and public history: Thomas, in his trip up river to the North, takes part in this century's huge exodus of blacks from America's southern states to those of the North. Heading out in hopes of work and the new life it might afford, Thomas partakes in what has been called the "Great Migration," 1915-60, during which nearly five million African-Americans from the rural South migrated to the cities of the industrial North. The movement's root cause lies first in the failure of blacks to receive the "forty acres and a mule" promised after the Civil War, but by the beginning of the century a more insidious cause was to blame as racial violence often culminated in lynchings. In addition to the usually cited wage differentials and "expansion of employment opportunities in the North," and the general disenfranchisement of black voters in the South, [in "Rethinking the Role of Racial Violence in the Great Migration," in *Black Exodus: The Great Migration from the American South,* 1991] Stewart Tolnay and E. M. Beck point to a possible and surprising "reciprocal relationship between black migration and racial violence, that is, that violence induced migration, which in turn moderated the level of violence." What is clear is that blacks chose to leave the South generally as last recourse, as is evident in an editorial published in the militant *Atlanta Independent* and addressed to white Southerners in 1917: "This is our home and . . . we are not going to leave, unless we are driven by want and lack of freedom." Elsewhere, the editorial asks that whites welcome blacks into the social and economic infrastructure, arguing that whites ought to "open the doors of the shops, of the industries and facilities for our children; because we love them as they do their children." Such social change, history tells us, proceeded at a snail's pace.

Whatever the reason for his departure in 1919, Thomas's personal motives become part and parcel of historical fact when he leaves Tennessee and settles later in Akron. Thomas is one of those responsible for the North experiencing a net population gain of over 500,000 blacks in the decade of 1910-20, a rush of migration no doubt accelerated by the industrialization accompanying the country's war effort.

On the riverboat, drunk from the heady effects of both possibility and cheap wine, Thomas sings to the accompaniment of his "inseparable" friend Lem's mandolin. The scene is exotic with moonlight and "tarantulas" among the boat's cargo of bananas, and one "boast" leads to another. Lem dives overboard for chestnuts crowning a river delta island, but tragically

> the island slipped
> under, dissolved
> in the thickening steam.

Lem drowns, disappearing from the poem but not from Thomas's psyche. He looms large in Thomas's life, presiding like a revenant returning from death on numerous occasions—all of which lends itself to Dove's strategy to build the book's narrative in lyric pieces and thus by accrual. Thomas feels Lem's presence or hears his words when he and Beulah buy a new car (**"Nothing Down"**), when, after his working at the zeppelin factory, he sees the Goodyear blimp "Akron" float over (**"The Zeppelin Factory"**), and when in dream he imagines the dead Lem "naked and swollen / under the backyard tree" (**"The Charm"**). Lem evokes such strong presence in Thomas's sensibility that when a stroke threatens to end his life, Thomas believes the pain was simply "Lem's knuckles tapping his chest in passing" (**"The Stroke"**).

Because Dove is, as I've suggested, a poet who envisions history as lives in motion, it's curious that in the midst of so much movement there is relatively little overt reference to great events in The Movement—black America's movement for racial and social equality. In fact, Arnold Rampersad, noting [in "The Poems of Rita Dove," *Callaloo,* Winter, 1986] that Dove writes "few poems about racism today," argues that she "apparently declines to dwell on the links between past history and present history." However, Dove's linking of past and present racial history is, as we've seen, implicit and understated. Admittedly, Dove's work lacks racial pungency, but much like Yusef Komunyakaa's poems of racial history, her poems work implicitly to link past and present grievances. It is precisely in the common and day-to-day experiences of African-Americans that Dove deals with racial bigotry, and often in subtle terms. Dove shows a fondness for "small" history as opposed to "big historical events," choosing, as she explains, to "talk about things which no one will remember but which are just as important in shaping our concept of ourselves and the world we live in as the biggies, so to speak." Take, for example, **"Nothing Down,"** in which Thomas and Beulah venture south to Tennessee in a new car, a "sky blue Chandler!", which ought to signal their success on the literal and figurative road to achieving the American Dream. (The automobile is, of course, the American symbol of freedom and mobility as well). Instead, in an incident tart with irony, the car breaks down outside Murfreesboro and a jeering

> . . . carload of white men
> halloo past them on route 231.
> "You and your South!" she shouts
> above the radiator hiss.

And then there's **"Roast Possum,"** a delightful poem showing Thomas reading to his grandchildren from the 1909 edition of the Werner encyclopedia, telling tales of possum hunting and embellishing the story of "Strolling Jim," a horse "who could balance / a glass of water on his back / and trot the village square / without spilling a drop." In the midst of this quaint domestic scene, Thomas considers telling the children another, more disturbing item from the Werner: "He could have gone on to tell them / that the Werner admitted Negro children / to be intelligent, though briskness / clouded over at puberty, bringing / indirection and laziness." Thomas says nothing of the above, choosing to continue his story of possum hunting, but Dove's poem says it for him—his silence speaking more loudly than her words.

These "small" events demarcate the pressures of "big" history on our lives, engraining its very texture into the day-to-day activities we often pass off with hardly a shrug. Occasionally, one of those events stands out in relief from the casual backdrop of our lives, and the light of our attention strikes at just the right angle to bring it forth into consciousness. We are then made suddenly aware of the strangeness of the apparently normal. Precisely this occurs in Dove's **"Wingfoot Lake,"** where the pattern of Beulah's personal life on July Fourth 1964 becomes portentously intermingled with public history on a grand scale:

> Now this act of mercy: four daughters
> dragging her to their husband's company picnic,
> white families on one side and them
> on the other, unpacking the same

> squeeze bottles of Heinz, the same
> waxy beef patties and Salem potato chip bags.

The repetition of "the same," of course, accentuates what's simply not the same for the two groups, whites and blacks absurdly minding the color line while dishing out identical picnic lunches at Good-year's Wingfoot Lake. Despite the similar menus, the two groups surely don't see themselves—their social lives as well—as equal, as "the same." Considering that the poem is set, perhaps none too subtly, on Independence Day, only emphasizes the point. In a rare gesture of overt acknowledgment of larger historical events, Dove allows Beulah to reflect on the scene in the context of the 1963 Civil Rights March on Washington:

> Last August she stood alone for hours
> in front of the T.V. set
> as a crow's wing moved slowly through
> the white streets of government.
> That brave swimming
> scared her, like Joanna saying
> *Mother, we're Afro-Americans now!*
> What did she know about Africa?
> Were there lakes like this one
> with a rowboat pushed under the pier?
> Or Thomas' Great Mississippi
> with its sullen silks?. . . .
>   Where she came from
> was the past, 12 miles into town
> where nobody locked their back door,
> and Goodyear hadn't begun to dream of a park
> under the company symbol, a white foot
> sprouting two small wings.

The poem's lines of demarcation between the races are apparent, though nonetheless compelling. The black "crow's wing" of marchers moving through the "white streets" of our federal government; the white wings and foot of the Goodyear symbol set alongside the segregated black picnickers. What's equally striking is the line marking sides of the black experience. The line between the terms "Negro" and "Afro-American" implies a disparate fashioning of self both invoked and embodied by language. In a nod to the powers of language reminiscent of **"Ö"** and **"Parsley,"** the poem speaks to the ability of a people to rename and thus remake themselves.

Such change can be disquieting, even within the affected group itself. It implicitly strikes a line between old and new—between Beulah, the old woman of a rural "past" of unlocked back doors, and her children, inhabitants of an urban present. Inexorably, the movement for social equality, "slowly" as it's destined to move, has begun to evoke change in the lives of older blacks like Beulah, for whom new pride in her African heritage is understandably both exciting and somewhat unsettling. Beulah surely knows less of Africa than she does of the rural South she and her family fled in 1906 during the early stages of the Great Migration, less of the Nile than of "Thomas' Great Mississippi." Thus Beulah feels doubly uprooted, doubly removed from her origins. Where has the incessant movement of her race—and of history in general—brought her, and more importantly, to what has it delivered her children? Nearly fifty years after the *Atlanta Independent*'s call for whites to "open the doors" of industry to black children, Beulah's children have found that economic equality in the North. They have not, however, found social equality. It is the stubborn constancy of that fact, rooted in racial bigotry, that gives depth and measure to the kind of restless motion that permeates Dove's poetry. The poem suggests that in 1964, one year after the march on Washington, much marching remains to be done, much "transport" toward a goal still distant in 1996. For a poet not usually associated with pungent racial commentary, Dove has fashioned a poignant statement on the notion of social change.

If, as Helen Vendler argues [in "In the Zoo of the New," *New York Review of Books,* October, 1986], Dove's is poetry of the "disarticulated," it is in her presentation of the inchoate and unspoken histories of these individuals that Dove gives them voice. It is almost painful to witness Thomas and Beulah, two people clearly devoted to each other, continually misinterpret each other's behavior. Even the intimate act of courting carries with it high stakes, a gamble in which one's acts or those of fate can be misread for good or ill, as **"Courtship"** examines when Thomas sets aside his mandolin and

> . . . wraps the yellow silk
> still warm from his throat
> around her shoulders. (He made
> good money; he could buy another.)
> A gnat flies
> in his eye and she thinks
> he's crying.

What follows reminds one, in both image and idea, of **"Ö"**; suddenly, the future's sail is taut with the intoxicating breezes of possibility:

> Then the parlor festooned
> like a ship and Thomas
> twirling his hat in his hands
> wondering how did I get here.

Still, the distance between Thomas's and Beulah's perspectives on this scene proves chilling; it sighs like an inarticulate gulf stretching between them. Beulah's version of these events, given in **"Courtship, Diligence,"** takes the wind out of Thomas's solicitude:

> Cigar-box music!
> She'd much prefer a pianola
> and scent in a sky-colored flask.

> Not that scarf, bright as butter.
> Not his hands, cool as dimes.

Occasions such as these give Dove the opportunity to replay one of her favorite tunes: the unreliability of fact, whether historical or familial—and thus the daunting task of interpreting static truth from events fraught with multiple perspectives.

The restless motion that characterizes the subjects of Dove's poems animates Beulah's yearning to break free of her circumscribed roles of wife and mother. If Thomas continually yearns for a place to go fishing (see, for instance, **"Lightnin' Blues"** and **"One Volume Missing"**), Beulah fretfully wishes to escape to a more exotic location, namely, France. In **"The Great Palaces of Versailles,"** she irons alterations in the "backroom of Charlotte's Dress Shoppe" while musing on what she'd once read in the library:

> how French ladies at court would tuck
> their fans in a sleeve
> and walk in the gardens for air. Swaying
> among the lilies, lifting shy layers of silk . . .

The agent of her travel is, of course, not literal but literary, and unsatisfyingly brief as well. Such travel requires a turn of mind, a "rehearsed deception," as the poem **"Magic"** refers to it. With concerted practice in evasions of reality, she convinces herself that a picture of the Eiffel Tower in the Sunday paper amounts to a "sign / / she would make it to Paris one day."

She makes it only as far as the backyard. In **"Daystar,"** Beulah successfully creates space for herself, "a little room for thinking," by toting a chair out back "behind the garage" while the children nap. It is perhaps the most disconcerting of Dove's "travelogue" poems. On most days, Beulah's trip offers highlights as mundane as a "floating maple leaf" or a dead cricket; on others, she closes her eyes to see "her own vivid blood." Each day her flight ends with a violent crash:

> She had only an hour, at best, before Liza appeared
> pouting from the top of the stairs.
> and just what was mother doing
> out back with the field mice?

That coming and going, the frenetic fleeing of one moment into another is the very stuff of Dove's view of public and private life: history as lives in motion. The wish to still that cease-less motion could well have been the impetus behind the mostly nostalgic and autobiographical poems of her recent collection **Grace Notes,** a book replete with memories of childhood sum-mers, youthful math proficiency, and the animated behavior of parents, sisters and brother, and assorted aunts. I say *wish* be-cause the book acknowledges the futility of that urge by its very celebration of times long gone. In the poem **"Ozone,"** even the present lurches ineluctably into the past, into "history." One can detect both the momentary longing for stasis and an equal awareness of its unavailability in the conditional "If only" which opens the closing movement of the poem:

> If only we could lose ourselves
> in the wreckage of the moment! Forget
> where we stand, dead center, and
> look up, look up,
> track a falling star . . .
>   now you see it
>   now you don't

"Daystar" aptly suggests the goal of much of Dove's poetry: to recognize, within the vagaries of personal and communal his-tory, our "own vivid blood." It is perhaps her best response to the "ultimately unanswerable" human question of "where I come from." Dove acknowledges history's multiple perspectives and encodings and its perpetual flux. If historical fact and family tale and even personal experience shudder with indeterminacy, if history "as it actually was" must elude her, she settles for what might have happened, how, and why—all from multiple van-tage points. She searches equally for origins and endings and yet distrusts both. In the end, if indeterminacy is our only claim, she answers the unreliability of history with the "truth" of po-etic imagination.

FURTHER READING

Criticism

Cook, Emily Walker. "'But She Won't Set Foot / in His

Turtle-Dove Nash': Gender Roles and Gender Symbolism in Rita Dove's *Thomas and Beulah.*" *College Language Association Journal* 38, No. 3 (March 1995): 21-36.

> Examines Dove's treatment of gender in *Thomas and Beulah,* and illustrates how the gender-specific expe-riences and perspectives determine the nature and form of the poetry.

Georgoudaki, Ekaterini. "Rita Dove: Crossing Boundaries." *Callaloo* 14, No. 2 (1991): 419-33.

> Illuminates Dove's challenging of traditional poetic topics, voices, characters, and perspectives, and ex-plains how circumstances in Dove's personal life in-form her tendency to cross barriers of gender, race, class, society, culture, and literature.

Neilen, Deirdre. Review of *The Darker Face of the Earth,* by Rita Dove. *World Literature Today* 71, No. 2 (Spring 1997): 389.

> Offers a laudatory review of *The Darker Face of the Earth,* calling it "an important play."

Rampersad, Arnold. "The Poems of Rita Dove." *Callaloo* 9, No. 1 (Winter 1986): 52-60.

> An often-cited essay in which Rampersad surveys Dove's works and characterizes her as "surely one of the three or four most gifted young black American po-ets since LeRoi Jones . . . and perhaps the most disci-plined and technically accomplished black poet to arrive since Gwendolyn Brooks. . . ."

Shoptaw, John. "Dove's *Thomas and Beulah.*" In *Reading Black, Reading Feminist: A Critical Anthology,* edited by Henry Louis Gates, Jr., pp. 374-81. New York: Meridian, 1990.

> Explores the poems in *Thomas and Beulah.*

Interviews

Cavalieri, Grace. "Rita Dove: An Interview." *The American Poetry Review* 24, No. 2 (March/April 1995): 11-15.

> Dove discusses her works and career.

> **Additional coverage of Dove's life and career is contained in the following sources published by Gale:** *Black Writers,* **Vol. 2;** *Contemporary Authors,* **Vol. 109;** *Contem-porary Authors Autobiography Series,* **Vol. 19;** *Contemporary Authors New Revision Series,* **Vols. 27 and 42;** *Contemporary Literary Criticism,* **Vols. 50 and 81;** *DISCovering Authors Modules: Multicultural Authors* **and** *Poets; Dictionary of Literary Biography,* **Vol. 120; and** *Poetry Criticism,* **Vol. 6.**

Leon Forrest
1937-1997

American novelist, essayist, and playwright.

INTRODUCTION

Forrest, a critically acclaimed African-American writer, is recognized primarily for his epic-length, stream-of-consciousness novels that explore the African-American experience. Although he tells the story of a particular people, his themes and characterizations, his eloquent, jazz-like prose, and his wry sense of humor have universal appeal. Like his contemporaries Toni Morrison, Albert Murray, Gayl Jones, and James Alan McPherson, he embodies in his works the rich oral traditions of storytellers and songwriters. Critics have compared his innovative style to James Joyce, William Faulkner, Ralph Ellison, and Dylan Thomas. He has received several literary awards, including the Chicago Public Library Carl Sandburg Award for his novel *Two Wings to Veil My Face* (1985), and *The New York Times* Notable Book of the Year Award for his novel *Divine Days* (1992). Stanley Crouch has called *Divine Days* "an adventurous masterwork . . . [a] virtuoso fusion of idiomatic detail and allusions to the worlds of literature, religion and folklore."

Biographical Information

The only child of Adeline Green Forrest and Leon Forrest, Sr., Forrest was born and raised on the South Side of Chicago. His father was a bartender on the Santa Fe railroad who composed lyrics, and his mother, a short story writer, admired the great jazz vocalists of the time. His parent's literary and musical sidelines, his exposure to the Scriptures and to the Roman Catholic and the Protestant faiths, and his friendship with numerous storytellers on both sides of the family fueled his literary development and interest in oral tradition. Forrest attended Wilson Junior College, Roosevelt University, and the University of Chicago before he was drafted into the Army in 1960. He was sent to Germany where he served as Public Information Specialist on the newspaper *Spearhead*. After returning to civilian life, he worked first as a bartender, then as a writer and editor for several South Side weekly newspapers, but he dreamed of becoming a playwright or poet. To that end, he took literature and creative writing courses at the University of Chicago from 1962 to 1963. In 1966, he published his first short story, which would later become part of his first novel. He married in 1971 while working for the newspaper *Muhammad Speaks*. Serving as the last non-Muslim editor of this Nation of Islam newspaper (1969-1973) gave Forrest a close-up look at the complexity of African-American life.

In 1973, Random House published his first novel, *There Is a Tree More Ancient than Eden,* for which Ralph Ellison wrote the foreword. That fall, he was appointed professor of African-American studies and English literature at Northwestern University in Evanston, Illinois. He would later become chairman of African-American studies (1985-1994). From 1974 to 1979, he was a visiting lecturer at Yale University, Rochester Institute of Technology, and Wesleyan University. Forrest was one of four Chicago-area novelists to be awarded the Chicago Public Library's gold medallion in 1978. He was elected to membership in the Society of Midland Authors in 1979 and became vice president of that society in 1980. He authored an opera libretto commissioned by the Indiana University School of Music in 1980, and a play. Of his four published novels, his award-winning *Divine Days* is considered his masterpiece. Forrest died of cancer in 1997.

Major Works

Forrest's first novel, *There Is a Tree More Ancient than Eden* (1973), concerns the relationships between the illegitimate children of a former slave-owning family. The story blends American cultural myth, black American history, black fundamentalist religion, and Catholicism. His second novel, *The Bloodworth Orphans* (1977), expands on the first, and several characters from the first novel, notably Nathaniel Witherspoon, reappear in this story. Central to this novel is the theme of abandonment and lost connections. In both novels, secular and spiritual oral testimony play a major role. In *Orphans,* the author has included recurring thematic motifs to help the reader sort through the multitude of characters and sequences of events. Forrest continued to probe the literary possibilities of oral tradition in *Two Wings to Veil My Face* (1984). Once again Nathaniel Witherspoon appears, this time to record the life story of Momma Sweetie Reed, a former slave, also seen earlier in *There Is a Tree.* As he transcribes her memories, Nathaniel is forced to redefine his own identity. Forrest's fourth and best-received novel is his 1,135-page epic, *Divine Days,* in which an aspiring playwright from Chicago's South Side, Joubert Jones, sets out to find the missing legend among South Side blacks, Sugar-Groove. In the process, Forrest explores African-American history through vivid characterization, literary and religious allusions, and punful wordplay. Forrest himself has described the book as "the *Ulysses* of Chicago's South Side." *Relocations of the Spirit* (1994) is a collection of Forrest's essays on the lives of prominent African-Americans, including Toni Morrison, Ralph Ellison, and Billie Holiday, as well as white writers, especially William Faulkner.

Critical Reception

Critical assessment of Forrest's work has been mostly favorable in literary and academic circles, although his popular audience is still relatively narrow. Critics have compared him to James Joyce, William Faulkner, Ralph Ellison, and Dylan Thomas. He is best known for his epic novels. With the publication of his first, *There Is a Tree More Ancient than Eden,* critic Robert Bone named it one of the important works by a black writer to appear in the 1970s. In particular, critics praised Forrest for his innovative style, "like an artist working in mosaic," according to George Cohen. Others commented on the wide range of individual and collective experience covered, and his memorable characters. *The Bloodworth Orphans* received mixed reviews. Although *Orphans* was praised for its eloquence, vivid characterization, and humor, some critics felt the story was overly complex and its thematic structure vague. On the other hand, an excerpt of *Two Wings to Veil My Face,* submitted as a work-in-progress, won the 1980 Illinois Arts Counsel Literary Award. Bernard Rodgers of the *Chicago Tribune Book World* concluded that the completed novel is for readers "who can recognize the magic beneath the mundane, as Forrest does . . . extraor-

dinary and unforgettable." Joseph Coates of *Chicago Tribune Books* has compared Forrest's fourth novel, *Divine Days* to James Joyce's *Finnegans Wake;* and Stanley Crouch of *The New York Times Book Review* has called it his masterpiece.

PRINCIPAL WORKS

There Is a Tree More Ancient than Eden (novel) 1973
The Bloodworth Orphans (novel) 1977
Two Wings to Veil My Face (novel) 1984
Divine Days (novel) 1992
Relocations of the Spirit (essays) 1994

CRITICISM

Joel Motley (review date 1974)

SOURCE: A review of *There Is a Tree More Ancient than Eden,* in *The Harvard Advocate,* Vol. CVII, No. 4, 1974, pp. 59-60.

[*In the following review, Motley describes Forrest's novel* There Is a Tree More Ancient than Eden *as a spiritual and historical odyssey that builds on William Faulkner's style.*]

For those of us who struggle to grow as individuals—tied to history yet constantly peering into the future, self-impressed but ashamed, self-centered though socially committed, finished with church-going and yet always seeking faith, ***There Is a Tree More Ancient than Eden*** is a welcome companion. To read it is to travel with the author on his spiritual, historical and personal odyssey—moving through a series of intense descriptions and responses, drawn from life in the streets, in the home and in black history. Using dialogue, testimony (the personal and religious kind), stream of consciousness and brief narratives, Forrest has produced a powerful work of literature. The book is written like a jazz composition: it begins with a core theme and then moves on to elaborations and explorations of the theme's possible variations. All the tensions of personal growth, race and religion which Forrest later treats are presented in a six-page self-portrait at the beginning of the book. The resolution, the book's conclusion, is one of themes rather than plot. . . .

Forrest's descriptions of people and places present a wealth of details from the black and the American experiences. The "lives" which follow the first self-portrait are brief but amazingly comprehensive portraits of people who have influenced Forrest's life. Each portrait has a completeness which is characteristic of other parts of the book; they can be read and appreciated separately. The book is held together, however, by Forrest's spirit which searched on all the levels of his experience and imagination for a place, a coherence, on this "faithstripping, long journey road that life is. . . ." The artistic achievement of this book lies in Forrest's mastery of a wide variety of forms which accompany his many changes of subject and mood. The language and rhythm of each section are beautifully suited to its subject.

Forrest's expression of spiritual searchings is particularly fine. The sense of a black man's spiritual odyssey—an odyssey with historical causes and deeply personal effects—is communicated in several moving passages. . . .

The mixture of contemporary and historical vision, the transcending symbols and images all combine to produce a new form of expressing the black, and indeed the human, experience. Faulkner mastered a writing style which used long, expansive sentences to convey the weight of history on his characters. Forrest borrows heavily from Faulkner, but he builds on Faulkner's mode. By infusing it with new rhythms and subjects he expands that writing style into a new medium for conveying the black, and particularly the urban-black, experience.

Anatole Broyard (review date 1 May 1977)

SOURCE: A review of *The Bloodworth Orphans,* in *The New York Times Book Review,* May 1, 1977, pp. 12, 55.

[*In the following review, Broyard faults Forrest's* The Bloodworth Orphans *for its stale story line and ethnic egocentrism.*]

Leon Forrest's first novel, ***There Is a Tree More Ancient than Eden,*** was like a rendering of one of the great old standard blues songs by a modern jazzman. The tension between past and present in Southern black life was expressed through the way Mr. Forrest interpreted the melody: using the moods and mocking them too, mixing nostalgia and irony, jubilance and rage, croon and staccato.

The Bloodworth Orphans resembles one of those post-bop renderings of an original composition by a member of the band, something with almost no melody, a mere excuse for harmonic toying and empty pyrotechnics. It's hard to know where you are in such a performance: even the soloists lose themselves from time to time and gargle meaningless runs while they try to get their bearings. In his first book, Mr. Forrest was firmly rooted in his culture, while in the second he, too, is as homeless and parentless as the orphans of his title or the illegitimate children who stud his pages.

In the earlier book, the author's passion was social; in this

one, it's literary. You might say that his rhetoric has become rhetorical. According to the dust jacket, ***The Bloodworth Orphans*** is "about the lives and interconnected relationships of the bastards and orphans—both black and white—sired by members of a slave-owning family named Bloodworth." This results in such stale stuff as a brother and sister falling in love before they know that they are related and then suffering the fury of their half-brother. Other sisters are raped by their respective unrecognized brothers, and so on. Sid Caesar used to do a wonderful parody of the Victorian novel, in which everyone turns out to be related at the end. Mr. Forrest, however, seems to be dead serious, and the tragedy of black life under slavery is reduced to a sensationalized incestuous gang-bang.

There was a time that Jewish intellectuals struggling with their alienation came to be called parochial, and perhaps the same charge could be laid at Mr. Forrest's door. His book suffers from ethnic egocentrism, an unexamined assumption that *anything* about blacks is interesting. These characters may not even be blacks: they seem more like caricatures, forcing language for attention much as an old-fashioned Negro waiter forced a smile in order to get a tip. Mr. Forrest's people use "lord" to pivot a sentence as Samuel Johnson used "sir." They soup up their speech with "blood" and "death" and "glory." As if they were all traumatized by reading Gerard Manley Hopkins, they share a passion for hyphenation too. Here is a typical sample: ". . . beast-of-burden body, tower-tolling and bell-delivering whole-note-lost-ness, in quest, in flight, climbing climbing climbing and back back back inside a bubble-babble, and vanishing body of recharged, violin-souring, joy romping canyons. . . ."

Years ago, in a nightclub, Harry Belafonte sang a melodramatic song about lynching, all the while holding his head on one side as if he was dangling from a rope. Considering his crooner's voice, his spoiled-darling face and easy sophistication, the number could only be regarded as a collusion with the predominantly white audience, an in-joke. Inasmuch as Mr. Forrest is no Belafonte, his book might be called an out-joke.

Joseph Coates (review date 2 August 1992)

SOURCE: "A Vast Swirl of Voices," in *Chicago Tribune Books,* August 2, 1992, Sec. 14, p. 3.

[*In the following review, Coates commends Forrest's novel* Divine Days, *comparing it to James Joyce's* Finnegans Wake.]

The book at hand—both hands, actually, because it has the heft as well as the ambitions, and some of the accomplishments, of a classic—is the fourth and probably capstone novel by a Chicago writer of immense talent who has been officially recognized in various ways but remains almost unknown even in his native city, even though in this book the black South Side attains an immortality as palpable as the Irish-immigrant version in James T. Farrell's Studs Lonigan trilogy. Such writers as Saul Bellow, Ralph Ellison and Toni Morrison have known about Leon Forrest for years, and one hopes *Divine Days* finally will establish him in the minds of the people he has been chronicling for almost a generation.

Divine Days is organized, as much as such a massive work can be, into the seven-day journal of Joubert Jones (the first entry is dated Wednesday, Feb. 16, 1966, 6 a.m.). An aspiring playwright recently returned from a two-year army stint in Germany, Joubert hopes to use his journal-keeping "as a springboard for my dramatic ventures," especially a play about the recently deceased "Sugar-Groove, the mythic soul of Forest [read Cook] County, whose early memory was forged mainly in Mississippi," from which Joubert hopes "to discover a meaning of existence out of this man's divine days upon this planet."

Though the critic John Cawelti and Forrest himself call this novel "the *Ulysses* of Chicago's South Side," the real model for *Divine Days* is *Finnegans Wake,* with its shifty cast of multi-masked selves, its intent to encapsulate the history of a people in the endless swirl of their personal and social identities and its playfully punful language, all organized around a death or deaths and at least one funeral.

To be sure, halfway through this huge book the mysterious and misidentified "McIntosh" from Paddy Dignam's funeral in *Ulysses* does make a cameo appearance as witness to a violent street incident. But about 70 pages later we hear Joubert bemoaning "Oh, conflicted me . . . Not [W. E. B.] Du Bois' formula of double-consciousness, but rather one of a hundred headed hog-cheese voices of madness from my literary genesis" and then quoting from the "Wake" Shaun's denunciation of his brother Shem the Penman for his scurrilous depictions of holy Ireland: "You were bred, fed, fostered from holy childhood up in this two easter island . . . and now, forsooth, a nogger among the blankards of this dastard century . . . you have reared your disunited kingdom on the vacuum of your most intensely doubtful soul."

That passage is appropriate both to Forrest's theme and the black experience of America: "this two easter island" referring to America, land of the second and third chance, except, perhaps, for those brought here in chains, while "the disunited kingdom" reared by the "nogger [nigger] among the blankards [white, worthless, as in blanks/drunkards of America's reigning race] points to the difficult creation of a whole alternative culture embodied in jazz, rap and religion.

Incidentally, the novel's trickster/prophet, W. A. D. Ford, clearly is a warts-and-all portrait of a real man of many names who founded the Black Muslims in Detroit in 1930, Wali Farad, a.k.a. Wallace D. Fard Muhammad, Professor Ford, or simply the Prophet. As managing editor of *Muhammad Speaks* in the early 1970s, Forrest probably heard a good deal about the man who had handed over the reins of the Temple of Islam to Elijah Muhammad.

Joubert's seven-day quest—which echoes the plan of Creation in Genesis and thus comprises the stages of his own self-creation—subjects him to a whole orchestra of voices as he tracks down the various people who have pieces of the puzzle that is Sugar-Groove, who in turn is the key not only to Joubert's individual identity but also to the whole black experience in America. Each of these encounters, and its accompanying sermon/speech, is an initiation, an imparting of secrets that connect up with his own childhood memories of Sugar-Groove, his mythical father, which are then resurrected into our experience of Joubert's fateful week.

This is a perilous journey indeed, because Joubert is not only obsessed but also possessed by voices, and has to tape his mouth shut while he writes lest one or more of them take charge of his project and of him as well. Just such a disaster occurs on the evening of Joubert's first day home, when he gets drunk while tending bar in his Aunt Eloise's Night Light Lounge, which happens to be the site where the phony prophet W. A. D. Ford once had his mission, and this ambient evil spirit speaks through Joubert with disastrous results.

Retailing homosexual slander about another preacher, as Ford had often done, Joubert almost gets shot by one of the rival preacher's devoted, if alcoholic, parishioners, a little old lady with a .44.

"If you can make them believe and live out your fantasy of their realities," Ford had once told Joubert, "you've already taken them to heaven. . . . Ah, divine days." Thus, when mad Daisy Dawes, who also knew Ford, comes up with her pistol, she tells Joubert, who punctured her fantasy: "NIGGER, I'M CALLING YOU OUT TO FLY YOU ON HOME!"

This original sin on Joubert's part (sexual slander arising from alcoholic rhetorical riffing) echoes through all the novel's ensuing divine days of talk and obsessive monologue in much the same way that HCE's alleged sexual misbehavior in Phoenix Park resonates through the "Wake." In both cases a bar is involved, as well as a Promethean assumption of godlike power.

"Was I, by God, engodded?" Joubert inquires of himself, as with a drunken writer's eloquence he orchestrates the minds of the 12 disciple/customers on the other side of the bar, who themselves are drunk enough to take his words as Gospel.

And just as HCE changes shape and role with protean speed to embody in succession the primal figures of the Western world, so the sublime and mythical Sugar-Groove, the incarnate voice not only of Forest County but also of the black South itself, dissolves into a sea of contradictory identities and voices.

In the same way that a reader of Joyce's classic conundrum needs such help as Adaline Glasheen's "A Census of *Finnegans Wake*," which includes a chart titled "Who Is Who When Everybody Is Somebody Else," so the new reader of Forrest should approach *Divine Days* with a copy of one of his previous novels, *The Bloodworth Orphans,* which contains an introduction from Cawelti to all Forrest's interlocked novels along with capsule biographies of the key characters who appear in them.

Fun as it is to read (in carefully measured doses), and vivid as is its portraiture and strong its atmospheric pressure, how well does this choir between covers work? It seems to me that Forrest, with a number of stellar exceptions, has a tin ear for any voice but his narrator's—i.e., his own—and what keeps the reader going is what he says, which to be sure is often very good stuff.

Also, Forrest's reliance on jazz for his prose riffs raises problems, for how "musical" can a novel be and still be fiction? Joubert's admitted failure "to run a ladder up the hieroglyphics of Charlie Parker's tortured soul, then transform this experience of his voice into a one-act play" often fails here even to sound like speech of any kind.

Even his natural prose voice too often flags when it should soar, as when Joubert apostrophizes: "Oh America may be a lighthouse-rescue beacon for the world's homeless, and she may cast forth thousands of beams of light; but for this native son, she has such a limited vision."

And though Forrest is as daring as Joyce in his puns—he refers to the catamite of Daisy's homosexual preacher as "canon versus cannon fodder"—he seldom achieves the chordlike complexity of Joyce's "fadograph of a yestern scene" to evoke the decline of the West, or of his reference to Anna Livia as being "jung and easily freudened."

Nevertheless, the book is wonderfully entertaining, and we have lots of fun at what might be called "pun-again's new take." And perhaps we should not be "astoneaged," like Joyce's archaeologists, if this late, brave attempt at Modernism no longer works quite so well in a Post-modern world.

Sven Birkerts (review date 31 May 1993)

SOURCE: "Invisible Man," in *The New Republic,* Vol. 208, No. 4089, May 31, 1993, pp. 42-5.

[*In the following review, Birkerts praises* Divine Days *and suggests why Forrest's critical reception has been minimal.*]

Leon Forrest is the invisible man of contemporary African American letters. Born in Chicago in 1937, raised and educated there, Forest has been publishing novels since the early 1970s, including *There is a Tree More Ancient than Eden* (1973), *The Bloodworth Orphans* (1977) and *Two Wings to Veil My Face* (1983). But public and critical reception have been minimal, to say the very least. Forrest's name does not come up much in discussions of writing; the indexes of scholarly studies march blithely forward without him.

I don't know that the publication of *Divine Days,* his megalithic novel, will change the situation much. I have not seen the book reviewed, or even mentioned, anywhere. That it is a third again as long as *The Brothers Karamazov* is not likely to recommend it to readers short on time and stamina. This would be a shame, and an enormous loss. *Divine Days* is unlike anything else in our recent literature. At once a comic opera and a metaphysical tract, this great wordy beast stamps and blinks in the glittering light of the marketplace like something kidnapped from a more expansive age.

Unfolding over the course of seven days in February, 1966, the novel carries us deep into the life of its narrator Joubert Jones, and at the same time layers around us the stories and the myths—the great fabric of polyphonic talk—of an entire community. The place is a Chicago-like city in the author's own Forest County. Joubert, a would-be playwright whose work thus far has only met with rejection, has returned from a stint of military service in Germany. He plans to set himself up and resume his writing, but for the short run he has moved in with his feisty aunt Eloise, who raised him after his parents died. Joubert also takes on the job of managing her bar, Eloise's Night Light Lounge, a place that he comes to see as a kind of stage for the tragedies and the comedies of neighborhood life. For all his determination to get on with his own work, Joubert finds himself utterly immersed in the human swirl around him. He tells himself that just by being present he is serving a dramatist's apprenticeship.

Joubert has been blessed with a special gift. He is susceptible to voices, and each one that he hears or remembers serves him as a pipeline to the speaker's soul. This is the source of his playwriting itch: he can hardly turn around without colliding with another inspiration. Once, he tells us, he thought of "trying to run a ladder up the hieroglyphics of Charlie Parker's tortured soul, then transforming this experience of his voice into a one-act play." His current fancy, which will occupy him increasingly as the book progresses, is to write a play "about the soul within the voice of Sugar

Groove." Traveler, talker, ladies' man, Sugar Groove (also known as Sugar Grove, Sugar Shit and a dozen other "sugar"-based monikers) is a Forest County legend. Joubert knew him years ago and has been fascinated ever since. Reports that Sugar Groove's body was recovered from a faraway mountain top will activate Joubert's memories; the man's enigmatic story will eventually give him answers about his own life.

Eventually, *Divine Days,* it must be said, gets underway slowly, like a great long freight train clattering its couplers out of the yard. Joubert's world, past and present, is thickly settled. Both he and his aunt are vital agents in the life of the community. The cast of characters takes some time to assemble. And for a spelunking temperament like Joubert's there is a good deal more involved. Every person—waitress, lounge lizard or community stalwart—is not just a presence, but a history; and every history is for him a kind of root system stretching back years, even decades.

But Joubert feels no compulsion to narrate quickly. Why, when narration is so interesting? Consider the excitements of the very first day, when Joubert finds himself embroiled in a knock-down shouting match with one Daisy Dawes, a sad, bewigged, dog-toting, spike-heeled old woman who has taken offense at an aspersion cast by Joubert at W. A. D. Ford. Ford, another legend, is the now-vanished huckster preacher, a "hermaphroditic" saver of souls who practiced his orgiastic messianism in his church, Divine Days, which is now the site of the lounge.

The Daisy Dawes confrontation begins as a "dirty dozens" trading of insults and jibes, with many of the onlookers chipping in. One of the regulars, Roy Ruffins, says of her dog Tosca: "that dog pisses perfumes, shits caviars and farts wine sauce . . . and if I'm lying, I'm flying." Joubert speeds and slows his report, taking time to fill us in on Daisy's past and on certain peculiarities of Ford's ministry. By the time we reach the climactic moment, with Daisy brandishing a .44 from her purse and then falling backward off her stool, we have taken the first of many tours of the human labyrinth that is Forest County. What's more, we have taken our first measure of the elusive Ford, the man who will emerge as Sugar Groove's great antagonist and an emblem of the collective superstitions of the community.

In scene after scene, the pattern repeats. Nearly every one of Joubert's encounters is a point of departure for an anecdotal history. At first, naturally, there is some confusion. The reader keeps checking the back of the book to see whether a chart of identifications might not have appeared. But after a while the root systems begin to grow together. Characters start showing up in each others' stories, and we relax into the meandering momentum of Joubert's talk, bunching our brows perplexedly only when he offers some new piece

of Ford apocrypha, such as his much bally-hooed Easter ascension at the end of a levitating umbrella, or an inventory of the cache he left behind in his storefront church, which included

> the mighty egg-shaped shell and oval coffin box (he himself was known to take a ten or fifteen minute catnap there, only to rebound with the agility of an antelope); the stockpile of African masks about the wall; the seven sacred Hopi Masks; the one hundred bottles of snake oil . . .

Forrest, word-glutted as Rabelais, is a master of the list, ticking off objects and names in endless catalogs, serving serial adjectives as appetizers to his nouns and contriving insult choruses that would scorch the wimple on the most liberal nun.

Characters, too, traipse before us in a vast processional. In what we must think of as the early pages—though many another novel would be in end-game at this point—we meet and hear from, among others, Galloway Wheeler, a one-time teacher and Shakespeare scholar who peppers the proceedings, whatever they may be, with appropriate citations from the Bard; Williemain, the garrulous barber who presides over a select men's conversation society that Joubert has been invited to pledge; McGovern McNabb, a Falstaff-sized boozer who stops the action for thirty pages when he crashes unconscious to the barroom floor, to be revived only by a vigorously administered ice-pack on the privates; and a beautiful but haunted young painter who calls herself Imani, and who, in addition to covering canvases with the likenesses of her African American heroes—Martin, Malcolm and others—conducts desperate searches for the many members of her family who have gone missing. Joubert longs for Imani, believes he could love her, but cannot seem to find the path to her heart. Imani thinks that Joubert is denying his African origins and is turning his back on the struggles of his people; in one scene she gets so upset with him that she chases him from her apartment.

The reader trained to the expectations of the Anglo-American novel waits for the rising action, for some sustained engagement or conflict to develop between the principal characters. That reader may wish to shop elsewhere, for this is an altogether different sort of enterprise. So different, in fact, that we begin to understand why the critical establishment has not caught on to Forrest. If Ellison's *Invisible Man* can be seen as the liberation of the African American novel, a claiming of new speculative and expressionistic options, then Forrest's work represents the transposition of these initiatives into the key of orality. What may from one vantage look like a sprawl of chatter and association looks from another position like a heroic effort to plant the African American novel in its original soil.

In his recent study, *To Wake the Nations: Race in the Making of American Literature,* Eric J. Sundquist has observed that "Just as anthropologists are likely to misperceive the 'sounds' of another culture they attempt to record or analyze, so readers and literary critics . . . are likely to misperceive and misunderstand the signs generated by another cultural tradition when they force unfamiliar signs into familiar and hence potentially inappropriate paradigms. . . ."

Something of the sort, I suggest, has been happening with the work of Forrest. The largely white critical establishment seems to be missing the man's music. *Divine Days* is not a clomping foray into mimesis, it is a sluicing of the energies of black speech. It looms as a tour de force carnival of tongues. References to Rabelais, Shakespeare and Joyce are not misplaced. Here is the soul of a community, and to a degree of a whole culture, exposed by way of speech—with Joubert Jones, hearer and interpreter of voices, as our guide. Now the presentation makes sense—its length, its anecdotal entanglements, its startling juxtaposition of kinds of talk, everything from insult to oratory to late-night philosophizing.

Forrest himself, in an essay titled **"In the Light of Likeness—Transformed,"** directs us to a central source of his vocal inspiration. "As a writer who comes out of a culture steeped in the eloquence of the Oral Tradition," he explains, "I've come to see the Negro preacher as the Bard of the race; and throughout my novels, that rich lodestone of eloquence has provided me with an important springboard." This is certainly the case in *Divine Days,* a novel that not only takes its name from the defunct church of the scurrilous W. A. D. Ford, but that features at intervals long passages of both religious and secular sermonizing. Forrest gives more than a few preacher characters a platform for their verbal strutting. And Joubert, attending, is rapt:

> Deep within their voices I heard that old genesis grain—over, under, around and through; in and out of the window of the time—of the Negro singing voice: bone plucked, hardy, harp-haunted, accusational, grieving, roped off, roped in; fiddle-cracking, grief instructed; time greased, woe-weary, wound-salted down; drum telegraphing, blues baked, hoe-cake fired; lightning mangled, fat-back foxy, bruised-blooded, merriment jangling; box-car coming, whistling and hushed over in Trouble.

So open is Joubert to what he hears that on one occasion, while at a service at the Anchor of Zion Missionary Baptist Church, he jumps to his feet, delirious, fully taken over by what he believes is the spirit of one Reverend Connie Dixon Rivers, all but stealing the show (and thunder) from the Reverend Lightfoot at the pulpit:

> . . . and suddenly I am, me, Joubert Jones outdoing the visiting preacher's voice (with bloody testifying and confessing Rivers' conversion in tongues of flames, like a man drowned up to his gills in fire water) just as Lightfoot took his sermon to another shrieking layer of climax and tried to razor me down with the signifying bad-eye look in order to offset my gradual takeover of his invitational sermon . . .

The scene builds and builds, finally exploding into the richest comedy as Joubert faints, and then wakes to find himself in the solicitous hands of the seven Lockhart Laudermilk sisters, each fatter than the next, and each more covetous of securing Joubert for some extra-ecclesiastical comfort giving.

But while Forrest mines church speechifying for its humorous elements, he also uses the sacred idiom to tap into the reservoir of black spirituality. Indeed, it is finally of first and last rulings—of the soul entrapped in the confusions of flesh—that he would speak. As he writes in that same essay, trying to come to terms with an epiphany he experienced once while listening to Mahalia Jackson, "all great literature was and is and ever shall be, world without end, amen, about man's spiritual agony and ascendancy. A spiritual agony that I seemed steeped in, like a child baptized in the chilly waters of the Jordan." And from its middle on, *Divine Days* mobilizes its vast anecdotal energies on behalf of ultimates.

Taking a few hints from Dostoyevsky, one of the deities in Joubert's pantheon, Forrest sets up what finally proves to be an epic confrontation between good and evil—between the arduous and solitary search for genuine spiritual understanding and the temptations offered by false prophets. The two principal contenders in the drama, which unfolds in the thoughts and conversations and written meditations of Joubert, are Sugar Groove and W. A. D. Ford.

Years ago, when Joubert was still an adolescent, Sugar Groove had come to Williemain's barbershop to get his shoes shined: Joubert, then making his money with brushes and rags, was alone in the shop, and Sugar Groove, for whatever reason, chose him to be the hearer of his extraordinary tale. For decades Joubert has kept a lid on what Sugar Groove told him. But now, after his experience in the Anchor of Zion church and his many homecoming encounters, he is ready to puzzle out the story and its implications.

Sugar Groove's narrative is convoluted—a Faulknerian agon from the deep South—and could not possibly be summarized here. Sugar Groove, we learn, was the illegitimate son of a white landowner and his black servant; the mother died in childbirth. We read of legacies and ghosts, of a beloved half-sister murdered by a jealous brother. Sugar Groove, afraid he will be blamed for the crime, flees North, carrying an illegitimate daughter from his own liaison. But before he leaves he is the victim of a cruel hoax perpetrated by none other than W. A. D. Ford, who in the guise of a medium tells him where he can meet the spirit of his mother—the first salvo in what will turn into a deathly rivalry. Once he arrives in Forest County, Sugar Groove gives his daughter to a woman named Sweetie Reed to be raised. He sends money but refuses to show his face. Self-exiled from fatherly love, he becomes a rolling stone and ladies' man, hunting for a connection that continues to elude him.

The conclusion of Sugar Groove's fabulous story is supplied by hearsay, as well as by a set of revealing documents. Joubert learns that after a long career, at once a search and a piracy, Sugar Groove betook himself to a mountain top:

> Sugar Groove up there sought out the meaning of his life. . . . Sought the radiance of not only the face of God; but more—sought out the radiance from whence all creation poured from, and out of which the Maker Himself was but a manifestation. Sugar Groove also sought to cast off that old skin of aggression and violence too. Sought to strip himself down to the bone bare essentials so that he could come alive to something that went beyond the bestial to the beautiful to the sublime that is lodged away in the vow of pure poverty.

Sugar Groove dies on the mountain top. At any rate, a body is found—a body from which the eyes have been plucked. Then we learn that Ford himself was known to be on the mountain, and that the two, authentic seeker and spiritual con, had a final stand-off. As Joubert begins to sort this information, pondering it as one would ponder a runic inscription, he gets the news that Imani has killed herself. He is stunned. When he goes to her apartment, he finds her diary. There, in grievous syllables, is depicted another kind of struggle, not so much with spiritual ultimates as with a legacy of violence and personal loss. Imani, he sees, was striving, so long as she could, to transmute her pain, to put it somehow in the service of her people. But then, irony of ironies, the "brother" she had deemed to be one of the genuine keepers of the cause arrives to rescue his cocaine cache from some tribal masks he had given Imani. The face-off, we see, writ large and writ small, is between ideals and their perversion at the hands of the wicked, between the upwardly inclining soul and the terrible gravity of sordid circumstance.

By now it must be clear that no short appreciation can begin to encompass the fugal architectonics of Forrest's vast work. One after another the voices—aspirant, corrupt, fierce and sorrowful—vie for a place in the would-be dramatist's comprehending perspective. But while Shakespeare may have possessed an absolute negative capability, Joubert does not. He is not merely gathering material, he is looking for

his own answers, laboring to forge his own identity. He understands at last that he must step aside from the chaotic plenitude of lounge life and face the silent page. He will let himself be guided by the example of Sugar Groove, by his will to remake himself into a vessel for higher truths and by his openness at the end to the guiding powers of love. He will also heed, as much as he is able, the words of Dostoyevsky's Father Zossima: "Above all, avoid falsehood, every kind of falsehood, especially falseness to yourself. Watch over your own deceitfulness and look into it every hour, every minute."

Divine Days is that rare thing in our self-conscious and ironic age—a full-out serious work of art. Cumbersome, complex and all-consuming, it asks the reader for a massive commitment. Forrest makes no concessions, apparently thinks nothing of tracking an encounter or a conversation over fifty pages. As if we had nothing better to do! But do we have something better to do, really? How better pass the time than by exposing the soul to a good buffeting, a mighty word storm? Here is a work that runs the octaves, carries us from street jive to the mysterious whisperings of the self in spiritual consultation. The world of the novel—the lore, the histories, the speech idioms—is African American, but its reach, like that of the great literature its author so much admires, extends to all. Forrest may be, as yet, an invisible man, but invisible, as every believer knows, does not mean absent.

Andy Solomon (review date 7 August 1994)

SOURCE: "Ceaseless Remaking," in *Chicago Tribune Books*, August 7, 1994, Sec. 14, p. 6.

[*In the following excerpt, Solomon lauds Forrest's collection of essays,* Relocation of the Spirit, *which profiles outstanding African Americans.*]

America's myth structure is like no other. Having severed roots in exchange for hope, those who left old worlds for this new one mortgaged their past to buy a future. New Americans abandoned the old gods of tradition and stability in favor of Proteus, the personification of change that fits any new condition. And no newcomers brought less hope or developed a greater capacity for reinventing themselves than those dragged from Africa, who faced the enforced redefinition of their human spirit by those who had forged their chains.

A focus on that aptitude for transformation links the 27 essays in Leon Forrest's engaging new collection [*Relocation of the Spirit*]. Chair of Northwestern University's African-American Studies Department, novelist Forrest divides these pieces into four groups, dealing in turn with Chicago, authors, athletes and entertainers. Unifying all the essays is his homage to reinvention, both personal and societal:

> We must be a people forever remaking our country, if we are to conserve consistently what's best and valid in the Democratic spirit and use our rich angularity of character as a springboard for new initiatives of cultural and intellectual fulfillment.

Within his guiding concept, Forrest employs a broad variety of voices, as these occasional writings include book reviews, articles from *Muhammad Speaks* (for which Forrest was associate editor), speeches before scholarly gatherings and previously unpublished think pieces. His tone ranges from the coolly analytical when assessing James Baldwin and Elijah Muhammad to the reverential when discussing Ralph Ellison and Jackie Robinson to the rhapsodic when celebrating Michael Jordan and Billie Holiday.

The Chicago South Side where Forrest was raised offered perhaps greater diversity of role models than it does today, as housing segregation kept middle-class and professional-class blacks from leaving the community. He recognized early the eclectic keys to self-transformation: a bit of the hustler's initiative, the guts and discipline of the athlete, the imaginative soaring of the jazz musician. Chicago was "a hustlers' town, where there weren't the rigid restrictions on who you were and what you were. . . . You could get busted, broken down, and defeated, but not necessarily destroyed—you could always get off the canvas and make a come-back."

Of his confessed "love-hate relationship" with Chicago, Forrest shares here mostly what he loves, especially Chicago's black preachers, "the Bards of the race," whose sermons became "a seminal source" of his own writing. He recalls Rev. J. C. Austin of Pilgrim Baptist Church, whom Franklin Roosevelt himself said had "the greatest speaking voice of any public man in America." He re-creates the call-and-response "throb of rapture and confirmation" in Rev. Carroll J. Thompson's West Point Baptist Church, how Thompson inspired the sublimation of "the furious rhythms of body and soul" into shared spiritual experience. He pays a possibly hyperbolic tribute to Rev. Joseph Wells of Mount Pisgah, with his voice "husky, vibrant and gruff one moment and mellow the next, like the combined voices of Jimmy Rushing, Louis Armstrong, Ray Charles and James Brown."

Forrest's literary observations, in these days of self-referential critical rhetoric, are cogent and illuminating. He justly elevates some writers above the limited recognition they've received, such as the enigmatic Jean Toomer, whose hauntingly lyrical *Cane* Forrest calls "the finest novel to come out of the Harlem Renaissance." Of more recent icons Richard Wright and Ralph Ellison, Forrest draws this provocative

distinction: "Wright's black male and female characters were often empty of substance and humanity and, like the author, were dominated by self-hatred and by a vicious, racist caste system. . . . Ralph Ellison is one of the most river-deep militant race men I have ever met. His very soul is anchored to black pride and excellence."

At all points, Forrest's literary remarks are astute and "old-fashioned" in the best sense, recalling a time when criticism meant public teaching written to deepen appreciation.

Forrest offers essays on only two sports figures—Michael Jordan and Jackie Robinson—but he chooses two of the most electrifying athletes of this half-century. That he includes none on Muhammad Ali seems a palpable gap, for Ali's lightning within boxing's world of thunder, like Robinson's quickness on the base paths, most often provided what Forrest says we observed in Michael Jordan: the "miracle of momentary self-transformation, in which the soul celebrates the possibilities of the body." And while his Jordan essay pays appropriate dues to superstars Bill Russell, Elgin Baylor, Jerry West, Dr. J, Magic and Bird, Forrest inexplicably scants Wilt Chamberlain and omits the nearly perfect Oscar Robertson. Despite regrettable omissions, however, Forrest captures the kinetic art of sport, the majesty and Van Gogh-like swirl of color and line that was Air Jordan and the "epic odyssey of Jackie Robinson's swift but significant half-century of living."

Forrest never seems more inspired by his subject than when describing his "romance" with Billie Holiday's singing. He wears Lady Day's voice like a coat of many colors whose spectrum includes Ray Charles' synthesis of gospel and blues, the "cutting edge of the bitch's tongue," Lester Young's "absolute attention to lyrical phraseology," the "borderline of madness. . . . the furious yeast of personal chaos" and mostly the blues singer's "eternal search for . . . true words to capture the ever-changing conditions of life upon the highly vulnerable heart."

Poetic in herself, Lady Day is the cause of poetry in Forrest: Her voice was "a small incandescent lyrical light, reedy and fragile as candlelight illuminating an echo chamber into the solitude and secret prisms of the soul"; her listeners were "made privy to the unburdening of grief on an individual basis, as expressed and revealed by one's best girlfriend, seated next to you at your favorite bar."

There are gaps and arguable judgments here, as well as repetitiveness and a grating addiction to the adjective "keening." But Leon Forrest's erudite commentaries provide an engrossing blend of wisdom and wonder, like a long fireside evening with a perceptive friend who's spent a lifetime reinventing himself, and now offers you the chance.

Stanley Crouch (essay date 1995)

SOURCE: "Beyond American Tribalism," in *The All-American Skin Game,* Pantheon Books, 1995, pp. 113-18.

[*In the following essay, Crouch extols Forrest's* Divine Days *for taking an unblinking, often humorous, look at American and African-American culture using literary and religious allusions.*]

Like our economy, our cities, and our universities, our long fiction has been in trouble for years. The problem is as much spiritual as intellectual, for we need a far, far richer sense of the inner lives that give our nation its particular complexity. And because all Americans make their elevating to wacky variations on a set of essences, those essences need to be delivered with high and subtle style, a feeling for the labyrinths of our history, and a sense of the shifting dialogue across race and class, sex and geography, myth and fact. Most novelists duck the job, preferring to sink down into explications of ideology and statistics; or they hop the latest cattle car of academic convention from France; some even embrace the least revealing aspects of our popular culture, never determining what the relationship of the street is to the truly sophisticated expression of our protean national consciousness. If nothing else, they bush-whack the reality of our lives from behind barricades of ethnic and gender franchises.

But Leon Forrest has accepted the task of capturing our culture and has produced a novel that provides a signal moment in our literature, one that was largely missed when it arrived last year. With an equal level of ambition, he responds to the standards of fiction and the breadth of thought found in the work of Ralph Ellison, Albert Murray, Saul Bellow, William Faulkner, Herman Melville, James Joyce, Thomas Mann, and Marcel Proust. The resulting success of *Divine Days* is as startling for its narrative risks as for the sustained power of its author's literary will. Having spent twenty years working his way to this point through three earlier novels—*There Is a Tree More Ancient than Eden, The Bloodworth Orphans,* and *Two Wings to Veil My Face*—Forrest has now moved to the forefront of American literature. All of the previous experiments and partial successes now read as a triptych of an overture to this masterwork.

Not one to satisfy himself with an imposing gift for mashing together the rural and urban sensibilities that make epic the Afro-American language of our cities, Forrest has a big feeling for literature at large, and this 1,135-page novel reads the way a whale eats, swimming forward with its massive mouth open to ensure the continued substance of its bulk. Forrest gives us characters, tales, set pieces, sermons, rhythms, images, jokes, and a vision of our culture's mythic size we rarely encounter in this day of the little world, the

little thought, and the devotion to a defeatist vision imported from Europe in the wake of the one-two punch of the world wars.

Even so, Forrest is no New Age Good Humor Man. He understands how we are duped by color, how unexamined or hysterical ideology often blinds us like intellectual mustard gas. But rather than crawl into that trench where engagement lies traumatized, Forrest successfully captures the struggle for the Afro-American soul that took place during the middle sixties. That soul has the feeling of multitudes and is a prism through which the spectrum of our nation at large appears: no matter how accurate the Afro-American texture, *Divine Days* provides us with a metaphor as resonant in its general meanings as it is commanding in the nuances of the particular.

Through the world Forrest summons with one brilliant thematic variation after another, we are able to see the struggles our democracy has in facing up to the prickly relationship between the individual and the masses. He artfully shows that the resentment we feel when faced with inevitable tragedy is what sets us up for the "happy endings" promised by purveyors of snake oil in every arena from the religious to the secular, the political to the psychoanalytic. The popularity of the intellectual, economic, spiritual, and physical surgery guaranteed to produce a "new you" is also fresh meat for the leaders of cults that stretch from the academy to the street corner. Our difficulty in combining intellect with style and style with intellect results in our accepting eloquent but empty-headed theories or being overly impressed by manner when we should also be looking for content. Our shallow, hand-me-down revisions of history and culture tear us from the transcendent grandeur of our human heritage, deny the endless miscegenations that complicate our national identity, and set us up for so many sucker blows that we end up culturally punch drunk. Finally, we can become so sanctimonious that we feel engagement is below us, or we can sneer at engagement because we have become convinced that every horror and disappointment is held in place by an invincible conspiracy.

These national themes come forward in the novel as the profane and empathetic flexibility of the blues spirit does battle against the various puritanical visions that stem from either the most restrictive versions of Christianity or the totalitarian cults that combine ethnic nationalism with religion. In one corner is Sugar-Groove. Sugar-Groove is a Mississippi-born half-caste and road runner whose mutating legend is a gift to the Chicago black people ever willing to spin a tale about him or listen when a fresh one arrives. Though it is not immediately apparent, Sugar-Groove dies seeking the meaning of life. He wants to get next to the light that symbolizes both the bittersweet richness of his cultural background and the courage to face the burdens of existence with tragic optimism. That affirmative courage sells out neither to innocence nor cynicism; it is the source of the wounded and optimistic love call heard in the pulsive swing of blues and jazz. That wise and enlivening principle has made the people as charismatic as the music.

In the other corner is W. A. D. Ford. Ford is the demonic force that rises from the recesses of black American culture. Through Ford, *Divine Days* looks without a blinking eye into mad orders and confidence men such as the Nation of Islam, Father Divine, Daddy Grace, and Jim Jones. Ford possesses ominous charm and knows that those black people who feel most intimidated by the intricacies of a society demanding great sophistication often harbor the desire to be part of an elite at any cost. Their rage, insecurity, envy, and bitterness can be manipulated to the point where they will end up accepting every repression of vitality in the interest of order. Overwhelmed by so many choices equaled by so many responsibilities, they will submit to one source for all direction. "They were absolutely mindless before his powers," Forrest writes of two potential Ford followers, a borderline street walker and a waiter, both marvelously drawn in their sass, pretensions, sorrow, and paranoia.

Though the spiritual contestants are quite clear, nothing functions very simply in *Divine Days.* The novel takes place over a week in the night world of Chicago's South Side, but much more is going on than a few guppies warring in the miniature aquarium of a pimp's platform shoe heel. Forrest weaves his complexities with a multihued fishing tackle that will not break under the demands of his epic ambition. His people have complicated family lines, and their experiences, their educational backgrounds, their interests, their terrors, and their hopes cross many different lines of color and class, religion and career. Freed from the small talk of the contemporary provincial, the characters of *Divine Days* move across the country and around the world. Having done or wished for or failed at many things, they have much on their minds and memory trunks full of corkscrews and bent objects.

Joubert Jones is perhaps the hero, at least the narrator, a playwright just returned from two years of military service in Germany. Joubert intends to write a play about Sugar-Groove and has previously worked at bringing Ford's evil to the stage. This conceit allows the many literary allusions to work naturally, and Joubert's job as a bartender in his Aunt Eloise's watering hole supplies the novel with the rich breadth of characters either met during visits to the Night Light Lounge or remembered through the hooks of association.

The characters function in a narrative that is built upon *Invisible Man* in as original a way as that novel was built upon Richard Wright's *American Hunger.* (That is: the published *Black Boy* and the then-unpublished second half, which took

the narrator to a disillusioning North, the book ending with his decision to become a writer and an allusion to the last lines of Tennyson's *Ulysses.*) Forrest is taken by Southern experience and the seditious elements in the North that also infringe on individual identity. For Wright and Ellison, the conservative and brutal demon of racism was extended by the radical Northern demon that dismissed human specificity in favor of rote political theory. Setting his novel in 1966, Forrest brings us to the brink of the destruction of the Civil Rights Movement by the politics of black power. The writer revels in the vitality, humor, religious depth, sensuality, and lyricism of black American culture but sees its radical enemies as black nationalism and the romance of Africa, both of which are finally so disappointing that they destroy one of his characters, just as bitterness over the shallowness of The Brotherhood did in Ellison's Todd Clifton.

The work's exceptional strength arrives through the virtuoso fusion of idiomatic detail and allusions to the worlds of literature and religion. Though the playwright narrator will push his own sound into the mouths of people when he feels like it, Forrest knows so well the diction, the living patterns, the aspirations, the courtship styles, the dangers, and the brands of humor from the alley to the penthouse that he is quite free to deliver his black American world with three-dimensional authenticity, while creating an antiphony between that universe and—to give but a *few* examples—Shakespeare (especially *Othello, Hamlet, Macbeth,* and *King Lear*), Poe, Hawthorne, Joyce, Melville (*Moby Dick,* "Benito Cereno," and *The Confidence Man*), Homer, Cain and Abel, Osiris and Sel, Oedipus, Icarus, and Saint Paul. Having done a marvelous variation on it earlier, Forrest even tips his hat to Ellison's short story "Flying Home" for his finale. Those allusions allow Forrest to layer his renderings of the weights and wages of identity, murder, manipulation, greed, exploitation, ruthlessness, irresponsible uses of power, madness, and the heartbreak of the doomed romance. There are also copious references to black American writing, opera, boxing, popular songs, blues tunes, movies, cartoons, and the various kinds of technology that either support or destroy memory, threaten or sustain life.

As Joubert observes, interacts with, and contemplates the condition of the world he's in and the worlds he's known, Forrest critiques as often as he celebrates. In a masterful sequence, Forrest brings together criminals, church ritual, and the honoring of dubious martyrs. However much Joubert might be moved by the singing at the funeral of Aaron Snow, a scurrilous black drug addict shot to death by a black policeman, the narrator doesn't mistake the hot rhythm for substantial reflection: "They had all gone too far with this mushy-minded-mercurial palaver, in which the punk was elevated to a man on stilts, and turned into a kind of outlaw, as hero. I found myself disdaining the eulogizers, by and large, and pitying the blindness of the kids in the audience. . . . Oh, well, it is some burden to be known as a soulful people. Whoever heard tell of such chosen people, as also known for moderate lamentation? This was mindless celebration!" But it doesn't stop there. Soon "even the life of Emmet Till was echoed out here in the chapel in several statements concerning Aaron Snow." The concluding speaker announces the establishing of a scholarship "to do honor to Aaron Snow."

Joubert's pursuit of the facts about Sugar-Groove, the folk hero at war with the dictatorial W. A. D. Ford, makes *Divine Days* a Melvillian detective story of shifting styles. The following of clues opens up the novel to much irony and humor, erotic attraction and sexual repulsion, tragic disillusionment and hard, ruthless violence. The literary flat-footing pulls in elements of the gothic, the tall tale, the parable, the philosophical argument, the novel of ideas, the history lesson, the novel of manners, and the sort of close observation Balzac, Mann, and Hemingway would admire. The technique of the novel is as musical as it is bold. Forrest prefers to lay his symbols out clearly so that the reader consciously watches him do his stuff the way an audience listens to jazz inventions on a standard song. He often sets up motifs—phrases, characters, colors, natural elements, conflicts, images, and so on—that form a chorus structure. With each successive chorus, the variations become more and more complex until they are either resolved or abruptly come to a conclusion, only to be picked up later. He also likes the extended dialogue, calling upon the precedents of Plato, Doestoevsky, Mann, Faulkner (especially "The Bear"), and the competitive invention of two jazz players foaming their creations at each other in four-bar units or entire blues choruses. Lengthy passages of evocative narrative in which the symbols are carefully submerged make obvious how well Forrest knows that the surreal nature of American experience often declares itself best when rendered accurately. The

orchestral control from the first chapter to the last is apt to make our most serious novelists both grateful and envious.

As with every very long and great novel, there are passages that don't sustain force, fall into excess, or blubber into sentimentality. But, like a liberating hero who must rise over interior shortcomings, Leon Forrest never fails to regain his power and take on the details necessary for a difficult victory. *Divine Days* should capture the souls of all who truly love books and feel our national need for freedom from the rusty chains of an intellectual and aesthetic slavery that maintains itself by adding link after link of clichés.

FURTHER READING

Criticism

Byrne, Jack. A review of *Divine Days. The Review of Contemporary Fiction* 14, No. 1 (Spring 1994): 210-11.
    Praises Forrest's novel *Divine Days* as a meaningful translation of African-American oral tradition.

Taylor-Gutherie, Danille. "Sermons, Testifying, and Prayers." *Callaloo* 16, No. 2 (Spring 1993): 419-30.
    Discusses Forrest's novel *Two Wings to Veil My Face* as an expression of his own belief in the artistry of African-American survival in America.

Warren, Kenneth W. "Thinking beyond Catastrophe." *Callaloo* 16, No. 2 (Spring 1993): 409-18.
    Interprets the style of Forrest's novel *There Is a Tree More Ancient than Eden* as comparable to the seamless juxtapositions of dream, reality, history, and prophecy seen in motion pictures.

Additional coverage of Forrest's life and career is contained in the following sources published by Gale: *Black Writers,* **Vol. 2; Contemporary Authors, Vols. 89-92;** *Contemporary Authors Autobiography Series,* **Vol. 7;** *Contemporary Authors New Revision Series,* **Vols. 25, 52;** *Contemporary Literary Criticism,* **Vol. 4; and** *Dictionary of Literary Biography,* **Vol. 33.**

Henry Louis Gates, Jr.
1950-

American critic and essayist.

INTRODUCTION

Gates is one of the most controversial and respected scholars in the field of African-American studies. Beginning in the late 1980s, when he was a professor of English at Cornell University, Gates helped redefine the American curriculum as a strong proponent of what has become widely known as multiculturalism, defending the study of the literature and arts of cultures outside the traditional Western canon.

Biographical Information

Gates was born in 1950 in Keyser, West Virginia, to Henry and Pauline Gates. As a child entering recently desegregated public schools, he experienced an insidious racism that discouraged him from "overachievement." Nevertheless, Gates enrolled in Yale University in 1968, majoring in history. From 1970 to 1971, Gates won a Carnegie Foundation Fellowship and a Phelps Fellowship to travel to Kilimatinde, Tanzania, to work as a general anesthetist with the Anglican Mission Hospital. He traveled throughout Africa, familiarizing himself with various aspects of African culture. After graduating summa cum laude from Yale in 1973, Gates earned fellowships to study at Clare College, Cambridge University, in England. There he met the Nigerian playwright and Nobel laureate Wole Soyinka, who encouraged Gates to study the black literatures of the United States, Africa, and the Caribbean. Gates earned his Master's degree at Clare College in 1974 and his Ph.D. in 1979. From 1973 to 1975 he was a staff correspondent at the *Time* magazine London bureau. He was a professor of English, and later the director of undergraduate Afro-American studies, at Yale University from 1976 to 1985, when he left Yale to become professor of English, comparative literature, and African studies at Cornell University. In 1983 Gates made his first major impact on African-American studies with his painstaking research on and republication of Harriet E. Wilson's *Our Nig* (1859), the first novel published by an African-American. Ignored for decades, and then considered the work of a white man, the novel's true authorship was proven by Gates, who was credited with adding thirty years to the tradition of African-American literature. From there Gates moved to Duke and then Harvard Universities, publishing numerous essays and books and becoming an important player in the controversial movement to redevelop the American curriculum with a focus more inclusive of non-Western cultures. In 1990 Gates placed himself in the midst

of controversy when he testified for the defense in the obscenity trial of the rap group 2 Live Crew. Arguing that the group's lyrics, while shocking on the surface, are actually well-crafted parody in the black mythic vernacular tradition, Gates defended the group's first amendment rights as artists, thereby incurring for himself the censure of many who found his highly publicized participation in the trial little more than self-promotion. Gates continues to teach, publish books and essays, and edit anthologies of African-American literature, and is involved in many organizations promoting multicultural study.

Major Works

The central concept in Gates's literary criticism is "Signifyin(g)," which forms the basis for *Figures in Black: Words, Signs, and the Racial Self* (1987) and *The Signifying Monkey: Towards a Theory of Afro-American Literary Criticism* (1988). Rooted in the African literary tradition of myths and folktales, the "signifying monkey" of these works is conceived as Èsù, a mythic African trickster figure who uses verbal play in the form of parody, irony, hyperbole, and reversals of meaning to educate, entertain, or outsmart listeners. With the parenthetical "g" representing black vernacular speech patterns, "Signifyin(g)" indicates an African-American literary technique of "playing" with language to gain verbal mastery over white oppressors. This technique evolved as slave owners used threats of torture and death to force blacks to abandon their native African languages, thereby preventing slaves from covertly organizing revolts. In *Loose Canons: Notes on the Culture Wars* (1992) Gates argues for greater tolerance and diversity in American arts and letters from both the political right and the left on issues of gender and multiculturalism. *Colored People: A Memoir* (1994) recalls Gates's childhood in small-town West Virginia during the birth of desegregation. While affirming the progress brought by desegregation, Gates also laments the loss of the strong, united community feeling that segregation created among blacks. Some reviewers found this nostalgia too noncritical of the momentous events it evokes, but the book was overall well-received. *The Future of the Race* (1996), which Gates wrote and edited with the African-American critic Cornel West, contains essays by Gates, West, and the early-twentieth-century black social theorist W. E. B. DuBois that explore the question of how best to raise the status of lower- and working-class blacks in America. *Thirteen Ways of Looking at a Black Man* (1997) is a collection of biographical and critical sketches of black literary and intellectual leaders, including such diverse figures as Louis Farrakhan, Anatole Broyard, James Baldwin, and O. J. Simpson.

Critical Reception

At the forefront of the most significant reappraisal of African-American critical thought since the 1960s, Gates opened himself up to harsh criticism as well as praise for his opinions on multiculturalism and gender diversity. Detractors have accused him of focusing too narrowly on Afrocentric curricula—an accusation Gates has called "ridiculous," and insists that what he is advocating is greater inclusion of and education about the many cultures that make up American society. Other critics have questioned Gates's use of poststructuralism, a predominantly Western and academic theory they consider inappropriate for criticism of texts by black authors. Gates has answered this charge by pointing out that, with his idea of Signifyin(g), he is not merely applying pre-constructed abstract theories to texts, but is transforming and adapting post-structuralism through careful study of the African literary tradition, creating an original tool for reading African-American literature.

PRINCIPAL WORKS

Figures in Black: Words, Signs, and the Racial Self (nonfiction) 1987

The Signifying Monkey: Towards a Theory of Afro-American Literary Criticism (nonfiction) 1988

Reading Black, Reading Feminist [editor] (nonfiction) 1990

Loose Canons: Notes on the Culture Wars (essays) 1992

Colored People: A Memoir (memoir) 1994

The Future of the Race [with Cornel West] (nonfiction) 1996

The Norton Anthology of African American Literature [editor] (anthology) 1996

The Dictionary of Global Culture [coedited with Kwame Anthony Appiah] (criticism) 1997

Thirteen Ways of Looking at a Black Man (essays) 1997

CRITICISM

Andrew Delbanco (essay date January 1989)

SOURCE: "Talking Texts," in *The New Republic,* Vol. 200, Nos. 2 & 3, January 9 & 16, 1989, pp. 28-34.

[*Delbanco is an American critic and educator. In the following review of* The Signifying Monkey: Towards a Theory of Afro-American Literary Criticism *and* Figures in Black: Words, Signs, and the Racial Self, *Delbanco examines Gates's theory of "Signifyin(g)."*]

In the late 1930s a young writer named Richard Wright charged that virtually all black American writers before him had approached "the Court of American Public Opinion dressed in the knee-pants of servility." Having addressed themselves for too long with a schoolboy's eagerness to impress "a small white audience rather than . . . a Negro one," black writers, Wright declared, should henceforth stop catering to white tastes, and turn instead to their own religious and folk traditions in America:

> There is . . . a culture of the Negro which is his and
> has been addressed to him; a culture which has, for
> good or ill, helped to clarify his consciousness and
> create emotional attitudes which are conducive to
> action. This culture has stemmed mainly from two
> sources: (1) the Negro church; (2) and the folklore
> of the Negro people.

Wright issued this manifesto as a Marxist who believed that "a Negro writer must create in his readers' minds a relationship between a Negro woman hoeing cotton in the South and the men who loll in swivel chairs in Wall Street and take the fruits of their toil." He was committed to the urgent project of raising his people's political consciousness, and he believed that the black religious and folk heritage in America could become instruments toward that purpose.

Now, more than a half century later, Henry Louis Gates Jr., in a series of loosely connected essays on topics ranging from the West African god Esu-Elgebara, a deity of fertility and knowledge "who interprets the will of the gods to man," to the fiction of Alice Walker, has set out to expose the common roots of black consciousness in Africa and America, and thereby to "identify a theory of criticism that is inscribed within the black vernacular tradition" from its beginnings in tribal myth. Gates . . . [in *The Signifying Monkey: Towards a Theory of Afro-American Literary Criticism*], is concerned with some of the same issues as was Wright: with the pain of self-recognition for black children; with the continuing struggle (even after the emergence of a black middle class) against the subhuman black image in the white mind; with the restorative power of humor in the face of degradation. Wright, of course, believed in Soviet socialism as the best model for social justice in America; those were the heady days before the Molotov-Ribbentrop pact and Stalin's show trials. Gates, by contrast, is writing from within the American academy at a time when the idea of revolution seems mainly an abstraction to be debated in arcane journals by tenured literati.

It is unfair, perhaps, to hold a critic accountable to a rhetorical standard set by a great writer. Wright was looking for the language that would most effectively represent intolerable experience, while Gates is trying to represent the ways in which blacks in America have written about that experience. But Gates is also working within a tradition that tends to doubt the distinction between critical work and creative work, that endows both with comparable homiletic power. In confronting the delicate and highly charged question of cultural continuity between Africa and America, Gates believes that what is needed now are "black, text-specific theories" whose genealogies lie in African and Afro-American folk culture, where they are waiting to be discovered. He is committed to "the authority of the black vernacular tradition, a nameless, selfless tradition, at once collective and compelling, true somehow to the unwritten text of a common blackness," which, if traced back to its origins, serves as a "signpost at that liminal crossroads of culture contact and ensuing difference at which Africa meets Afro-America."

Beginning with a long chapter ambiguously titled "A Myth of Origins: Esu-Elegbara and the Signifying Monkey," Gates surveys some of the forms in which this "one specific trickster figure . . . recurs with startling frequency in black mythology in Africa, the Caribbean, and South America." Gates approaches the works of Afro-American literature, too, with this premise of its continuity with the African past. He is committed, moreover, to the idea of a natural linkage between texts and the exegetical method by which their inner spirit can be revealed. This is an attractive, if anachronistic, notion. It implies that the responsible critic ought to

honor the spirit of his subject by emulating it—a worthy imperative that seems to have a certain urgency for Gates, since he goes so far as to apologize, in the preface to *The Signifying Monkey,* for having written a book that his parents and brother are unlikely to understand. What he apparently means by this disclaimer is that, despite his inclination to meet the texts on their own terms, he has written his study largely in the hermetic language of contemporary literary theory, and wishes it could be otherwise. Many of his readers will wish so, too.

By "signifying," Gates most often means something close to the idea, made familiar by Walter Jackson Bate and Harold Bloom, that writers throw off the oppressive weight of their predecessors by first incorporating, then transforming, them. Although black writers have performed this revisionary activity on both black and white texts, Gates is mainly interested in defining an Afro-American tradition by showing the ways in which (as Bloom might say) it willfully misquotes itself.

For Gates, this collapse of the past and the future into a continuous literary present takes place within the familial boundaries of Afro-American writing itself. Thus (although she is not one of Gates's examples) Toni Morrison, in *Beloved,* may be said to have in mind certain excruciating precedents in the slave-literature for her tale of infanticide, or perhaps the terrible moment in a novel by Chester Himes when the narrator reflects that it might be better for a screaming baby if "they'd cut his throat and bury him in the backyard before he got old enough to know he was a nigger." Morrison, of course, also "signifies" the texts of Faulkner; but Gates applies his literary-historical definition of "Signifyin(g)" mainly to the relations between blank texts and other black texts.

The "Signifying" of Gates's title is what is nowadays called "multivalent." Its primary meaning is simply "denoting," or "representing." But its concurrent meaning (as suggested by an alternate spelling that capitalizes "S" and brackets "g" to indicate the consonant that tends to get dropped in colloquial black speech) is quite different. As Gates explains, with a monologue from H. Rap Brown:

> A session [of Signifyin(g)] would start maybe by a
>   brother
> saying, "Man, before you mess with me
> you'd rather run rabbits, eat shit and
> bark at the moon." Then, if he was talking
> to me, I'd tell him:
>
> Man, you must don't know who I am.
> I'm sweet peeter jeeter the womb beater
> The baby maker the cradle shaker
> The deerslayer the buckbinder the women finder

. . . . .

I'm the man who walked the water and tied
the whale's tail in a knot
Taught the little fishes how to swim

. . . . .

I might not be the best in the world, but I'm in the
top two and my
brother's getting old.
Ain't nothing bad 'bout you but your breath.

This catalog of extravagances is assembled (by H. Rap Brown) with an exhilarating inventiveness and a boastful joy. It is an inner-city version of verbal one-upmanship that is both cruel and respectful toward its audience, in the way that only certain forms of antagonistic performance can be. The word "bad" in the final line is perhaps the purest example of what Gates means by "Signifyin(g)"—it is simultaneously an endorsement and a reversal of the conventional meaning of the word in white usage. Both meanings, white and black, are present. The word is thereby enriched.

There are many other entertaining examples of "Signifyin(g)" in Gates's book. Here is a brief one that is closer in its diction to the norms of academic discourse: "Nigger, your breed ain't metaphysical," says Robert Penn Warren in his poem "Pondy Woods." "Cracker," Sterling A. Brown replies some years later, "your breed ain't exegetical." In this case, the repetitive and parodic energy of "Signifyin(g)" is paramount, which is what Gates has chiefly in mind when he explains that "Signifyin(g) is my metaphor for literary history." Gates means that repetition, revision, and usurpation are as integral to black street talk as they are to the history of Western poetry. Thus he establishes a connection between what is now called "intertextuality" (it was formerly known as allusion) and a particular black folk tradition that involves parodic mimicry.

As Gates recognizes, "Signifyin(g)," whether verbal or wordlessly dramatic, is a human activity, not a black one. Rap Brown's banter, for instance, in its hyperbolic appropriation to the self of fertility myths and creation myths borrowed from the dominant culture, is remarkably akin to the tradition of Southwestern humor that culminated in Twain, and to the poetry of Whitman. As a form of creative play somewhere between sadism and ceremony, it is also close to the old vaudeville routine of stepped retaliation: one thinks of the Laurel and Hardy skit in which, as traveling salesmen, they break a prospective customer's flower pot after he slams the door on them. What follows is a stately sequence of symmetrical reprisals: headlights, then houselights smashed; bumpers, then trellises ripped out—until, after a crescendo of mutual destruction, car and house lie in ruins.

When Gates uses "Signifyin(g)" to mean something like the ferocious language-game of Rap Brown, he is intent on establishing an indigenous black tradition. He is a lively observer of its manifestations in various forms of black expression, from the Yoruba myths of the trickster god Esu to the Afro-American folktales of the "Signifyin(g)" monkey, who taunts the proud lion and the obtuse elephant with his wit. But Gates is aware, I think, that neither his observations on literary influence nor his explorations of folk traditions finally constitute an inductive inquiry into the roots of Afro-American literature. "Each of us," he concedes, "brings to a text an implicit theory of literature," rather than finding it there. *The Signifying Monkey* is really about the search for legitimizing precedents in black culture for a literary theory that Gates learned mainly at Yale.

Gates is au courant in his deployment of the latest literary technologies. But he is somewhat out of step with the historicism that has come to inform literary criticism in the last decade or so. His sense of the relations between texts is oddly ethereal. They seem to exist for him in some kind of timeless continuum, in which they exert mutual attraction and repulsion. He talks about the slave narrative, for example, as a "countergenre, a mediation between the novel of sentiment and the picaresque, oscillating somewhere between the two in a bipolar moment." This is a way of saying that the slave narrative combines elements of piety, the deliverance plot, swashbuckling, and even deflating humor at the master's expense. But the remark attends very little to the complex genealogy of the texts.

Gates's framework for understanding black texts is essentially that of European romantic fiction. That is arguably one universe in which the slave narrative can be placed. But surely one must ask whether those narratives were forced into that mold by the abolitionist editors who in many cases supervised their transcription and publication, and may have, in the process, imposed a known form upon unknown experience. Were the generic conventions of European fiction imposed upon the minds of barely literate ex-slaves? Or is Gates talking about structural resemblances that cannot be causally explained? These fundamentally historical questions do not arise much in Gates's work.

Similarly, Gates wants not to stress the roots of certain black texts in white traditions (the slave narratives are rich in biblical, especially Old Testament elements), but he sees them resolutely through European literary perspective. There is within this new-style critic an old New Critic, who values in a text the qualities of ambiguity, irony, allusiveness, structural intricacy—the very features emphasized by T. S. Eliot, John Crowe Ransom, Cleanth Brooks, and Allen Tate, but nowadays condemned as expressions of the withdrawal of literary modernism from the scene of progressive political struggle. Gates is in the singular position of sharing the vocabulary, the style, and the political disposition of his critical contemporaries while facing a literature that he wants to celebrate rather than debunk.

This, I think, is the central problem for Afro-American literary criticism, of which Gates's work is the most ambitious example to date. Despite the bad reputation that close formal analysis has acquired among critics who consider it an evasion of political analysis, it can still claim to be in the service of a radical social criticism when applied to texts that can be shown to be fundamentally at odds with the social order. Thus it is possible for Gates to gloss Frederick Douglass's statement to his readers that "you have seen how a man became a slave, you will see how a slave became a man" with the rather professorial remark that Douglass's "major contribution to the slave's narrative was to make chiasmus the central trope."

Here is my favorite example from the slave literature of the subversive force within an apparently deferential text. It is an apparently benign dialogue between a slave named Pompey and his master, who is preparing for a duel:

> Pompey, how do I look?
> O, massa, mighty.
> What do you mean "mighty," Pompey?
> Why, massa, you look noble.
> What do you mean by "noble"?
> Why, sar, you just look like one *lion*.
> Why, Pompey, where have you ever seen a lion?
> I see one down in yonder field the other day, massa.
> Pompey, you foolish fellow, that was a *jackass*.
> Was it, massa? Well, you look just like him.

These slave texts, in other words, are simultaneously dependent on, and free of, white models; and despite the many wonderful instances of sly "Signifyin(g)," their paradoxical relationship to white texts is not easy to resolve.

Gates writes of Frederick Douglass, for example, with a reverential passion that is as moving as it is virtually unknown in contemporary writing about other 19th-century American figures. (Andrew Jackson, once treated by mainstream scholars as a populist hero, is now chiefly represented as an Indian-killing demagogue; Herman Melville, once thought of as the epic poet of democracy, is now often described as a witting apologist for corporate expediency.) And yet Gates, even as he wants to represent Douglass as a liberator who escaped the racist categories in which he was imprisoned, must recognize Douglass's assent to other crippling assumptions imposed on him by the same culture that enslaved him: the Enlightenment premise, for instance, that only literacy denotes civilization. . . .

Gates's problem, the problem of Afro-American literary criticism today, is that he wishes to combine a critical advocacy of certain literary works with a spirit of opposition toward the culture that produced them. The problem has been resolved by other black critics through the practice of literary biography, which has the capacity to describe the inhibiting context within which the dissenting imagination in America has managed to flourish. Others, such as Houston Baker Jr., have pointed out that the difference between the spirit of the Harlem Renaissance (which remains the authorizing moment for Afro-American letters) and the larger modernist movement of which it was a part has to do with this same distinction between attacking the regnant culture and generating an alternative: "Rather than bashing the bourgeoisie," Baker has written, as the Anglo-American modernists were doing, black writers in the 1920s and '30s "were attempting to create one."

In the 1980s, rather than dismantling the received literary canon (as many of their white counterparts are doing), many black critics are attempting to build one. Despite the delicacy and the constructive nature of this task, however, Gates tends to fall back into the portentous jargon of a literary criticism that is ill-suited to it. His analysis is murderously dissecting, a reductive translation of the living language of Ralph Ellison and Zora Neale Hurston into the taxonomies of Mikhail Bakhtin and Jacques Lacan.

It is also frequently downright silly. After noting, for example, the distinction between white and black uses of "signifying," Gates generalizes his observation into the statement that "all homonyms depend on the absent presence of received concepts associated with a signifier." Now, it is true that the force of the word "Signifyin(g)" derives in part from the differences between its familiar linguistic sense (to denote) and the more playful sense (to make parodic fun) that Gates is interested in. Still, Gates's generalization about "absent presence" is somewhere between rhetorical exaggeration and sheer nonsense. Does the word "squash," when used to signify an indoor racquet game, always carry with it the subliminal suggestion of a yellow vegetable?

Once one gets used to this sort of thing, *The Signifying Monkey* turns out at heart to be a poignant book. It is continuous with an important discussion that has always been central to black intellectual life—Alain Locke's suggestion, for instance, that a "New Negro" was emerging in the 1920s, whose cultural identity, fostered by the rediscovery of the African past, was now secure, and that "our poets have now stopped speaking for the Negro—they speak *as* Negroes." Gates is reentering territory that was fought over by black intellectuals a half century ago. There is a certain horror in the fact that, more than 60 years later, he must still press this same case.

Of course, not all black intellectuals granted the premise that a prehistorical black identity could or should be recouped. Some thought that, by insisting on their African identity, blacks were merely confirming the image of a titillating savage that lurked in the white mind. . . .

The trouble with the Harlem Renaissance was that it became, at least for some of its white enthusiasts, a kind of anthropological festival. It partook of the same spirit that allowed for a long time in America that the only breasts permitted to be bared publicly were black breasts in the pages of *National Geographic,* the same spirit that lured white men north on "safari" into Harlem in search of "specialty sex." Embarrassment and prudery can only exist as a relation between two human consciousnesses: if one is judged subhuman by the other, then all is permitted. There is no such thing as a naked animal.

The willed connection of black Americans to the African past, in other words, has remained not only tenuous, but also suspect in its effects. Gates sees the difficulties, but he puts them mildly: "The degree to which the [Afro-American] figure of the Monkey is anthropologically related to the figure of the Pan-African trickster, Esu-Elgebara, shall most probably remain a matter of speculation." He acknowledges the fragility of the oral tradition with which he is working, but he pays little attention to the brutal deformation that African culture suffered in its forced translation to the New World.

Still, whatever the pitfalls of pursuing that past, or the obstacles to furnishing the sense of that past with an empirical basis, it has never been far from the center of black intellectual life. It was the occasion for James Baldwin's eloquent insistence that the effacement of the slave experience by substituting "X" for the slavemaster's name was as much a mutilation of memory as a gesture toward freedom. It has since been the cause of a number of powerful anthropologists and historians to show the tenacity of tribal and familial identities, even under the corrosive effect of the black diaspora, even under slavery itself.

The African past may have been an ungraspable phantom, but the idea of it was not. The idea of a retrievable black history that predates slavery has been an inescapable force in the lives of black Americans. It is everywhere attested by the extraordinary literature they have produced. In this sense, Gates's books, like the prolific output of young black fiction writers in the last decade, are alive to contemporary experience, certainly more so than most academic criticism. The stakes are real for Gates, as real as they once were for those who believed that critical writing could actually further social reform or political change. This may explain his ambivalence toward the exclusionary language in which he

feels compelled to write. He understands that it is not much of a political or affective instrument.

Gates is contending with one of the fundamental problems that have engaged Afro-American writers for a long time. Like the literature of other immigrant peoples, black writing in America has never strayed far from the problem of assimilation. It is important to remember that assimilation has been more painful for blacks than for other immigrants, because the sense of loss can never be quite attached to a recoverable past, and the sense of gain in consenting to the new American identity can never be complete.

At the end of his *Autobiography of an Ex-Coloured Man* (1912), which tells the story of a light-skinned black who marries a white woman, James Weldon Johnson writes that "I cannot repress the thought that I have sold my birthright for a mess of pottage." This fear, imprecise but visceral, is present from the earliest black texts, such as William Wells Brown's account, written in 1865, of his being "scraped, scrubbed, soaked, washed" on his way from fieldwork to service in the plantation house, to Malcolm X's harrowing tale of his burning the kinks out of his hair by soaking it in lye. Anguish over the racial self-hatred of American blacks must have reached a peak 20 years ago, when Eldridge Cleaver accused James Baldwin of "shameful, fanatical, fawning, sycophantic love of the whites."

Yet once the scrubdown has been refused and the hair "relaxer" thrown away, the great problem for the black intellectual remains the forging of an independent identity within a white culture that is hostile and seductive. Black reformation of white language has been one means toward that end. In the '30s the young anthropologist (and incipient novelist) Zora Neale Hurston recorded with delight the variations on standard English that she found among rural Southern blacks, who made old words like "feature" and "ugly" and "confidence" and "beaucoup" into new verbs. Forty years later, Malcolm reported the bewilderment of a downtown Negro when a hustler walks by on a Harlem street and announces his intention to pawn some clothes: "I'm going to lay a vine under the Jew's balls for a dime." The man from downtown, Malcolm remarks, looked "as if he's just heard Sanskrit."

It was not Sanskrit. Gates would call it "Signifyin(g)." However one names such reformulations of the coercive white language, they are expressions of the impulse toward black freedom. It is an impulse given impetus, as Baldwin once put it, by the fact that "the American Negro has the great advantage of never having believed that collection of myths to which white Americans cling." If this has been an advantage, however, it has also been a great deprivation. It was because of this suspension between worlds—the one ungrounded and inchoate, the other forbidding and closed—

that the black novel was stalled, even as it emerged as a mature genre after the Civil War. It was blocked by its contradictory impulses to conserve the memory of apartness for the former slave while helping to lift him into the civic life of his country.

That is why the first black novelists were obsessed with the figure of the mulatto, who embodied the condition of suspension between worlds. When Malcolm, a hundred years later, repudiated his Stepin Fetchit self and asserted the vigor of his blackness, he came back to the sanctification of the individual and the colorblind vocabulary of human rights. Even these angriest of black writers came to doubt that "Signifyin(g)" on Mister Charlie is ultimately the best means toward real freedom. They have looked instead for a transcendent language into which race might disappear.

Gates is caught, I think, in something like the same pincer. His own language, to borrow a term from his preferred lexicon, tends to deconstruct itself. He is talking about universal habits of mind that operate within all literary texts; but he is also intent on identifying a unique black tradition that he believes has been slighted by (mainly white) critics. At one point he declares that "a vernacular tradition's relation to a formal literary tradition is that of a parallel discursive universe." Parallel lines, however, never meet; and most of Gates's work is devoted to showing, with valuable results, the many points of collision between black folk traditions and the "high" texts of Afro-American literature. Gates pays little attention to the points of intersection between white and black texts, but could just as well attend, say, to Ralph Ellison's allusive use of Emerson and Whitman as to his reprise of Booker T. Washington.

Eventually Gates concedes that "parallel universes . . . is an inappropriate metaphor; *perpendicular* universes is perhaps a more accurate visual description." The correction is apt. Perpendicular lines, if they are sufficiently extended, do meet. Black folk tales meet black fiction; but black texts, oral and written, also meet white texts. When Gates keeps these interracial transactions out of view, one recalls Ellison's infuriated response to Irving Howe's essay "Black Boys and Native Sons" in 1963, in which Howe argued Ellison's indebtedness to Richard Wright:

> It requires real poverty of the imagination to think that [a sense of life and possibility] can come to a Negro *only* through the example of *other Negroes,* especially after the performance of the slaves in recreating themselves, in good part, out of the images and myths of the Old Testament Jews.

Ellison had insisted in *Invisible Man* that blacks must find and keep their history in America, that to obliterate the slave-memory would be to duplicate one of the crimes of slavery

itself: the destruction of a people's past. The terrible fact is that the predominantly oral traditions of West Africa *did* almost completely disappear in the decades after the Middle Passage. Gates's work, like the work of all serious black writers in America, is raised against the debilitating knowledge of this loss. It also flirts with the compensatory, but potentially insidious, idea of a residual race-consciousness that somehow survives in the blood.

In one of his more affecting sentences, Gates remarks, about the sometimes unbridgeable space between black and white expression, that "to learn to manipulate language in such a way as to facilitate the smooth navigation between [the white linguistic realm and the black] has been the challenge of black parenthood and remains so even today." Such is the crossing that we witness when W. E. B. DuBois, having written with immense respect about the black "sorrow songs" to which he was introduced in the post-Reconstruction South, nevertheless comes back to an oratorio of Handel as equally "real" music that moved him in the chapel of Fisk University. . . .

Wahneema Lubiano (essay date December 1989)

SOURCE: "Henry Louis Gates, Jr., and African-American Literary Discourse," in *The New England Quarterly,* Vol. 62, No. 4, December 1989, pp. 561-72.

[*In the following excerpt, Lubiano examines the political implications of Gates's theory of "Signifyin(g)."*]

Henry Louis Gates, Jr., is both one of the most read and misread figures within African-American literary discourse in this century. To some extent his work has generated more heat than light, the ubiquitousness of his written and public presence having rendered him and his work phenomena more talked about than read, more excoriated than understood, more inveighed against than engaged. The terrain of his work has been largely literary history; his sorties into literary criticism and theory, however, also provide a basis for much productive critical work in the future. The implications of *The Signifying Monkey*—in "blue-print" form ("The Blackness of Blackness: A Critique of the Sign and the Signifying Monkey") widely disseminated in manuscript form over the past five or six years and periodically in lectures given around the country—have already transformed discussions and work within the field.

Being awarded a MacArthur Foundation Fellowship thrust Gates into the public arena at a time when debates over deconstruction and other forms of post-structuralist theories, as well as post-colonialist critiques and a reenergized Marxist literary discourse, were generating interest in texts by writers from marginalized groups. Tracing the influence of Gates on African-American literary discourse as well as its influences on him, however, extends beyond the confines of the present project. What I intend to do here, rather, is to delineate the agendas Gates sets himself in **Figures in Black** and **The Signifying Monkey** in order to underscore something of the importance and open-endedness of the two studies.

Gates has put together a spectacular piece of "native informacy" which is even more useful because it is addressed to both "natives" (practitioners of African-American literary criticism) and those on the "outside" (who know nothing of the field). He covers the terrain of African-American literary history with his own formalist and historical interests very much uppermost, but in neither book does he close down discussion in order to raise a monolithic African-American point of view, either of criticism or of literature. His work is, rather, part of the reclamation project about which Frantz Fanon theorizes [in *Wretched of the Earth*]. . . .

The first two chapters of **Figures in Black** historicize the confrontation of the first writings of African-Americans with Euro-American dominance. Gates intervenes in that history by re-narrating the paradigms of that discourse. He explains the writings' position as political cannon fodder in the context of North American ideology and its support of slavery. Further, Gates describes the complexities of the position that he and other critics of African-American literature occupy— the difficulty and demands of speaking to a split audience.

From the beginning Gates has asserted that he wants to change the perception, held by critics of both Euro-American texts and African-American texts, that African-American texts are transparent reflections of the history, sociology, and psychology of African-Americans. He argues that "Blackness" as a Western Enlightenment formulation was and is a metaphor for the metaphysical anomaly or non-metaphysicality of African-Americans. By the late 1960s, Black militants set out to dethrone the Euro-American hegemonic aesthetic and to crack its hold on African-American literary production. The Black Aesthetic critics who took responsibility for the initiative, reclaimed "Blackness" as a privileged "essence" for Black art. Each time it is reenacted, however, this reclamation project begins as a defensive position and all too often proceeds to exhaust itself in critical, often ahistorical, tautologies. Nonetheless, Gates recognizes that the work of the Black Aesthetic critics "determined the nature and shape" of his own critical response, and he understands that his insistence on the primacy of a "repressed" African-American formalism has been "somewhat excessive and too polemical" when he meant it to be "*corrective* and polemical."

Gates's work has been read as consciously apolitical, as an attempt to divorce texts from their historical and political contexts, the politics of their production and reception, and the politics—both implicit and explicit—of their content. Surely such a criticism is unwarranted, however, as evidenced by his reading of the Harlem Renaissance, which concerns itself with the short-sighted (and middle-class-centered) dismissal of dialect, and by his reading of Wright's reactionary race and art politics. In such cases, and others, Gates demonstrates his commitment to reading African-American texts vis à vis historically specific cultural practices. Nonetheless, I do have a problem with his assertion that "a poem is above all atemporal" and "must cohere at a symbolic level if it coheres at all," for logic as well as Bakhtin—"it is not, after all, out of a dictionary that the speaker gets his words!"—tells us that symbols evoke different meanings in different circumstances. Moreover, one can agree with Gates's use of Wittgenstein's admonishment "not to forget that a poem, even though it is composed in the language of information, is not used in the language of giving information" without necessarily supporting or giving comfort to the idea that poetry exists apart from its times—especially when one is armed from the arsenal of historicity that Gates puts in the services of one's reasoning.

In fact, Gates's concern that a historicized formalism has been neglected in past epochs prompts his criticism that African-American literature has been put to uses not primarily aesthetic. It is crucial to understand the distinction, however, between Gates's recognition that African-American texts weren't being read for aesthetic features and some spurious admonition that the terms of the Euro-American aesthetic be adopted by the marginalized group. Gates is not so naive. He realizes that it is possible, rather, to rethink a marginalized group's project to eschew "aesthetics" as a basis for privileging cultural production; that is to say, one can re-create the grounds for "aesthetic" judgment from *within* a marginalized group in order to do justice to, to appreciate, "intentionality" or "craft" among members of that group. It is this project that Gates and the Black Aesthetic critics have in common.

On the other hand, viewing African-American literature as simple sociological and historical reflection is a reductionist exercise whether it is practiced by Euro-Americans dismissing the writing of African-Americans or by Black Aesthetic critics privileging it. It is precisely at this point that Gates sees his agenda diverging from the Black Aesthetic critics'. Whether from the comfortably racist Thomas Jefferson, who would have it believed that African-Americans could not produce anything of cultural value, or the friendly American Marxist critic Max Eastman, who praised Claude McKay's *Harlem Shadows* because it was the work of a "pure-blooded negro," Gates recognizes the damage that "essentialist" theory inflicts on African-American cultural production. While Black Nationalist and Aesthetic critics of African-American literature and Black Marxist writers and critics—preeminent among them Richard Wright—privileged the "treatment" of the African-American proletariat and street caste, they did so generally within terms only of content, not of form: the African-American "lumpen" were the shapeless "stuff" of the art of the literary worker and were the site of politically engaged art and work. Such critics did not theorize about the possibility of the lumpen (rural or urban) being themselves engaged in art-making except in their unconsciously lived lives. Wright could not even give a name to the artistic production of those people; for him, what they did was "the form of things unknown."

Another of Gates's reservations about the Black Aesthetic critics is that they treat "Blackness" as an entity rather than a metaphor. But since the Western discourse on race postulates biology as a signifier of metaphysical being, the "race" critics may be privileging biology in a manner more complicated than Gates has acknowledged: What if "Blackness" as a positive essentialist biological category is evoked not only as a corrective to racist essentialist formulations but also as a corrective to a racist metaphorical confusion of race and being? If such is the case, Addison Gayle, Stephen Henderson, and the other Black Aesthetic critics have been using "Blackness" as their site for rhetorically subverting the racist metaphor with full knowledge that such an act is fraught with danger. In other words, while Gates states, accurately, that "Blackness" is not a material object but a metaphor, within a racist discourse "Blackness" has been treated as a material presence subsumed by its negative force as a metaphor for debasement. . . .

According to Gates *The Signifying Monkey* is "more precisely a theory of literary history." I would add that, in common with other seminal historical and interpretive studies, it also provides an extremely valuable critical apparatus useful in approaching all kinds of texts. In his study, Gates discusses "explicitly that which is implicit in what we might think of as the logic of the tradition," in other words, he makes visible what was previously invisible both within the marginalized group and to the dominant group outside. This theory of African-American literature has its genesis in the first two chapters of *Figures in Black* and the manifesto apparent therein, a manifesto that stresses the importance of attending to form, which, according to Gates, is the neglected "other" of African-American literary discourse. The program Gates called for in *Figures in Black*—to connect the fictiveness and literariness of African-American literature to its own culture—is made manifest in this study. In the first three chapters of *Signifying Monkey* Gates gathers together a vast amount of material across a wide spectrum of scholarly domains. He assembles a cast of hundreds. He brings into African-American literary discourse the work of anthropologists, historians, and linguists of the New and Old World. As he molds this material, Gates re-historicizes the African literary presence in the New World and broadens our appreciation of the cultural practices that survived the diaspora.

Gates's insights owe much to the work done during the 1960s and 1970s by Black Nationalist scholars, many of whom were in graduate school during the period of the Black militancy upheavals, and to other scholars who served as fellow travelers with the Black Nationalist cultural workers. That time marked the biggest outpouring of cultural production and revisionist scholarship since the other great revisionist period that began right before, and continued during, the Harlem Renaissance (generally considered to be the decade between 1919 and 1929).

Gates outlines the historical and geographical evolution of the Signifying Monkey, the New World descendant of the Old World god/goddess Esu-Elegbara, the trickster of Yoruba, Fon, and Dahomey cultures, and that figure's place in African and African-American cultures. While the name and specific descriptions of the figure vary from culture to culture, similarities are numerous and distinct enough that anthropologists, linguists, and historians have developed an incredibly large body of work to which Gates lays claim in his argument that within African, Caribbean, and South American cultures the figure embodies the principle of indeterminacy and interpretation; in other words, Esu embodies "the uncertainties of explication." The divine trickster Esu-Elegbara, tied to the Ifa system of divination, does not survive the journey to North America intact, primarily because African religious and cultural practices were proscribed there, but an important representative of his attributes, the Signifying Monkey, does. The Signifying Monkey, a key player in a group of animal tales and, therefore, in folklore, would certainly have been less threatening than a divine trickster and, as a result, could have escaped the repressive apparatus of the slave system's otherwise quite stringent and comprehensive policing.

In exploring the value of the Signifying Monkey for theorizing about African-American cultural production, Gates must analyze how "signifying" functions in the vernacular. Whereas in standard English, "signification" refers to *meaning,* by contrast, in the vernacular it refers to engagement in rhetorical games; in other words, that which standard English refers to as figuration or figurative language corresponds to signifying in the vernacular. The difference, however, is both more powerful and more subtle than the instrumental difference between the denotative meanings generated by the two practices of language suggests. Although figurative language in standard English is tied to particular kinds of extra-normal usage—such as occasion or other clearly understood and demarcated organized usages as poetry, lyrical prose, or dramatic license—within the dynamic of the vernacular, figurativeness is a mode of speech or conversation as well as a mode of "reading" that speech and "capping" or "revising" it. Vernacular signifying, according to folklorist Roger Abrahams, "emphasizes 're-figuration,'" or "repetition and difference," or "troping" as a matter of *conversational* interplay. So while "signification" refers to "meaning" in standard English, in the vernacular it means "ways of meaning."

Vernacular signifying concerns itself with the *suspension* of meaning and the chaos that ensues. It is a playful mode, full of puns and substitutions that are humorous or functional in a "telling manner." It "luxuriates in the *inclusion* of the free play of associative rhetorical and semantic relations"; in short, "everything that must be excluded for meaning to remain coherent and linear comes to bear with the process of signifying." By contrast, standard English "signification" depends for order and coherence upon *some* attempt at a restraint of "unconscious" associations.

Vernacular signifying always deliberately replaces what is being said, asked, understood with something else—as though the utterance itself were only the departure point for an artistic rearrangement of signs. That the vernacular exists as a discourse parallel to standard English is important, but equally important is the *manner* in which it exists. Vernacular language moves along lines of alteration, maintaining contradictory, ironic, oblique stances vis à vis experience, narration, or even assumptions about reality. Thus, as Claudia Mitchell-Kernan points out [in "Signifying," in *Mother Wit from the Laughing Barrel,* edited by Alan Dundes], one can "signify on" something or someone and redress a power imbalance.

Vernacular signifying is to me an *attitude toward* language fully as much as it is a use of language; as much a reminder of possibilities of meaning as it is a vehicle of meaning. As such, the vernacular is perfectly constituted to undermine ironically whatever dominant language form it employs. In other words, it stands in deconstructive relation to the dominant language whether by using the dialect and syntactical structure of the African-American "other" or by subverting standard English. In this way, the vernacular reflects the defensive status and indirect stance of its users.

While explorations of the vernacular and of signifying as the dominant mode within that system have occupied numerous linguists and anthropologists for at least two decades, Gates draws together their findings and its implications for literary discourse. Following the work of Mitchell-Kernan, Geneva Smitherman, and others, he further elucidates the varieties of rhetorical strategies available in order to put to rest the notion that verbal signifying is only the rhetorical victimage of one powerless person by another equally powerless person in the form of either ritualized insult ex-

changes—such as the "dozens"—or more specific and momentary insults and verbal manipulations.

The political implications for discussions of race and culture are tremendous. Signifying is equivalent to both form and content and serves to mark their relationship to historical context. When one signifies in the public domain—with an owner, employer, or Euro-American readership (within the pages of a text)—one intervenes politically as well as artistically. As the basis of a critical apparatus, signifying allows us to debunk the fallacy that it is only the "stuff" of African-American lies that is art; signifying is a mode of vernacular artistic production as well as a mechanism for "on-site" meta-commentary. As the linchpin of a critical theory, signifying restores the fictiveness and politicalness of verbal indirection, a holdover not just from slavery but from African cultural practice.

Furthermore, signifying is a collectivist mode of artistic production. Within its dynamic, revision is not necessarily always and only an act of individual competition. Gates describes the activity of signifying revision by means of an analogy to jazz: "The most salient analogue for this unmotivated mode of revision in the broader black cultural tradition might be that between black jazz musicians who perform each other's standards on a joint album, not to critique these but to engage in refiguration as an act of homage. . . . This form of the double-voiced implies unity and resemblance rather than critique and difference." Mitchell-Kernan provides another interesting example with her account of her interaction with some of her male signifying respondents, a highly orchestrated exchange with a bit of a bite on her part that keeps the gendered power differential destabilized.

Signifying is both practice and theory since each speaker takes as his/her raw material the previous utterance, then decodes it across a wide spectrum of possibilities, and in finally "capping" it remaps the rhetorical strategy. Signifying also embodies the refusal to be defined, the refusal constantly and consistently to identify oneself and one's position. In short, it marks the refusal . . . to answer as if a problem, to be defined in terms of the categorical imperative, to be "policed" in language.

Finally, signifying reinscribes racial difference as cultural difference, with all of the complexities entailed in such a categorization. Even more significant, racial difference played out in language also marks an interesting nexus of class difference, for while signifying is a "game" activity that cuts across class lines within the African-American group, it was supported in the New World first by the manner in which slavery enforced illiteracy which in turn bolstered an oral tradition, and later by political and economic segregation and continued power differentials. African-Americans have been uni-class for most of their history in the United States, and even now in the late twentieth century, when class divisions are more apparent, not only do class differences among African-Americans continue to be less salient than class and other differences between Euro-Americans and African-Americans, but African-American cultural structures, which have to a great degree survived the Black diaspora, remain steadfast and uniform.

The implications of signifying criticism include the possibility of transforming dominant Euro-American theorizing about African-American culture and the African diaspora, discussing the relationship of language to a political world, and understanding the relationship of an African-American working-class and street people to self-intentioned literariness and self-consciousness within the field of language—a project to which Zora Neale Hurston addressed herself in "Characteristics of Negro Expression" (reprinted in *Voices from the Harlem Renaissance* [1976]).

Gates's contribution to our appreciation of the extent of African "holdovers" in the New World is profound. . . . African-Americans were not a blank slate, despite the intention and efforts of the slave system to make them so. . . .

Gates's vernacular signifying theory provides at once a way into particular texts, a way to rethink the relationship between African-American texts and other discourses, and a way to chart the political possibilities tied into writers' uses of the vernacular. On a broader field, what Gates is signaling "within the group" is that our tradition is much more varied than our critical apparatuses have been able to account for; but, more important, he is signifying, in the presence of Euro-America, that we do not have to repeat its mistakes about us. . . .

Jerry W. Ward, Jr., with Henry Louis Gates, Jr. (interview date Autumn 1991)

SOURCE: "Interview with Henry Louis Gates, Jr.," in *New Literary History,* Vol. 22, No. 4, Autumn 1991.

[*In the following interview, Gates discusses his views on the primacy of Western culture to the neglect of the study of non-Western cultures.*]

[*Ward*]: *Professor Gates, let us begin with something specific. In* The Future of Literary Theory, *a book edited by Ralph Cohen, the director of the Commonwealth Center, you have an essay entitled* **"Authority, (White) Power, and the (Black) Critic."** *That essay generates, at least for me, some questions about responsibility. To be specific, I want to quote some assertions you make about (black) critics. You wrote:*

We critics of the 1980s have the especial privilege of explicating the black tradition in ever closer detail. We shall not meet this challenge by remaining afraid of, or naive about, literary theory; rather, we will only inflict upon our literary tradition the violation of the uninformed reading. We are the keepers of black literary tradition. No matter what theories we seem to embrace, we have more in common with each other than we do with any other critic of any other literature. We write for each other, and for our own contemporary writers. This relation is a critical trust.

What does the phrase "a critical trust" mean? How does it operate for people who are neither critics nor writers if we interpret those words strictly? Might this idea of a critical trust produce fundamental changes in how we read in the future? How we institutionalize reading in the academic world?

[Gates]: I think it may be best not to interpret that phrase too strictly, but the "critical trust" I had in mind was one shared by those of us who write about African American and African literatures, whatever our "race" or ethnic background might be. I think what I had to say should have gone without saying, but at the time I was writing, I had noticed a great deal of resistance among critics of African American literature to theorizing about that literature. Some of the most exciting developments in the analysis of literature in the past couple of decades—at least to my mind—were dismissed out of hand as "white" and thus alien, foreign, intrusive, an affront to the putative integrity of "our" literature. And I thought it was very important to turn that rhetoric on its head and encourage people to rethink that kind of reflexive repudiation. African American culture was "impure," relational from its inception, whether the relation between cultures was conflictual or cross-fertilizing. And since I take this to be one of the most interesting and compelling features of diasporic cultures, I find it strange that some would try to make of black culture a sump of essentialism. Like most people who take the study of culture seriously, I distrust boundaries, I distrust border patrols, I don't want to be told that something is "outside." If you're a critic, know the tools of your trade so you can make an informed choice about them. So much posturing goes on in the profession that it makes some academic critics uncomfortable when you point out that their first and primary audience is other critics. Maybe that's good, maybe it's bad, and let's face it, that's the way it is. Who do you think reads *Critical Inquiry* or *PMLA* or *New Literary History*? But—and I think this is particularly the case for African American literature criticism, because of the "advocacy" role that's historically been thrust upon it—we're also part of a conversation with our artists and writers. What we have to say matters to them, and more than you might think. Third, I think there's a responsibility to translate obscure academic jargon into language accessible to a broader audience. Which is one of the reasons I do so much literary journalism: I think it's important to be able to move between discursive realms, and if we're onto something, we should try it out in a larger, more public forum. Finally, there's no denying that black critics—and this is probably a case where ethnicity isn't irrelevant—have, willy-nilly, a special relationship with what the media call the "black community." We're in a position to heighten interest and awareness in black history, to raise literacy, to encourage people to read more. We can make a difference to the way basic literature training is done in the public schools, by integrating the subject matter of anthologies and teaching guides, something which is important to people of the inner city. And this, too, I see as part of our larger cultural function.

I appreciate your clarifying the various levels at which criticism might operate with regard to a mass of people, which I hesitate to call the black community. That might be a misunderstood construction. Let us say among people of African descent in this country who need to broaden their access to discourses. The critical trust is something we should respect and do more to develop.

And we can't pretend that the nature of the subject matter is irrelevant to this. I remember when I was at an Episcopal church camp when I was fifteen years old. We didn't get daily newspapers there, but we did get the Sunday paper. And one Sunday, the headline read: "Negroes Riot in Watts." I didn't know what this meant. Did it mean white people were killing black people? Were black people killing white people? And where in the world was Watts? A very sensitive Episcopal priest from New England gave me a copy of *Notes of a Native Son* by James Baldwin. I had always read voraciously, and I kept a commonplace book where I had written down paragraphs that named things I felt deeply but couldn't yet articulate. Well, when I read James Baldwin, I transcribed virtually the whole book in my commonplace book. It fueled a love of literature like nothing I had ever experienced before. I began to *engulf* books written by black authors. I began to read everything that I could order through the local newspaper store in Piedmont, West Virginia. I'd gather up bottles and get coins, then spend them all on books.

You bring up nostalgia. I recall the only book I have ever read aloud to another person is Baldwin's The Fire Next Time.

It's a book I love. Which isn't to say that I wasn't as deeply moved by *Pride and Prejudice, Little Dorrit, Hamlet,* or what not, like any other kid in high school. But I think that, given the way ethnic identity is socially constructed, one as it were, learns how to be "black" in this society. It happens through the tutelage of one's parents and relatives, through the examples of one's friends, and particularly in adolescence through the written examples provided by other people of color writing precisely, about discovering that they were black, discovering that being black put them at a disadvantage in American society, and learning how to cope with that complexity.

Doesn't that also operate for learning to be American? I'm not sure that what it is to be an American has been fully identified. I think of projects in canon reform or revolution that encourage us to have a very different view of what American literature is, a composite of various tradition. The process you described may be related to learning to be an American.

Absolutely. I think that one of our most eloquent commentators on this is James Baldwin. In his famous essay "The Discovery of What It Means to Be An American" he said that as soon as one leaves the United States one realizes one has more in common with all those people one thought one hated than one does with anyone else in the world. For an African American, it can be disconcerting to discover this, whether in Paris or Lagos or Nairobi or Manila. But one does discover Americanness. Which isn't to say that we have a genuinely public culture yet. The regnant myth of a common public culture is based on the fiction of an Anglo-American regional culture that has passed itself off as universally American. We have, in effect, forced underground the various cultures of color that are proliferating now—Native American, Asian American, Hispanic American, African American, et cetera—depicting them as "parochial," "tribal," "local," and somehow not truly American. What we are seeing—and this is causing great anxiety in many quarters—is a fundamental redefinition of what common public American culture might and in fact will be in the twenty-first century, a culture that is embracive of the excluded voices of those various cultures of color.

Part of the resistance to such a move is illustrated by today's editorial "The Politics of Culture" in The University Journal, *which refers to your lecture* **"Goodbye Columbus: Public Culture in an Age after Empire."** *While the editorial is generally commendatory, the very last paragraph suggests a fundamental misunderstanding of what you were trying to say. The editor insists that you fail "to adequately appreciate the central role Western culture must take in formulating a global culture." Would you comment on that reading of your lecture?*

It is an interesting misreading, since, as you know, nothing I said in the speech was derogatory about so-called Western culture and its remarkable achievements. That's not to say that this tortoise-shell thing called "Western culture," like every other culture I know about, can't and shouldn't be taken to task for its failings, and indeed, the strain of self-criticism is a strain found within "Western culture" itself. But I did want to emphasize that the notion that the cultures of the West are the only ones worth studying and learning from is simply untenable. We are woefully ignorant of much of the achievements of the world's great civilizations. I believe that, without diminishing the role of Western culture, we can stop pretending that it has an exclusive claim on truth and beauty.

I'd also like to know about other works-in-progress, especially your book on canon formation and the black tradition and the collection you are doing with Kimberly Benston, **The Language of Blackness: Reading the Afro-American Literary Tradition.** *What is the focus of each?*

The book really charts the debate over multiculturalism from the very beginning when I was determined to establish a case for it, using examples from the African American and African traditions, to the critique of the excesses of the multiculturalist movement, which I do in **"Goodbye Columbus."** While I've ended up as something of a gadfly to both the left and the right, I firmly believe in an academic arena that is culturally plural; I think this is inevitable. We are who we are because of complex historical forces: we're not trying to make anyone feel guilty about it. But it's important to see the West not as a mythical, integrative whole, but as part of a larger whole. That doesn't mean that we have to pretend we're Martians without our own biases and preferences. It's neither possible nor desirable to suspend the faculty of judgment. Patriarchy isn't any prettier in Yorubal and than in Europe. Ethnic hatred isn't any nobler in Burundi than in Bensonhurst.

And **The Language of Blackness** *will contain essays by a variety of critics?*

The Language of Blackness is a Festschrift, a collection of essays dedicated to the career and contributions of the late Charles T. Davis, who was both Kimberly Benston's and my own mentor at Yale University. Kimberly Benston is the chair of the English Department at Haverford College. We were undergraduates together at Yale; we were junior faculty members at Yale, and, in fact, we both left Yale at the same time. Charles Davis was a subtle critic, a generous person, and a very distinguished teacher who functioned as a midwife to a younger generation of critics of African American literature. He was the first person of African descent to serve on the faculty at Princeton. A number of his essays were collected in the book, *Black is the Color of the Cosmos.* We invited several colleagues and critics to write essays in honor of his memory. This book should be published next year by the University of Illinois Press.

Let's consider briefly the matter of terminology. Some terms seem so embedded in our thinking about culture that despite our best efforts we can't get rid of them. I have in mind the terms *minority and* majority. *Would you agree that these are in a family relationship with the term race, being very ambiguous, slippery, divisive? Can you envision a future in which we might have fruitful analysis of culture, society, and literature without these terms?*

All these terms are indeed slippery, ambiguous, and potentially dangerous. I'm not fond of the words *minority* and *majority,* because they seem to bias the formula from the very beginning. In the same way, *race* comes with a lot of historical baggage. I try to be careful when I use them, though I realize I don't always succeed. But if you ask what other terms we might substitute for these terms, I'm not sure what they might be. I do think it's important to give specificity to concepts of ethnicity, rather than eliding the differences between Asian Americans, African Americans, Hispanic Americans by subsuming them under the master rubric of *minority.* That does great disservice to the differences among these cultures, as well as their different positioning within the larger society. But the violence of our conventional vocabulary of the "minority" is to pretend that a non-Anglo-Saxon culture has something interesting in common with another non-Anglo-Saxon culture.

Yes. And the language itself allows for this. I am indeed interested in what terms we might evolve. I return to the metaphoric images that emerge for me when one talks about "margin," "center," "mainstream." We are trying to deal with movement, but we fail to deal with it. We just cover it over.

There's a danger that by privileging the rhetoric of the margin, we only reinscribe this relation of marginality. We know that the boundaries between black culture and white culture in America have always been fluid, have always been porous. To pretend otherwise really perpetuates a racist fiction about American culture.

Speaking of racist fictions and clarification of mythologies. . . . Well, would you explain the grounds upon which you served as an expert witness in the 1990 trial of 2 Live Crew?

Thank you for asking. I was approached by a correspondent at *The New York Times* who asked me if I would comment about the censorship of 2 Live Crew in Florida. I told him I couldn't comment because I hadn't heard the tape. He suggested I get the tape, and we spoke the next day. Listening to the album, I was struck by two things. First, much of the album was self-consciously parodic; one of the songs is called the "2 Live Blues," which takes the classic blues stanza form and turns it inside out in an obvious and heavy-handed parody:

My baby left me,
and I've never been so happy in my whole life,
and yesterday I slept with my neighbor's wife
and broke up their happy home.

Or something like that. It's the reverse of what the blues are all about. Second, I felt that it took racist stereotypes of black men and black women, particularly their supposed hypersexuality, and exaggerated them to the point where you could only laugh at how ridiculous it all was. I was also struck by the album's sexism and misogyny, which reflected elements of vernacular black culture, certainly, but which was pushed to such an extreme that its effect was, again, parodic. I didn't think Luther Campbell was an advertisement for black macho, I thought he made it seem silly. I compared it to Archie Bunker's blatant racism on "All in the Family," which was hardly meant to reinforce those attitudes. More worrisome, I wondered why it was that of all performances in this country, whether on the comedy stage or popular American music, the only people to be arrested for "talking dirty" were these young black men. The racial aspect of this bothered me. Dirty rap was seen as peculiarly inflammatory, because black people were seen as peculiarly inflammable. So I did what I could to stop their conviction. Unfortunately, many otherwise sophisticated people do not understand the status of censorship and free speech in this country, and frankly, my involvement in the trial was pretty unpopular. *Of course,* it's a problematic case. *Every* first amendment case is "problematic." But all these right-thinking people were saying, "It goes without saying that Luther Campbell's first amendment rights must be protected, *but. . . .* " And nobody was willing to lift a finger to see that these first amendment rights *were* protected. People preferred to keep their hands clean, so nobody could reproach them for being politically incorrect or whatever. But under the law, it's not enough to cry "First Amendment." Right now, the law of the land is the Supreme Court ruling in *Miller v. California* (1973), according to which speech offensive to the local community standard is only entitled to first amendment protection if it has significant political, scientific, or artistic value, as established by "objective" standards, hence the juridical role of the "expert testimony." Me, I think *Miller v. California* is obscene, but what can you do? As a witness for the defense, I talked a little about the black traditions of signifying and playing the dozens, which were "filthy dirty," as my mother would say. If you have much familiarity with that kind of thing, then 2 Live Crew is nothing new. Which doesn't exempt us from the need to critique the sexual politics of much black "street culture" today, including the work of rap artists.

Your ending the explanation with matters of historical understanding ties into other commitments you have, whether literary or cultural, to the history of African American products. That is important, because we have a dangerous loss of genuine historical memory in this country. What critics

can do might help. I can't know how effective it will be. There is another aspect of your defense that interests me. We need to think about morality or its absence in American society. In your address **"Goodbye Columbus,"** *you did mention, with trepidation as you put it, "that it's worth distinguishing between morality and moralism" and, in what I take to be a gloss, comment that "the critical hair-shirt has become more of a fashion statement than a political one." Can we turn that back to our utterances as critics? How do we treat a distinction between morality and moralism in public affairs, which I would distinguish from literary critical affairs in the community of interpreters? What effect might our utterances have in a much larger, less controllable arena?*

We can never control completely how what we say will be used, no matter who we are, no matter where we are. One of the reasons I like to give talks is that it gives me a chance to explain "what I meant." That is very important; it's important to continue the dialogue, because these are issues that matter to people. Who would have thought five years ago that the politics of culture would be so important? At the same time, we've developed a whole rhetoric of academic interchange where one comfortable, middle-class academic decides that another comfortable, middle-class academic is complicitous with Larger Oppressive Structures because he or she failed to "acknowledge" some theoretical nicety or other. I think this kind of rhetoric is beginning to strike our ears as hollow, bumptious, and unhelpful. The unglamorous truth is that we are all teachers, first and last; rather little of what we say in this country, even if cast in the most explicitly political tones, has an appreciable political effect. It's time to move beyond the windy self-righteousness that's so cherished both on the left and on the right—and I don't exempt myself from this critique, either. Nor is this to trivialize what we're about. America is at a point of transition, and there really is great confusion about it. I think a lot of people are looking for commentators to help them understand what is happening in our society and to our society. So I think this is a time for care in our public discourse, not a time for either feel-good rhetoric or threatening, accusatory rhetoric that preempts real conversation. I can understand very well why people feel embattled, feel they must fight to defend the primary role of this thing called Western culture. What I have tried to make clear is that the primacy of Western culture is not at issue. It's just that we owe it to ourselves to try to account for and understand the contributions of other cultures as well. To do this, we need to move beyond ethnic absolutism of any kind. A proliferation of narrow ethnic chauvinisms isn't the objective; a genuine conversation among the different voices very much *is.*

Gerald Early (essay date 21 April 1996)

SOURCE: "Black Like Them," in *New York Times Book Review,* April 21, 1996, pp. 7, 9.

[*Early is an American author and educator. In the following review, he notes contradictions and inconsistencies in* The Future of the Race.]

Indeed, for the first time in African-American history there is a powerful, thoroughly credentialed and completely professionalized black intellectual class, something wished for since March 5, 1897, when the American Negro Academy was formed in Washington by Alexander Crummell, Francis Grimk and W. E. B. Du Bois for the express purpose of providing such a cadre of minds and pens. Today's generation of black intellectuals has been well publicized; in fact, it has access to the entire machinery of intellectual self-promotion. There is all sorts of deconstructionist, postmodernist talk about the representation and colonialization of the black body, but our culture is perhaps more than a little ironically enjoying a romance with the black mind. In the end, books like *The Bell Curve* may only succeed in intensifying the thrill. That the race question has become a near-manic intellectual concern is less surprising than the intellectual establishment's need to have a phalanx of highly educated blacks who are experts on the race question—in essence, experts on the meaning of themselves and their presence. But what is the meaning of their ambition, and what is its end?

The Future of the Race is a short volume consisting of an essay by Mr. Gates, an essay by Mr. West and two essays by the father of the modern black intellectual, W. E. B. Du Bois, preceded by an informative preface by Mr. Gates. The subject is what Du Bois called the Talented Tenth, or the very class of black folk that Mr. Gates, a professor of humanities and chairman of the department of Afro-American studies at Harvard University, and Mr. West, a professor of Afro-American studies and of the philosophy of religion there, typify—gifted, ambitious black thinkers who wish to lead the race. For the authors represent not only a black intellectual class but a black middle class of the best and brightest. If, in America, the middle class is the most anxiety-ridden, then the black middle class is in an absolute quagmire of insecurity. Members of the black middle class sweat over whether they are sell-outs, if they have succeeded on merit, how much their race may still hold them back, if they are authentically "black." Now that an expansionist, self-reflective black middle class is an object of curiosity for whites as well as for itself, it is no wonder this book exists. If it is a truism that each American generation has been promised more than its predecessors can ever hope to deliver, then it is clear that this generation of blacks—promised so much more by the civil rights movement than what was ultimately delivered but finally given more than any generation of blacks ever had in the United States—should wish

to be in touch with the meaning of it all, should wish to ask itself that grand bourgeois question: How are we doing?

Like Du Bois, Mr. Gates and Mr. West are writing essays about not only why they exist but, in essence, why they should. Naturally, wishing to demonstrate their racial solidarity with and their concern (and relevance) for those less fortunate, they are rather predictably liberal in their political views. After all, they, like all black Americans, are the products of reform gone right (or awry). In their joint introduction to the book, though, they manage to strike just the right centrist note: social reform must be accompanied by personal initiative.

The question, inescapably Victorian in its aspect, that the authors wish to answer—what is their duty to the lower or less fortunate class of blacks?—indicates the black bourgeoisie's inability to understand precisely what their success means to themselves or to blacks generally. The fact that a certain number of people had to suffer, even die, for this class to have its success seems, as much as anything, the occasion for this book: both Mr. Gates and Mr. West want to show that they are sufficiently aware of, and humbled by, the circumstances of their good fortune.

Mr. Gates and Mr. West respond to both Du Bois's original essay, written in 1903, and his revisions on the subject, written in 1948. Both have written essays reflecting their individual temperaments, one supposes, as much as their writerly artifices: Mr. Gates is engagingly witty and journalistic, and uses dollops of statistics and an occasional arcane word or literary reference to let us know he is, after all, an academic; Mr. West paints on a larger canvas, grasping for prophecy, sermonic by turns as well as performing something of an intellectual tour de force, never allowing his reader to forget for one instant that he, too, is an academic.

Neither essay represents its writer at his best. The pieces seem hastily written. Mr. Gates's is an autobiographical sketch of his undergraduate days at Yale during the early 1970's. He draws a touching, vivid picture of being a black student at a prestigious white school, of ungainly political posturing arising mostly from a sense of enormous fear and, paradoxically, from expectations that were both too great and not great enough. I was a student at the University of Pennsylvania from 1970 to 1974, and reading this I felt the shock of recognition.

The weaknesses of this essay come in the sections where Mr. Gates decides to become something like a public policy analyst or where he talks about the black arts—all too sweeping and too superficial to be taken seriously. But the entire essay is informed by a subtle intelligence, a sense that Mr. Gates understands the true contradiction here: that the very measures of assimilation that were used to free blacks from their alienation, both within and beyond their group, simply intensify it. The other major question—why are there so many blacks at risk when there are so many successful blacks?—arises not simply from guilt but from sheer befuddlement. But Mr. Gates seems to think the answer is taking more good-will money from white pockets; at the end of his essay, he recounts his student-days attempt to sucker his dean into sending him to Africa to find himself. In the land of the Yankee peddler, it is not a bad thing to be a "hustler."

In this regard, one might have thought he would have been a bit fairer to Booker T. Washington, a quintessential hustler, in his preface to the Du Bois essays in this volume. He promotes Du Bois at Washington's expense. Washington on more than one occasion tried to hire Du Bois, and he financially backed Du Bois's research for years. Moreover, Washington, far from being an ogre on black liberal arts education, was responsible for Fisk University getting its Carnegie Library when he served on Fisk's board of trustees. He obtained libraries for several other black liberal arts schools as well. Washington was devious but not cruel or uncaring.

Mr. West's essay is not so charming and coherent as Mr. Gates's. He is a more strident believer in "transformational politics," so his essay suffers from being earnest. The first part, largely an analysis of Du Bois as a thinker, is fair enough, although some of the criticism seems not to consider him as a person of his times (as Mr. West is unquestionably a person of his). In the end, it seems that Mr. West condemns the turn-of-the-century Du Bois for being insufficiently left-wing and not politically correct enough. He hadn't read his Marx and Freud. He believed too much in the Enlightenment, rationalism and the like. But Du Bois had read his William James, his Hegel, his Descartes, his Schopenhauer and his Herder. He had also read his Horace Mann and his J. L. M. Curry, contemporary educators, and since Du Bois's essays are very much theories of education, talking about Du Bois in this context would have been more useful than in the context Mr. West employs. Between the publication of Du Bois's two essays was John Dewey's landmark "Democracy and Education" in 1916. How did Dewey affect Du Bois? How did Jane Addams influence Du Bois? Mr. West never considers these questions.

The major problem with this essay, especially in its second part when things really get sermonic and moralistic, is that there is too much free association and not enough in-depth analysis. Mr. West speaks, for instance, of the moans and cries of certain African-American musicians, writers and ministers. But what does this mean? Are there not profound moans and cries in opera, in bel canto, in Shaker hymns, in the works of the metaphysical poets? Mr. West quotes a long passage from Toni Morrison, saying that it "depicts in a concrete and graphic way the enactment and expression of black love, black joy, black community and black faith that bears witness to black suffering and keeps alive a vision of black hope." What does this sentence mean? How does putting "black" in front of a string of nouns clarify anything? Moreover, the entire sentiment seems in contradiction with his concern about the white racist tendency to lump blacks together and not understand them as individuals. Isn't he guilty of the same thing when he writes such maudlin sentences?

The Future of the Race provides the great service of reprinting the Du Bois essays, which still make singular reading—better reading than Mr. Gates's or Mr. West's pieces. The very Victorian idea of a social mission described in the 1903 essay—which was written at a time when college-educated blacks were articulating social mission through the formation of Alpha Kappa Alpha and Alpha Phi Alpha, through the formation of women's clubs, through the formation of professional baseball teams all called "giants"—is still compelling, still worth emulating. Neither Mr. Gates nor Mr. West approaches anything like the verve and candor of Oscar Wilde's 1891 masterpiece, "The Soul of Man Under Socialism," although Mr. Gates is far more honest than Mr. West is about the rank opportunism concealed in his (and all) bourgeois ambition. Would that some black might say, "I have little interest in speaking to the poor and absolutely none in speaking for them, so how am I to be my brother's and sister's keeper as I must be?" Old-fashioned Victorian mission might be the best way to rid ourselves of the stigma of the poor, by never forgetting how much we, the bourgeoisie, owe them for what we are and what we aren't.

Vince Passaro (essay date July 1997)

SOURCE: "Black Letters on a White Page," in *Harper's Magazine,* Vol. 295, No. 1766, July 1997, pp. 70-75.

[*In the following essay, Passaro discusses the* Norton Anthology of African American Literature, *of which Gates served as an editor, considering the paradoxical nature of African American art and social and economic status.*]

To understand the machinery of contemporary African American cultural studies, one might look at the back cover of the recent *Norton Anthology of African American Literature,* edited by Henry Louis Gates Jr. and Nellie Y. McKay. Across the top, in gold type dropping out of a dark green band, stands a blurb from Cornel West: "A classic of splendid proportions," he announces, leaving the reader to wonder whether he is referring to the book's large size or to its contents. What only specialized observers will know is that Gates, the more prominent and influential of the volume's two editors, is Chair of the Afro-American Studies Department at Harvard University, where West, when not busy writing content-free blurbs for Gates's books, reports to him as one of the department's best-known professors. The world of African American studies is a small one, but over the last twenty years it has become enormously influential within American universities and, more recently, in the culture at large.

Henry Louis Gates Jr. sits atop that world. *The Norton Anthology* in the first month of its publication sold more than 30,000 volumes, making it the fastest-selling anthology in the illustrious history of Norton literary textbooks. Gates, a promotional wizard, can be at least partially credited with the book's enormous success. Glowing reports of its achievement appeared in such forums as Frank Rich's op-ed column in the *New York Times,* in that paper's culture pages, and on a *Charlie Rose* show largely dedicated to Gates that aired in February. On other fronts in the Gates empire, one could read almost universally favorable reviews of his recent collection of essays and profiles entitled *Thirteen Ways of Looking at a Black Man* and, not long after, similarly positive reviews of *The Dictionary of Global Culture,* co-edited with Kwame Anthony Appiah. And although he was not one of the editors of *The Oxford Companion to African American Literature,* also published this year, Oxford turned to him for his imprimatur in the form of a foreword to the book.

Having one's name on four major books in a couple of months is impressive work. Gates's memoir of three years ago, *Colored People,* was similarly well-reviewed, his pieces are regularly published in *The New Yorker,* and he is quoted and called upon by journalists in most significant commentaries about black America. Gates resides now in a position almost unimaginable three decades ago, when he was a young intellectual working shrewdly beside rather than within the Black Arts movement.

To attain such a position of authority requires several well-developed skills. Hard work certainly helps: Gates has written six books of his own, including four earlier, well-received works of literary and cultural criticism; co-written another with West; edited not only *The Dictionary of Global Culture* and *The Norton Anthology* but the collection *Reading Black, Reading Feminist;* and served as series editor for such monstrous projects as the complete works of Zora Neale Hurston, the forty-volume *Schomburg Library of Nineteenth-Century Black Women Writers,* and the thirty-volume *African-American Women Writers 1910-1940.* In other words, Gates has made himself the most prolific and influential mainstream scholar in the most popular academic subject of our time.

For the most part this is a fortunate thing. Gates ranks as the most able writer and critic in his field, and one of the best in literary academia. He is a smooth prose stylist and a

reliably intelligent if rarely skeptical critic, one whose strength resides in the convincing advocacy of certain literary figures, movements, and forms rather than in diagnosis or deconstruction. Nevertheless, maintaining the position of chief spokesman for such a heavily institutional movement as multicultural literary studies also demands a continual, quick-footed dance with political orthodoxy—an orthodoxy now less obviously tilted toward a distinct ruling class than it once was, yet more often riddled with internal contradictions. Gates thrives in these gray zones, as his own writing demonstrates.

In *Thirteen Ways of Looking at a Black Man,* a collection of Gates's profiles published largely in *The New Yorker* over the last few years, one may see the personal and political passions that animate him and stand central to his career as a critic and a scholar. The title of the collection—a play on the title of Wallace Stevens's poem "Thirteen Ways of Looking at a Blackbird"—captures Gates's main interests, which have evolved over the last ten years or so from the issue of authentic black expression to the larger question of what is authentic "blackness," especially for black men. The problem is a personal one. He mentions it in interviews, in *Thirteen Ways,* in *Colored People,* and elsewhere. Focusing on such a question puts Gates in a difficult intellectual position, for it posits, and then balefully argues against, the assertion that legitimate and authentic culture in America is perceived only as white culture. Therefore, the black artist, writer, scholar, or politician cannot define himself freely but must work within a complex role that already has been established for him—that of the outsider, the outlaw, someone heroically disadvantaged and separate. This issue of an enforced and disempowering identity haunts black American writers, of course, but for the best of them it remains secondary. Growing up in more hateful times, writers such as Ralph Ellison, Albert Murray, and James Baldwin forced themselves beyond the constraints of white culture; they understood in a deeper sense their true relation to it (thus can Murray openly admire Thomas Mann and Ellison can praise William Faulkner); they came to value their own worth and to recognize the highly individual and essentially nonracial difficulty of knowing their own souls. No one has yet analyzed in any extensive way why a later generation of black American thinkers and artists often lacks this essential artistic self-confidence. Gates himself touches on the issue, especially in writing about Murray and Baldwin, but ultimately does not meet it head on. To begin to assess the problem would be to impute a failure, to condemn certain black writers of his generation.

And condemn he does not. Only in Gates's "outing" of Anatole Broyard, a writer who denied his black parentage and spent his life passing as white (the payoff being a job as a book critic for the *Times*), does one sense in Gates a hardness of sentiment and a streak of intellectual disapproval. Interestingly enough, the Broyard profile is one of the most absorbing and elegantly written pieces in *Thirteen Ways.*

The essay about the great critic Albert Murray forms the book's most striking contrast between black writers and critics of Gates's generation and those born earlier. Much of Murray's thinking and writing is aimed at challenging conventional assumptions. He is suspicious of the reaction to such lovable black literary figures as the poet Maya Angelou and even asks what no other prominent commentator, black or white, has asked about Toni Morrison's Nobel Prize—whether it was not "tainted with do-goodism." Of course, the Nobel Prizes were invented as "do-goodism"; they have always been "tainted," to use Murray's word, with politics, and the politics have always been left-of-center. Morrison's work will last, I suspect, at least as long as Hemingway's or Steinbeck's. On the issue of Morrison, Gates politely puts down his foot, "agree[ing] to disagree" and associating himself with her in the ways major critics traditionally have endorsed certain writers as emblems both of their era and of the critic's own aesthetic principles.

In Maya Angelou, however, we have something else together. In the Murray profile, as elsewhere in these essays, when something negative is to be said, Gates lets other people do the talking while he stands by making no comment and offering no defense. Murray describes Angelou's performance at Bill Clinton's first inaugural as a kind of traditional black entertainment, dazzling the white folks. Gates includes the accusation but lets it sit there, like a burning car in an otherwise empty parking lot. In such silent moments, one realizes that black radicalism, now tenured, has been utterly marginalized, its critical discourse so deadened that a literary figure of Gates's intelligence and stature cannot bring himself to say anything bad about, or leave out of his pantheon, even the most mediocre black artists. At the inaugural, Bill Clinton, whose signature on welfare "reform" would follow three years later, used Maya Angelou, a very weak poet, as a new, mediagenic form of lawn jockey, and no one in the new black-culture orthodoxy, as far as I know, has uttered a word of criticism about her willingness to play the part.

Given the complexity of Gates's role within the black intellectual community and his relationship with the white culture, *The Norton Anthology,* as he initiated it eleven years ago and as it appears with him as co-editor, becomes that much richer an emblem of the multicultural-studies movement. Gates has a unifying sensibility in a field that is fractious by definition. His aesthetic, I suspect, has helped lend the book its tone of distant and established authority, and guided its effort to conceive of African American literature as a coherent development over the last three centuries. But it has also meant the inclusion of work that is not up to

par and a suffusion of editorial sentimentality and weak politics.

Nonetheless, the anthology is an immensely interesting and valuable work. It will change the teaching of American literature in the classroom, spotlighting certain works that, because they were once difficult to find, only occasionally made their way onto university reading lists.

Moreover, the volume may provide the happiest marriage of chronology with theme that I have seen in an anthology. The book is arranged with an introductory section, "The Vernacular Tradition," that moves across all major periods and concentrates on music and the spoken word. Six main sections follow, each informed by the thematically overarching "Vernacular" section: "The Literature of Slavery and Freedom: 1746-1865"; "Literature of the Reconstruction and the New Negro Renaissance," which takes one through 1919; "Harlem Renaissance: 1919-1940"; "Realism, Naturalism, Modernism: 1940-1960"; "The Black Arts Movement: 1960-1970"; and "Literature Since 1970." Within these capacious rooms are stored amazing treasures: the fascinating early slave narratives, for example, and, closely related to them, what can be described as didactic tracts on slavery, which are extraordinary documents insofar as they detail the very mechanisms of repression constructed to prevent such writing. A reader cannot help but recognize something miraculous in these early texts, not for any "defect overcome" by the Africans who produced them but for the lengths to which their overseers went to keep their slaves from mastering the English literary arts. Not only did the government of a given population of slaves depend on this repression; the entire underlying presumption of black inferiority was threatened as well, a fact that the early writers unmistakably recognized and exploited. Among the slave narratives, one of the first and most direct, Olaudah Equiano's "The Interesting Narrative of the Life of Olaudah Equiano, or Gustavus Vassa, the African, Written by Himself," is fascinating for its clarity of expression and its self-confident good humor. Victor Séjour's short story, "The Mulatto," the first known work of fiction by an African American, appears here in the first widely available translation from the French, and it is a small masterpiece. Also included are Harriet Jacobs's "Incidents in the Life of a Slave Girl," Frances Harper's poems and essays, and what is considered to be the first African American novel, Harriet E. Wilson's *Our Nig.*

Frederick Douglass's extraordinary *Narrative of the Life* is reprinted in full, as is W. E. B. Du Bois's equally seminal later work, *The Souls of Black Folk,* published in 1903 and containing the prophetic (and starkly beautiful) lines: "The problem of the twentieth century is the problem of the color-line,—the relation of the darker to the lighter races of men in Asia and Africa, in America and the islands of the sea." Later, in the Harlem Renaissance section, is Jean Toomer's

"Cane," a breathtaking Modernistic prose construction, beautifully and powerfully charged:

> Karintha is a woman. She who carries beauty, perfect as dusk when the sun goes down. She has been married many times. Old men remind her that a few years back they rode her hobby-horse upon their knees. Karintha smiles, and indulges them when she is in the mood for it. She has contempt for them. Karintha is a woman. Young men run stills to make her money. Young men go to the big cities and run on the road. Young men go away to college. They all want to bring her money. . . . A child fell out of her womb onto a bed of pine-needles in the forest. Pine-needles are smooth and sweet.

In the period of intense literary experimentation in Europe and the United States, corresponding roughly to the second generation of liberty for African Americans, black writers were in a position of unusual freedom in their language and narrative sensibilities; they drew on the cadences, idioms, and vocabularies of both black and white America, and were less hindered by the traditional forms that often bound their European counterparts. By the early twentieth century, African American writers were not only able but eager to "make it new," to use Ezra Pound's exhortation. Especially in the early twentieth century and the Harlem Renaissance period, writers such as Hurston and Claude McKay and Toomer, among many others, moved gracefully into a powerful form of Modernism, echoing the aesthetic sentiment of one of T. S. Eliot's early titles for *The Waste Land:* "He Do the Police in Different Voices." Their essential historical experience, that of exile and debasement, is the Modern artistic experience. The anthology goes on and on, more than 2,600 pages featuring many, many fine writers, each sharing a culture and a language both permanently separated from and yet passionately defining something, often discussed but never satisfactorily captured, called "America."

The introduction of African Americans to the United States constituted in most cases an introduction to Christianity, and to American Protestant Christianity in particular. From the mélange of biblical narratives made available in that tradition, African Americans quickly appropriated for their own special purposes the central Christian narrative of prolonged suffering, isolation, imprisonment, and eventual redemption and release. Thus did Exodus, as one example, become their tale—slavery, escape, trial, justification.

"The Vernacular Tradition" as articulated by the editors, with its overwhelmingly Christian atmosphere ("Spirituals," "Sermons," even "Blues"), stands over the rest of the volume, giving meaning not only to the language of the African American tradition but to its philosophical foundations as well. The "Sermons" section, also within the introductory

"Vernacular Tradition," moves from early verse sermon to Malcolm X. The highlights include Martin Luther King's "I've Been to the Mountaintop," which I have always preferred to his "I Have a Dream" speech, also included here, because the former is personal and anguished, and improvisationally explains the meaning of King's entire ministry:

> I remember in Birmingham, Alabama, when we were in that majestic struggle there we would move out of the 16th Street Baptist Church day after day; by the hundreds we would move out. And Bull Connor would tell them to send the dogs forth and they did come; but we just went before the dogs singing, "Ain't gonna let nobody turn me round." Bull Connor next would say, "Turn the fire hoses on." And as I said to you the other night, Bull Connor didn't know history. He knew a kind of physics that somehow didn't relate to the transphysics that we knew about. And that was the fact that there was a certain kind of fire that no water could put out. And we went before the fire hoses; we had known water. If we were Baptist or some other denomination, we had been immersed. If we were Methodist, and some others, we had been sprinkled, but we knew water.

Unfortunately, though, there is an introduction to the section.

> The African American sermon is a complex oratorical form with significant differences from religion to religion, denomination to denomination, region to region, and era to era. Sermons heard in a northern Nation of Islam mosque differ significantly from those heard in a down-home Southern Baptist church. Those flattening out all of these differences to expound on *the* black sermon deny this pulchritudinous variety and do a serious injustice to history and its unfurling.

Hyperbole and jargon rule the day. Repeatedly, and nowhere more than in the "Sermons" section, is the theme of "the vernacular tradition" abused in service of a favorite social theory of contemporary academics: a denial of the efficacy of actual individual authorship and a new definition of literature as a form of cultural production, the result of "call and response" between speaker and listener, the expression of whole communities. I, for one, have always preferred the late Harold Brodkey's definition of literature, pure and explicit in its hegemonic tendencies: "I speak, you listen."

Fortunately we have the writers themselves. The nineteenth-century poetry and commentary by black women would make a fascinating volume of its own (or forty volumes, as noted above); the early slave narratives and slave poetry are composed of a language that feels immediate and, in the way that only Southern American writing can be, both elegant and colloquial in describing a circumstantial horror, often taking a surprisingly long historical view. Also to be visited in this volume are the incomparable greats of black literature in this century, including Du Bois, Langston Hughes, Ellison, Richard Wright, Hurston, Baldwin, Murray, Chester Himes (though not enough of him), and Gwendolyn Brooks. Among contemporary authors, there are arrayed some of the best American writers working today, including John Edgar Wideman, Jamaica Kincaid, James Alan McPherson, and Walter Mosley.

But perhaps most astonishing are the folktales, which constitute the single most entertaining and splendid portion of the anthology. I am a particular fan of "Deer Hunting Story":

> You know Ole Massa took a nigger deer huntin' and posted him in his place and told him, says: "Now you wait right here and keep yo' gun reformed and ready. Ah'm goin' 'round de hill and skeer up de deer and head him dis way. When he come past, you shoot."

> De nigger says: "Yessuh, Ah sho' will, Massa."

> He set there and waited wid de gun all cocked and after a while de deer come tearin' past him. He didn't make a move to shoot de deer so he went on 'bout his business. After while de white man come on 'round de hill and ast de nigger: "Did you kill de deer?"

> De nigger says: "Ah ain't seen no deer pass here yet."

> Massa says: "Yes, you did. You couldn't help but see him. He come right dis way."

> Nigger says: "Well Ah sho' ain't seen none. All Ah seen was a white man come along here wid a pack of chairs on his head and Ah tipped my hat to him and waited for de deer."

This comes from Zora Neale Hurston's collection of folktales heard, collected, and remembered, *Mules and Men.* Unfortunately, in a fit of caution, perhaps necessary given the passionately un-ironic audience that has created such a large market for this book, the editors add a footnote: "Note the deliberate spoofing of the white 'Massa' by the ostensibly respectful 'nigger.'" If there is a vernacular tradition in African American literature, there is an equally significant tradition of multilayered irony, and these tweedy, altogether Caucasian editorial moments do their best to undermine it.

Like every Norton anthology, the present volume also houses a whole family of cultural and political assumptions that the genre cannot acknowledge. Convention dictates that one must call this an "Anthology of Literature," but literature as defined by most readers outside the university makes up only a portion of its entries. Documents of exclusively historical interest take up what seems an unprecedented share of the cabin space, and for reasons that are obvious but not always compelling, more pages here are devoted to song lyrics, by a good deal, than in any other serious literature anthology I have seen. (In a new twist, Norton also offers, through a mail-in card, an accompanying CD for $15.99.) The reader quickly understands that "the vernacular" was established in music and in other forms of public discourse and that its particular tropes and rhythms unify African American cultural experience and absolutely dominate its literary sensibilities. A fifth or a quarter of the songs appearing here would have done just as well. The inclusion of rap songs doesn't particularly help; they are not on the whole very interesting to *read,* and their relationship to contemporary African American writing, or within the increasingly fractionalized African American culture, is not explained. As is, we are left to assume that "Tell old Pharaoh / Let my people go" and "All the jealous punks can't stop the dunk" are both simply parts of the same vital cultural experience.

On the level of strictly literary particulars, the anthology contains many choices that one has to question: Alice Walker, Terry McMillan, and Amiri Baraka are overrepresented here, and overrespected, for that matter. Walker, for instance, is given three times the space of one of the best writers in the country, Jamaica Kincaid, and considerably more room than a host of other, better writers. A fine author of short stories, Edward P. Jones, is not here at all, surprisingly. Even looked at charitably, at least a dozen contemporary writers do not deserve to be in this volume.

Take, for example, this excerpt from Walker's *The Color Purple.*

> Sinners have more good times, I say.

> You know why? she ast.

> Cause you ain't all the time worrying bout God, I say.

> Naw, that ain't it, she say. Us worry bout God a lot. But once us feel loved by God, us do the best us can to please him with what us like.

> You telling me God love you, and you ain't never done nothing for him? I mean, not go to church, sing in the choir, feed the preacher and all like that?

But if God love me, Celie, I don't have to do all
that. Unless I want to. There's a lot of other things
I can do that I speck God likes.
Like what? I ast.

Oh, she say. I can lay back and just admire stuff.
Be happy.

This is like Zora Neale Hurston sent to a Hallmark indoctrination camp.

The paradoxical position of the professors who edited the
Norton Anthology of African American Literature (there
are eleven in all, plus dozens of professors and graduate students who assisted in research), curating and to some degree mummifying black American culture in the process, can
be imaginatively reconstructed in their choice to reprint the
words of Gil Scott-Heron's "The Revolution Will Not Be
Televised," which they claim, interestingly, had a "vital impact" on rap.

I have heard the recording many times but never read its
lines stark on the page: "The revolution will not be televised.
/ The revolution will not be brought to you by Xerox in four
parts without commercial interruption . . . " Clearly, Scott-
Heron didn't foresee PBS's "Eyes on the Prize." In the full
musical performance, one hears Scott-Heron's voice, anger,
adamancy, and ominous rhythm. What struck me while reading the lyrics was that Scott-Heron, wrongly predicting victory where there would be only defeat, nevertheless puts his
finger on exactly the mechanisms by which late-twentieth-
century, high-tech capitalism absorbs and nullifies any idea,
gesture, word, or image. The revolution was, in fact, beautifully televised, packaged on video, and African American
literature has now itself been packaged, bound, priced, and
marketed. The condition of American blacks worsens inexorably. As Gates himself observes in ***Thirteen Ways of Looking at a Black Man,*** "Thirteen decades have passed since
Emancipation, and half of our black men between twenty-
four and thirty-five are without full-time employment. One
black man graduates from college for every hundred who go
to jail. Almost half of black children live in poverty." One
looks up from the page with this in mind, and there is little
comfort left in the collection. Are we all supposed to join
in the national book party, rejoice with Charlie Rose? Sure.
Norton has published the ***Anthology of African American
Literature;*** Gates and Cornel West are entrenched at Harvard
and are doing very well indeed. But ***The Norton Anthology of African American Literature,*** filled with genuine
American treasure, remains a painfully paradoxical volume,
for the politics that drive it are profoundly insufficient both
to honor what lies in the book or the problems those politics were once invented to address.

FURTHER READING

Criticism

Begley, Adam. "Henry Louis Gates, Jr.: Black Studies' New
Star." *The New York Times Magazine* (1 April 1990): 24-5,
48-50.
    Overview of Gates's career and main ideas about Afro-
    American studies.

Clarke, Breena. "A 'Race Man' Argues for a Broader Curriculum." *Time* 137, No. 16 (22 April 1991): 16, 18.
    Interview with Gates in which he briefly discusses his
    opinions on creating an American public school curricu-
    lum inclusive of a variety of cultures.

Helmling, Steven. "Recent African-American Biography and
Criticism." *The Sewanee Review* C, No. 4, (Fall 1992): 684-
99.
    Includes Gates's *The Signifying Monkey: A Theory
    of Afro-American Literary Criticism* in a review of
    works on African-Americans, concluding that the
    book is a "rich, suggestive, funny, often brilliant
    performance–of a kind, to be sure, that hardly any-
    one outside a university literature department will be
    able to enjoy."

Newman, Richard. "Henry Louis Gates, Jr.: The Scholar of
African-American Culture Has Written a 'Storytelling' Memoir of Growing Up in the South," in *Words Like Freedom:
Essays on African-American Culture and History,* pp. 29-
34. West Cornwall, Conn.: Locust Hill Press, 1996.
    Biographical sketch of Gates, based on his memoir *Col-
    ored People.*

Preston, Rohan B. "Survival Guides: The Possibilities and
Limitations for Black Men in America." *Chicago Tribune,*
Sec. 14 (16 March 1997): 6.
    Praises the essays in *Thirteen Ways of Looking at a
    Black Man,* noting, however, that most of them would
    benefit from a longer treatment of their subjects.

Rowell, Charles H. "An Interview with Henry Louis Gates,
Jr." *Callaloo* 14, No. 2 (Spring 1991): 444-63.
    Interview in which Gates discusses trends in literary
    theory, African-American academics and literature, and
    his own scholarly work.

Smothers, Bonnie. "The Booklist Interview: Henry Louis
Gates, Jr." *Booklist* 93, No. 12 (15 February 1997): 972-73.
    Interview in which Gates discusses the conception of his
    book *Thirteen Ways of Looking at a Black Man.*

Additional coverage of Gates's life and career is contained in the following sources published by Gale: *Black Writers,* **Vol. 2;** *Contemporary Authors,* **Vol. 109;** *Contemporary Authors New Revision Series,* **Vols. 25, 53;** *Contemporary Literary Criticism,* **Vol. 65;** *DISCovering Authors: Multicultural Module;* **and** *Dictionary of Literary Biography,* **Vol. 67.**

bell hooks
1952-

(Born Gloria Watkins) American essayist and memoirist.

INTRODUCTION

Known as one of the new African-American intellectuals, along with Cornel West, Michael Eric Dyson, and Derrick Bell, hooks reaches a wider audience than most academic essayists because of her non-didactic writing style and her inclusion of personal reflection in her scholarly work. hooks, who addresses such subjects as feminism, civil rights, and the place of black women in American culture, raises important questions about the tension between black women and white women in the feminist movement and analyzes how the media and popular culture portray African Americans.

Biographical Information

Born Gloria Watkins in Hopkinsville, Kentucky, hooks chose to write under the name of her great-grandmother to honor her foremothers; she often refers to a household full of strong black women as one of her greatest influences. hooks received her bachelor of arts degree from Stanford University in 1973 and her Ph.D. in English from the University of California at Santa Cruz in 1983. Throughout her years of study, hooks had difficulty reconciling her small-town Southern roots with her academic life. This disparity later became a subject in her essays. In the mid-1980s, hooks became an assistant professor of Afro-American Studies and English at Yale University. Later she became a professor of English and Women's Studies at Oberlin College and then moved to City College in New York as a professor of English. hooks had always been interested in expressing herself through writing, and a friend finally convinced her to write her first collection, *Ain't I a Woman* (1981). In 1991 hooks was presented the Before Columbus Foundation's American Book Award for *Yearning* (1990).

Major Works

The major theme of hooks's first two works, *Ain't I a Woman* and *Feminist Theory* (1984), is that of black women finding a place within mainstream feminism. She explores this issue by tracing the oppression that African-American women have suffered since slavery. Arguing that domination is at the root of racism, classism, and sexism, and that black women are at the bottom of the hierarchical struggle in the United States, hooks asserts that mainstream feminism is interested in raising only white women up to the level of white

men. According to hooks, real equality can only be gained by overturning the whole hierarchical system. In *Talking Back* (1988), hooks begins to infuse more of her personal background into her work. In this collection she combined her experience as an African-American woman with theory and analysis to show that feminist perspectives can be useful to assess the position of African-American women in American society. In several of her works hooks discusses how portrayals of African Americans in the media have hurt black women. *Breaking Bread* (1991) is a dialogue with African-American social critic Cornel West in which hooks and West discuss the crises many black communities face, and how the media have contributed to these problems. hooks also asserts in *Black Looks* (1992) that mass media has denied the existence of a critical black female subjectivity. In addition to criticizing the media's complicity in racism and sexism, hooks excoriated the educational system in *Teaching to Transgress* (1994) for its role in perpetuating the hierarchical system in the United States. The focus of all of hooks's work, including her 1995 publication *Killing Rage,* is to heal the divisions in American society by creating a dialogue that respects all people and leads the way to building a new society. In *Bone Black* (1996) hooks changes gears to produce a memoir of her childhood in rural Kentucky. Centering again on the black woman's place in white America, hooks concentrates on her formative years, noting the damage to self- esteem that can occur very early in the lives of young black women.

Critical Reception

hooks has received varied critical response throughout her career. Many reviewers praise her for her insight and boldness. However, while most agree that her arguments are strong and challenging, many disagree with her opinions. The flaw most often noted by critics is her flouting of academic style. Many are uncomfortable with hooks's lack of footnotes and scholarly references and her reliance on self-help rhetoric and pop psychology. They also argue that she shows contempt toward black men and what they have suffered, and that she appears to be homophobic. Many of her reviewers, however, praise her for bringing a balance to feminist theory by including nonwhite, poor, and working class women into feminist discussions. Patricia Bell-Scott has observed that "we must keep in mind [hooks's] goal, to enrich feminist discourse and 'to share in the work of making a liberatory ideology,' as we struggle with the uncomfortable issues she raises."

PRINCIPAL WORKS

Ain't I a Woman: Black Women and Feminism (essays) 1981

Feminist Theory: From Margin to Center (essays) 1984

Talking Back: Thinking Feminist, Thinking Black (essays) 1988

Yearning: Race, Gender, and Cultural Politics (essays) 1990

Breaking Bread: Insurgent Black Intellectual Life [with Cornel West] (essays) 1991

Black Looks: Race and Representation (essays) 1992

A Woman's Mourning Song (essays) 1992

Sisters of the Yam: Black Women and Self Recovery (essays) 1993

Outlaw Culture: Resisting Representations (essays) 1994

Teaching to Transgress: Education as the Practice of Freedom (essays) 1994

Art on My Mind: Visual Politics (essays) 1995

Killing Rage: Ending Racism (essays) 1995

Bone Black: Memories of Girlhood (memoirs) 1996

CRITICISM

Dorothy Randall-Tsuruta (essay date January-February 1983)

SOURCE: "Sojourner Rhetorically Declares; Hooks Asks; Kizzy Spits in the Glass," in *The Black Scholar,* Vol. 14, No. 1, January-February 1983, pp. 46-52.

[Randall-Tsuruta is an American writer and educator. In the following essay, she expresses disappointment with the lack of documentation and the abundance of unsubstantiated opinions in Ain't I a Woman, *stating that "the book is a disgrace to American publishing."]*

A startling foretelling of Bell Hooks' *Ain't I a Woman* comes in the Acknowledgements and Introduction. She begins by sharing how when out to dinner she discussed with companions the subject of the book in question and "one person in a big booming voice, choking with laughter exclaimed, 'What is there to say about black women!' Others joined in the laughter." The author does not tell us if these were friends or strangers, but the liberties they take, and the fact that she dines with this sort is an indication of what she can stomach.

The excellent thing about Hooks' book is that it pinpoints annoyances over which many black American women daily sigh, yet repress, in an attempt to get through the work day without flying off the handle. Then just as we begin to vent our rage through Hooks', she confounds us by drawing conclusions, to her experience, which are either damaging to black women or unsupported by black experience in America.

Point in fact. In the introduction Hooks' own chagrin belts to crescendo her "white sisters" for among other things feeling:

> . . . comfortable writing books or articles on the "woman question" in which they drew analogies between "women" and blacks. . . . By continuously making this analogy, they *unwittingly* suggest that to them the term "woman" is synonymous with "white women"

> [Italics added by Randall-Tsuruta]

Any black woman who has ever had to deal with white women in an organizational setting, or neighborhood, or friendship, knows that whites—women and men—do not "unwittingly" assert a racial complex. However cathartic Hooks' anger is at times, she nonetheless reasons wildly—thus the troubled complexion of her study.

Hooks is so mad at her white sisters that she cannot sit still; yet prefers them to black feminist thinkers who "responded to the racism of white female[s] . . . by creating segregated feminist groups . . . and structured their groups on racist platform." Hooks expounds:

> White women were actively excluded from black groups. In fact the distinguishing characteristic of the black "feminist" group was its focus on issues relating specifically to black women.

Besides being flabbergasted that Hooks should think it wrong for black feminists to organize independently, I find it scandalous that Hooks places in quotes the word "feminists" referring to black women. Is this a slip of tongue, a scoff of sorts, a denigration translated, "if you ain't white (nor under white umbrella), you sho ain't no feminist?" But most incredible is Hooks' wording which singles black feminists out, for "creating segregated feminist groups." This despite her own words denouncing white feminists as "reactionary." Half the time while reading this book I kept asking the author if she was for real—and not rhetorically either.

According to Hooks, slavery was worse for black women than for black men because while black men may have had their testicles cut off this was not as frequent as rape, nor were they forced to perform homosexual acts. (Hooks' way of knowing this last suggests she is reincarnated with a clear memory and omnipresent.)

Ain't I a Woman contains five chapters: 1—Sexism and the Black Female Slave Experience; 2—Continued Devaluation of Black Womanhood; 3—The Imperialism of Patriarchy; 4—Racism and Feminism: The Issue of Accountability; and 5—Black Women and Feminism.

The historical data on slavery provided in chapter one is bereft of documentation, and is further reduced by argumentation which begs the question; specifically whether slavery was worse for women or men. The author plays down the suffering of black male slaves saying, that "individual black men were castrated by their owners or by mobs" for the purpose of setting "an example for other male slaves so that they would not resist authority." But she contends that white "women and men" were not "obsessed by the ideal of destroying black masculinity" for they did not force "black men to assume 'feminine' attire or perform so-called 'feminine' tasks." And she argues, comparatively, that they were obsessed with destroying black femininity for they forced "black women [to] perform the same tasks as black men," plowing, planting, and harvesting crops. When I was approaching graduate school, the noted scholar St. Clair Drake counseled a gathering of black students, saying when it comes time for dissertation, don't waste your time researching where slavery was worse—Brazil or the United States: it was horrible in both to the extent that figuring the degree is ludicrous.

In this chapter Hooks also criticizes black parents for their failure to "warn their daughters about the possibility of rape or help them to prepare for such situations." On and on she controverts. She concludes:

> The slave parents' unwillingness to openly concern themselves with the reality of sexual exploitation reflects the general colonial American attitude regarding sexuality.

Hooks has the galling habit of allowing enslaved ancestors choices of action no master allowed them. Further she demeans her ancestors, without benefit of documented evidence. Who told her this about slave parents?

Hooks singles out slave men for chiding, reasoning they did not move to protect female slaves from rape because in Africa they were socialized to aid only the women of their own tribe. No mention of how in America they were restrained. Alas, more global reductionism for Western anthropologists out to prove the heathen's halo is an Afro. Hooks thus aptly reads down the white sister's ancestor for her role in all this.

Chapter three plunges into "The Imperialism of Patriarchy." Here Hooks wins my applause for taking on Baraka and Jim Brown for their rationalizations bereft of admission that the white woman fills their dreams. Hooks submits for review, almost as an effigy, Baraka's response to the question concerning militant black men and white women:

> Jim Brown put it pretty straight and this is really quite true. He says that there are black men and white men, then there are women. So you can indeed be going through a black militant thing and have yourself a woman. The fact that she happens to be black or white is no longer impressive to anybody, but a man who gets himself a woman is what's impressive. The battle is really between white men and black men whether we like to admit it that is the battlefield at this time.

While no footnote is provided, the bibliography implies that Baraka's quote is taken from *Black World,* 1970. Seeing as how this is dated material, its purpose is limited, but does attest to what yet pains black women.

In chapter four, "Racism and Feminism," the author returns to her overriding contention with white feminists, taking on black feminists as well. Here the book succeeds in painting a graphic, and in this informative, sketch of her coming to grips with her "white sisters" as well as black feminist sisters who split off into race related groups—she calls the latter "Others." Considering the chapter—indeed the entire book—reads in large like an angry cry to white feminists, it smacks of a letter from an unrequited love. The reader feels at times like an eavesdropper, seeing the author seated miserably amongst "white sisters" whom she depicts as coolly indifferent to truths with which she confronts them. She exclaims they are just apt to turn on such as herself, snorting, "We won't be guilt tripped."

Yet Hooks bad raps black women who, "to express their anger and rage at white women" evoke "the negative stereotypical image of the white woman as passive, parasitic, privileged being living off the labor of others as a way to mock and ridicule the white women liberationists [sic]". In this chapter poet Lorraine Bethel is singled out for chastisement because of her poem "What Chous Mean We White Girl? Or, The Cullud Lesbian Feminist Declaration of Independence." (No reference given for this work.)

Interestingly here, Hooks suggests that hostilities between blacks and whites involved in the women's liberation movement, were not only due to disagreements over racism, but were also due to "jealousy, envy, competition, and anger, which took root during slavery." She explains how, as she sees it, slavery provided white women with creatures who were more denigrated by white men than they themselves. She seems to be saying this drove white women to sadistic acts, resorting "to brutal punishment to assert authority," which yet "could not change the fact that black women were not inclined to regard the white female with the awe and respect they showed the white male." She seems to be saying black slave women preferred their male torturers to their female torturers—you remember, those men who brutally raped them, beat them harder than they did men, hung their babies upside down until dead if they did not eat their food, and made them harvest the ground along with the men to the loss of their femininity. The point here is Hooks' penchant for arguing the degree of difference in the face of unmentionable horrors.

Hooks romanticizes slave owners much as Capote does criminals in *In Cold Blood.* Pretty soon these sadists start to emerge as personalities. If they were alive they might be able to turn a pretty profit from their crimes as did the John Deans and Richard Nixons, and presently the Dan Whites (George Wallace convinced a needed black votership of having changed for the better).

Finally in chapter five, "Black Women and Feminism" Hooks returns to the theme begun in her introduction, that black women passively stand outside the women's movement because they lack sexual esteem. She also returns to her witness of what whites "unwittingly" do, this time rendering the white man who yelled at Sojourner, "I don't believe you really are a woman." Hooks reasons he "unwittingly voiced America's contempt and disrespect for black womanhood." Since Hooks again offers no documentation for this quote, one can only assume it is hearsay across generations. But in

what context and at what event was Sojourner being thus read down? Hooks' book would be better if such documentation were supplied. It leaves one wondering at the publishing motive which dumps on the public such poor black scholarship.

Besides not documenting evidence, Hooks, throughout the book, works quotes which do not even serve her intent—like a puzzle piece forced into a pattern. For instance, referring back to her discussion of white women flaunting a "women and blacks" analogy, in her introduction, Hooks asserts that:

> When black people are talked about sexism militates against the acknowledgment of the interests of black women; when women are talked about racism militates against a recognition of black female interests. When black people are talked about the focus tends to be on black men; and when women are talked about the focus tends to be on white women.

But then for proof she offers (from William O'Neill's book *Everyone Was Brave*):

> Their shocked disbelief that men would so humiliate them by supporting votes for Negroes but not for women demonstrated the limits of their sympathy for black men, even as it drove these former allies further apart.

Whatever the point she was trying to make becomes lost in the scathing "humiliate" (in this reference) incites.

But Hooks has some interesting things to say about black women's organizations—how they changed over the course of history from being concerned with social *services* to focus instead on social *affairs* like debutante balls and fundraisers. In this she is instructive, and given a second attempt might even embed this information in a book more carefully organized, researched and edited. Yet, even as she sounds promising, in chapter five, she also reduces Angela Davis to "a poster pinup" who Hooks says was not admired for her intelligence but for her beauty. Again Hooks shows herself not contained by her own opinion, but wallowing in the stew whites would make of blacks. She offers further antagonism toward black women who dared deem themselves free, criticizing now black sociologist Joyce Ladner, and essayists Ida Lewis and Linda LaRue. Even charging this she insists that black women today are afraid to "openly confront white feminists with their racism." Deaf and dumb to her own conflicting charges, priding herself on being able to turn the other cheek, Hooks closes the book on the hope that black women everywhere will take courage from her pioneering in feminist ideology and follow suit.

While the book straddles five chapters, it is the essence grasped in the Introduction that essence recalls its passion long after the book is closed. For it is here that the author springs an admirable spirit let down by a sputtering intellect. The section also alerts the reader to Hooks' summation of blacks, that lack of racial esteem which so intrigues social scientists rent with wicked purpose. If the black reader approaches the book with the understanding it is addressed to Hooks' "white sisters," she or he may only wince seeing red when coming across such fabricated confidences as:

> Contemporary black women could not join together to fight for women's rights because we did not see "womanhood" as an important aspect of our identity.

and further along:

> When white men supported giving black men the vote while leaving all women disenfranchised, Horace Greeley and Wendell Phillips called it "the Negro's finest hour" but in actuality what was spoken of as a black suffrage was black male suffrage. By supporting black male suffrage and denouncing white women's rights activists, white men revealed the depths of their sexism—a sexism that was at that brief moment in American history greater than their racism.

Is Hooks serious? Is she really so naive as to believe white men ever embraced the needs of black men in preference to those of white women, suffragette or not? And could this mean she actually believes white men neglected to build into the system control of black men—vote or no vote?

What emerges here is the embarrassing probability that Hooks derives hope for a united women's movement by drawing analogy from white males' support of black males which she contends for a brief moment relegated sexism more important than racism: thus if white men can do this perhaps their womenfolk can as well.

This glimmer of hope lurks in the shadow of her voice, when vicariously reliving the words of toxic pig Elizabeth Cady Stanton whom she quotes cringing aghast that "'niggers' should be granted the vote while 'superior' white women remained disenfranchised." Though purporting to be alerting her sisters to racism, her voice betrays something akin to despising what the enemy despises, a condition sadistic biographers report gave strut to Hitler's walk, and entertained him in idle moments.

Concluding observations turn first to Hooks' title. As the words are Sojourner Truth's, taken from her famous speech it does us well to review them in context:

> That man over there say that woman needs to be helped into carriages, and lifted over ditches, and to have the best place everywhere. Nobody ever helped me into carriages, or over mud puddles, or gives me a best place . . . And ain't I a woman? Look at me. Look at my arm! I have plowed and planted and gathered into barns, and no man could head me . . . And ain't I a woman? I could . . . eat as much as a man when I could get it, and bear the lash as well . . . And ain't I a woman? I have borned thirteen children and seen them most all sold off into slavery. And when I cried out with a mother's grief, none but Jesus heard . . . And ain't I a woman?

Speaking this, Sojourner stepped into the limelight asserting the will of a visionary disgusted with the charade before her eyes. Clearly in her phrasing "ain't I a woman?" she is not asking a question but asserting indeed I am! Here we are presented with a wonderfully proud woman. She was no tail along feminist-hopeful, but a leader who as Hooks admits "could refer to her own life as evidence of woman's ability." Her patience, desire for certain comforts, sturdy arms firmed by plowing, equal footing with men, motherhood, and sufferings which none but Jesus heard are strengths she claimed. Sojourner delivered this speech in 1852 before a group of white women who Hooks informs, "deemed it unfitting that a black woman should speak on a platform in their presence screamed: 'Don't let her speak! Don't let her speak! Don't let her speak!'" Seeing as how that was 131 years ago, yet the picture Hooks paints of white feminists reveals them significantly unchanged today, it seems this would suggest something to her—other than that her patience is meritorious.

For many black women Sojourner's message has been instructive as they grew keen on living embraced by a compassion which yet never undermines that spirit of fight Sojourner resounds. You see these black women everywhere; some grouped for action in clubs or organizations which bear witness to our having come a long way since the only organization addressing female concerns was a band of white women. My early years as a teacher in a community college in Northern California saw my coming into a newly built school and helping to form a women's organization concerned with directions for black women, though open to other Third World women and working class women of all races who joined us from time to time in a common cause. Our group served the entire campus and community, providing model to middle class whites who that first year were enlightened at our conference, and the second year started a women's program of their own—then commenced to fret because we were separate. But we yawned perplexed by their behavior, continuing purposefully and intact until their tactics debilitated those in our ranks who believed "white folks water wetter and their ice cooler." A reading of Hooks' book leaves the impression she knows only of black women organizing in reaction to negative treatment from white women. The group I helped form, typical of many in this nation, came together quite naturally as a first impulse.

In contrast to the firm declaration Sojourner's "ain't I a woman?" sounds, Hooks' adaptation is marked by uncertainty. In the latter's delivery neither contextual clues, nor content reveal a sense of self. Indeed it is a sob in her mouth, revealing one painfully in doubt which could be eased if only her white sisters would mend their ways.

Hooks defines feminism, then goes on, ignoring the connotation, to label so many of our black female ancestors "feminist." While a fine title for contemporary women who self proclaim this attuned to problematic aspects, it is not fair to those dead who cannot be consulted. She goes on and on about "black feminist Mary Church Terrell," when here I sat holding that woman's autobiography aptly titled, *A Colored Woman in a White World.* The pervasive theme of the work is injustice endured, fought, and survived by blacks, with much focus on the black family. Here and there is constructive analysis of purposeful uses of suffragette agitation, but in no way does she paint her life as one given to feminist impulse. Black women have long been organized in the silent manor of prisoners of war—signaling when conversation meant death, and passing on to daughters ideas and remembered models that kept them from going mad; from standing on the corners burning bras. Much of what black women have long known about how to raise a family while holding down a job, white women are presently celebrating as some new discovery. In her introduction Terrell states, "this is the story of a colored woman living in a white world." Note she does not qualify it solely a white male world. In fact the first paragraph suggests an analogy of "women and whites." The second sentence reads, "It cannot possibly be like a story written by a white woman."

Terrell continues the paragraph with:

> A white woman has only one handicap to overcome—that of sex. I have two—both sex and race. I belong to the only group in this country which has two such huge obstacles to surmount. Colored men have only one—that of race.

Since Terrell speaks posthumously telling the group to which she belongs—black women—her example serves better black feminist groups (which Hooks decries) than white feminist groups (though Hooks ignores history insisting otherwise). In the page before the last of *Colored Woman in a White World* Terrell boasts being made an honorary member of the black sorority Delta Sigma Theta, and how she happily complied with that organization's request for her to write their creed. Thus further proof of the racial group with which she identified, and felt significant impact on her womanhood. The final thought Terrell leaves us with, however, in her autobiography focuses not on sex but race. The final paragraph reads:

> While I am grateful for the blessings which have been bestowed upon me and for the opportunities which have been offered, I cannot help wondering sometimes what I might have become and might have done if I had lived in a country which had not circumscribed and handicapped me on account of my race, but had allowed me to reach any height I was able to attain.

When referring to contemporary black feminists, as shown, Hooks is not very kind. She is particularly competitive with Michelle Wallace (*Black Macho and the Myth of the Superwoman*), saying of Wallace's book:

> While the book is an interesting provocative account of Wallace's personal life that includes a very sharp and witty analysis of the patriarchal impulses of black male activists, it is neither [sic] an important feminist work nor an important work about black women.

To this condescending assessment of Wallace and her work, Hooks adds (inadvertently perhaps), "All too often in our society it is assumed that one can know all there is about black people by merely hearing the life story and opinions of one black person." Yet in her acknowledgement she admits *Ain't I a Woman* is about her own "lived experiences."

Of Wallace's book "sister" Steinem has praise. Hooks, however, is miffed that Steinem could value Wallace's book comparable to Kate Millett's *Sexual Politics.* (Seems ole Steinem makes out the report cards.)

As stated in the outset *Ain't I a Woman* gives vent to much that is daily suppressed by black women who look askance on white feminists, while accepting of black feminists as exercising their right to join the movement which best attends their needs. Given time to rethink some of her conclusions, to add documentation, to have edited, and to reconfront her identity, Hooks might just write a book we all can be proud of. As is the book is a disgrace to American publishing. One wonders the motive backing its release.

Michele Wallace (essay date November 1995)

SOURCE: "For Whom the Bell Tolls: Why America Can't

Deal with Black Feminist Intellectuals," in *VLS,* No. 140, November 1995, pp. 19-24.

[*Wallace is an American educator and author of* Black Macho and the Myth of the Superwoman *(1979). In the following excerpt, she complains that hooks's work has become increasingly "self-centered, narcissistic, and even hostile to the idea of countervailing perspectives."*]

It's interesting to visit different bookstores in Manhattan just to see how they handle the dilemma posed by the existence of a black female author, who is not a novelist or a poet, who has 10 books in print. At the Barnes & Noble superstore uptown, they are getting perilously close to having to devote an entire shelf to hooks studies, in the manner that there are presently multiple shelves on MLK and Malcolm X.

And yet she might prefer it if instead I compared her to the white male Olympians of critical theory—Barthes, Foucault, Freud, and Marx—and that it was only conformity to what she likes to call "white supremacist thinking" that prevents me from classing her with the founding fathers.

In the past 14 years, as the author of 10 books on black feminism, bell hooks has managed to corner the multicultural feminist advice market almost singlehandedly, bell hooks is the alias of Gloria Watkins, who is now Distinguished Professor of English at the City College of New York. Raised in the rural South of Hopkinsville, Kentucky, Watkins collected her B.A. at Stanford, going on to finish her Ph.D. in English at UC Santa Cruz over a decade ago. We've been hearing from hooks regularly ever since.

Much like her previous work, *Killing Rage: Ending Racism,* consists of a collection of unconnected essays, some of them recycled from earlier books. As usual, the writing is leftist dogmatic, repetitive, and dated. For instance, in the book's penultimate chapter, called "Moving From Pain to Power: Black Self-Determination," Watkins offers the following turgid explanation of the failure of black struggle in the '60s:

> Revolutionary black liberation struggle in the United States was undermined by outmoded patriarchal emphasis on nationhood and masculine rule, the absence of a strategy for coalition building that would keep a place for non-black allies in struggle, and the lack of sustained programs for education for critical consciousness that would continually engage black folks of all classes in a process of radical politicization.

But then it was never in the expectation of beautiful writing, or subtly nuanced analysis, that we turned to bell hooks. With chapters bearing titles like "Healing Our Wounds:

Liberatory Mental Health Care," "Where Is the Love?" and "Overcoming White Supremacy," we are being offered, simultaneously, a series of potentially contradictory solutions to what ails us.

Hooks suggests that a black feminist analysis of "race and racism in America" is the essential missing component in current mainstream perspectives on race, at the same time that she offers a defense of black rage, in all its masculinist appeal, as inherently liberatory. "I understand rage to be a necessary aspect of resistance struggle," she writes. Meanwhile, interspersed with the rage and the feminist analysis, she is also slipping us a kind of hit-or-miss guide to self-healing, self-recovery, and self-actualization.

The new hooks began to emerge, like a butterfly from a chrysalis, about a year or two ago when Watkins abandoned the leftist rigors of the South End Collective in Boston and her post as associate professor at Oberlin College, more or less at the same time, moved to New York and CCNY, published *Outlaw Culture* and *Teaching to Transgress* with Routledge, and *Art on My Mind* with the nonprofit New Press, only to turn around a few months later to publish *Killing Rage* with Holt, her first major mainstream publisher, this fall.

Using cultural analysis of popular culture, film, visual art, and pedagogy, with occasional outbursts of self-help rhetoric (to which hooks had already devoted an entire book—*Sisters of the Yam*), *Teaching to Transgress, Outlaw Culture,* and *Art on My Mind* all continue in the direction hooks's work has taken the past few years, as amply demonstrated in *Black Looks, Yearning: Race, Gender, and Cultural Politics,* and *Talking Back: Thinking Feminist, Thinking Black.* However, with *Killing Rage,* hooks is clearly trying to drive a wedge into the current white market for books on race and the recent upsurge in the black market for books on spirituality and self-recovery.

Given this onslaught of publication, accompanied by an alarming dearth of explanatory or analytic criticism about her work, either in mainstream or alternative venues, perhaps it should come as no surprise that the poorly researched cover story in *The Chronicle of Higher Education* (the *New York Times* of academics) on the hooks/Watkins phenomenon considers her not only the most viable voice of black feminism, but also the only acceptable black female candidate for inclusion in the roster of the "new black intellectuals," whose emergence has been repeatedly announced in the pages of *The Atlantic Monthly, The New Republic, The New York Times, The New Yorker* and even the *VLS.*

"When black feminism needed a voice, bell hooks was born," *The Chronicle* proclaimed a few months ago. Which makes her a candidate for the only black feminist that matters? Not. Perhaps the dominant discourse is given to these lapses of amnesia because some ideas are so repugnant to Western culture that they are forced to emerge, again and again, as if new.

There hasn't been much resistance lately to the idea of a mainstream feminist discourse or even to a left-wing alternative and/or academic feminism. But what continues to boggle the minds of the powers that be is that black feminism has been around for a long time. . . .

All of this black feminist activity preceded the publication of bell hooks's first book, *Ain't I a Woman: Black Women and Feminism,* in 1981, as Gloria Watkins well knows. Indeed, Watkins begins the book she now claims to have actually written years before by chastising Gloria Steinem for her blurb on the jacket of *Black Macho.*

> Steinem makes a such narrowminded, and racist, assumption when she suggests that Wallace's book has a similar scope as Kate Millet's *Sexual Politics* . . . One can only assume that Steinem believes that the American public can be informed about the sexual politics of black people by merely reading a discussion of the 60's black movement, a cursory examination of the role of black women during slavery, and Michele Wallace's life.

I wouldn't go so far as to suggest that hooks is deliberately and maliciously attempting to obliterate the vast and subversive history of black feminist discourse. In *Ain't I a Woman* hooks does a fine job of providing the historical overview of black feminist thought. But progressively her analysis has become more and more self-centered, narcissistic, and even hostile to the idea of countervailing perspectives. Given more to the passive-aggressive approach in dealing with black women, she is never direct.

For instance, in an essay called **"Black Intellectuals"** in *Killing Rage,* while she claims for herself an exemplary humility, simplicity, open-mindedness, and commitment to revolutionary struggle, she also distances herself from the rank and file of black intellectuals with comments like "Most academics (like their white and non-white counterparts) are not intellectuals" and "Empowered to be hostile towards and policing of one another, black female academics and/or intellectuals often work to censor and silence one another."

In *Black Looks,* hooks repeatedly rails against those pseudo-progressive whites who would "eat the other" in their perpetual attempt to appropriate the transgressive energies of artists, writers, and theorists of color. But then hooks is also capable of writing, "When patriarchal support of competition between women is coupled with competitive academic longing for status and influence, black women are not em-

powered to bond on the basis of shared commitment to intellectual life or open-minded exchange of ideas. . . . Since many women in the academy are conservative or liberal in their politics, tensions arise between those groups and individuals like myself, who advocate revolutionary politics."

What hooks is doing here is what I call eating the other. Yes, people of color can eat each other, too.

Those of us who first became black feminists in the early '70s knew so little about the black women—the artists, intellectuals, and feminist activists—who had come before us. It took a long time to find the record they had left. However, this wasn't because the record didn't exist. Rather, the documentation was either destroyed or mouldering in dusty attics and rare-book collections, and it was no simple matter to retrieve them. It no longer surprises me that Zora Neale Hurston, Nella Larsen, and Jessie Fauset all had to be rediscovered.

And it should come as no surprise to anyone that, not only was there a black feminism before bell hooks, there was a black feminism long before most of us were born. There were black feminist abolitionists before the Civil War and there were black women suffragettes, whose works are now preserved and annotated by the Schomburg Collection of 19th-century black women writers, as well as by other publishing efforts such as Florence Howe's Feminist Press.

But when I was a kid, the only one I knew was Sojourner, and I didn't know much about her.

The black feminist historian Nell Painter, professor of history at Princeton, is currently working on a biography of Sojourner Truth and has already published several excerpts from her research in which he suggests that the famous "Ain't I a Woman" which so many feminists have clung to over the years, might have been a historical conflation of a number of different events and speeches, none of them anything like the speech we've come to know and love.

Since Truth was illiterate, not an intellectual but a charismatic itinerant preacher who wandered about the countryside expecting strangers to provide her next meal and her next place to sleep, she wasn't exactly into knowledge production.

Moreover, Painter suggests that part of the legacy of the racisms of the period comes down to us in the iconography of Sojourner Truth. All of her portraits were carefully posed to confirm the myth of her unlettered, inborn, commonsensical strength, and as such, to confirm, as well, the peculiar and essential otherness then considered characteristic of the black woman—an "otherness," not coincidentally, that also served to highlight the beauty, delicacy, and intelligence of the women of the "superior race."

Meanwhile, Truth's "Ain't I a Woman" speech has been institutionalized as the originary moment of black feminist discourse. Many works—hooks's first book, as well as Deborah Gray White's history of slave women, *Ar'n't I a Woman,* and even *Black Macho*—bear witness to her presumed power as a black feminist foremother. But suppose Painter has uncovered a nasty little paradigmatic secret about black feminism: that the iconic status of Truth is much like the iconic status of Hurston, or indeed any single black female figure, in that it is meant to stand in for the whole. Its primary function is to distract us from the actual debate and dilemma with which black feminist intellectuals, artists, and activists are really engaged.

In fact, I would even go so far as to say that the media success of *Black Macho* placed me in possible danger of the same instant iconic status. But I was 27, naive, inexperienced, and had no concept of the big picture that Painter is outlining. Whereas hooks has had a long, steady climb, from the publication of her first book to her present position, poised to enter the mainstream. Is she being manipulated by the structural racism and misogyny of the mainstream media or is she an opportunist trying to turn a fast buck? I think perhaps a little of both. Frankly, she can't begin to make a dent in this structural thing by herself. As for the opportunism, how do you suppose revolutionaries will occupy themselves in these reactionary times? And the timing is perfect.

In case you hadn't noticed, there's a black book boom. It has many dimensions, from the apartheid of the publishing industry itself, to the phenomenon of the black public intellectual, to *Time* magazine's construction (with Henry Louis Gates Jr.'s help) of a new black cultural renaissance. But one aspect of the boom that is grossly underreported is the accelerating interest in a New Age kind of spiritualism and the rhetoric of self-recovery. When this tendency is combined with a public black intellectual component—such as in the case of the works of bell hooks, Cornel West, and a host of others—it can be unfortunate indeed.

Watkins is openly and proudly religious, or what she would call spiritual, which is a euphemism for religious. Nobody has ever accused black folk of not being religious enough. But it may be precisely this religiosity that not only serves to fuel the overreported anti-Semitism but also the much more prevalent anti-intellectualism that is fast becoming the only thing that most dark peoples splattered around the tristate area have in common.

Watkins's **Killing Rage** suggests that we bury the racial hatchet in places like New York through spiritual growth. But in the title essay, hooks still has a long way to go. Her

story begins with the words, "I am writing this essay sitting beside an anonymous white male that I long to murder." She and her traveling companion had sought first-class upgrades in exchange for their coach airline seats at a New York airport, but when they got on the plane, there was a white man sitting in the friend's first-class seat. Watkins immediately reads this situation as deliberate racist sabotage on the part of the airline representative at the counter.

A stewardess was called to clear up the dilemma of whose seat it was, but anybody who flies on airplanes with any regularity knows who won. If there are two people with the same seat assignment, the butt in the seat has the right of way.

But not without Watkins going ballistic. "I stared him down with rage," she writes, "tell him that I do not want to hear his liberal apologies . . . In no uncertain terms I let him know that he had an opportunity to not be complicit with the racism and sexism that is so all-pervasive in this society" by voluntarily giving up his cushy seat in first class to her black friend now condemned to the cramped conditions of coach.

I guess I'm just hard-hearted Hannah, but somehow I'm not weeping for Watkins here. I can remember the insanity that began to grip me in the midst of the whirlwind of publicity around *Black Macho* when, all of sudden, it became desperately important to me whether or not I traveled first class or coach. I am quite familiar with this illness. I call it first-class-itis, or, more simply, celebrity-itis. Given the symptoms, you shouldn't be surprised at all that there is no hint in Watkins's narrative of the seemingly obvious antibourgeois alternative of joining her friend, in solidarity, in coach.

Black feminist intellectuals generally kowtow to hooks and dutifully quote her numerous books, but they don't like her and they don't trust her. She doesn't represent the views of black feminist academics (most of whom she would dismiss, in any case, as privileged members of the bourgeois academic elite), and yet we go on mumbling under our breath.

Released in her last books from the rigor of the South End Press collective—where editorial decisions are made jointly—what was once merely typically bad leftist writing has become self-indulgent and undigested drivel that careens madly from outrageous self-pity, poetic and elliptical, to playful exhibitionism, to dogmatic righteous sermonizing. Sometimes as I read some of this stuff, I can't believe that I am reading what I'm reading.

For instance, in **Outlaw Culture** hooks sets an *Esquire* reporter straight about the notion that the women's movement was prudish in the '70s. "We had all girl parties, grownup sleepovers," she told him. "We slept together. We had sex. We did it with girls and boys. We did it across race, class, nationality. We did it in groups. We watched each other do-ing it."

Or, hooks will say, "the vast majority of black women in *academe* are *not* in revolt—they seem to be as conservative as the other conservatizing forces there! . . . I've been reread-ing Simon Watney's *Policing Desire,* and thinking a lot about how I often feel more policed by other black women who say to me: 'How can you be out there on the edge? How can you *do* certain things, like be wild, inappropriate? You're making it harder for the rest of us.'"

Watkins knocks everybody. She has done everything and known everything, long before it was fashionable to do so. Yet she is rarely specific or precise about her experiences or her references.

She can also be a chameleon, taking on camouflage colors in different environments, as in her interview with the rap-per Ice Cube. In talking with him about *Boyz'n the Hood,* she says of the lead character, Tre, falling into the vernacu-lar.

> You don't want to be him 'cause he didn't have no humor hardly, he didn't have much. Part of what I try to do as a teacher, a professor, is to show people just 'cause you're a professor and you got a Ph.D., you don't have to be all tired, with no style and with no presence.

Constantly citing her experience of child abuse at the hands of her family, physical abuse by her former lover, as well as the "racist" and/or "sexist" reaction of the "white feminist" and/or "black male" and/or "white supremacist patriarchal" establishment, she epitomizes the cult of victimization that Shelby Steele, Stanley Crouch, and Jerry Watts have writ-ten about so persuasively.

While I have no desire to play into the hands of the right, everybody knows that p.c. rhetoric has become a problem, and hooks has made herself queen of p.c. rhetoric. Without the unlovely code phrases, "white supremacy," "patriarchal domination," and "self-recovery," hooks couldn't write a sen-tence.

Hooks reminds me of the young people in my youth who would come from the suburbs, dress up like hobos, and hang around in the Village for the weekend. You just sprinkle these words around and you're an automatic academic left-ist.

In *Manufacturing Consent,* Noam Chomsky reminds us that the principal function of mass culture is to distract most Americans, perhaps as many as 80 per cent, from issues of real power, domination, and control. The other 20 per cent,

whom Chomsky identifies as the educational/intellectual elite, votes, runs the media and academic, and, as such, is actively, although probably not consciously, engaged in manufacturing consent. Although it's not all that important how the 80 per cent chooses its poison, the predilections of the 20 per cent elite can be crucial.

According to Chomsky's vision, the correct information is almost always out there, but it is literally buried under the continuous and overwhelming flow and bombardment of mass cultural noise and distraction.

In an imperceptible shift from automatic leftism to Cultural Studies, most of what hooks chooses to write about—Ma-donna, *The Crying Game, The Body Guard,* Camille Paglia, shooping, and so forth—is noise. Part of the distraction of mass culture, and now the most popular mass cultural com-mentary (sometimes called cultural critique or cultural stud-ies) as well, is that its function is increasingly continuous with that of its object of study. At best, it is becoming mind-fuck candy for the intellectually overendowed. In other words, much of it has become just high-falutin noise.

As for what there ever was to value about hooks's work, I am not the ideal person to say since I have never felt com-fortable with the world according to bell hooks. Yet it should be said that hooks/Watkins has a saucy, mischievous, and playful side, which is fascinating. It emerges occasionally in her affect and intonation as a public speaker, but rarely makes it to the page. Although that edge peeks out in some of the riskier moments in **Outlaw Culture**—when she is dissing Camille Paglia, or in some of her speculations about rap—for the most part, hooks grossly underestimates the willingness of her reader to comprehend her particular jour-ney.

In black feminism, two clearly divergent paths are emerg-ing: Either one travels the high road, the intellectual-creative route, out of which such women as Walker, Morrison, and Bambara have carved their path—every step earned and co-piously contextualized so that you know exactly where you are all the time; or one travels the low road, the gospel ac-cording to bell hooks firmly in hand, the path etched in the vertiginous stone of rhetoric, hyperbole, generalizations, platitudes, bad faith, phony prophetism, and blanket condem-nation.

Inspired though we may be by the Morrisons, the Walkers, the Fannie Lou Hamers, the June Jordans, most of us don't have it in us to be them. And you can't really follow them because they're not leaders. I don't mean this as criticism. They don't present themselves as leaders. Whereas hooks is all too happy to present herself as your leader, if you just have to have one.

But, in fact, black feminists don't have any leaders, if you mean by leaders people who will stand up and say that they are leading black women down one independent and autonomous path because black women—whether they are lesbian, intellectual, married to white men, or considered atypical in any other way—have no desire to put more distance between themselves and black men, either individually or collectively. It has to do not only with romance, but with a political commitment to black identity, black struggle, and the painful lessons of black history.

On the other hand, if one stops looking for leaders who claim to know the direction black women should follow and looks instead for black female role models, for lack of a better term, who know their stuff and who have spent their lives conquering a particular field, there are tons of potential "leaders" all over the place.

If you think of an ideology as a religion, then the church of black feminists is not one that you have to attend or even declare yourself a member of. In fact, it is better if you don't. Like the Quakers, black feminists don't proselytize or seek converts, and they hold very few meetings. The history of organized women's movements and their symbiotic relationship to the dominant discourse is nasty indeed: see the work of Davis, Giddings, or any feminist historian worth her salt for details.

Also, it is precisely the point of black feminism, or any feminism on behalf of the dispossessed, to empower the disenfranchised—both women and men—what Gayatri Spivak has called the subaltern. Subalterns are not necessarily defined by race (although their skins are usually dark), gender, sexuality, or geography (although they are concentrated in certain parts of the world), but by their relationship to global issues of class, poverty, and power.

Their problem is their lack of symbolic power and agency in the dominant discourse. The subaltern speaks but it doesn't speak to us. hooks is not the link. The subaltern doesn't write books. As for whether or not Ice Cube can speak for the subaltern, I'll leave it to you to figure that out.

George M. Fredrickson (essay date 18 April 1996)

SOURCE: "Far from the Promised Land," in *New York Review of Books,* Vol. XLIII, No. 7, April 18, 1996, pp. 16-20.

[*In the following review of* Killing Rage, *Fredrickson questions the practicality of hooks's proposals to end racism, but*

nonetheless finds her "a force to be reckoned with in the debate on race in America."]

Hooks's ***Killing Rage*** is an angry book that pulls no punches. The first essay recalls the author's intense fury when a white man, assigned the same first-class seat on an airliner as hooks's black female traveling companion, pulled rank to get the already seated companion consigned to coach class. This was on a day filled with incidents of white rudeness and insensitivity. Hooks uses her reactions to such experiences to explain and justify black rage against white arrogance, and abuse, and she takes the press and television to task for their assumption that when blacks get angry and strike back, they are being "pathological." Although hooks disassociates herself from what she considers to be the dominant values of the black middle class, her reactions to discriminatory treatment might have provided supporting evidence for [Jennifer] Hochschild's contention that middle-class blacks feel the sting of racism more directly and acutely than do the more isolated members of the lower class. A poor black woman would hardly ever be in a position to be bumped from first class.

When she is being prescriptive rather than autobiographical, however, hooks criticizes the black middle class for concentrating on racism as the sole source of black disadvantage and for ignoring the role of class domination in a capitalist society.

Class divisions among blacks in a racially desegregated society have been the breeding grounds for those who are privileged to internalize contempt and hatred of the black poor and underclass. The connectedness of capitalism and the perpetuation of racist exploitation makes class a subject privileged blacks seek to avoid. More than other groups of black folks, they emphasize racism as a system of domination without drawing attention to class. . . . It is in their class interests to emphasize the way racism inhibits their progress.

Rarely, at least since the days of E. Franklin Frazier, has any black writer been so sharply critical of the black middle class. It seems at times that hooks's rage is directed as much at elite African Americans as at white racists. Bourgeois blacks, she charges, have sold out to a capitalist system that oppresses the African-American majority. She excoriates them for buying into the American dream of personal success that is the subject of Hochschild's inquiry [in *Facing Up to the American Dream*]. Her analysis of black values in general is in fact quite consistent with Hochschild's findings, except that hooks deplores what she sees, instead of viewing it as a basis for eradicating racism. "The ethic of liberal individualism," she writes, "has so deeply permeated the psyches of black folks in America of all classes that we have little support for a political ethic of communalism that promotes the sharing of resources."

For hooks, therefore, the fact that many blacks have been "eagerly embracing the American dream of wealth and power" is an obstacle to racial justice rather than a possible basis for it. She advocates coalitions for radical change between blacks who have become aware of their true situation and other people of color in this society who also suffer from "neocolonial white supremacist domination." She also believes that blacks can make alliances with well-intentioned whites and encourage them to combat racism. (She deplores black anti-Semitism and writes that "working to eradicate anti-Semitism, we are equally working to end racism.") Blacks, she writes, can construct "a practical model for social change" that will induce progressive whites to surrender their privileges and join in the struggle for a just society. How such a model might be constructed and then become persuasive, however, remains unclear in *Killing Rage.*

Hooks is a feminist as well as a socialist, and much of her book expresses a black woman's anger at the sexist attitudes that she finds pervasive in the black community. She believes that up to now the struggle for black freedom has been waged on patriarchal principles—the emphasis was always on making it possible for blacks to act like "men"—and she is especially critical of the subordination of women in black nationalist movements and ideologies. Whatever one thinks of the practicality of her hopes, her frankness and willingness to face up to the divisive issues that refuse to go away make her a voice to be reckoned with in the debate on race in America.

Thulani Davis (essay date 15 December 1996)

SOURCE: "Native Daughter," in *New York Times Book Review,* December 15, 1996, pp. 32, 34.

[*In the following review of* Bone Black: Memories of Girlhood, *Davis finds the memoir of hooks's childhood lacking her usual vibrant language and narrative style.*]

The only woman in recent years who is readily identified as a member of that select group known as "black public intellectuals," Bell Hooks is probably the most provocative and prolific of them all. For 15 years Ms. Hooks has been writing catalytic essays on cultural politics, teaching, feminist theory and issues of representation, as well as publishing interviews with and musings on pop culture icons. (She is Distinguished Professor of English at City College and the author of 10 previous nonfiction books—two last year alone—and a volume of poetry.) Her essays, like her public appearances, are an uninterrupted flow from the personal and anecdotal to the theoretical and the radical proposition.

From Ms. Hooks, therefore, one might expect memoir of ut-ter clarity, rendered without sentiment, that shows us the startling counterpoints of a female upbringing. *Bone Black: Memories of Girlhood* is more of a work in progress, ruminations on how one learns gender and acquires rage, notes from which to build a solid autobiography.

In Ms. Hooks's other writings, one encounters references to growing up in a racially segregated small town and a gradual immersion into larger, predominantly white bourgeois worlds. *Bone Black* is situated in one such Southern town and moves by small steps toward a young girl's departure from home. This journey from a Southern town at the end of segregation to a place in the "white" world is the subject of a number of modern memoirs. These days the story often marches from working-class roots to middle-class career success, and the urge to look back comes ever earlier as some professional pinnacle is reached.

Most black writers cling to the traditional model, rooted in slave narratives, which charts a set of passages from slavery to freedom, or from a latter-day oppression to personal deliverance. The earliest accounts make for gripping reading: from the violence and privation of slavery to perilous escape to the toils and triumphs of life in "free" society. Some, like those by James Baldwin, Maya Angelou and Malcolm X, all with powerful tales to tell of extraordinary people who were nearly lost through harsh but ordinary travails, became part of black iconography.

Bone Black is a departure not only from these models but from Ms. Hooks's other work as well. It contains the recollections of a woman who was a curious, often too-bold child who loved books, caught up in a world that taught she would end up "crazy, locked up, alone." It is written in an awkward prose that tries for the qualities of fiction and seems trapped by an experiment in style. Ms. Hooks adopts a youthful voice; thus, the houses are "white white with green grass," and a woman is "the color of warm honey, with straight jet black hair." She writes that she "saw women and men all around in distress, feeling pain, waiting for the rescue that never came. She saw herself as one of them. She was one of those children who had come to believe that it was somehow all a mistake that she had been born into this family, into this life of never being able to do anything right, of endless torment."

Writing of herself in both the first and the third person, Ms. Hooks creates an awkward tension—as if comfortable one moment to use "I" and then uncomfortable, shifting to the more distanced "she." The writing lacks the ease and energy of Ms. Hooks's other prose, the exuberance of her engagement with rich texts and conversation and solitude. Reading *Bone Black* raised questions about the power of personal exploration to halt the tongue and impoverish an elegant vocabulary. I wondered if it was by design or by mishap that

Ms. Hooks has created here a language devoid of the sensuality she so amply displays elsewhere.

She does point us to ideas that take shape in her later thinking: the humiliation of "the pretend Tom Thumb wedding she had to participate in during first grade," the enjoyment of a grandmother's tales, the labeling of jazz as a black man's music. But the isolation she endeavors to share yields only the plainest words—"pain," "punishment," "betrayal"; sometimes these words appear in multiples on the page.

The great wealth of detail that usually grounds the reader in a past time and place, and the dramatic incidents that allow characters to show what they can never properly explain, have been discarded in favor of an elliptical narrative, a reverie that circles round important moments. Ms. Hooks's world is one of close spaces where one tries not to touch. One of her childhood chores was to spend the night with elderly women who liked a companion in bed or in another room during the night. She writes of being there and trying not to be heard or felt. There are no particulars. One can only guess at the narrator's age throughout the book, and though one learns that money is tight and the children must not incur expenses for the family, one has no idea how people in her life made a living.

As the chapters, of two to three pages each, are usually without major incident, these snapshots of sweet elders and childhood confusions are like youthful photographs, somewhat sentimental, muted, maybe a little blurred. They are also memories of discomfort, and the reader too begins to feel reluctant to climb into the writer's subjective space. Of seeing a baby picture of herself, she recalls: "I know this is not me and has never been for this baby has no hair. Her skull is smooth and shiny like polished silver with black jade for eyes—this cannot be me. The grown-ups identify it as me, happy baby, smiling baby, baby with no hair. I know who I am, the one not seen in the photo, the one hiding under the bed, hiding in the dark, waiting for the camera monster to go away."

Much of *Bone Black* seems to be an effort to write of times she has chosen to forget. Ms. Hooks's readers will probably not share these reservations, and go forward undeterred. But for the new reader, Ms. Hooks's memories of girlhood may seem no more than moments safely told of the ordinary days of an extraordinary person who might have been crushed by harsh but common circumstances, moments that one can only sense, not inhabit.

FURTHER READING

Criticism

Rothenberg, Paula. Review of *Teaching to Transgress: Education as the Practice of Freedom,* by bell hooks. *Signs* (Spring 1997): 739-40.
    Rothenberg praises hooks's pragmatic and rational approach to education theory.

Additional coverage of hooks's life and career is contained in the following sources published by Gale: *Black Writers,* **Vol. 2;** *Contemporary Authors,* **Vol. 143; and** *Contemporary Literary Criticism,* **Vol. 94.**

C. L. R. James
1901-1989

(Full name Cyril Lionel Robert James; has also written under the pseudonym of J. R. Johnson) West Indian nonfiction writer, journalist, novelist, short story writer, essayist, dramatist, and critic.

INTRODUCTION

James was a pioneering intellectual and historian. He is known for his emphasis on recognizing the importance of the masses and the common man in political movements. As a middle-class, black intellectual, James felt alienated from the largely uneducated black population of his native land, Trinidad, and much of his work focuses on this alienation. James's work analyzed African, Caribbean, and Soviet revolutionary movements. Pan Africanism and Marxism both profoundly shaped his political thinking. He was also unique in his focus on popular culture, but he did not dismiss the value of classical literature and philosophy. James was well-read and often combined elements of different genres to illustrate his points. Known for his balanced portrayal of events and characters, James proved his assertions by presenting all sides of an event or character in his work.

Biographical Information

James was born in the British colony of Trinidad on January 4, 1901. The son of a black school teacher, he won a scholarship to Queens Royal College, the local government secondary school in Port of Spain. He was an accomplished student and cricket player. James graduated in 1918 and began teaching at the college, and later taught at the Government Training College for Teachers. During these years James wrote several successful short stories, and in 1932 he wrote his first book, *The Life of Captain Cipriani* (1932). That same year he departed for Britain. In 1934 James became a lifelong member of the Revolutionary Socialist Party. Throughout his life, James loved the game of cricket and was the cricket correspondent for several English newspapers. He also wrote books about the sport, including *Beyond the Boundary* (1963). James went to the United States in 1938, where he wrote for the Workers Party and then the Socialist Workers Party, both branches of the American Trotskyist movement. In addition to his writing duties, he helped organize tenant farmers in the South and automobile workers in Detroit, Michigan. He married writer Constance Webb in 1950, and his letters to her were later published in the *C. L. R. James Reader* (1992) and *Special Delivery* (1995). In 1953, James was expelled from the United States as an "undesirable alien." He returned to Trinidad where he lived

until 1968 when he was able to re-enter the United States, lecturing there and abroad. In the 1980s he moved to England, where he died in 1989.

Major Works

James's first book, *The Life of Captain Cipriani,* is a combination of biography, social history, and political theory, which is characteristic of much of his writing. On the surface it is a biography of Arthur Andrew Cipriani, a white West Indian who opposed colonial rule in Trinidad. Beyond the biography of this one man, the book provides a survey of West Indian social history; an analysis of the area's political, social, and economic problems; and an argument for West Indian self-government. James's writing is usually concerned with one or all of the themes of race, color, and class. The majority of his books deal with subjects relating to the lives of black people living in Africa and the Caribbean. *The Black Jacobins* (1938) is a history of the African slaves in the French colony of San Domingo (later called Haiti) and their struggle for freedom. The revolution lasted twelve years and in the end the slaves were victorious. The book focuses on the slave leader Toussaint L'Ouverture, but also examines the conflicts among various members of the colony; the politics of revolutionary France; and British and Spanish involvement in the events in San Domingo. In *Beyond the Boundary,* James wrote about the sport of cricket, but the book goes beyond sportswriting. James uses social history, social and political analysis, and biography and autobiography to show how cricket is an art as well as a game. *Beyond the Boundary* presents the importance of cricket to West Indian life and provides biographical sketches of cricketers, including the author himself. James did not employ the genre of fiction often in his career. He wrote a few short stories and a novel, *Minty Alley* (1936). The novel tells the story of an educated, middle-class Trinidadian, Mr. Haynes, who rents a room with a lower-class family in Port of Spain. Haynes narrates the activity of the household around him. The main themes of the novel are racial tension, class rivalry, and color discrimination. In *Mariners, Renegades and Castaways* (1953) James wrote about Herman Melville and modern civilization. James asserted that Melville was primarily concerned with world revolution and the future of American democracy.

Critical Reception

Most critics laud James's intellect, immense scholarship, and the quality and scope of his research. William E. Cain asserts that "James's view of the world was shaped . . . by his capacious, optimistic intellect." Many also praise his objectivity in presenting all sides of an event or issue. F. M. Birbalsingh states that the "combination of balanced objectivity and deep conviction greatly enhances the persuasiveness of James's writing." He also states that "Seldom before or since have race, colour, and class, as they relate to the English-speaking Caribbean, been examined with such analytic clarity and precisely organized logic." Many reviewers point out James's innovative emphasis on the importance of the masses in political change. Cynthia Hamilton states that James recognizes this by "affirming first that the masses are the creators of their own history; the mass party and the 'barefoot men,' the peasants, workers, and unemployed must be exalted, elevated to a primary position as a force in history." Concerning the importance James places on popular culture, she says, "Not often is he or she [the intellectual] able to challenge his or her own right of privilege and status by looking to mass expression as the arbitrator of ideas." James gave an insider's view into what was then a little-known West Indian society. Reviewers laud James for his immense contribution to the understanding of West Indian life under slavery and during its emerging independence.

PRINCIPAL WORKS

The Life of Captain Cipriani: An Account of British Government in the West Indies (nonfiction) 1932

Cricket and I [with L. R. Constantine] (nonfiction) 1933

Minty Alley (novel) 1936

Toussaint L'Ouverture (drama) 1936; revised as *The Black Jacobins,* 1967

World Revolution, 1917-1936: The Rise and Fall of the Communist International (nonfiction) 1937

The Black Jacobins: Toussaint L'Ouverture and the San Domingo Revolution (nonfiction) 1938; revised edition, 1963; revised edition, 1980

A History of Negro Revolt (nonfiction) 1938; revised as *A History of Pan-African Revolt,* 1969

Mariners, Renegades and Castaways: The Story of Herman Melville and the World We Live In (nonfiction) 1953

Facing Reality [as J. R. Johnson; with Grace C. Lee and Pierre Chaulieu] (nonfiction) 1958

Modern Politics (lectures) 1960

Party Politics in the West Indies (nonfiction) 1962

Beyond a Boundary (nonfiction) 1963

State Capitalism and World Revolution (nonfiction) 1969

Notes on Dialectics: Hegel, Marx, Lenin (nonfiction) 1971

The Books of American Negro Spirituals [as J. R. Johnson] (nonfiction) 1977

The Future in the Present (nonfiction) 1977

Nkrumah and the Ghana Revolution (nonfiction) 1977; revised edition, 1982

Black Nationalism and Socialism [with Tony Bogues and Kim Gordon] (nonfiction) 1979

Fighting Racism in World War II [with George Breitman, Edgar Keemer, and others] (nonfiction) 1980

Spheres of Existence (nonfiction) 1980

At the Rendezvous of Victory (nonfiction) 1984

C. L. R. James's 80th Birthday Lectures [edited by Margaret Busby and Darcus Howe] (lectures) 1984

Cricket (nonfiction) 1986

The C. L. R. James Reader [edited by Anna Grimshaw] (essays) 1992

American Civilization [edited by Grimshaw and Keith Hart] (nonfiction) 1993

Special Delivery: The Letters of C. L. R. James to Constance Webb, 1939-1948 (letters) 1995

C. L. R. James on the "Negro Question" [edited by Scott McLemee] (nonfiction) 1996

CRITICISM

F. M. Birbalsingh (essay date 1984)

SOURCE: "The Literary Achievement of C. L. R. James," in *The Journal of Commonwealth Literature,* Vol. XIX, No. 1, 1984, pp. 108-21.

[*In the following essay, Birbalsingh discusses the scope and style of James's writing.*]

Cyril Lionel Robert James was born in the British colony of Trinidad in 1901. The son of a negro schoolteacher, James won a scholarship to Queens Royal College, the local Government Secondary School, where he distinguished himself as a scholar and cricketer. In 1932 when James went to Britain, he had already written his first book *The Life of Captain Cipriani* which combined biography, social history, and political theory in a blend that proved characteristic of his later writing. *The Life of Captain Cipriani* was the start of an astonishingly productive and still unfinished literary career to which James has already devoted more than fifty years as biographer, historian, journalist, novelist, editor, playwright, literary critic, lecturer, and much else. The sheer volume of James's writing, the scope of its subjects and the multiplicity of its genres defy detailed assessment in a single essay or even in a single volume. In a short essay all that may reasonably be attempted is to examine James's technique, broadly define the scope of his achievement as a man of letters, and in terms of the literary history of the English-speaking Caribbean, give an account that may serve as an introduction to detailed and comprehensive studies of his writing that will undoubtedly follow.

Despite its volume, scope, and diverse genres, James's writing reveals a recurring political theme concerned with amelioration of the social, economic, and cultural conditions of those he would later describe as "the vast majority of living men." For James is an international socialist, and has been a member of the Revolutionary Socialist Party since 1934. Whether he is writing about the fiction of Herman Melville, or the cricketing exploits of his friend, the late Sir Learie Constantine, whether the form he employs is biography or history, some aspect of James's broad theme invariably emerges. And although his subjects deal with living conditions in Europe, Asia, America, Africa, and the Caribbean, James's writing concentrates predominantly on the last two of these regions.

James's theme usually emerges from his treatment of three main topics—race, colour, and class. Although he has written a substantial history of the Third Communist International, *World Revolution,* together with such essays as **"Dialectical Materialism and the Fate of Humanity,"** and **"Every Cook Can Govern: A Study of Democracy in Ancient Greece,"** the bulk of his writing deals with subjects related to black people, the vast majority of living men in Africa and the Caribbean. His preoccupation with black people is illustrated in the very titles of his books; for example, *The Black Jacobins*—a history of the San Domingo revolution—and *Nkrumah and the Ghana Revolution.* His numerous essays also include such titles as **"British Barbarism in Jamaica: Support the Negro Worker's Struggle," "Parties, Politics and Economics in the Caribbean,"** and **"The Atlantic Slave-Trade."**

The Life of Captain Cipriani is ostensibly a biography of Arthur Andrew Cipriani, a French Creole, that is to say, a white West Indian who, first as an officer in the West India Regiment during World War Two, then as mayor of Port of Spain, voiced loud disapproval of colonial rule in Trinidad. Yet the book is not biography alone, nor a simple, self-righteous diatribe against colonial oppression and injustice. It gives an informed survey of West Indian social history, and such a lucid analysis of political, cultural, and economic problems in the region, that it becomes a work of scholarship, as well as an argument for West Indian self-government. The argument was persuasive enough for three chapters to be later republished separately as a second book—*The Case for West Indian Self-Government.* The appeal in both books lies in the peculiar authority of James's scholarship and the fluency of his writing, which cooperate successfully and make his achievement appear less distinguished than it actually is. *The Life of Captain Cipriani* is, in fact, a pioneering work, one of the first serious attempts to examine living conditions in a completely new society, a young Caribbean culture, born out of the frenzy of European Imperial ventures in the New World.

Four centuries of European Imperial rivalry in the Caribbean had produced, by the end of the nineteenth century, a complex mixture of languages, cultures, races, and in the English-speaking territories, at any rate, a society without a satisfactory sense of its historical origins and development, or a clear awareness of its political and economic prospects in the modern world. Such self-awareness as existed came from detached and often unsympathetic reports, journals, or travelogues by itinerant British men of letters like Matthew Gregory Lewis, James Anthony Froude, Anthony Trollope and Charles Kingsley. James's book therefore satisfied a real need: it provided a sympathetic and articulate commentary by someone with authoritative, inside knowledge of his subject:

> With emancipation in 1834 the blacks themselves
> established a middle class. But between the
> brown-skinned middle class and the black there
> is a continual rivalry, distrust and ill-feeling,
> which, skillfully played upon by the European
> people, poisons the life of the community. Where
> so many crosses and colors meet and mingle, the
> shades are naturally difficult to determine and the
> resulting confusion is immense. There are the
> nearly-white hanging on tooth and nail to the
> fringes of white society, and these, as is easy to
> understand, hate contact with the darker skin far
> more than some of the broader-minded whites.
> Then there are the browns, intermediates, who
> cannot by any stretch of imagination pass as

white, but who will not go one inch towards mixing with people darker than themselves. And so on, and on, and on.

Seldom before or since have race, colour, and class, as they relate to the English-speaking Caribbean, been examined with such analytic clarity and precisely organized logic. Not only is the information clearly organized, the insights and judgments are expressed in a bold, natural, and lively style. Most of all, James is able effectively to convey his reformer's zeal for change: he analyzes the weaknesses of West Indian society with such indisputable logic that the reader is wholly persuaded to the need for change. The passage illustrates a general pattern in James's writing whereby general issues of race, colour, and class are analyzed in order to reflect a political theme; in this case, the establishment of self-government in the English-speaking West Indies, and the radical social reorganization that must follow. The intention, as always, is to remove oppression and achieve greater social and political justice.

Although James's sympathy for self-government is based on explicit opposition to colonial rule, he appears to present his preference for self-government with objectivity. While he condemns the Crown Colony system of government, and the British officials who administer it, he admits the usefulness of the Crown Colony system at a certain stage of history; he also attributes the faults of British colonial administrators to the corrupting effect of colonial life on the "admirable characteristics" which they possessed in Britain. His sympathy for those he perceives as victims of oppression does not blind him to the circumstances of the victimizers. This enables him to give a more complete view of his subject, and achieve balance and objectivity:

> It [the Crown Colony system] was useful in its day, but that day is now over. It is a fraud, because it is based on assumptions of superiority which have no foundation in fact. Admirable as are their gifts in this direction, yet administrative capacity is not the monopoly of the English; and even if it were, charity begins at home, especially in these difficult times. The system is wicked, because to an extent far more than is immediately obvious it permits a privileged few to work their will on hundreds of thousands of defenceless people. But most of all is the system criminal because it uses England's overflow as a cork to choke down the natural expansion of the people.

James is obviously not one to mince words. But his opinions are not unbalanced or impulsive; one feels they are the product of long study and careful deliberation, and as such, carry the weight and power of deep conviction.

This combination of balanced objectivity and deep conviction greatly enhances the persuasiveness of James's writing. In expressing his outrage against the slave trade, for example, when he was almost seventy years old, James wrote:

> This then, was the slave trade. It was not easy on the slavers or on the slaves. It is notable that probably as many crew members as slaves died during the voyages. African leaders, if not ordinary free Africans, often willingly collaborated in the trade; and if they and the Europeans were out to get what they could from each other where possible, it remains those who were actually enslaved who suffered the greatest miseries and hardships, and who died in vast numbers.

The passage conveys an impression of total open-mindedness, of all the facts being laid squarely on the table. If the reader is convinced by the author's open-minded disclosure of the facts of the case, he is likely to believe his argument based on the same facts. Nothing distinguishes James's writing more than this ability to convince his readers of his integrity, and persuade them to accept his preferences and convictions: it contributes a combative, polemical vigour that is probably the most enduring element of his style.

The Black Jacobins is a typically Jamesian compound of history, biography, and political analysis, not to mention its success as a narrative of gripping adventure and high drama, acts of public heroism and personal failure, and description of war, with its attendant cruelty and human degradation. The story begins during the period of the French Revolution, and describes the struggle for freedom by African slaves in the French colony of San Domingo, today's Haiti. The slaves struggle against their local masters, soldiers of the French monarchy, and against armies from Spain, Britain, and Napoleonic France. In the end, after twelve years of conflict, they win a victory which has been called by one reviewer "perhaps the most glorious victory of the oppressed over their oppressors in all history." The entire enterprise is indeed extraordinary, a feat so utterly without exact parallel that, but for James's convincing documentation, it might not be believed by some readers. As James himself describes the feat in his preface to the first edition of the book:

> The transformation of slaves, trembling in hundreds before a single white man, into a people able to organize themselves and defeat the most powerful European nations of their day, is one of the great epics of revolutionary struggle and achievement.

Perhaps the achievement itself was too extraordinary for sober historians. In any case, this marvellous success story of the slave leader Toussaint L'Ouverture and of his successors Dessalines and Henri Christophe was never given extensive treatment until *The Black Jacobins,* testifying once more to the pioneering boldness of James's mind and the righteous depth of his convictions.

The Black Jacobins is profusely documented with facts and figures from a variety of sources, and crowded with verbatim quotations from speeches, letters, military despatches and proclamations—all marshalled into a fluent and coherent narrative. The natural fluency of his writing again belies the complexity of James's material, the diversity of his sources, and the prodigious effort of organizing intelligence required to translate everything into some order. He had to resolve the conflicts between various factions of French colonists in San Domingo, and between these colonists and their mulatto countrymen. In addition, James found it necessary to examine the shifting politics of Revolutionary France, with its deep-seated complications involving aristocrat, bourgeois, and the French masses. He had to consider interaction between metropolitan French policies and events in San Domingo; and he could not forget the intrigues of the British and Spanish. Only after disentangling all this, and the volatile situation of the slaves on San Domingo, could James relate with any degree of coherence the story of Toussaint L'Ouverture and the San Domingo revolution.

If James did no more than disentangle chaotic threads of social, political, economic, and military history in *The Black Jacobins,* the book would be a remarkable achievement in historical scholarship. In addition, he recreates the living actuality of people and events in the context of their historical period. His sketches, for example, of black, brown, or white characters, masters or slaves, are fully fleshed out. The author's fine psychological insight imparts great human interest and vividness to a narrative that might otherwise have been a sterile, routine account of cold, historical events. Instead, here is James's description of one of the leaders of the French Revolution:

> Barnave is one of the great figures of the French Revolution. He was bourgeois to the bone, a lawyer with a clear, cold intellect. For him, once the bourgeoisie had gained the Constitution and limited the franchise, the revolution was over. Like a good bourgeois he had an immense respect for royal and noble blood.

The paragraph continues to give a full portrait of Barnave as a debater and politician; but his distinguishing trait, as far as James is concerned, is his implicit support of slavery, despite his revolutionary views. It is a perceptive and discriminating portrait, enlivened by the author's discussion of Barnave's inner motives and personal concerns. Short

sketches of this sort abound in *The Black Jacobins,* and endow the narrative with personal interest and human warmth. James's history of the San Domingo revolution is thus transformed from a purely factual record that might have been just intellectually rewarding, to a dramatic and deeply moving story that is both intellectually and emotionally stimulating.

The most complete portrait in the book undoubtedly is that of Toussaint; but there is no need to describe it in detail, or to relate the main events of the revolution. Suffice it to say that Toussaint joined the revolution at the late age of forty-five, and proved to be a remarkable leader, before he was tricked and captured by the French, who transported him to imprisonment and eventual death in Europe. Of Toussaint, James says: "But men make history, and Toussaint made the history that he made because he was the man he was." Before the revolution, as a steward of livestock, Toussaint had had some experience in administration. By James's account he also had a "superb intellect," and had read Caesar's Commentaries and a volume by the Abbé Raynal, which gave him much insight into colonial economics and politics of the period. His feats of leadership and military prowess cannot then be regarded as merely freakish.

James's description of Toussaint's background and explanation of his abilities and motives constitute a credible and realistic portrait of an actual human being with virtues as well as faults. While his main purpose is to celebrate Toussaint's genius, James does not neglect his faults:

> In nothing does his [Toussaint's] genius stand out so much as in refusing to trust the liberties of the blacks to the promises of French or British Imperialism. His error was his neglect of his own people. They did not understand what he was doing or where he was going. He took no trouble to explain. It was dangerous to explain, but still more dangerous not to explain.

The last sentence amply illustrates James's profound understanding of Toussaint's character and the events in which he was involved. His book presents a fully rounded dramatization of Toussaint's career and these events, illuminated by the author's immense scholarship, and insights and judgments blessed with the happy benefit of hindsight.

The Black Jacobins provides many examples of James's ability to communicate his sympathies and preferences with polemical skill. Part of his technique, as mentioned earlier, is to create an impression of objectivity. He usually does this by admitting evidence that contradicts his own preferences, then by demolishing that evidence. The technique incorporates lucid thinking, cogent argument, and perhaps the most stimulating of all aspects of James's writing—its enduring combativeness:

> The slaves destroyed tirelessly. Like the peasants in the Jacquerie or the Luddite wreckers, they were seeking their salvation in the most obvious way, the destruction of what they knew was the cause of their sufferings; and if they destroyed much it was because they had suffered much. They knew that as long as these plantations stood their lot would be to labour on them until they dropped. The only thing was to destroy them. From their masters they had known rape, torture, degradation, and, at the slightest provocation, death. They returned in kind. For two centuries the higher civilisation had shown them that power was used for wreaking your will on those whom you controlled. Now that they held power they did as they had been taught. In the frenzy of the first encounters they killed all, yet they spared the priests whom they feared and the surgeons who had been kind to them. They, whose women had undergone countless violations, violated all the women who fell into their hands, often on the bodies of their still bleeding husbands, fathers and brothers. "Vengeance! Vengeance!" was their war-cry, and one of them carried a white child on a pike as a standard.

How skilfully James is able to persuade the reader of the justice of the slaves' cause and the rightness of their actions without concealing their own atrocities and abuses! All the facts are laid on the table with scrupulous integrity. Or so the reader believes.

The passage begins by stating the fact of destruction perpetrated by the slaves. But these destructive actions are quickly compared with those of other oppressed groups (the Luddites in nineteenth-century England, and the Jacquerie in fourteenth-century France), who were similarly motivated. By placing their actions on a universal plane of human activity shared by other similar groups, the comparison tends to moderate whatever natural resentment the reader might feel towards the slaves. This is followed by a telling point: that the cruelty of the slaves was reciprocal, because they were responding to cruel actions which their masters had perpetrated on them during two centuries. If their destructive actions are the result of what they were taught, they cannot be held entirely responsible for them. James then lists atrocities previously inflicted on the slaves by their masters and teachers. He saturates the reader's mind so thoroughly with examples of the slaves' victimization, that by the time the last sentence is reached, the reader is more or less disposed to accept the slaves without demur in their new role as victimizers.

James preserves historical accuracy by reporting facts that reflect badly on the slaves as well as on their masters. Yet he is able to celebrate the heroism of the slaves, which is his chief theme. His general argument is that "like revolutionary peasants everywhere" the slaves "aimed at the extermination of their oppressors." If he does not fully succeed in justifying the cruel actions of the slaves, he successfully neutralizes their negative effect on the reader. This enables him effectively to communicate his theme of revolutionary political action which has the capacity to eradicate injustice and oppression.

By any standard, *The Black Jacobins* is a superlative literary achievement. It vividly dramatizes complex issues of war and peace, freedom and oppression, by means of a narrative that is always instructive, and sometimes intensely moving; and whether one agrees with the author or not, his book successfully conveys his uncompromising opposition to injustice, especially when it is generated by racial discrimination, colour prejudice, class distinction, or as in *The Black Jacobins* by all three together. The eradication of such injustice is the principal theme in James's writing. It is present in *The Black Jacobins* to the extent that the book condemns the injustice of slavery, and celebrates the revolutionary action of the San Domingo slaves who successfully eradicate it from their island. While James's opposition to injustice may not be based on belief in the equal ability of all human individuals, his writing reflects belief in the equality of all racial groups. Most often it reflects abiding faith in the equality of black and white people, particularly those who belong to racial groups that originate in Africa and Europe.

James's books and essays contain an undercurrent of assertiveness implied by an almost compulsive desire to convince his readers that blacks, historically, have shown themselves to be capable of at least the same level of accomplishment that the best whites can boast. One may recall his claim in his first book that an English administrator would find in the West Indies (in 1932) "a thoroughly civilised community . . . with its best men as good as, and only too often better than himself." Similar echoes pervade his later writing, for example his memoir of Paul Robeson:

> As I think of many ideas prevalent today, it is important to remember that while Paul was insisting that the Black man had special qualities which were the result of his past in Africa and of his centuries of experience in the Western world, he was equally aware of the fact that this Black man was able to participate fully and completely in the distinctively Western arts of Western civilisation.

Echoes of this sort encourage the view that James's writing was partly stimulated by the outrage he felt towards those who denied or ignored Robeson's claim of full and complete participation by black people in the distinctively Western arts of western civilisation. Hence the combative vigour of his style, and his tireless assault on the manifold injustices of a Eurocentric world order, which had become so entrenched and institutionalized by centuries of world-wide European domination, that it had come to be accepted as normal or natural, by Europeans and non-Europeans alike.

The Black Jacobins is the peak of James's writing and probably the finest piece of non-fiction writing to come out of the English-speaking Caribbean. James's subsequent writing deals with broadly similar subjects and concerns which portray race, colour and class—essential factors in the political problems of injustice which he wishes to solve; for example, *Modern Politics* and *Party Politics in the West Indies.* It must be remembered that James's associations were predominantly political. Apart from West Indian leaders like Eric Williams, George Padmore and Sir Learie Constantine, James knew Kwame Nkrumah and Jomo Kenyatta. He was familiar with the work of Marcus Garvey and Aimé Césaire, and wrote an essay on W. E. B. Dubois. His associations conditioned his writing, and placed him in the vanguard of social and political change in emerging nations that were later to be called the Third World. His writing should be viewed within the political context of this whole pioneering achievement.

James's literary interest in cricket may come as a surprise in someone so intimately connected with politics and other serious subjects including the arts. The point is that James considers cricket to be serious—both a sport and an art. He was cricket correspondent for several English newspapers over many years; his cricket journalism is extensive. Two of his most outstanding shorter works are individual essays on Sir Garfield Sobers and Sir Learie Constantine. Constantine was reputed to be one of the greatest fieldsmen in the game of cricket. Some idea of James's treatment of cricket may be conveyed by his description of Constantine's fielding. In order to illustrate the exact quality of Constantine's greatness as a fieldsman, James quotes from the nineteenth-century English literary critic William Hazlitt, in two passages which eulogize the performance of the great actress Sarah Siddons. Similarly, in order to illustrate the extraordinary contribution of Sobers to cricket, James makes lengthy reference to William Wordsworth's *Preface to Lyrical Ballads,* published in 1798. These two illustrations demonstrate James's bold, freewheeling, and intellectually catholic approach toward cricket, as indeed to every other subject of his writing.

Among his works on cricket, this approach is most comprehensively illustrated by James's book *Beyond a Boundary,* a typical compound of autobiography, social history, cultural and political analysis, as well as sportswriting. To support his argument that cricket is an art as well as a game, James elicits references from the visual arts, from English litera-

ture, from the Greek and Roman classics, and from his specialist's knowledge as an experienced cricket journalist. If cricket is an art, the West Indies has produced more than its fair share of cricket artists. No doubt this is because of "the intimate connection between cricket and West Indian social and political life." Thus James's cricket writing also reveals the familiar undercurrent of assertiveness in celebrating the careers of black men who have distinguished themselves in one or other of "the distinctively Western arts of Western civilisation." *Beyond a Boundary* is rich in cricket reminiscences and sketches of cricketers: a pure delight for the cricket aficionado. But the wider interest of the book lies in the author's account of his early life and education, in his treatment of cricket as an intrinsic feature of West Indian culture, and in his display of learning drawn from every branch of knowledge that is relevant to his main theme.

If volume is anything to go by, fiction is not James's favourite form: his fiction consists of the novel *Minty Alley* and a few short stories, which together add up to a mere fraction of his total output as a writer. *Minty Alley* tells the story of Mr Haynes, an educated, middle-class Trinidadian who takes lodgings in a lower-class household in Port of Spain. Haynes stays for three years, and with a suspect combination of benignity and detachment, coolly observes the uninhibited, brawling manners of the people around him. The characters of the novel are stereotypes; the plot is a linear account of chronological events; and the dialogue is rather mechanical. The main interest of the novel is its impartial display of racial animosity, colour discrimination, class rivalry, superstition and other features of Trinidadian society. Perhaps it is James's impartial stance which robs his fiction of the full vigour and provocative vitality that his expressed preferences and convictions lend to his non-fiction. Or perhaps his literary gifts are weighted more in the skills of commentary and exposition, rather than of evocation and moral speculation. In any case, his non-fiction adds more to his literary achievement than his fiction.

One feature of James's writing, however,—its buoyant optimism—survives in every form he employs. Whether it comes in the early, middle or later stages of his career, James's writing is invariably directed against wrongdoers or perpetrators of injustice, and it is invariably sustained by a firm belief that racial wrongs can be righted, complications of history satisfactorily explained and all problems solved. As an international socialist, James regards Imperialism as the great enemy, which in its contemporary guise appears as foreign economic domination. But however strong the enemy, or entrenched its injustice, James's writing never betrays doubt, uncertainty, or the possibility of failure. His outlook is always positive, confident, absolutely certain of success—if not immediately, then in the future.

James's optimistic vision is clearly expressed in *Mariner, Renegades and Castaways,* a book which bears the subtitle, "The story of Herman Melville and the world we live in." As the subtitle suggests, the book is as much about Melville as about modern civilisation:

> Melville wrote *Moby Dick* in 1851. Yet in it today can be seen the anticipations of Darwin's theory of man's relation to the natural world, of Marx's theory of the relation of the individual to the economic and social structure, of Freud's theory of the irrational and primitive forces which lie just below the surface of human behaviour.

According to James, the two things that are of greatest interest to Melville are world revolution and the future of American democracy. He sees Melville's novel as prophesying the doom of modern industrial civilisation, because it has become outworn through its emphasis on material wealth, rather than on the legitimate needs of the human spirit. James cites many twentieth-century writers who confirm the fulfillment of Melville's prophecy—Eliot, Céline, Koestler, Hemingway, Gide, Proust. But James's point is that unlike Melville, these writers "know nothing about work and workers, the living experience of the vast majority of living men." He dismisses their collective despair as completely alien to Melville's vision—and his own.

After mentioning famous twentieth-century literary works such as *The Waste Land, Journey to the End of the Night, Darkness at Noon, The Naked and the Dead* and *From Here to Eternity,* James continues with his objections to their authors:

> Some of them are men of very great gifts, but for all of them, human beings are the naked and the dead, for whom there is nothing between here and eternity, life is a journey to the end of the night, where in the darkness of midday, the neurotic personality of our time escapes from freedom into a wasteland of guilt and hopelessness. Melville describes the same world in which they live, and Ishmael and Pierre are sick to the heart with the modern sickness. Yet how light in the scales is the contemporary mountain of self-examination and self-pity against the warmth, the humour, the sanity, the anonymous but unfailing humanity of the renegades and castaways and savages of the Pequod, rooted in the whole historical past of man, doing what they have to do, facing what they have to face.

The passage expresses exactly the cool, practical optimism of James's writing, which derives from single-minded concern with what the author has to do and what he has to face.

The difference between James's and Melville's characters is that much of what he has to do and face is specifically related to black people, who form one of the groups most oppressed by modern civilisation.

Because of its preoccupation with the eradication of injustice, as experienced primarily by black people, James's writing must ultimately be seen as the work of a black, Caribbean intellectual, whose fundamental ideas were shaped during the first three decades of this century. James's name has been linked, in one way or another, with those of Nkrumah and Kenyatta, Williams, Garvey, Constantine, Césaire, Padmore, and with the black Americans Robeson, DuBois and Richard Wright. These men all belonged to a generation in which what they had to do, and what they had to face, was to try to secure for black people—the citizens of Africa, the Caribbean and black America—their rightful place in the modern world. Like James, they tended to see the world through political rather than artistic glasses, and their achievement consequently is largely political. The more literary of these men—James, Césaire, Wright—can also boast of achievement as writers who made a contribution to the thought and culture of their time, by questioning the dominant Eurocentric image of twentieth-century man, and asserting an equally positive image of the black man. Part of James's literary achievement derives from the role his writing has played, world-wide, in this reversal of images of black and white.

Although the English-speaking Caribbean has produced novelists superior to James, *Minty Alley* remains one of the first novels to provide a serious examination of important social, cultural, and political issues in the region. Similarly, professional economists, historians, political theorists, each in his own discipline, have produced scholarly studies which today supersede James's contribution in these fields; but it was James's writing in the first place which helped to stimulate interest in all these fields. To acknowledge this pioneering achievement in separate disciplines, however, is to ignore the comprehensiveness of James's achievement as a writer, and his intellectual gifts as a genuine polymath. Despite his concentration on issues of race, colour, and class, James belongs to a select band of intellectuals whose literary achievement is intimately related to the problems and struggles of new nations in establishing themselves. This places him not only alongside Commonwealth writers such as Nirad Chaudhuri of India and Northrop Frye of Canada, but also alongside a nineteenth-century American like Ralph Waldo Emerson. Like all these men, James brings his encyclopaedic knowledge and versatile writing skills to bear upon fundamental problems of social and cultural evolution in territories emerging out of British colonialism. His pioneering literary achievement must therefore be acknowledged for its double contribution, firstly to a reassessment of the role of black people in the modern world, and secondly to the evolution and growth of social, political, and economic ideas and strategies mainly in the English-speaking West Indies, but also in the Third World.

It tends to confirm his claim of an intimate connection between cricket and West Indian social and political life, when we turn finally to cricket for the best explanation of James's motives and achievement as a writer. James's description of Sobers the cricketer is often curiously self-revealing. He describes aspects of Sober's game as "aggressive" and "demonic," and he compares Sobers to a West Indian hurricane. He also calls him a genius and concludes his essay:

> He [Sobers] being what he is (and I being what I am), for me his command of the rising ball in the drive, his close fielding and his hurling himself into his fast bowling are a living embodiment of centuries of a tortured history.

The phrase in brackets hints at recognition by James of similarities between his writing and the cricket of Sobers. Sobers's excellence in every aspect of cricket except wicket keeping, may be compared with James's own comprehensive mastery of writing in different forms and genres.

The style of both men offers an even closer comparison. James observes Sobers's "rage" when he has missed opportunities on the playing field; he compares the cricketer's disappointment to the "gleam of a damped-down furnace." As we have seen, James's writing is no less combative in spirit. The combativeness of his writing reflects a similar rage over the victimized condition of black people, following centuries of tortured history. This history which inspired Sobers and James

> is governed by two factors, the sugar plantation and Negro slavery. That the majority of the population in Cuba was never slave does not affect the underlying social identity. Wherever the sugar plantation and slavery existed, they imposed a pattern. It is an original pattern, not European, not African, not a part of the American main, not native in any conceivable sense of that word, but West Indian, *sui generis,* with no parallel anywhere else.

Perhaps this is why Sobers's cricket has never been matched anywhere else; and this is probably why James's writing, for all its association with the work of non-Caribbean black or ex-colonial writers, is nowhere fully matched in scope, vigour, and fluency. It is the righteous rage engendered in him by the torture of Caribbean his-

tory, which continues to sustain James's writing after fifty years, and lifts it to peaks of excellence of which *The Black Jacobins* is the most prominent and lasting example.

Derek Walcott (review date 25 March 1984)

SOURCE: "A Classic of Cricket, A Legend of Baseball," in *The New York Times Book Review,* March 25, 1984, pp. 1, 36-7.

[*In the following review, Walcott praises James's* Beyond a Boundary, *a book about cricket players of African descent. Walcott asserts that the book "is both a chronicle of the sport and the decline of an empire, from colonialism to independence."*]

George John, Arthur Jones, Josh Rudder, Piggott, Wilton St. Hill, Matthew Boardman—the roll is like a chronicle of fallen yeomen in a Shakespearean battle, but they were cricketers of African descent who brought glory to an English game in the West Indies. Their battlefields were ringed with quietly clapping spectators. Most fell victim to prejudice and neglect. They have found a grateful chronicler in C. L. R. James, whose book, *Beyond a Boundary* (published in England in 1963 but not here until now), should find its place on the team with Izaak Walton, Ivan Turgenev, A. J. Liebling and Ernest Hemingway, unless its author suffers the same fate as his black subjects.

Beyond a Boundary is a book about grace, about slow-bowlers with the wrists of anglers and fast-bowlers with the thunder of fighting bulls, and every one of its sentences, deftly turned, is like a lesson in that game, whose criterion is elegance. . . . [But] this book goes further afield than cricket. It goes behind the rusted tin forces of the barrack yards of West Indian life as far as the Periclean archipelago. And the Greek past is a lesson that Mr. James appropriates as authoritatively as blacksmiths, yardboys and groundsmen dominated the sport of their masters. He sees no difference between their achievements and those of the Athenian athletes.

Portentous as this sounds, it is what Mr. James means by civilization. It is, for him, that sweetness of disposition and that clarity of intellect that Matthew Arnold defined as culture, and Mr. James's book dramatizes its ironies as accurately as Arnold or Henry Adams did and does it not through contemplation but through action.

"It's just a book about cricket, for God's sake." It isn't. It is a book about cricket for the gods' sake as well. It is a book about treachery, despair and the fate of some of the best for being black, and still it is written without bitterness. Anger, yes, but no rancor. It is a noble book about poor, beautifully built but socially desperate men (one of whom begged his captain to be allowed to play the game barefoot because shoes slowed down his delivery) who made this game the next thing to religion. Mr. James radiantly celebrates this blend of African prowess with Victorian codes. He sees how those Victorian ideals of gentlemanly conduct were ethics, even tribal ethics, regardless of race, and not a trap.

But Mr. James was never blinded by the plaster casts and hypocritical marble copies of the Victorian ideal. He always had a hard mind, and this book does not try to make marble from ebony. It would be laughable if it were yet another paean of gratitude, a fake pastoral with classical echoes, but it would also be incredible, since Mr. James has been a Marxist (who has broken with Russia) and, in a politically active life, has been interned on Ellis Island, out of which degradation he wrote his *Mariners, Renegades and Castaways;* he has also been a pamphleteer, a pioneering West Indian novelist and in *Black Jacobins* a historian of the Haitian Revolution. All of his life he has been known in the islands, by trade unionists as well as by writers, as a controversial humanist. But he loves cricket above everything else, not because it is a sport, but because he has found in it all the decencies required for a culture.

Then how can one be as passionate about the Russian Revolution as he is and still idealize a sport practiced by "gentlemen"? In his long life Mr. James has arrived, through this book, at a calm center. His calm is that of a meridian between two oceans, two cultures, even between radical and conservative politics, without mere neutrality. His calm is not neutrality. It has the passion of conviction, for decent conduct is the first and last thing required of men, as it is of states. He has arrived at that calm as quietly as a knight concludes a pilgrimage, and his quest has been that cup called "The Ashes," that grail of Test Cricket for which teams from South Africa, New Zealand, Australia, Pakistan, India and the West Indies have fought so that one of their captains, many of them knighted later, could hold it up to the world.

It is Mr. James's belief that there is a difference between discipline and natural grace, between relentless practice and genius. But he cherishes obedience in the Sophoclean sense, or even in the Roman way of not questioning the emperor's thumb of the umpire, if not of the empire. For him, obedience irradiates the most belligerent stroke-maker; he is appalled at the commercial anarchy of American sport. But things have changed. Cricket teams, through a certain entrepreneur, can now be bought or rented for high salaries, and black West Indian cricketers now play in South Africa. But it is the ideal that remains untarnished, not its vandals.

Mr. James's ancestors are African; why does he not find mi-

mesis in African not Periclean sculpture when he describes the grace of his cricketers? Bodily movement is not a principle of African art, and the game is not played there on the scale of its other arenas. Proletarian in politics, patrician in taste, Mr. James should be a contradiction, but he was never a target for black radicals, rather one of its legislators, like Frantz Fanon, Léopold Sédar Senghor, Aimé Césaire and Kwame Nkrumah. His history as a polemicist, his campaigns for African and West Indian nationalism have often caused him to be black-listed, interned and put under house arrest in his native Trinidad. And, in fact, if one thinks carefully again, *Beyond a Boundary* can be thought of as subversion; it undermines concepts that feel safe, it beats tradition by joining it, and its technique is not bitterness but joy.

Writers who worship a sport can sublimate their mediocrity into envy. Mr. James, who was a good bowler, has no envy. He sounds like a better bowler than Hemingway was a bullfighter or Mailer is a boxer. He had real promise and was going to make cricketing his profession. He chortles with unaffected boasting about bowling out Learie Constantine, but what remains in this book is the shadow that stained the heroes of his boyhood with colonial prejudice—the darkening future when the "gentleman's game" is over, and his blacksmiths and roundsmen split from their teammates to go their own ways.

This sense of dusk in *Beyond a Boundary* provides it with history, gives it a tragic enchantment, since it is both a chronicle of the sport and the decline of an empire, from colonialism to independence, from the days when black and brown cricketers had different clubs to the days of the black captaincy of Frank Worrell. It is also a book, then, about twilight, about the turning of an epoch, and yet its tone is triumphal. Most of all, for a third of its length, it is like an excellent novel. Its characters are more than biographical asides. They have their own arc, no matter how minor their roles.

[Any] boy today as keen on cricket as Mr. James was then would be already a writer if he appreciated this passage by Mr. James himself:

"My grandfather went to church every Sunday morning at eleven o'clock wearing in the broiling sun a frock-coat, striped trousers and top-hat, with his walking stick in hand, surrounded by his family."

Fair enough, Victorian in meter, decorous in memory, then the right tingle comes: "The underwear of the women crackling with starch."

This is simply one stroke from a book whose light is as clear as a summer game's and which, as the highest tribute I can offer, every writer should read, because there, in one phrase, like the broken bottles on a moonlit wall in Chekhov, is the history of a colonial epoch: its rigors, its deprivations and its pride.

Cynthia Hamilton (essay date March 1992)

SOURCE: "A Way of Seeing: Culture as Political Expression in the Works of C. L. R. James," in *Journal of Black Studies,* Vol. 22, No. 3, March, 1992, pp. 429-43.

[*In the following essay, Hamilton discusses James's approach to political analyses and his historical perspective.*]

Left on the bookshelves to collect dust on their yellowing pages, the literary works of political activists are often forgotten to history. Rarely are they taken seriously, but rather, are seen as quaint relics of the author's past. We have done ourselves, as well as these individuals, a great disservice. For writers of the African diaspora in particular, literary work is often the form in which political ideas and analyses appear first. These writers have often, in the words of St. Clair Drake, "transmuted sociological data into lyrical prose and turned controlled observations and more casual impressions into convincing generalization and perceptive predictions." We must learn, as have these writers, to understand ourselves and our history through an appreciation of the ordinary. We must see in everyday life the manifestations not simply of exploitation, but of the struggle for authenticity among ordinary men and women. The culture of the masses of people can tell us much about historical events if we learn to see clearly that which surrounds us daily.

This article takes a closer look at the literary works of C. L. R. James as the first expression of the sensitive social observation that forms the basis for much of his political and historical analysis. His early work must be seen as instruction in the use of the "method" that James employs to analyze history. He gives us a real sense of how ordinary people make extraordinary history.

The social sciences have not been able to present us with an adequate picture of everyday life and popular culture. They fall short of this task because of the assumptions and hypotheses that underscore research. These include assumptions about man and human motivation, as well as established definitions of culture and institutional structures. Because social scientists have traditionally been concerned with stability and continuity, they have missed—intentionally or unintentionally—the adaptive quality and resilience of the masses that manifest themselves in varying environments. Because social scientists have focused on elites and their organized efforts of social transformation, they have failed to

see the nameless multitudes whose creativity and imagination have been the source of all human history.

Because of the shortcomings of traditional social science analysis, James begins his most famous work, ***Black Jacobins,*** the history of the Haitian Revolution, by distinguishing his work from existing historical analysis:

> The propagandists of the time claimed that however cruel was the slave traffic, the African slave in America was happier than in his own African civilization. Ours too is an age of propaganda. Men will say anything in order to foster national pride or soothe a troubled conscience.

In an effort to understand and analyze the contributions of societies and people ignored by the social science of the day, James, of necessity, rejected the starting point of the established disciplines. He did so by affirming first that the masses are the creators of their own history; the mass party and the "barefoot men," the peasants, workers, and unemployed must be exalted, elevated to a primary position as a force in history. As one writer has said with regard to James's work:

> [He] established for the first time the historical importance of the self-activity of the oppressed colonial peoples. The wretched of the earth, to use Fanon's term, were no more passive objects of administrative control. They were men who resisted and in their resistance, proved as creative if not more so, as any other set of men.

This is the starting point in the works of C. L. R. James. There is no attempt to romanticize, but rather he points to ordinary people as the force in history, the tiny levers of change that normally go unnoticed. He thereby gives us new planes of analyses. We are not to bear witness to a great chain of triumphs, but by focusing on mass action generated at the bottom of the society, we see history in a new light.

W. E. B. DuBois pioneered the application of the recognition of the role of the masses in history, which began with the realization of the shortcomings of early sociological and historical analyses of Blacks in America. He expressed his concern in a chapter in *The Souls of Black Folk.* He wrote:

> We seldom study the condition of the Negro today honestly and carefully. It is so much easier to assume that we know it all. And yet how little we really know of these millions and of their daily lives and longings, of their homely joys and sorrows, of their real shortcomings and the meaning of their crimes! All this we can only learn by intimate contact with the masses, and not by wholesale argu-

ments covering millions separated in time and space and differing widely in training and culture.

DuBois developed for us this alternative approach that placed the action of ordinary people at the center stage of history. James concurred and wrote in recognition: "All thinking about Black struggles today and some years past originates from him [DuBois]." In particular, James was referring to *Black Reconstruction in America, 1860-1888,* which DuBois wrote in 1935. It was here that DuBois employed the recognition of the role of the masses as creators of history; in particular, he set out to document the role of slaves as central to the outcome of the Civil War. His chapter, "The General Strike," has never been surpassed in this regard.

This is also the starting point for C. L. R. James. In his short stories and his novel, as well as in his historical work, the "yard" (the residential environment of the working poor) is the locus of activity of ordinary men and women who rise to extraordinary triumphs as well as defeat: Toussaint, Boukman, and Matthew Bondman. In all of his work, it is the recognition of the "vitality and validity" of the independent Negro struggle that serves as James's guide.

James's life work has been devoted to what we might call "a way of seeing." He recognizes the plight of consciousness resulting from the fragmentation in society, while at the same time, he identifies the ways in which ordinary people struggle to make their lives whole. He wrote in this regard:

> The whole world today lives in the shadow of state power. . . . This state power, by whatever names it is called, one-party state or welfare state, destroys all pretense of government by the people, of the people. All that remains is government *for* the people.

> Against this monster, people all over the world, and particularly ordinary working people in factories, mines, fields, and offices, are rebelling every day in ways of their own invention. Sometimes their struggles are on a small personal scale. More effectively they are the actions of groups, formal or informal, but always unofficial, organized around their work and their place of work. Always the aim is to regain control over their own conditions of life and their relations with one another. Their strivings, their struggles, their methods have few chroniclers. They themselves are constantly attempting various forms of organization, uncertain of where the struggle is going to end. Nevertheless, they are imbued with one fundamental certainty, that they have to destroy the continuously mounting bureaucratic mass or be themselves destroyed by it.

James's recognition of the political significance of the independent and daily initiative of working people is in many ways a continuation of the social observation he employed in his earliest work as a fiction writer and social historian. In his semiautobiographical work *Beyond a Boundary,* we get a sense of the source of James's skills of social observation and his early acknowledgment of the power of ordinary men and women in shaping events. He wrote in his opening pages:

> Our house was superbly situated, exactly behind the wicket. I doubt if for some years I knew what I was looking at in detail. But this watching from the window shaped one of my strongest early impressions of personality in society. His name was Matthew Bondman and he lived next door to us. . . . He was generally dirty. He would not work. His eyes were fierce, his language was violent and his voice was loud. For ne'er-do-well, in fact vicious character, as he was, Matthew had one saving grace, Matthew could bat. . . . Matthew dropped out early. But he was my first acquaintance with the genus Britannicus, a fine batsman, and the impact that he makes on all around him, non-cricketers and cricketers alike. The contrast between Matthew's pitiable existence as an individual and the attitude people had towards him filled my growing mind and has occupied me to this day.

Matthew Bondman is James's model of the "barefoot man." He is a metaphor for the extraordinary that is a product of the ordinary, the unpretentious skill most often left undeveloped, so often unrecognized or even despised by the bourgeoisie.

Although there may be great acceptance of the literary value of the ordinary today, it was not always so. James's early fiction, his short story **"Triumph,"** and his novel *Minty Alley* presented a picture of West Indian life that the middle classes would have preferred to ignore. It was the same in the United States when writers like Zora Hurston, Langston Hughes, and Wallace Thurman published their magazine *Fire!!* inspired by Black street life and the "folk," only to have it met by hostility from those who demanded more "respectable" images.

James does include the Black middle class in his novel. In fact, he makes such a character his narrative voice. Thus the reader gains appreciation for the strength and character of ordinary folk along with the narrator as he comes to recognize *his* alienation and their authenticity.

James did not leave the people of the yard when he developed politically. To the contrary, his appreciation for the barefoot men and women is the starting point of his political analysis. He wrote in the first chapter of **Black Jacobins,** "The Property":

> The difficulty was that though one could trap them like animals, transport them in pens, work them alongside an ass or a horse and beat both with the same stick, stable them and starve them, they remained, despite their black skins and curly hair, quite invincibly human beings with the intelligence and resentments of human beings. To cow them into the necessary docility and acceptance necessitated a regime of calculated brutality and terrorism.

In spite of such brutality, something remained that allowed these "servants" to maintain a secret pride and feeling of superiority to their masters.

> One has to hear with what precision of ideas and accuracy of judgement, this creature, heavy and taciturn all day, now squatting before his fire, tells stories, talks, gesticulates, argues, passes opinions, approves or condemns both his master and everyone who surrounds him. It was this intelligence which refused to be crushed, these latent possibilities, that frightened the colonists, as it frightens the whites in Africa today. "No species of men has more intelligence," wrote Hilliard d'Auberteuil, a colonist, in 1784 and had his book banned.

The key in James's analysis is the emphasis on struggle, the tension between the demands made by the society and the human need for expression. Despite the obstacles created to separate men from themselves, they struggle to overcome them and create normalcy in their lives, consciously and unconsciously. It is James's ability to see so clearly through the problem and a way to a solution that makes him important for us today. His method of perception is paramount; more important than the "what" is the "how" of his analysis. That, I believe is his greatest legacy.

Because of his own way of seeing the world, it was quite natural that James would always view phenomenon in its totality. The artificial fragmentation that is so common to Western and Western-influenced societies has resulted in the separation of beauty and art, the separation between politics and history, of economics and ethics, and of our individual selves from ourselves as citizen, worker, mother—whatever role we perform. This fragmentation was rejected by James. But more important, he saw in the daily lives of ordinary people their own mighty struggle to reject fragmentation. Only when our entire life, our character, ideals, morals, jobs, social life, and our culture become one, can we claim to have achieved real political consciousness, for only then will we have recognized the whole. It is this

totality of vision which constitutes the historical method of James's work.

James himself made this point about his work to a small group of people invited to his home to share part of his personal history in 1972. He said that he wanted to present to us the climax of his political ideas during the past 40 years that he had been in politics, the summation of where he stood and certain perspectives for the future of "speculative truth." He emphasized that in order to understand the present, we had to understand the past, that is, the totality. For this type of understanding, he said, we needed a philosophical method—a method unlike empiricism, which recognizes only bits and pieces of phenomenon by taking things as they come, but rather, a method that forged a unity of all the separate parts. This totality of vision was no easy assignment; it required more than just fitting the pieces together. To emphasize this, James read to us from Hegel and concluded:

> It is in this dialectic, and in the comprehension of the unity of opposites or of the positive in the negative, that speculative knowledge consists. This is the most important aspect of the dialectic but for thought that is as yet unpracticed and unfree it is the most difficult.

Without this method of history, we take things as they come. We see political struggles, for example, as isolated and fragmented bursts of energy that die out after the crisis. We lose the message because we are unexpecting spectators. We are conditioned to view social phenomena as an evolutionary process: Little by little, things happen. But we must begin to see differently: These phenomena have been there all along and then simply "explode," the opposites joining to form something new. The dialectic is the only methodological tool that allows us to truly understand sudden disruption or change; it allows us to understand and know that what existed before will never be possible again. Sudden explosions of mass action do not surprise James, because always he had an eye on the people, what they are and what they do from day to day.

James was a product of the history of the Caribbean: of slavery, colonialism, European cultural dominance and influence, and mass struggles against such. He lived that history in its totality; it is reflected in his writings and speeches; it has been the determinant behind his action and motives. It is the Caribbean of his birth that provides the lens through which James views phenomena. And as George Lamming, the West Indian novelist, has said, what a person thinks is very much determined by the way a person sees. However, we must see, as James did, that this was not a static history, that is, one of dominance and exploitation alone. The Caribbean was simultaneously the antithesis of the West. The very life and culture of the people of the Caribbean has been a reaction against the West, as alternative to the West. It was through a recognition of the function of mass culture, the popular culture of peasant and proletariat alike, that gave James a focal point for his political analysis. He wrote in an introduction to J. J. Thomas's work, *Froudacity:*

> We of the Caribbean are a people more than any other people constructed by history, and therefore any attempt not only to analyze but to carry out political or social activity, in connection with ourselves and in relation to other peoples, any such attempt has got to begin and constantly to bear in mind how we came into being, where we have reached, who we are and what we are. We were brought from Africa and thrown into a highly developed modern industry and a highly developed modern language. We had to master them or die. We have lived. We are not dealing with abstractions that concern people who are intellectuals and historians. We are dealing with concrete matters that penetrate into the very immediate necessities of our social existence.

The cultural expressions of Africans in the New World are manifestations of the methods and tools of survival, as well as a critique of what they found. For this reason, culture is central to James's work.

When one looks back at the chronology of James's publications, some might comment that there are two Jameses, the James of criticism and the *Manchester Guardian* and the James of politics. Such a remark would have its origins in the fragmented thinking of our day. Sometimes it is hard for us to see and understand the relation between politics and culture. But in fact it is one that makes the other possible, grounds it in reality. When James reported on cricket, when he wrote of cricket, it was as an expression and representation of everyday life. Cricket was much more than a game; it was reflective of social structure and values. It embodied and expressed the social relations of an entire island. In cricket, the battle was one of hierarchy and status. The art and skill of the game would manifest themselves in these terms, as well as sportsmanship, according to James. The bowlers and batsman worked out in practice the very attitudes of the people, not simply with respect to the obvious English influence of manners or style but the very complex feelings about economics and politics. In his analysis of cricket, James has forged the "unity of opposites"; he has put cricket into its proper political perspective and traced the interplay of the game itself to present an image of popular culture.

Quite possibly one of the reasons for James's success in projecting everyday life and consciousness so well was also the very motivation for his writing. He wrote about everyday life, not just because it was the closest thing at hand but because

it *was* the reality of the audience he wished to address. According to Kenneth Ramshaud, it was a way of encouraging his countrymen to read, while at the same time teaching them *how* to read. James expressed this same motivation 39 years after his first short story, in the newspaper he edited in Trinidad in 1965, *We The People.* In response to a question regarding his intention to write an autobiography, James commented that he would indeed write one, but only under one condition.

> This condition is that I publish it week by week in fifteen or twenty thousand copies to be given away free. That means the ordinary man will be able to get it and read it week by week. I will not write any autobiography that he will see in the show window at $6.95 a copy. This is where I stand.

James did not have to turn to politics to recognize the barefoot men. It was just a matter of years and historical circumstances that distanced the men and women of his novel, *Minty Alley* from the peasants of the Haitian Revolution. James presents culture as a weapon, a tool of preservation. In particular for those who survived the "middle passage" cultural attitudes and symbols, the essence of the culture was resistance, opposition to everything that denied and denigrated the past. History was that which progressed from day to day within this cultural context of resistance. James presents this interpretation of history, the history of oppression and the struggle against it. This view of history also introduces a view of consciousness. While the characters in the novel, Maisie, Mrs. Rouse, Philomen, and Mr. Haynes, the intellectual, work out their social relations of consciousness on Minty Alley, in Europe the subject of consciousness was also under scrutiny. James and the participants of the Harlem Renaissance and the Negritude Movement worked out in poetry and fiction the conditions of consciousness of the colonized, while European Marxists like Georg Lukacs and Karl Korsch introduced the same concern in their theoretical work. Lukacs and Korsch insisted that Marx's idea of the proletarianization of philosophy be taken seriously, and this meant essentially that ideas would have to be sought and addressed among the mass of the population. These ideas would most certainly be manifest in culture and social relations. This emphasis on culture was continued by those who recognized that not only oppression but resistance may take a very spontaneous and unorganized form, and we will fail to see this if we confine our standards to those set by bourgeois society. To recognize new forms, it was necessary to acknowledge the creativity of the masses and reintroduce the subject of culture as a determinant of political consciousness and action. This is where the colonized had to begin. Any conscious or unconscious rejection of bourgeois style and culture was simultaneously a revolt against bourgeois political and social systems and thereby a challenge to the West. Sometimes it was conscious and sometimes not, but it was left to persons like James to expose the imagination that produced these rejections, and in the process, allowed the colonized to view themselves. For James, both his subjects and his audience were one and the same. The challenge for him was the review that would be written in action.

Not often does the intellectual make such a choice. Not often is he or she able to challenge his or her own right of privilege and status by looking to mass expression as the arbitrator of ideas. James in 1936 used his character, Mr. Haynes in *Minty Alley,* to point out the dilemma of the intellectual, whose alienation can be overcome only through interaction with and respect for the masses. It was a very personal comment for James. Forty-two years later, at the Cultural Congress in Havana in 1968, he would reiterate the same idea by proposing to the delegates that they, intellectuals all, prepare the way for the abolition of the intellectual as an embodiment of culture. To be truly conscious of themselves, they (like the character in *Minty Alley*) had to reject all of the artificial trappings of Western society, including the very artificial hierarchy that ranked them in relation to the masses. The intellectual must recognize the source of his alienation, that which separates him from the "barefoot men." Only if he is willing to disarm himself of those trappings can he be reunited with his kind. Only then can he face himself.

It is important to know exactly what we mean by mass or popular culture if we are to see it as a true measure and expression of consciousness. The simple ability to define culture is a major triumph in this era, however, because of the efforts made to both destroy and obscure it by the professional image-makers. Mass popular culture is that which existed "before the word," before it had been transformed into commodity: Blues, spirituals, work songs, and the calypso of the Might Sparrow are all examples of mass culture that are able to express so freely the public mood, the spirit of resistance. These expressions belong to the people. Their forms are the basis for expression: personal, social, political, and economic. Culture is a tool that facilitates action, allowing personal initiative and spontaneity without hindrance, because it exonerates opposition. The significance of culture was certainly not overlooked by the colonizer, and cultural assimilation was as essential as economic domination for control. To overcome the alienation resulting from this cultural domination, it was imperative to review a vision of the peoples' culture. This was the only way to remove the blinders on consciousness that colonialism had produced. As James wrote in *Beyond A Boundary* about his own early development:

> It was only long years after that I understood the limitation on spirit, vision, and self respect which was imposed on us by the fact that our masters, our curriculum, our code of morals, everything began

from the basis that Britain was the source of all light and leading, and our business was to admire, wonder, imitate, learn; our criterion of success was to have succeeded in approaching that distant ideal— to attain it was of course, impossible. Both masters and boys accepted it as in the very nature of things. The masters could not be offensive about it and, as for me, it was the beacon that beckoned me on.

While James's conception of history was rooted in his recognition of mass culture, he does not romanticize it. As we see from the quote, this culture of the folk may have a twin character: It is both the culture of Caliban and Prospero, of the colonized and the colonizer, of oppression and resistance concurrently. He writes further in *Black Jacobins:*

> There was therefore in West Indian society an inherent antagonism between the consciousness of the black masses and the reality of their lives, inherent in that it was constantly produced and reproduced not by agitators but by the very conditions of the society itself. It is the modern media of mass communication which have made essence into existence. The cinema presents actualities and not infrequently stirs the imagination with the cinematic masterpieces of the world. Every hour on the hour all variations of food, clothing, household necessities and luxuries are presented as absolutely essential to a civilized existence. All this to a population which over a large area still lives in conditions little removed from slavery.

Alienation is a constant for the Black masses. Theirs is, therefore, a living dialectic: The master/slave relation persists in all things, social as well as economic. There is the constant contradiction that the colonized must live with what writers like DuBois, Fanon, and Cesaire have captured so well. Only when the consciousness of the colonized corresponds with their reality is this antagonism resolved.

Only with the rejection of the West, of the master, of materialism, can the colonized regain themselves as fully human. This is the most important example that the Haitian revolution provides, and this, no doubt, was one of the reasons why James selected it as the area for his first historical treatise. Therefore, when he writes of revolt, it is in the same way that he has recognized mass culture; revolts begin not with self-denial, but rather with self-expression. James wrote in *Black Jacobins:*

> Toussaint L'Ouverture and the Haitian slaves brought into the world more than the abolition of slavery. When Latin Americans saw that small and insignificant Haiti could win and keep independence they began to think that they ought to be able

to do the same. The West Indians have brought something new. Passion not spent but turned inward. Toussaint tried and paid for it with his life. Torn, twisted, stretched to the limits of agony, injected with poisonous patent medicines, it lives in the state which Fidel started. It is of the West Indies, West Indian. For it, Toussaint, the fir`.:` `~nd` greatest of West Indians, paid with his life.

Revolt, then, must be viewed as a necessary expression of consciousness for the masses of the population. The change that it brings is most importantly a change in social relations that forms the basis for all expression, collective and individual. What the West Indian, the Blacks, have brought in cultural innovations is the idea of dissent, the feeling of resistance that they have integrated into the very nature of cultural expression: in our music, form and instrumentation; in our folklore, speech, myths; in our very attitudes. As James says, "The mass of the people are not seeking a national identity, they are expressing one."

In summation, James might be best described in the words of Kant, which he used to describe another West Indian writer, John Jacob Thomas:

> one who sees the issue clearly and who has a command of language in its wealth and its purity, and who is possessed of an imagination that is fertile and effective in presenting his ideas and whose heart, turns with lively sympathy to what is truly good.

What James has awakened in me, he has aroused in no less a person than George Lamming, that it is a responsibility to pay attention, to know and understand. The understanding that he imparts is expressed best by the words of Aime Cesaire, which James used to close *Black Jacobins:*

> For it is not true that the work of man
>   is finished
> that man has nothing more to do in the
>   world but be a parasite in the world
> that all we need is to keep in step
>   with the world
> but the work of man is only just beginning
>   and it remains to man to conquer all
>   the violence entrenched in the recesses
>   of his passion
> and no race possesses the monopoly on beauty,
>   of intelligence, of force, and there
>   is a place for all at the rendezvous
>   of victory.

William E. Cain (review date 15 November 1992)

SOURCE: "Race, Revolution and Cricket," in *The New York Times Book Review,* November 15, 1992, p. 23.

[*In the following review, Cain calls* The C. L. R. James Reader *"an intellectual event of the first order."*]

The breadth of C. L. R. James's interests was extraordinary. The Trinidadian writer, historian, critic and editor loved Shakespeare and soap operas, Hegel and calypso. He read Aeschylus, Sophocles, Milton, Rousseau, Thackeray, Dickens, Dostoyevsky, Melville and Whitman, even as he delighted in detective stories, gangster films and Hollywood comedies.

James (1901-89) made contributions in a host of fields—literature, criticism, cultural studies, political theory, history, philosophy. His brilliant account of the Haitian revolution of the 1790's, *The Black Jacobins,* is regarded by scholars as one of the seminal texts about the history of slavery and abolition, along with W. E. B. DuBois's *Black Reconstruction* and Eric Williams's *Capitalism and Slavery.* And his semi-autobiographical meditation on the game of cricket, *Beyond a Boundary,* which beautifully blends witty recollection and shrewdly appreciative insight, is a classic of sportswriting, political analysis and esthetic theory.

While James had many admirers in his lifetime, he remains too little known. He did not have an academic appointment or a network in which to circulate his ideas, and he traveled from one subject to another with a freedom that defied the modern tendency toward specialization. His books are provocative and empowering, especially in their complex demonstrations of the ways in which exploited, oppressed peoples act creatively and resolutely. But the books themselves have flown in and out of print, and a good deal of James's finest writing—including a book-length meditation on American civilization written in the late 1940's—has never been published, passing from one reader to the next only in photocopied form.

James also contributed to small-circulation newspapers, magazines and journals, was the co-author of pamphlets and monographs, and maintained an elaborate correspondence. He was a spellbinding lecturer and orator. But these texts and the transcripts of his lectures have also not been widely available, and in some cases have not been published at all.

For this reason, *The C. L. R. James Reader* is an intellectual event of the first order. It is a rich, diverse gathering of James's work that extends from short stories done in the late 1920's to a discussion of three black women writers (Toni Morrison, Alice Walker, Ntozake Shange) that James presented in the early 1980's. *The Reader* is expertly organized and edited by Anna Grimshaw, a lecturer in anthropology and film at Manchester University and his assistant during the final years of his life, when James, in ill health, was living in the Brixton district of London, "in a small room filled with books, music and art." Through her lucid introduction and well-chosen selections, Ms. Grimshaw highlights and clarifies the scope of James's achievements, the passionate intelligence of his prose, and his ability to describe the twists of Hegel's *Logic,* the splendors of Melville's *Moby-Dick* and the baffled warmth of Charlie Chaplin's Little Tramp.

Born in Port of Spain, Trinidad, James was a fierce critic of imperialism. Yet he recognized the value (as well as the limits) of the British colonial education that he received. Encouraged by his mother ("She read everything that came her way," he said), James quickly acquired command of the classic texts of the Western tradition. He seems to have harbored high aspirations as a creative writer himself, producing short stories and a novel, **Minty Alley.** Upon his arrival in London in 1932, he became a columnist on cricket for *The Manchester Guardian* and involved himself in Pan-African politics and programs. James was a great believer in the need for people of African descent to unify in pursuit of justice. In England during the 1930's, he was also a stalwart, exacting foe of Stalinism.

James was such an uncompromising radical, according to Paul Buhle, the author of the biography *C. L. R. James: The Artist as Revolutionary,* that most of his British comrades welcomed his wish to visit the United States. His forthright critiques had both impressed them and made them uncomfortable.

James arrived in America in 1938. He labored and wrote for two branches of the American Trotskyist movement (the Workers Party and, later, the Socialist Workers Party), lived among sharecroppers in Missouri, and completed two books, **Notes on Dialectics: Hegel, Marx, Lenin** and **Mariners, Renegades and Castaways: The Story of Herman Melville and the World We Live In.** In 1953 he was expelled from the United States as an "undesirable alien."

In 1968, James (who had spent the intervening years in Trinidad) was allowed to re-enter the United States, and in his remaining years he lectured here and abroad. In the mid-80's he returned to England.

The C. L. R. James Reader includes essays on the Soviet Union, Lenin's political thought, dialectical materialism, "the Negro question in the socialist movement," and Kwame Nkrumah's Ghana. It also includes the text of a play James wrote on the Haitian revolutionary leader Toussaint L'Ouverture, which was performed in London in 1936 with Paul Robeson in the leading role. James's critical powers are displayed compellingly here in sharp scrutinies of Whitman, Melville, Shakespeare and Lincoln; masterly commentaries on D. W. Griffith, Charlie Chaplin and Sergei Eisenstein; and

eloquent letters that he wrote throughout the 40's to the writer Constance Webb (whom he married in 1950) and to such scholars as Maxwell Geismar, Jay Leyda and Frank Kermode.

James is an attractive figure, but also a challenging one. Cultural conservatives will be gratified by his loyalty to the Western tradition, but they may not share his tender, inquisitive regard for popular culture. Populists will appreciate his praise of common folks and factory workers, yet may be impatient with his demand that everybody read Plato and Aristotle. Scholars of the black experience will value James's pioneering accomplishments in African and Caribbean history. But James was opposed to compartmentalized research and teaching, concluding that "I do not believe that there is any such thing as Black Studies."

James's view of the world was shaped, I think, by his capacious, optimistic intellect. James perceived the barbarism of Stalinism and Nazism, but he had no true vision of evil, no real sense that there might be something starkly wicked at the heart of things. He did not even confront and weigh the fury and malice evident in Shakespeare and Melville. He shielded himself from something cruel and unforgiving that their art had revealed to them. James retained his faith in the positive direction of history by keeping distant from some of the truths that the writers he cherished had dared to voice.

For James, the goal was always to enlarge the frame of reference, in order to move from specific texts, literary periods, racial and ethnic conflicts and political crises to larger, universal lessons. He was intensely curious and open-minded, heartened and intrigued by what people of all races and ethnicities had produced—evidence, for him, of the manifold variety of creative human effort and expression.

Kara M. Rabbitt (essay date 1995)

SOURCE: "C. L. R. James's Figuring of Toussaint-Louverture: *The Black Jacobins* and the Literary Hero," in *C. L. R. James: His Intellectual Legacies,* edited by Selwyn R. Cudjoe and William E. Cain, University of Massachusetts Press, 1995, pp. 118-35.

[*In the following essay, Rabbitt analyzes the way in which James makes Toussaint-Louverture a dramatic figure in addition to a historical one in* The Black Jacobins.]

As the extensive amount of recent work on C. L. R. James shows, the richness and variety of James's oeuvre solicit critical inquiry at many different levels of analysis. Yet the length of James's career, the intellectual and political development apparent in his writings, his ability to respond to the actualities of the day (to "face reality"), the very dialectical nature of his work, all invite diachronic analyses of their significance and problematize any synchronic reading of a given text. The numerous and excellent overviews of James's life and works that have appeared in recent years, however, allow more particular attention to be given now to the unique strengths and contradictions of individual works, and C. L. R. James's *The Black Jacobins* is one work that benefits greatly from such individual attention. While the rapport among *The Black Jacobins* and many of James's later works is highly significant and will be touched upon in this study, the historical study stands alone as a site for the intersection of many of James's diverse literary capacities and interests—narrative, political, philosophical. Originally published in 1938, just a few years after James's only novel, *Minty Alley,* and reissued by James in 1963 with new notes, preface, and appendix, this historical account of the Haitian Revolution offers a unique glimpse into a multifaceted James, as the layered nature of the work (the two editions) offers us a different view of the figure of James the writer than we find in later works: a view not only of his perceptions of the figure of Toussaint, but also of his perceptions of history and of writing itself.

James's focus on Toussaint-Louverture in his work on the Haitian Revolution is perhaps a prime factor in the intersection of genres indicated above. Over the two past centuries, Toussaint-Louverture, leader of the Haitian Revolution, has become an allegorical figure, the focus of myth, legend, and moral. As Percy Waxman noted, it requires a "gift for fiction" to write this figure into history, a quality that C. L. R. James appears to seek consciously in writing this epic story of a former slave who created a free nation. Indeed, James first addressed the subject of Toussaint and the Haitian Revolution in the form of a play, produced in 1936 under the title *Toussaint L'Ouverture* and revised by James in the 1970s as *The Black Jacobins.* James's awareness of the narrative and dramatic aspects of a historical work seems to create a tension of purpose in his exhaustive study of the figure of Toussaint-Louverture as he freely combines a self-conscious literary style with the historical account of the Revolution. This potential conflict is one that James explicitly introduced in his preface to the first edition of *The Black Jacobins* as the intersection of literature and history—"art" and "science"—for the writer:

> The writer [James] believes, and is confident the narrative will prove, that between 1789 and 1815, with the single exception of Bonaparte himself, no single figure appeared on the historical stage more greatly gifted than this Negro, a slave till he was 45. Yet Toussaint did not make the revolution. It was the revolution that made Toussaint. And even that is not the whole truth.

> The writing of history becomes ever more difficult. The power of God or the weakness of man, Christianity or the divine right of kings to govern wrong, can easily be made responsible for the downfall of states and the birth of new societies. Such elementary conceptions lend themselves willingly to narrative treatment and from Tacitus to Macaulay, from Thucydides to Green, the traditionally famous historians have been more artist than scientist: they wrote so well because they saw so little. To-day by a natural reaction we tend to a personification of the social forces, great men being merely or nearly instruments in the hands of economic destiny. As so often the truth does not lie in between. Great men make history, but only such history as it is possible for them to make. Their freedom of achievement is limited by the necessities of their environment. To portray the limits of those necessities and the realisation, complete or partial, of all possibilities, that is the true business of the historian.

The "traditionally famous historians have been more artist than scientist: they wrote so well because they saw so little." How, then, does one maintain historical perspective, refrain from relying on the clichéd tropes of "the weakness of man, Christianity or the divine right of kings to govern wrong," and yet not reduce great figures to "mere . . . instruments in the hands of economic destiny"? James is engaged in a tenuous, genre-challenging enterprise: "Great men make history, but only such history as it is possible for them to make. Their freedom of achievement is limited by the necessities of their environment." Working within a Marxist paradigm, he cannot reduce Toussaint-Louverture to "elementary conceptions" of grandeur, to an idealized figure who "made history." Yet in creating a historical narrative, James is also "making history": the literary dimension of such an endeavor disallows the more "scientific" reduction of Toussaint to the product of an economic system, while his own "freedom of achievement is limited by the necessities" of addressing that system in a more profound fashion that did those "traditionally famous" and methodologically indicted historians. James appears highly conscious of this tension throughout the text and almost apologizes for it at various moments in his "narrative":

> Toussaint was attempting the impossible—the impossible that was for him the only reality that mattered. The realities to which the historian is condemned will at times simplify the tragic alternatives with which he was faced. But these factual statements and the judgments they demand must not be allowed to obscure or minimise the truly tragic character of [Toussaint-Louverture's] dilemma, one of the most remarkable of which there is an authentic historical record.

The tensions between a materialist analysis of history and a portraiture of a powerful individual are readily apparent in James's endeavor; this study proposes, then, to examine the methods by which James creates a dramatic figure of the historical one of Toussaint-Louverture in *The Black Jacobins* and to explore the tensions and the strengths that such a choice creates within the text.

In the passage from his preface cited above, James states that "between 1789 and 1815, . . . no single figure appeared on the historical stage more greatly gifted than this Negro, a slave till he was 45." Toward the end of his narrative James states that, "There is no drama like the drama of history," and it is indeed a drama—and, we will argue here, a classical Aristotelian one at that—that he unfolds before us on "the historical stage." Reinhard Sander has stated in regard to the play *The Black Jacobins* that James essentially used the "characters" of the historical figures in order to present "particular ideological position[s]," with little attempt to create of them dramatic individuals. The same observation could not be made as accurately of the historical study. While Napoleon and the Haitian leaders do serve therein as foils for the figure of Toussaint, or as embodiments of contrasting political positions, the "characters" of Vincent, of Leclerc, and most particularly of Toussaint are rendered in full dramatic detail and given full voice by James, making their positions and tactical choices ultimately all the more tragic. Indeed, James appears to make full and conscious use of Aristotelian tragic structure, allowing a *mimesis* of the historical events of the Haitian Revolution to point toward the universals regarding the fall of colonialism and repressive hegemonic systems that he will underline in his 1938 conclusion and the 1963 appendix. At a more mundane level, this move also allows James to assume, much like the classical dramaturgists, that the drama that took place on the "historical stage" of eighteenth-century San Domingo is one intimately known to his readers, his task thus being to fill in the important details and to offer analyses of events rather than to provide a historical timeline.

James explicitly refers to the underlying structure of classical myth of which he has been making use at several moments in the text. On the same page on which he makes reference to the mythological and literary figures of "Prometheus, Hamlet, Lear, Phèdre, [and] Ahab," for example, he refers directly to his characterization of Toussaint as the "tragically flawed" hero:

> The hamartia, the tragic flaw, which we have constructed from Aristotle, was in Toussaint not a moral weakness. It was a specific error, a total miscalculation of the constituent events. Yet what is lost by the imaginative freedom and creative logic of great dramatists is to some degree atoned for by the his-

torical actuality of his dilemma. It would therefore be a mistake to see him merely as a political figure in a remote West Indian island. If his story does not approach the greater dramatic creations, in its social significance and human appeal it far exceeds the last days at St. Helena and that apotheosis of accumulation and degradation, the suicide in the Wilheimstrasse. The Greek tragedians could always go to their gods for a dramatic embodiment of fate, the *dike* which rules over a world neither they nor we ever made. But not Shakespeare himself could have found such a dramatic embodiment of fate as Toussaint struggled against, Bonaparte himself; nor could the furthest imagination have envisaged the entry of the chorus, of the ex-slaves themselves, as the arbiters of their own fate. Toussaint's certainty of this as the ultimate and irresistible resolution of the problem to which he refused to limit himself, that explains his mistakes and atones for them.

As James himself notes, such a characterization clearly corresponds to Aristotle's ideal tragic hero as "a man who is neither a paragon of virtue and justice nor undergoes the change to misfortune through any real badness or wickedness but because of some mistake . . . of great weight and consequence." However, this self-referential passage, in which James makes clear both the strategy of his narrative and its limitations, points to a paradoxically realistic mythography building upon the "recognition" Aristotle deemed requisite for identification and catharsis and for comprehension of the universals at play. The portrait James develops for us of Toussaint-Louverture is truly that of a mythological hero with a "tragic flaw"—the hubris that makes him blind to the need to communicate with his people—and thus of a real, human-size, leader in a crisis that we can comprehend and with which we can sympathize.

James builds on this mythological structure throughout the historical study as he dramatically develops Toussaint's hamartia by warning us repeatedly of the hero's inevitable fall:

> His error was his neglect of his own people. They did not understand what he was doing or where he was going. He took no trouble to explain. It was dangerous to explain, but still more dangerous not to explain . . . it is no accident that Dessalines and not Toussaint finally led the island to independence. Toussaint, shut up within himself, immersed in diplomacy, went his tortuous way, overconfident that he had only to speak and the masses would follow.

From these repeated references to Toussaint's errors and his eminent downfall, James creates, much as Sophocles does in *Oedipus Rex,* a mounting tension for the "spectator" of the drama. We already know the historic events that took place, but we are made to feel in James's work the inevitability of their occurrence, their tragic nature. Moreover, James underlines Toussaint's error that will lead him to that inevitable end by demonstrating to us that Toussaint's blindness to the necessity of communicating with his people is ironically emphasized by his paradoxical overconsciousness of the French. His concern for the support of the white settlers and of France offers a bitterly ironic contrast:

> [Toussaint] still continued to favor the whites. Every white woman was entitled to come to all "circles." Only the wives of the highest black officials could come. A white woman was called madame, the black woman was citizen. Losing sight of his mass support, taking it for granted, he sought only to conciliate the whites at home and abroad. As always now, he was thinking of the effect in France, and not of the effect on his own masses, feeling too sure of them.

> Toussaint did not trust the French Government as Christophe says. He would not have armed to the extent and in the manner he did if he had. But he allowed the people to think that he trusted the French.

James links this "weakness" on Toussaint's part to a moral ("Always, but particularly at the moment of struggle, a leader must think of his own masses") for revolutionary leaders, a moral marked even more strongly by "good" examples:

> [W]hereas Lenin kept the party and the masses thoroughly aware of every step, and explained carefully the exact position of the bourgeois servants of the Workers' State, Toussaint explained nothing, and allowed the masses to think that their old enemies were being favoured at their expense.

> Moïse's bitter complaint about Toussaint and the whites came obviously from a man to whom Toussaint had never explained the motives of his policy. They would not have needed much persuasion to follow a bold lead. Moïse was feeling his way towards it, and we can point out Toussaint's weakness all the more clearly because Dessalines had actually found the correct method.

Toussaint's misplaced concern, the inevitable fall toward which such an error in judgment was leading him, the contrasting examples of other leaders, James paints with them all a clear picture for us of Toussaint's mistake and its consequences, building upon this classic dramatic tension toward a clear analysis of "what Toussaint should have done": having clearly mapped the path of Toussaint's error, James

is able to enunciate all the more clearly the warning to be drawn from it. Yet James portrays for us a Toussaint who, again like a tragically flawed Greek hero, though fallen is immensely heroic, much more so in James's narrative than the more pragmatic leaders who will follow him, and more so than a quantitative analysis of Toussaint's career might indicate.

Paradoxically, James argues for this singular importance of Toussaint-Louverture by linking him with other significant figures. In his preface James states that, "with the single exception of Bonaparte himself, no single figure appeared on the historical stage more greatly gifted than this Negro," and he continues to mythologize and universalize the figure of Toussaint throughout the text by identifying him with other mythicized figures, historical or fictional. "Not Shakespeare himself could have found such a dramatic embodiment of fate as Toussaint struggled against, Bonaparte himself," and James particularly exploits this dramatic figure, repeatedly comparing Toussaint with Napoleon, as apparently did Toussaint himself. (At one point, James cites a letter of Toussaint-Louverture in which the latter declared, "If Bonaparte is the first man in France, Toussaint is the first man of the Archipelago of the Antilles.") James ensures that this conflation is not unidirectional ("Like Toussaint, Bonaparte did everything himself and he wrote out the plan of campaign with his own hand") and explicitly links their connection, moreover, to Toussaint-Louverture's "hamartia"—the intensely solitary nature that both gave him strength and brought about his downfall: "He had that curious detachment and inward scorn of men which distinguished Bonaparte." The final effect of the comparison of these two historic figures is thus equally as equivocal: both powerful and dynamic leaders, Toussaint-Louverture and Napoleon Bonaparte pursued unrealistic dreams at the expense of their subjects, with their final days in exile forming a far too ironic parallel; yet the figure of Toussaint could be seen as suffering in the equation with such a personally ambitious demagogue.

James also compares Toussaint to Lincoln, Pericles, Paine, Marx, and Engels, and centuries of epic heroes (the "black Spartacus"; or a Roland-esque hero whose devotion gives him strength). And he reminds us that Toussaint-Louverture, in being compared to these great figures, is made all the greater in that these others "were men of a liberal education, formed in the traditions of ethics, philosophy and history. [Whereas] Toussaint was a slave, not six years out of slavery, bearing alone the unaccustomed burden of wars and government, dictating his thoughts in the crude words of a broken dialect." While the Eurocentric biases implicit and unproblematized in this description do both point to James's own cultural tensions and undermine somewhat the glory of the portraiture, James's point is clear. Toussaint's actions *are* the more significant for the difficulties of his circumstances; the Marxist stage defines the classical character.

James, moreover, appears continually conscious of the complexity of real heroes: the Toussaint he portrays does hold back from those he is fighting for and does appear too conciliatory toward those whom he is fighting against; in the name of freedom, he is forced to reinstate a form of slavery; he becomes, indeed, "afraid of the contact between the revolutionary army and the people, an infallible sign of revolutionary degeneration." ("His splendid powers do not rise but decline. Where formerly he was distinguished above all for his prompt and fearless estimate of whatever faced him, we shall see him, we have already seen him, misjudging events and people, vacillating in principle, and losing both the fear of his enemies and the confidence of his own supporters.") If Toussaint the man, though a heroic fighter and an amazing diplomat, was as fallible, as complex, as human as any other, however, the *figure* of Toussaint stands alone—literally within the text and figuratively beyond it.

> It is also clear that the poet's job is not to report what has happened but what is likely to happen: that is, what is capable of happening according to the rule of probability or necessity. Thus the difference between the historian and the poet is not in their utterances being in verse or prose . . . ; the difference lies in the fact that the historian speaks of what has happened, the poet of the kind of thing that *can* happen. Hence poetry is a more philosophical and serious business than history; for poetry speaks of universals, history of particulars.

In creating a universal figure of Toussaint-Louverture through the use of dramatic character development and comparisons with other legendary figures, James seems to be attempting to move from a potentially limiting historic paradigm to a more "poetic" one—to create of a historical situation a more general warning. Indeed, his emphasis on the tragedy inherent in the historical account of Toussaint's life allows him to develop one of the strongest arguments for hegemonic accountability and revolutionary pluralism possible out of a powerful tribute to a historical leader. His 1938 conclusion underlines this argument and its "universal" application, and his 1963 appendix develops its relevance for contemporary Caribbean politics; in these parts of James's text we can see the attempts to draw "the kind of thing that *can* happen" out of "what has happened."

The most immediate demonstration of James's argument against an elite power can be found in the violent and repressive aftermath of the Haitian Revolution, as he makes clear in his conclusion. The actions of the leaders who followed Toussaint, when not in accordance with the wishes and needs of the masses, also had counterrevolutionary and tragic consequences for the Haitian people. James sees Dessalines's moves toward elitism and submission to British and American interests, for example, as having created a "tragedy" for the Haitian populace:

> The massacre of the whites [called for by the British and carried out by Dessalines' new Haitian government] was a tragedy; not for the whites. For these old slave-owners, those who burnt a little powder in the arse of a Negro, who buried him alive for insects to eat, who were well treated by Toussaint, and who, as soon as they got the chance, began their old cruelties again; for these there is no need to waste one tear or one drop of ink. The tragedy was for the blacks and the Mulattoes. It was not policy but revenge, and revenge has no place in politics. The whites were no longer to be feared, and such purposeless massacres degrade and brutalise a population, especially one which was just beginning as a nation and had had so bitter a past. *The people did not want it*—all they wanted was freedom, and independence seemed to promise that. Christophe and other generals strongly disapproved. Had the British and the Americans thrown their weight on the side of humanity, Dessalines might have been curbed. As it was Haiti suffered terribly from the resulting isolation. . . . [T]he unfortunate country, ruined economically, its population lacking in social culture, had its inevitable difficulties doubled by this massacre. That the new nation survived at all is forever to its credit for if the Haitians thought that imperialism was finished with them, they were mistaken. (italics added)

The tragedy was for the people whose needs were not addressed and opinions not listened to: "the masses had shown greater political understanding than their leaders." The "tragic flaw" that James has developed in his portrait of Toussaint can now be seen amplified in later leaders: whereas Toussaint was blind to the need to communicate with the masses, Dessalines was blind to the need to consider them, and the cycle became only more vicious. "That the new nation survived at all is forever to its credit," for the seeds of further betrayal are to be found even in the heroic figure of Toussaint-Louverture, whose vision for the nation blinded him to the power of the people who formed it.

James (and his colleagues) would reiterate the implicit warnings that he develops in *The Black Jacobins* later in *Mariners, Renegades and Castaways* and in the astute analysis of the Hungarian Revolution found in *Facing Reality*. The latter study's collective of writers saw in the Hungarian tragedy a "true" revolution being crushed by an institutionalized revolutionary party—much the same division created between the leaders of the Haitian Revolution and the revolutionary people. In the former, the Workers Party could have been "the political form in which the great masses of the people would be able to bring *their* energies to fulfill *their* destiny, in accordance with *their* economic structure, *their* past history, and *their* consciousness of *themselves*" (italics added). Likewise, the Haitian Revolution could perhaps have developed into a true revolution, rather than a reproduction of the systems of oppression, had the people been allowed to pursue that same dream. This is a lesson that James underlines when he predicts in his 1938 conclusion and reiterates in his 1963 preface the manifestation of African independence movements and calls for leadership arising from the masses:

> Finally those black Haitian labourers and the Mulattoes have given us an example to study. . . . The imperialists envisage an eternity of African exploitation. . . . They dream dreams.

> From the people heaving in action will come the leaders; not the isolated blacks at Guy's Hospital or the Sorbonne, the dabblers in *surréalisme* or the lawyers, but the quiet recruits in a black police force, the sergeant in the French native army or British police, familiarising himself with military tactics and strategy, reading a stray pamphlet of Lenin or Trotsky as Toussaint read the Abbé Raynal.

The arguments that James will later build against the concept of a vanguard party, against that of an educated elite leading a passive mass, are thus already apparent here: "From the people heaving in action will come the leaders." From the exploited will come the call for the end of oppression: a call from the people that has too often been ignored by its leaders.

Yet it should be noted that James's poetic and dramatic rendering of Toussaint in *The Black Jacobins* ironically seems occasionally to efface that very element: the people. References to the impressive force of slave resistance, for example, so strongly underlined in Fick's *The Making of Haiti: The Saint Domingue Revolution from Below,* though present, particularly early in James's study (for example, chap. 4), are occasionally underplayed. As Consuelo Lopez Springfield has stated in reference to some of James's later work, "in the drama of human history, . . . [the 'common folk'] were its leading protagonists." James's stated focus on the figure of Toussaint in *The Black Jacobins,* however, seems to create in the work the same problem that he underlines in the leader. His figuring of Toussaint into a tragic archetype, important for his development of the morals to be learned from the "story," precludes an in-depth analysis of the "lesser figures"—the vital "chorus"—who surrounded and defined him. (It is occasionally startling to read in his

text, for example, such casual comments as, "No doubt the poor sweated and were backward so that the new ruling class might thrive. But at least they too were better off than they had been.") While one could hardly accuse even early James of being blind to the complex issues of class and oppression or of being an apologist for repression on the part of otherwise admirable figures or systems, there is a clear tension between a "literary" portrait of a powerful individual and an analysis of historical materialism that remains unresolved in this work. In his preface to *The Invading Socialist Society,* James quotes Marx's preface to *The Critique of Political Economy* in order to point out the significance of the social for the individual: "The mode of production of material life conditions the social, political and intellectual life process in general. It is not the consciousness of men that determines their being, but, on the contrary, their social being that determines their consciousness." While such an analysis of the relation of the individual to society is not antithetical to the figure of Toussaint-Louverture as developed by James in *The Black Jacobins,* neither is it fully developed: the tensions pointed to in the original preface of that work remain throughout the text. Thus, James's emphasis on the figure of Toussaint in *The Black Jacobins* may obscure the importance of the elements of resistance James himself will later celebrate in *Facing Reality*—the workers (the slaves) themselves and their repeated demonstrations of the capacity for self-government (the maroons, plantation survival, etc.).

This tension between a dramatic building up of a single historic figure—that of the complex and courageous hero who led the world's only successful slave revolt and one of the first successful anticolonial revolutions—and a more "scientific" account of a historic period and a people does not, however, deter James from developing some important "universal" arguments. In the 1963 appendix to *The Black Jacobins,* he steps outside of the narrative he has developed to elucidate its significance. James sees the Haitian Revolution, as embodied by the figure of Toussaint, as a pivotal point in West Indian history: "West Indians first became aware of themselves as a people in the Haitian Revolution." James's view is that the "people," again as exemplified by the figure of Toussaint-Louverture, is a very modern—and "Western"—one. He focuses the appendix on the development of a West Indian identity from the period of the Haitian Revolution to his present: a portrayal of the struggle against an "old colonial system . . . [that] was not a democratic system, was not born as such . . . [and that] cannot live with democracy." This struggle becomes "an inherent antagonism between the consciousness of the black masses and the reality of their lives . . . constantly produced and reproduced . . . by the very conditions of the society itself." Each of the stages of identity that he portrays is inextricably linked with the figure of Toussaint-Louverture, the modern hero battling an "ancien régime," "the first and greatest of West Indians." For James posits explicitly, both in his original conclusion in reference to Africa and in this appendix concerning the West Indies, that the Haitian Revolution serves as an example: pulling from what has happened "the kind of thing that *can* happen," he offers of Haiti a symbol of the revolt of a people oppressed. This is a theme that James had already touched on implicitly in his earlier essay **"The Case for West-Indian Self-Government"** wherein he refers to West Indians as "modern wage-slaves," thereby linking contemporary capitalistic colonialism to the earlier slave structures that led to the Haitian Revolution. But he renders this theme more "poetically" powerful here through the figure of Toussaint-Louverture who becomes, in such analogies, an epic figure of liberation.

In 1939 (one year after the original publication of *The Black Jacobins*), Aimé Césaire wrote of Haiti in his *Cahier d'un retour au pays natal* (*Notebook of a Return to the Native Land*): "Haïti où la négritude se mit debout pour la première fois et dit qu'elle croyait à son humanité" ("Haiti where negritude rose for the first time and stated that it believed in its humanity"). Haiti, site of "the only successful slave revolt in history," becomes in James's work as in Césaire's the figure of the possible, the necessary. It is where a successful "subaltern" revolution occurred "for the first time" and as such can be mythologized as the promise that it will not be for the last. The dramatic symbol that the figure of Toussaint-Louverture becomes in *The Black Jacobins,* while obscuring some of the force of the people, does allow James to pull from his narrative of the Haitian Revolution accurate predictions regarding African independence and to analyze the possibilities for economic and political independence for the West Indies. Like Césaire's driving image in *Notebook of a Return to the Native Land* of the "la négraille . . . inattendument debout" ("the . . . nigger scum unexpectedly standing"—in reference to the revolt against slavery and the slave trade as well as to the concept of Negritude), James finishes his 1938 study of the figure of Toussaint-Louverture with the image of the colonized standing up to systems of exploitation and carrying him/herself beyond them:

> Imperialism vaunts its exploitation of the wealth of Africa for the benefit of civilisation. In reality, from the very nature of its system of production for profit it strangles the real wealth of the continent—the creative capacity of the African people. The African faces a long and difficult road and he will need guidance. But he will tread it fast because he will walk upright.

Such, perhaps, is the lesson of *The Black Jacobins:* the rising up of a creative capacity of the people, overlooked by, yet epitomized in, the figure of Toussaint-Louverture. "Great men make history, but only such history as it is pos-

sible for them to make. Their freedom of achievement is limited by the necessities of their environment." Toussaint's ultimate failure of "obstinately persisting in [his] own reasons," of not "confront[ing] the issues of [his] own self-limitation," was a tragedy for democracy and arguably a direct result of "the necessities of [his] environment." Toussaint's vision, whose breadth did not include a true appreciation of the potential of his own people, was not a democratic one; his nation, though liberated, did not become a democratic one. As James emphasizes in his appendix to *The Black Jacobins,* "within a West Indian island the old colonial system and democracy are incompatible. One has to go." Toussaint was a product of the old colonial system that is still in place, in economic if not in political structures, in many areas of the Caribbean. Perhaps, then, Toussaint's tragic flaw was both the limit and the full import of his significance, his hubris being the hubris that must be addressed for democracy to succeed. His tragedy, just as much as his heroic stance, is the legacy that he has left the Haitian people.

In focusing on the "poetic" characters more than on the "scientific" stage of the drama of the Haitian Revolution, James does succeed in taking his work beyond the limits of the strictly historical genre to lead us to understand the power of the literary imagination of historical figures. This choice seems to have required that the "stage," the Marxist analysis of the economic and political reality of the Haitian revolutionaries that underpins the whole text, not be as fully articulated in this work as it will be later in James's oeuvre (the James of *Facing Reality* might not have written *The Black Jacobins* in the same fashion). While James thus does not confine himself to his own vision of the "true business of the historian" ("to portray the limits of those necessities and the realisation, complete or partial, of all possibilities"), his narrative does show how a more "nonscientific" approach can create of a historic figure a tragic and epic hero whose fall then carries as many lessons as does his glory. The presentation of a dramatic narrative such as *The Black Jacobins,* if it does not provide a complete and accurate portrayal of the Haitian Revolution, does make powerfully clear why one of the greatest Caribbean poets might proclaim in his manifesto of Negritude identity,

> What is mine also: a little
> cell in the Jura,
> a little cell, the snow lines
> it with white bars
> the snow is a jailer mounting
> guard before a prison
>
> What is mine
> a lonely man imprisoned in
> whiteness
> a lonely man defying the
> white screams of white death

(TOUSSAINT, TOUSSAINT
LOUVERTURE)

FURTHER READING

Criticism

Buhle, Paul. "The Making of a Literary Life: C. L. R. James
Interviewed by Paul Buhle." In *C. L. R. James's Caribbean*,
edited by Paget Henry and Paul Buhle, pp. 56-62. Durham,
NC: Duke University Press, 1992.
    Discusses with James the influences on his work and
    events of his life.

Casey, Ethan. "In the Company of C. L. R. James." *Callaloo*
17 (Fall 1994): 1262-64.
    Praises James's *American Civilization* and asserts that

the book "shows vividly and indisputably that
America is a unique phenomenon in world history,
with at least latent potential . . . to be a genuinely free
and benign society."

McLemee, Scott. "A Trotskyite in Love." *The New York
Times Book Review* (8 September 1996): 12.
    Complains that *Special Delivery: The Letters of C.
    L. R. James to Constance Webb, 1939-1948* is "an
    editorial disaster," but asserts that "there is the soul
    of a good book here. . . . And the reader who perse-
    veres may be able to dig that book out of *Special De-
    livery.*"

San Juan, Jr., E. "Beyond Postcolonial Theory: The Mass
Line in C. L. R. James's Imagination." *The Journal of
Commonwealth Literature* XXXI, No. 1 (1996): 25-44.
    Analyzes the work of C. L. R. James in its relation-
    ship to postcolonialism.

Additional coverage of James's life and career is contained in the following sources
published by Gale: *Black Writers,* Vol. 2; *Contemporary Authors,* Vols. 117, 125, and
128; *Contemporary Literary Criticism,* Vol. 33; *Dictionary of Literary Biography,* Vol.
125; and *Major 20th-Century Writers.*

June Jordan
1936-

American poet, novelist, essayist, playwright, and writer of children's books.

INTRODUCTION

Although best known as a poet June Jordan has published a substantial number of children's works, novels, essays, plays, and librettos. Jordan's works explore the African American experience, focusing on a wide range of topics including conflicts in Nicaragua and Africa and more personal issues of love and self-awareness. Critics have praised Jordan for uniting in poetic form the personal everyday struggle and political oppression of African Americans.

Biographical Information

Jordan was born in 1936 in Harlem, the only child of immigrants from Jamaica. When she was five, the family moved to the Bedford-Stuyvesant area of Brooklyn, where she grew up. Jordan's father, a post-office clerk, introduced her to poetry, from the Scriptures to the writings of African American poet Paul Laurence Dunbar, and her mother, a nurse, provided an example of community service. Jordan's parents jeopardized their daughter's developing sense of identity, however, with harsh treatment—beatings from the father, and the mother's failure to intervene—and by opposing Jordan's ambition to become a poet. Coming to terms with her parents and her childhood became a major biographical theme in Jordan's writing. For a year, Jordan was the only African-American student in the high school she attended; she then spent three years at the Northfield School for Girls in Massachusetts before entering Barnard College in 1953. At Barnard she met Michael Meyer, a white student at Columbia University, and they were married in 1955. The marriage ended in divorce in 1965, but the couple's child, Christopher David Meyer, provided another biographical theme in Jordan's writing: motherhood and, by extension, nurturing for the broader African-American community. Her first book, *Who Look at Me* (1969), was dedicated to Christopher, as was her autobiographical essay collection *Civil Wars* (1981). Jordan has also enjoyed a distinguished university teaching career, including positions at the State University of New York at Stony Brook and the University of California-Berkeley.

Major Works

Who Look at Me is a long poem that turns on the image of eye contact between the races to treat the history of African

Americans in a prejudiced white America. Twenty-seven paintings of African Americans from Colonial days to the present complement the poem and reinforce the theme of looking at others as individuals rather than stereotypes. In her first poetry collection, *Some Changes* (1971), Jordan explored her efforts to find her poetic voice despite her troubled relationship with her parents. While continuing to address the African-American experience, she elucidated her artistic ideals, appealing for a revision of the literary canon that would incorporate African-American writers and writing on social consciousness. *His Own Where* (1971) is a novel for teens in which a young man and woman make themselves a place to live in the midst of urban ruin. This book is noteworthy in part for Jordan's use of black English, which she fervently espouses and promotes through her work. Jordan's second poetry collection, *New Days* (1974), deals with the civil rights movement and returns to the poet's evolving perception of her mother, for whom she had found a kind of surrogate in Mrs. Fannie Lou Hamer during trips to Mississippi in 1969 and 1971. A poem in the collection is addressed to Hamer, who is also the subject of a 1972 biography for young readers. A major collection, *Things That*

I Do in the Dark (1977), contains poems from earlier works as well as pieces never previously published; subsequent collections include *Passion* (1980) and *Living Room* (1985). The essays collected in *Civil Wars* are a good source of information on Jordan's life, thought, and development as a writer. Jordan's books for children and young adults include, in addition to *His Own Where* and *Fannie Lou Hamer* (1972), the novels *New Life, New Room* (1975) and *Kimako's Story* (1981). In *Naming Our Destiny* (1994) Jordan achieves unity between her lyrical poetic voice and the political voice of her essays. She uses a variety of voices and personas to convey her investigation of the "we/us" versus "they/them" rhetoric which she sees as central to the divisiveness of American culture.

Critical Reception

Critics have found Jordan a powerful and important voice in contemporary African-American poetry. Darryl Pinckney, reviewing *Passion* in the *New York Times Book Review,* remarked that "Jordan serves the [oral] tradition well, with a sensitive ear for the vernacular, for the ironic tone. . . ." He found both these poems and the essays in *Civil Wars* "the work of a writer of integrity and will." Though several critics considered her earlier work strident and despairing, others deemed it optimistic. As Toni Cade Bambara stated in *Ms.,* "What is fundamental to [Jordan's] spirit is caring, commitment, a deep-rooted belief in the sanctity of life."

PRINCIPAL WORKS

Who Look at Me (juvenile fiction) 1969
Some Changes (poetry) 1971
His Own Where (juvenile fiction) 1971
Dry victories (juvenile fiction) 1972
Fannie Lou Hamer (biography) 1972
Poem: On Moral Leadership as a Political Dilemma (Watergate, 1973) (poetry) 1973
New Days: Poems of Exile and Return (poetry) 1974
New Life, New Room (juvenile fiction) 1975
Things That I Do in the Dark: Selected Poetry (poetry) 1977
Passion: New Poems 1977-80 (poetry) 1980
Civil Wars: Selected Essays 1963-1980 (essays) 1981
Kimako's Story (juvenile fiction) 1981
Freedom Now Suite (play) 1984
The Break (play) 1984
The Music of Poetry and the Poetry of Music (play) 1984
Bobo Goetz a Gun (essays) 1985
Living Room: New Poems 1980-1984 (poetry) 1985
Bang Bang UberAlles (play) 1986
On Call: New Political Essays 1981-1985 (essays) 1986
Lyrical Campaigns: Selected Poems (poetry) 1989

Moving Towards Home: Political Essays (essays) 1989
Naming Our Destiny: New and Selected Poems (poetry) 1989
HARUKO/Love Poems, New and Selected Love Poetry (poetry) 1994
Technical Difficulties: African-American Notes on the State of the Union (essays) 1994
I Was Looking at the Ceiling and then I Saw the Sky (opera libretto) 1995

CRITICISM

Hayden Carruth (review date 9 October 1977)

SOURCE: "Politics and Love," in *The New York Times Book Review,* October 9, 1977, pp. 15, 35.

[*In the following review Carruth finds some of Jordan's poems too self-consciously poetic, but deems that others have a strong, unique lyrical sense.*]

June Jordan's selected poems [***Things That I Do in the Dark: Selected Poetry***] . . . fall into three classifications: political, personal and experimental.

Jordan's experimental impulses fall . . . into two varieties. One is technical, arty, formalistic, *avant-gardiste,* in the manner of the New York poets of the 1950's (of whom she was one). I don't mean her work isn't her own or sounds anything like Ashbery or even LeRoi Jones. . . . But the same self-conscious poeticizing is observable. One section of her book is called, for instance, **"Towards a Personal Semantics,"** and it contains many poems of this sort. . . . They are full of polysyllabic abstractions, images pulled out of nowhere, themes that appear and disappear and never quite define themselves. Maybe these poems would be comprehensible if one heard the poet read them. . . . They do possess a cadential vigor, reinforced by excited, onrushing word associations, that might be effective if chanted in the manner of a black sermon, with antiphonal responses from the auditors. Perhaps then they would be lively and if not rationally then intuitively intelligible. But on the page they are the opposite—flat and murky.

Jordan's other variety of experimentalism may not be experimental at all, narrowly speaking. It is much less self-conscious, almost unconscious—spontaneous and natural [as in **"Sunflower Sonnet Number Two"**]. . . .

Supposing we could just go on and on as two
voracious in the days apart as well as when
we side by side (the many ways we do
that) well! I would consider then
perfection possible, or else worthwhile

to think about. Which is to say
I guess the costs of long term tend to pile
up, block and complicate, erase away
the accidental, temporary, near
thing/pulsebeat promises one makes
because the chance, the easy new, is there
in front of you. But still, perfection takes some
   sacrifice of falling stars for rare.
And there are stars, but none of you, to spare.

[This is] a sonnet as surely as anything from Petrarch to Cummings, with that unmistakable movement, that lyric play. Yet it is changed. Notice the interpermeation of black idiom, her own voice and literary English. What it produces is not merely verbal effect but an augmentation of poetic (human) feeling.

Even in free poems Jordan is best when she retains this hint of tradition, working creatively, newly, with the span of poetry. . . . Just as black musicians have changed, augmented and reformed Western music, making it functionally their own without quite abandoning it, so Jordan and other black poets are taking to themselves, rightly, the formal impulse that was Shakespeare's, Wordsworth's, Browning's. But *taking* it, *commanding* it; not imitating it.

Marilyn Hacker (essay date 29 January 1990)

SOURCE: "Provoking Engagement," in *The Nation,* Vol. 250, No. 4, January 29, 1990, pp. 135-39.

[*In the following essay, Hacker discusses* Naming Our Destiny: New and Selected Poems. *She generally praises the collection, but feels that some of the poems illustrate a problem the poet sometimes has in letting her political ideology get in the way of her artistic sensibilities.*]

June Jordan's new book [*Naming Our Destiny*] is an anthology of causes won, lost, moot, private and public, forgotten and remembered. Anyone who doubts the relevance and timeliness of poetry ought to read Jordan, who has been among the front-line correspondents for almost thirty years and is still a young and vital writer. So should anyone who wants his or her curiosity and indignation aroused, or wants to read a voice that makes itself heard on the page.

There are as many kinds of poetry as there are novels and plays. But some critics, who would not fault a novel of social protest for failing to be a novel of manners or a nouveau roman, seem to want all poetry to fit one mold. June Jordan epitomizes a particular kind and strength of American poetry: that of the politically engaged poet whose commitment is as seamlessly joined to her work as it is to her life.

What makes politically engaged poetry unique, and primarily poetry before it is politics? Jordan's political poetry is, at its best, the opposite of polemic. It is not written with a preconceived, predigested agenda of ideas and images. Rather, the process of composition is, or reproduces, the process of discovering how events are connected, how oppressions are analogous, how lives interpenetrate. Jordan's poems are strongest when they deal with interior issues, when she begins with a politics of the personal, with the articulate and colloquial voice of, if you will, "a woman speaking to women" (and to men) and ranges outward to illustrate how issues, lives and themes are inextricably interconnected. One of the most powerful examples is **"Poem About My Rights,"** first published in 1980, which begins as an interior monologue of a woman angry because, as a woman, the threat of rape and violence keeps her from going where she pleases when she pleases:

> . . . without changing my clothes my
> shoes
> my body posture my gender identity
> my age
> my status as a woman alone in the
> evening/
> alone on the streets/ alone not being
> the point
> the point being that I can't do what
> I want
> to do with my own body because I am
> the wrong
> sex the wrong age the wrong skin

But she moves from the individual instances to the laws defining rape, and from rape to other questions of violation:

> which is exactly like South Africa
> penetrating into Namibia penetrating
> into
> Angola and does that mean I mean
> how do you know if
> Pretoria ejaculates

then deftly to Nkrumah and Lumumba, also in the wrong place at the wrong time, and to her own father, who was at once "wrong" himself as a working-class black male in his daughter's Ivy League college cafeteria and an oppressor who defined his child by her deficiencies. When Jordan concludes this poem with a defiant challenge to anyone seeking to physically or ideologically circumscribe her, we believe her and have made leaps—possibly new ones—of consciousness.

She uses a similar technique of accumulating incident/fact/detail in **"Gettin Down to Get Over,"** a poem for her mother which swells to a litany of praise for black women and the African-American family. **"Free Flight,"** another late-night stream of consciousness, though it stays closer to the "personal," builds momentum and depth with Whitmanesque inclusiveness to consider the humorously identical possibilities of consolation by a female or a male lover before settling on self-respect as the best way to get through the night.

Where Jordan is unlike Whitman is in her creation of a quirky, fallible persona (apart from her creation of personae that are clearly different from that of the poet), an alter ego by which readers accustomed to identifying the poet with the speaker of a poem may sometimes be taken aback, if not shocked.

Jordan plays skillfully with this post-Whitman, post-Williams but also post-Romantic expectation in **"Poem from Taped Testimony in the Tradition of Bernhard Goetz,"** an ironically issue-oriented dramatic monologue which transcends its headline-bound issue. Jordan's speaker breathlessly appropriates to a black perspective the reasoning Goetz used to justify arming himself and firing on black youths in the New York City subway. Is a black woman who has suffered every kind of violence from ridicule and exclusion to invisibility, battery and rape at the hands of whites also justified in assuming the worst and acting accordingly? Justified if she carries a gun and fires not on a racist cop or armed rapist but on the white woman beside her at an artists' colony dinner table whose loose-cannon talk was the last straw? The poem is at once horrifying and funny, as a tall tale is meant to be, and hard to dismiss (even if, "logically," a reader who rejected Goetz's reasoning would reject that of Jordan's speaker as well).

The inevitability and passion of this poem, as well as its wit, will keep it valid and readable after the "issue" of Goetz is forgotten. The connection between being spat at on the way to third grade, seeing a neighborhood friend beaten by the police, being ignored in a New England drugstore and being raped in a college town may not necessarily be apparent to all white (or even black male) readers. It's to Jordan's credit that she concretizes the link by juxtaposition, with the accelerating energy of deceptively ordinary speech. From her opening she establishes not only her speedy and frenetic "I" but the "they" that is, more than any "I," the opposite of "thou": the "they" that, be its antecedent "blacks," "whites," "Jews," "Muslims," "women" or "men," is the essential evil agent in any prejudiced discourse. Describing an incident that was perhaps only an eye contact made or avoided, the speaker here is confused—paranoid, the reader might think—or is she?

> . . . I mean you didn't
> necessarily see some kind of a smile
> or hear them laughing but I could

> feel
> it like I could feel I could always
> feel this shiver thing this fear take
> me over when I would have to come
> into a room
> full of them and I would be by myself
> and they would just look at you know
> what
> I mean you can't know what I mean
> you're not Black.

Of course Jordan's proposition is farcically surreal, exaggerated to show the fallaciousness of its white equivalent, absurd (as the murder of twenty-two black children in Atlanta, the murder of fourteen women students in Montreal, the murder of one homeless man in New York's 103d Street subway station, are absurd; they all died for being "they" to someone). Nonetheless, a reader somewhere will categorize Jordan as a rabble-rousing reverse racist, missing the point of her "Modest Proposal": the quantum leap from grievance to slaughter and the culturally triggered impulse to jump it.

How can a white critic say that a black poet has a spectacular sense of rhythm? Modestly, or courageously. Jordan writes (mostly) free verse. Many writers of free verse produce a kind of syntactically disjointed prose, expecting line breaks to provide a concentration and a syncopation not achieved by means of language. In Jordan's best poems there is a strong, audible, rhythmic counterpoint to the line breaks, a rhythm as apparent to the reader as it is to the auditor who hears the poet deliver them. This is true of her poems that have been set to music by Bernice Reagon of the a cappella group Sweet Honey in the Rock (**"Alla Tha's All Right, but"** and **"A Song of Sojourner Truth"**), but it's equally true of dramatic monologues like **"The Talking Back of Miss Valentine Jones"** and **"Unemployment Monologue,"** and of the interior monologues evolving into public declaration, like **"Poem About My Rights."**

The fluid speech-become-aria quality of Jordan's free verse poems also makes them difficult to quote, though never difficult to remember. They are not made of lapidary lines and epigrammatic stanzas. They gather momentum verbally, aurally. Most often, the effects of the voice and the statement are cumulative.

Why is this important? Because it fixes the poems in the reader's memory; because it makes these poems, even those on the most serious subjects, paradoxically fun to read. It is a reason for these texts to be written in verse, to be poetry. They are not fiction, journalism, essays or any other form of prose, even when they share qualities with these other genres. When Jordan's poems are unambiguous and straightforward, as well as when they are figurative, ironic or complex, her words create a music, create voices, which readers must hear the way they were written: Her poems read themselves to us.

Like many contemporary poets, Jordan sometimes ventures back into fixed forms. There are five sonnets and a loose ghazal sequence among the forty-three new poems here. Unfortunately, in the new sonnets the poet too often uses grandiose statement and inflated diction as if they came with the form:

> From Africa singing of justice and
> grace
> Your early verse sweetens the fame
> of our Race.

> **("Something Like a Sonnet for Phillis Miracle
> Wheatley")**

Or she seems tone-deaf to the meter, which may always be broken, but for a purpose:

> I admire the possibilities of flight and
> space
> without one move towards the ending
> of my pain.

> **("A Sonnet from the Stony Brook")**

She can also come up with a gem of a line like "A top ten lyric fallen to eleven" to refer to a fading love affair. Still, it's a long way from her best work, such as **"The Reception,"** which depicts vividly imagined characters and action in iambic pentameter quatrains:

> Doretha wore the short blue lace last
> night
> and William watched her drinking so
> she fight
> with him in flying collar slim-jim
> orange
> tie and alligator belt below the navel
> pants uptight.
> " . . . I flirt. Damned right. You
> Look at me."
> But William watched her carefully
> his mustache shaky she could see
> him jealous "which is how he always
> be
> at parties."

Some of Jordan's most successful poems are the farthest from polemic. They are vignettes, short dramatic monologues, observations of characters who may or may not be in some interaction with the narrator, like **"Newport Jazz**

Festival," "Patricia's Poem" and "If You Saw a Negro Lady":

> sitting on a Tuesday
> near the whirl-sludge doors of
> Horn & Hardart on the main drag
> of downtown Brooklyn

> solitary and inconspicuous as plain
> and neat as walls impossible to
> fresco and you watched her self
> conscious features shape about
> a Horn & Hardart teaspoon
> with a pucker from a cartoon
> she would not understand

> would you turn her treat
> into surprise
> observing

> happy birthday

"The Madison Experience" expands this quick-take technique into a fourteen-part sequence that is a tender and surprising love song to one swath of Middle Western America. Its clean primary colors and color-blind courtesy impress the poet (who nevertheless "went out / looking for traffic") as much as the juxtaposition of rain-washed fresh produce, a rally for Soweto and "fathers / for Equal Rights." As much as anything, Jordan appreciates an untroubled solitude:

> Above the backyard mulberry tree
> leaves a full moon
> Not quite as high as the Himalaya
> Mountains
> not quite as high as the rents in
> New York City
> summons my mind into the meat and
> mud
> of things that sing

Jordan hints at but does not politicize an "incorrect" sexuality. There are love poems to men and love poems to women, to black and to white partners, poems in the aftermath of loving, poems on the erotic edge of friendship, love poems that (no surprise) broadcast mistrust, question the accepted definitions of relationships. There has been pressure in the past three decades on black writers and on feminist writers to put their personal lives on the line, or to make them toe one (revolutionary black heterosexual monogamy; radical feminist lesbian ditto). "The subject tonight for / public discussion is / our love," Jordan writes ironically in "Meta-Rhetoric." Her only manifesto on her private choices has been her refusal to let them be the subject of discussion, at once revealing and sufficiently circumspect to make either name-calling or roll-calling impossible.

Often the glancing, yearning glimpses through language are more suggestive, more erotic than a clear depiction would be. (The word "lesbian" occurs only once in Jordan's book: the poet "worried about unilateral words like Lesbian or Nationalist." The word "gay," usually but not always in reference to men, is positively stated and vindicated.)

Rape is a subject about which Jordan is unambiguous. It is not sexual in nature but violent, and it is, she illustrates, analogous to other forms of violence motivated by lust for power, by "thou" becoming "they." She is not speculating. She reveals that she has been raped twice: "the first occasion / being a whiteman and the most recent / situation being a blackman actually / head of the local NAACP" (**"Case in Point"**). Her poems re-examine these violations through description, through metaphor (**"Rape Is Not a Poem"**) and through theory (**"Poem About My Rights"**). If there is a "silence peculiar / to the female" (**"Case in Point"**), it is that of the forcibly silenced. **"Poem on the Road"** reiterates, through other women's stories, that no racial combination explains or excuses sexual violence. I think the double betrayal of black-on-black assault makes her angriest.

Another depiction which is mercilessly specific is that of one particular black nuclear family: the poet's own, beleaguered from without, reproducing the conditions of oppression within. West Indian strivers (a postal worker and a nurse), her father tried to beat his "Black devil child" into submission while making sure she was educated for rebellion, while her mother personified both submission and endurance to her daughter. We meet these people on the first pages of *Naming Our Destiny* and are back in their kitchen in the last poem, written thirty years later. The effect is much that of reading a novel in which new points of view reveal different, complementary truths about a character or situation, culminating in **"War and Memory,"** which delineates how the dynamics of what we now call a dysfunctional family woke a bright child to the power of words and the possibility of dissent.

A Selected Poems is a second chance for an author and for readers. Work gone out of print can be rediscovered, the development and evolution of themes and style underlined. Poems bound too closely to an outdated topicality, or ones which are simply not good enough, can be cut out, thus placing the best-realized work into sharper relief. There are deleted poems I miss in this book: from *Things That I Do in the Dark*, **"Uncle Bullboy"** and the second **"Talking Back of Miss Valentine Jones"**; from *Passion*, **"For Lil' Bit"** and especially the two **"Inaugural Rose"** poems; from *Living Room*, **"To Sing a Song of Palestine"** and **"Notes Toward Home."** There are also texts that upon rereading seem

to be occasional pieces whose occasion has passed: **"On Moral Leadership as a Political Dilemma," "Some People," "What Would I Do White?"** (wear furs and clip coupons; this reader optimistically thinks a white June Jordan would still be more June Jordan than Ivana Trump) and **"Memo."** In the newer work, **"Poem Instead of a Columbus Day Parade," "The Torn Sky"** and **"Take Them Out!"** pose the same problem. The events are current, but the poems don't transcend the level of chants, captions or slogans:

> Swim beside the blown-up bridges
> Fish inside the bomb-sick harbors
> Farm across the contra ridges
> Dance with revolutionary ardor
> Swim/Fish/Farm/Dance
> Nicaragua Nicaragua

> (**"Dance: Nicaragua"**)

Likewise, printing the word "chlorofluorocarbons" nine times down a page, with an odd simile in the middle, is less informative about the destruction of the ozone layer than was last week's exchange of letters in The New York Times, and less productive of thought and action on the issue.

There are, in short, too many propaganda poems, where the activist's desire to touch every base, to stand up and be counted on every current issue, took precedence over the poet/critic's choice of what ought to be published, not in a newspaper or a flyer but in a book that will be kept, read and reread. One need only compare Jordan's elegy for Martin Luther King Jr., which is entirely, though musically, public, with her poem for Fannie Lou Hamer—also a public figure, but this time a person Jordan knew well and worked beside. There's a life, a voice, no hagiography but a lively portrait in **"1977: Poem for Mrs. Fannie Lou Hamer"**:

> Humble as a woman anywhere
> I remember finding you inside the
> laundromat
> in Ruleville
> lion spine relaxed/hell
> what's the point to courage
> when you washin clothes?
> . . .
> one solid gospel
> (sanctified)
> one gospel
> (peace)
> one full Black lily
> luminescent
> in a homemade field
>
> of love.

This could have been a poem for an aunt/sister/mother (the feeling of blood tie is so strong) as well as a poem about any brave friend. The fact that its subject was also a public (now historical) figure gives it another dimension, and the poet a status she or he has rarely held in this country: someone who writes as an intimate of the makers of history, as an actor in significant events—and who also reminds us that the face of history can be changed to a familiar, to a family face.

One public issue with which Jordan has been closely associated in recent years and which has become a recurrent subject of her poetry is the conflict in the Middle East, including Lebanon, and the struggle of the Palestinian people for self-determination in the West Bank and elsewhere. It's an issue that has at times polarized some readers' responses to her work. I too have stopped myself to examine my own responses to texts like **"Apologies to All the People in Lebanon," "Living Room"** and **"Intifada."** What I find is that Jordan does in these poems what she satirizes and exposes in the Bernhard Goetz monologue: She creates an undifferentiated "they" with no stated antecedent, which embodies evil or at least the evil done to the Palestinians. A reader familiar with the events will know that Jordan's "they" sometimes refers to the Lebanese Christian Phalangist militia, sometimes to the Israeli Army, sometimes to the present Israeli government. Because these names do not appear, what the "they" represents becomes unspecified, a monolith. Once a name has been written it is more difficult to use it unilaterally: There is the Lebanese Army and the Israeli Army, and also the Israeli opposition and the Israeli peace movement. There is a poem in Jordan's previous collection, *Living Room,* that expresses confusion and dismay at the paradox of Lebanese-on-Lebanese violence. There is also one envisioning peace and cooperation, dedicated to an Israeli peace activist. These weren't included in the present collection. A poet, a worker with words, should use those words to clarify, not to obfuscate.

The best American writing I've read about Vietnam has been by black and white vets who were there (Yusef Komunyakaa's *Dien Cai Dau* is a moving recent example), not by antiwar activists who weren't. I think the best poetry of the intifada will be written by Palestinians, and by Israelis—and that a writer who is neither, who hasn't been there except by analogy, runs the risk of letting exhortation and indignation replace observation and introspection. Adrienne Rich's recent poems about the Middle East are essentially the meditations of an American Jew who finds herself implicated in the conflict whether she chooses to be or not. Therein lie the tension and interest of the poems. The source of Jordan's involvement may be equally specific, but we don't know what it is. She gives us catalogues of the atrocities "they" performed; she seems to have no questions and to know all the answers. I think it is necessary to add that I write this as a Jew who is sickened by the Likud-led government's historically overdetermined version of apartheid, who is also opposed to and frightened by the conflation of that government with "Israelis" and "Jews" too easily made by right- and left-wing lobbyists and politicians.

Jordan's Palestinians and Nicaraguans are too often one-dimensional hero/victims. Jordan's African-Americans, small-town Middle Western whites and long-distance Brooklyn lovers of any race or sex are complex, even when glimpsed quickly in a hardware store or from a cab crossing a bridge at midnight. In spite of rage and outrage, even a rapist is not "they" but "thou":

> . . . considering the history
> that leads us to this dismal place
> where (your arm
> raised
> and my eyes
> lowered)
> there is nothing left but the drippings
> of power and
> a consummate wreck of tenderness/I
> want to know
> Is this what you call
> Only Natural?

("Rape Is Not a Poem")

The desire to reread and to pass a book on to others are two strong strands of a writer-reader connection. I don't know how many times I've read Jordan's work to myself and out loud to friends and students. At a writers' conference in Grenoble last November I read **"Poem About My Rights"** to illustrate that North American feminist poetry could not be segregated from a tradition of politically engaged writing, and also to show how a poet could create a voice that would be heard as intended, no matter who was reading the poem. What is it about June Jordan's work that I like as much as I do? Its capacity to unsettle and disturb me, for one thing, to make me want to pursue the discussion, write something in response. In **"War and Memory"** she recounts that, as a child, she related the suffering of Jewish concentration camp prisoners—described factually by her father and symbolically, in terms of women's pain, by her mother—to the war and internal bleeding in her home. The two-way trajectory between reporting and metaphor, between personal and global politics, is floodlit in Jordan's writing. Engaged as she is with the issues of the day and the irreducible issues of human life, her work provokes engagement with the reader, something too few readers now expect of poetry, something June Jordan gives back to poetry generously.

Adele Logan Alexander (review date April 1993)

SOURCE: "Stirring the Melting Pot," in *Women's Reviews of Books,* Vol. X, No. 7, April, 1993, pp. 6-7.

[*In the following review Alexander examines the feminist and leftist politics of Jordan's writing.*]

"I am one barbarian who will not apologize," June Jordan shouts. (Because I can hear her voice's clarion call, I'm sure that she shouts these words, although I only read them on the printed page.) "Two weeks ago my aunt called me a Communist," she confides, acknowledging the outrage that her opinions have caused her kin. "Calling someone a Communist," she continues, "is an entirely respectable, and popular, middle-class way to call somebody a low-down dirty dog." Yes, Jordan often must have outraged her relatives because she is such an unapologetic "barbarian," so piercing in her analysis, often so provocative beyond apparent reason. Yet after all, reason prevails in *Technical Difficulties,* this new collection of essays. Kinfolk notwithstanding, Jordan scarcely could be considered anyone's cup of tea (warm, sweet, milky—if that's what one seeks) or even their meat and potatoes; she is, rather, the very finest bitter vetch, the best champagne or straight shot of Stoly.

Technical Difficulties is a book about America—subtitled, as it is, **"The State of the Union."** This is America observed and found both noble and nurturing, brutal and malformed—often at the same time—by a brilliant and mature African American scholar who has looked at our country with her own unique clarity of vision and focus. Her subjects include affectionate tributes to her own Jamaican heritage (**"For My American Family"**) and that of those other immigrants, not the Poles, Russians, Irish, or Germans but the too-often invisible and darker-skinned newcomers whose journeys through New York harbor, past the Statue of Liberty and Ellis Island, have been largely overlooked in our romantic imaging of the American melting-pot.

Although these less chronicled voyagers harbored dreams much like those of America's white immigrants, they came not from the *shtetls* of Eastern Europe, but rather from places like "Clonmel, a delicate dot of a mountain village in Jamaica." They settled their families down in black communities such as Brooklyn's Bedford-Stuyvesant that sociologists in the 1950s characterized as "breeding grounds for despair," where teachers taught Jordan "all about white history and white literature." Yet there, in her parents' "culturally deprived" home, she "became an American poet." In her essays Jordan combines love and respect with scorn and mistrust for this America where her parents—her "faithful American family"—created a new life and nurtured this "barbarian" of a writer.

In another essay, **"Waking Up in the Middle of Some American Dreams,"** Jordan directs her attention to an analysis of her own deliberate self-isolation and the intrusions upon it by a lifetime of memories, a single ring of the telephone, and then, violently, by a rapist. She inserts this brutal assault into her narrative with just three words, but those words carry the potency of a drop of paint splashed into a bucket of water—spreading out to infuse the entire pail with its livid pigment. Questioning "American illusions of autonomy, American delusions of individuality," she had created her own "willful loneliness," designed to nurture her own creative process. She had sought and found an isolated spot where she could ask herself such questions as "what besides race and sex and class could block me from becoming a clearly successful American, a Great White Man," only to have her illusions of Eden-like solitude shattered by violence. Her conclusion, "I do not believe that I am living alone in America," is countered by the fearful question, "Am I?"

"Dont you talk about My Momma" and **"No Chocolates for Breakfast"** both traverse Jordan's familiar home ground—the lives of African American women. With wit and steel, she lashes out at men such as Daniel Patrick Moynihan who would endlessly analyze and put down her "Momma." "If Black women disappeared tomorrow," she argues persuasively, "a huge retinue of self-appointed and *New York Times*-appointed 'experts' would have to hit the street looking for new jobs." Her own 1965 **"Memo"** to Moynihan elegantly encapsulated her opinion of these self-righteous analyzers and experts:

> You done what you done
> I do what I can
>
> Don't you liberate me
> from my Black female pathology
>
> I been working off my knees
> I been drinking what I please. . .
>
> But you been screwing me so long
> I got a idea something's wrong
> with you
>
> I got a simple proposition
> You take over my position
>
> Clean your own house, babyface.

"When and Where and Whose Country is This, Anyway?" continues in this vein. Fannie Lou Hamer's declaration at the 1964 Democratic Convention that "We didn't come all the way up here for no two seats," provides the essay's keynote. As an African American woman, Jordan wants to know just what she and other intruders at the great American banquet have to do to get more than just the "two seats" they have been told they deserved. In **"No Chocolates for Breakfast"** she reiterates her conviction that Black women have been doing for others while no one has been doing for them—with the near-perfect observation that "I can't think of a single Black woman who has a wife." Combining this point with her observations about Moynihan, Jordan revises Aretha Franklin's familiar lyrics: "Don't Send Me No Experts; I Need a Man Named Dr. Feelgood—and I could also use me a wife."

Moving along from the experts to the icons, Jordan tries to develop a revised perspective on a deeply admired but nonetheless flawed Martin Luther King in **"The Mountain and the Man Who Was Not God."** "Any time you decide to take on a mountain," she observes, "you just better take good care." (Take on Dr. King? No wonder her aunt called her a Communist.) But Jordan only wants to demythify King, not dishonor him, and she urges us to remember and revere others as well. She recalls "Jo-Ann Robinson, Diana Nash, Rosa Parks, Ruby Doris Robinson, Septima Clarke, Bernice Reagon, Ella Baker, Fannie Lou Hamer, and, of course, Angela Davis"—all of them stalwarts of the civil rights movement—calling them "just a handful of the amazing components of The Invisible Woman whose invisibility has cost all of us an incalculable loss." As they struggled in the movement without the continuing domestic support enjoyed by men such as King, who knows how often Hamer and Parks might have thought "I could also use me a wife"?

Jordan tackles and dissects familiar themes: family, race, neighborhood ("two-and-a-half years ago," she writes, "I . . . returned to my beloved Brooklyn where, I knew, my eyes and ears would never be lonely for diversified, loud craziness and surprise"), the love of men, women and children, the mutable American Constitution, education, creativity and politics (of nations and of sexuality, the "correct" and the "incorrect"). For many years she has been a teacher and writer, with several books of essays, including *Civil Wars, Moving Towards Home* and *On Call* to her credit, as well as collections of her poetry, including the less well-known *Who Look at Me?*—poems for children about African American artists and their work. These new essays, though they cover a variety of topics, come together into a unified and consistent whole. Adapting the Cubists' technique of viewing a subject from many different perspectives at once, Jordan sees all sides and then reassembles the fragments into a consistent, if multifaceted, whole. One should not say *Technical Difficulties* is "better" than what preceded it, but it is surely "more," and though a little of Jordan's well-muscled prose goes a long way, in this case it is also true that "more is better."

June Jordan has a prolific intellect and a vast reservoir of extraordinary and broad-based knowledge, yet her writing maintains its solid grounding in everyday experience. (The frustrating disempowerment of Black women, for example, is captured in the impossibility of getting a taxi on a rainy afternoon.) The luminous accessibility of these essays keeps them well clear of the murky pits of obfuscation that trap those scholars who write for the purpose of garnering accolades from others in the academy. Jordan's is an intricate and often jarring patchwork collage of Americans and American life. Attempting in her "Alternative Commencement Address at Dartmouth College" to define this "American," puzzling over how to characterize that slippery and complex essence, Jordan observes that "*He* was not supposed to be an Indian. *He* was not supposed to be a *she*. He was not supposed to be Black or the African-American descendant of slaves. And yet, here we are, at our own indomitable insistence, here we are, the peoples of America."

"Finding the Haystack in the Needle" is one of the more intriguing titles I've come across recently, but it surely fits the skewed perspectives, insolent assumptions and refreshing ambiguities of Jordan's work. "Why would you lose the needle in the first place?" she wonders. Perhaps we have worried too much about that minuscule, even insignificant, needle, while failing to notice the importance of the hay: "How come nobody's out looking for that common big messy thing: that food, that playground that children and lovers enjoy?" she asks, and now, so do I. And hungry as I sometimes find myself, I look forward to more of Jordan's intellectual "food" and more recess time spent in her "playground."

Jordan vigorously rants at our familiar "emperors," from George Washington to Ronald Reagan. She reminds us of the meaty, but non-mainstream, substance that has been deliberately omitted and obscured from our educational, cultural and political lives. I look to her not only to rail at the way things have been ("if you're not an American white man and you travel through the traditional twistings and distortions of the white Western canon, you stand an excellent chance of ending up *nuts*," she says) but to knock our white, male-centered world cockeyed from its moorings and provide more of the revised visions that we need.

For my next feast, I would like to order from June Jordan a little less Dr. Spock and more Dr. May Chinn; less Martin and more Fannie Lou; less Jesse and more Sojourner; less Clarence ("whose accomplishments as former head of the Equal Employment Opportunity Commission do not cleanly distinguish him from David Duke") and more Anita; less Thomas Jefferson and more Sally Hemings—and more Aretha, more Marys (Magdalene, Church Terrell, McLeod Bethune and many others come to mind) and more Josephines (both Empress and Baker, perhaps) as well.

I admire what you've given us here, Ms. Jordan. It's quirky enough to make us giggle out loud, and then in turn it's heart-wrenchingly sad. It's always provocative. To employ the new argon, you're really "pushing the envelope." It's great stuff—but please, come back soon and feed us some more.

Michelle Cliff (review date June 1994)

SOURCE: "The Lover: June Jordan's Revolution," in *Village Voice Literary Supplement*, No. 126, June, 1994, pp. 27-29.

[*In the following review Cliff praises the revolutionary politics of Jordan's poetry.*]

Enter the African American intellectual, suddenly celebrated in *The New Yorker*, on the front page of the *Times Book Review*, the full-color cover of the *New York Times* Sunday magazine, in the offices of multinationals dressed up as publishing houses, in the halls of ivy and the groves of academe. People who have never read a word of W. E. B. Du Bois, never heard of J. A. Rogers or George Schuyler, are snapping up Cornel West like crazy. Whether they champion his thoughts is another matter.

As usual, those in power have no respect for history, are ignorant of the minds that contribute to the African American continuum of ideas. Have no sense of the relationship between the African American intellectual and other thinkers of the African diaspora: Frantz Fanon, Edouard Glissant, Sylvia Wynter, for example. Or the relationship between the African American intellectual and the intellectuals of Africa: Chinua Achebe, Ama Ata Aidoo, Leopold Senghor, for example. Most probably think the African American intellectual is a Johnny-come-lately, or worse, merely a response to the white American intellectual.

The African American intellectual, the Black thinker, has always existed in the American landscape, where being white is a state of complacency, while being Black demands understanding; being Black in this landscape clamors for something to explain it, to explain the ideology of racism, among other things. *Among other things* is important; Black thought is not monolithic, does not exist solely in response to racism, although it may be impelled by it.

Neither is Black thought formally limited, presented only through the essay, for example. It is also embodied in poetry, in the novel. Think of the conceptualization of time in *Beloved*, the historiographic sense of Walcott's "The Star-Apple Kingdom." The Black thinker is not limited formally or linguistically.

June Jordan is among the company of African-descended intellectuals. In her prose and her poetry, she defines and redefines the African person, female and male, in relation to the American landscape, her thought radiating outward to the First World and all of its inhabitants. A note to Jordan's essay collection *On Call: New Political Essays* states: "Given that they were the first to exist on the planet and currently make up the majority, the author will refer to that part of the population usually termed Third World as the First World."

Jordan's thought, her expression of it, is not facile. She does not assuage. She challenges the reader to understand the workings of the world as she describes them, and in between her written lines the question lies: What are you, we, going to do about it? She is not facile, and yet she never gives in to despair. She writes with a radical grace, a verbal relationship with change, a sense of immediacy. Jordan's poetic, intellectual gaze is incisive, expansive, embracing Agostinho Neto and Fannie Lou Hamer, Phillis Wheatley and Mike Tyson.

Her loving and furious gaze settles on the universals of Black existence in this world.

> How many of my brothers and my sisters
> will they kill
> before I teach myself
> retaliation?
> Shall we pick a number?
> South Africa for instance:
> do we agree that more than ten thousand
> in less than a year but less than
> five thousand slaughtered in more than
> six months will
> WHAT IS THE MATTER WITH ME?
> I must become a menace to my enemies.

. . . .

> And if I
> if I ever let love go
> because the hatred and the whisperings
> become a phantom dictate I o-
> bey in lieu of impulse and realities
> (the blossoming flamingos of my
> wild mimosa trees)
> then let love freeze me
> out.

> I must become
> I must become a menace to my enemies.

Throughout Jordan's writing one thing rings clear: the necessity for love in the spiritual and practical course of revolution, and in the lives of individuals, like the revolutionary Fannie Lou Hamer.

> You used to say. "June?
> Honey when you come down here you
> supposed to stay with me. Where
> else?"
> Meanin home
> against the beer the shotguns and the
> point of view of whitemen don'
> never see Black anybodies without
> some violent itch start up.
> The ones who
> said, "No Nigga's Votin in This
> Town . . ."

To live in a loving way against such lovelessness is an existential triumph, and I am not talking about praying for and loving those who persecute you, those with their foot planted on your neck. That is neither triumphant, nor revolutionary, I doubt it's same. The triumph derives from recognizing the enemy, facing him, while maintaining an existential love.

Love begins with the individual; in its multiplying begins the revolution. And I am not talking, nor is Jordan, in some sort of touchy-feely Calspeak, of that grotesque self-involvement (*self* being the operative word) that passes for love in our miserable culture. The "inner child" for one takes up a lot of space.

Love is most useful, most transformative, when it becomes an ethical drive. "Love should be put into action!" Elizabeth Bishop has a hermit shout in her poem "Chemin de Fer," expressing a fierce longing, perhaps to end his isolation.

In the '60s June Jordan embarked on a plan for the redesign of Harlem; her collaborator was Buckminster Fuller. The two were serious about, for example, building new structures over and above existing dilapidated housing, then demolishing the substandard housing, having residents move up into new space, while the spaces below would be transformed into areas of communal use.

> This project, we thought, would have enormous, national, showcase impact. It would demonstrate the rational feasibility of beautiful and low-cast shelter integral to a comprehensively conceived new community for human beings.

> We conceived of this environmental redesign as a form of federal reparations to the ravaged peoples of Harlem. We fully expected its enactment. In this spirit, we worried over every problem and detail related to maximal speed practically, and economy.

When the article appeared in the April 1965 issue of Esquire with the results of our collaboration ascribed entirely to Fuller, the editors referred to it as "an utopian plan." These same editors called the piece "Instant Slum Clearance." My title had been "Skyrise for Harlem."

When love is absent, the imagination is shut down. Things that should be are disingenuously labeled "utopian." As in streets swept clean of crack. As in a city that cherishes and amplifies the human experience of life. We live in a society in which the unimaginative becomes the solution. More police, more prisons, more guns. It's the natural order, apparently, that so many of us inhabit dystopia.

In her collection ***Living Room,*** the poem from **"Sea to Shining Sea"** describes the dystopia in which we find ourselves.

> This was not a good time to be against the natural
> order.
>
> This was not a good time to rent housing
> on a completely decontrolled rental market.
>
> This was not a good time to be a Jew
> when the national Klan agenda targets
> Jews as well as Blacks among its
> enemies of the purity of the people.
> This was not a good time to be a tree
> This was not a good time to be a river
> This was not a good time to be found with a gun
> This was not a good time to be found without one

There is a constant and consistent resonance in Jordan's writing—a tension between telling it as it was, is, and apparently will ever be, and the longing expressed by Bishop's hermit, to activate love, to realize, concretely, that we are all in this together, and that the natural order—of separation, hierarchy; quantification, purification—is as unnatural as they come.

> This is a good time
> This is the best time
> This is the only time to come together
>
>   Fractious
>   Kicking
>   Spilling
>   Burly
>   Whirling
>   Raucous
>   Messy
>   Free

Exploding like the seeds of a natural disorder.

And which poet sings that kind of America? Who is the poetic exponent of a natural disorder, a celebrator of wildness? Jordan writes of him as the father of public New World poetry in her essay **"For the Sake of People's Poetry: Walt Whitman and the Rest of Us"**.

> Trying to understand the system responsible for every boring, inaccessible, irrelevant, derivative and pretentious poem that is glued to the marrow of required readings in American classrooms, or trying to understand the system responsible for the exclusion of every hilarious, amazing, visionary, pertinent and unforgettable poet from the National Endowment for the Arts grants and from national publications, I come back to Walt Whitman. What in the hell happened to him? Wasn't he white man? Wasn't he some kind of father to American literature? Didn't he talk about this New World? Didn't he see it? Didn't he sing this New World, this America on a New World, an American scale of his own visionary invention?

Whitman was the true American, New World poet, spilling, burly, whirling, raucous, free (and, of course queer), responding to the American, New World landscape not with the prim exclusively of the Eurocentric, but with an imaginative wildness.

"New World," as Jordan reminds us, "does not mean New England." New World should reference the aboriginal, the native.

> who know obliteration
> who arise from the abyss
> the aboriginal
> as definite as heated through as dry
> around the eyes
> as Arizona
> the aboriginal
> as apparently inclement as invincible
> as porous
> as the desert
> the aboriginal
> from whom the mountains slide
> away
> afraid to block the day's deliverance
> into stars and cool air lonely
> for the infinite invention of avenging
> fires

"New World means non-European," Jordan writes, "it means new . . . big . . . heterogeneous . . . unknown . . . free . . . an end to feudalism, caste, privilege, and the violence of power." Or so it should. "It means *wild* in the sense that a tree growing away from the earth enacts a wild event. It means *democratic* . . . "

Whitman, a witness to the auction block, wrote:

> A man's body at auction
> (For before the war I often go to the slave-
> mart and watch the sale.)
> I help the auctioneer, the sloven does not
> half know his business . . .
> Gentlemen look on this wonder
> Whatever the bids of the bidders they
> cannot be high enough for it . . .
> This is not only one man this the father
> of those who shall be fathers in their turns
> In him the start of populous states and
> rich republics, Of him countless
> immortal lives with countless
> embodiments and enjoyments

Jordan acknowledges herself a descendant of Walt Whitman, "that weird . . . white father"; she also descends from Phillis Wheatley. Whitman, big, burly, queer, white, male, roving the American landscape, and Phillis, small, African, enslaved, captive in a drawing room in Boston. What does each bring to the poet who descends from them?

Each knew the auction block. From Whitman's vantage point a poem may be written, the democratic, New World poet decrying the transaction, regarding the male body about to be sold. But what of the African child, the girl "standing on the auctioneer's rude platform: Phillis for Sale."

Here, as elsewhere, Jordan is brilliant, seeing into Phillis Wheatley's apparently straitened sense of her African self, seeing through her poetry. Jordan speaks of the poem **"On Being Brought From Africa to America."** Past Phillis Wheatley's assertion that the theft of her was merciful, Jordan finds something surprising, something beyond the "iniquitous nonsense" assimilated by the poet.

> . . . this first Black poet presents us with something wholly her own, something entirely new. It is her matter of fact assertion that, "Once I redemption neither sought nor knew," as in: once I existed beyond and without these terms under consideration. Once I existed on other than your terms.

A friend sends me a gift. An ex-library copy of *The Image of the Indian and the Black Man in American Art 1590-1900*. She knows I have an interest in the visual, its use, its impression in our minds. One image captures me. It is a stereograph, the double photograph which fit a stereopticon, a 19th-century device used to bring the outside world inside. This particular double image shows a blindfolded man hanging from a wooden scaffold. It is captioned "Execution of a Colored Soldier." On the reverse is printed.

> In the month of June 1864, a colored soldier in the Union Army . . . attempted to commit a rape on a white woman whose house chanced to be within our lines; the woman's husband was absent from home, serving in the Rebel army. This colored soldier, named Johnson, was caught, tried by Court-Martial, found guilty, and sentenced to be hanged. A request was made of the Rebels, under a flag of truce, that we might be permitted to hang Johnson in plain sight of both armies, between the lines. The request was granted and this is a photograph of him hanging where both armies can plainly see him.

Soldiers look on this wonder. What was it like between the lines? Did they pass around a jug? Sing a song or two? Did anyone weep? Was the atmosphere carnivalesque like a lynching? Or heavy with military ceremony?

Who cut him down?

Between the lines the colored soldier has effected a peace; the situation is absurd, one war is stopped so another may have a moment. And another—

> I am a woman searching for her savagery
> even if it's doomed
>
> . . .
>
> They found her face down
> where she would be dancing
> to the shadow drums that humble,
> birds to silent
> flight
>
> They found her body held
> its life dispelled
> by ice
> my life burns to destroy
>
> Anna Mae Pictou Aquash
> stain on the Trail of Broken Treaties
> bullet lodged in her brain/hands
> and fingertips
> dismembered
>
> who won the only peace
> that cannot pass
> from mouth to mouth

What is most heartbreaking is the isolation, the aloneness of these figures in the American landscape: of the man on the auction block, the poet and slave Phillis Wheatley, the Union soldier Johnson, the mutilated being of Anna Mae Aquash.

> Tell me something
> what you think would happen if
> everytime they kill a black boy
> then we kill a cop
> everytime they kill a black man
> then we kill a cop
>
> you think the accident rate would lower
> subsequently?
>
> . . . . . .
>
> I lose consciousness of ugly bestial rabid
> and repetitive affront as when they tell
> me
> 18 cops in order to subdue one man
> 18 strangled him to death in the ensuing
> scuffle (don't
> you idolize the diction of the powerful
> subdue and
> scuffle my oh my) and that the murder
> that the killing of Arthur Miller on a
> Brooklyn
> street was a "justifiable accident" again
> (again)

Jordan is relentless as she refuses to turn from the streets, from the dystopic state of things, describing again and again the consequences of lovelessness.

In her most recent collection of essays, *Technical Difficulties,* subtitled *African-American Notes on the State of the Union* Jordan writes about Mike Tyson, the spectacle of his rise and fall.

Tyson was, as all heavyweights have been, an entertainer, descended from the Black men who engaged in "battles royal" for the pleasure of the white master and his cronies at ringside. Tyson's capacity for violence, learned on the streets, nurtured by poverty, honed by his trainers and handlers, was the essence of his performance. He learned his lessons well. He learned as Jordan says, he had "the choice of violence or violence: the violence of defeat or the violence of victory."

Who taught Mike Tyson anything about love? "What was America willing to love about Mike Tyson?" Not much, unless you count his ability to beat someone's brains out. He was never cherished. And yes, he was probably guilty, and yes, he also took the fall.

> But did anybody ever tell Mike Tyson that you talk different to a girl? Where would he learn that?

Would he learn that from U.S. Senator Ted Kennedy? Or from hotshot/scot-free movie director Roman Polanski? Or from rap recording star Ice Cube? Or from Ronald Reagan and the Grenada escapade? Or from George Bush in Panama? Or from George Bush and Colin Powell in the Persian Gulf? Or from the military hero flyboys who returned from bombing the shit out of civilian cities in Iraq and then said, laughing and proud, on international TV "All I need, now, is a woman"?

The eye that is unwilling or unable to look away, the voice that refuses to stop describing what the eye sees, the intellect driven to understand text and subtext, the spirit insisting love is possible, the thing that can save us, the anger that fuels it all, taking issue with human waste and self-destruction—these belong to June Jordan.

And then there is her wit.

> Poem for Etel Adnan Who Writes:
> "So we shall say: Don't fool
> yourselves.
> Jesus is not coming.
> We are alone."

—1983

1

I am alone
I am not coming not coming to Jesus not
coming to
the telephone
not coming to the door not coming to my
own true
love I am alone
I am not coming

2

Jesus forgot
Jesus came and then he left for then he
forgot
He forgot why he came
He forgot to come back
And this is written in the water by the
dolphins
flying like rice-paper submarines

Jesus forgot

3

Nobody died to save the world

4

Come

5

Let us break heads together.

FURTHER READING

Criticism

Brown, Marie D. and Greene, Cheryll Y. An interview with June Jordan and Angela Davis. *Essence* Vol. 21, No. 1 (May 1990) pp. 92-94, 96, 190, 193.
    The two writers and activists discuss the history of Black women's progress and directions for the future.

Emanuel, James A. A review of *Who Look at Me. The New York Times Book Review* (November 16, 1969) p. 52.
    Emanuel favorably reviews Jordan's collection of children's poetry, illustrated with paintings of Black artists from Colonial times to the present.

Erickson, Peter. "The Love Poetry of June Jordan." *Callaloo* Vol. 9, No. 1, (Winter 1986) pp. 221-34.
    Comparing work from several volumes of Jordan's poetry, Erickson traces the development of love themes in her work.

Martz, Louis L. "New Books in Review-Recent Poetry: Established Idiom." *The Yale Review* Vol. LIX, No. 4, (June 1970) pp. 551-69.
    Jordan's *Some Changes* is included in a review of recent books of poetry.

Smith, Dale Edwyna. "The Mother Tongue." *Belles Lettres* Vol. 10, No. 2 (Spring 1995) pp. 68-9.
    Jordan's *Technical Difficulties* is included in an analysis of Black Women poets.

Additional coverage of Jordan's life and career is included in the following sources published by Gale: *Authors and Artists for Young Adults,* **Vol. 2;** *Black Writers,* **Vol. 2;** *Contemporary Authors,* **Vols. 33-36R;** *Contemporary Authors New Revision Series,* **Vol. 25;** *Children's Literature Review,* **Vol. 10;** *Contemporary Literary Criticism,* **Vols. 5, 11, 23;** *DISCovering Authors Modules: Multicultural Authors Module; DISCovering Authors Modules: Poets Module;* *Dictionary of Literary Biography,* **Vol. 38;** *Major Au-*

Yusef Komunyakaa
1947-

(Born James Willie Brown) American poet.

INTRODUCTION

Komunyakaa's reputation as a poet has grown steadily since his work first appeared in small magazines and poetry journals in the mid-1970s. His acclaim has culminated thus far with his receipt of the 1994 Pulitzer Prize in poetry for his volume of new and selected poems, *Neon Vernacular* (1993). In the same year, he also received the largest award bestowed on a single work of poetry, the $50,000 Kingsley Tufts Poetry Award given by the Claremont Graduate School. The judges described Komunyakaa's work as "almost electrically compelling," and they were "excited by the way he combines colloquial language with poetic language and uses images and themes from jazz music." From the outset, critics have found Komunyakaa's work intensely personal and representative of his generation. While presenting the unique perspective of a black man in America and a Vietnam veteran, Komunyakaa's works also address universal themes of the human condition that transcend social and political boundaries.

Biographical Information

Born in Bogalusa, Louisiana, the oldest of five children, Komunyakaa was named James Willie Brown, after his father, a carpenter. Growing up in the segregated South, he turned early to books. As he recalled in a 1986 interview, James Baldwin was an early influence: "I remember first checking out *Nobody Knows My Name* at the black library in Bogalusa . . . in the late '50s. I read that book about twenty-five times." His grandmother remembered that "he was always reading something or writing something." Komunyakaa has traced his love of poetry to elementary school and his introduction to the verse classics of English literature. In his early teens, he read the Bible twice on his own initiative. Not long after graduating from small, segregated Central High School in 1965, Komunyakaa joined the Army. He was sent to Vietnam in 1969, where he served as a front-line correspondent and editor of the military newspaper, *The Southern Cross,* and received the Bronze Star. After his tour of duty, Komunyakaa entered college, earning a B.A. from the University of Colorado in 1975, an M.A. from Colorado State in 1979, and an M.F.A. from the University of California, Irvine, in 1980. During this period, his works first appeared in print. Stints at the University of New Orleans as an instructor, in New Orleans public schools as Poet-in-the-Schools, and Indiana University as a visiting pro-

fessor followed. He married Australian novelist and short story writer Mandy Jane Sayer in 1985. Since 1987, Komunyakaa has been a professor of African-American Studies and English at Indiana University at Bloomington.

Major Works

Komunyakaa's first two volumes of poetry appeared while he was still in graduate school: *Dedications and Other Darkhorses* (1977) and *Lost in the Bonewheel Factory* (1979) are short collections that were published in limited editions. His first full book, *Copacetic* (1984), focuses on his childhood and youth in poems that borrow the idioms and rhythms of jazz and blues. *I Apologize for the Eyes in My Head* (1986) presents ironic and satirical accounts of Komunyakaa's experience as a black man in American society, examining the effects of the past on the present. *Magic City* (1986) continues this focus on personal history, concentrating on his childhood. *Dien cai dau* (1988) collects Komunyakaa's poems about his experiences in Vietnam. He did not write about the war until 1983, fourteen years after his tour of duty, and the long gestation period resulted in poems with a unique combination of surrealistic imagery and journalistic precision in their examination of the psychological effects of the war. *Neon Vernacular* includes selections from all of Komunyakaa's previous volumes along with a number of new poems. The collection integrates the various personas of the earlier works, while the new poems speak in the mature voice of the black child from Louisiana who survived Vietnam and made himself into a spokesman for his generation.

Critical Reception

Komunyakaa's first volume to receive national attention, *Copacetic,* attracted mixed reviews. Critics commented favorably on his blending of colloquial and poetic language, but faulted him for needless obscurity and a superficial treatment of themes. With each succeeding volume, however, the balance has shifted in the poet's favor. In reviewing *I Apologize for the Eyes in My Head,* critics celebrated Komunyakaa as a "talented surrealist" whose "fierce yet mysterious" style makes him "one of the important poets of his generation." Komunyakaa's reputation further solidified with *Dien cai dau,* a volume of poems covering his Vietnam experiences. Critics received it as one of the most articulate expressions of the moral ambiguity and the psychological consequences of that conflict, lauding it for imaging the agonized dilemma of black and white soldiers alike. The wide acclaim for Komunyakaa's rehearsal of his life and career in *Neon Vernacular* put him in the front rank of contemporary poets. With this prize-winning book, Alvin Aubert said Komunyakaa "makes a great contribution to one of the newest genres in the canon: the black male epic of self." Many critics now view Komunyakaa as the current incarnation of the tradition embodied in the works of musicians like Duke Ellington and John Coltrane and writers James Baldwin and Ralph Ellison.

PRINCIPAL WORKS

Dedications and Other Darkhorses (poetry) 1977
Lost in the Bonewheel Factory (poetry) 1979
Copacetic (poetry) 1984
I Apologize for the Eyes in My Head (poetry) 1986
Magic City (poetry) 1986
Dien cai dau (poetry) 1988
February in Sydney (poetry) 1989
The Jazz Poetry Anthology [editor, with Sascha Feinstein] (poetry) 1991
Neon Vernacular: New and Selected Poems (poetry) 1993
Thieves of Paradise (poetry) 1998

CRITICISM

Alvin Aubert (essay date Spring 1993)

SOURCE: "Yusef Komunyakaa: The Unified Vision—Canonization and Humanity." in *African American Review,* Vol. 27, No. 1, Spring, 1993, pp.119-23.

[*In the following essay, Aubert discusses Komunyakaa's "quest for a unified vision, his bid for literary canonization, and his push for the completion of his humanity."*]

In an interview in the journal *Callaloo,* Yusef Komunyakaa, author of seven collections of poems, expresses his admiration for poets whom he considers to have achieved a "unified vision" in their poetry, an achievement he apparently strives for in his own work. A closely associated, if not identical, goal and a source of tension in Komunyakaa's poetry is his desire to gain admittance into the American literary canon, but not at the expense of surrendering his African American cultural identity.

At the core of Komunyakaa's pursuit of a unified vision and literary canonization is his stern resistance, textualized formalistically as well as thematically in his poems, to those forces in the hegemonous counterculture aimed at excluding him as an African American from the ranks of humanity. Indeed, in the singularity of his perseverance and in both the high quality and quantity of his poetic output, Komunyakaa approaches the intensity of no less a figure than prototypical canonization quester Ralph Ellison in his bid for mainstream American literary status. Komunyakaa, however, lacks the irritability Ellison sometimes displays in his attitude toward other African American writers, in particular the young black writers of the culturally insurrectionary 1970s.

The unified vision Komunyakaa seeks involves the integration and aesthetic instillation in his poetry of cultural material from both his African American and his European American sources. A useful sampling of Komunyakaa's artistry at work—including his quest for a unified vision, his bid for literary canonization, and his push for the completion of his humanity—can be found in two poems from his ironically titled fourth collection, *I Apologize for the Eyes in My Head* (1986): **"When in Rome—Apologia,"** the last two lines of which supply the title of the book, and "I Apologize." I will also refer briefly to **"The Music That Hurts."**

A particularly illustrative passage appears in **"I Apologize,"** a dramatic monologue that intertextualizes Robert Browning's prototypical dramatic monologue "My Last Duchess": "I'm just like the rest of the world: / No comment; no way, Jose . . . " After staking his claim for unqualified status in the human race and issuing his somewhat tongue-in-cheek declaration of no comment (ironically noting the extent to which further comment might implicate him in the negatives as well as the positives of the humanity he holds in common with his white auditor), the persona comments anyway. Addressing the person designated as "sir," who occupies the position of the implicit, silent auditor of the traditional dramatic monologue, the persona observes that he "want[s] spring always / dancing with the pepper trees," etc.

Like most of Komunyakaa's poems, **"I Apologize"** is markedly obscure. On first reading, the persona might be the typical, racially or ethnically unspecified, Peeping Tom, but we soon realize that he is the archetypal reckless eyeballer, the fated African American male in the U.S. South of not too many years ago who is accused of looking too long, and by implication with sexual intent, at some white woman, a tabooistic infringement for which he is likely to be lynched. The accused's only defense, his only recourse in such a predicament, is a desperate and futile excuse. This is typified in the poem's opening lines, which also encapsulate the kind of redemptive humor black people engage in among themselves: "My mind wasn't even there / Mirage, sir I didn't see / what I thought I saw. / . . . I was miles away, I saw nothing!" Then there is the sheer desperation of the poem's concluding line and a half—"This morning / I can't even remember who I am"—an apparent plea of insanity.

"When in Rome—Apologia" aptly intertextualizes Browning's monologue as well. Both of Komunyakaa's poems allude to the fate of the wife of Browning's jealous persona, the Duke who had his spouse killed for smiling excessively at other men. In Komunyakaa's poems, however, an ironic readjustment of roles takes place, for it is the would-be suitor whose life is at stake, prompting his desperate plea:

> Please forgive me, sir,
> for getting involved
>
> in the music—
> it's my innate weakness
> for the cello: so human.
> Please forgive me
> for the attention
>
> I've given your wife
> tonight, sir.

We note the gap posited by the interstanzaic enjambment between "involved" and its complement "in the music," suggesting a deliberate, playful withholding of the right information from the "sir" of the poem—the sense being *I won't say it but it's not music I'm talking about, it's life: Excuse me, just a dumb nigger, for insisting on being involved on an equal basis with you in life.* Ironically, the speaker's "innate weakness" is the humanity he has in common with his auditor, as expressed in the phrase "so human." And the use of a highly prized wife to epitomize the cultural exclusion that diminishes the persona's human status is an appropriate choice in view of the idea that enjoys considerable currency among African American artists and intellectuals that, not only are women co-creators with men of culture, they are singularly carriers and dispensers of it as well. Furthermore, the irony informing the speaker's plea borders on sarcasm, thus implying that irony may be too exalted a sentiment to spend on the insensitive "sirs" of this world.

The petitioner's final, desperate plea evidences a loss of control which is due to intoxication: "I don't know / what came over me, sir. / After three Jack Daniel's / you must overlook / my candor, my lack of / sequitur." In a statement that engenders the title of the book, the poem concludes: "I apologize for / the eyes in my head," an ambiguously metonymical reference to the outer (physical) and inner (intuitive) facilities of sight that interact in the process of creating poems. *Forgive me,* the implication goes, *not only for insisting on seeing all that there is humanly possible to see in the world but also for being so presumptuous in my reputed inhumanity as a person of African descent to aspire to write poetry of a quality and comprehensiveness equal to your own.*

Who is the forbidden woman in these poems? Is she the same as the "white wife" of the surrealistic poem **"The Music That Hurts,"** personified there as "Silence"? Although Komunyakaa's poems incline toward nonreferentiality, they are not characterized by the nonfigurativeness nonreferential poetry reputedly strives for. Thus, viewed in the context of Komunyakaa's work as a whole, music in these three poems is metaphorical of life; its opposite, "Silence," signifies outsiderness, comprehending an absence of humanity. Add to this the act of seeing as literally and figuratively a means for fulfilling one's humanity, and Komunyakaa's ironic apology may be stated as *Sorry, but have I not eyes to see all that there is to be seen in the world, which accords with my right as an American citizen and, preeminently, as a human being?* In the very act of laying claim to and pursuing canonical status in his poems, Komunyakaa demonstrates his "qualification" for it in rhetorical and aesthetic maneuvers that include a repudiation of racial or ethnically based limitations or boundaries. He comes across as a person who is well-versed in the poetic traditions of Anglo-Europe and Anglo-America, and who is also aware of the abundant technical and material properties that are available for the advancement of the art of poetry in America, especially the rich resources that abound in African American life and culture.

Not all of Komunyakaa's poems contain African American cultural material, and in some of those that do, the material is not always easily recognizable, possibly identifying these poems as exemplary achievements of Komunyakaa's unified vision. These are among the numerous poems by Komunyakaa that occupy the right end of an accessibility continuum that ranges from obscure on the right to clear on the left, and they provide a unique glimpse into Komunyakaa's artistry, especially in the extraordinary challenge the poems present to the reader who must work to discover, process, and integrate the works' African American cultural material into the fabric of meaning of the poems. The poem, **"I Apologize"** is a case in point, with its subtle inscription of the persona's African Americanness in a poem not easily identifiable as the work of an African American author. Clues to the persona's identity appear in one of a sequence of desperate alibis he concocts in his apologetic response to the person he addresses as "sir," who implicitly has accused him of reckless eyeballing. "I was in my woman's bedroom / removing her red shoes & dress," he pleads, adding in cadences reminiscent of Browning's poem and in mildly contradictory terms as he attempts to extricate himself, that he could not have committed the "crime" because

> I was miles away, I saw nothing!
> Did I say their diamond rings
> blinded me & I nearly lost my head?
> I think it was how the North
> Star fell through plate glass.
> I don't remember what they wore.

The "sir," as indicated earlier, is a white man; the "they" of the last line quoted above are white women, the reputed objects of the defensively comedic African American male persona's reckless eyeballing. The white women, whom he denies having seen at all, yet whose attire he contradictorily indicates he cannot "remember," are identified with diamonds and refined attire, in contrast with the "red shoes & dress" worn by the person whom we justifiably assume to be the persona's African American woman, with whom he was supposedly, and perhaps actually, too preoccupied in her bedroom to be paying attention to anyone else. The red shoes and dress allude ironically to the reputed fondness of black women for the color red and to the disparagement to which they were subjected in white society's stereotyping of them as sexually promiscuous, as scarlet women.

Another, possibly less obscure, allusion is to the North Star, a symbol of freedom derived from its use as a guide by fugitive slaves on their journeys out of slavery. The persona claims he was more concerned with the star than the white women's diamond rings. Throughout the poem the persona is portrayed as a ludicrously bumbling trickster figure, offering one lame excuse after another in his effort to escape the lynching he is likely to receive for his reckless eyeballing. For all its comedic trappings, however, **"I Apolo-**

gize" is a serious dramatization of the obstacles confronting the African American poet who wants his humanity acknowledged—and a rightful place in the American literary canon.

Also of particular interest are some of Komunyakaa's Vietnam war poems, which appear in the chapbook *Toys in a Field* (1987) and the full-length *Dien cai dau* (1988). In my review of the latter work for *Epoch* magazine [Vol. 38, No. 1 (1989)], I noted the appropriateness of Komunyakaa's use of surrealism for depicting the absurdity of Vietnam combat experiences, especially as they involved black and white American GIs together in situations where, despite the combat survival value of camaraderie, the African American soldier had to contend with the differential burden of racial, and ofttimes racist, inequities (which is not to say that one should overlook the absurdity that frequently surfaces in relations between whites and blacks generally).

Especially relevant to the present discussion is the poem **"Tu Do Street,"** from *Dien cai dau,* with its titular punning on "two door." The persona is an African American GI and is immediately identifiable as such, but he also has a penchant for invisibility. He is a quester of sorts for whom invisibility, or at least a certain neutrality, is prerequisite, since he is intent on testing out the waters of racial interfacing along a Saigon bar strip frequented by black and white GIs who enter the area, as it were, through separate doors as they seek relief from the stress and strain of combat among the mamasans and their attendant bar girls.

An implicit distinction is drawn in the poem between the GIs' quest for sexless or pre-sexual socialization in the bars and their quest for sex in other rooms, for although the black GIs are shunned by the mama-sans and bar girls in the bars frequented by the white GIs, "deeper into alleys," in off-limits areas, the black soldiers have access to prostitutes whose services are available on a nondiscriminatory basis. These assignations take place in "rooms" that invoke a transformational combat landscape: They "run into each other like tunnels / leading to the underworld." Implicit in these conduits is a common humanity, linked to a common death, figuratively in sex and literally in war, for black and white GIs alike:

> There's more than a nation
> inside us, as black & white
> soldiers touch the same lovers
> minutes apart, tasting
> each other's breath . . .

What's "more than a nation / inside" the GIs, black and white, is of course their shared humanity.

The persona knows about the two doors, but impelled by

purposes of the persona behind the persona—the poet in quest of a poem and, consequently, of his equalization and literary canonization—he goes in through the opposite door anyway, purposefully and perhaps ritualistically subjecting himself to the rejection on racial grounds he knows he is sure to get. When he enters the bar frequented by the white GIs, where the music is different from that in the bars where the black GIs go, the bar girls "fade like tropical birds" in their evasiveness. The experience triggers a memory involving an ironic representation of music that separates rather than unites by virtue of its inherent harmony:

> Music divides the evening.
> I close my eyes & can see
> men drawing lines in the dust.
> America pushes through the membrane
> of mist & smoke, & I'm a small boy
> again in Bogalusa. *White Only*
> signs & Hank Snow.

The impulse that motivated Komunyakaa as a small boy in his Louisiana hometown of Bogalusa impels him now as a GI in Vietnam, both personae laying claim to their humanity. And as it was at home, so it is on the war front—at least in the rear echelon in Saigon where the soldiers go for rest and recuperation. In the combat zone, where "only machine gun fire brings us / together," where interracial camaraderie has immediate survival value, a different code of behavior prevails:

> Back in the bush at Dak To
> & Khe Sanh, we fought
> the brothers of these women
> we now run to hold in our arms.

The surface implications of the last two lines quoted are apparent, but just as we should not miss their function in expressing the common humanity that is the object of the persona's quest, we should not overlook the note of respect the passage affords women in its emphasis on the humanistic aspect of the embrace, virtually annulling the sexual import of the situation and betokening the generally humanistic portrayal of women we find in Komunyakaa's work as a whole.

The bar girls and prostitutes of Saigon are metonymically depicted in **"Tu Do Street"** as victims, their "voices / wounded by their beauty and war." These women are also a part of the "nation / inside us" quoted and commented on above, for it is they—"the same lovers" touched by black GIs and white GIs alike, implicitly by virtue of their capacity for motherhood, for bringing life into the world, and as the primary sources of nurturing—who are the conferers and common denominators of the universal, of the common humanity that populates Komunyakaa's projected socio-literary commonwealth and makes material his "unified vision."

Michael Collins (essay date 1993-94)

SOURCE: "Staying Human," in *Parnassus,* Vol. 18, No. 2, 1993-94, pp. 126-50.

[*In the following essay, Collins provides a retrospective of Komunyakaa's career, giving particular attention to the poet's Vietnam and jazz poems.*]

> "I went to Vietnam as a basic naive young man of eighteen. Before I reached my nineteenth birthday, I was an animal. . . . They prepared us for Vietnam as a group of individuals who worked together as a unit to annihilate whatever enemy we came upon . . . There was this saying: 'Yeah though I walk through the valley of death, I shall fear no evil, 'cause I'm the baddest motherfucker in the valley' . . . I collected about 14 ears and fingers. With them strung on a piece of leather around my neck, I would go downtown, and you would get free drugs, free booze, free pussy because they wouldn't wanna bother you 'cause this man's a killer. It symbolized that I'm a killer. And it was, so to speak, a symbol of combat-type manhood."
>
> —Specialist 4 Arthur E. "Gene" Woodley, Jr.
> (aka Cyclops and Montagnard)

> " . . . There seems to be always some human landscape that creates a Paul Celan. . . ."
>
> —Yusef Komunyakaa

Reading the Vietnam poems of Yusef Komunyakaa, one is reminded that culture is made as often on battlefields as it is in the thinker's notebook, or in the schoolroom; that heroes, those bloody-handed fellows, are the originals of our great men. There are days when the sun seems to rise for no other purpose than to illuminate some killer of genius: to make his uniform glow like a nation's stained glass windows on Sunday. True, Michelangelo is the equal of Napoleon in fame, but it is Napoleon's example that is most often followed: More men aspire to populate tombs than to carve them.

Komunyakaa is more the Michelangelesque carver than the populator of tombs. Yet though his *Neon Vernacular: New and Selected Poems* ranges far and wide in its subject matter, it turns willy-nilly round his battlefield epiphanies and traumas, round the question of survival when that question is, in Emily Dickinson's phrase, "at the white heat." **"At the Screen Door,"** for instance, one of the "new" poems in *Neon Vernacular*, chronicles Komunyakaa's return after many years to his Louisiana home town; yet its true subject is the question of survival and survival's cost in coins of madness. In this poem, Komunyakaa, at what appears to be his mother's door—at the fountainhead of his life—wonders, as any bemused prodigal son would, "Is it her?" But in the next clause war rears its head: "will she know / What I've seen & done, / How my boots leave little grave-stone / Shapes in the wet dirt . . . ?" At that door he recalls a buddy who ended up in "a padded cell . . . After all the men he'd killed in Korea / & on his first tour in Vietnam, / Someone tracked him down. / That Spec 4 he ordered / Into a tunnel in Cu su Chi / Now waited for him behind / The screen door, a sunset / in his eyes, / a dead man / Wearing his teenage son's face. . . ." In the poem "Please," Komunyakaa reports an occasion when he gave a similar order—an order that so haunts him that in the midst of lovemaking he cries out, "Hit the dirt!" This arduous journey into the self recalls the climbs in the Tour de France that, too difficult to rate, are called "beyond category."

As both **"Please"** and **"At the Screen Door"** demonstrate, Komunyakaa often chooses as his subject experiences painful enough to destroy the personality, not so much to exorcise them as to connect them to insights that, like certain icons and kings of the old religions, might heal the halt and the sick. The bridges he strives to build between pain and insight are those of the jazz musician—that improviser's leaping among epiphanies on which, Komunyakaa has said, his consciousness, was nurtured: "I think we internalize a kind of life rhythm," he told an interviewer [Vince F. Gotera]: "The music I was listening to when I was seven or eight years old and the music I listen to today are not that different . . . I listen to a lot of classical jazz, as well as European classical music. I think you do all those things side by side" [*Callaloo,* 1990]. Discovering rhythms that tie two moments or two traditions of music together, Komunyakaa pulls the one thread of pleasure in the valley of death and unravels, one poem at a time, that dour place woven from suffering. This unraveling can disorient and blind those grown accustomed to the Valley of the Shadow, and it is something like the disorientation and still earthly rage that salvation brings that one finds in the last image of **"At the Screen Door,"** where Komunyakaa writes of "Watching a new day stumble / Through a whiplash of grass / Like a man drunk on the rage / Of being alive."

The "rage" of being alive but limited—whether by society, by the other army's bullets, by your bloodguilt, or by the borders of the human itself—can make even the dawn's light harsh, as if not a new day, but flakes of brimstone were sifting down upon all human effort. The rage to live beyond limitation is nowhere more compelling than in the heart of a warrior. From Alexander and Hannibal to Powell and Schwarzkopf, the man who spills blood has been loved, looked upon as a shaman who knows death by heart, who can recite it or swallow it like a secret code. Not without reason, people assume that the man of blood is the best protector: General de Gaulle and General Eisenhower led their nations after World War II. America's last President reached the heights of public approval as a warlord; its current Vice President is a Vietnam veteran, and President Clinton's Achilles heel is his ignorance of warfare. The generals can talk back to him, and their talk carries weight.

The talk of the man of action *always* carries weight. It fascinates, for who doesn't want to know the workings of the mind of war, from whose every detail spring whole trees of language and metaphor? General Schwarzkopf's memoirs conquered the best-seller list. Homosexuals and many women have begun to clamor for their right to validate themselves in battle: In modern (and ancient) culture, it often seems that killing is the one royal route to proving oneself human and noble. All this makes the best poetry of Yusef Komunyakaa—the poetry in which he directly describes his Vietnam experiences, and the poetry for which that experience acts as a kind of antimatter power source—an invaluable resource. It gives even some of Komunyakaa's lesser work and apprentice efforts the patina of the man of action's recollections of his formative kneescrapes and triumphs. For Komunyakaa is the real deal twice over—a brilliant poet in his best work and a hero who came back from Vietnam not only with a Bronze Star like a piece of the firmament on his chest, but with a knowledge of what it is to live without vanity, without any tradition but the Darwinian one that says: first survive, *then* return to history and its haze of manners and names. He told Vincente F. Gotera [in *Callaloo*] that when he began to write the Vietnam poems he remembered many faces from his tour of duty, but few names:

> I suppose that's all part of the forgetting process, in striving to forget particular situations that were pretty traumatic for me. Not when I was there as much as in retrospect. When you're there in such a situation, you're thinking about where the nearest safest place is to run, in case of an incoming rocket. You don't even have time to think about the moral implications. . . .

The poems he produced about Vietnam are a deliberate and painful reconstruction of those missing—one might say vaporized—implications. Komunyakaa has said it took him "about fourteen years to start getting" the poems down on paper. One of the most moving of the group is **"We Never Know,"** in which Komunyakaa recalls how a man he shoots

> . . . danced with tall grass

for a moment, like he was swaying
with a woman. Our gun barrels
glowed white-hot.
When I got to him,
a blue halo
of flies had already claimed him.
I pulled the crumpled photograph
from his fingers.
There's no other way
to say this: I fell in love.
The morning cleared again,
except for a distant mortar
& somewhere choppers taking off.
I slid the wallet into his pocket
& turned him over, so he wouldn't be
kissing the ground.

The portrait of tenderness in reverse, of understanding in reverse—indeed, of *time* in reverse, for the whole is remembered, like that past-backwards solo Jimi Hendrix devises
for "Are You Experienced?"—drives home the irreversibil-
ity of violence and understanding. Its great poignance and
power derives from the fact that it shows us the moral wilderness of the Vietnam war and the way out, inaccessible in
this poem, but not forever. It shows also one of the characteristic sonic patterns of Komunyakaa's free verse, which
sometimes, as in this poem, looks to the eye like a thousand
magazine poems. This formal signature has to do with the
way the end words communicate with each other: not so
much through rhyme or slant rhyme as through the more
mysterious language of echoes—the reincarnation of vow-
els which, unlike men, do return. Thus the "a" in "grass" alters slightly, but changes its spots in "barrels," whose "e"
surfaces, cropped but visible, a ghost of itself, in the hyphen-
ated incandescence of "white-hot." "Hot" of course rhymes
with "got," and that uncloseable "o," like the mouth of a man
hit by gunshot, draws its circle in the dead man's nightmare
halo of flies. Komunyakaa has fashioned from the banqueting flies the ancient sign of the blest, and he sees, too late,
that the man he has killed is a blessed thing—a human, deserving of the company of whatever angels he believed in
when alive, and, even in death, commanding love.

That same sonic pattern is at play on a larger scale in the
gorgeous **"Starlight Scope Myopia,"** which, unlike **"We
Never Know,"** approaches strict formality and manages a
virtuoso incorporation of rhyme and slant rhyme:

Gray-blue shadows lift
shadows onto an oxcart.

Making night work for us,
the starlight scope brings
men into killing range.

The river under Vi Bridge
takes the heart away

like the Water God
riding his dragon.
Smoke-colored

Viet Cong
move under our eyelids,

lords over loneliness
winding like coral vine through
sandalwood & lotus,

inside our lowered heads
years after this scene

ends. The brain closes
down. What looks like
one step into the trees,

they're lifting crates of ammo
& sacks of rice, swaying

under their shared weight.
Caught in the infrared,
what are they saying?

Are they talking about women
or calling the Americans

beaucoup dien cai dau?
One of them is laughing.
You want to place a finger

to his lips & say "shhhh."
You try reading ghost talk

on their lips. They say
"up-up we go," lifting as one.
This one, old, bowlegged,

you feel you could reach out
& take him into your arms. You

peer down the sights of your M-16,
seeing the full moon
loaded on an oxcart.

In this poem Komunyakaa achieves his chronic ambition to
be a jazz poet with a lineage as traceable to Louis
Armstrong's trumpet as a Roman centurion's would have
been to the sea foam from which Aphrodite rose. The alternating two-and three-line stanzas, with a pattern of three
beats that Komunyakaa now and then expands to four or tele-

scopes to two, combines with the end-word pattern of slant rhyme, assonance, and consonance that chimes throughout the poem to mime the magnifying powers of a starlight scope. The poem itself is a kind of starlight scope to which the reader presses his eye and sees ordinary words and terms under extreme magnification, like genetic proteins brought to light by some unblinking microscope: The Vietcong, appearing all alone in their two-beat line (# 11), are scarier, larger, more vulnerable than life.

The "myopia" facet of the starlight scope makes itself felt in the fact that the Vietcong, technologically cut off from space and time and fixed to astral coordinates "inside our lowered heads / years after this scene / ends," are easier to shoot; having been transformed into creatures of the starlight scope, gathered at the wrong end of the technological rainbow, they are already dead:

> Are they talking about women
> or calling Americans
>
> *beaucoup dien cai dau*?
> One of them is laughing.
> You want to place a finger
>
> to his lips & say "shhhh."
> You try reading host talk
>
> on their lips. They say
> "up-up we go," lifting as one.

Mao Tse-tung wrote that the theory that "'weapons decide everything,' which is a mechanist theory of war, [is] a subjective and one-sided view," since in war there are "not only weapons but also human beings" and "the contest of strength is not only a contest of military and economic power but also of human power and morale." Mao, a strong influence on Communist Vietnam's General Vo Nguyen Giap, according to the historian-general Philip B. Davidson, would seem to have been proven right by the decades of military success during which Giap drove first France and then the United States out of his small country. **"Starlight Scope Myopia"** exposes both the power and the myopia of the "mechanistic" view, while suggesting a third view: that "human power"—the power of being "lords over loneliness," of *speaking* ("Caught in the infrared, / what are they saying?" Komunyakaa asks in the poem)—may be incompatible with weaponry, which is designed to expand the empire of silence. Writing his poems, Komunyakaa tries to steer clear of the world's starlight scopes, to correct their imposed myopias, to reinfuse them with what he says poetry is: "in essence . . . the spiritual and emotional dimension of the human animal," a source of spontaneous communication that "can link two people together, reader and poet. . . ."

The two-and three-line stanzas, with their haiku terseness, provoke a kind of double vision through their invocation of the Water God—from a *believer's* point of view—and the paradox of traditional Vietnamese reverence for the old man at the moment he is killed ("you feel you could reach out / & take him in your arms."). They enact the deep cultural exchange that might have gone on between the American soldiers and the Vietcong under other circumstances. (Such exchanges did and do occur, even in the midst of war, despite the propaganda on both sides thick as wax dripped in the ears.) Yet they suggest that when the chips are down, such exchanges make no difference. What the American soldiers know of the Vietnamese does not foster mercy. It "takes the heart away." Mercy and humor ("One of them is laughing") are foolhardy in a combat zone. In fact, with the help of high-tech weapons they can be twisted to detach a soldier from his actions. In the heat of battle or the cover of ambush, such feelings are best kept locked up in a mind patrolled by fear mounted on anger. The Vietnamese, after all, are loading ammunition meant to kill Americans along with their rice. The flickering identification with them—before, during, and after their deaths—must contend with the fingers of history moving to snuff it out.

In **"Starlight Scope Myopia,"** this unexpected empathy is best expressed by the words Komunyakaa puts into the mouths of the Vietnamese who may be "calling the Americans / *beaucoup dien cai dau*" (very crazy). This multicultural insult begins with a word the Vietnamese took from the French, whom they defeated, then switches for exactitude into Vietnamese to characterize the Americans, whom they are in the process of defeating. (The ironic phrase spans all the relevant cultures in the long Vietnam nightmare. That an American is wondering whether the Vietcong are using this phrase demonstrates both discomfort and a certain muted triumph at having them in his sights. Even a battlefield is a society with rules and language games.)

It also crystallizes a point Komunyakaa suggests in his interviews with Gotera, that societies of strangers, or even of traditional enemies, can be ever so delicately held together by infinitely recycled bits of language, by clichés:

> [Among American] soldiers, for some reason—individuals coming from so many backgrounds: the deep South, the North, different educational levels—clichés are used many times as efforts to communicate, as bridges perhaps. And soldiers often speak in clichés. . . .

Clichés, like tatoos on the bodies of languages, are useful decorations of places where a common vision is hidden, or being brought to light. The cliché *"Beaucoup dien cai dau"* is Komunyakaa's assessment of the war itself and perhaps of America's role in it. True, his Vietnam lyrics display none of the sense of outrage, of being pierced by betrayal, so evident in the testimony of some black Vietnam veterans. Gene Woodley, who gives this essay its first epigraph, told journalist Wallace Terry of being transformed into an "animal" by his boot camp training and by the brutality of Vietnam and insisted that in shipping him and other "bloods" off to its rice paddy war, America

> befell upon us one big atrocity. It lied. They had us naive, young, dumb-ass niggers believin' that this war was for democracy and independence. It was fought for money. All those big corporations made billions on the war, and then America left.

On the other hand, Komunyakaa is no indestructible patriot like the blood Terry interviewed who narrated the following anecdotes about his experience as a prisoner of war in Vietnam:

> They would read things in their behalf about the Communist way and downgrading the United States, blah, blah, blah, all the time. . . . When Dr. King was assassinated, they called me in for interrogation to see if I would make a statement critical of the United States. I said no, I don't know enough about it. . . . My personal feeling is that black people have problems and still have problems in America. But I never told them that, because I had no intention of helping them to defeat us. We deal with our problems within our own country. Some people just do not live up to the great ideals our country stands for. . . .

Komunyakaa's poetry conveys the pain and grace involved in maintaining not so much the middle ground *between* these two positions as the shifting ground of possibilities that lies under them both. He illuminates these and other positions in part by creating a "tension between levels of diction," as Gotera has said, by deploying what he himself calls a "neon vernacular" in which argots and forms of life blink on and off like those neon signs with which a cityscape expands and contracts, caressing and reshaping the night. Consider the masterful **"Hanoi Hannah"**:

> *Ray Charles*! His voice
> calls from waist-high grass,
> & we duck behind gray sandbags.
> "Hello, Soul Brothers. Yeah,
> Georgia's also on my mind."
> Flares bloom over the trees.
> "Here's Hannah again.
> Let's see if we can't
> light her goddamn fuse
> this time." Artillery
> shells carve a white arc

> against dusk. Her voice rises
> from a hedgerow on our left.
> "It's Saturday night in the States.
> Guess what your woman's doing tonight.
> I think I'll let Tina Turner
> tell you, you homesick GIs."
> . . . . "You know you're dead men,
> don't you? You're dead
> as King today in Memphis.
> Boys, you're surrounded by
> General Tran Do's division."
> Her knife-edge song cuts
> deep as a sniper's bullet.
> "Soul Brothers, what you dying for?" . . . .

One of the many heartbreaking nuances of this poem is its suggestion that when people at last learn each other's language, they will do so the better to hook and destroy each other with narcotics of commiseration, gossip, trust, half-truth, or, unkindest cut of all, some inaccessible sweetness, some Tina Turner dancing in the mind's high grass. Hannah's questions are, as she well knows, also the questions asked by the bloods and, by the time of Komunyakaa's 1969-1970 tour, by most Americans: "what you dying for?" She also suggests to the "soul brothers" that they are fighting on the wrong side—*against* a people of color that has suffered colonial oppression. Her grains of truth, for all the soldiers' resistance to them ("Let's see if we can't / light her goddamn fuse / this time"), must sooner or later call up those emotions dangerous to bring to the battlefield. One of the veterans quoted above spoke of joining the Black Panthers after the war because they were a semi-military group ready to prolong what General Giap would have called the "armed struggle."

Komunyakaa, who served as a correspondent and editor for *The Southern Cross* in Vietnam, illustrates the black soldier's agonized dilemma in **"Report from the Skull's Diorama."** Here he writes of

> . . . . a platoon of black GIs
> back from night patrol

> with five dead. . . .

> These men have lost their tongues,

> but the red-bordered
> leaflets tell us
> *VC didn't kill*
> *Dr. Martin Luther King.*
> The silence etched into their skin

> is also mine. . . .

What can be more unnerving than to find your lost voice coming back to you through the leaflets of an enemy? As General Giap knew, no weapon is more powerful than the weapon that cuts the mind. Thus Hanoi Hannah uses the "moonlight-through-the-pines" beauty of Ray Charles' voice to kindle, amid the gun barrels and starlight scopes and killing, "the spiritual and emotional dimension of the human animal" at exactly the time that soldiers most strive to remain machines. The healing voice is thus made into its opposite: a kind of psychological napalm that sets fires in the ganglia and carries out General Giap's "strategy of revolutionary war [which] totally integrated two principal forms of force: armed force and political force . . . , military *dau tranh* (struggle) and political *dau tranh*." According to Philip B. Davidson [in *Vietnam at War: The History 1946-1975*, 1988],

> their combined use created a kind of war unseen before: a single war waged simultaneously on several fronts—not geographical fronts, but programmatical fronts—all conducted by one and the same authority, all carefully meshed. It was a war in which military campaigns were waged for political and diplomatic reasons; economic measures . . . were adopted to further political ends; political and diplomatic losses were accepted to forward military campaigns; and psychological campaigns were launched to lower enemy military effectiveness.

By showing how all this works in his poetry, Komunyakaa engages in an equal and opposite *dau tranh*. With poetry as his weapon and tool, he seeks to rebuild the psyche that war and other social traumas disorder. He recalls reading poetry avidly in Vietnam, before he himself became a poet, in order to keep "in contact with [his] innermost feelings" and not be mummified by the starlight scopes or caught on the hook of some perfectly-baited propaganda broadcast: in other words, to keep thinking, to keep being human, to keep humming the rhythm of life. "The real interrogator," he writes in **"Jungle Surrender,"**

> . . . . is the voice within.
> I would have told them about my daughter
>
> in Phoenix, how young she was,
> about my first woman, anything
>
> but how I helped ambush two Viet Cong
> while plugged into the Grateful Dead.
>
> For some, a soft windy voice makes them
> snap. Blues & purples. Some place between
>
> central Georgia & Tay Ninh Province—

> the vision of a knot of blood unravels
> & parts of us we dared put into the picture
> come together. . . .

This daring to put the unbearable first into memory, then into the poem, reconstructs the war-broken rhythms losing track of which, as a Thelonious Monk sideman once said of Monk's asymmetries, would mean plunging down a kind of elevator shaft away from sanity, but even more from the ability to speak, to play. Climbing the precipice of memory, the soldier-poet proves his mettle in peace. He is like an amputee who feels his missing hand and looks down to find that it is there.

Not only Komunyakaa's war poems, but also his peacetime poetry is obsessed with recovering what is lost, with scope and possibility and with jazz, the music of possibility—the noise freedom makes when it moves through the nerves. The peacetime poems in *Neon Vernacular* and *Magic City* display the conceptual and emotional range that is available only to a man who has been to the lip of the abyss and looked around. High-school football, horniness, warfare, sex, torture, rape, racism, loneliness, yellow-jackets, history—Komunyakaa probes them all. In a *Magic City* ballad about prepubescent interracial hijinks called **"Albino,"** Komunyakaa milks everyday incidents for their drops of revelation:

> . . . Some summer days
>   We shot marbles with ball bearings
> For hours before the first punch
>   & the namecalling
>
> Erupted. But by dusk
>   We were back to quick kisses,
> Hollering *You're It & Home*
>   As we played hide & seek.
>
>   . . . . .
>
> She led me to their clubhouse
>   Beside the creek, a betrayal
>
> Of the genes. . . . .
>
>   . . . . .
>
> An odor in the air made its own
> Laws, as if the tongue was a latch
>   Holding down a grace note.

If Komunyakaa finds his way to the kingdom of things past in such *Magic City* reveries, it is because he put in his hours of dusty apprenticeship. The early books excerpted in *Neon Vernacular* are certainly uneven, and some of the poems, such as **"Light on the Subject"** from *Lost in the Bonewheel Factory,* would have been better left unselected. *That* poem dates from a period when Komunyakaa was struggling to find his "own voice." He began writing poetry in a University of Colorado workshop in 1973 and continued taking workshops throughout the seventies, studying under such luminaries as Charles Wright, C. K. Williams, and Howard Moss before landing a fellowship in 1980 at the Provincetown Fine Arts Work Center. "Well, in essence," Komunyakaa admitted to Gotera,

> one's voice is already inside, but a sort of unearthing has to take place; sometimes one has to remove layers of facades and superficialities. The writer has to get down to the guts of the thing and rediscover the basic timbre of his or her existence.

This unearthing is what must be done in the writing of *every* poem. Like ditch digging or distance running, it builds up a poet's strength. Komunyakaa's "basic timbre" is not so much a "voice" as the meter-making arguments that Emerson espoused, where the heart beats out time on the brainstem.

In Komunyakaa's weak poems, he is simply "not in form," as the athletes say. **"Light on the Subject"** finds Komunyakaa pumped up, like a blood doper, with an exaggeration of a "voice": "Hello, Mister Jack / The Ripper, come on in / make yourself at home." Most of Komunyakaa's poorer efforts follow the glib workshop technique in which tones of voice clash together to make brassy ironies, and verb phrases are paired with nouns not to make meaning, but to startle, like the marriage of the three-foot midget and the 1000-pound giantess in a circus. Komunyakaa writes, "In this gray station of wood / our hearts are wet rags, / & we turn to ourselves, / holding our own hands / as the scaffolds / sway." Despite their authenticity of feeling, these lines betray a paint-by-numbers imagery.

None of this criticism is meant to deprecate Komunyakaa's "pre-war" volumes. Even when most weighed down by ill-considered borrowings, the early poems rarely fail to display flashes of Olympian form. **"Chair Gallows,"** from his first book, *Dedications & Other Darkhorses,* is a fine elegy for the folksinger Phil Ochs, only mildly flawed by its soft-focus Bob Dylan ending and the somewhat forced imagery of its fourth line:

> Beating wind with a stick.
> Riding herd on the human spirit.
>
> It's how a man slips his head into a noose
> & watches the easy weight of gods pull down
> on his legs. I hope this is just another lie,

> just another typo in a newspaper headline.
> But I know war criminals
> live longer than men lost between railroad tracks
>
> & crossroad blues, with twelve strings
> two days out of hock.
>
> I've seen in women's eyes
> men who swallow themselves in mirrors.

The poems in *Copacetic* (1984), Komunyakaa's strongest pre-war "set," have their flaws, like bumpy light aircraft, but they do sooner or later lift off. In **"Back Then,"** Komunyakaa, like one of his acknowledged literary fathers, Aimé Césaire, manages to give surrealism a political backbone:

> I've eaten handfuls of fire
> back to the bright sea
> of my first breath
> riding the hipbone of memory
> & saw a wheel of birds
> a bridge into the morning
> but that was when gold
> didn't burn out a man's eyes
> before auction blocks
> groaned in courtyards
> & nearly got the best of me
> that was when the spine,
> of every ebony tree wasn't
> a pale woman's easy chair. . . .
>
> . . . . .
>
> at the pottery wheel
> of each dawn
> an antelope leaps
> in the heartbeat
> of the talking drum

Here the collective memory of an entire people is caught in the poem's talking drum. Komunyakaa makes all that history contemporaneous. He boldly casts his rhythmical net from the "the bright sea/of my first breath" to the slave trade (the "auction block") to the results of age-old economic apartheids ("the spine/ of every ebony tree [is] /a pale woman's easy chair"). Like a jazz musician playing a standard such as "When the Saints Come Marching In," he composes a talking poem out of the major chords (sea, slavery, economic injustice). The escape from history that Stephen Daedalus could not achieve is managed on the page: The antelope on whose skin—the poem's "drumskin"—the enjambed rhythms are beaten out suddenly lives again, leaping. Even more than the enjambments in **"Starlight Scope**

Myopia," the ones here resist death by burning its endstops. "There's a completeness about a line," Komunyakaa told Gotera,

> a completeness and yet a continuation. It's the whole thing of enjambment, what I like to call "extended possibilities." The line grows. It's not a linguistic labyrinth; it's in logical segments, and yet it grows. It's the whole process of becoming; that's how we are as humans. There's a kind of fluid life about us, and it's how poetry should be. . . . I would like to write poems that are just single lines. That is, a continuing line that doesn't run out of space because of the margin. . .

This sort of perpetual motion, the ability to play notes that orbit forever in the mind's outer spaces, is clearly what Komunyakaa is after in **"Back Then."** This is what he admires in the jazzmen—Thelonious Monk, Louis Armstrong, Duke Ellington, Ray Charles, and Charles Mingus—about whom he writes. Strangely, poems or passages tendered as tributes to his musical fathers—an elegy for Thelonious Monk, for instance—are among his weakest riffs; sprung from the will, or a sense of filial duty, they give the impression that the poet is intimidated, like a piano student auditioning before some severe master. Komunyakaa seems to feel, too, the long shadow of Auden's twentieth-century elegies. In the backsliding Monk elegy, Komunyakaa writes what he thinks his readers want to hear: an impersonation of angry grief. "Damn the snow. / Its senseless beauty / pours hard light / through the hemlock. / Thelonious is dead." These lines work against the anguish they seek to express.

More successful are the poems in which jazz appears like an angel that wanders into the lines and breaks into song. In its blues feeling, **"Audacity of the Lower Gods"** (from the 1986 collection *I Apologize for the Eyes in My Head*) is a jazz ballad. The pronoun "I" is not a site of anxiety or drama, but a place where the reader can rest without discomfort, a leaping off point for the ride down the long, vowel-extended, mostly iambic beats:

> I know salt marshes that move along like one big
> trembling wing. I've noticed insects
> shiny as gold in a blues singer's teeth
> & more keenly calibrated than a railroad watch,
> but at heart I'm another breed.

> The audacity of the lower gods—
> whatever we name we own.

> . . . . .

> I'd rather let the flowers
> keep doing what they do best.

> Unblessing each petal,
> letting go a year's worth of white
> death notes, busily unnaming themselves.

In a volume as cynical as *I Apologize for the Eyes in My Head,* the fat tone of these drawling iambs offers a seemingly anti-poetic paradox: that the happiest world may be a world left alone, untroubled by so much as a curse or a blessing or a name, all of which limit possibility, Komunyakaa's muse and first love.

That such a world is not for humans, but for angels and flowers in their haze of death notes, means that the search for possibility, and the eternal rediscovery of it, goes on, as it does in **"Copacetic Mingus"** (from *Copacetic*) and **"Changes; or, Reveries at a Window Overlooking a Country Road, with Two Women Talking Blues in the Kitchen"** (a "new" poem in *New and Selected.*) These poems are proof that pleasure, as much as any dour war god, can dominate and set its stamp on a life. **"Copacetic Mingus"** is made from two-to four-beat lines that hover like notes under Mingus' fat fingers and from punctuation that comes in now a little ahead, now a little behind the movable beat (made not from stresses so much as from whole words and phrases: whole notes of "hard love . . . hard love"):

> Heartstring. Blessed wood
> & every moment the thing's made of:
> ball of fatback
> licked by fingers of fire.
> Hard love, it's hard love.
> Running big hands down
> the upright's wide hips,
> rocking his moon-eyed mistress
> with gold in her teeth.
> Art & life bleed
> into each other
> as he works the bow.

> . . . . .

> . . . Here in New Orleans
> years below sea level,
> I listen to *Pithecanthropus.*
> *Erectus:* Up & down, under
> & over, every which way—
> thump, thump, dada—ah, yes.
> Wood heavy with tenderness,
> Mingus fingers the loom
> gone on Segovia,
> dogging the raw strings
> unwaxed with rosin.
> Hyperbolic bass line. Oh no!

Hard love, it's hard love.

Here the jazzman's and the poet's vision of time meet, like the two sides of some fantastic commemorative medal. This is possible because there is so much delight and devotion in Komunyakaa's portrait, so much diamond-hard love. If the poem has a flaw, it is that it lacks the metaphysical edge—the at times stark terror—of the grand war poems that begin two volumes later.

The question arises whether the peacetime poems can achieve the intensity that their "mighty subject" gives the wartime ones. The answer, inevitable for a poet of Komunyakaa's gifts, is yes. In the new poems with which **Neon Vernacular** begins and in the poems that evoke the neighborhoods of **Magic City,** Komunyakaa taps a seam of memory deep into his childhood in Bogalusa, Louisiana—at the time a complicated spot roamed by both the Ku Klux Klan and anti-Klan civil rights organizers—and up into the untappable future.

In **"Changes,"** Komunyakaa sets two columns of text parallel on the pages, just as one might place two old friends and one stranger between two mirrored walls and then sit back to be instructed by the infinite series of reflections on either side. In the mostly three-beat lines of the left hand column Komunyakaa writes a conversation between two women whose subject is the losses, like some dyslexia of the fates, that make life unreadable. In the right hand column, Komunyakaa sets down what appear to be his own historical reveries, his own rearrangement and orchestration of the unreadable. The effect he achieves is that of a vast conceptual rhyme, the written equivalent of harmonics in music. Possibility is extended and made equal to what Komunyakaa calls the "psychic domain" of his speakers:

> a blues environment . . . . [like that] in New Orleans . . . [where] there are so many layers of everything . . . [where] you have the traditional and the modern side by side . . . . [to create] an existential melancholy based on an acute awareness . . . I admire that to an extent, because linked to it is a kind of psychological survival. How one deals with life: to be on this plane one moment and the next moment, a different plane. . . .

In the same interview Komunyakaa speaks of the necessity of keeping "one foot in history, and the other in a progressive vision." Thus, in **"Changes,"** the country women, one's voice italicized, the other's voice in plain text, speak of death while the poet, in a smaller typeface to indicate the unspoken stream of consciousness, probes like Miles playing with his back to the audience and muses on beginnings:

Joe, Gus, Sham	Heat lightning jumpstarts the slow
Even, George Edward	afternoon & syncopated rainfall
Done gone. Done	peppers the tinroof like Philly Joe
Gone to Jesus, honey.	Jones' brushes reaching for a dusky
Doncha mean the devil,	backbeat across the high hat. Rhythm
Mary? Those Johnson boys	like cells multiplying . . . language &
Were only sweet talkers	notes made flesh. Accents & stress
& long, tall bootleggers.	almost sexual. Pleasure's knot; to wrestle
Child, now you can count	the mind down to unrelenting white space,
The men we usedta know	to fill each room with spring's contagious
On one hand. They done	changes. Words & music. "Ruby, My Dear,"
Dropped like mayflies—	turned down on the cassette player. . . . .

A full analysis of this fabulous poem would require another long essay, but even in this short excerpt one can see Komunyakaa achieving some of that jagged grandeur that the old man of strangeness, Thelonious Sphere Monk, set down in tunes such as "Ruby, My Dear," which Komunyakaa here conjures up like a familiar spirit. The poem is clearly an *ars poetica* of sorts: an ode to Komunyakaa's beloved possibility and poetry's enacting of it. Again, Komunyakaa finagles his way around death and destruction:

It's a fast world	dragging up moans from shark-infested
Out there, honey	seas as a blood moon rises. A shock
They go all kinda ways.	of sunlight breaks the mood & I hear
Just buried John Henry	my father's voice growing young again,
With that old guitar.	as he says, "The devil's beating
Cradled in his arms.	his wife": One side of the road's rainy
Over on Fourth Street	& the other side's sunny. Imagination—
Singing 'bout hell hounds	driftwood from a spring flood, stockpiled
When he dropped dead.	Furies. Changes. Pinetop's boogiewoogie
You heard 'bout Jack	keys stacked against each other like syllables
Right? He just tilted over	in tongue-tripped elegies for Lady Day
in prayer meeting.	& Duke. Don't try to make any sense
The good & the bad go	out of this; just let it take you
Into the same song.	like Pres's tenor & keep you human. . . . .

If an ex-warrior's meditations on death are always of interest, his meditations on life are specially revelatory. To have the two meditations joined together in this tour-de-force arrangement makes for the "extended possibility—what falls on either side of a word—" that Komunyakaa explicates later in the poem. The columns are like two numbers multiplied together, generating something larger. Like that ferocious Max Roach-Cecil Taylor encounter in which the drummer and the pianist go to war on their instruments, aurally sprouting extra arms like a pair of Shivas, all the while creating spontaneous and phantasmagorical harmonies, Komunyakaa in his two columns reaches the goal he proclaims at the end of the poem. He gets "beyond the tragedy / of always knowing [as in the starlight scope poem] what the right hand / will do." As is only feasible from a poet whose right hand really does know what his left hand is doing, we can read straight across the page ("Right? He just tilted over in tongue-tripped elegies for Lady Day" or "The good & the bad go out of this; just let it take you"). The crossover lines enact little resurrections: The man who tilts over comes up singing. The good and the bad slip out of ordinary ethical perception, as if they found a world of pure beauty on the other side, where evil is as unthinkable as the violation of the laws of physical symmetry. Death, as some scientists like to tell us, is nothing to be afraid of. It is only change. It is on death as change that Komunyakaa rings his **"Changes."** The columns of the poem end up wrapping suggestively around each other, like strands of DNA: strands of hope, of humanity. Don't let your fear of death lock you up in hurt and bloodshed, they seem to say: "just let it take you / like Pres's tenor & keep you human."

In our day Hamlet's question is "Shall we be human, or not be human?" Technology and foolishness have ordained this choice. Komunyakaa's Bogalusa memories, collected in *Magic City* and at the beginning of *Neon Vernacular,* include a double portrait of the town's Ku Klux Klansmen and their African American opponents, the "Deacons of Defense." In the first stanza of the poem, entitled **"Knights of the White Camellia & Deacons of Defense,"** the dragons and all the Klansmen gather "in a big circle / Beside Mitch Creek, as it murmured / Like a murderer tossing in his sleep. . . ." Shrouded in their robes and hoods, like small tepees possessed by the ghosts of lunatics, the Klansmen choose to become a color: to *not* be human. The conscience of the river is deeper and faster-flowing than theirs. As the poem progresses, Komunyakaa manages the considerable feat of teaching the reader about politics without resorting to diatribe. The Ku Klux Klan as an evil institution is remarkable mainly for what it shares with many a "mainstream" organization:

> The sacrament. A gallon
> Jug of bootleg passed from hand to hand . . .
>
>   . . . . .
>
> Bibles, icons, & old lies. Names
> Dead in their mouths like broken
> Treaties. . . .

In the poem's second stanza, describing the nonviolent resistance of the "Deacons" on the day after the Klan assembly, Komunyakaa sips the mead of troubled warriors: "a radiance / Not borrowed from the gleam / of gun barrels. . . ." Radiance, after all, has always been a great teacher. It was the study of radiance that led Copernicus to conclude that the earth was not the center of the universe. The Deacons and the other freedom marchers prove among humans what Copernicus' observations proved among the stars; and all those mythical beings—shining knights and dragons and thoroughbred whites to whom the bursting wood of burning crosses speaks—cannot get used to the idea that they no longer exist. And ghosts walk the earth.

Kevin Stein (essay date 1996)

SOURCE: "Vietnam and the Voice Within," in his *Private Poets, Worldly Acts,* Ohio University Press, 1996, pp. 90-107.

[*In the following essay on* Dien cai dau, *Stein emphasizes Komunyakaa's unique African-American perspective.*]

The haunting locale of Yusef Komunyakaa's *Dien cai dau* (1988) is as much the domain of the human heart and mind as the jungles of Southeast Asia. Based on Komunyakaa's Vietnam War experiences, the book details an inward turning, "a way of dealing with the images inside my head," as Komunyakaa tells an interviewer, a means to put in order a private history that exists as much outside of history as within it. Komunyakaa abjures the war's "objective" history that flickered in America's living rooms on the nightly news, objectivity figured most shockingly by the daily body count fulgurating behind Walter Cronkite's head like heat lightning on a steamy July evening. Instead, Komunyakaa's *Dien cai dau* operates within an essentially dialogic structure in which he carefully directs a dialogue between such communal history and the more personal accounts of those who took part in these events. As an African-American veteran, Komunyakaa exists on the margins of official war history, grouped with those Wallace Terry has called the forgotten "fact" of the war—the "Black Americans who fought there." His collection provides a perspective on the war that other fine poetry collections by Vietnam vets—John Balaban's *After Our War* and Bruce Weigl's *The Monkey Wars* come to mind as perhaps the best—simply can't offer. Komunyakaa creates a soldier's history of Vietnam from an African-American perspective, and not surprisingly, our view of what it was to be an American in Vietnam, particularly a Black American, alters considerably. Komunyakaa relies on elements of the very media we most closely associate with the war's communal experience—music, television, drama, and film—to reveal how these elements were perceived, often quite differently, by white and African-American soldiers.

Perhaps by virtue of this marginalization, Komunyakaa is acutely aware of the disparity between the history recorded in books and the history one immediately experiences. In fact, Komunyakaa's implicit recognition of the distinction between objective history and a personally felt history resembles Martin Heidegger's distinction between "Historie" and "Geschichte." For Heidegger, in his study of temporality, *Being and Time,* "Historie" is roughly what is "recorded," the course of events that chronicles the rise and fall of nations, the wars these nations prosecute, the fate of civilizations on a large scale. It amounts to a "science" of history. On the other hand, "Geschichte" has more to do with the individual's own inward and "authentic" sense of life, the way what is recorded may pale in comparison to the individual's own immediate experience of those very outward events that shape "Historie." In "Geschichte," time becomes an ontological category, the historical-being of the individual. Thus, each individual must take responsibility for his/her own life and push ahead into the "possibilities" of a future not bound to historical time. In Komunyakaa's work, these two senses of the individual's place in history are often in dialogue, for while the actual events of history possess a real presence, the speaker nearly always subordinates them to a more intuited, felt, and existential sense of what it meant (and still means) to experience the Vietnam War.

Because his quest is inward and subjective, the war's actual events frequently serve as mere backdrop for Komunyakaa's obdurate, private search for meaning. As a result, time collapses and expands within the journey as the speaker moves from past to present to a tentative future. Thus, time itself attains a kind of mutability in Komunyakaa's work, for what we assume to be past, and therefore gone, feverishly reasserts itself in the speaker's mind. The past simply will not stay put. And neither will the dead—as the speaker of **"The Dead at Quang Tri"** laments when the Buddhist boy whose head he'd rubbed "for luck" comes floating by "like a white moon" one dark night, "He won't stay dead, dammit!" Komunyakaa's goal is a careful thinking and rethinking that will simultaneously revivify such events and enable him to come to peace with them. He does so, as Heidegger believes all poets must, through the natural agent of memory, through the second "coming of what has been":

> . . . thinking holds to the
> coming of what has been, and
> is remembrance.

This amalgam of public and private history, hauntingly persistent and deeply pooled in Komunyakaa's memory, spills out in these poems in sometimes unexpected effluences. Komunyakaa says as much when, in an interview, he describes his brain as "sort of like a reservoir," containing "all the frightening images and what have you" associated with the war. Komunyakaa realizes that writing the book was an actual process of "letting go" of those images, a release of the perilous waters of memory. In the poetic process, Komunyakaa combines actual history and his own inward response to historical events, then subjects both to the filter of his artistic sensibility. What results is a different kind of history that makes use of external, historical events to produce an inward, aestheticized history flushed with personal values and interpretations. Jeffrey Walsh summarizes this

process for any veteran who attempts to present an artistic "vision of Vietnam": "the writer needs to order and recreate his own memories, and then to communicate an aesthetic 'version' of the realities he faced." Still, Komunyakaa's **_Dien cai dau_** differs considerably from earlier poetic texts devoted to the war. Because the book comes thirteen years after the war's close, its manner is more retrospective and ruminative than collections published while the war raged in Southeast Asia, volumes such as Michael Casey's *Obscenities* (1972), D. C. Berry's *saigon cemetery* (1972), and the anthology of poems by Vietnam veterans, *Winning Hearts and Minds* (1972). It is less a book "against" the Vietnam War, the claimed purpose of much poetry published during the War, and more a book *about* the War and the experiences it held for soldiers and innocents alike.

Like revenants returned from death, these ghostly images conspire in Komunyakaa's work to make the past discomfitingly present. A good example of the collapse and expansion of time in these poems is **"Starlight Scope Myopia,"** which opens with a nearly surreal memory of an ambush aided by the nightscope's deft technology of death:

> Gray-blue shadows lift
> shadows onto an oxcart.
> Making night work for us,
> the starlight scope brings
> men into killing range.

Not only does the scope make the enemy visible in the dark night of that distant past, but it also serves as the agent of their return to the speaker in the present, as the ironic use of "[m]yopia" in the title indicates. If anything, the speaker's vision is farsighted, stretching from the past to the moment of his present.

Even though the speaker tells the story in past tense, he acknowledges, later in the poem, the event's continuing presence in his life "years after" the war. In this way, the speaker alters the poem's radical of presentation, rhetorically shifting himself and his reader from the past into the present. Moreover, he calls attention to himself as speaker and storyteller, and thus breaks the willing suspension of disbelief many poems demand of their readers:

> Viet Cong
> move under our eyelids,
> lords over loneliness
> winding like coral vine through
> sandalwood & lotus
>
> inside our lowered heads
> years after this scene
>
> ends.

The distance between poet and poem and between poet and reader further collapses when the speaker suddenly begins to identify with these "shadows" and begins painfully to see them as human beings it is his job to kill. The essential dialogic structure of the poem, and of much of the book, first manifests itself here, enabling the speaker both to address his past "self" and to engage his reader in the chilling scene. In the selection quoted below, the speaker's dialogue between duty and moral humanism is expressed in his choice of the pronoun "you," which enables the speaker to distance the self who is speaking from the self who years ago experienced this incident in Vietnam. At the same time, the pronoun "you" collapses the reader's distance from the poem and entwines that reader in the scene's moral ambivalence:

> You try reading ghost talk
> on their lips. They say
>
> 'up-up we go,' lifting as one.
> This one, old, bowlegged,
>
> you feel you could reach out
> & take him into your arms. You
>
> peer down the sights of your M-16,
> seeing the full moon
> loaded on an oxcart.

If violence against combatants brings moral questions to the fore, it's no wonder that the speaker finds violence against innocents especially disturbing. In **"Re-creating the Scene,"** the speaker details the circumstances surrounding the rape of a Vietnamese woman by three American soldiers. Komunyakaa, who served as a journalist in Vietnam, uses those skills to narrate the incident with ostensibly detached, journalistic precision. This rhetorical strategy helps the reader understand that, while the speaker did not actually witness the incident firsthand, he recounts it much like a journalist whose job is to recreate "the scene" of a crime for his readers. The poem's speaker seems to understand, as must Komunyakaa, that the incident inheres with the potential for exploitative use of language as disturbing in its own way as were the government's obfuscations regarding "kill ratio," "protective reaction strikes," and "pacification." Such an understanding issues from what James Mersmann describes as the poet's "awareness that war (the ultimate insensibility and untruth) is itself an abuse of language (the ultimate vehicle of sensibility and truth), or at least an occasion for its abuse." Here, the speaker pieces together a narrative replete with careful details that enlarge the context of the incident:

> The metal door groans
> & folds shut like an ancient turtle
> that won't let go

> of a finger till it thunders.
> The Confederate flag
> flaps from a radio antenna,
> & the woman's clothes
> come apart in their hands.
> Their mouths find hers
> in the titanic darkness
> of the steel grotto,
> as she counts the names of dead
> ancestors, shielding a baby
> in her arms.

The language, though restrained and measured, strikingly contrasts the relative condition of the empowered and disempowered characters it describes. Torn from her largely agrarian society, the woman is pulled through the "metal door" of an armored vehicle representing at once the best and worst of a powerfully mechanized culture. Not only is the woman desecrated by the men's actions, but so too are her past, in the figure of the ancestors she recalls, and her future, embodied by the child she protects in her arms—all of them simultaneously wounded inside "a machine / where men are gods." One subtle but telling detail enlarges the context of the woman's fate: the "Confederate flag" that flies above the vehicle. Given that the poem's speaker, one assumes, is African-American, this one enumeration evokes the implicit racism of the incident and makes it more than a discrete, if obscene, aspect of the spoils of war. Surely the speaker recognizes in the woman's plight a version of his own struggle for respect and equality, and just as surely he sees that skin color—black, white, yellow—silently undergirds much of the politics of this war.

This one detail—the Confederate flag flapping above the rape scene—offers a trenchant and disturbing irony which belies its nearly offhand inclusion. The flag itself is an emblem of an agrarian society similarly crushed in the nineteenth century by the North's powerful military-industrial complex. That war was ostensibly fought to free the oppressed African-American slave population of the South (notwithstanding Lincoln's desire to maintain the Union). However, no sooner than the war was concluded—the slaves freed and democratic principles upheld—did trouble begin to brew in the western United States. When miners violated treaties by moving into Sioux country looking for quick wealth, the same government which had fought for the human dignity of slaves now sent soldiers to subjugate the Sioux by lethal force. The Sioux responded violently by slaughtering Captain W. J. Fetterman's contingent of eighty-two soldiers near Fort Kearny in 1866. The Sioux War (1865-67) raged in the western territories, ending with the inauguration of a new governmental policy of "small reservations" meant to segregate Indians in out-of-the-way and often desolate areas spurned by whites.

White governmental policy toward those with red skin thus stood in stark contrast to its treatment of blacks. Although Congress had approved Radical Reconstruction in an attempt to assure equality and integration for black Southerners, at the same time it sanctioned inequality and segregation for Native Americans in the West. Gen. William T. Sherman, seen by many Northerners as the savior of Southern slaves, directed a decade-long war against Plains Indians who would not meekly accept the reservation system and forego their nomadic way of life. When Kiowa, Cheyenne, Sioux, and other tribes resisted, Sherman vehemently urged General Sheridan to "prosecute the war with vindictive earnestness against all hostile Indians, till they are obliterated or beg for mercy." Numerous pitched battles ensued over the following years, including Custer's infamous "last stand" and concluding with the horrific and misnamed "Battle of Wounded Knee," where U. S. troops killed two hundred Dakota men, women, and children. As a southern black man, Komunyakaa is surely familiar with how such brutal ironies complicate the history of race relations in America. That his poem would extend these ironies to Southeast Asia is therefore not surprising.

As with **"Starlight Scope Myopia,"** time shrinks and swells in **"Re-creating the Scene,"** both for the woman whose story has been told and for the speaker who tells it. Once released from the APC, the woman turns her attention to filing a complaint, and she's momentarily filled with the promise of justice as "for a moment the world's future tense." Here too the speaker enters the poem in his position as journalist, interrupting the narrative to claim his role in the incident he's retelling, "I inform *The Overseas Weekly.*" Although he tells the story in present tense to increase the immediacy of the incident, the speaker, of course, knows the story's ending as well as he knows the previous events he's already related to his readers. Again the past-and-present-self implicitly engage in dialogue, in this instance pitting the soldier-self's belief in justice against the present-day speaker's knowledge of what has become of such innocence. At the poem's close, he conflates time as a means to emphasize this dialogue between temporal versions of the self, both his and hers, in which a difference in time demarcates the line between innocence and experience:

> on the trial's second day
> she turns into mist—
> someone says money
> changed hands,
> & someone else swears
> she's buried at LZ Gator.
> But for now, the baby
> makes a fist & grabs at the air,
> searching for a breast.

Komunyakaa's poem makes disconcertingly apparent that the

Vietnam War involved more than the all too familiar arguments about Communist expansionism that characterized America's "objective" history of the conflict. In fact, as early as 1968, political commentators such as George Liska haggled over the salient "domestic implications" of the war, asserting that the domino theory had real and pertinent influence over issues in the United States. In *War and Order: Reflections on Vietnam and History* (1968), Liska asserts that the "key" domestic issue affected by the war at that time is quite simply America's "racial" turmoil, a situation he describes as a "crisis." Liska explains at length why opposing camps of "interventionists" and "anti-interventionists" disagree vehemently on what is at stake domestically through America's foreign policy initiatives in Vietnam. He then offers this summary of the interventionist or "imperial" viewpoint, one which he shares:

> There is an interdependence between affirmation of American prestige and power vis-a-vis Hanoi and its allies and the prospect for semi-orderly integration of American society in the face of Black Power. In the last resort, whatever order exists in the United States depends on the government's known will and ability to deal firmly with hostile force. A collapse of this reputation abroad would strengthen the appeal and increase the credibility of domestic advocates of violence as a safe and profitable way to "racial equality." Any administration conspicuously threatened abroad would be bound to have the greatest difficulty in dealing with domestic crises. The consequence of default in the exercise of the imperial role might very well be a Second American Revolution for the "independence" of a hitherto "colonized" group.

Liska's *War and Order* overtly defends, as the chilling oxymoron of its title implies, a relationship between the judicious prosecution of war and the maintenance of amenable social order. If America doesn't show the Viet Cong who's boss, Liska argues, America will never squash the Black Power movement for equality at home. Perhaps the "hostile force" Liska has rightfully in mind is the Black Panthers, who sought the violent overthrow of government structures they regarded as oppressive. Still, it's not difficult to see such an argument as a means both to justify the war and to maintain the then-current distribution of power at home, or to alter it only so much as not to disrupt its imbalance. Even the phrase "semi-orderly integration" implies the kind of glacial progress toward equal rights that contributed largely to the civil unrest Liska sought to forestall. For most Americans, this interrelationship between domestic and foreign policy remained well beyond the horizon of their attention, and equally beyond the periphery of their knowledge. Many of Komunyakaa's poems, to the contrary, address these larger ideological issues and their effects on Black Americans, whom Liska sarcastically refers to above as an internally "colonized" group seeking "independence." As a result, the social situation back in the States in the late sixties insistently reappears in the text of these poems, and, as one would expect, the issue often revolves around race. True enough, these poems refuse overt racial and political anger. Alvin Aubert, in fact, regards Komunyakaa as "cautious in dealing with his ethnicity." But these poems' resolute will is the source of their rhetorical power. Komunyakaa's speaker looks his readers in the eye and does not blink. When Vicente Gotera argues, in an otherwise cogent essay, that the fact "Komunyakaa is black hardly matters in many of the poems in *Dien cai dau,*" he diminishes a substantial number of poems that gain their ability to scald and instruct from the fact of Komunyakaa's being African-American. Those poems offer a viewpoint attainable best, and perhaps only, from a source conversant with the politics of race in America.

In fact, Komunyakaa takes some of our easy assumptions about the war, oftentimes garnered from film and music, and turns them on ear. How frequently in films devoted to the war, for example, is music shown as a kind of unifying force among American soldiers? How many scenes out of a film such as *Good Morning, Vietnam,* for instance, use music as the common denominator linking our troops in a shared cultural heritage? While it's difficult to deny that music itself was a crucial part of the experience of the war, both in Vietnam and at home, notice how Komunyakaa's African-American experience illuminates incidents in the poem **"Tu Do Street"** where music is not the unifying element we might have thought it to be:

> Music divides the evening.
> I close my eyes & can see
> men drawing lines in the dust.
> America pushes through the membrane
> of mist & smoke, & I'm a small boy
> again in Bogalusa. White Only
> signs & Hank Snow. But tonight
> I walk into a place where bar girls
> fade like tropical birds. When
> I order a beer, the mama-san
> behind the counter acts as if she
> can't understand, while her eyes
> skirt each white face, as Hank Williams
> calls from the psychedelic jukebox.

In this instance, music, instead of unifying, "divides" as surely as those "lines" drawn in the dust by men behaving like schoolyard from another, and likewise dividing one country into separate and unequal parts. The irony proves to be trenchant for America, a country founded on the doctrine of equal rights to all, and especially poignant when that country has called its citizens, both black and white, to of-

fer themselves in sacrifice at war. The speaker gives the betrayal of these political and moral dogma a Biblical context:

> We have played Judas where
> only machine gun fire brings us
> together.

And lest the reader miss the careful choice of the pronoun "we" above, the speaker clarifies and broadens the culpability for such racism:

> Down the street
> black GIs hold to their turf also.

Racism is answered, not surprisingly, by racism, though it's unarguable that one of these groups holds more power to act upon this prejudice. Still, and this illustrates Komunyakaa's tenacious will and intellectual honesty, the poem does not stop here, at this ironic sense of brothers-in-arms at war amongst themselves. To his credit, Komunyakaa pushes the poem further into the darkened recesses of human relationships, discovering in the Saigon brothel neighborhood an even greater irony:

> Back in the bush at Dak To
> & Khe Sanh, we fought
> the brothers of these women
> we now run to hold in our arms.
> There's more than a nation
> inside us, as black & white
> soldiers touch the same lovers
> minutes apart, tasting
> each other's breath,
> without knowing these rooms
> run into each other like tunnels
> leading to the underworld.

In this brothel scene, hardly the most promising site for such revelations, the poem's black speaker comes to an epiphanic understanding of "shared humanity" that, for the American combatants, runs deeper than their skin color. More importantly, the speaker recognizes a common humanity whose roots cross the superficial boundaries of nations, connecting those of black, white, yellow, and, recalling Komunyakaa's **"Recreating the Scene,"** red skin. Surely the Vietnamese women these soldiers "run to hold," as well as their brothers who fight the Americans, understand what it is to be human upon this green globe and what sentence awaits each of us in death's "underworld." However, this revelation does not come without its share of ominous undertones, for the figurative "tunnels" that link these men and women in their humanity also have a literal reality in the deadly maze of tunnels the Viet Cong used to ferry supplies, to fight and quickly disappear, and into which many American soldiers ventured never to return (as "Tunnels," the book's second poem, memorably describes). Such ironies did not escape the attention of the Viet Cong, who employed every tactic available to them to undermine the morale of the American troops. Vietnam's version of Tokyo Rose is the spritely **"Hanoi Hannah,"** who, in a poem bearing her name, strives to induce homesickness among the American troops by playing their music and reminding them of women left behind:

> Ray Charles! His voice
> calls from waist-high grass,
> & we duck behind gray sandbags.
> "Hello, Soul Brothers. Yeah,
> Georgia's also on my mind". . . .
> "It's Saturday night in the States.
> Guess what your woman's doing tonight.
> I think I'll let Tina Turner
> tell you, you homesick GIs."

Hannah's tactics are predictable, as predictable as the American soldiers' reaction to them: they unleash "a white arc" of artillery fire in vain attempt to silence her. The poem might easily fall prey to cliché if it ended here, but Komunyakaa surprises his readers by presenting an account of these tactics that has, for the most part, gone unnoticed in other poetic descriptions of the war. His poems become politically charged, though always understated, as he offers a Black American's perspective on psychological warfare strategies that accentuate racial division. Here the racial undercurrents of the war produce the unpleasant, dull shock of nine-volt batteries held to the tongue, as Hannah, having used Ray Charles and Tina Turner to attract the black soldiers' attention, then spews forth her cynical punch line while lamely attempting to mimic black dialect:

> "You know you're dead men,
> don't you? You're dead
> as King today in Memphis" . . . .
> "Soul Brothers, what you dying for?"

The question, of course, preys upon African-American soldiers' ambiguous position in the war, for they know the "King" who has died in Memphis is not Elvis, as some of my culturally impaired students have suggested, but Martin Luther King, Jr., assassinated at the hands of a white man. The question also calls to mind Muhammad Ali's curt retort when asked his reasons, other than religious, for not fighting in Vietnam: "No Viet Cong ever called me *nigger.*"

Komunyakaa seizes this issue and examines it via a wide variety of media, employing television, drama, and even painting as portals to the human psyche. What's most interesting about each of these examples is the location where these events take place—inside an individual soldier's, or ex-soldier's, mind. The paradoxical effect of this existential

mode, rather surprisingly, is to interrogate the reader's own assumptions about the interplay of this war and racial politics, and its results are startling. One piece in particular, **"The One-legged Stool,"** makes clear that the Viet Cong realized the potential value of America's own latent racism and used it with terrifying results. A rambling dramatic monologue set in prose and prefaced by stage directions, the poem reads like a one-man play invoking all of the racial politics and psychological warfare tactics the book alludes to elsewhere. Forced to squat all day on a one-legged stool and "partly hallucinating," as the stage directions indicate, a black soldier bravely attempts to subvert his captors' tactics by standing up, literally and figuratively, for himself and America:

> Don't you know I'll never cooperate? No, don't care what you whisper into the darkness of this cage like it came out of my own head, I won't believe a word. Lies, lies, lies. You're lying. Those white prisoners didn't say what you say they said. They ain't laughing. Ain't cooperating. They ain't putting me down, calling me names like you say. Lies. Lies. It ain't the way you say it is. I'm American. (Pause.) Doctor King, he ain't dead like you say. Lies. . . . You didn't see that. I'm still sitting on my stool.

The piece moves at a frenetic pace, as the speaker himself lurches from reality to fantasy, from present to past, from Vietnam to home—all of it punctuated by the periodic appearance of a shadowy-faced Viet Cong at a peephole in the hut's only door. Near the breaking point, reduced to eating "dung beetles" pinched from the floor, the man repeats his name, rank, and serial number as if they are a mantra, a way to pull back so far inside of the self as to become unassailable. Defiantly, the speaker refuses to give in to the enemy's psychological manipulation, and in the end he sees it as a kind of racism even worse than that he experienced in the American South:

> Yeah, VC. I've been through Georgia. Yeah, been through 'Bama too. Mississippi, yeah. You know what? You eye me worse than those rednecks.

This sense of the perilous nature of American racial and national identity pervades the book. It appears in one form in **"Communique,"** where African-American soldiers quickly tire of the dominant culture's offering of Bob Hope's shopworn routines and the Gold Diggers' "[w]hite legs." (They wait instead for "Aretha" Franklin, who never appears.) These black soldiers "don't wanna see no Miss America," no doubt because in the sixties she was sure to be white, and even reject "Lola" Falana because she "looks awful white" to them. Elsewhere, it serves as fulcrum in **"Report from the Skull's Diorama,"** through which the poem's black GIs, back from night patrol "with five dead," confront both the reality of their loss and "red bordered / leaflets" printed with the reminder, "*VC didn't kill / Dr. Martin Luther King.*"

Balancing these expressions of ethnic isolation, several poems stitched throughout the collection insist that a shared cultural heritage does exist for the American soldier and that this heritage can bind rather than divide. A good example is **"Eyeball Television,"** in which a captured soldier, whose race is never an issue, conjures up images from American television's more or less universal popular culture, lurching from "Spike Jones" to "Marilyn Monroe" as a way to endure his fate. One show the soldier replays in his head—Robert Culp and Bill Cosby's *I Spy*—carries particular cultural significance as American television's first to feature a black co-star:

> He sits crouched in a hole
> covered with slats of bamboo,
> recalling hundreds of faces
> from *I Love Lucy, Dragnet,*
> *I Spy, & The Ed Sullivan Show.* . . .
> When he can't stop laughing
> at *Roadrunner* on Channel 6
> the sharp pain goes away.

In the same fashion, these soldiers, once removed from the battlefield, are shown to share interests that blur lines of color, age, class. In **"A Break from the Bush,"** for instance, a mixed-race platoon of men with names like "Clem," "Johnny," and "Frenchie" relax as a group on R & R. The men play volleyball together, get "high on Buddha grass," and jam to the great black guitarist Jimi Hendrix's "Purple Haze," a song which came to be regarded, among the drug culture anyway, as an anthem to LSD. Another poem, **"Seeing in the Dark,"** plays upon the serviceman's long-standing appreciation of "skin / flicks." Regardless of race, a randy mob of infantry men "just back from the boonies" gathers together to watch "washed-out images / thrown against a bed sheet." The image of the bed sheet provides a ghostly means to join two things that surely dominate these soldiers' thoughts: the poetic, figurative death found on the sex bed and the literal death had on the battlefield.

The core of this loose series and a key to its structure, as well as the clue to the existential mode of the entire book, lies in **"Jungle Surrender,"** a poem based on Don Cooper's painting of the same name. In the poem, the speaker imagines himself in the place of the captured American soldier the painting portrays, and he wonders how he would have fared under such interrogation. Would he tell them of the ambush he sprung while "plugged into the Grateful Dead"? Would he suffer and break, only to return "almost whole"? In Cooper's painting, as within the human mind, the speaker recognizes:

> Love & hate
> flesh out the real man, how he wrestles
> himself through a hallucination of blues
> & deep purples that set the day on fire.
>
> He sleep walks a labyrinth of violet,
> measuring footsteps from one tree to the next,
>
> knowing somehow we're all connected.
> What would I have said?
>
> The real interrogator is a voice within.

Yeats once said that while rhetoric involves an argument with another person, true poetry requires an argument *with*—or perhaps, *against*—the self. Throughout the book, the poem's speaker has engaged in a lively debate with the self, invoking complex issues of morality and race and politics and basic humanity. In the process, the reader, because "we're all connected" (a line which echoes the epiphany of **"Tu Do Street"**), has necessarily been drawn into this dialogue between public and private history.

The book has at its core the quest for a personal and authentically meaningful sense of history that, while acknowledging the presence of "Historie," is not burdened by it. Perhaps the book seeks a concrete instance of Heidegger's "Geschichte" that enables an African-American poet to deal with his past, accept the present, and forge ahead into the possibilities of the future opening before him. It's arguable that such a sense of history, once achieved, is actually *ahistorical,* bound more to an immediate experience of time than that provided by objective history. One final poem in *Dien cai dau* best delineates the dialogic process in Komunyakaa's work in which "Historie" and "Geschichte" come to be juxtaposed. As such, the poem serves as a good illustration of the Russian theorist M. M. Bakhtin's contention that an individual can indeed hold a "dialogic relationship" with his/her own words: ". . . dialogic relationships are also possible toward one's own utterance as a whole, toward its separate parts and toward an individual word within it, if we somehow detach ourselves from them, speak with an inner reservation, if we observe a certain distance from them, as if limiting our own authorship or dividing it in two."

In **"Facing It,"** the speaker appears to be very much in dialogue with himself, intensely divided "in two." The speaker is torn between the dialectics of power and powerlessness, racial difference and human universality. Given the context of the book, its melding of personal and collective history, it's difficult to see the speaker as anyone but Komunyakaa himself. Here, the science of recorded history confronts the poet's inward experience of "what happens," as the opening lines reveal:

My black face fades,
hiding inside the black granite.
I said I wouldn't,
dammit: No tears.
I'm stone, I'm flesh.
My clouded reflection eyes me
like a bird of prey, the profile of night
slanted against morning. I turn
this way—the stone lets me go.
I turn that way—I'm inside
the Vietnam Veterans Memorial
again, depending on the light
to make a difference.

The terms of Komunyakaa's dialectic are many and obvious: stone vs. flesh, night vs. morning, release from memory's cold cell vs. imprisonment inside the memorial which represents it. The most compelling expression of this dialogue, of course, is figured in the racial dialectic of the speaker's "black face, a "profile of night," fading and reappearing in the recurrent white "light" of "morning." It is a version of the argument which animates the book as a whole, extending beyond the mere question of race to larger and more fundamental questions of basic humanity that seek to know what we share, why, and to what end? Which ask what it means to be human and therefore intellectually capable of carrying forward a past, and yet willing to seize one's future? The poem demonstrates what the speaker of **"Jungle Surrender"** has already come to know, namely that the "real interrogator" is always the "voice within." Komunyakaa seems to understand, as does Heidegger, that our past is never truly gone until our future is complete, until the future has exhausted its endless possibilities to alter and realign the way we view the past which has led us to this present moment. That past, thus, must stay with him, ineluctably present. The book represents the poet's way of coming to terms with it, "a way of dealing with" its horrific images.

Curiously enough, **"Facing It,"** the final poem in the collection, was the first poem written for this book, and it became the "standard" by which Komunyakaa judged those that followed. It's not difficult to see why. The poem enacts the kind of transformations sought throughout the book and then coldly denies them, as when Komunyakaa touches the "name of Andrew Johnson," hoping to conjure up a vision of the man's face, his life, but instead sees only "the booby trap's white flash" of death. And later, when the names of the dead "shimmer on a woman's blouse," releasing them from the role of dead inscribed there, this release is short-lived, for "when she walks away / the names stay on the wall."

Near the poem's close, this same disenchanting pattern of promise followed by disappointment appears again:

A white vet's image floats
closer to me, then his pale eyes
look through mine. I'm a window.

These lines promise the kind of mingling and transformation that the speaker has fervently sought through the book's interior dialogues. When the white vet comes "closer," his eyes momentarily "look through" those of the black speaker, unifying their presence and value. This, an uncautious reader might conclude, is just the point of the book, its ultimate achievement. Note, though, how Komunyakaa problematizes this scene of racial unity by following it immediately with the realization, "I'm a window." Two powerfully conflicting interpretations, held in juxtapose, result: that the white vet has indeed learned to see things empathetically "through" the black speaker's eyes, or more discomfitingly, that the white vet simply "looks through" the black speaker as if he were merely a window, an inhuman object hardly worth noticing.

If the poem were to end here, mired in ambivalence, the quest would barely seem worth the trouble, either for poet or reader. The speaker's dialogue with himself, with his reader, and with "Historie" is splendidly realized in the image of the window. He looks silently backward and forward in time, both toward his reader and away. He is at once visible and invisible, colorless as glass, neither black nor white. He serves as both sign and signified of the essential dialogic structure of the book, a window to history nailed in place, immovable and unmoved, both outside and inside of its margins—all of which, of course, refuses resolution in its ambiguity, in its very muteness.

However, the poem's (and the book's) closing image reverses the usual pattern and frees the speaker from his static, nearly deathlike trance:

In the black mirror
a woman is trying to erase names:
No, she's brushing a boy's hair.

The woman's thoughtful, nurturing, thoroughly quotidian act of love closes the book on perhaps the most redemptive note imaginable for such a text. Her gesture focuses the book's ending on the future that young boy embodies, a future outside of the glass-like surface of the memorial and ahead of the faceless window the speaker has imagined himself to be. What's more, the question of whether this mother and son are black or white matters not at all. The touch of her hands is a kind of blessing, a simple but profound sacramental act enriching the lives of mother, son, and the poet who observes them. Komunyakaa's speaker comes to understand the existentialist Heidegger's concept of *"Dasein,"* the "givenness" of human existence from which we cannot stand apart and of which the fabric of our lives is spun. His speaker discovers human existence is always founded on being-in-the-world, bound up with others in the beautiful and frightening relations that constitute our very lives. "Dasein" places the individual out in the world, connects his/her being to others' being. In such a view there is no retreat, no escape into the separate realms of "subject" and "object," for these categories overlap and contain each other. Thus immutably bound up with others and the material world through which he moves, Komunyakaa closes his dialogue between private and public history. In the end, the recognition that issues from this dialogue and enables him to move resolutely forward, neither erasing the "names" of the past nor failing to seize his future, proves to be fittingly "authentic" and revivifying.

FURTHER READING

Criticism

Aubert, Alvin. "Stars and Gunbarrels." *African American Review* 28, No. 4 (Winter 1994): 671-73.

A very favorable review of Komunyakaa's *Neon Vernacular.*

Gotera, Vicente F. "Killer Imagination." *Callaloo* 13 (Spring 1990): 364.

Brief, highly favorable comments on *Dien cai dau.*

Jones, Kirkland C. "Folk Idiom in the Literary Expression of Two African American Authors: Rita Dove and Yusef Komunyakaa." In *Language and Literature in the African American Imagination,* edited by Carol Aisha Blackshire-Belay, pp. 149-65. Westport: Greenwood Press, 1992.

A comparative study of the use of colloquial language in poetic imagery.

Ringnalda, Don. "Rejecting 'Sweet Geometry': Komunyakaa's *Duende.*" *Journal of American Culture* 16, No. 3 (Fall 1993): 21-28.

Lauds Komunyakaa's war poems for speaking in a voice that avoids the "sameness and tameness" of much Vietnam war literature.

Interviews

Kelly, Robert. "Jazz and Poetry: A Conversation." *The Georgia Review* 46, No. 4 (1992): 645-61.

A conversation with Komunyakaa and William Matthews on the use of jazz rhythms and idioms in poetry.

Alex La Guma

1925-1985

(Full name Justin Alexander La Guma) South African novelist and short story writer.

INTRODUCTION

La Guma is considered a major South African writer, journalist, and anti-apartheid activist. He is best known for his short stories, novels, and essays that deal with the oppressive conditions of people of color living under the apartheid system in his native Cape Town. His stories are somewhat autobiographical and his protagonists reflect an increasingly militant stance. Although his active opposition to the South African government's racist policies sent him to prison for several years, he completed the novel *And A Threefold Cord* (1964) during his imprisonment. In 1966, he went into self-imposed exile in London, England, where he continued to work as a novelist and journalist. He has been honored for both his writings and political activism by several national governments. *In the Fog of the Season's End* (1972) is considered his finest novel. Although his works were once banned in South Africa, his readership is worldwide.

Biographical Information

Born in Cape Town, South Africa, La Guma was the son of Jimmy La Guma, president of the South African Colored People's Congress and a member of the Central Committee of the Communist party. His mother, Wilhelmina Alexander La Guma, worked in a cigarette factory. From an early age, Alex learned of the racism that segregated his country and of the poverty that most children in his neighborhood, District Six (mixed race), experienced. He attended Cape Technical College (1941-1942), but did not complete his studies because of his desire to fight fascist forces in Spain or to see combat in World War II. However, he was too young and underweight to volunteer. Instead he found jobs at a furniture factory and at the Metal Box Company. He became active in the union movement and the South African Colored People's Organization. When the Afrikaner Nationalist party won the 1948 election on the apartheid platform, he joined the Communist party. In 1954, he married Blanche Valerie Herman; they later had two sons. In 1955, he helped draw up the Freedom Charter, a declaration of rights which caught the attention of the government. He also began work at the leftist newspaper *New Age,* which provided material on the plight of black and colored South Africans for his novel *A Walk in the Night* (1962) and later fiction. In 1956, he and 155 other antiracist leaders were put on trial for treason. That same year, he published his first short story, "A

Christmas Story," in the journal *Fighting Talk.* Government legislation kept La Guma in prison (including time in solitary confinement) or under twenty-four-hour house arrest for a number of years. Yet he finished his novel *And a Threefold Cord* during this period. La Guma left South Africa for London in 1966, where he remained until 1979, working as a novelist and free-lance journalist. While in London, he completed his best-received novel *In the Fog of the Season's End.* At the time of his death in 1985, he was serving as the African National Congress representative to Cuba.

Major Works

Some of La Guma's most important short stories appear in the anthology *Quartet* (1963) and include "Nocturne," "Out of Darkness," "A Glass of Wine," and "Slipper Satin." In 1967, *A Walk in the Night* was enlarged to include "The Gladiators," "At the Portagee's," "The Lemon Orchard," "Coffee for the Road," "A Matter of Taste," "Tattoo Marks and Nails," and "Blankets." The title work of *A Walk in the Night* focuses on a Cape Town slum in District Six, the poor colored neighborhood of La Guma's childhood. La Guma explores how the apartheid system turns the protagonist Michael Adonis from a law-abiding citizen into a desperate, angry "skollie," or local thug. *And a Threefold Cord* also looks at the plight of Cape Town's poor, represented here by the Pauls family. Ma Pauls, who is pregnant, lives in the near-collapsed squalor of a "pondokkie cabin" with her husband and children during the cold of winter. Their hopelessness is deepened by family quarrels, sickness, and police raids. *The Stone Country* (1967) defines the South African prison as a "stone country" where guards and prisoners are "enforced inhabitants." George Adams, the strong, if unsuccessful, protagonist shows his fellow inmates that by demanding his rights and defying the prison guards, it is possible to oppose injustice. La Guma's critically acclaimed *In the Fog of the Season's End* tells of the South African resistance movement and the events preceding it. The protagonist Beukes is largely a portrait of La Guma, the political activist, and his other characters are based on real figures who worked with him in the resistance. Unlike his first three books, *In the Fog of the Season's End* closes with the triumphant vision of a liberated South Africa. *Time of the Butcherbird* (1979), La Guma's last published novel, is actually two major, interconnected stories and some shorter ones. The major stories build on the theme of the time of the butcherbird (a time of cleansing) and the author's belief that the time for cleansing South Africa of its negative customs has arrived. The novel relies heavily on symbolism and historical narrative instead of the immediate experiences that are characteristic of La Guma's other novels.

Critical Reception

Although La Guma's writings have been banned in South Africa, they have been well received by critics and readers worldwide. His short stories were first published in Cape Town newspapers in 1956. All but two of these were published between 1956 and 1966 while he was still living in South Africa. Robert Green praised La Guma's gift for understating the atrocious in "The Lemon Orchard" and commented on the dignity of his characters "despite hideous external pressures" in such stories as "Tattoo Marks and Nails," "A Glass of Wine," and "Nocturne." Critic Shatto Arthur Gakwandi praised *A Walk in the Night* for its "powerful impression of that rhythm of violence which characterizes South African life" and for its lack of sentimentality. *And a Threefold Cord*—a powerful statement against the cruelty of apartheid—is the least known of La Guma's works, partially because it was not reprinted until 1988. John Updike claimed *In the Fog of the Season's End* to be a social protest against the "brutal regime of apartheid" and noted that the work is reminiscent of the novels of Theodore Dreiser and Emile Zola. Leonard Kibera described the novel as La Guma's finest work and a "major achievement in African literature." It has outsold his other books and like many of his works, has been translated into twenty languages. La Guma's last novel, *Time of the Butcherbird* (1979), which relies largely on symbolism and historical narrative, was not as well received as earlier works which relate immediate experiences, although it is still widely read. Several national governments have honored La Guma for addressing the central questions of life in South Africa. He received the Afro-Asian Lotus Award for literature in 1969.

PRINCIPAL WORKS

A Walk in the Night (novella) 1962; enlarged as *A Walk in the Night, and Other Stories* (short stories) 1967
Quartet (short stories) 1963
And a Threefold Cord (novel) 1964
The Stone Country (novel) 1967
Apartheid: A Collection of Writings on South African Racism by South Africans [editor] (essays) 1971
In the Fog of the Season's End (novel) 1972
A Soviet Journey (travel) 1978
Time of the Butcherbird (novel) 1979

CRITICISM

David Rabkin (review date June 1973)

SOURCE: "La Guma and Reality in South Africa," in *Journal of Commonwealth Literature,* Vol. VIII, No. 1, June 1973, pp. 54-61.

[*In the following review, Rabkin discusses several of La Guma's works, noting the author's consistent departure from the typical structure of the novel which is especially evident in* In the Fog of the Season's End.]

La Guma is a committed opponent of the South African system of government, and his writings reflect this political stance. At the same time, they avoid the pitfalls of South African writing on the colour question, which Lewis Nkosi has accused of being 'journalistic fact parading outrageously as imaginative literature'. Nkosi considers that black South African writers have failed to satisfy the requirement of literature as a 'maker of values'. On the other hand, La Guma's novels, especially [*In the Fog of the Season's End*], would satisfy Dr. Gurr's request for 'Third World' writers who 'help us to change the world'.

A Walk in the Night is about crime, not politics. A robbery is planned, an innocent bystander is robbed and two murders are committed, one by the hero and one by the police. Yet these events are not the heart of the story, and their impact is muted, even casual. The cause of this effect is the limited subjectivity which La Guma imparts to his characters. The inhabitants of the slum live almost at the level of instinct, and their mental processes are minimal. Even Mike Adonis, the hero, is restricted to the simple emotions of anger, lust, truculence, and a dogged pride. La Guma's purpose is to enlarge our understanding, not of the characters, but of their situation. The basis of this situation is a power equation. . . . This power, to which the powerless hardly dare raise their eyes, defines the whole *locus* of the story. It is the external force from which the characters seek redemption. The form of their struggle is for the retention of their fundamental humanity, which is also the emotional centre of La Guma's writing. The characters are morally evaluated according to this minimal scale, each being tested how far he or she remains humane, in their instinctive self-defence.

The impact of the power imbalance cannot simply be resisted, however, for La Guma realizes that brutalization corrodes the moral faculties of the poor. Two distinct reactions on the part of the powerless can be noted in all his writings: that of the brutal gang leader who exerts an equivalent dominance over his fellow blacks, at once thug and lackey; and the self-assertive basically decent character, often a worker, who attempts to exercise a humane influence and preserve his residual dignity. These alternative reactions are present, though muted, in *A Walk in the Night,* in the petty crook Willie-Boy, and the hero Michael Adonis. In La Guma's later work they are more broadly drawn, as in Butcher Boy, who terrorizes the inhabitants of the prison in *The Stone Country,* and George Adams, the quiet but courageous hero of the same novel.

La Guma is unsentimental about his characters, and acknowledges that a superior quality of reaction is usually the product of superior education, or of political experience. He distinguishes consistently between those who live parasitically off the slum people, and those whose work has given them a wider conception and extended standards of comparison. These standards may be crude, as in the case of Freda, in *And a Threefold Cord,* whose job as a domestic servant provides her with a simple comparison between her life and that of her employers. For the individual character, the capacity to understand the situation enables him better to resist it.

In La Guma's novels, the characters reflect the situation of the society, enabling the reader to perceive more fully its moral dynamics. Moral action is defensive and passive, rather than active and assertive.

Although the primary function of the characters is to reflect the present reality, La Guma also employs a more symbolic approach to character. It is most clear with Joe, in *A Walk in the Night,* but can also be seen in 'Dronk 'Ria' and George Mostert in *And a Threefold Cord,* and Solly in *The Stone Country.* . . . As a representative of the earliest forebears of the Cape Coloured people, [Joe] speaks with the voice of the tribe: 'I'm your pal. A man's got a right to look after another man. Jesus, isn't we all people?' This instinctive force, which allows him to claim a right, is shown to be related, in a semi-mystical fashion, to his traditional closeness to the sea.

The white character, George Mostert, serves a similar function, in *And a Threefold Cord.* His isolation, his inability to form human relationships and his desperate clinging to an outmoded and crumbling petrol-station, is contrasted to the living warmth of the shanty-town community. George expresses the spiritual impoverishment of the whites and, schematically, their ultimate dependence on the blacks. La Guma uses this type of static character . . . to bring out the relatively unchanging aspects of the total situation which the novels illumine. In this way an historical dimension is added.

In the novels of Alex La Guma the physical setting is rigorously selected and meticulously drawn. *The Stone Country,* a loosely-knit narrative of prison life, is set in the stone and iron world of the prison, 'a small something of what they want to make the country'.

The effective creation of a physical setting is one of La Guma's characteristic technical strengths. It is one in which he remains close to the classical conceptions of the novelist's technique. Yet the function of La Guma's settings is not primarily to give verisimilitude to the moral progress of his characters. Nor is it to create . . . a 'totality of objects' through which the protagonist must struggle in order to gain an authentic sense of self. Because of the very character of the South African situation . . . , the material environment of the novels has a force and function of its own. It is thus akin to the function of place in the social novels of Dickens, where the Marshalsea, or Tom-All-Alone's, for example, exercise the moral function of major characters. The surface of slum life in an under-developed country differs from that of civil society, in being not a veneer, but the most direct expression of the quality of that life.

La Guma clearly sees the South African situation as being wholly conditioned by its social and political problems. Character is subordinated to the task of portraying the specifics of that situation, while the physical setting is so composed as to describe its material basis. Nevertheless, the function of character as the bearer of personal truth is not entirely negated; it is merely reduced, in accordance with the author's view of the situation. In his short stories, La Guma is able to give greater scope to the examination of personal experience. Even here, however, we find that political realities cannot be wholly excluded, although the balance between personal and social concerns can be varied. The substance of the story, **"A Glass of Wine"**, consists of the shy courtship of a young coloured girl by a white boy. The anguish of an adolescent relationship is thrown into relief by the drunken comments of an onlooker at the cafe where the lovers meet. The onlooker is hustled outside by his embarrassed friend, the narrator of the story, who tells him: 'You know that white boy can't marry the girl, even though he loves her. It isn't allowed.' Here La Guma is using the short story for the same ends as the novel. The point of the story is to demonstrate, in human terms, the content of the Immorality Act. The author's method is to use the typical device of the short story, the final twist which alters the context of the tale, and thus brings home the point.

In another of La Guma's stories, **"Out of Darkness"**, . . . the balance between the personal and the political is even more finely pitched. The love of a dark-skinned Coloured school teacher for a near-white girl, Cora, ends in murder.

In these and other stories, La Guma examines the more fugitive repercussions of the South African reality upon the sensibilities of those who are part of it.

The moral action of La Guma's characters has been described as essentially defensive. There is evidence, however, that the author has found this method increasingly inadequate, and in the succession of his leading characters can be traced a development towards an outright political posture. Thus, while Mike Adonis is shown in moral retreat, from the dignity of a factory worker to the questionable status of a petty criminal, Charlie Pauls, in **And a Threefold Cord,** is an occasional worker, in whom the roots of class consciousness have taken a precarious hold. . . . In this train of development can be perceived the emergence of a technical obstacle derived from the author's hardening attitude to the reality which he confronts. It has become increasingly difficult for La Guma to allow to the fictional material itself the responsibility of political statement. In this most recent work the problem has become acute.

In the Fog of the Season's End differs in many respects from La Guma's earlier work. The subject matter is directly political, an account of underground activity. . . . More ambitious in scope than the earlier novels, it centres on two main characters, an African, Elias Tekwane, and a Coloured man, called Beukes. However, in this novel, character is the exhibition of alternative responses to the political situation. The rich variety of what La Guma earlier described as 'the human salad', is replaced by a set of typical figures: the frightened middle-class Coloured person, the worker who assists the political organizers, the simple people who help out of personal friendship, and the committed politicals themselves. Personal details are largely subordinated to this scheme. Where characters are provided with a personal history, its function is to illustrate how they came to adopt their present stance. The characters are necessarily static, since the author's concern is here not with the quality of their response, but with the actions that flow from the choices they have *already made.* The novel is permeated with a sense of a new era, a post-critical phase in which, with the battle lines already drawn, the action has become mechanical. Whatever one may think of La Guma's analysis of the political situation, it is clearly not one which will readily assist the novelist's art. Unlike the earlier novels, **In the Fog of the Season's End** gains little from La Guma's profound sense of atmosphere and locale.

The decisive transition which has been made in the writing of this novel, is the move from a concern to illuminate the moral character of the society through a delineation of its effects upon its members, to an illustration of the specific actions taken by those who represent the society, and those who oppose it. The book is about the play of pure forces. Since the vision of the principal characters is the vision of the author himself, no additional insight can be gained by refraction through their eyes. Thus the heuristic functions of the novel form become redundant. The technique of documentary will serve as well, indeed better, since the artifices of fiction obscure where they do not further clarify.

The writings of Alex La Guma, therefore, show a consistent departure from the typical procedures of the novel form, being concerned rather to illuminate the moral character of

South African society, than to portray the personal and moral development of individual characters. In his latest work there appears to be a departure from the concerns best served by fiction as such. It has naturally affected the quality of the writer's artistry. Clearly a crisis has arisen in the relation between form and content.

Samuel Omo Asein (essay date March 1978)

SOURCE: "The Revolutionary Vision in Alex La Guma's Novels," in *Phylon,* Vol. XXXIX, No. 1, March, 1978, pp. 74-86.

[*In the following essay, Asein relates the assertiveness of La Guma's protagonists to his development as an activist.*]

> Step by step our people must acquire both the techniques of war and the means for fighting such a war. It is not only the advanced ones, but the entire people that must be prepared, convinced.'

"I, as a South African writer," La Guma affirmed in 1967, "am prepared to run guns and to hold up radio stations, because in South Africa that is what we are faced with, whether we are writers or whether we are common labourers." The occasion was the African-Scandinavian Writers' Conference held at Hasselby, Stockholm in February of that year. Having in 1966 gone into exile in London, it was appropriate for La Guma to seize the opportunity of an international audience to redefine his position in relation to the struggle for freedom in his South African homeland. Moreover, the conference theme—"the writer in African Society, his individuality and his social commitment"—more than justified La Guma's self-assertive comments which had been prompted by Soyinka's earlier remarks in his own paper about "Poets (who) have lately taken to gun-running and writers (who) are heard of holding up radio stations."

In making that public pronouncement, La Guma attempted to justify not only his self-assigned role as a revolutionary theorist but also, and perhaps more important, the literary ethics which underlies his own works, namely: that literature cannot be divorced from the realities of a writer's life and environment. Because of the compulsive force of the historical moment, it is, in La Guma's view, imperative that a writer should play a purposeful and vital role in the human drama of his times. From these premises he went on in his *extempore* contribution to propose a program for South African writers. It was on the basis of that program that he offered this highly restrictive definition of South African literature as that which embodies the contemporary political and social realities of apartheid as its main integrative theme:

. . . South African literature, I am prepared to say, is that literature which concerns itself with the realities of South Africa. And what are the realities of South Africa? When we sit down to write a book, I or any of my colleagues around me, we are as writers faced with the reality that 80% of the population lives below the breadline standard, we are faced with the reality that the average daily population of prisoners in South African prisons amounts to 70,000 persons. We are faced with the reality that half the non-white people who died last year were below the age of five years.

These are the realities. Even if we want to ignore these gruesome details and think in terms of culture and art in South Africa, we are faced with the fact that in South Africa today people are not allowed to develop their minds along the lines which they prefer.

If writers elsewhere in Africa do not feel the need for social commitment in their writings, for South African writers the imposition of that responsibility by the social environment is their unique literary reality. It is, indeed, the basis of the only tradition in which La Guma grew up. And in spite of the discomforts of exile, he has never expressed regrets for his actions. In fact, he considers his participation in the struggle as one of his most rewarding experiences as an individual and as a writer whose central concerns are the cause of social justice and the need to restore reason to an errant humanity. In an address which he delivered at a conference in Moscow about a year after Stockholm, La Guma explained his position in this regard:

> When I write in a book that somewhere in South Africa poor people who have no water must buy it by the bucketful from some local exploiter, then I also entertain the secret hope that when somebody reads it he will be moved to do something about those robbers who have turned my country into a material and cultural wasteland for the majority of the inhabitants. But this is already being done in South Africa, and I would be satisfied to know that I had something to do with it.

La Guma's position in relation to contemporary South African society can be explained by this strong belief in the close correspondence which ought to be maintained between literature and life, and his ardent pursuit of the cause of social justice. At the same conference in Moscow, La Guma not only reaffirmed his conviction about the functionality of literature, he also endorsed Gorky's definition of literature and its role in shaping human destiny. "Literature," Gorky had said, "is the heart of the world; . . . (it) shares the unity of the emotions, thoughts and ideas common to all men, the unity of the sacred striving of man towards happiness and freedom of the spirit, the unanimous hope for better forms of life. . . ." Not only did La Guma adopt this precept, he further contended that most writers of the Third World are in fact engaged in this humanistic pursuit. While La Guma approves of the preoccupation of some of his fellow writers with basically humanistic goals, he insists that it is not enough for the writer to merely record the events of his times; he should in addition participate actively in the struggle to liberate man and to realize that vision of a new world order which will guarantee mankind "happiness and freedom of spirit": "All writers worth their salt," La Guma pontificated, "are among the ranks of those struggling for human happiness and progress in all parts of the world." And South African writers, one might add, are no exception. Indeed, it would be hazardous to act differently by attempting to "separate literature from life, from human experience and human aspirations." It has been and still is the nature of literature to further, rather than retard, man's progress towards a better form of life; and therein lies its ultimate social value. For, as La Guma rightly asserts,

> by deepening our consciousness, (and) widening our feeling for life, it reminds us that all ideas and all actions derive from realism and experience within social realities. . . . Literature, art, culture, civilization, these are not abstract conceptions as some would imagine. They define the direction and basis of our actions at a particular time. They must therefore be understood and interpreted on their revolutionary paths as the ethos which drives man forward or retards his progress according to the dynamism of that civilization.

In spite of these persistent and somewhat platitudinous comments on the interplay of literature and life and the social responsibility of the writer, it must be stressed that La Guma is far from being an idle armchair theoretician. In fact, for close to thirty years before going into exile, La Guma was an ardent and unrelenting advocate for social justice. During that period he had his fair share of the injustices and indignities of South African public life. Born in Cape Town, the son of Jimmy La Guma, one-time President of the South African Coloured People's Congress, Alex La Guma lived through his childhood in very close contact with the politics of apartheid and the Resistance. He grew up in District Six, as one might expect, a toughened militant. He had been persecuted and victimized for his single-minded dedication to the ideals of social justice and racial equality. In 1956, along with a hundred and fifty-five others, La Guma was arrested for treason and was not released until after four years of prolonged harassment. Defying, as it were, the extreme repressive measures adopted by the authorities to crush the supposedly subversive elements in that racially segregated society, La Guma found the indomitable energy to survive the ordeal of a five-year detention and house arrest during the emergency period that followed the Sharpeville shootings. Twice, under the 90-day and 180-day regulations, La Guma was again the target of the South African Secret Service. Finally, like many others before him, he was literally hunted into exile in 1966 and now lives in London, a refugee from a troubled homeland.

This action-packed span of life is hardly separable from La Guma's works as a creative writer. As a matter of fact, his four novels to date grew directly from his experiences during the crucial decade immediately preceding his exile. This fact explains in part the functional value which he attaches to literature and the quality of engagement of his works right from his earliest short story to his latest novel, *In the Fog of the Season's End.* The short stories demonstrate La Guma's interest in the various and crucial aspects of South African life, the most central among which are: the continual struggle of blacks and coloureds alike against the crippling social laws in South Africa, the tensions which arise from interracial love, racial violence and murder, and the harrowing experiences of convicts in South Africa's overcrowded prison cells. However, it is from his novels that we get his most impressively articulated appraisal of the South African situation. They tell a long continuous story of oppression, exploitation and dehumanization of blacks by a ruthless social machine.

La Guma's appraisal of the agony of South African blacks and coloureds is well represented in two suggestively dramatic and symbolic situations in *And A Threefold Cord* and *The Stone Country,* respectively, accounts of a fly trapped in a cup, and of a prison cat sadistically chasing a mouse. In the first, we are given an insight into the gruesome struggle against the stifling, almost elemental, force of apartheid. In the second, La Guma attempts to capture the life of haunted blacks as they enact their tragic drama against the parched background of "the stone country":

> The cat was watching the mouse crouched between its paws. It lay on its belly again, breathing on the dusty-gray creature with the bright beady eyes and tiny panting jaws. The mouse had its body drawn into a ball of tensed muscles, waiting for another opening, refusing to give up hope. A clubbed paw reached out and nudged it. To the mouse it was like the charge of a rhinoceros. Pain quivered through the bunched muscles and the hide rippled, but it remained balled up, waiting with tiny, beating heart for another chance to escape the doom that waited for it with horrid patience.

> Then the cat made a mistake. It rose on all fours. Without hesitation the mouse streaked straight forward, under the long belly and out past the swishing tail. There was a vast roaring sound in its ears. It was the laughter of the onlookers.

> The cat spun round; too late. The time taken to turn by the cat gave the mouse a few seconds headway and it was off, hurtling across the square again. Something huge and shiny—it was the boot of a guard—tried to block its passage, but it swerved skillfully, and its tiny muscles worked desperately, and it headed into the shade.

> The cat was a few inches behind it, but it swerved again and then the blurred, dark hole of a drainpipe loomed somewhere to its right, seen out of the corner of the pain-wrecked eye. The mouse dodged a slashing, sabred paw by a hair's breadth, and gained the entrance to the hole.

> The paw struck again, just as the mouse dashed in, taking the slender tail, but the mouse was gone, and outside the spectators were chuckling over the disappointment of the cat as it crouched waiting at the hole.

> Inside, in the cool, familiar darkness, the mouse lay panting to regain its breath.

La Guma's main success in this passage lies in the sympathetic relationship which is established between the prison inmates and the mouse in this symbolic confrontation with the prison cat. In the tripartite relationship which is thus established, the cat becomes synonymous with South Africa's authoritarian rule, while the mouse signifies the oppressed downtrodden black and coloured community in its desperate struggle for survival. The point is clearly indicated in George Adams' reflections on the symbolic value of the event within the story:

> You were on the side of the mouse, of all the mice, George Adams thought. The little one who gets kicked in the backside all the time. You get punched and beaten like that mouse, and you had to duck and edge to avoid the claws and fangs. Even a mouse turns, someday. No, not a mouse, it's a worm that turns, okay. But he was glad the mouse had won out eventually, had managed to escape the slashing claws. You were on the side of the little animals, the weak and the timid who spent all their lives dodging and ducking.

> Well, that mouse must have been bloody punch-drunk, slap-happy, after that mauling it received. People get knocked slap-happy by life, too, and did funny things.

Whether it is the mouse or the worm that turns does not really matter; the point is that ultimately the common man will need to rise against the authority and assert his humanity and essence. George Adams' perceptive comment that "even a mouse (will turn) someday" reveals that latent revolutionary impulse in La Guma's leading characters which can be found in George Adams' defiant nobility, in Gus' and Morgan's fearsome courage in their abortive midnight escape bid in *The Stone Country,* and also in Elias' indomitable zeal in *In the Fog of the Season's End.* Even Michael Adonis' murder of Mr. Doughty in *A Walk in the Night,* as much as Charlie's instinctive but vengeful murder of the guard at the square in *And A Threefold Cord,* are manifestations in La Guma's fiction of the dormant rebelliousness which was to characterize his later creations.

In gradually building up self-assurance and a self-assertive urge in these characters, La Guma seeks to establish the basis for a radical ideological principle which is sustained in his four novels. From the probing precepts of *A Walk in the Night* to the assertive and compulsive ideological statement of *In the Fog of the Season's End,* a recognizable pattern of radical thought finally emerges. In his first novel, La Guma concerns himself primarily with the everyday reality and violent rhythm of life in District Six: racial injustice, the enigmatic nature of South African authority, the life style and human agony of the oppressed black population. In the story, Michael Adonis, a young black South African, is fired from his job in a sheet metal factory because he dares to answer back his white foreman. He goes home and, under a sudden impulse coupled with frustration, he kills Mr. Doughty, his old Irish co-tenant. His friend, Willieboy, comes in shortly afterwards and discovers the corpse of the Irishman. In trepidation, Willieboy flees from the house to avoid suspicion for the crime. Ironically, he does so in circumstances which later lend credibility to the evidence of John Abrahams, who testifies that Willieboy was in fact the killer. A hunt for Willieboy begins. In the meantime Michael Adonis, the unsuspected murderer, goes on to join Foxy's robber gang. The story ends with the two action lines brought close together as the shooting of Willieboy coincides with Adonis' admission into the gang.

The story in *And A Threefold Cord* is based on the premise that under the prevailing state of constant fear, uncertainty and insecurity such as that presented in *A Walk in the Night,* black South Africans, as well as the coloureds, can only survive the assault of apartheid by sheer force of will and collaborative efforts. "We all got to stand by each other," says old Nzuba of *And A Threefold Cord,* a novel whose main theme is the solidarity of the group; and true enough, the only member of the family who scorns this attitude turns out to be a victim of the system. In the main story itself, La Guma leads us into the heart of a black location where we watch the pathetic struggle of the Pauls family in a social setting which denies the individual a purposeful existence and a cosmic setting symbolically alienated from its human inhabitants. In their struggle with apartheid and the soggy landscape, we witness the frustration of aspirations, momentary indulgence in cheap love, and the wreckage of Dad Pauls and George Mostert. In the end, Charlie's sister is delivered of her baby; Fredda loses her two sons in a blaze but she is finally restored in the Pauls' household, which goes to prove that beyond this gloomy landscape is La Guma's land of hope and ultimate redemption. Ronnie, who scorns the ethos of communal solidarity, is arrested for the murder of his flirtatious girl-friend Maysie Myer, convicted and sent to the gallows.

In *The Stone Country,* the scene shifts from a domestic setting to a typical South African prison. La Guma focuses on the commonplace experience of South African convicts who are locked up in cells for crimes ranging from "subversion" to murder. In the course of the action, we see George Adams, a political activist and first offender, engulfed in a strange and sensitively metallic country with its disorganized sects, heterogenous community of ideas, conviction, and criminal propensities. In spite of the characteristically factious way of life of the prisoners, we are nevertheless made aware of an operative code of conduct and a certain degree of solidarity which bind the group together. In this novel also, there exists a firm statement of the revolutionary ideology which is exemplified by George Adams' grounding in Marxist egalitarian ideas.

In his fourth and latest novel, *In the Fog of the Season's End,* La Guma further schematises the theme of revolt, which is his primary concern in *The Stone Country.* In the action-packed story of *In the Fog of the Season's End,* *l'homme revolté* Elias is arrested and tortured to death in a South African prison for no other reason than his participation in the fight against apartheid and his refusal to betray the cause of the Resistance. Told in a series of flashbacks, the novel presents a grim account of the South African situation. In the story of Elias and his friend Beukes, we follow the careers of two highly dedicated leaders of an underground resistance movement whose sole aim is to topple the machinery of white oppression. In the end, the two revolutionaries are taken unawares by the Secret Police in a midnight raid on Elias' house. Beukes manages to escape with a gunshot wound on his shoulder; Elias is arrested and led away to the prison cell where he is tortured to death. Through flashbacks, we are given an insight into the social scene outside the cells. There is the omnipresent shadow of the South African Secret Police alongside the absorbing accounts of nocturnal committee meetings and various other clandestine anti-government activities which remind us too well of Adams' professional attachment to the resistance movement in *The Stone Country.* There are also gruesome accounts of strikes and demonstrations which are broken up with brutal ruthlessness by the police. One is struck by the distressing reality of the dwindling force and perpetual exposure of the freedom-fighters to the harshness of South African life. These various odds notwithstanding, Beukes and his collaborators persist in their struggle. In the end we are enabled to take a long view of things to come as we stand beside Beukes on the threshold of a new dawn. The crackdown on the underground force, La Guma indicates, is a temporary setback. For although a disastrous blow has been struck at the backbone of the resistance, there is a strong indication that the task force will re-group and continue its fight against apartheid.

In the formulation of this militant ideological principle, La Guma presents four major protagonists whose performances reflect in a progressive order the changing phases of his own experiences and opinions as an activist: Michael Adonis, the evasive oppressed worker with his limited horizon of ideas; Charlie Pauls, the struggling and psychically battered product of the South African situation, striving towards political awareness; George Adams, the underground militant, politically motivated and extremely courageous in the firmness with which he bears the burden of a communal reformist cause; and the arch-militant Elias whose politically mature mind and clear-headedness endear him to us even after his death in the hands of South African prison guards.

There is an underlying ideological view which provides a link among these novels, that religion cannot solve the problem which faces the blacks in South Africa, nor will it alleviate the plight of the poor dispossessed members of that community. The first clear statement of that view comes after an elaborate account of the daily struggles of black South Africans against stringent racial laws in *A Walk in the Night.* Significantly, in *And A Threefold Cord,* Charlie Pauls dissociates himself from his mother's naive reliance on capricious Fate: "Ma read the Bible every night. It don't make the poor old toppy any better." He identifies, instead, with the more pragmatic egalitarian view of his colleague who helped him to gain the revolutionary insight which he builds upon later in the novel:

> "There was a burg working with us on the pipe. When we was laying pipe up by Calvinia. Know what he say? Always reading newspapers and things. He said to us, the poor don't have to be poor. . . . This burg say, if the poor people all got together and took everything in the whole blerry world, there wouldn't be poor no more. Funny kind of talk, but it sounded all right," Charlie said. He continued warming up: "Further, this rooker say if all the stuff in the world was shared out among everybody, all would have enough to live nice. He reckoned people got to stick together to get this stuff."

Later in the novel, Charlie recalls the insightful comments of one of his fellow workers, once again on the formidable power of solidarity among an oppressed and struggling people:

> "There was this other *rooker* I worked with when we was laying pipe up country. A *slim* burg, I reckon. A clever fellow. Always saying funny things. He said something one time, about people most of the time takes trouble hardest when they alone. I don't know how it fit here, hey. I don't understand it real right, you see. But this burg had a lot of good things in his head, I reckon. . . . Like he say, people can't stand up to the world alone, they got to be together. I-reckon may be he was right. A *slim juba.* May be it was like that with Ronny-boy. Ronald didn't ever want nobody to he'p him. Wanted to do things alone. Never was a part of us. I don't know. May be like Uncle Ben, too. Is not natural for people to be alone. Hell, I reckon people was just *made* to be together. I." Words failed him again, and he shook his head, frowning.

By the time we come to **The Stone Country** La Guma's groping protagonists have found a foothold in Marxist ideological principles. There is neither the apolitical, evasive introvert of *A Walk in the Night* nor the meditative and ideologically immature Charlie of *And A Threefold Cord,* whose only source of intellectual nourishment is the incidental "facktry" asides of his fellow workers. A new man of action emerges in George Adams, a communist underground worker who dares to talk back at white prison guards. In the story, George Adams is arrested and cast into the bare wasteland of a South African prison community where he is utterly bewildered by its grotesque pattern of life. Initially, we are told, he felt "like an immigrant in a strange country, ignorant of the habits and customs of its violent people."

In this "stone country," he meets other victims of apartheid. They include: the jocular Solly, the wiry and violent Joseph the Turk, who subdues the prison bully, Butcherboy Williams, in a gruesome fight, and the crack, reticent, enigmatic Casbah kid, "wrapped up in his own personal armour of silence, hiding his secret thoughts under invisible layers of dispassionate blankness," but with whom Adams' human sympathies are ultimately reconciled. These characters represent various forms of defiant arrogance and the "solidarity of the underworld." Through the relationship which exists between George Adams and the Casbah Kid, we get to know the latter's ideas and La Guma's attempt to organize these ideas into a coherent ideological statement. Their first major encounter reveals the Casbah Kid's indifference to the racial struggle as well as his resignation to the situation in South Africa, both attitudes deriving essentially from his own experiences and family background, as the following dialogue clearly illustrates:

> George Adams looked at him, and then asked softly:
>
> "Don't it worry you, old son?"
>
> "Whetter?"
>
> "I don't mean about heaven and hell. But . . . but . . . " He did not want to say it. "If they . . . "
>
> The Casbah Kid said, "Like if they give me the rope?"
>
> "Well, ja, ma."
>
> "Crack. Look, mister, you going to die some day, don't I say? We all got to die. Hear me, mister, I put a knife in a *juba*. He went dead. Is put out, like. Everybody got his life and death put on, reckon and think." He bit at a finger-nail and looked at it. "Like me and you, and . . . and that basket, Butcherboy."
>
> "Put out?" George Adams asked. "You reckon so? Man, if our life was laid out for us before hand, what use would it be for us to work to change things, hey?"
>
> "Right, mister. You can't change things, *mos*" He chewed the cuticle of thumb.
>
> "But hear me, chommy. People's trying to change things all the time."
>
> "*Ja*. So what do they get? Crack."

Later in the novel we notice a shift in the position taken by the Casbah Kid as his response to the reformist hopes of George Adams becomes increasingly more sensitive. In fact, the ideological barrier, which had hitherto separated the two, begins to crumble. At this time we see La Guma attempting to resolve the conflict between the Casbah Kid's deterministic world order and the revolutionary pragmatism of George Adams, with whom we more readily identify.

> "You's funny people, mister." The child-face with the ancient, bitter eyes, frowned. "Hear me, mister. All this stuff about our people getting into the government, too. You reckon it will help people like us? People in prison, like?"
>
> George Adams said to this strange boy who was also a murderer: "There will certainly be more sympathy, I reckon."

> "You reckon that time will come?"
>
> George Adams said, feeling sad: "You'll see."

And, of course, it is this understanding and consequent affiliation of the aspirations of the two characters which makes their intimacy the more touching.

Although there is the promise of a new dawn, we are too well aware that the Casbah Kid will not live to witness it and that George Adams himself may not participate in that great ritual which he envisions. In spite of the pervasively bleak and parched landscape which La Guma depicts in this novel, he manages to leave an escape route from this sombre enclosure. Adams' relationship with the condemned Kid and the pathos of the scene of separation mark the triumph of those who have chosen to live by standards other than those dictated by apartheid. In these final moments the stature of the Casbah Kid is amplified, and with dignified solemnity he goes through the rites of separation from the only inmate who has had a fairly intimate knowledge of him:

> George Adams saw the boy come up. The guard made no move to stop him, and George Adams saw him on the other side of the wire screen. Fingers with bitten nails touched the screen, and for an infinitesimal instant there was a flicker of light in the cold, grey eyes, like a spark of faulty electricity. The bitter mouth cracked slightly into one of its rare grins.

> "So long, mister," The Casbah Kid said.
> George Adams nodded, he said, "So long, mate."

In order to win ultimate victory the revolutionary, I presume, must demonstrate a complete dedication to the cause, and above all a clear understanding and acceptance of the consequences of his actions. Elias, in *In the Fog of the Season's End* demonstrates these traits. Not only do we find in him a clear indication of his awareness of the full implications of his subversive acts, there is evidence of his anxiety to ensure that the cause is in no way compromised. The scene at the police station after his arrest provides a good example of his steadfast pursuit of the cause of social justice:

> "Now, we know that you (Elias) are in charge of a section in these parts. You are in touch with others, like that fellow who got away. But we will soon have him too. I want you to tell me who that other one is, his name, where he lives, et cetera. Everything. I want you to tell us the names of who work with you, where you meet, and so on. Who is your contact with the central committee or the high command—is that what you call it? If you speak now, you will be okay, you will save yourself a lot of

trouble. If you don't talk now, you will later on, but then all the trouble you go through, and the damage, will have been for nothing. You know we need not bring you to court; we can hold you indefinitely, merely on suspicion."

The small blue eyes scanned the prisoner like the points of surgical flashlights, bright and without expression. The prisoner smiled a little and said: "But if, as you say, we are wrong and only making trouble, and that nobody believes us, why are you so concerned with us?"

The sportsman shouted angrily; "We don't want to hear that nonsense. Just tell the Major what he wants to know."

The prisoner ignored him and said to the Major, "You want me to co-operate. You have shot my people when they have protested against unjust treatment; you have torn people from their homes, imprisoned them, not for stealing or murder, but for not having your permission to live. Our children live in rags and die of hunger. And you want me to co-operate with you? It is impossible."

Here is a bold confrontation with authority, and Elias' protest against the outrageous excesses of the South African police stuns his erstwhile liberal conscience. We are immediately reminded of a similar incident in *The Stone Country* involving George Adams and the law agents. After the encounter, we are told, Elias had a traumatic experience of pain and was unusually exalted for the simple reason that he could look the law straight in the face and defy inscrutable authority: "There was a dryness in his throat and he was surprised at himself for being able to say these words so directly to the man behind the desk. His cheek burned where the skin had been scraped off; he felt harassed, lonely, hunted, but he carried with him a sense of great injustice and desperate pride." This is a fine example of that resolve on the part of some of La Guma's heroes, especially the later ones, to assume full responsibility for their actions. There is not even the slightest indication of remorsefulness in George Adams after his arrest.

> (He) did not have any regrets about his arrest. You did what you decided was the right thing, and then accepted the consequences. He had gone to meetings and had listened to speeches, had read a little, and had come to the conclusion that what had been said was right. He thought, falling into dreamless sleep, There's a limit to being kicked in the backside . . .

Similarly, even when Elias knows the terrible ordeal that awaits him in the prison cell, he does not succumb to remorse or despair. Indeed, it is his past experiences with the police which help to rekindle his anguish and dedication to his cause. "He had no regrets, and knew that he would have done everything over again, given the opportunity." This is a state of mind which Michael Adonis wishes to attain, but cannot, after the murder of the Irishman because it takes a clear perception of events in their proper political context to arrive at the position of a George Adams in *The Stone Country* or Beukes and Elias in *In the Fog of the Season's End*. The revolutionary always has in view a terrain which promises hope and ultimate liberation from the scorge of the oppressor. But it is a fight which demands group cooperation. In other words, he must be able to, or at least attempt to, reach out to the masses and make his message register in their minds as he waves his banner for freedom.

He read the hand bill. "We bring a message . . . you will wonder that men and women would risk long terms of imprisonment to bring you this message. What kind of people do these things? The answer is simple. They are ordinary people who want freedom in this country. . . . From underground we launched the new fighting corps . . . sent youth abroad to train as people's soldiers, technicians, administrators. . . . We will fight back. . . . To men who are oppressed freedom means many things. . . . Give us back our country to rule for ourselves as we choose. . . . Many ways to fight for freedom."

After the crackdown by the secret police, Elias remains undaunted. He is convinced that there is an urgent need to alter their strategy and to rededicate themselves to the cause:

> "Well, we have started," Elias said, "We are beginning to recover from earlier setbacks. Step by step our people must acquire both the techniques of war and the means for fighting such a war. It is not only the advanced ones, but the entire people that must be prepared, convinced."
>
> He sucked at his pipe and the smell of tobacco deadened the paraffin fumes.
>
> "Anyway, on Monday they must be off, Peter, Paul and Michael. Here is part of our work to convince the people."

In the end, Beukes comes in the manner of an epilogue to make the final pronouncement of the underlying combative spirit of the resistance movement. We have witnessed the end of a brief skirmish; the force is routed but still the fight continues as another advance party of liberationists prepare to launch a counter-attack against apartheid:

> Beukes stood by the side of the street in early morning and thought, they have gone to war in the name of a suffering people. What the enemy himself has created, these will become battle grounds, and what we see now is only the tip of an iceberg of resentment against an ignoble regime, the tortured victims of hatred and humiliation. And those who persist in hatred and humiliation must prepare. Let them prepare hard and fast—they do not have long to wait.

The earlier novels prepare us for this proclamation. In the gradual formulation of a revolutionary strategy, emphasis is placed on violent confrontation as a means of neutralizing the force of the secret police and the establishment, and also of guaranteeing ultimate recognition of the essence of blacks in South Africa. The pervasive note then in La Guma's novels is not that of despair and flight into a protective world of political negativism, but that of hope in the eventual overthrow of the oppressive regime in South Africa.

Robert Green (review date Spring 1981)

SOURCE: "Chopin in the Ghetto: The Short Stories of Alex La Guma," in *World Literature Written in English,* Vol. 20, No. 1, Spring 1981, pp. 5-16.

[*In the following review of La Guma's short stories, Green lauds the author's depictions of everyday violence against blacks in South Africa, asserting that the portrayals "show the dark without sensationalism, the bright without sentimentality.*]

A gang of burglars is planning a robbery in a pub in District Six, Cape Town. One of them, Harry, is captivated by the music coming from a nearby house, in particular by a Chopin nocturne, and he goes to listen for a while before rejoining his criminal colleagues. He is momentarily touched by Chopin, but not reformed; the music overpowers him, but ordinary life, crime as an escape from poverty and racial discrimination, soon reasserts itself.

This episode from one of the short stories of Alex La Guma, the coloured South African writer now in exile in London, illustrates the two most common themes in his stories: the brutalizing effect of apartheid and of poverty on people and places, and man's ability to survive the resulting impoverishment and indeed to erect some monument, however slight or evanescent, to his stamina. Thus in **"Nocturne"** the world of the pub and streets is demeaning, crippling and corrupt-

ing, yet at the same time, a young girl is there playing beautiful, dignified music. This combination of brutality and humanity might seem incompatible in some writers, but it causes no tension in La Guma's stories. The pessimist, determinist or Social Darwinist might claim that environment is all powerful, bending and fracturing the naked individual. The optimist or idealist, on the other hand, might assert that human nature is capable of rising above all onslaughts upon its integrity. As a humane socialist—he was a member of the Communist party until it was banned in 1950—La Guma provides a third account of the relations between the individual and a harsh, totalitarian world. In La Guma's stories such relations are, in effect, dialectical: the noxious power of the environment is rendered in full, unsparing detail, yet within the crevices of that cruel world love, charity, affection and humanity still bloom. Like Bruno Bettelheim, another writer uncrushed by genocide, La Guma believes in man's power of "surviving" in the "abyss." As a result of their intermingling of defeat and resistance, horrors inflicted and victories won, La Guma's stories show the dark without sensationalism, the bright without sentimentality. The convent girl playing the Chopin nocturne in the ghetto wins our credence because the bleak surroundings are so fully drawn; yet the latter's power is acknowledged when the burglar forsakes the girl's music to return to his friends in the pub.

The final effect of **"Nocturne"** is a delicate equilibrium between culture and crime, decency and depravity. The sordid streets are drawn briefly and economically:

> Drab and haunted-looking people sat in doorways looking like scarred saints among the ruins of abandoned churches, half listening, gossiping idly, while the pinched children shot at each other with wooden guns from behind over-flowing dustbins in the dusk.

At the same time the young girl playing her piano is an entirely believable creation. La Guma's choice of music to stand for the survival of culture within such poverty is itself of interest, for no music could perhaps be less "relevant" than a nocturne from the world of nineteenth-century European romanticism. Other voices have lately been arguing that European culture is of limited utility in Africa; La Guma's story implies that exploited people can find human sustenance in very unlikely places. There is no trace of betrayal or dilettantism in the young pianist's choosing to play European rather than South African music. Her rendering of Liszt, Tchaikowsky, Beethoven and Schubert is quite simply and unironically a monument to her ability to transcend her surroundings.

Like **"A Glass of Wine"** and **"Out of Darkness," "Nocturne"** indicates that La Guma is not afraid of approaching sentimentality. In **"Nocturne"** he avoids this through the ending, in which the burglar pulls himself away from the music to rejoin his mates, and in the materialistic comment given Harry in the final sentence. Walking down the street with his associates, "he thought, sentimentally, that it would be real smart to have a goose [girl] that played the piano like that." In one sense "sentimentally" is the right word here, for Harry's notion is unreal, impractical. Yet, paradoxically, the effect of this last sentence is in fact to jerk the whole story away from sentimentality, since the episode between Harry and the girl is now seen clearly for what it is—an intermission, a relaxation from the world of petty crime. The word "sentimentally," then, only serves to confirm that this indeed is not the emotion generated by **"Nocturne."**

This story is told by a spectator uninvolved in the action, and its only flaw is one brief, unnecessary and clumsy intervention: "It was the Nocturne No. 2, in E flat major, by Chopin, but Harry did not know that." Perhaps we don't need to be told that a man who cannot pronounce "nocturne" would be unable to identify the piece the girl is playing. This awkward authorial intervention—found occasionally, too, in Hardy's fiction—is rare in La Guma, for one of his strengths is the displacement of himself from the text, the selfless management of the narrator's persona, the creation of an authentic voice for each story. Thus **"The Gladiators"** is narrated by one of a coloured boxer's "seconds," and the language of the first few sentences establishes the persona of that tough, uneducated man:

> You know mos how it feel when you waiting for your boy to go in and you don't know how he's going to come out. Well, we was feeling the same way that night. We had the bandages on and wait around for the preliminaries to make finish, smoking nervous like and looking at Kenny. He just sit on the table with his legs hanging down, waiting like us, but not nervous like, only full up to his ears with his brag. He's a good juba awright.

The shady, sadistic world of professional boxing is authenticated by the voice of the narrator, his sporting idioms and grammatical errors.

Though this environment is perhaps almost as rough as the prison of **"Out of Darkness,"** the latter story is narrated by a quite different personality—an educated man, sensitive, alert to nuance and others' feelings, perhaps a political prisoner like George Adams of *The Stone Country:*

> I could make out the dim shapeless bulge of his body curled up on the mat. He had entered the seventh year of his ten-year sentence for culpable homicide, and being shut up so long had unhinged him somewhat. He was neither staring mad nor violent. His insanity was of a gentle quality that came in

spells. It was then that he would talk. Otherwise he was clamped up tight and retired, like a snail withdrawn into its shell. He was friendly enough, but it was the friendliness of a man on the other side of a peephole.

The narrator's early description here of one of his fellow prisoners, Old Cockroach, evinces a sensitivity to feeling and environment not possessed by the earthy narrator of the boxing story. The narrator becomes curious about the older man and the story is climaxed by Old Cockroach's revelatory account of his enduring love for the worthless Cora. This story again is constructed around the contrast between the brutality of prison life and the survival of a gentle, idealistic, hopeless passion. The nameless narrator refrains from offering any kind of cynical comment on Old Cockroach's misdirected love, and his respectful, sensitive narration is further proof of man's ability to retain his decency despite all the external pressures in the prison.

Many years earlier Cora, a coloured girl light enough to pass as white, had rejected the adopting schoolmaster, who then killed a man who had criticized Cora as "a damn play-white bitch." **"Out of Darkness,"** the title of this story, alludes to Cora's passage from the coloured to the white world. Like Morris in Athol Fugard's *The Blood-Knot,* Cora is fatally drawn, as a moth at night, towards the "light" of white society. The tragedy of this story, the schoolmaster's killing of Cora's critic, is generated by the tensions implicit in a racially divided country, for Cora's rejection of her lover had been motivated solely by the higher social and economic status attached to membership of white society. Many of La Guma's stories are similarly built around the human losses that attend apartheid, for, although this word is nowhere mentioned in his fiction, racial segregation is its keystone, determining all human responses in patterns of limitation, restriction, impoverishment and frustration. Man's separation from man on grounds of pigmentation alone is as central to La Guma's fictional world as is, say, the class stratification in Jane Austen. Furthermore, if apartheid determines human behaviour in these stories, it is also a shaping, controlling force on their form. In **"A Glass of Wine,"** for instance, a white boy is in love with a coloured shebeen-girl, their relationship virginal and innocent despite its sordid setting. An intoxicated customer teases the two lovers about their approaching wedding, too drunk or too insensitive to perceive the impossibility of the white boy's marrying the coloured girl. The story ends abruptly, as their love must, the conclusion reflecting the inability of the young lovers to marry and raise a family "across the colour bar." The story cannot proceed because the lovers' relationship, too, is terminal. The fondness of black South African writers for the short-story form has been linked with the physical pressures on the writer himself, but the form of **"A Glass of Wine"** suggests that there is also a powerful analogy between the ellipses and discontinuities of the short-story form and the disruptions imposed by apartheid. **"A Glass of Wine"** must be a short story because the story of the two young people can only, in the context of the Immorality Act, be short.

There is a powerful impression of inevitability, too, in **"Coffee for the Road,"** in which an Indian woman, rich and sophisticated, strikes a crude white cafe owner before continuing with her car journey towards Cape Town. Under the petty restrictions of apartheid, the woman is unable to stop for rest or refreshment; tired and harassed by her children, she loses patience with the cafe owner's refusal to refill her thermos. At the inevitable road-block which awaits them the Indian driver and her children are turned back and escorted for trial. Again, as in **"A Glass of Wine,"** the story cannot continue past the police check. La Guma is careful to generate no trace of suspense in the remaining few paragraphs, the decelerating rhythm of the story being powerfully suggestive of the inevitability of arrest.

Similarly, several other stories deal with aspects of apartheid's effect on private life in South Africa. In **"Slipper Satin"** Myra, a coloured girl, has just been released from a jail sentence under the Immorality Act. Her white lover had committed suicide upon their discovery by the police. (This story indicates the potentially tragic outcome of the situation sketched in **"A Glass of Wine."**) Her home and neighbourhood appear unchanged but Myra herself has altered, having become harder, tougher, coarser as a result of her stay in prison:

> The bitterness inside her [was] like a new part of her being. She had finished with crying, and crying had left the bitterness behind her like the layer of salt found in a pan after the water had evaporated.

The female neighbours and Myra's own mother, accepting the definitions implied by racist laws, call the girl, whose only crime has been to love the wrong man, a "whore." Myra's sister requires eight guineas for a new wedding dress, and Myra promises to raise this money through, it is implied, prostitution. **"Slipper Satin,"** then, shows how a person's whole personality can be changed by the experience of arrest and imprisonment. In this story the environment has succeeded in shaping an individual into a quite new mould. The effect of the Immorality Act has been to transform a decent girl into a potential whore. The irony of this transformation is both mordant and implicit.

Racism is equally deforming in **"The Gladiators,"** in which the coloured boxer, Kenny, who was "sorry he wasn't white and glad he wasn't black," is so contemptuous of his black opponent that in a few moments of overconfidence he al-

lows himself to lose the fight. Once more an individual's racist perceptions, his acceptance of the state's stratification of value by colour, pervert his natural reactions. La Guma is indeed honest enough to accept that some coloured people effectively support the very system that decrees their inferiority. The attractions of whiteness are too strong for Kenny here, as for Cora in **"Out of Darkness."** The final irony is that the crowd at the boxing hall don't care who wins, black or coloured, so long as they see blood spilled.

"A Matter of Taste" is a metaphor about freedom in South Africa. A white man, assisted by a couple of coloured railway workers, jumps a goods train bound for Cape Town, where he hopes to secure his passage to the United States. The white, though dirty and ragged, is able to leave South Africa; the two coloureds are left behind on the embankment. Earlier, discussing the kind of food they liked, the white had claimed this was all "a matter of taste," to which one of the coloured men replied that what one ate was rather "a matter of money." The story's dénouement, the white's departure into the night, only confirms the coloured's view that human behaviour is limited by economic pressures. The two coloured workers don't choose to remain as labourers in South Africa; their poverty imposes this life upon them, and this limitation is, in its turn, the consequence of racist laws about employment, education and trade unionism in South Africa. In this story, as in all La Guma's fiction, the balance between racio-economic determinism and individual resistance, between victimization and survival, has swung away from the individual's power of assertion. The long powerful goods train to which the white leaps seems to embody the monstrous juggernaut of apartheid, thundering through the night, hospitable to the white's ambition but deaf to any black aspirations.

"At The Portagee's," a slighter story, makes a similarly deterministic point: two boys able to afford to buy soft drinks and feed the jukebox can stay in the restaurant as long as they wish; a poor man who merely wants sixpennyworth of fish is kicked out of the cafe. The violence meted out here to a man whose only crime is poverty is indeed endemic to most of La Guma's fiction, Key scenes in his novels—the human bonfire at the end of **And a Threefold Cord,** the internecine brutality of **The Stone Country,** the torturing of Elias, the political prisoner of **In the Fog of the Seasons' End**—describe murder and physical confrontation. However there is no evidence that such scenes are included by La Guma from base, sensationalist motives; no savouring, such as is evident in Western pulp fiction or in lesser Kenyan novelists, Mangua and Ruheni for instance, of violence for its own sake. The sobriety of La Guma's fiction attests, rather, to the fearful ordinariness of brutality in South Africa, whether that licensed by the state or the kind that erupts spontaneously from frustration and impotence.

"The Lemon Orchard" is a good illustration of La Guma's partiality towards the understatement of the harsh and the atrocious. Here a vigilante group of rich Afrikaner farmers is frog-marching a coloured school teacher to an isolated location in order to *sjambok* him for his "impudence" to two pillars of the white community. The racist contempt of the farmers for the educated coloured man is well conveyed, but the story stops short of the beating itself, ending when the group reaches the rural "amphitheatre" selected for the assault. La Guma chooses not to describe the increasing blows of the *sjambok* or the psychological humiliation borne by the cultured, sensitive teacher. Instead, he emphasizes the beauties of the landscape, the bracing winter air and the perfume of the lemon bushes. **"The Lemon Orchard"** is the only evocation in La Guma's fiction of a rural setting:

> They had come into a wide gap in the orchard, a small amphitheatre surrounded by fragrant growth, and they all stopped within it. The moonlight clung for a while to the leaves and the angled branches, so that along their tips and edges the moisture gleamed with the quivering shine of scattered quicksilver.

This, the final paragraph, illustrates the basic dislocation within the story, and indeed within South Africa itself: the contrast between a magnificent physical environment and the bestiality of the inhabitants.

Shortly before this paragraph La Guma had accorded the night an immense organic presence:

> The blackness of the night crouched over the orchard and the leaves rustled with a harsh whispering that was inconsistent with the pleasant scent of the lemon.

The crouching night, like a leopard about to spring, may evoke the celebrated passage in Book I of *The Prelude* (1805/1806), where Wordsworth recalls the awesome physical presence of Black Crag, a peak overlooking Ullswater, and its effect on the young rower. The lemon orchard has something of the magisterial power of Wordsworth's lakeland landscape, but La Guma uses this not as a romantic embodiment of the power of nature, but as an implicit commentary upon the tawdriness of the human beings who besmirch the grove. The criticism of Afrikaner racism is thus implicit, the irony achieved by the disjunction felt between the romantic imagery and the human squalor.

A similar implicit, understated irony is at work in another story, **"Blankets."** Here Choker has been wounded in a fight and is being transported to hospital in a non-white ambulance. He is unconscious but the "thick and new and warm" ambulance blanket evokes in him images of earlier scenes

in his life—his first day in prison, childhood with his elder brother, married life with his wife. All these brief memories merge imperceptibly into each other, but are linked by the sensuous impression of the blanket that is a part of each image. The ambulance blanket—Choker's last, since the story implies that he is mortally wounded—is, ironically, the cleanest and warmest, for all the earlier blankets, in childhood, prison and at home, had been dirty and thin. Such is the degradation of Choker's life that even the facilities provided in the segregated ambulance are superior to those experienced before. In its manipulation of the chronology of Choker's memory and its mordant, buried irony **"Blankets"** is one of the most effective of La Guma's stories.

Most of these stories are spare, just a few pages long, their brevity contributing to their power. The writer himself never enters into the stories to inveigh directly against apartheid. Instead he allows his invented characters and episodes in the bars, prisons and homes of South Africa to speak for him. **"A Walk in the Night,"** the longest story in the volume of that title, is unique as La Guma's only attempt at the novella. A fiction that is, in a sense, an amalgam of the short story and the more leisurely novel, **"A Walk in the Night"** raises certain problems of interpretation. The short stories, on the one hand, are not difficult to read, for their form permits La Guma, if he wishes, to leave an ending open—as, for example, in **"Tattoo Marks and Nails,"** in which the identity of Ahmed's tattoo remains unresolved, or in **"Blankets,"** where the point of the story is unaffected by the reader's ignorance of whether Choker lives or dies. La Guma's three novels, on the other hand, arouse quite different expectations: that the fiction will embrace some kind of resolution and completeness, tying up all the loose ends and clarifying relationships established across the spokes of the text. Hence in *The Fog* the development of the narrative finally links the two characters, Elias and Beukes, who at the outset had appeared disconnected. **"A Walk in the Night"** is more difficult to read than either the stories or the novels, because it doesn't quite satisfy either of the reader's two expectations—for brevity and the episodic, or for amplitude and coherence. It is worth examining this in more detail, for the problem of how it is to be read is central to the achieved meaning of **"A Walk in the Night."**

At the beginning **"A Walk"** implies that Michael Adonis is its hero, situated in the same dominant place in the text as Adams in *The Stone Country* or Beukes in *The Fog*. The novella's first five sections—there are nineteen altogether—narrate the movements of Adonis soon after he has been dismissed from a sheet-metal factory for cheek to the white foreman. His "feeling of rage, frustration and violence, swelled like a boil, knotted with pain," is powerfully conveyed and the reader's initial expectation is that the novella will attend to the development of this emotion until it is finally released at the end. The three criminals Adonis meets in the restaurant (section 1) are looking out for someone to make up a foursome in that night's robbery, and La Guma invites the reader to believe that the novella may well be concerned with this crime as its dénouement, as a catharsis for Adonis' legitimate anger and as the fiction's point of conclusion. Adonis' accidental killing of Doughty, the alcoholic Irish actor (section 4) provides, apparently, a digression to what the reader assumes at this point will be the central narrative line, the relationship between Adonis and the three burglars. These early sections, then, suggest that **"A Walk in the Night"** will tell a story of which Adonis will be the hero. The epigraph, from *Hamlet,* confirms such an expectation, linking, as it does, Adonis with the Ghost and hinting that the "foul crimes," his unjust dismissal from the factory, will be "burnt and purged away." The *Hamlet* quotation, so prominently displayed at the beginning of the text, implies that La Guma's story, too, will be an individual tragedy.

The progress of the narrative, though, frustrates this expectation, for it turns out that **"A Walk in the Night"** is more concerned with Denmark than with Hamlet; that the story is focussed on the community of District Six—itinerant white policemen, stranded white flotsam, struggling coloureds, streets, shops and apartments—than on any single individual. From section 6 onwards the primacy of Adonis in the story withers and the text becomes less and less centripetal, seemingly fragmented into a series of unrelated cameos, a group of embryonic short stories bereft of the centralizing narrative thrust of a novel. The formal principles of its construction seem less and less obvious as the novella proceeds.

This fragmentation of the narrative begins in section 6, with the sudden shift from Adonis to the white policemen cruising around District Six in their patrol car. Of the following twelve sections (7 to 18), five are narrated from Willieboy's point of view, one through Franky Lorenzo, three more through the white policemen, and only three (10, 13 and 15) from Adonis' point of view. The latter, the assumed hero of the first five sections, has been relegated to the status of simply being another stone in the mosaic, one of the many characters of all races whose lives momentarily touch one evening in Cape Town's District Six. By the end of **"A Walk in the Night"** the reader sees that the novella is about a community, the people of one particular place, more than about any single individual. This is confirmed in the final phase, section 19, which tersely summarizes the activities of the various characters after the death of Willieboy, shot for a murder he has not committed. Adonis, it is true, appears briefly in this section, when he and the gangsters set off for the break-in, but our earlier anticipation that La Guma will indicate the outcome of the robbery remains unsatisfied.

Most of La Guma's short stories are driven, as we have seen, by the narrative impulse to tell a story. Most end at a point

different from where they begin yet anticipated at the outset. **"A Matter of Taste,"** for example, is bounded at the beginning by the white joining the two coloured plate layers and at the end by the former's departure as he jumps the goods train. The shape of this story, with its introduction, development and conclusion, satisfies conventional expectations for a short story. **"A Walk in the Night,"** though, is patterned quite differently, not lineally but spatially, as the story itself seems to move through the streets and bars of District Six, stopping to create characters who have no role to play in the plot—the cab-driver of section 3 who tells a story of a local *crime passionnel* before disappearing from the novella, or young Joe, "a wreck of a youth," the beachcomber whose appearances in the story seem quite as random, as undirected as his own profession.

Randomness, the good (or, more usually, bad) fortune that brings together isolated lives and then quickly spins them apart, is really the subject of **"A Walk in the Night."** The story's only, and slight, narrative thread is a collection of accidents and mistaken identities: Adonis accidentally murders an Irishman, Willieboy is mistaken for the murderer and then shot by a white policeman in irrelevant revenge on his troublesome wife. The fortuitous, the random and the contingent lie at the heart of the novella's content just as these same qualities define the tale's form, its circularity and jerkiness. La Guma, though, does not suggest that these mishaps result from the working of any supernatural or metaphysical force: there is no malignant extraterrestrial destiny at the back of **"A Walk in the Night,"** no President of the Immortals to sport with Adonis or Willieboy in the manner of Hardy's *Tess.*

Instead La Guma's story suggests that life's randomness directly results from the urban environment. The first few paragraphs of **"A Walk"** evoke the impersonal, anonymous feeling of the streets of Cape Town as Adonis alights from the train which has brought him in from his suburban factory:

> The young man dropped from the trackless tram just before it stopped at Castle Bridge. He dropped off, ignoring the stream of late-afternoon traffic rolling in from the suburbs, bobbed and ducked the cars and buses, the big, rumbling delivery trucks, deaf to the shouts and curses of the drivers, and reached the pavement.

> Standing there, near the green railings around the public convenience, he lighted a cigarette, jostled by the lines of workers going home, the first trickle of a stream that would soon be flowing towards Hanover Street. He looked right through them, refusing to see them, nursing a little growth of anger

the way one caresses the beginnings of a toothache with the tip of the tongue.

Around him the buzz and hum of voices and the growl of traffic blended into one solid mutter of sound which he only half-heard, his thoughts concentrated upon the pustule of rage and humiliation that was continuing to ripen deep down within him.

These early sentences feel more like New York of Saul Bellow or the London of Angus Wilson than any African environment. Or, to recall an earlier parallel, they aim at evoking an impression similar to the celebrated descriptions of London in Book VII of *The Prelude.* Part of the "great city" yet also alienated from it, Wordsworth there recorded how often amid the unnumbered throng had he said "Unto myself, 'The face of every one/ That passes by me is a mystery.'" These two lines might have stood alongside the *Hamlet* quotation as an epigraph to **"A Walk in the Night,"** which, in both content and form, establishes the vast, un-African, antlike quality of life in one of Africa's larger cities.

La Guma's Cape Town reads as if it were an American or European city, save in one notable respect. Although Wordsworth, in *The Prelude,* is as hard pressed to find verbal forms for the outlandishness of London as Dickens in *Bleak House,* a turbulent energy pulses through the London of Dickens or Wordsworth as through the Western cities of much twentieth-century literature. In **"A Walk"** La Guma's environment, oddly, mixes anonymity with the regimented inertia of people under a totalitarian regime. Cape Town is a Western city without the driving energy. Individuality, ambition, hope, optimism have all been throttled in La Guma's city. Here everyone, irrespective of race, is a victim: even the white policeman is the harried, frustrated victim of his own wife. La Guma's poor come in many shapes, sizes and colours, their defeated status defined by class, not race alone. In these circumstances the rolling of a joint, a dagga cigarette, is described in minute detail (p. 76) because it is only through such private, ritual acts that the external world may briefly be stilled.

"A Walk in the Night" is La Guma's fullest, harshest picture of the miseries of urban life, the grim marriage of urban impersonality with totalitarian repression, for the poor in South Africa. As such it is rightly placed at the head of his volume of short stories for it does establish the context in which the lives of urban blacks are played out. But the rest of his stories hint that perhaps **"A Walk in the Night"** wasn't intended to portray the whole truth. The *Hamlet* epigraph suggests that all the novella's characters inhabit some bleak limbo, condemned to "walk the night" until apartheid has been "burnt and purged away," yet several of the short stories testify to the survival of human dignity despite hideous external pressures. Notable here are the insouciance of Ahmed in **"Tattoo Marks and Nails,"** the brave dignity of the schoolmaster in **"The Lemon Orchard,"** the tender affection of the lovers in **"A Glass of Wine,"** or the delicacy of the pianist of **"Nocturne."** La Guma's shorter fiction generates an admiring respect for his survivors, and a feeling of helpless despair for his victims. Perhaps it is no surprise that this mixture also characterized one of the classic Victorian statements about urban and race victimization—Engels' *Conditions of the Working Class in England, 1844.*

FURTHER READING

Biography

Santos, Daniel Garcia. "Alex La Guma: Revolutionary Intellectual." *The Black Scholar* 17, No. 4 (July/August 1986): 55-6.

> Eulogizes La Guma's life as writer and anti-apartheid activist.

Criticism

"Eastern Europe Speaking English." *Times Literary Supplement* (January 1965): 52.

> Praises La Guma's novel *And a Threefold Cord,* a protest against apartheid written between two terms of imprisonment.

Additional coverage of La Guma's life and career is contained in the following sources published by Gale: *Black Writers,* Vol. 1; *Contemporary Authors,* Vols. 49-52; *Contemporary Authors New Revision Series,* Vol. 25; *Contemporary Literary Criticism,* Vol. 19; *Dictionary of Literary Biography,* Vol. 117; *DISCovering Authors Modules: Novelists;* and *Major 20th-Century Writers.*

Spike Lee
1957-

(Full name Shelton Jackson Lee) American director, producer, screenwriter, nonfiction writer, and actor.

INTRODUCTION

Known for his outspokenness as well as for his films, Spike Lee has attracted much controversy and critical attention. Since the mid-1980s, when his first feature film *She's Gotta Have It* (1986) won an award at the Cannes Film Festival, Lee has proven himself as a successful screenwriter, director, producer, and actor. Tackling such topics as racism, the life of slain African-American activist Malcolm X, interracial relationships, and inner-city life, Lee's work has been both largely applauded and harshly criticized. Lee has sought to present a different picture of African Americans to the moviegoing public, and his success has created opportunities for other African-American directors.

Biographical Information

Lee was born on March 20, 1957, in Atlanta, Georgia, to William and Jacqueline Lee. His father was a musician and composer, and his mother was a teacher. While he was still a baby, Lee's mother nicknamed him Spike for his toughness. His family moved to Chicago and then to Brooklyn when he was very young, and many of his films are set in Brooklyn neighborhoods similar to the ones in which he spent his youth. From the beginning of his career, Lee has involved his family in his film productions. Lee's father scored several of his films, and his sister has acted in several of his movies. Lee attended his grandfather's and father's alma mater, Morehouse College, where he received a B.A. in 1979. He first became interested in filmmaking during college, and after graduation he attended New York University film school. His first film, a short parody of D. W. Griffith's *The Birth of a Nation,* was not well-received by the faculty. In the film he criticized Griffith's condescending portrayal of African Americans. He went on to win the Student Director's Award from the Academy of Motion Picture Arts and Sciences for *Joe's Bed-Stuy Barbershop* (1982). To make ends meet after film school, Lee worked at a movie distribution house cleaning and shipping film. His first movie after graduating from N.Y.U. was the low budget *She's Gotta Have It,* which won the Prix de Jeunesse from the Cannes Film Festival and the New Generation Award from the Los Angeles Film Critics. After the success of his first film, Hollywood's interest in Lee enabled him to make pictures with larger budgets. Even with backing from Hollywood, however, Lee has had to procure much of the

financing for his films on his own. Because he does not solely rely on major studios for financial support, Lee has managed to retain creative control over the final cuts of his films.

Major Works

Lee's films focus on various aspects of contemporary African-American life. *She's Gotta Have It* centers on the life of Nola Darling, a young woman with strong sexual desires who does not believe in restricting herself to one man to fulfill them. Nola represents a modern, independent woman who makes her own choices about her sexuality, yet in the conclusion of the film she discovers that she loves the man who rapes her. Lee's second major film was *School Daze* (1988), a musical which parodies the conflict between light-skinned and dark-skinned African Americans at an all-black college in the South. *Do the Right Thing* (1989) follows a day in the Bedford-Stuyvesant section of Brooklyn on the hottest day of the summer. Racial tensions rise, culminating in the murder of a young African-American man by the police and the burning of a local pizzeria. In *Mo' Better Blues*

(1990), Lee explores the world of a jazz musician and the conflicts between his creative life and his love life. Lee's next project, *Jungle Fever* (1991), centers on an interracial affair between an African-American architect and his Italian-American secretary. The relationship is met with scorn and violence from the respective families and members of the neighborhood. *Malcolm X* (1992) was one of Lee's most ambitious projects, depicting the life of African-American activist Malcolm X. *Crooklyn* (1994) is a semi-autobiographical movie that Lee wrote with his sister and brother. The story follows a few months in the life of a family in the 1970s. The Carmichael family lives in Brooklyn; the father is a musician, the mother a teacher. The film is told from the perspective of the 10-year-old daughter and follows her as she deals with the death of her mother and her journey toward adulthood. In *Clockers* (1995) Lee tells the story of an African-American teenager who gets involved in the world of drug dealing. The character is able to rationalize his decision to sell crack cocaine until he witnesses a murder and the black-on-black violence that drug use creates. With *Girl 6* (1996) Lee returned to a female protagonist. The heroine is an actress who becomes disenchanted when a director asks her to take off her top during a reading. She turns to the phone sex business to make a living and is quite successful. When a sadistic customer reveals that he knows where she lives, Girl 6 decides to leave the business, move to California, and resume her acting career. In *He Got Game* (1998) Lee examines the world of professional basketball and the exploitation of young sports stars. The protagonist, Jesus Shuttlesworth, is the top-ranked high school prospect in the nation. The governor of New York arranges a furlough for Jesus' father from a state prison in an attempt to persuade Jesus to sign with the governor's alma mater. The film addresses many of the temptations encountered by young athletes and the corrupt practices that have become commonplace in professional sports.

Critical Reception

Critics who review Lee's work often digress into discussions of Lee's persona in addition to or instead of his films. Some assert that Lee is a keen commentator on contemporary society and a cinematic innovator. Others describe him as an untalented commercial sellout. Lee is typically criticized for his lack of technical virtuosity. Reviewers point to his use of a moving screen behind two still characters to make them appear to be walking as a sign of his amateurish preoccupation with cinematic gadgetry. Feminists often complain about Lee's portrayal of women. Bell hooks states that "Like many females in Lee's audience, I have found his representation of women in general, and black women in particular, to be consistently stereotypical and one-dimensional." The female protagonist of *She's Gotta Have It* came closest to a portrait of a modern, independent woman, but critics assert that the rape scene subverted the character Lee had created. Re-

viewers point to Nola's rape as a punishment for her sexual independence, and the scene has caused many reviewers to accuse Lee of sexism and misogyny. Lee is sometimes compared to Woody Allen because New York City plays a pivotal role in both directors' films, and because both directors act in their own movies. Lee resists the comparison, however, citing the lack of African Americans in Allen's films as an unrealistic portrayal of the racial makeup of New York. Some reviewers complain that Lee's work is superficial and that his plots lack focus. Bert Cardullo, writing in *The Hudson Review,* asserts that Lee "prefers to do the easier thing: cram his film with incident rather than exploration, with texture rather than subtext." Most critics mention the ambiguity in Lee's films, including the question of what the right thing is in his *Do the Right Thing.* Reviewers are divided on the success of the ambiguity. Some praise Lee for refusing to give his audience simple Hollywood answers, while others complain that his films are unstructured with unfocused plots. Despite the controversy surrounding the filmmaker, most critics agree that Lee's portrayal of the everyday lives of African Americans is new and refreshing, and his success will make it possible for other African-American directors to make further contributions.

---

*PRINCIPAL WORKS

Joe's Bed-Stuy Barbershop: We Cut Heads (film) 1982

She's Gotta Have It (film) 1986

Spike Lee's "Gotta Have It": Inside Guerilla Filmmaking (nonfiction) 1987

School Daze (film) 1988

Uplift the Race: The Construction of "School Daze" [with Lisa Jones] (nonfiction) 1988

Do the Right Thing (film) 1989

"Do the Right Thing": The New Spike Lee Joint [with Lisa Jones] (nonfiction) 1989

Mo' Better Blues (film) 1990

"Mo' Better Blues" [with Lisa Jones] (nonfiction) 1990

Jungle Fever (film) 1991

Malcolm X [with Arnold Perl and (uncredited) James Baldwin; based on the book *The Autobiography of Malcolm X,* written by Alex Haley] (film) 1992

By Any Means Necessary: The Trials and Tribulations of the Making of "Malcolm X" [with Ralph Wiley] (nonfiction) 1992

Crooklyn [with Joie Lee and Cinqué Lee] (film) 1994

Clockers [with Richard Price; based on Price's novel of the same title] (film) 1995

Girl 6 [written by Suzan-Lori Parks] (film) 1996

Get on the Bus [written by Reggie Rock Bythewood] (film) 1996

Best Seat in the House: A Basketball Memoir [with Ralph Wiley] (nonfiction) 1997

4 Little Girls (documentary film) 1997
He Got Game (film) 1998

*In addition to directing the films listed here, Lee has also
  directed numerous television commercials and music videos.
  Bracketed information refers to screenwriting credit only.

CRITICISM

Spike Lee with Marlaine Glicksman (interview date September/October 1986)

SOURCE: "Lee Way," in *Film Content,* Vol. 22, No. 5, September/October, 1986, pp. 46-9.

[*In the following interview with Lee, Glicksman discusses his first feature film,* She's Gotta Have It, *his budget limitations, family involvement, and the future of African American-made films.*]

"You so fine, I drink a tub of your bathwater." "You need a man like me. . . . What's your number?" "I love you. . . . " "Please baby, please baby, please baby, please." "You know the minute you get fat, I'm leaving you."

So cajole, plead, woo, and threaten the men—the decent ones and the dogs—in 29-year-old filmmaker Spike Lee's first feature film, *She's Gotta Have It.* The focus of their attention is Nola Darling. Nola possesses what we have come to know as a man's desire, but is cursed (in society's eyes) with a woman's body. "Some people would call me a freak," she explains at the film's beginning, meaning she's a woman who likes to get down. The story unfolds through Nola's eyes and through the multiple perspectives of those men and women who long to see into and possess them. It is a comedic commentary on the frazzled rules of cat-and-mouse, with Nola as the mouse who scores.

Set entirely in Brooklyn, the film is, like the borough's namesake bridge, laced with the tangles and crossed wires of love and its accompanying emotions, as well as a warm and generous sense of humor. Black and white and in the confession style of Akira Kurosawa's *Rashomon, She's Gotta Have It,* was shot in 12 days with a New York State Council of the Arts grant of $18,000. Lee worked closely with Ernest Dickerson ("my ace cameraman") as well as a cast and crew with whom he has worked on past films, some whom he has known since undergraduate days at Morehouse College, where he first began "dibbing and dabbing" in film.

Lee also involved almost his whole family in the production. ("If you have a talented family," he says, "you should be shot if you don't use them.") This is the third film that his well-known jazz musician father, Bill Lee, has scored. His sister, Joie, plays Clorinda Bradford, Nola's ex-roommate. And his brother, David, acted as still photographer on the shoot. His straightforward, grainy stills are interspersed throughout the film, contrasting their sense of vanishing time and place with the film's sassy tone, as well as setting the scene for the story. Spike himself plays one of Nola's three main men, the aptly named Mars Blackmon, the four-eyed, hiphopper B-boy who hilariously woos Nola and wars with her other suitors: Jamie Overstreet as Nola's serious and stable suitor, who sees himself as Nola's soulmate; Greer Childs as her self-possessed Buppie beau; and finally the seductive Opal Gilstrap as Nola's lesbian admirer.

All of the characters in the film are black. Unlike Steven Spielberg's *The Color Purple, She's Gotta Have It* neither needs white context nor white audiences to-which-blacks-have-been-invited. This time, black women talk to black men, and whites are invited—to learn something about blacks, and also about themselves.

Nola shares her birthday with Malcolm X and paints a commemorative mural, pasted with headlines such as "Honor Student Shot by Cop." Mars wears hi-top sneakers (even when making love to Nola) sports an extra-large 18-karat gold nameplate around his neck, and street-talks and jives, repeating himself incessantly. Greer is a *GQ* model who plays scrabble with a dictionary. Jamie is, well, always decent and stable, very predictable. When Nola invites all three to Thanksgiving dinner, the feathers fly. "Chain snatcher," Greer sniffs at Mars. "Pseudo black man," Mars retorts. When Jamie attempts to quiet the ruckus, Greer cuts, "What are you? Henry Kissinger?" In another scene, Nola and Mars share a nice moment after lovemaking and she greases his hair. The film's final credits include the statement "This film contains no *jerri curls* and no *drugs.*" These characters are well-grounded in a largely black neighborhood and, unlike black characters in most other films, speak black dialect *intelligently.* The blacks in Lee's film are real people. And as real people, they speak to us all.

Each lover offers a lover's reason why he isn't Nola Darling's number one man. "To Nola," says Jamie, "we're all interchangeable." Accuses Greer, "I think you are sick. I'm not saying you're a nympho, slut, or whore, but I do think you are a sex addict." When bike-conjoined Mars encounters Jamie on a parkbench he opines, "Nola is about as dependable as a ripped diaphragm." But soon the discussion veers off into sports—stopped dead by a female passerby— before the two return to their thoughts about Nola, providing yet another universal observation on the ways men and women navigate and collide. It is Mars who finally figures it out, that all three men comprise an integrated whole for Nola, that it was the men who were really at fault. "We let her create a three-headed, six-armed, six-legged, three-penis monster." In the end, Nola ditches them all and, content to be alone in her bed, reveals the decisive verdict, "It's about control. My body. My mind. Whose gonna own it, them or me?"

She's Gotta Have It uniquely tackles an age-old controversial topic, the discrepancies that exist not only between the sexes but also in the judgments rendered by society. Ironically, the film's willingness to investigate the hot spot where love meets sex landed it in hot water. The MPAA thrice gave the film an X rating. Since the film features a woman and her three lovers, naturally there are sex scenes. But there is no more to be seen than the breasts and butts that grace the lovemaking of white mainstream R-rated films. Spike had to recut his film three times, plus cut in half an overhead shot of Greer and Nola in bed, to get down to the R rating dictated by his Island Pictures contract for its domestic release. "It'll be shown the real way in Europe and on tape," Spike said.

Spike is no stranger to trouble. Outspoken, he was almost not asked back after his probational first year at NYU graduate film school when he submitted *The Answer.* The 20-minute short portrayed a young black screenwriter hired to do a rewrite on a $50 million remake of *Birth of a Nation.* Lee eventually graduated with a Student Academy Award for *Joe's Bed-Stuy Barbershop: We Cut Heads,* about a numbers-running barbershop in the Bedford-Stuyvesant section of Brooklyn. This film also earned him a screening in the New Directors/New Films festival at the Museum of Modern Art in 1983.

It is no surprise, then, that *She's Gotta Have It* this year achieved a spot in the director's fortnight at Cannes, as well as the Prix de Jeunesse. (We got robbed of the Camera d'Or," Lee says, "but I'm not complaining.") Still, it is often the comments on the long line to the ladies room which serve final judgment on the success of a film, and in the case of this film, perhaps one of the most appropos places to listen. "I want three men, too," said one line-stander. "Yeah but I want 'em all at the same time," said another. Perhaps Mars was wrong; perhaps it is Spike Lee who has created the monster.

[*Glicksman:*] *The MPAA originally gave* **She's Gotta Have It** *an X rating.*

[Lee:] The MPAA said it was filled with gratuitous sex, that it was—and this is an actual quote—'Saturated with sex.' I edited the film three times and each time they said it was better. But it was still given an X rating. The film will be released unrated in New York, but I have to cut an R rated film for me to get money, because that is in my contract.

I don't think it's out-and-out racist, but the film portrays

blacks outside stereotypical roles, and they don't know what to do with blacks in films. They never have any love interests. Nick Nolte is the one who has a relationship in *48 Hours.* And when it comes to black sexuality, they especially don't know how to deal with it. They feel uncomfortable. There are films with more gratuitous sex and even violence. *91/2 Weeks* got an R. And look at *Body Double.*

Why did you set and film **She's Gotta Have It** *in Brooklyn—because you're from there?*

I was born in Atlanta, Georgia, but I've lived in Brooklyn all my life. When you are doing independent filmmaking, you don't have the means to go anywhere else. *She's Gotta Have It* was really shot in a one-mile radius, the whole film, in the neighborhood where I lived. That's the only way we could shoot a film in 12 days, only if locations are within a block from each other.

How did the film come about?

In the summer of 1984, I attempted to do a film called **Messenger.** We were in pre-production for eight weeks, but I had to pull the plug because it just never really came together with all the money and stuff. So out of that devastation and disaster, we came up with the idea, out of desperation, to do *She's Gotta Have It.* I was determined do another film the next summer for as little money as possible. Small cast, small crew. I had a grant from NYSCA [the N.Y. State Council on the Arts] for $18,000 for **Messenger.** NYSCA was kind enough to let me move that money to *She's Gotta Have It.* I also got a grant from American Film Institute for $20,000, but those mother fuckers took the money back. They wouldn't let me move the money. Print that too.

You had no private funding?

When we started out, there wasn't. But the whole game plan was to raise the money stage by stage. The next stage was to get the film out of the lab. I had the confidence that if we could get it shot, cut, and show it to people, I would be able to raise enough money.

Was the $18,000 to shoot enough?

No. Monty Ross, the lead actor in *Joe's Bed-Stuy Barbershop,* who I went to school with at Morehouse, was production supervisor on this film. After we would shoot, everyday, Monty would come home, get on the phone, and call and write everybody we knew in the world asking them to please, please, please help us out, to please, please, please send money, their hundreds, fifties, whatever. So we raised the money at the same time we were shooting. I remember a number of times while Monty, during the shoot, would leave the set and I would fill out the deposit slip and he would run to the bank and deposit the checks. So that's the kind of duress we made this film under. But I'm not complaining. That's the only way that this film could be done.

It's wonderful that you had the confidence to go ahead and do the film.

Well, I've never lacked confidence [*laughs*]. It's just money. And I've been fortunate that I've had people around me like Ernest Dickerson and Pam Jackson, who went to school with Monty and me. She was associate producer of the film.

You shot the film on a very small ratio.

It's just my style. There's really no need to take eight million takes of everything. We were well-rehearsed. And we try to just get it within the first or second take, move it on to the next shot.

Why did you decide to shoot the film in black and white?

Well, the images came to me in black and white. This had nothing to do with the budget. I just felt that the subject was a black and white movie.

You used color for the birthday scene.

Well, we wanted to make that scene, which is a present that Jamie is giving to Nola, a very imaginable scene, to make it different. A little homage to *The Wizard of Oz* . . . Jamie says to her, 'Close your eyes and repeat after me,' 'There's no place like home, there's no place like home.' And she says, 'There's no place like home, there's no place like home,' and you cut to the close-up of her clicking her heels.

What is it like to act in your own film?

I never acted before. Well, halfway through writing this film, I decided, hey, I should play this role. It was hard. The first day, it was horrible because I was trying to direct and act, and Michael Hunter, who was the gaffer, says to me, 'When you're in front of the camera, let Ernest be the director,' because I was still saying 'Everybody ready, roll sound, action,' all that, and then I'd try to go and act. You can't do that. So when I was in front of the camera, Ernest assumed the reins of the director as far as getting the crew ready, the action, cut, that stuff.

Did you ever take acting lessons?

I'm really not an opponent of those acting schools. My sister has never acted before either and I think that she's very natural. That stuff—Mars repeating everything—that wasn't scripted.

Why do you feel a particular affinity toward the character of Mars?

There are a lot of them out there, especially in Brooklyn, a lot of young black youths, and they don't have such a good reputation. Look at the Bernard Goetz situation. That's why I had stuff like Greer calling him a "chain snatcher." I knew I couldn't attempt to clear their reputation, but I could portray them more positively.

Was it difficult for you to shoot and direct the sex scenes?

That is why I used Tracy as an actress. I could have had a known actress, but it was important that I use somebody who was comfortable with the love scenes, someone at ease, because her ease would make the audience more at ease.

The script was written remarkably from a woman's point of view.

I'm a good listener. And I think I really try to be honest. And if you really try to go about the truth and honesty in your work, then you can hurdle my not being a woman. But you have to understand, I have not attempted to make a feminist film. For me, it is about a woman who has three lovers. My friends are always boasting and bragging about how many women they have. But when word gets back to them that one of the women in their stable is even thinking about seeing somebody else, they go berserk. That's insane, that double standard. So I decided, let's make a film about a woman who is actually living her life as a man.

How did "black" figure into it?

Another reason I did this film was because there are hardly any films about black people. When you do see films about black people, they're either musicals or comedies. You know, ha-ha, chi-chi, and dancing. Eddie Murphy and Richard Pryor, don't even kiss or have any romantic interests in their films.

They don't have a home, no wife, no lovers. And I knew that black people would kill to go into the movie theater and see black people hugging and kissing and, you know, loving each other.

There is so much catching up to do, I know I'm not going to have any problems, for the next three or four films, just dealing with stuff within a black genre. This film has shown a lot of people, especially at Cannes, that black people are just as diversified as any other race. People have been shocked by just how universal this film is, by how they had never seen black people portrayed like this before. I guess all their experiences have been with Hollywood films.

Is it harder for blacks to work in the industry?

It is harder for blacks in the industry. But we have to create our own jobs and make our own films. That is why it is important to find close working associates that have the same goals and aspirations that you do.

Is this film about blacks or men and women?

I think my love of women is reflected in the work. But I think this film should be the antidote to how the black male is perceived in *The Color Purple*. See, nobody is saying that black men haven't done some terrible things, and what Jamie does to Nola at the end of the film is a horrible act. But Jamie is a full-bodied character, unlike Mister in *The Color Purple* and the rest of that film's black men, who are just one-dimensional animals. I'm not going to blame it all entirely on Steven Spielberg, because if you read Alice Walker's work, that's the way she feels about black men. She really has problems with them. I think people should really analyze why *The Color Purple* this film was made.

Why?

Within recent years, the quickest way for a black playwright, novelist, or poet to get published has been to say that black men are shit. If you say that, then you are definitely going to get media, your book published, your play done—Ntozake Shange, Alice Walker.

Do you feel the same way about black male playwrights?

To me, Toni Morrison could write motherfuckin' rings around Alice Walker. If you look at Toni Morrison's body of work—*Sula, The Bluest Eye, Tar Baby, Song of Solomon*—*Song of Solomon*, I mean, I would like to do that one day. That's going to make a great movie. But still, till today, not one of Toni Morrison's works has been made into film. Why hasn't she won a Pulitzer prize? That's why they put Alice Walker out there. That's why she won the Pulitzer Prize. That's why Hollywood leaped the pond to seize this book and had it made. To me, it's justifying everything they say about black people and black men in general: that we ain't shit, that we're animals. That's why this film was made. Of all the black novels, it's not just coincidence that this was the one that they chose. And then they turn around and get some Dutch guy to write the script and get Spielberg to direct it. He knows nothing about black people.

And Whoopi Goldberg—you've got to print this—I've seen her on *Phil Donahue* and she was getting all defensive about the flak that she's getting about *Color Purple*, telling black men that if they can't take a joke, fuck it, and shit like that, and then she's going to try to defend *The Color Purple* by saying, what about *Purple Rain?* What about when Prince had women thrown in garbage cans? Hey, I didn't like that shit either, but that doesn't have a goddamn thing to do with *Color Purple*. And Whoopi Goldberg says that Steven Spielberg is the only director in the world who could have directed that film. Does she realize what she is saying? Is she saying that a white person is the only person who can define our existence? And now, even something more stupid, she's running around with goddamn blue contact lenses in her eyes, telling everybody that she has blue eyes. And that's sick . . . to me. And I hope people realize, that the media realizes, that she's not a spokesperson for black people, especially when you're running around with motherfucking blue contact lenses telling everybody that your eyes are blue. Tell her to read Toni Morrison's book, *The Bluest Eye*.

It was a wonderful idea to have "the dogs" speak.

I'm just amazed at the things men tell women. And when you think about it, the only reason why they say that stuff is that is must work some of the time, because if it never worked, they wouldn't keep on saying that dumb stuff.

And what do women say to men?

I don't think they're as. . . . I don't know about that. It might work. But it never happened with me! [*laughs.*]

Whose work are you influenced by? You quote Zora Neale Hurston in the beginning of your film.

I think it's a very good book [*Their Eyes Were Watching God*], and she's a person that all black female novelists quote. Alice Walker, Toni Morrison, all talk about the influence Zora Neale Hurston had on them. But for film, I like the work of Scorsese, Kurosawa, Coppola. I also like musicals, too, and my next film is going to be a musical.

She's Gotta Have It *was shot in the style of* Rashomon. *Was that scripted?*

Yeah. I called it confessions with people facing the camera. It also was very economical. It doesn't take a whole lot of time to light. And you just shoot. That really helped us to shoot in 12 days.

Were you very influenced by your dad? Does his music influence your work?

Yeah, his music, jazz. . . . We were raised in a very artistic family. So he was taking me to see him play at the Village Gate, at The Bitter End, at the Blue Note, when I was four, five years old. See him play with Odetta, Judy Collins, Leon Bibb, Peter, Paul, and Mary. I really strive to make music play an important part in all my films. This is the third film that my father has done the music for. And this is the first where the soundtrack is going to be released." [*Island Records is releasing.*]

What's it like working with him?

It's hard [laughs]. Because he's a perfectionist and a non-conformist, and I love him because he's my father, but he's not the easiest person to work with.

At what stage do you start working with him? In the script?

Yes. I knew I wanted a theme for Nola played throughout the whole film and I had a lot that had to be recorded before we shot for playback, for the choreography, for the dance scene, and some other stuff. Then I went and shot it, cut it, and when I had a rough cut, that's when we sat down and decided when we wanted music, the type of music, the color of the instrumentation, the length of it. Then he went away and came back and played an idea on the piano. Then we decided what piece was appropriate for each particular scene.

What is the balance of power, working with your father?

Well, I don't want to sound like a dictator, but film is a director's medium. I try to listen to everybody's suggestions, but the final outcome ultimately is going to be my decision.

Do you feel like jazz has influenced your writing or editing?

That's a hard question. Well, I guess it has in the sense that I never try to restrict myself. I just let my imagination go very free. And I like to improvise. So you could say maybe like that.

Are you a perfectionist?

No. I haven't been in a situation where I could afford to be a perfectionist.

What is your next project?

The next film is a musical called *School Daze* for Island Pictures. I hope to begin shooting in March on a $3 million budget, which feels good. It is set at a black college in the South, during homecoming, on the Spellman/Morehouse campuses. I intend to include a whole spectrum of black music, from funk to jazz.

You know, what we're doing now, people are saying,"Spike, this is great, this is great, aren't you excited? You look so blasé." And I say, "Everything we're doing now, Monty, Pam, and I talked about when we were in school eight or nine years ago. So this is what we're supposed to be doing. It's no shock."

Spike Lee with Gary Crowdus and Dan Georgakas (interview date December 1992)

SOURCE: "Our Film Is Only a Starting Point: An Interview with Spike Lee," in *Cineaste,* Vol. 19, No. 4, 1993, pp. 20-4.

[*In the following interview, which took place in December, 1992, Lee discusses the making of the film* Malcolm X, *and explains his reasons for excluding certain material.*]

In addition to our Critical Symposium on **Malcolm X,** Cineaste *felt it was important to talk to Spike Lee and incorporate his comments in our overall perspective on the film. In the following interview, Lee explains his primary desire to introduce Malcolm X to young viewers and his awareness that the time limits of even a nearly three and a half hour movie prevented him from producing anything more than a "primer" on one of America's most charismatic black leaders. His additional comments about the difficulties of attempting to produce an epic political film within the budgetary constraints imposed by Warner Bros. and in light of the many other pragmatic and political considerations involved are important aspects in arriving at a fully informed appraisal of the artistic achievement and political significance of* **Malcolm X.** *Spike Lee spoke to* Cineaste *Editors Gary Crowdus and Dan Georgakas in mid-December 1992, just three weeks after the film's nationwide premiere.*

[*Cineaste:*] *What sort of research did you do for the film? And what was the role of your Historical Consultant Paul Lee?*

[Lee:] I read everything that I could, including a new book by Zak Kondo about the assassination that was very important in helping us re-create the assassination in the film. Paul Lee was a great help because he's someone who's really devoted his life to Malcolm X. Paul, who lives in Detroit, was in the Nation, I think, when he was twelve years old. As far as scholars go, I don't think there's anyone who knows more about Malcolm X than Paul Lee.

I also talked to a lot of people, including Benjamin Karim, who's Benjamin 2X in the film, Malcolm's brothers—Wilfred, Omar Azziz, and Robert—his sister Yvonne, Malcolm's widow, Betty Shabazz, and Malcolm Jarvis, who's Shorty in the film. I also went to Chicago and talked to Minister Farrakhan. That's where a lot of the good stuff came from, going around the country and talking to people who knew Malcolm. Not just his relatives, but people who were in the Nation with him, in the OAAU, and so on.

Have you had any dealings with the Socialist Workers Party? They got to Malcolm early, gave him podiums numerous times, and published a lot of his speeches.

Pathfinder Press? No, I just used their books, because they're fine documents.

Of the various screenplay adaptations of The Autobiography *that had been written, why did you feel that the James Baldwin/Arnold Perl script was the best?*

I read 'em all—the David Mamet script, Charles Fuller's two drafts, Calder Willingham's script, and David Bradley's script—but the Baldwin/Perl script was the best. James Baldwin was a great writer and he really captured Harlem and that whole period. He was a friend of Malcolm's.

What did your rewrite of the Baldwin/Perl script involve?

What was lacking, I felt, in the Baldwin/Perl script was the third act—what happens during the split between Malcolm and the Nation, between Malcolm and Elijah Muhammad. A lot of stuff about the assassination had not come out then. William Kunstler was a great help on that. He represented Talmadge Hayer and gave me a copy of Hayer's affidavit where he 'fessed up to the assassination. I mean, if you look at the credits of the movie, we name the five assassins, we *name* those guys—Ben Thomas, William X, Wilbur Kinley, Leon Davis, and Thomas Hayer.

I also wanted to tie the film into today. I did not want this film just to be a historical document. That's why we open the film with the Rodney King footage and the American flag burning, and end the film with the classrooms, from Harlem to Soweto.

The speeches in the Baldwin/Perl script were not really Malcolm's best speeches, they did not really show the growth politically of Malcolm's mind, so we threw them all out. With the help of Paul Lee, who gave us copies of every single speech that Malcolm gave, Denzel and I chose and inserted speeches. Baldwin had stuff out of order. He had Malcolm giving speeches at the beginning of the movie that didn't really come until 1963 or 1964, so we had to get rid of those.

So Denzel was involved somewhat in working on the script?

Yeah, Denzel was very involved. He has a good story sense. We both knew a lot was riding on this film. We did not want to live in another country the rest of our lives. We could not go anywhere without being reminded by black folks, "Don't

fuck up Malcolm, don't mess this one up." We were under tremendous pressure on this film. We can laugh about it now, but it was no joke while we were doing the film.

Given the difficulty of portraying about forty years of a man's life in any film, even one nearly three and a half hours long, are there some aspects of Malcolm's life you felt you weren't able to do justice to?

No, this is it, this is the movie I wanted to make. Our first cut was about four hours and ten minutes, I forget exactly, and we had more speeches and stuff, but this is the best shape the film can be. Of course, people say, "Why did you leave this out and why did you leave that out?," but you cannot put a man's whole life in a film.

People have told us, "The most important year in Malcolm's life was his final year," and "Why didn't you show his whole pan-Africanism thing?" But it's limited. We've never said that anyone who sees this film doesn't need to know anything else about Malcolm X. I mean, the man had four or five different lives, so the film is really only a primer, a starting point.

But don't you think that showing him meeting heads of state in Africa would have added to his dimension at the end, especially for people who don't know?

But people don't know who Kwame Nkrumah is anyway. Besides, we didn't have the money. I mean, we just barely got to Egypt. We shot in the U.S. from September 16, 1991, up to the Christmas holiday and after the holidays we did what we had to do in Cairo and then we went to South Africa. But I don't think we would have gained anything by showing him meeting with Nkrumah or others. Besides, at that point in the film, we're trying to build some momentum.

Cassius Clay/Muhammad Ali is sort of dropped from the film, too.

What, and get someone to impersonate him? I think it was important to have Muhammad Ali in the movie, but we show him in a newsreel clip in the montage at the end.

You don't think it dissipates some of the anti-Vietnam War feeling that was in the Nation?

They weren't really anti-Vietnam. Malcolm was, but Elijah Muhammad never said anything about the Vietnam War. And by the time Malcolm spoke out against the Vietnam War, he had already been kicked out of the Nation.

Do you feel a film of this financial scale has built-in 'crossover' requirements in terms of its audience?

We felt so. We felt that everybody would want to see the film and we've received a large white audience to date. This is my first PG film—the previous five have all been rated R—because we wanted to get a young audience. We feel this is an important piece of American history and people, especially young kids, need to see this.

Is that why the few sex scenes in the film are considerably milder than those in the published screenplay?

Yes, because we made the decision for a PG-13 rating. We did not want to give teachers, schools, or parents an excuse why they could not take their children to see this film. I think when you weigh it, it's much more important for young kids to be exposed to Malcolm X than to see that other shit. We're preparing a classroom study guide on the film that'll be out in January.

It's amazing, I've seen this film with ten, eleven, and twelve-year-olds and they're just riveted in their seats. You know the attention span of young people at that age—they're usually throwing popcorn at the screen—but there's not a sound, they're riveted for three hours and twenty-one minutes. A whole generation of young people are being introduced to Malcolm X and people who've heard of him or had limited views of him are having their views expanded. Above all, we hope that black folks will come out of the theater inspired and moved to do something positive.

What sort of message would you like white viewers to come away with from the film?

I think that, as with any film I've done, people will take away their own message. For a large part of the white audience, however, I think we're helping to redefine Malcolm X because for the most part their view of Malcolm came from the white media which portrayed him as anti-white, anti-Semitic, and pro-violence. It's funny, when we had the national press junket for this film, many of the white journalists said they felt they'd been robbed, that they'd been cheated, because they'd never been taught about Malcolm X in school or they had only been told that he was anti-white and violent. A great miseducation has gone on about this man.

In that regard, we heard that Warner Bros., presumably concerned about defusing any controversy about potential violence at screenings, held advance showings of the film for police departments around the country.

That was Barry Reardon's decision. I did not agree with that. I thought it was inappropriate. I mean, if they do that to us, they should do it to *Terminator.* How many cops got killed in those films? Actually, it was the exhibitors. Before the film came out, exhibitors were calling Warner Bros., they were scared shitless, they were requesting extra police protection. One theater in Chicago even installed metal detectors!

What was the response at the police screenings?

Oh, the cops loved it. In Los Angeles, they showed it to Willie Williams, the new Police Commissioner there. It was the exhibitors and also the press who were waiting for that violence so they could destroy the movie. **Do the Right Thing** was really hurt at the box office when the press—people like David Denby, Joe Klein, and Jack Mathews—predicted that the film was going to create riots. In Westwood, in Los Angeles, for example, nine police were at the theater on the opening weekend, some mounted on horseback.

What's interesting for me now in reading a lot of the reviews of **Malcolm X** is how so many critics had predetermined that the film was going to be inflammatory.

To a great extent that's because of their unfamiliarity with Malcolm X other than what they've read in the mainstream press.

And with me, with the combination of Malcolm X and Spike Lee. They were expecting a film that for three hours and twenty-one minutes would be saying, "C'mon, black folks, let's get some guns and kill every single white person in America," but in the end the critics were saying, "This film is *mild.*"

In the published screenplay, there are two sort of 'dramatic bookends' scenes. In the first scene, Malcolm brushes off the well-intentioned young white woman outside Harvard who asks how she might be of help in his struggle. The second scene, which occurs later at the Hilton Hotel in New York, involves the same type of encounter but this time Malcolm has a completely different response. The two scenes emphasizes Malcolm's evolution on this question, but only the first scene appears in the film. Why?

We shot that other scene, but the acting just didn't work. Anyone who's read the book knows that Malcolm's response to that young woman was one of his biggest regrets. I wanted to give Malcolm a chance to make up for it, so I wrote the scene where he could answer that same question again, but it just didn't work.

Are you concerned with how the dramatic weight has now shifted to that first scene? At the two screenings we've attended, that scene always gets a big laugh.

Who's laughing? Black viewers or white viewers?

They've been mixed audiences.

White people don't laugh at that because for the white audience that young white woman is *them*. We shot the second scene, but it just didn't work, so what were we supposed to do? In any case, I think we see Malcolm change when he comes back from Mecca.

In terms of The Autobiography's *portrayal of Malcolm's youthful criminal career and the extent of his drug abuse, Malcolm was much more critical of himself in the book than the film is. Do you think that aspect of the book is exaggerated?*

I've talked to Malcolm's brothers and they said that he was not that big of a criminal. He was a street hustler and not even a pimp, just a steerer. I think he was a wannabe, a wannabe big-time gangster, but he wasn't. The description in the book was not so much to build himself up but to lower the depths from which he rises. That's OK, but I don't buy this Bruce Perry bullshit that Malcolm was a homosexual, that he used to crossdress, or that Malcolm's father burned down their house in Omaha or that Malcolm fire-bombed his own house in Queens. That's bullshit! He did a lot of research, and some of the interviews were good, but Bruce Perry's book reads like *The National Enquirer*.

Many feminists are critical of the Nation of Islam's sexist attitudes towards women. In fact, one of their well-intentioned slogans refers to women as "property."

We didn't make that up. That was an actual banner.

No, we understand that was historically accurate, but since you've taken so much heat from feminists in the past . . .

Hey, you know who should be taking more heat than me? Oliver Stone!

Oh, he has taken a lot of heat.

Not as much as me, though, about women.

In a historical film like this, the dilemma seems to be whether one can—or should even attempt to—deal with such an issue by presenting an anachronistic, retroactive 'politically correct' perspective on the Nation's attitude towards women.

We just showed it the way it was.

We thought you dealt with this issue well in at least one scene where you intercut Elijah Muhammad's various strictures against women with Malcolm's conversation with Betty where he parrots pretty much the same line.

Yeah, he's a mouthpiece. [*Lee at this point does a pretty good impersonation of Al Freeman as Elijah Muhammad*] "She should be half the man's age plus seven. She must cook, sew, stay out of trouble." [*Laughs*] Sure, I've been at some screenings where women go, "Ugh!," but, look, those are not my views.

You often have scenes where there's no obvious interpretation, you leave it up to the viewer.

A lot of my work has been done that way. Some things I'll slant, but a lot of time I let people make up their own minds.

We're thinking especially of the scene where Denzel is watching television, and you intercut newsreel footage of police repression of civil rights demonstrations with a slow zoom into his face.

Yeah, and with John Coltrane's "Alabama" on the soundtrack.

There are a couple of different levels of interpretation there. You can think that he's despising Martin Luther King, Jr. and his nonviolent approach, or you can think that he's regretting that he's not involved in action like that. In this regard, we also wondered about the little smile you see briefly on Malcolm's face just before he's shot.

That was Denzel's idea.

I guess that's also open to interpretation.

Well, Denzel and I felt that he just got tired of being hounded. In actuality, you know, there were several assassination attempts. The CIA tried to poison him in Cairo, and the Nation tried to kill him numerous times. There was a big assassination attempt in Los Angeles, another in Chicago, and one night he had to run into his house because guys with knives were chasing him. So he was hounded for a year, the last year of his life, and Denzel and I thought about it and just felt that, you know, he was happy to go. It was Denzel's idea to smile right before he gets the shotgun blast—like, "You finally got me," and it was over.

Malcolm knew that he was going to die—even in the book he says, "I'll be dead before this comes out"—and that idea is played through that montage where Malcolm, his aides, and the assassins are all driving in separate cars to the Audubon Ballroom—an idea we got from *The Godfather*, by the way ('props' to Francis)—accompanied by the Sam Cooke song, "A Change Is Gonna Come."

In terms of FBI and CIA involvement in the assassination, do you think it was more a case of them letting it happen rather than actually doing it?

In my opinion they definitely stirred things up between Malcolm and the Nation. The FBI's COINTELPRO operation had infiltrated the Nation and was writing letters back and forth. Then I think they just stood back and let it happen. I don't think the FBI or CIA needed to assassinate Malcolm because, if you read *Muhammad Speaks* at that time, the Nation was going to do it themselves.

The FBI did the same thing on the West Coast, fomenting a rift between the Black Panthers and Ron Karenga.

Oh yeah, they're great at that. A very important book in this regard is *Malcolm X: The FBI File*. Two new books coming out—*The Judas Factor: The Plot to Kill Malcolm X* by Karl Evanzz and *Conspiracies: Unraveling the Assassination of Malcolm X* by Zak Kondo—both say the Nation was responsible. Of course, Amiri Baraka's saying that I'm part of some great government conspiracy and that the reason the studio let me make the film is because I was going to pin the assassination on black people. That's bullshit!

The five assassins were from Temple No. 25 in Newark, New Jersey, and the orders came from Chicago. I don't know if they came from the Honorable Elijah Muhammad, but it was from somewhere high up. That's the truth. I mean, Baraka should talk to Betty Shabazz, he should ask her who killed her husband. She told me the same thing. I'm not part of some conspiracy to turn black folks against the Nation of Islam. That's bullshit!

Has the Nation had a response to the film yet?

The Thursday before the movie opened we had a special screening in Chicago for Minister Farrakhan.

How did that go?

He was there, and I got a note from his secretary saying he was going to respond by letter, but we haven't heard from him since. But Minister Farrakhan has been supportive. While we were shooting the film, he said, "Look, Spike, I support your right as an artist." That's been it.

Do you think they'll make an official pronouncement, one way or another?

I think they'll just let it blow over.

In making this film, did you arrive at a more sympathetic understanding or appreciation of Islam?

Yeah, I mean you had to have respect. Denzel and I were reading the Koran before we began to shoot. We *had* to. If we didn't have a sympathetic attitude toward Islam, why would the Saudi government allow us to bring cameras into Mecca to shoot the holy rite of *hajj?* You have to be a Muslim to enter Mecca, so we had two second units, Islamic crews, who in May 1990 and June 1991 were permitted, for the first time ever in history, to film in Mecca.

I think the Saudi government realized this film could be good publicity for Islam. I mean, Islam and the Arabs in general have been taking a bashing in the West—what with Khomeini and the Gulf War and everything—and in Islam Malcolm is considered a martyr. That's why they let us bring cameras in.

Will the Islamic countries be an important overseas market for the film?

Yeah, we're going to try. We've got to be careful, though, because the same people who gave us the stamp of approval, the Islamic Court, are the same cats who sentenced Salman Rushdie to die, so we don't want to fuck around.

Some felt that the film's Mecca scenes were a little saccharine, somewhat like Christian movies of Jerusalem.

If the man says this was a deeply religious experience, you have to be true to that, no matter how you feel personally about religion. I mean, if up until that point the man felt that every single white person was a blue-eyed, grafted devil, and he no longer believed that after his visit to Mecca, something must have happened.

A very powerful scene in the film is when the young man, after seeing Malcolm and other members of the Nation confront the police, approaches Malcolm and says he wants to become a Muslim. It showed the power of the Nation to influence people and change their behavior.

People can talk about Elijah Muhammad all they want, but there's never been a better program in America for black folks to convert drug addicts, alcoholics, criminals, whatever. Elijah Muhammad straightened those guys out and, once they were clean, that was that.

A lot of people felt Malcolm would have left Islam, but we always thought he was as devout a Muslim as King was a Christian.

No, he would never have left Islam. He would have moved on to other stuff, but he would have remained a Muslim. He would not have made it a requirement to join his organization because he saw it was too regimented. He wanted to include as many people as possible. People wanted to follow him but they weren't willing to give up pork, or sex, or whatever.

There was always this tension between Malcolm and King

which some people saw as a contradiction but which we saw as more of a dynamic tension.

I agree. At the end of **Do the Right Thing,** when I use the statements from Malcolm and King, I wasn't saying it's either one or the other. I think one can form a synthesis of both. When Malcolm was assassinated, I think they were trying to find a common ground, a plan they could both work on.

Some people felt I took a low blow at King in the film in the scene where John Sayles, as an FBI agent listening in on a phone tap on Malcolm, cracks, "Compared to King, this guy is a monk." I don't think that's low blow. J. Edgar Hoover had made tapes of King with other women and he confronted King with them, saying, "If you don't commit suicide, I'm going to send these tapes to Coretta," and he did. Afterwards things weren't the same between Coretta and Dr. King, but I'm not taking a low blow at King. The low blow was the FBI doing this to Dr. King. But some black people told me, "Spike, you know, you shouldn't have done that."

They have a hard time dealing with King as a sexual being. Baldwin also thought that there was this dynamic, this dialectical tension, between Malcolm and King. Toward the end, Malcolm seemed to be saying, "You'd better deal with King, because, if you don't, you'll have to deal with me." It's the Ballot or the Bullet.

He said that all the time. He told King, "I'm good for you."

Some people would have liked for you to have included the scene where Malcolm went down to Selma and spoke to Coretta King. Did you think of putting that in?

[*Covers his head in a defensive manner and laughs uproariously*] We couldn't do everything! We knew going in that, at best, we'd just get the essence of the man, that's the most we'd be able to do. Besides, Henry Hampton of Blackside—you know, the guy who did *Eyes on the Prize*—he's preparing an eight hour series on Malcolm. They'll be able to do a lot more than we did, and I'm glad.

We've also heard that there are plans to re-release, at least on video, the 1972 feature documentary on Malcolm.

Marvin Worth's film. It's good. I think if more people can learn about Malcolm X, that's cool.

We thought you might have done more with Ossie Davis's eulogy.

What, you mean see him delivering it? Then we'd have to restage the funeral and I didn't want to see Denzel in a cas-

ket. Besides, by that time we show footage of the real Malcolm X. I gotta give my props here to Oliver Stone. Barry Brown [*the editor who cut* **School Daze** *and* **Do the Right Thing**] and I saw Oliver Stone's *JFK* the first day it came out, and I said, "Barry, man, look what they're doing. C'mon!" That film gave us great inspiration.

You remember the opening newsreel montage in *JFK?* Well, we tried to do the same thing, or better it, with our montage at the end where Ossie Davis delivers the eulogy. We also had some of the black and white thing going, like newsreel footage.

So you were directly influenced by JFK?

Yes. There are other similarities between **Malcolm X** and *JFK* but what makes our film stand out is the performance of the lead actor. I think Kevin Costner is an OK actor, and I know that's probably the only way Oliver could have gotten the film made with the amount of money he wanted to, but I love that film *despite* Kevin Costner's performance. In **Malcolm X,** Denzel is the film, he's in every single scene. I hope he gets nominated for the Academy Award and I hope he wins.

Another thing we're really proud of with this film is the craft. Far too often with my films the craft is overlooked, but I think everything here—Barry Brown's editing, Ruth Carter's costume design, Terence Blanchard's score, plus the source music we used, and Ernest Dickerson's cinematography—is outstanding.

The cameo appearances in your film are another similarity to JFK. *In some ways they're amusing, and people love them, but, on the other hand, they seem to disrupt the dramatic intensity, because people are saying, "Hey, that's Al Sharpton," or "There's Bill Kunstler," or "Did you see Bobby Seale?"*

Not that many viewers know who these people are, and for me it just added weight to the stuff. I don't think I was making jokes or trying to make it campy or funny. I actually wanted Clint Eastwood to play the cop in the Peter Boyle scene, but he was shooting *Unforgiven*.

Has Warner Bros. been supportive in terms of the advertising campaign and the national release?

Yes, ever since they saw the rough cut. I mean, for a while there during production we went at it toe to toe, but since they've seen it they've been behind the film. We're on 1600 screens nationwide. I have no complaints.

In terms of the highly publicized dispute during production between yourself, Warner Bros., and the Completion Bond Company, to what extent do you feel racism was involved?

Racism is part of the fabric of American society, so why should the film industry be exempt? I think it's a racist assumption that white America will not go to see a black film that's not a comedy, or that doesn't have singing and dancing, or that doesn't star Eddie Murphy. I think there are racist tendencies that keep this glass ceiling on the amount of money that is spent on black films, to produce them or to market and promote them. I mean, how is it that Dan Aykroyd, a first-time director, can get $45 million to do *Nothing But Trouble?* $45 million! They're willing to give more money to these white boys right out of film school than they are to accomplished black directors.

In terms of the controversy, films go over budget all the time, so why I am on the front page? I wasn't calling up these newspapers and saying, "I'm over budget and the Completion Bond Company is taking the film over."

Wasn't there some sort of misunderstanding about the delivery date of the film?

No. Here's what happened. Any time a director and the lead actor are shooting, that is first unit, that is principal photography. The Completion Bond Company tried to say that what we did in Africa was second unit. But Denzel and I were shooting, so that's principal photography. We finished shooting in Soweto in late January 1992, and five weeks later they wanted a first rough cut!

The Bond Company was mad because they were getting stuck by Warner Bros. and were having to deal with a $5,000,000 overage. Usually the studio will help out the bond company, but in this case Warner Bros. said, "Fuck you. We paid you a fee and this is your job." So the Bond Company said to us, "Look, until we work this agreement out with Warner Bros., we're not paying you anything." So they fired all our editors. We had no money coming in to complete the film, so that's when I made the phone calls to these prominent African-Americans—Oprah Winfrey, Bill Cosby, Magic Johnson, Michael Jordan, and others.

And their contributions were gifts.

These were gifts—not loans, not investments. So for two months we continued to work and neither the Bond Company nor Warner Bros., knew where the money was coming from. That really fucked 'em up. I chose to announce what we had been able to do on May 19th, Malcolm's birthday, at a press conference at the Schomburg Center. *Miraculously,* two days later, the Bond Company and Warner Bros. worked it out. They say it was just a coincidence, that it would have happened anyway. I say bullshit.

But I hope this will be a precedent. Next time, maybe myself or some other filmmaker will bypass Hollywood altogether for financing and go directly to people like Oprah or Bill or Magic or Michael who'll finance the production, and then just go to Hollywood for distribution once the film is done. There are plenty of black people with money, plenty of black entrepreneurs. It can be done.

Are there other major black historical figures that you'd like to do films on?

Yeah, Walter Yetnikoff and I are working to acquire the rights to Miles Davis's life story. I heard that Robert Townsend may direct and star in a film on Duke Ellington. Right now, Touchstone is getting ready to do the Tina Turner story, with Angela Bassett, who plays Betty Shabazz in *Malcolm X,* as Tina and Larry Fishburne as Ike Turner. What we hope, what we're praying for, is that with the success of *Malcolm X,* you'll be able to eventually see films about Miles Davis, Paul Robeson, Harriet Tubman, Sojourner Truth . . . you can go right on down the line.

bell hooks (essay date August 1994)

SOURCE: "Sorrowful Black Death Is Not a Hot Ticket," in *Sight and Sound,* Vol. 4, No. 8, August, 1994, pp. 10-14.

[*In the following essay, hooks asserts that Lee's* Crooklyn *presents an "anti-woman, anti-feminist vision of black family life."*]

Hollywood is not into plain old sorrowful death. The death that captures the public imagination in movies, the death that sells, is passionate, sexualised, glamorised and violent. Films like *One False Move, True Romance, Reservoir Dogs, Menace II Society, A Perfect World* bring us the sensational heat of relentless dying. It's fierce—intense—and there is no time to mourn. Dying that makes audiences contemplative, sad, mindful of the transitory nature of human life has little appeal. When portrayed in the contemporary Hollywood film, such deaths are swift, romanticised by soft lighting and elegiac soundtracks. The sights and sounds of death do not linger long enough to disturb the senses, to remind us in any way that sorrow for the dying may be sustained and unrelenting. When Hollywood films depict sorrowful death, audiences come prepared to cry. Films like *Philadelphia* advertise the pathos so that even before tickets are bought and seats are taken, everyone knows that tears are in order, but that the crying time will not last long.

The racial politics of Hollywood is such that there can be no serious representations of death and dying when the characters are African-Americans. Sorrowful black death is not a hot ticket. In the financially successful film *The Body-guard,* the sister of Rachel Marron (Whitney Houston) is accidentally assassinated by the killer she has hired. There is no grief, no remembrance. In most Hollywood movies, black death is violent. It is often trivialised and mocked—as in that viciously homophobic moment in *Menace II So-ciety* when a young black male crack addict holding a fast-food hamburger while seeking drugs tells the powerful drug dealer, "I'll suck your dick", only to be blown away for daring to suggest that the hard gangsta mack would be at all interested. Pleased with the killing, he laughingly offers the hamburger to onlookers, a gesture that defines the value of black life. It's worth nothing. It's dead meat.

Even black children cannot be spared Hollywood's cruelty. Audiences watching the film *Paris Trout* witness the pro-longed, brutal slaughter of a gifted southern black girl by a powerful, sadistic, racist white man. The black males who are her relatives are depicted as utterly indifferent. Too cowardly to save or avenge her life, for a few coins they will-ingly show the lawyer who will defend her killer the blood stains left by her dragging body, the bullet holes in the walls. Her life is worth nothing.

Violent slaughter

Audiences are so accustomed to representations of the bru-tal death of black folks in Hollywood films that no one is outraged when our bodies are violently slaughtered. I could find no Hollywood movie where a white child is the object of a prolonged, brutal murder by a powerful white male—no image comparable to that of *Paris Trout.* Yet no group in the United States publicly protests against this image—even though the film is shown regularly on Home Box Of-fice, reaching an audience far wider than the moviegoing public, finding its way into the intimate spaces of home life and the private world of family values. Apparently the graphic representation of the murder of a little black girl does not shock, does not engender grief or protest. There is col-lective cultural agreement that black death is inevitable, meaningless, not worth much. That there is nothing to mourn.

This is the culture Spike Lee confronts with his new film *Crooklyn.* On the surface, the movie appears to represent issues of death and dying in black life as though our sur-vival matters, as though our living bodies count, yet in the end the usual Hollywood message about black death is re-affirmed. Lee has made a film that is both provocative and controversial. To introduce it to consumers who do not take black life seriously, advertisements give little indication of its content. Huge billboards tell consumers "The Smart Choice is Spike Lee's hilarious *Crooklyn*", suggesting that the film is a comedy. The seriousness of the subject matter must be downplayed, denied.

Expecting to see a comedy, moviegoers I talked to were not so much disappointed as puzzled by the fact that the come-dic elements were overshadowed by the serious representa-tion of a family in crisis that culminates with the mother's death. When the movie ended, the folks standing around the theatre in Greenwich Village were mostly saying: "It wasn't what I expected. It wasn't like his other films." But *Crooklyn* differs from Lee's previous work primarily because the ma-jor protagonist is a ten-year-old-girl, Troy (Zelda Harris). Positively radical in this regard—rarely do we see Holly-wood films with black female stars, not to mention child stars—*Crooklyn* invites audiences to look at black experi-ence through Troy's eyes, to enter the spaces of her emo-tional universe, the intimate world of family and friends that grounds her being and gives her life meaning.

Lee's magic as a film-maker has been best expressed by his construction of an aesthetic space wherein decolonised im-ages (familiar representations of blackness that oppose rac-ist stereotypes) are lovingly presented. But this radical intervention is most often framed by a conventional narra-tive and structure of representations that reinscribes stereo-typical norms. The laughing darky family portrait that advertises *Crooklyn* is just one example. Moviegoers want to see this image rather than those that challenge it. This con-tradictory stance tends to undermine Lee's ability to subvert dominant representations of blackness. His radical images are usually overshadowed by stock characterisations and can be easily overlooked, particularly by audiences who are more accustomed to stereotypes. Even progressive, aware view-ers may be so fascinated by the funky, funny 'otherness' of typical Spike Lee black images that they refuse to 'see' rep-resentations that challenge conventional ways of looking at blackness.

J. Hoberman's review of *Crooklyn* in *Village Voice* is a per-fect example of the way our standpoint can determine how we see what we see. Hoberman did not see a film that high-lights issues of death and dying—to his mind's eye, "the grit-tier specifics of the Lee family drama" are exemplified by arguments at family dinners and witty disagreements over television programmes. Indeed, he saw the movie as having "no particular plot"; never mentioning the mother's death, he did not see the film as constructing a context in which this event, more than any other, leads to a ten-year-old black girl's coming of age. Hoberman is more engaged with the comedic aspects of the film, especially those that centre on the eldest child in this family of four boys and one girl, Clinton (Carlton Williams), the character who most re-sembles Lee himself. Not unlike other moviegoers I talked to, Hoberman seems more fascinated with the antics of Spike Lee, controversial film-maker, than with the content of his film. By deflecting attention away from *Crooklyn* and on to Lee, Hoberman and others do not have to interrogate the film on its own terms. To do that would require looking at

Crooklyn's treatment of death and dying, and the way this aspect of the film fails to excite and challenge our imagination.

Play and pleasure

Crooklyn is most compelling in those moments when it offers fictive representations of black subjectivity rarely seen in mainstream cinema, depictions that counter both racist stereotypes and facile notions of positive images. The property-owning, artistic, progressive 70s black family portrayed is one that dares to be different. The Carmichaels in no way represent the conventional black bourgeoisie: they are not obsessed with being upwardly mobile, with the material trappings of success. Counter-cultural—a mixture of the nationalist movement for racial uplift and a bohemian artistic subculture—they represent an alternative to the bourgeois norm.

The father Woody (Delroy Lindo) is an aspiring jazz musician and composer, the mother Carolyn (Alfre Woodard) a non-traditional schoolteacher. Their five children are all encouraged by progressive, hands-off parenting to be individuals with their own interests, passions and obsessions. These are not your average kids: they take a democratic vote to see which television show will be watched and are made to participate equally in household chores. Though black nationalist thinking shapes the family politics, the world they live in is multicultural and multi-ethnic—Italians, Latinos, gays and straights, young and old, the haves and have nots are all part of the mix. This is the world of cultural hybridity and border crossing extolled by progressive contemporary critics. And much of the film depicts that world 'as is', not framed by the will to present images that are artificially positive or unduly negative.

Beginning in the style of a fictive documentary (enhanced initially by the cinematography of Arthur Jafa), the film's opening scene offers a panorama of visual images of black community that disrupts prevailing one-dimensional portrayals of urban black life. Highlighting scenes of play and pleasure, the beauty of black bodies, the faces of children and old men, we see joy in living as opposed to the usual depictions of racial dehumanisation and deprivation. These representations signal heightened creativity, an unbridled imagination that creates splendour in a world of lack, that makes elegance and grace so common a part of the everyday as to render them regular expressions of natural communion with the universe.

Northerners in drag

This opening sequence acts like a phototext, calling us to be resisting readers able to embrace a vision of blackness that challenges the norm. Lee engages a politics of repre-sentation which cultural critic Saidiya Hartman describes in 'Roots and Romance', an essay on black photography, as "a critical labor of reconstruction". She explains: "It is a resolutely counterhegemonic labor that has as its aim the establishment of other standards of aesthetic value and visual possibility. The intention of the work is corrective representation." At rare moments through the film this strategy is realised. And it is marvellous to follow where the camera leads—to catch sight of such empowering images. Seduced by this initial moment of radical intervention—by the way it shifts paradigms and requires new ways of seeing—the enthralled viewer can sit in a daze of delight through the rest of the movie, failing to experience how the cinematic direction and narrative structure counteract the initial subversive representations.

A distinction must be made between oppositional representations and romantically glorifying images of blackness which white supremacist thinking as it informs movie-making may have rendered invisible. Visibility does not mean that images are inherently radical or progressive. Hartman urges cultural critics to interrogate this distinction, to ask necessary questions: "Simply put, how are redemptive narratives of blackness shaped and informed by romantic racialism, the pastoral and sentimental representation of black life? How is the discourse of black cultural authenticity and Afrocentrism shaped and informed by this construction of Africanism and do they too maintain and normalise white cultural hegemony?" *Crooklyn* is offered as a redemptive narrative. The counterhegemonic images we see at the beginning serve to mask all that is 'wrong' with this picture.

From the moment we encounter the Carmichaels at their dinner table, we are offered a non-critical representation of their family life. Shot like docu-drama, these early scenes appear innocent and neutral; the ethnographic day-in-a-life style of presentation demands that the viewer see nothing wrong with this picture. The camera aggressively normalises. These family scenes are presented unproblematically and so appear to be positive representations, fulfilling Lee's quest to bring to the big screen 'authentic' black aesthetic subjects.

Since Spike Lee's cinematic genius is best revealed during those moments when he documents familiar aspects of a rich black cultural legacy wherein collective internal codes and references that may or may not be known to outsiders converge, it is easy to overlook the fact that these counterhegemonic representations are constantly countered in his work by stock stereotypical images. When these are coupled with Lee's use of 'animal house' type humour appropriated from mainstream white culture, a carnivalesque atmosphere emerges that seems directed towards mainstream, largely white, viewers. This cultural borrowing, which gives the movie cross-over appeal, is most evident in the scenes where Troy travels south to stay with relatives in a Virginia suburb. Though the cinematography didactically demands that the audience detach from a notion of the 'real' and engage the 'ridiculous and absurd', these scenes appear stupid, especially the mysterious, not really comical, death of the pet dog Troy's aunt dotes on. Lee works overtime to create a comedic atmosphere to contrast with the seriousness of the Carmichael household, but it does not work; the switch to an anamorphic lens confuses (no doubt that is why signs were placed at ticket booths telling viewers that this change did not indicate a problem with the projector). In these scenes Lee mockingly caricatures the southern black middle class (who appear more like northerners in drag doing the classic Hollywood comedic rendition of southern life). Lee gives it to us in black face. It is predictable and you can't wait to return home to the Carmichael family. However, while he strategically constructs images to normalise the dysfunctions of the Carmichael family, he insists on making this family pathological. This attempt at counterhegemonic representation fails.

Anyone who sees the Carmichael family without the rose-coloured glasses the film offers will realise that they are seriously dysfunctional. The recurrent eating disorders (one of the children is coercively forced by verbal harassment to eat to the point where on one occasion he vomits in his plate); an excessive addiction to sugar (dad's pouring half a bag of the white stuff into a pitcher of lemonade, his cake and ice-cream forays, his candy-buying all hint that he may be addicted to more than sugar, though he is not overtly shown to be a drug-user); the lack of economic stability, signified by the absence of money for food choice, shutting off the electricity, as well as dad's mismanagement of funds, are all indications that there are serious problems. By normalising the family image, Lee refuses to engage with the issue of psychological abuse; all interactions are made to appear natural, ordinary, comedic, not tragic. The autobiographical roots of *Crooklyn* may account for Lee's inability to take any stance other than that of 'objective' reporter; working with a screenplay written collaboratively with his sister Joie and brother Cinqué, he may have felt the need to distance himself from the material. Certainly emotional detachment characterises the interaction between family members in the film.

Joie Lee stated that to write the screenplay she "drew from the few memories I have of my mother", who died of cancer when she was 14. Yet the children in *Crooklyn* are much younger than this and are clearly deeply ambivalent about their mother. Portrayed as a modern-day Sapphire with direct lineage to the *Amos n' Andy* character, Carolyn responds to economic crisis by constantly nagging and erupting into irrational states of anger and outrage that lead her to be mean and at times abusive. Even though the problems the family faces are caused by Woody's unemployment, he is depicted

compassionately—an aspiring artist who just wants to be left alone to compose music, always laid-back and calm.

Sexist/racist stereotypes of gender identity in black experience are evident in the construction of these two characters. Although Carolyn is glamorous, beautiful in her Afrocentric style, she is portrayed as a bitch goddess. Her physical allure seduces, even as her unpredictable rage alienates. In keeping with sexist stereotypes of the emasculating black matriarch, Carolyn usurps her husband's authority by insisting that as the primary breadwinner she has the right to dominate, shaming Woody in front of the children. These aspects encourage us to see her unsympathetically and to empathise with him. His irresponsibility and misuse of resources is given legitimacy by the suggestion that his is an artistic, non-patriarchal mindset; he cannot be held accountable. Since Carolyn's rage is often over-reactive, it is easy to forget that she has concrete reasons to be angry. Portrayed as vengeful, anti-pleasure, dangerous and threatening, her moments of tenderness are not sustained enough to counter the negatives. Even her sweetness is depicted as manipulative, whereas Woody's 'sweet' demeanour is a mark of his artistic sensibility, one that enhances his value.

As the artist, he embodies the pleasure principle, the will to transgress. His mild-mannered response to life is infinitely more compelling than the work-hard-to-meet-your-responsibilities ethic by which Carolyn lives. Being responsible seems to make her 'crazy'. In one scene the children are watching a basketball game when she encourages them to turn off the television to do schoolwork. They refuse to obey and she goes berserk. Woody intervenes, not to offer reinforcement, but rather to take sides. Carolyn becomes the bad guy, who wants to curtail the children's freedom to indulge in pleasure without responsibility. Woody responds to her rage by being physically coercive. Domestic violence in black life is sugarcoated—portrayed as a family affair, one where there are no victims or abusers. In fact, Carolyn has been humiliated and physically assaulted. But her demand that Woody leave makes him appear the victim and the children first attend to him, pleading with him not to go. Her pain is unattended by her male children; it is Troy who assumes the traditional feminine role of caretaker.

In contrast to Carolyn, the ten-year-old Troy is concerned with traditional notions of womanhood. Her mother expresses rage at not being able to "take a piss without six people hanging off my tits", repudiating sexist thinking about the woman's role. Flirtatious and cute, Troy manipulates with practised charm. It is she who advises her dad to take Carolyn on a date to make up. Troy embodies all the desirable elements of sexist-defined femininity. Indeed, it is her capacity to escape into a world of romantic fantasy that makes her and everyone else ignore her internal anguish. When she lies, steals and cheats, her acts of defiance have no consequences. As the little princess, she has privileges denied her brothers; when her mother is sick, it is only Troy who is sheltered from this painful reality and sent down south.

In the home of her southern relatives, Troy meets a fair-skinned cousin who is portrayed as conventionally feminine in her concerns, though she is eager to bond with her guest. By contrast Troy assumes a 'bitchified role'. She is hostile, suspicious, until charmed. Representing the light-skinned female as 'good' and Troy as 'bad', *Crooklyn,* like all Lee's films, perpetuates stereotypes of darker-skinned females as evil. While her cousin is loving, Troy is narcissistic and indifferent. When she decides to return home, it is her cousin who runs alongside the car that carries Troy away, waving tenderly, while Troy appears unconcerned. This encounter prepares us for her transformation from princess to mini-matriarch.

Taken to the hospital to see her mother, Troy is given instructions as to how she must assume the caretaker role. Contemporary feminist thinkers are calling attention to girlhood as a time when females have access to greater power than that offered us in womanhood. No one in the film is concerned about the loss of Troy's girlhood, though her brothers remain free to maintain their spirit of play. Clinton, the eldest boy, does not have to relinquish his passion for sports to become responsible; he can still be a child. But becoming a mini-matriarch because her mother is sick and dying requires of Troy that she relinquish all concern with pleasure and play, that she repress desire. Sexist/racist thinking about black female identity leads to cultural acceptance of the exploitation and denigration of black girlhood. Commenting on the way black girls are often forced to assume adult roles in *In the Company of My Sisters: Black Women and Self-Esteem,* Julia Boyd asserts: "Without fully understanding the adult tasks we were expected to perform, we filled shoes that were much too big for our small feet. Again, we did not have a choice and we weren't allowed to experience the full developmental process of girlhood." Lee romanticises this violation by making it appear a 'natural' progression for Troy rather than sexist gender politics coercively imposing a matriarchal role via a process of socialisation.

Television times

Carolyn did not make gender distinctions about household chores when she was well, and the movie fails to indicate why she now has an unconvincing shift in attitude. As if to highlight patriarchal thinking that females are interchangeable, undifferentiated, the film in no way suggests that there is anything wrong with a ten-year-old girl assuming an adult role. Indeed, this is affirmed, and the mother's dying is upstaged by the passing of the torch to Troy. The seriousness of her illness is announced to the children by their father, who commands them to turn away from their gleeful watching of *Soul Train* to hear the news (even in her absence, the mother/matriarch spoils their pleasure). Throughout *Crooklyn* Lee shows the importance of television in shaping the children's identities, their sense of self. While the boys panic emotionally when they hear the news, bursting into tears, Troy's feelings are hidden by a mask of indifference. That the children obey their father in their mother's absence (not complaining when he tells them to turn off the television) suggests that he is better able to assume an authoritative parental role when she is no longer present. Woody's transformation into a responsible adult reinscribes the sexist/racist thinking that the presence of a 'strong' black female emasculates the male. Carolyn's death is treated in a matter-of-fact manner; we learn about it as the children casually discuss the funeral. We never see the family grieve. Troy, who is emotionally numb, only confronts the reality of this death when she is jolted from sleep by what she imagines is her mother's raging voice. Bonding with her father in the kitchen, her suppressed grief does not unleash tears; instead she vomits. This ritual cathartic cleansing is the rite of passage that signals her movement away from girlhood.

Taking her mother's place, Troy is no longer adventurous. She no longer roams the streets, discovering, but is bound to the house, to domestic life. While the male children and grown-up dad continue to lead autonomous lives, to express their creativity and will to explore, Troy is confined, her creativity stifled. Since she is always and only a mother substitute, her power is more symbolic than real. We see her tending to the needs of her brothers, being the 'little woman'. Gone is the vulnerable, emotionally open girl who expressed a range of feelings; in her place is a hard impenetrable mask. Just as no one mourns the mother's death, no one mourns the erasure of Troy's adolescence. In their book *Failing at Fairness: How America's Schools Cheat Girls,* Myra and David Sadker document the pervasiveness of a "curricular sexism" that turns girls into "spectators instead of players". Troy becomes a spectator, standing behind the gate looking out at life, a stern expression on her face.

Silent losses

Though dead, Carolyn reappears to reassure and affirm her daughter. This reappearance is yet another rejection of loss. The controlling, dominating mother remains present even when dead, visible only to her girl child, now the guardian of patriarchy who gives approval to Troy's subjugation. Powerful black mothers, who work outside the home, the film suggests, 'fail' their families. Their punishment is death. When she is dying Carolyn gives lessons in sexism to her daughter in a way that runs counter to the values she has expressed throughout the film (she does, however, encourage her daughter to think about a work future, if only because it is her own career that ensured the family's economic survival).

The Sadkers conclude their introductory chapter, which exposes the way sexist socialisation robs girls of their potential, with a section called 'Silent Losses' that ends with the declaration: "If the cure for cancer is forming in the mind of one of our daughters, it is less likely to become a reality than if it is forming in the mind of one of our sons." Whereas *Crooklyn* attempts to counter racist assumptions about black identity, it upholds sexist and misogynist thinking about gender roles. Order is restored in the Carmichael house when the dominating mother-figure dies. The emergence of patriarchy is celebrated, marked by the subjugating of Troy, and all the household's problems 'magically' disappear. Life not only goes on without the matriarch, but is more harmonious.

Crooklyn constructs a redemptive fictive narrative for black life where the subjugation of the black female body is celebrated as a rite of passage which is restorative, which ensures family survival. Whether it is the grown woman's body erased by death or the little girl's body erased by violent interruption of her girlhood, the sexist politics embedded in this movie has often gone unnoticed by viewers whose attention is riveted by the exploits of the male characters. In failing to identify with the female characters or to bring any critical perspective to these representations, audiences tacitly condone the patriarchal devaluation and erasure of rebellious black female subjectivity the film depicts. Oppositional representations of blackness deflect attention away from the sexist politics that surfaces when race and gender converge. The naturalistic style of *Crooklyn* gives the sense of life-as-is rather than life as fictive construction.

Lee is indeed fictively re-imagining the 70s in this film and not merely providing a nostalgic portrait of the way things were. In his ahistorical narrative there is no meaningful convergence of black liberation and feminist politics, whereas in reality black women active in nationalist black power groups were challenging sexism and insisting on a feminist agenda. In *Crooklyn* Lee's aggressively masculinist vision is diffused by excessive sentimentality and by the use of Troy as the central embodiment of his message. Writing about the dangers that arise when excessive emotionality is used as a cover-up for a different agenda, James Baldwin reminds us that: "Sentimentality is the ostentatious parading of excessive and spurious emotion. It is the mark of dishonesty, the inability to feel." Such emotional dishonesty emerges full force in *Crooklyn*. The focus on Troy's coming of age and her mother's death is a non-threatening cover for the more insidious anti-woman, anti-feminist vision of black family life that is the film's dominant theme.

It is used to mask the repressive patriarchal valorisation of black family life, in which the reinscription of sexist idealised femininity symbolically rescues the family from dissolution. Death and dying are merely a subtext in *Crooklyn,* a diversionary ploy that creates a passive emotional backdrop on to which Lee imposes a vision of the black family that is conservative and in no way opposed to the beliefs of white mainstream culture. The aspects of the film that are rooted in Lee's own life-story are the most interesting; it is when he exploits those memories to create a counter-worldview that will advance patriarchal thinking that the narrative loses its appeal.

Women's work

Testifying that writing this script was cathartic, that it enabled her to confront the past, Joie Lee declares: "The emotional things that happen to you as a child, they're timeless, they stay with you until you deal with them. I definitely cleaned up some areas in my life that I hadn't dealt with before—like death." But the film Spike Lee has made does not confront death. In *Crooklyn,* death and dying are realities males escape from. There is no redemptive healing of a gendered split between mind and body; instead, *Crooklyn* echoes the patriarchal vision celebrated in Norman O. Brown's *Life Against Death,* where the hope is that "unrepressed man" "would be rid of the nightmares . . . haunting civilization" and that "freedom from those fantasies would also mean freedom from that disorder in the human body."

The messiness of death is women's work in *Crooklyn.* Expressing creativity, engaging pleasure and play is the way men escape from the reality of death and dying. In the space of imaginative fantasy, Lee can resurrect the dead female mothering body and create a world where there is never any need to confront the limitations of the flesh and therefore no place for loss. In such a world there is no need for grief, since death has no meaning.

Kent Jones (essay date January/February 1997)

SOURCE: "The Invisible Man: Spike Lee," in *Film Comment,* Vol. 33, No. 1, January/February, 1997, pp. 42-7.

[*In the following essay, Jones discusses Lee's body of work.*]

The proof of Spike Lee's insight is the clamor of opposing rash positions around his films—how difficult is it to imagine a scene from a Lee movie in which a gaggle of film critics scream their opinions about the relative worth of a young African-American filmmaker's oeuvre in each other's faces, shot in contrasting off-angles and perfectly sculpted light? His less sophisticated admirers, in other words those who are unwilling to apply the same sort of hardworking analysis to his work that he applies to American society, have never done him any favors by pushing him as an "innovator." (Some innovator: his actor-on-the-dolly move, cribbed from *Mean Streets* and monotonously reprised in every film from *Mo' Better Blues* through *Girl 6,* is numbingly off-key and gives the impression to the unsuspecting viewer that certain sidewalks in the New York area are equipped with conveyor belts.) Then there are those who claim that he is basically reheating old-fashioned social consciousness in a rock video microwave. But the classic social consciousness of, say, *To Kill a Mockingbird* begins with an abstraction—Racism, and How It Can Be Overcome—and structures its narrative accordingly: a racist malefactor and a good and righteous man square off against the backdrop of an amorphously indifferent populace that could be swayed either way and finally listens to reason. Lee, on the other hand, always starts from the specifics that make up the fractured consciousness of African-American males. "Hey daddy, I'll suck your big black dick for two dollars!" drawls the teenaged whore to Wesley Snipes's Flipper Purify before he screams with indignation and takes her in his arms at the end of *Jungle Fever.* It's one of the few sweepingly rhetorical moments in modern cinema that earns its weight and self-importance because it's the culmination of a whole battery of anxieties, horrors, disappointments, and subterfuges that have all been laid out by Lee with his typical block-by-block, hard plastic clarity.

There is also the overgrown-film-student charge, somewhat easier to fathom but essentially wrong and recklessly dismissive. What I understand people to mean by this is that Lee is a showoff, which is true enough. His camera never gets comfortable, and no stroll down the block is complete without at least six changes of angle. He is also constantly throwing aesthetic blankets over large chunks of his movies: changes of film stock for different locales in *Clockers* and *Get On the Bus,* high-def video for the images of the phantom callers in *Girl 6,* the infamous (and truly maddening) squeezed anamorphic image for the Southern section of *Crooklyn.* That's not to mention the liberal application of pop songs ladled over large portions of his films. There are few filmmakers whose work seems less organic and more the sum of their aesthetic choices.

Moreover, there are few filmmakers who are less interested in (or less adept at?) giving us the rhythms of quotidian existence. The world of Spike Lee is almost completely devoid of the everyday tasks and actions that make up the backbone of most films. When he does have a go at everyday life, it is often editorialized to a level beyond absurdity. Annabella Sciorra's family in *Jungle Fever* is so heavily singularized and lacking in nuance that "Italian Family" seems to be a new flavor of salad dressing. The opening scenes of *Malcolm X* are the most embarrassing, a fifth-hand evocation of zoot-suit culture. Lee's relentless, never-ending con-

trol leaves you with the feeling that when his good actors (Snipes, Denzel Washington, Angela Bassett, Alfre Woodard, Giancarlo Esposito) score a few points, they're getting one over on their director.

The fact is that legibility and visibility are more important to Spike Lee than anything else. Every film has its own eye-catching design and every moment is held only as long as it takes to register as a sign; everything beyond that feels like a holding action. Lee is a completely arrhythmic filmmaker in this sense: tempo and nuance are always sacrificed for clarity. It's fascinating to watch one of his attempts to render abandon because of his complete unwillingness to surrender his lock on the visuals. (Image and sound often seem like two separate categories with their own energies: while the visuals feel uptight, cramped, and fixated on the center, the soundtrack is always a mighty river of words and music.) When Denzel Washington's Bleek is composing a tune in *Mo' Better Blues,* Lee puts his poor actor on the dolly and spins the room around him. It's very similar to Troy's dream of a glue-induced flight over the block in *Crooklyn* because of the way that both actors are all but stapled to the camera. What is supposed to play as a sense of flight, artistic in the first instance and psychosexual in the second, is instead tidy and tight as a drum. On close inspection, though (and close inspection of Lee's cinema is always rewarding), there's something conceptually right about the *Mo' Better* scene, since the story deals with the way that artistic expression can be the unhealthy result of a transferral of guarded aggression from mother to son, a mask of mastery to wear in a racist world.

Which is pretty close to a self-portrait, at least based on the evidence of Lee's films (and his acting: in all of Lee's performances his voice and his body seem to be going in two different directions, which plays like a bizarre and quite intriguing evasion technique). His detractors make an enormous leap when they lazily insist that there's nothing but a vacuum behind all that "style." How ridiculous: what other filmmaker has been more adept at delineating the process of American racism and treating it as a living organism rather than a frozen entity? It's no small achievement, even when the film is as artistically pallid and mushy as *School Daze* or *Mo' Better Blues.* The insistence on leaving nothing to chance, which often flattens out his representations of jazz clubs, city blocks, and middle-class homes to the point that they feel like computer art, has a painful, extracinematic edge. You can feel Lee's desire to loosen up, but it's always checked by his fear of making a move without the protection of his agile mind. His films are personal in the strangest sense: the artist is revealed by the many ways with which he chooses to constantly camouflage his personality.

The film school complaint is the other side of the coin from the more absurd charges of "reverse racism," divisiveness, and separatism, all of which are hogwash, and all of which start from the wrongheaded assumption that Lee is some kind of "special interest" filmmaker. Aside from the fact that people are constantly attributing sentiments voiced by Lee's warring characters to Lee himself, what's so striking about the frequent criticisms and judgments of his work is their eagerness to reduce it to a lowest "cinematic" denominator and sweep it under the rug. The idea that Lee is a propagandist grows out of what can only be understood as fear of encroachment on the sacred territory of American cinema and its myths. It's the same kind of fear that once prompted a friend of mine to make the following remark to an acquaintance on the neighboring barstool who said he was afraid to go to Harlem: "Let me get this straight—you're afraid to be a white man in America?"

Lee goes against the grain of the model well-rounded filmmaker, balanced between the thematic and the organic, between action and emotion. As an artist, he has firmly positioned himself midway between didacticism and dialectics. The didactic side is his tireless effort to keep the desires, frustrations, looming terrors, and class diversity among African-American men visible and viable within mainstream, i.e. white, i.e. racist American culture. (He is less interested in women but willing to keep his films democratically open to their viewpoints, as in the interminable but informative improvised discussion in *Jungle Fever.*) The dialectical side is the rigorous manner in which he breaks down and presents the warring components of American society, a pot in which nothing melts and everything congeals (he has never been interested in the currently fashionable Hollywood idea of "positive images of black people," in which Wesley Snipes or Samuel L. Jackson is afforded the same golden opportunity as Bruce Willis or Harrison Ford to play the lead in idiotic action movies). The ensuing tension, which catches characters in a grid between the personal and the societal, is palpable in every one of his films, from the throwaway *Girl 6* to the hymnlike *Get On the Bus,* from the synthetically delicate *She's Gotta Have It* to the grandiose *Malcolm X,* from the awful yet shaggily lovable *School Daze* to the magnificent *Do the Right Thing* and *Jungle Fever.* And that tension makes something odd but undeniably beautiful out of *Crooklyn,* an autobiographical reminiscence filtered through his sister Joie (he co-authored the script with her and brother Cinqué) that all but denies the possibility of Proustian reverie in favor of a systematic and seemingly exhaustive survey of the focal points, obsessions, and imagery of an early-Seventies African-American childhood. It's a haunting film in which the action is interestingly dispersed across a more delicate visual palette than the burnished tones of Ernest Dickerson would have allowed (courtesy of *Daughters of the Dust* cinematographer Arthur Jafa), suggestive of public-school mural art.

Placing Lee as a filmmaker rather than as a public figure or

a provocateur has been somewhat set aside over the years. An instructive comparison would be Claire Denis, another essentially cold and precise filmmaker intent on rendering the multicultural makeup of modern life, who also strategically casts her films in warm, convivial tones and atmospheres. Denis is also a filmmaker of choices: a handheld camera for *S'en fout la mort,* interlocking narratives in *J'ai pas sommeil,* extreme closeup sensuality spread dolloped all over *Nénette et Boni.* But there are moments of comfort and reflection for her characters, and none whatsoever for Lee's—the people in his films are just as guarded and wary as their creator, who may never be relaxed enough to make a spontaneously generated autobiographical work like *U.S. Go Home.* A better precedent for Lee in world cinema is Nagisa Oshima, in whose films the patient accumulation of dry detail and opposing forces bursts open with an emblematic action at the film's climax. The ending of *Jungle Fever* or Mookie's garbage can in the window at the end of *Do the Right Thing* are kissing cousins to culminating moments like the eating of the apple in *Cruel Story of Youth* or the moment in *Dear Summer Sister* when the girl says, "They should never have given Okinawa back to the Japanese." Oshima is a more naturally elegant and economical filmmaker than Lee—more than he would probably have cared to admit in his angrier days—but they are both children of Brecht with a shared obsession with clarity, specificity, and the abandonment of personal concerns in favor of political directness. An interesting cultural divide: where one might say that Lee "likes" all of his characters, one might in turn say that Oshima "hates" all of his, at least in early films like *The Sun's Burial* (perhaps it's more correct to say that he equalizes them to a uniform unpleasantness). In any case, the net effect is virtually identical.

Lee may be even bleaker than his relentlessly tough Japanese cousin. There is always a lot of high spirits, Fifties-style sentimentality, and verbal jazz in Lee's work. But they hide what is in the end a despairing vision of existence, in which the backdrop of divisiveness and polarization not only never gives way to transcendent action and understanding (the way it does with the kiss at the end of Oshima's *Merry Christmas, Mr. Lawrence*) but shadows his characters mercilessly. When it's not felt in the restless visuals or through the neurotically inert characters—Lee's people, like Fassbinder's, are forever making small, tightly circumscribed movements across a limited selection of folkways that make them look like rats in a maze—it's there in the oppressively heavy atmosphere, a side effect of turning every field of action (Morehouse College, a movieish jazz club located in some unimaginably bland netherworld, the life of Malcolm X, a project courtyard, a Brooklyn block) into a metaphorically charged space. There's an uncharacteristic moment in *Jungle Fever* when Lee suddenly cuts to Flipper standing on a bad corner of Harlem a split second before he consorts with some unsavory characters in search of his crackhead brother

(Samuel L. Jackson). You can feel his tension, distaste, and angry confusion in the way he mills around, his body tight. It's an unusual moment because it hands over the reins to an actor, no matter how short the duration. The entire Harlem—swanky-architectural-firm—Bensonhurst social grid that Lee has set up seems to be pressing down on Flipper.

There are appalling things in *Jungle Fever,* but it remains his most devastating film, perhaps for the crazy reason that it's the one most packed with interlocking thematic material. That's the paradox of Lee as an artist: the more linear and streamlined his films are, the duller they get and the more they flounder. The Tim Robbins-Brad Dourif yuppie tag team, the Italian family scenes (Anthony Quinn's performance as a supposedly prototypical Italian father—"Your mother was a *real woman!*"—is like an industrial disaster in an olive oil factory), the floating conversations between Lee and Snipes all just sit there, but their place in the grid that Lee sets up, the way they counterpoint, amplify, and bruise one another, give the film a remarkable fullness and social three-dimensionality. As in *Do the Right Thing* (which has some similarly awful moments that are nonetheless vital cogs in the machinery, like Lee and Turturro's conversation about niggers), Lee achieves something rare in American cinema, which is an illustration of the degree to which people are products of their environment, a far cry from the bogus individualism of so much American cinema. Flipper and Angie (Sciorra) are ciphers at the center of *Jungle Fever,* surrounded by a range of far more vivid characters: Ossie Davis's terrifyingly stern, separatist, Old Testament father and Ruby Dee's pathologically genteel mother, John Turturro's haloed candy store proprietor, and Samuel L. Jackson's horrifying crackhead. And on reflection what seems like an artistic miscalculation turns out to be a dialectical strategy. Lee is speaking to middle-class people like Flipper (and himself, presumably) who keep things status quo by avoiding the cacophony of warring voices in their ears, just as in *Do the Right Thing* he is speaking to layabouts like Mookie who try to float through the world and eventually act out of sheer psychic exhaustion. When Mookie throws that garbage can through the window, he is egged on by his neighborhood friends, as Jonathan Rosenbaum has correctly pointed out, but he is also making a fruitless and mindless gesture that is the result of so much heat, aggravation, and sloganeering. It seems appropriate that the characters are diminished by the confusion that makes up their world (was this the reason Wim Wenders made his insane and now legendary comment that Mookie was not enough of a hero?) and that they have no time or room to analyze calmly.

In his less successful work, the striking moments come unmoored in a sea of heady aesthetic choices. Since Lee films every moment with equal weight and at an unvarying rhythm, his hyperbolic clarity can backfire on him when the focal points are reduced in number. *Clockers* is an unsatisfying film because the sheer immersion technique of Richard Price's novel is antithetical to Lee's aesthetic strengths. If any of his films does actually follow the old social-consciousness model it's this one, in which every character represents not a societal force but a different symbolic aspect of The Drug Problem In The Ghetto. (Lee is about as good a candidate for an in-depth study of life in the projects as Richard Attenborough.) But there are impassioned moments, particularly the montage in which a slow track away from Strike (Mekhi Phifer) playing with his trains is intercut with terrifyingly immediate shots of real crackheads scoring and getting high. There's nothing terribly wrong with *Malcolm X* beyond the fact that it drains a lot of the flashfire anger and drama out of the autobiography to give us a good, sturdy, dignified tour through the subject's life (the most striking passages of the film move with the slow and stately rhythm of Washington and Angela Bassett's immaculately acted mutual respect). *Girl 6,* which seems to enter a more playful mode, devolves into nothing much by the end (although it does have one of Lee's most physically frank moments: Isaiah Washington's shoplifter sweet-talks ex-wife Theresa Randle into an alley and shoves her hand down his pants).

Get On the Bus marks a turning point for Lee, a move towards a valid, tempered feeling of uplift and more faith in his actors and away from so much fanatical control. Lee finds myriad ways of exploring the faces of his uniformly magnificent actors in worried contemplation, to the point where his film takes on a singing beauty and a simple closeup of the great Charles Dutton carries real weight. There have been some ridiculous things written about this buoyant, defiantly old-fashioned movie, far from a song of praise to Louis Farrakhan. The Million Man March does not take on ideological but symbolic import: the simple and joyous fact of one million African-American men congregating in one place is what motivates everyone to get on the Spotted Owl to Washington, and the feeling is echoed by the actors as they bite into their meaty roles. The makeup is standard WWII bomber crew stuff: an old failure, a young upstart actor, a gentle cop, a reformed gangbanger, a homosexual couple, a silent Muslim, a Republican businessman, an estranged father reunited with his gangbanger son and chained to him by court order, a Jewish relief driver, an aspiring filmmaker/witness ("Spike Lee Jr.," as one of the characters calls him), and the bus driver-spokesman hash out what seems like every conflict that currently besets the African-American community in a more musical version of vintage Rod Serling or Reginald Rose. But as always, Lee short-circuits any answers beyond a lonely self-respect. There is a painfully beautiful moment midfilm when the cop, whose father has been killed by gang members and whose beat is the ghetto, listens to the murder confession of the former gangbanger-turned-counselor, a moment made possible by the fellowship of the bus ride. And the cop suddenly turns the tables and tells him he'll have to arrest him when they get back to L.A. Lee cuts away from the standoff to a shot of the moon seen from the front window. This is presumably one of the moments in the film that's been called a cop-out, but is it a cop-out to illustrate a hopelessly divisive issue and refuse to put a Band-Aid on it? Lee isn't turning away from the conflict but turning towards the sad flow of time.

Get On the Bus may be his most heart-felt movie, but it still has the protective coating of every other Lee film—its materials are just more human. As he slowly loses his audience in the increasingly foul atmosphere of corporate culture (*Bus* disappeared from theaters with ruthless speed), it's puzzling to imagine how Lee will evolve. As a filmmaker he is caught between a rock and a hard place: he is too resolutely anti-American for the self-satisfaction of the current political climate, and he is too tightly coiled an artist to generate new enthusiasms now that the first flush has been over for some time. As much as I admire his abilities as a dialectician, the most penetrating moments in his enormously complex cinema are the small, instinctive ones. There is a moment at the end of *Crooklyn* when three of the children are walking up a public staircase, two of them holding hands and the other straggling behind, and they are lackadaisically singing a song that is gently echoed by a harmonica in Terence Blanchard's score. When they stop they wonder what they'll be wearing to their mother's funeral. The heartbreak—and the moment is heartbreaking like few moments in recent cinema—is in the high oblique angle that places the kids in a vast expanse of concrete, a detail that feels as if it comes straight from the filmmaker's memory. And it's in the stoic trudge up the steps, the sense of a burden that must be shouldered with dignity at all costs.

And then there are two moments in *Jungle Fever* and *Get On the Bus,* almost identical. In *Jungle Fever,* during the crushing scene where Snipes and Sciorra are fooling around on the hood of a car, Lee makes a brief cut to a shot from the point of view of an apartment window looking down on them. We never see the inhabitant and the shot is over quickly, but once Lee cuts back to his interracial couple we just wait for the sirens to start blaring. And in *Get On the Bus,* amidst the guarded but real camaraderie of a Memphis bar (exemplified by a lovely moment in which Davis and the proprietor bridge their racial divide with a shared passion for rodeo, reminiscent of the scene in Powell's *A Canterbury Tale* in which the Oregonian G.I. and the Kentish car-

penter talk woodworking), Lee makes an almost subliminal cut to a shot of a random white face staring. We don't see what he's staring at, but we don't have to. In both instances, a whole range of anger and fear is shot right into the heart of the film. It's during moments like these that I feel another, more vulnerable Spike Lee lurking beneath the quicksilver intelligence and stoic demeanor of the one we know. The question is: does he really want to reveal himself to those staring faces and open windows, positioned throughout American culture, even in the supposedly generous world of cinephilia?

FURTHER READING

Criticism

Denzin, Norman K. "Do the Right Thing: Race in the USA." In *Images of Postmodern Society: Social Theory and Contemporary Cinema,* pp. 125-36. London: Sage Publications, 1991.

    Extols Lee's controversial film *Do the Right Thing* for its exposure of racism in postmodern America.

Handelman, David. "Insight to Riot." *Rolling Stone,* No. 556/557 (13-27 July 1989): 104-9, 174-5.

    Gives an overview of Lee's films, especially *Do the Right Thing,* and its reception at the Cannes Film Festival.

Perkins, Eric. "Renewing the African-American Cinema: The Films of Spike Lee." *Cineaste* XVII, No. 4 (1990): 4-8.

    Praises Lee's films for their look at African-American culture against the wider American sociopolitical milieu.

Williams, John. Review of *By Any Means Necessary: The Trials and Tribulations of the Making of "Malcolm X,"* by Spike Lee. *The Black Scholar* 23, No. 1 (Winter 1993): 35-6.

    Reviews favorably Lee's candid making-of-the-film companion volume.

Williams, Lena. Review of *Best Seat in the House: A Basketball Memoir,* by Spike Lee with Ralph Wiley. *The New York Times Book Review* (8 June 1997): 24.

    Faults the book, saying it sounds too much like television commentary, with too little personal insight.

Additional coverage of Lee's life and career is contained in the following sources published by Gale: *Black Writers,* **Vol. 2;** *Contemporary Authors,* **Vol. 125;** *Contemporary Authors New Revision Series,* **Vol. 42;** *Contemporary Literary Criticism,* **Vol. 105; and** *DISCovering Authors Modules: Multicultural Authors.*

Alain Locke
1886-1954

American philosopher, critic, and editor.

INTRODUCTION

A lifelong advocate for African-American arts and letters, Locke is best known as the editor of *The New Negro* (1925). This book was one of the earliest anthologies of works by authors of the Harlem Renaissance, an important cultural movement of African-American artists and writers. Locke is generally recognized as the greatest influence on the writers and artists of the Harlem Renaissance, even by his intellectual opponents such as W. E. B. Du Bois. Locke's aesthetic theories concretized the role and objectives of many African-American artists of the 1920s and were a virtual manifesto for artists involved with the Harlem Renaissance, while his writings on the relationship between culture and aesthetics continue to act as a catalyst in African-American art and literature today.

Biographical Information

Alain Locke was born in 1886 in Philadelphia, Pennsylvania. He attended Central High School and the Philadelphia School of Pedagogy. In 1904 he left to attend Harvard University, where he received the Phi Beta Kappa Award his junior year. While at Harvard, Locke studied under the psychologist and philosopher William James, the author and critic Charles Eliot Norton, and the philosopher George Santayana. Locke was the first African American to be awarded a Rhodes Scholarship to study at Oxford University, and then the first African American to graduate from Oxford with a bachelor's degree in literature. Locke left England for Berlin to pursue his interest in the philosophical movement known as the Austrian School of Value, which comprises the works of philosopher Franz Brentano and psychologist Alexius von Meinong. Locke later studied at the College de France in Paris, where he attended lectures by the French philosopher Henri Bergson. In 1912 Locke returned to the United States and became assistant professor of English and philosophy at Howard University in Washington D.C. He returned to Harvard in 1916 and completed his dissertation entitled "The Problem of Classification on the Theory of Value." Then in 1918 he returned to Howard University to become professor of philosophy. Locke was a visiting professor at several other American and Caribbean universities, but he remained at Howard until his retirement in 1952. While still living in Washington, D.C., Locke was involved with several literary journals in New York City, including *Opportunity,* edited by the sociologist Charles S.

Johnson; *Crisis,* edited by the writer and activist W. E. B. Du Bois; and *Survey Graphic,* where as a contributing editor Locke first published the material that would later become *The New Negro.* In addition to his book-length studies of African-American culture and literature, Locke published numerous annual literary reviews and critical essays in these and other journals. He died in 1954.

Major Works

Insisting on the intimate relationship between aesthetics and ethics, Locke based his writings on the sociopolitical relevance of the reclamation by the African-American community of the right to self-representation, a task best achieved, according to Locke, through literary expression. Locke's philosophy rejects all authoritarian and absolute principles, whether political or philosophical, in favor of a value-relative philosophy that privileges the experiences and beliefs of the individual. Locke's emphasis on the individual in value relativism led to his studies of the historical and cultural factors that contribute to the experiences of African-American artists. Locke's *The Negro in Art* (1940) is divided into three sections: the first about the African American as artist; the second about the African-American theme in art; and the third about the African's ancestral arts. Locke asserts that African Americans are cut off from the arts of their African ancestors. He argued that the tradition of African art should be better understood by African Americans, a process labeled "ancestralism," in order to have a greater influence on their work. Concomitant with his role as a cultural critic, Locke was also a proponent of "art for art's sake" who believed that critics must utilize aesthetic rather than racial standards in assessing works of art. However, Locke's philosophy, which stresses the intimacy of art and identity, considers race a factor in all aesthetic categories. Throughout his works Locke produced socially engaged and aesthetically discerning discussions of politics and art, such as "The Dilemma of Segregation" and "The Contribution of Race to Culture." Locke's later career is characterized by works that qualify his early idealist belief in the power of a few privileged artists, the "talented tenth," to revolutionize the thinking of the masses.

Critical Reception

W. E. B. Du Bois asserts that *The New Negro* "is in many respects sprawling, illogical, with an open and unashamed lack of unity and continuity, and yet it probably expresses better than any book that has been published in the last ten years the present state of thought and culture among American Negroes and it expresses it so well and so adequately, with such ramification into all phases of thought and attitude, that it is a singularly unifying and inspiring thing." Many critics credited Locke with fostering the artists and writers of the Harlem Renaissance. H. M. Kallen states that Locke "made himself the philosophical midwife to a generation of younger Negro poets, writers, artists." Many critics took exception to Locke's focus on the "talented tenth" of the African-American community. Critics asserted that since Locke's work was aimed at the intellectual elite, he failed to understand the problems facing the majority of the African-American population. Others asserted that Locke was just politically naive. Receiving both credit and blame for the success and eventual demise of the Harlem Renaissance, Locke is remembered today as a critic and philosopher who applied his thinking to a variety of fields and whose works continue to contribute to current issues concerning the nature and function of an African-American aesthetic.

PRINCIPAL WORKS

The New Negro: An Interpretation [editor] (criticism) 1925
Four Negro Poets [editor] (criticism) 1927
Plays of Negro Life: A Source-Book of Native American
Drama [editor with Montgomery Gregory] (criticism) 1927
A Decade of Negro Self-Expression (criticism) 1928
The Negro in America (criticism) 1933
The Negro and His Music (criticism) 1936
Negro Art: Past and Present (criticism) 1936
The Negro in Art: A Pictorial Record of the Negro Artist and of the Negro Theme in Art [editor] (criticism) 1940
When People Meet: A Study in Race and Culture Contacts [editor with Bernhard J. Stern] (criticism) 1942

CRITICISM

W. E. B. Du Bois (review date January 1926)

SOURCE: A review of *The New Negro,* in *The Crisis,* Vol. 31, No. 3, January, 1926, pp. 140-41.

[*An American educator and intellectual, Du Bois was the founder of the National Association for the Advancement of Colored People (NAACP) and the editor of that organization's periodical,* The Crisis, *from 1910 to 1934. In the following review, Du Bois lauds Locke's scholarly editorial work in* The New Negro, *but disagrees with his thesis.*]

[*The New Negro*] in many ways marks an epoch. It is in many respects sprawling, illogical, with an open and unashamed lack of unity and continuity, and yet it probably expresses better than any book that has been published in the last ten years the present state of thought and culture among American Negroes and it expresses it so well and so adequately, with such ramification into all phases of thought and attitude, that it is a singularly satisfying and inspiring thing.

It has, too, more than most books, a history. The well-known magazine, *The Survey,* which represents organized social reform in America, has always been traditionally afraid of the Negro problem and has usually touched it either not at all or gingerly. Even last year one of the editors at a great meeting of social workers in Los Angeles succeeded in talking over an hour on the social problems of America, dividing and examining them exhaustively both geographically and qualitatively, and yet said no word on the race problems.

Notwithstanding this *The Survey* has grown and developed tremendously in the last few years. I remember vividly being asked by *The Survey* to furnish it for the New Year 1914 a statement of the aims of the N. A. A. C. P. I did so and said among other things:

Sixth—Finally, in 1914, the Negro must demand his social rights. His right to be treated as a gentleman when he acts like one, to marry any sane, grown person who wants to marry him, and to meet and eat with his friends without being accused of undue assumption or unworthy ambition.

No sooner had the editors of *The Survey* read this than they telephoned frantically to some of the directors of the N. A. A. C. P. and they found easily several who did not agree with this statement and one indeed who threatened to resign if it were published. *The Survey* therefore refused to publish my statement unless this particular paragraph were excised. The statement was not published.

Since then much water has flowed under the bridge and it happened last year that the editor of *The Survey* was sitting next to Mr. A. G. Dill, our business manager, at a dinner given to Miss Fauset in honor of the appearance of her novel, *There Is Confusion.* The editor looked at the company with interest and Mr. Dill began to tell him who they were. It occurred to the editor of *The Survey* that here was material for a *Survey Graphic;* still he hesitated and feared the "social uplifters" of the United States with a mighty fear. But he took one step which saved the day: He got a colored man to edit that number of the *Graphic,* Alain Locke, a former Rhodes scholar and a professor at Howard University. Locke did a good job, so good a job that this Negro number of the *Survey Graphic* was one of the most successful numbers ever issued by *The Survey.*

It was a happy thought on the part of the Bonis to have the material thus collected, arranged and expanded, combined with the painting and decoration of Winold Reiss and issued as a book which states and explains the present civilization of black folk in America. Mr. Locke has done a fine piece of editing. The proof reading, the bibliographies and the general arrangement are all beyond criticism.

With one point alone do I differ with the Editor. Mr. Locke has newly been seized with the idea that Beauty rather than Propaganda should be the object of Negro literature and art. His book proves the falseness of this thesis. This is a book filled and bursting with propaganda but it is propaganda for the most part beautifully and painstakingly done; and it is a grave question if ever in this world in any renaissance there can be a search for disembodied beauty which is not really a passionate effort to do something tangible, accompanied and illumined and made holy by the vision of eternal beauty.

Of course this involves a controversy as old as the world and much too transcendental for practical purposes, and yet, if Mr. Locke's thesis is insisted on too much it is going to turn the Negro renaissance into decadence. It is the fight for Life and Liberty that is giving birth to Negro literature and

art today and when, turning from this fight or ignoring it, the young Negro tries to do pretty things or things that catch the passing fancy of the really unimportant critics and publishers about him, he will find that he has killed the soul of Beauty in his Art.

Roi Ottley (review date 7 September 1941)

SOURCE: "Art and Social Record," in *New York Herald Tribune Books,* September 7, 1941, p. 17.

[*In the following review, Ottley discusses Locke's theories about African American art as presented in his* The Negro in Art.]

With the announced object of documenting pictorially the Negro's creative career in the fine arts, Alain Locke, for many years a large figure in the cultural world of the Negro, has published an important collection of art, tracing the Negro's cultural history. With proper perspective, he has divided his volume into three sections: the first is concerned with the Negro as an artist; second, the Negro theme in art; and third, the Negro's ancestral arts. Thus the reader is able to see clearly the Negro's vital part in the occasional works of the early European masters and later the modernists; his contemporary vogue in the development of a native American art; the rapidly increasing maturity of the Negro artist in the recent decades; and the fluctuating interests and influences.

In the formal fine arts the path of the Negro has been distinctly limited. Here and there a chance contact or a liberal-minded patron encouraged a few rare talents. Centuries ago, when Seville was an art center, Juan Pareja and Sebastian Gomez, Negro servant-apprentices, respectively, of Velasquez and Murillo, were competent echoes of their masters, later rising to the stature of fellow artists and disciples. Less auspicious was the American Negro's beginnings. Yet, in spite of an imitativeness which was common in early American painting generally, the Negro artist did creditable work. Joshua Johnston, the first authenticated Negro artist in the United States and a slave belonging to a prominent Baltimore family, did thirteen competent family portraits. It took three or four generations before a Negro was recognized for his technical excellence This occurred at the turn of this century when Henry O. Tanner won recognition in Paris, at a time when it was the world capital of art. Not until the mid-twenties did anything approaching a movement in Negro art take place. In 1928 the Harmon Foundation, recognizing the Negro as suffering from neglect, specially promoted exhibitions of the work of Negro artists, which caused a sharp rise in interest and racial self-expression. This so-called New Negro movement was, of course, underscored by the French modernists.

African art, the fountain head of modernist style, is a lost cultural heritage for the Negro. For up to the present century, the American Negro, cut from his African art traditions and skills, had only his body as an artistic instrument, so that dance and song provided the only outlet for creative expression. Since there is no continuity between the American Negro and his African sources, there is only a sentimental kinship to African art, both in its use and understanding. Locke believes that if this tradition was properly understood by the American Negro. It would have greater influence on his work. Yet the Negro has come under its influence, if only vicariously, by way of the French modernist, not as a Negro to be sure, but as an artist. There is this difference, however, the Negro artist, influenced as he is by the modernists, seeks the idea of self-expression, originality and art as a separate tradition: whereas the African, largely a folk artist, is essentially a "functionalist." According to Locke, this "African art embodies and vindicates one of the soundest of all esthetic principles—beauty in vital application to life and use."

The emphasis of *The Negro in Art* is placed upon the contemporary artist, who, under the encouragement, sponsorship and support of the Federal Art Projects, gives a panoramic survey of Negro life. Much of the contemporary work is obviously social analysis and criticism. For the Negro artist appears to have turned his back on mere picturesqueness of the Negro color, form and features, and has entered a period of penetrating social vision, in which he goes deeper than the surface and the jazzy overtones of Negro life. The vital problems of religion, labor, housing, lynching, unemployment and social reform form the broad canvas of this collection.

"We must not expect the work of the Negro artist to be too different from that of his fellow artists," writes Locke. "Product of the same social and cultural soil, our art has an equal right and obligation to be typically American at the same time that it strives to be typical and representative of the Negro; and that, indeed, if the evidence is rightly read, we believe it already is, and promises even more to be. The American Negro, it begins to seem clear, is destined to make as distinct a contribution to the visual arts as he has made in music."

H. M. Kallen (essay date 28 February 1957)

SOURCE: "Alain Locke and Cultural Pluralism," in *The Journal of Philosophy,* Vol. LIV, No. 5, February 28, 1957, pp. 119-27.

[*In the following excerpt, Kallen discusses Locke's essays "Values and Imperatives" and "Pluralism and Ideological Peace," and the effect that racism had on Locke's philosophy.*]

The expression "cultural pluralism" must now be familiar. . . . It has figured in the public prints. It has come to denote one of the alternatives of foreign policy for our State Department. Even members of the Security Council and the General Staff are reported as talking about the importance of the Bill of Rights and the intercultural relations which the Bill of Rights implies as against those implied by totalitarian creeds. It is not possible to implement any of the propositions of our American Bill or of the Universal Declaration of Human Rights of the United Nations without assuming the primacy and the irreducible plurality of the cultures of mankind and their impact on one another.

As an expression in the American language "cultural pluralism" is about 50 years old. I used it first around 1906 or 1907 when Alain Locke was in a section of a class at Harvard where I served as assistant to Mr. George Santayana. It has taken these two generations for the term to come into more general use and to figure in philosophical discourse in this country. Locke, you may remember, refers in one of his philosophical essays to a book by F. C. S. Northrop of Yale, entitled *The Meeting of East and West,* and indeed since the First World War the expression has recurred in public discussion more and more frequently and more diversely.

In my mind, here is what it fundamentally signifies: first, a concept that social science and social philosophy can and do employ as a working hypothesis concerning human nature and human relations; second, an ethical ideal—an article of faith which challenges certain prevailing philosophical conceptions about both. Those conceptions are fundamentally monistic. There persists in the sciences of man and nature and in philosophies as they have developed in our country, a disposition to assert and somehow to establish the primacy of totalitarian unity at the beginning, and its supremacy in the consummation, of all existence. It is, of course, conceded that multitude and variety seem pervasive, always and everywhere. But it is denied that they are real. It is the One that is real, not the Many—whether we regard many things or many men. Men come and go but Man goes on forever, and it is in their eternal and universal Manhood that all men are brothers. That this brotherhood involves the blood rivalry of Cain and Abel perhaps much more commonly than the relationship between David and Jonathan seems not to affect this monist creed, nor the cliché regarding the fatherhood of God and the brotherhood of Man, which is one of its commoner expressions. A better word for what is intended by "brotherhood" is the word "friendship." For this word carries no implication of an identical beginning and common end that are to be attributed to the event that two persons or two peoples or a thousand peoples who are different from each other and must perforce live together with each other, seek such ways of togetherness as shall be ways of peace and freedom.

Now, the expression "Cultural Pluralism" is intended to signify this endeavor toward friendship by people who are different from each other but who, as different, hold themselves equal to each other. By "equal" we commonly mean "similar" or "identical." Cultural Pluralism, however, intends by "equal" also parity of the unequal, equality of the unlike, not only of the like or the same. It postulates that individuality is indefeasible, that differences are primary, and that consequently human beings have an indefeasible right to their differences and should not be penalized for their differences, however they may be constituted, whatever they may consist in: color, faith, sex, occupation, possessions, or what have you. On the record, nevertheless, human beings continually penalize one another for their differences. This is how they exemplify the brotherhood of man and the fatherhood of God; how the South Africans are brothers to their dark-skinned victims, the Chinese to the Koreans, the Arabs to the Israelis, and the Russians to non-Communist mankind. Each demands of his sibling, "Agree with me, be my brother—or else! And so that you may become completely a brother, you must offer up your own different being to be digested into identification with mine. You must replace your purposes with mine, your ways and means with mine. Unless you do this you refuse brotherhood." Contrast this requirement with the requirement of friendship, which says to the other fellow not "Be my brother" but *"Be my friend.* I am different from you. You are different from me. The basis of our communion is our difference. Let us exchange the fruits of our difference so that each may enrich the other with what the other is not or has not in himself. In what else are we important to one another, what else can we pool and share if not our differences?" The valuations here postulated should be obvious. If for example, in coming here today, we had expected merely a repetition of what we already know and feel, it is unlikely that even our reverence to a notable friend and beautiful character would have brought us. We expected something somehow still unknown and unpossessed. We do not care to seek what we already sufficiently have. We want what we don't yet have. This is how we achieve spiritual abundance, which consists in the free and friendly barter of different things and thoughts and neighborly relations. It lives in untrammeled communication between the different on all levels. It signalizes the idea of civilization that the expression "cultural pluralism" denotes.

Now this is what Alain Locke envisioned from the time that he became reconciled to himself. He became a cultural pluralist. It took him some time.

In 1935 Sidney Hook and I got out a collection of essays by younger United States philosophers entitled, *American Philosophy Today and Tomorrow.* Alain Locke contributed to this collection a paper on the theme, **"Values and Imperatives."** Each contributor accompanied his essay with a short autobiographical note. I will read you Locke's note which, I suspect, is not as familiar to his friends as it should be, and then ask what it postulates *en philosophe.* How did the author get this way? How came Locke—a proud and sensitive man who was penalized by "whites" for his darker skin, in matters of spirit an incidental difference—to give up the idea of equality as identification, as sameness with whites, and to urge equality as parity in and of his difference from the whites; hence to see the human enterprise as free, friendly, creative intercommunication between differents and their reciprocal enrichment thereby?

> I should like to claim [he wrote] as life-motto the good Greek principle, *"Nothing in excess,"* but I have probably worn instead as the badge of circumstance,—*"All things with a reservation."* Philadelphia, with her birthright of provincialism flavored by urbanity and her petty bourgeois psyche with the Tory slant, at the start set the key of paradox; circumstance compounded it by decreeing me as a Negro a dubious and doubting sort of American and by reason of the racial inheritance making me more of a pagan than a Puritan, more of a humanist than a pragmatist.

> Verily paradox has followed me the rest of my days: at Harvard, clinging to the genteel tradition of Palmer, Royce and Munsterberg, yet attracted by the disillusion of Santayana and the radical protest of James: again in 1916 I returned to work under Royce but was destined to take my doctorate in Value Theory under Perry. At Oxford, once more intrigued by the twilight of aestheticism but dimly aware of the new realism of the Austrian philosophy of value; socially Anglophile, but because of race loyalty, strenuously anti-imperialist; universalist in religion, internationalist and pacifist in worldview, but forced by a sense of simple justice to approve of the militant counter-nationalisms of Zionism, Young Turkey, Young Egypt, Young India, and with reservations even Garveyism and current-day "Nippon over Asia." Finally a cultural cosmopolitan, but perforce an advocate of cultural racialism as a defensive counter-move for the American Negro, and accordingly more of a philosophical mid-wife to a generation of younger Negro poets, writers, artists than a professional philosopher.

> Small wonder, then, with this psychograph, that I project my personal history into its inevitable ratio-

nalization as cultural pluralism and value relativism, with a not too orthodox reaction to the American way of life.

Locke presents himself here with the passions and powers of his individuality. His singularity is evident, and he gives hints of his idiosyncrasy. But he accepted neither, although he couldn't reject them. He felt, in sense and intellect, a human being the same as other human beings, especially white ones who denied the sameness. He knew that in his ideals, his intentions, and his works and ways he was not inferior, nor otherwise different from those people who held themselves to be better than he was, and there were intervals—one was certainly his undergraduate days at Harvard—when he did not appear to live under any penalty for his difference. He seems not to have in Philadelphia. I know that at Oxford—I was there at the time—he was penalized. There were among the Rhodes scholars at Oxford gentlemen from Dixie who could not possibly associate with Negroes. They could not possibly attend the Thanksgiving dinner celebrated by Americans if a Negro was to be there. So although students from elsewhere in the United States outnumbered the gentlemen from Dixie, Locke was not invited, and one or two other persons, authentically Americans, refused in consequence to attend. You might say it was a dinner of inauthentic Americans. Now, the impact of that kind of experience left scars. The more so in a philosophic spirit. For the dominant trend among philosophers is always to prove unity and to work at unifications—to assert *one* humanity, *one* universe, *one* system of values and ideals which somehow is coërcive of the many and somehow argues away the actualities of penalization for one's being oneself into unimportant appearances, without in any way relieving the feelings of dehumanization, the pain and the suffering; and without lessening the desire never again to expose oneself to them. There were times that year when Locke thought never to return to the United States. In fact, he deeply wanted not to. He was at ease in Europe. The penalties for "color," especially in France and on the continent, were not apparent. They were not as apparent in England as they are today. But however or wherever the penalties were laid, Locke felt he could not expose himself to their indignities. As a human being with an individuality of his own, he knew that no commitment or obligation could be laid on him heavier than anybody else's, and that the necessities of vindicating his integrity and realizing his own potentialities in his own way had the first claim and the last.

It took him some time to find his way to that acquiescence in unalienable right to his difference, which became the core of his value-system. This acquiescence is not primarily defensive, not a struggle for political or economic or other form of equalization. It expresses itself in affirming the integral individuality of one's person, of taking on freely the obligations that go with it; of insisting not on becoming *like* anybody else, but on having one's singularity recognized and acknowledged as possessing a title equal with any other's to live and grow.

Now this sort of self-acquiescence is the personal premise—whatever be the pattern of grouping—for the group belongingness, the group identification for which one name is cultural pluralism. Alain Locke made this choice as a grown man, just as Walter White made this choice as a boy in Atlanta, when he experienced the violence of a mob of whites.

For Locke's disposition had been first monistic or universalist. Pluralism and particularism imposed their reality upon him by the exigent harshnesses of experience. It is these which convinced him of the actuality of difference, which brought him to recognize that difference is no mere appearance, but *the* valid, vital force in human communication and in human creation.

The transvaluation had never seemed to me to be quite complete. As you can see from his "psychograph," Locke chooses to speak of it as a rationalization. He would have preferred reality to be basically a One and not a Many, and human relations to be expressive of this Oneness. His preference interposed an active reservation to the actuality of the plural. It long kept him from completely committing himself. Philosophically, it led him at last to the concept of ideological peace.

I have spoken of Locke's essay, **"Values and Imperatives."** There is another he wrote and, apart from his doctor's thesis, I don't know of any more philosophical studies by him. The second he called, **"Pluralism and Ideological Peace."** As I read the essay, which he contributed to a collection entitled, *Freedom and Experience,* edited by Sidney Hook and Milton Konvitz, "ideological peace" again involves an association of the different which requires our making a distinction between unity and union. The import of Unity is liquidation of difference and diversity, either by way of an identification of the different, or by way of a subordination and subjection of the different to the point where it makes no difference. *Per contra,* the import of Union is the teamplay of the different. Union resides in the uncoërced, the voluntary commitment of the different to one another in free coöperation; and ideological peace, as Locke had expounded it in this essay, is a conception denoting fundamentally this free intercommunication of diversities—denoting the cultivation of those diversities for the purpose of free and fruitful intercommunication between equals.

To the American Negro it presents the idea of an authentic Negro cultural community sensitive not only to the positive values of all the present, but aware also of the immemorial African past and rendering it presently a living past. Of course, this past is not in the memory of any living American Negro. He must need to create that memory, by means of exploration and study, as Locke did and just as every white must; indeed, as the record shows, identification with African cultures and arts can be more passionate and more complete among white men than among Negroes. To many, perhaps to most, the import of the term "Afro-American" is unwelcome. For Negroes tend to reject such an identification because they perceive themselves to be penalized on account of this same African difference. So long as a person thinks of himself as being penalized as African, so long as he is not self-acquiescent, just so long will he resist identification with those presumed sources or conditions of his imposed inequality. The hyphen represents a bondage, not a resource or power. Let him absorb and digest the condition, turning it from a limiting handicap into a releasing endowment, and he frees himself.

This, it seems to me, is what Locke did. And hence, in his discussion of the New Negro, Locke was able to talk about the Negro problem as a creation of non-Negroes which they imposed on the Negroes. As anybody knows who has lived through the abominations of Senator Eastland's Mississippi in the past few months, Locke's analysis is correct.

The Negro, Locke held, is not a problem. The Negro is a fact, an American fact, but not merely because he has lived and labored in America since Colonial times. He is American in virtue of his commitment, in common with non-Negro Americans, to the essential American Idea, the idea that human beings, all different from each other, are equal to each other in their inalienable rights to life, liberty, and the pursuit of happiness, and owe each other participation in the joint endeavor "to secure these rights" on which the institution of government rests in free societies. All "these rights" may be comprehended as the right to be different without penalty, without privilege, and with each of the different maturing its own excellence, the excellence expressive of its individual or associative singularity in willing coöperation with all. Believing this, Alain Locke gave expression to his own commitment to the Negro fact by undertaking to disclose to Americans, especially to Negro Americans, the Negro, not the problem. He made himself the philosophical midwife to a generation of younger Negro poets, writers, artists.

However it is a very delicate and difficult undertaking to separate any existence from the problems of this existence. This challenge confronts all communities everywhere, not alone the American Negro community. And it is far harder to effect this separation where a community is penalized for merely existing. Hence, one cannot be sure that Locke succeeded. But one can be sure that, without the affirmation of Negro as Negro in terms of what cultural and spiritual production Negro as Negro can achieve, without the manifes-

tation of inner strength based on self-knowledge, developing without tutelage from anybody, the Negro cannot begin to accept himself as a fact instead of a problem to himself. One can be sure that where such a process eventuates, the Negro problem transvalues into a white problem, both south and north. And one may observe that the problem "gets liquidated" wherever communities of diverse identity do thus accept themselves. An orchestration of their diversities follows, a teamplay of their differences. The concept "race" wouldn't apply to these differences since any species whose members can breed together may be said to belong to the same race. First and last the differences are the specific differentiations of personal and group existence that make cultures, that make systems of ideas, creeds and codes about which human beings fight. "Race" is one such fighting word. Color constitutes no problem when it is not appraised in racist terms. Transactions between peoples of different colors in the same culture and different cultures in the same color, and different colors and cultures have gone on freely enough throughout recorded time. Alain Locke urged that they can go on here at home. He held that they would have to be postulated on what he called ideological peace. In his essay on **"Values and Imperatives"** he urged that this peace might be attained by the conceptions and the methods of science. There is, he declared in that essay of 1935, "an objective universe," whose unity is broken up into a pluriverse by human behavior.

I think that in the twelve years between the first essay in 1935 and the second in 1947, he decided that primarily there is a pluriverse, and that ideological peace is the endeavor to establish a universe, not as a unity, but a union. His pluralism reshaped into a primary, a fundamental pluralism—a value pluralism, a metaphysical pluralism, and the reshaping may have involved something like a religious conversion. As he believed, it is a way of changing your own attitude toward yourself, and your own attitude toward the different. First one needs to recognize the integrity and autonomy of difference; then perhaps one can also peaceably do business with it. In point of fact, Locke had already done so in *The New Negro,* although his philosophic realization seems to have come later.

There are two current words which signify ideas that have a present bearing on this notion of free coöperation of the different, or ideological peace. One of these words, signifying an American policy, is "containment." And what does "containment" mean? It means forcefully holding back the different. Why did we have to have a national policy of containment? Because of Communist aggression against what is not Communist. Perforce it is to be held back, and unless the resistance were equally strong or stronger it could not be held back. Outer containment depends on inner moral and material strength. Whether or not we achieve the political end, it continues morally and culturally on the agenda for the American people, and of our Negro fellow-Americans *vis-a-vis* certain categories of non-Negroes.

The second word is a word that came into vogue after "containment" had become a policy. The word is "co-existence." There are different ways of co-existence. There is the co-existence of cold toleration signalized as balance of power; here powers stand over against each other at alert and ready to shoot—the way the South Koreans had to stand against the North Koreans, the Israelis stand against the Arabs, and the entire West stands against the Soviet and its satellites.

In another phase, co-existence signifies passive toleration. Each existent says to the other: You're there and I've got to recognize you are there, but I don't like you and I won't have anything to do with you. You may be a brother, but you're no neighbor and no friend.

In still another phase, co-existence signifies what we now usually mean by toleration—that is, not an inimical endurance or suffering of the different, but a recognition that the different can live and let you live and that you can live and let the different live. Co-existence means live and let live.

The mature phase of co-existence comes whenever existent pass from this sort of *laissez-faire* into a free, a voluntary coöperative relationship where each, in living on, also helps, and is helped by, the others in living. This is the co-existence that cultural pluralism signifies. It is the consummation of the system of ideas and the philosophic faith that Alain Locke became a notable spokesman for.

Eugene C. Holmes (essay date Summer 1963)

SOURCE: "The Legacy of Alain Locke," in *Freedomways*, Vol. 3, No. 3, Summer, 1963, pp. 292-306.

[In the following essay, Holmes discusses Locke's essays in The New Negro *as a manifesto for the Harlem Renaissance.]*

The rise of a genuine New Negro Movement was fostered and encouraged by one person, Alain Leroy Locke, who became its creative editor and its chronicler. It may be true that the term Renaissance, as Sterling Brown has so perceptively pointed out, is a misnomer because of the shortness of the life span of the Harlem movement. Also, the New Negro writers were not centered only in Harlem, and much of the best writing of the decade was not always about Harlem, for most of the writers were not Harlemites. Yet Harlem was the "show window," the cashier's till, though it is no more "Negro America" than New York is America. The New Negro had temporal roots in the past and spatial roots elsewhere

in America and the term has validity only when considered to be a continuing tradition.

It may be argued that the so-called Negro Renaissance held the seeds of defeat for a number of reasons, among them being the general anti-intellectualism of the new Negro middle class. But it was, by every admission, a representation of a re-evaluation of the Negro's past and of the Negro himself by Negro intellectuals and artists. For the rise of the New Negro Movement coincided with an ever-increasing interest in Negro life and character in the twenties. American literature was being re-evaluated and overhauled as a revolt against the genteel tradition and the acquisitive society of the last decades of the nineteenth century.

Charles Johnson characterized Alain Locke as "the Dean of this group of fledgling writers of the new and lively generation of the 1920's." Johnson wrote, "A brilliant analyst trained in philosophy, and an esthete with a flair for art as well as letters, he gave encouragement and guidance to these young writers as an older practitioner too sure of his craft to be discouraged by failure of full acceptance in the publishing media of the period." Johnson referred to Alain Locke as "an important maker of history" of a "dramatic period in our national history." Locke had this to say about these young writers being launched on their careers: "They sense within their group—a spiritual wealth which if they can properly expound, will be ample for a new judgment and re-appraisal of the race." This, then, is only a part of the backdrop of what has been called the Negro Renaissance. What Charles Johnson referred to as "that sudden and altogether phenomenal outburst of emotional expression unmatched by any comparable period in American or Negro American history."

No one, not even the older Du Bois, could have been better equipped to have been the architect of the New Negro Movement and maker of history. Philadelphia, Locke's birthplace, was the one city where one could speak of a culture. Negro artists were encouraged and Negro literary, musical and painting groups were encouraged. Young Locke was aware of this personally and always kept these artists in mind as reminders of the awakening of Negro art in America. The literary movement had many of its origins in Philadelphia, but, because of social, economic and political reasons, it flowered in New York. For a racial dilemma in Negro art, a racial solution was necessary. This came in the mid-twenties from the inspiration of the New Negro Movement with its crusade of folk expression in all of the arts, the drama, painting, sculpture, music and the rediscovery of the folk origins of the Negro's African heritage.

The racial dilemma was a distinct carryover from the same dilemma encountered by the Negro writers of the late nineteenth century. In most of these writers, there was to be found the same tendentious, pedestrian and imitative style as observed in many of the painters. There was the dialect poetry of Dunbar and his later English poems in which he was the exponent of the romantic tendencies which were to be decried by the next generation of Negro poets. There were the propaganda novels of Frances Harper, Martin Delany, Frank Webb and William Wells Brown. The novels of Charles Chesnutt were outstanding for their genre, style and impact. The political essays, the pamphleteering, the autobiographical slave accounts, the polemical essays were all to be merged with and channelized into that renascence which came to be known as the New Negro Movement.

As a burgeoning critic and student of Negro life in Philadelphia, in Boston and New York, at Howard University where he had gone to teach in 1912, Locke had been working in his way, in concert with many friends, to help lay to rest the mawkish and moribund dialect school of poetry. William Stanley Braithwaite, Locke's friend and mentor while he was at Harvard; William Monroe Trotter, the editor; W. E. B. Du Bois, all helped in hastening the demise of Negro dialect poetry. Friendly critics such as Louis Untermeyer also helped by labeling the traditional dialect as "an affectation to please a white audience." And, along with James Weldon Johnson, who had genuine poetic talent, this critics' coterie saw that dialect poetry had neither the wit nor the beauty of folk speech, but was only a continuation of the stock stereotypes about gentility, humility and buffoonery, and an evasion of all of the realities of Negro life.

One counteraction, however, to this dialect poetry was a conscious reverting to Romanticism and neo-Romanticism which reflected a middle-class recognition of Europeanized esthetic values. In some ways, this was a result of the rejection of the minstrel-buffoon stereotype. In addition, as the middle-class Negro became better educated, there was an increase in his desire to share in the legacy of general culture, to participate in it, even though in a lesser fashion. As Sterling Brown put it, in too many instances "these poets were more concerned with making copies of the 'beauty' that was the stock-in-trade of a languishing tradition." These imitators were, for the most part, only too anxious to avoid any mention of a Negro tradition or to look into their own experiences as Negroes. The result, in their poetry, was escapist, without vitality or understanding.

Along with this counteraction there developed in the same period, the movement which assisted in the Negro writer's spiritual emancipation. As Locke himself put it in his last published account (1952) of the movement: "For from 1912 on, there was brewing the movement that in 1925, explicitly became the so-called Renaissance of the New Negro. The movement was not so much in itself a triumph of realism, although it had its share of realists, but a deliberate cessation by Negro authors of their attempts primarily to influence majority opinion. By then, Negro artists had outgrown the handicaps of allowing didactic emphasis and propagandist motives to choke their sense of artistry. Partly in disillusionment, partly in newly acquired group pride and self-respect, they turned inward to the Negro audience in frankly avowed self-expression."

Langston Hughes, one of their number, thus phrased this literary declaration of independence:

> We younger Negro artists who create now intend to express our individual dark-skinned selves without fear or shame. If white people are pleased, we are glad. If they are not, it doesn't matter. We know we are beautiful. And ugly too. If colored are pleased, we are glad. If they are not, their displeasure doesn't matter either. We build our temples for tomorrow, strong as we know how, and we stand on the top of the mountain, free within ourselves.

Once again, there was a common denominator between the advance-guard elements of the majority and the minority. The anti-slavery collaboration had forged a moral alliance; this was an esthetic one, which spelled out a final release from propaganda and its shackling commitments both for Negro materials in American art and literature and for the Negro artist and writer. And from 1925 to the present, realism and Southern regionalism on the one side, and the promotion of racial self-expression on the other, have informally but effectively combined to form a new progressive atmosphere in American letters.

No one could have been better equipped for the leadership and sponsorship of the New Negro Movement than Locke, who described himself "more of a philosophical midwife to a generation of younger Negro poets, writers and artists than a professional philosopher." For years he [encouraged] . . . artists and musicians to study the African sources at first hand. He was an avid collector of Africans. He wrote expertly about the lost ancestral arts of Africa and traced the influence of African art on European artists in the early twentieth century. He knew a great deal about African influences in Haiti and other Caribbean islands and he consistently pointed out African influences on the Negro American, both before and after the abolition of slavery.

Alain Locke did not make many original researches into American Negro history or into the golden lore of African history, but he grew in stature as he learned more and more of this history. It taught him that the Negro scholar's ability to withstand the infirmities of the American scene is a dialectic phase of the democratic process. And this dialectic must necessarily aid in bringing into fruition the dream of a community of Negro scholars. This was his sensitivity about American history and it led him to an identity with the great leader, the self-taught Frederick Douglass, about whom he wrote a biography. Locke was deeply appreciative of Du Bois' scientific approach to history and Carter G. Woodson's pioneer scientific work in the history of slavery and the Negro past. His contributions to the New Negro Movement always turned out to be re-evaluations of Negro history as it affected the Negro writer, the Negro scholar, and the lives of all sensitively aware Negroes.

As an author, Locke knew that the story of the Negro writer had to be told, because of the social history involved. He came to see that the position of the Negro in American culture had come to mean a great deal more than merely the artistic activity of the Negro minority. It came to mean for him a pointing toward a goal of a "natively characteristic national literature as being one of the crucial issues of cultural democracy." And this had to be evaluated against the slavery and anti-slavery background from which this literature emerged.

The harsh effects of slavery had to be viewed as contributing to the recognition of the Negro's role as participant and contributor to American culture. "Just as slavery may now (1952) in perspective be viewed as having first threatened our democratic institutions and then forced them to more consistent maturity, the artistic and cultural impact of the Negro must be credited with producing unforeseen constructive pressures and generating unexpected creative ferment in the literary and artistic culture of America. In cutting the Negro loose from his ancestral culture, slavery set up a unique and unprecedented situation between the Anglo-Saxon majority and the Negro minority group. The peculiar conditions of American slavery so scrambled Africans from the diverse regions and culture of our entire continent that with the original background culture, tribal to begin with, neither a minority language nor an ancestral tradition remains. The American Negro was left no alternative but to share the language and tradition of the majority culture."

The Negro had never set up separate cultural values, even though he had been forced on many occasions to take on defensive attitudes of racialism, "an enforced, protective, counter-attitude, stemming the worst of proscription and discrimination." Locke believed that, despite historical interludes, the Negro's values, ideals and objectives, have always been integrally and unreservedly American. He wrote, "The crucial factors in group relationships are social attitudes and literature—recording and reflecting these in preference even in social fact—becomes the most revealing medium."

Locke wrote more than a dozen books and articles since 1921 on Negro art, music and literature, tracing these developments from the earliest times, from 1760 up to 1920. He began with the first Negro poets, essayists and novelists, showing that the earliest indictment of slavery from the ar-

ticulate free Negro displayed signs of a strong race consciousness. He showed that if slavery had molded the emotional and folk life of the Negro, that also it was the anti-slavery movement which developed the intellect of the Negro and pushed him forward to articulate, disciplined expression. The edifice of chattel slavery was shaken to its foundation by the combined efforts of the literary and oratorical efforts of Negro leaders and self-taught fugitive slaves. The emergence of the "slave narrative" supplied the incandescent spark, to be added to the abolitionist tinder.

In making America aware of the Negro artist and his work, an important part was played by the *Harlem Number* of the *Survey Graphic* which was edited by Locke. This issue of the *Survey* contained a hundred pages. There were twenty contributors, fifteen Negro and five white and twelve belonged to the Harlem group. Among the articles were, "Enter the New Negro," "The Making of Harlem," "Black Workers and the City," "Jazz at Home," "Negro Art and America," "The Negro Digs Up His Past," "The Rhythm of Harlem," and many others appertaining to Harlem. This issue of the *Survey* had the largest circulation of any in its history. Several editions had to be run off before the demand was satisfied. In *Black Manhattan,* James Weldon Johnson in 1926, wrote, "It was a revelation to New York and the country. Later the symposium, somewhat enlarged, was brought out as a book, entitled ***The New Negro,*** under the editorship of Alain Locke. It remains one of the most important books on the Negro ever published."

The movement, for a while *did* thrive in Harlem. Then the "influence of Locke's essays and of the movement in general, spread outward over the country, touching writers in Missouri, Mississippi, in Boston, Philadelphia and Nashville and Chicago."

Unknowingly, there was being cultivated a middle-class nationalism within the protective folds of the capitalist ethos. The majority did not rebel, but rather hearkened to the voice of bourgeois authority. American capitalism had prospered in the redivision of the profits and spoils of the war. In too many instances, the "New Negro" had served in too large a measure as a means of amusement, to be fawned upon and idolized. Many of the New Negroes were unwilling victims of an inverted racialistic nationalism, looking upon themselves as having arrived, and priding themselves that they could sing, paint and write as well as their white-skinned patrons.

But, the movement was a true "renaissance" in another sense—the antiquity which Negroes wanted to revive from a "lost" African past. However they might share in the leavings of their new-found prosperity, if they were to rediscover their racial souls, they had to go back, at least mentally, to the African past. There were the successes and the failures of Du Bois' leadership in the 1921, 1923 and 1925 Pan-African Congresses. The efforts of Locke to instill in the younger poets, artists and musicians, some sense of this African heritage bore fruit in the work of Toomer, Cullen, McKay and Hughes.

The most developed poet and literary figure of the New Negro movement, Langston Hughes, wrote on all manners of subjects and always movingly of Africa. In 1926, *Weary Blues* and in 1927, *Fine Clothes to the Jew*, Hughes displayed his artistry of particular power and beauty pursuing his own course more than any other of the New Negroes. Hughes' antecedents were bound up in a family tradition where the struggle for freedom was always a strong memory and inspiration. A grandfather died fighting beside John Brown. An uncle was a Reconstruction Congressman and the first Dean of the Howard Law School. Even Hughes' blues, melodious and rhythmic are full of African feeling as in *Homesick Blues:*

> De railroad bridge's
> A sad song in de air
> Every time de trains pass
> I wants to go somewhere.

The black world of America and Africa came to have a new meaningful nationalistic pride for so many of these poets. It was not always very deep or couched in any scientific anthropological understanding, but no matter, there was precious little understanding at the time for anyone. What mattered was that this flowering was a true renaissance of feeling, a prideful evocation of the dark image of Africa, germinated from a fructified seedbed but one which took on a new form and content.

The Harlem Renaissance, substantively, transformed the Negro as subject and as artist from the old stereotype into the New Negro, militant, no longer obsequious, more of a paragon because he had shown that he was nearly on equal terms with his white counterpart. He won coveted prizes, fellowships, he was being published and he won his spurs the hard way in creative writing. These artists were not organized but theirs was a strong spirit of cohesion, a bond of group consciousness, toward some goal of achievement which would make the Negro artist proud of his work. It was a self-confidence which grew and proliferated into an outburst of emotional expression, never matched by any comparable period in American history. The new generation of writers began to carve out a niche in the hitherto impermeable walls of American literary culture. Hence the self-confidence, the self-assurance and the pride of craftsmanship.

The New Poetry Movement embraced every facet of Negro experience from lyricism, African heritage, social protest, folk song and blues, Negro heroes and episodes, lynchings,

race riots, treatment of the Negro masses (frequently of the folk, less often of the workers), and franker and deeper self-revelation, social injustice and intolerance. Claude McKay's famous *If We Must Die* became the touchstone for the dynamics of the social forces and conflicts of the twenties. His was an answer to the growing crescendo of race riots and lynchings which characterized the times. Toomer's eloquent outcries in *Cane* were race conscious and challenging. In Cullen's *Shroud of Color,* his sense of race is one of loyalty, pride and group consciousness, "almost the tone of a chosen people."

> Lord, I would live persuaded by mine own
> I cannot play the recreant to these:
> My spirit has come home, that sailed the doubtful
> seas.

Hughes' *Brass Spittoons* tells of the distasteful tasks of menial labor:

> Hey, Boy!
> A bright bowl of brass is beautiful to the Lord
> Bright polished brass like the cymbals
> Of King David's dancers
> Like the wine cups of Solomon.

These poets, in their different ways, were all influential in the twenties and thirties, influencing an entire generation of younger poets. Cullen and Toomer in New York and all over America, Hughes in New York and all over the world, McKay in New York and the socialist world, Sterling Brown at Howard and all over the south, all expressing ideas that were representative of the Negro movement. In *Strong Men,* Brown pens:

> They dragged you from your homeland,
> They chained you in coffles
> They broke you in like oxen
> They scourged you
> They branded you
>   You sang:
>   Keep a-inchin' along
>   Lak a po' inch worm . . .
>   You sang:
>   Walk togedder, chillen,
>   Dontcha get weary
> The strong men keep a comin' on
> The strong men get stronger.

After Frederick Douglass' fictionalized *Madison Washington* and the short stories of William Wells Brown and Chesnutt, the Negro as short story writer could only emerge from a vacuum even though the short story as literary genre had taken creditable form in America. Negro writers were unable to gain any entree into the magazines. Charles

Chesnutt's experiences in 1887 with the *Atlantic Monthly* when the editors did not wish to publicize his racial identity was an infamous blot on American literature. Chesnutt's story *The Goophered Grapevine* was accepted by Walter Hines Page and later Page accepted *The Wife of His Youth,* and only belatedly admitted that the author was a Negro, claiming to the editor of the magazine *Critic* that he did not want to do damage to the author's reputation. Dunbar's stories were popular because of the plantation tradition of his dialect style and they did not offend.

In the late twenties, Langston Hughes faced the problem when *Esquire* published *A Good Job Gone.* Hughes wrote about this in *Fighting Words:*

> Here are our problems: In the first place, Negro books are considered by editors and publishers as exotic. Negro material is placed, like Chinese material or Bali material into a certain classification. Magazine editors will tell you, "We can use but so many Negro stories a year." (That "so many" meaning very few.) Publishers will say, "We already have one Negro novel on our list this fall."

> When we cease to be exotic, we do not sell well.

These have been the circumscriptions placed on the Negro short story writer on all sides in the publishing world.

When the Negro writer published in either *Crisis* or *Opportunity,* the pay was paltry and the stories were typed. The stories were concerned with lynchings, race riots, race praise or passing. Rudolph Fisher's *High Yaller* won the first prize in the 1925 *Crisis* contest. Later in the same year, *Atlantic Monthly* published his story, *The City of Refuge.* Many other new writers of the Movement wrote well-constructed stories which won *Crisis* and *Opportunity* prizes—Arthur Huff Fauset, John Matheus, Eugene Gordon, Marita Bonner, Edwin Sheen and Jean Toomer. Unlike Fisher, most of these writers did not continue their careers of writing. Eric Walrond's *Tropic Death,* Langston Hughes' *Ways of White Folks* came close to penetrating into the innermost workings of Negro life which were overlooked by the racial idealists who wrote cloyingly of the new Negro middle-class escapists.

Perhaps the novel as an art form was grist to the mill of the Negro writer at any time or place, whenever he began to write about his own experiences or those of others. The earliest Negro novelists, William Wells Brown and Martin Delaney, wrote as pleaders for a cause and as Sterling Brown wrote, "their successors have almost followed their example." The inferior propaganda novels such as Frances Harper's *Iola Leroy* or *Shadows Uplifted* and Dunbar's four conventional novels were not comparable to Chesnutt's novels of social realism.

James Weldon Johnson's *Autobiography of an Ex-Coloured Man* was a purpose work, the first "passing novel," Du Bois' *Quest of the Silver Fleece* had virtues but it was not artistic. Nella Larsen's *Quicksand,* Jessie Fauset's *Plum Bun* and Walter White's *Flight,* all written in the twenties, were "passing" novels. White's *Fire in the Flint* had the virtue of being the first anti-lynch novel written by a Negro in the twenties. Du Bois' *Dark Princess* part fantasy and part fiction, called for a union of the darker nations and also criticised the weaknesses of the Negroes' struggles for freedom and America's handling of the race problem.

The New Negro Movement produced the first really competent novelists—Fisher, Walrond, Cullen, McKay, Thurman and Hughes. The forefield of this New Negro literature was an artistic awakening. Publishers may have had only one Negro on their lists, but as the late E. Franklin Frazier pointed out, the audience was not Negro, but white. These writers were very important in the development of the Negro novelist as a craftsman. With these new writers there was great fire and enthusiasm, a creative dynamism of self-conscious racialistic expression which at the time was a healthy manifestation of the problems which beset the Negro people. Thurman, in *Infants of the Spring* satirized the exaggerations and Bohemian aspects of the movement. Fisher, a physician, the first Negro to write a detective story and a writer of social comedy, in *Wall of Jericho,* wrote of Harlem jive, a socially intelligent satire of the foibles of the new Negro middle class.

The Negro had come to stay as a novelist and the novelists of the New Negro Movement prepared the way for all of those who were to come later. The genius of Wright burgeoned out of the thirties. Many, like Ellison, relied heavily on the New Negro novelists' experiences. The writers of the Federal Writers Project of the thirties looked back only a decade to their New Negro precursors. As Sterling Brown wrote in his essay, *The New Negro in Literature (1925-1955),* "Negro authors of the thirties, like their compatriots, faced reality more squarely. For the older light-heartedness, they substituted sober self-searching; for the bravado of false Africanism and Bohemianism, they substituted attempts to understand Negro life in its workaday aspects in the here and now. . . . Alert to the changing times, a few critics—Alain Locke among them—charted new directions."

In 1930, James Weldon Johnson in *Black Manhattan* wrote: "Harlem is still in the process of making. It is still new and mixed; so mixed that one may get many different views—which is all right so long as one view is not taken to be the whole picture. This many-sided aspect, however, makes it one of the most interesting communities in America. But

Harlem is more than a community, it is a large-scale laboratory experiment in the race problem and from it a good many facts have been found."

And Alain Locke, more prophetic and Cassandra-like than he could have ever known, in the last article written before his death said, "It is to this mirror that I turn for the salient changes of majority attitudes toward the Negro, and equally important, for a view of the Negro's changed attitude toward himself. For the Negro seems at last on the verge of proper cultural recognition and a fraternal acceptance as a welcome participant and collaborator in the American arts. Should this become the realized goal, the history of the Negro's strange and tortuous career in American literature may become also the story of America's hard-won but easily endured attainment of cultural democracy."

Ernest D. Mason (essay date December 1979)

SOURCE: "Alain Locke on Race and Race Relations," in *Phylon: The Atlanta University Review of Race and Culture,* Vol. XL, No. 4, December, 1979, pp. 342-50.

[*In the following essay, Mason analyzes several of Locke's essays to delineate the author's ideas about race and race relations.*]

As in the cases of so many of his ideas, Alain Locke's thinking on race and race relations is not always clearly understood. A typical example of misunderstanding is provided by literary critic George Kent, who, though praising Locke for his critical and practical services during the Harlem Renaissance, speaks of Locke's "essentially middle-class sensibility and somewhat simplistic integrationist orientation." In view of the current ambiguity of the words *middle-class* and *integration,* this statement, while not actually wrong, is most unfortunate since it obscures the deep differences that separate a man like Locke from others who cherish middle-class values and call themselves integrationists in an attempt to deny their own racial and cultural heritage. It seems reasonable then to apply the labels primarily to those who prefer them, and not to Locke who was more concerned with race than with class and who constantly referred to himself as cultural pluralist, as opposed to an integrationist.

Locke's interest in the idea of race stems primarily from his attempt to combat notions of national, racial, and cultural superiority. In one of his earliest writings, **"The Concept of Race as Applied to Social Culture,"** Locke expresses the urgent need to shift from the anthropological perspective, with its emphasis on the biological and physical aspects of race, to the ethnological perspective, with its emphasis on social and historical factors. "If," he says,

instead of the anthropological, the ethnic characters had been more in the focus of scientific attention, . . . Race would have been regarded as primarily a matter of social heredity, and its distinctions due to the selective psychological "set" of established cultural reactions. There is a social determination involved in this which quite more rationally interprets and explains the relative stability or so-called permanency that the old theorists were trying to account for on the basis of fixed anthropological characters and factors.

When we speak of race in the social or ethnic sense, a theoretical reversal takes place. Instead of culture being viewed as expressive of race, as certain anthropological theories would have it, race itself becomes a sociocultural product. The practical implication of this shift, in terms of cultural and racial relations, is that each individual should be considered as a product of his or her culture and judged accordingly. This means, specifically, that in relating to individuals of a different race, we should make an honest attempt to understand the social and historical factors that determine that race's "stressed values which become the conscious symbols and traditions of the culture. Such stressed values are themselves factors in the process of culture making, and account primarily for the persistence and resistance of culture-traits."

One of the many social consequences of the refusal to adopt the sociocultural interpretation of race is the idea of biracialism or racial segregation. In a debate with Locke concerning equality in 1927, Lothrop Stoddard, then a teacher at Harvard, argued for biracialism in the following manner:

> The basic reason for White America's attitude and policy toward the Negro is,—not belief in the Negro's inferiority,—but the fact of his difference. True, most whites today believe the Negro to be their inferior. On the contrary, it springs largely from realization of racial difference and all that it connotes. White Americans feel that to incorporate the many millions of this widely differing stock into our racial life would profoundly change our national character, temperament, and ideas. And since these matters are supremely cherished, we do not propose to jeopardize them, either for ourselves or for unborn generations who have an indefeasible right to their racial heritage.

What is at stake, according to Stoddard, is the preservation of the purity of the white race: "Therefore, if we desire to perpetuate *our* America, we white Americans must absolutely refuse to countenance the spread through our stock of racial strains so different and so numerous that they would undermine our ethnic foundations. In other words, we are dealing, . . . with an imperative urge of self-preservation.

And self-preservation is the first law of nature." Locke, in response, points out that the person who argues that race prejudice is primarily the instinct of race preservation and that intimate relations between blacks and whites pose a danger to white America is the very same person

> whose social regime and life most depend upon close personal relations with Negroes,—in familiar and household relations at that,—and whose chief delight is to be instantly and widely familiar with Negroes provided he can protect sentimentally his caste pride and personal egotism, to which, as a matter of fact, such relations are the chief sustaining foil. It is this type of man who in open or clandestine relations, by the sex exploitation of the socially and economically unprotected Negro women, has bred a social dilution which threatens at its weakest point the race integrity he boasts of maintaining and upholding.

> In the light of this active contradiction of its own social creed by its own social practice, White orthodoxy on the race questions becomes not a consistent creed of race superiority and inner conviction, but the social self-defense of a bad conscience, the hysterical ruse of a self-defeatist vice. It fumes about keeping society closed at the top and insists on keeping it viciously open at the bottom. It claims to eliminate social contracts between the races, but actually promotes race mixing. Under conditions and habits such as these contradictions have bred, a rabidly "White America" can not refuse to recognize the Negro and long remain White.

Furthermore, adds Locke, blacks themselves have no desire to be mixed racially with whites. "Race fusion," he says, "is in our minds too tainted with the assumptions of White dominance and aggression, too associated with the stigma of inferiority rather than equality, for race amalgamation to be the social ideal and objective of an intelligent and self-respecting race consciousness such as we are now developing. In brief, the progressive Negro of today wants cultural opportunity and cultural recognition, and wants it as a Negro."

Stoddard's doctrine of biracialism aims at separating the races not only physically but culturally as well. Yet cultural fusion is inevitable. As Locke states it:

> What is "racial" for the American Negro resides merely in the overtones to certain fundamental elements of culture common to white and black and his by adoption and acculturation. What is distinctively Negro in culture usually passes over by rapid osmosis of the general culture, and often as in the case of Negro folklore and folk music and jazz becomes nationally current and representative. The Negro culture product we find to be in every instance itself a composite, partaking often of the nationally typical and characteristic as well, and thus something which if styled Negro for short, is more accurately to be described as "Afro-American," . . . there is little if any evidence and justification for biracialism in the cultural field, if closely scrutinized and carefully interpreted.

At the bottom of Locke's attack on biracialism lies his conviction that race, culture, politics, and equality are all intimately related. At one point he writes: "Ultimately a people is judged by its capacity to contribute to culture." Elsewhere he states: "there is no way of putting a social premium upon a product and at the same time putting a social discount upon its active producers. . . . The man who contributes to culture must fully participate in its best and most stimulating aspects." Such statements clearly explain why Locke devoted so much of his energy to cultural and artistic problems—it was his way of fighting the social and political battle:

> Cultural recognition, . . . means the removal of wholesale social proscription and, therefore, the conscious scrapping of the mood and creed of "White Supremacy." It means an open society instead of a closed ethnic shop. For what? For making possible free and unbiased contracts between the races on the selective basis of common interest and mutual consent, in contrast to what prevails at present,—dictated relations of inequality based on caste psychology and class exploitation.

Locke's rejection of biracialism also helps to explain why he favors DuBois's position as opposed to the views of Booker T. Washington.

> Never [says Locke], up to the time of his death in 1915, was he [Washington] able completely to disavow the interpretation put upon his program as an acceptance of the principle of opportunism and of the policy of biracial segregation. The equal rights reformist wing of the Negro thought under the leadership of DuBois so interpreted it; and later, reactionary and conservatively halfway white opinion seized upon the same interpretation, with approval, for condoning separatism, the double standard of unequal treatment, claiming the endorsement of an outstanding Negro leader.

The tension between Washington and DuBois is, in Locke's view, one between the

> necessity for practical compromise and radical as-

sertion of rights and principles. In one phase you have a person like Booker T. Washington attempting a practical program which manifestly is a compromise with an unfavorable situation and in another a person like Dr. DuBois who, as an intellectual and crusader, comes out foursquare for what he knows is right in principle, what everybody admits is right, but what he and everybody also knows is not going to be immediately conceded by a majority that is in power, and that has back of it a tradition of discrimination.

At a time when blacks were living in abject poverty and being lynched daily, it had to be, according to Locke, one's heart and sense of justice that dictated the rejection of accommodation. Although fully aware of the dangers, Locke insists that blacks "be taught to see and regard as paramount the long-term interests, which is another way of saying that principle rather than expedience must decide if constructive progress is to be made." In making this statement, Locke acknowledges that suffering and even death are sometimes the price of equality and freedom. Although Locke called himself a pacifist and favored legal pressure through the courts, he was not so unhistorically minded or blind to the limitations of legal action to see that violence might be necessary to produce significant changes in race relations. It is, in fact, Locke's recognition of the limitations of legal action that leads him to reject the theory of "gradualism" in race relations:

> Nothing is more contrary to fact than the rather widespread policy and program of gradualism. This theory of slow accumulative growth, of the slow reform of public opinion, of "the education of public sentiment" is a fallacy; the lines of social reform are not smooth gradual curves but jagged breaks, sudden advances and inevitable setbacks of reaction. . . . There may be a period for the gradual extension of a right, but not for the creation of a right or its recognition; this holds both for races and classes. Even though the values may exist for others, a revolutionary introduction or vindication of them as applying to the new group is always or usually the case.

The essence of Locke's critique of gradualism lies in his distinction between the "extension" of a right which is already in existence for at least some members of an exploited race or class and the "creation" of a right for that race or class. It is a distinction which discloses an important element of the relations between means and ends. Specifically, Locke argues that the creation of rights often requires radical or militant means:

> The compromise phase makes its characteristic

gains, the militant phases make certain other gains. It is a matter of temperament as to which you interpret as the more important. I myself (and I think in this I speak for a goodly section of Negro thinkers at this time) believe that we have made more substantial gains in militant phases than in others. In other words, we regard the anti-slavery and Civil War period as a period of great permanent gain. . . . We regard the civil rights, equal rights movement of the first decade of the nineteen hundreds that has been carried on in organizations like the N.A.A.C.P. . . . as another phase of militancy calculated to recover lost ground and gain fresh advances. We regard the after-World-War reaction as another period of militancy on a cultural and to an extent a social front, . . . And we regard the stage when the New Deal measures of social reform began to link up with the Negro cause, as the beginning of another phase of militancy and reform which probably is at its peak today in the Second World War.

To speak of the militancy of the N.A.A.C.P. and the New Deal is hardly to speak of violence. But notice that Locke also considers the Civil War period to have been a "great permanent gain" and both World Wars instrumental in producing militant phases of great social value. Thus the question is not whether or not Locke himself advocated war, racial or otherwise, but whether or not he condoned it as a means of reinforcing the legal or political efforts to achieve racial equality. As a genuine pacifist he could not possibly do so, but as a value relativist he could.

Although Locke defends blacks wholeheartedly, he is by no means blind to the dangers of excessive racialism. He was confronted with this problem most directly in his efforts to make blacks aware of the international dimension of their struggle. Given that race interest on an international scale is an essential factor in the development and survival of a culture, should one deliberately emphasize and perpetuate racial unity at the risk of more chauvinistic prejudice and sectarianism? As Locke himself states the matter, "if we argue for raciality as a desirable thing, we seem to argue for the present practice of nations and to sanction the pride and prejudice of past history. Whereas, if we condemn these things, we seem close to a rejection of race as something useful in human life and desirable to perpetuate." In an effort to solve this dilemma, Locke attempts to avoid the extremes of both universalism and race chauvinism by way of emphasizing their interrelation. His alternative is stated most clearly in his article **"Jingo, Counter-Jingo and Us."** Here, in response to an article by Benjamin Stolberg, Locke makes clear the nature of minority jingo:

> Like Mr. Stolberg, I also say: "Good Lord deliver

us from jingo." But unlike him, yet like a philosopher, I must begin with the beginning. And "minority jingo" isn't the beginning, and so, not the root of the evil, evil though it may be. Minority-jingo is counterjingo; the real jingo is majority jingo and there lies the original sin. Minority jingo is the defensive reaction, sadly inevitable as an antidote, and even science has had to learn to fight poison with poison. However, for cure or compensation, it must be the right poison and in the right amount. And just as sure as revolution is successful treason and treason unsuccessful revolution, minority jingo is good when it succeeds in offsetting either the effects or the habits of majority jingo and bad when it reinfects the minority with the majority disease. . . . The minority is entitled to its racial point of view provided it is soundly and successfully carried through.

Concluding, Locke says,

As I see it, then, there is the chaff and there's the wheat. A Negro, or anyone, who writes African history inaccurately or in a distorted perspective should be scorned as a "black chauvinist," but he can also be scotched as a tyro. . . . Or the racialist to whom group egotism is more precious than truth or who parades in the tawdry trappings of adolescent exhibitionism is likewise to be silenced and laughed off stage; but that does not invalidate all racialism. There are, in short, sound degrees and varieties of these things, which their extremisms discount and discredit but cannot completely invalidate. I am not defending fanaticism, Nordic or Negro, or condoning chauvinism, black or white; nor even calling "stalemate" because the same rot can be discovered in both the majority and the minority basket.

It should be clear then that, for Locke, minority chauvinism need not be a necessary constituent of race pride. Rather, it must be understood as a position which is forced upon minorities because of majority pressures. It is precisely because counter-claims of minority jingoism are externally determined that Locke concludes in favor of minority jingoism, provided of course that it is reasonably held. In his article, **"Unity through Diversity: A Baha'i Principle,"** Locke poses and answers the following question: "Can anyone with a fair-minded sense of things, give wholesale condemnation to the partisanship of Indian Nationalism, or Chinese integrity and independence, of Negro proletarian self-assertion after generations of persecution and restriction? Scarcely,— and certainly not at all unless the older partisanships that have aroused them repent, relax, and finally abdicate their claims and presumptions." In other words, "we feel and hope in the direction of universality, but still think and act particularistically."

Locke's interest in the problem of race and race relations throughout the world has led some of his commentators to a number of false conclusions. In *The Mind and Mood of Black America,* S. P. Fullinwider, for instance, maintains that

Locke was unique in that he was able to turn his critical faculties to things other than the race question—it was not his all-consuming passion. In fact, he tended to see the solution of the Negro's problem in the broader terms of curing the ills which trouble Western civilization. DuBois had plenty to say about the ills of Western civilization but it was always with the Negro as the referent—to solve the Negro's problem would solve the problems of civilization. For Locke it was rather the other way around: the problems of his race were part of the larger problems of modern civilization.

Fullinwider is somewhat off the mark in stating that Locke "tended to see the solution of the Negro's problem in the broader terms of curing the ills which trouble Western civilization." For according to Locke, the ills which trouble Western civilization are precisely those ills created by the race question in America, namely, the lack of respect for racial and cultural differences. In his own words,

I think the Negro situation has perpetuated the psychology, the social habit of discrimination and that other minorities have indirectly suffered from its presence. It seems to me, as I study it, that the psychology of prejudice—that the habit of social group discrimination—is a very infectious and vicious thing which, if allowed to grow, spreads from one group to another; and I also feel that in talking against American racial prejudice we are at the same time talking against religious prejudice, cultural prejudice of all kinds, and even social class prejudice to a certain extent. The same psychology seems to feed them all.

On the surface, it may appear that the distinction is a trivial one. Its seriousness emerges only when we realize that Fullinwider's interpretation gives the false impression that Locke subordinated the social, economic and political struggles of black Americans to his concern for international affairs. Such an interpretation is perhaps merely the outgrowth of Fullinwider's conviction that Locke "reflected the inability of the middle class truly to empathize with the city masses." "Much derision," he continues,

was directed at Locke by Renaissance poets and writers—as often as not he was set up as a symbol of what the writers were in revolt against. . . . He did not try to hide the polish usually associated with a Rhodes Scholar and Harvard Ph.D. In short, he was easily stigmatized as—"dicty"—he stood apart from the masses—by those writers who were in a great lather to escape from that category themselves.

It is true that Locke, like DuBois, was a strong advocate of a "talented tenth" and felt little could be expected, politically, from the economically deprived masses. Thus one is likely to encounter in his writings such expressions as "exceptional few," "nationally representative classes," "leaderless masses" and "vulgar crowd." For example, [in] **"The High Cost of Prejudice"** he writes: "Both as an American and as a Negro, I would so much prefer to see the black masses going gradually forward under the leadership of a recognized and representative and responsible elite than see a frustrated group of malcontents later hurl these masses at society in doubtful but desperate strife." In no way, however, do such statements prove that Locke had contempt for the masses or that he deliberately sought to distance himself from them. On the contrary, Locke's "elitism" and advocacy of the "talented tenth" represents a devotion to the causes of the black masses, and he esteems elitism only insofar as it furthers political, economic and cultural net gains:

> By recognizing the talent and the representative types among Negroes, an easing and vindicating satisfaction can be carried down into the Negro masses, as well as the most quickening and stimulating sort of inspiration that could be given them. Their elite would then become symbols in advance of expected justice and of a peaceful eventual solution. They would be literally an investment in democracy. . . . Not only great satisfaction, but great social incentive can be created for the masses in the recognition of the outstanding few,—*as a group representative,* however, and *not* with the reservations to which Negro talent of a previous generation had to submit, namely, of being regarded as a prodigy, a biological sport. [my italics]

The clear inference is that to bridge the gap, to bring the level of the masses' sense of appreciation and understanding closer to the consensus of the best qualified opinion, to stop claims of black inferiority, and to eventually stop racism were Locke's only intentions in advocating a black elitism. This education in appreciation and understanding is, for Locke, most essential:

> As a race group we are at the critical stage where we are releasing creative artistic talent in excess of our group ability to understand and support it. Those of us who have been concerned about our progress in the things of culture have now begun

to fear as the greatest handicap the discouraging, stultifying effect upon our artistic talent of lack of appreciation from the group which it represents. . . . Here is our present dilemma. If the standard of cultural tastes is not rapidly raised in the generation which you represent, the natural affinities of appreciation and response will drain off, like cream, the richest products of the group, and leave the mass without the enriching quality of its finest ingredients. This is already happening: I need not cite the painful individual instances. The only remedy is the more rapid development and diffusion of culture among us.

It should be stressed, by way of conclusion, that it is Locke's understanding of the nature of man and of the nature of culture—rather than the "middle-class sensibility" so often attributed to him—that leads him to take the position he does on the nature of race and race relations. Specifically, it is his view that cultural interchange enables people to come together in ways mutually stimulating and functional that determines the direction of his thinking. Such an interchange should in no way result in the weakening of a race's cultural traditions and values, but rather in a more profound consciousness of them. Race, says Locke,

> seems to lie in that peculiar selective preference for certain culture-traits and resistance to certain others. . . . And instead of decreasing as a result of contacts this sense and its accumulative results seem on the whole to increase, so that we get accumulative effect. It intensifies therefore with contacts and increases with the increasing complexity of the culture elements in any particular area. A diversity of culture types temporarily at least accentuates the racial stresses involved.

Locke's thinking on race and race relations seems to me to be both sound and healthy. Those who wish to maintain that his position is faulty cannot adequately do so by merely pointing to his personality or lifestyle; they must show the untenability of one or more of the views on which his position depends. So far this has not been done.

Clarence E. Walker (review date 1992)

SOURCE: "Two Black Intellectuals and the Burden of Race," in *African American Review,* Vol. 26, No. 4, 1992, pp. 675-82.

[*In the following excerpt, Harris discusses* The Philosophy of Alain Locke, *edited by Leonard Harris; and J. Saunders*

Redding's Stranger and Alone, *and how American racism affected the two intellectuals.*]

To be black, male, and an intellectual has not been an easy task in a society where, historically, African American men have been more valued for their strength than for their intellect. To be an African American intellectual, regardless of gender, has also meant occupying a precarious position between black and white America. Some whites fear and despise black intellectuals because they confound their racism and do not fit society's stereotype of black people as mentally incompetent. Similarly a number of blacks think their peers have betrayed the "race" and fail to "think black" if they are not racial romantics or chauvinists. In the past this tension caused problems between W. E. B. Du Bois and Marcus Garvey and between Malcolm X and the Martin Luther King wing of the Civil Rights Movement. More recently it has surfaced in the racial ruckus pitting New York City's black shoppers against Korean merchants, Mayor Dinkins, and the black political leadership of the city. These disputes among American blacks indicate that ideas about race have divided the community as much as they have divided black and white Americans.

The word *race* as I use it here is not the social construct neo-Marxists conveniently invoke to explain the growth of capitalism, maintaining that there was no race or racism before the rise of the market economy. I eschew the Marxist and neo-Marxist technique of folding or incorporating racial dynamics into economic dynamics, for to do this minimizes the relative autonomy of racial conflict in the United States. "Race," for me, refers to a deeply ingrained cultural sensibility varying over time; "racism" arises when that sensibility is ignored, attacked, or undervalued by members of a different race.

The works by Alain Locke and J. Saunders Redding reviewed here reflect the impact of American racism on two black intellectuals. What the books tell us is that these two men transcended the burden of race. They never lost their faith in human progress and at the same time remained true to the critical task of intellectuals. That is, they posited, because they were black and cosmopolitan, an alternative to the American racial status quo. At a time when the United States has entered into another cycle of racial crisis, the republication of Locke's and Reddings' works is timely. This is particularly true for those of us in the academy who are black and believe in the ideal of racial integration; Locke and Redding are examples of black intellectuals who never compromised their individuality by becoming either racial apologists or chauvinists.

Although both men were proud of their race and its accomplishments, neither was entombed in blackness. They took pride in being both black and American. This duality was the source of their intellectual strength and enabled them to see paradox, contradiction, and irony in the society that surrounded them. Locke expressed this ironic sensibility when he wrote: "Hitherto, it must be admitted that American Negroes have been a race more in name than in fact, or to be more exact, more in sentiment than in experience." With the exception of Stanley Crouch, Ralph Ellison, Martin Kilson, Robert O'Meally, Adolph Reed, Jerry Watts, Cornel West, and William Julius Wilson, few black intellectuals writing today would express in print the "imagined" nature of being black in contemporary America.

Alain Locke, who served for forty years as chair of the Howard University philosophy department, was born in 1885 and died in 1954. His life spanned the age of accommodation, World War I, the great migration, black urbanization, World War II, and the first stirrings of the Civil Rights Movement. For Locke and his generation of black Americans, "white supremacy" was not just a slogan, as one Southern historian has recently claimed. Between 1885 and 1894, for example, 1,700 blacks were lynched in America. These brutal ritual acts of terror were designed to intimidate the black population and dissuade them from exercising their democratic franchise. Moreover, lynching was aimed at both politically active blacks and those who opted for the politics of accommodation as preached by Booker T. Washington.

Washington ultimately failed because he confused culture with politics. Blacks' major problem in the late nineteenth century was not a deficient culture but a lack of political power. Washington's failure forced black Americans to re-evaluate their struggle for racial equality. Some black people, including Locke, opted for the program of racial integration championed by W. E. B. Du Bois and the NAACP. The clearest statement of Locke's commitment to an integrationist or cosmopolitan culture for the United States may be found in his essay **"The New Negro,"** in which he remarked with favor on "the re-establishment of contact between the more advanced and representative classes" of black and white America.

Locke's transcendence of the American racial morass derived from his education and travels abroad. As Michael Winston has noted, he "was nurtured in a genteel and cultivated environment that shaped his interests and choice of career." After graduating from Harvard, Locke in 1907 became the first black American to win a Rhodes scholarship and study at Oxford University. Later he studied at the University of Berlin. Study abroad gave Locke a "new perspective for viewing American society and culture." In Europe, the young black American "developed a global conception of the race problem and a corresponding interest in Africa and the problems of nonwhite colonies elsewhere." This broadened perspective of the race problem made him an advocate of "cultural pluralism," committed to the development of an American society that cultivated difference.

When he returned from Europe and began teaching at Howard University in 1913, it was to embark on a career of promulgating his ideas about race and cultural pluralism. Locke thought that Howard should be a center for the study of "race, 'culture contact,' and colonialism." At the heart of this program was Locke's belief that the "study of race contacts [is] the only scientific basis for the comprehension of race relations." Study, travel abroad, and his experience as a black American all stimulated Locke to urge social scientists studying humankind to "abandon as altogether unscientific the conception of physical race groups as basic in anthropology, and throw the category of race into the discard as another of the many popular misconceptions detrimentally foisted upon science." Race, to Locke, was a social definition, not an immutable biological fact: "We must consider race not in the fascist, blood-clan sense, which also is tribal and fetishist, but consider race as a common culture and brotherhood."

Cultural pluralism was for Locke a way of melding together a heterogeneous nation. As a black American he saw the danger of making culture a "proprietary doctrine," as whites had done in the United States. The primacy accorded Anglo-Saxon culture in the United States contributed to the intolerance and bigotry which pervaded American society after World War I. The growth of the Ku Klux Klan and the rise of religious fundamentalism reflected the inability of some white Americans to conceive of their country as a cosmopolitan state, or what Randolph Bourne has called "Trans-National America." Writing in 1930, Locke observed: "Civilization, for all its claims of distinctiveness, is a vast amalgam of cultures. The difficulties of our social creeds and practices have arisen in great measure from our refusal to recognize this fact."

Locke's perceptive and cosmopolitan intellect enabled him to see the limitations of fetishizing race and culture, a talent that distinguished him from other black intellectuals of his day. His volume *The New Negro* proclaimed the birth of a new racial awareness among black Americans and a sense of cultural renewal for black people. Yet despite his prominent role in disseminating the ideas of the Renaissance, in later years Locke distanced himself from that movement and pointed out its failings and limitations. In an article published in *Opportunity* in 1939, he savaged the phrase *New Negro*. A badge of honor and pride in 1925, the name *New Negro* had, after nearly a decade and a half, become "a slogan for cheap race demagogues who wouldn't know a 'cultural movement' if they could see one, a handy megaphone for petty exhibitionists who were only posing as 'racialist'

when in fact they were the rankest kind of egoist, and a gilded fetish for race idolaters who were at heart still sentimentalist seeking consolation for inferiority." This sense of betrayal and loss persisted in later years. In an essay published in 1950, Locke observed that the "New Negro" movement had died "of a fatal misconception of the true nature of culture."

Locke's ability to think critically about the nature of race and culture enabled him to see the multifaceted nature of black life in America. Unlike either Marcus Garvey or Malcolm X, Locke was not a racial essentialist—that is, he did not think in terms of an undifferentiated, singular Negro. His essay **"Who and What is Negro?"** stated eloquently Locke's understanding of the variety of Negroness in the United States:

> There is, in brief, no "The Negro." More and more, even as we stress the right of the mass Negro to his important place in the picture, artistically and sociologically, we must become aware of the class structure of the Negro population, and expect to see, hear and understand the intellectual elite, the black bourgeoisie as well as the black masses. To this common stratification is added in the Negro's case internal splits resulting from differential response to particular racial stresses and strains, divergent loyalties which, in my judgment, constitute racial distinctiveness, not by some magic of inheritance but through some very obvious environmental conditionings. For just as we have, for comparative example, the orthodox and the assimilate, the Zionist and anti-Zionist Jew, so in Negro life we have on practically all of these levels, the conformist and the non-conformist strains,—the conformist elite and the racialist elite, the lily-white and the race-patriotic bourgeois, the folk and the ghetto peasant and the emerging Negro proletarian. Each is a significant segment of Negro life. . . .

Locke's advice to racial and cultural essentialists regardless of their color was quite direct: ". . . we must abandon the idea of cultural truism as a criterion . . . just as we have abandoned the idea of a true race under the most scientific and objective scrutiny of the facts of history." Locke's advocacy of cultural pluralism did not mean that he felt his people were inferior, as black nationalists have often alleged in their critique of integrationists. Integral to his commitment to America as a culturally pluralist society was his belief that the culture and history of black people in the United States was of equal value to those of other groups. Moreover, the propagation and enrichment of their culture was for blacks an important weapon in the struggle against racism—a concomitant to political assertion. This involvement in black culture was the twentieth-century continuation of a crusade begun by free blacks in the eighteenth and nineteenth centuries to "elevate the race." One of its key components was education.

Although he was an advocate of African Studies at Howard University, Locke was not an Afrocentrist. He did not think that black people were "best fitted for" a particular type of college education. Blacks, according to Locke, "like any other constituency, needed all types of education that were not actually obsolete in American educational practice." Locke thought that the black college of the 1920s was "reactionary" and "old fashioned" in its educational philosophy. The Negro college in the United States, he wrote in 1925, had failed to "produce its own leadership to give it a vital and distinctive program . . . to justify it according to its true relation to racial development and advance." This type of college, Locke went on to say, had "failed [to produce] recognized social leadership and reform." As an educator with a cosmopolitan vision of the world, Locke urged black colleges to be self-determining centers of "spiritual autonomy." For Locke, "the highest aim and real justification of the Negro college should be the development of a racially inspired and devoted professional class with group service as their integrating ideal."

But Locke's hope for black higher education was only partially realized. During the 1920s the campuses of black colleges in the North and South were scenes of student and faculty protest. The black students and faculties of these institutions wanted their colleges to be more responsive to the needs of black people. As Raymond Wolters has documented, they resented the fact that their alma maters were run by white boards of trustees, and in some instances had white presidents. The background of these protests, as well as the reasons for their partial failure, is beautifully illuminated by the novel *Stranger and Alone*. . . .

FURTHER READING

Criticism

Brown, Kevin. "Harlem Shadows." *American Book Review* 15, No. 4 (October/November 1993): 17-8.
> Discusses the Harlem Renaissance and its portrayal in *The New Negro,* a volume of essays edited by Locke.

Calverton, V. F. "The Latest Negro." *The Nation* 121, No. 3156 (31 December 1925): 761.
> Discusses the cultural growth of African Americans since the Civil War as presented in *The New Negro,* a volume of essays edited by Locke.

Ellison, Ralph. "Alain Locke." In *The Collected Essays of Ralph Ellison,* edited by John F. Callahan, pp. 439-47. New York: The Modern Library, 1995.
> Discusses Locke, his idea of cultural pluralism, and what it means to be an African American.

Mencken, H. L. "The Aframerican: New Style." *The American Mercury* 7 (1926): 254-55.
> Praises *The New Negro,* and Locke as the book's editor, for its portrayal of the new African American.

> **Additional coverage of Locke's life and career is contained in the following sources published by Gale:** *Black Writers,* **Vol. 1;** *Contemporary Authors,* **Vols. 106 and 124;** *Dictionary of Literary Biography,* **Vol. 51; and** *Twentieth-Century Literary Criticism,* **Vol. 43.**

Terry McMillan

1951-

American novelist and editor.

INTRODUCTION

Terry McMillan is an American novelist whose works often depict the lives of economically successful African-American women. Her novels focus on the problems professional African-American women have in finding romantic relationships with professional African-American men. Her emphasis on love and sexual relationships, her urban, successful characters, and her depictions of genuine friendships between women have garnered her a wide audience.

Biographical Information

McMillan was born and reared in Port Huron, Michigan, a blue-collar community north of Detroit. She was one of five children cared for primarily by her mother, Madeline, who worked as a domestic and at an auto factory; McMillan's father was an abusive alcoholic. At the age of sixteen McMillan took a job at the local library and it was there that she was first introduced to literature by African Americans; she became inspired to write fiction herself after reading the works of such authors as James Baldwin. After moving to Los Angeles, McMillan attended writing courses at Los Angeles Community College. She earned a degree from the University of California at Berkeley in 1979 and moved to New York City to attend Columbia University, where she received a master's degree. For several years she lived with her lover, a drug dealer, and endured her own three-year period of drug and alcohol addiction; she eventually joined Alcoholics Anonymous and ended her substance abuse. McMillan has taught writing at Stanford University, the University of Wyoming, and the University of Arizona. She has a son, Solomon Welch.

Major Works

McMillan's novels focus on African-American women who are struggling to find a suitable lover or husband, to succeed in the business world, and to raise their families. Her first novel, *Mama* (1987), is based largely on her own family, and relates the story of Mildred Peacock, a woman who divorces her philandering husband to raise their five children on her own. Mildred overcomes alcohol and drug addiction and financial difficulties and ultimately prospers. *Disappearing Acts* (1989) reveals the challenges within a relationship between a professional woman and a blue-collar man. One of McMillan's most popular and widely read

novels is *Waiting to Exhale* (1992), which traces the lives of four women friends as they discuss the difficulties they encounter in finding and preserving romantic relationships. *How Stella Got Her Groove Back* (1996) relates the experience of the title character, a highly successful businesswoman in her 40s, who finds love along with her lost sense of joy and fun during a vacation in Jamaica.

Critical Reception

Critics have praised McMillan's realistic, believable depiction of urban African-American women, and have applauded her frank and fully-developed approach to her characters' language and concerns. Although some commentators have asserted that McMillan's use of profanity and mention of popular commercial names and products is gratuitous and detracts from the effectiveness of her narratives, she has been credited with creating a unique niche in American literature: the urban romance novel. Liesl Schillinger remarked that because of her portrayals of empowered, successful female characters, "Terry McMillan is the only novelist I have ever read, apart from writers of children's books, who makes me glad to be a woman. . . . [Maybe] fiction at last is about to understand that women are ready to read about themselves not only as schemers or sufferers, but as the adventurous heroes of their own lives."

PRINCIPAL WORKS

Mama (novel) 1987
Disappearing Acts (novel) 1989
Breaking Ice: An Anthology of Contemporary African-American Fiction [editor] (short stories) 1990
Waiting to Exhale (novel) 1992
How Stella Got Her Groove Back (novel) 1996

CRITICISM

Thulani Davis (review date May 1990)

SOURCE: "Don't Worry, Be Buppie: Black Novelists Head for the Mainstream," in *Village Voice Literary Supplement,* May, 1990, pp. 26-29.

[*In the following excerpt, Davis provides a synopsis of* Disappearing Acts, *commenting on McMillan's characters and her treatment of race and the human condition.*]

Disappearing Acts, like Terry McMillan's first novel, *Mama,* is an energetic and earthy book that takes place wholly within the confines of an intense relationship. While the narrator of *Mama* sounded like a character in the story, in this book McMillan uses two alternating voices that speak directly to the reader. The whole world is filtered through the self-naming, self-mythologizing first-person monologue—from racism to masturbation, parental conflicts to staying on a diet. And because there's no one obvious for Zora Banks or Franklin Swift to tell it to—they are loners in every way—the question is whether these folks are for real. In many ways they are quite ordinary, in other ways they are hardly tangible.

Zora is a young black woman on the lookout for the right man while she pursues singing ambitions; Franklin is a construction worker frustrated by his inability to get steady work in a closed industry. Zora sounds a lot like the narrator of *Mama,* in spite of her *Essence*-style self-improvement rap: "When I started visualizing myself less abundant, and desirable again, that's how I think I was able to get here—to 139 pounds." She likes to tell you straight up how it is: "I've got two major weaknesses: tall black men and food." Though reviewers have said that Franklin dominates the book, he has

the same brassy, up-front, I'm-gon'-tell-you-exactly style as Zora. "Don't ask me why I did some stupid shit like that. Ringing that woman's doorbell at that time of morning. And with a lame-ass line like, 'You drink coffee?' . . . She was still pretty, though, even with no makeup. Her skin looked like Lipton tea. I saw them thick nipples sticking out through that pink bath-robe, and I felt Tarzan rising." Yes, a tall black man whose swinging thing was made in Hollywood.

Even though Zora and Franklin are last-week contemporary, they are also like classic folklore characters come to life in Brooklyn. She's the wily black woman of yore, smart-talking Eve who's always got a little something on the rail for the lizard, as we used to say. She's also a sophisticated shopper who likes fancy cheeses and bottled water, and she says shit all the time. Zora has all the pulls and tugs of feminism versus the feminine that a modern black woman who's read Walker and Shange is supposed to have. She's not unlike Zora Neale Hurston's sassy folk women—characters *Cosmo* would never dare to pop-psychoanalyze.

Complicated as Franklin is supposed to be, he is a savvy urban John Henry—he don't take no tea fo' the fever. An intellectual Tina Turner meets a hardhat Ike. They are both bricks and though they may chip each other, they ain't never gonna blend. They live and work in New York City, but are in a very insulated world; their problems are completely personal. Their relationship is doomed by mutual expectations and ended by an outburst of gratuitous male violence. Let's just say it wasn't needed for the love affair to fall apart.

These two are as they are; like other folk heroes, they don't change much, or drag skeletons out of the closet, and they learn their lessons the hard way. They've been created by years of past mythologizing, drawn their images from popular culture, black and white. They are black, sho' nuff—the last thing I would say about McMillan's people is that they ain't black—but they're black in big, bold strokes. And that means her work will continue to raise questions among African Americans about the fuzzy line between realism and popular misconception. And at the same time, McMillan is, as she said, less race-conscious. She confines herself to the day-to-day life struggle, as told from behind the mask Claude McKay so poignantly described. McMillan uses, almost exclusively, the performance side of black character, emphasizing the most public, most familiar aspects of us. If you smell a little song and dance in the self-sufficient ribaldry, it's there.

Still, hard as it may be to imagine, for me at least, I suppose the time had to come when race would cease to be the obsession of African-American writers, and in its place would be some form of ordinary life—stripped in varying degrees of "context," depoliticized. If I can feel it in the street—the dislocation that can no longer be healed by inspiring leaders—I shouldn't be surprised to find it in our literature. I hope for some understanding from novels about African-American life, but perhaps it isn't there to be had. Welcome to the '90s.

Susan Isaacs (review date 31 May 1992)

SOURCE: "Chilling Out in Phoenix," in *The New York Times Book Review,* May 31, 1992, p. 12.

[*In the following review, Isaacs offers a favorable assessment of* Waiting to Exhale, *describing the novel as humorous and engaging and the characters as well drawn and captivating.*]

Was I upset about Robin! Thirty-four years old, an insurance company executive, comes from a lovely family, great sense of humor. But promiscuous. And the men she picks! Terrific looking, smooth-talking fakes and frauds. What also had me worried was Gloria's weight and high blood pressure—to say nothing of the stress she's under, being a single mother and running a beauty salon, Oasis Hair. She's popping Mylanta like mad and the minute the pain in her chest subsides what does she do? Goes out to dinner and orders pot stickers, foil-wrapped chicken, twice-cooked pork, Mongolian beef and Yangchow fried rice. It's not only Robin and Gloria that got to me. If I hadn't read *Waiting to Exhale* in one long sitting, I would have lost sleep over Savannah's loneliness and Bernadine's divorce settlement, too.

But relax. All is not angst in Terry McMillan's hilarious, irreverent novel about friendships among four Phoenix women. Like the best of its predecessors—*The Group* by Mary McCarthy, *The Best of Everything* by Rona Jaffe, Consuelo S. Baehr's *Best Friends*—this book about female buddies is full of good times as well as bad. The genre has been enormously popular through the years; the pleasure of sharing a friendship among women seems to be so great we can't get enough of it.

The four women in *Waiting to Exhale* are black, but aside from that distinction (and the fact that the author brings a wicked wit to this often sentimental form of fiction), no new literary ground is broken. But going over the old ground is still great fun with Ms. McMillan's characters for company. Savannah Jackson, a public-relations executive, is, like the others, in her mid-30's. She is cool, competent and shrewd, the strongest of the group. But her private relations with men are singularly unsatisfying. "What I want to know is this," she asks. "How do you tell a man—in a nice way—that he makes you sick?"

Savannah decides she's had it with cold Denver. Her col-

lege roommate, Bernadine Harris, who is living the ideal black urban professional life, complete with an entrepreneur husband, two children, pastel-perfect interior décor and a BMW, urges her to come to Phoenix. It's warm. It's beautiful. It's the good life. But by the time Savannah arrives, Bernadine's marriage is in ashes and her husband has flown off—with his beautiful, young and exceedingly blond bookkeeper.

As Gloria, hairdresser to them all, notes: "I don't know which is worse, trying to raise a teen-age son or dealing with a husband who leaves you for a white woman." Gloria is worried about her 16-year-old son, Tarik, a smart, talented kid who, overnight, has turned sullen, secretive and stunningly hostile.

She should relax. Gloria is a great mother, a straight-talker ("I never really expected you to come up to me one day and say, 'Yo, Ma, I'm doing the wild thang now,' but my Lord, Tarik. This is just one reason why I've always wanted you to have a father. Let me ask you something. And don't lie to me. Are you using condoms?"). She is also a shrewd businesswoman and a loving friend: a super woman. But Savannah, Robin and Bernadine are distressed that she is hiding behind a wall of fat, endangering her health as she protects herself from men, from love—from the possibility of pain.

Pain? Robin, the eternal optimist, is the expert. She looks for love in all the wrong places and, naturally, never finds it. Well, Michael, the "human submarine sandwich," a pudgy, upper-level executive with her insurance company, is smitten with her. Nevertheless, she still finds the strength to throw over good-hearted Michael (big deal, so he isn't the world's greatest lover), who adores and respects her. Then she takes up again with handsome, slothful (albeit harmless) Russell, *and* brings home a man she picks up in a supermarket, the gorgeous, charming Troy, who turns out to be a crack addict. Robin's liaison with Troy made me so nervous I chewed off most of my nail polish.

Terry McMillan's heroines are so well drawn that by the end of the novel, the reader is completely at home with the four of them. They observe men—and contemporary America—with bawdy humor, occasional melancholy and great affection. But the novel is about more than four lives; the bonds among the women are so alive and so appealing they almost seem a character in their own right. Reading *Waiting to Exhale* is like being in the company of a great friend. It is thought-provoking, thoroughly entertaining and very, very comforting.

James Robert Saunders (essay date 1995)

SOURCE: "A Missing Brother: The Ultimate Inadequacy of the Reverend Jasper," in *The Wayward Preacher in the Literature of African American Women,* McFarland & Company, Inc., 1995, pp. 125-44.

[*In the following essay, Saunders examines McMillan's portrayal of male black characters as incompetent and unreliable in her novels, focusing particularly on the character Reverend Jasper in* Mama.]

In a 1992 interview, fellow author Quincy Troupe asked Terry McMillan, "What do you think that men have to learn?" Her response was, "They need to understand something about passion. . . . A lot of men don't have enough convictions about things." *Waiting to Exhale* (1992) provides several good examples of what McMillan means because in this novel she presents us with a wide variety of men who are lacking in dedication and are willing to abdicate crucial responsibilities. What these men have in common is the ability to live selfishly notwithstanding the fact that others are depending on them for emotional and financial sustenance.

But we can go back to McMillan's first novel, *Mama* (1987), to see this particular theme of male inadequacy played out to its fullest extent. In the small town of Point Haven, Michigan, Mildred (Mama) has suffered indignations varying from a public beating administered by her husband, Crook, to the day-to-day ordeal of having to raise and provide for their five children by herself. Mildred's oldest daughter, Freda (the alter ego of McMillan herself who was raised in Port Huron, Michigan), has very distinct feelings about what is going on:

> She didn't like seeing her mama all patched up like this. As a matter of fact, Freda hoped that by her thirteenth birthday her daddy would be dead or divorced. She had started to hate him, couldn't understand why Mildred didn't just leave him. Then they all could go on welfare like everybody else seemed to be doing in Point Haven.

Mildred does indeed eventually divorce her husband and finds herself going on and off welfare, in between stints of menial employment, as she goes through the process of raising her children alone.

In *Labor of Love, Labor of Sorrow* (1985), author Jacqueline Jones has drawn certain conclusions about the interplay of black women, family, and work. She finds that "despite great difficulties in making ends meet, many mothers derived extraordinary pride and satisfaction from the well-being of their children, and they viewed life according to the options available to their offspring." This would explain how Mildred, a high school dropout, can nevertheless demand of her children, "Every last one of y'all is going to college." As

McMillan tells us, "These kids were her future. They made her feel important and gave her a feeling of place, of movement, a sense of having come from somewhere." Mildred is the major reason why each of her children will find some degree of success in their lives.

McMillan is not unsympathetic with regard to the plight of black men in America, however. The time is 1964, and the author concedes, "Most of the black men couldn't find jobs, and as a result, they had so much spare time on their hands that when they were stone cold broke, bored with themselves, or pissed off about everything because life turned out to be such a disappointment, their dissatisfaction would burst open and their rage would explode." The artist there reveals the same concern that Haki Madhubuti expresses in his introductory comments to *Black Men: Obsolete, Single, Dangerous?* (1990) as he describes "young black men in their late twenties or early thirties living in urban America, lost and abandoned, aimlessly walking and hawking the streets with nothing behind their eyes but anger, confusion, disappointment and pain." And certainly, McMillan will reinvestigate this theme through the character of Franklin Swift, who at one point in *Disappearing Acts* (1989) bemoans the subway "full of black men who looked mad at the world." He himself fails to overcome the crippling self-perception that he is little more than a common day laborer.

One cannot help but believe, however, that Crook would be better off if he had even a modicum of the passion Mildred shows toward their children. True, he is only a sanitation worker. But Mildred has been at various times a maid, a waitress, a cook, a factory worker, or a caretaker for the elderly. What is the essential difference between Crook's occupation and the tasks Mildred has had to perform? The types of employment are in fact quite similar. Any difference has to do with how society demands prestige from men. Men are expected to perform more dignified labor that in some sense reflects who they are. If this is not possible, then it has an effect on their egos. They may even reach the point where they consider themselves less than "real" men. Such social perspectives are even more devastating for black men, who over the years have consistently received the worst of employment opportunities.

The detrimental impact of social attitudes was not lessened with the publication of Daniel Moynihan's 1965 report on the black family. He believed, as Michelle Wallace interprets the document, that "if you increase the black *man*'s educational and employment opportunities—the implication was that you would ignore the black woman, who had too much already—you will increase the numbers of black status quo families with principal male providers and thus eliminate or substantially diminish the problems of blacks—in other words, unemployment, juvenile delinquency, illiteracy, fatherless households." Moynihan truly believed that the black community's major problem was that there were too many female-dominated households. But even as he criticized the overabundance of black matriarchs, he failed to acknowledge the danger of black patriarchy. Furthermore he took too much for granted in assuming that once black men had power it would as a direct consequence trickle down and filter into the overall black community.

Author bell hooks is enlightening as she renders the following assessment:

> Many black men who express the greatest hostility toward the white male power structure are often eager to gain access to that power. Their expressions of rage and anger are less a critique of the white male patriarchal social order and more a reaction against the fact that they have not been allowed full participation in the power game. In the past, these black men have been most supportive of male subjugation of women. They hoped to gain public recognition of their "manhood" by demonstrating that they were the dominant figure in the black family.

The point that hooks makes here is especially important because she is in essence saying that from a black woman's perspective, it matters little whether the oppressor is a white male or a black male, her well-being will not be substantially altered. Many black men in pursuit of power have not been especially concerned about the very specific problems that black women face. Moreover, the circumstances of impoverished black children have not really been their priority.

Mildred's brother Jasper is one of these men with whom hooks finds fault. Early on in his life he was a frequenter of the local pool hall and was in fact shot for having stolen a beer. Now, however, he is a preacher with "so many kids he had to keep adding rooms onto his house so he could have somewhere to put them." One immediately notices the tone with which McMillan describes that housing necessity. He did not *want* to add rooms. He "had to." Not to be able to provide better shelter for them or raise them better or care for them. But "so he could have somewhere to put them." It might be argued that this particular phrasing is just indicative of McMillan's writing style. *Publishers Weekly* writer Wendy Smith observes that the author has a tendency to use "salty, often profane language." So it is conceivable that when McMillan says, "so he could have somewhere to put them," she indeed means "so he could have somewhere to love them."

I would submit, however, that McMillan means to say what she says in the particular manner that she says it. The author knows how to write so that it is clear when one person loves another. And this is not the sense we get from Jasper.

Nor is it just his own children that he regards as objects. At one point in the novel when Doll and Angel, two of Mildred's daughters, have returned from California to visit yet another sister, Bootsey, they all "didn't want to go see him, because he'd never been very friendly." Again, some might wish to defend Jasper. We all, at one time or another, have seen images of the self-possessed, respectable minister, aloof from everyday happenstance. Such men are often regarded as being above the ordinary fray of what consumes so much of other people's lives. But to have an uncle who has *never* been friendly—and is a preacher—is something to which we must pay attention. Indeed we must wonder just how far he has come since those days when he might have been shot for stealing beer in a pool hall. What manner of thief is he now?

In her essay entitled "Black Women and the Church," Jacquelyn Grant contends that "if Black theology speaks of the Black community as if the special problems of Black women do not exist, it is no different from the white theology it claims to reject precisely because of its inability to take account of the existence of Black people." Grant's comment reminds us of what hooks has to say about the false distinction whether black women are being oppressed by white men or black men. hooks emphasizes the desire of black men to prove their manhood through the acquisition of economic power. What Grant does, in her essay, is explain how the black church has facilitated what have been the efforts of black men to participate in the patriarchy even to the detriment of black women.

Early on in *Mama,* we get a sense of where McMillan will lead us in terms of how black theology is promulgated by the religious leaders of Point Haven. There is much to consider in her story about another preacher who when he

> put on his white robe and walked through waves and over stones to baptize people, he wouldn't go out too far. Once he dropped his Bible in the water after dipping Melinda Pinkerton backward into salvation and a wave clipped his sleeve, sweeping his Bible away. He didn't try to go after it, either.

The preacher cannot be very far out in the water, but he will not bend down to retrieve an item so sacred as his own personal Bible. We can just envision this "apostle" jumping back from the wave as though at any second it might destroy him. "Forget God," he must be saying to himself. Forget the Bible. It is evident his faith is not genuine.

Although Mildred may appear on the surface to be one of the most irreverent characters in the annals of American literature, that presumed irreverence merits a close look. Curly, her sister-in-law, criticizes Crook for drinking too much, confiding to Mildred, "Abusing hisself like he do ain't nowhere in the Bible, is it?" Mildred responds, "Honey, I wouldn't know, been so damn long since I read it." We could conclude that these are simply the words of an unabashed nonbeliever.

On another occasion, Freda asks Mildred why most black people are poor. Mildred answers, "They thank they can get something for nothing and that that God they keep praying to every Sunday is gon' rush down from the sky and save 'em." In that answer we can begin to understand that Mildred is not an atheist at all. She just has her own beliefs about how faith in God should be pursued. Although she is acquainted with the Bible, she is nevertheless not now an avid Bible reader. And she does not accept the notion that regular church attendance by itself is the means to earthly success or other worldly salvation.

Mildred has had such a rough life that her particular faith has to be structured around the cold, hard reality of her very practical existence. She has had to raise five kids alone, and then when it seems that she has pretty much accomplished this feat, her father has a heart attack. She is in California when her sister Georgia calls her with the details. The doctors do not know if he will survive, but Georgia cavalierly proclaims, "The Lord is watching over him." In another one of her seemingly irreverent responses, Mildred tells Georgia, "I'll be on the next plane out of here. My daddy need me more than he need the Lord." Mildred remembers how eager Georgia was to move in with their father when their stepmother died. It had been Georgia's intention to take advantage of their father's pension and the life insurance payments he would be receiving as a consequence of his wife's death. It was Mildred in that instance who had stopped Georgia dead in her tracks, threatening, "If I have to come back there and put padlocks on the doors myself, you ain't using my daddy."

As already mentioned, Mildred is living in California. Another brother, Leon, resides in Arizona, so Georgia is free to take advantage of her father's circumstances. But where is the other brother, Jasper, who has been residing in Point Haven all along? Why is it that he can do nothing to prevent Georgia from exploiting their father? One can only fathom that this son does not care. In fact, Jasper can be said to have a great deal in common with Georgia, who has "turned her soul over" to God for the purpose of sheer convenience. Georgia tells the story of how her husband returned from the grave to get her to drive back and watch her house burn down. Not only will she get insurance money but also a chance to move in with her father. Similarly, Jasper has undergone a "conversion" that will allow him to take advantage of others' unfortunate circumstances. In spite of the widespread poverty suffered by blacks, he has positioned himself to acquire wealth. And we are left with the question

of just how concerned he really is when it comes to the community for which he is presumed to be a spiritual steward.

Jasper is not available for his father in time of need, and certainly not for Mildred and her children as they negotiate a plethora of precarious events. His sister struggles through furnace breakdowns, utility cutoffs, and finally eviction, and never once do we see him appear and offer assistance. If nothing else, one would think he could show concern for Mildred's only son, Money. After that child has fallen prey to drug addiction and been incarcerated, the narrator contemplates a succession of causes that amounts quite simply to his having had to assume the responsibilities of manhood far too early in his adolescent development. In one of the more poignant sections of the novel, McMillan conveys:

> When Mildred and Crook split up Money had become the man of the house at eleven years old. It was Money who picked up the dead mice because everybody else was too scared. It was Money who drained the water from the basement when it flooded. Waded through three inches of water just to put the clothes in the dryer so the girls could wear matching knee socks to school. It was Money who learned how to put a penny in the meter to get the lights and gas back on when they'd been cut off. It was Money who pulled the trash barrels out to the street to be picked up. And when things broke, Money fixed them. No one had taught him; his instincts told him what to do. . . . They all took it for granted that this was his role. He had never had any options.

Money got his name because by the time "he was barely old enough to tell you his address," he had become a beggar. He would ask, "You got a dime?" If the person he was asking said no, then Money would ask, "You got a nickel?" If the person still said no, then the child would implore, "Well you got *any* money?" Before long, this habit of begging became one of stealing, as a downward spiral continued.

But the main point is that while all this is going on, Jasper is nowhere to be found. In some ways he resembles Kristen Hunter's the Reverend Bird, for whom his congregation "contributed enough to the church collections to provide him with all the antiques . . . he required for his happiness. And since *their* happiness required that their pastor be transported in a large, elegant car and the Reverend Bird did not drive, they could hardly object to his series of chauffeurs." We have seen in my earlier chapters how comfort and prosperity for the preacher can take priority over even the basic needs of church members. Bird does at least fight government officials when it seems that the interests of his congregation are in jeopardy. There is absolutely no evidence, however, that Jasper is inclined to project himself into the forefront in defense of the interests of those he would acknowledge as his flock.

Keep in mind that Jasper is for the most part an artistically effective preacher. He knows how to deliver a "fire and brimstone" sermon. As Curly confirms, "Jasper still preaching like ain't no tomorrow. The words be like music filling up your body." On the one occasion we see him elocuting, the congregation as a whole is awe-inspired, following along in the same "call-and-response" manner that characterizes black preaching at its best. The "Tell its," "Amens," and "Ain't that the truths" are a testament to the speaker's undeniable force.

Still, the sermon is problematic. It is useful here to consider another Jasper—the John Jacob Jasper who was my own grandmother's minister. This preacher is especially famous for having sought to convince his listeners that the sun revolved around the earth instead of vice versa. "De Sun do Move" was the title of that sermon he delivered over and over again from one Virginia church to another. In his talks he relied on Malachi 1:11, where it says, "For from the rising of the sun even unto the going down of the same my name *shall* be great among the Gentiles." But we immediately see the flaw in that Jasper's interpretation. Even today, televised weather reports include the times of sunrise and sunset. But this is not to say that those who use the terms believe that the earth is the center of the universe. Galileo proved the opposite four centuries ago.

John Jasper found it useful to proliferate a contradictory theory of his own devising, however, and he was a gifted enough speaker to be utterly persuasive. One need only put himself in the position of an illiterate former slave to comprehend how easy it might have been to be swayed by the famous preacher's words:

> Has I proven my point? Oh, ye whose hearts is full of unbelief! Is you still holding out? I reckon de reason you say de sun don't move is cause you are so hard to move yourself. You is a real trial to me, but, never mind, I ain't given you up yet and never will. Truth is mighty; it can break de heart of stone and I must fire another arrow of truth out of de quiver of de Lord.

John Jasper spoke in brilliant metaphoric terms as he depicted himself shooting arrows from the Lord's quiver in order to pierce hearts that resisted his versions of the truth. As was the case with Hurston's John Pearson, and indeed all of the preachers we have covered in this study, the power of words can have a blinding effect that impedes the listener from realizing the deeper truths about humanity and the world.

McMillan's preacher is similarly fallible. Jasper, like his historical namesake, can enrapture an audience with wonderful metaphors, asking on one occasion, "Do it feel like you in a boat rowing backwards when the island you trying to get to is up ahead?" Jasper understands the psychology of this small factory town where "women usually did day work" and for more than a few, welfare checks were "steadier and went a lot further" than what regular employment would provide. In fact, Freda, who has no idea where she will move, nevertheless cannot wait until the day when she will graduate from high school and leave this town because "she knew that there had to be a better place to live than here." Not everyone will be so singleminded as Freda is in their efforts to get out of Point Haven. But Jasper is aware of the deep-seated misery festering within the black population. "*Sometimes*," he exhorts his congregation, "you can get so full of sorrow and so heavy-hearted, that you feel like you in a jail run by Satan." He touches their emotions in a way that places special emphasis on the torment he knows is being suffered.

But why is it Jasper seems to give so little help in ameliorating the awful societal conditions? We will remember how Paule Marshall has suggested that there is no difference between the preacher and the rum seller. Interestingly enough, McMillan raises the same issue when she notes that "drinking was the single most reliable source of entertainment for a lot of people in Point Haven. Alcohol was a genuine elixir, granting instant relief from the mundane existence that each and every one of them led." In addition to the many McMillan characters who possess a "salty" vocabulary, there are also quite a few who are hard drinkers, including Mildred. But such characters are meant to be admirable. They are survivors. And as they move from the church to the barroom, we witness a capacity to persevere, notwithstanding life's problems. There evidently are times when the obscurities and contradictions that are lodged in Jasper's words simply are not enough.

For example, Jasper tells the story of a teenage girl who, having injured her ear, "couldn't hear nothin' but a roaring sound" for two solid years. Now Jasper is eager to get to the part where he talks about God completely restoring the girl's hearing. The preacher speaks of her unwavering faith and tells how she prayed persistently. In the story, the girl's hearing is restored. Yet anyone paying careful attention to the story's details would have to ask how someone who hears only a roaring noise can sleep "so very sound" over the course of the same two-year period. An all-powerful God could of course provide for a person to sleep peacefully through such a roaring sound, even if it is deafening. But considered from another perspective, it makes little sense. God will not answer her prayers for two years, but He allows her to be at peace with the roar, making her premiracle condition not all that drastic as the preacher would have us believe.

Jasper goes on to tell these "healing stories for what felt like hours to Mildred." The entire sermon has really become an ordeal for her as she eases the high-heeled shoes off her feet and dreams of being able to get even more comfortable and smoke a cigarette. "The power of Almighty God is *Swift. Immediate*," says the preacher in his sermonic commentary on the girl with the ear problem. If taking two years to accomplish something could be called swift and immediate, then perhaps Mildred would be swayed by her brother's reasoning. Under the circumstances, however, she is not impressed.

Jasper says, "*desire* is prayer," and that "in order to find God, you must first have discernment." McMillan tells us that Mildred does not even know what that last word means. But this is not to say the author would have us believe that the hardworking mother is stupid or in some other way lacking in necessary intelligence. Mildred does not know what the literal definition of *discernment* is, and those of us who do know what the definition is find ourselves wondering what Jasper himself wants to convey in saying what amounts to "In order to find God, you must first have found God." Mildred's confusion is but a reflection of the confusion we should all have at hearing such a statement.

I will refrain from even attempting to interpret the reverend's statement that desire is prayer, other than to say that the lack of any information with regard to what is being desired makes a virtual plethora of possibilities exist for what prayer is being equated with. We are reminded of how John Jacob Jasper sought to convince his congregation that the sun revolved around the earth. That Jasper convinced numerous listeners he was correct. McMillan's preacher wants to have that same kind of oratorical power. In fact, he does have such power, for there are many who will do whatever he says and follow him anywhere. Mildred, on the other hand, is the type of person who never will be deterred from the scientific findings of Galileo.

Considering the methodology of John Jacob Jasper, it is very likely that he would have been unsuccessful in attempting to convert Mildred to Christianity. At the conclusion of her brother's sermon, she mulls over what he has said but is ultimately disappointed. The author tells us, "She did not feel an inch closer to God." Mildred needs the kind of hard, cold facts that are implicit when she admonishes her son, "Money, boy, where you thank that bike you ride all over town come from? God?" She knows first hand of the day-to-day strivings required if people like her are to achieve anything. In fact, a strong sense of inappropriateness is conveyed by the author as she has the main protagonist drop "one of her last five dollars into the brass plate" when Jasper asks for donations. We cannot help but believe that it is he who should be contributing to her social betterment instead of the other way around.

It is not only because Jasper espouses himself to be a man of God that we think he should be making some more tangible contribution to Mildred's life. We believe this because he is also her brother. But in a dramatic chapter near the end of the novel, we are confronted with a stark reality. Jasper will never be available for Mildred. In the scene where Mildred walks out into snow and zero-degree temperature to get to her sister-in-law who has been hospitalized for a stroke, this long-suffering woman is in dire need of some kind of support. When she first gets the news of Curly's illness, she "considered going to the hospital, but she felt so tired she sat back down in the chair by the window." Several hours pass before she attempts again, but "she hadn't had a drop of strength left in her."

It would seem logical here for Mildred to phone her brother and ask if he could drive her to the hospital. Such duties fall under the rubric of pastoral responsibilities anyway. Since Curly is a member of Jasper's congregation, perhaps he has already visited her. If such is the case, then Mildred could simply call him to inquire about her best friend's condition. But she does not call. And we do not get the sense that Jasper has visited Curly at either the hospital or her home, where even Mildred "couldn't stand being . . . too long because it depressed her" with its "dark, rickety furniture." No, if anyone was going to be there for Curly, it would have to be Mildred. Support from the Reverend Jasper is tenuous at best.

Maybe Curly joined church for the wrong reasons anyway. Earlier she had poured out her troubles to Mildred:

> Shelly most likely gon' spend the rest of her life in and out of prison, Chunky half crazy from them drugs, and last night, chile, some boy beat Big Man in the nose with a poolstick and he up in Mercy Hospital right now. . . . My husband don't even touch me no more, Milly, so you turn to whoever gon' make you feel the most glory and peace. And for me, right this minute, it's God. If it weren't for him, I don't know if I'd even have the strength to get up in the morning and face daylight.

Curly for some time now has been mourning the circumstances of her immediate family. Her children are a disappointment, and she is unable even to receive solace from her husband. For her, God is a last resort, a crutch, a diversion from the reality which would otherwise drive her to despair.

After listening to Curly's explanation for why she joined the church, Mildred offers that friend her best wishes, saying, "Well, more power to you, Curly." But then when Curly asks Mildred to attend church with her the following Sunday, Mildred defers, maintaining, "Last time I went to church I got depressed." Curly presses further in the fashion of an evangelist herself, insisting, "That's 'cause you didn't give yourself a chance to let God in. Once you let him in, it feel so good . . . you won't want to turn back." "I'd love to sit here and chitchat with you all day," Mildred says, as she abruptly ends the conversation, "but I got thangs to do."

Mildred is primarily a doer in spite of her limited resources. This is why later in the novel, after struggling against her own weariness, she is finally able to lift herself up out of the chair and go outside to the car she has borrowed from Bootsey. She is determined to get to the hospital. Relying on God is not enough. The author had told us at the beginning of the book that when it came to acquiring money, Mildred "didn't think he was such a reliable source." When it comes to looking out for her friends, Mildred is not willing to turn that mission over to God either.

Driving through the snow, Mildred skids and gets trapped in a snowbank, but she is not injured. In fact, she reserves most of her remorse for Curly rather than for herself or her immediate predicament. But it is during this incident that we see Mildred at her most introspective. One might even be inclined to say that she is praying as she talks out loud to some unknown entity:

> If you up there, I hope the hell you can hear me. I wanna know what the hell you trying to prove? . . . Why can't you do something right for a change? I thought you was supposed to be so big and bad, could do anything anytime anywhere. Are you there or am I just wasting my damn time?

The language is sometimes profane as she asks whoever she is speaking to whether this is "some kind of damn test." She wavers back and forth between giving up (at one point she says, "I've had it") and being determined to overcome this adversity, proclaiming, "I'm gon' tell you something, buddy. I'm gon' make it past the finish line." In the final analysis, she will not give up, and in the process of this struggle, we are witness to the blossoming of a faith that is nothing like what occurs in the rarefied atmosphere of a church sanctuary.

Carlene Hatcher Polite, in *The Flagellants* (1967), presents us with a character named Ideal, who as a child witnesses the verbal power of the minister at her great-grandmother's church. The response of the congregation is identical to what the McMillan's Reverend Jasper is able to evoke from his parishioners. Polite's preacher is so effective that "brothers and sisters of the church whooped and hollered for release." Meanwhile, Ideal, sitting beside her great-grandmother, observes all the commotion and silently questions:

> Where was the God who had created the flowers, the light, the heart of this place called Black Bot-

tom? Who was the God who had chosen our mothers to bring us into the world? Where was the God who is love?

After thus contemplating, the child "cried tears of ignorance." This protagonist has legitimate questions about how the world is composed, particularly her segregated, less affluent side of town. That she is ignorant about the status of God should not be viewed as evidence of any flaw in her character. Remember that her name is "Ideal," and the questioning search that she is conducting may be meant to serve as a model for others who would seek to investigate the deeper meanings of life.

There are those who look at J.D. Salinger's *The Catcher in the Rye* (1951) and find in Holden Caulfield only the musings of a disturbed adolescent who can make neither heads nor tails of the world other than to condemn all adults for being phoney. Perhaps this young man is being overly sensitive. But perhaps the kind of analysis he is conducting is essential for an understanding of those things that many others have been willing to take for granted without any true understanding at all. He is not to be taken literally when he says, "I'm sort of an atheist." The operative phrase there is "sort of." How is someone sort of an atheist? An atheist does not believe in God or Jesus. Maybe agnostic would be a better word to describe Holden. But if he is agnostic, why does he go on to talk about Jesus as though he really existed? And he has harsh words for the disciples. "They were all right after Jesus was dead and all," contends Holden, "but while He was alive, they were about as much use to Him as a hole in the head." Blasphemy some might say. I, on the other hand, argue that this is the kind of straightforward analysis that both Ideal and Mildred are capable of conducting. Theirs is the methodology by which answers are obtained.

In the snow, Mildred gets out of the car to examine her situation. She immediately discovers that she has a flat tire, which was what caused her to skid. But she does not know how to change a car tire. It so happens that Jasper lives only a half mile down the road. But Mildred still has on her indoor shoes, and the author uses this fact as the reason why she cannot walk to his house for help. It is rather intriguing that Mildred has brought along her coat and gloves but somehow neglected to put on boots. In walking across the snow to the car at her house, it should have dawned on her that some type of outdoor footwear would be needed.

We should consider the precise language McMillan uses in depicting Mildred at her residence walking "across the hard snow" that "crunched under her house shoes." For indeed the snow may be so hard that it basically holds her weight, giving in, as the author tells us, only to a limited extent and then only under her shoes. Had snow been engulfing her feet at every step, it seems she would have noticed a need for boots. So if the snow was that hard right outside her house, why is it not just as hard on Fortieth Street where the car has run off the road? She would not have to trudge through wet snow to get to Jasper's house. She should be able to glide there just as easily as she had walked out to Bootsey's car in the first place.

The narrator posits the question thusly: "Why hadn't she put her snow boots on when she left? Jasper's house was damn near a half mile down the road." Considering that the word "damn" is used here, we can assume that this is how Mildred contemplates her situation. But rather than having Mildred's dilemma being a mere quirk of fate, the author is intentionally placing obstacles to prevent her from reaching her brother. And thereby the point is emphasized just how distant this brother is. He is in essence much more than just a half mile away. He is entirely unreachable. He was not available for Mildred's son. He was not available for his own father. And now while Mildred undergoes her ordeal out in the snow, his availability looms once again as a question.

The physical barriers between Mildred and her brother are not formidable. Even if the snow was wet and sloshy, she could have warmed her feet upon her arrival at his home. Moreover, she could have walked in the paths created by car tires in the middle of the road. But the author wants to convey that it was easier for Mildred to change the tire herself (something she had never done before) than receive any kind of satisfactory help from Jasper. One wonders how satisfactory is the help that he would give anyone.

During his sermon, Jasper urged the congregation to believe that "God is within you." It sounds like a revolutionary notion along the lines of what Shug, in *The Color Purple,* tells Celie. "God is inside you," Shug says, "and inside everybody else." Yet while Shug encourages self-identification and explains how the search for God should be conducted, Jasper succumbs to contradiction. God is inside people according to the preacher, but he also says, "*God* alone lessens the sum total of all evil." Jasper first joins God in a physical mutuality of responsibility and then separates Him based on sermonic convenience. His congregation apparently adheres to the message in spite of it being inherently flawed.

Mildred needs more than shallow words, especially at this point when Bootsey's car is hopelessly trapped in the snow. As if in direct response to this need, a communion takes place that is unlike anything she could have achieved in Jasper's church. Whereas at one point during her ordeal, she questioned God's existence, now she is talking to Him as though He will give concrete help. "Look," she beseeches, "it's a lot of thangs I could've done differently, I know that. And I ain't never asked you for much." There is remorse in those words, but she is not quite apologetic. Rather, she has

accepted the circumstances of her life, asking little help from God until times arise when she absolutely needs it.

For Mildred, "*faith* in God alone" is not enough. In her case Jasper would have been well advised to draw from Thessalonians II, where Paul reminds the crowd that those who follow him do not "eat any man's bread for nought; but wrought with labour and travail night and day, that we might not be chargeable to any of you. . . . If any would not work, neither should he eat" (3:8 and 3:10). Mildred would have been able to identify with the substance of those passages. That mother went through torment when she was laid off from two housekeeping jobs she held simultaneously. As a consequence, she had to sign up for welfare. The author informs us that "this humiliated and embarrassed the hell out of her—Mildred hated the idea of begging, which is what she thought it boiled down to. . . . She had always prided herself on being self-sufficient and self-reliant." But with five children to support, she needed the assurance of a steady income. Pride would have to be sacrificed.

In verse 11, Paul criticizes those who "walk among you disorderly, working not at all, but are busybodies." Jasper seems not to be bothered so much by the large number of blacks in the community who are on welfare. Just as long as he gets a certain percentage of their income, whatever its source, he is satisfied. Mildred, however, has a different vision that ironically enough is more in line with Paul's teachings than anything Jasper has thus far offered. McMillan may well have drawn this aspect of Mildred's character from her own mother. In an interview with Molly Giles, McMillan recalls that her mother was

> one of the strongest women I've ever met in my life, and I think what I learned from her was how not to be afraid. . . . She taught us to test ourselves in every way. If I got a *B* on my report card in math, she'd say, "That's great; next time get an *A*." . . . We never got any Happy Face stickers. But she made all five of us strive to outdo ourselves, always. She never finished high school herself. . . . She was a domestic and worked for a lot of rich white people.

The evidence is strong that Mildred is the alter ego of the author's own mother. Mildred has five children, just like McMillan's mother. In addition, the two mothers are high school dropouts who have had to work off and on as domestics. But neither mother wants our pity. They regard life as a test to be passed or failed in proportion with the amount of effort they have exerted.

So when Mildred goes on welfare, she must exert even more energy, now in the effort to get off the public dole. Toward this end, she garners all her inner resources and in the process of doing so, she refuses to go to church because she "didn't like the nosy people in town knowing all her damn business." How little has changed in the 2000 years since Paul delivered his message in Corinth. The "busybodies" that he spoke of are now the "nosy people" of McMillan's novel, who are, Mildred would have us believe, substantially to blame for the persistence of problems in the black community. Rather than contributing to the betterment of their social environment, they spread malicious gossip and thus make us want to examine their moral code.

In her volume of poetry entitled *Bronze* (1922), Georgia Douglas Johnson included a poem that embodies the spiritual selfanalysis that Mildred will undergo a full 65 years after that poem was written. Even the poem's title reflects the vacillating tendencies that are sure to exist in the psyche of anyone who seriously ponders the extent to which God influences people.

MOODS

My heart is pregnant with a great despair
With much beholding of my people's care,
'Mid blinded prejudice and nurtured wrong,
Exhaling wantonly the days along:
I mark Faith's fragile craft of cheering light
Tossing imperiled on the sea of night,
And then, enanguished, comes my heart's low cry,
"God, God! I crave to learn the reason why!"
Again, in spirit loftily I soar
With winged vision through earth's outer door,
In such an hour, it is mine to see,
In frowning fortune smiling destiny!

Within the first two lines of that poem is the concern for a race of people who have been much maligned. McMillan's mother inculcated in her children her belief that blacks should push themselves even harder to overcome that adversity. "She taught us," McMillan states in the Giles interview, "that we could be anything we wanted to be. And if we didn't believe it, then she was going to ram it down our throats until we did." One hears echoes of Paul addressing the Galatians, entreating them to "not be weary in well doing: for in due season we shall reap, if we faint not." Mildred has this understanding about life as she, like McMillan's mother, has accepted the value of hard work.

Mildred is capable of a certain callousness about the issue of faith. As she reflects on God early in the novel, we are told, "she didn't think he was such a reliable source." Yet we must consider the context within which she expresses that sentiment. A paragraph earlier in the novel, we were presented with the scene where women realized they would receive more money from welfare than from working a job. These particular women "spent their afternoons watching

soap operas." Mildred, however, tries to keep working, knowing that for her, "nobody was coming by to drop off a bundle of dollar bills unless it was God." And this is when she calls God unreliable since she believes He will do no such thing.

Still, like the narrator in "Moods," Mildred is intrigued by the prospect of understanding the fiber of real faith. Of what does it consist? What is the nature of her responsibility in the bargain? In Johnson's poem, faith is personified, "Tossing imperiled on the sea of night." Therein lies a crucial question: Will faith survive? It is the same question Mildred subconsciously entertains during a thunderstorm when, while sitting on the sun porch with Spooky Cooper, she issues the maxim, "My daddy always saying a thunderstorm is the Lord doing his work and we should be quiet." While it is true that she says this because she is "unable to think of anything else to say" while she and Spooky are "listening to the thunder and the rain falling in the drain pipes," it is significant that she even thinks of this. It is as though faith was lurking in her all along like a wellspring that was waiting to be tapped.

Although she had never changed a flat tire before, Mildred determinedly goes to the trunk, pulls out a jack and lug wrench, and proceeds to remove the flat tire and replace it with the spare. She has never asked much of God and now largely due to her own efforts, she accomplishes what she never imagined she could. She concludes, "Hell, this wasn't as hard as she thought it was." In Johnson's poem, the narrator evolves through her spiritual dilemma with the newfound power of a bird in majestic flight. "In spirit loftily I soar / With winged vision through earth's outer door," the poet writes. By the time she has completed the tire-changing job, Mildred likewise is filled with supernatural exhilaration, feeling "like she could probably fly if she flapped her arms fast enough."

The car is still stuck in the snow, but we are not as worried as we were earlier when it first ran off the road. It has now become evident that a contract of sorts is in effect between Mildred and the God who has helped her throughout the years she raised all those children. Here in the middle of the night, after first trying to drive the car out of the snowbank and then unsuccessfully trying to push it out, she addresses God, imploring, "I'm gon' ask you to help me one last time, and I swear I'll do everythang else myself." Having uttered that request, she strains with all her might against the car, loses her balance, and falls in such a mysteriously awkward way as to cause the car to roll out of the snowbank with her lying prone on the hood. As the car glides loose, we are left in a quandary about which of the partners is most responsible for that success.

When Jasper is preaching, one woman in the congregation blurts out, "All I see is fog." Like Mildred and the speaker in the poem "Moods," she may be involved in intense spiritual self-analysis. Jasper's brusque response, rendered in midsermon, is, "It's the devil causing all that fog." But how can he be sure that the vagaries of life have not been caused by God pressing people to test their fortitude? McMillan, in the Giles interview, was concerned that "any time you give men power, they will abuse it." This theme is certainly apparent in the artist's other novels. In *Disappearing Acts,* Franklin exploits Zora's undying love. In *Waiting to Exhale,* the vast majority of men prey on women like hawks pursuing frantic field mice. One would assume that a reverend would be considerably better than the men who appear in those other two works. Instead, in Jasper we see yet another man misappropriating the devices available to him. This preacher does not have all the answers. Needless to say, no one human being does. But behind Jasper's high-sounding words lies a sordid mentality incapable of helping where help is needed most while he impedes the progress of those who come to God on their own.

Liesl Schillinger (review date 5 May 1996)

SOURCE: "Beneath a Jamaican Moon," in *Washington Post Book World,* May 5, 1996, pp. 1, 8.

[*In the following review, Schillinger provides a highly favorable assessment of* How Stella Got Her Groove Back.]

Is a happy woman in charge of her own fate de facto an unsympathetic character—someone people don't want to read about and cannot empathize with? If so, the defenders of serious literature will no doubt join in unison to eject Terry McMillan's rip-roaring new book, *How Stella Got Her Groove Back* from the Eden of politically and academically correct approval. Because, in *How Stella Got Her Groove Back,* no women weep; and Stella, in fact, revels. She revels and even gloats at being a woman, revels in being in solitary possession of her mind, her body, her child, her house, her finances, her beauty, her creativity and finally, of her sexy, strapping young dream lover, whom she finds and triumphantly lashes to her side. If this is unserious literature, it is unserious literature of the most serious kind, perhaps even, in its own way, revolutionary.

Terry McMillan is the only novelist I have ever read, apart from writers of children's books, who makes me glad to be a woman. Children's fiction overflows with examples of authoritative girls who control their worlds, fictional and real; from Laura Ingalls Wilder's own Laura, to C. S. Lewis's Lucy, to E. E. Nesbit's Anthea, Lloyd Alexander's Eilonwy, and of course L. Frank Baum's Dorothy—or, perhaps more remarkable, Baum's Ozma of Oz, who actually chose to be

transformed from a boy to a girl to claim the Emerald City throne. But the moment the cloak of girlhood is thrown off, and writers choose to write about grown-up girls, any sense of empowerment, opportunity or strength in the female characters is bestowed only to be smashed sooner or later, as the women run through such hurdles as pleasing men, struggling to find a mate, supporting children and, more often than not, coping with emotional, physical or intellectual bullying of some kind, or paying the wages of their own sentimentalized sin.

I was afraid at first that this impression might have been an absurd exaggeration; but then I looked at my bookshelf of favorite books—books I have read and reread, and care about deeply—and was astonished to find my theory amply confirmed. In the A's to F's alone—Amis (both), Austen, Bronte, Cervantes, Dickens, Dostoevsky, Dos Passos, Duras, Eliot, Faulkner, Fitzgerald and Forster—I remembered female characters who, however interesting their tales might have been, principally sought male sanction or suffered, one way or another. Further down the alphabet, in Shakespeare and Wharton, Graham Greene, Hemingway, Virgil, and Maugham, I recalled doomed Lady Macbeth and Lily Bart, prostitutes and spurned wives, the weeping women of the Trojan wars, weeping women, in fact everywhere. (In fairness, I submit, Trollope also makes me glad to be a woman; the exception proves the rule. But then, in his time, and even now, he was often dismissed as an unserious writer). This seems to beg the question: Does serious literature want women to be subject or else abject? McMillan abundantly proves that if it does, it shouldn't.

Fans of McMillan's previous novels, the hugely popular *Waiting to Exhale* and the more critically esteemed *Disappearing Acts* and *Mama,* will recognize McMillan's authentic, unpretentious voice in every page of *How Stella Got Her Groove Back.* It is the voice of the kind of woman all of us know and all of us need: the warm, strong, bossy mother/sister/best friend. Fans and enemies alike will also get their share of the brand names that McMillan uses to signify arrival into this country's upper-middle class: BMW and Calvin Klein, Nordstrom's and Macy's. Having just spent an evening with a friend who crowed ecstatically all night over a new pair of Gucci loafers, which did in fact seem to lend her some special glow, I don't find the product emphasis fatuous or crass. Even Emerson recognized that for a woman, which McMillan indubitably is, "the sense of being perfectly well dressed gives a feeling of inward tranquillity which religion is powerless to bestow." But readers of this book will find more than wise words and icons of wealth; they will find the rare and perhaps unique example of a courtship in which the woman hunts down her own love object herself— and finds the man willing to be wooed.

At the outset of the book, we learn that Stella, 42, an affluent single mom in San Francisco, has gone a little stale, like champagne that's been uncorked and not tasted for too long. She's content, but she spends more time taking care of business and conducting lengthy Molly Bloom-like internal harangues with herself and external harangues with her sisters than trying to find happiness for herself. So, defying her stagnation, she packs herself off to a luxury resort in Jamaica, where from get-go, every young stud's eyes swing appreciatively in her direction. Sure enough, Stella soon finds the "real thing" in the form of a noble, gentle, fine 20-year-old man, Winston Shakespeare. When McMillan describes Stella's first vision of the boy wonder, you want to howl with laughter at her audacity, and shout, "Go, girl!":

> When I look at him I almost have a stroke. He is wearing baggy brown shorts and has to be at least six three or four and he is lean but his shoulders are wide broad and as he walks toward my table all I can think is Lord Lord Lord some young girl is gonna get lucky as I don't know what if she can snag you . . . when he smiles he shows off a beautiful set of straight white teeth that've been hiding behind and under those succulent young lips.

Name another time you've read a man objectified by a woman in this way, if you can. Stella, of course, turns out to be the lucky girl, and soon finds that she's hooked. Back in California, her sister Vanessa encourages her, while her sister Angela moans in despair at the folly of a May-December romance in which her sister is not May. Vanessa boldly comes to Stella's defense: "Men have been dating younger women for [expletive] centuries and does anybody say anything to them?" she sputters. Women may talk like this to each other, but few of us write like this.

To those who say this could never happen in real life, I of-

fer the evidence of the young divemaster I met last summer in Belize under an apricot moon, whose gallantry and open-hearted effusiveness restored my own faith in romance, even if he was no Winston Shakespeare. McMillan's book may be the stuff of fantasies, not reality; but if fantasies could be bought whole, every woman in the country would be lining up to buy them from Terry McMillan. And maybe then other writers would dare to write them, too. And maybe this is happening right now—and fiction at last is about to understand that women are ready to read about themselves not only as schemers or sufferers, but as the adventurous heroes of their own lives.

FURTHER READING

Biography

Skow, John. "Some Groove: With Her New Book, Money and Man, is Terry McMillan Going All Happy On Us?" *Time* 147, No. 19 (6 May 1996): 77-8.
    Article in which Skow surveys McMillan's life and career following the publication of *How Stella Got Her Groove Back.*

Criticism

Peck, Dale. A review of *How Stella Got Her Groove Back,* by Terry McMillan. *London Review of Books* 19, No. 3 (6 February 1997): 25-6.
    A negative assessment of *How Stella Got Her Groove Back.*

Pinckney, Darryl. "The Best of Everything." *New York Review of Books* 40, No. 18 (4 November 1993): 33-37.
    Praises *Waiting to Exhale* for its sincerity.

Additional coverage of McMillan's life and career is contained in the following sources published by Gale: *Authors and Artists for Young Adults,* **Vol. 21;** *Black Writers,* **Vol. 2;** *Contemporary Authors,* **Vol. 140;** *Contemporary Authors New Revision Series,* **Vol. 60;** *Contemporary Literary Criticism,* **Vols. 50 and 61; and** *DISCovering Authors Modules: Multicultural Authors, Novelists,* **and** *Popular Fiction and Genre Authors.*

James Alan McPherson
1943-

American novelist, short story writer, and memoirist.

INTRODUCTION

McPherson is best known for his short story collection, *Elbow Room,* (1977), for which he won the Pulitzer Prize in 1978. Like the stories in his earlier collection, *Hue and Cry* (1969), these stories examine issues of race, class, and culture, challenging stereotypes and recognizing the dangers of prejudice. McPherson's stories typically delineate the experiences of African Americans and illuminate the effects of poverty, violence, and racism on working-class individuals. However, McPherson's skill at portraying complete, well defined characters gives his work universal appeal. Irving Howe has stated, "James McPherson has a strong sense of injustice, almost a boy's sense, and he knows how disproportionately large a share of that injustice black men must bear; yet he manages to take human beings one at a time, honoring their portion of uniqueness."

Biographical Information

McPherson was born on September 16, 1943, in Savannah, Georgia. The son of James Allen and Mable (Smalls) McPherson, he grew up in a lower-class black community where he attended segregated public schools. Savannah, a historic city comprised of French, Spanish, Indian, English, and African ethnic groups, exposed McPherson to an atmosphere of multiculturalism, and he was acutely aware of class and color delineations. However, he learned early in life how to transcend racial and social barriers and dedicated his writing career to celebrating individuality. As a youth, McPherson worked as a grocery clerk, a waiter on a train, a janitor, and a newspaper delivery boy—experiences that later helped shape some of the characters in his fiction. McPherson attended Morgan Sate University, earned a bachelor of arts degree from Morris Brown College in 1965, and a law degree from Harvard in 1968. He never practiced law, instead devoting himself to his writing career. He began working at the University of Iowa Law School as a writing instructor while pursuing a master of fine arts degree, which he completed in 1969. He was an instructor in Afro-American literature at the University of California, Santa Cruz, from 1969 to 1970, and instructed at Morgan State University, from 1975 to 1976, and at the University of Virginia from 1976 to 1981. He is currently a professor in the Writer's Workshop at the University of Iowa.

Major Works

In 1965, McPherson won first prize in the *Atlantic Monthly*'s short story competition for "Gold Coast," a sympathetic look at an elderly black janitor in Harvard Square. In 1968, the story was selected for *Atlantic Monthly*'s "Firsts" award, and subsequently published in the magazine. In the same issue, the publishers announced McPherson's selection for an *Atlantic Monthly* grant for his forthcoming collection *Hue and Cry* (1969). This signalled a long-standing relationship between McPherson and the *Atlantic Monthly*. Many of his stories and non-fiction articles were first published in the magazine, and he was listed as a contributing editor in 1969. The title for his collection *Hue and Cry* comes from a text of English Law: "When a felony is committed, the hue and cry should be raised." *Hue and Cry* was praised for its insightful stories and accomplished prose style. Ralph Ellison, a mentor of McPherson's, stated that "McPherson will never, as a writer, be an embarrassment to such people of excellence as Willie Mays, Duke Ellington, Leontyne Price—or, for that matter, Stephen Crane or F. Scott Fitzgerald." In *Hue and Cry* McPherson addresses the themes of injustice, loneliness, and self-identity. Facing such obstacles as racism, economic exploitation, and age discrimination, the characters in this collection are unable to alleviate the pain and frustration in their lives and frequently suffer in silence. McPherson's *Elbow Room* won the Pulitzer Prize in 1978. The collection is generally considered more optimistic than *Hue and Cry* because of its emphasis on social improvement, personal development, and racial harmony. The characters in *Elbow Room* range from college professionals to ex-convicts and are willing and able to struggle for survival. While some of the stories in this work focus specifically on African-Americans trying to gain respectability and status in contemporary American society, the collection as a whole addresses the concerns of all individuals who are limited by social injustices. McPherson also emphasizes the importance of communication, critical thought, and the ability to understand others as complex and unique human beings rather than stereotypes. In "Just Enough for the City," for example, the narrator questions conventional views of religion, love, language, and race as he seeks to identify and appreciate the humanity in all people. In "Elbow Room," an unidentified narrator wrestles with the moral, aesthetic, and social issues related to interracial relationships. Like the other stories in this volume, "Elbow Room" demonstrates McPherson's belief that racial stereotypes are insidious. Robert Phillips has observed that the stories in *Elbow Room* are "not so much about the black condition as the human condition." McPherson published two books in 1998, *Fathering Daughters,* an anthology he edited with DeWitt Henry, and *Crabcakes,* a memoir. One reviewer stated that *Crabcakes* was written with "an astonishing range of language and emotion," and that the book constitutes a highly personal and revealing look at McPherson's life and work.

Critical Reception

McPherson has been praised for the artful prose and precise language of his stories. His well-crafted characters are constructed with a combination of meticulous prose and realistic dialogue. Some critics, however, have found the plots of his early work to be a weak point. In a review of *Hue and Cry,* Irving Howe noted plot deficiencies while praising the writing style. He says, "Though sometimes lacking in a culminating tension—his stories begin more strongly than they end—Mr. McPherson's writing is beautifully poised." McPherson's next collection, *Elbow Room,* drew stronger praise for its storylines and merging of style and plot. In "The Story of a Scar" and "The Story of a Dead Man," the language becomes a character of the story, a strong force acting on the unfolding of events. In both cases, the narrator uses precise language as a barrier to intimacy with the other characters. Commenting on "The Story of a Scar," Jon Wallace stated, "Within the story proper, the narrative of physical events, we see a narrator behaving in ways wholly at odds with his intellectual insights: intimidating people with his precise but distancing and at times baffling language." In *Crabcakes,* McPherson's literary approach to

the issues of individuality moves in another direction. One critic claimed: "Having previously addressed the black experience in America on many levels, he [McPherson] now tells a profoundly personal tale of displacement and discovery that is poetic and universal." The book is divided into two parts. The first deals with McPherson's attempts to prevent the eviction of an elderly black couple in Baltimore. The second is an ongoing correspondence with two Japanese friends, one a scholar of black literature, in which McPherson attempts to describe his life and American culture in terms his friends could understand. Overall, critical reaction to McPherson's work has been positive. Throughout his career he has been the recipient of numerous honors, including a National Institute of Art and Letters grant, a Rockefeller grant, a Guggenheim Fellowship, and a MacArthur Foundation Award. Ralph Ellison reflected the opinion of most critics when he asserted: "[McPherson is] a writer of insight, sympathy, and humour and one of the most gifted young Americans I've had the privilege to read."

PRINCIPAL WORKS

Hue and Cry (short stories) 1969
Railroad: Trains and Train People in American Culture [editor, with Miller Williams] (short stories) 1976
Elbow Room (short stories) 1977
Crabcakes (memoirs) 1998
Fathering Daughters [editor, with DeWitt Henry] (essays) 1998

CRITICISM

Irving Howe (review date December 1969)

SOURCE: "New Black Writers," in *Harper's Magazine,* Vol. 239, No. 1435, December, 1969, pp. 130-46.

[*Howe is a longtime editor and frequent magazine contributor. In the following review, he praises McPherson's short story collection* Hue and Cry.]

At twenty-six James Alan McPherson has written a book of short stories, **Hue and Cry,** that one can read with pleasure and respect, caring only for the calm assurance with which he penetrates the lives of Negro train waiters, black students, white janitors. Though sometimes lacking in a culminating tension—his stories begin more strongly than they end—Mr. McPherson's writing is beautifully poised. He possesses an ability some writers take decades to acquire, the ability to keep the right distance from the creatures of his imagination, not to get murkily involved and blot out his figures with vanity and fuss. He doesn't reach as deeply into the entanglements of black life as Hal Bennett occasionally can, nor is he as familiar with the psychic lesions of plebeian blacks; but he is a more controlled writer, able to turn out a finished piece of work.

His hue and cry is over life's incompleteness, the small betrayals we all enact. James McPherson has a strong sense of injustice, almost a boy's sense, and he knows how disproportionately large a share of that injustice black men must bear; yet he manages to take human beings one at a time, honoring their portion of uniqueness. Some writers have the psychology of inquisitors, and some of victims; Mr. McPherson has none of the former and not too much of the latter, which for a black writer these days seems exactly right. In **"Gold Coast"** he writes with a shudder of sympathy about the feebleness and loneliness of an old white janitor in Harvard Square; in **"A Solo Song: For Doc"** he speaks a low-keyed paean of affection for an aging black waiter expert at "the service" on railroad dining cars. (James McPherson isn't so foolish as to suppose that all older Negroes must have been shuffling Toms, and he even knows that those who were probably had no choice and deserve their mite of respect too.) The title story is a touching portrait of a bright and sensitive black girl who has an affair with a bright and sensitive white boy; slowly the affair disintegrates ("I don't know," says Margot to Eric, "if I'm a person to you or an idea. Right now, back there, I felt like a damn cause"). The girl starts losing her nerve, she can no longer summon that shrug of independence which had set her above all the cults and causes of campus life.

James McPherson's stories need a sharper articulation, and his language could with advantage be given a freer idiomatic lilt. But he is a born writer—which means a writer who works hard on every sentence, thinks lucidly about his effects, and knows that in art meaning, even salvation, depends finally on craft.

William Domnarski (essay date Spring 1986)

SOURCE: "The Voices of Misery and Despair in James Alan McPherson," in *Arizona Quarterly,* Vol. 42, No. 1, Spring, 1986, pp. 37-44.

[*In the following essay, Domnarski analyzes the recurring themes in McPherson's work and shows how they also appear in less obvious ways in some of his short stories.*]

James Alan McPherson's two collections of short stories, *Hue and Cry* and *Elbow Room,* have established him as an important writer interested in illustrating the effects of ra-

cial prejudice on blacks. The two collections are integrally related, with the second expanding and defining more precisely McPherson's bleak vision of blacks seeking respectability and self-identity. A sense of misery, which sometimes develops into rage, controls McPherson's work. Through explosive moments of insight into the black experience, he enables us to know and feel the frustration and despair of his characters.

Critics have praised the diversity of McPherson's stories and noted a conscious attempt to repress the blackness of the characters, suggesting the two characteristics are complementary. This is ironically misleading, however, because the wide range of stories reflects McPherson's broad focus on the very issue critics have tended to lead us away from: the blackness of the characters. At first the handful of stories about blacks working at various jobs does not seem to have much in common with other stories about the law or the search for self-identity, yet a careful working out of the themes of McPherson's fiction reveals his attempt to analyze comprehensively the difficulties blacks face at every turn.

To outline the plight of blacks trying to establish themselves within the mainstream of American society, McPherson examines the underlying premise of the American dream—that individuals can rise socially by working hard—and shows how this premise often does not apply to blacks. McPherson's characters, instead of demonstrating through their hard work that they are no different from anyone else, find that no matter how well they do their jobs, they cannot escape those holding racial prejudices.

Thomas, the shy, insecure boy in **"A Matter of Vocabulary,"** discovers, for example, that the work he does in the local supermarket creates a dilemma he will always have to endure. His work brings praise from the owners and gives him a sense of responsibility, pride, and even superiority, but the job's impact cuts both ways for him, as the benefits are balanced against the stereotypical role he must assume to please the owners, who expect Thomas, like all the other blacks in the neighborhood, to drop out of school.

The supermarket owners will not accept Thomas if he fails to conform to his role. To show this, McPherson has Thomas's brother Eddie, who also works in the supermarket, show his intelligence and antagonize the owners by using a precisely appropriate word in an argument. The lesson Thomas learns is clear. If he does not act in the expected manner, he threatens his job and the sense of pride and identity that goes with it. As a result, Thomas must give up part of himself to keep part of himself.

In a brilliant stroke, McPherson gives Thomas's internal misery an external equivalent by linking Thomas with the beggar woman crying desperately in the night. Her scream is "a painful sound, lonely, desperate, threatening, impatient, angry, hungry." Thomas comes to realize they share the experience of being in misery and not being able to do anything about it, yet we recognize that Thomas's agony is greater because he cannot release his frustrations by wailing at night. He must keep his anguish within him and continue with the work that paradoxically creates the anguish.

Thomas suffers quietly, as does the railroad porter in **"On Trains."** By connecting the two, McPherson expands his theme and gives us a sense of what lies ahead for Thomas. We see the porter as a man who takes great pride in his work, who wants the respect that accompanies a job well done, but instead he gets passengers who see only his color, which makes prejudice, not competence, the controlling issue. The result is that the job both builds up and tears down the porter. We are compelled to think of young Thomas when we read of the porter's broken spirit after an argument between the conductor and a woman who objects to the porter because he is black.

> The porter, who stood all the while like a child waiting for punishment, seemed to droop and wither and grow smaller; and his eyes, which had only minutes before flashed brightly from the face of the conductor to the enraged face of the lady, now seemed to dull and turn inward as only those who have learned to suffer silently can turn their eyes inward. He was a very old man and he grew older, even older than his occupation or the oldest and most obsequious Pullman Porter.

McPherson wants us to associate the painful cry of the beggar woman in **"A Matter of Vocabulary"** with the old porter. When we then reexamine the description of her cry we recognize that it contains inchoate elements of rage, some of which can be seen in **"A Solo Song: For Doc,"** the third story in *Hue and Cry* focusing on work. Here McPherson varies his theme to show a black unwilling to act obsequiously. The black railroad waiter eventually loses his battle with a vengeful, threatened management, but only after a tense, heroic struggle. In two subsequent stories in *Elbow Room,* McPherson takes his developing theme further to detail the disappearance of obsequiousness and the emergence of violence.

"A Sense of Story" and **"The Story of a Scar"** are important to McPherson's vision partly because each story depicts job related frustrations leading to explosions of violence. Equally important, the stories widen McPherson's focus yet further to show additional forces working on the characters. In **"A Sense of Story,"** McPherson includes a comment on a legal system that cannot find sympathy for a mechanic who kills his boss because he is convinced the boss has not given

his invention the consideration it deserves. The judge handling the case has little difficulty convincing himself that the mechanic is guilty—it was cold-blooded murder. But as readers we have ambivalent feelings. We realize that the mechanic is guilty, yet we demand more for him. We want the court at least to recognize the frustration the mechanic endured knowing he was deprived of something due him. The stories about work in *Hue and Cry* have prepared us to understand not just the mechanic's frustration but also the dimensions of the problem. We leave the story feeling there have been two injustices. The first is the white boss's successful repression of the black mechanic's talents and ambitions. The second is the judge's reaction to the case: the facts are interesting, but nothing more. His summary conviction thus symbolizes a general dismissal of this problem of a blighted version of the American dream for blacks.

Billy's slashing of his girlfriend's face in **"The Story of a Scar"** comes to symbolize a reaction to yet another aspect of the problems associated with work and social mobility for blacks: peer pressure and the difficulty of being ambitious within the black community. McPherson uses the contrast between Billy and Teddy, both postal workers, to illustrate the differences between those planning for the future and those living for the present. **"The Story of a Scar"** suggests the extent of the friction between the two groups, with those living for the present avoiding and resenting their opposites, attributing to them a sense of aloofness and superiority.

"The Story of a Scar" shows that the apparently sincere interest Billy's girlfriend has in him, an interest grounded in her respect for his ambition, is not strong enough to withstand the dreaded feeling of isolation she will experience at work in the post office if she continues making Billy and what he represents her choice. Her ultimate rejection of Billy for Teddy and his view of life comes to mean much more than a failed romance. When Billy viciously attacks his girlfriend in a moment of rage, he is symbolically attacking an attitude within his own cultural niche that represses and frustrates him.

The recognition that elements within the black community can paradoxically retard blacks seeking social mobility enables us to understand **"Of Cabbages and Kings,"** one of McPherson's most disturbing stories. It involves The Brotherhood, a black power organization that harms rather than helps those adhering to its principles by espousing a kind of reality-distorting mysticism and by failing to deal effectively with the problem of self-identity for blacks.

"Of Cabbages and Kings" depicts two pathetic figures. Claude is torn apart by paranoia, prompting him to sleep with an endless number of white women in an attempt to ease his anxiety. The result, however, is continued self-hatred. He responds to the real world around him by believing in flying saucers and his own supernatural powers. McPherson's point that The Brotherhood contributes to Claude's evolving destruction is clear. Equally clear is the mood of despair McPherson evokes by having Howard, the story's narrator, succumb to his fascination with Claude and willingly accept his teachings. The path the once rational Howard follows thereby highlights McPherson's comment on black splinter groups that ultimately divert blacks from the real problems facing them.

By illustrating the deleterious effects ostensibly positive forces can have on blacks, **"Of Cabbages and Kings"** heightens our awareness to the problem blacks may face of aligning themselves with social forces in an age in which forces and attitudes change quickly. The Afro haircut represents one of these forces, and John Butler's refusal in **"The Faithful"** to offer it in his barbershop suggests the broader issue of blacks being forced to make decisions about themselves and their place in the community. The decisions are difficult to make, illustrating McPherson's point that blacks may be forced to turn their backs on their cultural pasts to embrace the forces of the future.

Butler sees the schoolboy, the old style haircut, as important to black pride and identity. Those around him, however, argue that blacks must now avoid the schoolboy because the very values Butler ascribes to it have come to characterize Uncle Toms. The Afro, they point out, gives a new sense of identity to the black seeking to assert himself in a new age. Butler's decision to oppose the Afro shows the depth of the conflict within him, as his shop will be unable to survive without the trade brought in by the Afro. In this conflict of forces, Butler does not trust the future enough to give up the past.

McPherson inverts the problem of blacks choosing between old and new values in **"The Silver Bullet."** Instead of an older man desperately clinging to the values of his generation, we see a young man trying to make his mark in the world by enlisting the aid of a community organization he feels is the force of the future. His is a foolish choice, however, because the community organization is actually a toothless extortion operation disguised by rhetoric featuring the latest sociological jargon. McPherson has pulled our sympathies both ways in these two stories, giving us both young and old failing to recognize what is best for them. By doing this, McPherson gives us a sense of the dilemma that blacks might face in trying to sort out the forces operating on them.

When we distance ourselves from individual stories and see McPherson's two collections of short stories as general statements, we see the pervasive bleakness of his vision. The stories about a callous legal system, such as **"A Sense of Story"** and **"An Act of Prostitution,"** complement the group of stories focusing on work and its paradoxical effect on blacks to show layers of entrenched forces affecting blacks. McPherson then goes further to expose elements within the black community itself that complicate the existing institutional forces.

Important to McPherson's short stories is the mood of despair, a mood illustrated well in **"A Loaf of Bread."** The story, which at first makes us feel anger and indignation toward the white grocery store owner for charging more at his store in a black neighborhood than at his suburban store, concludes with the recognition, both by us and the story's principal black character, that the higher overhead costs created by the crime in the black neighborhood justify the higher prices. The story details an economic system adversely affecting blacks and then, almost without comment, acknowledges the logic supporting the system.

Despair strikes at the characters and destroys them from the inside. In the end, the social and economic conditions that McPherson's characters collide with rob them of their self-respect and identity. Indeed, the theme of self-identity runs through many of the stories in both *Hue and Cry* and *Elbow Room*. We see it, for example, in **"The Faithful," "A Solo Song: For Doc," "Of Cabbages and Kings," "The Story of a Scar,"** and **"Private Domain."**

But of course not all of McPherson's stories fit within the scope of themes I have outlined. There are some stories about the search for self-identity in which homosexuality, not race, plays a dominant role, while other stories present blacks who are successful at their jobs. The diversity of McPherson's work has the ironic effect of buffering the sound of the angry, tormented, and despairing voices in his fiction. My contention is that once we recognize these voices in stories such as **"A Matter of Vocabulary"** and **"The Story of a Scar,"** we begin to hear them in an increasing number of stories, leading us to conclude that they are the true voices of McPherson's work.

An analysis of **"Why I Like Country Music,"** McPherson's often-anthologized tale of first love, bears this out. If we come to the story with the understanding of McPherson's work I have suggested, we see that the black narrator's silent suffering, and not the delightful account of his youthful love, controls the story. The narrator's lengthy digression to explain why he likes country music serves on one level as a means of discrediting stereotypical beliefs, such as the idea that blacks cannot like a type of music traditionally associated with rednecks or that blacks have a natural sense of rhythm. More important, though, the story points to the narrator's wife as the unlikely source of the stereotypical thinking he must contend with.

The narrator's memory of country music, Gweneth, and his love for her is important to him. Yet he finds that his wife's staunch belief that blacks should not like country music comes between him and his fond memory of Gweneth. As a result, the narrator feels that his wife is telling him to bury that part of himself. This is the crux of the issue, as the conflict between the forces attacks the narrator's sense of self. A public-self/private-self dichotomy develops, with the narrator keeping his fondness for country music to himself. He, like Thomas in **"A Matter of Vocabulary"** and the old porter in **"On Trains,"** has learned to suffer silently, a connection made clear by the emphasis in all three stories on the words "silently" or "quietly."

The connections between **"Why I Like Country Music"** and McPherson's other stories depend more on an understanding of just what troubles the narrator. Like Billy in **"The Story of a Scar,"** the narrator in **"Why I Like Country Music"** finds that the woman closest to him cannot give him what he needs most, an acceptance of him as he is. Thus, the narrator's frustration shares a common theme with Billy's frustration and with the frustration of the other characters encountering layers of resistance in their attempts to achieve fulfillment, whether it be economic or personal. Fulfillment, they all learn, is harder to come by because they are black.

Edith Blicksilver (essay date Winter 1987-Summer 1988)

SOURCE: "Interracial Relationships in Three Short Stories by James Alan McPherson," in *The CEA Critic,* Vol. 50, Nos. 2-4, Winter 1987-Summer 1988, pp. 79-89.

[*In the following essay, Blicksilver examines McPherson's portrayal of interracial relations in the short stories "Hue and Cry," "Gold Coast," and "Elbow Room."*]

During a question-and-answer session at Iowa State University in March 1980 after Ralph Ellison talked about "The Concept of Race in American Literature," a student asked if miscegenation was a necessary ingredient of racial integration. Ellison responded by saying:

> I don't think that any of us Americans wants to lose his ethnic identity. . . . The existence of such strong Negro-American influences in the society, the style, the way things are done, would indicate that there's never been the desire to lose that. . . . There are individual decisions which will be made by a few people. . . . There is enough of a hold of tradition, of ways of cooking, of ways of just relaxing, which comes right out of the family circle, to keep us in certain groups.

The individual decisions involving interracial relationships

and marital concerns preoccupy modern blacks and figure prominently in three short stories of James Alan McPherson. **"Gold Coast," "Hue and Cry,"** and **"Elbow Room"** will be discussed in this paper through an analysis of the personality characteristics; motivations; actions and coping techniques of those involved; the influence of the geographical setting and historical period; parental reactions; society's acceptance or condemnation; and the outcome.

Because Ellison is a generation older than McPherson, their versions of black/white relationships were influenced by different young adult experiences, the former's taking place during the Depression and Second World War, the latter's during the 1960s civil rights movement. McPherson's background is essential because his works are semi-autobiographical. Born in Savannah, Georgia in 1943, the writer attended all-black Morris Brown College in Atlanta and Morgan State in Baltimore where he was chosen by a Harvard Law School recruiter for admission. Graduating in 1964, he never practiced law, choosing instead to become a writer and winning a Reader's Digest prize for his second story.

At Harvard, the setting for **"Gold Coast"** and **"Hue and Cry,"** the sensitive Southerner together with fellow blacks went through an adjustment period, frequently a debilitating struggle—among blacks, between whites and blacks, men and women, Northerners and Southerners, and poor and rich—for status, power and love. Later, while, ironically, recruiting for Harvard at a black southern college, McPherson describes talking to a student more insecure than he himself had been. Finally, losing patience, the writer asserted: "I went to a white law school and I survived it. . . . I'm still sane." But, the student, he continues, "sat looking at me, and his eyes were so close to accusation that I almost felt compelled to add, 'I think.'"

McPherson taught at the University of California at Santa Cruz, the University of Virginia, and now teaches creative writing at Iowa State, admitting that he experienced discomfort at the Charlottesville school where black men often are viewed as janitors or retainers. He felt like a trapped outsider, similar to some of the characters in his stories, only remaining in Virginia because of his former wife's urgings. Now single, his young daughter's education will be subsidized by a 1981 MacArthur Foundation grant. In 1961 McPherson became a contributing editor to Atlantic where a version of **"Gold Coast"** first appeared and won the best short story prize a year earlier. He was awarded the Pulitzer Prize in 1978 for *Elbow Room,* his second short story collection; the first, *Hue and Cry,* was published nine years before.

The historical period of all three works is the 1960s which McPherson calls "a crazy time."

Opportunities seemed to materialize . . . and if you were lucky . . . you could become a doctor, a lawyer . . . an engineer. Achieving these things was easy if you applied yourself.

But a very hard price was extracted . . . because certain institutional forces . . . threw together black peasants and white aristocrats . . . people who were peasants/frightened, threatened, and felt inferior, . . . there were idealists and opportunists, people who seemed to want to be exploited and people who delighted in exploiting them. Old identities were thrown off. . . . People from backgrounds like my own, those from the South, while content with the new opportunities, found themselves trying to make sense of the growing diversity of friendships . . . of the differences between their values and those of their parents . . . thinking of themselves in new and different ways. We never wanted to be 'white,' but we never wanted to be 'black' either. And . . . there was the feeling we could be whatever we wanted. But . . . unless we . . . accepted some provisional identity . . . for defining and stabilizing what it was we wanted to be . . . , this was an individual problem, and . . . one had to go inside one's self.

McPherson's experiences shaped many of his stories, and **"Gold Coast"** narrates a young man's maturing process during a summer job as a janitor similar to one the writer had in an apartment house near Harvard Square. Because Rob, the youthful protagonist, believes he is "gifted," his writing is going well, and he has "the urge to acquire . . . and youth besides . . . ," he finds himself a rich white girl to love. McPherson's tale deals in part with the tension between white and black, in its delineation of the course of the affair between the narrator and his girlfriend Jean.

Rob's youthful optimism is evident. He is ambitious, self-confident, dreaming of future success, "lulled by sweet anticipation of that time when his potential would suddenly be realized." He egotistically believes he can immortalize any of the tenants with the "magic" of his pen. Loving a white woman is an extension of his self-esteem.

Another janitor Sullivan, dislikes his choice of a white mistress because she is not a flower child and "liberal people will tolerate two interracial hippies more than they will an intelligent, serious-minded mixed couple." The former liaison is dismissed because they are inferior folk deserving each other and the contempt of both races, but the latter poses a threat to racial purity. Sullivan, bigoted and hostile to those better off than himself, questions Robert about Jean's refined breeding and philosophizes that "the Colonel's Lady and Nelly O'Grady are sisters under the skin." The self-assured younger man replies: "that's why you have to maintain a distinction by marrying the Colonel's Lady." Rob's optimism reflects the changes in interpersonal contacts taking place, among young people, across race lines. These interactions became broader and deeper as individuals shared educational opportunities and traveled to liberated social climates. But provincial New England was not the setting in which their affair could flourish and survive.

The turmoil that Rob and Jean experience due to the intimidation from the community are overwhelming. At parties, blacks attempt to enchant Jean "with skillful dances and hip vocabulary, believing her to be community property," while she remains politely aloof. The affair ends after a subway incident where "one side of the car was black and tense and hating and the whites tense and hating on the other side . . . . " There was not enough room on either side for them to sit and they would not separate; and so they stood, holding on to a steel post "feeling all the eyes . . . ," and "there was nothing left to say."

An interracial couple creates a political and an emotional reaction, fostered by black consciousness and white racism, which makes it different from a normal love affair. Too many implications cannot be blocked out, and during the stressful subway incident communication and understanding are replaced by defeated, silent acceptance. Rob and Jean do not have an intense enough commitment to each other in order to challenge the critical value system of their New England environment. They are unable to find the strength to overcome society's judgmental hostility which destroys their love. They permit intolerance and aggressiveness to shatter their relationship, becoming victims of cultural arrogance.

Before these "social forces" disrupted their love affair, Rob pridefully internalizes looking back on the episode, that Jean "belonged to me and not to the race . . . I did not have to wear a beard or be especially hip or ultra-Ivy Leagueish. I did not have to smoke pot or supply her with it, or be for any other cause at all except myself." Rob's defensiveness is contrasted with his pity for and condescension toward Sullivan, the old, worn-out Irishman. But their relationship is different from that of the young black writer with his white girlfriend. Given the widespread historical attitude on the part of American society that blacks are inferior, it is not difficult to understand the complexity of Rob's reaction to his role in Jean's life. He faces a new situation for which his past has given him little guidance, so he charters new territory in exploring how to carry on this intimate contact. Internal stress results for both young people, but it is less difficult for a member of a dominant majority to adjust than for a sensitive individual from an oppressed minority. Jean's superior social and financial situation is an additional hurdle her janitor-lover faces.

Rob's illusions of instant success, his naive belief in his

"boundless perception" and most importantly, his self-deception in trying to ignore his race are shattered. His fantasies that an interracial couple can find easy happiness are replaced by a maturing reality. As the narrator observes looking back on his younger self, "In those days I had forgotten that I was first of all a black. . . ." But after the relationship disintegrates, Rob's character growth is reflected by his changing attitude toward both Sullivan and Jean. He is more compassionate toward the old janitor who, although outwardly a failure is "well-read in history, philosophy, literature and law." With youthful resiliency, after "that desperate look had finally gone somewhere deep inside," Rob can love another girl, and at the end of the summer his values change. He abandons his superficial idea of happiness personified by a girl and a stereo. He shares a common bond of brotherhood with Sullivan. Both have suffered loss; he, Jean's love, the Irishman, his dog. When the young black man moves away, he places Jean's picture under some clothes in a trunk that he does not plan to open for quite some time. With the elderly man's fate awaiting him, Rob matures enough to realize that "nothing really matters except not being old and being alive and having potential to dream about, and not being alone."

McPherson's other stories **"Hue and Cry"** and **"Elbow Room"** also depict the dilemma confronting the displaced black intellectual during the 1960s in America, showing the tensions between brotherhood and separateness, between the emotional and the rational, especially where explosive interracial interactions are involved. He delineates minorities attracted to the power that whites symbolize and repelled by their racist record. Even lovers faced confrontations of bigoted injustice which vitiated American life, and nullified the attempts of those seeking to ignore or overcome ethnic barriers.

McPherson is not a revolutionary, however, and he deals with people and feelings, not masses nor slogans. His racially mixed couples, in particular, are drawn with sympathy and with respect for their suffering. Langston Hughes once wrote that "the relationships between mixed couples is always more graciously accepted by the viewers when related by a white author than by a Negro," but McPherson's artistic sensitivity will not offend readers of any color; the climate of opinion has changed.

The last two stories tell about affairs of black women with white men and the love relationship between Margot Payne and Eric Carney in **"Hue and Cry"** shows a male/female power struggle, also evident in Paul Frost's magnetic attraction for Virginia Valentine, in **"Elbow Room,"** resulting in a shaky marriage. All four young people fear entrapment and identity loss. McPherson's thematic development in these works is to show that some interracial couples are motivated to become lovers because it is a source of approval by their peer group; i.e., among so-called "hip" types and/or nonconformist liberals, much of whose behavior is a reaction or protest against anything associated with the conservative establishment. The affairs of Rob and Jean, that of Margot and Eric, and the marriage of Paul and Virginia can be interpreted, in part, by exploring the individuality of each character.

Cleveland-born Margot, for example, is a studious nonconformist from early girlhood, who rebels against her mother's admonition to make her intelligence as imperceptible as possible because black men would resent it and her. She blames her family for teaching that life's greatest goal is smug security, and at her Ivy League college she decides to have a love affair with a New Hampshire Quaker idealist, clinging to him even after she admits that the relationship had become stagnant. Vulnerable Margot yearns to be loved as a woman and not as a symbolic moral issue. "I don't know," she says to Eric, "if I'm a person to you or an idea." After a stress-filled trip to his New Hampshire home, Margot tells her lover that "back there, I felt like a damn cause."

In Eric's case, McPherson implies that it is unlikely that he will marry Margot because his primary attraction to her is his desire to make a social contribution to better race relations. Margot senses his self-righteous attitude which adds an additional burden to the relationship. She realizes that this idealistic Quaker is trying to impress blacks with how liberal he is, and she resents being used to foster his missionary zeal. The young woman is too independent to be grateful, hardly a prideful attribute.

With so much potential, the girl starts losing her nerve due to social and parental condemnation. She no longer is able to summon that shrug of independent action which has set her above the cults and causes of campus life during the '60s when the events transpired. She drops out of school, dragged down in a tragic round-robin of mistakes and misfortunes such as sexual encounters, described in tones of sardonic understatement and controlled irony. Margot enjoys manipulating awe-struck black men such as Eric's roommate, Jerry. She taunts him when the young man boasts about his affair with an Anglo-Saxon: "Next time she calls, before you go running over, ask her to describe your face." Jerry becomes insulted because his girl is the liberated daughter of three generations of money invested in his car and in his clothes.

In the past, according to a study by Irving R. Stuart and Lawrence E. Abt entitled Interracial Marriage, black men married white women far more than white men married black women. The explanation is that the white woman "exchanges her superior class position over the black man for his personal traits, superior to those of white men available to her." However, because historically white men have had sexual access to black slave women without permanent commitments, they do not so often marry black women. In addition, because black men have been barred by law and by custom from intimate associates with white women, they find this relationship an exotic one and marriages result even though the female's class position and personality characteristics are inferior to available black women. In the case of Jerry, McPherson implies that the epitome of being a real "stud" is to show off a white mistress.

Margot believes that her affair with Eric is different from Jerry's indifferent liaisons with white women and that they will get married eventually. After all, Eric assures her that only people over thirty-five do not approve of their courtship. Slowly the affair disintegrates, and Margot loses her self-confidence where men are concerned. In a last attempt to find security, she accepts the devoted attention of a fellow black named Charles. Actually, Margot never appreciates his good qualities until he ceases to remain faithful and turns into a playboy. In desperation, she becomes another of Jerry's easy conquests, and the story ends with Margot begging Charles to marry her because she is spiritually wounded by Eric's final rejection. She was used as a source of private purgation by the white man, mistaking exploitation for love.

For both Eric and Paul, an interracial relationship represents a cleansing process. Paul is attracted to Virginia, in part, because "he felt the need to redeem the family": the narrator saw "dead Indians living in his eyes." Both idealistic men are Quakers and come from small towns in New Hampshire and Kansas with few black contacts. Both are rebelling against conservative middle-class families, who oppose the prospect of black daughters-in-law. When Eric tells his parents that he is bringing home "a special girl," his father chooses to go hunting, while his mother politely serves them tea, "close to tears."

McPherson explores what motivates a person of a particular culture to cross racial boundaries and have an affair or marry outside his group. Eric and Paul were brought up within a parochial social setting with parental prejudice instilled toward different ethnic groups, but after going to college, both young men became liberated during the 1960s and rejected the preconceived, stereotypical opinions of their families. They are motivated, in part, to love black women because of profound guilt feelings resulting from the physical exploitation which was historically characteristic of the sexual relationships between whites and blacks. They are seeking affection from a member of a former slave society to redress this abuse.

McPherson's gift for characterization and his mastery of dialogue are evident in **"Elbow Room"** as he describes Virginia's attempts to make the marriage work, sketching her personality more thoroughly than any of his other women

with the exception of Margot by working hard on every nuance of her individuality. During the 1960s, as McPherson himself witnessed, blacks left southern cultural pockets moving north and west as did Virginia who

> had come out of Warren, Tennessee . . . on the crest
> of jailbreaking peasants. To people like her, impris-
> oned for generations, . . . the outside world seemed
> . . . full of sweet choices. Many could not cope with
> freedom. . . . Some committed suicide. Others, seek-
> ing safety, rushed into other prisons. But a few like
> Virginia rose and ranged far and wide in flight, like
> aristocratic eagles seeking high, free peaks on which
> to build their nests.

Virginia herself is exposed to different cultures as a Peace Corps volunteer, living in Ceylon, India, Kenya, Egypt, and Syria. Returning to America, she leaves the confines of provincial Tennessee and after marrying Paul in San Francisco, recreates the cosmopolitan environment in their home that Virginia had experienced abroad, with friends who are Chicanos, Asians, French, Brazilians, and black and white Americans.

An interracial relationship invites attack from society, encouraging people to reveal their prejudices in a self-righteous manner. It is easier for Paul and Virginia to be accepted by friends in a cosmopolitan city than by parents in a small town because it doesn't threaten strangers who don't have to make commitments. On the other hand, adjustments are necessary when the members of this marriage share the home. Some families, McPherson observes, accept and love the young people while others merely tolerate an unchangeable situation.

Seeking parental acceptance of their union is difficult, and Paul's parents do not attend the wedding. Virginia's kinfolk, after failing to dissuade her, fly to San Francisco from Tennessee bringing country-cured hams and a wedding gift sewn by the bride's full-blooded Cherokee grandmother. Virginia's father with the facial features of an Indian, feels ill at ease during the reception. His face reveals "fear and pride and puzzlement" because he has assumed that "color was the highest bond," having come from a long line of family. Virginia, however, "has moved away from that small living room in which conventional opinion mattered."

Both families fear racial pollution, preferring ethnic purity. Fernando Henriques in *Children of Conflict* suggests that those hostile to miscegenation are influenced by the belief which originated when societies were divided into communities based upon self-sufficiency and isolation. To project the values of primeval hunters and food-gatherers into the modern world as a justification for racist theories is challenged by several of McPherson's characters.

Virginia, more worldly, forceful and self-confident than Margot, has a better chance of overcoming parental and group hostility because Paul wants to marry her, and the young woman, impressed with the patience and faith of the Indians, shows an outward display of strength that masks vulnerability. When she introduces Paul, she says, "' . . . meet my fiance, and if you don't like it you can go to hell!',", watching closely for reactions, with her dark eyes saying "'I hurt easily.'" She has to convince herself that she is desirable, not secondary to a white woman.

Paul's father, as a good businessman, believes that "his son had made a bad investment that was bound to be corrected as soon as Virginia's stock declined." Unlike Eric, Paul courageously defies his family, and faces social slander, but he pays a price for his decision to marry the black woman. He cuts himself off from the company of most white males, denounces his father as "a moral coward . . . struggling and abysmally along, with large brown eyes desperately asking, 'Who am I?'" Since he is not socially sterile, Paul is aware of people's reactions, and giving up family ties is emotionally draining.

In a supermarket lot, a carload of children call Paul a nigger and an incident at a New Year's Eve Mass proves his loyalty. Virginia is wearing her usual mug's cap, popularized by movie gangsters in the forties, when a voice behind them breaks the church stillness: "'Young man, if you're too drunk to take your hat off in church get out! . . .'" The usually gentle Paul turns fiercely toward the old man and retorts, "'This is my wife. If you don't like what she's wearing, that's tough!'" He then puts his arm around Virginia.

Finally, when both sets of parents learn that the young wife is pregnant, they start making conciliatory gestures. Her Tennessee folk propose treasured family names for the baby; Paul's mother sends money for a bassinet and hints that "more than European bloodlines ran in her veins."

The trauma of Paul's father's refusal to acknowledge the baby she will soon have provokes Virginia to speak freely with the narrator about her own self-identity:

> "I'm black. I've accepted myself as that. But didn't I make some elbow room though?" She tapped her temple ". . . . I mean up here! . . . When times get tough, anybody can pass for white. Niggers been doing that for centuries . . . But . . . wouldn't it of been something to be a nigger that could relate to white and black and everything else in the world out of a self as big as the world is?"

Since Virginia feels that their relationship is contributing to better race relations, her attitude solidifies the marriage. But as the black partner, the young woman is more defensive be-cause of the widespread historical attitude on the part of the white society that negroes are inferior. However, the hostility from the outside world brings Virginia and Paul closer together. They are individualists, not conformists, able to cope with parental and community rejection. McPherson implies that a person who doesn't have to depend upon kinship or group approval is more likely to get involved in an interracial relationship than one who has to depend upon familial and societal acceptance and conform to their thinking. A peripheral personality doesn't need external reinforcement.

Margot feels that Eric is having the liaison because he is committed to a liberal philosophy, and at first the affair is an exotic one. But since the obstacles come from within the relationship, it soon disintegrates, since neither person has the courage or the strength to overcome these problems. As a result, the romantic involvement of Eric with Margot and of Jean with Rob ended. Virginia has a better chance of overcoming parental hostility because Paul has married her, and the birth of a son helps heal the breach between two sets of parents. Her search for a more inclusive, universal identity is emphasized at the story's conclusion when the narrator admonishes Virginia, "For the sake of your child, don't be black. Be more of a classic kind of nigger." The woman takes his advice and later sends a picture of her new-born baby with the inscription, "He will be a classic kind of nigger." The photo shows a brown baby in his Kansas grandmother's arms; the grandfather looks serious; Paul, "defiant, has a familiar intensity about his face"; Virginia "smiling triumphantly," is still wearing her mug's cap. She never compromises with her ideals, or with her unique personality. The narrator pays tribute to her as "a magic woman," and this final scene symbolizes McPherson's aspirations for greater interracial harmony.

The author writes that the model he was depicting in **"Elbow Room"** was epitomized by Albion Tourgee's argument in the Plessy vs. Ferguson case in 1896 interpreting the Fourteenth Amendment. Its purpose was to "create a new citizenship of the United States, embracing new rights, privileges and immunities, . . . in a new manner controlled by new authority, having a new scope and extent, depending on national authority for its existence and looking to national power for its preservation." McPherson believes that Virginia and her baby embody the best ideals of this representative American, which he states "can be achieved with or without intermarriage, . . . a product of culture and not of race." His people in **"Elbow Room"** support the belief that "most of us are products of much more complex cultural influences than we suppose" and McPherson agrees with Ellison that the identity of the black American is "a blending of both cultures."

In all three of his stories, **"Gold Coast," "Hue and Cry,"** and **"Elbow Room,"** McPherson describes these love relationships from the viewpoint of a black observer. In the last narration, he plays the role of a family friend engaged in a battle of his own to free himself of the "caste curtains" that he is aware has resulted in "resegregating all imagination." A recurrent theme in his second tale deals with the difficult options people have, with those choosing easy ones either pitied or hated because they betrayed loyalties, doomed to unhappy lives.

His story **"Elbow Room"** personifies what every character wanted: space enough to break free from a stereotyped life, a hollow role, a restraining sensibility. Like Hemingway, McPherson uses controlled dialogue to let his people speak eloquently for themselves, and his technique in handling introspection and psychological realism is similar to Kafka's. The tensions of American life produced by the psychic and spiritual alienation of interracial lovers and their attempts to find parental and community acceptance are some of the themes that vitalize these three memorable stories by a gifted contemporary writer, giving his works timeless, universal applications with whom the lonely and the exiled outsiders of all races, ethnic groups and classes can identify.

Jon Wallace (essay date Spring 1988)

SOURCE: "The Politics of Style in Three Stories by James Alan McPherson," in *Modern Fiction Studies,* Vol. 34, No. 1, Spring, 1988, pp. 17-26.

[*In the following essay, Wallace shows how the narrators in three of McPherson's stories use Standard English as a weapon and a barrier to intimacy.*]

"I'm black," declares Virginia Frost in the title story of James Alan McPherson's **Elbow Room:**

> "I've accepted myself as that. But didn't I make some elbow room though?" She tapped her temple with her forefinger. "I mean up here!" Then she laughed bitterly and sipped her tea. "When times get tough, anybody can pass for white. Niggers been doing that for centuries, so it ain't nothing new. But shit, wouldn't it of been something to be a nigger that could relate to white and black and everything else in the world out of a self as big as the world is?" She laughed. Then she said, "That would have been some nigger!"

As a seeker of personal space, of the elbow room she needs to develop herself and a sympathetic understanding of other human beings, Virginia represents one end of a psychological continuum within the book. At the opposite end stand other characters who also seek elbow room—but for antithetical reasons. My intention is to show that, unlike Virginia, who wants room to grow, the narrators of **"The Story of a Dead Man," "The Story of a Scar,"** and **"Just Enough for the City"** seek a space within which they can defend themselves against the claims of intimacy, human involvement, and personal history. The tool they use to accomplish this goal is language. Masters of what is primarily a white linguistic code, these narrators attempt to look out at the world from deep within the safety of conventional institutions and ideologies that implicitly justify their failure to see beyond them. In their mouths Standard English becomes a defensive weapon—a means of self-protection that, like Standard English in the mouths of defensive Whites, enables them to "hold the floor" at the expense of speakers of other codes (language varieties or dialects) who want, and often desperately need, to be heard. As a consequence, these characters avoid developing, or even considering, Virginia's admirable ideal of a self "as big as the world."

"It is not true," declares William, the narrator of **"The Story of a Dead Man,"** "that Billy Renfro was killed during that trouble in Houston." Thus begins a narrative designed to accomplish in fiction what the dramatic monologue accomplishes in poetry: unconscious self-revelation. The difference between most first-person fiction and the dramatic monologue, however, is that in the latter the identity of the audience is clear—and of course relevant to what the speaker is saying and why he is saying it. In **"The Story of a Dead Man"** McPherson does not identify William's audience, but he continually reminds us that William is speaking, or writing, to someone and that his motive is self-defense. Indeed, the narrative is William's response to stories told by Billy about his own heroic adventures on the road and to rumors about William's mistreatment of Billy. Both the stories and the rumors threaten William: the rumors for obvious reasons, the stories because they reveal, by implication, the staid pointlessness of William's very conventional life. "Neither is it true," William tells us in the second paragraph, "as certain of his enemies have maintained, that Billy's left eye was lost during a rumble with that red-neck storekeep outside Limehouse, South Carolina." At this point, William seems to be interested in establishing the truth about his cousin Billy. He says as much shortly thereafter: "I bother to refute these rumors because the man is my cousin, and I am honor-bound to love him as I know he really is." In this wonderfully rationalized construction, we discover William's underlying motive and the identity of the audience he is addressing. He speaks not of love here but of an obligation that requires love. He speaks also of Billy as "he really is." Given his "honor-bound to love him" construction, his casual fusing of love and obligation, we have to infer that William is both unable and unwilling to give us his wildly mythic cousin as "he really is"—that what we will get instead is a formal attempt to de-mythify Billy in the interests of William's very unmythical values.

And this is indeed what William proceeds to do. Thus, when he asserts at the end of the story that "it is not true, contrary to rumors circulating in my family, that Billy Renfro is unwelcome in my home," we appreciate the distinction between "not unwelcome" and "welcome"; and we know that William does also, for he is nothing if not a stickler for distinctions—a highly literate explainer resorting to the precisions of a standard code in an attempt to defend his bourgeois commitments, and a personal identity based on them, against the claims of the past and the present. His presumed audience is those who would not find anything the least objectionable in the candid but cautious fluency of the following lines:

> In contrast to [Billy], I moved westward [sic], but only as far as Chicago, and settled in against this city's soul-killing winter winds. I purged from my speech all traces of the South and warmed myself by the fire of my thirty-year plan. Employment was available in the credit reference section of the Melrose Department Store, and there I established, though slowly, a reputation for efficiency and tact. Because I got along, I began moving up. In my second year in Chicago, I found and courted Chelseia Raymond, a family-backed, efficiency-minded girl. She was the kind of woman I needed to make my children safe. Her family loved me, and had the grace to overlook the fact that I had once been a poor migrant from the South. Third-generation Chicagoans, they nonetheless opened their hearts and home to me, as if I had been native to their city. With their backing, I settled into this rough-and-tumble city and learned to dodge all events detracting attention from the direction in which I had determined to move. From time to time, trudging through the winter slush on Michigan, I would pause to explore a reflection of myself in a store window. By my fifth year in Chicago, I became satisfied that no one could have mistaken me for a refugee from the South.

> This was my situation when Billy Renfro came to visit.

Here the basic social and linguistic issues of the story are made clear. In the second sentence, William explicitly notes the relevance of language to identity, or at least to social success; moreover, his metaphor reveals how willingly he yielded his native dialect in order to succeed in Chicago—a sacrifice we can understand, even endorse, except, perhaps, in cases where such a sacrifice, made in the interests of "ef-

ficiency and tact," leads to a more costly sacrifice of human feeling.

That William has made such a sacrifice is implied throughout **"The Story of a Dead Man,"** more or less explicitly in the passages in which he attempts to justify his handling of Billy and implicitly in the language of the above paragraph. Consider, for example, the way William himself unknowingly modifies, at his own expense, the meaning of such honorific words as "loved," "grace," and "hearts." The context establishes the relationship between William and the Raymonds as a contingent and convenient one based on a mutual respect for efficiency, tact, and social status. "Loved," "grace," and "hearts" therefore mean something less here than they mean in most religious contexts—something significantly less spiritual and more commercial. It is a distinction easily missed in a paragraph in which the words seem to purr so naturally. But just as we can hear lines such as "let's not be so philosophical" without being aware of the enormous difference in meaning between the adjective in this sentence and the same word in, say, Plato, so we can easily miss the secularization of William's terms. To put the point another way, his words seem descriptive, but they are in fact argumentative: implicit predications intended to affirm the middle-class values that William and the Raymonds live by.

At the end of the paragraph, William returns to the identity issue—to acknowledge his determination "to dodge all events detracting attention from the direction in which I had determined to move." His narrative gives us every reason to believe that some of the events he dodged involved love, grace, and matters of the heart in less commercial senses.

After establishing William as the voice of black middle-class propriety, McPherson goes on to dramatize the primary conflict of the story: William's struggle to de-mythify (which is to say, to kill, make into a dead man) Billy within a net of Standard English and the presuppositions it affirms. In reference to Billy's losing his eye in a rumble, William writes: "That eye, I now have reason to believe, was lost during domestic troubles." In the minds of most middle-class readers, especially those interested in efficiency and tact, a man who has a "reason to believe," who can make such a point in the form of a nonrestrictive clause and then follow it with alliterative and euphemistic phrases such as "during domestic troubles," is certainly going to seem more reliable than a man allegedly given to rumbling with red-neck storekeeps outside Limehouse, South Carolina. Such readers would also be inclined to accept William's conclusion that Billy was essentially nothing more than a liar. Here is a passage in which William seeks to justify this claim:

> "We are no longer young men," I said. "The foam has settled down into the beer. I, myself, no longer chase women, speak hotly, challenge opinions too

far different from my own. I have learned it is to my advantage to get along . . . . In short, Billy, in my manhood I have become aware of complexity. You owe it to the family, and to the memory of your mother, to do the same."

Billy swished his Scotch and drank it down, then rapped the glass on the table to alert the barmaid. When she looked, he pointed two fingers downward toward our glasses and kissed at her. Then, turning to focus his single, red-rimmed eye on my face, he said, "Bullshit!"

He was dressed in the black gabardine suit of an undertaker. Dried purple-black blood streaked his coat sleeves, his black string tie, and the collar of the dirty white shirt he wore.

"People change, Billy," I said.

"Bullshit!" Billy Renfro said.

I looked closely at him and saw a gangster. He was not the kind of man I wanted to meet my family. I glanced at my watch and sipped my drink. I listened to his stories.

Billy spun his usual lies.

We do not know how many of Billy's stories are pure fiction and how many are authentic. The blood he carries on his clothes suggests that some of the violent ones must be based on fact, but it doesn't matter which. It doesn't even matter if Billy is all lies, as William believes—at least not as far as our reading of the story as a whole is concerned, because what distinguishes William and Billy is not their allegiance to truth but their relation to white middle-class values. As they stand, they are both partial men: two halves of a whole that would presumably add up to Virginia's "self as big as the world." One half, William, has defined himself in collective terms; the other, Billy, has defined himself in opposition to them. By so doing, each has exaggerated a truth: William the truth that we need to be a part of something, Billy that we need to be apart—individualized, to some extent alone. In a moral sense, then, they are equally limited. Linguistically, however, they are not, for William controls the power code: Standard American English, the "transparent" language of American industry and government, the means by which the middle- and upper-class do business and, at the same time, keep alternative realities or, more specifically, alternative stories from being heard as anything but lies.

In the last lines of the story, William hopes that he and Chelseia will one day be able to "reconstruct" Billy:

I say it is just a matter of time. We are, after all, the same age. Yet I have already charted my course. I have settled into Chicago, against the winter whippings of this city's winds. He can do the same. But as things stand now, he is still someplace out there, with a single eye flickering over open roadways, in his careless search for an exciting death. Ah, Billy!

The last words recall the last words of another upholder of the ideological status quo: the narrator of Melville's "Bartleby," who was equally eloquent ("Ah, Bartleby! Ah, Humanity!") and equally determined to live a safe and easy life. In both stories, the outsider is abandoned not merely in favor of commercial interests, as a casual reading might suggest, but also in favor of spiritual security. Billy might not symbolize the existence of a Melvillian "organic ill," but he does represent a radical spiritual as well as social alternative to William's thirty-year plan. He represents not just a way of living but a dimension of the self that must, or so the story implies, be accommodated if human beings are ever to become fully human.

In **"The Story of a Scar"** we meet a man as pompous as, but even more presumptuous than, William:

Since Dr. Wayland was late and there were no recent newsmagazines in the waiting room, I turned to the other patient and said: "As a concerned person, and as your brother, I ask you, without meaning to offend, how did you get that scar on the side of your face?"

The sentence reveals the narrator for what he is: a liar who uses language as a mask with which he attempts to protect himself by intimidating others. By demonstrating a fluent command of standard-to-formal English, he asserts what he presumes to be his superiority to most of his auditors: speakers of black dialect. Safely ensconced within it, he can look out upon a world of inferiors to whom, or so he believes, he owes nothing.

The quotation mark that precedes his utterance above draws the line between the private reality and public appearance. The narrator is interested in accumulating "information," preferably in print form, in isolation from others. Unable to find it, he resorts not to social intercourse but to interrogation. This form of discourse enables him to speak without involvement, risk, or concern. Contrary to his claim, therefore, he is not speaking as a brother, and he does intend to offend—in order to put his auditor on the defensive and so avoid the risks of intimacy. In another formulation, he speaks as a detached reader of human texts:

I studied her approvingly. Such women have a natural leaning toward the abstract expression of themselves. Their styles have private meanings, advertise secret distillations of their souls. Their figures, and their disfigurations, make meaningful statements. . . . Such craftsmen must be approached with subtlety if they are to be deciphered.

It is probably no coincidence that the narrator describes the woman as a "craftsman," thus missing, in language anyway, one of the most important facts about her. It is probably no coincidence, because although everything he says is true, he has neither the subtlety nor the sensitivity to "decipher" anyone's soul. And she knows it, as she knows his type: "I knowed you'd get back around to that," she says, when he asks again about her scar. "Black guys like you with them funny eyeglasses are a real trip. You got to know everything. You sit in corners and watch people." Unfazed, he continues to press for an answer. But shortly after she begins to talk about where she was when it happened and about the men she had been working with, the narrator interrupts what he calls "her tiresome ramblings" to demand "Which one of them cut you?"

> Her face flashed a wall of brown fire. "This here's my story!" she muttered, eyeing me up and down with suspicion. "You dudes cain't stand to hear the whole of anything. You want everything broke down in little pieces."

In a sense, she is wrong. The narrator isn't as interested in breaking things down as he is in discovering and imposing patterns on the world around him—patterns that suit his needs, his story about himself, and his relation to everyone else. Put another way, what he wants is the continual validation of the assumptions that confirm his presumed superiority. This becomes clear later when he again interrupts to answer his own question. While listening to the woman tell about her growing disenchantment with Billy Crawford, a bookish, Williamesque boyfriend, and her growing interest in a jive-talking newcomer to the post office named Teddy Johnson, whom she describes as "the last true son of the Great McDaddy," the narrator loses control:

> "Sister," I said quickly, overwhelmed suddenly by the burden of insight. "I know the man of whom you speak. There is no time for this gutter-patter and indirection. Please, for my sake and for your own, avoid stuffing the shoes of the small with mythic homilies. This man was a bum, a hustler and a small-time punk. He broke up your romance with Billy, then he lived off you, cheated on you, and cut you when you confronted him." So pathetic and gross seemed her elevation of the fellow that I abandoned all sense of caution. "Is your mind so dead," I continued, "did this switchblade slice so deep, do you have so little respect for yourself, or at least for

the idea of proportion in this sad world, that you'd sit here and praise this brute!?"

What the narrator means by proportion is that quality of coherence and meaning that his ideological presuppositions and stereotypes provide him—presuppositions and stereotypes that, among other things, identify him as superior intellectually and spiritually to practically everyone else. He himself is a more sophisticated Billy Crawford threatened by the physical (primarily sexual) power of the Great McDaddys of the world—and by earthy, voluptuous women who know what he is beneath his elaborate, carefully-articulated verbal shell. This is why he is so unnerved by her response. He tells us that while she looked at him through the smoke of her cigarette, he "watched her nervously, recognizing the evidence of past destructiveness, yet fearing the imminent occurrence of more. But it was not her temper or the potential strength of her fleshly arms that I feared." What he fears is her insight through his intellectual defenses into his frail, impotent heart.

For unspecified reasons, the narrator cannot, or will not, love. Language is his means of masking this fact, of keeping it from others and from himself. When the woman does finish the story, does reveal that it was Billy Crawford and not Teddy Johnson who knifed her, he is predictably unnerved. The situation is made worse by the fact that the woman then begins to speak to him as a "sister," as a human being in need:

> "This here's the third doctor I been to see. The first one stiched [sic] me up like a turkey and left this scar. The second one refused to touch me." She paused and wet her lips again. "This man fixed your nose for you," she said softly. "Do you think he could do somethin' about this scar?"

The narrator's subsequent behavior reveals him for what he is: a fearful wordman whose last refuge is print and abstract, impersonal rights—forms designed to compensate for the absence of human feeling:

> I searched the end table next to my couch for a newsmagazine, carefully avoiding her face. "Dr. Wyland is a skilled man," I told her. "Whenever he's not late. I think he may be able to do something for you."

> She sighed heavily and seemed to tremble. "I don't expect no miracle or nothin'," she said. "If he could just fix the part around my eye I wouldn't expect nothin' else. People say the rest don't look too bad."

> I clutched a random magazine and did not answer. Nor did I look at her. The flesh around my nose be-

gan to itch, and I looked toward the inner office door with the most extreme irritation building in me . . . . I resolved to put aside all notions of civility and go into the office before her, as was my right.

Needing desperately to escape the threat of intimacy, the narrator at first seeks protection behind a magazine. Then another idea occurs to him, a question that seems personal, that in fact can be personal, but that in context is merely another defensive tactic—the narrator's way of keeping his distance by reducing intimate discourse to mere form:

> And then I remembered the most important question, without which the entire exchange would have been wasted. I turned to the woman, now drawn together in the red plastic chair, as if struggling to sleep in a cold bed. "Sister," I said, careful to maintain a casual air. "Sister . . . what is your name?"

For all interpretive purposes, the narrator of **"The Story of a Scar"** is the narrator of **"Just Enough for the City,"** who meets with various fundamentalist proselytizers, speculates on the nature of love, and concludes that just enough love for the city and the people therein is not very much—or much more than he is willing to give. Appropriately enough, he has an ear for language. Were it not for their accents, he tells us, he would not let the Germans into his house. Once in, however, they accomplish little, because he has nothing to give them but questions—to which he expects no answers; for he too is an interrogator trying to avoid self-revelation: "They both watch and wait for me to disclose myself. Backed into a corner, I have no choice but to shift their focus. 'Where do you get your money?' I ask them. 'Who finances your operation?' They go away." On this occasion, the narrator accomplishes his goal of self-defense through intimidation with relatively simple, factual questions. On other occasions, he resorts to elaborate conundrums designed to end uncomfortable discussions that he made possible by admitting fundamentalists into his apartment in the first place. By means of such elaborate verbosity he avoids living the basic truths that most of his visitors present. "Der simple problem," one German lady tells him, "is dat vee do not luff one anudder." Faced with such a simple but demanding fact, the narrator does what so many of McPherson's protagonists do so well, or at least so often: transform a spiritual or interpersonal issue into linguistic or aesthetic categories: "I agree with this. But I insist that they define for me the term."

Developing a simple definition of love, it turns out, is a goal the narrator has set for himself. Here is his first attempt:

> I think love must be the ability to suspend one's intelligence for the sake of something. At the basis of love therefore must live imagination. Instead of

thinking always "I am I," to love one must be able to feelingly conjugate the verb to be. Intuition must be part of the circuitous pathway leading ultimately to love. I wish I could ask someone.

Within the story proper, the narrative of physical events, we see a narrator behaving in ways wholly at odds with his intellectual insights: intimidating people with his precise but distancing and at times baffling language. Together, his meditations on the theme of love, and his narrative of his human relations, reveal him to be a sensitive and intelligent but emotionally sterile man who knows what he should be but who cannot be it—despite the depth and apparent sincerity of his conclusions. "Love must be a going outward from the self," he writes, "from the most secret of safe positions. God is no more than the most secret place from which such emanations can be sent." The idea seems promising, thoroughly consistent with the speculations of, for example, Thomas Merton. His grammatical metaphor seems equally insightful:

> If one is not too strict in his conjugation of the verb to be, he might wind up with a sense of living in the present. I believe that love exists at just that point when the first person singular moves into the plural estate: I am, you are, he is, she is, we are . . . . The saying of it requires a going out of oneself, of breath as well as confidence. Its image is of expansiveness, a taking roundly into and putting roundly out of oneself. Or perhaps another word should be used, one invented or one transported from another context: I am, you are, he is, she is, we be. . . . Or again, perhaps a beat of silence alone could best bear the weight of it, a silence suggesting the burden of subjectivity: I am, you are, he is, she is, they are. . . .

The possibilities proliferate, as defensive speculation always must, into a substitute for the experience speculated about; and the narrator's meditations become empty, idle, and destructive. Eventually he decides that he need not entertain proselytizers at all: "I am refusing these days to bow on my knees and cry holy." It is the beginning of the end. In response to the realization that he has seen deep into the eyes of a young, haunted woman, he is tempted to speak:

> I want to say, but do not dare to say, that I saw briefly in her face the shadow of a human soul.
>
> I am. . . .

Although still unable to conjugate feelingly the second-person singular, he nevertheless comes to realize that there is more to human experience than artful formulations. In an exchange with two ministers, he tells the story of a man who, "suspecting now that words were of little importance, he found himself watching gestures and facial expressions, listening to the rhythms of voices and not to the words spoken, for telltale insights into the true nature of reality. . . ." But like the man in his story, who later became "unable . . . to believe in any words" and who "retreated into a room, questioning even the character behind his own name," the narrator ends up isolated within a semantic universe that protects him against love by a wall of metaphor:

> Something breathes quickly against the cobwebs inside me. But because I fear what I feel is love, I turn my face away.
>
> Tu es. . . .
>
> I am becoming sufficient.

Read as correct French, tu es indicates that the narrator is once again attempting to conjugate the verb "to be"; read as incorrect Spanish (a second-person pronoun and a third-person verb), tu es indicates that the narrator cannot, or will not, "go outward from the most secret of safe positions," which in his case is not God, apparently, but his own fragile self: a matter of words contrived as defense. The disjunction expresses his inability to connect with the human world. In either interpretation, he is not really in the world of human relations; he is somewhere else, making use of what Joseph Chilton Pearce sees as a distinguishing characteristic of literate culture: an "infinite capacity for rationalization." It is just about all he has, and is: words, words, words, spoken not to connect but to separate and protect a profoundly insufficient self.

At the conclusions of **"The Story of a Dead Man," "The Story of a Scar,"** and **"Just Enough for the City,"** McPherson leaves us with characters who might, but probably will not, break through the walls they have made to protect themselves against human involvement. Theirs is a problem that is inevitable in cultures—black or white—that value the individual as such. Within them, most sensitive human beings are alternately haunted and invigorated by the tension between the desire simply to be themselves in the narrow sense of "apart from the human community" and the desire to be a part of it, to connect with others in satisfying and yet necessarily self-effacing ways. Although this is a common problem inside and outside books, McPherson deepens our understanding of it by showing what a crucial role language can play as a means of protecting a self that is not "as big as the world" but as small—and as tenuous—as an ego.

Kirkus Reviews (review date 15 November 1997)

SOURCE: A review of *Crabcakes,* in *Kirkus Reviews,* November 15, 1997.

[*In the following review, the critic praises the universal humanity of McPherson's memoir,* Crabcakes.]

McPherson, author of the Pulitzer Prizewinning short-story collection **Elbow Room** (1977), writes here with an astonishing range of language and emotion. Having previously addressed the black experience in America on many levels, he now tells a profoundly personal tale of displacement and discovery that is poetic and universal. The life described in this volume comes into focus in a moment of retrospection, in a bitter season of doubt. "Life itself' had become his enemy, he writes: "I sought to control its every effort at intrusion into my personal space"—space that was almost entirely confined to his bed, "in which I perfected my escape from life into an art." Remembering the seasons of pain and repair in a lifetime of missed opportunities, he returns repeatedly in this account to Channie Washington, his longtime tenant, a nurturing, self-reliant, and deeply religious woman who represented sanctuary—"the place where you pause to get your bearings for the road." For McPherson, the present beckons to memory slowly, seductively, revelation then coming into Proustian clarity with a crabcake or the sensual gait of a brown-eyed woman descending a stair. The fish market of a Baltimore neighborhood where he first savored crabcakes, the fields of Iowa, where he now teaches, and the streets of Japanese cities, where he sojourned awhile, all gather into a personal monologue that invites us to understand the crossroads he has reached. Ultimately, McPherson finds renewal in simple sentiments. Late in a long conversation-letter to a Japanese friend that runs through the second part of the book, he reminds us that "if nothing in the future of the present seems permanent . . . one can always focus on . . . the future enjoyment of a Maryland crabcake. Such exercises of the imagination keep hope alive." Although its ever-shifting form is sometimes unsettling, this is a thoughtful and life-affirming memoir, unforgettable for its humanity, its gentle pace. McPherson has traveled the world and never lost sight of the inspirational lure of one's origins.

FURTHER READING

Criticism

Christ, Ronald. Review of *Hue and Cry,* by James Alan McPherson. *Commonweal* XC, No. 21 (19 September 1969): 570-71.

Faults McPherson's language in *Hue and Cry* as flat and awkward. The critic also states: "McPherson is a Negro writer who admittedly has tried to keep the question of race far in the background, and his stories show (and suffer from) this repression."

Shacochis, Bob. "Interview with James Alan McPherson," edited by Dan Campion. *Iowa Journal of Literary Studies* (1983): 7-33.
    An interview with McPherson.

"Scenes before Themes." *Times Literary Supplement* (25 December 1969): 1465.
    Praises the realistic depiction of urban life in Elbow Room, but states McPherson's "hip idiom" sometimes overpowers his themes.

Sullivan, Walter. "Where Have All the Flowers Gone?: The Short Story in Search of Itself." *The Sewanee Review* LXX-VII, No. 1 (Winter 1970): 530-42.
    Brief review in which Sullivan aruges that McPherson's political views on racial issues compromise the literary qualities of *Hue and Cry.*

Additional coverage of McPherson's life and career is contained in the following sources published by Gale: *Black Writers,* **Vol. 1;** *Contemporary Authors,* **Vols. 25-28R;** *Contemporary Authors Autobiography Series,* **Vol. 17;** *Contemporary Authors New Revisions,* **Vol. 24;** *Contemporary Literary Criticism,* **Vols. 19 and 77;** *Dictionary of Literary Biography,* **Vol. 38; and** *Major Twentieth Century Writers.*

Walter Mosley
1952-

American novelist.

INTRODUCTION

Walter Mosley has emerged as one of the premier African-American novelists of the 1990s. As a writer of detective fiction, he has been compared favorably with the masters of the genre and recognized for the added dimensions of racial and interpersonal relations included in his mystery stories. His first novel, *Devil in a Blue Dress* (1990), was an immediate success. He has followed with an average of one novel per year, firmly establishing his main character, Ezekiel "Easy" Rawlins, as the African-American member of the "hard-boiled, California" school of detectives founded by Raymond Chandler's Philip Marlowe and Dashiell Hammett's Sam Spade. As Mosley told critic Bob McCullough in 1994, "I'd like my name to be mentioned with Raymond Chandler, Hammett, Ross McDonald, people like that. If people mention my race, I won't be unhappy." In addition to the six novels in the Rawlins series, Mosley has broadened his range with *R. L.'s Dream* (1995) and *Always Outnumbered, Always Outgunned* (1997), novels that focus on representative figures of the black underclass in America.

Biographical Information

Born in 1952 in the Watts section of Los Angeles, Mosley grew up listening to stories from both sides of his mixed heritage. His mother's family recounted old Jewish stories about the czars and life in Russia; from his war-veteran father's side came tales of the black experience in the South. Eager to leave racially tense Los Angeles upon his high school graduation in 1970, Mosley enrolled at Goddard College in Vermont. He spent more time hitchhiking around the country than studying, however, and was expelled from Goddard. Mosley finally earned a degree in political science from Johnson State College in Vermont in 1977. After brief graduate work at the University of Minnesota, Mosley settled in Boston, where he met his wife-to-be, Joy Kellman, in 1979. Moving to New York in 1982, Mosley worked as a computer programmer and began attending creative-writing classes at the City College of New York. In 1989, Mosley showed a finished work to his teacher, Frederic Tuten, who sent the work to his own agent. Shortly after, the agent sold the work to W. W. Norton Company, and *Devil in a Blue Dress* appeared to an enthusiastic reception the next year.

Major Works

Set in 1948 Los Angeles, *Devil in a Blue Dress* introduces Easy Rawlins, a recently unemployed war veteran who turns to private detective work out of economic necessity. The novel presents a fairly conventional, convoluted mystery plot with the added dimension of Rawlins' race to complicate his sleuthing and, especially, his relationship with the local police. Rawlins is hired by a pale man in a white suit to find a "white" woman who frequents black bars. Mosley employs perceptions about race to add twists to the plot as well as to comment upon the social conditions in which Rawlins' quest takes place. *A Red Death* (1991) begins in 1953 and finds Rawlins more prosperous as a result of his first case. The ambitious plot of this second installment includes elements from the Holocaust, Garveyism, McCarthyism, black-Jewish social relations, and domestic violence. Unlike many detective series, in which an essentially unchanging picaresque character moves from one adventure to the next, Rawlins ages and his circumstances change with each book. In *White Butterfly* (1992), set in 1956, Easy has become a family man, hiding his prosperity and much of his earlier life from his young wife. *Black Betty* (1994) shifts the action to 1961; the Kennedy era and growing civil rights unrest provide the backdrop against which a more mature Rawlins, whose earlier prosperity has evaporated, searches for the title character. After a detour outside the detective genre with *R. L.'s Dream,* a story of a blues musician who travels back in time to play with the legendary Robert Johnson, Mosley returned to Rawlins in *A Little Yellow Dog* (1996). In this work, an aging, reputable Rawlins is drawn back into the L.A. underworld to help a woman escape her abusive husband. *Gone Fishin'* (1997) is the prequel to the Rawlins mysteries, introducing readers to the 19-year-old Easy and recounting the beginning of his relationship with Mouse, his companion in the series. Also in 1997, Mosley published *Always Outnumbered, Always Outgunned,* featuring aging ex-convict turned social activist Socrates Fortlow. Mosley plans to complete his Easy Rawlins series in a total of nine or ten books.

Critical Reception

Mosley's immediate popular success was mirrored by broad critical acclaim. *Devil in a Blue Dress* was nominated for an Edgar Award from the Mystery Writers of America and won the Shamus Award from the Private Eye Writers of America. Reviewers likened his character portrayals, authentic locales, and crisp dialogue to such masters of the genre as Chandler, Hammett, McDonald, and his predecessor in black detective fiction, Chester Himes. Critics also noted his ability to create a complex and sympathetic main character who struggles with moral ambiguity in a hostile social environment. As the Rawlins series has developed, Mosley has been criticized for predictable and overly complicated plot lines, but at the same time, critics have lauded his increasingly dark and probing focus on social issues. Joseph Ferrandino has said: "Beneath the conventional and trite mystery plot lies a subtext in which the author exhibits the sinewy moral intellect of James Baldwin at his best. . . . Mosley is a social critic posing as a mystery writer."

PRINCIPAL WORKS

Devil in a Blue Dress (novel) 1990
A Red Death (novel) 1991
White Butterfly (novel) 1992
Black Betty (novel) 1994
R. L.'s Dream (novel) 1995
The Walter Mosley Omnibus (collection) 1995
A Little Yellow Dog (novel) 1996
Always Outnumbered, Always Outgunned (novel) 1997
Gone Fishin' (novel) 1997

CRITICISM

Theodore O. Mason Jr. (essay date Fall 1992)

SOURCE:"Walter Mosley's Easy Rawlins: The Detective and Afro-American Fiction," in *The Kenyon Review,* Vol. 14, No. 4, Fall, 1992, pp. 177-83.

[*In the following essay, Mason applies the critical theories of George Lukács and M. M. Bakhtin to Mosley's first novel,* Devil in a Blue Dress.]

> I was surprised to see a white man walk into Joppy's bar. It's not just that he was white but he wore an off-white linen suit and shirt with a Panama straw hat and bone shoes over flashing white silk socks. His skin was smooth and pale with just a few freckles. One lick of strawberry-blond hair escaped the band of his hat. He stopped in the doorway, filling it with his large frame, and surveyed the room with pale eyes; not a color I'd ever seen in a man's eyes. When he looked at me I felt a thrill of fear, but that went away quickly because I was used to white people by 1948.

With these words Walter Mosley begins his first detective novel *Devil in a Blue Dress.* Mosley's narrator is his detective/"hero" Ezekiel "Easy" Rawlins, a black World War II veteran, now occupied with trying to make a living in the Los Angeles of 1948. Rawlins's narration makes clear from the very first paragraph that *Devil in a Blue Dress* will, among other things, concern itself with the borders between "races" and between genders, configuring these borders as the site not only of the criminal act, but also as the site of culturally transgressive possibility.

Devil in a Blue Dress concerns Rawlins's search for a woman named Daphne Monet. He is hired by a gangster, DeWitt Albright, first simply to search for her, then to recover both her and a considerable amount of stolen money. This search for Monet takes Easy Rawlins on a journey bringing him in contact not only with the police, but also with highly placed members of the political and financial community of Los Angeles, to say nothing of members of the "underworld." In many respects, Mosley's work seems of a piece with a great deal of crime fiction. What distinguishes *Devil in a Blue Dress,* as well as Mosley's second novel *A Red Death,* is the implications of its decision to represent the black community as the dominant site of the novel's action, rather than simply being the locus of exotic difference into which the white detective occasionally stumbles.

Joppy Shag's bar is one of the many places figured in the novel as a black site. In these sites Afro-American cultural identity becomes outlined, represented, and acted out by Mosley's characters. There they can find a space insulated for the most part from the intrusions of the white world, such as DeWitt Albright, even if "the odor of rotted meat filled every corner of the building." We learn later that Joppy's landlord is the only white face usually seen in the bar, and generally only on collection day. So in the first paragraph Albright's entrance into the bar is disruptive, if only by way of its rarity.

Mosley, though, makes certain to emphasize this particular intrusion because Albright ("all bright") becomes represented as whiter than white. From his "bone shoes" and silk socks to the Panama hat, Albright's hulking presence figures the overriding power of the white world. The discordant note to his appearance is the eye color Easy Rawlins has never seen despite his wide experience. Presumably, Easy has never seen Albright's eyes in any black man either. Significantly for the patterns of symbolism and imagery in the novel, the gangster seems the incarnation of evil, a real white devil—from his "great white shoulders" to the even more indicative identifying white business card on which he scribbles his address with "a white enameled fountain pen." Albright's significant attribute in the opening chapter is a sinister seductiveness Mosley indicates by recourse to the fairly standard symbolism of the serpent—DeWitt's grip was "like a snake coiling around my hand." His language, like his handshake, finds itself equally undercut. There, in the middle of post-World War II Watts, the gangster speaks "a light drawl like a well-to-do Southern gentleman."

Rawlins's relative equanimity in the face of the white devil derives from his thorough familiarity with whites and with death. He "was used to white people by 1948," because he had killed them in the war. Rawlins's familiarity gained in the war extends also to the realm of the sexual, since Easy on at least one other occasion refers to his sexual experience with white women—in Europe "all they got is white girls." Placed against DeWitt Albright's representation as the devil with the drawl, the experiences occasioning Easy's equanimity indicate Mosley's intention to play out at least part of his drama on the ground of racial and cultural transgressiveness.

This emphasis on transgression makes a consideration of *Devil in a Blue Dress* more important than it might otherwise seem. The "popularity" of detective fiction frequently militates against its being taken seriously. A different view, however, holds that the emphasis on transgression moves the detective fiction closer to the center of the novelistic tradition. As a genre, the novel might well be characterized as frequently concerned with the relation between the social whole and the possibility of transgression, or the maintenance of social norms. Some of the more significant and influential theoreticians of the novel form have tended to emphasize the role society plays as a totalizing structure in

relation to the formal and thematic components of this dominant fictional genre.

If we shift the ground of the inquiry to the Afro-American novelistic tradition specifically, then the figure of the detective becomes, I think, even more central. This centrality derives from the experience of *difference* explored and represented by this body of fiction. In the context of a racist society, *difference* becomes encoded within cultural discourse as one of the chief signs of transgression (if not criminality)—so that the emphasis on transgression characteristic of the novel form generally becomes historicized and concretized in distinctive ways within the specific category of the Afro-American novel. In this way, protagonists in many of these novels, given their necessary engagement with transgression, begin to resemble detectives such as Easy Rawlins.

In this essay I want to bring some versions of the theory of the novel to bear on Mosley's *Devil in a Blue Dress*. Rather than taking the road likely more traveled, that is, reading Mosley in relation to the work of Chester Himes or even Rudolph Fisher, I prefer to study Mosley's novel within the context of Georg Lukács's *Theory of the Novel* and M. M. Bakhtin's "Epic and Novel," to shed some light on what I take to be the centrality of Mosley's work to much that is generally considered in the Afro-American novelistic tradition.

Invoking two critics and theorists such as Lukács and Bakhtin in an essay on Afro-American detective fiction may seem something like overkill. After all, the logic might go, the subgenre of detective fiction falls rather readily into the categories of popular literature. Further, these categories seem removed from the provinces of "high theory."

While I sympathize with the inclinations behind such an objection, I find myself unable to agree with it, for there is a fashion in which the theories of Lukács and Bakhtin center rather than marginalize detective fiction, even if they do so in rather different ways. But even more significantly, both Lukács and Bakhtin provide us with the foundation for a reading of Afro-American detective fiction that moves this form of writing far closer to the center of the Afro-American literary tradition taken as a whole than one might suspect. Both Lukács and Bakhtin achieve this special value by emphasizing the novel's role in engaging a world that is inherently fallen, or the site of the potentially transgressive.

Lukács consistently reads the novel as the epic of a fallen world. In one of his earliest published works, *Theory of the Novel* (1920), Lukács conceives of the novel in the following terms. "The novel is the epic of an age in which the extensive totality of life is no longer directly given, in which the immanence of meaning in life has become a problem, yet which still thinks in terms of totality." Though he is obviously a critic of enormous strengths, one of Lukács's consistent weaknesses is his inclination to romanticize the social ground of the epic, in a fashion perhaps somewhat surprising for a Marxist literary theorist and critic. The wholeness of the epic world sharply contrasts with the inherent brokenness of the novelistic universe. While this brokenness may well be seen as the result of a Fall, it is a fortunate Fall (in a limited sense) into the realm of history. From Lukács's perspective, the absence of *totality* in the novelistic world provides the novel with its fundamental impetus—the desire to reform some version of epic totality, even if that version is historical and contingent, rather than transcendent and necessary.

The novel's hero, then, is a seeker, a status that implies a world in need of ordering, a social whole of considerably greater fluidity than that of the epic world. The epistemological implications of this shift in worldview cannot be overlooked, for if philosophy in the epic world is not a "problem," then presumably neither is epistemology. But the fall into fluidity and history tends to locate the philosophical problem precisely as an epistemological one, at least in its origins. For that reason, I want to suggest further that the epistemological problem is necessarily grounded within the realm of the social. The seeking done by the novel's heroes and heroines centers inevitably on the nature and substance of *social* knowledge within the context of a developing and dynamic social whole. Consequently, totality here is ever shifting. Furthermore, this concept of totality is impossible to separate from larger questions of power and politics, issues that in a culturally and "racially" heterogeneous scene (such as that undertaken by the Afro-American novel) inevitably involve the construction of self within the context of historically charged categories developed in the interest of the larger and controlling white society.

M. M. Bakhtin's engagement with the same kinds of issues that concern Lukács in *Theory of the Novel* moves us closer to a fuller appreciation of detective fiction as a subgenre. One of Bakhtin's central advantages over Lukács is his disinclination to read the epic world as the site of grace from which we all have fallen. Rather, Bakhtin sees in the very fluidity of the world a set of conditions perfect for representation by the novel. Throughout the pages of "Epic and Novel," he celebrates the novel's very incompleteness, a condition mirroring the condition of "reality" the novel takes as its field of representation. "The novel comes into contact with the spontaneity of the inconclusive present; this is what keeps the genre from congealing. The novelist is drawn toward everything that is not yet complete." This incompleteness mimics and is mimicked by a similar condition in the representation of characters, particularly the "hero." As Bakhtin states it, "one of the basic internal themes of the novel is precisely the theme of the hero's inadequacy to his

fate or his situation." The combination of a highly unstable "field" of representation and the instability of the hero's relation to the task before him or her underscores the novel's status as a highly problematized project.

But where Lukács may have seen this condition as defective (if perhaps inevitable), Bakhtin embraces this instability as a site of multiple possibility. Part of this enthusiasm we can grasp as a recognition of the understandable indeterminacy or indeterminate-ness of historical existence. Unlike the epic world, the novelistic world's absence of "totality" causes reality to be always in process, always somehow unequal to our categories of understanding. For precisely this reason, Bakhtin centers *epistemology* as the fundamental subtext of the novel form. "When the novel becomes the dominant genre, epistemology becomes the dominant discipline." But we should understand that this emphasis on epistemology of course does not indicate a rather easy assignment of everyday phenomena into a static set of categories. Instead, epistemology itself is a highly problematized site, a form of inquiry that looks forward in the novelistic world in process, rather than backward to a highly static universe, as in the epic world.

Perhaps even more significantly, Bakhtin points us in a direction that seems inordinately fruitful for a "reading" of Mosley's Afro-American detective fiction. From its origins, the novel takes as part of its developmental impetus a significant engagement with questions of difference. The development of the novel is "powerfully affected by a very specific rupture in the history of European civilization: its emergence from a socially isolated and culturally deaf semi-patriarchal society, and its entrance into international and interlingual contacts and relationships. A multitude of different languages, cultures and times became available to Europe, and this became a decisive factor in its life and thought." This historical rupture becomes incorporated even in the novel's conception of its own world as "already opened up; one's own monolithic and closed world (the world of the epic) has been replaced by the great world of one's own plus 'the others'."

Now, assuredly, the history of Europe's engagement with the "other," even the white "other," has most often been less than salutary. Important here is less the outcome of this engagement, and more Bakhtin's centering of the engagement with the other in an epistemologically indeterminate scene as characteristic of the novel form. For what Bakhtin does, I believe, is historicize the novel's interest in epistemology in such a way as to put cross-cultural, potentially hybridized engagements at the heart of the form's genealogy. The search characteristic of novelistic heroes, then, becomes fundamentally grounded in the sociology of knowledge and identity, set within a dynamic set of social categories. And this ground is identical, I believe, to the ground of Afro-American detective fiction (and by implication Afro-American literature generally considered).

I am convinced this is true, even if so influential a writer as Raymond Chandler has it otherwise. His famous essay, "The Simple Art of Murder," on detective fiction ("hard-boiled" and "standard") reads the genre as principally involved with the righting of wrong. "The emotional basis of the standard detective story was and had always been that murder will out and justice will be done." The "hard-boiled" story differs from Chandler's perspective only insofar as the reinstitution of the "right" is less probable, "unless some very determined individual makes it his business to see that justice is done." These individuals tend to be "hard men" doing "hard, dangerous work." Rather than emphasizing the restoration of justice and order, this characterization of the detective actually centers the reality of transgression as *the* informing issue, not only in terms of the criminal, but also in terms of the detective. One need only think of Hammett's description of Sam Spade as a "blond Satan" in *Maltese Falcon,* or the characterization of some of Chandler's own protagonists, even Philip Marlowe, to say nothing of the generally recognized tendency of the detective's behavior to replicate that of the criminal. The "dark street" to which Chandler refers in "The Simple Art of Murder" is the site of moral ambiguity, frequently on the part of all concerned. It can also be a site of informing cultural conflict regarding not only questions of justice, but also questions of social identity (racial, sexual, and the like) and cultural formation in a novelistic world characterized generically by a dynamic instability. The presence of these kinds of conflicts makes *transgression* a central issue, not so much in terms of criminality in the legal sense, but more generally in terms of the crossing of categories or the violation of social protocols about social, cultural, and historical identity. This is the dark street Walter Mosley takes us down in *Devil in a Blue Dress.*

Even though Mosley chooses to work the dark street, he complicates his presentation by figuring Easy Rawlins as having an interest in middle-class respectability. Contrasting with the emphasis on the potential for seeing *Devil in a Blue Dress* within the context of the transgressive alone is Mosley's insistence on the significance of Easy's *house.* It is, after all, a desire to ensure his mortgage payment that inclines him to accept Albright's offer of a "little job," even as the detective is aware of Albright's criminality. Put more accurately, it is precisely and ironically Easy's love for his house that propels him into the role of detective and into the zone of potential transgression.

> Maybe it was that I was raised on a sharecropper's farm or that I never owned anything until I bought that house, but I loved my little home. There was an apple tree and an avocado in the front yard surrounded by thick St. Augustine grass. At the side

of the house I had a pomegranate tree that bore more than thirty fruit every season and a banana tree that never produced a thing. There were dahlias and wild roses in beds around the fence and African violets that I kept in a big jar on the front porch.

Here the house works in both conventional and unconventional ways. Rawlins figures his home as a zone of safety and pastoral retreat away from the urban scene of Los Angeles. This is particularly clear given his inclination to use the garden and the trees surrounding his house as emblems of its "value" for him. Just as clearly the house is also a sign of stability and worth, and as such corresponds with a tradition in the novel (dating to its early origins) of symbolically negotiating and mediating the nature of middle-class life. The house as emblem or sign defines membership in the middle class and presumably indicates laudable stability and solid citizenship—contrasting starkly with the vision of the "hard-boiled" detective of Chandler and Hammett as liminal figures.

On the other hand, Mosley is inclined to historicize and problematize the symbolism of Rawlins's house in at least two ways. By making Rawlins a veteran, Mosley historicizes his hero within the context of a major cultural movement or problem—the reintegration of World War II soldiers into the fabric of American life. The figure of the veteran here, both as incarnated by Rawlins and in general, is seen as someone possessing knowledge different from that of his fellows—a knowledge deriving from contact with death that tends to dislocate the veteran not only from the sphere of middle-class safety, but also from a set of assumptions about the nature of life, the nature of society, and the nature of human connection. The house, then, assuredly signifies the attempt to fold its owner back into the realm of the "everyday," but the fact that such a transformation is required casts doubts on its ultimate success.

The doubts are reinforced by Mosley's representation of Easy's war experiences as insistently making him unable to conform with prewar protocols about race. Having killed blue-eyed "Aryans" and therefore unpacked the mythology of whiteness, Easy does not imagine himself inclined to reinstall the racial understandings of the 1930s in 1948. The fashion in which Rawlins engages DeWitt Albright from the beginning of the novel (and all the other white characters) suggests that he recognizes their power, but that recognition hardly moves him toward abject obedience. In this regard the house works in ways more transgressive than not, for while it remains an emblem of entrance into middle-class life, that zone of safety and stability does not belong to Afro-Americans. In *Devil in a Blue Dress,* Easy's ownership of a house leads him to claim an equality with whites—"I felt that I was as good as any white man, but if I didn't even own my front door then people would look at me like just another poor beggar." This assertion of his value moves Easy into a more unstable realm by violating the "inviolable" metaphorical and literal spaces and categories a racist society requires to get on with its business. The house as an emblem of transgression works to expand this novel's examination of the nature of cultural knowledge in a scene informed by extreme fluidity, even as that fluidity remains unacknowledged.

Cultural knowledge within the universe of *Devil in a Blue Dress* becomes represented initially as racial knowledge, or more precisely, the negotiation of racial protocols. At nearly every step Mosley foregrounds race, but takes pains to set the issue of race within the context of culture, language, and history. Rawlins places himself early at the site of conflict between race and class phrased as a problem of language. "I always tried to speak proper English in my life, the kind of English they taught in school, but I found over the years that I could only truly express myself in the natural, 'uneducated' dialect of my upbringing." Proper English works here very much in the same fashion as Easy's house. Like the house, grammatical English is a site of convention, of stability, of safety. Identified with formal education, it can readily be seen as Easy's entry into a realm previously denied him and those like him. But here the fit is imperfect, for proper English is not the dialect of Easy's personal history, nor is it represented in the novel as the dialect of his culture or race. The emphasis on language is repeated throughout the novel when Easy strays into "white" territory—especially the offices of Albright and the other businesspeople.

Easy's verbal articulations of self are always conceived of as inappropriate or disjunctive. In Chapter 17, Mosley describes his hero's search for a white banker, Mr. Carter, who may be involved in the developing mystery. The difficulty Easy experiences in gaining access to Carter revolves around protocols of language—who speaks to whom on whose terms, and in what language. Easy slides from formal English into "dialect" as his interview with Carter's receptionist proceeds. But more important than whether Easy violates the conventions of verb forms is the question of whether he is allowed to speak the language of power, or whether his "race" ought to prevent him from doing so. Usurping white language resembles owning a house, insofar as both acts move one into the realm of transgression, the zone of dangerous instability. Even verbal conventions in the police station affirm this insistent transgressiveness. The drama of "discipline and punish" played out by the police is interpreted by Easy as yet another version of "cops and niggers," even if it does not play out exactly to form. The obvious play on "cops and robbers" signifies the essential condition of blackness as the ground of transgression.

Even more significant, the ground of race is given an im-

portant twist by invoking the no less problematic issue of sex. The devil in the novel's title is Daphne Monet, whose patterns of signification suggest how fluid and how complicated the discursive cultural universe represented in *Devil in a Blue Dress* really is. Daphne first appears to us as a variable signifier, indicating a range of "feminine" types from fearful potential victim to knowing seductress. As such, one is tempted to read her in much the same light as Hammett's Bridget O'Shaughnessy or Chandler's Carmen Sternwood. But Daphne's patterns of signification involve more than simple questions of truth and falsehood, or sexual innocence and sexual knowledge, once Mosley puts her particular form of masquerade at the culturally charged crossroads of race and sex.

Throughout the text she changes identities. "Her face was beautiful. More beautiful than [her] photograph. Wavy hair so light brown that you might have called it blond from a distance, and eyes that were either green or blue depending on how she held her head. Her cheekbones were high but her face was full enough that it didn't make her seem severe." From this initial description of Daphne Monet, Mosley frames her identity as shifting and changing. Neither hair color nor eye color remains constant. The character of each depends entirely on the perspective of the viewer and on Daphne's own "positioning" of herself. The variable effect is part and parcel of Mosley's larger intention to unpack the categories governing cultural knowledge within the discursive field of *Devil in a Blue Dress* by creating characters who constantly violate the borders of those categories.

Daphne first represents herself as French, bringing Easy metaphorically back to his experiences of interracial sex during the war. But under stress, her accent noticeably slips away, sliding from French into something likely southern. She says to Rawlins after a passionate kiss, "Too bad we won't have a chance to get to know each other Easy. Otherwise I'd let you eat this little white girl up." The explicit invitation to enter this most unequivocally transgressive zone, is given yet another turn by Easy's inclination to see her (and Mosley's inclination to construct her) as shifting her identity even more radically. Her sexual aggressiveness is read as somehow even more than masculine—"I never knew a man who talked as bold as Daphne Monet." Mosley goes so far as having her urinate as loudly as a man. This gender shifting is set within the context of Daphne's indeterminate identity. "Daphne was like a chameleon lizard. She changed for her man. If he was a mild white man who was afraid to complain to the waiter she'd pull his head to her bosom and pat him. If he was a poor black man who had soaked up pain and rage for a lifetime she washed his wounds with a rough rag and licked the blood till it stanched."

Mosley gives Daphne's character yet another turn by revealing that in fact she is not "a little old white girl," but rather is "black." Her "true" identity is Ruby Hanks, the half sister of Frank Green, one of the novel's "heavies," a man as "black" as Daphne seems "white." "He was wearing a dark suit, so dark that you might have mistaken it for black. He wore a black shirt. His black shoe was on the cushion next to my head. There was a short-rimmed black Stetson on his head. His face was as black as the rest of him. The only color to Frank Green was his banana-colored tie, loosely knotted at his throat." This play of colors in Frank's description anticipates the familial conjunction of Frank and Daphne, for she is the high "yellow" in a field of black (and no doubt the offspring of another transgressive sexual union).

When Rawlins finally understands who (and what) Daphne/Ruby really is, he phrases that revelation in language consistent with the novel's decentering of conventional categories informing identity and cultural knowledge. "I had only been in an earthquake once but the feeling was the same: The ground under me seemed to shift. I looked at her to see the truth. But it wasn't there. Her nose, cheeks, her skin color—they were white. Daphne was a white woman. Even her pubic hair was barely bushy, almost flat." Daphne's straight pubic hair becomes a sign for the intentionalized indeterminateness of her identity. Significantly, given the cultural perspective on questions of race in the novel's represented world, this ultimate sign is sexual—the site of the most powerful form of transgression. But Easy Rawlins (Mosley, too) figures identity here as an absence. The shifting ground to which Easy refers indicates the entire set of understandings about "race" that the novel has sought to problematize and to deconstruct. There is no "truth" there, at least no truth in the social text that fetishes the outward signs of difference.

Just as in Bakhtin's view of the novel, the social text of race is incommensurate with what it seeks to represent or to signify. The detective, like the novel's seeker/heroes, discovers not only his (in this case) inadequacy, but also the profound inadequacy of the whole range of social matrices that presumably have constructed cultural knowledge. The mystery here is finally not about money or murder. Rather the mystery revealed here concerns the shifting nature of racial "being" and cultural knowing. By constructing *Devil in a Blue Dress* in this fashion, Mosley moves us into the realm of a socially constructed epistemology that is ever in motion.

In a larger sense this novel seems absolutely at home with much of the general trajectory of Afro-American fiction, particularly recent work with its emphasis on genealogy and origin. Perhaps better said, much of Afro-American fiction seems quite possibly to be following the trajectory of detective fiction, culturally encoded or conceived. The only sig-

nificant difference here is that Mosley actively embraces what in other venues is merely gestured at.

If one of the fundamental signs of the experience of difference is a disjunction between experience itself and the categories imposed on that experience, then such a condition mirrors the hybridized world outlined by Bakhtin. In a fictional work, this fundamental instability necessitates the kind of protagonist who seeks the resolution of the various tensions occasioned by this cultural instability. It seems to me that searchers in Afro-American fiction approximate the condition of detectives precisely because the assertion of the authentic self constitutes a transgressive act in a racist and sexist society—even if the self advanced is figured as multiple or shifting or indeterminate.

One thinks here of Milkman in Morrison's *Song of Solomon,* where the search is figured as a form of *genealogy.* Significantly, the final outcome of the dramatic action of the novel is represented as indeterminate. Not only is it indeterminate, but the indeterminacy is not a problem. Morrison's narrator reminds us that "it did not matter which one of them [Guitar or Milkman] would give up his ghost in the killing arms of his brother." Similarly, David Bradley's protagonist in *The Chaneysville Incident* (1981), John Washington, is a professional historian whose search for the truth about his father's death leads him to a fuller understanding of his own identity. In the process of seeking, Washington ultimately discards the intellectual tools of the historian, forsaking formal categories of intellectual discourse for an act of imaginative reconstruction that recreates the past, perhaps more than reconstructing it—so that the method of the search dismantles one of Washington's identities as it constructs another.

One thinks here, too, of Ishmael Reed's *Mumbo-Jumbo* (1972), where the search is for the text of blackness, the *Book of Thoth.* But the book itself is a variable signifier, elusive, almost Protean, as is the blackness it signifies. What Reed's HooDoo detective Papa LaBas finds is the indeterminacy of identity, a condition certified when the book itself is burned, leaving only a hybridized and multifaceted blackness, without even a variable or floating signifier. Reed's version of the seeker and the search, as well as Morrison's and Bradley's, have a great deal in common with the ones represented in the pages of *Devil in a Blue Dress.* The experience of transgressive difference deconstructs the idea of totality; and the novel form's inclination to engage in exactly such a project facilitates the aims of Afro-American seekers both in explicitly detective fictions such as Mosley's *Devil in a Blue Dress* and in much of the recent Afro-American novelistic tradition as a whole.

Greg Tate (essay date October 1992)

SOURCE: "Ain't That a Shamus," in *Village Voice Literary Supplement,* No. 109, October, 1992, p. 41.

[*In the following essay, Tate identifies the elements of Mosley's writing that give it literary weight in its examination of racial and interpersonal issues.*]

What makes Walter Mosley's mysteries so compelling isn't his man Easy Rawlins's powers of ratiocination but the black dick's racial metaphysics. Race politics foreshadow the action in these books the way decadence foreshadowed everything that happened in Raymond Chandler's. Mosley doesn't just raise the race card to thicken the plot. He beats you down with spades, then rubs your nose in ethnic stool. Says Easy Rawlins:

> I had played the game of "cops and niggers" before. The cops pick you up, take your name and fingerprints, then they throw you into a holding tank with other "suspects" and drunks. After you were sick from the vomit and foul language they'd take you to another room and ask why you robbed that liquor store or what did you do with the money? [*Devil in a Blue Dress*]

The spotlight Mosley throws on race as power game and psychoanalytic tool makes him matter more than his being a black guy writing detective fiction straight outta 1950s Compton. Mosley is a savvy observer-philosopher first, and a mystery writer second.

His black literary forebears are everywhere in evidence. Baldwin broke the Foucauldian ground Mosley likes to work, interrogating white supremacy everywhere, from the corridors of power to the souls of black folk; race is not so much Mosley's "theme" as the grid set on top of his American characters. Ellison's influence shows as Mosley works the paradox of how black folks' retarded social position provides certain intellectual and moral advantages. Rawlins tells the story:

> Mr. Todd Carter was so rich that he didn't even consider me in human terms. He could tell me anything. I could have been a prized dog that he knelt to and hugged when he felt low.
>
> It was the worst kind of racism. The fact that he didn't even recognize our difference showed that he didn't care one damn about me. But I didn't have the time to worry about it. I just watched him move his lips about lost love until, finally, I began to see him as some strange being. Like a baby who, grows to man-size and terrorizes his poor parents with his strength and his stupidity. [*Devil in a Blue Dress*]

In all of American fiction, only Richard Wright treats America's race problem more savagely as the shaper and breaker of men, women, and children. The black mystery's avant-garde—Chester Himes and his hoodoo stepchild, Ishmael Reed—would smile with recognition at every cartoonish plot turn, and at Mosley's wealth of exaggerated working-class character types. But Mosley's work is more psychologically insightful, empathetic, and pathos-ridden than that of Reed or Himes, and merely a hair less crazed with invention. In bridging the gap between naturalism and Negro-ism, Mosley creates queasily poignant moments that bring to mind his fellow Los Angelenophile, filmmaker Charles Burnett. . . .

Mosley writes in a page-turning style filled with tough, terse, sucker-punch sentences. *White Butterfly,* his third book in the Easy Rawlins series, lacks *Devil in a Blue Dress*'s big surprises, and *A Red Death*'s Herculean kitchen-sink subplotting. (Book two had tangents sprung loose from such fact-totems as the Holocaust, Garveyism, McCarthyism, black-Jewish relations, and black-church soap-operatic skullduggery all woven into a demented plot of domestic violence, madness, and murder.) However, for all the riches that preceded it, *White Butterfly* is the Easy Rawlins book with the heaviest heart, the deepest soul, the most boiling-over racial brain matter. Rawlins is so color-sensitive in this book that not even his librarian is spared the African-centric ire:

> To her Shakespeare was a god. I didn't mind that, but what did she know about the folk tales and riddles and stories colored folks had been telling for centuries? What did she know about the language we spoke?
>
> I always heard her correcting children's speech. "Not 'I is,'" she'd say. "It's 'I am.'"
>
> And, of course, she was right. It's just that little colored children listening to that proper white woman would never hear their own cadence in her words. They'd come to believe that they would have to abandon their own language and stories to become a part of her educated world. They would have to forfeit Waller for Mozart and Remus for Puck. They would enter a world where only white people spoke.

Easy Rawlins was born emotionally complex, ethically confusing, intellectually enraged, and engaged. In *A Red Death,* Rawlins is revealed as a property owner who pretends he's a handyman to throw black and white folks off his well-endowed hide. He is a college-educated war veteran who speaks mushmouth black English to stay down with the folk and to divert white anxieties about smart niggas.

As Rawlins matures in the first two books, his deceits seem

less strategic than eccentric, unanalyzed, maybe even counter-productive. *White Butterfly* pushes at Rawlins's existential doubt by way of the blues strains that turn up in his relationship with his younger, apprehensive wife. Even in the wake of raising an infant with her, Rawlins has told his hardworking spouse—a nurses' aide at the local hospital—nothing of his hidden wealth or his secret life as the 'hood's resident private eye. But she knows he's hiding something, denying her access to his life. The serial murders of prostitutes that are ostensibly the mystery element in *White Butterfly* are really just props for Mosley's handling of the Rawlinses' misshapen marriage:

> "If you love me you just take me like I am. I ain't never hurt you, have I?"
>
> Regina just stared.
>
> "Have I?"
>
> "No. You ain't laid a hand on me. Not that way."
>
> "What's that s'posed to mean?" . . .
>
> "You don't hit me but you do other things just as bad."
>
> "Like what?"
>
> Regina was looking at my hands. I looked down myself to see clenched fists.
>
> "Last night," she said. "What you call that?"
>
> "Call what?"
>
> "What you did to me. I didn't want none'a you. But you made me. You raped me."
>
> "Rape?" I laughed. "Man cain't rape his own wife."
>
> My laugh died when I saw the angry tears in Regina's eyes.

What emerges within Mosley's fluent mystery is a subtle essay on black male anxiety about openness, intimacy, and vulnerability. Mosley deftly meshes Rawlins's domestic troubles with the standard pulp fare: brutal cops, homicidal patriarchs, wicked sirens, surrealist nightmares. His crisp and writerly sleight-of-hand won't let you be distracted from the pulp by Rawlins's failure as a husband—but you know that is where Mosley's heart lies. In fact, the contrast between the profane and the profound dimensions of the story makes you wonder if Mosley will opt next to further deepen the genre with these sorts of interpersonal issues, as Chandler did around male-bonding in *The Long Goodbye*—or whether he'll move outside the genre altogether.

Madelyn Jablon (essay date 1997)

SOURCE:"Metafiction as Genre," in *Black Metafiction: Self-Consciousness in African American Literature,* University of Iowa Press, 1997, pp. 139-65.

[*In the following excerpt, Jablon examines Mosley's Easy Rawlins as a contemporary example of the archetypal figures of the American literary tradition.*]

Walter Mosley is a master magician who juggles the conventions of the [detective fiction] genre with issues of race. Tossing an array of items—history, politics, current events, and a detective in a dashiki—into the magician's hat assists Mosley in recasting the "whodunit" crime story. Although unique in its composition, *Black Betty* is the fourth novel in Mosley's Easy Rawlins Mystery Series, and like the others in the series, it contains everything that readers of hard-boiled detective fiction expect.

Although scholars may disagree about the origins and development of the detective novel, they agree about its central characteristics. Hard-boiled detective fiction is most often identified by the character of the detective who is driven by a personal commitment to right wrongs. Speculating on the origins of the genre, Richard Slotkin suggests that James Fenimore Cooper's Hawkeye or Natty Bumppo is the prototype of the modern-day hard-boiled detective. Such characters are "out to rescue people—usually women—from some kind of threat" and "they achieve the rescue by following a path of clues to a hidden goal." In addition to the characteristic detective, there is usually a "detective process." Stephano Tani explains this process as an "attempt to discover by rational means the solution to a mysterious occurrence—generally a crime—usually a murder." Finally, there is the anticipated solution to the mystery, a principal ingredient in detective fiction: the women are rescued, the murderers are discovered, the mystery is solved. In addition to detective, process, and solution, the genre is renowned for action-packed plots, sensationalistic violence, and gratuitous sex.

Several features of *Black Betty* fit these descriptions. Like the Cooper prototype, Mosley's detective rescues a woman by pursuing a series of clues concerning Betty's whereabouts to a hidden goal. In this novel, the goal is a servant's secluded house surrounded by a maze of shrubbery, resembling the house in Charles Chesnutt's *The House behind the Cedars*. Consistent with the genre, it is a fastpaced adventure story, both violent and sexy. Easy's memories of Elizabeth are riddled with a desire that ignites his passion for Elizabeth's daughter, Gwen. Easy makes amorous advances to Gwen in the cab of his truck. Several pages later, he is driving home with a pickax in his back. Solutions are proffered to several murders and the usual motive—greed—is disclosed. Order and justice are restored at the close of the novel.

While detective process and solution fit the mandates of the genre, the black detective differs from the prototype in several important ways. Unlike most detectives, Easy—Ezekiel—Rawlins is not a member of the Los Angeles police force. Instead, Rawlins works for himself: writing, directing, and producing "little pieces of history" that have previously been "unrecorded." The story that Easy tells is unrecorded because in 1961, "there wasn't a Negro in the world worthy of an article." The events that made history—the inauguration of President John F. Kennedy, above-and below-ground nuclear testing in the United States and Russia, the building of the Berlin Wall, the Bay of Pigs, and the trial of Adolf Eichmann—reflect the prejudices of those who wrote the news that made history. This record of historical events excludes black people. Easy knows that what passes as the truth is a fiction that denies black reality. Easy's truth is nowhere in this account, so he assumes the responsibility of telling it himself. With Martin Luther King, Jr., as his hero and inspiration, Easy shares his story, believing that "the world was changing and a black man in America had the chance to be a man for the first time in a hundred years." Being a man means telling the story that has been excluded and denied its reality. Like the Freedom Riders, Easy believes it is his responsibility to make the changes that might cost him his life and still not make the history books: "I didn't pay dues in the Southern Christian Leadership Conference or the NAACP. I didn't have any kind of god on my side. But even though the cameras weren't on me and JFK never heard my name, I had to make my little stand for what's right."

What's right for Easy is not the peaceful resistance of Martin Luther King, Jr., nor the steadfast determination of those who conducted voter-registration drives or desegregated schools. Nevertheless, Easy is incarcerated in a jail cell "designed to take the overflow on those special days when there was some kind of protest or other civil unrest." Although he may appear to have nothing in common with the heroes of the civil rights movement, upon closer scrutiny his actions reveal an affinity. He is jailed by the police for what he knows of their corrupt activities. He knows which ones of them are moonlighting from their jobs as police officers to work as hired gunmen. His brutal beating and illegal detainment are some of the routine scare tactics used by the police. Unable to uncover a warrant for his arrest, Faye Rabinowitz, an attorney who feels that "the people who run this world" are "the ones who should die," and state supreme

court judge Mellon, "outspoken critic of racism and champion of the rights of the poor," secure his release. Police records show no evidence of his arrest, but when Rabinowitz urges Easy to press charges, he says, "Maybe later. . . . Right now I got too much already to do." When she accuses him of shirking responsibility, he explains: "That man up there is a stone killer. You can't stop him with a writ and a lawsuit." Like the attorney, he knows of the corrupt activities of those who represent the law, but while Rabinowitz believes in legal recourse, Easy knows what every black man in 1961 knew, what Huey Newton, Eldridge Cleaver, and the Black Panthers tried to defend the community against: the law could not protect a black man who had been wrongfully beaten by the police. This reality affects the conclusion of the novel. Although the formulaic detective novel ends with justice restored, justice cannot be restored in the unjust society depicted in Mosley's novel.

Saul Lynx, a private investigator employed by a wealthy client, gets Easy involved in the case, but Easy refuses the generous and much-needed financial reward offered at its conclusion. A monetary reward would compromise his role of savior and guardian of the underprivileged. Such moral scruples are typical of detectives, but one of the things that distinguishes Easy from most detectives is the skillful way he synthesizes his private and public lives. Unlike the Chandlerian heroes, "detached" loners who seek and find "individual integrity," African American detectives like Easy Rawlins discover that "Chandlerian heroism is not an option." Like Grave Digger Jones and Coffin Ed Johnson, the heroes in Chester Himes' Harlem Detective Series, Easy is personally involved in his work. He has known Elizabeth since childhood, and he sees himself as a part of the community rather than as a loner.

Beside this "personal involvement," he is unique in his approach to the crime. It is a part of his busy day, which involves him in the multiple roles of detective, entrepreneur, father, and friend. Each day is orchestrated to take care of his personal business as well as the business of others. His own business includes several real estate ventures. As the story unfolds, we learn of his investment in Freedom's Plaza, a mall of shops "owned and patronized by black people." The building permit has been granted, but the city has issued an injunction to build a sewage treatment plant in its place. The city forecloses on the development and pays the "Negro investment group," Freedom's Trust, only "what the land is worth." Freedom's Trust goes bankrupt, the injunction is suspended, and the land is purchased from the city at cost by a white realtor who will profit from building the proposed mall. Easy uncovers the collaboration of Clovis, a secretary at Freedom's Trust, and Mason LaMone, the white realtor. A second investigation has him looking for the witness who called the police on Mouse. Mouse is determined to kill someone in retaliation for his prison sentence, so Easy arranges for him to kill a friend whose illness has made him eager to die. Easy is a family man despite his failed marriage. Although his wife has left him, he has found a family, one made up of people who need and want each other: Easy says, "The only agreement between us was love and mutual need." Easy's family consists of Jesus, or "Juice," a child rescued from prostitution, and Feather, whose white mother was murdered by her grandfather for "bearing a black child." Easy brags about his found family, even going so far as to suggest it is superior to biologically determined families: "He was my son. A son of preference. We weren't blood, but he wanted to live with me and I wanted to have him—how many fathers and sons can say that?" His concern for his business enterprises, his friends, and his family distinguishes Easy from most detectives. The detective in the dashiki is a community man whose story is told because it is typical. He frequently refers to the invisible poor and "men like me"—inserting them into history, recording their presence and explaining their lives:

> Men like John and me didn't have lives like the white men on TV had. We didn't roll out of bed for an eight-hour day job and then come home in the evening for *The Honeymooners* and a beer.
>
> We didn't do one thing at a time.
>
> We were men who came from poor stock. We had to be cooks and tailors and plumbers and electricians. We had to be our own cops and our own counsel because there wasn't anything for us down at City Hall.
>
> We worked until the job was done or until we couldn't work anymore. And even when we'd done everything we could, that didn't mean we'd get a paycheck or a vacation. It didn't mean a damn thing.

This life insists on its own telling. The episodic plot structure duplicates the multifarious quality of Easy's life. Not only will he write into history the story of a black detective, the "righter of wrongs," but he will make the effort to tell the whole story and include the untold stories of others. His story encompasses the stories of his friends and the stories of those who live in his neighborhood. The importance of this locus is not to be overlooked. Theodore O. Mason, Jr., notes that though the detective element and the search make Mosley's fiction of "a piece with a great deal of crime fiction," Mosley's decision to "present the black community as the dominant site of the novel's action rather than simply being the locus of exotic difference" makes his work unique to the genre of detective literature.

Easy assembles the pieces of an intricate puzzle to uncover Elizabeth's whereabouts and the murderers of her brother and two children. His act of deciphering the mystery of Elizabeth's whereabouts parallels the reader's act of deciphering text. Psychoanalytic readings of crime fiction explain this correspondence between reader and detective. According to Geraldine Pederson-Krag, the detective story is a non-threatening replay of the primal scene. In this family drama, the reader identifies with the child who is cast in the role of detective. The parent is the victim of the crime, and the secret crime is the sex act. According to this analysis, the child learns of his or her parent's sexual activity via detective work. Easy's search for Elizabeth (or Betty) fits this pattern because she introduces him to sex, and he fantasizes about her. The rescue is interspersed with memories of his desire. His longing for her is transferred to her daughter. This act of incest is avoided by Gwen's murder, which recasts Easy as surrogate parent and nurturer to the grieving Elizabeth. The story allows for the vicarious resolution of the reader's oedipal complex. The identification with Easy takes the reader through the stages of the child-parent relationship, which begins with the desire for the parent and ends with the child assuming the role of the parent's guardian or protector. This transition is evident in the passage below:

> For years after her kiss, I dreamed of it, yearned for it. And there she was, filled with passion and calling out for love. But not my love. Not me.
>
> I held her and ran my flat palms over her back and head. We slid down to the porch and she tucked up her legs so I could run my hands from her head to her feet; not a lover's stroke but a mother's, a mother's whose child has come awake from a terrible nightmare.

In the closing scene, Easy chooses to obey protective impulses and suppress sexual ones. Readers have been escorted through the oedipal complex and its resolution. Gwen's murder and his decision to parent Elizabeth rather than act a lover toward her enable Easy to maintain the "loner" stance typical of most detectives. Like most detectives, Easy finds that women distract his attention from his work.

As scholars of the African American detective novel note, race alters the genre in important ways. In his study of the ethnic detective, Peter Freeze identifies a "cultural mediator," or a narrator who introduces the reader to an unfamiliar ethnic culture. This cultural mediator allows the novel to "fulfill the function of anthropological handbooks" by introducing readers to a foreign culture. Similarly, by relying on the theories of Bakhtin and Lukács, Theodore Mason describes the interplay of cultures in the Rawlins mysteries as an act of *transgression,* a "crossing of categories or the violation of social protocols about social, cultural and historical identity." In his analysis, "cultural knowledge" becomes represented initially as racial knowledge or, more precisely, "the negation of racial protocols." Regardless of whether it is intended to challenge or educate, cultural knowledge affects the character of the detective and the solution of the crime-story by precluding the return to order and justice that serves as the standard close for detective fiction. In ***Black Betty,*** the police are criminals, the lawyers are motivated by self-interest, and courts are at the disposal of those who have money. In a two-page final chapter, Mosley describes the trial and its outcome. Some, but not all, of the police are indicted. The wealthy son, an accomplice to murder, goes free. Elizabeth is destroyed by the trial, and the accusation of her working as Cain's concubine is used to break the will that made her heir to a fortune. Mofass wrests his business from the hands of a conniving secretary, Clovis. Mouse kills terminally ill Martin, and Easy signs on to the construction crew to lay the foundation for the shopping plaza. In this instance, Easy decides to do what the courts don't by taking justice into his own hands and enacting revenge: "No one ever suspected that it was me who put the extra sand in the cement that made it crumble only one year after the opening ceremonies." This is revenge for being cheated out of Freedom's Plaza. The message isn't that the right will be victorious or that the system of justice will punish the guilty. Instead, Easy employs an Islamic code of justice that includes self-protection and retaliation. When laws fail to protect and punish, Easy accomplishes these things on his own. Mosley rewrites the message of the detective genre and makes it relevant to the lives of those who are denied power by the legal, judicial, and social institutions.

Easy says that though he had his foot on the chest and a shotgun pointed at the temple of the man who called him "nigger," he "didn't enjoy it." Although this may seem a peculiar moment for genuflection, he adds: "One of the problems with so many oppressed people is that they don't have the stomach to give what they get. I hurt that simple white man because I was scared of him. If he'd called me boy or nigger one more time I might have started gibbering myself." Mosley explains the fear that leads to violence—for those who haven't experienced it themselves—but this information is coupled with the observation that most oppressed people can't "give what they get," an implicit admonishment to toughen up. Its irony is evident, given that the genre is founded on the assumption that ethics is a virtue. Outside a boxing parlor, an old man approaches Easy, who has just been knocked down. The old man offers assistance and remarks: "It's always a black man out there hittin' another black man so all the white folks could laugh: 'look at that fool . . . beatin' the blood outta his own brother'." Regardless of whether we agree with this sociology of "black-on-black" violence, remarks such as this alter the usual message of detective fiction, extending its scope beyond platitudes about crime and punishment, truth and justice, to encompass the complex realities of life.

In "Literature under the Table: The Detective Novel and Its Social Mission," Ernest Kaemmel argues that the genre is a "child of capitalism." According to Kaemmel, the crime represents an attack on private property. Authorized institutions are incapable of bringing it to justice, but an individual representing the oppressed classes can. This interpretation is validated by Mosley's novel, which shows in the character of Easy and in the observations concerning oppressed classes that the hope for ethics resides in the lower classes and oppressed peoples. Although rooted in historical analysis rather than Marxism, Slotkin argues similarly when he says that the present-day detective hero is like Sam Spade, "a person who finally ends up doing the work of the law—but who stands finally outside the law as well."

Like the real world, both our understanding and the events are colored by attitudes toward race, toward trying to second-guess people because of who they are and where they come from. Easy sees the cruelest forms of racism and oppression not just in the effects on the community—poverty, drugs, and gambling—but in the effects on individuals such as Elizabeth Eady (Black Betty), a servant sought by her affluent employers, the Cains. She has been employed by an affluent white man who attempts to make amends for his sexual exploitation of her by naming her his heir. His widow, son, and lawyer kill her son and daughter and will do anything necessary to claim the estate. They hire a detective, Saul Lynx, who in turn hires Easy, who is known "for finding people in the colored part of town." Easy certainly seems to know everyone, but his investigation reveals that he has been hired by the master to punish the slave. The Cains want to murder Elizabeth to reclaim the estate that has been bequeathed to her by the repentant Mr. Cain.

While Easy's almost instinctual distrust of white people saves his life repeatedly, a message about blue-eyed devils and the evil inherent in whiteness is too simplistic for Mosley. To erase whatever doubt the reader may have concerning Mosley's intent on this matter, he has Easy's life saved by the white detective who hired him. Saul Lynx puts himself between his buddy and the bullet intended for him. At the hospital, awaiting a report on his condition, Easy meets Saul's black wife and infant son, who, Rawlins says, "has very little of Saul in his dark features." This episode complicates what Easy has learned about white people from Elizabeth's ordeal. The descendants of Cain are momentarily redeemed. What Easy says about the Horns, the neighbors who care for Juice and Feather, is further evidence of his stubborn, ironic disavowal of racial stereotypes: "The [Horns] were real people and so I rarely thought about them being white."

Black Betty is told from the first-person point of view, and while there is no reference to the writing of the text or the assembling of the story for literary production, it is a "speakerly text," which reads as if it is being spoken. The cadence and inflection of Easy's speech reveal his character, and it is largely by his voice that we know him. Easy addresses an audience unfamiliar with the world he inhabits. His voice chaperons the reader on a guided tour through the "bad" part of town. This voice is that of the "cultural mediator" discussed earlier. A clue to the fact that he is talking to outsiders is his repeated efforts to explain life on the street. Reference has already been made to his explanations of the working life of a "poor man." Additional examples provide insight into other aspects of a poor man's life: "Poor men are always ready to die. We always expect that there is somebody out there who wants to kill us." Insight into his friendships: "One of the reasons I was broke is that I gave my money away to friends who had less than I did. That's a poor man's insurance: Give when you got it and hope that they remember and give back when you're in need." And his attitudes toward war and death: "Behind every poor old man there's a line of death. Siblings and children, lovers and wives. There's disease and no doctor. There's war, and war eats poor men like an aardvark licking up ants."

Easy serves as an interlocutor, a narrator who uses standard English to bracket dialogue in the vernacular. He even interrupts conversations among characters to instruct his readers in what is going on. When Jackson Blue opens the door with a mean "What the fuck you think you poundin' on, motherfucker?" Easy's "Who axin'?" is preceded by this explanation: "One of the things the street teaches you is that if you bend over you're bound to get kicked." He interrupts another anecdote to explain his use of the expression "down home":

> I always talk about down home like it really was home. Like everybody who looked like me and talked like me really cared about me. I knew that life was hard, but I hoped that if someone stole from me it would be because they were hungry and needed it. But some people will tear you down just to see you fall. They'll do it even if your loss is their own.
>
> They will laugh at your misfortune and sit next to you at misery's table.

In both passages the narrator's explanation of events illustrates his skill with both formal English and the vernacular. Easy moves easily from the language that he uses to address his audience to the language of the street. His explanation of "down home" provides the pick necessary to mine the rich vein of ironic street talk. Here Easy tells his uninitiated audience that things aren't really what they are said to be and that "down home" is a place where people don't act like family, but act instead out of malice and evil. Easy knows that words deceive and he knows how to use that to advantage.

Moreover, he knows when to use the vernacular to his advantage in conversation with whites: "Marlon wasn't nowhere to be seen. I spoke in a dialect that they would expect. If I gave them what they expected then they wouldn't suspect me of being any kind of real threat." Easy knows the power of language. He learned it when Elizabeth chided him for saying she was *almost* the prettiest woman he had ever seen. Easy remembers this lesson so well, he assumes the role of teacher with others. When Lynx refers to Elizabeth as a girl, Easy is quick to correct him: "She's almost fifty years old, man. She's a woman." Education, language, and politics are interwoven in this conversation between Easy and Jackson:

> "Did you ever get that degree from UCLA?"
>
> "Shit. Motherfuckers wanted me to study some kinda language.
>
> Uh-uh, man. I walk on the ground an' I talk like my people talk."
>
> "But you could do somethin', Jackson. You're smart."
>
> "Naw, Easy, I cain't do nuthin'."
>
> "Why not? Of course you could."
>
> "Naw, man. I been a niggah too long." He said it as if he were proud of the fact.
>
> "You think that Martin Luther King is down south marchin' an' takin' his life in his hands just so you could be gamblin' and actin' like a niggah?"
>
> "I ain't got nuthin' to do with him, Easy. You know I be livin' my life the onliest way I can."

Jackson's refusal to speak formal English, to enter the world outside the black community, is respected by Easy. Although Easy speaks whatever language is necessary, he respects the person who chooses to speak only in the vernacular. Hence passages like the above, rich in street talk, dwarf the bidialectism of Easy. What is usually represented negatively in detective fiction is presented as a positive here. The reader respects Jackson for his decision, just as he or she comes to respect Bruno, Mouse, and all the other characters who are part of Easy's world. This community is neither more nor less violent or irrational than the world that detective literature has traditionally portrayed as its apotheosis.

Easy tackles the subject of language and then moves on to the latest controversies in education and censorship. At the beginning of the second chapter, he picks up a copy of *Huck-*

leberry Finn and says, "A few liberal libraries and the school system had wanted to ban the book because of the racist content. Liberal-minded whites and blacks wanted to erase racism from the world. I applauded the idea but my memory of Huckleberry wasn't one of racism. I remembered Jim and Huck as friends out on the river. I could have been either one of them."

The novel indulges this similarity. As first-person narrator, Easy resembles Huck, but when he puts a white sheet over his head and lies down in the back of his car so Lynx can gain access to a high-security Hollywood neighborhood, he evokes an image of Jim lying on the bottom of the canoe. Whereas the duke and king double-cross Jim by trying to sell him, the people who hire Easy—Lynx and the Cains—are the very people who wish to kill Elizabeth. Like Jim's floating down the Mississippi, Easy's involvement in the case proves increasingly dangerous as the police try to pin the murder on him. A final similarity is the episodic structure. Just as the first part of *Huckleberry Finn* contains repeated episodes of Huck and Jim interacting with people on land and retreating to the community of two aboard the raft, the first part of the novel contains repeated episodes of Easy pursuing information about Betty's location. Finding Elizabeth is like reaching Cairo. If, as Easy says, "Mr. Clemens knew that all men were ignorant and wasn't afraid to say so," Mosley knows it too. He shares Twain's cynicism when he observes the effects of racism. He addresses a favorite subject of Twain's when he writes: "Law is just the other side of the coin from crime . . . they're both the same and interchangeable. Criminals were just a bunch of thugs living off what honest people and rich people made. The cops were thugs too; paid by the owners of property to keep the other thugs down."

Huckleberry Finn isn't the only work of literature implicated in the novel. If Easy is a composite of Huck *and* Jim, he is also the invisible man. This affinity is suggested in the opening pages of the novel when Saul Lynx approaches Easy asleep on his porch: "I didn't want him to see me with no clothes on. It was still in a dream, as if I was vulnerable if someone could see my skin. I wanted to linger in the shadows, but I'd learned that you can't hide in your own house— if somebody knows where you live you've got to stand up." Like the invisible man, Easy realizes that he is invisible and that it is impossible to hide, even in his own home. Like the invisible man and his predecessors, he has tried to fit into white society but comes to realize that he can never be the successful businessman he aspired to be: "I had reached out for the white man's brass ring and got caught up short. . . . I knew the world wasn't going to let me be an upright businessman. It was just that I had worked so hard. Since I was a child I worked the daylight hours; sweeping, gardening, delivering, I'd done every kind of low job, and I wanted my success. I wanted it—violently."

He also realizes that his life will be filled with "violence" and "insanity" and "that feeling of anger wrapped tight under [his] skin." Like the invisible man, he realizes that, to the police, "all blacks were criminals," and he is haunted by nightmares that reflect his fear:

> I was running with a mob of black men. In pursuit of us were ravens and dogs followed by rabid white men and white women—the white people were naked and hairless. Horses with razor hooves galloped among them and a searing wind blew. We were all running but every black man trying to get away was also pushing his brothers down. And every man that fell was set upon by dogs with hungry rats dangling down from between their legs.

Toni Morrison concludes her theoretical treatise on American literature, "My project is an effort to avert the critical gaze from the racial object to the racial subject; from the described and imagined to the describers and imaginers." Within this purview, the absence of the African presence in American literature becomes as significant as the presence of it. Elizabeth Eady epitomizes this absence. She is the missing subject of the novel, the empty center that acts as a centrifugal force controlling characters and events. She explodes beyond the boundaries in the imaginings of others. Although many of the characters have nicknames (Bluto gets his from wearing the blue shoes he won in a bet from a white man who was so angry about having to give them up that he dyed them blue; Ed Sullivan for the funny way his head sits on his shoulders—no neck), Elizabeth Eady's nickname, Black Betty, makes her color and race the foremost thing about her, a pronouncement that precedes her given name. Black Betty may be a play on brown betty, a sweet, fruity dessert, for all regard her as a "dish" to be consumed and discarded. Easy may correct Saul's word choice when he refers to her as a girl, but when he mentions Elizabeth Eady to Easy her name strikes a "dark chord" in the back of his mind, one that fit with "the humid September heat—and with my dreams." Saul presents a photograph to Easy, who focuses on her blackness and sexuality:

> Its colors were rose-brown and tan instead of black and white. It wasn't a posed portrait, but a kind of snapshot. A young woman on the front porch of a small house. She was smiling at the time, leaning awkwardly against the doorjamb. She was tall and big-boned and very dark, even the rose coloring couldn't hide Betty's blackness. Her mouth was open as if she were smiling and flirting with the photographer. It brought a sense of intimacy that few amateur photographs have. Intimacy but not warmth. Black Betty wasn't your warm sort of home-making girl.

Easy's description begins with what he sees in the photograph, moves to what he imagines, and concludes with what he knows about Elizabeth from direct experience. All three of these ways of knowing contribute to his sense of her identity. Even his actual experiences with Elizabeth are affected by his imaginings and his memory. He knew her when he was a twelve-year-old boy growing up in the Fifth Ward of Houston, Texas. She was the woman every boy fantasized about. He followed her around and was flattered when she asked him to do errands for her. This childhood infatuation prompts Easy to pursue the case: he wants to be her rescuer. The protective feelings he has toward Elizabeth are identical to those he feels toward his orphaned children, Feather and Juice. This desire to protect, to father, is complicated by what he knows about the life of this beautiful woman. He knows that she will be used by men like Rufus, a Houston beau who assaults her on a mattress between two buildings, and Cain, the wealthy employer who exploited her and deprived her of her children.

Everyone is searching for her, and while her life illustrates to Easy the tragic fate of too many beautiful black women, it takes on a different significance for others. She is maid and servant to Mrs. Cain. She is concubine and means of redemption for Mr. Cain. She is friend in need to her brother, Marlon, who dies in an effort to save her. She is the unknown mother of Terry and Gwen, children who are murdered by those looking to kill her. Easy's remark—"Miss Eady is a black woman and there's a whole lotta people wanna see her"—suggests that she is the African "other" that Toni Morrison recognizes in American literature:

> This African other became the means of thinking about body, mind, chaos, kindness and love; provided the occasion for exercises in the absence of restraint, the presence of restraint, the contemplation of freedom and of aggression; permitted opportunities for the exploration of ethics and morality, for meeting the obligations of the social contract, for bearing the cross of religion and following out the ramifications of power.

Elizabeth embodies sexuality and in so doing signals an absence of restraint for Cain and its presence for Easy. She serves as a means of sin and redemption for Cain and an opportunity for Easy to test his self-control. Finally, she represents freedom from Cain's wife and the unwritten and ongoing history of the black woman's bondage and persecution for Easy.

When Easy gives Elizabeth the news that her children have been murdered, he has to restrain her. In this scene, readers witness the confusion of paternal and sexual roles. The introduction of the mirror, a renowned symbol in detective literature and metafiction, further complicates the description:

> I was holding Betty in front of a long slender mirror that was attached to the door leading to her tiny bedroom. Both of her breasts were out and she struggled with the strength of a mother fighting to save her child. With a great heave she pulled one arm free and let fly with a china cup that she'd grabbed. The mirror shattered in place, our images froze for a second in a thousand slender shards, and then fell to the floor giving me the distinct impression that it was both of our lives that had been splintered and destroyed.

The shattered mirror reflects the inseparability of Elizabeth and Easy, the victim and the rescuer. It also suggests the inseparability of the black man's and black woman's fates. The mirror does more than reflect the entanglement of two lives, however; it also reminds readers that the story is Easy's and that Elizabeth can never escape the role of the object. We never know her without his vision and understanding filtering her image. The postmodern symbol has added significance in detective fiction. Tani reads its presence as an indication of the relationship between the detective process and time. According to Tani, the mirror is the present distorted view of the crime, which occurred in the past. Easy's view of the past and his efforts to resurrect it culminate in the breaking of the mirror, asserting freedom from the past. The shattering of the mirror gives rise to a view beyond the boundaries of fiction, an acknowledgment of the stories that will go untold:

> In the early sixties nearly everybody was working. On the bus there were mainly old people and young mothers and teenagers coming in late to school.
>
> Most of them were black people. Dark-skinned with generous features. Women with eyes so deep that most men can never know them. Women like Betty who'd lost too much to be silly or kind. And there were the children, like Spider and Terry Tonce were, with futures so bleak that it could make you cry just to hear them laugh. Because behind the music of their laughing you knew there was the rattle of chains. Chains we wore for no crime; chains we wore for so long they melded with our bones. We all carry them but nobody can see it—not even most of us.
>
> All the way home I thought about freedom coming for us at last. But what about all those centuries in chains? Where do they go when you get free?

This subtext on freedom transforms the genre of detective fiction, taking it one step beyond the hard-boiled detective story. If the trend has been to move from a simplistic good versus bad, law versus criminal, to a more complex vision that questions fixed definitions of these terms as well as their dialectical relationships, the African American detective novel projects the genre further down the path of ambiguity, so that the idea of right and wrong as fixed categories seems a distant memory. The interjection of race and class in Mosley's **Black Betty** illustrates the relativity of such terms as "good" and "bad" and demonstrates that different codes of behavior operate in different contexts. It topples the belief in universal values and encourages the audience to reconsider the role of the individual in taking justice into his own hands, in acting in socially responsible ways, in choosing not to interact with the alien, imperfect, dangerous world outside the black community.

FURTHER READING

Criticism

Birkerts, Sven. "The Socratic Method." *The New York Times Book Review* (9 November 1997): 11.
   A highly complimentary review of Mosley's eighth novel.

Ferrandino, Joseph. Review of *A Red Death,* by Walter Mosley. *San Francisco Review of Books* 116 (Fall 1991): 38.
   Notes the literary weight of Mosley's second novel.

Friedman, Robert. "Walter Mosley Gets Platonic with His Thoughtful Ex-Con, Socrates." *The Detroit News* (6 December 1997): 34D.
   A favorable review of Mosley's second novel outside the Easy Rawlins series, *Always Outnumbered, Always Outgunned.*

Hitchens, Christopher. "The Tribes of Walter Mosley." *Vanity Fair,* 56, No. 2 (February 1993): 46.
   Discusses Mosley's career, especially his attention to relations between blacks and Jews in his novels.

Jones, Malcolm. Review of *Devil in a Blue Dress,* by Walter Mosley. *Newsweek,* 116 (9 July 1990): 65.
   A favorable review of Mosley's first novel.

Klett, Rex. Review of *Black Betty,* by Walter Mosley. *Library Journal,* 119 (1 May 1994): 141.
   Identifies Mosley as a top-ranking writer of mysteries.

Ott, Bill. Review of *R. L.'s Dream,* by Walter Mosley. *Booklist,* 91 (1-15 June 1995): 1684.
   Finds Mosley's first novel outside the Easy Rawlins series as distinctive as the detective stories.

Additional coverage of Mosley's life and career is contained in the following sources published by Gale: *Authors and Artists for Young Adults,* **Vol. 17;** *Black Writers 2,* **1994;** *Contemporary Authors,* **Vol. 142;** *Contemporary Black Biography,* **Vol. 5; and** *Contemporary Literary Criticism,* **Vol. 97.**

Flora Nwapa
1931-1993

(Full name Flora Nwapa-Nwakuche) Nigerian novelist, poet, short story writer, and children's author.

INTRODUCTION

The first African woman novelist, as well as the first to publish her works in English, Nwapa examined in her novels and short stories the evolving status of women in modern Nigerian society. In a country torn by brutal civil wars, social conflict, and economic hardship, Nwapa's female characters are able to move beyond the traditional Igbo, or east Nigerian, roles of wife and mother to establish themselves as significant social, economic, and spiritual forces within their culture. While early critics of African literature tended to ignore Nwapa's contribution to the canon, later commentators recognized in her work an important use of folk language and the oral tradition as well as a vivid depiction of village women's lives.

Biographical Information

Nwapa was born in Oguta, in eastern Nigeria. The eldest of six children, she grew up listening to the folk songs and stories of the women in her region, an experience she later used in her writing. Nwapa left Oguta to finish her education in Port Harcourt and then Lagos. In 1957 she graduated with a bachelor's degree from the University of Ibadan, and then attended Edinburgh University in Scotland, where she earned a degree in education in 1958. When she returned to Nigeria, Nwapa served as an education officer in Calabar and taught English and geography in eastern Nigeria. In 1966 civil war broke out in Nigeria, forcing many citizens to relocate. Nwapa and her husband were made to leave their home in Lagos and return to Oguta. At this time, she began seriously pursuing a career in writing, publishing her first two novels, *Efuru* (1966) and *Idu* (1970), with the English company Heinemann's African Writers Series before moving to a Nigerian publisher with *This Is Lagos, and Other Stories* (1971). Although she was able to reach more Nigerian readers this way, Nwapa found that promotion of her work outside the country was severely limited. Unsatisfied, Nwapa founded her own publishing company, Tana Press, in 1975, and its offshoot, Flora Nwapa and Company. Nwapa continued writing and publishing, as well as holding a number of government and university posts, until her death from pneumonia in 1993.

Major Works

Nwapa's first novel, *Efuru,* takes place in Oguta, Nwapa's home community, and tells the story of Efuru, a beautiful, intelligent, and successful woman who cannot bear children. In a society where motherhood is seen as the fundamental purpose of women, Efuru is considered a failure despite her many accomplishments. After two disappointing marriages, Efuru finds her place in the community as the worshiper of the lake deity Uhamiri (known in Igbo culture as the lady of the lake) although she continues to struggle with a sense of deficiency. In her next novel, *Idu,* Nwapa further explored the plight of a childless woman trying to fit into her society. Happily married, Idu eventually gives birth to a son and is pregnant again when her husband dies. Unable to face life alone, Idu wills herself to die. After *Idu,* Nwapa began publishing short stories and children's books. *This Is Lagos, and Other Stories,* which appeared in 1971, focuses largely on young people who move from village life to the larger city of Lagos. In this collection, Nwapa also began examining in fiction the civil war that devastated Nigeria beginning with a military coup in 1966. She further explored themes related to the war in her novel *Never Again* (1975)—which reflects Nwapa's antiwar sentiments—and in *Wives at War, and Other Stories* (1975), in which Nwapa examined the effects of the war on the women of Nigeria. In her next novel, *One Is Enough* (1981), Nwapa returned to the theme of a childless woman negotiating an independent life for herself despite societal strictures. Her heroine in *One Is Enough* is Amaku, who leaves her derisive husband and his family to move to Lagos. There she becomes a successful, if somewhat shady, businesswoman, and falls in love with a priest. When he offers to leave the church and marry her after she becomes pregnant with twins, Amaku refuses, telling him she has had enough of marriage and wifehood. In *Women Are Different* (1986), Nwapa continued to examine the place of women in Nigerian society and the constant tension between individual and community in modern Africa.

Critical Reception

Critical response to Nwapa's work was initially lukewarm to negative. Early critics of African literature tended to consider her focus on the lives of village women narrow and lacking in substance. But with the rise of feminist literary criticism and African studies, Nwapa began receiving recognition as an important chronicler of women's experience in postcolonial Africa, as well as of the scourge of civil war and its effects on the people of Africa. Critics have pointed to her use of the Igbo dialect, folktales, and to the influence of the oral tradition to emphasize her significance as a Nigerian writer. While virtually ignored upon its initial publication, *Efuru* is now considered a classic of African literature. Many commentators have objected to Nwapa's apparently amoral authorial distance from her heroines' actions--particularly Idu's seemingly needless death at the end of *Idu* and Amaku's triumph as a woman of uncertain repute both in business and her personal life in *One Is Enough*—but Nwapa defended her options as a writer in an interview: "If the evils are relevant to the stories I am telling, I will include them; it does not mean that I approve of it." As both a writer and a publisher, Nwapa is highly regarded as a gifted contributor to African literature, and her works are considered by many scholars to be classics.

PRINCIPAL WORKS

Efuru (novel) 1966
Idu (novel) 1970
This Is Lagos, and Other Stories (short stories) 1971
Emeka: Driver's Guard [illustrated by Roslyn Isaacs] (juvenilia) 1972
Never Again (novel) 1975
Wives at War, and Other Stories (short stories) 1975
My Animal Number Book (juvenilia) 1977
My Tana Colouring Book (juvenilia) 1978
MammyWater [illustrated by Obiora Udechukwu] (juvenilia) 1979
The Adventures of Deke (juvenilia) 1980
Journey to Space [illustrated by Chinwe Orieke] (juvenilia) 1980
The Miracle Kittens [illustrated by Emeka Onwudinjo] (juvenilia) 1980
One Is Enough (novel) 1981
Cassava Song and Rice Song (poetry) 1986
Women Are Different (novel) 1986

CRITICISM

Naana Banyiwa-Horne (essay date 1986)

SOURCE: "African Womanhood: The Contrasting Perspectives of Flora Nwapa's *Efuru* and Elechi Amadi's *The Concubine*," in *Ngambika: Studies of Women in African Literature,* edited by Carole Boyce Davies and Anne Adams Graves, Africa World Press, Inc., 1986, pp. 119-29.

[*In the following essay, Banyiwa-Horne examines the differing views of female identity in Africa as portrayed in* Efuru *and Elechi Amadi's novel* The Concubine, *arguing that Nwapa presents a more fully developed characterization of womanhood than Amadi's.*]

The question of African womanhood, though not given much consideration in critical evaluations of African literature until recent years, is one of the subjects that often finds its way into the writings of both male and female authors from the continent. Images of African womanhood abound in the literature, with some male authors giving as much exposure to the subject as female ones. In fact, some of the most fascinating and exotic women in fiction have been created by male writers. Cyprian Ekwensi's Jagua Nana is a novel by that name, and Wole Soyinka's Simi in *The Interpreters* readily come to mind.

A close look at the various images of African womanhood provided in the literature reveals that, to a considerable extent, depictions of African women in the literature by African woman writers differ from the images presented by their male counterparts. By virtue of their shared gender experiences, women writers are inclined to depict female characters in more realistic terms, with a great deal of insight, and in meaningful interaction with their environment. Also women writers tend to create a woman's world in which women characters exist in their own right, and not as mere appendages to a male world. There are exceptions, of course, but in the main, women authors explore alternate possibilities for self-actualization outside the sexual roles that are open to their women characters.

On the other hand, male depictions of female characters are often from a fiercely male perspective, reflecting male conceptions, or rather misconceptions, of female sexuality. Men writers tend to overplay the sexuality of their female characters, creating the impression that women have no identity outside their sexual roles. Their women are seen primarily in relation to male protagonists and in secondary roles. These characters usually serve to enhance the images of the male protagonists who occupy the central positions in the works. Furthermore, male images of African womanhood tend to be idealized and romanticized. There is little or no psychological growth in such portraitures which seems to suggest they are largely male fantasies of womanhood. The above does not suggest that every African male writer dabbles in stereotypes of African womanhood. There are brilliant exceptions. But generally, male depictions of African womanhood conform to the above stated observations.

These contentions are brought home forcefully when one examines two works that share a lot of superficial similarities—Flora Nwapa's *Efuru* and Elechi Amadi's *The Concubine.* The term superficial is employed here to qualify the similarities between the two novels, because they are apparent mainly in the surface structure of the two works but cannot be sustained in any in-depth analysis of the themes, particularly as they reveal Nwapa's and Amadi's perspectives of African womanhood.

The titles of both novels suggest that a female character is central to each work. Nwapa's novel revolves around Efuru, whose name provides the title for the work. In Amadi's novel too, Ihuoma, a woman, plays a central role. Efuru and Ihuoma have a lot in common; they are exceptional in many respects. Moreover, both works are set in rural Igbo villages, and in both, the supernatural plays a dominant role in the lives of the women. The similarities, however, only apply to the raw materials the two authors employ in their works. Nwapa and Amadi utilize their materials in very distinct ways resulting in contrasting portrayals of their main female characters.

The following exploration of the attitudes of the two authors to the worlds they create, to their characters, and to their use of the supernatural reveals the two very different perspectives: Nwapa's *Efuru* provides a feminine perspective of African womanhood and gives a more complex treatment of the female character, while Amadi's *The Concubine* provides a perspective that is male and limiting.

In rural Ibgoland, where *Efuru* and *The Concubine* are set, close-knit family structures predominate, and everyone knows and is related to everyone else either by blood or by marriage. Each person's business is that of the entire community. No occurrence is sacrosanct. Both Amadi and Nwapa excel in creating the fabric and texture of their rural communities, bringing their characters and their worlds vividly to life for the reader. One leaves both novels with the feeling of having intimate knowledge of the fictional worlds and their inhabitants. The attitudes, beliefs, fears, loves, strengths and weaknesses of both individuals and the community at large are made apparent through the descriptions and the dialogue employed. There is very little authorial commentary in either work, though Amadi utilizes this technique a little more than Nwapa.

Nwapa depends almost exclusively on dialogue to reveal Efuru's world, and she proves very successful at it. Her novel is filled with the daily conversation mainly of women, a technique that captures most effectively the oral-aural nature of the world she unfolds. The constant banter of women reveals character as much as it paints a comprehensive, credible, social canvas against which Efuru's life can be assessed. The total world view is brought to life through dialogue. In commenting on this technique Maryse Condé observes that

> . . . by making her heroine unique among her fellow-villagers and by reporting the unanimously hostile and adverse comments of the other women on every one of Efuru's decisions and actions, Flora Nwapa gives, in fact, a disturbing picture of narrow-mindedness, superstition, malevolence, and greed and fear in traditional Africa and might go contrary to what she has thought to defend. In depicting her minor characters, she conveys a very poor impression of her society. Her men are weak, dissolute and irrational. Her women, a formidable gallery of malicious gossipers.

Condé, apparently disturbed by Nwapa's frankness in bringing to life her women characters with their idiosyncrasies and their entire baggage of attitudes, concludes that the result of Nwapa's technique goes contrary to her objectives. She is of the impression that Nwapa is not a conscious craftsperson. But on the contrary, what she interprets as Nwapa's weakness is one of her fortes—a conscious manipulation of dialogue in the revelation not so much of individual personality as in the creation of a tableau against which social values and attitudes can be evaluated.

The "formidable gallery of malicious gossipers" as Condé sees Nwapa's women, is definitely more than just that. They enable Nwapa to portray her world from the perspective of women. She brings out quite clearly the ways her women view the world in which they live, and their reactions not only to the other womenfolk, but to those aspects of life that touch directly on their lives as women. The thought patterns of the individual personalities as they comment on and react to Efuru are revealed. Of course, the comments of the women on Efuru's life reveal their envy, their own shortcomings, and their aspirations; but that is human nature, and Nwapa does a good job of revealing character. After all, who among the village gossips would not want to be beautiful and prosperous? Which of the married women would not bask in the attention Efuru's husband lavishes on her? Above all, which woman would not wish to be appreciated for herself rather than for her childbearing ability? Even as the women decry Efuru's beauty, her leaving her child with a maid in order to pursue her profession as a trader, or her going to the stream with her husband, their reactions reveal the restricted, limited sense of accomplishment in their own lives.

Efuru's infertility is a source of concern, yes, and the constant lamenting of her condition, more by other women than by herself, reveals the importance her society attaches to childbearing. But, at the same time, Efuru's undaunted effort to live her life as fully as possible, regardless of this shortcoming, is striking. Her misfortune does not diminish the awe in which the other women hold her, and this is equally reflected in the envious comments they pass on her. What Nwapa achieves through her setting, therefore, is a lifelike recreation of the world of women in her rural Igbo community.

Elechi Amadi also employs similar tools in depicting his world and its attitudes. The world he projects, however, is a male world, and the voices heard are mainly male voices. The statements made by these voices and even by the authorial voice reflect not just a masculine attitude to women but a chauvinistic one. When friends and relatives assemble to celebrate the second burial of Ihuoma's husband, Amadi portrays his men as a dignified group while his women are bunched together as a cantankerous lot—"The old men were served. As they crunched their kola nuts slowly they talked to each other with a dignified buzz, an octave lower than the high-pitched, piping, market-chatter of the women."

His male characters consistently pass disparaging comments about their women. Madume dismisses his wife with the statement, "Women argue forwards and backwards." Wakiri confides in his friend Ekwueme, "when it comes to nagging I treat all women as children." Wigwe, a dignified elder, advises his son to regard his wife as "a baby needing constant correction." Ekwueme, the major male protagonist, sees all women as stupid and horrible and dismisses them as unworthy of him. Even Ihuoma, who is acknowledged as being superior to other women, does not escape Ekwueme's deprecations. He perceives her as "just a simpleton with as much heart as a chicken." Furthermore, the exemplary behavior of Amadi's heroine is acknowledged in highly chauvinistic terms. Wigwe admits reluctantly: "True, you are only a woman but your good behavior has placed you a little above many other women in the village."

What emerges from the world Amadi creates, then, is a reinforcement of stereotypical male chauvinistic impressions about African womanhood. All of his women characters are depicted as inferior and subordinate to men with even Ihuoma portrayed in subordination to the dominant male characters. The story begins, in characteristic male fashion, with a fight between two men, Emenike and Madume. Ihuoma's introduction into the story is tied to her position as Emenike's wife and as a woman on whom Madume has designs with these factors aggravating the conflict between the two men. Amadi informs the reader: "Perhaps Madume's hatred of Emenike might not have been so great if only the latter had not snatched Ihuoma from him."

Amadi's depiction of Ihuoma is dehumanizing. She is not portrayed as a human being with a will of her own. She is more like a piece of land, or a house, or some form of property that is there to be grabbed. Clearly, the only significance that women have in Amadi's novel is sexual. All exist in a man's world, to be used by the men as sexual vehicles. Amadi's sexism circumscribes his heroine's entire existence, and the very title of his novel, *The Concubine,* reveals the rigidly sexual mold in which Ihuoma is cast. Whether in the spirit world or in her life on earth, Ihuoma's relevance is thus limited by the machinations of a man: "in the spirit world she was the wife of the Sea King, the ruling spirit of the sea." Though reincarnated, her life on earth is still governed by her status as the wife of the Sea King. Before this information is disclosed at the end of the novel, we already know that Ihuoma is being manipulated by the author to reveal only her circumscribed role. She is always either the devoted wife and mother, the pitiable widow of highly commendable behavior, or the prospective wife to be wooed. The plot of *The Concubine* revolves around her successive attempts to seek fulfillment in marriage and on the attempts made by three successive men to woo and marry or bed her. After the death of her first husband, her mother continuously advises her to think of remarrying because a woman needs a man to survive. The impression one gets is that Ihuoma can have no independent life; she must always be attached to a man, as she has little or no relevance beyond her role as a sexual object.

At the same time, Amadi spares no effort in idealizing his heroine. Most of the novel concentrates on her physical and moral superiority to the other women in her world and on her relentless efforts to be an ideal wife and mother. Amadi's main preoccupation in *The Concubine* seems to be to portray a character who will epitomize female perfection from a sexist perspective, and he is highly successful in that respect. His heroine is all that such a man would wish a woman to be. She is endowed with the kind of physical attractiveness that makes a man proud to possess her.

> She was a pretty woman: perhaps that is why she married so early. Her three children looked more like her brothers and sisters. She was young . . . she was just about twenty-two.

> Ihuoma's complexion was that of the ant-hill. Her features were smoothly rounded and looking at her no one could doubt that she was 'enjoying her husband's wealth.' Nothing did a husband greater credit than the well-fed look of his wife.

Ihuoma's attractiveness is emphasized over and over again. She seems impressed by her own beauty, gazing at herself in the mirror every little chance she gets. Calamity, the most notorious agent of premature aging, adds only an ameliorating quality to her beauty. It gives her a "softly alluring, deeply enchanting . . . bewitching subtlety that only deep sorrow can give . . . young men and even the old gazed at her . . . irresistibly." The matured Ihuoma is even more fascinating; she is "confident without being brazen, self-respecting yet approachable, sweet but sensible."

Ihuoma is, above all, a model traditional wife; she shows "her great devotion to her husband in every way she could think of." She is always polite and never gives offense. She is submissive and very understanding. In short, she has none of those qualities that make a woman threatening to a man. She's no good at invectives and other women talk much faster than she does. She does not talk in parables; therefore, she cannot infringe on the male prerogative of verbal excellence. She is a staunch upholder of her society's values, and her high sense of morality matches her high physical endowments. She is so preoccupied with maintaining her good name as a woman that she readily sacrifices her happiness to her good name. For example, she declines to marry Ekwueme, a man she is in love with, because such behavior would be considered improper in her society. She takes it upon herself to remind him that tradition requires him to marry a young maiden who would obey him and give him the first fruits of her womb.

Elechi Amadi's portrayal of Ihuoma fits five of seven stereotypes catalogued by Roseann Bell. Ihuoma is the "Earthmother, the concubine, the loyal doormat of a wife, the sacrificial lamb, [and] the willing mechanism in a polygamous drama."

Compare Flora Nwapa's approach to her heroine, Efuru. She is at the center of the world Nwapa creates. There is no event or situation in the novel that does not stem from her. The novel is Efuru's story, and her life provides the materials for plotting it. Other characters are brought in only as what they do and say leads to revealing or clarifying aspects of Efuru's life. Her presence controls the action, unlike Ihuoma whose actions are reactions to male-initiated actions. While Ihuoma becomes prominent in Amadi's novel only when her presence is required to complete the story of one of Amadi's male protagonists, Efuru is always present in Nwapa's novel in her own right. And this is significant because Amadi's work purports to deal principally with a female character.

Efuru is exceptional in many respects. She is beautiful, the daughter of one of the last survivors of a vanishing age of traditional valor and grandeur, and a highly successful businesswoman. She is prosperous; it is as though anything she touches literally transforms into riches. She is also very compassionate and unassuming, qualities that couple with her beauty to give her a striking resemblance to Ihuoma, Amadi's heroine.

However, Nwapa's Efuru is no paragon of female submissiveness. She demonstrates a marked sense of independence and a determination to lead a fulfilling life. From an early age she reveals a resolve to control her own life rather than to submit blindly to tradition. She is by no means a revolutionary because she does not completely abrogate tradition, but neither is she enslaved by it. Whenever traditional stipulations stifle her individuality, she steps out of them to adopt alternative means that best enable her to express her personality. For example, she contravenes the mores governing male-female relationships and declares herself married by moving in with her lover who is of low social status and too poor at the time to afford her dowry. But later, through her enterprising nature, she makes enough money with her husband to pay her dowry. Also when her first husband deserts her, she continues to live in his house for a considerable length of time—two years. She even goes in search of him. But after waiting long enough to avoid accusations of impropriety, she returns to her father's house, an indication that she is ready, among other things, to consider other possible suitors. She marries again, shortly after moving back to her father's house and enjoys a period of near total marital bliss with her new husband. Not only do they work together, they do everything together. She acts as his counselor, advising him on what projects are ripe for pursuit. In addition, they enjoy a closeness that is not quite usual in the rural setting within which they live. They even go to the stream together to swim and thereby attract a lot of gossip from envious women bound by unexciting lives and the values of their rural world.

Nwapa, like Amadi, highlights her heroine's physical attributes—the village gossips always comment on her beauty. Both women are exceptional in their communities. But Nwapa emphasizes Efuru's other characteristics as well, some of them not totally complimentary, and by so doing, prevents the idealization of her heroine's image. Nwapa's approach to Efuru's beauty in no way reduces the heroine to being a sex object. In fact, the manner in which her beauty is depicted often plays down its positive nature. While there is no question about Efuru's great beauty, the village gossips always juxtapose it, her wealth, and her closeness with her husband to her childlessness, thereby attempting to diminish her endowments.

Above all, Nwapa's portrayal of her heroine presents an in-depth study of womanhood. Her novel is a study of the growth of Efuru, and both her physical and psychological development are brought to light as she searches for options for self-actualization. Efuru begins by accepting the traditional sexually-oriented prescriptions for defining a woman's identity, but she moves gradually towards a new definition of a sense of self, a better option for self-definition. Initially she attempts to find fulfillment both as a wife and a mother, hence her two marriages and her striving to make them work. Also in the early years of her married life she agonizes over her childlessness and goes to some length to remedy this anomaly. She goes to see a *dibia* who assures her she will bear a child. After this assurance, she is still alarmed by her tardiness and becomes overjoyed when she finally bears a child. She feels fulfilled, at last, as a woman.

> Efuru lay there thinking of it all, "Is this happening to me or someone I know. Is that baby mine or somebody else's? Is it really true that I have had a baby, that I am a woman after all. Perhaps I am dreaming. I shall soon wake up and discover that it is not real."

Her sense of fulfillment is threatened when her only daughter falls ill. "'What will I do if I lose her?' she thought. 'If she dies, that will mean the end of me'.'

The above image is that of the growing Efuru, still struggling to come to terms with her identity. The death of her child, however and the grief it brings, does not reduce her to a non-person; neither does the failure of her two marriages. She continues with her trade and proves herself a serious and successful businesswoman. Moreover she becomes a special worshipper of the woman of the lake when she is still married to her second husband. Thus even when she was still married, her other roles played down her sexual one, pointing her in alternative directions for self-realization.

Efuru's life is in some ways wryly ironic. With all her endowments, she fails miserably to find fulfillment within the sexual modes prescribed by her society. She fails both as a wife and a mother. She ends up each time, after two brief spells of marital bliss, back in her father's home. There is no question about her possessing qualities that make men proud to be her mate. Her beauty and the prosperity she brings to her husbands, in themselves, should enamor them to her. Her strong love for her mates and her unflinching devotion to them more than compensate for those qualities such as her strong will and determination that, when unrestrained, can threaten their masculinity. Still, her first husband deserts her for a woman who is Efuru's inferior physically and morally. Her second husband maintains an enviable relationship with her for two years, then becomes inattentive and mistrusting, believing a rumor about Efuru's infidelity. Appalled by her husband's lack of faith in her, Efuru leaves him to return to her home of birth.

Efuru's matrimonial failures, in a superficial way, recall those of Ihuoma, who loses two husbands and ends up a widow at a relatively early age. However, Efuru's life is a failure only within a very limited sexual framework, on which unfortunately her society places so much importance. Her life is not a failure when seen through her own eyes and from a broader perspective. That she is a remarkable human being is communicated even more strongly than the sense of failure projected mainly through the comments of the village gossips. Her generosity, her wealth, and her general sense of worth to her community at large is as much a reality as her failed marriages and childlessness. The sense of accomplishment of Nwapa's heroine is no less strong because of her unsuccessful stint as wife and mother, a point which sets her off from Amadi's Ihuoma, whose life crumbles around her once she fails to lead a fulfilling sexual life.

The supernatural element plays a vital role in both novels. However, once more, Nwapa's use of the supernatural differs markedly from the way Amadi uses it. In Efuru's case, the supernatural becomes an extension of her sense of self while in the case of Ihuoma, it assumes a masculine form and hinders her development as a successful woman. In direct opposition, Uhamiri, the woman of the lake, the supernatural element in Nwapa's novel, is a symbolic representation of Nwapa's heroine, who is chosen as a special worshipper of this deity. Uhamiri becomes the alter ego of the matured Efuru who is invested with all of Uhamiri's qualities. Both of them are rich, beautiful and worshipped by those who appreciate their worth, but they have no children. Significantly, Uhamiri lavishes on her favorites wealth and not children, and she is worshipped even though she does not have children or give her worshippers children. Efuru's acceptance of her role as a special worshipper of the woman of the lake, therefore, becomes a symbolic representation of her acceptance of herself as a person in her own right. The novel's end supports this contention.

> Efuru slept soundly that night. She dreamt of the woman of the lake, her beauty, her long hair and her riches. She had lived for ages at the bottom of the lake. She was as old as the lake itself. She was happy, she was wealthy. She was beautiful. She gave women beauty and wealth but she had no child. She had never experienced the joy of motherhood. Why then did women worship her?

This passage is the crux of the story of Efuru, capturing well her final acceptance of herself, her coming to terms with her life, and her determination to live happily and reject those traditional prescriptions of the identity of women, which only diminish their sense of personal worth.

Maryse Condé is right in her observation that the closing lines of *Efuru* provide the clue to the whole book, but her interpretation of it reflects her limited understanding of Efuru's identification with the woman of the lake. Condé's interpretation of *Efuru* is that:

> No happiness can be achieved for a woman unless in childbearing. . . . Efuru, for all her qualities and gifts, considers her life as valueless since she fails to have a child. She can deliberately and willfully decide to leave her husband and therefore live by herself, but she cannot follow the logical consequences. She cannot find in herself enough resources to counterbalance her sterility and never thinks of devoting her energies to something else.

Ms. Condé's statements present a gross misreading of Nwapa's heroine. Nwapa makes it quite clear that, far from feeling that her life is valueless, Efuru seeks new alternatives through which to realize her life. There is no question that Efuru finds in herself enough resources to counterbalance her sterility and devotes her energies to the pursuit of other things, symbolically represented by her becoming a devoted worshipper of the woman of the lake, the spiritual embodiment of her own identity.

Nwapa's use of the supernatural is not dissimilar from Amadi's in so far as it bears directly on the life and identity of her heroine. But in this regard too, there is a marked difference. While Nwapa's supernatural being is a woman and functions to promote her heroine's search for identity, Amadi's supernatural being provides another means of confining his heroine to her sexual identity. It is a further projection of his male perspective of African womanhood. Ihuoma's chain of unsuccessful marriages, like Efuru's, stem from her special relationship to the supernatural. However, in her case, the supernatural thwarts her life rather than offers her alternatives for self-actualization. Being a human reincarnation of the spirit wife of the Sea King, a highly jealous male deity, who refuses to relinquish his hold on her, Ihuoma can at best be only a concubine to human men, but can never marry in her life on earth. So Ihumoa's relevance even in the spirit world is limited to a sexual one. She is bound body and soul to the Sea King.

This study therefore supports Lloyd Brown's evaluations of these two works. The difference between Ihuoma's total sense of doom and despair at the end of *The Concubine,* and Efuru's ability to devote herself to something other than seeking fulfillment in the traditionally instituted female roles illustrates a basic difference between the perception of females from a strictly male perspective and from a female one.

While Amadi's character never becomes more than an instrument in someone else's scheme, Nwapa's Efuru transcends those proscriptions, becoming an actor in her own, in woman's right.

Flora Nwapa with Marie Umeh (interview date December 1992)

SOURCE: "The Poetics of Economic Independence for Female Empowerment: An Interview with Flora Nwapa," in *Research in African Literatures,* Vol. 26, No. 2, Summer, 1995, pp. 22-29.

[*The following interview was conducted in 1992, several months before Nwapa's death. In it she discusses her literary influences and her opinions on the evolving place of women in Nigerian society.*]

Flora Nwapa-Nwakuche, popularly known as Flora Nwapa, Africa's first internationally recognized female novelist and publisher, died of pneumonia on 16 October 1993, at the age of 62 in Enugu, Nigeria. She was buried at Amede's Court

in Ugwuta. In what was to be my last conversation with Flora Nwapa-Nwakuche in December 1992, in Scarsdale, New York, when she was on tour in the United States, the renowned author spoke not only of the glory she received as the first African woman to be published internationally, but also unashamedly of her position as a writer globally, coming from a formerly colonized state. Very much in tune with her Ugwuta heritage, Nwapa applauded the androgynous nature of her society. Conversely, she decried the "multiple marginality" she experienced with her Western publisher who regarded her as a "minor writer." Regarded as a Third World writer, her London publisher did not bother to print and distribute her books locally and internationally when they were in demand as they would have if she came from a so-called "first world" country. According to Nwapa, Heinemann's placing her in the literary backwaters resulted in the piracy of her books in Africa and the death of her voice globally. And as Ama Ata Aidoo once said, when the canonical establishment refuses to promote, print, distribute, read, and critique your books, they kill you creatively. Recognizing her status as "other," Nwapa took it upon herself to distribute her books herself and established Tana Press Limited in 1977 for this purpose. It is my contention that Nwapa's resistance to the canonical politics of her erasure is behind her distancing herself from the term "feminist" to describe her ideological position in global letters. Certainly, Nwapa x-rayed and analyzed her own realities and concluded that sexism is a secondary problem that arises out of race, class, and the exploitation of people of color. Hence, she preferred to identify with Alice Walker's term "womanist," which reflected the African reality of effacement based on racial difference.

The Eurocentric popular view of the position of African women is one of subordination to husbands, and the repression of talents outside the domestic realm. Despite the asymmetrical nature of some African societies, gifted African women in pre-colonial times were not deterred from playing significant roles exercised by female leaders, such as Moremi, Queen Amina of Zaria, and Olufunmilayo Ransome-Kuti. Similarly, Flora Nwapa contends that if she is considered the doyenne of African female writers, the glory goes to the oral historians and griottes who mesmerized her with stories about the mystical powers of Ogbuide, the mother of the lake, her family members of industrious women and men who served as role models, as well as her penchant for service and the pursuit of excellence. Accordingly, in opposition to the belief that women in the Igbo area of Nigeria do not break kola nut, Nwapa informs us that a woman in Ugwuta society who has achieved because of her industry and talent is indeed recognized for her accomplishments and has the privilege of breaking and sharing kola. Of course, this *modus operandi* points to the complexity and complementary nature of sex roles of some Igbo societies in pre-colonial Africa, which ensured kith and kin that a woman who has distinguished herself would not have her gender mitigated against her. The Ugwuta community is therefore one of those special communities in that status and recognition are not biologically based. Ugwuta society, it appears, subscribes to Victor Uchendu's view that "a child who washes his/her hands, eats with elders." Indeed, the unit of analysis is the individual. For her courage in exploiting the complementary sex-role system in Ugwuta society, despite the obstacles pioneers must confront and overcome, Flora Nwapa is certainly a phenomenon.

By breaking the silence of women in Nigerian letters, Flora Nwapa has made a name for herself as a major twentieth-century African woman writer. Since the publication of her first novel, *Efuru* (1966), she had gained an impressive readership in both African and international circles, as well as critical acclaim for her novels: *Idu* (1970), *Never Again* (1975), *One Is Enough* (1981), and *Women Are Different* (1986). Her two collections of short stories are entitled *This Is Lagos, and Other Stories* (1971) and *Wives at War and Other Stories* (1975). She has also published a book of prose poems, *Cassava Song and Rice Song* (1986). Apart from her creative works for an adult readership, Nwapa held the reputation of a fine creator of children's books: *Emeka: The Driver's Guard* (1972), *MammyWater* (1979), *My Tana Colouring Book* (1979), *My Animal Number Book* (1979), *The Miracle Kittens* (1980), *Journey To Space* (1980), and *The Adventures of Deke* (1980). Her manuscript, *The Lake Goddess,* will be published posthumously. For her achievements, she received The Officer of the Order of the Niger (OON) Award in 1982 from the Federal Government of Nigeria and the University of Ife Merit Award for Authorship and Publishing in 1985, to name only two of the distinguished prizes accorded her. She was also the President of the Association of Nigerian Authors (1989) and a member of PEN International (1991) and the Commonwealth Writers Awards Committee (1992), among the many positions she held during her lifetime.

With the characterizations of her female protagonists in her adult fiction, she complicated female identity as delineated in the literature of Chinua Achebe and his brothers by critiquing both their gender conventions and power relations between men and women in the homestead. Thus, the female literary tradition she initiated was rooted in resistance, a protest against the one-dimensional images of Nigerian women either as wives, mothers, *femmes fatales,* or rebel girls. Although she has not been given the critical acclaim she deserves, Nwapa's work represents a monumental effort to invent an African female personality and attitude and to define an African female subject narrativistically. Indeed, her explorations of the female psyche link her works theoretically and thematically with womanist writers such as Alice Walker, Toni Morrison, Ifeoma Okoye, and Zaynab Alkali, to name only a few, whose aim is not only to present the

female point of view but also to subvert patriarchal authority over women in world literary history. Her canonical contribution to Nigerian letters is, then, a "poetics of economic independence and self-reliance for female empowerment." Nwapa sets the record straight by the power of the pen. She actually feminizes Nigerian letters as she realistically fictionalizes the shrewd, ubiquitous market women, energetic female farmers, sagacious wives and mothers, and astute women chiefs and priestesses as an integral part of quotidian existence. It is in her fiction that the enterprising African woman takes a stand and demands her rightful place in the halls of global literary history.

Nwapa would have agreed that African men wield a great deal of power in African society. On the other hand, her honest portrayal of Ugwuta women insists on the complementary nature of Ugwuta society beginning with a mixed-gender age grade system, a mystical Lake Goddess, who guarantees women, as well as men, power, prominence, and peace. Indeed, woman is something, an achiever, a go-getter in Ugwuta, not only for her special child-bearing and child rearing abilities, but also for her potential to benefit her community spiritually, educationally, economically, and psychologically. As Mgbada, the diviner in Nwapa's last novel, *The Lake Goddess,* tells Ona's husband: "We believe that the Goddess protects us and inspires us to great heights. We believe that no invader from any part of the world can destroy us. We believe that the deity is a beautiful and ageless woman who is partial to women." Coming from this rich tradition where women paddle canoes up, down, across, and beyond Ugwuta Lake, transporting passengers and their wares for a nominal fee, where women are leaders in trade and commerce, where a democratic gender system recognizes talent, regardless of one's sex, where confidence and perfection are nurtured in both females and males, is it any wonder that Flora Nwapa was able to touch the hand of the goddess?

[Umeh:] Congratulations on the publishing and launching of a number of your books with Africa World Press in New Jersey. How does it feel to be so successful? How does it feel to be Africa's first internationally published female writer in the English language?

[Nwapa:] Thank you very much, Marie. It feels good. It feels fulfilling.

What are the rewards and difficulties of being the first African woman writer and publisher in Nigeria?

I've had my ups and downs. In 1966, when Heinemann published *Efuru,* I did not receive much publicity because Nigeria was in a turmoil. There was a *coup d'état* in 1966 and the whole system had broken down. And in 1967, I had to go back to Eastern Nigeria, where all the Igbos returned from all over Nigeria. The war was fought for thirty months and when we came back we had to start all over again. It was at this time when I was a minister in East Central State, which is what Enugu was called in those days, that I continued to write again. But my second novel, *Idu,* was also published by Heinemann in 1970. These are the two books published by Heinemann. After that I thought I should have some African publishing companies distribute my books. That was when Nwamife Publishing Company came out. They were the first to publish *This Is Lagos* and *Never Again.* It's been fulfilling. I must say there's been a lot of hard work. There's been a lot of frustration all the same. But the problem in Nigeria is the problem of having a reading public, the people who will appreciate your work. In the '80s and '90s things have been accelerating. But, you discover that not many people can afford to buy books. I was lucky because for the past five years the West African Examination Council, called WAEC, had *Efuru* on its reading list. It was something that I should have been congratulated for. It should have brought in a lot of money. However, the problem was piracy. Heinemann Publishing Company could not bring out the books on time. Therefore, pirates took over so that writing and publishing didn't make any impact. The school system did not make an impact at all on my earnings.

What advice would you give to women who would like to write?

The advice that I would give to them is, one, they should read and read and read. You have to be a good reader. And you have to be a good listener to be able to write. I think this is the advice that I would give to them. When you hear people asking writers, "Where do you find the time to do all of this?" I tell them that time has little to do with it. If you have a story to tell, the story is there in you and it will haunt you until you tell it. So I would advise them to read and listen.

What circumstances in your life are responsible for the writing of both your adult novels and your children's books?

I read a lot of books. As a child before I went to high school, I listened to a lot of stories, moonlight stories told by the women in Ugwuta. As a child I would call on anybody who promised to tell me a story. I would sit down and listen. And when I went to high school, I had read practically everything that I could find, so that contributed again to my writing. After graduating from Ibadan University in Nigeria and Edinburgh University in London, I came home to Nigeria and I taught at a girls' secondary school. While I was teaching, I discovered I had plenty of time on my hands. I didn't know what to do with it. So, I began to write stories about my schooldays. It

was in this process that I began the story of *Efuru.* It just happened. I started writing the story of this woman and then I went on and on and I discovered that I had a good story to write and a good story to tell. I continued to write until I finished it. There was nothing in me when I was in school that made me feel I was going to be a writer. It was one of those things that just happened. I didn't have the ambition to say, "Oh, Flora, you are going to be a writer, so work towards it." No, it didn't happen that way. But having written *Efuru* and having published it, I continued to write. It is difficult to write children's books. But I remember that Christopher Okigbo, in those days when he was working for Cambridge University Press, had asked me to write a children's book. I told him, "OK, Chris, I will do something about it." I began to write *Emeka: The Driver's Guard,* and I finished it. Chris had died during the war. So I sent my manuscript to London University Press and they published it in 1971. Now when I had my own publishing company, I decided that I needed good books for my growing children. When I went to the book stores, I didn't see anything that was good for my children. That was when I started writing more children's books. I wrote *Mammy Water* in 1979.

Flora, what year did you start your publishing company, Tana Press?

Tana Press was opened in 1976 and business started in 1977 and I published *Mammy Water* in 1979.

Out of all your creative works, which one has given you the most satisfaction? And why?

This is a difficult question to ask, Marie. Similar to Buchi Emecheta, I too feel that books are like your children. It's not easy for one to say that you love one and not the other. They are all good books. I cannot tell you that I like this one or that I like that or, that I prefer this one. It is difficult for me to say.

My favorite novel is **One Is Enough.** *What was the audience's reaction to* **One Is Enough***?*

Hmmm. It is hard to say. But let me tell you what happened. *One Is Enough* was published in 1982. And a friend of mine who read the book came to me and told me that *One Is Enough* was a true story of a friend. I did not know her friend. It was three years after this, when I was at a funeral, that another friend came along and said, "Look, the lady you wrote about in that story is in this audience." I couldn't believe it. So the lady came over, shook my hand, and said, "Mrs. Nwakuche, I heard so much about this book. People say it is my story. I haven't read it; so I don't know whether it's my story or not." But she didn't feel bad about it. What I want to say is this: after the war in 1970, things changed a great deal in Nigeria. During the war, that is the Nigerian Civil War, women saw themselves playing roles that they never thought they would play. They saw themselves across the enemy lines, trying to trade, trying to feed their children and caring for their husbands. At the end of the war, you could not restrict them any more. They started enjoying their economic independence. So what they tolerated before the war, they could no longer tolerate. For example, if you discovered that your marriage is not giving you satisfaction or that your in-laws are worrying you because you have not produced a male child or a female child, whatever the case may be, you can just decide to leave that family and go to the big city. The big city at that time was Lagos, where you were anonymous, where nobody seemed to care what you do for a living. So I think I wouldn't presume that **One Is Enough** had an impact on Nigerians. I would presume that all **One Is Enough** is about is the story of what is happening in male/female relationships in Nigeria today.

You are indeed a prolific writer: eight adult works and seven children's books. Have your books been translated into other languages?

Yes, **Efuru** has been translated into French. Unfortunately, up to now, I do not have a copy. **Efuru** has also been translated into the Icelandic language.

Which writers do you admire? And outside of your literary foremothers who expressed themselves in the oral tradition, which literary artists have influenced your writings?

I would say that Chinua Achebe influenced me a great deal. He influenced me in my adult life. But as a young girl in school, many writers, such as Ernest Hemingway and Charles Dickens, also influenced me a great deal.

In addition to your enthusiasm for storytelling, do you have a sense of mission? What is your purpose in writing?

I write because I want to write. I write because I have a story to tell. There is this urge always to write and put things down. I do not presume that I have a mission. If you continue to read my books, maybe you could find the mission. But I continue to write because I feel fulfilled. I feel satisfied in what I'm doing.

Are there any autobiographical elements in your creative writing?

None! I am not like Efuru, neither am I like Idu, neither am I Amaka in any way.

What do you think of Léopold Sédar Senghor and Ali Mazrui's statements that "African women have always been

liberated"? In other words, is there any truth in the statement?

For me, yes! In Ugwuta, women have certain rights that women elsewhere, in other parts of the country, do not have. For instance, in Ugwuta, a woman can break the kola nut where men are. If she is old, or if she has achieved much or if she has paid the bride price for a male relation and that member of the family is there, she can break the kola nut. And everybody would eat the kola nut. But in certain parts of Igboland, a woman is not even *shown* a kola nut, not to talk about *breaking* it.

Now we know why you're a first. It's because the Ugwuta tradition certainly nurtured you into being an independent thinker. It appears that you don't even wince before you perform a task.

Thank you, Marie.

The critic Katherine Frank, in an article entitled "Women Without Men: The Feminist Novel in Africa," describes you as a radical feminist. What is your opinion of this assessment?

I don't think that I'm a radical feminist. I don't even accept that I'm a feminist. I accept that I'm an ordinary woman who is writing about what she knows. I try to project the image of women positively. I attempt to correct our menfolks when they started writing, when they wrote little or less about women, where their female characters are prostitutes and ne'er-do-wells. I started writing to tell them that this is not so. When I do write about women in Nigeria, in Africa, I try to paint a positive picture about women because there are many women who are very, very positive in their thinking, who are very, very independent, and very, very industrious.

What do you perceive to be the major ideological difference between male and female writing in Nigeria?

The male writers have disappointed us a great deal by not painting the female character as they should paint them. I have to say that there's been a kind of an ideological change. I think male writers are now presenting women as they are. They are not only mothers; they are not only palm collectors; they are not only traders; but they are also wealthy people. Women can stand on their own. My example is Beatrice in *Anthills of the Savannah* by Chinua Achebe. In that novel, Beatrice stands out. She was the one who really understood what was going on. The men were too ideological. They were not actually down to earth. It was Beatrice who was practical.

Certainly, Chinua Achebe's attitude towards women in Ant-

hills of the Savannah, *published in 1988, is a far cry from his portrayal of women in* Things Fall Apart, *published in 1958. What do you feel about Elechi Amadi's female character in his latest novel,* Estrangement?

Estrangement is another story which I enjoyed a great deal because Elechi Amadi tried to portray this unfortunate woman in a true picture. He has sympathy for the Nigerian woman. In *Estrangement* you could see that the heroine was treated very, very positively by the author. All her misfortunes were clearly stated. And the way the author portrayed her showed understanding.

Africa has produced three Nobel Laureates in literature—Wole Soyinka, Naguib Mahfouz, and Nadine Gordimer. What was your immediate reaction to each writer's winning the Nobel Prize for literature?

I was very pleased. I was very excited. I was delighted.

Do you recognize Nadine Gordimer as an African writer? Who is an African writer?

Nadine Gordimer is a white South African. She has been writing for a very long time; she has sympathy for the black South African. She is an African writer.

More and more people, even those in Muslim countries, are moving away from polygamy and polygyny. But in Nigeria they are still common. What do you think about this, since they are affecting the Nigerian family as a unit?

Well, I think it is the society. It is the age that we are in. I think it's going to pass. It started in the '70s and it is going on and on. There is this stigma on a woman who elects to be single. Mothers bring up their daughters telling them that they have to marry. In my own language we say, "No matter how beautiful one is, if she doesn't get married she's nothing." It's left for us who have received a Western education to de-emphasize this tradition. However, you discover that a woman who has gone to college, who is working, who has a profession, who is a lawyer or a doctor, who doesn't have a husband, then she will not mind being a second wife. In fact, polygamy is becoming very fashionable in Nigeria these days among Western-educated women.

Do you think it's right for people to say that every woman should have a husband and a child?

No! However, I'm telling you about the tradition. If you had a child out of wedlock in those days in the community that I grew up in, your child was not legitimate. Nevertheless, things are changing; people are now accepting it. In fact, when I was growing up, if a young girl became pregnant,

we viewed her with horror. The child was not baptized. Now when these things happen, the baby is baptized.

Nowadays, do you think a woman would elect to have a child, if a husband is not forthcoming, rather than enter into a polygamous marriage?

Many women are doing this, Marie. Many women are saying that they don't want a husband but they want a child.

So your female character, Amaka, who has twin sons and refuses to marry the father, in **One Is Enough,** *is prophetic?*

I think she is, because she, like many women, has had experiences in her married life, with men generally, which were nothing but war.

Do you have a specific message for women? Do you have an ideology or some words of advice?

Yes, I do. I feel that every woman, married or single, must have economic independence. If you look at *One Is Enough,* I quote an Hausa proverb which says, "A woman who holds her husband as a father dies an orphan."

My interpretation of the proverb is that a woman should be economically independent. One should not rely on inheritance or men for survival?

Exactly.

Thank you very much.

Elleke Boehmer (essay date 1992)

SOURCE: "Stories of Women and Mothers: Gender and Nationalism in the Early Fiction of Flora Nwapa," in *Motherlands: Black Women's Writing from Africa, the Caribbean and South Asia,* edited by Susheila Nasta, Rutgers University Press, 1992, pp. 3-23.

[*In the following essay excerpt, Boehmer contends that Nwapa's portrayal of women as strong, independent mother-figures in her early novels is symbolic of African nationalism.*]

Published during the first decade of Nigerian independence, a time featuring robust and cocksure, if also embattled nationalisms, Nwapa's novels represent the first narrative appearance from a woman on the broader African literary stage. This in itself was a significant voicing, yet added to this was Nwapa's specific focus on women's community and colloquy in Igbo culture.

Like Elechi Amadi or Nkem Nwankwo, her male counterparts of the first post-independence decade, Flora Nwapa has written 'after Achebe', both chronologically and in terms of literary influence. Nwapa's narratives, like Amadi's and Achebe's, remember and recreate the Igbo village past in the colonial period. Period generalisations, however, tend to obscure the significant differences that exist between Nwapa and her male cohorts.

Her writing is situated outside of conventional male narrative history; she chooses to engage neither with the manly adventures and public displays of patriarchal authority described by male writers from her community nor with the narrative conventions of their accounts. Instead she concentrates, and at length, on what was incidental or simply contextual to male action—domestic matters, politics of intimacy.

In both *Efuru* and *Idu,* Nwapa's interest is in the routines and rituals of everyday life specifically within women's compounds. Women press into Nwapa's narrative as speakers, actors, decision-makers, brokers of opinion and market prices and unofficial jurors in their communities. But Nwapa's specific intervention as a writer goes beyond her interest in women subjects. What also distinguishes her writing from others in the 'Igbo school' are the ways in which she has used choric language to enable and to empower her representation, creating the effect of a women's verbal presence within her text, while bringing home her subject matter by evoking the vocality of women's everyday existence.

Though it may have attracted a certain amount of negative comment, the apparent lack of conventional novelistic complexity in *Efuru* and *Idu,* I would argue, far from being a deficiency, instead clears the space for the elaboration of another kind of narrative entirely—a highly verbalised collective women's biography—'transsubjective, anonymous', transgressive, a narrative method which bears comparison with Zora Neale Hurston's recreation of porch-side comment and of gossip on the road.

The precise contribution represented by Nwapa's writing can perhaps be more clearly demonstrated when set in contrast on the one side with a historical narrative by Elechi Amadi, and on the other with an anthropological account of a Nigerian Igbo community by a woman researcher, Ifi Amadiume. In his novel *The Great Ponds,* written in 1969, Elechi Amadi has depicted the life of an Igbo village as strongly determined by the forces of war, rumour and disease. Over war and rumour, it soon becomes clear, men hold undisputed sway; of disease, the gods decide, but they, like the village leaders, are all male. As with Achebe's writing, *The Great Ponds* is not uncritical of the 'masculine' social values which may contribute to and exacerbate community crises. Yet, unlike in Achebe, no locus of value is suggested which might

form the rallying point of a new order: the male characters represent different types and degrees of manliness, but their actual position of authority is not called into question. It is thus quite within the terms laid down by the novel that the women in the community form a completely marginal and passive group. Their existence is affirmed by male subjects—they are desired, taken in marriage, captured as booty in male wars and are heard speaking when spoken to. For the rest, they are ignored.

Superficially this arrangement would seem hardly to differ from conventional gender divisions of power and cultural space. Upon closer scrutiny, however, it would appear that in Amadi the gender separation is perhaps more pronounced. The physical distance of the gender groups and their extreme social and political non-equivalence both suggest that they may well be independently reproduced and regulated. It is this view of a society radically split by gender that allows Amadi in *The Great Ponds* to represent the male side of Igbo life as though it were not only normative and authoritative, but self-sufficient and entire.

Yet, the writer's individual bias aside, it does not necessarily follow that this sort of exclusivity is the sign of a lack of power or self-determination on the part of women. It may just as well be the case that the distance between genders signifies and allows an autonomy and also a social validity for women. The women possess jurisdiction and authority over an area of village life which, though separate, is only *apparently* marginal; women conduct the business of their lives convinced of the validity of their activity.

Contrary to appearances, then, the representations of writers such as Amadi and Achebe, rather than defining the whole compass of the Igbo world, describe only one section of it. That another independent sphere of social existence exists is intimated only once, and then very briefly, in the Amadi text. It does, however, represent a significant break in the narrative when, in confrontational tones reminiscent of some of Nwapa's speakers, a senior wife, though nameless, comments on the folly of the protracted war and its goals;

> Why can't men take advice? . . . They think they are
> wise but they are as foolish as a baby in arms. Look
> at all the suffering of the past month. What good
> will that pond [the site of the contention] do us?

Ifi Amadiume offers a corroborative perspective on the self-reliance of Igbo women, and on one of the chief conditions of that self-reliance—what might be called the mutual exclusivity of gender groups. In her study *Male Daughters, Female Husbands,* she shows that women obtain a great deal of power in Igbo—and specifically Nnobi—society because of the separation of gender from sex roles. Amadiume does not always deal satisfactorily with the continuing predominance of *de facto* patriarchal authority in the community, and the status commanded by the roles of son and husband. Yet she does present evidence not simply for the existence of a clearly demarcated women's 'sphere' (which in itself says relatively little), but also for the independence and self-coherence of women's lives within that 'sphere'. She indicates that in precolonial times political and economic roles, as well as compound space and village ground, were divided according to the conventional sex dualities, with family units being matricentric. She argues, however, that these socially constructed dualities were mediated by the cross-gender roles available to women. Women were thus granted a range of powers with the appeal to Idemili, the water goddess, as offering the highest sanction of their authority.

It is the autonomous women's world delineated by Amadiume which Nwapa embodies in *Efuru* and *Idu:* Nwapa thus extends the boundaries of the African novel to include the women's side of the compound, a domain of village life which writers like Amadi have neglected for reasons not only of patriarchal lack of interest but also perhaps (a fact not given sufficient attention) of ignorance. Nwapa refracts a women's presence into her text through creating the conceit of women representing themselves in voice. Dialogue dominates in both novels, especially in *Idu,* as numbers of partly curious, partly phatic and frequently anonymous women's voices meet, interact with and interpellate one another. This vocality, rambling and seemingly unstoppable, pulls against the confinements of the women's lives—their market rivalries, their anxieties about husbands, families and children. Therefore, if, as Nwapa portrays it, though not always overtly, male values in the society remain normative, women's talk can be interpreted not only as a way of life but as a mode of self-making. The impression of the fullness and autonomy of women's lives which Nwapa creates must remain partially qualified by their acquiescence in patriarchal views and values. Yet, at the same time, in their discourse, even as they speak, not only do the village women share their woes and confirm female bonds, they also transpose their lives into a medium which they control. The reader is made privy to the women representing and so, in effect, recreating their lives in speech. The narrative result is that most of the (non-discursive) action in *Idu* and *Efuru* happens offstage and is more or less incidental to the 'spoken' text. Nwapa's writing is thus a decisive vindication of that congenital fault of garrulousness often attributed to 'the sex' (for example, in *The Great Ponds* pp. 23, 42 and 45). As Idu bemusedly observes: 'You know women's conversation never ends.'

How does this method of verbal self-representation work in practice? *Efuru* and *Idu* unfold as conversations; both are loosely chronological and markedly lacking in the temporal framework of conventional narrative. *Efuru* begins at the

time that the heroine marries Adizua without parental consent; 'one moonlit night' they make plans; the next Nkwo (market) day she moves to his house. With this information in hand the gossip-mongers can have their say, and, sure enough, by the second page of the novel speculations are afoot regarding Efuru's movements. These form the first soundings of that hum of conjecture that will run throughout the novel, commenting on Efuru's fortunes, her barrenness, her second marriage, her second barrenness. Against the background of this flow, trade seasons, other moonlit nights, gestation periods come and go with their accustomed regularity, but have significance in the conversational narrative largely as arbitrary starting points for new fragments of chatter. In *Idu* the verbal presence of the community would seem to be even more pervasive. Of the novel's 22 chapters, 14 including the first begin in mid-dialogue, and then usually à propos of events mentioned in some earlier conversation, the dialogue thus propagating itself across the pages of the novel.

The social setting Nwapa has chosen for her novels enables this self-generating orality. In each, the women occupy a self-enclosed, stable domestic domain—custom and environment are known to all the speakers and few characters are unfamiliar. Where these may be physically gestured at or taken as understood, reference to external objects or to habitual activity is elided or abbreviated. From the non-Igbo reader's point of view, this is emphasised when in both novels Igbo words and concepts are left unexplained and cannot always be elucidated by context—*ganashi, obo, nsala* soup. Within the community, the meanings of such words would not require elucidation. The insularity of the community is also suggested by the frequent repetitiveness of the conversation; comments are echoed, opinions reiterated, events retold, and it would appear that the point of talking is often simply the interaction, confirming contact, and not an exchange of information. Or as Uzoechi in *Idu* says, 'Sometimes, after discussing something, I like to come back to it and talk it over again'.

So much is action a function of what is spoken that, especially in *Idu,* 'plot' developments take place off-stage as the conversation passes. At one moment in *Idu,* for example, Adiewere and Idu think of sending their new wife away; within a few paragraphs it is said that 'Adiewere had already sent her away'. In chapter 13 of *Efuru,* Eneberi, Efuru's husband, expresses interest in taking a new wife; in the next chapter, during a chat between his mother and her friends, we learn that she (the mother) has a new daughter-in-law. Thus a particular state of affairs may change into its opposite after a few pages, almost in the course of a few fragments of dialogue: here Idu observes that market is bad, there that it is good. With dialogue constituting the main action and medium of community life, narrated or conversational time predominates over chronological time. Gossips summarise changes that have taken place over a span of years while also running through community opinion of those changes. One of the clearest examples of this occurs in *Efuru* when the heroine hears of her husband's desertion through overhearing gossip at market.

Though Nwapa's dialogic approach appears as the dominant feature of her narrative, its prominence should not detract from that other important aspect of her writing which in fact enables the vocality of her style—her focus on women's affairs. Nwapa's women represent themselves in voice, yet their spirit of pride and self-reliance is manifested also in the relative diversity of their quotidian activity.

Efuru and *Idu* document in some detail women's customs, business preoccupations and worries: certain sections, in particular the chapter on childbirth in *Efuru* (chapter 2), read like extracts from an almanac of women's simples. Through recreating a sense of the fullness of Igbo women's lives during the time of colonisation, Nwapa thus begins to chart out the neglected gender dimension in the grand narrative of nationalist historical literature as told by male writers. She questions, if only implicitly, the gender-bound space-time coordinates of that narrative. More specifically even than this, however, she delivers her riposte to a male-dominated nationalist tradition and its iconography of womanhood by making available for her women characters roles and symbols of identity which diverge from the mother stereotype. Nwapa's women characters are concerned about bearing children and being good mothers, yet their lives are not defined solely through their maternal function. Especially in *Efuru* Nwapa delineates the 'clearly expressed female principle' in Igbo life where 'fecundity [is] important, not entire'.

Efuru opens with the heroine marrying without parental consent, defiant and unafraid. Later, when her husband proves unworthy, she leaves, just as defiant. Though her action is more problematic, *Idu* ends with the heroine willing her own death so as to join her husband: she resolves that the relationship provided by the marriage was more important to her than bearing children. Both heroines are admittedly exceptional figures, yet it is important to note that they are not unique. Characters like the older woman, Ajanupu, in *Efuru* and Ojiugo in *Idu* exemplify comparable qualities of decisiveness, outspokenness and self-sufficiency.

In Igbo society, as Amadiume shows, it is in trade as much as in marriage and childbirth that women obtain power. Accordingly, both novels focus on marketing as the chief dynamic of women's lives and the means whereby they obtain status. Attracted by the lure of a good business reputation, women like Idu and Efuru structure their lives around market days and keep out a vigilant eye for profit. In this way, as well as through sheer audacity and hard labour, they de-

velop the trading prowess for which the community respects them. Two important qualifications should perhaps be made here. One, that the economic abilities shown by Nwapa's women characters are compromised in her later writing when, in a capitalist cash system, marketing heroines turn exploitative and conspicuously consumerist. And two, that, even while women command power through economic means, patriarchal law is never challenged, even in matters of trade.

It is therefore only when women take on spiritual power, thus discarding their sex roles, that they are able to enter a sphere where male authority has little effect. Nwapa's Woman of the Lake deity in *Idu* and especially *Efuru* bears a strong resemblance to the water goddess, Idemili, described by Amadiume. In Amadiume's account, women wield considerable power as the worshippers and representatives of this water spirit: ritual elites develop from groups who worship her; successful market women are seen to be blessed by her. So too, in Nwapa, Uhamiri, the Woman of the Lake, is held in high regard, as are her followers. At the end of *Efuru,* the heroine is chosen to represent the deity in recognition of her status in the community. As infertility is a necessary condition of the goddess' chosen followers, Uhamiri's intercession gives Efuru's barrenness new meaning—in a way, makes it fruitful.

Where Amadi recognised only male deities, Nwapa thus puts the community's shrines in order, setting the female goddess back in her rightful place. This readjustment reflects on what I have argued is the more general effect of her writing—that of counterbalancing both in language and in character iconography a post-colonial literary patriarchy and a matrifocal nationalism. In the crucial decade of the sixties, Nwapa in *Idu* and *Efuru* re-angled the perspective set by male writing, showing where and in what ways women wield verbal and actual power. If nationalism has typically been embodied in patriarchal formations and fraternal bonding, and involves the exclusion of women from public political life, then Nwapa, in choosing not to engage with 'big' national themes, dealt with the exclusion first by reproducing it—by situating her narratives in another place entirely—and then by making of that occlusion a richness. By allowing a women's discourse apparently to articulate itself in her writing, she elaborates the text of national experience. Yet even more importantly than this perhaps, Nwapa also uncovers the practical, lived reality of motherhood—she digs into the muddy, grainy underside of nationalism's privileged icon. The mothers of Africa, Nwapa shows, also have voices, anger, rival aspirations, their own lives. Most of all, they are as much the subjects of communal history as their nationalist sons.

FURTHER READING

Criticism

Berrian, Brenda F. "In Memoriam: Flora Nwapa (1931-1993)." *Signs* 20, No. 4 (Summer 1995): 996-99.

Eulogy of Nwapa that recalls Berrian's first meeting with the writer.

Emenyonu, Ernest N. "Who Does Flora Nwapa Write For?" *African Literature Today* 7, (1975): 28-33.

Emenyonu discusses the chief characteristics of African literary criticism and the place of *Idu* within African literature.

Nnaemeka, Obioma. "Feminism, Rebellious Women, and Cultural Boundaries: Rereading Flora Nwapa and Her Compatriots." *Research in African Literatures* 26, No. 2 (Summer 1995): 80-113.

Contends that Western feminist criticism has misinterpreted many women's issues in Africa, leading to a vast misrepresentation of African women's literature, including that of Flora Nwapa.

Ogunyemi, Chikwenye Okonjo. "Introduction: The Invalid

Dea(r)th, and the Author: The Case of Flora Nwapa, aka Professor (Mrs.) Flora Nwanzuruahu Nwakuche." *Research in African Literatures* 26, No. 2 (Summer 1995): 1-16.

Considers Nwapa as an authorial presence in the post-structuralist sense.

Sample, Maxine. "In Another Life: The Refugee Phenomenon in Two Novels of the Nigerian Civil War." *Modern Fiction Studies* 37, No. 3 (Autumn 1991): 445-54.

Places Nwapa's novel *Never Again* and her short story collection *Wives at War, and Other Stories* within the literature of the Nigerian Civil War of 1966, noting that Nwapa captures the psychological trauma suffered by individuals caught between national pride and their own survival instincts.

Zongo, Opportune. "Rethinking African Literary Criticism: Obioma Nnaemeka." *Research in African Literatures* 27, No. 2 (Summer 1996): 178-84.

Praises African literary critic Obioma Nnaemeka's paper "Feminism, Rebellious Women, and Cultural Boundaries: Rereading Flora Nwapa and Her Compatriots" as a groundbreaking rethinking of African women's studies.

Additional coverage of Nwapa's life and career is contained in the following sources published by Gale: *Black Writers,* Vol. 2; *Contemporary Authors,* Vol. 143; and *Dictionary of Literary Biography,* Vol. 125.

Orlando Patterson

1940-

(Full name Horace Orlando Lloyd Patterson) Jamaican novelist, nonfiction writer, and essayist.

INTRODUCTION

A writer of fiction and sociological works that explore slavery and its ramifications, Patterson draws on West Indian history to bring new insights to his subjects, whether they be the Caribbean characters of his novels or the slave societies of his sociological studies. Patterson's unique application of historical research and critical techniques have pointed the way for new, interdisciplinary approaches to sociological research. Although many critics find his conclusions controversial, many praise Patterson's scholarship and mastery of secondary sources, noting the significant contribution he has made to the field of social history.

Biographical Information

Patterson was born on June 5, 1940, in Jamaica, West Indies, to Charles A. and Almina (Morris) Patterson. He received a Bachelor of Science degree from the University of the West Indies in 1962 and wrote his first novel, *The Children of Sisyphus*, in 1964. In 1965 he received a Ph.D. from the London School of Economics. After publishing another novel and a sociological study in 1967, Patterson immigrated to the United States in 1970. He received a Master of Arts from Harvard University in 1971 and became a professor of sociology at Harvard. Since then Patterson has written several sociological studies analyzing slavery and the concept of freedom. His nonfiction work *Freedom* (1991), an examination of the concept of freedom, won the 1991 National Book Award.

Major Works

Patterson's first novel, *The Children of Sisyphus,* is set in the slum world of Kingston, Jamaica, and traces the attempts of Dinah, a prostitute, to free herself from her situation and find happiness. *Die the Long Day* (1972) is set on a colonial Jamaican sugar plantation and focuses on the attempts of a slave, Quasheba, to save her daughter from the syphilitic advances of the plantation owner. By focusing on the character of Quasheba, Patterson sheds a unique light on West Indian society and the master-slave relationship. Patterson augments his fictional treatment of slave societies with sociological studies of slavery and ethnic issues. Although his scholarly works concern social issues, Patterson uses historical research and techniques to analyze them. In

The Sociology of Slavery (1967) Patterson uses this interdisciplinary approach to analyze the structure of slavery in his native Jamaica. *Slavery and Social Death* (1982) establishes the universality of the institution of slavery by tracing its existence in different civilizations throughout history. In this book Patterson looks at two types of slavery: institutional, in which there are cultural, economic, and/or political reasons for slavery; and slavery that is a secondary and nonintegral factor in a society. Patterson describes three vital elements to the institution of slavery: force or coercion, "natal alienation" (alienation from the rights enjoyed by the members of the social order), and the loss of honor. Furthermore, Patterson concludes that the institution of slavery gave birth to our recognition and concept of freedom. Patterson develops this conclusion further in *Freedom,* in which he also credits women with playing an important role in the development of the concept of freedom in Greek and Roman societies. Patterson identifies three notes which combine to create "the uniquely Western chord of freedom": personal (to act as one pleases, limited by others' desire to do as they please); sovereignal (to act as one pleases, regardless of what others want); and civic (to participate in a community's governance).

Critical Reception

Patterson has impressed some reviewers with his ability to look at slavery with historical objectivity. Mary Lefkowitz asserts: "Unlike many recent critics of antiquity, Mr. Patterson writes without condescension, observing that we carelessly ignore certain distressing aspects of our own society." Critics praise Patterson's blending of different specialties, including history and economics, in his studies of social history. Although he is admired for the scope of his work, several critics have questioned the authenticity of Patterson's more obscure sources and the validity of some of his conclusions. Robert Nisbet, for example, comments that "In many ways the most provocative and perhaps controversial element in *Slavery and Social Death* is the author's contention that slavery has been indispensable not only to the great civilizations of the past where it flourished but also to the rise of ideas of freedom." While praised for the variety of his sources, Patterson is sometimes accused of drawing unwarranted conclusions from his data. D. A. Miller finds that Patterson's "willingness to chance his hand and venture his opinion can lead to some very strange and maladroit statements." Despite this criticism, however, reviewers note Patterson's intellectual ability and great contribution to the field of sociology.

PRINCIPAL WORKS

The Children of Sisyphus (novel) 1964

An Absence of Ruins (novel) 1967

The Sociology of Slavery: An Analysis of the Origins, Development, and Structure of Negro Slave Society in Jamaica (nonfiction) 1967

Die the Long Day (novel) 1972

Ethnic Chauvinism: The Reactionary Impulse (nonfiction) 1977

Slavery and Social Death: A Comparative Study (nonfiction) 1982

Freedom: Freedom in the Making of Western Culture (nonfiction) 1991

The Ordeal of Integration: Progress and Resentment in America's Racial Crisis (nonfiction) 1997

CRITICISM

Robert Nisbet (review date April 1983)

SOURCE: "The Unfree," in *Commentary,* Vol. 75, April, 1983, pp. 74-6.

[*In the following review of* Slavery and Social Death, *Nisbet expresses reservations about some of Patterson's "concepts and generalizations," but praises his "major contribution, which is the assembling in logical and readable form of data drawn from dozens of cultures and civilizations."*]

Slavery, this book demonstrates, far from being a "peculiar institution," comes very close to being, along with kinship and religion, a universal one. "There is no region on earth that has not at some time harbored the institution. Probably there is no group of people whose ancestors were not at one time slaves or slaveholders." Moreover, slavery has been not only compatible with but indispensable to some of the greatest, most creative civilizations in world history.

Despite the abundance of scholarly writing on slavery during the past several decades, until now no serious work has been addressed to its global dimension. Orlando Patterson, who is a professor of sociology at Harvard and the author of a highly regarded study of slavery in the Caribbean, deals with slavery in all the types of society in which it has been present—pre-literate, Asian, and Western European, from ancient Greece to the American South. Although I have reservations about a few of his concepts and generalizations, I have none about the book's major contribution, which is the assembling in logical and readable form of data drawn from dozens of cultures and civilizations. This is a work of solid

scholarship that will undoubtedly stand a long time before any effort is made to supersede it.

Two major types of slavery are distinguished by Patterson. The first is found in societies in which "slavery attained marked structural significance, ranging from those in which it was important for cultural, economic, or political reasons, or a combination of all three, through those in which it was critical though not definitive, to those in which it was the determinative institution." These are the societies on which the greatest abundance of information exists; they include ancient Greece and Rome, the deep South in the United States prior to the Civil War, many of the Arabic cultures, the African states of the Sudan, the Caribbean nations (whether under Spanish or British rule), Thailand, and Korea. As Patterson shows us in detail, there have been a great many such societies in world history.

The second kind of slave society is one in which slavery, though highly visible, does not play such a strong institutional role as in the first. It is more of an eddy than a main current. Why study slavery in such a small compass? Patterson's answer is interesting: "If one confines oneself to major cases only, to the structurally important cases, one remains unable to answer what is perhaps the most serious structural problem, namely how and under what conditions the process in question ceases being unimportant and becomes important." Among the many examples of small-scale slavery dealt with are the Hebrews of the Kingdom of Judah, the Aztecs, the Comanche Indians, the Ifugao of the Philippines, and the Ibo of central Nigeria.

There is one form of slavery that Patterson should not have omitted: the penal slave systems of the totalitarian states of the 20th century. The Soviet Union leads them, and has done so since the very beginning of Soviet Communism. What Lenin commenced, Stalin brought to fullness. Patterson does deal with penal slavery, and refers to its incidence in 17th- and 18th-century Russia, but that slavery was moderate compared with the Gulag Archipelago. Moreover, totalitarian penal slavery meets most of Patterson's criteria for the identification of the phenomenon: the ruthless uprooting of individuals from normal existence and condemnation to slave labor under limitless power; the forced separation of individuals from all contact with families and neighborhoods; absolute segregation from the social order; and the relentless degradation of persons and the destruction of individual identity—in short, the calculated manufacture of non-persons. If, as Patterson believes, the metaphor of "social death" is useful in the understanding of historic slave societies, it is no less useful in our appreciation of the lot of the tens of millions of Russians and others who have been forced into a horrifying oblivion for alleged crimes against the state. One of the greatest achievements of Patterson's book is the rigorous comparative method. He is no pseudo-evolutionist, using comparison for the sole purpose of contriving balloonlike stages or epochs through which "mankind" is said to have evolved. For Patterson, the purpose of comparison is to illuminate the analysis of some distinctive feature of slavery, and thus make it possible to discern genuine types of slavery and the varied mechanisms within them.

Three elements are, for Patterson, vital in true slavery. Each corresponds to a facet of domination generally—the larger social category in which he locates slavery—and is vivid wherever slavery is found. The first element is force or coercion, exerted whenever it is needed. Absolute power over the slave may be muted, camouflaged, or trivialized by a given master, but it is always there, waiting to be used. Second is what Patterson calls "natal alienation": alienation, that is, from all the rights and immunities enjoyed by members of the social order; alienation indeed from life in the full social and cultural sense. The third element is the loss of honor, or rather the subjection of the slave to a perpetual process of "dishonoring." The slave can have no honor in the historic sense of the word because of the origin of his status, but most of all, Patterson stresses, because he is utterly without power in society save through his master.

Thus honor and power are inseparable. Patterson is well aware of the ostensible exceptions to this pattern, and gives substantial treatment to the eunuchoid slaves who at various times, as in the Ottoman empire, have exercised extraordinary power directly over individuals, indeed over masses of subjects. He is aware too of the seemingly privileged place slaves can have, as in the status of long-time house servant, of craftsman, artist, and musician, even in the deep South where slavery was perhaps more potent a force and less trammeled by any protective law than even in ancient Rome. The literature of comedy in the ancient world has a full share of portraits of the pampered, fawned-upon slave, male and female, and of the sly ways in which the slave, technically under domination by master, is in fact the master of the master. And, finally, Patterson registers his understanding of the kinds of limitation upon complete domination of one being by another which Hegel highlighted, followed by Georg Simmel in his magisterial study of superordination and subordination, a work Patterson makes little use of though it is highly pertinent to his main argument.

But these apparent exceptions or inconsistencies notwithstanding, the fact remains, as Patterson argues forcefully, that they can only mask the residual power that is confirmed by law and custom for the master alone, a power that can at any time be activated to terminate completely whatever limited powers and privileges may have been conferred upon a slave.

In many ways the most provocative and perhaps controver-sial element in *Slavery and Social Death* is the author's contention that slavery has been indispensable not only to the great civilizations of the past where it flourished but also to the rise of ideas of freedom. We commonly assume, Patterson argues, that slavery by its very nature could have nothing to do with freedom. But it was the existence of two classes of people, those in slavery and those not, that first led to stirrings of recognition of something that might be thought of as freedom. Moreover, in the act of freeing a slave, of making a freedman of him, as in ancient Greece, the vital difference between being unfree and free was dramatized; in time, contemplation of this difference evolved into the awareness of freedom.

Patterson states the paradox:

> Before slavery people simply could not have conceived of the thing we call freedom. Men and women in premodern, non-slave-holding societies did not, could not, value the removal of a restraint as an ideal. Individuals yearned only for the security of being positively anchored in a network of power and authority. . . . The first men and women to struggle for freedom, the first to think of themselves as free in the only meaningful sense of the term, were freedmen. And without slavery there would have been no freedom.

> We arrive then at a strange and bewildering enigma: are we to esteem slavery for what it has wrought, or must we challenge our conception of freedom and the value we place upon it?

But all this is surely too much to claim for slavery and liberation from slavery. There are other, far more substantial and widespread historical forces involved in the rise of awareness of freedom. There is, to begin with, the absolute authority of the household father in ancient times, the power to which the Romans gave the label, *patria potestas*. Among Greeks, Romans, and a good many other peoples this power was fundamental, extending as it did to matters of life and death. There were times, as in war, when sons knew the undoubtedly heady experience of liberation from the *patria potestas*, and frequent experience of this kind must have had more than a little to do with the evolution of the consciousness of freedom. Even more important, perhaps, was religion, and claims by innumerable peoples of rights to worship their own gods.

The concept of rights, especially religious rights, is vital to the emergence of the separate but closely related idea of freedom. To be given or otherwise to win the right to one's own religious practices is, in substance at least, to be given or to win the freedom to worship as one desires. I do not question the argument that liberation from slavery generated, in the minds of those liberated, some awareness, however dim, of freedom. But it is not necessary to endow slavery with the unique capacity of being the setting or necessary prelude to the human consciousness of freedom. To answer the question with which Patterson concludes his book, we are not at all obliged to "esteem slavery for what it has wrought"; we may continue to loathe it and regard it as an ugly blot on human history. Nor are we in any respect obliged to "challenge our conception of freedom and the value we place upon it."

Mary Lefkowitz (review date 17 November 1991)

SOURCE: "Liberty for Whom?" in *New York Times Book Review,* November 17, 1991, p. 23.

[*In the following review, Lefkowitz raises certain questions about Patterson's* Freedom, *but asserts that "it is a tribute to Mr. Patterson that as one reads his interesting book one wants to ask and try to answer these and many other difficult and even painful questions."*]

When the founding fathers of this country looked to ancient Athens as their model of a democratic state, it was not their concern to point out that Athenian democracy, like their own, allowed the power of government (*kratein*) to only a small portion of its people (*demos*), namely, male citizens who owned property. Excluded by definition were women, foreigners and slaves. Surprisingly, perhaps, for all of us who live in a democracy where every adult citizen has the right to vote, during most of history these disenfranchised groups made up the majority of the population. How could they have contributed to the notions of freedom, both personal and political, celebrated and guarded by the enfranchised minority? Or how did they?

In the first of his projected two volumes on the origins of the idea of freedom, Orlando Patterson, a professor of sociology at Harvard, argues that it was "slavery, and slavery alone, which made it possible to enjoy a certain kind of freedom." After briefly surveying the role of slaves in other early societies, he concentrates on the Greeks and Romans, and concludes with a brief discussion of notions of freedom in the Middle Ages. In virtually all early societies, about a third of the population, both male and female, whether they were born within a slaveholding household or captured in war or at sea, were in effect chattel, liable to be bought and sold by their owners, who had the power to treat them well and even allow them to buy their freedom, or to abuse and torture them and even put them to death.

Mr. Patterson shows it was only in Western societies that the institution of slavery produced a new awareness of the value of freedom. Certainly the Greek invention of rationalism and philosophy made the crucial difference, for Greek men (as opposed to men in Egypt or Mesopotamia), the ideal existence was not perfect obedience, but (as Socrates put it) the "examined life," which left choice and moral judgments up to each individual.

But, according to Mr. Patterson, Greek males became uniquely aware of the privileges of their personal freedom through the insistence of the women in their society. In Greek literature, even though most of it is written by men, women continually make critical decisions and speak out on significant issues. It is the Trojan women (not their men) who, as survivors of the war with the Greeks, are left to complain that now as slaves they are as good as dead. In *The Trojan Women* of Euripides they describe what it is like to live as captives and mental servants in a foreign land. It is Antigone who rebels against orders that she considers wrong; as a woman she is powerless to change them, so she chooses, however reluctantly, to die rather than obey. In Sophocles' play her attitude is contrasted with that of the slavish guard, whose main concern is not to be punished by King Creon; to save his own skin he carries out the King's orders, even though he knows they are wrong.

Other recent scholars have not credited women with a decisive role in the development of the Greek and Roman concept of freedom. Mr. Patterson says he himself did not expect to arrive at that discovery, and it is not an easy proposition to maintain, because of the nature of the surviving evidence. So long as he has at his disposal source materials in which women's voices can be heard, such as fifth-century B.C. Athenian drama, he can show how women, both slave and free, could make husbands and captors keenly aware of the limitations of their status. But once he is compelled to leave the confrontational world of drama and concentrate on philosophical treatises, women inevitably recede into the background.

Plato either ignored women or sought, in *The Republic,* to make the most capable of them into quasi-males, thus effectively avoiding the question of slavery altogether. Aristotle took care of his female dependents in his will, but on the basis of his writings it would be hard to claim that he gave much thought to reforming their condition. In his *Politics* he disagrees with Plato and insists that "the courage and justice of a man and of a woman are not the same; the courage of a man is shown in commanding, and of a woman in obeying." To him, slaves and women are analogous, except that a woman retains "the deliberative faculty," although without authority.

Later philosophers, like Plato and Aristotle, also used the notion of slavery as a metaphor for dedicated and unceasing service to particular causes or systems of values, and it is this metaphorical application, and not the actual practice of slavery, that is their most important legacy to the Christians and to later Western thought. In Socrates' discussions, and in the moral discourse that derived from them, freedom becomes an internal quest: how can I live without being a slave to my basest passions? As Mr. Patterson observes, in late antiquity and in the Middle Ages the search for the liberation of the soul provided (although inadvertently) new independence for women who could choose to practice celibacy under the auspices of the Christian Church.

It was the Romans, in fact, who gave women and slaves the greatest opportunities for literal freedom, as Mr. Patterson shows. In Hellenistic Egypt, women could write wills and own property. Unlike other peoples, including the ancient Greeks, the Romans allowed freed slaves (though not women) to have full citizen rights. As gravestones attest, these freed men and women seemed to have been proud of their status. In a poem addressed to his patron, the rich nobleman Maecenas, Horace boasts of his freedman father, and in Petronius' novel *Satyricon* the nouveau-riche Trimalchio has on the walls of his palace a mural that depicts the story of his life, including his beginnings as a slave. As Mr. Patterson observes, such open references to their slave origins are best understood as declarations of the value of independence.

If Roman men had a finer appreciation of the value of liberty, why did they not allow women to have the same political rights as freed male slaves? The sources (mostly written by men) are silent. Was it that they had sufficient material rights and so much influence on their men that the subject did not come up? Women in Rome, as in Mediterranean societies today, had great power over the men in their families, and could exercise considerable influence over their sons. Quasi-official powers and, on occasion, considerable financial resources were accorded to the wife or the mother, or even the mistress, of a Roman emperor.

I wish Mr. Patterson had tried to explain why, as it seems, more female than male babies were "exposed" (abandoned at birth by their parents) if in the Roman world a new sensitivity to women's condition had made men aware of the inhumane treatment of other human beings. He might have commented on the ways in which some women slaves (such as prostitutes) were actually freer to determine the course of their own lives than ladies in propertied households. But it is a tribute to Mr. Patterson that as one reads his interesting book one wants to ask and try to answer these and many other difficult and even painful questions.

Unlike many recent critics of antiquity, Mr. Patterson writes without condescension, observing that we carelessly ignore certain distressing aspects of our own society. In the same way, the ancient philosophers, in other respects so high-minded, assumed that slavery was a virtually necessary component of any civilized system of government. Mr. Patterson's book is among the finalists for the 1991 National Book Awards. Read it if you need to understand why we still need to know about the Greeks and Romans, even if you come away from it unsatisfied, or without the admiration (or contempt) that you have been taught to have for the complex legacy of civilization.

Karl F. Morrison (review date April 1992)

SOURCE: A review of *Freedom,* in *American Historical Review,* Vol. 97, No. 2, April, 1992, pp. 512-14.

[*In the following review, Morrison compares Patterson's approach to the concept of freedom in his* Freedom *with that of Donald W. Treadgold's in his* Freedom: A History.]

Reading a book on freedom in the West is often like revisiting a well-loved house. The furniture is the same, perhaps a bit rearranged, a new acquisition here or there, an old standby relegated to the attic. Still, one is consciously at home.

The almost simultaneous publication of two scholarly essays on freedom reminds us how long this sense of place has taken to develop, how essential it is in the artificial structure known as Western culture, and how uncongenial and disorienting it has been, and is, to some within and to nearly all outside the household of the West.

Donald W. Treadgold's book has the wider chronological span, from pre-history to 1990. For him, freedom is equivalent with political pluralism, incorporated above all in democratic forms of government and social orders that safeguard the independence of the individual in person and property. Freedom is optimistic; it is "everlasting" in the human spirit. His numerous and distinguished studies of Russia and China during the last two centuries anticipated the later chapters in this book. He describes how ideals and institutions of freedom, which continuously developed from the beginnings of Western civilization through the Enlightenment, expanded with quite checkered and precarious results into Latin America after 1492 and, also with entirely distinct careers, during the Age of Colonialism, into India, China, and Japan. In their diffusion, they left no traces on other parts of Asia "east of Turkey and Israel."

Transmutations of the state system, which began their onslaught suddenly between completion and publication of this book, have rendered some conclusions more provisional than the author could have foreseen, certainly those concerning Yugoslavia and the former Soviet Union. Possibly events will have cast a strange light over other conclusions before the publication of this review. The rare breadth of learning and the intellectual boldness of Treadgold's book are demonstrated most strikingly in the concluding chapters, where the author surveys with great concision the entire histories of India, China, Japan, and Latin America (the last chiefly since Columbus). The earlier chapters provide an incremental account of the formation of ideals and ideologies of freedom in three great sources of Western civilization (Old Testamental Judaism, Athens, and Rome). Treadgold goes on to chronicle their assimilation to the pluralistic institutions of medieval Europe, refinement (notably by means of doctrines on the freedom of conscience) in the Renaissance and Reformation, and vindication under the challenge of absolutism, with the resulting establishment of constitutional, democratic forms of government.

As a genre, the encyclopedic history of freedom is poetic, and the life mimicked by its art is normally that of the author. Thus, Hegel, Engels, John Stuart Mill, John Bagnell Bury, and John Dewey all refracted quite different ideals of freedom through the prism of personal experience and commitment. Possibly because Treadgold's autobiographical traces in the book have recognizable precedents in the tradition of writings about liberty in Western culture, his inventory of the house of freedom is also familiar. He was able to omit Africa and to relegate slavery to an incidental role.

The life mirrored by Orlando Patterson's art is a different, and rather less familiar, kind. Africa is present, pretextually, in the original inspiration that this book received from studies of the African slave trade and the antislavery movement and, textually, in the normative role assigned to slavery throughout the entire history of freedom in this account. It is present subtextually in the sociological coordinates with which Patterson frames the study and contextually in his earlier, celebrated, investigations of slavery.

For Patterson, slavery is the precondition of freedom. In fact, freedom and slavery become conceivable and intelligible dialectically, through one another, much as do good and evil. His interpretation is a variation on the older dialectic of liberty and authority, which characterized authority as tyranny of magistrates, religion, or dominant class interests and opinions. Patterson's substitution of slavery for authority in this dialectic came about through the experience and reflection that led him to conclude that "at its best, the valorization of personal liberty is the noblest achievement of Western civilization," but one that, from the beginning of European civilization, was imprinted with "Europe's most loathsome heritage of racism." Patterson's interpretation took shape in a gap, unknown to Treadgold, between what he calls "the Western past" and what he calls "my past." The method by which Patterson unfolds the stages of this contaminated and contaminating heritage combines history with sociology.

Patterson ends his account in this first volume with the fourteenth century, reserving "the modern history of freedom" to "a later, shorter work." The expansion of ideologies of freedom outside the boundaries of Europe has not yet entered his narrative, but, considering that the valorization of freedom was complete by the fourteenth century, he has had occasion to explain, from the beginning, why the universal institution of slavery did not engender a universal dialectic with freedom. It was essential, he maintains, that personal freedom be valued and endowed with the capacity of self-determination, and that it have prerogatives and worth beyond those demanding obedience to the group, class, or corporation. Such personal freedom must be cherished and defended by a critical mass, an articulate and powerful subclass of society. It must confer rights to participate in the conduct of political affairs. Thus were combined what Patterson calls the three notes in "the uniquely Western chord of freedom": personal (freedom to act as one wills and can), "sovereignal" (freedom to act as one wills, reserved in autocracies to the ruler alone), and civil (freedom to participate in governance of a centralized political order). In different degrees, these converged (with their dialectical opposite, slavery or serfdom) in classical Athens, the Roman empire, and, with increasing completeness, medieval Europe, but not elsewhere.

Patterson holds that slavery belonged to an artificial, or "unnatural," social and political order that men imposed on nature. Coercive power was the basis of that order. As a social value, personal freedom defied the artificial hierarchy of compulsion and had to be intruded on by agents other than dominant male elites. In his consistent effort to recover the voices of the historically voiceless, Patterson concludes that this was first done by women in classical Athens, as portrayed by tragic dramatists, appealing beyond the changeable limits of law to the universal order of natural justice and, heedless of penalty, enacting the unwritten obligations to self and kindred even in defiance of human law. Their empathy with slaves enabled Athenian women to be "the first creators of Western freedom" by shifting the valorization of freedom from social order to nature. Throughout later periods, in other societies, women continually reconstructed "a distinctively feminine version of the value" after men had assimilated and modified the "note" of personal freedom in prevailing social ideologies.

Much of Patterson's subsequent argument depends on his hypotheses regarding the dialectic of slavery and freedom. Are these foundation stones securely laid? One is aware from the outset that Patterson's subject is morphology rather than phenomena. Diverse, and diversely gathered, data are collated to identify "culture-characters" that transcend differences "in time, place, and levels of sociocultural development." Thus, the materials with which he frames his conceptions come from the ancient Near East (including the enslavement of Hebrews in Egypt), from recent studies of pre-Columbian Cherokees, and from anthropological research in Africa, the South Seas, Polynesia, and Brazil.

Morphology has its own freedom from detail, but there is reason to wonder whether artistic license of brilliant, darting eclecticism tends to deny evidence its own voice. Inevitably, examining Greek tragedians through Patterson's lens produces some novel interpretations of classical texts. Euripides provides the bulk of his proof. Euripides has long been known as not typical but eccentric, the one Athenian tragedian who gave prominence to the suffering of women, the exceptional writer who (in Edith Hamilton's judgment) was daring enough to set "a poor ignorant peasant beside a royal princess and show him at least her equal in nobility." Before Hamilton, others regarded Euripides as "the first modern mind" because of his compassion for those who suffered the consequences of male ideals. She, and they, also acknowledged Euripides as an "archheretic" writing against the prevailing values of his time. Patterson's assertions that women drew empathetic associations of themselves with slaves are occasionally hypothetical reconstitutions rather than readings of ancient texts. Moreover, it would be difficult to imagine that a reader of this book heard a woman's voice in a late-twentieth-century man's interpretation of dramas written more than two millennia ago by men to be performed by men before audiences of men.

There is much to admire in Patterson's boldness, in his wide and comprehensive knowledge, in his regard for analytical distinctions, and in his ability to draw vast and disparate materials into an intelligible and intriguing exposition. As the study moves from antiquity on, however, the dominant morphology does not allow one willingly to suspend disbelief. Where is the evidence that conceptions of freedom in Christianity were framed without reference to theodicy, and that this indifference to human understanding of how there could be evil if God were omnipotent and omniscient (and thus perfectly good) "goes back to Paul," when, in fact, so much reflection about the freedom of the will began with the Apostle Paul's queries on why the Jews were first chosen and then reprobate, why God elected the foolish things of the world to confound the wise, why He had mercy on some but sent "strong delusion" to others "that they should believe a lie," and why the righteous suffered tribulation?

It is no small matter to omit the theodical component from a system of thought preoccupied with suffering and cursed human nature as made in the image and likeness of God, particularly regarding intellective and volitional freedom. Patterson thereby draws a great divide between his morphology and the patristic and medieval materials to which he refers. This omission is, however, of a piece with the discount that he places on the connection between freedom and wisdom and on the regard for the pursuit of wisdom and education, as a process of emancipation that was cherished from antiquity onward. The values that he imposes on patristic texts are not the ones that their authors deposited in them.

According to Patterson, the culminating moment in the formation of the ideology of freedom came in the Middle Ages. European civilization was complete; freedom was its lodestar. Many specialists would argue that generalizations about liberty become increasingly difficult to draw from the twelfth century on. With the development of professional classes, meanings proliferated. Regional practices imposed quite distinctive modifications on teachings inherited from ancient and patristic cultures. As earlier, Patterson gives precedence to unprivileged social orders that were excluded from what used to be called the great humanist tradition.

Although he refers to learned authors, he rests his case largely on his own interpretation of serfdom, burgeoning into new hybrids of slavery, and on the status of degraded and oppressed members of society other than serfs, including heretics. While this emphasis assists the development of his overarching interpretation, it does distract him from a more easily established fulcrum of emancipation. In medieval texts the word "liberty" commonly denotes property—the "liberty" to collect a toll, to build a bridge, to hang a man. To receive a "liberty" established obligations, notably toward its grantor. In such instances, exercising freedom entailed discharging obligations. Frequently, the sign and guarantee of a liberty was a charter or contract. Without expecting this volume to violate its chronological limits by providing a discussion of the social contract's place in the history of freedom, one does rather miss an account of its origins.

The coordinates of the received scholarly tradition concerning the range of medieval speculation have hardly varied from the account given by M. C. D'Arcy in "Authority and Freedom in Medieval Europe." Certainly there is room for zealous, even iconoclastic, analysis to supplement those coordinates or place them in a wider constellation.

Patterson's inventory of the house of freedom includes more unfamiliar entries than Treadgold's. There is reason to ask that some of the more surprising ones be verified. There is no question, however, that Patterson's lens has also refracted more obviously than Treadgold's the suffering that the ideology of freedom has brought with it through war, persecution, enslavement, and oppression. This, too, is a familiar theme (although not in the variations conferred on it by Patterson), arising in the satires of Voltaire and passing through many stages to Franz Fanon's arraignment of humanism as the antithesis of humanity, and now formally lodged in historiography. It inspires some with hatred for the grandeur and beneficence canonized in Western ideals of freedom; from others, it calls forth improvisations on theodicy, in a human key.

D. A. Miller (review date Summer 1993)

SOURCE: A review of *Freedom*, in *Journal of Social History*, Vol. 26, No. 4, Summer, 1993, pp. 877-80.

[*In the following review, Miller asserts that Patterson deserves all praise for a complicated, ambitious, merciless book with many excellences. . . .*"]

Orlando Patterson's first volume on *Freedom* is easy enough to read, and the very devil to review. The reader is drawn on by Patterson's simple but orderly chronological plot, and by a style that is energetic and occasionally elegant, despite the odd sociological obfuscation. The difficulty comes in the task that every honest reviewer must put for him- or herself: to fairly estimate the validity of Patterson's central thesis, that the Western concept of individual freedom must be causally attached to the appearance and the essence of its ancient opposite, chattel slavery.

So baldly stated, it is easy to react almost viscerally—in one's "intellectual viscera," if such an organ can be imagined—to Patterson's thesis, and to reactively denounce the possibility of such a causal connection, of one of the noblest statements of individual right to the most ignoble state of personal rightlessness, impotence, social separation and dependence. It is to Patterson's considerable credit, and because of his considerable scholarly talents, that he can persuade a reader to be patient, to modify that original reaction, to give this author time and space enough to deploy and fully develop his arguments. Since Patterson intends this to be the first volume in a series devoted to proving his thesis, we will have a large body of evidence and opinion to work through, and in this volume we already have a dense and thorny thicket of this evidence and opinion. Here, after setting aside the non-Western social contexts as fundamentally outside and inimical to any true concept of individual freedom, the author devotes the bulk of this book (about two hundred and fifty pages) to the phenomenon of freedom in the Classical context and thoughtworld, that is, to Greek *eleutheria* and Roman *libertas*. This is where his argument is founded, and here is where he must either convince us or fall and fail. And like any scholar, he must not only prove that he is right in the main, in the large strategic plan, but that he is not that often wrong in detail. But Patterson gives us a very large target, and the tendency of the close-reading critic to reach for that potent Latin legal tag *falsus in partibus, falsus in toto* can, to speak frankly (and perhaps predicting one of my reactions to the book), make its appearance here.

Stripped down to its core, Patterson's argument is this: that the fact and presence of a large servile population in the Greek *polis* produces by reaction what he calls a "chordal triad" or "tripartite value," of "personal, sovereignal and civic freedoms," all developed out of a sense of oppositeness to the slave's state and condition. The first two elements of the triad are to a degree related dialectically, as personal freedom is conscious of possible limitations, while "sovereignal" freedom completely empowers the individual in relation to others and stands, in Patterson's theory, at the grim center of the slave-master relationship. Civic freedom is political (and social). To take his musical image onward from this triple chord, the author then plays with theme and variation: adding a Greek woman's voice (as she feels herself essentially in tune with the slave), investigating the bass notes of Greek philosophy, discovering the martial blare of Rome where *libertas* concentrates in the freedman's knowledge of where he once was, and passing on to the cantorial psalmody of Paul and the early Christian "community of urban freedmen." He ends with the plainsong of the early Middle Ages where, to make his point, he must posit that a great many singers (or more correctly, a muttering or grumbling ground-base) are still powerless slaves or near-slaves.

Patterson is a brave man. He is never afraid to reassess and reestimate, to barge into another controversy and churn his way energetically through the evidence, to (returning to that musical image) add his own experimental chords and riffs and the occasional shrill but attention-getting dissonance. But does he convince, and not just entertain, us? The answer has to be a resounding "maybe." Many of his conclusions depend on our acceptance of that putative "large servile class" dominating both agriculture and "trade" in the Greek *polis,* and Patterson dodges around the opinions of Moses Finley and Ellen Meiksins Wood on this essential point. Beyond this, I think that he neglects or misreads two important aspects of the problem. First, there is the matter of the subjective reaction of the free (the Greek, especially the Athenian) to the slave. Patterson sees and must see a permanent and perpetual obsessive attention and consequent tension; I think that the most apparent and consistent attitude of the free Greek to the slave was to ignore him, *not* to be conscious of him. We might call this a moral blindness, but that is *our* view, in our *aeon*. Second, Patterson appears to ignore an objective political element capable of serving as a guide and component in the Greek concept and ideal of freedom, and that is the idea that the *polis* itself served as a powerful communal model for a developing sense of private or individual freedom: I refer to the ideal state of absolute 'political' independence, of identity, with the indelible marks of *autarcheia* and *autarkeia,* sovereignty and self-sufficiency, that were supposed to underpin and define the city-state.

These two points can be debated, and Patterson's positions are certainly worth our serious attention. To estimate his effectiveness and the validity of his argument we must make our own conclusions on the size of the slave component in Greek and Roman society, and to mark as well that point where an arguable quantitative mass was converted to, effected, a qualitative, intellectual-psychological shift. Here we remain in the ambivalent realm of "maybe." What also has to affect our opinion of this book is the niggling but continuous damage done to the author's case by errors, missteps, and excesses of enthusiasm, all combining to make one reader wonder if Patterson knows his subject as well as he might, or ought to. Of course, his subject is immense. And an excess of enthusiasm at least presupposes enthusiasm. Despite the provocative simplicity of his original formula, Patterson is not a reductionist but an expansionist, willing to follow his nose into any byway, however dangerous. And his willingness to chance his hand and venture his opinion can lead to some very strange and maladroit statements. I have already noted those passages and conclusions, a great number of them, that elicit a "well, maybe . . ." from the reader, but in addition and *en passant* Patterson mauls Hesiod (and includes and misuses a bad translation of a passage from the *Works and Days*); makes the poet Archilochos (!) a model for hoplite "courage"; forgets that Athens built the bulk of its empire on the tribute-treasure of the Delian League; conflates the slave and the metic; wonders why Perikles' Funeral Oration doesn't mention the gods; assigns a "superman doctrine" to Plato and for that matter is confident that he can separate Socrates' thinking from that of Plato. And further on: the "massive slave risings" "shook the [Roman] system" (the point is that they did not); the Roman mob's opinion of Cicero, the Outsider, is based on the fact that "his concept of freedom was so much at variance with their own"; Mithraism is called "a kind of early Calvinism." And so on; this is neither an unfair nor an unrepresentative selection.

Some of these missteps are more significant and potentially damaging to his argument than others. In the end, I have to say that Patterson's book itself is more important than, and can probably survive, these gaffes, and as irritating, as tin-eared (especially in his use of Classical literary materials), and as fond of the scatter-shot assault as he sometimes is, he deserves all praise for a complicated, ambitious, merciless book with many excellences—not the least his combative and unbuttoned style, the very style that leads him to the excesses I have listed in part. As for his thesis, I think that it falls toward the Scots verdict: *nil probandum,* or at least not yet. Perhaps before he advances on to other volumes in his project, he should pause to take in, meditate on, and respond to the criticism directed at this one.

Thomas L. Haskell (review date Summer 1994)

SOURCE: A review of *Freedom,* in *Journal of Interdisciplinary History,* Vol. 25, No. 1, Summer, 1994, pp. 95-102.

[*In the following review, Haskell questions Patterson's methodology in* Freedom, *but asserts that the author "has embarked on a daring project of undoubted relevance to us all."*]

Brave fellow, Patterson. Never before have I read a scholarly book as ambitious as this one. Patterson's aim is nothing less than to write the history of freedom, "the supreme value of the Western world." A large order on anyone's premises, Patterson's make it especially daunting. A historically minded sociologist, he cannot rest content with impressionistic description and eclectic, unsystematic evocation of the sort that many historians are taught to regard as the highest aim of their guild. He wants his historical account to have explanatory force, and unlike many scholars of the present generation, he does not imagine that explanation can be separated from causal analysis. The four questions that organize this study are all explicitly causal:

> First, how and why was freedom initially constructed as a social value? Second, how and why, after having been invented, did it emerge as the supreme value distinct from any number of other important values? Third, why did this rise to cultural supremacy happen only in the Western world, and for so many centuries remain confined to this civilization? Finally, having achieved preeminence, what forces maintained its status as the core value of Western civilization throughout the course of its history?

The project is immense and requires so much trespassing on the turf of specialists that few scholars would ever dream of attempting it. Patterson takes no short cuts. Because he believes that freedom developed in ideological counterpoint to the institution of slavery, his history of freedom comes close to being a history of slavery as well. Since he believes that individual liberty and personal freedom are not recent cultural inventions, but go all the way back to ancient Greece—*contra* Berlin and a host of others—the main narrative thread of the study has to be spun out over a period of two millennia, from the time of Homer to the high Middle Ages (and beyond in a forthcoming volume or volumes.) Can the thread stretch that far, readers wonder, without parting under the strain?

The cultural and geographical scale of the study is as breathtaking as the span of time it covers. Patterson begins with an examination of slavery and its cultural concomitants in ancient and preliterate societies: Egypt in the era of Akhnaton, the Tupinamba of pre-European South America, the Imbangala and Kasanje of Africa, the Toradja of the South Pacific, among others. Having drawn from these exotic cases some important preliminary conclusions about the reasons for the "stillbirth" of freedom everywhere but the

West, he turns to Greece, where between the seventh and the fifth centuries B.C., he believes freedom in its current, distinctly Western, form took shape for the first time. The heart of his story, he devotes a full nine chapters to it, ranging panoramically across the social and economic history of ancient Greece and carefully examining cultural monuments usually regarded as the province of classicists, literary critics, and philosophers. Pericles' funeral oration, the plays of Sophocles, Aeschylus, and Euripides, the philosophical writings of Plato, Aristotle, the Sophists, and other less well-known figures: all are great for his mill, and all give evidence, sometimes oblique, of a growing preoccupation with the paradoxes of freedom and servitude.

He covers ancient Rome in four chapters. He finds it striking that Stoicism, a philosophy that was especially intent on distinguishing between inner and outer freedom, took root in a society numerically dominated by freedman. The same resonance between social condition and cultural preoccupation paved the way for Jesus and the emergence of Christianity, a religion that blossomed into a full-blown "theology of freedom" in the hands of Paul of Tarsus. Christians found slavery to sin more degrading than physical bondage, and they won many converts in societies like Rome that were strongly marked by large-scale urban slavery. To Christianity, which he credits with the institutionalization of freedom in Western culture, Patterson devotes four of the book's most interesting chapters.

Three final chapters assemble what little knowledge we have about the gradual and irregular transition from slaves to serfs to peasants after the collapse of the Roman Empire, and then carry the story of freedom in a somewhat halting and perfunctory way up into the Middle Ages. At every stop along this remarkably long and academically treacherous path, Patterson displays an impressive grasp of the local specialist's literature and actively enters into debates, pulling no punches and acting for all the world as if he were on his home turf.

Plainly the book is intended as a *tour de force*. Does it come off successfully? One hesitates to judge. As a scholar whose expertise extends only narrowly back into the seventeenth century (and becomes perishingly thin when pushed back before the sixteenth), this reviewer can only say that Patterson has done an extraordinary amount of homework and put his cards on the table. In view of all that he has done, it seems petty to ask for more. But bravery is no substitute for being right. Although the specialists will have their day, and properly so, no particular tribe of specialists deserves the last word on a project as broadly conceived as this one. The hoops that specialists will ask Patterson to jump through are not the only barriers in his path. Some of the most severe challenges to the success of this project are of a con-

ceptual and methodological nature. What, for example, is this thing called "freedom," the history of which he claims to trace all the way from the fifth century B.C. to the medieval world and beyond? Over a period that long, can anything remain stable enough to serve as a subject of historical inquiry—especially something as abstract, intangible, and open to interpretation as the idea of freedom? Did freedom have any common reference for people as remote from one another temporally and culturally as Pericles, Aristotle, Paul, and, say, Marcilius of Padua, not to mention their innumerable less articulate contemporaries, or more recent writers? Think of Nietzsche's aphorism: "only that which has no history is definable." Two thousand years is a lot of history, enough to wear away the edges of almost anything in a kaleidoscopic torrent of permutations and appropriations, leaving the subject undefinable—and the historian in pursuit of a will-o-the-wisp.

Although Patterson walks where angels fear to tread, he is no innocent. His methodological sophistication is most clearly exhibited in his definition of freedom as a tripartite value, the parts of which bear the same relation to the whole as the notes of a musical chord. The musical metaphor is well-suited to his needs: the strength and timbre of each of the constituent notes of a musical chord can vary with the instrument, the player, and the occasion; one does not expect to hear exactly the same sound each time the chord is played. Still, the same three notes always produce the same chord. A nice touch: the metaphor preserves identity and insists on a measure of sameness, even as it accommodates a good deal of change and variation.

The first of the three notes comprising Patterson's "chord of freedom" is *personal freedom*, simply the absence of coercion or restraint such that one feels able to do as one pleases, limited only by the desire of others to do as they please. Its familiarity deceives us, Patterson warns. Far from being inherent in human nature, the wish to do as one pleases has been and continues to be ranked lower than honor, status, and other forms of social connection in many of the world's cultures. So fundamental, however, is this component in Western thinking that it might easily be mistaken for the whole of the idea of freedom, and it is another token of Patterson's sophistication that he treats it only as one vital part of the story.

The chord's second note is *civic freedom*, which Patterson defines as the capacity of the adult members of a community to participate in its life and governance. Here, not autonomy, or immunity from the will of others, but recognition and participation are of the essence. Although democracy and universal suffrage represent advanced stages of civic freedom, Patterson recognizes that participation comes in many degrees and forms and can be authentic without being either as complete or as literal as modern Western sensibilities demand.

The third of the three notes that make up Patterson's chord, *organic* or *sovereignal freedom,* is by far the most complex. His deceptively straightforward definition does not adequately prepare readers for the far-reaching implications that he draws from it as the text proceeds. Still, this is the source of much that is original and provocative about the book. Sovereignal freedom is a deliberately dissonant note that introduces tensions throughout the chordal triad, reflecting the author's conviction that good and evil are inextricably intertwined. Patterson appears to believe that good not only coexists with evil, but requires it. Indeed, this pessimistic conviction lies at the heart of the book, which is devoted in its entirety to exploring the tragic interdependence that links freedom intimately to its seeming negation, slavery.

Patterson defines sovereignal freedom as "simply the power to act as one pleases, regardless of the wishes of others." It superficially resembles, but on reflection contrasts sharply with, the first note of the chord, personal freedom, which is "the capacity to do as one pleases, *insofar as one can* [given the necessity of respecting the legitimate aspirations of others]" (emphasis in the original). The sovereign disregards the aspirations of others, seeing in them no legitimate limits to the exercise of his freedom. Because sovereignal freedom for some plainly entails exclusion and domination for others, it is the note of the chordal triad held in lowest repute today. So low, indeed, that most of us would probably be inclined to treat it, not as one of the notes of which the chord of freedom is constituted, but simply as a threat to freedom, an obliteration of it. Patterson warns us away from this easy assumption because of its presentist bias, to which he believes Russell succumbed. Keenly aware that "most human beings . . . desire to control not only their own lives but the lives of others," Russell did not regard such desires as an expression of the wish to be free, and did not consider them worthy of philosophical examination. "But this is precisely where sociology and history differ from philosophy," writes Patterson. "It may be illogical and immoral to desire for oneself the absence of obstacles, only to be able to restrain others, but, as this work will demonstrate, it is a sociohistorical fact that human beings have always sought to do just that, and have often succeeded in doing so. What is more, they have, until quite recently, found no problem calling such constraint on others 'freedom.'"

According sovereignal freedom co-equal status with the other two elements of the chord has curious consequences. It means, for example, that the abolitionist's altruistic dedication to the liberation of the slave is no more authentic, as an expression of the conception of freedom that first took shape in seventh- to fifth-century Greece, than the slaveholder's self-serving dedication to his own freedom (or that of his family, his class, or his race). The complex of cultural values that comprise the ideal of freedom and constitute the subject of this book shape the master's motives, not only at the end of history's story, when the master emancipates his slave, but also at the beginning, when he liberates himself by acquiring another human being to till his fields and drudge for him.

For Patterson, then, the disapprobation for efforts to control the lives of others that has grown in the West ever since the Enlightenment does not represent the advance of freedom over nonfreedom; it is instead a shift of emphasis within the chordal triad. Two elements of the chord, personal and civic freedom, are being played so loudly nowadays that the third, the sovereignal variety, is virtually drowned out. Its contribution has become so faint that we have difficulty even thinking about it. But it lingers on, loathed in some cases, unnoticed in others. We have no reason to think it is on the road to extinction.

Patterson bends over backwards to be especially respectful to one variation on the theme of sovereignal freedom that he associates with Plato: the "organic" notion of freedom, in which the individual submerges his or her personal freedom in willing obedience to a master, whether divine or temporal, but *in so doing* is understood to have achieved the highest and truest form of freedom (think of Christian doctrines of personal rebirth through commitment to Christ, or the way the idea of "History" functions for Party members, as depicted in Arthur Koestler's *Darkness at Noon*). Modern, secular thought has tended to dismiss this variety of freedom as an outright delusion, but Patterson insists upon both its authenticity and its historically creative role.

Patterson's ambivalent respect for the organic and sovereignal varieties of freedom, in spite of their dangers and their partial eclipse by the other two notes of the chord, puts him out of step with current fashion. He recognizes that some of the manifestations of these forms of freedom, such as the rise of the Nazis, have been appalling. But with characteristic tough-mindedness, he makes the analytical knife cut both ways. Horrifying as the Nazi phenomenon was, it was an authentic expression of freedom, the keystone of Western culture. Although admirable, freedom shares in the moral complexity of all sublunary things. Patterson offers no escape from ambivalence and ambiguity.

Patterson has deep reservations about Plato and he will not accept the idea that the Nazis were a freak of nature, with no cultural roots. But he is firmly convinced that Western culture, for all its warts, blemishes, crimes, and villainies, is genuinely preferable to its competitors, and that freedom is the key to its achievements. "Individually liberating, socially energizing, and culturally generative, freedom is undeniably the source of Western intellectual mastery, the engine of its extraordinary creativity, and the open secret of the triumph of Western culture, in one form or another, over the other cultures of mankind."

The central question for Patterson is why the natural obstacles to freedom's development did not prevail in ancient Greece as they did elsewhere. The sovereignal variety of freedom, being inherent in slavery, was not unique to the West, and neither was civic freedom. Personal freedom is a different story. Patterson believes that slaves were the first to get the "unusual idea" that freedom was the most important thing a person could possess, but valuing personal freedom in a culture that assigned it no value would have been like "jumping from a slave ship into a shark-filled ocean. Only where the possibility existed for the isolated individual to fend for himself economically, and to survive the hostility of the freeman socially and culturally, could the slave even began to think about his freedom as the absence of personal restraint and as doing as he pleased. No such social space ever existed before the rise of slavery in ancient Greece."

Before personal, civic, and sovereignal freedom could fuse into the trinitarian unity that constitutes "freedom" in the full, Western sense, Patterson argues, freedom had to become a collective value or norm, capable of powerfully shaping perceptions and channeling conduct. Before that could happen, it had to be socially constructed out of brutal interactions between masters, slaves, and nonslaves. Masters would find freedom valuable only as a means of inducing higher productivity from skilled slave craftsmen in an urban setting; nonslaves would discover the virtues of freedom in their resentment of the slave-masters, as they strove to distinguish their status from that of the slave.

What overcame the usual barriers to the development of freedom as a social value was an extremely complex and long drawn out concatenation of events, running from the seventh century to 431 B.C., when Patterson finds freedom as a fused chordal triad fully articulated for the first time in Pericles' famous funeral oration. Two streams of events converged to produce this result. In the first, personal and civic freedom won unprecedentedly strong support from two different nonslave constituencies, one female, the other male. This occurred just as an expansion of slavery, along with favorable military and economic conditions, made masters receptive to the sort of concessions that could create the "social space" that personal and civic freedom required if they were to thrive and fuse with the sovereignal variety. Slavery was the "decisive factor" precipitating the fusion. Nothing that the men who instituted the breakthrough to democracy were nearly all aristocrats, Patterson argues in terms reminiscent of Edmund S. Morgan in *American Slavery, American Freedom* that "slavery had rendered the independence of the mass

of native Greeks possible, not by making them a leisure or idle class, as was once naively thought, but by making their independence tolerable to their former masters by providing them with an alternative, more flexible labor force."

From the outset, slavery as a social value was sustained by an exceedingly uneasy alliance of diverse interests, each party to the alliance interpreting the value differently. The receptivity of masters made possible the expansion of civic freedom, but the propelling force, Patterson suggests, came from nonslave males who feared the slavemasters, envied the gains their slaves were bringing them, and thus wrung concessions from them in the form of citizenship and a rough political equality. In contrast, Patterson believes that the expansion of personal freedom was initially carried out by women, whose "freedom consciousness" was more acute than that of men because of fear that they themselves would be enslaved, at a time when most slaves were women. Men as well as women dreaded forced obedience, but when men defended themselves against enslavement they fought for honor, family, status, and life itself, not personal freedom, which had little cultural significance for them. Since women were not expected to defend themselves, they were not caught in this "honorific trap." "In other words, gender expectations in early Greece, made freedom a possibility for women, even as they closed it off for men." Only gradually, Patterson argues, as the threat of enslavement was increasingly masculinized, did personal freedom take on value for males as well as females.

Patterson's argument, for all its dialectical intricacies, remains skeletal. The book sometimes reads more like the musings of a scholar who is self-consciously reading and taking notes outside his field, than a text designed either to inform the uninitiated, or to persuade specialists. Schematic formulations and sweeping generalizations abound, perhaps inevitably. Evidence for some claims, especially the priority of women in the development of personal freedom, is skimpy and wide open to alternative readings. There is room to wonder if slavery were really as indispensable to the promotion of "freedom consciousness" as Patterson claims. After all, every child moves through stages of dependence and independence on the way to adulthood. These psychological passages are culturally mediated and can be more or less wrenching, depending on circumstances; but the same could be said of slavery. These developmental dilemmas, even if not psychological universals, have some bearing on the wish to be free. Patterson never considers them. Nor could he readily do so, within his strongly sociological perspective.

Admirably supple as Patterson's chord metaphor is, the most fundamental of his claims—that freedom emerged full-blown in the fifth century B.C. and has not changed in any essential way over the intervening centuries—can be doubted. "Essentialism" is not in good odor today, making it difficult to sustain the distinction between important and unimportant changes upon which all claims of continuity necessarily depend, but anyone who believes that the civilization of the West originated in ancient Greece needs an explanatory scheme that insists, as Patterson's does, on continuity in the face of all changes. The success of Patterson's formulation remains to be demonstrated in subsequent volumes, as he shows us how well the metaphor can handle such far-reaching changes in the meaning of freedom as those that accompanied the Protestant Reformation, the American and French Revolutions, the rise of market society, and the bitter debate between Liberal and Socialist conceptions of freedom that has preoccupied the West for the past century and a half.

The question is not which is "true," change or continuity, or even which "prevailed," but how best to represent the shifting balance between them. My own guess is that the development of the idea of freedom after 1750 cannot be fully accounted for without reference to changes in the perception of human agency, causality and, finally, personhood itself, for which the chordal metaphor has no place. But that remains to be seen. In the meantime, Patterson's achievement is a considerable one. At a time when plodding timidity passes for wisdom in some academic circles, trendy iconoclasm is mistaken for deep insight in others, and conformity to orthodoxies of both left and right wins undeserved rewards all around, he has embarked on a daring project of undoubted relevance to us all, under the impulsion of a genuine and independent-minded curiosity about how things came to be the way they are. The project deserves a wider and more thoughtful audience than it is likely to receive.

FURTHER READING

Criticism

Diggory, Terence. "'Neo-Puritan' or 'Legalistic'? Orlando Patterson's Critique of Feminism." *Salmagundi,* No. 101-102 (Winter-Spring 1994): 142-50.
    Discusses Patterson's relationship to contemporary feminism.

> **Additional coverage of Patterson's life and career is contained in the following sources published by Gale:** *Black Writers,* **Vol. 1;** *Contemporary Authors,* **Vols. 65-68; and** *Contemporary Authors New Revision Series,* **Vol. 27.**

Caryl Phillips
1958-

English novelist and playwright.

INTRODUCTION

Phillips is perhaps better known today for his novels, particularly *Cambridge* (1991) and *Crossing the River* (1993), than for his plays, which have been produced for the stage, television, radio, and cinema. In both his drama and awarding-winning fiction, Phillips consistently has related the experiences of the African diaspora in the Caribbean, Europe, and America. His works offer a historical and an international perspective on the themes of immigration (forced and otherwise), cultural and social displacement, and nostalgia for an elusive "home" that often exists in mythical proportions in the minds of his characters. Yet Phillips adamantly has refused the label "black" writer. In the preface to his play *The Shelter* (1983), he said: "In Africa I was not black. In Africa I was a writer. In Europe I am black. In Europe I am a black writer. If the missionaries wish to play the game along these lines then I do not wish to be an honorary white."

Biographical Information

Born March 13, 1958, in St. Kitts, West Indies, Phillips was brought to England when he was only twelve weeks old. He was raised in Leeds and attended The Queen's College, Oxford, from which he received a B.A. with honors in 1979. Phillips's first stage play, *Strange Fruit,* was produced in 1980, followed by *Where There Is Darkness* (1982) and *The Shelter.* He then pursued other media for his dramatic productions. In 1984 he produced the radio play *The Wasted Years,* which was published in Best Radio Plays of 1984, and the television plays *The Hope and the Glory* and *The Record.* In 1985 Phillips was awarded the Malcolm X Prize for his first novel, *The Final Passage* (1985) which encouraged him to write another novel, *A State of Independence* (1986), and a collection of three novellas, *Higher Ground* (1986). Upon returning from a European tour during 1986, he wrote *The European Tribe* (1987), a collection of travel essays for which he received the Martin Luther King Memorial Prize. With the publication of his third novel, *Cambridge* (1991), Phillips was recognized by the London Sunday Times as "Young Writer of the Year" in 1992 and was listed among GRANTA's "Best of Young British Novelists" of 1993. His novel *Crossing the River* was nominated for the respected Booker Prize. Phillips was appointed writer-in-residence at Mysore, India, in 1987 and at Stockholm University, Sweden, in 1989. Since 1990 he has

been Visiting Professor of English at Amherst College in Massachusetts.

Major Works

The dominant theme in most of Phillips's works is the human displacement and dislocation associated with the migratory experience of blacks in both England and America. His first play, *Strange Fruit* explores the lives of West Indian immigrants pulled between England and their Caribbean homeland; his later dramas focus on historical situations concerning the African slave trade in America and England. Much of Phillips's fiction expands the issues presented in his plays. For example, *The Final Passage* tells of a West Indian family that gains passage to England during the 1950s, while *A State of Independence* relates the return of a man who had left his native island twenty years earlier for an Oxford scholarship. *Cambridge* juxtaposes the journal of Emily, a nineteenth-century English woman living at her father's West Indian plantation, with the story of Cambridge, an educated slave there; it reflects the situation portrayed in the play *The Shelter,* in which a white widow and a freed slave are shipwrecked on a desert island at the end of the eighteenth century. *Crossing the River,* like Phillips's radio play of the same name, addresses the human cost of the African slave trade, but the novel is narrated by several voices, including a father who sold his children, a slave-ship captain, and an English shopgirl who loves an African-American soldier stationed in England during World War II. *Higher Ground* voices the separate tales of an African operative in the slave trade, an African-American convict during the 1960s, and Irene, a Jewish Pole exiled in London after World War II. Notable among the travel essays in *The European Tribe* are studies of the Shakespearean characters Othello and Shylock, made while the author was in Venice, and reminiscences of a dinner party with James Baldwin and Miles Davis in France.

Critical Reception

Critics almost universally acclaimed Phillips's first novel, *The Final Passage,* which revealed to David Montrose the author's "clear potential as a novelist." But detractors began to appear with the release of *A State of Independence.* According to Adewale Maja-Pearce, the novel suffers from "appalling prose style and indifferent characterisation." *Higher Ground* generated confusion about whether the individual stories were meant to be linked thematically; nonetheless, Charles P. Sarvan called it "a moving and disturbing book." The racial theme in *The European Tribe* made this work "too important a book to be ignored," according to Charles R. Johnson, but most critics concurred with Merle Rubin, who found the collection "significant but uneven." Phillips reached a considerably larger audience with the publication of *Cambridge,* "a masterfully sustained, exquisitely crafted novel," according to Maya Jaggi. Following the appearance of this work, certain commentators noted Phillips's adept handling of female voices in his fiction, while others detected an undercurrent of pessimism in his novelistic vision. Recently, scholars have started exploring Phillips's texts within the context of postcolonial literary theory. Many critics found significance in the "multi-voiced chorus" of *Crossing the River;* as John Brenkman indicated, "the global awareness of the [black] diaspora has stimulated a writer like Caryl Phillips to find the languages and the stories in which [our] complex fates can be told."

PRINCIPAL WORKS

Strange Fruit (play) 1980
The Shelter (play) 1983
The Wasted Years (radio play) 1984
The Final Passage (novel) 1985
A State of Independence (novel) 1986
The European Tribe (essays) 1987

Higher Ground (novel) 1989
Cambridge (novel) 1992
Crossing the River (novel) 1994
The Nature of Blood (novel) 1997

CRITICISM

Charles P. Sarvan and Hasan Marhama (essay date Winter 1991)

SOURCE: "The Fictional Works of Caryl Phillips: An Introduction," in *World Literature Today,* Winter 1991, pp. 35-40.

[*The following essay examines three works by Phillips:* The Final Passage, A State of Independence, *and* Higher Ground. *Sarvan and Marhama provide an introduction to Phillips' fiction and some conclusions about its essential characteristics.*]

Caryl Phillips was born in St. Kitts in 1958 and was brought by his parents to England in that year. He grew up in Leeds, studied at the University of Oxford, but returned recently to St. Kitts and the Caribbean. (Of course, there are no real returns but always and only onward journeys.) He has traveled extensively in the United States and Europe and has visited Africa.

The Final Passage (winner of the Malcolm X Prize) is the story of Leila, who comes to England, bringing her husband Michael (more burden than baggage) and infant son Calvin. Left alone by her unfaithful husband, living without hope or happiness in slum conditions, she decides to return to her little Caribbean island. However, by this time Leila has suffered a breakdown, is unemployed, and one wonders if she will be able to give the decision practical, financial expression. It is not that Britain has opened her eyes to previously overlooked positive aspects of her island home; return is merely the lesser of two unattractive alternatives. The author, who himself was taken to England as a baby and who as an adult has made the journey back, writes about "the West Indian wave of immigration" into Britain, the so-called mother country, in the 1960s. Through Leila we gain an inkling of understanding as to why people left the Caribbean and what life was like for those immigrants in Britain, where at that time it was legal and normal to display signs that read, "No coloureds [or 'blacks']. No dogs." (Wole Soyinka records his experiences in the satiric poem "Telephone Conversation.") The novel thus has wider dimensions—of a historical, economic, and cultural nature.

In 1962 V. S. Naipaul published a collection of essays titled *The Middle Passage.* The phrase "the middle passage" comes down from the days of slavery. The "first passage" was when a ship left England for Africa, carrying baubles, cheap industrial products that were bartered for slaves. Then began the dreadful "middle passage," to the American and Caribbean plantations, during which voyage many died and were thrown overboard. (It is estimated that as many as twenty million Africans were abducted from the continent.) The survivors were sold at auction; with the money realized, raw materials were purchased to feed the voracious industrial machines back home, and the ship began "the final passage," so much the richer for the "enterprise." Leila wishes to make her final passage back to the Caribbean, although, as already indicated, she may end up marooned and captive for the rest of her life: a different form of life imprisonment from that experienced by Rudy in **Higher Ground** (more on this later). On the other hand, the first section of the novel bears the subtitle "The End," describing Leila's departure from the Caribbean: the end may also be the beginning of a return after all. Her mother, dying in a London hospital, says, "London is not my home. . . . And I don't want you to forget that either." Naipaul, in *The Middle Passage,* observes with detachment the subdued, bewildered immigrants herding onto the ship for England. Phillips presents us with the case of one out of those anonymous thousands, one from the historical statistics.

In the same collection of essays Naipaul describes St. Kitts as "an overpopulated island of sixty-eight square miles, producing a little sea-island cotton, having trouble to sell its sugar, and no longer growing the tobacco, the first crop of the settlers. . . . We were . . . watching the lights of the toy capital where people took themselves seriously enough to drive cars from one point to another." He records his nightmare, "that I was back in tropical Trinidad," a land indifferent to virtue as well as to vice. History, he argues, is built around achievement and creation, and nothing was created in the West Indies. (The epigraph of **The Final Passage** is from Eliot: "A people without history / Is not redeemed from time.") Slavery has bred self-contempt, and the "West Indian, more than most, needs writers to tell him who he is and where he stands." Phillips undertakes a telling, and absence becomes the essence of the novel: absence of history and achievement, of scope in the present and hope for the future.

The second and longer section of the work is "Home." Michael's grandfather uses a metaphor to convey the island's cultural hybrid: yams from Africa, mangoes from India, and coconuts from the Pacific. The men almost miraculously find money to go drinking day and night, but it is not a glorious riot, a Bacchanalian celebration of life, but rather a drinking through boredom and hopelessness to a state of stupor. The island is a place where the sound of a motorcycle starting up is a sufficient event to attract adult spectators: "There's nothing here for me to do, nothing! . . . Nothing,

man!" Michael falls back on physical vanity: great care is taken over the length of his shirt sleeves and trousers; the motorcycle gives him the illusion of power, and he possesses the "freedom" that is a total denial of responsibility. In sleep, with pose and posturing set aside, his tired face crumbles like a bridge collapsing into rubble. He gets drunk on his wedding day and spends the night with Beverley, by whom he already has a son. As Leila's pregnancy advances, he moves into Beverley's shack and sees the baby for the first time when it is six weeks old.

In order to escape from the life in which she was trapped, Leila decides to emigrate to England. Michael's preparation for the challenges of this new life is to wonder whether or not to grow a moustache. Leila does all the packing; Michael drinks—and almost misses the ship. Leila's beauty, discipline, and determination attract Michael, but he feels inferior and, as a consequence, resentful. He has no understanding of himself, of the forces that have shaped him and account for his circumstances and behavior. He is an unthinking victim: his situation is all vague and confused but, nevertheless, real and damaging. His grandfather had advised, "You must hate enough, and you must be angry enough to get just what you want," but disgruntled, destructive Michael is not clear about what he wants, much less how to set about getting it.

Unqualified, unskilled, and unprepared, Michael and Leila move into a depressed part of London, initially to a boardinghouse, where men sleep "head to toe" for want of space. The house they later rent is squalid.

> Two of the upstairs window panes were broken in, and the door looked like it had been put together from the remains of a dozen forgotten doors. . . .
>
> The light switch did not work. The house was dark and smelled of neglect. . . .
>
> Upstairs there was a solitary bedroom. A soiled double mattress lay prostrate in the middle of an otherwise naked floor. . . . The small bathroom consisted of a toilet bowl and a wash basin. . . . There was no bath, and the door to this room hung from its hinges.

Michael's reaction is to walk out (escape), saying he expected to find the house in better shape on his return. Whether describing scene, house, character, or conduct, the narrator impassively, "factually" gives us the details.

> Michael forced his hand down between her legs and pried them open. Then he hauled himself on top of her, unable to take any of the weight himself. . . . But it was no good. He leaned over and vomited

beside her head, catching the edge of the pillow and running back some of the vomit into her hair. Then, having emptied his stomach for the third time, he lay unconscious and draped across her. . . . She looked at the side of his head and waited until morning came. . . .

Leila had booked passage on a ship, but a passage is also a path, an initiation, as in Forster's *Passage to India.* Having learned, she would rather retrace her steps and come to terms with life back home: there she has a friend who loves and understands her. Her experience is one that was shared by many: "home" is a plantation economy in dilapidation, with an imported population (the descendants of slaves and indentured laborers) without history or hope. Attempting to fashion a more meaningful life, they leave their stagnant societies and come to Britain, only to find that she can be as cruel as the heartless stepmother in fairy tales. Lacking education, training, and (especially the men) inner resources, encountering racial prejudice, reduced to mean employment, and restricted to certain areas for accommodation, they neither find nor are able to create opportunities. Since individuals like Michael are unaware of the impersonal forces that have damaged their lives, they continue the pattern: irresponsible, violent, fantasizing, trying to find temporary escape from a reality they do not comprehend and cannot combat. It is the reader who reaches an understanding.

The title of Phillips's second novel, *A State of Independence,* recalls Naipaul's *In a Free State.* Bertram Francis returns to his Caribbean home (having lived the last twenty years in Britain) three days before the country gains its independence. The island has turquoise coral and green forests, but outside the capital the houses are small fragile boxes with roofs of corrugated-iron sheets: "People seem just as poor as they always been" (*sic*). In the naïve rhymes there are shades of Naipaul's perception of Caribbean politics: "Forward ever—backward never"; "Proud, Dignified and Black / None Can Take My Freedom Back!" There is a touch of satire in the doctor and the funeral director's joint ownership of a rum distillery, in the fire-brigade station's catching fire and burning down. And, as in most of what is hopefully called the "developing" world, there is exploitation: "Our finest minds . . . who all been overseas [*sic*] . . . are so bored with how easy it is to make money off the back of the people that they are getting drunk for kicks and betting on who can lap up the most sewage water from the gutter."

Much of this is embodied in Jackson Clayton, once a close friend of and almost a brother to Bertram and now deputy prime minister as well as minister of agriculture, lands, housing, labor, *and* tourism. Among the things Clayton proudly claims to have done for his country is the bringing in of the luxury liner *Queen Elizabeth II* (with her affluent tourists),

Pan American Airlines, and Hollywood films. In short, this man who once referred to himself as Jackson X, following the example of the radical Malcolm X, is a representative of Western capitalism rather than of the island's people. Made calloused and smug by wealth and power, Jackson now advocates closer ties with the United States, not because of a rejection of Britain and her imperial past but because the United States is commercially more promising to him. (Jackson imports Japanese cars via the U.S.) Independence means that, in addition to economic "clout," complete political power will now pass into such hands. To the people, celebrating independence is a patriotic excuse to drink more and longer than usual. It is an inefficient, poor, and polluted island, "And what is the response from the people with the money? The Rotary Club decide to donate a dustbin to every village. . . . As a people we come like prostitutes." The people are not angry, not even cynical, but only apathetic. (Cynicism implies understanding.) Enter Bertram Francis.

Francis went on a scholarship to England but, after two years, was asked to leave college. Thereafter he drifted: "My time just slide away from me . . . there's plenty more just like me. . . . People who went there for five years, then one morning they wake up with grey hair and wonder what happened." Bertram returns with guilt and apprehension, after an absence of two decades. The airport runway is his welcome carpet, but otherwise, to adapt the words of Christopher Okigbo, he was the sole witness of his homecoming. It is not that Bertram has been away so long; it is not that he slacked in his studies and returns with nothing to show for all those years, but that during his absence he did not write to anyone—not to his mother, his brother Dominic, his girlfriend Patsy, or his friend Clayton—much less send the odd bit of money to his long and silently struggling mother. Bertram returns unaware that his brother, who had become an alcoholic, was killed by a hit-and-run driver. This failure in human relationships, and the obligations which go with them, is paralleled by our misgivings about his political stance.

Bertram returns because the country is about to become free. He did not help in the hunt and, in fact, showed no interest in it, but has come to see if he can get a share of the meat. He seems to think that the mere fact of his having lived in Europe is qualification enough, something that makes him superior. An obnoxious Clayton demands, "What do you have to offer us? What is it about yourself that you think might be of some benefit to our young country?" All he has is a vague notion of setting up a commercial venture that will not depend on the white man. It is significant that he wants to "seize the opportunity" by going into business: he does not think of a cooperative project, or rural development, or of education, but only of making money for himself. Neither in personal relationships nor in public matters is he any different from Clayton, and his sense of moral superiority is baseless. Most of the time between arrival and independence (three days later) he spends drinking bottle after bottle of beer. The positive characters are the minor ones (and all female): Bertram's mother; Mrs. Sutton, who, though old herself and having no obligation to do so, cares for Bertram's mother; and Patsy, who loves, forgives, is quietly cheerful, and takes back the failed and directionless man.

Bertram has lived "in a free state," one without commitment and duties, but now accepts his "mediocrity," resumes his relationship with Patsy, and begins to wonder what he can do for his bedridden mother. (Perhaps nineteen-year-old Livingstone is his son.) As Bertram moves away from his selfish, sterile "freedom," the country is moving into *its* state of independence under the likes of the Honourable Jackson Clayton. Are the rains which disrupt the celebrations inauspicious or a sign of fertility and promise? A similar enigma is also faced at the end of Ngugi wa Thiongo's novel *A Grain of Wheat.*

Higher Ground, subtitled "A Novel in Three Parts," consists of three stories. The first, **"Heartland,"** is told by a "collaborationist" (an anachronistic term), an African who assists in the slave trade: "It is moments such as these . . . marooned between [the European traders and the enslaved Africans] . . . that the magnitude of my fall strikes me." Circumstances have distorted the narrator—"If survival is a crime then I am guilty"—and there is a diminution of human feelings to the point of extinction. Because **"Heartland"** is a first-person narrative, the reader is situated within the consciousness of this man, and contradictory impulses result: between identification and sympathy, on the one hand, and recoil on the other. The reader must constantly remind her- or himself of the appalling wretchedness the slave trade inflicted, of the terror and misery. The brutality is heightened by the neutral tone of the narrator: "In the corner trading equipment is temporarily stored: whips, flails, yokes, branding-irons, metal masks." Women are kept separate because they often attempt, mercifully, to take the lives of their children. The European slavers, who equate literacy, technological (military) superiority, and fine clothes with "civilization," are barbarous in conduct, often perverted and sadistic; but the African chiefs are also guilty of selling their own for baubles and beer.

This holocaust is little remembered because it was visited upon "natives" long ago, at a time when that graphic recorder of human cruelty, the camera, had not yet been invented. In the end the narrator resists and is himself transported to the United States as a slave. Beyond degradation, there is regeneration and moral recovery. He decides to feign ignorance of English, for competence in the language is a liability and has led to his being a tool in the exploitation of his own people. Caliban ostensibly forgoes Prospero's language yet is subversive in that he writes his memoir in it, using the language of the slave masters to indict them, to return, if not to his home across the ocean, then to himself: "We are promising ourselves that we will return to our people. . . . And the promise comes from deep inside of our souls."

"Heartland" is told throughout in the present tense, which accords with the narrator's determination to keep the past alive and thus to "return" to it, yet it is more a memoir than a diary. As with that earlier African novel, *Houseboy,* apart from literary conventions and a willing suspension of disbelief, the impact is such that we do not query how the narrator, given his circumstances, contrived to write, and preserve, his testimony.

Prisons have sometimes proved to be places of education, reflection, writing. At random, one thinks of Pandit Nehru of India and, from more recent times, of Kenya's Ngugi and Nigeria's Soyinka. The letters that constitute **"The Cargo Rap"** (the longest and the most central of the three stories) are the direct descendants of the prison letters of George Jackson, published in 1970 as *Soledad Brother.* In 1960, at the age of eighteen, Jackson was misadvised to plead guilty to a charge of robbery and was sentenced to an indeterminate prison term of one year to life. In Soledad Prison he was accused of the murder of a white prison guard and transferred to San Quentin, pending trial. He was killed there on 21 August 1971 in circumstances that have never been satisfactorily explained. "Rudy," who writes the letters of **"The Cargo Rap,"** is very similar to Jackson. He did not enter prison because of a politically motivated act, and his consciousness developed while he was in prison. As Jackson wrote, "I have almost arrived but look at the cost."

Both Jackson and the fictional Rudy arrive at an understanding of society and what it has done to them, but too late. Indeed, because of their awareness, consequent stance, and political influence, the system does not release them. Jackson's letters were to his parents, whom he loved (but about whose limitations—their mental shackles and timidity—he remained bitter and upbraiding); to his younger brother (shot dead while attempting to free him); to his lawyer Fay and to Angela Davis, the black activist. Rudy, also serving a "one year to life" sentence for robbery, writes to his parents, his sister, and two female lawyers. However, unlike in Jackson's case, finally it is not Rudy's life but his sanity that is killed. In style too, the letters—in one instance real, in the other fictional—are similar, for Jackson's correspondence ranges from sardonic, terse, and witty to impassioned protests of tremendous rhetorical power. Jackson belongs to history, however, and what is interesting in **"The Cargo Rap"** is the fictional Rudy: the processes by which character is created, the character himself, and his perceptions. Unlike *Soledad Brother: The Prison Letters of George Jackson,* **"The Cargo Rap"** must provide its own context, its own external data, necessary for an understanding of the fictional present.

The narrator of **"Heartland"** lived inside a fort, a stockade; Rudolph Leroy Williams is in prison, and prison becomes the metaphor for an unfree society and for captive lives: "It is only logical that two hundred years of exposure to the idea of a 'natural' (inferior) position should have nappied your mind," Rudy writes to his mother. His teacher had told him that he had talent and could, one day, become a clerk: "He did not mention doctor, lawyer, judge, professor, or nuclear physicist. . . . He wanted me to make peace with my mediocrity." Black Americans are released from the womb "only into the greater captivity of American society," and prison brutality is but a reflection of that brutality which is present in society. Rudy describes himself as follows: "Name: Homo Africans; Occupation: Survivor; Age: 200-300 years; Parents: Africans captured and made slaves; Education: American school of life." The reader wonders whether this survivor will survive. Will he succeed in being moved from solitary confinement to the main block? Will he win parole? "In the bosom of this country there is a man who is being stretched and tortured for forty dollars."

Rudy's passing references to a broken arm, a concussion, and to spitting blood indicate that the letters do not tell everything; this is an epistolary story, and the letters are all we have to go by: "I am once again down here on Max Row. I apologize to you for the disappointment that this will no doubt cause you." What happened? Why is he back in the "maximum" (solitary) wing of the prison? His struggles are protracted, and there are increasing signs of irrationality. Don't let mother work so hard and physically, he writes, without confronting the reality that the family needs the money, that his mother cannot find other work. Has his sister lost her virginity? Can he pay his lawyers with fruit from Africa, once he is released and "returns" to that continent? And, writing to his father, he asks whether the latter still derives sexual pleasure from sleeping with Mother or whether he masturbates. Rudy's last letter, poignantly, is addressed to his mother, whose death a month earlier represented the proverbial final nail.

Since there is no narrator other than himself and the replies he receives are not included, Rudy is characterized solely through his letters. These can be direct, with a conversational casualness: "Come a Saturday night Mr Charlie likes nothing better than to go out and crack a coon [black man] or two." Rudy educated himself politically, relying on books, and the language of these works enters his vocabulary with incongruous effects, so that in writing to his family we have "I'll amplify upon this in my next communication. . . . She is being malprogrammed in a hostile and alien culture." He uses words and phrases such as "peruse" or "your senescent body" and pellucid disquisitions, but he can be succinct: "For

half an hour each day, I breathe fresh, if not free, air." Life in prison is like being inside not a boxing ring but the boxing glove itself: one passively and helplessly encounters pain. Rudy uses irony ("I tried to liberate some money"), puns ("We are trying to make the white Americans change their attitudes but are we getting any change [results]?"), and paradox ("I sit here in the darkness of constant light")—the last phrase also possessing biblical overtones of a people who sat in darkness and then saw a great light. He can be warm and persuasive, as when writing to his mother—"You describe yourself as an invalid. . . . In-valid . . . . You are a very valid part of our world"—or sardonic and bitter: "In the mornings, grandfather would get up, take down his cap and jacket, hang up his dignity and his mind, and slope out to slave and giggle for the white man." He can rise to tremendous verbal power, reminiscent of protest and revivalist rhetoric: "Do you want mustard for your hot dog, flowers for your hair or bullets for your gun?"; "Hang in or hang up." Black women in prison are there "for whoring, not warring." The black man needs "your support, not your scorn. . . . I am a literal and metaphorical prisoner, Moma. I need you to stand by me, not sit on me." His perceptions and his power point to potential, and thus to the waste.

Rejecting the society in which he is a prisoner, Rudy turns (in order to fill the void) to the original home of his people, to Africa and to a "Negro Zionism": "Is this America, the civilized country of satellites and color television? . . . We must flee and burn bridges behind us as we leave. . . . The dice are loaded, the terms are unacceptable, the American odds too long." It is here that the setting (in terms of time) throws a cruel irony on Rudy: his (fictional) letters were written between January 1967 and August 1968; *Higher Ground* was published in 1989, and, seen from the perspective of the latter date, Rudy's vision of Africa is undercut and mocked. His heroes are Lumumba Nyerere, and Kenyatta; he wishes to visit Egypt and Ethiopia, and then settle in Ghana. Patrice Lumumba of the Congo was killed before he could implement his policies, but Nyerere's long experiment with village socialism led Tanzania to economic ruin; indirectly admitting his mistakes and failure, he resigned from office. Jomo Kenyatta "hijacked" the Kenyan revolution and created an exploitative society, with his family and supporters being the beneficiaries—the structures Ngugi condemns and opposes. Egypt has grave economic difficulties; so does Ghana, which has the added bane of military coups and violence. As for Ethiopia, it is now associated with extreme poverty, mass starvation, and the attempt to raise money through international music concerts. These are Rudy's ideal leaders and countries: the irony is gained by placing the story two decades back in time. Events and developments of the seventies and eighties subvert and mock Rudy, even as we are moved by his predicament and words, and leave the reader to make her or his own way out: a disturbed character, and a work that is disturbing in more ways than one.

The third story, **"Higher Ground,"** begins with the narrator telling us that Irene did this, Irene did that, Irene, Irene, Irene. It is winter and the trees are naked; when they put on their clothes, so will Irene. We move from an outer observation of Irene to what she thinks and feels, and we realize that she has passed beyond what is termed normality. A headache is an iron handcuff around her head—again, the prison image. "Stop talking to yourself, you crazy Polish bitch," shouts the incontinent old man next door, throwing a shoe at the dividing wall as an added expletive.

We gradually make sense of it all. Rachel and Irina were daughters of a Jewish shopkeeper in Poland: decent, caring parents; a frugal flat but well stocked with books; a close relationship between the sisters; prospects of university studies. Then Nazism reaches out, Rachel is beaten up and takes to her bed, and the sisters no longer attend school. There is talk of mother and daughters escaping while father remains to tidy up and sell the shop. (How can one abruptly abandon a shop slowly built up over the years? And he could not have known the virulence of the evil coming closer.) The ominous minutes of history tick by, and suddenly it is too late. Time only to hustle Irina, clutching the family photographs, to Vienna and so to England. Working in a factory, she meets and goes out with Reg, gets pregnant, and miscarries; relieved of responsibility in this way, he abandons her. She meets Louis from the Caribbean; he has been in London ten days and has already decided to return home, on the reasoning that "it was better to return as the defeated traveller than be praised as the absent hero and live a life of spiritual poverty." There is a strong affinity between them; but Louis is determined to return, and Irene is left to her loneliness. In the face of her alienation and total loss (parents, sister, home, language, and even name, with *Irina* Anglicized into *Irene*), destruction seems inevitable. In his book-length essay *The European Tribe* Phillips writes that the exploitation and sufferings of black people were not in his school curriculum, nor did they find articulation on television and in the media: "As a result I vicariously channelled a part of my hurt and frustration through the Jewish experience."

Joseph Conrad in his "Author's Note" to *Youth* wrote that the three stories "lay no claim to unity of artistic purpose"; *Higher Ground* is described as a novel in three parts. However, one expects a degree of integration within a novel, and if, for example, the work produces new characters, we assume they will be related, however tenuously, to the preceding characters. The three parts of *Higher Ground* take us from Africa and the slave trade, to the United States of the 1960s, and finally to Britain during and shortly after World War II. The characters are an African, a black American, and a Polish-Jewish woman. Therefore, to claim that *Higher Ground* is a novel—not short stories on the same theme—is to urge readers to see the stories as a unity. The work is a triptych, and it is not only that when we place the three parts together they form a unity—of damaged and hurt lives—but that there emerges a significance which no one part by itself can communicate with such clarity and force: "If one takes a piece of banal journalistic prose and sets it down on a page as a lyric poem, surrounded by intimidating margins of silence, the words remain the same but their effects for readers are substantially altered." So too, by the simple device of asserting that *Higher Ground* is a novel, Phillips makes us approach it as a single, unified work, and to respond and draw significance accordingly.

Can Phillips be described as a British (or a black British) writer? In the bulk of Conrad's work, Poland—in terms of setting—is not significant, yet his Polish life shaped a part of his basic awareness. So too with Phillips, and even if little of his work thus far is set in England, his British years, from infancy to manhood, have given him great advantages. The term *advantages* may surprise, given the degree of racism—covert or overt, suave or crude—that pervades contemporary Britain. Still, I would argue that having grown up in Britain has heightened Phillips's awareness and fine (in the two meanings of *sharp* and *excellent*) sensitivity. This is not to suggest that Phillips is some bruised plant trembling delicately in unkind winds. His difference and exile have positively defined him; they make up his essential being, and, if often a source of hurt or anger, of alienation and loneliness, they also constitute his awareness and strength. It is the turning of what a hostile society and a denigrating culture would impose as misfortune and limitation into advantage and a wonderful broadening out of understanding and sympathy, a turning of prisons into castles (with acknowledgment to George Lamming and his novel *In the Castle of My Skin*), a moving from pain to knowledge and beyond to joy, pride, and thence to celebration.

To return to the question, can Phillips be labeled "British" despite his "return" to the Caribbean? Not to do so would leave our taxonomic lust unsatisfied. If anything, his latest work, *Higher Ground,* shifting from the days of slavery somewhere on the coast of black Africa to a contemporary maximum-security prison cell in the United States and then to a Polish-Jewish woman suffering incomprehension, loneliness, and a breakdown in Britain during World War II, shows a liberated Phillips, a writer who can penetrate the inner being of people vastly different from himself in time, place, and gender, yet people very much like us all in the common and eternal human inheritance of pain and suffering. In a recent essay Phillips writes that his "branches have developed, and to some extent continue to develop and grow, in Britain" but that his "roots are in Caribbean soil." Eluding labels that will seize and fix him, he finally remains Caryl Phillips.

If one were to ask what unifies the fictional works of Phillips, I would turn to the words of the Spaniard Camilo José Cela (winner of the 1989 Nobel Prize in Literature), who said that he is on the side not of those who make History but of those who *suffer* History. In Phillips's work there is a strong sense of historical violence and its consequences, of resulting journeys and alienation, but also the effort to find (or make for oneself) a little peace. As Rudy urged from prison, don't let anyone take away your dreams.

Claudia Roth Pierpont (review date 10 August 1992)

SOURCE: "English Lessons," in *The New Yorker,* August 10, 1992, pp. 74-9.

[*In the following excerpt, Pierpont outlines and assesses the features of Phillips's novel* Cambridge *and traces the origins of its themes.*]

In the introduction to his play *The Shelter,* produced in 1983, when he was twenty-five, the British writer Caryl Phillips described a postcard photograph that he had kept pinned to the wall above his desk for over a year: "A white woman's face, probably that of a woman of thirty or thirty-five, who had probably just cried, or who would cry; and curled around her forehead, with just enough pressure to cause a line of folds in the skin above her eyes, were two black hands; obviously power and strength slept somewhere within them but at this moment they were infinitely gentle, describing with eight fingers that moment when a grip of iron weakens to a caress of love." The story of the relationship between this white woman and this black man—"perhaps the most explosive of all relationships, seldom written about, seldom explained, feared, observed, hated"—seemed to the author impossible to get down on paper, and many times, Phillips tells us, he wanted to quit: "The responsibility was too big, I would say, to myself only; and I would wait until I was more mature." It was with what he thought to be a final, regretful glance at the image that he experienced at last a clearing of the mind and with it the knowledge that "the postcard was a part of me and if I did not acknowledge it I would be haunted. . . . I clearly saw in it, perhaps for the first time, something that had made me what I was."

What Phillips was at the time—besides a budding playwright—was a recent Oxford graduate, brought up in Leeds, who was born in the West Indies and taken to England before his first birthday. He was just moving toward the discovery of his voice—the voice of an England not often heard, far from sweeping lawns and university quadrangles. Phillips has written elsewhere of the depths of exclusionism and ignorance which continually challenged his right to feel himself English, from the deliberate humiliations of boyhood to the questions of a BBC television producer as to "what African languages I spoke, and if I spoke them when I'm with other West Indians." At Oxford, he envied the African students for having "a home to which they could return"; he implies almost as much about black Americans. Two years after *The Shelter,* which dealt with the impossible relations of a black man and a flesh-and-blood Britannia, Phillips began writing novels on the subject of West Indian rootlessness—of in-betweenness, of pained unacceptance and categorically enforced un-Englishness—set forth in the measured and evocative prose of a natural master of the language.

Both Phillips' insistent early theme and his developing virtuosity of style are brought to an extreme pitch in his most recent novel, *Cambridge.* Set in the British West Indies before the victory of abolitionism, under a system of slavery carried out half a world away from its masters and beneficiaries, the story concerns the voyage of an Englishwoman, a near-perfect representative of the formative conventions of her class—"I am simply a lady of polite status with little talent, artistic or otherwise"—directly into the heat and confrontation of an island where her countrymen have painstakingly raised up a hell in the bower of paradise. Miss Emily Cartwright, come to inspect the running of her father's sugar plantation, is the proverbial drawing-room mirror, silvered and polished and transported over an ocean in order to capture in reflection the unthinkable English beast of slavery. Caryl Phillips, like Pat Barker, approaches the evils of history through the trials of individual conscience. His book, too, seems to set up a challenge of will against will, and a promise of transformation—in this case, through the presence on the plantation of a highly educated and articulate slave, called Cambridge. Yet as the story progresses these apparent promises grow dimmer and dimmer, until Phillips fatally reverses every prospect, every expectation. He leads where no one could expect who does not know his painfully divided earlier work.

Phillips' first novels centered on the physical beauty and social squalor of the Caribbean, the tiny islands of sizzling tin roofs and sleep and beer, "overburdened with vegetation and complacency," offering nothing, without future. This splendorous desolation he set against the cold, gray refusal of the great mother island, where what is offered is always out of reach, and where the past is all the comfort left. His people sailed away from their homes with a pity for all those "satisfied enough to stay," and they inevitably returned, defeated—in *The Final Passage* after several months; in *A State of Independence* after twenty years—and at once grateful and unfitted for the slow, eventless life they had thought to abandon.

In 1989, Phillips published a collection of three novellas under the title *Higher Ground,* in which he seemed not only to have become a new writer but to have become several writers. The growth and the range were remarkable, and the command of voice—with narrators belonging to different sexes, races, countries, and times—was uncanny. The strongest of the stories was a dramatic monologue in letters called **"The Cargo Rap,"** which records a black American's seventh year in prison during the nineteen-sixties. Here Phillips captures an era and a way of thinking and speaking with line-for-line precision, and renders a particular human personality with almost unbearable penetration: a young man of mental complexity and blanketing self-deception, whose belligerence and naive schemes slowly give way to a seeping, cracking desperation. All of this hundred-page story is told in the singular and ever-recognizable voice of one Rudolph Leroy Williams, although Phillips manages to create—over the teller's shoulder, as it were—an array of other characters. And it is characteristic of the author's temperament that the tale begins in prison, with his narrator's crime obscured in the past, barely relevant, and all his actions cut off at the level of thought. Even rage is something that the reflective and rather gentle Phillips explores rather than releases.

The narrator of Phillips' third novella is an educated and privileged slave employed by the British military at an African trading post, whose job it is to translate between English and the dialects of captured tribes. The story, again, is delivered as a monologue, but eighteenth-century speech is alluded to rather than reproduced; something other than historical accuracy is intended. This nameless figure is marooned between his two peoples, "knowing that neither fully trusts me, that neither wants to be close to me, neither recognizes my smell or my posture." In the end, despite his Christianized learning and civility, he is turned upon by his masters and shackled to the latest group of captives; in a vortex of self-realization and terror, he is sold, in a distant country, on the block. This is a potent nightmare, as hard and irreducible as myth. In varied forms, it is at least as old as Stowe's Uncle Tom. For Phillips, its gospel seems to be especially urgent, and it reappears, elaborated in detail and consequence, at the ambitious and inscrutable heart of *Cambridge.*

The familiar Phillips gifts are much in evidence in the new novel, and its early sections have an intoxicating vocal grace. Here is the Englishwoman's story, told in her own steady voice, a brief prelude of dishevelled memory quickly bound up into the ordered form of a journal: "I shall have a record of all I have passed through, so that I might better recount for the use of my father what pains and pleasures are en-

dured by those whose labour enables him to continue to indulge himself in the heavy-pocketed manner to which he has become accustomed."

A great part of the delight of these early pages lies in the secret of high and risky artifice shared between author and reader—the perfect balance with which Phillips has summoned up this nineteenth-century Emily. But there is also the simple appeal of the woman herself, with her dartings of bitter knowledge and need beneath the dutiful pose of the lady, with her wry intelligence and her distinctive way of trying out a new thought or expression—restyling the conventional inflections of an even earlier period—as though pressing the taste of it up against her palate, as when she notes of a seasick cabin boy: "Merely a few years hence he will have *sea legs* as opposed to *land legs,* and find it difficult to reside in a world that is devoid of motion." One believes in this Emily, and cares for her, as she broods and italicizes her way across the ocean.

Confusion sets in soon after her arrival, however, and slowly expands throughout the book. At first, we lose our hold on who Emily is or might be. Simultaneously appalled and seduced by tropical languor, the woman who left England with the bold hope that she might one day "encourage Father to accept the increasingly common, though abstract, English belief in the iniquity of slavery" is converted with startling immediacy—through plainly expressed disgust with black features and habits, with violations of "laws of taste"—to a stony conviction of the natural rightness of the slave system. The character closes up, becomes merely priggish, loses the Brontë-like sense of mettle beneath apparent mildness; even in giving herself over to island delicacies and sensualities, she is reduced to the hard and casually abusive England she had so recently sought to escape.

While there is no requirement, of course, that the heroine of a novel be also a political or moral heroine, and while the brutalization of this woman's mind is as potentially valid and perhaps more devastating a subject than its liberation, the reversal here is carried out without struggle or question, or even transition. More, the tight airlessness of that diminishing mind becomes stifling for the reader, who is, after all, trapped inside it, craning to locate a clear fact or another human face, to escape a monologue that turns into a drone long before its hundred and twenty-plus pages are out. Phillips' extraordinary control of tone never wavers, but the cost is great.

It was perhaps part of the author's rhythmic plan to have the plot rush in so late and so wild: a love affair, a baby, a murder. Emily's lover is the cruel plantation foreman, whose killer is the "black Hercules" called Cambridge, the sole slave who would not back down, who sought justice. We have seen the two men facing off in the fields—the result is the first whipping that Emily witnesses—and have seen Cambridge sitting outside Emily's sickroom reading his Bible:

> I asked if this was his common form of recreation, to which he replied in highly fanciful English, that indeed it was. You might imagine my surprise when he then broached the conversational lead and enquired after my family origins, and my opinions pertaining to slavery. I properly declined to share these with him, instead counter-quizzing with enquiries as to the origins of his knowledge.

Learning nothing of these origins, Emily "quickly closed in the door, for I feared this negro was truly ignorant of the correct degree of deference that a lady might reasonably expect from a base slave."

The history of this "base slave" is given at last by his own testimony, some thirty pages written out on the eve of hanging. Cambridge, born Olumide, was captured and taken to England, and there renamed, reclothed, reëducated, and eventually freed—"Truly I was now an Englishman, albeit a little smudgy of complexion!"—before the final and irrevocable betrayal back into slavery, aboard a ship travelling to Africa to convert the heathen. But his tale resolves the plot in only the most cursory way, and the book not at all. Where is Cambridge's voice? Far from sounding particularly fanciful, as Emily hears him, he sounds to us hardly different from Emily herself. It is soon apparent that Cambridge is less a man than an archetype, as isolated from sources of life as, finally, Emily is—or as she comes to be, it seems, once she has chosen, in the fields, in some mysterious and unexplored way, to set her heart toward the whip-wielding foreman rather than his steadfast opponent.

It is presumptuous to claim that an author should have stayed true to intentions that he may not, after all, have possessed. But everything that goes wrong with *Cambridge*—the sudden moral reduction of the heroine, the plot too sketchy and immaterial to contain, or even occupy, the characters, and the lack of conviction in the presentation of Cambridge himself—suggests a change of direction, the uprooting of a vital motivation: the meeting of this complex woman, white and free, and this complex man, black and enslaved, in a world set apart. Such is the magnetism of these twin poles of the narrative that just the anticipation of their mutual discovery is sufficiently charged to hold the story in tension, until the prospect is, chance by chance, eliminated. That there will be no connection made between these two people, no recognition, is emphasized more than once, as a kind of refutation, a warding off. ("That I might have conversed with her at ease, perhaps even discussed acquaintances in common, undoubtedly never occurred to her," Cambridge muses near the story's end.) This is not to say that these characters need to have become lovers but that the reader feels led in-

exorably toward some greater awareness, some eruption of sympathy, or of any emotion that would fertilize the sterile grounds in which the pair have been planted.

It is difficult to know whether this negative choice reflects technical restrictions or philosophical ones. On the simplest level, Phillips has chosen to retain his monologue form, his passive and dissociated poise, his tight control. But the choice encompasses, too, a backing away from the assailable cliché of black man and white woman—that "most explosive of all relationships," the exploration of which Phillips once regarded as part of his "inevitable task" and the responsibility for which he had feared. The image on the postcard that so obsessed the young writer remains one of essential division. Phillips' insistence that we are forever separate in our skins, that every voyage out is a foundering, is manifest in *Cambridge*—which begins by promising so much more—through the cutting back of dimension in the characters and of freedom in the author. Yet if *Cambridge* is a smaller book than it might have been, and more self-protective, it leaves one with the conviction that Phillips has it in him to write books that are larger and bolder. One would not require of the artist a different conclusion, or a feigned optimism—or, for that matter, a real optimism—but only the breath of possibility, without which the most meticulous creation is still-born.

William H. Pritchard (essay date Autumn 1992)

SOURCE: "Tradition and Some Individual Talents," in *The Hudson Review,* Autumn, 1992, pp. 481-90.

[*In the following excerpt, Pritchard briefly reviews* Cambridge, *comparing the novel to Jonathan Swift's* Gulliver's Travels.]

Caryl Phillips' novel [*Cambridge*] is short but dense and needs to be read a second time before the full beauty of its design is apparent. *Cambridge* consists mainly of two narratives: the longer one by Emily Cartwright, an Englishwoman who is visiting her father's sugar plantation in the West Indies; the shorter by a black slave, Cambridge (this name pressed upon him when he was brought to the Caribbean), about to be executed for the murder of the plantation's estate manager who has been revealed as the lover of Emily and father of her stillborn child. Mr. Phillips' own career as a man born in St. Kitts, growing up in Leeds, educated at Oxford, traveling widely, is wholly relevant to the sense of place and of displacement in *Cambridge*. (He has written a very interesting memoir, *The European Tribe,* 1986, about his education and travels and his ambiguous relation to western civ.) But the really impressive thing about the new novel is the style he has concocted to express both Emily's leisurely, devoted, anthropological fascination with life in the tropics, and Cambridge's compressed, urgent account of the disruptions of a life that includes Africa, America, London, Warwickshire and the West Indies.

Although the time of the novel is early nineteenth century, the written style contrived for both characters reminded me of nothing so much as *Gulliver's Travels,* really an apt predecessor in many ways. Emily observes a "traditional West Indian dinner"

> where the table labored under a burden of ostentatious and substantial dishes. Gentlemen predominated numerically. Many brought with them their servants, some in livery, some not so, some with shoes, some barefoot, but all truly exemplified the type of the unprepossessing negro. They buzzed and swarmed around us like flies, and the lack of any formal arrangement among them created a vast disorder—excepting, of course, the arrangement whereby they might attempt to steal from beneath our very gaze whatever might be carried off.

Like Gulliver in Books I and II, Emily tries hard, means well, is comparatively "enlightened"; also, like Gulliver and the rest of us, she is trapped within the limits of her perceptions and the language available to express them. Cambridge's style is more like Gulliver's in Book IV, caught between the Houyhnhnms and Yahoos, increasingly isolated the more he tries to speak and act humanly. Cambridge's final words to the reader assert that his only interest has been to speak the truth in the service of the Christian faith to which he was converted: "Praise be the Lord! He who 'hath made of one blood all nations of men for to dwell on all the face of the earth'." The bitter irony of such idealistic talk about "blood" is fully apparent by now to the reader, since at the end of the novel the main characters have been as effectively killed off as the heroes and villains of a Jacobean tragedy. There is indeed a tragic quality to *Cambridge,* but it's leavened and qualified by the power, and sometimes the beauty, of its language of enlightenment, of the Enlightenment. It is an impressive instance of what a remarkably individual talent can achieve because of, not despite, tradition—in fact, because of traditions.

Carol Margaret Davison (interview date 14 February 1994)

SOURCE: "Crisscrossing the River: An Interview with Caryl Phillips," in *Ariel,* October, 1994, pp. 91-9.

[*In the following interview conducted on February 14, 1994, Davidson questions Phillips on the development of his work, his influences, and the writer's responsibilities.*]

Taken to England at the "portable" age of 12 weeks from St. Kitts, one of the Leeward Islands in the Caribbean, 35-year-old Caryl Phillips grew up in Leeds, was educated at Oxford, and has spent his literary career probing the ramifications of displacement, a complex condition that he claims characterizes the twentieth century and "engenders a great deal of suffering, a great deal of confusion, a great deal of soul searching." Describing writers as "basically just people who are trying to organize their confusion," he has opted, it would seem, for the right calling. The rapidly growing list of honours for his prolific output certainly validates his choice. The author of five novels, Phillips was the recipient of the Malcolm X Award for his first novel, *The Final Passage* (1985), and the Martin Luther King Memorial Prize for his travel-commentary *The European Tribe* (1987). While *The Final Passage* and *A State of Independence* (1986) were "written out of a sense of great elation at having 're-discovered' the Caribbean," his third novel, *Higher Ground* (1989), encompasses everything from Africa in the days of slave trading to post-World War II Europe and the Black Power Movement. With the publication in 1991 of his fourth novel, *Cambridge,* which chronicles the story of Emily, a nineteenth-century woman who escapes an arranged marriage by travelling to her father's West Indian plantation where she is exposed to the effects of slavery and colonialism, Phillips garnered more serious attention in North America. Back "home" in England, he was subsequently named (*London*) *Sunday Times*' Young Writer of the Year in 1992 and listed among GRANTA's Best of Young British Novelists of 1993. He is also a well-established playwright and currently is Visiting Professor of English at Amherst College in Massachusetts, USA.

Phillips's fifth novel, *Crossing the River,* shortlisted for Britain's prestigious Booker Prize in 1993 and published in January 1994 by Knopf, Canada, is a sophisticated, sometimes-sorrowful meditation upon the painful dislocations, longings, and "weird" relationships borne of the aptly named "peculiar institution" of slavery. Three years in the making and spanning 250 years of the African diaspora, *Crossing the River* is a fragmented work plagued by questions of identity, paternalism, and spiritual growth. The novel is framed by an African father's melancholic reflections on his desperate act of selling his three children into slavery following his crop's failure and relates their life stories. In each instance, Phillips conjures up largely unchronicled moments in black history: Nash becomes a Christian missionary repatriated to the new land of Liberia in the 1830s; Martha, at the end of the nineteenth century, accompanies some black pioneers west in search of her beloved daughter; and Travis is stationed as an American GI in a small Yorkshire village during the Second World War.

This interview was conducted by telephone on 14 February

1994, when Phillips was engaged to read from *Crossing the River* at Harbourfront, in Toronto, Canada.

[*Davison:*] **Crossing the River** *has been called your most ambitious work to date. Do you think that's an accurate description?*

[Phillips:] Not really. I think they're all pretty ambitious. When you sit down with an idea—to turn it into a novel, it's always a big risk, it's always a danger. So there's an element of ambition always. In the formal sense, however, it probably is my most ambitious work. But it's not in the more specific way of looking at the desire to write a book and the ambition. They're all as hard as each other.

What was the seed of this book?

Originally, I had lots of ideas in my mind, including doing a piece about something in the Second World War. That was the idea to start with and then it just got out of control.

The novel reminded me somewhat of your 1983 play **The Shelter.** *You span a great deal of time there too, moving from Act One, set in the eighteenth century, to Act Two in the 1950s. You also deal there with interracial relationships.*

That's interesting. Most people haven't made any references to **The Shelter;** a play I wrote back in 1982-83, because they don't know of it. It's not as easily accessible as most of the novels, but if I were to look at one piece of work of mine which has the beginning of this structural paranoia and schizophrenia, that would be it. You could say that I've been writing or exploring the way of writing and connecting across centuries for ten years.

What was your principal aim in writing **Crossing the River?** *What did you feel you wanted to do here that you hadn't done in your earlier work?*

Well, I wanted to make a connection between the African world which was left behind and the diasporan world which people had entered once they crossed the water. I wanted to make an affirmative connection, not a connection based upon exploitation or suffering or misery, but a connection based upon a kind of survival. This is an unusually optimistic book for me. I don't have a deliberately downbeat feel, but there's never been a redemptive spirit to the things that I've written. There's always been a sense that things have been rough and people have just about managed to limp by and survive, but I don't think there's any reason why one should be "positive." I have never really had a very optimistic view of things.

In some of your earlier interviews, however, you have expressed surprise about being pegged as a pessimist.

I have been surprised because I've never really considered myself to be a pessimist, but I've never really given people any good reason to think otherwise.

As your wonderful portraits of the elderly Western pioneer, Martha, and the restrained British housewife, Joyce, attest in **Crossing the River,** *you have a tremendous ability to do cross-gender writing. By that I am referring to the ability to enter the consciousness of a woman—and in the case of Joyce, here, and Emily in* **Cambridge,** *you have the added difficulty of traversing racial difference too. Do you have any thoughts about assuming a female voice? Do you think this involves a special ability at all?*

I don't feel it requires any particular strengths. The deal is really that we all play to our own strings, and you find out where you feel most comfortable. Women's position on the edge of society—both central in society, but also marginalized by men—seems to me, in some way, to mirror the rather tenuous and oscillating relationship that all sorts of people, in this case, specifically, black people, have in society, and maybe there is some kind of undercurrent of communicable empathy that's going on. Again, I don't want to make too much of anything because I don't really see it as that much of a mystery. It doesn't appear to be that way to me, and I don't want to find a logical reason in case the ability to do so somehow goes away. I do think that to write only from the point of view of a male is to exclude half of the world and I obviously want to include as many different points of view as I can, so I'm very pleased that I've never really felt a problem doing that.

There are certainly many different literary influences in **Crossing the River.** *Several critics mention the echoes of Toni Morrison's* Beloved *in the Martha Section. It also seems to me that the father figure here whose voice frames the four narrative segments encompasses the voices of the African diaspora just as Saleem Sinai encompasses the whole of India in Salman Rushdie's* Midnight's Children. *Could you speak a bit about the various literary influences at work here?*

I haven't sat down and thought too clearly about what books have perhaps influenced me in putting this novel together, but you have certainly named some authors who are big influences. *Beloved* has been particularly influential. It's always easier for an author to see these things in retrospect and, looking back, yes, I can see the influences of all of these people. It's a novel which is fragmentary in form and structure, polyphonic in its voices, which means that a lot of my reading and a lot of the people whose work I've enjoyed have made their way in. Obviously there's ample room for echoes of all sorts of people. It's great for me as a writer because it allows me to switch gear or switch direction, shift perspective, and at each new turn I'm able to employ something else which, obviously, I have learned by reading other people's work.

Another book that kept coming to mind while I was reading **Crossing the River** *was Edward Brathwaite's jazzy Caribbean poem-trilogy,* The Arrivants. *I decided finally to pull it off the shelf and, lo and behold, I discovered that Chapter Five is entitled "Crossing the River."*

Is it? I know him. He's going to murder me. Is it really? I'm going to write that down. That's probably where I got the original title because I first thought of this title 10 or 11 years ago.

There is a haunting, reiterated Biblical question throughout this novel, namely, "Father, why hast thou forsaken me?" Nash mentions this about his white "Father" Edward; Martha seems to be addressing God when she repeats the same phrase in Section Two. In the larger picture, of course, they are addressing their flesh-and-blood father who has sold them to the slave traders. The connected issues of paternalism and responsibility are often meditated upon here. What exactly fascinates you about these subjects?

It seems to me that the very nature of the relationship between the master and the slave, the colonizer and the colony, Britain and the Caribbean, is paternalistic. The whole question of relationships between black and white historically has tended to be paternalistic and perhaps enshrouded in some air of patronage at times, and so I've always been interested in those kinds of power relationships. It has such Biblical overtones as well because it is also a reference to religious themes. In the immigrant experience in Britain, the father was often pretty absent from the home. There are so many broken families in the black community in general, not just in the migrant community. There tends to be a preponderance of single mothers. I'm very interested in the whole question of how, on the personal level, that has emerged out of the larger development of slavery and all of those kinds of diasporan movements. There is a very commonly held theory that one of the reasons there is such a preponderance of single mothers is *because* of slavery, an institution which greatly disrupted the black family. There is an idea that if you take away a man's responsibility for his children, which is what happened in slavery when the man was replaced by the master as head of the family, it does something to the psyche of the man of African origin. It induces an irresponsibility. I don't know whether this is true or not. I'm not a sociologist or an anthropologist, but all of these issues make me interested in that whole power-father-paternalistic-patronage issue. They all seem to be pretty linked.

I want to ask you about your changing ideas about the writer's responsibilities. In the introduction to your play **The Shelter,** *you speak of the various burdens on the writer; in particular, you state that you were then motivated by the luxury of inexperience and felt that your "only responsibility was to locate the truth in whatever piece I was working on, live with it, sleep with it, and be responsible to that truth, and that truth alone." In* **The European Tribe** *[1987], written a few years later, you seem to be more aware of the power the writer has along political lines. You state towards the end of that book: "I had learnt that in a situation in which history is distorted, the literature of a people often becomes its history, its writers the keepers of the past, present, and future. In this situation a writer can infuse a people with their own unique identity and spiritually kindle the fire of resistance." What do you feel today about your responsibility as a writer?*

I think that the second piece from **The European Tribe** is a development from what I thought earlier. It doesn't displace what I thought earlier, because I do think that that remains true—your first responsibility is to locate the truth and to deal with the truth, particularly as it relates specifically to the characters—but I think that by travelling and writing a bit more and becoming hopefully a bit more knowledgeable about writing and the world and about other writers' lives in other communities, I did realize—and I think that I already knew it, but I wasn't able to articulate it—that there is a particular responsibility in *certain* situations for the writer to take up. He doesn't have to become a politician, but the writer has to be aware of the writer's power, his capacity for good as well as his ability to duck larger social responsibility. I agree with the position I had in *The European Tribe,* but I would go further than that and say that it seems to me increasingly important since then that one, as a writer, does try to locate the truth in one's work. You do become aware of the possibility of being somebody who can identify a history and perhaps do something about redressing the imbalance of some of the ills and falsehoods that have been perpetrated by others about your own history. But beyond that, I think a writer really has a responsibility to at least acknowledge that he was produced by very specific social circumstances. We weren't, any of us—male, female, black, white, whatever—immaculate conceptions dropped out of nowhere without a history. One shouldn't feel a guilt for one's history and one shouldn't feel ashamed of one's history, one should just take responsibility for it.

Do you ever feel, though, that you have to compromise conveying your own personal "truths" because they clash with your responsibilities as a writer, or is it your primary responsibility to tell the truth, the whole truth, and nothing but the truth, so help you God?

The latter. I don't think I could actually write properly if I felt that in any way, even in any small way, that I was somehow in my life as well as in my writing, not tackling issues of injustice and speaking up when they appear. I just don't think I could do it, because I think that eventually those kinds of lies and that kind of self-deception do seep into your work. It has honestly never occurred to me to pull a punch a little bit or change gears. I don't think you can do that. I mean I just don't see how you can. You just have to continually risk coming up against irate people.

As you are certainly aware, today is not only Valentine's Day. Today marks the fifth anniversary of the fatwa *declared against Salman Rushdie. Do you have any comments about Rushdie's situation and the issue of censorship and writing in general?*

I just got off the phone with him. He and I speak a lot. To tell you the truth, I don't think that I have got anything to say that hasn't already been said and maybe said better by others, but I was talking to somebody earlier today about his situation. It seems to me clearly that one of the most unfortunate things in the *fatwa* is the way a lot of people in the West have taken it as a convenient excuse to hammer Islam, and it's not Islam that needs to be hammered. It's a particular extreme branch of Islam. It really is like judging the whole of Christianity on the actions of the Spanish Inquisition. It doesn't really make any sense. That has nothing to do with Salman personally. That is just my own discomfort at watching writers and other people, including a lot of people who should know better, who claim to be defending Salman Rushdie making incredibly sweeping and stupid comments about Islam, but not taking into consideration that this isn't Islam. There are many Muslims all over the world who think this is an outrage.

What were your feelings about being nominated for the Booker Prize? Were you surprised?

That's a good question. Was I surprised? Well, I suppose I was a little bit. To tell you the truth, I was more surprised that **Cambridge** wasn't nominated because everyone kept telling me it would be. So by the time this came around, I was pleased but I just didn't care because I realized how much of a lottery it was. I wondered about it in the days leading up to it when it was **Cambridge.** This time I didn't even know that it was the day of the announcements or anything. I came into my office and there was a message from Salman on the machine. I was pleased because of the sales.

What were your feelings when Roddy Doyle received it?

Oh, that was fine, I know Roddy. I was sitting right at the next table. I didn't mind you see because it wasn't really about winning it. I was just pleased to be on the shortlist. After a while, you need to get sales because the more sales you get, the more money you get. The more money you get, the more time you have, and that's the deal. I'm not sure that I would want to be like Miss World for a year, which is

what you would be if you won. I was pleased that Roddy won because he is a nice guy. At the Booker Prize dinner everybody talked to everybody. The person that I knew the best was David Malouf and, in some ways, I would have liked David Malouf to have won simply because he's 25 years older than Roddy and I who are both 35. I'll get another chance as will Roddy, even though he doesn't really need another chance, but I would have liked David Malouf, whose work I really admire, to have won it and gained this recognition at this stage of his career. As Kazuo Ishiguro, who called me up the morning of it, said: "Just remember, it's an exercise in public humiliation."

Speaking of influences, taking into consideration both their life and their work, who stands out as the most important single literary influence on you?

I would probably have to say, if it's a combination of their life and their work, James Baldwin. I hesitated because there's no other person who I've ever met who is a writer who has been as important to me. I think that this is partly because at the time when I met him I was a sort of "wannabe" writer. To meet a real and a great writer, I was incredibly lucky. He was also incredibly generous with his time.

The novel seems to have a firm hold on you. Would you ever consider writing another play?

Oh yes, I'm probably going to write another play next year or later this year. I prefer the theatre to film. There are just too many people involved in television and film. I have worked in both mediums, and I don't particularly enjoy them that much.

Have you ever been approached by anyone about adapting one of your novels for the screen?

I have often been approached by people who have wanted to do that. I'm afraid that I'm not usually very good at replying. I get my agent to speak to them, but it's not a world that I feel particularly comfortable in anymore. A number of my friends have had bad experiences having their novels adapted or even adapting them themselves. I'll tell you the truth. I look upon adaptations of my work for the screen as something that I would like to be involved in and I would like to see happen at a time when I don't feel quite so fertile about producing original work. There may be a time down the line, whether it's in 5 or 25 years' time, when I just feel I don't have anything else to say, or I dry up, then it would be fun to go back and look at some of the early work and try to find new ways of saying that stuff and working on the screen. But right now, I'm too keen and eager and hungry to write prose, so I don't want to waste time on screen work.

Marina Warner (review date 20 March 1997)

SOURCE: "Its Own Dark Styx," in *London Review of Books*, March 20, 1997, p. 23.

[*In the following review, Warner traces the threads of history and layers of plot in Phillips's* The Nature of Blood.]

'Memory says: Want to do right? Don't count on me.' So writes Adrienne Rich in a poem from *An Atlas of a Difficult World,* opening an unpunctuated sequence of horrors: lynchings, pogroms, Auschwitz, Berlin, Palestine, Israel:

> I am accused of child death of drinking
> blood . . .
> there is spit on my sleeve there are phone-
> calls in the night . . .

She concludes: 'I am standing here in your poem unsatisfied / lifting my smoky mirror.' Memory's smoky mirror, like the witch's crystal, or the burning glass of the Aztec god who demands human sacrifice, has become the prime instrument turned on history by several of the most powerful recent or contemporary novelists. In its shadowed and unreliable depths Toni Morrison, Kazuo Ishiguro, Leonardo Sciascia, Alejo Carpentier have searched out their material, reflections of ourselves; and from *A State of Independence* his second novel (1986), to *The Nature of Blood,* Caryl Phillips, too, has been scrying for glimpses of troubled histories.

The Nature of Blood opens in a Displaced Persons camp in Cyprus after the Second World War, where the British are holding Jews before releasing them in quotas to travel to Palestine; a boy asks, emblematically, the name of the country to which they will be going. Israel, replies the doctor-soldier, Stephan Stern. Dr Stern threads through the story like the implied key of a sonata; for Phillips's construction is musical, and his predominant motif—of an unsparing minor starkness—is provided by Eva, Stern's niece. In her parallel story, she's liberated from another (Nazi) camp; having lost her much-loved sister Margot and her parents somewhere unnamed in Germany, she goes mad in the aftermath. The novel's phrasing strikes echoes across different movements, as the several stories and characters twist through time and place, until Phillips brings the various themes together in a beautifully poised, tender and melancholy coda. The Holocaust and its victims (among whom Phillips counts the survivors: this is a novel in which no one escapes damage) occupy the foreground, but it is Israel as the dream of the Promised Land that provides the book's tragic core. For Israel, in the sense of home, cannot exist except as yearning. However clearly it appears on the atlas, it eludes the explorer and the refugee alike in the restless involutions of the mind's desires. In the closing scene, a nurse from Ethiopia, one of

the Falasha invited 'home' to Israel, meets Dr Stern at a dancing club; they make love, the single act that attaches; she can't find work in racist Israel; he has become a lonely old pensioner, a stranger without moorings in the country he gave up wife, child and birthplace to create.

Both in its contemporary theme—the desolate condition of diaspora and the impossibility of a resolution—and in its diachronic approach, *The Nature of Blood* extends the methods Phillips developed in *Cambridge* and *Crossing the River,* his most recent novels. Both of those, however, explored black identity directly. *Cambridge* returned to the Caribbean, to an 18th-century slave plantation where a young woman from England voyages in order to set her father's estate in order. Phillips tells much of the story in her words, unflinchingly voicing the plantocracy's assumptions of racial superiority, and setting up against them the figure of Cambridge, the dignified, literate, ironically named slave who unsettles her received ideas. It is as if Sir Bertram had died and Fanny Price had slipped through the gates of Mansfield Park to see for herself what the family's fortunes entailed in Jamaica: Phillips drew for his portraits on the literature of abolition, including such powerful witnesses as Olaudah Equiano, who wrote one of the most eloquent and detailed accounts of life as a slave. *Crossing the River,* Phillips's last novel, and his most intense to date, took up an even less familiar corner of black history, and explored the failure of the American experiment in Liberia, the West African nation that 'enlightened' citizens sent freed slaves to settle after the Civil War.

He has distinguished himself in these three works by his refusal of pieties; there's a quiet dourness and cussedness in his handling of the material; he pits himself against any kind of received wisdom, including the prevailing feel-good tendency of some black American writing. His ironies work at everyone's expense: no one, black, white, patrician, serf, is spared. He is a sympathetic impersonator of women (Eva in *The Nature of Blood*) and white idealists (Stern the well-meaning terrorist/freedom fighter), but his pitiless irony projects their self-deceptions, too: Eva, befriended in the camp by an English soldier who gives her chocolate, follows him to London after the war, where he turns out to be married. He jilts her, abandoning her in a pub with a gin and tonic. But before we can align ourselves against this betrayal, Phillips discloses, in one of his fingertip asides, that in her dazed condition, she had forged the letter of invitation from him with which she arrived in the country.

By setting out, in *Cambridge,* the beliefs that underpinned slavery, by playing parts far beyond the borders of his own autobiography, by choosing to write about the Holocaust when he is not Jewish, Caryl Phillips is making a political statement, angled strongly at the United States, where he lives and teaches for half the year. But he's not simply flouting the parish boundaries of PC, in which only a woman may write as a woman, or only a black may address the themes of race. Phillips's contumaciousness arises from a more philosophical view of identity, which his fictions propose in their ventriloquism and polyphony, without assistance from the authorial voice. Much current writing takes up similar issues, but it is dominated by the confessional or advocacy mode, reflections of America's legal and religious culture. Hilton Als's recent essays, *The Women,* Henry Louis Gates's *Colored People,* the reportage of Keith Richburg in *Out of America: A Black Man Confronts Africa* square up to the way in which the black individual is the perceived representative of his race, and of 'being black'; the writers fight against it, plead furiously as they realign the co-ordinates and propose re-evaluations (for example, Ebonix, or black street slang). Phillips sets aside this direct mode of address in order to avoid group labelling and the corral of designated racial character. The regulation of difference, *The Nature of Blood* seems to tell us, has excited more hatred and bloodshed than the weaving and binding of societies according to elective affinities between persons. The blurb on the jacket—and authors are routinely asked to provide this nowadays—says: 'What emerges through these inextricably linked stories is the realisation not only of how we define ourselves but also, shockingly, that we sometimes determine who we are by destroying others.'

Questions of national place, of roots, of where one belongs, depend on psychic identifications: where hostility and contempt are projected, where fear springs. Conversely, affinities are elected where sympathy rises, where love happens. Narrative, when it throws its voice, can dissolve hatreds by deepening understanding: *The Persians,* in which Aeschylus dramatises the terrible grief of the enemy Xerxes's mother, represents an early instance of this potential.

In pursuit of this possibility, Phillips contrasts in *The Nature of Blood* two stories taken from the past and plaits them into his Holocaust theme: a blood libel occurring in the small town of Portobuffole near Venice in 1480 and the story of Othello, the African general who, according to a glancing reference in the 16th-century Venetian drama that inspired Shakespeare, served the Serenissima and thanks to his 'good qualities' won the love of one of the Republic's most nobly born daughters. With his love of helical structures, Phillips twists together the story of a fair-haired child beggar's disappearance and the subsequent trial, torture and execution of a group of Jews charged with his sacrifice; his Othello crosses into this world when he enters the ghetto—that stifling, overcrowded, indeed concentrated city within the city—in search of a scribe who will write a love letter to Desdemona for him. Labelling is libelling; only personal contact can efface the characteristics attributed to groups: Desdemona's father reacts with furious bigotry to his daughter's choice, but she is steadfast; Dr Stern, looking

at the colour of the nurse Malka's skin as she sleeps beside him, sees her as someone who has made him a belated gift, not a representative of her Otherness, her tribe, her race. The choice of Othello leads to some richly worked passages on Venetian courtship rituals, on the lore of gondolas, on oligarchical banqueting, as well as on the harsh expediency of the Republic's politics. But Shakespeare's tragedy necessarily throws its long shadow over the steadfast love that grows between Desdemona and the older stranger. Phillips has decided not to trace their story to its conclusion, nor to revise it. Given the harshness of the novel's general music, the reader cannot dare hope for a happy ending, though the couple are last seen in Rhodes feasting. Two brief passages, in an external, anonymous voice, then interpellate Othello:

> And so you shadow her every move, attend to her every whim, like the black Uncle Tom that you are. Fighting the white man's war for him / . . . The republic's grinning Satchmo hoisting his sword like a trumpet / You tuck your black skin away beneath their epauletted uniform, appropriate their words (*Rude am I in speech*), their manners, worry your nappy woollen head with anxiety about learning their ways . . . O strong man, O strong arm, O valiant soldier, O weak man. You are lost, a sad black man, first in a long line of so-called achievers who are too weak to yoke their past with their present; too naive to insist on both; too foolish to realise that to supplant one with the other can only lead to catastrophe. Go ahead, peer on her alabaster skin . . . My friend, the Yoruba have a saying: the river that does not know its own source will dry up. You will do well to remember this.

This passage, and another that comes soon after it and closes, 'Brother, jump from her bed and fly away home,' are hard to interpret, and in their apparently direct and rootsy Afrocentrism, run counter to the disillusion recorded by Phillips as far back as *A State of Independence,* in which his protagonist returns to St Kitts, the island where Phillips himself was born, tries to rejoin the society of his extended family, but fails. The taunting of Othello by this unanchored late 20th-century voice is disruptive in a book whose title implies, surely, that blood of its nature is common. Yet the discomfort it produces reintegrates itself into the novel, which refuses comfort from any source; these cries from outside the narrative express Phillips's sense of the futility of his general enterprise as he tries to locate homelands outside the formal geography of the difficult world. Novelists can't be shut out of exclusion zones, but novels, it turns out, can't be charters for newfoundlands.

There is, however, another clue to the way Phillips sees this existential and perpetual displacement: his prose. He belongs to the current school of ironists who button their lip; his sentences mimic the histories he's excavating: indecipherable fragments are picked out of the mud in which they were buried and handed over to be pieced together, making the reader work to read them. (We are only allowed to suspect that his Dr Stern is the Stern of the Stern Gang.) This is also Ishiguro's unemphatic method, and to some extent, Graham Swift's, both of them contemporaries of Phillips. It could not be more different from Rushdie's method, or Angela Carter's: they are baroque ironists, for whom the interest swirls and flares on the mobile and sumptuous surface of the prose. Ishiguro and Phillips are elliptical encrypters: what is happening is not what you see, but what you can't see, until you adjust your perception—Wittgenstein's duck/rabbit. Both writers perform quasi-autistically as they draw the rabbit and make the duck at the same time. Phillips's storytelling manner is flat, his sentences short and bare of ornament; the rhetorical finesse exists entirely in the mimicry of voices (as it does in Swift and Ishiguro). How this reflects—and indeed extends—his inquiry into history and belonging can be seen in the effect of paralysis that the flatness creates. History itself—in this book the Holocaust; in the earlier novels, other great themes, slavery, emancipation, utopias—gives up its evidence grudgingly: a damaged child in a casestudy whose rare and enigmatic utterances must be carefully collected and examined and pressed to yield meaning; which often enough they stubbornly refuse. The lacunae between them open, but meanings hide.

The temperature of this latest novel runs a little low. The several lost lives and loves that crowd the banks of its own dark Styx are too numerous to bind the reader emotionally in the way his three dominant protagonists did in *Crossing the River.* The effect is a little remote, the method a little schematic, and here and there the research still pokes through the extreme reticence. But in a blur that itself reflects lost history, the maimed subjects of events—Eva maddened by surviving her sister and the camps, Dr Stern desolate in Zion, the murdered Jews of Renaissance Venice, Othello travelling ineluctably towards Iago, the novel's population of exiles and immigrants, so many of the undone and unbelonging—appear in the cracks that fissure the clouded mirror Caryl Phillips is holding up as he stubbornly wills memory to articulate something we can maybe count on, in spite of everything.

James Shapiro (review date 25 August 1997)

SOURCE: "Diasporas and Desperations," in *New York Times Book Review,* August 25, 1997, p. 7.

[*In the following review, Shapiro explains the historical settings in Phillips's* The Nature of Blood *and discusses the novel's themes.*]

In the early 1980's the novelist Caryl Phillips, a West Indian raised in England, spent a year traveling through Europe. In *The European Tribe,* his nonfiction account of that journey, Mr. Phillips relates that wherever he went he was confronted by expressions of racist and nationalist sentiment so strong that they amounted to a kind of tribalism.

Literature offered Mr. Phillips a way into the darker currents of this European obsession with cultural difference. His experience of Venice is filtered through those of Othello and Shylock; his Amsterdam is also the Amsterdam of Anne Frank. Mr. Phillips recalls that the first story he wrote as a teen-ager was about the deportation of a Dutch Jewish boy; the boy, who thought he was just like everybody else, didn't understand why he had to wear a yellow Star of David. The Holocaust made a powerful impression on the young Mr. Phillips: "If white people could do that to white people," he remembers thinking, "then what the hell would they do to me?"

In his sixth novel, *The Nature of Blood,* Mr. Phillips returns to the problem of European tribalism and the awful price it exacted of the Jews. His earliest novels, *The Final Passage* (1985) and *A State of Independence* (1986), focused on modern Britain and the Caribbean. In *Higher Ground* (1989), *Cambridge* (1992) and *Crossing the River* (1994), his scope has steadily widened. As a black, Oxford-educated writer who finds himself both inside and outside European culture, who has also written penetratingly and from personal experience of diaspora and racial hatred, Mr. Phillips brings an unusual sympathy and understanding to the fate of European Jewry. Moreover, in taking the Holocaust as his subject, and in writing much of the novel in the voice of a white Jewish woman, Mr. Phillips also challenges the current literary tribalism, pervasive in this age of identity politics, that would mark off black experience as the domain of blacks, restrict the telling of women's lives to other women, and leave the Holocaust to the Jews.

This ambitious historical novel is constructed of several interwoven plots, set in a number of locations—Germany, Venice, London, Palestine, Cyprus—that are revisited at various points in time, from the Renaissance to World War II to the present. The central character is a young German Jew, Eva Stern, whose life we follow from the mid-1930's up through her liberation from the death camps. In the course of the narrative Eva loses her home, her parents, her sister, her few friends and, finally, her sanity. Mr. Phillips is particularly adept at capturing her psychic disintegration and estrangement. To "remember too much," as he repeatedly makes clear, "is, indeed, a form of madness." Eva's story, one imagines, is what Anne Frank might have left behind had she survived and continued her diary from where it abruptly ends.

We also follow the life of Eva's uncle, Stephan Stern, who escapes Nazi Germany at the cost of losing his wife and child, sacrificing family in order to help found an underground military force in Palestine (perhaps, as his name suggests, the ruthless Stern Gang).

Mr. Phillips goes back to the Renaissance, a golden age of European culture, in search of the historical roots of intolerance. In one subplot he recounts the story of a small group of 15th-century Jews who had fled persecution in Germany and settled in the Venetian Republic in the town of Portobuffole. These Jews "arrived as foreigners, and foreigners they remained." Though tolerated in Italy for their moneylending, they were, in local eyes, still feared for their strange customs.

Shortly after Easter 1480, neighbors accused the Jews of Portobuffole of murdering a Christian boy who had been seen walking through town and was never seen again. The blood libel emerges bit by bit as a communal story, with various inhabitants of Portobuffole contributing elements of the plot until the accusation emerges as a coherent and terrifying narrative. The finishing touches are offered by a Jewish boy who converted to Christianity (and who will later be punished along with the other Jews). Though initially skeptical, the Venetian authorities find it politically prudent to put some of these Jews to death, following confessions induced by torture. In July 1480, three of them—Servadio, Moses and Giacobbe—are rowed across the Grand Canal to their execution: "As the blaze consumed flesh and blood, the spectators, on both land and water, were deeply moved by the power of the Christian faith."

Renaissance Venice is also the site of another subplot: Mr. Phillips retells the story of Othello, brought to Venice to wage war against the infidel Turks. Venice needs the Moorish general, as it does its moneylending Jews, to secure its empire—but does not expect him to violate its ironclad racial and religious boundaries; it was "important to keep the bloodlines pure." In Mr. Phillips's revision of Shakespeare's tale, Othello has left behind a wife and child in Africa and imagines that his marriage to Desdemona will provide the social acceptance he so badly craves.

Othello is destroyed by Venetian racism, but he is nonetheless culpable, as an unforgiving 20th-century narrative voice is quick to remind us, for having been a "black Uncle Tom" fighting the "white man's war for him." One senses that for Mr. Phillips, no less than for his narrator, Othello is in the end "a sad black man, first in a long line of so-called achievers who are too weak to yoke their past with their present." The force of endogamy, here and elsewhere in the plot, is strong. Eva, upon learning that her neighbor Rosa has "married outside of her people," is given to understand by her mother that this was "the greatest crime that a person could

commit." Tribalism, even—and perhaps especially—among those living in an unrooted diaspora, punishes all violators. The novel ends, as it begins, in an elusive vision of Zion. The conclusion brings together two Jews—one white, the other black. Stephan Stern, having outlived his usefulness to the country he helped found, has survived into old age and lives as a lonely pensioner outside Tel Aviv. He seeks companionship at a dance club, where he meets a young and beautiful unemployed nurse named Malka (the Hebrew word means queen, suggesting that like the other black African in the novel, Othello, she is of royal blood). Malka has arrived in the Jewish homeland from Ethiopia unprepared for the racism that has left her feeling humiliated and outcast: "This Holy Land did not deceive us. The people did." She remembers wondering on her flight to Israel: "In this new land, would our babies be born white? We, the people of the House of Israel, we were going home. No more wandering." In a novel alert to all fantasies of racial purity, one suspects that Mr. Phillips's unspoken subtext here is the recent scandal in Israel that arose when blood donated by Ethiopian Jews serving in the army (like the fictional Malka's brother) was dumped for fear that it would contaminate the national blood supply. There is no monopoly on tribalism; it infects even those who ostensibly share the same blood.

The Nature of Blood is at times a difficult novel to read. The style often feels flat; the narrative control is sometimes shaky; the interpolation of definitions of "ghetto," "Venice," "suicide" and "Othello" is unwarranted and distracting. But it is also an extraordinarily perceptive and intelligent novel, and a haunting one. Mr. Phillips succeeds in making one feel anew the force of tribalism and the terrible strangeness of Europe, Zion and the Holocaust.

FURTHER READING

Criticism

Burroway, Janet. "Slaves to Fate." *New York Times Book Review* (30 January 1994): 10.

> Presents a close reading of *Crossing the River*'s narrative qualities and a discussion of its themes.

Lezard, Nicholas. "Facing it." *London Review of Books* (23 September 1993): 21.

> A detailed, perceptive and inspired review of *Crossing the River* that relates Phillips's concerns with the formal and thematic features of the novel.

Miller, Lucasta. "Passages." *New Statesman and Society* (23 March 1993): 34-35.

> An appreciative review of *Crossing the River* that examines Phillips's use of voices and varying perspectives.

> **Additional coverage of Phillips's life and career is contained in the following sources published by Gale:** *Black Writers,* **Vol. 2;** *Contemporary Authors,* **Vol. 141;** *Contemporary Literary Criticism,* **Vol. 96;** *Discovering Authors: Multicultural Authors Module; Dictionary of Literary Biography,* **Vol. 157.**

Sol T. Plaatje
1876-1932

(Full name Solomon Tshekisho Plaatje) South African novelist, diarist, linguist, translator, newspaper editor, journalist, and political activist.

INTRODUCTION

Plaatje was a writer whose works are deeply rooted in the traditions and culture of native black African peoples. He aimed both to preserve and to disseminate his cultural heritage, working to promote civil rights for the native people of South Africa during the time when white political supremacy was being established. Perhaps best remembered as an activist in the movement for government reform, Plaatje is also noted for making literature in the European tradition more accessible to an African audience as well as bringing awareness of African culture to Europeans. His efforts to bridge cultural conflicts and to represent his culture as the equal of any in the world make him a major figure in the long struggle for democratic rule in his homeland.

Biographical Information

Plaatje was born in the Orange Free State, Republic of South Africa, into an atmosphere of growing social and political tension. Both the Boers, descendants of the early Dutch settlers, and the British laid claim to the originally Bantu lands. His family descended from some of the earliest converts to Christianity. He was raised speaking Tswana (Sechuana) and showed a remarkable facility for African and European languages during his education at Pniel missionary school. At seventeen, he left school and took a job as a postal messenger in Kimberley, the center of British diamond mining operations, in Cape Town Province. Here he added English to his linguistic accomplishments and in 1898 became a court interpreter for the Cape civil service in Mafeking. During his tenure here, the Boers, chafing at British interference, declared war on Britain and laid siege to a number of Cape cities, including Mafeking. Plaatje served as interpreter and signal man for the British army during the siege and kept a diary, in English, of his experiences. While many British diaries appeared not long after the siege ended in 1900, Plaatje's sole African account was apparently "lost" and was not published until 1973 after it was "discovered" in Mafeking. After the Anglo-Boer War, Plaatje began his newspaper career as editor of the Tswana-English newspaper, *Koranta ea Becoana (The Tswana Gazette)*. In the years before World War I, he became an increasingly active and articulate defender of native rights against the segregationist policies of the British. His courage and commitment made him one of

the most respected newspaper editors in the country. In 1914, Plaatje was named secretary general of the African National Congress, an organization he had helped to form the previous year. As a spokesman for the cause of black equality, he traveled to England in an unsuccessful effort to persuade the British government to repeal the Natives' Land Act of 1913, a law viewed as one of the keystones of South Africa's apartheid government. Plaatje remained in England, where he wrote and published three books in support of his people and culture. Plaatje returned to South Africa in 1917. He made subsequent trips to Great Britain and the United States, continuing his crusade for black South African civil rights with little effect. Upon resettling in South Africa in 1923, Plaatje was unsuccessful in resuming his career as an editor, and his political influence waned, but he did continue to write for newspapers with both black and white audiences. During the final years of his life, Plaatje concentrated on works that would preserve Tswana language and culture. An English-Tswana dictionary, a collection of Tswana folk tales and poems, and a revised edition of *Sechuana Proverbs* (1916) were never published. The first novel in English by a black African, *Mhudi* (1930), was written during Plaatje's stay in England in 1919-20 but was not published until 1930. At the time of his death, Plaatje left another African historical novel unfinished.

Major Works

Plaatje's commitment to racial equality, cultural tolerance, and democratic government provides the dominant themes of his works. *The Boer War Diary of Sol T. Plaatje* (1973) demonstrates his interest in and knowledge of African, British, and Dutch languages and cultural intricacies. It also provides the otherwise forgotten perspective of a native black African in events that had a tremendous impact on his people. *Native Life in South Africa* (1916) likewise gives voice to the people who suffered most from the Land Act of 1913 that relegated the native population to less than second-class status in their own homeland. Two translations of Shakespeare plays into Tswana, *Diphosho-phosho* (1930; *A Comedy of Errors*) and *Dintshontsho tsa bo Juliuse Kesara* (1937; *Julius Caesar*), were the first appearance of Shakespeare in any African language and received critical acclaim for their language facility. Plaatje's lone novel *Mhudi* presents a cautionary tale drawn from black African history that shows the cyclical nature of conflicts arising from autocratic rule, cultural chauvinism, racism, and gender inequality. The heroine, Mhudi, exemplifies the value of women in creating and maintaining social harmony. The friendship between a native African and a Boer depicts Plaatje's belief in racial equality. The bloody battles the story recounts arise from tribal leaders' flouting of the democratic principles of their own tradition.

Critical Reception

Critical response to Plaatje's work during his lifetime reflects the cultural and racial condescension dominant in his British and European audience. *Mhudi*, for example, was admired for the facility of its language. As the first black African to write in English, Plaatje drew praise for that accomplishment, but the novel's political and social critique was overlooked or deprecated as a pale imitation of European literary technique. These attitudes help to explain why it took him ten years to find a publisher for the work. Appreciation for his writing has grown steadily since the publication of his *Boer War Diary* in 1973. Critics now praise his blend of Western literary devices and African oral traditions. Reviewers laud his work for the feminist and culturally diverse themes of *Mhudi*, and the articulate voice of protest and representation of the "other" in his nonfiction. His historical position as one of the founders of the instrument of democratic government in South Africa is now being matched by his central importance as the predecessor of modern black African literature.

PRINCIPAL WORKS

Native Life in South Africa (nonfiction) 1916; revised edition, 1983, 1991
Sechuana Proverbs, with Literal Translations and Their European Equivalents (proverbs) 1916
A Sechuana Reader, in International Phonetic Orthography [with Daniel Jones] (dictionary and folklore) 1916
The Mote and the Beam (nonfiction) 1920
Diphosho-phosho [translator; from the drama *A Comedy of Errors* by William Shakespeare] (drama) 1930
*Mhudi: An Epic of Native Life a Hundred Years Ago (novel) 1930; revised edition, 1978, 1996
Mabolela a ga Tshikinya-Chaka [translator; extracts from the works of William Shakespeare] (extracts) 1935
Dintshontsho tsa bo Juliuse Kesara [translator; from the drama *Julius Caesar* by William Shakespeare] (drama) 1937
**The Boer War Diary of Sol T. Plaatje (diary) 1973; also published in revised form as *Mafeking Diary: A Black Man's View of a White Man's War,* 1990

*This work was written in 1919-1920.
** This work was written in October 1899-March 1900.

CRITICISM

Sol T. Plaatje (essay date 1930)

SOURCE: A preface to *Mhudi: An Epic of South African Native Life a Hundred Years Ago,* Negro Universities Press, 1970.

[*In this brief preface to* Mhudi, *Plaatje presents his rationale for writing the novel.*]

South African literature has hitherto been almost exclusively European, so that a foreword seems necessary to give reasons for a Native venture.

In all the tales of battle I have ever read, or heard of, the cause of the war is invariably ascribed to the other side. Similarly, we have been taught almost from childhood, to fear the Matebele—a fierce nation—so unreasoning in its ferocity that it will attack any individual or tribe, at sight, without the slightest provocation. Their destruction of our people, we were told, had no justification in fact or in reason; they were actuated by sheer lust for human blood.

By the merest accident, while collecting stray scraps of tribal history, later in life, the writer incidentally heard of "the day

Mzilikazi's tax collectors were killed." Tracing this bit of information further back, he elicited from old people that the slaying of Bhoya and his companion, about the year 1830, constituted the *casus belli* which unleashed the war dogs and precipitated the Barolong nation headlong into the horrors described in these pages.

This book should have been published over ten years ago, but circumstances beyond the control of the writer delayed its appearance. If, however, the objects can be attained, it will have come not a moment too soon.

This book has been written with two objects in view, viz., (*a*) to interpret to the reading public, one phase of "the back of the Native mind"; and (*b*), with the readers' money, to collect and print (for Bantu Schools) Sechuana folk-tales, which, with the spread of European ideas, are fast being forgotten. It is thus hoped to arrest this process by cultivating a love for art and literature in the Vernacular. The latter object interests not missionaries alone, but also eminent scholars like Dr. C. T. Loram, Dr. C. M. Doke and other Professors of the University of the Witwatersrand, not to mention commercial men of the stamp of Mr. J. W. Mushet, Chairman of the Capetown Chamber of Commerce.

The last time I wrote a booklet, it was to pay my way through the United States. It was a disquisition on a delicate social problem known to Europeans in South Africa as the *Black Peril* and to the Bantu as the *White Peril*. I called it, **The Mote and the Beam.** It more than fulfilled its purpose, for, by the time I left the States, over 18,000 copies had been sold and helped to pay my research journeys through several farms and cities of nineteen different States; and it is the author's sincere hope that the objects of this book [*Mhudi*] will likewise be fulfilled.

Tim Couzens (essay date 1973)

SOURCE: "Sol Plaatje's *Mhudi,*" in *The Journal of Commonwealth Literature,* Vol. VIII, No. 1, June 1973, pp. 1-19.

[*In this essay, Couzens contends that early, indifferent reviews of* Mhudi *failed to consider the social and historical background of the work and therefore undervalue it as literature and as a statement of political dissent.*]

One of the first novels written in English by an African, *Mhudi,* which was published in 1930 but probably largely written about 1917 or 1918, has not been considered worthy of major critical attention. In 1952, J. Snyman could dismiss the book fairly quickly and attack Plaatje for a lack of imagination:

In *Mhudi* (1930), Plaatje deals with the times of Mzilikazi, and especially with the war between the Matabele and Barolong. He has examined the causes of this war and finds that its origin lay in the murder of Mzilikazi's tax-collectors by the Barolong. He shows also that the Matabele had justification for some of their deeds. Plaatje takes pride in his people, and attempts here to interpret to the reading public 'one phase of the back of the native mind', as well as to gain sufficient money to arrest the lack of interest of his people in their own beliefs and literature, by collecting and printing Sechuana folk-tales which are in danger of being forgotten through the spread of European ideas.

Although *Mhudi* would seem to be authentic, it lacks the spontaneity of Mitford's Untúswa series. The reader is aware that the writer is recounting events which occurred a hundred years ago, and it seems as if Plaatje is unable to span the gap and live in the period about which he is writing. Little fault can be found, however, with his account of life at Mzilikazi's kraal in the Matabele capital.

Martin Tucker remains somewhat non-committal:

Plaatje's novel, **Mhudi: An Epic of South African Native Life a Hundred Years Ago,** written at least ten years before its publication by Lovedale Press in South Africa in 1930, is an attempt at blending African folk material with individually realized characters in the Western novelistic tradition; the result has been both admired and denigrated by commentators. Plaatje's story of the two Bechuana natives who survive a raid by a warring Zulu tribe, fall in love (one episode describes the admiration which the hero inspires in his female companion when he subdues a lion by wrenching its tail), and triumph over the mistreatment they endure from the Boers whom they have aided, is leavened by humour and sense of proportion. Although the novel contains idyllic scenes of native life, the hero Ra-Thaga, and Mhudi, who becomes his wife, are not sentimental Noble Savages but peaceful citizens forced to accept the harshness of the invading white world.

Tucker says too that 'Plaatje is not highly regarded by his fellow African writers today'. Janheinz Jahn has categorized *Mhudi* as being 'hedging or half-and-half' writing and as 'mission' literature:

No hard-and-fast line, of course, can be drawn dividing 'apprentice' and 'protest' literature. Between them there is a wide field of 'hedging' or 'neutral'

works. For, to avoid having to approve their tutelage, many writers glorified the traditional life of
the tribe and the tribal chiefs and heroes: this can
be interpreted as a form of indirect protest. The
novel *Mhudi,* for instance, by Solomon Tzhekisho
Plaatje (1877-1932), is a love story which has as its
background the battles between Mzilikazi's Ndebele
and the Baralong.

Jahn has also written of *Mhudi* that it is 'weak in comparison with other works, for Plaatje tries to individualize his
characters in the European fashion and thus the African pathos of the dialogue becomes empty'. When critics largely
ignore the social-historical milieu from which a work
springs, the unfortunate situation can arise that a book is
written off for its poor 'quality of writing' or for what at first
sight seem to be clichaic ideas. Not only do arbitrary and
vague (and often ethnocentric) ideas of 'taste' lead to hasty
dismissals, they also conveniently allow the critic to avoid
the attempt to find out the author's intentions in writing the
book. *Mhudi* seems to be such a novel, which has been neglected for the lack of a little extra-novel research.

To characterize *Mhudi* as in any way being 'neutral', as Jahn
does, may be in the interest of categorization, and may be
the reasonable expectation set up by works of Plaatje's contemporaries, but it certainly cannot seriously be maintained
in the light of Plaatje's character, his beliefs, his actions, and
his other writings. This article argues that a study of these
matters throws new light on *Mhudi.*

Since biographical information on Plaatje is not easy to come
by, it seems desirable to quote a pen-sketch which Plaatje
probably played a large part in writing:

> Mr Sol. T. Plaatje was born at Boshof and educated
> at Pniel Lutheran Mission school. Married Eliza-
> beth, daughter of the late Mr Mbelle, and sister of
> Mr I. Bud Mbelle, of Pretoria. Was interpreter to the
> Court of Summary Jurisdiction under Lord Edward
> Cecil. Rendered much service to the British Gov-
> ernment during the siege of Mafeking in the Anglo-
> Boer War. Was editor of *Koranta ea Becoana* and
> *Tsala ea Batho,* Kimberley. Was war correspondent
> during the Anglo-Boer War. Foundation member
> and first general secretary of the South African Na-
> tional Congress when Rev. J. L. Dube was presi-
> dent. Went abroad twice on deputations in 1914 and
> 1919. Toured Canada and the United States during
> 1920-23. Founder and president of the Diamond
> Fields Men's Own Brotherhood. On attaining 50
> years of age, in 1928, a group of Bantu, Coloured
> and Indian admirers started a Jubilee Fund and pur-
> chased his residence, 32, Angel Street, and gave it
> to him as a present in appreciation of his lifelong

unsalaried work in the Non-European cause. Mr
Plaatje is now engaged in writing Sechuana Readers for Native schools. He is the author of the famous book *Native Life in South Africa.* Has also
written *Mhudi*—a novel, *Sechuana Proverbs and
their European Equivalents, The Mote and the
Beam, Native Labour in South Africa,* also
Sechuana Reader in International Phonetics (the
latter in conjunction with Professor Daniel Jones,
M.A., University College, London). The latest of Mr
Plaatje's books is the translation of Shakespeare's
works in Sechuana. Is one of the best writers and
speakers among Africans in S.A.

A founder member of the African National Congress (he refused its presidency on one occasion), a writer of a famous
political book (*Native Life in South Africa*) and of two linguistic texts, Plaatje, the uncle of Z. K. Matthews, was in
the forefront of the political defence of his people throughout his life and was certainly no Uncle Tom of the missions.
Indeed, in a letter to the Administrator of Rhodesia in which
he attacks the hypocrisy and knock-kneed quality of English
liberals (particularly John Harris, the Secretary of the Ab-
origines Protection Society), he describes himself with characteristic humour and irony:

> I am exceedingly sorry to encroach upon your pre-
> cious time but, as the following lines will show the
> above controversy [between Harris and the Rhode-
> sian Government] is of intense interest to me and
> the natives of the Union; you will perhaps be sur-
> prised to hear that I, a native of natives, immensely
> enjoyed reading the sound thrashing administered
> to Mr J. H. Harris by the logical pen of His Honour
> Sir Drummond Chaplin.

In this article I would like to examine three major issues relating to Plaatje's work in general and to *Mhudi* in particular: (1) the question of his language use, attempting a partial
defence of it; (2) his distinctive ideas of history, the portrayal
of which is virtually unique in South African literature; (3)
the question whether *Mhudi* is something more than a love
idyll with black heroes or an historical romance. I argue that
Mhudi is a sensitive political novel, in which the historical
moment of the 1830s was a carefully selected model for
Plaatje's own situation in the period after Union and the Natives Land Act of 1913.

Janheinz Jahn talks of Plaatje's 'padded "Victorian" style',
and it is true that Plaatje uses 'poetic' archaisms such as 'jo-
cund lambs', 'eligible swains', and 'native gallantry', but
these tend to be absent when Plaatje reaches the more significant moments in his narrative and, in any case, the
phrases often seem to be used with that distinctive sense of

irony which is seldom far from the surface in all of Plaatje's writing (as, for instance, in the probable pun in the last of the examples cited). This irony manifests itself in Plaatje's frequently used technique of reinforcing his argument by couching it in his opponents' own terms—whether their language or their beliefs. The technique can be illustrated by his use of a European (Scottish) proverb to illustrate the throwing-off from their land of two related 'native' families, described in his book *Native Life in South Africa.*

> The father-in-law asked that Kgobadi should try and secure a place for him in the much dreaded 'Free' State as the Transvaal had suddenly become uninhabitable to Natives who cannot become servants; but 'greedy folk hae long airms', and Kgobadi himself was proceeding with his family and belongings in a wagon, to inform his people-in-law of his own eviction without notice, in the 'Free' State, for a similar reason to that which sent his father-in-law adrift.

The passion here is in no doubt, for his hatred of the Natives Land Act is implicit in all Plaatje's public actions after 1913, and the irony is savage. It is the irony of adopting what many South African whites would call the 'cheeky Kaffir' stance, by answering the opponent in his own language. To miss Plaatje's tone, and often his irony, will almost inevitably lead to patronizing his language. It would be well to remember that the great linguist Daniel Jones, in his preface to *A Sechuana Reader* which he and Plaatje compiled, found Plaatje in possession of 'unusual linguistic ability'.

For his use of Biblical and epic language, though perhaps not completely successful, Plaatje does at least give a justification, whether adequate or not. In the introduction to his *Sechuana Proverbs* he writes: 'The similarity between all pastoral nations is such that some passages in the history of the Jews read uncommonly like a description of the Bechuana during the nineteenth century.' There is here a concept of decorum, and the use of the metaphor of the Garden of Eden at the beginning of the novel to describe African traditional life is not accidental—for he is showing an idyllic society about to be shattered by forces which were the genesis of South Africa's problems, as Plaatje saw them after the Natives Land Act. What is more, Plaatje comments on the limitations of his own use of language within the novel itself. He says of the speech of Chief Moroka:

> His speeches abounded in allegories and proverbial sayings, some traditional and others original. His own maxims had about them the spice of originality which always provided his auditors with much food for thought . . . The crowd pressed forward and

eagerly hung on to every word, but it is to be regretted that much of the charm is lost in translation.

Plaatje was fully aware of all the problems of 'translation' which still beset the African writer, but once his decision was made he did not fuss unnecessarily about it. One of his minor themes, however, is the tragedy which frequently arises because of the lack of communication through mutual ignorance of respective languages, whether between man and man, or man and beast or nature.

But Plaatje does not simply use clichaic English of suitable decorum. Part of the richness of literature lies in deviation. And Plaatje frequently gives us a fresh idiom, stemming often from 'translation'; for example, his description of lions as 'making thunder in the forest', or when one speaker rebukes another for dissenting, by saying 'his speech was the one fly in the milk'. The language of the novel abounds also in localized South African imagery. Most interesting in the field of the figurative use of language, however, is his deliberate distribution of proverbs.

In discussing proverbs in both their oral and written form, Ruth Finnegan has written:

> In neither case should they be regarded as isolated sayings to be collected in hundreds or thousands on their own, but rather as just one aspect of artistic expression within a social and literary context.

It is noticeable that in *Mhudi* there is a marked increase in the number of proverbs used by speakers during the crucial debate amongst the Baralong about whether they should help the Boers (five proverbs in five pages, three of them given to the man who is the ideal of justice, Chief Moroka, whose 'allegories and proverbial sayings' were both original and traditional). This debate reveals one of the major themes of the book, that the whites would scarcely have survived without the aid of the blacks, and the heightening of the language through proverbs, showing the traditional wisdom of the debaters, is both functional and significant. There is also, in the same scene, interesting confirmation of another of Ruth Finnegan's suggestions:

> Though proverbs can occur in very many different kinds of contexts, they seem to be particularly important in situations where there is both conflict and, at the same time, some obligation that this conflict should not take on too open and personal a form.

A conflict situation arises in the debate, but is de-fused through a humorous proverb:

> Some were for letting the Boers stew in their own

juice, as the Barolongs had perforce to do years before; others were for combining with the Boers against the Matebele; some again were for letting the enemy well alone as long as he remained on the far side of the Vaal River—that river of many vicissitudes and grim histories—yet many believed that a scrap with the Matebele with the aid of the Boers would give each one an opportunity of avenging the blood of his relations before he himself joined his forefathers. Such were the conflicting views that found expression among the waiting throng. One grizzly old man with small jaws and very short teeth, touching his shins said: 'Oh, that I could infuse some youth into these old bones and raise my shield! I would march against the vampires with spear in hand. Then Mzilikazi would know that among the Barolong there was a man named Nakedi—just as the pack of lions at Mafika-Kgocoana knew me to their cost.'

One man raised a laugh among the serious groups. 'What a truthful thing is a proverb,' he said. 'According to an old saying "Lightning fire is quenched by other fire." It seems a good idea then to fight the Matebele with the help of the women, for they always kill women in their attacks. If Sarel Siljay's women had not helped the Boers, they would not have defied Gubuza's army and Schalk would not be here to tell the tale.'

The 'sense of detachment and generalization inherent in proverbs' is clearly in evidence, mixed here with laughter in its conflict-avoiding function.

Plaatje's relationship with proverbs has yet one more interesting aspect. At the Matebele victory celebrations after the defeat of the Baralong near the beginning of the book, one man, Gubuza, stands out against the rest in warning of the possible consequences. His pessimism is rebuked by another speaker, but Mzilikazi defends Gubuza.

If Gubuza had not spoken I should have been very sorry. You see a man has two legs so as to enable him to walk properly. He cannot go far if he has one leg . . . For the same reason he has two eyes in order to see better. A man has two ears so as to hear both sides of a dispute. A man who joins in a discussion with the acts of one side only, will often find himself in the wrong. In every grade of life there are two sides to every matter.

In this idiomatic passage, which is Plaatje at his best, the near-proverbs express the idea of the two-sidedness of arguments. The idea seems to interest him. In his collection of Sechuana proverbs Plaatje writes:

The reader will here and there come across two proverbs that appear to contradict each other; but such anomalies are not peculiar to Sechuana . . . The whole truth about a fact cannot be summed up in one pithy saying. It may have several different aspects, which, taken separately, seem to be contradictory and have to be considered in connexion with their surrounding circumstances. To explain the connexion is the work of a sermon or essay, not of a proverb. All the latter can do is to express each aspect by itself and let them balance each other.

It seems to me that he extends this idea into both the theme and technique of the novel. Although the book is clearly an epic praising the Baralong, through the technique of shifting perspective, we come to have a certain sympathy with the Matabele; we see, in fact, the final battle through their eyes not through those of the favoured victors (this is a technique which is probably reinforced by his translation of several Shakespearian plays, for though the crimes of Claudius and Macbeth are very similar, our response is different, but only because of the amount we see of their inner thoughts). The technique, then, in the novel, is of shifting perspective; that both sides are given through this technique is a reinforcement of one of the major themes—that there *are* two sides in every argument.

The merit of Plaatje's novel also lies in other directions. Because South African written history has been dominated by white historians and most of South Africa's imaginative writers have been white, South African history and literature usually display a bias of historical interpretation which seldom escapes complete ethnocentricity. Writers have endlessly extolled the courage of the Voortrekkers and the 1820 Settlers, but Plaatje is one of the few, and certainly one of the very earliest, who dealt with the events from 'the other side', from the side of the people who had to face dangers just as great, if not greater, for they ultimately came into contact with a people who had the advantage of those conveniences of civilization, the horse and the gun. (Indeed, without these two benefits, with, according to some historians, the Bible as a supplement, it is difficult to see how the whites could have survived at all in South Africa.) In **Mhudi,** the Great Trek is put into perspective, and is seen as a mere part of a much greater complex of events and activity, so that, in **Mhudi,** the whites appear only a third of the way through the book, and the course of South African history had already been as much determined by interaction amongst the blacks as anything the whites could do in the future. In other words, the blacks *made history* in South Africa as much as, if not more so than, the whites. Plaatje perceived that the Boers were simply a fourth force added to the existing groups of Baralong, Matabele and Korannas—not to mention Griquas, Bakwena, Bangwaketse, etc. The world of the novel is that of the relatively peaceful tribes inhabiting the areas around Transorangia who are, after the initial idyllic setting, thrown into turmoil as a result of the 'Mfecane', the great upheaval caused by the transformation of the tribes of Northern Natal into the Zulu military state, when tribes were sent fleeing all over Southern Africa and the effects of the upheaval were felt in areas as far distant as present-day Tanzania. J. D. Omer-Cooper has written of the 'Mfecane': 'It far exceeds other comparable movements such as the sixteenth century migration of the Zimba and Jagas and it positively dwarfs the Boer Great Trek.'

Life before the 'Mfecane', though not without its intertribal conflict, was fairly peaceful, and it is this life which Plaatje is describing at the beginning of the novel. The introduction of the terrible and warlike Matabele is clearly meant to be a contrast to the picture of the relatively peaceful Baralong—relatively peaceful because Plaatje's image of the Baralong has two sides to it. In his *Sechuana Proverbs* he took pains to describe his disagreement with prevailing historians over the character of the Bechuana, particularly the Baralong:

> Historians describe the Bechuana as the most peace-loving and timid section of the Bantu. Their statements, however, do not seem to be quite in accord with the facts; for, fighting their way South, from the Central African lakes, some of the Bechuana tribes became known as 'the People with the Sharp spear'. And if I am not much mistaken they were the only natives who indignantly, though vainly, protested against the South African Defence Act which debars Native citizens from joining the Citizen Volunteer Force . . . But the proverbial phrases in this book do seem to support the view that they are by nature far from being bellicose.

Most of their proverbs, he points out, are of hunting or the pastoral and not concerned with war, but it is his clear intention to show that though the Baralong love peace they are brave if war is necessary. His concern here is not unreasonable. The leading historians of his time were explicit. G. W. Stow, for instance, wrote of the Baralong in 1905:

> They seem however to have possessed the same natural timidity as the rest of the Bechuana, and as a race were not a whit more warlike than the cowardly Batlapin themselves, who, as we have seen, were only brave when they found their antagonists weaker than themselves, or when they had defenceless women and children to deal with.

The historian Theal concurred in 1915:

> It is impossible to give the number of Moselekatse's warriors, but it was probably not greater than twenty thousand. Fifty of them were a match for more than five hundred Betshuana.

Plaatje's motive in showing the Baralong to be courageous when necessary was not only to counter white prejudice but also to indicate that the exclusion of his people from the army was one more sign of the inequality existing at the time of writing. (The whites' ability both to admire and condemn the bravery of the Zulu war-machine is a fascinating exercise in double standards; the whites' pride in 'bringing peace' yet their contempt for the Tswana 'cowards' is a similar contradiction and forces Plaatje to defend on two seemingly contradictory fronts.)

In keeping with this view of history, in which blacks contribute as much as whites, Plaatje does not sentimentalize the Boers as so many writers have done. Rather he views central South African history more in terms of what someone once described as 'a clash of rival cattle cultures'. De Kiewiet describes it in terms which would probably have appealed to Plaatje:

> The native wars, from major campaigns to unheralded skirmishes, were spectacular phases in a lengthy process of encroachment, invasion, extrusion, and dispossession. For the most part the wars were not caused by the inborn quarrelsomeness of savage and warlike tribes, but by the keen competition of two groups, with very similar agricultural and pastoral habits, for the possession of the most fertile and best-watered stretches of land.

Plaatje gives a view of a Boer search-party in *Mhudi* which few white writers would ever have thought of at the time.

> The search party looked foolish as they brought no news, but the climax of their incompetence came a few days later when a Basuto chief sent an ultimatum to the effect that the Boer party had killed two of his men and maimed two more who were peacefully hunting on the Vaal River . . . But thanks to the intercession of Chief Moroka, a satisfactory compromise was effected.

The only Boer who is sympathetically dealt with in *Mhudi,* Phil Jay, is described by the heroine, Mhudi, as 'the one humane Boer that there was among the wild men of his tribe', and even he, despite the general sentimentality used to describe him, is illiterate.

Not only is Plaatje able to correct what he regards as a mistaken bias in history, he is, at the same time, able to defend many traditional customs and beliefs of his people and to establish them as a coherent system within the novel. He praises his own people for the same things that Edward

Blyden praised Africans for in his *African Life and Customs* (1908)—for their religion and socialism, their system of marriage, and the absence of orphans and prostitutes. From the beginning of the book he emphasizes the religion of his people, with the ancestral spirits at its core, and contrasts it with the broken-down Christianity of the Boers. And throughout the book he contrasts the basic justice of the traditional society with the arbitrary, dictatorial justice of Mzilikazi (and, implicitly, of modern whites, as we shall see). In Chapter Fifteen of *Mhudi,* Chief Moroka is seen to dispense justice in a manner far superior to any of the other characters, including the white men, and the function of the chapter is somewhat similar to that of Chapter Ten in Chinua Achebe's *Things Fall Apart*—in both books justice is established as central to the society and is given a central place in the book. De Kiewiet has described the tragedy of the whites' failure to see any merit in African society:

> At least two generations of settlers grew up in ignorance of the ingenuity and appropriateness with which the natives in their tribal state met the many problems of their lives, in ignorance of the validity of many of the social and moral rules which held them together. European society most easily saw the unattractive aspect of tribal life. It saw the superstition and witchcraft and cruelty. But it failed to see, or saw only imperfectly, the rational structure of tribal life, the protection which it gave the individual, the comfort which it gave his mind, the surveillance which it kept over the distribution of food and land. European society condemned as stagnant and unenlightened a way of life in which happiness and contentment were, for the native, not difficult to find. Between soldier and settler, missionary and magistrate there was an unvoiced conspiracy against the institutions of the tribe.

Plaatje has clearly chosen to describe a time when these values and customs were most coherent, most unified, strongest, and yet also a time of transition when these values are about to change or disappear. He chooses a period where he can analyse both the values and the genesis of the causes of their disappearance.

It is Plaatje's view of history, then, which directs him to choose this particular period for his novel. But there is a possible further reason for his choosing this time. Omer-Cooper points to it:

> The events of the Mfecane have moreover impressed themselves indelibly on the consciousness of subsequent generations. The memories and traditions of this period serve to maintain the sense of identity of peoples who were vitally affected by it, influencing attitudes within and between groups in

many complex ways. In the context of white rule, this heritage has helped many peoples to keep alive a sense of pride and independence of spirit. Together with other factors it has contributed to that great reservoir of largely inarticulate feelings and attitudes which underlies the emergence of modern African political movements.

Plaatje returns to a time when (in the face of a common enemy, the Matabele) there are the beginnings of intertribal unity, when the seeds of the alliances of 1917 were first sown, when the possibility of a nationalism transcending tribalism was first conceivable (linked naturally to Plaatje's interest in the South African Native Congress). In this period of the 1830s Plaatje discovers 'a sense of pride and independence of spirit' whose incarnation is the heroine, Mhudi. Vladimir Klima has admirably hinted at these aspects of the novel:

> The novel is remarkable for memorable portraits of Negro characters (mainly female ones are well characterized), and for Plaatje's original interpretation of historical facts. Both the Zulus and the Boers are shown as violent invaders but the author's compassionate detachment helped him in presenting a well-balanced historical fresco in which human fates can easily be traced. Mhudi's love story is especially successful and would provide a good piece of reading even outside the historical framework of the novel.

Mhudi, however, is not a novel interesting only for its concept of history and its defence of traditional custom. It is also an historical document relevant to the time it was written in, relevant to that period immediately following the Natives Land Act. It is also a comment on the conditions which resulted from that Act. Plaatje attacked the Act directly in his best-known book *Native Life in South Africa,* and in his pamphlet on the legal disabilities of Africans. I believe that *Mhudi* and *Native Life in South Africa* should be read in conjunction for they were not only written within a short time of each other, but they also show Plaatje's consistent and persistent preoccupations. The Natives Land Act was devastating in its effect, rendering homeless large numbers of Africans throughout the Union and causing untold hardship. *Native Life in South Africa* is an explicit, and *Mhudi* an implicit, attack on the Act and the hardship it caused. *Mhudi,* I believe, is a political novel relevant to 1917 or thereabouts.

South African history largely revolves around two problems: land and labour. The whites have usually solved both problems simultaneously: take land away from the Africans and they then need to sell their labour. The labour shortage can often be helped, too, by the levying of a tax. And, throughout Plaatje's writings, a single theme constantly recurs—the loss of the land the African loves and needs. 'To lose land,' writes De Kiewiet, 'was to lose the most important foundation upon which tribal life was built.' (So Plaatje's defence of traditional custom described above is an integral part of what follows.)

In *Mhudi* Plaatje's people are deprived of their land (after refusing to pay taxes) by the Matabele; in *Native Life in South Africa* they are deprived of their land by the whites. It seems to me, therefore, that Plaatje intends *Mhudi* to be, in addition to the true perspective of history discussed above, a model for events including and after the Natives Land Act of 1913. For, in *Native Life in South Africa,* the whites are described in exactly the same terms as are the Matabele in *Mhudi.* The Natives Land Act, for instance, is called 'the plague law', 'this Parliamentary land plague', 'the land plague' and 'the Plague Act'. Furthermore, he quotes with approval a speech by Dr. A. Abdurahman:

> Now let us consider the position in the Northern Colonies, especially in the misnamed Free State. There a very different picture is presented. From the days that the voortrekkers endeavoured to escape English rule, from the day that they sought the hospitality of Chief Moroka, the history of the treatment of the blacks north of the Orange River is one long and uninterrupted record of rapine and greed, without a solitary virtue to redeem the horrors which were committed in the name of civilization. Such is the opinion any impartial student must arrive at from a study even of the meagre records available. If all were told, it would indeed be a bloodcurdling tale, and it is probably well that the world was not acquainted with all that happened. However, the treatment of the Coloured races, even in the Northern Colonies, is just what one might expect from their history. The restraints of civilization were flung aside, and the essentials of Christian precepts ignored. The northward march of the voortrekkers was a gigantic plundering raid. They swept like a desolating pestilence through the land, blasting everything in their path, and pitilessly laughing at the ravages from which the native races have not yet recovered.

In *Mhudi* the Matabele are described as continuing 'their march very much like a swarm of locusts', and Chief Moroka later asks for help 'to rid the country of this pest'. Both the whites and Mzilikazi levy taxes and give little in return, and both have systems of justice arbitrary in the extreme. The Matabele in *Mhudi* are particularly loathsome because they are 'impartial in their killing', women and children are not spared. In *Native Life in South Africa* the whites share this trait:

> When the Free State ex-Republicans made use of the South African Constitution—a Constitution which Lord Gladstone says is one after the Boer sentiment—to ruin the coloured population, they should at least have confined their persecution to the male portion of the blacks . . . and have left the women and children alone.

The implicit comparison in *Mhudi* is explicit in *Native Life:*

> 'This', says Mr Lüdorf, 'caused the Natives to exclaim: "Mzilikazi, the Matabele King, was cruel to his enemies, but kind to those he conquered; whilst the Boers are cruel to their enemies and ill-treat and enslave their friends."'

If there are doubts that *Mhudi* provides a model for the situation created by the Land Act they should be assuaged by the dedication of the novel, to 'Our beloved Olive, One of the many youthful victims of "A Settled System"', a dedication very much against the land settlement scheme. Indeed, the whole theory that *Mhudi* is a model for 1918 can be checked by reference to pages 105 to 111 of *Native Life* where the whole background plot of *Mhudi* is specifically recounted as leading up to and foreshadowing the Land Act.

What makes the behaviour of the Boers worse is the hospitality and generosity with which they are originally received by the Africans, in *Mhudi* and, according to Plaatje, in history. The leader of the Korannas for instance, says that for any man who enters his dominion: 'My home is his home, my lands are his lands, my cattle are his cattle, and my law is his shield.' And when the Boers arrive 'the Baralongs informed the Boers that the country round about was wide and there was plenty of land for all'. The Boers' hospitality does not show up well when Ra-Thaga tries to drink water from a vessel in the Boers' camp. Not only has the Boers' subsequent behaviour shown ingratitude towards original hospitality but it is shown to be even worse: for in *Mhudi* they even plead for help from the Baralong when hard-pressed by the Matabele. Their subsequent unification with the Baralong and Griquas against the Matabele also has its ulterior motive. 'Of course,' explains Plaatje in *Native Life,* 'Boers could not be expected to participate in any adventure which did not immediately lead to land grabbing.' The land question is not only vital in itself; it leads to another important problem, that of labour. As I have remarked, it has been a frequent device in South African history to cure labour problems by the confiscating of land, and allowing the Africans nothing to sell but their labour. This labour problem, too, has its model in *Mhudi* in the Boers' treatment of their Hottentot servants, as in the following episode:

> Outside one of the huts close by she observed a grizzly old Boer who started to give a Hottentot

maid some thunder and lightning with his tongue. Of course Mhudi could not understand a word: but the harangue sounded positively terrible and its effect upon the maid was unmistakable. She felt that the Hottentot's position was unenviable, but more was to come. An old lady sitting near a fire behind the wagon took sides against the maid. The episode which began rather humorously developed quickly into a tragedy. The old lady pulled a poker out of the fire and beat the half naked girl with the hot iron. The unfortunate maid screamed, jumped away and writhed with pain as she tried to escape. A stalwart young Boer caught hold of the screaming girl and brought her back to the old dame, who had now left the fireplace and stood beside a vice near the waggon. The young man pressed the head of the Hottentot girl against the vice; the old lady pulled her left ear between the two irons, then screwed the jaws of the vice tightly upon the poor girl's ear. Mhudi looked at Phil's mother, but, so far from showing any concern on behalf of the sufferer, she went about her own domestic business as though nothing at all unusual was taking place. The screams of the girl attracted several Dutch men and women who looked as though they enjoyed the sickly sight.

'Africa,' Plaatje writes in **Native Life,** 'is a land of prophets and prophetesses.' And the idea of **Mhudi** being a model for a future time fits neatly into the prophetic strain of much of the work. In fact, in a crucial prophecy, Mzilikazi specifically points to it. In one of Plaatje's most interesting and skillful adaptations of an oral literature technique, Mzilikazi takes a folktale from the past and says it applies to his own fate. He then says that his own story applies to the Baralong in the future:

> The Bechuana know not the story of Zungu of old. Remember him, my people; he caught a lion's whelp and thought that, if he fed it with milk of his cows, he would in due course possess a useful mastiff to help him in hunting valuable specimens of wild beasts. The cub grew up, apparently tame and meek just like an ordinary domestic puppy; but one day Zungu came home and found, what? It had eaten his children, chewed up two of his wives, and in destroying it, he himself narrowly escaped being mauled. So, if Tauana and his gang of brigands imagine that they shall have rain and plenty under the protection of these marauding wizards from the sea, they will gather some sense before long.

> Chaka served us just as treacherously. Where is Chaka's dynasty now? Extinguished, by the very Boers who poisoned my wives and are pursuing us to-day. The Bechuana are fools to think that these

unnatural Kiwas will return their so-called friendship with honest friendship. Together they are laughing at my misery. Let them rejoice; they need all the laughter they can have to-day for when their deliverers begin to dose them with the same bitter medicine they prepared for me; when the Kiwas rob them of their cattle, their children and their lands, they will weep their eyes out of their sockets and get left with only their empty throats to squeal in vain for mercy.

> They will despoil them of the very lands they have rendered unsafe for us; they will entice the Bechuana youths to war and the chase, only to use them as pack-oxen; yea, they will refuse to share with them the spoils of victory. They will turn Bechuana women into beasts of burden to drag their loaded wagons to their granaries, . . .

The folktale is seen as a model for Mzilikazi, and Mzilikazi in **Mhudi** is seen as a model for the twentieth-century black South African. Thus the folktale here is used not merely for its quaintness but for its model-like functions, a use which illuminates the technique of the whole novel.

There is a further and, I think, conclusive proof of this model-like function of the novel. Implicit in the model of **Mhudi** is the warning that, if a people like the Matabele oppress other peoples long enough, the oppressed will eventually unite and overthrow their oppressor, in open conflict if necessary—that such oppressors are, in a phrase from **Native Life,** 'courting retribution'. The whites are being warned in **Mhudi** that the kind of thing they are doing, as described in **Native Life,** could lead to ultimate revolution. What confirms it, I think, is his use of Halley's comet. Halley's comet appeared in 1835, and, though the Matabele were only driven out of the Transvaal at the beginning of 1837, Plaatje has conflated time so that the comet appears immediately before the Matabele exodus and is heralded by a 'witch-doctor' as presaging disaster:

> Picking up his bones once more, he cast them down in different positions, and repeating the operation a few times, he critically examined the lay of every piece and, having praised his bones again, he said 'Away in the distance I can see a mighty star in the skies with a long white tail stretching almost across the heavens. Wise men have always said that such a star is the harbinger of diseases of men and beasts, wars and the overthrow of governments as well as the death of princes. Within the rays of the tail of this star, I can clearly see streams of tears and rivers of blood.' Having praised his bones once more, the wizard proceeded: 'I can see the mighty throne of Mzilikazi floating across the crimson stream, and

reaching a safe landing on the opposite bank. I also perceive clear indications of death and destruction among rulers and commoners but no death seems marked out for Mzilikazi, ruler of the ground and of the clouds.'

Here probably is another reason why Plaatje chose the 1830s. For the next time Halley's comet appeared was in 1910, and it was specifically interpreted by many millenarian movements as heralding the overthrow of the whites (in the quotation above Plaatje uses the phrase 'overthrow of governments'). Not only that, but there were strong millenarian movements of this kind amongst the Baralong, which, as editor of a Sechuana newspaper and living in the area, Plaatje must have known about. *The Rhodesia Herald* newspaper reported events from Kimberley on the 18 April 1910. (Taungs is a town in the very heart of the country of the northern Baralong; it means 'place of the Lion' and is named after the great Baralong chief of the eighteenth century, Tau, mentioned in **Mhudi.** From his sons sprang the various subgroupings of the tribe):

> There are again rumours of unrest among the natives of Taungs, where it is stated two stores have been burned and a native, who was flogged as a result of the last disturbances, has been arrested for preaching sedition, the natives being told that when the comet appears is the time for wiping out the white man. The available police in Vryberg and Mafeking have been drafted to the district. Inquiry is being made into the truth of the statements going round.

This report tells of the persistence of the disturbance, the scale of it (to require so many police), and the unrepentant quality of its participants. The disturbances, which became known as the 'Bechuana Scare', continued. A report from Kimberley on 25 April went thus:

> *The Advertiser*'s Taungs correspondent reports that another native prophet has been arrested at Mogopella by the native headman. There is still one more prophet at large, but the police are vigilant.

In the same paper there is a further report:

> The special correspondent of *The Advertiser* at Taungs, in the course of a review on the position in Bechuanaland says the sentences of five and six-and-a-half years' hard labour on the two natives last October for seditious teaching have evidently not had a salutary effect. To deal with the problem he suggests (1) that the chief and headmen be called together to a meeting at which should be impressed

upon them their paramount duty of discouraging by every legitimate means seditious teaching; (2) a meeting should be called of all native missionaries, evangelists, and teachers in the affected area who should be appealed to to counteract the effect of seditious and superstitious teaching; (3) a strong, well-paid and efficient corps of native detectives should be organized and used to the utmost possible extent.

That the effect of Halley's comet was widespread and persistent and was interpreted as presaging the end of the white man is confirmed by events in 1921.

> The second train of events involved the 'Israelites'. Gathered around their religious leaders on Bullhoek commonage near Queenstown, they had been deeply impressed by the appearance of Halley's comet and accepted this as a sign to abandon the New Testament as the invention of the white man. Returning to the Old Testament, they became fanatically indifferent to the threat of modern weapons in the belief that Jehovah was about to liberate his chosen people from the foreign yoke. After repeated warnings to abandon their recently erected huts and return to their various villages, and after leading congressmen had backed this up with a plea that they obey and avoid impending violence from the State, a strong police contingent was despatched to assert government authority. When the Israelites charged with home-made weapons, 171 were shot dead.

This prophetic concern of Plaatje's may also be influenced by the ideas of Marcus Garvey.

The final question to be asked is what is Plaatje's solution. The revolutionary solution is to be tried as a last resort only, it seems. The prior hope lies in what is symbolized by the womenfolk. Plaatje shows himself in his writings to be fully aware of the female emancipation issue, which critics who have condemned his Europeanizing of his characters have not taken enough account of. The old life has been partially destroyed in **Mhudi,** a woman is thrown out into the wilderness on her own and she acquires an independence manifested in her ability to face lions and other dangers. Mhudi herself is a symbol of the pride and spirit of her people, and circumstances have forced her into a measure of independence. She is the 'cradle of the race', as sceptical of the Boers as she is of the Matabele. On the individual level she comes to friendship with the women who are symbols of what is virtuous in the other peoples—Umnandi, favourite wife of Mzilikazi (significantly this first lady of the children-slayers is childless) and Annetje, the Boer girl. By splitting the friendship of the individuals from the hostility of the people for one another, Plaatje has been able to give us a glimpse of the possible ideal as well as a view of the real situation. His final warning seems to be contained in an opinion quoted from the *Brotherhood Journal:* 'For Brotherhood is not only between man and man, but between nation and nation, race and race.' In a prize-winning essay written late in 1910 and published in the Johannesburg *Chronicle* (it is otherwise unpublished), Plaatje considered the desirability of the separation or segregation of races and came to the conclusion it was desirable but impossible. The events since the 1830s had led to an 'economic interdependence' (to use a phrase of Peter Walshe's) which was unalterable and irrevocable. In the final passage of the essay he considers first the self-governing black state, then he rejects its possibility and directs his plea to South African liberalism (reflecting something of the naivety of the early Congress leaders), advocating only the banning of the bar and the side-bar.

> They [the blacks] will not pay any taxes unless, as in Basutoland, the money is devoted solely for their use. This will result in a net loss to the Union Treasury of £2,000,000 annually and a large sum to the respective municipalities. Europeans will make the rude discovery that the Kafir was handy not only as a water carrier, but as the gold mine from which local and general exchequers drew heavily and paid the fancy salaries which helped to educate white children and keep white families in comfort. Millions of money now circulating amongst Europeans will be withdrawn to pay black officials and feed black storekeepers; the effect whereof will be wholesale dismissal of many white men, and then the trouble will begin. Oh, no! earlier still, for I am sure that when you tell the traders of the Transkei to relinquish their holdings and seek fresh pastures in white areas, they are not the Englishmen I took them for if they do not resist the order at the point of a bayonet. The ideal is sound, but how will you attain it? . . . Two things you need to give the native, and two things only must you deny him. Keep him away from liquor and lawyers; give him the franchise and your confidence, and the problem will solve itself to your mutual advantage.

Plaatje's plea is initially to reason, but if reason fails, there is his prediction.

Brian Willan (essay date 1984)

SOURCE: *"Mhudi,"* in *Sol Plaatje: South African Nationalist, 1876-1932,* Heinemann, 1984, pp. 349-71.

[*In this analysis of* Mhudi, *Willan views the novel as an effort to combine African oral forms and traditions with the written forms and traditions of English literature.*]

'After ten years of disappointment,' Plaatje informed his old friend, Georgiana Solomon, in May 1930, 'I have at length succeeded in printing my book. Lovedale is publishing it. I am expecting the proofs any day this week.' The book to which Plaatje referred was **Mhudi,** the title of the manuscript he had completed in London in 1920, and somewhat modestly described at the time as 'a love story after the manner of romances . . . but based on historical facts'.

The Lovedale Press was certainly not the leading international publishing house which Plaatje had once hoped would take on his book, but after 'ten years of disappointment' and numerous rejections from publishers in England and America—'circumstances beyond the control of the writer', so Plaatje described them—he was well pleased to have been able to come to terms with them over it. The Lovedale Press's decision to publish the book is attributable to the arrival at Lovedale, the previous year, of a new chaplain by the name of R. H. W. Shepherd. Up until then, the Lovedale Press had concentrated almost exclusively on publishing books and pamphlets, mostly in English and Xhosa, for religious and educational purposes. Shepherd, though, possessed a somewhat broader view of the literary responsibilities of a mission press, and believed that Lovedale should also concern itself with the provision of more general reading matter for the African population. Within a short time of his arrival at Lovedale he was taking a very active role in the affairs of the press, became convenor of the Press Committee in 1930, Director of Publications in 1932, and was thereafter—for better or worse—one of the most influential figures in the development of African literature in South Africa in the 1930s and 1940s.

The possibility of the Lovedale Press publishing **Mhudi** was raised when Plaatje himself once visited Lovedale. Shepherd recalled the occasion later: 'Into the writer's study came one day an African, Sol T. Plaatje. His object was to talk of a novel in English for which through eight years he had been seeking a publisher. Its title was **Mhudi: an epic of South African native life a hundred years ago.**' Plaatje's mission was successful, and a contract was duly signed in March 1930: it provided for a first edition of 2,000 copies, to be sold at 5s 6d each, with a 10 per cent royalty payable when 700 copies of the book had been sold. Considering that the overseas publishers Plaatje had approached had wanted him to make a prior payment to them if they were to publish **Mhudi,** the terms must have appeared satisfactory to him, and the price of 5s 6d per copy—for a hard-cover book that was likely to run to over 200 pages—not so high as to deter his potential readership.

Further evidence of Shepherd's personal interest and involvement in seeing *Mhudi* through to publication is to be found in the preface (dated August 1930) which Plaatje wrote for the book, which concludes with an acknowledgement of Shepherd's assistance, along with that of Michael van Reenen, in 'helping to correct the proofs'.

. . . . .

Even though *Mhudi*'s publication had been delayed for ten years, it was nevertheless the first book of its kind, in English, to have been written by a black South African. It was this fact which prompted Plaatje to offer a few words in justification and explanation at the beginning of the book: 'South African literature,' he noted, 'has hitherto been almost exclusively European, so that a foreword seems necessary to give reasons for a Native venture.' He went on:

> In all the tales of battle I have ever read, or heard of, the cause of the war is invariably ascribed to the other side. Similarly, we have been taught almost from childhood to fear the Matabele—a fierce nation—so unreasoning in its ferocity that it will attack any individual or tribe, at sight, without the slightest provocation. Their destruction of our people, we are told, had no justification in fact or in reason; they were actuated by sheer lust for human blood.

> By the merest accident, while collecting stray scraps of tribal history, later in life, the writer incidentally heard of 'the day Mzilikazi's tax collectors were killed'. Tracing this bit of information back, he elicited from old people that the slaying of Bhoya and his companion, about the year 1830, constituted the *casus belli* which unleashed the war dogs and precipitated the Barolong nation headlong into the horrors described in these pages.

The slaying of Bhoya, unrecorded in any of the written histories of the time, provided Plaatje with his point of departure for the book, and it is against this historical background of South Africa in the 1830s that Plaatje develops the action and the characters. There follows a dramatic account of the brutal destruction of Khunana, the Barolong capital, and an introduction to the two main characters, Mhudi and Ra-Thaga. Thereafter the scene shifts to the court of the victorious Matabele king, Mzilikazi. As his people celebrate their victory, Gubuza, commander of Mzilikazi's army, utters one of the prophetic warnings that build up an atmosphere of suspense and impending doom, predicting that the Barolong would not rest until they had their revenge.

Mhudi and Ra-Thaga, meanwhile, meet one another in the wilderness, fall in love, and after several encounters with lions, meet up with a band of Koranna, and join them in the

hope of discovering the fate of the rest of the Barolong people. Ra-Thaga then has a narrow escape at the hands of Ton-Qon, a Koranna headman who is intent on taking Mhudi as his wife, but the couple hear that the survivors of the massacre at Khunana, together with the other branches of the Barolong nation, have now gathered and made a new home in Thaba Nchu. They set out to find them, and arrive to a joyous reception from Mhudi's cousin Baile, each amazed to find the other alive. Soon their arrival is eclipsed by that of another group of newcomers, 'a travel-stained party' of Boers travelling northwards from the Cape Colony, who are offered hospitality by Chief Moroka, the senior Barolong chief at Thaba Nchu. In due course, a friendship develops between Ra-Thaga and De Villiers, one of the Boer trekkers, and after much deliberation, and the dispatch of a spying expedition, the Barolong and Boer leaders decide to form a military alliance and attack the Matabele.

The Matabele, for their part, prepare themselves for the onslaught; as they do so, a bright comet appears in the sky above them, an omen of defeat and destruction prophesied many times before by their witch doctors and seers. In the battle that follows, the combined forces of Boers, Barolong and Griqua (also enlisted as allies) prove more than a match for the dispirited Matabele forces, and their triumph is joyously celebrated. In the opposite camp Gubuza brings news of the defeat of his army to the king, and advises him to 'evacuate the city and move the nation to the north'. Only in this way, he said, mindful of an earlier prophecy, could the complete annihilation of the Matabele nation be averted.

From the tragic scene of the court of the defeated Matabele king the action returns to Thaba Nchu, where Mhudi has been left behind whilst her husband is away with the army sent out against the Matabele. It is not a situation she can long endure: having a premonition of an injury to Ra-Thaga, she decides impulsively to make her way to the allies' camp, setting out alone on the hazardous journey. On the way there she encounters Umnandi, the former wife of Mzilikazi, forced to flee his court as a result of the machinations of her jealous rivals, and they arrive together in the allies' camp. Mzilikazi, meanwhile, prepares to move northwards, bitterly regretting his failure to heed the warnings and prophecies that had been uttered so often before: 'I alone am to blame,' he acknowledges, 'notwithstanding that my magicians warned me of the looming terrors, I heeded them not. Had I only listened and moved the nation to the north, I could have transplanted my kingdom there with all my impis still intact—but mayebab'o—now I have lost all!' Then, in one of the most powerful passages of the book, Mzilikazi makes a prophecy of his own: the Barolong, he predicts, will live to regret the alliance they have made with the Boers.

After so powerful and haunting a prophecy the remaining two chapters of the book come almost as an anti-climax, and are devoted mostly to tying up loose ends in the personal relationships developed by the main characters. Umnandi rejoins Mzilikazi, welcomed back as his rightful queen; De Villiers, Ra-Thaga's Boer friend, marries the girl he loves, Annetje; whilst Mhudi and Ra-Thaga, after declining an invitation to stay on with their new-found friends, De Villiers and Annetjie, set off in an old waggon in the direction of Thaba Nchu: 'from henceforth', says Ra-Thaga to Mhudi, in the final lines of the book, 'I shall have no ears for the call of war or the chase; my ears shall be open to one call only—the call of your voice'.

. . . . .

In many ways the actual sequence of events, the development of the individual characters and the interaction of their relationships, is not of primary importance. For Plaatje did not conceive of *Mhudi* as anything approaching a realistic novel in the western literary tradition. He himself gave his book the sub-title 'An epic of native life a hundred years ago', and it is as an epic that *Mhudi* is best defined. Just as in Shakespeare, clearly an important influence upon Plaatje in writing *Mhudi,* he expected his readers to suspend a sense of realism to allow for the delivery of long set-piece monologues and dialogues; to allow him to bring historical events backwards and forwards in time as it suited him in the construction of the narrative, and exploit for dramatic purposes an assumed historical knowledge on the part of his readers; and he composed his characters not so much to reflect the way they might realistically have behaved, as to provide a vehicle for the expression of a variety of human qualities and ideas which Plaatje wished to explore.

Mhudi was the outcome of a quite conscious and deliberate attempt on Plaatje's part to marry together two different cultural traditions: African oral forms and traditions, particularly those of the Barolong, on the one hand; and the written traditions and forms of the English language and literature on the other. The full extent to which these African oral traditions have found their way into *Mhudi* may never be fully known, although if Plaatje's own collection of Tswana folktales had survived we would probably have been in a much better position to make some sort of assessment. But some of the ways at least in which Plaatje incorporated these traditions and cultural forms can be identified. The slaying of Bhoya, as Plaatje explained in his foreword, was one obvious example of the way in which he incorporated into his story what he had heard from old Barolong people he had talked to. His use of proverbs and African idiom was similarly a quite deliberate attempt to try and convey something of the richness of the cultural reservoir upon which he was drawing. Often the technique of literal translation was strikingly successful. 'I would rather be a Bushman and eat scorpions than that Matabele could be hunted and killed as freely as rockrabbits,' said Dambuza, one of Mzilikazi's warriors, at the Matabele court; and later he observes: 'Gubuza, my

chief, your speech was the one fly in the milk. Your unworthy words stung like needles in my ears.'

Plaatje was struck particularly by the way in which Tswana oral tradition and the written traditions of English literature—above all, Shakespeare, which he knew best—shared a common fund of literary and cultural symbols. In *Mhudi* he was concerned to explore the possibilities that this perception presented, above all in relation to omen and prophecy, and their association with planetary movements—characteristic both of Shakespeare and the oral traditions of his own people. It was something that had always fascinated him. 'In common with other Bantu tribes,' Plaatje had written in his newspaper at the time of the reappearance of Halley's Comet in 1910, 'the Bechuana attach many ominous traditions to stellar movements and cometary visitations in particular', and he had added: 'space will not permit of one going as far back as the 30s and 50s to record momentous events, in Sechuana history, which occurred synchronically with the movements of heavenly bodies'. Ten years later Plaatje did find time to do exactly this in writing *Mhudi,* even if he had then to wait a further ten years before the results of this literary exploration were published.

Plaatje's awareness of the literary possibilities that lay in the manipulation of symbols that had meaning in both Tswana and English cultures also found expression in the humorous lion stories that appear in the early part of the book. These serve as a means of testing the courage of both Mhudi and Ra-Thaga, and are contrasted later on with the cowardly reaction of Lepane, a traveller, faced with a similar dilemma. That lion stories of this kind were a familiar motif in Tswana tradition emerges from the story that Plaatje himself reproduced in his *Sechuana Reader:* like the lion story that appears in Chapter 5 of *Mhudi,* its central point is the way in which the protagonist proves his bravery by holding on to the lion's tail. At the same time, lion stories of this kind, serving a similar function of demonstrating bravery and cowardice, are a familiar motif in English literature as well—in Bunyan's *Pilgrim's Progress,* and Shakespeare's *Love's Labour Lost, Julius Caesar,* and *A Midsummer Night's Dream,* all of which Plaatje knew well.

In 1916, in his contribution to the *Book of Homage to Shakespeare,* Plaatje had expressed the view that he thought it likely that 'some of the stories on which his [Shakespeare's] dramas are based find equivalents in African folk-lore'. When he had looked into this question more closely he had found this prediction to be correct: the lion stories in *Mhudi* were one of the more humorous outcomes, and so too—in a more general sense—was Plaatje's exploration of the symbolism and meaning of planetary omens and prophecies. It was the kind of cultural borderland that Plaatje delighted in exploring. The tragedy was that so few people were in any kind of position to appreciate to the full just what it was that he was doing.

. . . . .

Plaatje had a number of other considerations in mind when he wrote **Mhudi.** Perhaps the most important of these he summed up in his foreword when he indicated that one of his main objectives in writing the book was 'to interpret to the reading public one phase of "the back of the Native mind"': essentially, to write of a particular historical episode from an African, and more particularly, a Barolong viewpoint, rather than from the more familiar white perspective. It had long rankled in Plaatje's mind that the Boers, to whom he attributed so many of the later misfortunes of his people, owed their survival to the succour and help which one section of the Great Trek had received at the hands of the Barolong Chief Moroka at Thaba Nchu. It was a point to which he had often drawn attention in his political writings. 'In the eyes of most Natives the Prime Minister's campaign of calumny,' Plaatje wrote in the year before **Mhudi** was published, 'lumping us all as a barbarian menace to European civilisation was nothing but colossal ingratitude,' and he went on to outline—as he had done in *Native Life in South Africa* and on several other occasions since—the way in which Moroka's Barolong came to their assistance and helped them defeat the Matabele. Even more disturbing for Plaatje was the way in which the historical record was distorted for political purposes, something he came up against again and again. It was not simply the politicians who exploited these distortions. 'It is a standing complaint among educated natives,' he wrote another time, 'that in South African history books (except where natives acted entirely under their own unaided initiative) tribal succour of Europeans is not even as much as mentioned, although tradition abounds with the stories of battle after battle carried by native legions in the cause of European colonisation in South Africa.'

In **Mhudi** it was one of Plaatje's main intentions to counter these kind of distortions by writing of a familiar historical episode from a novel perspective. One theme that recurs throughout the book is an assertion of the fact that Barolong society prior to its contact with 'European civilisation' was not in the state of savagery so frequently used to justify its subsequent conquest by white colonists. At the very beginning of the book Plaatje implicitly contrasts the communal values of pre-colonial Barolong society with its later transformation under the impact of white settlement:

> Strange to relate, these simple folk were perfectly happy without money and without silver watches. Abject poverty was practically unknown; they had no orphanages because there were no nameless babies. When a man had a couple of karosses to make he invited the neighbours to spend the day with him,

cutting, fitting in and sewing together the sixty grey jackal pelts into two rugs, and there would be intervals of feasting throughout the day. On such an occasion, some one would announce a field day at another place where there was a dwelling to thatch; here too the guests might receive an invitation from a peasant who had a stockade to erect at a third homestead on a subsequent day; and great would be the expectation of the fat bullock to be slaughtered by the good man, to say nothing of the good things to be prepared by the kind hostess. Thus a month's job would be accomplished in a day.

> But the anomaly of this community life was that, while the many seams in a rich man's kaross carried all kinds of knittings—good, bad, and indifferent—the wife of a poor man, who could not afford such a feast, was often gowned in flawless furs. It being the skilled handiwork of her own husband, the nicety of its seams seldom failed to evoke the admiration of experts.

The absence of extremes of wealth, a tradition of communal hospitality—both are portrayed as attractive features of Barolong society before its contact with white civilisation. Elsewhere in **Mhudi** other characteristics of traditional Barolong society are also presented in a favourable light. At Thaba Nchu, for example, Chief Moroka is called upon to make a 'Solomonic' decision in a case involving two married couples who have exchanged partners; contrary to the precepts of Christian morality, his decision is that the new arrangement should continue since it was now obvious that this was the judgment that would give satisfaction to all parties concerned. A kind of consensus justice, in other words, was preferable in certain circumstances to adherence to a rigid legal or moral code. In another decision made by Chief Moroka, the qualities emphasised were the seriousness with which physical assault was viewed in Barolong society, and the mercy bestowed in dealing with those guilty of this offence.

So Plaatje was concerned to offer something of a corrective to the predominant view in the literature and the stereotypes of white South Africans (and others) that his people were murderous savages, saved only by the coming of the white man. He also has a fresh perspective to offer upon the Boers themselves. In **Mhudi** they are viewed not as the embodiment of the advance of civilisation, but as a strange and far from heroic group of travellers who are obliged to turn to Moroka for succour and assistance. When they first make their appearance, over a third of the way through the book, they are seen from a novel Barolong perspective, their credentials somewhat open to question:

> They were mounted and each carried a rifle. It was

a travel-stained party, and the faces of the older men bore traces of anxiety. Apart from that they were well-fed on the whole, as the open air of a sunny country had impressed health, vigour, and energy on their well-clothed bodies, especially the younger men of the party. The spokesman of the riders was their leader, a Boer named Sarel Cilliers, who headed a large band of Dutch emigrants from Cape Colony. They were travelling with their families in hooded waggons, and driving with their caravans their wealth of livestock into the hinterland in search of some unoccupied territory to colonise and to worship God in peace.

'But,' asked Chief Moroka, 'could you not worship God on the south of the Orange River?'

'We could,' replied Cilliers, 'but oppression is not conducive to piety. We are after freedom. The English of the Cape are not fair to us.'

'We Barolongs have always heard that, since David and Solomon, no king has ruled so justly as King George of England.'

'It may be so,' replied the Boer leader, 'but there are always two points of view. The point of view of the ruler is not always the viewpoint of the ruled. We Boers are tired of foreign kings and rulers. We only want one ruler and that is God, our Creator. No man or woman can rule another.'

'Yours must be a very strange people,' said several chiefs simultaneously. 'The Bible says when the children of Israel had only one God as their ruler, they gave Him no rest until He anointed a king for them. We are just like them. There are two persons that we Barolongs can never do without: a wife to mind the home and a king to call us to order, settle our disputes and lead us in battle.'

It was a picture of the Boers far removed from the conventional image of the chroniclers of the Great Trek: it was no part of this, it need scarcely be said, that the Boers were met at Thaba Nchu by Barolong chiefs quoting the Bible at them, and disputing their arguments on the nature of freedom and justice on biblical grounds. Thereafter, Plaatje presents the Boers in a distinctly unfavourable light, and with several individual exceptions they are portrayed as greedy, cruel and deceitful. They mistreat their Hottentot servants, they fail to appreciate the hospitality accorded to them at Thaba Nchu, and they try to strike a very unfair bargain over the spoils of war during the negotiations with the Barolong over mounting a joint expedition against the Matabele. On other occasions they are almost figures of fun: "How long must it last,

O God?", they [a group of Boer women] demanded, as though expecting an answer by return post.' The Boers in Plaatje's **Mhudi,** in short, were far removed from the heroic image so carefully cultivated by their twentieth-century successors.

. . . . .

Mhudi also contains a more direct political message, or warning. Although the action of the novel does not extend beyond the 1830s or the 1840s it is perfectly clear that Plaatje expects his readers to draw a connection between the circumstances of the Barolong of the period covered in the book, and the position they found themselves in in the early part of the twentieth century when the book was written. In **Mhudi,** oppression and tyranny bring forth retribution with an inevitability emphasised throughout the book by the use of prophecy. When Bhoya is killed, it is prophesied that Mzilikazi will seek his revenge—even if, when this duly took place, the devastation and destruction was on a scale that none had imagined. Then, amongst the Matabele, Gubuza is the first to warn that the Barolong would never rest until they had secured their revenge for punishment which he believed went far beyond reasonable retribution for the offence they had committed. Ultimately, that prophecy, too, is fulfilled: the Barolong ally themselves with the Boers, defeat the mighty Matabele in battle, and Mzilikazi is forced to flee northwards with his people. But before he does so he himself utters the greatest prophecy of them all, recovering his dignity and stature in a magnificent, haunting exhortation to his people, warning the Barolong of the inevitable outcome of their fateful alliance with the Boers:

> The Bechuana know not the story of Zungu of old. Remember him, my people; he caught a lion's whelp and thought that, if he fed it with the milk of his cows, he would in due course possess a useful mastiff to help him in hunting valuable specimens of wild beasts. The cub grew up, apparently tame and meek, just like an ordinary domestic puppy; but one day Zungu came home and found, what? It had eaten his children, chewed up two of his wives, and in destroying it, he himself narrowly escaped being mauled. So, if Tauana and his gang of brigands imagine that they shall have rain and plenty under the protection of these marauding wizards from the sea, they will gather some sense before long.

> Chaka served us just as treacherously. Where is Chaka's dynasty now? Extinguished, by the very Boers who poisoned my wives and are pursuing us today. The Bechuana are fools to think that these unnatural Kiwas (white men) will return their so-called friendship with honest friendship. Together they are laughing at my misery. Let them rejoice;

they need all the laughter they can have today for when their deliverers begin to dose them with the same bitter medicine they prepared for me; when the Kiwas rob them of their cattle, their children and their lands, they will weep their eyes out of their sockets and get left with only their empty throats to squeal in vain for mercy.

They will despoil them of the very lands they have rendered unsafe for us; they will entice the Bechuana youths to war and the chase, only to use them as pack oxen; yea, they will refuse to share with them the spoils of victory.

They will turn Bechuana women into beasts of burden to drag their loaded waggons to their granaries, while their own bullocks are fattening on the hillside and pining for exercise. They will use the whiplash on the bare skins of women to accelerate their paces and quicken their activities: they shall take Bechuana women to wife and, with them, breed a race of half man and half goblin, and they will deny them their legitimate lobolo. With their cries unheeded these Bechuana will waste away in helpless fury till the gnome offspring of such miscegenation rise up against their cruel sires; by that time their mucus will blend with their tears past their chins down to their heels, then shall come our turn to laugh.

Thereupon, Mzilikazi exhorts his people to move northwards to find a new home, 'far, far beyond the reach of killing spirits, where the stars have no tails and the woods are free of mischievous Barolong'. In *Mhudi* there is an inevitability about the overthrow of oppression and tyranny: prophecies, once made, are always realised. Mzilikazi's prophecy was the only one not to have been fulfilled in the course of the book. But by the time Plaatje was writing his book it had been realised: in the South Africa of the early twentieth century the Barolong had become the oppressed, the Boers—as Plaatje saw it—the oppressors. In directing his readers to the lessons of history Plaatje's point was a straightforward one: unless tyranny and oppression were ended peaceably, it was inevitable that violence would then remain the only alternative. It was not an outcome that Plaatje either welcomed nor even wished to contemplate: his concern was simply to warn that this was what would happen. *Native Life in South Africa* had ended on exactly the same note.

Yet *Mhudi* also contains a message of hope as well as this fateful warning, and Plaatje made it perfectly clear how he felt so violent an outcome could be averted. One element of this message of hope is expressed in the bond of friendship that develops in the book between Ra-Thaga, the Morolong, and De Villiers, the Boer. In this friendship they

discover a common humanity, and as a result De Villiers is able to escape from the otherwise characteristic Boer attitudes towards black people, Matabele or Barolong. 'But to tell you the truth,' De Villiers eventually says to Ra-Thaga, 'I get on much better with you than with many of my own people.' For Plaatje, human brotherhood and individual, moral change provide the key to the resolution of South Africa's racial problems: the friendship between Ra-Thaga and De Villiers represents not only the 'literary wish fulfilment of what South African society could be if only the facts of the power struggle could conveniently be ignored', as one critic writing about *Mhudi* has it; in Plaatje's view, it is also the means of actually attaining such a society, the means of altering these facts of power by peaceful means, the means of avoiding the violent but inevitable alternative. No stable, just South Africa, Plaatje said on another occasion, could ever be built 'on the rickety foundation of a race discrimination, which takes everything from a subject race without giving anything for it'.

This theme of brotherhood provides one important strand which runs throughout *Mhudi,* even as the ideal of brotherhood sustained Plaatje throughout his own life. But its literary expression gains added meaning when it is recalled that the book was written at a time when Plaatje was particularly hopeful of what might be achieved for his own Brotherhood movement: he enjoyed the support and hospitality of members of the movement in England, he had promises of financial aid and support from the Canadian branch of the movement, and much of *Mhudi* itself may well have been written in the home of William Cross, president of the Southall Men's Own Brotherhood, and one of Plaatje's closest English friends. Having at that time just exhausted all constitutional options for bringing about change in South Africa through appealing for imperial intervention, Plaatje's commitment to the theme of brotherhood remained one of the few sources of hope left to him: *Mhudi* can perhaps be regarded as the literary expression of this theme, affirmation of a creed that was to be severely tested in the years to come.

Yet in *Mhudi* there is another, even more fundamental source of hope and inspiration: the character of Mhudi herself. She is the central, life-giving figure of the book, a woman of great beauty, courage, wisdom and determination. Her qualities stand in sharp contrast to the far weaker and less formed character of her husband, Ra-Thaga. Often Plaatje sets her qualities in a humorous way against the stereotypes of submissive female behaviour which he is intent on both making fun of and undermining as the book unfolds. Thus his conclusion to the first lion-killing episode:

> Leaving the dead lion, Ra-Thaga fetched his herbs
> and his buck, secured the openings to his enclosure
> with freshwag-'n-bietjie bush, and followed Mhudi

into the hut where he skinned his buck while sunning himself in the adoration of his devoted wife. Her trust in him, which had never waned, was this evening greater than ever. She forgot that she herself was the only female native of Kunana who had thrice faced the king of beasts, and had finally killed one with her own hand. Needless to say, Ra-Thaga was a proud husband that night.

Thereafter Mhudi completely dominates the relationship with Ra-Thaga. Immediately after the lion-killing incident Mhudi and Ra-Thaga discuss their attitudes towards Mzilikazi. Plaatje leaves no doubt whatever as to who emerges with the credit:

> At times Mhudi and Ra-Thaga found fruitful subjects for animated discussion. On one topic there was a sharp difference of opinion between man and wife. Ra-Thaga at times felt inclined to believe that the land on which they lived belonged to Mzilikazi, and that Mzilikazi was justified in sending his marauding expedition against Kunana. This roused the feminine ire of Mhudi. She could not be persuaded that the crime of one chief who murdered two indunas was sufficient justification for the massacre of a whole nation.

> 'But,' protested Ra-Thaga, 'all the tribes who quietly paid their dues in kind were left unmolested. Mzilikazi did not even insist that larger tribes should increase the value of their tax in proportion to their numbers. So long as each tribe sent something each spring in acknowledgement of its fealty, he was satisfied.'

> Mhudi, growing very irritated, cried: 'I begin to think that you are sorry that you met and married me, holding such extraordinary views. You would surely have been happier with a Matabele wife. Fancy my husband justifying our exploitation by wild Khonkhobes, who fled from the poverty in their own land and came down to fatten on us!'

Mhudi's judgement of people and character is also far superior to that of her husband. Ra-Thaga, Plaatje says, 'benefited much from the sober judgement of his clever wife', during their stay in the wilderness; but he nevertheless failed to heed her warnings about Ton-Qon, the Koranna leader, who in due course tries to kill him. As a result it is left to Mhudi to venture out and save his life, and then to nurse him back to recovery from his wounds. Later, when they encounter the Boers, Mhudi is sceptical of Ra-Thaga's somewhat uncritical enthusiasm for his new friends, and she is outraged by their cruelty; he, by contrast, came almost to turn a blind eye to instances of this cruelty, to pretend it did not exist.

Mhudi is also a woman of great courage. This is demonstrated at the beginning of the book in relation to the lion stories, and is expressed on numerous occasions thereafter—above all during the epic journey she undertakes from Thaba Nchu to the camp of the Barolong and Boer allies. Her qualities, in short, dominate the book. But they are paralleled and emphasised by the qualities and character of Umnandi, Mzilikazi's favourite wife who is forced to flee his court as a result of the jealousies of her rivals. She, too, was a woman of great beauty, excellent at every royal duty except providing royal heirs. And like Mhudi, she is the source of strength of her husband, and it is her disappearance that coincided with the change in his fortunes. 'That daughter of Mzinyato,' Mzilikazi exclaims to himself in his hour of defeat,

> was the mainstay of my throne. My greatness grew with the renown of her beauty, her wisdom, and her stately reception of my guests. She vanished, and with her the magic talisman of my court. She must have possessed the wand round which the pomp of Inzwinyani was twined, for the rise of my misfortune synchronised with her disappearance.

When Umnandi is reunited with her husband at the end of the book, the symbolism is clear: the rebirth of a nation beyond the reach of Boer and Barolong.

In the qualities displayed by these two women Plaatje seems to be offering a source of hope and inspiration for a South Africa of the future. As far as the character of Mhudi herself is concerned, it seems reasonable to assume that she is composite, created in Plaatje's imagination from a variety of people, ideas, and associations. One fundamental element was the historical figure of Mhudi. Although there is nothing in the book to indicate that Mhudi was a 'real' historical figure, in his account of his own ancestry Plaatje wrote the following: 'My mother is a direct descendant of a grandson of Tau from the house of his youngest and dearest wife, Mhudi.' Mhudi, in other words, must have been Plaatje's great-great-grandmother.

Family tradition therefore provided Plaatje with a knowledge of Mhudi's existence, and very probably he had heard from his mother and other relatives something of the character and the life of this woman from whom he was descended.

At the same time it is evident that Mhudi is invested, in Plaatje's book, with qualities and characteristics which flow very directly from his own experiences and perceptions of women during his own life. Perhaps first and foremost Mhudi stands as a tribute to his own wife, Elizabeth, 'without whose loyal cooperation' his previous book, *Native Life in South Africa,* so he acknowledged, would not have been written. But it would be surprising if Plaatje did not also conceive of Mhudi as a kind of literary testimony to those women who gave him so much support and encouragement when the book was being written in London in 1920—Georgiana Solomon, the Colensos, Betty Molteno, Jane Cobden Unwin, Alice Werner. From these women in particular Plaatje had derived a keen insight into the parallels between the racial and sexual discrimination, and through their actions and beliefs they had done much to strengthen his conviction that women, more than men, possessed the qualities from which a more just and humane society could emerge. He had once said as much, indeed, in a letter written to Mrs. Lennox Murray, another woman in this circle of friends, when congratulating her upon the birth of her baby: 'The mothers of a past generation', he had written, 'bequeathed to us a happy and beautiful subcontinent—the healthiest end of the Dark Continent: and it is the work of the mothers of tomorrow to save South Africa from degeneration if their dear ones are to live and enjoy the blessed privileges that once were ours.' *Mhudi,* in large measure, was the literary expression of this belief.

Plaatje's somewhat more humorous playing around with male/female stereotypes in the book followed from this same awareness of male dominance in the society in which he lived. Much of this is very tongue in cheek, and on occasions Plaatje simply reverses the conventional roles. When the Boers first arrive in the Barolong camp, for example, it is the men who are the first to flee in flight, the women who are the more curious to venture forth and meet them. Elsewhere, the stereotypes are contrasted ironically with Mhudi's own actions—her statement, 'Of course young women are timid and not as bold as men', for example, coming immediately after the account of her own bravery which directly contradicts this cliché; or later, when Mhudi first meets her long-lost cousin, Baile:

Baile (between sobs): 'And you escaped wholly unscathed?'

Mhudi (also sobbing): 'Yes, thanks to my husband.'

—the point being, rather, that it had been thanks to *her* that Ra-Thaga was still alive, not vice versa. Plaatje took great delight, in other words, in exploiting the humour implicit in contrasting reality and stereotype, as well as being concerned to make the more serious point about the potential role that women could play in South Africa's future. Just as he felt that individual, moral change was the key to the solution of South Africa's problems, so did he believe that women possessed particular qualities, transcending barriers of race, that gave them a special role in initiating these changes and bringing a more just society into existence. *Mhudi* stands as an eloquent, often amusing, testimony to this conviction.

So *Mhudi*—the book—was many things: the literary creation of a man of complex sensibilities, who found in writing it not only an escape from the day-to-day struggles that preoccupied him at the time he wrote in 1920, but also the opportunity to give expression to many of his underlying values and beliefs. Just as a knowledge of Plaatje's life makes possible a fuller appreciation of the book, so too does the book itself shed light upon the values and beliefs which sustained him throughout life. In this sense *Mhudi*'s particular value is that it brings all this together, and at a level of detachment from reality which provides a glimpse into an underlying character so often obscured by the many different guises Plaatje had to adopt in circumstances over which, as he often complained, he could exercise so little control.

In *Mhudi* it is different. Plaatje is in control of both his characters and their circumstances, released from the constraints, imposed upon his own activities and ambitions. There is scope for a much freer expression of his personality and beliefs, his fascination with the traditions of his people, his humour, his enjoyment in exploring the literary and cultural possibilities of mixing Tswana tradition and Shakespeare, his admiration for the qualities he believed women to possess, his vision of the consequences of continued injustice in South Africa, his hope that the ideals of human brotherhood might yet provide a solution to South Africa's evils; above all, perhaps, an optimistic faith, a generosity of spirit, a commitment to the idea of a South African nation—all these things are conveyed in *Mhudi,* and in a totality and coherence not expressed elsewhere. The result is both a revealing personal testimony and a pioneering, eminently readable novel, which anticipates in many of its themes the preoccupations of later generations of writers from the African continent.

In terms of the more technical qualities of the book, several other characteristics stand out: a breadth of vision and scope which more than justifies Plaatje's description of *Mhudi* as 'an epic of native life', a sense of grandeur which is conveyed in some of the great set-piece speeches—above all those of the tragic figure of Mzilikazi. Many of the descriptive passages, too, are finely drawn—the battle scenes, for example, but perhaps even more notably, Plaatje's descriptions of landscapes and natural phenomena, quite clearly the product of a man who knew and loved the countryside, who felt a closeness to nature, who spiritually was far more at home here than in the towns and cities where he lived for the greater part of his life.

. . . . .

By any standards *Mhudi* was a rich and complex novel. There was, though, little recognition of this fact in the reviews and comments that followed its publication in September 1930. These were generally favourable, although often rather patronising—as in the comment 'the style is wonderfully good for a native' from the review published in the East London *Daily Dispatch*. The same reviewer was somewhat critical of Plaatje's handling of the relationship between De Villiers and Ra-Thaga ('no one who knows Boer character will take in the story of an intimate relationship between a young Boer and a native which is enlarged upon in the latter part of the tale'), but felt that on the whole the book was 'a welcome contribution to South African literature, and is very pleasant reading'.

Other people who commented upon *Mhudi* generally emphasised the significance of the fact that it was the first novel in English to have been written by a black South African. Sir David Harris, Plaatje's old Kimberley friend, considered *Mhudi* to be 'as fascinating as it is enthralling' and 'a book of exceptional merit', and that anybody capable of such an achievement 'is capable of occupying high office in the Union'. Another of Plaatje's old friends, Vere Stent, still editing the *Pretoria News,* was likewise struck by the contrast between the achievement of having written such a novel and the status and disabilities faced by its author: 'If Mr. Plaatje was a French subject', he wrote, 'they would fête him and make him a member of the *Academie*. In South Africa he is only a Native, and may not even ride a tram in the capital of the Union.'

When the reviews and notices concerned themselves with *Mhudi* itself the opinions, like that of the East London *Daily Dispatch,* were mostly favourable, if not very penetrating. 'M.S.S.' in the *South African Outlook* advised that 'all who are in search of a thrilling and well-written book should make a point of reading this work'. The *Diamond Fields Advertiser* was similarly enthusiastic. Its reviewer, 'L.C.', thought Plaatje had accomplished his stated objective of 'interpreting one phase of the back of the Native mind' to Europeans 'with outstanding success', and had written 'a really readable narrative into the bargain which informs us of the conditions of life natives lived a century ago'. *Mhudi* was, moreover, 'a good honest tale told straightforwardly and without due artifice'; if any criticism was to be made it was of the dialogue which 'occasionally reads a little stiltedly'—an opinion echoed by several other reviewers. All in all, thought the *Advertiser, Mhudi* 'is a South African book for South Africans and it may cordially be commended to young readers whose parents, however, will probably refuse to hand *Mhudi* over till they have finished it themselves.'

Mhudi was not a great deal noted in more literary circles in South Africa, for it simply fell outside any recognised literary tradition. A characteristic exception to this general lack of interest, though, was Stephen Black, editor of the *Sjambok.* Shortly after *Mhudi* was published Plaatje was in Johannesburg and went along to see Stephen Black—probably the same occasion on which they discussed his Shakespeare translations. In the office that day was a young Zulu writer by the name of H. I. E. Dhlomo, whose brother, R. R. R. Dhlomo, was a regular and highly promising short-story writer for the *Sjambok.* 'I remember as if it were but yesterday,' H. I. E. was to recall, over fifteen years later,

> when that remarkable and talented man, Sol T. Plaatje (an admirer of Stephen Black), called at the *Sjambok* offices to get Plaatje's opinion on his (Plaatje's) novel, *Mhudi.* Black told Plaatje quite frankly that one of his faults was to make all his characters speak in high-sounding language and advised the grand old man to read some of the sketches of Dhlomo already published. Here, although the characters spoke in English, their language was natural.

Black was another, in other words, who treated *Mhudi* as a realistic novel in the predominant western literary tradition and judged its characters and their dialogue accordingly. In a letter to another literary friend of his, W. C. Scully, author of *Daniel Venanda* (the book which Black advised Plaatje to translate into Setswana), Black acknowledged that he was reading *Mhudi* 'with great interest and a good deal of pleasure' and that he thought there was 'a charming authority in this book'; but he added, as an afterthought, as though such praise was too excessive, 'Of course it is crude.' Stephen Black in fact had little liking for Plaatje's Shakespeare-like monologues and dialogues (nor indeed for Shakespeare himself) and little sympathy for the kind of cultural cross-fertilization which is at the essence both of *Mhudi* and Plaatje's Shakespeare translations; his preference, rather, was for the realistic short stories of contemporary African life of the kind that R. R. R. Dhlomo was busy writing for him.

Stephen Black then voiced further criticism via the columns of 'The Telephone Conversations of Jeremiah', a regular feature that appeared in the *Sjambok,* which took *Mhudi* as its subject in its issue of October 1930. The point Stephen Black sought to make, in the convoluted style of the 'Conversations', was inspired by a similar feeling to that which underlay his views on the suitability of Shakespeare in African translation. Plaatje had 'forgotten Bechuanaland sometimes', Jeremiah says, 'and remembered only the kingdoms of Shakespeare, and those two people, Mhudi and Ra-Thaga, speak like, like . . . literature'. *Mhudi,* Jeremiah goes on to say, 'is composed of two parts . . . Sol Plaatje, the Bechuana writer, and all the white authors whom he has been reading'. In future, Jeremiah concluded, Plaatje should concentrate upon writing a novel that was about black life alone, and did not involve whites in it at all.

Stephen Black was not alone in these views. When the *Times Literary Supplement* got around to reviewing *Mhudi* several years later the view it expressed was that while the book was 'definitely memorable—a torch for some other to carry on', Plaatje would have been better advised to steer away from 'Europeanism'. 'One wonders,' said the anonymous *TLS* reviewer,

> what secret fountain of African art might not have been unsealed if, in interpreting his people, a writer of Plaatje's insight had thought and written 'like a Native'. That might well have been the first authentic utterance out of the aeons of African silence.

There was an element of this line of thinking in Clement Doke's reaction to the book as well. Whilst he acknowledged (in a review in *Bantu Studies*) that 'Mr Plaatje has done a good service in writing this', he added that it was 'a great pity that for Bantu publications the demand is at present so small among the Bantu themselves that books such as this have to be written in English. *Mhudi* written in Chwana would have been a still greater contribution, and Chwana sadly needs such additions to its present meagre literature.' With this last comment about the state of Tswana literature Plaatje would have been in full agreement. Indeed, Doke need have read no further for confirmation of this than the Preface to *Mhudi,* wherein Plaatje says, amongst other things, that he hoped 'with the readers' money to collect and print (for Bantu schools) Sechuana folk-tales which, with the spread of European ideas, are fast being forgotten', and thereby 'to arrest this process by cultivating a love for art and literature in the vernacular.'

But with the earlier part of Doke's remarks—that *Mhudi* would have been 'a still greater contribution' had it been written in Setswana—Plaatje would have been rather uneasy, for it carried with it the implication, explicit in what both Stephen Black and the *Times Literary Supplement* said as well, that Africans should concentrate exclusively on interpreting their own people and culture. This was a view that Plaatje could never share: he contributed more to the development and preservation of Tswana literature than anybody else, but he could not accept that either he or his people should be denied the right to explore to the full the cultural possibilities of English (or any other language) if they so pleased. Quite apart from the unacceptable political connotations that were bound up in this, the whole basis to Plaatje's literary endeavours, in English or Setswana, was his insistence upon his right to interpret the one culture to the other as he wished. It was the inevitable consequence of such a position that he found himself being criticised on two fronts at the same time: and a sad paradox that it tended to be Africans who insisted upon the primacy of English, Europeans who sang the praises of concentrating upon Setswana.

. . . . .

Whatever the reactions *Mhudi* elicited, Plaatje himself was well pleased to have finally seen his book published after such a long delay. In the three months after publication he himself ordered 250 copies from Lovedale, most of which he must have then sold himself. But he also sent copies to old friends and colleagues—an appropriate way, he felt, of repaying past debts of help or hospitality. Ernst Westphal, the missionary at Pniel where Plaatje had grown up, had died in 1922, but his widow was still alive, and Plaatje sent her a copy for Christmas 1930, inscribed 'with the author's filial compliments and affectionate wishes for a blessed Christmas and a happy New Year'. Sir Ernest Oppenheimer also received a copy, inscribed—somewhat mysteriously—'with the author's compliments, in grateful recollection of courtesies during foggy nights in London'; so too did Mr. Morris, Kimberley's City Electrical Engineer, who had earned Plaatje's appreciation for persuading the City Council to pay for the installation of street lighting in No. 2 Location. To other people Plaatje sent copies of *Mhudi* in the hope of receiving books in exchange to add to his library. 'I should be glad to receive in exchange,' he wrote to Dr W. E. B. Du Bois, after sending him a copy of *Mhudi,* 'any Negro book—particularly *Darkwater* or *The Quest of the Silver Fleece,* as some sinners have relieved me of those two. I still treasure *The Soul, The Gift of Black Folk* etc.'

Not that this ploy was always successful. Professor Victor Murray, a well-known educationist at Selly Oak College in Birmingham, England, and author of a recent study on education in Africa, received an unsolicited copy of *Mhudi* from Plaatje but he was somewhat reluctant to send his own book in return (since it was more expensive), and so sent him another one instead. 'Poor old Sol,' he wrote afterwards, 'was very peeved, but what could he do? He wrote back very bad tempered but as he was 6d up on the transaction I doubt if he could convince anybody that he has a case against me!' It was not the most sympathetic of responses: Plaatje simply did not have the money to build up his library by purchasing the books he wanted, and sending copies of *Mhudi* to people who had written books themselves seemed, in the circumstances, one of the few means open to him of keeping up with subjects in which he had an interest. He may have had a further consideration in mind: while Plaatje would not have received royalties on copies of *Mhudi* which he obtained from Lovedale (at a 33 per cent discount), these would nevertheless have been taken into account in reaching the total of 700 copies which, according to his contract, had to be sold before royalties were payable. In less than a year after *Mhudi*'s publication Plaatje himself had purchased, so the Lovedale Press's records reveal, over 500 copies of his book.

Plaatje also took a keen interest in seeking to arrange an edition of the book for potential readers in England and the United States, a possibility which he raised in July 1931 in letters to both Dr Du Bois and Dr Robert Moton. To Dr Moton he wrote as follows:

> Can we not get a publisher over there to issue a SECOND edition? Any good publisher should successfully exploit the English and North American market with an overseas edition—2nd print. Lovedale not being commercial have no agencies abroad and the field here is so limited that I am afraid by the end of the year when this edition is exhausted, every South African reader will have a copy of *Mhudi*.

The response does not seem to have been encouraging: from Dr Du Bois there is no record of a reply at all, and G. Lake Innes, Moton's assistant, who replied to the letter in Moton's absence, could offer little hope. While Innes himself had enjoyed reading *Mhudi* (he found it 'delightful and informing', and was 'impressed with the fidelity of the narrative and particularly the sympathetic reflection of the heart and mind of the native people'), he wrote:

> I am doubtful, however, if *Mhudi* would find the circulation in America all that you would hope to achieve for it. It is true that Negro literature is in vogue at the present time, but not of the type which your book represents. I do not think any publisher would volunteer to issue it, but I am not sure that any of the Foundations would sponsor it. I think, however, that Dr Moton would be glad to feel them out and see what could be done.

Plaatje did not succeed in arranging an American edition of *Mhudi* in his lifetime. Forty years, indeed, were to pass before an American edition was published. After his own experiences with the dubious J. S. Neale Publishing Company in the United States in 1922 he would perhaps not have been wholly surprised that when an American edition did finally appear, it should have been a pirated edition from which neither the Lovedale Press nor his heirs benefited at all.

. . . . .

Mhudi was Plaatje's only English-language novel (if novel is the right word to describe it) to have been published. According to Isaiah Bud-M'belle, though, in an obituary notice written immediately after Plaatje's death, he had also written another novel in English with the intriguing title of 'Monkey Voodoo', which was, as Bud-M'belle said, 'as yet unpublished'. Bud-M'belle gave no further indication here or elsewhere as to what the book was about, and it seemed to have been lost for ever. But in 1977 an incomplete 70-page manuscript, partly written in Plaatje's hand, partly typed on his typewriter, came to light. Overall, it has the appearance of a rough, early draft, and does not have a title. But

from what has survived of the manuscript it is clear that Plaatje toyed with several possible alternative titles, and he set these out after writing some fifty pages in the notebook:

> 'A forty years romance in the life of the AmaBaca, a South East African Tribe'
>
> 'With Other People's wives: a Romantic Epic of the Baca, a South East African Native Tribe'
>
> 'The Other Fellow's Wives'   An epic
> 'Other People's Wives'   covering two
>   generations in
>   the history of the
>   Baca, a South East
>   African Tribe

There is no mention here of the term 'Monkey Voodoo', nor is it offered as a possible title anywhere else in the part of the manuscript that has survived. But it may well be that this was a thought which Plaatje had later on, and there is some evidence to suggest, as we shall see, that 'With Other People's Wives' and 'Monkey Voodoo' may well have been one and the same thing.

But the subject and source of inspiration of Plaatje's manuscript is clear: it is concerned with the dramatic history and migrations of the Ama-Baca tribe of the eastern Cape. Historically, the Baca originated in an area that was to become the colony of Natal. During the reign of the Zulu King Chaka in the early nineteenth century, so most accounts and traditions agree, they fled from that part of the country and then, under the leadership of their great Chief Madikane, travelled southwards, ultimately settling in the Mount Frere district of the eastern Cape. Madikane himself seems to have been killed in battle with the Tembu some time between 1830 and 1834. He was succeeded by his elder son, Ncapayi, another great warrior, who fought a further series of battles and acquired for his army a reputation which—in the view of the British naval captain, A. F. Gardiner, who visited Ncapayi's court in 1835—would rival that of Chaka himself, were their population more numerous. Thereafter the Baca entered into a short-lived alliance with the Mpondo against the Tembu, and clashed with a Boer commando sent down from Natal, before Ncapayi himself was finally killed in battle in the mid-1840s in an attack upon the Mpondo chief, Faku. Then, after a period of regency under Diko, Makhaula assumed the regency, and his people were peacefully incorporated into the Cape Colony, inhabiting the Mount Frere district where their descendants live to this day.

Their history was a dramatic and eventful one, and for Plaatje it held great fascination. He had some very interesting remarks to make about the reasons for this in a 'preface', although this does not actually appear at the beginning of the manuscript:

> Why did I do it?
>
> Outside the Baca tribe my limited reading has not disclosed another people whose history within living memory furnished miracles that approximate to Moses and the destruction of Sannacherib's army. The more I investigated their history the prouder I felt that this South Africa of ours can show a tribe whose history includes epical topics paralleled only by some of those found in the annals of the ancient Israelites and I have often wondered why, apart from occasional sketches by Mr. W. C. Scully, epical incidents like those of the Baca escaped the notice of all able writers.
>
> So while many stories are written to provide readers with a thrill or a shock and incidents are recorded to fill a gap in some narrative, this book is the expression of pride—race pride—in the fact that South Africa . . . [*incomplete*]

Despite being incomplete, Plaatje's remarks are a revealing indication of what was in his mind when he set out to explore the history of the Baca. He was quick to recognise the quality of an epic in what he had found, and with his knowledge of the Bible could not fail to be struck by the parallels between the historical experience of the Baca and the biblical story of the exodus of Moses and the children of Israel from the land of Egypt. And he had a fascination in any case with the period of the *mfecane* in South African history—the forced migrations of the 1820s and 1830s which did so much to create the identities of the different African peoples of the sub-continent. For this was the heroic age of African history: a time that saw great leaders arise, brave exploits performed, a time when nations could be created or destroyed; and from the perspective of subsequent South African history a time of independence, the era before the white man began to assert his control over the lives of those who lived in the interior of southern Africa. Plaatje was not alone in looking back upon these years—for all their violence and turbulence—as a kind of golden age. In literary terms he viewed these times very much as Shakespeare viewed the adventures of the medieval kings of England from the perspective of the late Elizabethan era: both looked back to a heroic past for inspiration. For a man who knew Shakespeare so well it would be surprising if Plaatje himself was not struck by the comparison.

So Plaatje perceived in the history of the Baca material for the construction of an epic: his stated intention was not 'to provide readers with a thrill or a shock', or simply to fill in some gaps to an interesting historical episode, but to dem-onstrate that in South Africa's own neglected past there lay traditions that could provide a source of 'race-pride' for the African people; to emphasise that they need look no further than their own past, in other words, for that sense of identity and pride which South Africa's subsequent history had done so much to destroy.

Perhaps the single most important phrase that appears in this 'preface' was the term 'within living memory'. When Plaatje talked of investigating Baca history he must have been doing so at first hand, for at the time his manuscript was written—during the course of 1931, judging from the evidence of a letter and several newspaper clippings interleaved in the pages of the notebook in which it was written—there were no comprehensive written sources available upon which his account could have been based. W. C. Scully's writings on the Baca—published in *The State* in 1909, and his *Further Reminiscences of a South African Pioneer,* published in 1913—may have provided Plaatje with the impetus to investigate the subject further, but what Scully has to say bears little resemblance to Plaatje's own account; and Bryant's *Olden Times in Natal and Zululand* and J. H. Soga's *The South-Eastern Bantu,* both of which Plaatje would have been familiar with, do not throw very much light on the history of the Baca either. And none of these accounts contain anything like the level of detail that Plaatje goes into.

Plaatje's manuscript must have been the product, rather, of his own first-hand investigations into Baca tradition, which he then re-worked in dramatic form: similar in this sense to *Mhudi,* but standing closer in both form and content to oral tradition. From what survives of 'With Other People's Wives' it seems Plaatje was much less concerned to work into it the degree of individual characterisation and the personal relationships that are developed in *Mhudi.* Individual characters there certainly are, but it is as though they are now subordinate in importance to the epic story of the Baca people as a whole; enough of 'With Other People's Wives' has survived to make it clear that history, or the Baca people generally, constitute the real hero. But there are similarities with *Mhudi* as well. As in *Mhudi,* prophecies play a vital part in carrying the tale along. At the beginning of 'With Other People's Wives' an old Baca woman, on her deathbed, prophesies the departure of the Baca from the land of Chaka, and exhorts them to be prepared for the tribulations that lie ahead: 'Great are the battles that you will fight with your son, Ncapayi,' she says to Madikane, the Baca chief, and she warns them to be ready to take in the women and children of other tribes whom they defeat in battle.

As in *Mhudi,* much of what follows sees the working out of these prophecies: Madikane and his people decide they can no longer endure the oppressive rule of Chaka; they plan secretly for their escape, and flee southwards. At the Tugela river they are saved from Chaka's pursuing army by a miracle. As the Zulu prepare to cross the river after them, a wall of water suddenly appears, blocking their route. They try to cross:

> The Bacas watched and the Zulus surged. Swarms of Zulus lined the water's edge with shields poised and spears aloft. In obedience to the orders of the commanders to swim across they plunged side by side in a straight line into the angry waters. This was the signal for a second line and third to follow suit in like formation—the fourth line came to the water's edge and halted. These did not plunge in, for in five minutes the billows, having completely disorganised the ranks of the surviving pursuers, heaved and tossed with them. Already some Zulus disappearing below the waves a myriad heads floated past . . . like balls, with the bodies drowning some fathoms below the surface of the water, while the surface was tossing with a myriad heads and bodies of dead and drowning Zulus and all rushing with the angry stream towards the Indian ocean with a thundering sound.

So the Baca are saved by the miracle of the Tugela river, 'an episode', Plaatje says, 'that in every respect resembled the flight of the Israelites at the Red Sea'. Then they press on southwards, celebrating their bloodless victory, composing praise songs to commemorate the event. In Chaka's court, in contrast, the loss of so many of his bravest warriors to the upstart Baca causes great consternation, for the example of their escape is bound to have consequences for other tribes under Chaka's dominion: 'the Baca became an abiding menace long after their exodus', Plaatje writes, 'for whoever mentioned them his tongue was forfeit because it mentioned a taboo, and whoever denied knowledge of their existence forfeited his tongue because it told untruths'.

Yet for the Baca their difficulties are far from over. Apart from the ever-present danger of Chaka despatching a further expedition after them, as they travel southwards they encounter opposition from other people along their route. Amongst these are the Ama-Hola and Ama-Lala, but the Baca escape defeat at their hands because the Ama-Hola and Ama-Lala, intending to attack Madikane and his people, mistake one another for the intruders, and attack and destroy themselves. The Baca are left instead with their enemies' womenfolk, and in fulfilment of the prophecy, incorporate them into their tribe, taking the young women as wives for the Baca warriors; hence it is 'with other people's wives' that the Baca build up their strength as a nation. They move on to find a place of settlement at Amoshonemi, but soon have to fight off further attacks from the people on whose land they now find themselves. Their survival is due to the ingenuity of their chief, Madikane:

The consistent luck of Madikane's armies had acquired for their King the fame of being a great witch doctor. Madikane, who knew that he was no doctor, but profiting by this reputation which made his neighbours fear him, had no intention of disillusioning them. His fertile brain was constantly devising methods of keeping the illusion alive. One day the [?] army . . . mouths watering for the possession of the numerous Baca herds prepared to attack them and raid the cattle.

Getting news of the impending attack, Madikane at once mobilised the Baca. They travelled across the mountains with outspread flanks and marching determinedly and arriving in due time they forced the enemy's hand before his plans had matured. The consternation can be imagined when a people had trained for a surprise attack on foreign . . . suddenly finding themselves compelled to give a defensive battle on their own home and within view of their women and children amidst their own cattle posts.

In the battle that follows Madikane displays his resourcefulness yet again when he turns to his advantage the ominous appearance of a troop of monkeys, thereby defying the 'monkey voodoo':

> The evening before the delivery of the fatal blow a troop of monkeys made themselves very conspicuous on the mountain side below which position Madikane's army was encamped.

> Now among Bantu races these mischievous animals are regarded as walking voodoos and the proudest witch doctor is he who can cleanse his path of any omen of evil and turn it to his enemy's detriment.

> The monkeys scampered and kept shouting at his men. So Madikane quickly thought of a plan. The Baca were really despairing as according to custom they knew that the die was cast against their enterprise and they were calmly awaiting the order to retreat and give up a hopeless battle. They had no faith that they could change the edicts of fate . . . [*unclear*] But Madikane, like a resourceful wizard, quietly thought of a plan without the aid of his [witch doctors].

The page containing the details of Madikane's scheme is missing, but as the narrative continues it is evident that it achieved the desired outcome:

> The running battle was swift and decisive, commencing with the race of the baboons by sunrise.

The afternoon had led Madikane . . . collected a rich booty and the next day began the march back to the banks [of] the Kinra with hundreds of women and their children too.

Once again Madikane is able to build up the strength of his nation 'with other people's wives'. Ultimately he meets his death in battle with the Tembu. And just as Madikane had himself defied the 'monkey voodoo' in their earlier battle, so now did his son, Ncapayi, the new chief of the Baca, turn to his advantage the awesome effects of the total eclipse of the sun which took place during the fighting between the two armies:

'They have killed Madikane!' yelled a leather-lunged Tembu, regardless of the orders of his army leader. 'They have killed Madikane and his spirit has stolen our sun. Madikane alive was always a dangerous being but Madikane dead—Hewu, he has blackened the sun.' This cry struck terror into the hearts of the bravest Tembu warriors. They could fight the Baca alive but an angry spirit that controlled the skies was surely too much.

The tide of battle was turned. Ncapayi's warriors, though they were 'also wondering what was the matter with the sky', took full advantage of the fear struck into the Tembu army by the eclipse of the sun, and pressed home their advantage. But at this point, the moment that saw both the death of the great Chief Madikane and the decisive victory of his army over his foes, Plaatje's manuscript comes to an abrupt end, having covered only one generation of the two that he seems to have envisaged.

. . . . .

It is impossible to reach any conclusive assessment of 'With Other People's Wives': at least half of it is missing, leaves are missing from the notebook in which it is written, parts are impossible to decipher or are very obscure, and virtually the whole of it is in a very early draft. Nor is there any way of knowing whether Plaatje had indeed completed the remaining part of the manuscript, or whether the death of Madikane was simply as far as he had got with it. While Plaatje's knowledge of the Bible, and Shakespeare, undoubtedly helped to give shape to his recognition of the epic character of the story of the Baca people, there is no indication of when and how he was able to collect the information upon which 'With Other People's Wives' is based: perhaps he had been to the Mount Frere district on one or more of his visits to the eastern Cape in the 1920s and had the opportunity of talking to old people there; possibly, too, his interest had been aroused by Isaiah Bud-M'belle, or Elizabeth, both of them descended from a Hlubi family and clan whose history was closely associated with that of the Baca.

But whatever the sources of Plaatje's interest and information on the Baca, even the incomplete, fragmentary manuscript that has survived provides an insight into the direction that Plaatje's future literary plans might have taken. It was significant, amongst other things, that these were not confined to exploring the traditions of the Tswana people alone: there was a wider body of historical tradition which Plaatje was already exploring. It was a great pity that H. I. E. Dhlomo never elaborated further upon the 'many literary plans' that Plaatje had told him about during the several hours' conversation they had on the last occasion they met. Perhaps then he could have provided some clue as the nature of another manuscript with the title 'Chicago in the Bush' which (so Dr Molema at least had reason to believe) Plaatje had also written. Of this no trace whatever survives.

J. M. Phelps (essay date 1993)

SOURCE: "Sol Plaatje's *Mhudi* and Democratic Government," in *English Studies in Africa,* Vol. 36, No. 1, 1993, pp. 47-56.

[*In this essay, Phelps examines the political dimensions of Plaatje's novel, so far overlooked by critics, that make its lessons particularly relevant to the democratic systems in the new South Africa.*]

Sol Plaatje's dramatization in **Mhudi** of political actions set within traditionally-established structures and procedures of leadership and representation is an aspect of this complexly-woven novel that has been largely overlooked in the criticism. We encounter in the narrative a tension between traditional African democratic arrangements and crucial political actions which directly contravene these arrangements. The manner with which Plaatje controls the political dynamic in the novel, acting faithfully as the scribe to the narrative voice of Half-a-Crown (assumed son of Mhudi and Ra-Thaga), to generate a complex experience of tragic outcome, heroic overcoming, wise reconsolidation, and, especially, critical detachment, deserves consideration not only so that the seminal status of this pioneering South African work may be more fully realised, but that its contemporary relevance be highlighted.

The scholarly and critical work of Couzens and Gray, and the biography by Willan, have played a crucial role in liberating Plaatje and **Mhudi** from obscurity, so that now the novel may be examined in new ways that are relevant to our time, rather than to the time of its composition, which was often the concern of the ground-breaking scholarship. Three recent essays, dealing respectively with **Mhudi** and the historical novel (with comparative reference to Fenimore Cooper), the romance of protest, and **Mhudi**'s feminism, bear this out. The purpose of this discussion is to further this direction by following up a hint Couzens threw out in his introduction to the republished and re-edited novel (Heinemann African Writers Series edition [1978]), but which neither he, nor other critics, so far as I know, have pursued.

Couzens says of one of the themes of **Mhudi** that "[c]onsensus politics, the role of counsellors, restraints on chiefs are all handled with subtlety." The particular focus of this discussion will be upon the two turning points early in the narrative which recount decisions by leaders which override the checks and balances on power within the traditional political structures of their communities, and upon the one contrasting case at the mid-point of the story where democratic process is given full effect. These are the three occasions where the traditional, pre-European political process is clearly identified.

Mhudi is acknowledged by Plaatje in his preface to the original edition to have, in a broad sense, an instructive purpose. In the context of the 1970s and 80s, when the revived interest in the novel arose, because Plaatje had stated that one of his important "objects" in writing **Mhudi** was "to interpret to the reading public one phase of 'the back of the native mind'," a sense tended to take hold that it was the white "reading public" especially who was being addressed. However, from our perspective now, when we consider the long view of a non-racial democracy for South Africa that inspired Plaatje (he was one of the founding fathers of the African National Congress initially called the South African Native National Congress); the broad, historical view in **Mhudi** that sees events from all sides ("In all the tales of battle I have ever read, or heard of, the cause of the war is invariably ascribed to the other side") and his keen awareness—enriched both by his closeness to oral tradition and by his wide reading, including Shakespeare—that fiction serves to give form to the inchoate consciousness of its audience and thereby helps to articulate and enlarge that audience's sense of the relations between self and society—when we consider these perspectives, the fact that he conceived of his "reading public" widely to include all South Africans, both his contemporaries and those in the future, should be duly recognised. Fortunately, the opportunity for this due recognition is better than it has ever been before because **Mhudi** has become increasingly prescribed reading in the changed South African educational environment.

That the political error which causes the destruction of the Tshidi clan of the Barolong is realised tragically is, I believe, the important issue to identify if we are to engage with the subtlety of the political theme. The error, the *casus belli*, as Plaatje calls it, is Chief Tauana's proud and impetuous decision to have Bhoya and Bangela, Mzilikazi's tribute collectors, summarily executed. The dramatization of this error

generates a powerful sense of doom, while simultaneously heightening a critical perspective. It is the feel of gripping inevitability in tension with a conviction of what contrarily ought to be that gives the event its tragic force.

The immediate reaction within the Tshidi clan to Tauana's command elaborates the political context. Messengers report to Notto, one of Tauana's wisest headmen, that "'Chief Tauana, . . . *without informing his counsellors in any way*, . . . commanded some young men to take the two to the ravine and *lose them*. The news of this unilateral action, as soon as it reached Notto, and the other counsellors whom he informed, was instantly realised for its terrifying implication:'" . . . the chief counsellors decided to take immediate steps to make amends. But as the chief [Tauana] would probably refuse to apologise, it was decided to summon home from the cattle-posts all men of influence, to attend a tribal picho and arrange a settlement before it was too late'," Traditional democratic process—the consultation of counsellors, and a picho—is urgently invoked to attempt to overturn the autocratic error. But the horror cannot be averted.

The violent conflict to come is foreshadowed by the contradictory impulses vented within the community. The young men anticipate with glee the impending battle, while "Notto held views of quite another character." The desperate corrective measures taken by the counsellors and headmen intensify the foreboding, and with terrifying inevitability the awful massacre of the Barolong swiftly follows.

It is not the narrative voice which criticises Tauana: rather, critical voices emerge from within the drama, from friend and foe alike. From the Matabele perspective, Tauana is described as "foolhardy" and is contemptuously dismissed for making his decision while "drunk with the brew of his wives." The enemy, by pointing up the flaws of a political system in which decision-making and human fallibility are concentrated in one person alone, identifies, though with an irony towards itself of which it is oblivious, the obvious dangers of autocratic rule. But the friends go further in their criticism as they judge the arbitrary action as tantamount to treason, because it overrode all the traditional checks and balances designed to prevent such actions and to ensure accountability. Tauana's decision was made without serious thought and without any preparation for the future. When the remnants of the Barolong eventually reassemble at Thaba Nchu it is significant that Tauana no longer plays a major role in political affairs, and it is instead to Chief Moroka, leader of the surviving Selenka clan, that the people turn.

Further qualifying perspectives on Tauana's action are presented in the narrative by the contrasting strategies chosen by other Bechuana chiefs. Sechele of the Bakwena, Makabe of the Bangwaketse, as well as leaders of the Baharutshe and Bafokeng, though seen in ignominious trepidation at

Mzilikazi's court, demonstrate that for their people, at this juncture at least, discretion is the better part of valour. Makabe of the Bangwaketse shows that pragmatic servility could buy time for later courses of action. This more subtle politics, so very different from Tauana's, is vindicated later by the clan's brilliant tactical retreat into the Kalahari desert, which results in the first defeat of the Matabele. By working within the traditional democracy of the polity, Makabe shows how even a less powerful people, by maintaining community cohesion and adhering to consultative decision-making, can not only physically survive but can also preserve its integrity.

Plaatje's portrayal of the Barolong's destruction shows, on the one hand, how individual agency, and the hubris from which it can derive, has a direct effect on history; and, on the other, how structures providing accountability and the scope for corrective criticism, though ignored, are inherent in the polity. We experience from the narrative's dynamic both the catharsis of tragic inevitability, and the critical perspective that suggest we can learn from history.

The subtlety of treatment is developed further by shifting the view to those on the other side of the massacre. Thanks largely to the outspoken views of Gubuza, Mzilikazi's military commander-in-chief, we discover how the Barolong massacre is the result, on the Matabele side as well, of a combination of hubris and impetuosity which overrides the traditional checks and balances that are in place within the polity to ensure, if not the accountability of the Barolong arrangements, at least a balance to decision-making.

Recent historical enquiry has provided some new perspectives on Nguni political organisation (exemplified in **Mhudi** by Mzilikazi's court) following from the emergence of Shaka and the changes that came with him. These changes were to some extent precipitated by Shaka, but were also a consequence of climatic, demographic and economic conditions. The consolidation of Zulu power into the Shaka monarchy hardened the lines of stratification within society, and reduced the traditional and corrective role of kinship ties and chief's counsellors at the clan level. But the transformation was not absolute, and there were still traditionalists who held to the earlier, more democratic structures that were being largely superseded. That these earlier correctives to power, though in attenuated form, are represented in Mzilikazi's court (by Subuza) attests to Plaatje's sensitive feel for the historical complexity of the African politics he sought to reclaim, and, more importantly here to dramatize.

In Chapter 4, "Revels After Victory," we see into both the causes of the Matabele retribution and the nature of Matabele political organisation. Firstly, we see that the Barolong massacre was conducted opportunistically in order to advance the ambitions of Langa, second son of

Mzilizkazi. Secondly, it emerges that in carrying out the lightning raid and the massacre as he did, Langa "exceeded his orders," and, furthermore, did so without conducting an inquiry into the reasons for Tauana's action. The narrative here renders a subtle critique of the centralization of power, exemplified by Mzilikazi, and the favouritism which can ensue from it.

Discussion by the Matabele about their attack on the Barolong occurs when it is already a *fait accompli*. The dominant rhetoric is fervently nationalistic. The one-sided praise of Langa is transparent, and we perceive it as a serious criticism even before the impact of Gubuza's demur. The speeches of Sitonga, Dambuza and others are clearly self-serving flatteries of the power of Mzilikazi, and also of Langa, who, in the flush of victory, has emerged as his most likely successor. The overall effect is not only to expose the limitations of the narrow nationalism which fuels the autocratic power of Mzilikazi, but, more cogently, to reveal how autocracy disrupts the body politic by fostering the autocratic ambitions of others. The scene of the revels exposes how personal and social relations in this society have become conditioned by the abuse, and the fear, of absolute power.

Only Gubuza's personal power and community stature allow him to express criticism during the proceedings. In the wild moment of the victory of the young prince and his predominantly young warriors, Gubuza's admonition—"'Old people are equally agreed that individuals, especially nations, should beware the impetuosity of youth'"—while courageous, is sensed as coming from a different, more traditional wisdom. He goes on to ask:

> "Are we sure Bhoya was guiltless? Was there provocation? Supposing there was, are we satisfied that the Barolong could have maintained order in any manner short of killing Bhoya and his companion?"

By appealing to reason in his audience, and by pointing to the need for inquiry before action—which he does by suggesting the possibility of arrogance on the part of Bhoya (he says "emissaries of the King . . . sometimes think that they are their own ambassadors")—Gubuza challenges them to question the unchecked concentration of power which has come into being. He alludes to the damaging effects on the lives of individuals, particularly the young, and on the social fabric, which arises from it. Gubuza, brief as are his appearances, is one of the towering figures in the novel. Most prophetic is his concluding statement: "'I am afraid we have made a fresh enemy'." Personal ambition, bolstered by the heated rhetoric, has blinded the people to the political realities of the world they live in.

At the meeting of the privy council after the massacre, Mzilikaze commends Gubuza, saying: "'A man who joins a discussion with the facts of one side only, will often find himself in the wrong'." Nonetheless, Mzilikazi in the end not only condones Langa's methods, but rewards him for his "daring." We conclude that his acknowledgement of the need for other views as a check against power is merely a sop to appease the remnant of tradition that Gubuza represents. He countenances the view of another side for the sake of expediency, not as a vital, correcting principle.

Later complications consequent upon the excessive concentration of power in Mzilikazi's hands emerge when, with his judgment impaired—by the disappearance of his favourite wife Umnandi, the challenge of the dire prophecies of his soothsayers, and the defeat of the expedition against the Bangwaketse—he orders the execution not only of the soothsayers (who have advised that the Matabele should move far to the north to escape the growing power of Barolong "magic"—advice which, of course, is later proved to be sound), but also of the few survivors of the army returning from the desert campaign against the Bangwaketse. Gubuza again steps in. He says, "Mzilikazi knows not what he does. I am told that he has lost his pet; his wife, Umnandi, vanished during the night, and he is not responsible for his actions'." Such a statement cuts through to the central flaw of autocratic power. The whole society turns on the competence, or diminished responsibility, of one man. In the circumstances Gubuza's stand is very brave, since the king's derangement could well envelop Gubuza himself. But Gubuza's stature holds at the crucial moment, and sways the king back to reality. "Mzilikazi . . . promptly countermanded the sentence of death upon the defeated warriors." The soothsayers, however, even Gubuza does not attempt to save. The critique which emerges from the novel is formidable. Such governance, apart from violating the rights and trust of the people, is clearly dangerously haphazard, contradictory and unstable.

Against the blatant contravention of the tradition procedures which had evolved with the purpose of decentralizing power, and the dire failures of autocratic government which flowed from these contraventions, the democratic practice followed later at Thaba Nchu by Chief Moroka stands in pointed contrast. The event which dramatizes the consensualist political process occurs when a decision is needed as to whether or not the clans should lend their cattle and their military support to the Boers, who have suffered a serious setback at the hands of the Matabele in the progress of their trek. Should they combine forces with the Boers, who are strange to them, against their enemy the Matabele?

The gathering of the people is auspicious.

> At sunset the crowd began to collect at the chief's court to hear the council's decision on Sarel's message. It was on the night of the full moon, and the powerful rays of the big round aerial ball, mingling

with the light of the passing day, seemed to dispel the setting dusk, and to prolong the twilight; and so it was not at all dark as old men and young men collected and sat down to hear the ominous decision.

The peaceful, embracing cosmic scene sets the mood. It is true that the traditional gathering does not apparently include the women, though it does bring the old and young men together, and that, at first, it seems that the council's decision is merely to be delivered to the people.

But an early sign that the decision will not come simply from the top down is revealed by the "little knots of debaters" discussing the issue as the people gather. Before the chiefs arrive a full range of alternatives is confidently aired. The women are not forgotten, and one speaker proposes that they should help in the battle against the Matabele. The arrival of the council of chiefs appears to be deliberately delayed in order to allow for the atmosphere of open discussion to be well established. Individuals clearly do not fear to speak their minds. The diversity of political constituencies, marked by the various clan chiefs, is detailed.

That there is to be considered deliberation is immediately apparent when the narrator admits us to the mind of Moroka: "[h]e knew he had no right to join hostilities without the consent of the tribesmen, yet he delivered a speech which, while leaving no doubt as to his personal sympathies, left the main decision in the hands of the assembly." His speech is carefully structured. First he explains the nature of the reemerging Matabele danger now that they have crossed the Vaal river southwards. Then he points up the Boers' recent setback at the hands of the Matabele, despite the power of their guns. It is a rousing but reasoned speech, and it builds steadily till it stirs "a feeling at the center of the crowd . . . and the various clansmen responded: 'We are with thee, O Chief.' 'We will be there at thy command'." The final decision to support the Boers, because of the full and open participation and consensus of the community, carries not only the legitimacy neither Tauana's nor Mzilikazi's decisions ever could, but also the strength that the many minds have given to it. Whereas Tauana's and Mzilikazi's decision lead to tragedy, the decision reached at Thaba Nchu leads to a just resolution.

The importance of these three cases of political process presented in *Mhudi* is that they are all firmly placed in the pre-European history—the Boers play no part in the Moroka-led proceedings. Plaatje shows that the fundamentals of democratic political process have deep roots in African culture, both the Barolong and the Matabele, and it is their solid African foundation which is the illuminating contemporary reference point to emerge from the novel.

A criticism, particularly as regards the third case, might be raised, on two points, against this view.

The first might be that Moroka had himself, by this time, been influenced by Christian missionaries, and that his approach to the decision-making process by the united clans regarding the alliance with the Boers against the Matabele, as told by the narrator in *Mhudi,* reflects this influence more than traditional African political process. It is true that a few missionaries, led by James Archbell, were already with the clans before they gathered at Thaba Nchu, and had accompanied them on their migration there in 1833. But it seems highly improbable that Archbell would have had the capacity significantly to alter political practises and organisation by late 1836, when the scene depicted in the novel would have occurred. Alternatively, had the narrator's and Plaatje's perspective of the decisive meeting at Thaba Nchu not been altered in the telling to reflect later, Europeanized and missionary views of it? Attention to the care taken to depict in this scene the very African quality of the drama belies this view.

The second criticism might be that Plaatje was imposed upon in the presentation of this specific scene to reflect a missionary-influenced or Europeanized politics by the Lovedale Press, who published the first edition of *Mhudi* in 1930. I do not know whether the scene was altered in the first Lovedale Press edition, but my reference has, in any case, been to the Heinemann edition, which Couzens and Gray explain has carefully restored the integrity of the original typescript. To persist with this view without manuscript authority, I believe, is to slight the integrity of purpose and the depth of creative skill in drawing on the oral tradition which Plaatje evidences in *Mhudi.*

The discussion, by focusing on the key political scenes, has argued that the novel, in its subtle and critical rendering of the action, successfully portrays how the pride of power works in destructive combination with the common human weakness of ascribing the cause of hostilities to the other side. Shown as particularly vulnerable to capture in the tangle of war's cause and effect are the young, eager to fight before they think. But against the failures led by the vanities and impetuosities of Tauana, Mzilikazi and Langa there is the democratic wisdom and courage of Notto, Gubuza and Moroka. The narrative effectively dramatizes the

countervailing resources in the various communities which can unite the generations, and which do prevail when they are fostered by tradition, democratic process, and respect for the freedom of speech.

FURTHER READING

Biography

Pampallis, John. *Sol Plaatje.* Cape Town: Maskew Miller Longman, 1992.
> Provides an overview of Plaatje's life and work.

Willan, Brian. *Sol Plaatje, South African Nationalist, 1876-1932.* Berkeley: University of California Press, 1984.
> The first definitive biography of Plaatje.

Criticism

Couzens, Tim. "Politics and the Novel: Black South African Writing." *Washington Post Book World* (24 November 1985): 15.
> Along with Modikwe Dikobe's *The Marabi Dance,* Couzens discusses Plaatje's *Mhudi* from the perspective of the political turmoil in apartheid South Africa.

Gray, Stephen. *Sources of the First Black South African Novel in English: Solomon Plaatje's Use of Shakespeare and Bunyan in* Mhudi. Pasadena: Munger Africana Library, California Institute of Technology, 1976, 28 p.
> Cross-cultural critical examination of the European sources of Plaatje's themes and techniques.

"Life in Mafeking." *Times Literary Supplement* (30 November 1973): 1472.
> A mostly neutral account of *The Boer War Diary of Sol T. Plaatje.*

Mzamane, Mbulelo Vizikhungo. "Colonial and Imperial Themes in South African Literature 1820-1930." *The Yearbook of English Studies* 13 (1983): 181-95.
> This historical survey of earliest South African literature discusses Plaatje as the dominant South African literary figure of the first three decades of the twentieth century.

Additional coverage of Plaatje's life and career is contained in the following sources published by Gale: *Black Writers,* Vol. 2; *Contemporary Authors,* Vol. 141; *Twentieth-Century Literary Criticism,* Vol. 73.

Simone Schwarz-Bart
1938-

Guadeloupean novelist and dramatist.

INTRODUCTION

Schwarz-Bart is regarded as a significant contributor to both the literature of colonized peoples and to literature exploring black women's identities as a doubly marginalized group. Her novels feature characters living in occupied territories in search of literal and figurative homelands. Schwarz-Bart's works are praised for their lucid and often lyrical explication of the experience of slavery and colonization in the West Indies and the subsequently painful search for heritage and identity.

Biographical Information

Schwarz-Bart was born in Goyave, Guadeloupe, an island in the French West Indies, in 1938. In 1961 she married Andre Schwarz-Bart, with whom she wrote her first two novels, *Un plat de porc aux bananes vertes* (*A Dish of Pork with Green Bananas;* 1967) and *La Mulatresse Solitude* (*A Woman Named Solitude;* 1967). Schwarz-Bart keeps a residence in Guadeloupe and in Lausanne, France.

Major Works

Schwarz-Bart's two collaborations with her husband, Andre Schwarz-Bart, earned high praise from critics upon publication. Like Schwarz-Bart's later publications, *A Dish of Pork with Green Bananas* and *A Woman Named Solitude* are both concerned with the spiritual struggles and suffering of black women. *A Dish of Pork with Green Bananas* is narrated by Mariotte, an elderly woman from Martinique who, crippled and half blind, endures her last days in an asylum for the aged in Paris. *A Woman Named Solitude* is the story of Rosalie, a mulatto woman, "transformed by horrors" into an automaton named Solitude, who wanders the Guadeloupean countryside attacking white slave owners. In 1972 Schwarz-Bart published her first solo novel, *Pluie et vent sur Télumée Miracle* (*The Bridge of Beyond*). The heroine, Télumée Lougandor, is a descendant of slaves in rural Guadeloupe who relates her life story and eventually finds her identity in the West Indies. Considered by many critics a quest narrative, *The Bridge of Beyond* explores the dilemma of blacks forced from their African homeland to live in the French-colonized West Indies, who find it nearly impossible to discover or create for themselves a heritage. For the women in Schwarz-Bart's novels, this experience is intensified, as they must establish their identities within the constrictions of a white- and male-dominated society. Schwarz-Bart's next novel, *Ti Jean l'horizon* (*Between Two Worlds;* 1979), recounts the adventures of the Guadeloupean folk hero Ti Jean, whose fantastic travels to other countries and worlds in search of his ancestry eventually lead him back home. In 1987 Schwarz-Bart produced her only play to date, *Your Handsome Captain*. Using the dramatic technique of off-stage voices to emphasize the often artificial construction of personal identity, the play tells the story of a Haitian couple, Wilnor and Marie-Ange Baptiste, who must cope with separation and adultery. Forced to leave Haiti to find work in Guadeloupe as a farm laborer, Wilnor communicates with his wife by sending and receiving cassette tapes. Marie-Ange has an affair with one of the men who deliver the tapes, however, and becomes pregnant. Desperate not to tell her husband, Marie-Ange tries to abort, but nearly dies from blood loss. Convinced her husband will be furious and leave her, she nevertheless records her news and sends him the tape. Wilnor initially blames his wife but, realizing that he loves her, subverts the expectations of the patriarchal social code and accepts both his wife and the child.

Critical Reception

Response to Schwarz-Bart's work has been predominately positive. Her use of the French language peppered with the Créolité of Guadeloupean blacks has been praised for adding to the particularly feminine and colonial atmosphere of her works. But it is Schwarz-Bart's attention to the problem of African slave descendants locating their own identity and genealogy within a French outpost in the West Indies that has garnered the most critical regard. Critics have praised Schwarz-Bart for probing the nature of white patriarchal rule and its devastating effects on native peoples, especially women.

PRINCIPAL WORKS

La Mulatresse Solitude [*A Woman Named Solitude;* with Andre Schwarz-Bart] (novel) 1967
Un plat de porc aux bananes vertes [*A Dish of Pork with Green Bananas;* with Andre Schwarz-Bart] (novel) 1967
Pluie et vent sur Télumée Miracle [*The Bridge of Beyond*] (novel) 1972
Ti Jean l'horizon [*Between Two Worlds*] (novel) 1979
Your Handsome Captain (drama) 1987

CRITICISM

Kitzie McKinney (essay date March 1989)

SOURCE: "Second Vision: Antillean Versions of the Quest in Two Novels by Simone Schwarz-Bart," in *The French Review*, Vol. 62, No. 4, March, 1989, pp. 650-60.

[*In the following essay, McKinney discusses Schwarz-Bart's novels* Pluie et vent sur Télumée Miracle *and* Ti Jean l'horizon *as "quest literature."*]

For centuries, quest stories have reflected the social, moral and spiritual concerns, the hopes, disappointments and wishes of those who create and share tales of trial and adventure. Quest literature has also expressed these problems and possibilities in specific ways. In his book *The Hero with a Thousand Faces,* Joseph Campbell identifies three themes that give structure and substance to traditional quest literature. First, there is the call to adventure which separates the hero from his community. Inspired by a supernatural force, the hero then journeys to unknown regions and engages in a series of trials, culminating in a ritual death and rebirth. He finally returns to his community, bearing with him a life-enhancing and universally significant vision.

On the one hand, this thematic pattern embodies a search for identity, both personal and collective. On the other hand, Campbell's study reflects three limits in the structure of traditional quest literature. His title makes it clear that the prototypical questor is a man. Women serve as temptresses, victims or metaphysical helpers routinely cast in secondary roles. Campbell's schema also emphasizes the importance of action and adventures of heroic, if not supernatural, proportions that occur in a sacred place outside the boundaries of the community. Thirdly, the quest privileges the spiritual realm. The physical reality of self and community are seen as incomplete points of passage on the way to spiritual enlightenment.

Expressed as a personal, social and spiritual search, the quest is not a new theme in Caribbean literature. Peoples uprooted from traditional communities and forced into exile and slavery were haunted by the idea of lost origins and redefined identity. At first, Antillean writers sought to emulate European colonizers; early West Indian literature is full of alienated characters who set off in search of their masters' culture and mythical homeland. But modern writers such as Aimé Césaire, René Depestre and Jacques Roumain redefined the notion of quest as the struggle to overcome cultural servitude, to create a personal and social identity from the painful history of repressed origins and to come to terms with islands that had become one's ambivalent, problematical "native land." Yet, both questor and writer remained male.

The two works of fiction studied here were produced by a woman who has found different ways and a voice of her own for exploring and expressing the special quest for identity of Antillean peoples. Simone Schwarz-Bart's novel *Pluie et vent sur Télumée Miracle* was written as a testimonial to a remarkable woman known by the author in her native Guadeloupe. The book details the everyday life of a poverty-stricken community around the turn of the century, as seen through the eyes of a woman who has lived through the winds and rains of life without surrendering her dignity. *Ti Jean l'horizon* was published seven years later in 1979. It presents the adventures of a Guadeloupean folk hero, Ti Jean, who journeys to other continents and even to other worlds in episodes directly comparable to those of fabled quest heroes. Written in two different registers about characters of different genders, these works both demythologize traditional quest patterns and offer new versions of the quest able to accommodate Antillean women and men who set out on different paths to seek the inner peace that comes when one has found one's rightful place in the world. In this very special way, Schwarz-Bart's works propose a fresh vision of humanity and a specifically Antillean "modernity" of spirit and language.

At first glance, Télumée Lougandor hardly seems to qualify as the heroine of a quest. We are told at the beginning of the book that the measure of her heart was always and remains linked to her island of Guadeloupe. Her life is resolutely grounded in the here and now, and the literal boundaries of her adventures are circumscribed by the rural villages in which she lives. The account of her life does not contain grandiose adventures, supernatural intercession, or any of the traditional thematic trappings of quest literature. Yet her story does offer a resolute and very poetic coming to terms with man and woman, self and community, material richness and spiritual treasure. This is, in short, a quest that moves full circle without ever leaving its point of departure. The basic truth, the language of identity, is there from the start, yet it takes Télumée a lifetime and us the fictive space of that lifetime in the text to grasp its full meaning.

It is not by chance that the rural villages described in the novel are called Fond-Zombi, La Folie and L'Abandonnée. These names are eloquent markers of spiritual and linguistic as well as physical place. They suggest the no-man's land or liminal space of those part-living, part-dead who retain their human form but who have lost their inner being. The villagers of La Folie call themselves "la confrérie des Déplacés." These souls have embarked on a centuries-long quest for their rightful place in the sun. It matters little that slavery as an institution was abolished long before Télumée's time. The dishonor and physical and spiritual displacement suffered by her ancestors leave psychological and social scars and interiorized, but no less damaging, shackles:

je pense à ce qu'il en est de l'injustice sur la terre, et de nous autres en train de souffrir, de mourir silencieusement de l'esclavage après qu'il soit fini, oublié. J'essaye, j'essaye toutes les nuits, et je n'arrive pas à comprendre comment tout cela a pu commencer, comment cela a pu continuer, comment cela peut durer encore, dans notre âme tourmentée, indécise, en lambeaux et qui sera notre dernière prison.

The quest which Télumée undertakes both for herself and for her community holds out the promise of release from the inner prison and proof that the self has value and meaning. Yet the village names remind us that if the promise and the proof exist, they do so with neither guarantee nor guarantor. God took to the sky long ago, notes the old sorceress Man Cia, and chose to take up residence in the great house of the whites: "C'est depuis longtemps que pour nous libérer Dieu habite le ciel, et que pour nous cravacher il habite la maison des blancs." No divine word of love and redemption intervenes in the history of the Displaced Ones, no metaphysical power ensures that the elect will find the Holy Grail at the end of the quest. In Télumée's world, the very notion of a quest risks becoming an ironic, if not perverse, game, still one more displacement for a soul that recollects only too well the voices which already judged and denied its existence.

All three of the men who play a role in Télumée's life story leave the familiar territory of the community at one point or another in the novel, but their wandering never brings them vision. They reflect but never transcend the drama of the Displaced Ones. Télumée's first lover Elie and her last companion Médard are cursed, driven men, condemned by birth or bad fortune to perpetual wandering. Télumée's second lover Amboise journeys to France and back again in search of an end to the punishment, a release from the inner prison, a word that will heal his alienated soul: "dans ses yeux il y avait alors une sorte de disponibilité perpétuelle, comme si à tout instant il risquait d'entendre la parole qui l'apaiserait pour toujours. . . . Mais elle ne venait pas, il ne l'entendait jamais, cette parole, car nul ici ne pouvait la prononcer."

It is Télumée who finds the word. Her insight and wisdom come from her own experience and the examples of courage she finds and celebrates in her own community. As a child, Télumée is taught by her grandmother Toussine to preserve her integrity and self-esteem, no matter what blows life delivers, just as a cathedral and a drum maintain their plenitude of sacred inner space. Toussine ends a folk tale not just with a warning that human trials never end but also with a pointed reversal that casts life as the beast and the self as the master: "derrière une peine il y a une autre peine, la misère est une vague sans fin, mais le cheval ne doit pas te

conduire, c'est toi qui dois conduire le cheval." These images constitute in essence the vision of life usually discovered at the end of a quest. Télumée receives them in childhood from women who offer them in wisdom and love. The words accompany Télumée through all the crises of her life. They return time and again to the text when she endures the condescending, racist insults of the white Desaragne family, the abuse of Elie, the degrading conditions of labor in the sugar cane field, the loss of her lovers and her adopted daughter, and the onset of old age. Each time, she draws language and experience closer together, allowing one to enrich and strengthen the other. It is the consequent growth—and centering—of her inner self that makes her a unique character and, I believe, an authentic heroine of quest.

Nor is her quest a solitary act. Télumée retraces in her own life the proverbs spoken and the situations experienced for centuries by her people in Guadeloupe and elsewhere in the Antilles, from the daily chores of a child in the countryside, to work as a housemaid, to labor in the cane fields, from the happiness of love to despair, abandonment and loss. Her grandmother also teaches her that the way in which she reacts to life's difficulties, her flair for living, her personal *panache*, indeed, the very way in which she speaks and carries herself, has a direct and profound influence on others in her community. Toussine's dying words to her granddaughter remind Télumée that Lougandor women have an inherent duty to live so as to keep self—and others—from despair:

> écoute, les gens t'épient, ils comptent toujours sur quelqu'un pour savoir comment vivre . . . si tu es heureuse, tout le monde peut être heureux et si tu sais souffrir, les autres sauront aussi . . . et si tu n'agis pas ainsi tu n'auras pas le droit de dire: c'est pas ma faute, lorsque quelqu'un cherchera une falaise pour se jeter à la mer.

According to Toussine, even the poorest of communities is filled with a network of tiny links which attach each dwelling to the others like the threads of a spider's web:

> saisissant un rameau desséché, elle se mit à tracer une forme à ses pieds. . . . On eût dit le réseau d'une toile d'araignée, don't les fils se croisaient sur de minuscules et dérisoires petites cases. Tout autour, elle traçait maintenant des signes qui rappelaient des arbres, et enfin, me désignant son œuvre d'un geste ample de la main, elle affirma . . . c'est Fond-Zombi. . . . Tu le vois, les cases ne sont rien sans les fils qui les relient les unes aux autres, et ce que tu perçois l'après-midi sous ton arbre n'est rien d'autre qu'un fil, celui que tisse le village et qu'il lance jusqu'à toi, ta case.

Just as Télumée gives strength to others, so does she receive it in time of need. When Elie beats and repudiates her and she is driven mad by grief, villagers pass by her dwelling, bringing songs, encouraging words, and small gifts, tossing out to her "un fil dans l'air, un fil très léger" so as to prove that "il ne pouvait y avoir de coupure dans la trame."

Télumée never leaves her community. She receives her name from villagers who recognize her victory over Médard, the man who caused her adopted daughter to leave her, destroyed her belongings, and almost killed her: "Médard a vécu en chien et tu l'as fait mourir en homme." Télumée's real miracle is not just that she remains faithful to herself in the face of overwhelming adversity; it is also that she calls back *les poursuivis*—the Pursued Ones—to their own place and to their own language. Her vision of the world and the words that she finds embrace natural forces both creative and destructive and the disparate lives of men and women who do both good and evil. Télumée herself grows with her increased understanding of the Other, and her words restore peace and identity, even to the most alienated of the Dispossessed. In so doing, she indirectly puts into question the notion of solitary heroism and the obsessive need to look elsewhere for what one finds lacking. Télumée finds plenitude and beauty in everyday events, and all of the heroic action described in this book takes place in the human heart. There is a different voice that speaks here, and it needs no supernatural Logos, no definite moment of death and rebirth to guarantee its authenticity. It inspires by power of will and, still more, by sheer force of generosity.

Simone Schwarz-Bart's second novel, *Ti Jean l'horizon*, goes farther afield in exploring the problems and possibilities of Antillean quest. It is not an easy book to read in that it shifts around layers of history and space, pieces of folk tales and popular legend, names, symbols, and cultural mythologies in a way that is both disorienting and provocative. In a brief introduction to the work, the author writes:

> On peut lire *Ti Jean l'horizon* comme une aventure extraordinaire, un conte d'amour, une histoire de sorcellerie, un ouvrage de science-fiction où le Bête jouerait le rôle de machine à remonter le temps: mais c'est aussi une quête de l'identité, un voyage que j'aurais fait au bout de ma nuit antillaise, pour tenter de l'exorciser. Comme mon héros, j'aimerais dire que je ne suis qu'un enfant et le monde un moulin à mystéres.

Ti Jean's plot follows the traditional thematic schema for quest literature, even down to the formal division of the story into seven episodes, each with a title announcing the adventure to come. The biological child of his good-natured Antillean father and the spiritual child of his African grandfather Wademba, Ti Jean moves in three spheres that make up the topography of his Guadeloupe: the hilly retreat of the

Old Ancestors who remember and celebrate the heroism of runaway slaves; the village below inhabited by Guadeloupeans who discard the old in favor of the new and the modern; and the mysterious domain of spirits who roam the woods—the dead and the souls partially transformed into animals. The call to adventure comes when a huge, cow-like beast appears on the island and swallows scores of inhabitants as well as the sun itself. When the Beast swallows Ti Jean's fiancée Egée, the young hunter returns to the Old Ancestors for counsel and his grandfather's magical arms: a belt of strength, a ring of wisdom, and an old musket from the times of the slave revolts. Once inside the Beast in search of Egée, Ti Jean journeys to other worlds: first, to Wademba's homeland in Africa, then to the Kingdom of the Dead, then around the polar seas to France, and finally back to Guadeloupe. Ti Jean returns with a full measure of *connaissance*, a deep understanding of all three domains. Having learned the secret of the Beast, Ti Jean uses the musket to kill it and restore both his people and the sun to their proper place. Ti Jean himself undergoes a final transformation from an old man back into a youth who finds his lost love waiting for him and assumes the wisdom and the destiny of his island.

Ti Jean's journey is fascinating in that it leads the reader to the farthest possible limits in what is not just a quest but also a questioning of the Antillean search for identity. The young hero's passage to the inside of the Beast triggers an ironic, other-worldly look at ideas and cultural experience normally accepted as a matter of fact. In this case, that look, like the laser gaze of the Beast itself, deconstructs four myths traditionally associated with Antillean quest: the return to Africa, the power of the spirit world, the Promised Land of France, and the heroic, linear dimensions of machismo.

As a boy, Ti Jean hears his grandfather's stories about Africa and the courage of the slaves who made the crossing, then chose to escape to the woods and fight to the death rather than remain in bondage. In particular, Wademba exhorts Ti Jean to return to the ancestral village of Obanishé on the Niger River: "si tu te présentes un jour là-bas, toi ou ton fils, ton petitfils . . . il vous suffira de dire que votre ancêtre se nommait Wademba pour être accueillis commes des fréres . . . car j'appartiens à un sang trés lourd et pesant, un sang de très longue mémoire et qui n'oublie rien." What in fact awaits Ti Jean when he drops down the Beast's gullet into Obanishé is a spear in the belly, just like that received by Wademba's spirit after the old man's death. The myth of return to Africa is shattered as Ti Jean learns that Wademba's tribe, the Sonanqués, will not accept a person who has ever been a slave. Having been sold into slavery by the Sonanqués themselves, Wademba is condemned to wander the Kingdom of the Dead in eternal shame, as a spirit repudiated by its kinsmen, the victim of a double irony of family betrayal and prejudice of Africans against Antilleans.

A second demystification that occurs during Ti Jean's sojourn in the belly of the Beast is that of the Kingdom of the Dead. Once Ti Jean passes through the legendary cavern separating the living from the dead, he finds that the shades of the Ancestors, objects of profound reverence for the living, take on an entirely different character. Those supposedly without whom nothing can be done on earth appear to Ti Jean as "marionnettes mues par des fils invisibles qui les reliaient au village d'en haut, à la face éclairée de la terre." Like the unhappy shades in Lucian's *Journey to the Underworld,* the souls in the Kingdom of the Dead mill about restlessly and nostalgically, remembering their time on earth, demanding proper respect for old customs, and longing for their next return to earth. Ti Jean is amazed to discover that the dead have power only over the dreams of the living. The rest of their legendary vast influence, he notes, is a "gaspillage de salive." Ti Jean's ironic demystification touches not just the Africans with whom he lives but also the Old Ancestors in Guadeloupe who, in wanting to gain godlike powers, acquire little more than the wretched forms and melancholic eyes of grotesque animals. While in the Kingdom of the Dead, Ti Jean also learns that in order to be reborn, a soul must find its way back to its home on earth. And Ti Jean realizes that for him "home" is not Africa but rather Guadeloupe, "une lèche de terre sans importance," but nonetheless the only legitimate place to which he can return.

Ti Jean has already learned that lesson when the magical boat which carries him out of the Kingdom of the Dead deposits him in the mecca of the francophone Antilles, France itself. Long the object of quest for expatriates cut off from their spiritual and cultural capital and for Antilleans taught to revere "Mother France" and her wonders, the Hexagon which Ti Jean discovers reveals its other side, facets not celebrated in French cultural mythology. Half-man, half-crow Ti Jean enters a city of "enfilades de vieilles rues malséantes, malodorantes, où stagnaient des blancs comme Ti Jean n'avait jamais vu, de vrais fantômes de blancs, osseux et pouilleux, en loques." While the upper part of town corresponds more closely to his preconceived idea of a bourgeois city, the French cityscape that Ti Jean experiences is composed primarily of metal enclosures, search lights, barbed wire, nets, soldiers and a solitary room suspended at the top of a staircase as if the rest of the building were bombed away. While the precise space and historical moment are never specified, the assiduity with which soldiers and gendarmes track down and try to capture the winged "Black Angel" cannot help but bring to mind the hunts and roundups during the Occupation, as well as those—more recent—of illegal aliens from African and Arab countries, when snares yielded an abundance of human quarry. It is in the cradle of culture that Ti Jean is transformed into a crow that can no longer fly. Like many of his compatriots who—far

more willingly than he—crossed the seas to France in search of their identity, he begins to rot, forgotten and abandoned in a dilapidated, freezing room.

Ti Jean is saved from death by the spirit of an old Guadeloupean named Eusebius the Elder, who seeks out and revives the dying hero by means of a ritual ceremony. And it is in the course of this ceremony of Vaudouesque "orientation" that the fourth and final object of false quest is repudiated. The boy who neglected his fiancée in order to hunt and pursue ancestral spirits in the forests, the young hunter who describes his vision of heroism as a "meteoric rise and even more fulgurous fall and demise", the man transplanted to Africa and named Ifu'umwâmi ("he-who-says-yes-to-death-and-no-to-life") must learn to reverse the meaning of his name and say no to death and yes to life. Ti Jean must transcend the macho version of heroism that looks at elsewhere and the Other as conquests to be made on the way to glory. He needs to develop a second pair of eyes which see beyond the linear progression of adventures and into the depths of the human heart.

All of the women whom Ti Jean encounters know this basic truth and, all heroism notwithstanding, Ti Jean makes progress on his quest only as he learns and lives this lesson. Ti Jean's mother Awa braves the wrath of the Ancient Ones in her search for love and silently bears her own anger and fear of her father Wademba out of love for her son. With a courage equal to his, the mysterious and beautiful Egée accompanies Ti Jean into haunted forests. She leaves her family to follow Ti Jean back into the woods and carries his child. Ti Jean's African wife Onjali, whom he suspects is the reincarnation of Egée, honors her husband and sees to his happiness by providing him with other wives. The deformed young woman who voluntarily maintains her own exile in the Kingdom of the Dead literally and spiritually guides Ti Jean by teaching him how to find the hideous old Queen who can help him leave the Kingdom of the Dead. The young woman also tells Ti Jean the story of the hero Losiko Siko, a fictional double of Ti Jean, who slays the Beast in a folk tale. But Losiko Siko also inadvertently slays many of the Beast's human victims by being too brutal and is himself transformed into a stone. The young woman's prophetic warning helps Ti Jean alter the outcome when his turn comes to slay the Beast. The difference is that by the end of his quest, Ti Jean has become just as mindful of preserving human life as he is about the glorious feat of returning the sun to its place in the heavens.

The last and most powerful of the women whom Ti Jean encounters is the sorceress named La Reine-aux-longs-seins, the Queen with the long breasts. It is in the company of this enchanted old hag cursed with a thirst for human blood that Ti Jean fully realizes that woman is free to give and to take away and that "l'homme ne déchoit pas en ouvrant son cœur." When he begins to love the old hag as much as the young beauty into which she is transformed at night, the Queen notes that Ti Jean has truly begun to see: "Vraiment, ils commencent à s'ouvrir, tes yeux, ceux qui sont à l'intérieur de la tête." She then sends him out of the Kingdom of the Dead. But Ti Jean is never sure if life or if death has claim to his body, his mind, his name, or his heart. Only when Death appears with the smile and the body of Egée does Ti Jean strike out at Death in indignation and anger and choose life. Having come to appreciate the very real sensual beauty of the physical world, as well as the spiritual richness of both his woman and his island, Ti Jean sees Egée both as a rainbow and as the island of Guadeloupe, while the reader realizes that Egée has in fact been present in all of the women whom Ti Jean meets. At the end of his journey, Ti Jean returns to Guadeloupe and kills the Beast. He finds Egée waiting for him, a young Negress sitting on the steps of his mother's house, singing of her good luck to come and the hope she keeps. As he salutes the young woman, he realizes that his real adventure has just begun.

Thus, Ti Jean's discovery of *connaissance* begins and ends at home, exactly as does that of Télumée. Despite their differences in content, both books demystify the false quests so tempting for Antilleans, the seductive "elsewhere" that leads to exile and the frustrating, futile search for an identity that has always been there, back home, unseen with the "eyes on the inside of the head" and undervalued in its richness. While it is true that the men in Schwarz-Bart's fiction have a harder time than the women in gaining access to the wisdom of the heart, this does not mean that men cannot and do not join women in true *connaissance*. Eusebius the Elder draws and offers the ritual blood of his own heart to help save Ti Jean from Death, and it is he who teaches Ti Jean the hunter to seek not just the linear unfolding of "woods behind woods" but also the hidden depths of "woods beneath woods": "on t'a appris qu'il y a des bois derrière les bois, et c'est la vérité. Mais je t'apprends qu'il y a aussi des bois à l'intérieur des bois." Ti Jean learns this lesson very well; he comes to see the island of Guadeloupe and its inhabitants with the same generosity of heart as Télumée. Like the protagonists of these stories, readers and authors of either sex are invited to contemplate and to follow a path that leads not just to "woods behind woods" but also to "woods beneath woods." Journeys to the farthest limits of Antillean night thus open into journeys behind journeys and journeys beneath journeys, all of which await women and men in search of *connaissance* and for whom each end is a new beginning.

Clarisse Zimra (essay date Summer 1993)

SOURCE: "In the Name of the Father: Chronotopia, Utopia, and Dystopia in *Ti Jean l'horizon,*" in *L'Esprit Createur,* Vol. XXXIII, No. 2, Summer, 1993, pp. 59-72.

[In the following essay, Zimra discusses the search for a mythical and ancestral homeland in Ti Jean l'horizon.]

Five hundred years ago (plus one), a bold voyager from Genoa sailed west into modernity by "discovering" a new continent. Five centuries later (give or take a few years), looking west from Europe in a blur of ethnocentric and phallocentric myopia, Tzvetan Todorov still pronounces "us all" heirs to Columbus—even though gallantly dedicating *La Conquête de l'Amérique* "to the memory of a Mayan woman devoured by dogs." Looking east from America, Edouard Glissant had already bypassed Europe whence, according to Todorov, all originated (their books were published within a year of each other by the same press). Searching for alternative beginnings, *Le Discours antillais* glimpsed an African history at once denied and erased. It would seem that the oppositional reading of the collision of two worlds was fated to continue indefinitely.

However, similarities are often more telling than differences: both the scholar from the Old World and the scholar from the New World defined "the question of America" as a circular quest that doubles back upon itself in time and space simultaneously. This movement constitutes the narrative "chronotope" of our thinking about the continent. To the historian of ideas, the voyage leitmotiv that marks our contemporary meditation on the "New" World comes as no surprise; the mysterious (is)land to the west has been a common *topos* from the Greeks onward. For the Ancients, this *locus classicus* reenacted radical beginnings in the characteristic gesture of Myth, Ur-time enfolding and enfolded into Ur-place. In its modern variations, the quest for the perfect place (*Eu-topia*) has uncovered either its non-existence (*U-topia*) or its transformation into the regimented structures of dystopia, unfolding a textual drama of containment played upon an obviously ideological stage. The modern Utopia, argues Fredric Jameson, is an attempt at circumventing the totalizing drive of History. It is the motif that I propose to examine in Simone Schwarz-Bart's ***Ti Jean l'horizon,*** a work published at about the same period, and one that excavates much of the ground that Todorov and Glissant sought to cover.

Denied a reality of their own making in the grand Hegelian scheme, the non-Europeans in the Americas were refused the right to their own historicity. It is therefore not surprising to see their writers coming back to the need, time and again, of repositioning the fractured self on the psychic map of the past—the Caribbean version of the "return of the repressed" as it were.

Negritude upended the fact of discovery and conquest, refiguring the Noble Savage and inverting the triangulation of the Middle Passage; to wit, Césaire's *Une tempête.* Was Negritude a utopia, the prophetic dream of the oppressed, as *Cahier d'un retour au pays natal* would have it? Or would it eventually self-destruct on its own repressed dystopia, as Caliban's increasing cruelty seemed to imply? Broached in Negritude's master-text, *Et les chiens se taisaient,* the question raises the specter of evasive textual strategies, a displacement constitutive of the Caribbean corpus for which the Bakhtinian chronotope serves as a structuring metaphor. This is the question Schwarz-Bart's last novel to date addresses.

The new generation of *Eloge de la créolité* now joyously claiming to be "tous fils de Césaire," an obvious response to Todorov's "tous descendants de Colon," does so without the reluctant ambiguity once exhibited by Glissant's first charting of "antillanité" in *L'Intention poétique,* or the gleeful causticity of Maryse Condé's shot across the ancestral bow in "Négritude senghorienne." This is not to imply that *créolité* could not have come about without Schwarz-Bart, but simply to observe that, *primum inter pares,* **Ti Jean l'horizon** signals a turn in the collective literary project that, in the French Caribbean, has recast all ideological moorings.

The novel seems to be a perfect illustration of what Joseph Campbell calls a monomyth, a linear quest that in the Western tradition is identified with male-oriented values and a narrowly gendered heroic self. I have argued that Schwarz-Bart's other works offer a polyvalent un-gendering vision of self-validation. In contrast, **Ti Jean** culminates in that most "male" of all mythic functions, the search for the Father. Embroidering on a simple tale from the oral cycle that has to do with Ti Jean's search for his real father's name ("Ti Jean et le nom de son père"), Schwarz-Bart enlarges it to mythic proportions. Voyaging into the African past, the peasant boy who might otherwise have remained village simpleton becomes not only his own Ancestor but that of a whole people.

If the novel still raises the question of elective (as opposed to biological) genealogy explored in the previous works, it does so in the opposite direction, opacifying rather than clarifying the quest for ancestors. As his birth name indicates, Schwarz-Bart's protagonist is the son of Jean l'horizon, a young man from Fond-Zombi, but this Caribbean allegiance is made immediately doubtful for the Lowlanders: "On l'avait baptisé du nom de son père, mais ceux de la vallée évitaient de l'appeler ainsi." For the Highlanders, there never is any doubt that the African is the child's father and that the child's claim to his father's name is legitimate: "Il vous suffira de dire que votre ancêtre se nommait Wademba." Yet there is plenty of doubt as to whose child Wademba is in African terms: i.e., whose clan he and his are allowed to claim. Evincing her own alternative and clearly non-Christian allegiance, the child's mother, who was once a Christian convert, insists that the newborn be given the name of his/her father-ancestor, Wademba, that would protect him.

C'est ton enfant, le vent du soir lui-même le sait, c'est ton enfant, et tu n'as pas de nom pour lui, rien à poser sur ses petites épaules . . . ? Tu veux donc qu'il soit à la merci des forces du mal, qu'il erre sans protection dans la vie, livré au premier qui voudra s'emparer de son âme et la jeter aux chiens: à l'injure du temps comme une bête, c'est ça?

This, of course, is precisely Ti Jean's fate. The old man sets up the conditions of the ordeal:

Il n'y a aucun nom que je puisse donner à ton enfant, car tu l'as dit toi-même, il sera dans la vie comme une bête, une bête sauvage qui trouve d'elle-même son chemin; et si je lui donnais un nom d'Afrique, ce nom s'enroulerait autour de sa gorge comme un collier et l'étranglerait . . .

Si je lui donnais un nom d'Afrique

The question of naming triggers the Caribbean voyage along the African memory trace and the first premonition of dystopia: "ce nom s'enroulerait autour de sa gorge." This image of the accursed necklace might evoke the captives' chains and stand as a metonym for slavery; in its serpentine connotation, however, it could be a veiled warning that the father, too, is lethal, for the green "congre" snake is Wademba's totem. However, the serpent is the ritual animal of Damballah Wedo as well, the rainbow *Loa* who spans the horizon—and "horizon" is, of course, one of Ti Jean's given names, that of his Caribbean father. The *vodun* god connects Africa to its diaspora across time and across space, the positive repository of immense spiritual knowledge in this life, as well as the final resting place of the soul's spirit in the next. What we have here is a demonstration of the polyvalence of symbols, simultaneous vectors of life and death. Not only will Ti Jean have to find his way (and choose a self) in their thicket, but, whatever his eventual name and eventual choice, he will have to earn it at the cost of his life.

Sent by the African father back to Africa, the son will die several times. What, then, is this name that kills? It is quite simply a name—hence, a past—that are not his to claim. Thus says the African elder who enlightens Ti Jean in Obanishé: "Les oiseaux vont avec les oiseaux, c'est bien connu, et les animaux à poil avec leurs semblables . . . *retourne parmi les tiens*" (emphasis mine). The warning is sounded: if Africa will not claim *him,* he may not claim *her.*

In the early novels, the multiplicity of name-passings and name-conferrings pointed to symbolic reenactments of the past. Still, they never reached further back than the first resistance on Caribbean soil. In *Ti Jean,* the people of Fond-Zombi refer to the Highlanders as "the Immortals," a clear inference that, even if they are physically mortal (and

Wademba's death triggers Ti Jean's quest), the memory they transmit is destined not to die, and so points—literally—to their own pre-history: descended from the resisting Maroons, the Immortels preserve that which the Lowlanders, descended of slaves, have willed themselves to forget. This claim to historical difference as self-validation reappears with equal aptness in most Caribbean writers, whatever their language or tradition. Its obvious socio-historical grounding has been commented upon at length by historians of slave societies.

The Immortels belong to the "time before time." This *temporal* moment of origins long forgotten—before the Middle Passage—embraces as well the *spatial* point of origins no less forgotten—the symbolic topography of a continent that is home. Not being able to read the terrain has dire consequences and confirms Wademba's grandson as an outsider. Because he fails to understand the difference between one bank of the river and the other, one tribe (Sonanqués) and the other (Ba'Sonanqués), Ti Jean loses his life. The Immortels, who sent him to his death, are the embodiment of a chronotope that articulates the inevitable passage from utopia to dystopia and signals the end of the African myth.

Ti Jean's quest is thus different from those undertaken in Schwarz-Bart's previous novels. It bypasses the mythical moment of Guadeloupean self-empowerment, Delgrès's resistance, Solitude's rebellion, memories that had structured the earlier works. *Ti Jean* now implies that to claim the Matouba, however legitimate the history, is not enough. With this ideological shift comes a corresponding change in the chronotope. The circumscribed space that had marked the previous novels (the carceral hell of the paupers' home in *Un plat de porc aux bananes vertes;* the shrinking of the island to a speck of garden in *Pluie et vent sur Télumée Miracle*) explodes across oceans and continents, as well as across physical and metaphysical limitations. In a corpus that had hitherto to conjoined and contained time and space, this is an intriguing shift.

In *Ti Jean,* the once nurturing island of *Plat de porc* and *Télumée* serves as point-and-moment of origins for an African quest that entraps and kills. It is precisely this Africa *dreamt of* (or, in Lacanian terms, "imaged") as-and-in the Caribbean, whose fragmented refracted memory survives in the Immortels, that Ti Jean must flee at the risk of his life. This mirroring effect calls forth its own deadly double: the Caribbean island imagined as-and-in Africa.

My interpretation runs against the grain. In particular with *Télumée Miracle,* most critics, from Makward to Ormerod (including Schwarz-Bart herself in several interviews), have stressed the final and triumphant image of the island as miniature ship and Télumée standing therein, Césairean "Négresse debout et libre." While I do not wish to invali-

date all positive interpretations, Télumée's short-term optimism does not necessarily invalidate my long-term circumspection. When considered as a dyad, the difference between *Télumée Miracle* and *Ti Jean l'horizon* becomes less a matter of kind than of degree.

In the former (*Télumée*), the disintegration of Elie's personality as well as the horrible death of Amboise, events that push Télumée into insanity, have to do with conditions on the island that make it impossible for one to preserve a measure of self-respect. They force Télumée herself into white service and eventually into field work, the ultimate humiliation. In the latter (*Ti Jean*), the whiteness of the beast is the color of death found in many non-western thought systems; but it is as well the deadly symbol of unconditional surrender to the white system. Frantz Fanon had said no less. The disappearance of the sun, starving cane cutters and factory workers parked inside fenced enclosures or rounded up in trucks like cattle for slaughter, the once fertile earth refusing to bear fruit—these scenes describe the irruption of technology and the disruption of modernity (this age of the book worshipped by the Lowlanders and scorned by Wademba) in a once stable agrarian world. It is a society further destabilized by the influx of new French people at the end of empire and the subsequent emigration of islanders to France, a Middle Passage in reverse upon which another Guadeloupean novelist, Jacqueline Manicom, has commented bitterly. There are also specific references to the cane riots of the 1960s and their bloody repression. Those readers (particularly the Caribbean public whom the 1979 interview addresses), who have come down on Schwarz-Bart for writing escapist tales, might reconsider. For it is the latent reality of the island's sociopolitics as they reproduce slavery that, undergirding and connecting *Télumée Miracle* and *Ti Jean l'horizon,* pushes the latter into a dystopian mode. The political subtext surfaces in a matricial scene that reaches far back into the insular past and beyond. Summoned for the ancestor's final moments, young Ti Jean has his mission spelled out; he must knock the knife from the white man's hand: "Retirer le couteau de la main des blancs." Nothing less than revolution.

The political grid reveals a familiar topography. *Ti Jean l'horizon* takes place in Fond-Zombi, the uphill village one encounters upon crossing Télumée's Bridge of Beyond, halfway up from the coast. Unlike *Ti Jean, Télumée* turns its back to the African sea, since one would have to cross through the white man's plain to reach the shore, a perilous journey; hence, Télumée's bondage as a maid down in the plain with the arachneid Desaragnes, pallid and predatory *békés*. Schwarz-Bart here operates a bit of "signifying" on the Capecian trope, down to the sickeningly "white" béchamel sauce (*sauce blanche*) her character must learn to serve and the fact that her main responsibilities entail *blanchissage*. But *Ti Jean* modifies the topography. Fond-

Zombi itself is only a half-way mark up the next higher hill that leads to the old Maroon settlement. Who, then, are the true "zombis," those living dead who have lost all memory of the past? *Télumée* sets up Fond-Zombi as the positive version of its own negative, the white man's cities of the plain (and the Biblical echo is there, too, of course). *Ti Jean* now identifies Fond-Zombi as the negative version of the Maroon settlement:

> Après l'abolition de l'esclavage, ils avaient tenté de parler à ceux de la vallée, les gens d'enbas comme ils les appelaient, pour leur dire la course des héros dans l'ombre et la chute finale et le foudroiement. Mais les autres avaient ri d'un curieux petit rire pointu, et ils avaient dit que ces événements n'en étaient pas, qu'il ne pouvait s'agir de vrais événements car, enfin, en quels livres étaient-ils écrits?

For the Highlander to surmount such contempt, initiate contact—and, even, miscegenation, through his daughter—with the Lowlanders, something must have changed between them, but Wademba is not able to pursue this brief insight. Ti Jean will do it for him.

Ti Jean's mother is Awa (African name for Eve, the primal Mother), daughter of Wademba (thus making him the original Father), whose loins contained her, as his name, too, contains hers (Wademb/Awa/demba . . .). In the Immortels' world, the name is a cipher of unbroken continuity. Wademba ritually initiates her sexually before sending her to the village below. For ten years she has remained barren or miscarried until Jean, bowing to the belief, "le maléfice où chacun avait reconnu la marque et la griffe, le coup de patte unique de l'Immortel," leaves her and immediately gets killed in a freak accident. Awa, who may or may not be pregnant by Jean, then hallucinates her own sexual repossession by Wademba. With this plural ancestry (what Claude Lévi-Strauss would, no doubt, call an overemphasis of blood ties bound to cause tragedy), we enter the domain of myth. This hero *par excellence* sports a biological father, Jean, and a bio-mythological father who is doubly his ancestor, Wademba: his mother's father. Moreover, since Wademba himself is the last in the chain of reincarnations, the child is the final avatar in a line reaching all the way across the sea. But unlike his mother's, Ti Jean's name neither contains nor is contained in that of his ancestor, the first hint that the chain may be broken, that something may, indeed, have changed.

The human link between two severed worlds, Ti Jean must find his way among many versions of the past. The narrative, divided into eight chapters (the ninth is a coda, a few pages long), moves through five initiation stages, each constituting a possible version of the self, each accompanied by a different name. (1) A Guadeloupean prehistory (Awa and Wademba), where Ti Jean is, first, refused an ancestral name ("Il n'y a aucun nom que je puisse donner à ton enfant"); then is given one that spells his future in the belly of the Beast ("si je pouvais te donner un nom d'Afrique, je t'appellerais Abunasanga, Celui-qui-semeut-dans-les profondeurs"). (2) Ti Jean's chronotopic fall takes him *up* the chain of successive reincarnations, *back* to Africa. (3) There is conferred upon him the name Ifu'umwami ("he who says yes to death," an expansion of "he who stirs-through-the-depths"), a second prophetic name, that symbolizes the temptation to remain within the house of the dead, safe within the chtonic body of Mother Africa, and eschew re-birth into historical contingency—a temptation to which Wademba will succumb. (4) An abortive, nameless return strands him on European soil. (5) The Guadeloupean home-coming; he finally assumes his full name as Ti Jean l'horizon, self-birthed from the belly of the Beast.

The emblematic animal coalesces Christian apocalyptic images of Revelation, a quasi-universal cosmogonic myth, and local folk beliefs ("la bête" being a vernacular term for snakes, Wademba's totem, and a reference to the Christian garden as well as to the African pantheon). The ordeal is not one of creation but of re-creation; for the Beast that swallowed the Sun is not the Creator, nor is its own creator. This initial scene foreshadows Ti Jean's postlapsarian African moves through a series of attempts and failures. Of even greater relevance to his quest is the fact that his fall is situated in a chronotopic moment that cannot be *anything but Caribbean:* topographically and historically.

We need only read the clues. The sacred animal occupies the grass swamp that separates Fond Zombi from the Maroons' hill. Neither solid nor liquid, this is the liminal space for negotiating identity between Highlanders and Lowlanders, an identity hitherto considered as oppositional. It will eventually turn into the birthing place of this new creature in whose veins courses the legacy and the knowledge of both ancestral groups: Ti Jean himself.

Something has gone awry in the balance of the universe for the island to be plunged into eternal darkness. Even the animal itself is described as more sad than angry, as if applying a cosmic sentence for a cosmic infraction over which it has no control. This infraction, as the hero will discover, is the scourge of slavery, a recurrent signature event in the text. Its consequence, the inability for the displaced self to take root elsewhere, eventually defines the difference between father and son, triggering Ti Jean's return and Wademba's eternal wandering. In a flash of insight, Ti Jean, entrapped in the African realm of the dead, muses on what has killed him: "Peut-être s'il avait aimé la Petite Guadeloupe *comme ça se doit*" (emphasis mine). "La grande Guadeloupe" being, of course, Africa, the inference is that not to love Guadeloupe "as one should" is to love Africa overmuch, a fixation that destroys the self. This discovery empowers the son's homecoming, but at the price of the father's eternal loss.

Reborn of the Ancestor's mistake, this son is a reluctant hero. The only acts he initiates are those that lead to his death (for instance, once as an African warrior; next, as an African slave). It is the mother who first seeks out Wademba, and the old man who sends for his grandchild, next. The Ancestor's dying words are, first, a warning: "Il n'y a plus de chemin, la route est arrêtée," then, a prediction: "il vous suffira de dire que votre ancêtre se nommait Wademba." The passage to self knowledge is blocked, cautions the ancestor, but, on the other side (Africa and/or Death, Africa as Death, again an ambivalent message), the son will only have to claim the father's lineage to be welcomed back into the fold:

> Il y a des temps et des temps que j'ai quitté mon village d'Obanishé, sur la boucle du Niger, et tous ceux qui m'ont connu dorment dans la poussière. Mais si tu te présentes un jour làbas, loi, ou ton fils, ton petit-fils jusqu'à la millième génération, il vous suffira de dire que votre ancêtre se nommait Wademba pour être accueillis comme des frères . . .

The name *is* the message but the message kills.

We need to consider the origins of the message and, with them, the messenger, in order to understand why this quest must fail. We must come back to the moment when Wademba finally acknowledges Ti Jean as his own. Of all the "miraculous arms" the old man entrusts him with (some will save his life), the most important is the old silver encrusted rifle with its silver bullet. It is the weapon that brings the Beast down and thus restores not only the individual but the community. The gift that saves him and his world is itself proof that the Ancestor is not deliberately plotting the son's death. Wademba may be as misguided as he is misguiding—malevolent by default rather than design.

Like all magic weapons this one comes with its own "past," a story of origins that must be retold as programmatic guidance through the ordeal, before the child can be sent on his quest. It belonged to Wademba's closest friend and alter-ego, Obé, the rebel who used it against the French before his execution. This matricial moment of retelling layers neatly spontaneous slave rebellions, Maroon revolts, and the famous last stand on Matouba, where, in 1802, Louis Delgrès and the last three hundred of his men blew themselves to bits rather than surrender to Napoleon's troops. Collective oral memory and occulted yet vivid history come together at this point in the text, in the multiple resurrected avatars of Obé (a truncated fusion of Caribbean "obeah," the occult protective powers, and Obanishé, the Niger village of ori-

gins). What is of interest, however, is the conflation (slaves equal Maroons equal free men of color) that simplifies and heroicizes the complicated power struggle among non-white and white factions at the time of the Matouba rebellion, colonials and French citizens, royalists and republicans, mulattoes, enslaved blacks, and "free men of color." The ancestor's mission, therefore, "to knock the knife from the white hand," is no less than a mandate to recreate the glorious days, and this time around do it right.

The sacrificial message, deconstructed by Ti Jean on African soil (Africa proves an endless cycle of capture and death, slavery and death), is further undercut along the sociohistorical axis on Caribbean soil. Obé's memory refuses to die. His Osiris-like presence appears each time cane cutters revolt, followed by their failure and his dismemberment. This cyclical rebirth of the heroic warrior is likewise reproduced along more playful lines with Ananzé, Ti Jean's own alter-ego, the last incarnation of the African trickster, Ananse (the myth-markers of synchronic doubles are everywhere). Ananzé eventually meets an early and violent death (a Césairean hero of pure revolt straight out of *Et les chiens se taisaient*). But die a useless death he does, as fail any and all of the pointless rebellions led by Obé. The glorious Caribbean past, handed down by Wademba as the path to African authenticity, proves a flawed model.

Ti Jean will have to figure out his legacy all by himself. This he does in a passage whose importance is underlined by its strategic position: dead center (chapter four of eight). For, in response to Awa's plea that he confer upon his son a name that would protect him, Wademba had insisted that his ultimate identity lay "ahead of him," and that his survival depended upon his reintegration of the ancestral clan. But which one?

Retourne parmi les tiens

In Africa, there is no welcome for him. Villages empty at his approach and dead animals are put in his path. Assaulted by his own kinsmen, Ti Jean is left for dead. Adopted by a neighboring prince whose life he had saved, he is finally told Wademba's true story; it is one that even the Ancestor himself does not know. In Obanishé there is not just one clan, but two, in perfect symmetry on either side of the great river and on either side of time: the Sonanqués, warrior group to whom Wademba would send him, his clan of origins; and the Ba' Sonanqués, their new name ("les Dévorants") and settling in for another thousand beknownst to himself, now belongs.

This new version of the myth of origins at the very point of origins signals a postlapsarian cosmogony reproducing itself endlessly. Defeated, the Sonanqués themselves were oppressed for a thousand years (a mythical "thousand years" that indicate near infinity), before acquiring their new name ("les dévorants") and settling in for another thousand years of gory terror upon the Ba' Sonanqués. For them, slavery is the unforgivable sin: "Il n'y pas de place ici pour ceux qu'on met dans les cordes." In bondage, the once Sonanqué Wademba has lost all claim on his own people.

To this, Ti Jean responds like the Caribbean he is, whose adequation to African beliefs is no longer unconditional. He argues that Wademba's sin is not his, but that of those who have sold him away: his own people. In gruff rebuttal, the old notable gives the (correct) African answer absolving the clan. It was Wademba's fate, since it was allowed to happen:

> Les oiseaux vont avec les oiseaux, c'est bien connu, et les animaux à poil avec leurs semblables . . . tes yeux se sont dessillés et tu as vu clair; retourne parmi les tiens . . . Wademba a été vendu avec l'assentiment des dieux. Hélas, jusque quand durera votre folie? Et combien de fils du néant renaîtront parmi nous, aveuglés par le désir de confondre leur sang avec le nôtre?

At the heart of the utopian dream, with "eyelids pulled wide open," Ti Jean has discovered a history of terror and slavery every bit as oppressive as any the Caribbean has known.

It is not until he has died several times, stages along the way of an initiation that take him progressively further from the Ancestor, that Ti Jean finally stumbles on the true meaning of his ordeal: he must birth himself. The Fall from grace that the arrival of the white Beast heralded on the island repeats the original Fall from grace in Africa. It is now repeated, one more time but in reverse, in this Caribbean text that recreates it. If the hero's return to the very moment and place of his disappearance seems nostalgic, it is a nostalgia with a difference. There is no bitterness toward the Ancestor who, clinging so tenaciously to the lethal belief in the redemptive return and the importance of keeping his African identity inviolate on Caribbean soil, shall drift eternally between two continents and two tribes. And yet, it is a belief he must have renounced for a too brief if crucial moment of insight when he decided to send his daughter down. As Ti Jean explains with his new self-knowledge to Wademba's grieving friends, it is the mark of Wademba's degraded self-knowledge that he should remain oblivious to his true "home," Guadeloupe:

> —Ça ne te semble pas qu'il soit en chemin, en chemin de la Guadeloupe?

> —Non, ça ne me semble pas, fit Ti Jean après un silence; et j'ai plutôt idée qu'il erre à travers les couloirs, *ne songeant guère à revenir au pays* . . .

> —Ah, je comprends, fit doucement le vieux, il est dans la honte . . .

> —La honte, dit Ti Jean. (emphasis mine)

For this ancestral "shame" that encompasses both Wademba's rejection by his own (African) people and Wademba's inability to embrace his new (Caribbean) people, the judgement of the son on the father is one of admirable compassion.

Schwarz-Bart's final message is eloquently simple. The return to Africa is no longer a viable political or cultural alternative; we already knew that. But neither is the unconditional return to its double, the glorious insular past itself—something which Maximin, who freely acknowledges his indebtedness to Schwarz-Bart, explores further in *L'Isolé soleil;* something with which Glissant has finally made peace in *Mahagony,* even if, as in Condé's *Les Derniers rois mages,* the wound is still throbbing.

Because it charts the movement back with such conviction, **Ti Jean l'horizon** has been found wanting. This is selling short a coda (part nine) that, with its homage to Jacques Roumain, invites us to expand Ti Jean's vision to the entire Caribbean. Still, the ending is ambivalent: positive and triumphant in the return to a regenerated land; negative or, at least, tentative in the lack of overt social change. But, unlike the father, the son knows exactly who he is at least. Lest we forget, in the original tale Ti Jean got the *béké*'s estate as well as his life, sending the white master to his death "to the end of the horizon." Nothing less than revolution indeed hidden within his name—and, for a Guadeloupean atuned to the oral tradition, it is hidden in full view. His new name, duly regained, chronotopically fuses the serpentine rainbow of his African forebears to the rebellious horizon of his Caribbean forebears, Highlanders to Lowlanders.

The new generation of writers celebrating their *créolité* has now turned to this trope of a plural encounter, expanding on what Glissant once called "poétique de la relation." They may not have been able to do so as felicitously had not Ti Jean made the trip ahead of them—and, without bitterness, chosen to come back. Home.

Judith Miller (essay date 1995)

SOURCE: "Simone Schwarz-Bart: Re-Figuring Heroics, Dis-Figuring Conventions," in *Theatre and Feminist Aesthetics,* edited by Karen Laughlin and Catherine Schuler, Fairleigh Dickinson University Press, 1995, pp. 148-59.

[*In the following essay, Miller discusses Schwarz-Bart's re-*

consideration of traditional gender roles in Your Handsome Captain.]

Since the mid-1960s, an impressive number of Guadeloupian and Martinican women writers have published prose narratives stemming from their experience as doubly marginalized figures. Not exactly "French"—although French citizens—not exactly represented as central to the body of oral tales which constitutes the literary tradition in the French Antilles—although present in most as "mother," "devilish temptress," or "empty-headed adolescent"—women of color have sought through their writing to forge a new, positive mythology. They wish on the one hand to valorize and explore Antillean culture. In so doing, they participate in a literary movement which traces its origins to the 1930s and the efforts of the Martinican poet, playwright, and statesman Aimé Césaire to recover metaphorically African roots and occulted Caribbean history. Like Césaire, women writers celebrate in their fiction both individual and collective achievements of slaves and free people of color, ancestors to the islands' contemporary population.

On the other hand, these women writers, very much products of their time, also examine the potentially untenable situation of the Antillean woman caught in the struggle for cultural and economic independence from France as well as for recognition of her *own* worth within a creolized form of patriarchy. They approach with caution the feminist theory and/or practice deployed by women of the dominant Western culture, aware of the danger of being co-opted by yet another version of a discourse which can be understood as positing race as the crucial dividing category of the human condition. Yet they recognize with Western feminists, and increasingly so since 1980, the necessity of placing women's issues squarely into legal and aesthetic representation. They too see many aspects of woman's experience as different from and often eclipsed by preoccupations which can be categorized as wholly male.

Foremost among the women authors seeking to express her Caribbean culture and also to refigure the role of women within it is the Guadeloupian Simone Schwarz-Bart. In her best-known and prize-winning novel, ***The Bridge of Beyond*** (1972), she hails in musical prose a matrilineal line of remarkable women, empowered by their passion for each other, their communal culture, and their mystical connection to the land. ***The Bridge of Beyond***'s main characters, Télumée and Toussine, together embody not only the richness of feminine connectedness but also the glory of an oral tradition brought to the Americas by the first African slaves, a tradition still fundamental to expressive pleasure in the Antilles. Moreover, Schwarz-Bart introduces creole phrases and syntactical structures into her French sentences, thereby proclaiming cultural specificity within the colonizer's language. Her efforts in ***The Bridge of Beyond*** partake of a

double consciousness and result in a double gesture of liberation—for the Antillean woman and for Antillean culture in general.

Schwarz-Bart's first and to date only play, ***Your Handsome Captain*** (1987), one of the few theatre pieces by women to emerge from France's former colonies, is also the most compelling. Unlike, for example, the violent denunciations of patriarchal culture in Lebanese-born Abla Farhoud's *The Girl from the Five and Ten* (1985) and Algerian Fatima Gallaire-Bourrega's *You Have Come Back* (1987), ***Your Handsome Captain*** presents an intimate and nuanced exploration of the rapport between an exiled Haitian agricultural worker and his wife. It neither ends, as Farhoud's and Gallaire-Bourega's pieces do, in the intolerable death of the female protagonist nor does it depend, as they do, on melodramatic realism to make its point. Rather, in the more experimental vein of plays by several women contemporaries in France, ***Your Handsome Captain*** dispenses with stable central characters and enraged indictments.

In ***Your Handsome Captain*** Schwarz-Bart, somewhat reminiscent of Simone Benmussa in *The Singular Life of Albert Nobbs* (1977) and Marguerite Duras in *The Eden Cinema* (1977) and *India Song* (1981), employs the technique of off-stage voices. She thus emphasizes, as Benmussa and Duras do, how a sense of self is "constructed" within patriarchy. Also, as in the early plays of Hélène Cixous (*Portrait of Dora*, 1974; *Le Nom d'Oedipe: Chant du Corps Interdit*, 1977 [The Name of Oedipus: Song of the forbidden body]) and in many Durassian pieces, a socially forbidden sexual act is introduced and unconventionally exploited. Schwarz-Bart's particular tack, similar to that of Cixous and Duras, problematizes the traditionally negative approach towards taboo sexual couplings which are thought to undermine the structure of society. In ***Your Handsome Captain***'s nontraditional treatment of adultery, Schwarz-Bart threatens—at least representationally–the omnipresent acceptable triangle of the nuclear family.

Like most of the exceptional feminist women (exceptional because still remarkably few) writing plays in French—for example Frenchwomen Duras, Cixous, and Andrée Chedid or Canadians Jovette Marchessault, Denise Boucher, and Louky Bersianik–Schwarz-Bart foregoes fourth-wall illusionism, an unambiguous message, and an ending which wraps up neatly the protagonist's problems. Her dramatic structure, like theirs, tends toward the ritualistic. And like theirs, her play invites discussion rather than catharsis.

Despite these similarities, it would be a mistake—and another example of Eurocentric tunnel vision—to place Schwarz-Bart's dramatic efforts uniquely within the realm of French or even Quebecois women contemporaries who seek an alternative form to express an alternative vision. In fact, like Martinican Ina Césaire in her play *Mémoires d'Isles: Maman N. et Maman F.* (1985) [Island Memories: Mama N. and Mama F.], Schwarz-Bart uses the extralinguistic and particularized creole languages of dance and song to convey her characters' inner drama. This allows her to insert a telling distance from what is most often recognizable, even in avant-garde pieces, as French cultural-expression. In *Your Handsome Captain,* Schwarz-Bart communicates a thematics of personal acts of liberation within neocolonialism through dramatic techniques which foreground concerns at once feminist and culturally specific to the Antilles. Her play thus encourages a reconceptualization of theatre and feminism which incorporates the reality and the effects of European (and American) colonization.

Your Handsome Captain tells, or better shows in one act and four tableaux, a crucial moment in the story of Haitian Wilnor Baptiste and his wife Marie-Ange. Self-exiled to Guadeloupe for the last several years and employed as a farm laborer in order to make enough money to keep his family afloat and assure himself and his wife a comfortable old age, Wilnor receives a cassette recording from Marie-Ange. Cassettes have been their only means of communication; but this time, the tape is very late in coming. Marie-Ange greets Wilnor with news of his family and the most recent tragic account of a Haitian friend drowned in his attempt to reach the United States by makeshift boat. Slowly, and after a series of hints and parallel narratives, she also discloses that she has had an affair with the last man who visited her on behalf of her husband. Returning to Haiti from Guadeloupe with money and presents, Wilnor's erstwhile comrade had talked himself momentarily into Marie-Ange's bed. She is now pregnant, and very much so, having unsuccessfully tried several times to abort the child she is carrying: "I tried everything to weaken my stomach. *(Pause.)* Finally, I lost half my blood and they took me to the hospital. *(Pause.)* But the child didn't leave with my blood. It didn't leave, Wilnor, it didn't."

This synopsis of Marie-Ange's confession hardly suggests what "happens" in the play. Nor does the term *confession* really apply to her recorded tale, which can also be read as a chronicle of the banal horrors which define women's limits. Throughout *Your Handsome Captain,* Schwarz-Bart underscores, without dwelling on any, certain common and often devastating aspects of the condition of being a woman in patriarchy. It is, for example, Marie-Ange who waits and is condemned to wait while Wilnor travels away. He has the right to "act" in order to try to provide for them. Marie-Ange is also victim to Wilnor's friend who at first coerces her into sleeping with him on the threat that he will not hand over Wilnor's savings. Finally, she nearly dies from a botched abortion because she is too distressed to seek help at the outset of her pregnancy.

These familiar terrors provide, however, a mere backdrop to the play, one which Schwarz-Bart ultimately erodes, or at least puts into a different perspective by focusing on liberating transformations in both Marie-Ange and Wilnor. In the manner of Marie-Ange's telling and in Wilnor's reaction to what he hears, Schwarz-Bart makes palpable both her feminism and her consciousness of oppression within the dominant culture. Through subversive gestures in staging and movement (as indicated in the didascalia) as well as through structuring and imagery, Schwarz-Bart demonstrates how a minority playwright can re-present positively new types of female and male characters and otherwise "hidden" (because out of mainstream representation) dimensions of her culture.

Paradoxically, what initially signals Schwarz-Bart's feminist sensitivity is the absence of the female character on stage. *Your Handsome Captain* would appear to be a one-man (plus cassette) show. Marie-Ange is apparently not meant to be the point of identification for the construction of a feminine heroics. Neither, however, does the actress playing her risk becoming the site of spectatorial desire. By metonymically displacing Marie-Ange to the cassette, Schwarz-Bart has uncannily side-stepped the difficult issue of the "male gaze," and the possibility that the public has learned to see as a gendered male, always positioning the staged female character as object of its desire. Wilnor becomes the "watched" character, displaying his body and baring his soul.

If Schwarz-Bart evacuates the problem of desire and the staged female body, she does not do away with the presence of Marie-Ange. Indeed her presence, through her recorded voice, dominates the first half of the play. Hers is the essential experience, the one on which Wilnor's reality is predicated. She is the original speaking subject, the weaver of the tale. Wilnor listens and reacts.

Furthermore, she is at hand not only every time Wilnor presses the "on" switch of his cassette recorder, but also and more constantly every time he plumbs his emotional depths. Towards the end of the play, when Wilnor debates how to handle the situation of her infidelity, Marie-Ange's voice emerges not from the cassette, but rather from his "mind." "Moin n'aime chanter, moin n'aime danser" [I love to sing, I love to dance]. Marie-Ange's voice challenges Wilnor to reject his original, and predictably outraged, response to her liaison. His final thoughts echo and develop her earliest explanation of how she came to be with another man:

> *Marie-Ange.* This is earth, Wilnor, and on earth everything is whirlwind and smoke. There are none of the straight, wide lanes of heaven.
>
> *Wilnor.* That's it, that's exactly it. Ah yes, separation is a big ocean, which muddles everything; it

shakes things up like a cupful of dice. You start seeing with your ears, hearing with your eyes and feeling with your hands things that are very far away, while the things nearby that surround you, you notice no more than a puff of smoke.

Understanding the legitimacy of Marie-Ange's desire and the needs of her body—something which Marie-Ange herself has admitted and never regretted—Wilnor takes back the epithet "tramp."

He advises her, instead: "Don't trouble your soul if you want the child to come into the world with a good start."

Inhabited by Marie-Ange's voice: "I heard your voice . . . and I saw the light . . . as though I had an electric light bulb in my throat," the Wilnor of the play's end refuses separation. He will continue to house her in a constant dialogue, neither subjugated by her voice nor attempting to silence it. He accepts the coming child as has Marie-Ange, metaphorically bridging the gulf which had nearly cut them off from each other for good. Unlike so many of his dramatic predecessors, Wilnor will not see his wife as solely whore or mother. She is not his "possession dispossessed" but rather an extension of what he also is. What might, then, have seemed like a masculine nightmare turns out to be a lifesaver. Theirs is a love story in which empowerment comes from recognizing similarity rather than establishing otherness.

Otherness, nevertheless, stakes out its claim in this play. But otherness in *Your Handsome Captain* is a matter of "national" or regional mythic structures—those which imprison as well as those which give strength. Wilnor and Marie-Ange are both enslaved by the white man's capitalist dream. Their physical apartness results directly from the terrible poverty of Haiti, plundered for generations by Europeans, Americans, and American-supported dictators. Their victimization also stems from Wilnor's integration of a consumer mentality. Marie-Ange chides him: "But you—whose soul was always full of marvels—you wanted daily bread, the whole loaf, and more. You spoke of striking it rich; you dreamed of buying land by the river and a cow. Every night you dreamed of that. I could hear you. And I got to like your dream. . . . That's why I let you get on that plane." Wilnor's desire to own things, to buy dresses for his wife, to lie about his prowess with the "jazzy mulatto" girls, speaks to Frantz Fanon's condemnation of "lactification," the colonized person's wearing of white masks, his or her interiorization of white hopes. Obsessed by his fantasy of wealth, Wilnor even pretends to live in what could easily be the replica of a colonial plantation: "a large white house with pillars, a big front door, and so many electric light bulbs that [you float] among the stars."

Marie-Ange's adultery gives Wilnor the chance to dig out

from under the weight of the myth of money and possessions. As he responds to her revelation, he gradually rids himself of the myth's trappings. He acknowledges that he has never seduced any other women at all. In a moment of extreme dramatic tension, he burns the secret cache of bills he has put aside to guarantee an even rosier retirement. And he finally comes to grips with the here and now, seeing the baby to come as no one's property, but rather as the sign of a different future. He seems to accept as his only real space the space created by his wife's voice.

That this voice sings in creole is singularly important, for it is through her song and Wilnor's dancing–that is, through two authentic cultural expressions of the Antilles—that Wilnor works out his liberation. In *Your Handsome Captain,* Schwarz-Bart thus uses the indigenous culture of the Antilles to articulate and structure her characters' emotional release. As noted earlier, Marie-Ange's last triumphant rendition of the creole beguine which resonates throughout the text finally releases Wilnor from his need to punish her. Filtered through his consciousness, the song helps him remember that he has always loved the "winged woman who sings like a dragonfly despite the tons of sorrow dragging on her skirts." Marie-Ange (Marie-Angel), the "generating angel," the "flying voice," permits Wilnor to fly too—to allow his imagination to take flight. Her song creates a space of liberty, a potential for a new text of their lives.

Since the early eighteenth century, dancing has been a way for Caribbean people of African descent to impose their own structure on an existence outwardly controlled by others. In *Your Handsome Captain,* Schwarz-Bart emphasizes this in her introductory didascalia: "This more or less secret means of expression is common in the Caribbean." Schwarz-Bart has Wilnor dance eight times in *Your Handsome Captain.* With each dance, he exteriorizes the process of decision making, drawing obvious strength from African roots as he comes closer to finding a solution to the chaos wreaked on him ostensibly by his wife, but, in fact, by the internalization of "foreign" ideals. As he does while listening to Marie-Ange's voice, Wilnor also "flies" while dancing, resembling more and more, according to Schwarz-Bart's directions, a "winged creature." Joining figuratively the radiant and radiating Marie-Ange, Wilnor appears in his penultimate dance to have conquered all worlds. Through dancing—and music in general—Schwarz-Bart proclaims that his African heritage as reinterpreted in local culture has saved Wilnor from complete surrender to the dominant values of the West.

Freedom from Eurocentric culture, including Eurocentric feminist culture, comes strikingly to the fore in Schwarz-Bart's handling of the title and informing image of the play, "your handsome captain." This is a variation on Marie-Ange's endearment for Wilnor, "handsome captain of my ship." With a nod in the direction of his wife, Wilnor also refers to himself in these terms. While he laughs at the beginning, his rendition grows more and more shaky as the play draws to a close. An initial interpretation might conclude that through her insistence on "your handsome captain," Schwarz-Bart merely perpetuates the conventional "woman as vessel / man as pilot and passenger" trope, achingly familiar to readers of, for example, Baudelaire's "exotic" poetry. Marie-Ange in one instance dreams aloud to Wilnor: "Wilnor, I wish I were a boat sailing to Guadeloupe. Once there, you'd climb inside me, you'd walk on my decks, you'd place your hands on my frame, you'd explore me from stem to stern. And then you would set sail and I would take you to a country far, far, far away."

A traditional reading of the phallocentric vessel-pilot sort would, however, ignore the fact that the characters of *Your Handsome Captain* are black, as is the author, and that for people of African descent everywhere in the diaspora, images of ships, captains, and the sea are irremediably marked by the experience of the middle passage—the deathly voyage of slave ships from Africa to the "New" World. Schwarz-Bart, through Marie-Ange, recodes the terms and thus attempts to counter the pain and trauma of imagery connected to the forced capture and exile of some fifteen million people. In establishing herself as "ship," Marie-Ange would shore up Wilnor by putting him again in contact with the reality of her material being as well as by transporting him to a place "where people don't look at you as though you were nothing, dried-out coconuts." They would thus simultaneously "be home" and find a home together.

Schwarz-Bart reinscribes, nonetheless, what can be understood as her own feminist slant in the way "your handsome captain" is put into question in the last short segment of the play. Wilnor has heard Marie-Ange's story and come to accept it. He expresses his hope that the child will be as "beautiful as an angel"; that is, like her—Marie-Ange. And he signs off once, "Your Handsome Captain." But he no longer knows either how to say the phrase or what it means. In four subsequent variations, he queries the truth of the possessive adjective, the descriptive "handsome," and the notion of captaincy. The experience of Marie-Ange's story has completely destabilized him. Whose captain is he? Is he a captain at all?

This destabilizing of Wilnor, rather than negative, should be construed as positive for both characters. It plays the crucial role among Schwarz-Bart's tactics of a double liberation. In the first place, if Wilnor is not Marie-Ange's captain and she is not at his command, then they are both free to negotiate a different and nonstatic relationship. In the second place, being "captain of one's ship" (or one's fate, as it were) inevitably brings to mind such bards of imperialism as Rudyard Kipling, who always quite jauntily disclose that in order to be captain someone else has to be chained to the galley and the oars. In the end, Schwarz-Bart's ironic rever-

sals torpedo the whole figurative constellation of commodores, repositories, and stewards. She would seem to reject any mode of power based on individual will (Will-no[t]), positing instead a vision which imagines the future in terms of community and dialogue.

Critic Françoise Lionnet's notion of *métissage* (understood here as the braiding of cultural forms in a work which simultaneously reevaluates Western concepts and rediscovers the value of oral and other cultural traditions) obtains directly to Schwarz-Bart's play. As is shown of the Francophone women writers Lionnet discusses in *Autobiographical Voices: Race, Gender, Self-Portraiture,* Schwarz-Bart also "articulates a vision of the future founded on individual and collective solidarities, respectful of cultural specificities, and opposed to all rigid, essentializing approaches to questions of race, class, or gender." Similar to the writers that Jonathan Ngaté analyzes in what he terms the "third" and most recent stage of Francophone literature, Schwarz-Bart is concerned to distance herself from Western models which themselves may reproduce the thought processes which make colonization possible. That she does so in a dramatic form which has been inspirational to the many Guadeloupian audiences who have seen *Your Handsome Captain* speaks eloquently to the evolving task of theater in the Antilles to supplement and question both mainstream French theater and the received wisdom of traditional story-tellers. It speaks, too, to the unending potential of theater to open spaces where multiplicity and diversity can be affirmed.

Karen Smyley Wallace (essay date March 1997)

SOURCE: "Créolité and the Feminine Text in Simone Schwarz-Bart," in *The French Review,* Vol. 70, No. 4, March, 1997, pp. 554-61.

[*In the following essay, Wallace examines Schwarz-Bart's use of language in* Pluie et vent sur Télumée Miracle *and the French feminist notion of "écriture féminine," or distinctly female writing.*]

Both to the casual reader of Simone Schwarz-Bart or to the more serious scholar, ***Pluie et vent sur Télumée Miracle*** stands out as a work which memorably captures the essence of the "univers créole" while paying hommage to the majesty of Caribbean women. Because it highlights the endurance of the "esprit antillais" and captures the colorful, folkloric richness of the rural Guadeloupean population, it stands as an acknowledged reflection of "créolité," at its very core. But what of the feminine aspect of this novel? How is the text conceived? What can be said about the feminine writing aesthetic? At first glance, there would appear to be little if any connection between the proponents of "créolité," as it is defined by current Antillean thinkers and writers, and the ideas expressed by modern French feminist literary criticism. Indeed, the author, herself, claims no particular allegiance to a school of literary thought or political action, and has quite simply said on occasion, "J'écris pour les miens: j'écris pour moi-même." Nevertheless, if one sets out to expand or reconfigure the definitions of "créolité," there is an unmistakeable link between the philosophical and cultural "calling to arms" of "créolité," on one hand, and the proponents of writing the feminine text, on the other.

The purpose of this article is to demonstrate how language serves as the nexus between these two seemingly unrelated concepts: the literary axel that stabilizes these two wheels and provides the dynamic force behind them. I am interested in how Schwarz-Bart accomplishes this. What linguistic magic does she use? I propose that it is the element of language-fusion which both enhances the narrative style and which is critical to the revelation of "créolité" and the female self. What we observe here is more than a superficial attempt at the "creolization" of French in this novel. Instead, the author seems to penetrate the French text, and to infuse within it creole patterns and rhythms which alter the original and result in a substantially new language. Neither synthetic nor decorative, this new language begins to take on the more complex properties inherent in cultural bilingualism. In *Le Discours Autillais,* Glissant defines "langue" as a certain "collectivité pratique": a mode of communication which can be learned at birth, borrowed, at times optional, at times imposed. There is a marked difference, however, between this mere tool of communication and the more psychologically complex notion of "language," which, according to Glissant, adds new dimensions, introduces subtleties and nuances which contribute to the cultural specificity of a people. If we look at this phenomenon as a type of visceral understanding of the symbols and meanings behind words, then, when Glissant says: "Je te parle dans ta langue," we understand the subtle connotations in the response "et c'est dans mon language que je te comprends."

From this perspective, Schwarz-Bart's work takes on a greater significance. The novel serves as a backdrop for the creation of this "language within a language" and the revelation of the female self. Revisiting this 1972 prize-winning piece will reveal some of these convergences of "créolité" within the feminine text, and will elucidate the novel in a new and fresher literary light. In order to provide structure to a somewhat elusive topic, I have focused this article around two central themes. First, how Schwarz-Bart depicts a certain "vision du monde créole" and how this converges with what the French feminist writer, Héléne Cixous [in *The Newly Born Woman*], calls "the inexhaustible feminine Imaginary." A second theme will explore the intimacy of the

text itself, in order to show how the author renders her work at once creole and feminine, through the subtleties of language.

Creole "Vision du Monde" and the Feminine Imaginary

While there is no one definition of the "vision du monde créole," the writers of the *Eloge de la Créolite* refer to it as a particular "attitude intérieure . . . une enveloppe mentale au mitan de laquelle se bâtira notre monde en pleine conscience du monde." Whether this "attitude intérieure" describes events of a past life or reflects the complexities of modern Caribbean society, at all times, it draws its strength and vitality from the richness of the rural populations: the tales that unfold up in the "mornes," in the small villages and hamlets, with the many memorable characters whose stories are shared in the musically rich creole language. At their best these literary pieces bring life to everyday events as they depict "nos manières de rire, de chanter, de marcher, de vivre la mort, de juger la vie . . . d'aimer et de parler l'amour." ***Pluie et vent*** uncontestably satisfies these requirements and, at the same time serves as a rich repository of what feminist writers call the "inexhaustible feminine Imaginary." Images of the feminine and "créolité" converge within the language of the text and are best reflected as they reveal woman as symbol and woman as metaphor.

One of the most prominent examples of symbolism which unleashes Schwarz-Bart's rich imagination as a female writer and also highlights the creole spirit of her characters is through the use of the elements of water, land and wind, as suggested by the very title. Through metaphor and language-fusion, the author is able to either describe or suggest a sense of the island women as they experience life. Toussine epitomizes this imagery, when the townsfolk call her "un morceau de monde, un pays tout entier, un panache de négresse, la barque, la voile et le vent." Often the phases of a woman's life are referred to as "les eaux de ma vie," as she, symbolized by "la barque enlisée" launched upon these waters. At all times a woman must learn to navigate successfully on these waters and to be prepared to face the constant currents of life itself, referred to as "une mer sans escale," "une vague sans fin."

Frequently, woman is metamorphosed into river; larger, more turbulent, a force trying to rock the boat while she attempts to keep it on course. On occasion, the image is one of rushing waters churning within the woman, exposing her to new experiences, unleashing new feelings. As Télumée passes from the innocence of girlhood, she comments: "l'école ne pouvait empêcher nos eaux de grossir et le moment vint ou elle ouvrit ses vannes, nous abandonnant au courant," and later, when she matures: "S'il n'y avait eu qu'Elie, je serais une rivière." At all times, the river is symbolically present. At other times, the image of water changes dramatically as it becomes a place for symbolic cleansing, "J'ai lâché mon chagrin au fond de la rivière," Télumée tells us, as she expulses Jérémie from her heart and mind and sets about to "reprendre mon voyage sur l'eau." Finally, the author uses the symbol of water to create the sense of peacefulness and repose as the older Télumée contemplates death and the notion that she, as "la barque" will soon undertake a longer spiritual journey into the hereafter.

As we continue this investigation of how Schwarz-Bart renders her text both creole and feminine, we note the variety of ways in which she has used the symbol of nature, or the land, to enhance this aspect of her work. Through the artistry of language and metaphor she has been able to fuse the notion of woman and land into one symbol, with three manifestations. First, when land represents the mother figure, it is all giving: the nurturer. In page after page, we encounter a veritable profusion of trees, flowers, herbs all acting as visual metaphors for woman. Through language-fusion, woman becomes "basilier rouge," "peau d'acajou," "un fétu de paille sèche," "une gousse de vanille," "fruit à pain," or the omnipresent "fleur de coco." At other points, Schwarz-Bart takes the woman/land symbol and renders it jealous, deceitful, able to take away what it had so bountifully provided. We recall the rainy season on Fond Zombi, which left the land and the people in desolation. We further recall Toussine's sense of devastation as a fire destroyed her house, gardens and took the life of her little girl, Méranée. At that point, the land unrelentingly sapped the strength of its men and women. Only time and patience would bring about a renewal of faith in nature, manifest in the act of woman's replanting:

> Toussine mettait des rideaux aux fenêtres, plantait des oeillets d'Inde autour de la ruine, des pois d'Angole, des racines, des touffes de canne congo . . . et un beau jour, elle mit en terre un pépin d'orange à colibris.

Just as we have observed in the symbolic use of water throughout the story, land also becomes a place of refuge and spiritual reverence. One remembers vividly how young Télumée is overwhelmed by the magic of Fond-Zombi as it unfolds before her, what she calls, "une lointaine éclaircie fantastique, mornes après mornes, savanes après savanes." Later, when Télumée is finally safe from the various winds, or "averses qui m'ont trempée et les vents qui m'ont secouée," she experiences ultimate peace within her surroundings once again: a type of cyclical return to nature as provider and nurturer. Here, land serves as the creative space for physical comfort and symbolic rebirth. As Télumée ends her days, she acknowledges that the island had given to her, had taken away and once again was providing her with the most essential yet simplest of needs: "mes grands bois . . . un arbre à pain, un groseiller, un citronnonier . . . un jardin

de vieille, une chaudière ou je fais griller mes cacahuètes que je vends sur la place de l'église."

Rendering the Text Creole

Scholars have already written and commented on Schwarz-Bart's remarkable ability to completely immerse the reader in a linguistic fictional space where the characters come to life and appear to communicate in creole; where French is syntactically preserved but takes on the music of spoken creole. While this is true, I believe that Schwarz-Bart's writing aesthetic involves a more complex literary technique. Her work gives meaning to what Glissant [in *Le Discours antillais*] called the creation of "un language" within "une langue," a process more intricate and subtle than simply reinventing or creolizing French. More accurately, Schwarz-Bart penetrates the linguistic space and reorders the language of the text so that simultaneously it reveals the oral nature of creole and the feminine as well. By using language in this way the author not only highlights the cultural specificity of the story being told but also celebrates creole as the mother tongue of the Caribbean: "le véhicule original de notre moi-profond."

While the inner Caribbean self is revealed through language, one wonders at what point it intersects with the feminine writing identity—how language is selected and rendered in order to produce the feminine text. Perhaps the most striking way, in feminist critical thinking, lies in the very notion of penetrating the language of the text and of taking it over: giving words a feminine palpability, what is called [in *New French Feminisms*] "la chair linguistique." When the writers of the *Eloge* discuss Caribbean bilingualism, they speak on the idea of inhabiting a language: a process which includes stretching it, bending it, twisting it yet ultimately enrichening the original language in its lexical and syntactical sense. In feminist critical thinking [in *The Body and the Text*], the process is similarly described as taking on a language and making it "stretch, shift or even swell as though it were matter and as though we could hear its working." Schwarz-Bart, therefore, enters the language of her text and inhabits it in two ways: as woman writer, as creole woman. She amplifies the original language and transforms it into something greater than itself through this language-fusion: reminiscent in many ways of a musical fugue: a composition in which the integrity of each voice is maintained while a new, altered musical pattern is produced combining them all. In fact the music of the text is a critical factor linking the orality of creole to the feminine language used in Schwarz-Bart's writing. Word choices and usage in both instances are enhanced through imagery, color, and particularly sound and rhythm.

In her call to women to immerse themselves in writing, Cixous [in *Newly Born Woman*] set forth a type of blueprint describing the multiple dimensions and shapes the feminine text could take. "Let her write!" she implored. "And her text knows in seeking itself that it is more than flesh and blood, dough kneading itself, rising, uprising openly with resounding, perfumed ingredients, a turbulent compound of flying colors, leafy spaces and rivers flowing to the sea." By broadening the interpretations contained within Cixous' message, we can see that Schwarz-Bart indeed excels in her descriptions of "perfumed ingredients," "flying colors," "leafy spaces," "rivers flowing." The entire world surrounding the Lougandor women calls upon the author's keen sense of the visual: recreating the lush, the verdant, the incredible pallet of colors. The "leafy spaces" described by Cixous are subtly rendered in Schwarz-Bart's hands and take various forms. Physical space is sensed in the passing through the hills and "mornes" from Fond-Zombi, to l'Autre-Bord, to Balata Bell Bois and back again. At other times language is crafted in order to create psychic or emotional space. Schwarz-Bart deftly enters small areas in the narrative and magnifies them creating an altered sense of depth and proportion. We are reminded here of the passage describing young Télumée's sense of safety as she contemplates the wonder and power of the protective folds in her grandmother, Toussine's, apron: "je me sentis comme dans une forteresse, à l'abri de toutes choses connues et inconnues, sous la protection de la grande jupe à fronces de grand-mère." This passage also reflects what is called the "feminine light"; that is, the light with which the female writer can see "the veins and nerves of matter."

While the language of the text can have visual or spatial connotations, it is in the area of movement, sound, and music that feminine writing and "créolité" most easily intersect in Schwarz-Bart's work. Examples of this are sometimes apparent in the tone or rhythm of the words themselves: "canne-congo," "biguine doux-sirop," "baguette de bambou." At other times there is syncopation within the dialogue or rhythmical placement of whole passages which enhance the musicality of the entire piece: "A présent, j'entendais et n'entendais pas, je voyais et ne voyais pas et le vent qui passait sur moi rencontrait un autre vent" or "la Reine, la Reine, qui dit qu'il n'y a rien pour moi sur la terre, qui dit pareille bêtise? . . . parle-moi de la vie grand-mère, parle-moi de ça." Again, all of these manifestations derive from Schwarz-Bart's creative ability to inhabit the language of her text, to slip inside of the words, thereby creating feminine zones, using the poetics of spoken creole, and ultimately crafting a special "language" within "une langue."

Rendering the Text Feminine

As we continue the exploration of the feminine in Schwarz-Bart's work, there are two themes which are critical to a broader understanding of the novel and of what is involved in the feminine writing identity: woman as sensual and woman as maternal.

When Hélène Cixous encourages woman to "write her body" [in *Newly Born Woman*], she focuses an intense, high powered light on the area of sensuality in the feminine text. Not the simple calling forth of erotic images designed to titillate, but instead a visceral, deeply rooted approach to unleashing and expressing female creativity. One might call this a kind of love making of words, images and ideas. In its celebration of the women of Guadeloupe, ***Pluie et vent*** offers many examples of the text as a sensual craft. What stands out in Schwarz-Bart's use of sensuality in the novel, is the manner in which she incorporates these elements and weaves them naturally into her work. First, there is the spatial zone of the body; sometimes observed by others, as when the women in the community make good natured references to Télumée's developing breasts. Sometimes rendered by a woman's own sense of her femininity, as when Télumée recognizes her own physical development and the accompanying new emotions: "J'avais quatorze ans sur mes deux seins et sous ma robe d'indienne à fleur, j'étais une femme." Throughout the novel Schwarz-Bart describes the various phases in a woman's life with specific reference to the body, "mes seins de femme," "ventre de femme," "femme libre à mes deux seins," "jambes de femme."

As one moves beyond the physical zone of the body, the author tactfully weaves the theme of sensuality throughout various scenes, highlighting the male/female relations in the story. Among these, some of the more memorable scenes take place between Télumée, as a young woman, with her first love, Elie, and later, as a mature woman, in what she calls "ma belle saison," with the older Amboise. In both instances the author evokes the eroticism in the passages by drawing upon what feminist literary criticism [in *New French Feminisms*] calls "the corporality of language." Here she makes clever use of a kind of love play illustrating the fusion of nature, woman and the sensual. A particularly vivid example begins with a poetic love language, a call and response pattern, reminiscent of the rhythmical "cric/crac" of creole storytelling: "Lorsque' Amboise me parlait de citrons, je lui répondais en citrons et si je disais coupe, il ajoutait hache." And then, expanding the symbolism in order to allow the words to vacillate among color, aroma, sound and movement, Schwarz-Bart writes: "A mesure que notre sueur pénétrait cette terre, elle devenait notre, se mettait à l'odeur de nos corps, de notre fumée et de notre manger, des éternels boucans d'acomats verts, acres et piquants." The association between lovemaking interwoven within the bountiful Guadeloupean produce, "gombos, malangas, bananes poteaux," symbolizes the fertility of both the land and the woman.

And what of the maternal? How can both the woman and

the text be defined as maternal in feminist critical thinking? For obvious reasons, we are not concerned here with the superficial number of female characters in the story, nor the motherly roles played by each. The maternal, in this instance, speaks to the interior of the text, that point at which the writer gives shape, definition and texture to the language; gives birth to feminine writing. Cixous [in *Newly Born Woman*] explains the maternal in the female writer as her way with words. They are a constant source of "repairing, feeding," what I refer to as the nurturing of the text.

> Text, my body: traversed by lilting flows; listen to me, it is not a captivating, clinging "mother"; it is the equivoice that, touching you, affects you, pushes you away from your breast to come to language . . . the one intimately addressed who makes all metaphors, all body . . . possible and desirable . . . the part of you that puts space between yourself and pushes you to inscribe your woman's style in language.

By the very fact that she has so artfully "inscribed her woman's style in language," at all times protecting the creole essence of her text and her characters, Schwarz-Bart, indeed, renders her work maternal. One could say that she has given birth to a specialized and intricate language. As a female writer, she has raised this language up, so to speak, and has carefully nurtured the words, symbols and the sheer poetry of the text. Just as we are assured that Télumée's strength and resilience will pass on from this life, only to be reborn in others, the language in this novel will continue to epitomize the feminine as well as the "permanence de l'esprit antillais" [Wallace attributes this quote to a Schwarz-Bart interview in *Textes et Etudes Documents 2,* 1979]).

In *Pluie et vent,* Schwarz-Bart has done more than amuse us with a creole tale. Through the artistry of language-fusion she has taken us inside a remarkable and specialized world, where she has expanded the confines of French and has created a thoroughly creole ambiance. By taking a simple island story she has developed it into a timeless act with universal implications. The idea of endurance and continuity is a critical point of intersection between "créolité" and the modern feminist aesthetic. The writers of the *Eloge* have placed great importance on the relationship between the "spécificité créole" and the broader world: what they refer to as "le Tout-Monde dans une dimension particulière." When Hélène Cixous reflects on the idea of endurance she speaks to the breadth and power within women's words; words, she says [in *New French Feminisms*], that "can only

keep going on without ever inscribing or discerning contours." She characterizes feminine language as the very voice of the text: mothers milk. Viewed from this perspective, Simone Schwarz-Bart's classic creole tale epitomizes what Cixous [in *Newly Born Woman*] would call "milk that could go on forever."

FURTHER READING

Criticism

Garane, Jeanne. "A Politics of Location in Simone Schwarz-Bart's *Bridge of Beyond*." *College Literature* 22 (February 1995): 21-36.
    Concludes that Télumée's turning her back to the ocean at the end of *Bridge of Beyond* indicates her severance of ties to both Africa and France, solving the identity crisis of colonized peoples by claiming her new homeland as her own.

McKinney, Kitzie. "Télumée's Miracle: The Language of the Other and the Composition of Self in Simone Schwarz-Bart's *Pluie et vent sur Télumée Miracle*." *Modern Language Studies* XX, No. 4 (Fall 1989): 58-65.
    Examines the connection between individual and community as represented by the poetic language of Schwarz-Bart in *Pluie et vent sur Télumée Miracle*.

Updike, John. "Saganland and the Back of Beyond." *The New Yorker* (12 August 1974): 95-8.
    Notes that *The Bridge of Beyond* is sometimes overly sentimental, but ultimately rewarding in its lyricism and the "generosity" with which the author tells the story.

Wallace, Karen Smyley. "The Female and the Self in Schwarz-Bart's *Pluie et vent sur Télumée Miracle*." *The French Review* 59, No. 3 (February 1986): 428-36.
    Examines various constructs of women's lives present in *Pluie et vent sur Télumée Miracle* and the ways in which women's relations with others and self come together to create a full self.

Wilson, Elizabeth Betty. "History and Memory in *Un plat de porc aux bananes vertes* and *Pluie et vent sur Télumée Miracle*." *Callaloo* 15, No. 1 (Winter 1992): 179-89.
    Discusses the ways in which Schwarz-Bart's novels attempt to reclaim a history for black West Indian women.

Additional coverage of Schwarz-Bart's life and works is contained in the following sources published by Gale: *Black Writers,* **Vol. 2;** *Contemporary Authors,* **Vol. 97-100; and** *Contemporary Literary Criticism,* **Vol. 7.**

Cornel West
1953-

(Full name Cornel Ronald West) American philosopher, educator, writer and social critic.

INTRODUCTION

A public figure who speaks frequently on issues of common concern for African Americans and whites alike, Cornel West has been called one of "the foremost modern intellectuals." As a thinker and chronicler of contemporary thought, West draws inspiration from Malcolm X and Martin Luther King, Jr., while expanding on the work of Richard Rorty and John Dewey to develop a philosophy he terms "prophetic pragmatism." West sees intellectuals as "cultural workers." To that end, he has committed himself to demystifying philosophy and applying it to practical issues that American society struggles with daily, such as multiculturalism and cultural diversity, Eurocentrism, race relations, socialism, sexism, and poverty. In his own words, West's objectives are to "uphold the moral character of the black freedom struggle in America." In his quest to achieve this goal West has combined a recognition of American society's moral failure with an optimism about the future.

Biographical Information

West was born June 2, 1953, in Tulsa, Oklahoma, the son of Clifton L., Jr., a civilian Air Force administrator, and Irene (maiden name Bias), an elementary school teacher. His grandfather was a Baptist minister, which later influenced West's emergence as a public speaker. West was raised in a black neighborhood in Sacramento, California. While in high school during the 1960s he participated in political demonstrations with family and friends and, in efforts to have courses in Black Studies added to his school's curriculum, he coordinated a strike with three other students. West graduated magna cum laude from Harvard (where he was a Du Bois fellow) with a Bachelor of Arts in 1973, and from Princeton with a Master of Arts in 1975. He earned a Ph.D. from Princeton in 1980. While a graduate student at Princeton he came under the influence of philosopher Richard Rorty, an authority on American Pragmatism, and Martin Luther King, Jr., who brought together ideas that West had embraced during his childhood. West has explained some of these ideas as "a Christian ethic of love-informed service to others, ego-deflating humility about oneself owing to the precious yet fallible humanity of others, and politically engaged struggle for social betterment." West recalls being very taken as a youth by "the sincere black militancy of Malcolm X, the defiant rage of the Black Panther Party,

and the livid black theology of James Cone," a writer and professor of religion at Union Theological Seminary in New York, where West was an assistant professor from 1977 to 1983. Politically West has been affiliated with the Democratic Socialists of America, becoming, in 1997, honorary co-chair. Currently a professor at Harvard, West has had previous appointments at Princeton, Yale University, and the University of Paris.

Major Works

In *The Ethical Dimensions of Marxist Thought* (1991), West explains that his descent from seven generations of Africans who were "enslaved and exploited, devalued and despised," by Euro-Americans, and three subsequent generations who were "subordinated and terrorized," has greatly influenced his views. West explores this mindset most prominently in *Race Matters* (1993), in which he envisions solutions to the seeming impasses of race relations and cultural misunderstandings. Ellis Cose writes that West "sees salvation in a renewal of love, empathy and compassion, in a radical redistribution of power and wealth." This observation identifies two tendencies in West's sensibility and background: that of the church and socialist politics. According to West, political solutions are only one part of the picture. "The liberal notion that more government programs can solve racial problems is simplistic," wrote West, "precisely because it focuses *solely* on the economic dimension." He also faults the conservative idea that change has to come from the attitudes of poor blacks in urban centers since this position sidesteps "public responsibility for the immoral circumstances that haunt our fellow citizens." West acknowledges the influence of Martin Luther King, Jr. and Malcolm X, although he "seems more comfortable with King's prophetic integrationism than with Malcolm's militant nationalism," observes Arch Puddington. Puddington asserts that West focuses on "spiritual values and the need to revive a sense of community as steps toward racial reconciliation." In *The American Evasion of Philosophy* (1989), West's concerns are more philosophical and ideological. Philosopher K. Anthony Appiah sees "a subtle polemic against the dangers of the highly influential new pragmatism." *Keeping Faith* (1993) takes an academic approach in its wide-ranging essays on culture and philosophy. In contrast, *Beyond Eurocentrism and Multiculturalism* (1993) incorporates a more popular frame of reference in its selection of thought-provoking interviews and speeches on politics and culture.

Critical Reception

While critics often praise West's analytical skills and his observations of American society, they sometimes find fault with his reasoning and the substance of his proposed solutions. Glenn C. Loury salutes West's influence on social and cultural policy, but complains that "because West writes more in the manner of the prophet than in that of the analyst, he never stays long enough with any one point." Arch Puddington, reviewing *Race Matters,* finds that West has "hazy and substanceless prescriptions for change." Puddington also objects to West's reliance on the rhetoric of progressive politics, because "by repeatedly stating that capitalism is the root cause of the American racial dilemma, and that little real change can be achieved without a fundamental reorganization of the economy," West "deflects many of the crucial and divisive issues over which America is now agonizing." West has many admirers, however, including Martin Kilson, a Harvard professor who applauds West's having "single-handedly fashioned a viable transracial style of intellectual discourse." K. Anthony Appiah echoes this sentiment, asserting that West "may well be the pre-eminent African-American intellectual of our generation." Furthermore, many see West's prophetic voice as one of his strengths. Norman Spencer compares West "to the black preachers, blues singers, and jazz musicians who have influenced him" and suggests that West's oratorical gift lies in the fact that he "manages to create hybrid modes of address that combine the abstract and the vernacular in such a

manner that each reinforces the other." Spencer also finds West's work "impressive because of its intellectual range and perceptive analysis," and states further that "what stands out above all is its provocative spirit, its conscious attempt to challenge preconceived notions and bring to light the often subtle interconnections between politics, culture, and society."

PRINCIPAL WORKS

Post-Analytic Philosophy (philosophy) 1985
The American Evasion of Philosophy (philosophy) 1989
Breaking Bread: Insurgent Black Intellectual Life [with bell hooks] (philosophy) 1991
The Ethical Dimensions of Marxist Thought (philosophy) 1991
Beyond Eurocentrism and Multiculturalism (philosophy) 1993
Keeping Faith: Philosophy and Race in America (philosophy) 1993
Race Matters (philosophy) 1993
The Future of the Race [with Henry Louis Gates, Jr.] (philosophy) 1996

CRITICISM

K. Anthony Appiah (review date 9 April 1990)

SOURCE: "A Prophetic Pragmatism," in *The Nation,* April 9, 1990, pp. 496-98.

[*In the following review Appiah explains the argument West presents in* The American Evasion of Philosophy, *namely that pragmatism offers more politically than philosopher Richard Rorty has claimed.*]

At least since Homer, in the European tradition, but surely everywhere and everywhen in societies both oral and literate, communities have fashioned themselves around stories of the past, chronicles that constitute "us" as Hellenes or Yorubas or Americans. And at least since Aristotle, Western philosophers have been constructing histories that place at the center of their ancestors' projects the very problems they now claim to be able to solve themselves. Both kinds of story often contain a fair degree of fancy, molding history into a usable narrative. One way of seeing Hegel's distinctive contribution to the philosophy of history is as a cementing of these two genres: Hegel understood the past of philosophy in protonationalist terms as a relay in which human self-understanding was the baton and the runners were historical communities. (It is not too much of a caricature to add that the historic task of the Germans was to cross the finish line and declare themselves the winners.) In this Hegelian conception philosophers are not merely accidental citizens of this or that nation, embedded in this or that culture. German philosophy, for Hegel, is not just the expression in the German language and by Germans of ideas and arguments that could just as easily have been made elsewhere. Not only is the core of German philosophy intimately bound up with German culture but the German people are bound together in part by German philosophy.

In recent years Richard Rorty has been conducting a campaign to persuade us that we should come to such an understanding of American philosophy. Rorty believes his own development of pragmatism—an unlikely melding of liberalism and postmodernism, of solidarity and irony—is the last best hope, not of man (nor even of humankind) but of America (or, sometimes, of something he calls European culture, in which he seems to include both himself and much of American "high" culture). If there is much that is appealing in Rorty's antifoundationalism, his liberal revulsion against human cruelty and his arguments for pluralism, there is something worrisome, too, in his deliberate ethnocentrism and the conservatism that flows from his political pessimism. Cornel West's engaging and engaged *The American Evasion of Philosophy* needs to be read as a subtle polemic against the dangers of the highly influential new pragmatism as it celebrates and expands Rorty's insights.

West, who has taught at Yale University and Union Theological Seminary and is now professor of religion and director of Afro-American studies at Princeton University, may well be the pre-eminent African-American intellectual of our generation. Highly influential as a theorist of postmodernism, West bridges cultural theory and the black community, inserting the issue of the progressive potential of the black church, for example, into debates about the politics of postmodernity, while transforming discussions in the black community with his sharp sense of the relevance of theory to its concerns. West's earlier books—*Prophesy Deliverance!*, *Prophetic Fragments* and a notable collection, *Post-Analytic Philosophy,* edited with John Rajchman—have ranged widely. Rooted in a sense of the continuing relevance of Christianity and socialism, his work displays an inexhaustible appetite for ideas and a compelling moral vision. But *The American Evasion of Philosophy* is the most ambitious and original project that he has undertaken.

West's argument is this: While mainstream American academic philosophers have been quietly practicing the epistemologically grounded inquiry that has dominated post-Cartesian philosophy in the West, a distinctive tradition of American philosophical work, pragmatism, has sought to evade this aspect of the Cartesian inheritance. "To evade modern philosophy means to strip the profession of philoso-

phy of its pretense, disclose its affiliations with structures of powers (both rhetorical and political) rooted in the past, and enact intellectual practices . . . that invigorate and unsettle one's culture and society."

Notice that what West seeks to achieve in this passage is an account of the "evasion" of philosophy that combines a poststructuralist demystification of philosophy's pretensions with cultural and political criticism. And while the latter is indeed central, though to varying degrees, in the pragmatism of Emerson, Peirce and James, and above all in the work of Dewey—who is, for West as for Rorty, the pre-eminent pragmatist—persuading us that the former is also a crucial part of the pragmatist inheritance is West's major task in this book.

The argument West makes begins, in essence, with Peirce's crucial formulation of pragmatism in "How to Make Our Ideas Clear": "Consider what effects, that might conceivably have practical bearings, we conceive the object of our conception to have." A philosophy that starts here is bound to undermine the pretensions of a philosophical tradition—the "modern philosophy" the pragmatists evade—whose epistemology is foundationalist, whose ontology is realist and whose understanding of meaning is atomistic. But once we begin to demythologize philosophy, West claims, we must end by "dragging in the complexities of politics and culture."

To pull off the kind of persuasive redefinition that West and Rorty seek requires above all a substantial marshaling of historical scholarship. And West's deployment of intellectual history—his account not merely of the figures most familiar in portraits of pragmatism but also of Sidney Hook, C. Wright Mills, W. E. B. Du Bois, Reinhold Niebuhr and Lionel Trilling—is impressive and compelling. More than this, West's position is not a simple-minded attack on academic philosophy. He argues, for example, that the contributions of the professional philosophers—Quine's holism, Goodman's antireductionism, Sellars's antifoundationalism—are part of what has made the contemporary resurgence of pragmatism possible.

But the heart of the book, its deeper argument, is West's insistence that Rorty has resurrected the wrong Dewey. "Rorty's Dewey," West observes at one point, "is much more intellectually playful and politically tame than the Dewey we examined." What, West asks,

> from an ethical point of view—the central point of view for pragmatists— . . . is the difference that makes a difference here? Rorty's neopragmatism only kicks the philosophic props from under liberal bourgeois capitalist societies; it requires no change in our cultural and political practices. What then are the ethical and political consequences of this

neopragmatism? On the macrosocietal level, there simply are none.

In arguing for his own "prophetic" pragmatism, West seeks to draw on the potentialities American pragmatism offers for radical political critique, and it is here that the work of the early Sidney Hook (Dewey's student but also, for a time, America's most original Marxist), of Du Bois and of C. Wright Mills, is central to his historical argument. No one can deny that these thinkers were self-consciously influenced by pragmatism. When West argues at the end of his book that his prophetic pragmatism, though "deeply indebted to the continental traveling theories such as Marxism, structuralism, and poststructuralism . . . remains in the American grain," it is a conclusion he has earned. *The American Evasion of Philosophy* is thus a gentle rebuke to the pragmatism without consequences of Richard Rorty, and a powerful call for philosophy to play its role in building a radical democracy in alliance with the wretched of the earth.

Arch Puddington (review date August 1993)

SOURCE: "Immoderate Moderate," in *Commentary,* August, 1993, pp. 62-64.

[*In the following review of* Race Matters, *Puddington presents a critical commentary on what he sees as biases underlying West's analysis of racial issues in America.*]

Cornel West has been acclaimed as one of the most important commentators on race relations in America. He has been the subject of feature profiles in major publications and appears frequently on televised public-affairs programs. Henry Louis Gates, Jr., chairman of the Afro-American Studies Department at Harvard, has described West as "the preeminent African-American intellectual of our generation"; according to Marian Wright Edelman, president of the Children's Defense Fund, his is "one of the most authentic, brilliant, prophetic, and healing voices in America today."

Until recently, West's audience has been limited to specialists in the culture and politics of black America. In *Race Matters,* however, West, a professor of religion and director of Afro-American Studies at Princeton, is writing for a much broader public. The essays here, all of which have previously appeared in magazines and books, deal with a number of the most controversial issues of the past several years, including the Los Angeles riots, the Clarence Thomas-Anita Hill confrontation, Malcolm X, affirmative action, and black-Jewish relations.

To a certain extent, the esteem in which West is held derives from his image as a man of moderation. He is not hostile to whites, he refuses to blame all the troubles of the inner city on white racism, and he is critical of black appeals to racial solidarity. Although he pays tribute to both Martin Luther King, Jr. and Malcolm X, West seems more comfortable with King's prophetic integrationism than with Malcolm's militant nationalism. He eschews the traditional liberal calls for urban Marshall Plans, focusing instead on spiritual values and the need to revive a sense of community as steps toward racial reconciliation.

West thus presents himself as steering a prudent centrist course among liberal statism, racial exclusiveness, and the conservative stress on personal conduct. As he puts it here:

> The liberal notion that more government programs can solve racial problems is simplistic—precisely because it focuses *solely* on the economic dimension. And the conservative idea that what is needed is a change in the behavior of poor black urban dwellers (especially poor black men, who, they say, should stay married, support their children, and stop committing so much crime) highlights immoral actions while ignoring public responsibility for the immoral circumstances that haunt our fellow citizens.

But passages like this notwithstanding, West is not, in fact, the centrist he would like us to think him. Although he can issue sweeping pronouncements that suggest a breaking of ranks with today's racial orthodoxies, in the next breath he is capable of blithely contradicting these same positions. An example is his rejection of race-specific solutions, which is followed by an unequivocal endorsement of affirmative action, one of the most divisive race-specific policies ever enacted. He also engages in polemical maneuver—by, for instance, denouncing arguments based on race solidarity and then outlandishly citing as his single case in point the support that many blacks gave to Clarence Thomas.

West engages in such posturing, I believe, in order to camouflage political beliefs which are well to the Left not only of the Center but of contemporary liberalism. Although the word "socialist" hardly appears in these pages, the assessment of American society that West sets forth owes more to the Marxist tradition than to the American civil-rights heritage. West, to be sure, does not focus on social class; rather, his radicalism is intermixed with a kind of New Age politics in which the dynamics of class recede while questions of race, gender, and sexual orientation are brought to the fore. (One laughable sign of West's embrace of the "diversity agenda" is the length to which he goes to be linguistically correct, as in his reference to "Jim and Jane Crow segregation.")

But West does not try to conceal his view that American

capitalism is evil. He writes of life in America as an "empty quest for pleasure, property, and power." Blacks, West contends, "reside in a jungle ruled by a cutthroat market morality" which breeds nihilism and leads, in the inner city, to an environment of utter despair.

It stands to reason that if the American economic system is intrinsically immoral, then those who accept the system have been touched by its corruption. And so it is, West believes, with the black middle class and black political leadership. He excoriates the former for having renounced the "vibrant tradition of resistance" fostered by the civil-rights movement while adopting a life based on "professional conscientiousness, personal accomplishment, and cautious adjustment." Likewise, West criticizes black political leaders for their "lack of authentic anger," and their general stance of accommodation with American ruling elites.

In both instances West's criticisms are unfair, extraordinarily so in the case of the black middle class. The traits he ascribes to black professionals are, in fact, precisely the traits required for successful lives and careers. If more Americans of whatever race were as committed to the work ethic and the idea of excellence as are West's black professionals, the country would be greatly strengthened and our racial climate vastly improved. It hardly needs to be pointed out, moreover, that these professionals represent the first mass black middle class in American history; the eyes of the nation are on their performance at work and at home, and they scarcely need the additional burden of civil-rights protest which West seeks to foist on them.

Much the same can be said for black political leaders. West presumably takes little comfort in the presence of Ron Brown, Mike Espy, Lee Brown, and other blacks in the Clinton administration, since these officials have risen to their current positions not as activist protesters but as professional politicians, and their success can thus be seen as reinforcing the notion that, in one area at least, American race relations are improving. It is precisely this idea—that the system might be working—which West seems least able to tolerate.

Given his treatment of black professionals and politicians, it will come as no surprise that West has little use for black conservatives. The idea, for example, that black conservatives have been the objects of *ad-hominem* attacks earns his scorn—West has evidently paid little attention to the many, many attacks on Thomas Sowell, Glenn Loury, and Clarence Thomas in which the major point has been to deny their credentials as authentic blacks. But more disturbing is West's accusation that "the widespread support black conservatives received from conservatives in the Reagan and Bush administrations and from Jewish neoconservatives has much to do with their views on U.S. foreign policies."

Here we have a perfect example of West's style of debate. As on a number of other issues, he plays loose with the facts: while black conservatives may have written critically of the tendency among black intellectuals to sympathize with authoritarian regimes of the Left, mostly they focus on domestic controversies like affirmative action, busing, and welfare. As for their specific foreign-policy views, West stops short of asserting explicitly that support of American policy is unworthy of a black intellectual, but the implication is unmistakable in his statement that black conservatives are "viewed in many black communities as mere apologists for pernicious U.S. foreign policies."

In a passage highly critical of the entertainment industry, West disparages the "reduction of individuals to objects of pleasure" and bemoans the way our culture has been polluted with "gestures of sexual foreplay and orgiastic pleasure." One might suppose that West, who repeatedly stresses the moral dimension of the racial debate, might find common ground here with conservative critics of the liberal ethos. Yet one will search in vain for any reference to such issues as rap music, the civil-liberties movement, First Amendment absolutism, or the cultural legacy of the 60's—although other black leaders of impeccably liberal reputations have spoken out about precisely such matters. Instead, West reduces all social ills to one issue alone: capitalism, with its "sexual and military images," its marginalized youth, ruined families, and ravaged communities.

One of the most controversial chapters in *Race Matters* deals with relations between blacks and Jews. West himself is very much in the tradition of interracial harmony, at least among those of a progressive political stripe, and there can be no question of his harboring anti-Semitic prejudices. Nevertheless, his attempts to explain the roots of black-Jewish division are deeply flawed, evasive, and less than honest.

West accurately cites affirmative action as a major point of difference between blacks and Jews. But while observing that hostility to preferential treatment is less pronounced among Jews than among other groups, he adds that Jewish opposition "seems to reek of naked group interest, as well as a willingness to abandon compassion for the underdog of American society." This is tantamount to saying that Jewish opposition to affirmative action has nothing to do with concerns about fairness, democracy, or fears of racial balkanization, but is due simply to moral blindness. Nor does West recognize the irony in his reference to Jewish group interests in discussing a policy which openly places one group, blacks, above all others in the apportionment of economic rewards.

An even graver problem emerges in West's treatment of Israel. He begins by acknowledging that some blacks, by failing to grasp the "deep historical sources of Jewish fears and anxieties about group survival," have been oblivious to the "visceral attachment of most Jews to Israel." But Jews, for their part, he writes, fail to recognize what "the symbolic predicament and literal plight of Palestinians in Israel means to blacks." Because of this, blacks see the Jewish defense of Israel as a "second instance of naked group interest" and an "abandonment of substantive moral deliberation."

West then pushes this symmetrical formulation further to the extreme by asserting that black-Jewish ties were especially damaged in the 1980's by the policies of Israel's Likud government: "When mainstream American Jewish organizations supported the inhumane policies of [Menachem] Begin and [Yitzhak] Shamir, they tipped their hats toward cold-hearted interest-group calculations." Blacks, he adds as a balancing afterthought, are not guiltless, either, as when they accept the various conspiracy theories about Jewish economic power.

On almost every point, West's analysis is inaccurate, and often obnoxious as well. The comparison he draws between Begin and Shamir on the one hand and Leonard Jeffries and Louis Farrakhan on the other is absurd, for the obvious reason that the Likud leaders neither said nor did anything inimical to the interests of blacks, while Jeffries and Farrakhan have issued blatantly anti-Semitic declarations and threatened Jews who opposed them.

Furthermore, by focusing on the Likud period, West has either forgotten or is unaware of a bit of relevant history. During the 1960's, it was Israel's Labor government under Golda Meir which was the object of savage attacks by black radicals for its alleged policies of racist genocide and imperialism. More to the heart of the matter, there is no evidence that black resentment of Jews has been significantly fueled by Israel's policies toward the Palestinians, or that black attitudes toward Begin and Shamir were much different from black attitudes toward Margaret Thatcher or Helmut Kohl.

West's observations on blacks and Jews conform to a clear pattern: he attributes a perspective to all blacks or many blacks or some blacks which in fact represents little more than his own opinion or an opinion limited to the relatively small fraternity of like-minded black leftists. And a similar tactic is evident in West's hazy and substanceless prescriptions for change. While he is under no obligation to provide his readers with a laundry list of policy ideas, we can surely expect more than, for example, the assertion that "Nihilism is not overcome by arguments or analyses, it is tamed by love and care." But here too there may well be deliberateness behind the vagueness. By repeatedly stating that capitalism is the root cause of the American racial dilemma, and that little real change can be achieved without a fundamental reorganization of the economy, West skillfully deflects many of the

crucial and divisive issues over which America is now agonizing.

Despite the artful packaging, West's ultimate message is neither new nor courageous. Indeed, were he to argue his case for socialism openly, "one of the most authentic, brilliant, prophetic, and healing voices in America today" might discover that very few were listening.

Norman Spencer (review date March-May 1995)

SOURCE: "Radical Prophesy," in *American Book Review,* March-May, 1995, pp. 21, 27.

[*In the following review of three collections of West's writing, Spencer appraises West's contribution to commentary on social and cultural issues.*]

During the 1980s, Cornel West emerged as one of America's preeminent left-wing intellectuals. A philosopher and theologian by training, a cultural critic by avocation, West has spent his entire academic career in elite institutions—the philosophy, religion, and African-American studies departments at Yale, Union Theological Seminary, Princeton, and Harvard—though by no means have his activities been restricted to this arena alone. Typical of a generation nurtured in the hot house environment of high theory, he is conversant with intellectual currents from both Europe and the Third World as well as with indigenous philosophical traditions, notably pragmatism and homespun variants of Marxism, feminism, and postmodernism. What sets him apart from most of his colleagues is that his perspectives and world view are guided by the oppositional framework of democratic socialism and the transcendent values of African-American religion. They serve as the inspirational wellspring and catalyst for his scholarship and his social and political commitments. Surprisingly, they also account for his recent popularity as a speaker and interpreter of American society. West's exposé of America's socioeconomic inequities, his critique of the imperatives of a consumer culture, his determinations on the conflicts surrounding race, class, and gender, combined with a radical vision of participatory democracy as a potential solution to societal ills, appeal to audiences skeptical of the glib pronouncements of media pundits and cautious politicians. They speak as well to those mystified by the abstract, disembodied rhetoric of experts propitiously removed from the important sites of conflict.

West has a public hearing today because his commitments are not restricted to the academy. He views his role as an intellectual as organically rooted in the struggles of ordinary people; and as a consequence, he consciously attempts to bridge the gap between the university and mainstream society by openly engaging in public dialogue and by reaching out and forging links with those groups and communities most afflicted by our current social morass. West's strength as an intellectual is his interpretation of complex ideas and experiences within the broad context of history, always careful to point out the continuities and ruptures between the past and the present, ever mindful to connect social movements for change to the overriding need for human emancipation and freedom. His credibility derives from his moral integrity and his willingness to listen to and empathize with the concerns of others. His lasting contribution resides in his ability to evoke the power, sophistication, and depth of African-American culture, verifying in the process the contributions and struggles of black people as beacons for the achievements and liberation of others.

Over the past year, four volumes of West's work have been published, making available essays, interviews, book reviews, and public lectures conceived during the last decade. Taken as a whole, they reveal West's stunning intellectual breadth and lay bare his views on politics, culture, and society. Interestingly, given his critique of consumerism, they appear to have been selected and organized with different audiences in mind. The best seller *Race Matters* (Beacon Press), with its timely subject, was put together for the American mainstream. *Keeping Faith* (Routledge Press) with substantial essays and selections on cultural criticism, philosophy, and politics and the emerging critical legal studies movement is geared to academics, while the two volumes *Beyond Eurocentrism and Multiculturalism* (Common Courage Press), a winner of the American Book Award, appeals to engaged intellectuals and community activists with its compilation of public addresses, personal interviews, and a focus on politics and culture. There is some overlap in subject matter in the four volumes, but they all warrant reading if one wants a sense of West's complete vision. Also, a comparison between the formal essay writing and the more informal interviews and public lectures is revealing; for despite the differences in format, there is an unmistakable, distinct voice. West's belief in the reciprocal relationship between the intellectual and society has influenced his style. Remarkably, like the black preachers, blues singers, and jazz musicians who have influenced him, West manages in his most successful and inspiring moments to create hybrid modes of address that combine the abstract and the vernacular in such a manner that each reinforces the other.

The best introduction to West's work is the seminal essay **"Nihilism in Black America"** from the *Race Matters* collection. Here West looks at the plight of America's black working class and poor first by pinpointing the limits and failings of the experts and then by offering an alternative angle of vision and point of reference. In the author's view, neither the "liberal structuralists" who stress institutional constraints on opportunities for African-Americans nor the "conservative behaviorists" who offer the Horatio Alger myth and free market as remedies for urban blight provide adequate analysis or solutions. Both camps overlook or underestimate what West sees as the most important issue facing black America—"the nihilist threat to its very existence." He warns that a new mood of nihilism, the experience of life as meaningless and hopeless, has infected African-American communities and diminished their capacity to thwart off the persistent legacy of racial degradation and devaluation. In the past, according to West's argument, black civil society, namely the church, unions, schools, and a wealth of social, political, and business organizations effectively resisted and challenged the status quo, keeping alive the possibility of overcoming oppression; but with important sections of the black middle class moving into the mainstream and the new global imperatives of a market driven economy, the jobs and networks of support that once sustained black communities are in decline. Add the emergence of a formidable drug subculture and the conditions for social disarray are inevitable.

Symptomatic of the current crisis is the pervasive cynicism and corresponding deep-seated rage that West finds so disturbing. Unchecked, without creative outlets, they threaten the very survival of once cohesive communities. For West, the challenge is to develop the sociopolitical, religious, and cultural institutions that can best address the need of those most under siege and inculcate in them a new sense of self-worth, achievement, and empowerment. West's depiction of anger and despair is not unlike that of James Baldwin's in essays published four decades ago. There is, however, an important difference. When Baldwin was writing, a potential solution existed in the emerging civil rights struggle and the black power movement that followed. In contrast, West is writing in a vacuum. Social, political, and cultural movements for change no longer exist. The individuals and groups who do speak out and openly challenge society do so at the margins without much of a following or base of operation.

The bulk of the selections from the four collections can be read as a response to this predicament. The important essay **"The Dilemma of the Black Intellectual"** (*Beyond Eurocentrism, Vol. I*) addresses the marginality of African-American intellectuals with respect to the life of black communities. Invoking the activist tradition of W. E. B. Du Bois, Paul Robeson, C. L. R. James, and James Baldwin, West calls on black writers and scholars and those involved in the arts to become socially and politically engaged, organically rooted as participants in collective efforts for social transformation. In **"The Paradox of African-American Rebellions"** (*Keeping Faith*) and **"Race, Class and Power in Contemporary America"** (*Beyond Eurocentrism, Vol. II*), West assesses prior African-American struggles for emancipation by signaling those acts of resistance relevant to current circumstances. In **"Theory, Pragmatism and Politics"** (*Keeping Faith*), **"Prophetic Theology"** (*Beyond*

Eurocentrism, Vol. II), and **"We Socialists"** (*Beyond Eurocentrism, Vol. II*), he points to specific philosophic, religious, and political traditions for inspiration and guidance in challenging the status quo. There are pieces interspersed throughout the four volumes that emphasize the importance of African-American culture as a site for struggle and contestation and a catalyst for the formation of a radical communal consciousness. In the process, West explores the hybrid nature of black artistic and religious expression, provides analysis for the shift away from European paradigms, and discusses the relevance of recent developments in popular culture.

In retrospect, West's published work is impressive because of its intellectual range and perceptive analysis; but what stands out above all is its provocative spirit, its conscious attempt to challenge preconceived notions and bring to light the often subtle interconnections between politics, culture, and society. These attributes are reinforced by a genuine seriousness, generosity, and respect for the general public that is missing from the work of many of his colleagues. But in spite of these strengths, there are definite limitations and weaknesses. Many of West's arguments require further elaboration. Consequently, there are times when his commentary results in half truth and exaggeration. His references to the black arts movement of the 1960s fall into this category. There are curious omissions as well. On a number of occasions, West calls for coalitions across race lines, yet he makes no attempt to assess the precedents for these alliances. Such an oversight is disturbing given the impressive scholarship on CORE, SNCC, the Highlander Folk School, and the interracial left-wing organizations of the 1930s and 40s.

Even in the area of African-American music, there are shortcomings. West offers some brilliant insights on the significance of black popular music and pays homage to the legacy of the towering figures Billie Holliday, Charlie Parker, and John Coltrane; but for all his engagement in the discussions surrounding modernism and postmodernism, black essentialism and black hybridity, there are no efforts to ground his arguments with examples from jazz, a black cultural tradition that is essential to the current intellectual debates on the politics of culture. Missing are the references to Ornette Coleman, Albert Ayler, Cecil Taylor, Archie Shepp, Anthony Braxton, Charles Mingus, Sun Ra, Art Ensemble of Chicago, David Murray, Julius Hemphil and Henry Threadgill. The list could be expanded endlessly. West is not alone in this respect. An entire generation of black cultural critics in the U.S. and England are remiss for not paying enough attention to jazz. Hopefully, the current crop of theorists will recognize their error and bring it into the forefront of their "discourse." Until that happens,

we will have to be content with the musings and theoretical speculations of the likes of Cornel West and make our own application.

Glenn C. Loury (essay date 1995)

SOURCE: "Preaching to the Converted," in *One by One from the Inside Out: Essays and Reviews on Race and Responsibility in America,* Free Press, 1995, pp. 217-24.

[*In the following essay, Loury questions the reasoning and values underlying West's views on race in America.*]

No one would likely dispute the claim that coming to grips with racial matters is fundamental to understanding American politics, history, or culture. But an argument is certain to arise if one ventures to be more specific. There is no common definition of the problem, no consensus historical narrative explaining how we have come to this juncture, no agreement about what should now be done. Perhaps most importantly, Americans lack a common vision for the future of our racial relations. We lack a common understanding of what we are trying to achieve—with our laws, through our politics, in our classrooms, from our pulpits—as we struggle with the legacy of African slavery. Indeed, Americans of all races seem to be confused about who "we" are.

In *Race Matters* Cornel West, professor of religion and director of Afro-American studies at Princeton, tries to bring order to our collective intellectual chaos on this vexing question. Sadly for all of us, he does not succeed. A philosopher, theologian, and social activist, Cornel West has emerged in the last decade as an important critical voice on the left of American public life. Though it may be an exaggeration to say, as one admirer boasts, that he is "the preeminent African-American intellectual of our generation," there is no arguing that he is a thoughtful, articulate, and quite influential social critic. His analyses of our "American dilemma" are studied in universities and seminaries across the country. His opinions on social and cultural policy were solicited by Bill Clinton in the wake of his 1992 presidential election victory. And shortly after his installment at Princeton, West acquired official academic celebrity status when he was profiled in the *New York Times Magazine*.

This new book is a collection of eight short essays that, taken together, sketch the outlines of an interesting, if problematic vision of race in America. West offers a stunning array of propositions about our economy, politics, and culture— each one elegant and provocative, and some possibly true. But because West writes more in the manner of the prophet than in that of the analyst, he never stays long enough with any one point to convince us that he has gotten it right.

West believes that public discourse about race matters in this society is pathetically impoverished. In this he is surely right. But his explanation is a good deal more controversial: the absence of an effective dialogue on the race question, he believes, derives from the fact that not all Americans are seen as equal members of the national community. This is a failure for which he holds both liberals and conservatives responsible. Both mistakenly define the "racial dilemma" in terms of the problems that black people pose for white people. Liberals see poor blacks as the historical victims of American racism, needful of government assistance, while conservatives see in the behavior of the black poor the need for moral reform. Both, however, look upon lower-class urban blacks as a people different in some elemental way from themselves. The problem for both is how to transform "them" so they will be more like "us." This, West believes, tragically misconstrues the problem:

> To engage in a serious discussion of race in America, we must begin not with the problems of black people but with the flaws of American society—flaws rooted in historic inequalities and longstanding cultural stereotypes. How we set up the terms for discussing racial issues shapes our perception and response to these issues. As long as black people are viewed as "them," the burden falls on blacks to do all the "cultural" and "moral" work necessary for healthy race relations. The implication is that only certain Americans can define what it means to be American—and the rest must simply "fit in."

West is talking here about hegemony, though (thankfully) he avoids the word. He has in mind the historical fact and ongoing reality of the oppression of black folk—our separation from mainstream American life for generations, even after the end of slavery, as well as the horrible conditions under which many blacks continue to live. The "cultural stereotypes" he mentions are negative ideas about the beauty, intelligence, moral worth, and even the humanity of Africans that, given the need to rationalize slavery in a putatively Christian democracy, evolved over the early years of the American experiment into an ugly antiblack ideology. He is asserting that we can get nowhere in our discussions of race until we unburden ourselves of the remnant of this ideological legacy. It is a superficially appealing position. But is it right?

Is it true that racial progress depends upon a more ecumenical, less judgmental approach to the question of which ways of life embraced by various groups of American citizens are worthy of tolerance and respect? Is it entirely obvious that certain Americans have no right to say to others that inclusion—if not in terms of legal rights, then in social, cultural, and moral terms—is contingent upon "fitting in" (that is,

upon adopting values more or less universally agreed upon)? Surely this was what we said to segregationists during the civil rights movement. Should it not also be our message today to an Afrocentric spokesman who insists on the moral superiority of blacks ("sun people") over whites ("ice people"); or to a black city councilman who states that, unless the needs of his constituents are met, urban guerrilla war will be waged against the white establishment; or to the black mayor of a drug-ridden metropolis who, when caught in the act of illegal drug use, declares himself a victim of racism in law enforcement?

Criticism of offenses such as these—offenses not simply against whites' sensibilities but against what should constitute core American values—are hard to find in *Race Matters*. This, in no small part, is due to the fact that West is usually preaching to the choir. His words collected here serve an emblematic function; they constitute for his like-minded readers banners of progressive sentiment. Few among the students and teachers of the humanities at the many universities where this book will be on the reading lists will need to be persuaded of the correctness of West's views. Not many of the black activists and intellectuals who will be energized by West's rhetoric are concerned about affirming core American values as a starting point for productive interracial dialogue. But out in the "real" America—the blue-collar districts of the industrial states that elected Bill Clinton last November; the suburban rings around the core cities where whites (and blacks) have fled from the problems of urban decay; in the South, where interracial coalitions must still be built—few doubts will be dispelled or souls converted to the cause by these essays. Yet without the engagement of these people in these places, true progress on racial problems is unlikely to be achieved. My concern is that these essays fail in their task of persuasion because they are too politically correct; they are so imbued with the peculiar ethos of the contemporary academy that they cannot provide a healing vision for our racial problems.

West does not deal evenhandedly with the conflicts of value and differences of perception that lie behind much of the racial tension in our country. A fitting metaphor for this split is the war of words that has raged over what to call the 1992 civil unrest in Los Angeles: "riot," or "rebellion"? This verbal struggle is really about the assignment of responsibility: Did we fail the minority poor of South-Central Los Angeles, or did they fail us? A respectable case can be made that both are true, but West primarily credits the former. He does not acknowledge that the fear, anger, and contempt felt by many whites in the face of urban violence perpetrated by blacks and Latinos are legitimate reactions. Nor does he consider the poisonous effect on race relations caused by the antisocial behavior of some among the urban poor.

It is not enough to note, as West does, that such behavior is the fruit of hopelessness and despair now rampant among poor blacks. Bridging the racial gap requires the affirmation by minority advocates of the legitimacy of those social norms that the hopeless and desperate are wont to violate. West mentions, for example, the "xenophobic" attacks directed at Korean-owned business during the Los Angeles disturbance, saying that this shows the extent of "powerlessness" felt by the poor. Yet blacks assaulting Koreans reveal something else—envy and resentment of the material success of hardworking people, success that stands as an indictment of the claim that the country affords little opportunity for non-whites to advance. This disparity between groups in their interpretations of and responses to the opportunity structure of American society may require us to make judgments about which viewpoint is the more reasonable. But this means challenging the progressive orthodoxy, something West is apparently reluctant to do.

One instance where West does challenge the conventional progressive wisdom, however, is in his discussion of the spiritual condition of the urban underclass. His willingness to confront this phenomenon head on, and to place it at the center of the crisis of urban black life, is admirable. He dares to peer into the vast emptiness and nihilism of the spirit that characterizes life at the bottom of our society, where one youth can kill another over a pair of sneakers or a disrespectful gaze, where children give birth to children amid multigenerational poverty and dependency, where the alienation is radical, the violence random, and the despair rampant. West understands that these conditions announce the arrival of "post-modern poverty," a truly new phenomenon on the American scene.

But what he has to say about the causes and the cures of these problems makes very little sense to me. The spiritual problems of the black poor, it turns out, are due to the predation of market capitalism. They have been infested—as have we all, West says—with a materialistic acquisitiveness fueled by profit-seeking manufacturers, distributors, and marketers of consumer goods. The poor have gotten the worst of this capitalistic onslaught on cultural stability because their civil institutions, churches, families, and community structures are too weak to provide a counterweight to the dictates of television advertising. West dismisses without an argument the possibility that the explosion of teen pregnancy, violent crime, family dissolution, and drug use among the poor might have something to do with the sexual revolution and subsequent liberalization of moral norms in American society that began in the 1960s and was (and still is) championed by liberal elites. Nor does he promote the restoration of "traditional values" as an antidote for the spiritual malaise. He simply asserts, without any support for the claim, that the root cause of the problem is the market.

One cannot dismiss this claim out of hand. There is a re-

spectable tradition, on both the left and the right, that is skeptical about the cultural results of capitalism. But it is far from clear, given the historically unprecedented severity of the problems that have emerged in urban black society during the last three decades, that West's explanation explains enough. After all, a television commercial may lead a youngster to desire a pair of sneakers, but only a pathological deprivation of moral sensibility will allow him to kill for them. In any event, placing responsibility on "market-driven corporate enterprises" tells us nothing about what must be done to reverse the decay.

West's answer to the underclass problem is rather to advocate an all-too-predictable "progressive" policy agenda: more money from the government for schools, investment in infrastructure, the creation of good jobs at good wages, the continuation of affirmative action, and so on. But there is no serious inquiry into why such efforts, which have been tried repeatedly, have had so little impact on the deteriorating condition of the urban black poor. To counter this decline, West proposes that spiritual renewal can be achieved through a "politics of conversion." As I understand it, he is implying a kind of communitarian democratic socialism, built from the grass roots. Through a collective effort to influence the economic structures affecting their lives, this "politics of conversion" would foster a "love ethic" among the downtrodden and promote their sense of agency. In advocating this new politics West seems to argue that spiritual emptiness can be vanquished through political struggle, if only that struggle is undertaken in a way that encourages self-respect among the poor: "Nihilism . . . is tamed by a turning of one's soul. This turning is done through one's own affirmation of one's worth—an affirmation fueled by the concern of others."

Yet one cannot help but observe that this vision, from a professor of religion and sometime preacher of the gospel, oddly makes no reference to the role of religious faith. The spiritual malaise is to be transcended not by a vertical relationship with the Almighty but through horizontal relationships with fellow combatants in the struggle against white supremacy and corporate greed. This sounds just a bit romantic. West offers little useful advice about how to put this new politics into effect, even as he ignores the ongoing ministries in the inner cities who are managing to "turn the souls" of some of those at the bottom.

About some of the more difficult questions that must be asked and answered if real change is to occur, West has even less to say. Why are the relations between black men and women so difficult, and why is the institution of marriage literally disappearing among African Americans? Why does black academic performance lag so in comparison with other students, even recent immigrants, and not just among the poor but at all levels of the income hierarchy? How can effective engagement in the lives of the alienated urban poor be promoted and achieved by middle-class Americans of any race, when the poor are seemingly so divorced from the social and political commonweal? And what practical political program, implementable in the here and now of American public life, can secure enough consensus to support concerted action on these problems?

Questions such as these cannot be answered by sloganeering, or with the clever deconstruction of our "patriarchal society" whose "machismo identity is expected and even exalted—as with Rambo and Reagan." It is no political program to call for the emergence of a "jazz freedom fighter" who will "attempt to galvanize and energize world-weary people into forms of organization with accountable leadership that promote critical exchange and broad reflection." It is an insufficient defense of affirmative action, which must be sustained by courts and electoral majorities, to invoke the need for an "affirmation of black humanity, especially among black people themselves . . . [that] speaks to the existential issues of what it means to be a degraded African (man, woman, gay, lesbian, child) in a racist society." This may be the rhetoric prescribed in the multiculturalists' handbook, but it is a rhetoric, I fear, that is largely irrelevant to the serious racial problems that continue to beset American society.

West talks about transcending race as, he asserts, blacks should have done when instead we rallied in large numbers behind the nomination of Clarence Thomas for the Supreme Court. Yet he mires himself in an essentially racialist vision that makes it difficult to see how such a transcendence can be achieved. Why, one wonders, does he find it necessary to equate the violence-promoting lyrics of rap performer Ice-T with the public statements of former Los Angeles police chief Daryl Gates? More disturbingly, how can a man whose claim on our attention here rests upon the morality of his denunciations of racism speak of "visible Jewish resistance to affirmative action and government spending on social programs" as "assaults on black livelihood," as if the fact that some American Jews hold some ideas is an offense properly ascribed to the entire group? This is the language of collective guilt. West would certainly, and rightly, be offended by a similar-sounding charge that blacks as a group should be judged as engaged in an "assault on Jewish survival" because some criminals who are black have murdered some victims who are Jews. He spends no time apologizing for "black criminality" in these pages. Why should Jews be held to account for what he regards as the intellectually indefensible writings of some of their ethnic fellows?

In the end, the moral authority of Cornel West's voice in these pages cannot be derived from the substance of his argument; it must be supplied by the reader. If you come as a true believer, you will be entertained and energized by the eloquence and commitment of this "preeminent black intellectual of our generation." As for the rest of us, perhaps we should take our lead from the current fashion in literary criticism and read this text not for what it seems to be arguing directly, but rather for what it can be understood to say about the curious disposition of power and authority in the contemporary American academy.

FURTHER READING

Criticism

Anderson, Jarvis. "The Public Intellectual." *The New Yorker* (17 January 1994): 39-48.

> Provides a thorough look at the form and substance of West as a thinker and public speaker and of reactions to and opinions on his work.

Pinsker, Sanford. "What's Love, and Gender, Got to Do with It?" *The Virginia Quarterly Review* 70, No. 1 (Winter 1994): 174-81.

> A review of *Race Matters* that looks at West's attempt "to stake out a higher moral ground" in dealing with issues of race.

Stephanson, Anders. "Interview with Cornel West." In *Universal Abandon,* pp. 269-86. Minneapolis: University of Minnesota Press, 1988.

> An interview in which West outlines and elaborates on many of the philosophical ideas basic to his work.

Wieseltier, Leon. "All and Nothing at All." *The New Republic* (6 March 1995): 31-36.

> A negative critical assessment of West's work, which the author deems "almost completely worthless."

Wood, Joe. "Who's the Boss?" *Voice Literary Supplement* (October 1992): 13-14.

> A conversation between West and author Patricia Williams on the questions of "whom does the black public intellectual serve, and to whom does he speak?"

Additional coverage of West's life and career is contained in the following sources published by Gale: *Contemporary Authors,* **Vol. 144;** *Contemporary Black Biography,* **Vol. 5.**

George C. Wolfe
1954-

American dramatist and director.

INTRODUCTION

By 1994, at the age of 40, Wolfe had become one of the most celebrated figures in contemporary American theatre and the most successful black dramatist and director ever. From his controversial major debut *The Colored Museum* (1986) to his long-running *Bring In 'da Noise/Bring In 'da Funk* (1995), Wolfe has attracted popular success and critical acclaim. His original productions and his staging of others' works have gained him numerous awards and recognition, including a position as principal director of the New York Shakespeare Festival since 1993.

Biographical Information

Born in Frankfort, Kentucky, in 1954, the third of four children of middle-class parents, Wolfe grew up in the black enclave of a white city and had little contact with anyone outside his race until after grade school. He proclaimed his intention to become an actor at the age of thirteen after seeing a Broadway production of *Hello, Dolly!* Wolfe joined theatre workshops in Frankfort and pursued acting in college, first at Kentucky State University and then at Pomona College in California. After receiving a bachelor's degree in theatre arts in 1976, he wrote, directed, and acted in plays in Los Angeles. In 1979, Wolfe moved to New York City and enrolled in the graduate program in musical theatre at New York University; he received an M.A. in 1983. His first play to be staged, *Paradise,* appeared Off-Off-Broadway in 1985 to very poor reviews, and quickly closed. With the subsequent productions of *The Colored Museum, Jelly's Last Jam* (1991), and the successful *Bring In 'da Noise/Bring In 'da Funk,* Wolfe established himself as a force in contemporary theatre.

Major Works

After struggling in New York for approximately seven years, Wolfe broke through with *The Colored Museum.* He has called this play a personal exorcism of black cultural myths. In a series of vignettes or "exhibits," Wolfe parodies stereotypical figures of the African-American community, from a black drag queen to cultural icon Lorraine Hansberry. The play sparked considerable controversy, especially among black critics, but proved so popular that it moved from its premiere in New Jersey to New York's Public Theater and was later broadcast as part of the *Great Performances* se-

ries on PBS. *Spunk* (1990) showcased Wolfe's skills as the adaptor of three Zora Neale Hurston short stories combined to present a strong affirmation of black women. His production of Bertolt Brecht's *The Caucasian Chalk Circle* in the same year also drew positive critical attention. In 1991, Wolfe mounted his most ambitious and riskiest production, the musical *Jelly's Last Jam.* Opening in Los Angeles, this play about jazz pioneer Jelly Roll Morton moved to Broadway in 1992 and starred Gregory Hines. *Jelly's* success led to Wolfe's selection as director for Tony Kushner's Pulitzer Prize-winning *Angels in America* and *Perestroika* in 1993. *Bring In 'da Noise/Bring In 'da Funk* continued Wolfe's run of successful productions.

Critical Reception

While some critics responded adversely to the acid satire of *The Colored Museum,* most agreed with John Simon that the work is a serious piece that shows artistic maturity. Wolfe's work on *Spunk* and *The Caucasian Chalk Circle* solidified his reputation, and garnered him an Obie Award in 1990. Reviewing *Jelly's Last Jam,* Edith Oliver said, "There has never been anything like it, on or off Broadway." E. R. Shipp also voiced high praise, calling Wolfe "the hope for the future of American theater." Official recognition followed critical accolades again in 1992 when Wolfe received the Dorothy Chandler Award and in 1993 when he won the Tony Award for best director for *Angels in America.* In recent years *Bring In 'da Noise/Bring In 'da Funk* has brought more popular and critical praise. While Wolfe's productions of Shakespeare for the New York Shakespeare Festival have been less well received thus far, his other works for the Public Theater continue to impress audiences and critics alike.

PRINCIPAL WORKS

Paradise (drama) 1985

The Colored Museum (drama) 1986

The Caucasian Chalk Circle [director and adaptor with Thulani Davis; play by Bertolt Brecht] (drama) 1990

Spunk [director, adaptor; from stories by Zora Neale Hurston] (drama) 1990

Jelly's Last Jam (musical drama) 1991

Angels in America: Millennium Approaches [director; play by Tony Kushner] (drama) 1993

Perestroika [director; play by Tony Kushner] (drama) 1993

Bring In 'da Noise/Bring In 'da Funk [with Savion Glover] (musical drama) 1995

CRITICISM

Thulani Davis (review date 11 November 1986)

SOURCE: "Sapphire Attire," in *The Village Voice,* Vol. XXXI, No. 45, November 11, 1986, p. 91.

[*In the following negative review, dramatist and critic Davis calls* The Colored Museum *a play in which "the serious is trivialized as the trivial is enlarged."*]

Near the beginning of *The Colored Museum,* as an Aunt Jemima clone appears stirring a cauldron and singing "First ya add a pinch of style / and then a dash of flair / now ya stir in some preoccupation / with the texture of your hair," you know not to be surprised that she's cooking "a batch of Negroes." When she ends by saying "but don't as' [sic] me what to do with 'em now that you got 'em 'cause child that is your problem," you have to wonder if the playwright knew what to do with them. I'm not sure he did.

George Wolfe's comedy is a smart collection of vignettes, some of them quite funny, displaying a mixed batch of black media stereotypes, many of whom were created by black

folks themselves. They are a very entertaining lot, the kind of plastic black folks we've all gotten too used to hearing from over the years. They know they're soulless, lost, and getting over, and so what about it? They parade through, doing monologues mostly, singing occasionally, and cracking jokes about what it takes to get by. The serious is trivialized as the trivial is enlarged, and the causes of their ugly transformations get lost right along with the victims.

I was told by someone I respect that *The Colored Museum* was a coon show, a nasty parody of black theater. I even expected to be offended. I also expected it to be well done and written with some facility—which it is—because I'd heard basically good things about Wolfe's work on the book of Duke Ellington's *Queenie Pie.* But the show is too slick to be really offensive. It's more like a satirical glimpse through Donald Bogle's film history *Toms, Coons, Mulattoes, Mammies, and Bucks,* with some other folks thrown in. Performed in a broad, vaudevillian style, the writing is smooth, effortlessly humorous, and wickedly stylized when Wolfe parodies other writers. At the end we are told that these stereotyped folks are "celebrating in their cultural madness." Perhaps this too is satire, but it seems to be soft-pedaling, calculated to keep anybody from getting mad. . . .

The most interesting moments here are visual: the stewardess fastening shackles on herself; the passengers in rags, looking every bit like slaves on an auction block, but crouched among the American Tourister luggage rolling by for collection. Miss Pat's description of the time passing is most alarming: "Oh look, now we're passing over the '60s. . . . 'Julia' with Miss Diahann Carroll—and five little girls in Sunday school—Martin Luther King—Oh no! The Supremes just broke up!" Here's where the trivial starts to get mixed up with the significant. . . .

Most of the characters in *The Colored Museum* are women—Sapphires to be exact—who, like Topsy Washington, are not fretting over the painful past, but have "everything I need to get over in this world." In a send-up of Lorraine Hansberry's *Raisin in the Sun,* we have several of these bloodless survivors: Mama, a Claudia McNeil parody; the Lady in Plaid, an Ntozake Shange cutout; and Medea Jones, who seems to be part Beneatha Younger (the daughter in *Raisin*), part Diana Sands, and who knows who else. The announcer passes each of these characters an award for her performance. . . .

I found myself laughing as these familiar sisters strode onstage. But I left feeling they were more the center of the author's intentions than he wants to let on. While the poor males are tormented, driven, sweating, and serving duty, the Lalas are all self-satisfied, reveling in their own glory, rewriting their bios, hiding mothers, abandoning daughters, tying up the rich white lover. Amos and Andy must have been out for lunch while these women were carrying on.

If Wolfe really wants to complain about the divas or Sapphires, he should just do so. The African slave trade resulted in more than minstrelsy, jheri curls, rap music, and naturalism in black theater, if these are his complaints. The process of transformation, the willful desire to shed the culture in order to "get over," seems to be his subject—*how* we have come to be pinups of decadence, if that is what we have become. Every time I think about Miss Roj, the disco habitué, crying out to her listeners, "Come on everybody and dance. A whole race of people gets trashed and debased. Snap those fingers and dance," I think somebody ought to bring Little Richard by so he can sit that child down and tell him a few things—Sapphire style.

Jack Kroll (review date 17 November 1986)

SOURCE: "Zapping Black Stereotypes," in *Newsweek,* Vol. CVIII, No. 20, November 17, 1986, pp. 84-5.

[*In the following favorable review, Kroll praises* The Colored Museum *as "a true satire, fiercely funny writing."*]

Playwright George C. Wolfe's savagely hilarious parody of the slave ships that brought blacks to America is the first "exhibit" in his *The Colored Museum,* a work that brings forward a bold new voice that is bound to shake up blacks and whites with separate-but-equal impartiality.

Wolfe is one black writer who's less concerned with castigating Whitey than with directing his razor-sharp shafts against the stereotypes and sacred cows of the black culture. Not that Wolfe is a New Conservative, the Thomas Sowell of the theater. He is as angry at racism as Richard Wright or James Baldwin. But he's just as angry at the worn-out cultural and psychological patterns that in his view prevent blacks from achieving and celebrating their own identities. *The Colored Museum* is true satire, fiercely funny writing that wraps Wolfe's anger and compassion in an effective theatrical structure.

That structure encompasses 11 sketches, the exhibits in Wolfe's museum of antic anthropology. Not all of these mini-plays are equally successful, but . . . they fuse into an organic whole. . . .

In an insanely funny section, [two] hairpieces (one Afro, one straight and flowing) . . . engage in a fiery debate over which one will adorn the head of their mistress . . ., who has gone bald through years of torturing her hair. The miracle is how Wolfe can be both merciless and loving while skewering his

characters, as in one sketch [which concerns] . . . LaLa, a Mississippi girl who's had to go to Europe and french-fry herself to become a star, just like "the Paul La Robesons, the James La Baldwins, the Josephine La Bakers" before her.

This loving mercilessness reaches a peak in the *Museum's* central exhibit, an all-out assault on "The last mama-on-the-couch play," which of course is *A Raisin in the Sun,* Lorraine Hansberry's breakthrough play that brought black revolt into the middle-class living room and created a genre that's still going strong. It's all here—the worn-out but indomitably religious mama; her son Walter-Lee-Beau-Willie, eternally imprecating against "the Man, Mr. Charlie, Mr. Bossman"; his wife, who sees herself as a degraded African princess; his sister, who talks in nonblack classical verse she's learned at Juilliard.

"Black American culture is a very fragmented thing," says Wolfe. "We're all trying to come up with some definition of what we are. My absolute definition of me is the schizophrenia, the contradiction." At the end of the play . . . [the character] Topsy Washington describes the ultimate party where all the contradictions meet—Bert Williams and Malcolm X, Angela Davis and Aunt Jemima. "I can't live inside yesterday's pain," says Topsy, "but I can't live without it."

Will Nixon (essay date April 1991)

SOURCE: "George C. Wolfe Creates Visions of Black Culture," in *American Visions,* Vol. 6, No. 2, April, 1991, pp. 50-2.

[*In the following essay, Nixon presents a favorable profile of Wolfe's career.*]

George C. Wolfe's friendly voice doesn't have any lower gears. It starts in fourth and accelerates. The only thing that slows him down is an occasional stutter when his words burn rubber for a moment before grabbing back onto his sentence and zooming off around the bend. "Half an hour?" he says incredulously when I get him on the phone during a rehearsal break at the Mark Taper Forum in Los Angeles, where he's directing his newest play, *Jelly's Last Jam,* about Jelly Roll Morton. "How about fifteen?" he asks. He's done in ten.

At 36, George Wolfe is a busy man. He's bi-coastal and bi-talented as a theater director and playwright. After *Jelly's Last Jam,* he flies back to New York and the Public Theater to present another new play, *Blackout,* in April. Asked what it's about, he promises, "It's funny, but most urban environments are comic nightmares that nobody knows how to wake up from. It's about madness, racism, people hating—

it all has to do with cities. New York City was designed for 27 fabulous chic people, and the rest of us are their entertainment." Enough said?

On February 1, PBS kicked off Black History Month with Wolfe's most famous play, *The Colored Museum*, which, among other things, makes it impossible to watch *A Raisin in the Sun* with a straight face ever again. Wolfe's satire on a Noah's Arkload of black stereotypes, from *Ebony* buppies to Aunt Jemima to Ntozake Shange's Soul Sisters, was one of the major black plays of the '80s. Some theatergoers were not amused—a few even climbed up on stage to attack one of the characters—but Wolfe means to blast the very idea that blacks could be typecast, whether by whites or by themselves. "I can't live inside of a museum, and I don't think a culture that's as vibrant as black culture can live inside of a museum," he says. "So I just found a way to tear down walls. . . . [Audiences] bring their baggage [to the theater] and some people are walking in with steamer trunks, and it's hard to sit there and enjoy a play when you've got a steamer trunk on your head loaded with all sorts of crap. I just say, 'How much longer are you going to carry that trunk on your head? But ultimately, that's their problem." I don't consider it my problem." The play ran for nine months at the Public Theater in 1986 and went on to major productions in London and Los Angeles.

"It's touching some truth," Wolfe says. "I did an interview on WLIB, and office workers, all these women who'd seen it eight, nine times, called and said they had come back and brought back 20 or 30 people. Actresses have come up to me to say, 'Doing that play was the most meaningful experience of my life."

In the late '80s a young novelist, Trey Ellis, coined the phrase "the new black aesthetic" to link Wolfe's theater, Spike Lee's movies, and his own satirical novel, *Platitudes.* Wolfe will buy the phrase, if he gets to define it for himself. "In the '50s black culture was more interested in explaining itself to white audiences; and in the '60s it was spent more in lashing out and claiming a territory of its own. My generation benefits from those two periods," he says. "I don't feel I have to explain anything or be defiant against anything. I am. I'm coming from a place of casual arrogance because I feel that black culture is one of—if not the—most dominant forces in American culture. Even if people don't admit to it, they snap to it, they watch it, they dress like it. So I don't have to translate it to anyone. I can just move forward and explore its peculiarities and complexities."

Wolfe grew up during the '50s in Frankfort, Ky., a white town with a black enclave. His father worked for the state government in the Department of Corrections, while his mother was the principal of a black private school, which he attended for eight years. He loved theater almost from the start, captivated by the possibilities of making his own little worlds. "I won't say I was born with it, because that sounds so mystical," he says, "but being attracted to it was part of my growing up. My reality was TV and going to the movies, but at school we always did plays, and I lived for that time." He went to Claremont College in Southern California to study acting and set design, but he soon took up directing and writing, which allowed him to control the whole theatrical experience—"creating the vision as opposed to executing the vision." In 1979 he moved on to the theater capital of New York, where he took a master of fine arts degree at New York University.

From the start Wolfe has shown a healthy disrespect for somber, realistic plays. In college he produced his first play, *Up for Grabs,* about a baby who is traded for a washer and dryer on a game show. The kid grows up in a soundproof booth, educated by cereal boxes and TV commercials. At 21 he's set free on the game show *Up for Grabs,* where he faces different futures behind each door: the corporate life, becoming a Hollywood superhero, joining a black revolution. "It was a strange show, but it was fun," Wolfe says. "And it got a very good reception and won an award, which foolishly encouraged me to write." He did six or seven more shows before *The Colored Museum* put him on the map.

In 1990 he revisited his Southern roots with *Spunk,* his adaptation of three short stories by Zora Neale Hurston. She, too, was from the South and found success in New York, and Wolfe finds her stories, set in the '20s and '30s, still vibrant today. "Her themes are classical, and so much about Southern black culture is classical, that I wanted to place black people in a timeless world," he says. He also wanted to bring the wonderful rhythms of Hurston's writing to life on the stage. "When I initially read the stories, I wanted to do them as an opera," he says. The second story especially— "Story in Harlem Slang"—becomes a verbal Super Bowl as two young men with mile-long watch chains dangling from their slick zoot suits vie for the attention of a passing young woman. Since it's the Depression, what they really want is the cash in her purse for a meal. They are cartoonish exaggerations, much like the characters in *The Colored Museum,* but as one critic noted in *American Theater* magazine, "Their rhymes, their boasts, their bluffs—their 'lies'—are still a source of true delight, and an unwitting testament to the strength of their oral traditions."

When asked where he gets his ear for vernacular, Wolfe says, "I like to talk. My family talks a lot, and I'm fascinated when people talk. I stuttered when I was little, and I still do sometimes. So maybe I listen to rhythms in a different way. What's fascinating about black people is that every language we spoke we no longer know. We lost the Rosetta stone. Somehow English is, in essence, a foreign language that we have made our own. The way we use language is very theatrical.

It's like wearing your neuroses and wearing your strengths and taking them everywhere you go. Some cultures will pack some things away and only pull them out periodically. Black people don't, in general, do that. They wear it all. And I think there's something incredibly healthy and incredibly exhausting about that."

Spunk had a successful run at the Public Theater in spring 1990. Several months later, Joseph Papp, the great patriarch of the Public Theater, decided his institution needed fresh blood. With the exception of Wolfe's plays and some recent Shakespeare productions, much of the excitement in off-Broadway theater had moved uptown to Lincoln Center and elsewhere. Papp chose JoAnne Akalaitis, a noted experimental director, to be his heir apparent and gave three young directors, including Wolfe, the Public's three stages for a year. "I'm in awe of Mr. Papp's generosity," Wolfe said soon afterwards.

Last November he presented Bertolt Brecht's *The Caucasian Chalk Circle,* which tells the story of a kitchen maid who rescues a royal baby during a bloody revolution, only to undergo the outrageous fortunes of a Stephen Spielberg movie before she can keep the child as her own. Brecht set the play in the Caucasus centuries ago, borrowing the story from medieval China; Wolfe moved it to an imaginary country much like Haiti with rulers much like the Duvaliers. "When I started reading this play, I realized that built into it are realities that totally fit into a Caribbean, colonial thrust," he says.

"The thing that Brecht does, which I think is very exciting," he continues, "is that his poor people, his peasants, know exactly how they fit into the scheme of things. They know exactly how foolish the rich people are and exactly how foolish they are. A lot of times, when plays are written about poor people and peasants, they're written as victims. Nobody in this play is a victim. They know how to get why they need, even if it's corrupt. They know how to survive."

Back in 1986, Wolfe described *The Colored Museum* as an exorcism and a party. The same could be said of all his plays, especially *The Caucasian Chalk Circle* With the aid of playwright Thulani Davis, who adapted Brecht's text to the Caribbean, puppeteers, who often transformed the stage into a mini-carnival, and a percussion band, Wolfe was able to create an entire world, from the fawning court around the governor's wife to the raggedy life on the streets. "I try to direct for children, but not 'children children,'" he says, "'adult children.' I create plays that make adults children in their receptiveness."

But *The Caucasian Chalk Circle* is already old news in George Wolfe's life. There's now *Jelly's Last Jam, Blackout,* and his long-held plans to write a trilogy of plays about

Kentucky. He obviously enjoys his busy success: the stream of interviews, the calls from Hollywood to write bad movies, the growing number of people who attend his annual New Year's Day party. "I love the shallow attention," he admits. "But, ultimately, it's getting more people to see the work. The more people I can share my work with, the more that fulfills a *real* drive inside of me."

Harry J. Elam, Jr. (essay date October 1992)

SOURCE: "Signifyin(g) on African American Theatre: *The Colored Museum* by George C. Wolfe," in *Theatre Journal,* Vol. 44, No. 3, October, 1992, pp. 291-303.

[*In the following essay, Elam discusses Wolfe's approach to his heritage in* The Colored Museum.]

How should African Americans confront their legacy, their heritage of struggle and survival? Heralded [by Jack Kroll in *Newsweek*] after its 1986 Off-Broadway debut as a "bold new voice in black theatre" *The Colored Museum* ponders this critical question. Playwright George C. Wolfe wraps his answer in contradiction and paradox, as *The Colored Museum* simultaneously celebrates, satirizes and subverts the African-American legacy. Wolfe calls his play both, "an exorcism and a party." *The Colored Museum* explores contemporary African-American cultural identity, while, at the same time revisiting and reexamining the African-American theatrical and cultural past. According to Wolfe the legacy of the past must be both embraced and overcome.

Implicitly and explicitly *The Colored Museum* "talks" to earlier African-American dramatic texts, critiquing and revising central themes, images and narrative strategies. Wolfe parodies earlier black plays, particularly works by black women. This parody questions and challenges the participation of black women in the cultural process. And yet, both the form and content of *The Colored Museum* are significantly informed by earlier efforts of African-American female playwrights. In addition, Wolfe's text encourages the audience to recognize and accept the contradictions and complexities of African-American culture. Wolfe's play writing is both fueled and frustrated by African-American dramatic traditions:

> People kept asking for a 'black' play. I kept asking, 'What's a 'black' play. Four walls, a couch and a mama?' I can't live within those old definitions.

Paradoxically, as Wolfe tries to escape certain definitions of black drama, he embraces others.

Through *The Colored Museum,* Wolfe is "signifyin(g)" on

the plays and traditions of African-American theatre. In his recent study on African-American literary theory, *The Signifying Monkey,* Henry Louis Gates argues that African-American literature is double voiced, with texts talking to other texts offering critique and revision. The process of repetition and revision with a signal difference Gates terms "signifyin(g)." According to Gates, through the process of signifyin(g) African-American literature is able to theorize about itself. Therefore, theory and criticism are implicit in the prose. Still, Gates writes only of African-American literature. He does not apply the theory of signifyin(g) to the theatre. The signifyin(g) of *The Colored Museum* is not limited to the dramatic text. Gestural and iconic symbols conveyed through the theatrical performance of the play are signifyin(g) on African-American cultural practices. *The Colored Museum,* because of its implicit and explicit critique of the African-American theatrical past, provides a striking opportunity to test the value of *The Signifying Monkey* as a model for African-American theatrical criticism.

Wolfe is immediately signifyin(g) on African-American theatre and cultural identity through the title, *The Colored Museum.* Gates maintains that signifyin(g) is a challenge to the meaning of meaning. The title, an important component in the overall rhetorical strategy of the play, challenges the connotative meanings of both colored and museum. Traditionally "museum" connotes a place where treasures of the past, important artifacts of the present are housed and exhibited. Far from a conventional museum, Wolfe's "colored museum" neither preserves nor displays venerated treasures. Virtually a "funnyhouse," this museum contains unusual and unexpected exhibits such as Miss Roj, an extraterrestrial drag queen and Normal Jean, a naive young woman who has given birth to a large white egg. Wolfe's exhibits challenge and disturb the audience's expectations. His choice of exhibits and use of stereotypes critique and question African-American cultural traditions and icons. In addition, pristine, *white* walls and a white revolving stage provide a symbolic and visually contradictory setting for Wolfe's "*colored* museum." The white environment encloses these colored exhibits, just as white American domination has constrained African-American cultural expression. Awakening from statue-like poses the exhibits come to life irreverently satirizing the African-American past, revising the meaning of museum and pressing the limits of white hegemonic control.

The term "colored" has both negative and contradictory connotations in contemporary African-American society. As a word used to label and define peoples of African descent, "colored" is outmoded and yet the term "people of color" is accepted and widely used. Concurrent with the shifts in social position, political strategy and ideological orientation, the designation for Americans of African descent has changed from Colored to Negro to Black and Afro-American to the more current term, African American. The pro-

cess has involved debate and dissension. Clearly, much is in a name. A sense of identity is contained in that label.

Wolfe's use of colored rekindles the debate over the appropriateness of any label. For Wolfe the problem resides not in choosing a politically correct label, but in the process of labeling itself. Wolfe claims external labels limit and confine creativity, expression and self-definition. Wolfe says the he wrote *The Colored Museum* "in order to undefine myself in relation to all these labels." Echoing Wolfe's sentiment, the character Topsy, in the final exhibit of *The Colored Museum,* **"The Party,"** admonishes the audience, "So honey, don't try and label or define me." African Americans have continually been categorized and defined solely by their color. Labelling denies the infinite variety, permutations and evolutions of the African-American experience. Wolfe's exhibits reject simple classifications and demand the power to define themselves.

The title, *Colored Museum,* is also signifyin(g) on two earlier works of African-American theatre which contain racial labels, *Funnyhouse of a Negro* by Adrienne Kennedy and *for colored girls* by Ntozake Shange. These two plays center around issues of racial and sexual identity. The use of "Negro" in the title of *Funnyhouse,* like "colored," carries negative connotations. When *Funnyhouse* opened Off-Broadway in 1964, "Negro" was being replaced in political rhetoric and public discourse by the term "black." In *Funnyhouse,* the color black both repulses and intrigues the focal character, Sarah, a young, middle class black woman. Sarah is unable to accept or cope with the pain of being a "Negro." She lives trapped in the "Funnyhouse" of her mind, a space that much like the "Colored Museum" contains a menagerie of characters ranging from Patrice Lamumba to Jesus Christ. These conflicting characters are Sarah's other selves. Overwhelmed by the contradictions of her cultural identity, she eventually commits suicide.

The black women in *for colored girls,* unlike Sarah in *Funnyhouse,* are not solely consumed by race, rather they must confront the compounded effects of gender and sexual oppression as well. Shange not only uses the racial label "colored" in her title but "girl," a word when used in reference to women, degrades and diminishes their status and achievements. Still, as the title and early lines in *for colored girls* suggest, the play has a message "for colored girls who," like Sarah, "have considered suicide when the rainbow is enuf." The title implies that for others facing the challenge of growing up as African-American women, there is an alternative to Sarah's unfortunate end. Shange inverts the negative implications of the title. From a position of marginality, her colored girls find strength through the recognition of their commonality and shared struggle. They break out from the subservient position implied by the label, "colored girls," and gain a new position of self-awareness. Suicide, the end chosen by Sarah, proves not to be a viable solution for the pain of these colored girls. The play affirms life and infinite possibilities because "the rainbow is enuf." Shange changes the label "colored girl" from being an undesirable and limiting designation to a source of pride and empowerment. The celebration of black women's lives achieved in *for colored girls* revises the self-denigration and destruction of the black woman, Sarah in *Funnyhouse.*

Clearly, the titles and texts of *Funnyhouse* and the later work, *for colored girls,* exhibit an implicit inter-textual communication and suggest a pattern of signifyin(g) revision. **The Colored Museum** continues the process of signifyin(g) by talking to and critiquing both of these earlier works through its own title and narrative content. In all three plays, the characters must confront the negative stigma implied by their titles. Labelling and racial identity are immediately called into question by these titles and then examined through the performance texts. Similar to *for colored girls,* **The Colored Museum** subverts and revises the negative connotations of the term "colored" and redefines it as an affirmation of African-American cultural diversity. With the ensemble cast gathered on stage for the final exhibit, the character Topsy assures the audience that her power lies in her "colored contradictions." Wolfe's exhibits explore the diversity of African-American culture and alter perceptions of African-American experience. Wolfe argues:

> Black American culture is a very fragmented thing. We're all trying to come up with some definition of what we are. My absolute definition of me is the schizophrenia, the contradiction.

The Colored Museum affirms the schizophrenia of African-American culture.

In the exhibit entitled, **"The Gospel According to Miss Roj,"** Wolfe presents the "extraterrestrial" drag queen Miss Roj. Historically, the drag queen has existed on the margins of black culture, a figure of ridicule and derision. With cross-gender dress, effeminate voice and attitude, the drag queen has been a very visible and derogatory symbol of black homosexuality. Despite the complexity of black homosexual experience, the effeminacy of the drag queen has become the representative image, a stereotypical comic figure. Miss Roj's first appearance on the stage affirms the comic stereotype. Wolfe's stage directions read, "He [Miss Roj] is dressed in striped patio pants, white go-go boots, a halter, and cat-shaped sun glasses. What would seem ridiculous on anyone else, Miss Roj wears as if it were high fashion." With his first appearance, the audience laughs and sighs with recognition. Still, in this exhibit, Wolfe revises, subverts and is signifyin(g) on the drag queen stereotype.

Miss Roj announces that he is a "Snap Queen" and that

"Snapping comes from another galaxy as do all snap queens." The gesture of the "Snap!" has been cultivated within the black gay community as a form of visual signifyin,' similar to the black tradition of playing the dozens on street corners. Within the black gay community, the Snap! is an integral part of the vernacular, a gesture replete with a multiplicity of "coded meanings." Black homosexual activist and cultural critic Marlon Riggs points out [in *Black American Literature Forum*]:

> The Snap! can be as emotional and politically charged as a clenched fist; can punctuate debate and dialogue like an exclamation point, a comma, an ellipsis; or altogether negate the need for words among those who are adept at decoding its nuanced meanings.

Recently the Snap! as well as the image of the drag queen have been appropriated and abused by more mainstream black media and culture. On the prime-time variety program *In Living Color* as well as the extremely successful touring black comedy, *Beauty Shop,* stereotypical gay caricatures swish, sashay and snap to the laughs and pleasure of the audience. According to Riggs,

> the particular appropriation of the Snap! by Hollywood's Black Pack deflates the gesture into rank caricature. Instead of a symbol of communal expression and, at times, cultural defiance, Snap! becomes part of a simplistically reductive Negro Faggot identity: It functions as a mere sign post of effeminate, cute, comic homosexuality. Thus robbed of its full political and cultural dimension, the Snap! in this appropriation descends to stereotype.

At first, Wolfe's representation of Miss Roj appears to support this comic misrepresentation of the Snap!. When Miss Roj cynically informs the audience of the power contained within his snap, the audience laughs at him as well as with him. Yet, his monologue changes from a tone of comic gentility to emotional attack and Miss Roj turns the power of her Snap! on the audience. Miss Roj chastises the spectators for their complacency, for not waking up to their own cultural blindness. Holding the spectators accountable for crimes, problems and poverty that they would rather avoid and ignore, Miss Roj ridicules black mainstream pretensions. "Snap for everytime you walk past someone lying in the street, smelling like frozen piss and shit and you don't see it." The presentational nature of the play compels Miss Roj to speak directly to the audience. The spectators can not avoid or ignore his attack. Transformed from a gay minstrel into a harrowing figure, Miss Roj now derisively laughs at the spectators.

Through Miss Roj, the drag queen is removed from the margins and placed in the subject position. Miss Roj is "Snapping" or "signifyin'" on the conventional, heterosexual world. While the world of the drag queen is commonly perceived as consisting of moral and spiritual degradation, sexual uncertainty and identity crisis, Miss Roj subverts these conceptions. Instead, he portrays the mainstream world as the one comprised of madness, confusion and decay. His community, on the other hand is self-aware, self-defined and conscious of its own identity. "We don't ask for your approval. We don't ask for your acceptance. We know who we are and we move on it." Miss Roj punctuates this line with a Snap!. In this exhibit, the gesture of the Snap! is once again politicized and empowered. Before he engages in a maddening final dance and disappears in a "blast of smoke," Miss Roj informs the audience, "I guarantee you will never hear two fingers put together in a snap and not think of Miss Roj. That's power baby."

Madness and cultural schizophrenia are central to the struggles for cultural, personal and racial identity in *The Colored Museum.* In considering the "madness" of race, Wolfe is again signifyin(g) on *Funnyhouse* as well as another play first produced in 1964, *Dutchman* by LeRoi Jones, the seminal work of the Black Revolutionary Theatre Movement. *The Colored Museum* shares an intertextual relationship with both of these plays. Gates writes that, "Signifyin(g) . . . entails formal revision and intertextual relation." Wolfe revisits and revises the definition of madness in both of these earlier plays.

In *Dutchman,* the character Clay and Playwright Jones identify "madness" as racial insanity fueled by years of racism and oppression. Clay, like Sarah in *Funnyhouse* is a middle-class black person who wishes to remove himself from the madness of the proletarian black masses. In his final apocalyptic speech to his nemesis/seductress Lula, Clay muses, "My people's madness, who needs it?" Still, despite his own desire to disassociate himself from the black majority, Clay understands and articulates the damage that this "madness" has caused in black culture: a collective psychosis that can only be exorcised and overcome through the murder of whites and violent black revolution.

> A whole people of neurotics, struggling to keep from being sane. And the only thing that would cure the neurosis would be your murder. Simple as that . . . Crazy niggers turning their backs on sanity. When all it need is that simple act. Murder. Just Murder!

Clay's words are a harrowing harbinger of the militancy and madness that would rise from the African-American urban enclaves in the late 1960s and early 1970s. However, Clay does not take his own advice and is subsequently murdered by Lula. His desire to be "left alone" goes unheeded. Jones

through Clay's inaction condemns and warns against middle class passivity in the struggle for black liberation.

Similarly, Wolfe in *The Colored Museum* bemoans the current black middle class complacency and the loss of revolutionary urgency. Miss Roj scolds the audience, "We've traded in our drums for respectability. So now its just words! words rapping, Words flowing instead of blood, 'cause you know that don't work." The middle class protagonists of *Dutchman* and *Funnyhouse* escape the "madness of race" through death. In several exhibits of *The Colored Museum,* the characters also attempt to escape the pain, the legacy of oppression, suffering and survival, the madness of African-American culture. However, Wolfe does not allow this option. In *The Colored Museum* embracing the "madness" becomes a coping mechanism critical to African-American survival in an irrational world.

In the exhibit entitled, **"The Photo Session,"** a black couple dressed in fabulous evening attire informs the audience that they "couldn't resolve the contradictions of our existence." As a result they have chosen to leave reality and live inside the artificial world of *Ebony Magazine,* where "everybody is beautiful" and "no one says anything profound." Through this exhibit, Wolfe indicts the lifestyle of bourgeois African Americans who insulate themselves from the plight of the masses. The plastic existence exemplified by this couple and glorified in the pages of black magazines ignores the urban blight, crime and poverty that is the reality for the majority of African Americans. Anesthetized from their African-American pain, this "fabulous" couple flaunt their vapid, unreal escapism. However, at the end of the scene, the couple reveals that they are starting to experience a different sort of pain, "the pain that comes from feeling no pain at all."

In another exhibit entitled, **"Symbiosis,"** a Wall Street executive, The Man, attempts to exorcize all vestiges of his earlier afrocentric identification by throwing away all his African-American cultural artifacts. Memories of a prior militancy, his first dashiki, his first afro comb, his autographed picture of Stokely Carmichael are all ceremonially discarded, as The Kid, The Man's former self, his anthropomorphized black rage, bears witness and raises dissent. When The Kid's protest evolves into violence, The Man symbolically strangles his own rage. He rationalizes his actions to the audience declaring "being Black is too emotionally taxing." Sounding very much like Clay, The Man argues that he "has no stake in the madness" of race. Rather than accepting the pressure, pain and problems of African-American heritage, The Man chooses to escape to the white, corporate world and resolves to be "black only on weekends and holidays."

The Man's dilemma not only recalls the crisis of the negro intellectual in the tumultuous sixties, but is critical to contemporary African-American discourse as well. Ambitious and educated African-Americans ponder the question: Must success in corporate America necessitate the sacrifice of African-American cultural identity? Wolfe answers in the final moment of this exhibit. The Kid rises from the dead and links onto The Man's arm flashing a malevolent smile and shouting, "What's happenin!" The rage cannot be left behind. The legacy of the past remains a part of The Man's contemporary identity.

The exhibit immediately following **"Symbiosis,"** entitled **"La La's Opening,"** reveals La La, an expatriate black female entertainer in her American debut. The presence of La La's real mother in the audience, a woman she has attempted to deny and forget, as well as the revelation that La La is the mother of a daughter abandoned years ago in Mississippi, disrupt her performance. Despite her adoption of a French accent, a fabricated life story, and a white French boyfriend, La La can not escape "the girl she left behind," her black roots, "the girl inside." Confronted by the reality of her child, La La recognizes the futility of her denial of the past and the fallacy of her current life. "It's all over for me," she says. This realization is visually reinforced as La La removes her long straight hair wig to reveal a head of African corn rows and then reaches out to accept her daughter in a loving embrace.

In neither **"La La's Opening,"** nor **"The Photo Session,"** nor **"Symbiosis"** do the characters escape from their African-American past. These exhibits establish that cultural denial or escape should not be a viable option for African Americans today. Without any connection to the past, the fabulous couple in **"The Photo Session"** experience a new, more unnerving pain that comes from "feeling no pain at all." Instead the legacy of past pain and achievement must shape and empower contemporary African-American cultural identity. Haunted by nightmares of assimilation, La La recognizes the need to reconnect with her past and embraces her daughter as well as her former self, while in **"Symbiosis,"** The Man's former self literally grabs hold of him. Continually in **The Colored Museum,** the past revitalizes the present. At the end of the play all the exhibits return to the stage and join in the refrain, "Whereas I can't live inside of yesterday's pain, I can't live without it."

In contrast, Sarah in *Funnyhouse* can not live with the pain of her undesirable heritage. Sarah condemns her very dark-skinned father for marrying her extremely light-skinned mother. Sarah even imagines murdering him, bludgeoning him with an "ebony head." Her suicide provides escape for the unresolved contradictions of her existence. As Genvieve Fabre notes [in *Drumbeats, Masks, and Metaphor*], "Her corpse balancing above a void is the image of a life that wavers between a rejected past and a confused present. There is no place for blacks to be somebody." Playwright

Kennedy asks the audience to appreciate the complex and contradictory nature of black identity, while Wolfe asks African Americans not only to recognize the contradictions but to embrace them.

The contradictions of race do not destroy the characters in **The Colored Museum** but, instead empower them. In the final exhibit of **The Colored Museum, "The Party,"** Topsy describes an amazing party she attended the other night, uptown, "somewhere between 125th street and infinity." At this ultimate party, the contradictions of African-American culture all interact together. Political figures and artists, past and present converge. As Larry Neal wrote [in *Drama Review*] about the Black Arts Movement of the 1960s, ethics and aesthetics function as one.

> In one corner we have Nat Turner sipping champagne out of Eartha Kitt's slipper. In another corner Malcolm X and Bert Williams discuss existentialism as it relates to the shuffle ball change. And in the kitchen Angela Davis and Aunt Jemima sharing a plate of greens and just going on about South Africa.

Just as the party started to move to "rhythm of its own madness" with everyone "dancing to the rhythm of their own definitions, celebrating their own cultural madness," the party lifts from the ground, flies off into space and finally lands inside Topsy's head. Topsy now understands that she "dances to the music of the madness in me."

Topsy's internal party acts as a conduit for her growing understanding of an African-American humanism. She realizes that she is connected to "everything and everyone that has come before." She proclaims that, "All this time I thought we'd given up our drums, but we haven't. They're still here." The drums, revolutionary retentions, voices of the African-American past remain an indelible part of the African-American present. No longer confused or enraged, reunited with her African-American heritage, Topsy now goes freely "about the business of being me." She explains that a key source of her new found power lies in her acceptance of her "colored contradictions."

"The Party" exhibit climaxes with the return to the stage of all the previous exhibits. Chaos ensues as they simultaneously shout important dialogue from their earlier appearance. In the background, Topsy sings, "There's a madness in me and the madness sets me free." This moment conveys the complexity as well as the overall significance of Wolfe's revised definition of "madness." For Wolfe African-American culture is madness. And each individual, like Topsy must discover and celebrate the madness within, the schizophrenia of African-American cultural heritage. Accordingly, all characters join together after the chaos has stopped and chant in unison, "My power is in my madness." Unlike the madness disdained by Clay, the insanity battled by Sarah, this madness is not to be overcome but embraced. Acknowledging and accepting the madness of the past and the present empowers African-American cultural survival.

Significantly, **"The Party"** exhibit is a pastiche, a motivated signifyin(g) on "The Bridge Across the Chasm" from *To Be Young Gifted and Black* by Lorraine Hansberry. In "The Bridge Across the Chasm," an elegantly dressed black woman at a party becomes oblivious to the external events and begins to tap her feet and respond to an internal party:

> I was patting my foot and singing my song. I was happy. I could see the bridge across the chasm. It was made up of a band of angels of art, hurling off the souls of twenty million. I saw Jimmy Baldwin and Leontyne, and Lena and Harry and Sammy. Johnnie Killens and—Lord have mercy, Paul was back! Langston and Julian Mayfield coming on the run . . . Oh it was a wondrous thing I could see. On and on they came, Sarah and the Duke and Count and Cannonball and Louis himself, wearing the crown that Billie gave him before she died. Oh, yes, there they were, the band of angels, picking up numbers along the way, singing and painting and dancing and writing and acting up a storm! And the golden waves rose from their labors and filtered down upon the earth and brought such heavenly brightness . . .

The similarity between this piece and Wolfe's exhibit are clearly evident. **"The Party"** with Topsy "attired in contradictions" rather than elegant evening attire, repeats and revises Hansberry's earlier vision. For Hansberry's elegantly dressed female party character, her internal party serves as a moment of consciousness raising and new self-awareness. She recognizes her connection to the individual, communal and earthly benefits derived from the gifts of these African-American artistic angels," such heavenly brightness." Topsy, too, appreciates the power of her internal party and its celebrants, who dance "to the rhythms of their own definitions. Celebrating in their cultural madness." While Hansberry's woman is "patting her feet and singing my song," Wolfe's Topsy is "dancing to the music of the madness in me." Not only black artists cross the chasm to Topsy's party, but important political and social leaders as well. All converging together, they form "a bridge across the chasm" of African-American culture uniting in celebration of "colored contradictions." Wolfe is signifyin(g) on Hansberry's party by creating a fusion of past and present, ethics and aesthetics.

Still, the most explicit use of motivated signification and parody occurs in the exhibit entitled, **"The Last Mama on the Couch Play."** The exhibit with biting sarcasm parodies Lorraine Hansberry's *Raisin in the Sun* and Ntozake Shange's *for colored girls.* Gates maintains that motivated signifyin(g) "functions to redress an imbalance of power, to clear a space rhetorically . . . This sort of Signifyin(g) revision serves, if successful, to create a space for the revising text." Wolfe created **"The Last Mama on the Couch Play"** precisely because he wanted to establish or clear a space for his own work. Wolfe explains:

> She's [Lorraine Hansberry] a wonderful playwright and it's a wonderful play, but every February all the regional theaters discover black people because its Black History Month and they pull out *Raisin in the Sun.* I want to remove these dead, stale, empty icons blocking me from my own truth.

The Colored Museum as revising text questions and attacks *Raisin in the Sun* and its position as model for African-American drama.

In his classic essay "No More Masterpieces," theatrical theorist Antonin Artaud argues that reverence for masterpieces of the past stifles the development of new drama relevant to contemporary society. Wolfe's irreverent treatment of *Raisin in the Sun* in **"The Last Mama on the Couch Play"** supports this contention. Through this signifyin(g) parody, Wolfe ridicules the limits that domestic realism has placed on African-American drama. Visually, the opening of this exhibit conveys the stultifying effects of convention and adherence to tradition in African-American theatre. The Mama sits reading her bible on the couch. Mama is literally rooted to this couch. The couch and Mama's dress are constructed of the same "well-worn" fabric. Together they symbolize the outmoded but recurrent themes of African-American drama. Just as this large unwieldy couch, situated center stage, inhibits the possibility for inventive staging, the recurrent Mama on the couch realism impedes the creative experimentation of African-American theatre. While Artaud called for the removal of "masterpieces," Wolfe asks that both the Mama and the couch be removed.

Gates notes that successful parody depends on "an intimate familiarity with the model of the parody." Wolfe's parody evidences his familiarity with both *Raisin in the Sun* and *for colored girls.* The visual images, language, symbols and situations are drawn directly from these works. The son's name in **"The Last Mama on the Couch Play"** is an amalgamation of the important male figures names from both of these earlier plays, Walter Lee Beau Willie Jones. Like his namesakes, he is caught up in never ending, psychologically damaging battle with, "The Man, Mr. Charley, The Bossman." The Mama in **"Last Mama,"** like Mama Younger in *Raisin,* symbolizes black matriarchal control and respect for time worn values. While Walter Lee wants to "be somebody" and to "take charge of his life," Mama patronizingly assures him that "You can do all that son, but first you got to wipe your feet." The well known and powerful scene from *Raisin* where Mama slaps daughter Benethea and reprimands her for blasphemy is comically recreated in this exhibit. In response to his blasphemy, **"The Last Mama"** Mama literally slaps Walter Lee across the room. Then with dramatic flare and fists clenched to the heavens she admonishes him, "Not in my house will you ever talk that way again!"

Walter Lee's wife, reminiscent of the seven black women in *for colored girls,* identified simply by the color of their costume dress, is called, The Lady in Plaid. Her speech and movement exaggerate the choreopoem style of Shange:

> And she asked herself, was this the life
> for a Princess Colored, who by the
> translucence of her skin, knew the universe was
> her sister.

Visually signifyin(g) on the tragic, climactic "Beau Willie" monologue performed by the Woman in Red in *for colored girls,* The Lady in Plaid screams and collapses to the floor in overwrought hysteria as Walter Lee Beau Willie throws two dolls representing her children out the window. Wolfe mocks the poetry and pretense of Shange's choreopoem format. In addition, this exhibit also satirizes socially vapid black musical comedies. After Walter Lee Beau Willie is shot by "The Man," his Mama muses "If only he had been born into an all-black musical. Nobody ever dies in an all-black musical." Then, she and the cast join in a rousing musical number that encompasses gospel and rhythm and blues as well as a "myriad of black dancing styles." This musical number includes the refrain, "Oh son get up and dance. We say get up this is your second chance," and literally raises Walter Lee Beau Willie from the dead.

Consequently, with its references to specific texts, the success of this parody depends not only on Wolfe's familiarity with the musical and classic African-American drama, but on the spectator's knowledge of them as well. In order for an audience to laugh with recognition and understanding of the parody, they, too, need to have knowledge of *Raisin in the Sun, for colored girls,* and black musicals. Thus, while **"The Last Mama on the Couch Play"** is signifyin(g) on African-American theatrical convention, the effectiveness of this exhibit depends on the spectators' awareness of African-American theatre.

Furthermore, this exhibit is inherently sexist. The women, Mama, the Lady in Plaid, Medea are all rewarded for their histrionics and their performances. They each receive an award from the Narrator and applause from the audience. Walter Lee, however, receives no award. Instead, "The Man" eventually demands Walter Lee's arrest for over acting. Walter Lee Beau Willie rails against these usurping women.

He snatches the award from his sister, Medea Jones and exclaims, "This is my play! It's about Me and The Man! . . . It's about me. Me and my pain! My Pain!" Walter Lee seeks to reclaim the dramatic voice, the subject position as his own. Contemporary literary criticism and public opinion have praised the works of black women writers, such as Alice Walker, Toni Morrison, Gloria Naylor. Some misinformed, chauvinistic black male writers have maintained that the recent and overdue notoriety of black women's literature has been achieved at the expense of their black male counterparts and has resulted in the denigration of black men in general. Walter Lee's tirade implicitly supports this sentiment. Wolfe's sexist attacks on black female writers (in the exhibit **"Symbiosis,"** he also caustically comments on *The Color Purple* replacing *Soul on Ice* on the bookshelves of the black middle class) dissipates his message of cultural diversity and inclusion. Walter Lee's exclamation that "this is my play!" symbolically negates the place for and role of black women. Through **"The Last Mama on the Couch Play,"** Wolfe is clearly signifyin(g) on the "icons" of the black theatrical past. However, in this exhibit, he limits his biting sarcasm to the works of black women. While Wolfe calls for a reorientation of African-American cultural perceptions and valorizes "colored contradictions," his diminution of the achievements of "colored girls and women" contradicts his own ideals. Throughout *The Colored Museum,* he decries essentialist perceptions of black experience. Wolfe rails against black middle class isolationism. With Miss Roj, he assails the limitations of heterosexual orthodoxy. However, his motivated signifyin(g) on, his negative refiguring parody of black female playwrights does not foreground their place within the matrix of African-American cultural diversity, but instead affirms the dominant and conventional patriarchal hegemony.

Still, not only the content, but the form of Wolfe's *The Colored Museum* is informed by the work of black women writers. Disdaining conventional realist structure, Wolfe creates a non-realistic form similar to those used by playwrights Adrienne Kennedy and Ntozake Shange. As in *Funnyhouse* and *for colored girls,* the exhibits in Wolfe's museum are not connected by linear causality. In almost every exhibit the actor/character relates a monologue, an individual story, to the audience and becomes the primary storyteller. The actors remain aware not only of the story they tell but of the performative dynamics of that story. Writing of Ntozake Shange's use of monologue, Deborah Geis observes that, "The monologue places the narrative weight of the play upon its spoken language and upon the performance of the individual actors." This quote holds equally true for *The Colored Museum.* Like *for colored girls, The Colored Museum* relies upon an adroit and flexible ensemble that must effectively create a variety of different personas. The actors in *The Colored Museum* must undergo a series of maddeningly rapid costume changes only to reappear as completely different characters with different physical and vocal attitudes. As the actors redefine themselves in each new role, they implicitly reflect on the wide variety of African-American experience.

Applying Gates's theory of signifyin(g) to **The Colored Museum** highlights the intertextual relationship between this play and earlier works of African-American theatre. Wolfe revisits and revises earlier discourses on the "madness of race." He challenges perceptions of African-American culture. His play celebrates the realization that the outdated cultural patterns from the past must be broken and yet the past can not be forgotten or forsaken. In the final exhibit, Topsy and the assembled cast proclaim "Whereas I can't live inside of yesterday's pain, I can't live without it." Still, a close reading of Wolfe's signifyin(g) text reveals that while he praises the contradictions of black experience, he is himself contradictory, particularly in his treatment of black women writers.

The play ends with the perky stewardess of the **"Celebrity Slaveship"** exhibit repeating a phrase she stated near the beginning of the play. She warns the audience "Before exiting, check the overhead as any baggage you don't claim we trash." When Miss Pat first delivered this line at the end of her opening monologue, she was signifyin(g) on the conventional informational warnings of flight attendants. More significantly, Miss Pat at that moment also forewarned the audience that none of the icons and images of black culture were safe from Wolfe's satirical assault. At the end of the play, the meaning of Miss Pat's statement is inverted. She is now signifyin(g) on her earlier statement, for it is a repetition with revision and a signal difference. Miss Pat now calls on African Americans to realize as Topsy does that the past, the present, the schizophrenia of culture must be carried out with them.

John Lahr (review date 4 December 1995)

SOURCE: "Big and Bad Wolfe," in *The New Yorker,* December 4, 1995, pp. 119-21.

[*In the following review, Lahr gives a rave notice for* Bring In 'da Noise/Bring In 'da Funk *and a much less enthusiastic response to Wolfe's production of Shakespeare's* The Tempest.]

"Showstopping" is a word that critics don't have occasion to use much these days. Once in a while, a song will arouse an audience to cheer or a comedian will rock a crowd so hard that it has to catch its breath or a star will strut his stuff so exuberantly that we lose all sense of gravity and jump out of our seats in glee. To get one of these moments in a

show is lucky; to get two is exceptional; but to get seven—which is what the director George C. Wolfe and the dancer-choreographer Savion Glover do at the Public Theatre in their fabulous *Bring In 'da Noise/Bring In 'da Funk*—is heroic. The show's heroic energy has its roots in the black experience. If you'd been sitting around the table with Wolfe at the beginning of rehearsals, you would have heard him expound on the historical context of the show's razzle-dazzle. *Bring In 'da Noise* tells the story of tap and of the wayward progress of the African-American beat that tap makes sensational. "One phenomenon of integration is that a whole lot of information has not been passed on," Wolfe told the cast, with his rapid-fire delivery. "The period from the end of the Civil War to the twenties was an unbelievable time for the black people in this country. During slavery, black people were somebody else's definition. Slavery ended, and black people came out of the starting gate. Phenomenal things were accomplished, including the invention of jazz. That history is what this piece is trying to celebrate. Black people took control of American culture. They had an influence during slavery, but afterward they took control, the way they still do to this day—with language, with the way they dressed." And with music, as Wolfe hardly needed to mention to the prodigiously talented Glover, the tappers who go by the name Real Tap Skills (Baakari Wilder, Jimmy Tate, Vincent Bingham, and Dulé Hill), and the street drummers Jared Crawford and Raymond King, who call themselves Drummin Too Deep.

Wolfe, who collects folk art, is a showman of folk expression. His best work is a kind of anthropological excavation of the buried treasures of the black experience: the tall tale, in *Spunk,* his adaptation of Zora Neale Hurston's short stories; jazz, in *Jelly's Last Jam;* and now the percussion of tap in *Bring In 'da Noise/Bring In 'da Funk*. Wolfe is attempting not only to return tap to black culture but to give black culture back to tap. "I want you guys to look at those pictures," he said at the rehearsal, pointing to a wall display that featured a Xeroxed quotation from the late black writer Henry Dumas: "One of the greatest roles ever created by Western man has been the role of Negro." Around the quotation, the wall was covered with pictures. Photographs of lynchings and riots juxtaposed with images of Bill Robinson (with Shirley Temple), the smiling Nicholas Brothers, and Billy Kersands' Minstrels, formed a kind of African-American time line of grief and gladness. "Each era had its sense of style," Wolfe told his cast. "The way they posed. The way they held their heads. There was Southern style, Northern style, I-got-a-lot-of-money style, I-got-no-money-but-I'm-gonna-act-like-I-got-a-lot-of-money style." *Bring In 'da Noise/Bring In 'da Funk* makes a drama out of these subtle shifts of presentation and rhythm as it charts the evolution of the black beat, from its rural Southern beginnings to its Northern urbanization and its present hip-hop incarnation in the choreography of Glover and his homeboy hoofers.

At one point in the show, Glover, dancing in front of a trip-tych of mirrors, performs a tap homage to the great rhythm tappers Jimmy Slyde, Chuck Green, Buster Brown, and Lon Chaney. Over Glover's astonishing moves, Wolfe plays a tape of the dancer's voice. "People think tap dancin' is arms and legs and all this big ol' smile," Glover is heard to say as he taps. "Naw, it's raw. It's rhythms, it's us. It's ours." Glover makes fierce, passionate, complex music with his feet. The lighting designers Jules Fisher and Peggy Eisenhauer sculpt his dynamism in subtle, moody pools of light. Glover and his troupe can "hit": their gorgeous clatter is their liberation, translating the fury of the black experi-ence into fun. Wolfe doesn't want to freeze the smile of tap, exactly; he wants to find ways for the dancers to be them-selves in their dance, to embrace the anger in tap's poetic show of aggression. He wants to deconstruct the tap dancer's smile, that emblem of both survival and submission. "As a person of color, you always have to send a signal that it's safe to come toward you," Wolfe said during the rehears-als. "You always have to put up this extraordinary signal that very often has nothing to do with the emotional complexity of what you're doing or who you are." Wolfe pushes the boundaries of this notion of safety and violates the arche-type of the dancer as a tap-happy figure of delight. Early in the show, as the beat starts to assert itself in ambling rural rhythms, the beaming Baakari Wilder does a shuffle on top of a bale of cotton. By the end of the dance, the bale has been transformed into a gallows, and he is no longer high-stepping but twitching. In one frenzied number, called "In-dustrialization," the dancers take their places on a stark steel scaffolding and are gradually transformed into interchange-able parts as mechanistic rhythms create a dehumanizing din. Here tap is not just the sound of joy; it's the tattoo of op-pression, and the dancers are captives sending back messages from their solitary confinement. This tone may irritate some white theatregoers who don't want their ecstatic cocktail laced with bitters, but it has a kick that comes straight from the streets.

Wolfe is most cogent when he lets laughter play off outrage. The show argues that the beat got lost when it was co-opted by the all-singing, all-dancing ballyhoo of Hollywood—where tap became a flashy vehicle of romance for white dancers, while a black man, if he had a female partner, danced with a child. Baakari Wilder, playing a character named Uncle Huck-a-Buck, sends up the Bill Robinson teeth-'n'-smiles stereotype, singing, "Who de hell cares if I acts de fool / When I takes a swim in my swimming pool?" He proceeds to dance with Lil Darlin, a blond doll operated from behind by Glover. (Her feet are attached to his pink tap shoes.) It's a clever image, but this satire is topped at the end of the evening, when Glover and his crew try to hail cabs, which won't stop for them. Wolfe's point about the way black people have to signal their non-threatening intentions is literally tapped out: one dancer waves; another, in jacket

and tie, holds up his credit card; a third, in military uniform, carries a copy of Colin Powell's autobiography. They stomp downstage together in a furious barrage of taps. "Taxi!" they yell before coming to a simultaneous halt and flipping the driver the bird.

Wolfe has titled one early section of his show "Som'thin from Nuthin'," which bears out Zora Neale Hurston's dic-tum about the black person's originality: "While he lives and moves in the midst of a white civilization, everything that he touches is re-interpreted for his own use." The show cel-ebrates the transformation of the ragtag into the glorious. In a section called "The Pan Handlers," the duo Drummin Too Deep wear vests festooned with pots and pans. They play one another before turning to make a marvelous racket on an array of kitchenware hung from ropes. Between the bra-vura exhibitions of drumming and dancing, Wolfe wedges in the fine jazz voice of Ann Duquesnay and the rapping of Reg E. Gaines. (Gaines's sharp words, when you can hear them, would be better served by an actor with an attitude than by a poet faking one.) "Be oxtails and pig cuts da boss toss down," he says. "We takes us den makes us da finest feast round"—another example of deprivation turned into delight.

The genius of Glover's choreography and the exhilaration of the experience distract the public and the performers from the realm of pain out of which the dance comes. Wolfe wants us to pay attention not just to the public show of mastery, however, but to the private sense of loss. At the finale, as the young dancers trade hits in their own, hip-hop style, their taped voices are played over their dazzling dance. Even as they triumph, we hear them struggling with a sense of being thrown away by the culture: "I didn't give up yet. I'm try-ing not to." "I'm not lost because: one, my mother, and two, tap dancing." "You know, a lot of people that I looked up to when I was younger and wanted to be like, now they dead or in jail or, you know what I mean?" "Tap—tap sorta like saved me. You know what I'm sayin'?" Words are not the dancers' chosen language, but by staging tap in this narra-tive way Wolfe makes the accident of their survival at once articulate, terrifying, and very beautiful.

In **Bring In 'da Noise/Bring In 'da Funk,** George C. Wolfe has used Glover to write a play and make his points about America. Wolfe does less well when he is trying to impose himself on a dead white male like William Shakespeare, who comes with a ready-made story and the vocabulary to tell it. Wolfe's acrylic version of *The Tempest*, a street-theatre production brought indoors (it had its début last summer at the Public's Delacorte Theatre, in Central Park), is billed as "a New World vision." But the vision on display at the Broadhurst Theatre consists largely of Old World avant-garde theatrics. We've seen these tricks before: the circle of sand (Peter Brook's *Carmen*); the storm at sea, complete with bobbing model frigate and waving bolts of cloth (Ingmar Bergman's *The Winter's Tale*); Ariel's robotic posturing (Meyerhold's biomechanics). "What kind of a Shakespeare production is this that smashes through Europe?" asks the polemical program note, referring to the map of Europe that is displayed on the stage before the shipwreck that strands the royal party is conjured up. "This is not the stuff of psychological theatre," the note continues. "This is bigger. It's a piece of spatial poetry that at once exposes the deep pain of cultural silence and celebrates the angry explosion of that silence." No, what it exposes is Wolfe's worrying glibness, his insecurity with Shakespeare's poetry, and his refusal to engage the text. Pyrotechnics like drumming, Indonesian shadow puppets, and Brazilian stilt walkers are intended to engage the intellect "through our viscera" (the jejune program note again). On the contrary, the technically skillful production never delivers an iota of the intellectual freight it claims to be carrying. Wolfe and his Prospero, Patrick Stewart, excite the audience without illuminating it; we leave the theatre remembering the sound of drums and the spectacle of gargantuan Brazilian saint-goddesses but not one vivid line of the poetry. With this *Tempest*, Wolfe, the

master of multicultural ceremonies, has his Broadway hit, but he also has an act of cultural brigandage on his hands.

FURTHER READING

Biography

Keene, John. "George C. Wolfe: A Brief Biography." *Callaloo* 16, No. 3 (Summer 1993): 593-94.
    Presents highlights of Wolfe's career.

Criticism

Brustein, Robert. "Cause Jelly Don't Shake Like That." In his *Dumbocracy in America: Studies in the Theatre of Guilt, 1987-1994*, pp.139-43. Chicago: Ivan R. Dee, 1994.
    A positive review of Wolfe's *Jelly's Last Jam.*

Scanlan, Dick. "Fall Preview: George C. Wolfe." *The Advocate*, No. 690 (19 September 1995): 53-4, 56.
    Focuses on Wolfe's sexuality and current projects.

Additional coverage of Wolfe's life and career is contained in the following sources published by Gale: *Contemporary Authors*, Vol. 149; *Contemporary Black Biography*, Vol. 6; and *Contemporary Literary Criticism*, Vol. 49

Black Literature Criticism
Supplement

Indexes

BLC Cumulative Author Index
BLC Cumulative Nationality Index
BLC Cumulative Title Index

How to Use This Index

The main references

Camus, Albert
1913-1960 ...... CLC 1, 2, 4, 9, 11, 14,
32, 69; DA; DAB; DAC; DAM DRAM,
MST, NOV; DC2; SSC 9; WLC

list all author entries in the following Gale Literary Criticism series:

BLC = *Black Literature Criticism*
BLCS = *Black Literature Criticism Supplement*
CLC = *Contemporary Literary Criticism*
CLR = *Children's Literature Review*
CMLC = *Classical and Medieval Literature Criticism*
DA = *DISCovering Authors*
DAB = *DISCovering Authors: British*
DAC = *DISCovering Authors: Canadian*
DAM = *DISCovering Authors Modules*
  DRAM = *dramatists;* *MST* = *most-studied*
  authors; *MULT* = *multicultural authors;* *NOV* =
  novelists; *POET* = *poets;* *POP* = *popular/genre*
  writers; *DC* = *Drama Criticism*
HLC = *Hispanic Literature Criticism*
LC = *Literature Criticism from 1400 to 1800*
NCLC = *Nineteenth-Century Literature Criticism*
PC = *Poetry Criticism*
SSC = *Short Story Criticism*
TCLC = *Twentieth-Century Literary Criticism*
WLC = *World Literature Criticism, 1500 to the Present*
WLCS = *World Literature Criticism Supplement*

The cross-references

See also CA 89-92; DLB 72; MTCW

list all author entries in the following Gale biographical and literary sources:

AAYA = *Authors & Artists for Young Adults*
AITN = *Authors in the News*
BEST = *Bestsellers*
BW = *Black Writers*
CA = *Contemporary Authors*
CAAS = *Contemporary Authors Autobiography Series*
CABS = *Contemporary Authors Bibliographical Series*
CANR = *Contemporary Authors New Revision Series*
CAP = *Contemporary Authors Permanent Series*
CDALB = *Concise Dictionary of American Literary Biography*
CDBLB = *Concise Dictionary of British Literary Biography*

DLB = *Dictionary of Literary Biography*
DLBD = *Dictionary of Literary Biography Documentary Series*
DLBY = *Dictionary of Literary Biography Yearbook*
HW = *Hispanic Writers*
JRDA = *Junior DISCovering Authors*
MAICYA = *Major Authors and Illustrators for Children and Young Adults*
MTCW = *Major 20th-Century Writers*
NNAL = *Native North American Literature*
SAAS = *Something about the Author Autobiography Series*
SATA = *Something about the Author*
YABC = *Yesterday's Authors of Books for Children*

Black Literature Criticism Cumulative Author Index

This index lists all author entries in *Black Literature Criticism* (BLC) and *Black Literature Criticism Supplement* (BLCS). Authors are listed under the names by which they are best known, with suitable cross-references. Volume numbers are given for each author.

Knight, Etheridge 1931-1991 .... **BLC 2**
See also BW 1; CA 21-24R; 133; CANR 23;
CLC 40; DAM POET; DLB 41; PC 14

Komunyakaa, Yusef 1947- .... **BLCS**
See also CA 147; CLC 86, 94; DLB 120

La Guma, (Justin) Alex(ander) 1925-1985
BLCS
See also BW 1; CA 49-52; 118; CANR 25; CLC
19; DAM NOV; DLB 117; MTCW

Lamming, George (William) 1927- .... **BLC 2**
See also BW 2; CA 85-88; CANR 26; CLC 2,
4, 66; DAM MULT; DLB 125; MTCW

Larsen, Nella 1891-1964 .... **BLC 2**
See also BW 1; CA 125; CLC 37; DAM MULT;
DLB 51

Laye, Camara 1928-1980 .... **BLC 2**
See also BW 1; CA 85-88; 97-100; CANR 25;
CLC 4, 38; DAM MULT; MTCW

Lee, Andrea 1953- .... **BLC 2**
See also BW 1; CA 125; CLC 36; DAM MULT

Lee Don L.
See Madhubuti, Haki R.

Lee, George W(ashington) 1894-1976 **BLC 2**
See also BW 1; CA 125; CLC 52; DAM MULT;
DLB 51

Lee, Shelton Jackson 1957(?)- .... **BLCS**
See also Lee, Spike
See also BW 2; CA 125; CANR 42; CLC 105;
DAM MULT

Lee, Spike
See Lee, Shelton Jackson

Little, Malcolm
See Malcolm X

Lorde, Audre (Geraldine) 1934-1992 **BLC 2**
See also BW 1; CA 25-28R; 142; CANR 16,
26, 46; CLC 18, 71; DAM MULT, POET;
DLB 41; MTCW; PC 12

Machado de Assis, Joaquim Maria 1839-1908
BLC 2
See also CA 107; 153; SSC 24; TCLC 10

Madhubuti, Haki R. 1942- .... **BLC 2**
See also Lee, Don L.
See also BW 2; CA 73-76; CANR 24, 51; CLC
6, 73; DAM MULT, POET; DLB 5, 41;
DLBD 8; PC 5

Major, Clarence 1936- .... **BLC 2**
See also BW 2; CA 21-24R; CAAS 6; CANR
13, 25, 53; CLC 3, 19, 48; DAM MULT; DLB
33

Malcolm X .... **BLC 2**
See also Little, Malcolm
See also CLC 82; WLCS

Mandrake, Ethel Belle
See Thurman, Wallace

Marshall, Paule 1929- .... **BLC 3**
See also BW 2; CA 77-80; CANR 25; CLC 27,
72; DAM MULT; DLB 157; MTCW; SSC 3

McKay, Claude .... **BLC 3**
See also McKay, Festus Claudius
See also DAB; DLB 4, 45, 51, 117; PC 2; TCLC
7, 41

McKay, Festus Claudius
See McKay, Claude

McMillan, Terry (L.) 1951- .... **BLCS**
See also AAYA 21; BW 2; CA 140; CANR 60;
CLC 50, 61; DAM MULT, NOV, POP

McPherson, James Alan 1943- .... **BLCS**
See also CA 25-28R; CAAS 17; CANR
24; CLC 19, 77; DLB 38; MTCW

Milner, Ron(ald) 1938- .... **BLC 3**
See also AITN 1; BW 1; CA 73-76; CANR 24;
CLC 56; DAM MULT; DLB 38; MTCW

Mofolo, Thomas (Mokopu) 1875(?)-1948

BLC 3
See also CA 121; 153; DAM MULT; TCLC 22

Morrison, Toni 1931- .... **BLC 3**
See also AAYA 1, 22; BW 2; CA 29-32R;
CANR 27, 42, 67; CDALB 1968-1988; CLC
4, 10, 22, 55, 81, 87; DA; DAB; DAC; DAM
MST, MULT, NOV, POP; DLB 6, 33, 143;
DLBY 81; MTCW; SATA 57

Mosley, Walter 1952- .... **BLCS**
See also AAYA 17; BW 2; CA 142; CANR 57;
CLC 97; DAM MULT, POP

Mphahlele, Ezekiel 1919-1983 .... **BLC 3**
See also Mphahlele, Ez'kia
See also BW 2; CA 81-84; CANR 26; CLC 25;
DAM MULT

Mphahlele, Ez'kia
See Mphahlele, Ezekiel

Mqhayi, S(amuel) E(dward) K(rune Loliwe)
1875-1945 .... **BLC 3**
See also CA 153; DAM MULT; TCLC 25

Myers, Walter Dean 1937- .... **BLC 3**
See also AAYA 4, 23; BW 2; CA 33-36R;
CANR 20, 42, 67; CLC 35; CLR 4, 16, 35;
DAM MULT, NOV; DLB 33; INT CANR-
20; JRDA; MAICYA; SAAS 2; SATA 41, 71;
SATA-Brief 27

Myers, Walter M.
See Myers, Walter Dean

Naylor, Gloria 1950- .... **BLC 3**
See also AAYA 6; BW 2; CA 107; CANR 27,
51; CLC 28, 52; DA; DAC; DAM MST,
MULT, NOV, POP; DLB 173; MTCW;
WLCS

Ngugi James Thiong'o
See Ngugi wa Thiong'o

Ngugi wa Thiong'o 1938- .... **BLC 3**
See also Ngugi, James T(hiong'o)
See also BW 2; CA 81-84; CANR 27, 58; CLC
36; DAM MULT, NOV; DLB 125; MTCW

Nkosi, Lewis 1936- .... **BLC 3**
See also BW 1; CA 65-68; CANR 27; CLC 45;
DAM MULT; DLB 157

Nwapa, Flora 1931- .... **BLCS**
See also BW 2; CA 143; DLB 125

Okigbo, Christopher (Ifenayichukwu) 1932-
1967 .... **BLC 3**
See also BW 1; CA 77-80; CLC 25, 84; DAM
MULT, POET; DLB 125; MTCW; PC 7

Ousmane, Sembène 1923- .... **BLC 3**
See also BW 1; CA 117; 125; CLC 66; MTCW

Parks, Gordon (Alexander Buchanan) 1912-
BLC 3
See also AITN 2; BW 2; CA 41-44R; CANR
26, 66; CLC 1, 16; DAM MULT; DLB 33;
SATA 8

Patterson, (Horace) Orlando (Lloyd) 1940-
BLCS
See also BW 1; CA 65-68; CANR 27

p'Bitek, Okot 1931-1982 .... **BLC 3**
See also BW 2; CA 124; 107; CLC 96; DAM
MULT; DLB 125; MTCW

Phillips, Caryl 1958- .... **BLCS**
See also BW 2; CA 141; CANR 63; CLC 96;
DAM MULT; DLB 157

Powell, Adam Clayton, Jr. 1908-1972 **BLC 3**
See also BW 1; CA 102; 33-36R; CLC 89; DAM
MULT

Randall, Dudley (Felker) 1914- .... **BLC 3**
See also BW 1; CA 25-28R; CANR 23; CLC 1;
DAM MULT; DLB 41

Reed, Ishmael 1938- .... **BLC 3**
See also BW 2; CA 21-24R; CANR 25, 48; CLC
2, 3, 5, 6, 13, 32, 60; DAM MULT; DLB 2,

5, 33, 169; DLBD 8; MTCW

Roumain, Jacques (Jean Baptiste) 1907-1944
BLC 3
See also BW 1; CA 117; 125; DAM MULT;
TCLC 19

Sanchez, Sonia 1934- .... **BLC 3**
See also BW 2; CA 33-36R; CANR 24, 49; CLC
5; CLR 18; DAM MULT; DLB 41; DLBD 8;
MAICYA; MTCW; PC 9; SATA 22

Schwarz-Bart, Simone 1938- .... **BLCS**
See also BW 2; CA 97-100; CLC 7

Sembène, Ousmane
See Ousmane, Sembène

Senghor, Léopold Sédar 1906- .... **BLC 3**
See also BW 2; CA 116; 125; CANR 47; CLC
54; DAM MULT, POET; MTCW

Shange, Ntozake 1948- .... **BLC 3**
See also AAYA 9; BW 2; CA 85-88; CABS 3;
CANR 27, 48; CLC 8, 25, 38, 74; DAM
DRAM, MULT; DC 3; DLB 38; MTCW

Soyinka, Wole 1934- .... **BLC 3**
See also BW 2; CA 13-16R; CANR 27, 39; CLC
3, 5, 14, 36, 44; DA; DAB; DAC; DAM
DRAM, MST, MULT; DC 2; DLB 125;
MTCW; WLC

Thurman, Wallace (Henry) 1902-1934 **BLC 3**
See also BW 1; CA 104; 124; DAM MULT;
DLB 51; TCLC 6

Tolson, Melvin B(eaunorus) 1898(?)-1966
BLC 3
See also BW 1; CA 124; 89-92; CLC 36, 105;
DAM MULT, POET; DLB 48, 76

Toomer, Jean 1894-1967 .... **BLC 3**
See also BW 1; CA 85-88; CDALB 1917-1929;
CLC 1, 4, 13, 22; DAM MULT; DLB 45, 51;
MTCW; PC 7; SSC 1; WLCS

Tutu, Desmond M(pilo) 1931- .... **BLC 3**
See also BW 1; CA 125; CANR 67; CLC 80;
DAM MULT

Tutuola, Amos 1920-1997 .... **BLC 3**
See also BW 2; CA 9-12R; 159; CANR 27, 66;
CLC 5, 14, 29; DAM MULT; DLB 125;
MTCW

Vassa, Gustavus
See Equiano, Olaudah

Walcott, Derek (Alton) 1930- .... **BLC 3**
See also BW 2; CA 89-92; CANR 26, 47; CLC
2, 4, 9, 14, 25, 42, 67, 76; DAB; DAC; DAM
MST, MULT, POET; DC 7; DLB 117; DLBY
81; MTCW

Walker, Alice (Malsenior) 1944- .... **BLC 3**
See also AAYA 3; BEST 89:4; BW 2; CA 37-
40R; CANR 9, 27, 49, 66; CDALB 1968-
1988; CLC 5, 6, 9, 19, 27, 46, 58, 103; DA;
DAB; DAC; DAM MST, MULT, NOV,
POET, POP; DLB 6, 33, 143; INT CANR-
27; MTCW; SATA 31; SSC 5; WLCS

Walker, Margaret (Abigail) 1915- ...... **BLC 3**
See also BW 2; CA 73-76; CANR 26, 54; CLC
1, 6; DAM MULT; DLB 76, 152; MTCW;
PC 20

Washington, Booker T(aliaferro) 1856-1915
BLC 3
See also BW 1; CA 114; 125; DAM MULT;
SATA 28; TCLC 10

West, Cornel (Ronald) 1953- .... **BLCS**
See also CA 144

Wheatley (Peters), Phillis 1754(?)-1784 **BLC 3**
See also CDALB 1640-1865; DA; DAC; DAM
MST, MULT, POET; DLB 31, 50; LC 3; PC
3; WLC

White, Walter .... **BLC 3**
See also DAM MULT

Black Literature Criticism Cumulative Nationality Index

This index lists all author entries in *Black Literature Criticism* (BLC) and *Black Literature Criticism Supplement* (BLCS) by nationality. Authors are listed under the names by which they are best known. Volume and page numbers are given for each author.

Black Literature Criticism Cumulative Title Index

This index lists all titles in *Black Literature Criticism* (BLC) and *Black Literature Criticism Supplement* (BLCS). Volume and page numbers are given for each title.

Title Index

Title Index

Title Index

Title Index

Title Index

Title Index